FIELDING'S
EUROPE
1992

Current Fielding Titles

FIELDING'S ALPINE EUROPE 1992
FIELDING'S AUSTRALIA 1992
FIELDING'S BENELUX 1992
FIELDING'S BERMUDA AND THE BAHAMAS 1992
FIELDING'S BRITAIN 1992
FIELDING'S BUDGET EUROPE 1992
FIELDING'S CARIBBEAN 1992
FIELDING'S EUROPE 1992
FIELDING'S HAWAII 1992
FIELDING'S ITALY 1992
FIELDING'S MEXICO 1992
FIELDING'S PEOPLE'S REPUBLIC OF CHINA 1992
FIELDING'S SCANDINAVIA 1992
FIELDING'S SELECTIVE SHOPPING GUIDE TO EUROPE 1992
FIELDING'S SPAIN AND PORTUGAL 1992

FIELDING'S ALASKA AND THE YUKON
FIELDING'S BUDGET ASIA Southeast Asia and the Far East
FIELDING'S CALIFORNIA
FIELDING'S FAMILY VACATIONS USA
FIELDING'S FAR EAST 2nd revised edition
FIELDING'S HAVENS AND HIDEAWAYS USA
FIELDING'S LEWIS AND CLARK TRAIL
FIELDING'S LITERARY AFRICA
FIELDING'S TRAVELERS' MEDICAL COMPANION
FIELDING'S WORLDWIDE CRUISES 5th revised edition

FIELDING'S
EUROPE
1992

BY
JOSEPH RAFF

FIELDING TRAVEL BOOKS
℅ WILLIAM MORROW & COMPANY, INC.
1350 Avenue of the Americas, New York, N.Y. 10019

Text design by Marsha Cohen/Parallelgram
All country maps by Mark Stein Studios

To Temple Fielding—A Tribute to a Friend
(1913–1983)

Joseph Raff

For many years Joe and his wife, Judith, have lived in Europe and crisscrossed their beat annually by car, train, boat, and plane to report on the latest trends and developments for readers of the Fielding guides.

Born in New York, Joe was graduated from the University of North Carolina at Chapel Hill, studied at Harvard, Ohio, and Indiana Universities, and then reported for the Associated Press and *Sports Illustrated* before moving overseas to edit the *Rome Daily American*. Since 1961 he has worked on the Fielding guides to Europe.

Travel writing for the Fielding publications requires almost six months of road work each year. Between times Joe is an avid sailor, an ardent tennis enthusiast, and an Alpine skier. He lives on Mallorca.

Photo credit: Maurice Fievet

Judith Raff

Judith shares with Joe the demanding research schedule that goes into the preparation of the Fielding European guides. Her specialty is the evaluation of merchandise and current fashions for the *Selective Shopping Guide,* but still she is involved totally in the gathering, weighing, and reporting on every major field of activity covered in the Fielding guides to Europe.

Born in Philadelphia, she was educated at Connecticut College for Women, the University of North Carolina, and New York University. When there is time for leisure, it is usually answered through downhill skiing, tennis, or sailing.

ABOUT THE STARS

Without the accustomed solemnity of some volumes, this guidebook employs a star-rating system for hotels and restaurants. The technique is meant to be not a substitute for the written report, but only a shortcut for the traveler who may be rushed and too busy to read the more detailed accounts. Furthermore, this ranking is highly subjective and personal, reflecting the attitudes of a rather small nucleus of reporters—not the consensus of scores of correspondents who have debated, weighed, and issued Solomonic judgments. In the hotel category, it has nothing whatever to do with "official" national ratings by the various lodging associations. Usually, in fact, these tourist bureaus disagree with me violently if I don't award the maximum number of stars corresponding to their own dicta. Clearly their purpose is to promote their own region.

In order to lend greater flexibility to my ratings, I am utilizing five stars. I could have used three, a scale ranging from one to ten, chef's hats, roosters, or whatever symbol the imagination could conjure up for each occasion. Stars, however, are universal, and, hence, have become the vehicle for this abbreviated expression.

In effecting this reader-aid, both hollow stars and solid ones appear in the text. The hollow ones symbolize superior quality while the solid ones indicate more of an impression of charm, warmth and visual appeal. One does not exclude the other, but in offering this shorthand judgment the aim is to submit a predominant impression. This will probably infuriate many hoteliers and restaurateurs, while others may be gleeful over these choices. Certainly you will not agree with all of the evaluations, but then, that is what subjectivity is in an impressionistic world.

My recommendation is that you skim the chapters that interest you, pick out some of the places that catch your fancy, and then read thoroughly the descriptive passages.

By failing to award any stars to a preponderance of establishments that are recorded, that is not to say that we have ignored them or feel indifferently about them. Indeed, to be in this book at all they must be of some importance—either because of their location, their size, their notoriety, their touristic popularity, or because we just plain like 'em or don't.

Moreover, the stars in each country are related only to the restaurants and hotels within that nation. In other words, a 5-star restaurant in Paris is not going to be the same as a 5-star restaurant in Greece and the 1-star hostelry in Switzerland, in fairness, should only be judged against another Swiss inn.

So here's the verdict:

xii · · · ABOUT THE STARS

☆☆☆☆☆ Impeccable quality
☆☆☆☆ Excellent in most respects
☆☆☆ Very good and probably superior value
☆☆ Meritorious and worth considering
☆ Better than average

★★★★★ Overwhelming beauty
★★★★ Splendid mood and visual appeal
★★★ Delightful to the senses
★★ Generally attractive
★ Pleasant

TEMPLE FIELDING TRAVEL AWARD

The precious air we like to breathe and the peace we all seek are becoming rarer commodities everywhere. Everywhere, that is, except in Zermatt, Switzerland, where air pollution does not exist (due to the banning of automobiles) and transportation is achieved entirely by clean, whisper-quiet electric and solar-powered vehicles. Zermatt has become the model resort that is being studied and, I hope, copied in other peace-loving communities where the air is recognized as a valuable asset and a human need. For this vital awareness and important contribution, this book is honored to dedicate the Temple Fielding Travel Award to:

ZERMATT (Switzerland)

Previous Recipients

Concorde SST
Freddie Laker
Conrad N. Hilton
Eurail
Greyhound
American Express

International Herald Tribune
Spanish Parador System
Pistolstraede (Copenhagen)
Frankfurt's Museum Bank
World Monuments Fund
Portuguese Pousada System
The "Other" Mallorca

The Temple Fielding Travel Award is a 64-pound sculpture of crystal created by Master Artist Vicke Lindstrand at the Kosta studios in Sweden.

Consultant: Eugene Raskin, Professor of Architecture, Columbia University, NYC.

FOREWORD: WHY EUROPE?

Europe is a different creature every year. In early 1989 who would have thought that the barriers between East and West were to tumble in 1990 and then become choke points again by 1991, responding to independence movements and the wrenching adjustments of power politics? And what further changes can we expect in 1992? Economies waver, democracies are born, coronations occur, borders open or close, fads evolve—but always with a pageantry, a zest and a glamour that makes Europe the ultimate travel destination.

As far as I know, my wife and I are the only American guidebook writers who actually live full time on European soil. And since we've covered this familiar ground for almost all of our journalistic lives, we have scores of friends and colleagues, both professional and casual, who keep us alerted to changes and nuances in their own particular regions. Consequently, we feel we can pass along the benefit of such information to you much faster and save you time, money and a lot of wasted motion, leaving you free to enrich your holiday with more important matters and to enjoy the fun of new experiences.

Our thanks go to the myriad readers who help (or scold) us by writing about their own travels. My wife and I as well as our esteemed Administrative Vice-President Jaime Sebastian check all of this correspondence and assign a follow-up.

From this zealous application of legwork, eyework and deskwork, all of us here hope we can provide you with a better time abroad.

Pollensa, Mallorca, Spain

J.R.

CONTENTS

LET'S GET READY

COSTS You'll find bargains if you know where to look. To a large degree that is the function of this book. If you are an *average* vacationer, you can save more than half of the total expenditure for your holiday by joining a tour. Because startlingly lower group rates are charged by most hotels for exactly the same rooms (this also applies in most restaurants and other facilities), because the lump transport of the baggage is a fraction of the same transfers by individuals, and because of a score of similar fiscal benefits built into them, simple economics dictate that they've *got* to be dramatically less. Along the same lines, if you are willing to buy a "package" that combines ground arrangements with your overseas flight, the relative price will be lower (perhaps 30%) than if you traveled entirely on your own. Air carriers are clued in to their clients' desires for flexibility; therefore, they are making it easier for you to fly cheaply, leave the flock if you wish, and even explore on your own once you've taken advantage of the special transatlantic ticketing. Some are even providing the option of a low-cost car rental during slow months.

We've included the top restaurants in this volume so that you may take your choice, but below the multistar listings of the stellar-grade chefs are many superb little "sleepers" where you might prefer to be anyway, because here is where you will find the real hometowners tucking in their napkins.

Another way to economize is to live out of the main centers. It is true that rural living is cheaper, but it is *still* rural. Since more visitors travel to Europe to sightsee, museum-hop, shop, and dine (rather than simply to relax in the country), think twice before embracing this mode of cutting back. Consider your motives for the trip and then decide.

Most expensive as we go to press (subject to changes, of course) are Norway, Sweden, Finland, Denmark, Germany, and Switzerland. Surprisingly, once-cheap Italy is becoming one of the more costly nations. Belgium, Austria, Monaco, Luxembourg, and the Netherlands come next, followed by Britain and France (where today you receive unusually good value for money relative to some of the others mentioned above). Least expensive are Spain, Ireland, Greece, and Portugal; the last (with Madeira) being the best buy of all.

PASSPORTS They are valid for 10 years for persons 18 years or older and cost $35; for those under 18, it's $20 and valid for 5 years. In addition, there's a $7 fee for applicants who are required to apply in person. However, that sum is waived for applicants whose latest passport was issued within the past 12 years, who were 16 or over when it was issued, and who are able to submit that passport with their new application. If you meet these requirements, you are eligible to apply by mail and should obtain Form DSP-82, "Application for Passport by Mail," which may be sent to one of the passport agencies mentioned below. Applicants who can't qualify under the rules above must apply in person.

Have two identical photos (2″×2″ and snapped within the last 6 months) ready to adorn the document. These must have a plain white or off-white background. For your first passport, you must present in person a completed Form DSP-11, "Passport Application," at one of the agencies located in Boston, Chicago, Honolulu, Houston, Los Angeles, Miami, New Orleans, New York, Philadelphia, San Francisco, Seattle, Stamford, and Washington, DC, or at one of the several thousand federal or state courts or U.S. post offices that accept passport applications. Be sure you have proof you are a U.S. citizen (birth or naturalization certificate) as well as proof of identity (driver's license). Forms are available from any of those offices.

For those abroad, petitions for new passports may be made by mail in numerous countries; otherwise, you'll have to appear in person at the nearest American Embassy or Consulate. Your old, dog-eared, canceled friend will be returned as a souvenir when the new one is issued.

As a precaution against loss or theft, have two photocopies made of your passport identification page. Leave one at home and carry the other with you, but separate from your passport.

MEDICAL ADVICE Immunization isn't required for European travelers. Europe has good public health officials, fine doctors, and the latest drugs; many of the last appear on pharmacy shelves years before they are put up for sale in North America—even when they may be produced by U.S. manufacturers. (Europeans often test the new products quicker than the FDA.)

Though shots are not required in Europe, information on foreign immunization laws for countries farther afield can be obtained from the U.S. Public Health Service. Check your phone book under U.S. Government, Department of Health, Education and Welfare. Also helpful is an organization called International Association for Medical Assistance to Travellers. IAMAT (736 Center St., Lewiston, NY 14092) can provide the names of English-speaking doctors in many foreign nations. I have had occasion to meet and use a few of its colleagues and feel the service is worthwhile. If you are moving on to hotter lands than Europe, be sure to read IAMAT's information on malaria prevention, still a major health problem in some areas.

World traveler and student of this specialized area of medicine (hodoiporiatrics), Dr. David Corwin of New York, offers some tips on staying in shape. Naturally, everyone is cautious about the drinking water in questionable places; this should include the water for brushing your teeth and ice cubes. Raw vegetables and fruits also require attention if your stay is to be a short one. If you are making a longer visit, it might be better, according to the doctor, to go ahead and live as the locals do unless the area suffers from extreme pollution. If the area is warm avoid mayonnaise, which might have been left in the sun. Factory-bottled dressings (made with preservatives) are usually safer than fresh ones, which may invite bacteria if they are not properly protected. More people are staying away from slightly cooked meat, poultry, fish, and eggs (also dressings made of raw egg). Beer is drinkable almost everywhere, but wines are more suspect.

"*Turista*" is likely to lurk anywhere, so nonprescription Polymagma or Pepto-Bismol are useful health aids in liquid or tablet form. We are also hearing good reports about Hoffmann-La Roche's Bactrim tablet. Diarrhea can cause loss of salts and fluids, so Dr. Corwin suggests having sugar in hot tea; it apparently enhances the absorption of salt. Imodium (also in liquid or capsule forms) is relatively new, fast-acting, and seems to be effective in keeping people on the tourist trails and worry-free.

Motion sickness, states Dr. Corwin, has many combatants in tablet form, some of which produce drowsiness, so it may be a trade-off as to whether you would prefer to be alert or queasy. Meclizine (generic), Antivert, Dramamine, and Bonine taken anywhere from a half to one hour before the motion begins are often effective. At the onset of nausea, lozenges, suppositories, or injections of Phenergan, Compazine, or Tigan are indicated. CIBA's Transderm-V (scopolamine) is a novel approach to relief. It's a dime-size adhesive patch that can be worn behind the ear or elsewhere on the body; the skin absorbs protective chemicals for up to 3 days—an easy way to wear instead of swallow your medication.

AIDS? Well, Europe suffers from it too. The causes are the same as elsewhere in the world and the precautions, of course, should be the same as those employed in the USA.

For the **handicapped** traveler, the American Automobile Association (AAA) distributes a guide. Another organization, Society for the Advancement of Travel for the Handicapped, offers further aid; it is located at 26 Court St., Brooklyn, NY 11242, Tel. (718) 858–5483.

Ambulance service? Three companies specialize in airlifting disabled travelers back to Stateside medical centers. Since their programs are tailored to specific needs, write to them for details. HOME and NEAR cater more to individuals while SOS works chiefly with corporate accounts. Here's how you reach them: HOME, International Travelers Association, 1100 17th St. NW, Washington, DC 20036, Tel. (301) 652–3150; SOS Assistance, P.O. Box 11568, Philadelphia, PA, Tel. (215) 244–1500. If your normal insurance does not include this expensive phase of assistance (and most will pay only for land ambulances) it is worth considering separate coverage.

Special diet? A friendly Iowa reader who could eat only certain foods prepared in special ways had instructions written in detail for the language areas she was to visit; these were shown to waiters along her travel path and she never heard even the slightest growl from a stomach which traveled over 5000 miles of foreign terrain.

Medic Alert Foundation renders an invaluable nonprofit service to travelers who suffer from any hidden medical problem. It furnishes lifesaving emblems of 10-karat gold-filled, sterling silver, or stainless steel to be worn around the neck or wrist. Should the patient be unable to talk, medical personnel or law-enforcement officials are instantly informed of dangers inherent in standard treatment. The tag carries such warnings as "DIABETIC," "ALLERGIC TO PENICILLIN," "TAKING ANTICOAGULANTS," "WEARING CONTACT LENSES," "NECK BREATHER," or whatever difficulty. It also bears the telephone number of the Medic Alert headquarters in California to which any-one may call "collect" from anywhere in the world at any hour of day or night for additional file material about the individual case. The organization also fea-tures an electric unit worn around the neck or wrist that alerts a telephonic standby facility if the wearer suffers a medical crisis. For more information about this splendid organization (donations are tax deductible), write to Medic Alert Foundation International, Turlock, CA 95380–1009.

LUGGAGE Buying quality in luggage really pays off. If you are frail and traveling alone, you might require a suitcase with wheels. Poor ones slither across airport lobbies crashing into vitrines and fellow passengers. So pick a good one, not the tail-wags-dog model. We find the stand-up type with the wheels on the short end of the rectangle and a guiding handle on top to be the easiest to manage. The vertical position allows you to push it along at about elbow level. A small foldup cart could also be the answer. Fashion and chic are other considerations. You'll pay plenty for these, but generally the materials are excellent. (Thieves are more often drawn to the finest luggage rather than to ordinary cases.) If you travel by car and handle your own pieces, leather is lovely. If you use the airlines, forget it; it will soon be nicked to shreds. Tough, light, and handsome synthetic materials are now readily available. Soft sides usually risk torn or jammed zippers, bottle-breakage and excessive wrinkling, but they are light. Hard siders are usually heavy. Semihard require careful at-tention to the frames. Any way you look at it, it's a compromise.

Cameras present special problems. Their complexity, accessory packs, and sheer bulk can be daunting. A new generation of pocket-size photo equipment is designed in the "smart" sense: with auto-set light values, adjusted focus and distance, with pop-up flash for dim situations, setting speeds, automatic wind-ing, rewinding, and even turning themselves off when the shooting is over. Have a look at brands such as Nikon, Olympus, Minolta, Canon, and Vivitar for these new micro-wonders. They are marvels at space-saving as well as pho-tography.

MONEY At this writing it no longer pays, in most cases, to try to beat other local rates of exchange by outside bank purchases in countries where the cur-rency is strong. The European market nowadays simply is too fickle for safe speculation in sizable amounts.

Most major European airports have 24-hour banks where you can exchange dollars or traveler's checks for local currency. (Even so, you should swap the bulk of your bucks at midcity banks, where the rates are usually better. For motorists, banks at frontier points are notorious for giving bad rates.) Banks usually pay a bit more for traveler's checks than for bills, and whenever you're ready to buy anything in a store ask first if the merchant will give you a discount for them. *Once abroad, always cash your checks at a bank,* not in your hotel or in a restaurant or shop. The last three's rakeoffs can be rapacious.

A few foreign currencies (subject to change) are mutually "convertible." This means, quite simply, that in exchange for your American traveler's checks within these nations, you may draw any hard monies including U.S. or Cana-dian dollars. You may also buy traveler's checks valid in francs, marks, or others at foreign-exchange houses in the major cities of the U.S. or Canada, or at most U.S. international airports.

For ordinary needs, you should carry about $300 in cash (either in U.S. currency or its foreign equivalent) and the balance in (1) traveler's checks, (2) free-market foreign currencies, and (3) personal checks. Internationally recognized credit cards (American Express, MasterCard, Diners Club, Visa, etc.) have become almost "must" items in these days of volatile currency reforms; with these you usually receive the exchange rate of the day your purchase was made. I frequently find that merchants prefer to take cards other than American Express; many say they have to pay a higher charge to Amexco than to other promoters of plastic money. Some claim they no longer accept Amexco, but if you point to the shield on their front door they will relent—often reluctantly—and write up your credit slip.

CUSTOMS OFFICIALS   If you're lucky, you could sail through your entire tour through the "Nothing to Declare" gates without one bag being checked. The speed of your clearance usually depends upon the inspector's state of digestion. Here are some helpful hints:

Be affable and cooperative, but don't be overly conversational. Their sole interest is to get rid of you; if you keep your mouth shut, things will move twice as fast.

Hold your passport casually in hand—don't flaunt it!—so that the inspector can identify you. (This might sound absurd, but sometimes it's surprisingly helpful.) And speak English solely, *not* a foreign language.

Liquor in your luggage: Break the seals before you get to Customs. In some lands (British Isles excepted) this may get around the import duty. Some countries forbid more than one. If you have an extra, stick it in the pocket of the topcoat or raincoat that hangs "carelessly" over your arm.

The Common Market nations permit 300 cigarettes, 1½ liters of hard liquor (2 "fifth" bottles should pass), 3 liters (¾-gallon) of wine, 1⅓ lbs. of coffee, and ¼ lb. of tea.

SHOPPING ABROAD   Today's duty-free allowance is $400 in *retail* value. (The next $1000 in value is taxable at only 10%.) These goods must accompany you personally on your return. Your free importation of wines or booze is 1 quart per person 21 years or over—a monument to the enormous power of the U.S. liquor lobby in Washington. Most states admit more than a quart if a modest duty is paid on the overage; others, such as California, confiscate all extra spirits.

Regarding other regulations, here are some key facts and suggestions: (1) Go easy on Coronas and champagne because 100 cigars and one quart per person are all you may import without fee (*foreign-made* cigarettes are limited to one carton). With certain limitations, booze may be "shipped to follow." (2) Foreign fruits, meats, plants, and vegetables might carry pests that could destroy millions of dollars in livestock, food, forests, or ornamentals; virtually all are confiscated. Most foreign-made eatables are banned unless all ingredients are printed on the label. (3) Your exemptions may include alterations or repairs on anything you originally took abroad; if your car throws a piston or your watch gets a dunking en route, charge off the cost of making them tick again. (4) Antiques 100 years old (exceptions: rugs and carpets made after 1700) are unrestricted. They include furniture, hardware, brass, bronze, marble, terra cotta, porcelain, chinaware, and "any object considered to have artistic value." Be sure to bring certificates of verification, if available. (5) Original works of art (*not* copies)—paintings, drawings, and sculptures of any age—and stamps are duty-free. So are books, prints, lithographs, and maps over 20 years old. (6) Gifts costing less than $50 may be mailed from abroad on a duty-free basis, with no effect on your exemptions. Alcohol, tobacco, and perfume are ineligible. No one person may receive more than one gift in one day; plainly mark the package "Gift—Value Under $50." (7) Certain trademarked articles—especially watches, perfumes, optical goods, musical instruments—require written permission of the foreign manufacturer or U.S. distributor before they may be cleared intact. (Accordions are especially hairy.) A few well-known manufacturers of cosmetics and beauty products are so stingy that nothing may be imported without their documentary consent. Most companies, however, allow bona fide tourists to bring back at least one unit as a souvenir. The way around it? Remove or obliterate the trademark. (8) If you sell some articles within 3 years after importation on a duty-free basis, you'll be fined double the normal quotation. But you *are* permitted to sell anything that was initially purchased for your personal or household use. Original intent is the key factor. (9) Everything in your baggage must be for your personal use or the use of your immediate family, or for gifts; samples and other merchandise will be taxed. (10) Finally, egret feathers, ammunition, narcotics, and various other commodities are contraband.

Be especially careful of items made from the skins of certain types of crocodile, spotted cat, or other endangered species. The list of God's creatures which are rapidly vanishing from our planet is too lengthy (and stretching day by day) to include here for purposes of up-to-the-minute accuracy. If you're considering this type of purchase, ask U.S. Customs before departure for a summary of those species; critters dispatched in a brutal fashion are also under protection and thus these pelts too can be seized by officials. Arrests for violations are not unknown; moreover, ignorance of the law is, as usual, no excuse.

On the European side, cigarettes are usually what officials look for first— if they look at all. Above the prescribed number, there's a fat duty to be paid. In some cases the excess will be confiscated, or (in England) the levy must be paid on the entire supply. Most wink at a reasonable excess. They *never* wink, however, at drugs, so these should never be transported across any frontier. Punishment for drug possession or use can be far in excess of U.S. norms.

If you have 3 or 4 parcels, your inquisitor has been trained to inspect the one wrapped with the greatest care. Likewise, if there is a choice between a bag and an independent package or case, he will usually examine the latter.

If the duty is too high, or if you're carrying a taxable item to a 2nd or 3rd country, the Customs will hold it in escrow at the border for your return, without charge—and it's usually safe. One or 2 lands won't do this.

U.S. CONSULAR SERVICES ABROAD If you should encounter serious trouble on your trip—anything from a lost passport to an arrest to death of a companion to a spectrum of other deep crises—communicate *immediately* with the nearest American consular office. They are, however, proscribed from extending loans to travelers in financial distress. Although they will give restricted aid in a dispute that could lead to legal or police action, furnish a list of reputable local lawyers, and try to prevent discrimination under foreign law, regulations prohibit them from participating on the *direct* level. If a citizen is arrested, they will visit him or her in detention, notify relatives and friends, provide a roster of attorneys, and attempt to obtain relief if conditions are inhumane or unhealthy. Here are some of their other duties: (1) Assistance in finding appropriate medical services, including English-speaking physicians. (2) Guidance on how to inform the local police about stolen funds or on how to inform the issuing authorities about missing traveler's checks. (3) The full extension of notary facilities. (4) Help in locating missing Americans. (5) Protection of U.S. voyagers and residents during civil unrest or in natural disasters.

It may be useful to leave behind at home the following direct Washington telephone numbers of the office of Special Consular Services:

- To find missing wanderers about whom there is special concern or to transmit emergency messages: (202) 647–5225.
- To transmit funds to foreign soil when commercial banking facilities are unavailable or to arrange medical evacuation: (202) 632–9706 or (202) 632–3529.
- For questions about members of your clan who have been arrested and how to get money to them: (202) 632–8089 or (202) 632–7823.
- For help when an American dies abroad: (202) 632–1423 or (202) 632–2172.
- For civil judicial inquiries and assistance: (202) 632–2400.
- Night and weekend emergency number for all of the above: (202) 655–4000. Ask for the Duty Officer.

The Overseas Citizens Services (202/632–5225) is a general helpmate for troubled travelers.

Don't ask these officials to do the work of travel agencies, information bureaus, or banks, search for missing luggage, settle disputes with hotel managers or shopkeepers, help get work permits, or find jobs.

TIPPING   Wherever you are and whatever you do, always carry a pocketful of assorted small change. Cash a large bill (or 2) each day before setting forth; by always having the *exact* tip on hand, the time and money you'll save will be phenomenal. In each country chapter we have described the specific tipping customs.

METRIC MEASUREMENT   The metric system used in every European country (usually dual systems in the U.K. and Ireland) is still confusing.

Here are a few translations. Conquer these 5 and you'll get along fine:

A kilometer (pronounced kill-OM-eter by the "mile"-minded British and Irish and KILL-o-meter by the continentals) is roughly 6/10 of a mile. Multiply by 6, knock off 1 decimal point, and you've got it in miles.

A kilo or kilogram (potatoes and onions) is 2.2 pounds.

A meter (dress material) and a liter (gasoline, beer) are both roughly 11/

10ths—one of a yard, the other of a quart. There are about 2½ centimeters to 1 inch.

A gram (airmail letters) is very tiny. There are about 28 to the ounce.

Above are some conversions that might come in handy. Since sizes are not standardized, this is a fairly rough yardstick. Try on the items whenever possible.

APPROXIMATE CLOTHING SIZES
(American-Continental)

Women's Clothing

American	6	8	10	12	14	16
Continental:						
France	36	38	40	42	44	46
Italy	38	40	42	44	46	48
Rest of Europe	34	36	38	40	42	44

Women's Shoes

American	4	5	6	7	8	9
Continental	35	36	37	38	39	40

Men's Sweaters

American	S	M	L	XL
Continental	48	50	52	54

Men's Shoes

American	8	8½	9½	10½	11½
Continental	41	42	43	44	45

APPROXIMATE CLOTHING SIZES
(American-British)

Women's Clothing

American	8	10	12	14	16
British	10	12	14	16	18

Women's Shoes

American	4	5	6	7	8	9
British	2½	3½	4½	5½	6½	7½

Men's Sweaters

American	S	M	L	XL
British	38	40	42	44

Men's Shoes

American	8	8½	9	9½	10	10½	11	11½	12	13
British	7	7½	8	8½	9	9½	10	10½	11	12

Last, here's a refresher on how to change Centigrade temperatures into Fahrenheit. The classic method is to take 9/5ths of the *Centigrade* temperature (the reading on European thermometers) and add 32. A much easier way is to double the Centigrade reading, deduct 10%, and add the same 32. Example: Let's imagine that the mercury says 15°. Twice 15 is 30, and 10% of 30 is 3. Taking 3 from 30 leaves 27. Add 32 to 27, and you'll have the Yankee version of 59°. In print it looks complicated—but in practice it's so simple that almost any traveler can do it in his head. Try it and see!

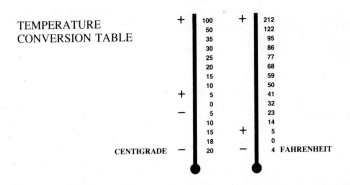

TEMPERATURE CONVERSION TABLE

CENTIGRADE	FAHRENHEIT
+ 100	+ 212
50	122
35	95
30	86
25	77
20	68
15	59
10	50
+ 5	41
0	32
− 5	23
10	14
15	+ 5
18	0
− 20	− 4

TRAINS AND PASSES **Eurailpass** ("Your-rail-pass") and **Eurail Youthpass** are 2 of the most rewarding bargains on that continent today. Any *resident* of North, Central, or South America may roam wherever and whenever desired on any continental train (not British; they have a separate Thrift Rail Plan) without further payment except for routine sleeper or *couchette* supplements. This more luxurious plan than its alternate for young people offers 15 days of unlimited *first class* travel for $390, 21 days for $498, 1 month for $616, 2 months for $840, or 3 months for $1042. Children under 12 are charged half-fare; those under 4 ride free. Including Trans-Europ Expresses (TEE) and all other extra-fare runs, it is valid on the national railways and many private trains, steamers, and ferry crossings in the following 16 nations: Austria, Belgium, Denmark, Finland, France, Germany (Federal Republic), Greece, Holland, Ireland, Italy, Luxembourg, Norway, Portugal, Spain, Sweden, and Switzerland, as well as on sea crossings that link Ireland into the continental system. (BritRail includes English Channel crossings.) You may choose its continuous usage period during 6 months following its purchase. Anyone under 26 (the limitation to students has been dropped) may opt for the **Eurail Youthpass,** which opens 1 month of unlimited roving in all of the same carriers in *second class* for a flat $425, or $560 for 2 months. Among its other alluring financial benefits is substantial savings on hotel bills by dozing sitting up, spending these nights in an inexpensive *couchette,* or, for slightly more, taking a tourist sleeper. Neither of these arrangements includes reservation fees (strongly urged always and compulsory for berths), meals, refreshments, nor with the latter, fees and supplements required to board certain trains. Both cards are personal and nontransferable, with the penalty of confiscation if another bearer is caught showing them. Your passport must always be produced when requested by conductors, gatemen, and other authorized personnel. Neither is refundable if lost or stolen. If you are traveling off season (Oct. 1–March 31), ask about the **Saverpass** ($240), which knocks off about 25% of the 15-day rate and applies only to couples or larger groups. There's also a **Flexipass,** $230 for any 5-day use over a 15-day span, $398 for any 9-day use over a 21-day span, and $498 for any 14-day use over a 30-day span.

Your Eurailpass, incidentally, is becoming increasingly valuable for **air-port-to-downtown rail connections.** Barcelona, Brussels, Dusseldorf, Frankfurt, Paris, Vienna, Amsterdam, Rome and Zurich are now on rails. If you have this card, why pay $30-or-so extra for taxi fare?

NOTE · · · *You must buy it before heading for Europe, because it is not sold abroad. To secure confirmed reservations booked through U.S. agencies is tricky unless application is made long in advance.* For further inquiries, see your travel agent or write to Eurailpass, P.O. Box 325, Old Greenwich, CT 06870-03255.

Intercity and **EuroCity** trains are gradually replacing the Trans-Europe-Express (TEE) network, which was more limited in scope. Simultaneously, second class is being upgraded; both first and second are being equalized in terms of air-conditioning, modern styling, and other basics. (The main difference today is in the size and comfort of the seats.) If your destination is within 250 miles, your door-to-door travel time will probably be less than if you bid for airline travel—and at nearly ¼ the cost! Moreover, in winter or foggy periods, rail is far more reliable; punctuality is assured. Average running speed is about 80 mph; as examples of their high-stepping gait, Paris-Brussels is only 2 hours, 22 minutes (3½ hrs. by air *et al.* from midtown-to-midtown), and Paris-Zurich is only 6 hours. Dining facilities are always on hand; frontier formalities have been streamlined to a minimum.

On all other trains abroad make sure *first* that there's a diner. Also check the times and reserve your place for the seating you prefer (see below). Advance knowledge can also give you time to improvise your own picnic—much better than the station platform vendors' snacks.

When you leave your seat for a meal, put some bulky possession (your spouse, for example?) on the cushion. Otherwise, the first incoming passenger is liable to take over, leaving you the worst place and lousiest view.

Dining cars? Here's the procedure: Usually there are 2 (sometimes 3) separate servings spanning more than 2 hours overall. First the steward will come to your compartment, learn your time preference, and give you a table-booking slip which must be returned when he greets you in his own domain. The closer your car is to the diner, the better your chance for getting the sitting that you wish. Although a few meager a la carte items are available (some trains offer cheese or coldcuts platters), probably 98% of the customers consume the standard, fixed meal at the standard, fixed price (usually $9 to $12 with some of the gourmet attractions in France topping out at over $65). Course after course is served on a 1-shot, universal basis; everybody eats the soup, the veal, the salad, and the fruit from the same service trays. When the whole car has finished, the cashier presents the check. Almost nobody tips.

Sleeping cars? The European railways offer 3 first-class and 2 second-class categories. First class consists of regular 1-berth or 2-berth accommodations, plus "Specials" for shorter runs (20 small single compartments per car). Second class offers the T-2 berthing with 18 double-decked twin compartments per car; these are gradually supplementing the older 3-bunk units. Finally, there's the second-class *couchette*—a minimum-price 6-seat (or 6-berth) compartment in which passengers may lie down without undressing. These are for the hardy.

Check the date of expiration of your round-trip ticket. On short rides in some countries they expire within 24 hours.

Orient-Express This is one of the greatest steps backward in recent generations—a delight in every way to recapture on wheels the nostalgia of the 1920s. The lifestyle recreated on the journey between Venice and London or Vienna and London (you can join or exit at other termini) is a moment shared with the Emperor of Austria, King Edward the VII, Menalik II, and other luminaries of that graceful era of elegance. With professional attention to cuisine, wines, presentation, and service, it is probable that today's reincarnation excels that of the original. Exquisite devotion to restoration and comfort is evidenced in every polished surface. To plan the exact adventure that appeals to you, check the myriad details with your travel agent or be in touch directly with Orient-Express, Tel. (800) 524–2420. Here has got to be one of the most beguiling and sybaritic anachronisms of today's Europe.

AUTOS If you're planning to ship your car across the Atlantic—a punishingly expensive exercise since auto rental agencies abound overseas—2 standard documents are recommended, apart from your vehicle registration, of course: (1) a valid U.S. driver's license, and (2) an International Driving Permit (in nine languages, no longer mandatory in all European countries but still useful for remote motoring) issued through the AAA. If the rental agency does not ask to see the latter (and usually it won't) that does not necessarily mean that a patrolman also will wink at your sin. The countries where an IDP is required (since a U.S. driver's license is not recognized) are: Bulgaria, Czechoslovakia, Greece, Hungary, Spain, and the USSR. Drivers in Austria, Germany, and Italy must provide "approved" translation (a function of the IDP). You should buy the AAA's one-dollar USA sticker, indicating the car is of North American registry. The AAA also can put you in the picture concerning the required insurance for driving abroad (see below) as well as with a policy for medical, legal, and other assistance features.

Third Party Insurance (Public Liability and Property Damage often called the "Green Card" or the equivalent in the local language) is compulsory throughout Europe. *Be sure to get complete coverage*—fire, theft, damage to yourself, the works—*wherever you go on the Continent*. If there's an accident, no matter how trivial, you'll be up to your neck in gendarmes, red tape, and A.D. 1066 legal procedures—and it's the devil to prove that the other fellow is wrong when you have to shout him down in a strange language.

If there isn't an AAA office nearby, write to **AAA Insurance Services, 1000 AAA Drive, Heathrow, FL 32746–5063.** The Foreign Motoring Insurance Section here is normally very patient and helpful. Your U.S. membership can be extremely valuable abroad because of the reciprocal agreements it has made with its foreign counterparts. When you show your card it is an open sesame to all of the benefits provided by various European clubs.

Purchase If you plan to buy an auto in Europe for shipment home or for eventual resale to the original foreign dealer on the guaranteed repurchase plan, make sure that your car meets American specifications (California is especially strict) for glass, safety features, emission standards, muffler, and headlights; later conversion can be costly.

With the **guaranteed repurchase** scheme, the agency buys back the vehicle at the termination of your journey, at a price mutually agreed upon in advance. Where the horse trading comes in, of course, is on the repurchase part of any agreement—and that's just routine business.

NOTE · · · With minor exceptions, road signs are standard. There are 3 basic categories: (1) triangular, to indicate danger (intersection, railway crossing, slippery road, etc.), (2) circular, to lay down prohibitions (road closed, 1-way street, no passing, etc.), (3) rectangular, to provide information (garage ahead, telephone ahead, first-aid station ahead, etc.).

Gasoline rings up at twice or triple the U.S. price—and, thank goodness, you can usually purchase it with major credit cards along important national routes. In most countries a top speed limit of 110 to 130 kilometers per hour (kph) is imposed for freeway traffic with 90 kph set for secondary highway runs, and 50 to 60 kph pegged for suburban cruising. Since the speed limits are not uniform, be sure to watch carefully or to ask at each frontier concerning that nation's rules.

Left-hand traffic? Only in Great Britain and Ireland. In all other countries you'll drive as you do at home. (At least that's their hope!)

In most European countries those in the front seats are required to buckle their safety harnesses; in many, this means only for highway driving, but a few sticklers (Switzerland, for example) enforce the edict full-time and on Sundays—front seats *and* back!

OTHER LIFESTYLES Not everyone plunks his or her suitcase down in a hotel while abroad. In our various national chapters programs are described that will expand your economy while broadening your experience. Excellent **parador** and **pousada** systems comprise networks of inns in Spain and Portugal. France has its **Federation Nationale des Agents Immobiliers,** where you can find accommodation in a chalet or a villa, and also the **Gite de France,** which turns on hospitality in farmhouses. England has its **Home From Home** collection of rectories, manses, and historic estates where you can become a part of the family for astonishingly low rates. A highly reliable London agency can find you a splendid villa with pool and private estate in Mallorca, Tuscany, Greek Isles, Turkey, Southern France, or other sunspots of Europe. Write to Richard Cookson at **C-V Travel,** 43 Cadogan St., Chelsea, London SW 32PR (Tel. 01–5890132 for 24-hour service). Germany has its **Gast im Schloss** assemblage for those who prefer to hobnob in castles. There is the superb **Relais et Chateaux** organization spotlighting intimate deluxe havens all over Europe and the U.K. Greece is guaranteeing that you can vacation in a "traditional settlement" that has not been spoiled by rampant tourism.

You can also do your thing on water. **Barge trips** through the Low Countries or through Burgundy, or even a 3-hour boat trip between Rudesheim and Coblenz can provide new perspectives of Old World scenery. **Floating Through Europe** (271 Madison Ave., NY, NY 10016, Tel: 212–685–5600) has launched a splendid fleet of comfortable hotels that roam for a week along the Thames, pause at exceptional restaurants for onshore dining, and provide nutrition for soul and body while cruising through the loveliness of England. There are ambles along continental canals too—and the prices are river-bottom low when compared with ordinary chartering rates in such high-cost regions. For details and tempting brochures write directly to Jennifer Ogilvie at the above address. Another purveyor of waterborne frolic is **Continental Waterways** (127 Albert Bridge Rd. London, S.W. 11). Their specialty is British canal cruising.

Want to go **ballooning** over French wine country, land at a chateau, dine on pate and champagne in a Gallic meadow? The one to write is The Bombard Society (6727 Curran St., McLean, VA 22101). I found the service at the Loire Valley site very poor, indeed, but if you phone often enough or pre-arrange your flight perhaps you'll have better luck than I did.

ODD FACTS—SOME IMPORTANT! **Classification** The North American term "first class" becomes "deluxe" abroad; "first class" is American "second class." Some hotels below the deluxe category do not furnish soap to guests— not poverty or stinginess, but a difference of customs. Try to have your own supply. Also, if you use a washcloth, bring your own. Most European hotels never have them.

Fire Safety Wherever you overnight, it's wise to be fire-conscious about your accommodations. In too many of the less-expensive places, you'll find open stairwells, inflammable furnishings, no fire escapes, or other potential hazards. In these. as a standard practice and small precaution which just might save your life, analyze in advance your possible escape route. If there is none, and if the building should look dangerous, accept only a lower-floor room.

Registration When you register in most European hotels you'll be given a form asking about you, where you've been and where you're going next. *Memorize the number and date of issue of your passport for just such occasions.* In some rural inns this document will be held overnight at the desk for registration with the local police. If so, don't forget to pick it up when you check out!

Dates are written differently in Europe: Our form of 6/30/92, for example, becomes 30/6/92.

Be sure to indicate your date of arrival *and* departure when you apply for accommodations abroad. Should you omit the latter, a little man in a large claw-hammer coat might step up, smile apologetically, and bounce you out into the cold, cruel world—routine European practice.

Concierge Practically every European hotel has one; in the U.K. and Ireland he is called the hall porter. He is the head contact man with the clients— boss of the bellhops, mail clerks, key clerks, nearly everybody on the street-floor service staff except the dining-room-and-bar help. He wears a pair of gold crossed keys ("Clefs d'Or") on his lapels—and he's not to be confused with the striped-pants, pearl-stickpin people at the reception counter in the lobby. Use him for everything—stamps, outside errands, complaints, reservations for trains, theaters, or restaurants, and, most important of all, questions and advice about what's what in the city. You are expected to tip him when you check out—a minimum of $1.50 per day per couple in deluxe or first-class houses, and from 50¢ to $1 per day in lesser ones. This tip is pooled for the whole desk (2 to 10 individuals who have served you). Incidentally, never tip the lofty reception gents.

Pension Plans A number of continental hostelries (especially in resorts) still offer the Pension Plan, which quotes room and board at one flat daily or weekly rate. It generally breaks down into 3 choices: full pension (room and all meals), demipension (room and 2 meals), and bed-and-breakfast. Some inn-keepers prefer that you state your choice on registration; some hotels such as those at beaches or ski stations require that you take full pension only. *Ask what is included and what is not included, as soon as you check in*—or you might be paying twice for your lunch or dinner, without being aware of it until they give you the bill.

Watch out for "supplements"—those devilish little sneak-charges. If you're operating under one of the pension plans, for example, most hotels give you the traditional continental breakfast as part of the contract—coffee or tea, toast, jam, butter. But when the waiter smiles and asks if Madame and Monsieur would like some fruit, some cereal, an egg perhaps?—these are on *your* bill, not the hotel's. (I just shelled out $16 for two glasses of fresh orange juice I thought were a part of a French breakfast offering.) Be sure to ask, too, if the breakfast is included in your bill. Today, many hoteliers are not making this clear; they invite you to a buffet table and when you check out, you find you've been lumbered with an additional $30 for two. The same croissant and coffee at the next-door cafe would have totaled $5 or so per couple. When you sit down to dine, they'll allow you only the dishes-of-the-day—a rigid list—and if you order *anything* extra, that's socked onto your account, too. If you don't watch these supplements carefully, they can absolutely murder any carefully planned budget.

Many hotel rooms have locks that demand 2 turns of the key instead of one. These must be twisted until both tumblers snap into place (easily audible); if only one is engaged, you have only 50% security against thieves. Some have electronically coded cards which are valid only for the length of your stay. Also it automatically advises the desk when you are in your room.

Foreign Table Etiquette (1) The man or the host (if it is a party) always leads the way to the table, following the Maitre and followed by his guest or guests. (2) The fish knife and fish fork are easily recognizable by their distinctive shapes. The former resembles a large butter knife, and the latter has a broad cutting edge on one tine. (3) When you're faced with a multiplicity of knives and forks, always reach for the outside ones, farthest away from the plate. (4) The dessert implements are placed *above* the plate—not to the sides. (5) The clamplike instrument sometimes presented with asparagus first captures the stalk and is then lifted directly to the mouth. (6) The special pincers for snails are employed to hold the shell firmly while forking out the beastie with the other hand. (7) You might be asked if you prefer your oysters to be served "without beard." The "beard" is the dark circumference surrounding the nugget; most North Americans prefer it "with beard." (8) The toothpick is used with abandon abroad. The more discreet diner at least has the grace to manipulate it with his napkin as a screen. When 2 people at the same table are engaged in this comic prophylaxis, it resembles the childhood game of peekaboo. (9) European hand-eating is just about confined to bread. Continentals almost always use knives and forks.

Here's an oddity of language, too: Corn (European) is the name for wheat (American), while corn (American) becomes maize abroad. Most restaurants abroad levy a special price for the bread you eat and don't serve drinking water unless specifically requested. At some places (normally either the costliest or cheapest ones) you'll also pay extra for the tablecloth and napkins—the origin of "cover charge."

Foreign Theater Etiquette Which way do you face when you try to slither unobtrusively into your center-of-the-row seats? Europeans consider it rude for the latecomer to force them to face *your* proscenium. They prefer the navel-to-eyeball confrontation. So go in facing the rear of the theater and the citizenry in your row.

Shoeshine Before retiring for the night, ask if it is customary in that particular hostelry to place shoes at your threshold in the hall. (This custom, which used to be universal, is now extinct in Scandinavia and is fast vanishing everywhere else.) If the answer is affirmative, they'll shine 'em free—part of the hotel-service charge (but you must add a small tip for the floor attendant when you leave).

Hotel Postage When you turn over your correspondence to the concierge's lads with instructions that it be airmailed, stand right there until they put on the stamps. Otherwise it might arrive by ordinary postage, with the desk people pocketing the difference. Always stamp postcards yourself, because too many go into the wastebasket.

Film While color film is now available even in most small villages, supplies are often spotty during the summer rush. The ultrahigh-speed types usually are available in big cities only. Take a few rolls of your own as insurance, especially if you are not going to be at any one stop long enough to have European-purchased film processed in Europe. (American developing of foreign negatives often gives blurry results due to differences in chemicals.) Strangely, black-and-white film is becoming more rare. It might be wiser to hand-carry all of your film (stills or even cinema types), since luggage x-raying equipment at international airports can alter the balance of unexposed *and* exposed keepsakes. Carry-on baggage also is subject to radiation damage, so if you see such a device coming up, ask the attendant to physically inspect your cameras and film supplies. For skeptics, keen amateurs, and professionals, lead-laminated pouches by a company called Film Shield are available through some photo-equipment dealers.

Long-Distance Telephone Except as specified below, *never make any international or transatlantic calls from your hotel, because you'll pay a surcharge of up to 300% if you do.* For decades it has been common and disgraceful tradition in virtually every hostelry abroad to tack its own "service fee" onto your bill for the casual, simple, normal use of its operator and the instrument. When checkout time comes, travelers are aghast to find that the $8.80 chat with the family in Connecticut has cost them $35.20 or that the $21.55 business talk with their Chicago partner has hooked them for $86.20. But there are methods for avoiding such heavy billings. AT&T pioneered **Teleplan,** a program whereby participating hotels agree to limit surcharges to one U.S. dollar or its equivalent for all USADIRECT and AT&T Card calls. The list of hotels and hotel chains offering AT&T Teleplan is constantly growing and changing. Current Teleplan participants include all Inter-Europe Hotels, the Irish Hotel Federation, the Ledra Hotel of Cyprus, and all Holiday Inn Asia/Pacific hotels. Another method for minimizing hotel surcharges and for cutting calling expenses is USADIRECT.

AT&T introduced USADIRECT service to Europe in order to provide U.S. travelers with an inexpensive, fast, and easy way to call home from overseas. With USADIRECT you just dial an access number from any phone in the country to reach an AT&T operator in the U.S. who completes your call. The USADIRECT access numbers are usually toll-free or, in some countries, may be charged as local calls. Just charge your calls to an AT&T Card or call collect. The USADIRECT access numbers for Europe include Belgium (11–0010), Denmark (0430–0010), Finland (9800–100–10), France (19–0011), Germany (0130–0010), Netherlands (06–022–9111), Norway (050–12–011), Sweden (020–795–611), and the United Kingdom (0800–89–0011). What to do if USADIRECT service or Teleplan is not available? Phone your party in the U.S. and quickly ask that they call you back. (Since calls are charged on a time basis, even a high surcharge is bearable when the call is for less than a minute.) A second method is to use an AT&T Card so that the charges are billed to your U.S. number at the American rate (even if the call emanated from Europe). A third way is to phone from a local telephone office where the charges are at the official rate only. With USADIRECT service and Teleplan or if you "shop" wisely and knowingly before you call, you could save a bundle on what you spend to keep in touch with the folks back home.

For more information on international calling while you're in the U.S., dial 1–800–874–4000.

AIR TRAVEL

SCHEDULED FARES Nobody needs guidance to buy standard fare tickets. APEX reduces that ridiculous astronomic sum somewhat, but as the initials stand for "advance purchase," you must know well ahead of departure when you want to go, pay for your passage in full, and stick rigidly to your flight plan. If you can take off on short notice, one of the best fly-buys of all will remain the standby rate for scheduled services. But each season fewer carriers offer these last-minute bargains.

Domestically, in order to link up with airports that service foreign destinations, low fares sometimes are offered under names such as Super Saver, Super Coach, Twosome, Liberty, Super Grouper and the like. A later trend (but not a cheaper one) is the urge to merge, which domestic services are realizing with foreign carriers. The alliances produce, more or less, continuous handling by one company from departure point to destination. There is a certain convenience in this, but I doubt if it will result in substantially lower prices unless the carriers are in the midst of an air-fare war. It will take a few seasons of use to find out.

Some airline reservation clerks can be louts by not offering all the options for connecting flights. In spite of today's more regulated "deregulation" (or possibly because of it) their computers are "fixed" to favor certain routes, dates, and similar details so that you may feel you are forced to book with that primary carrier. If you have a good agent and insist on knowing all of the possibilities you can significantly enhance your travel program.

Internationally, cut-rate passage between London and New York can sometimes be picked up for as little as $275 one way or $375 between Great Britain and Los Angeles. (Eastbound passage—that is, going to Europe—is about 35% higher.) If there's a price war (usually off season or during times of international crisis), these figures might decline. I've seen bucketshop (also called consolidator) notices for transoceanic or transcontinental flights for as low as $102! It's also a bit cheaper to fly on weekdays than on weekends. Under the APEX plan the ticket must be purchased 21 days before departure and the passenger must spend from 7 to 180 days abroad—and *you* specify the flight and dates. Standard excursion out-lays require 14 to 60 days at your destination. An APEX link between NY and London ranges between $479 and $749 roundtrip (seasonal variations); with Los Angeles as your starting point, it will cost between $665 and $865. Some carriers are now trying to cut your overall vacation expenses through "independent packaging." The air ticket remains unchanged but they can realize savings for you in hotels (up to 50% off), car rentals, and other ground arrangements.

My opinions on European airlines that fly the Atlantic as well as cover the home ground and other world destinations will be found under the respective national chapters in the "Transportation" subheadings. You'll also find helpful tips on getting to and from the airports of the gateway cities. If you opt for an American carrier, **TWA** and **Pan Am** are (at this writing) up in the air, so to speak, about routes and even about their futures. If they continue to operate as they did for many decades, both offer excellent service and fine interconnections. Pan Am has boosted transoceanic capacity substantially over the past two years but it is likely that by the time you read this it will have sold off much of its transoceanic network. **Delta** is noteworthy for its smooth ground and air operation. Now it not only calls on 156 American cities, but it wings into London, Amsterdam, Hamburg, Frankfurt, Paris, Stuttgart, Munich, Dublin, and Shannon. It features an alliance with Swissair and Singapore Airlines, which can be one of the greatest bonuses of flying Delta internationally. Delta has 10 other European landing requests pending, so ask before you start to travel if it offers one-line service to your destination. **American** impressed me with its Paris linkage between North America and the Middle East, but it will be more useful to you to know its European termini: London, Gatwick, Manchester, Paris (Orly), Frankfurt, Munich, Dusseldorf, Geneva, and Zurich; Madrid-Dallas also can be practical as will be its European link from Raleigh/Durham. **Air Canada** has a splendid northern network connecting from Saskatoon or Moose Jaw to a host of European capitals. **Northwest** is beavering away at establishing a European network. Their flights call on Amsterdam, Copenhagen, Frankfurt, Glasgow, London, Shannon, and Stockholm. Travelers seem to like its renewed spirit.

For years industry executives have juggled terminology relating to the fare structures. The public relations hotshots have injected additional legerdemain into the top hat by pulling out such rabbits as "Club class" (better meals than "Economy" but only rarely with larger size seats), "Business class" (cheaper than first class), and other slick nomenclature (*eg.* Preference, Galaxy, Super Executive, Gold) that chiefly refers to where the air-hostess hangs a gauze curtain between the high-priced customer and the bargain seeker. Some hint (but can't promise) that if bookings are light, you'll get an empty seat on either side of you, but these factors are largely left to the whims of traffic, world economy, or even the weather on the day of takeoff. In this specialized field, I think SAS and KLM do the best jobs of living up to (and beyond) their promises. TWA's Business Lounger provides generous space on transatlantic 747 crossings. As for first class within Europe, it's a *rara avis* now being offered only by Swissair, Lufthansa, and Iberia. The Swiss and Germans do it a lot better than the Spanish, in my view.

CHARTERS Here too the skies are rumbling with innovations. In fact, today it is becoming more and more difficult to distinguish between a charter and a standard fare. Airlines—regular scheduled ones too—may now sell individual charter tickets directly to the public rather than having to go through middlemen; hence, a whole new marketing approach has been formed.

Discounts are appearing for every imaginable category: preferential dates of departure, children, families, one-way travel, where you sit in the airplane, the color of your eyes, or the flatness of your feet. There are still charters that incorporate your hotel, a car rental or other goodies. These, of course, will vary with the quality and character of the holiday you desire.

Space doesn't permit us here to spell out in further detail the many options that are available, but the chock-filled *How to Fly for Less* is a splendid compendium assembled masterfully by travel expert Jens Jurgen. Write to him at P.O. Box 105, Kings Park, NY 11754. Another excellent source (this one free) is *A Question of Class,* issued by Hogg Robinson Travel (71 Kingsway, London).

SUPERSONIC CONCORDE Though necessarily expensive and not designed to provide the same wide-angle comforts you'll find aboard larger aircraft, the benefits of alighting absolutely fresh at your destination and in half the time expended on subsonic jets are puissant, joyful, and incontestable.

Strictly speaking, the Concorde is selling speed. Every erg is expended on terra firma to shave milliseconds off check-in time, baggage handling, customs, processing, and boarding. These Air France and British Airways SSTs have become so ultra-efficient and so smoothly coordinated, I'd wager that no chief of state could be transferred from throne room to gangway with greater swiftness than that accorded any ordinary ticketholder darting from midcity to tarmac. V-V-VIP lounges are available, where friends or clients may enter—and become appropriately impressed; there are phones, seas of beverages, magazines, and smiles of welcome; bulky coats are hung on racks and loaded neatly into cabin stowage; there's a special tax-rebate desk for travelers who have made purchases abroad; and for last-minute dashers, a standby rate has been initiated for any latecomers who are lucky enough to find an empty seat. For the hurry-up voyager, in other words, all systems are "go."

BAGGAGE IATA rules allow first-class passengers on flights of U.S. origin 2 free bags, but the length, width, and height of each bag must total no more than 62 inches. Business-class is usually the same. Economy-class travelers are permitted 2 bags, one with dimensions that total no more than 62 inches, and both bags totaling a maximum of 106 inches. From some airports you may carry aboard as many pieces of hand luggage as you like as long as their combined lengths, widths, and heights do not exceed 45 inches. (Tighter security restrictions today, however, often limit this to only one on-board item per person.) Beyond this you are charged by the piece according to a scale of flat amounts determined by the distance you are flying.

LOST BAGGAGE About 1% of the world's personal cargo (15 million pieces) will be misplaced this year. Approximately 90% of that luggage is recovered by the owner within 24 hours of loss. While airlines permit 7 days for notification, you should report your misfortune while you are still at the airport. If you are with a tour, then collar your group leader as soon as you are aware that your bundle has not followed you to your hotel. Some airlines, when they know they cannot retrieve the pieces quickly, provide emergency overnight kits to defrocked travelers; others hand out modest sums of money for basic necessities.

A "property irregularity" form must be filled in describing all the particulars of your loss. If you put some identification inside your suitcase, it will help tremendously should the outside tag have been ripped off. You are required nowadays to have your own personal luggage card on every piece. (All airlines, incidentally, have keys to every sort of luggage.) If it finds your baggage, the carrier will deliver it to you promptly.

After a week has passed and your caboodle still hasn't been located, you should then begin the process of extracting a settlement. Experience reveals that you won't get anything near like the value of your carryall or wardrobe (not to mention valuables such as cameras or jewelry—which should have been among hand luggage anyway). I was once offered $25 for a suitcase and contents worth a hundred times more than that "settlement" sum, and after going to the top of the executive ladder managed to pry only $50 out of the company!

The best protection, in other words, is your own insurance policy.

BUMPING OR BOUNCING (Artistically labeled "involuntary boarding denial" by the airlines.) These are the names of a widespread game played by airlines which use you as the ball. It goes like this: The 747 that's supposed to wing you to, say, Paris has 352 seats. Because Carrier X knows from experience that a number of people with reservations will be "no-shows," it covers itself when its loads reach capacity by overselling perhaps 20 extra passages. (Usually airline officials figure that 15% of the registrants on the computer won't arrive at the airport.) Sure enough, 19 inconsiderate individuals fail to appear— but what if you are customer number 353? "Sorry," says the clerk, "no more room." You have been bumped.

What to do?

Know your "fly-rights" and use them.

Provided you hold a confirmed reservation plus a properly validated ticket on a regularly scheduled flight and have shown up on time, the airline must deliver you to your overseas destination by other means *within 4 hours* of your planned arrival time. If unable to do so, it is required to give you at least partial compensation, depending upon the distance, of not less than $37.50 (or the one-way fare) or more than $200, plus free passage on the next available flight. If they don't get you to your destination within 6 hours of the scheduled time, their apology must be doubled, to a maximum of $400 plus overnight expenses. This is *in addition* to the price of your original ticket, which you can turn in for a 100% refund. Moreover, you must be paid this "denied boarding compensation" within 24 hours; if you aren't, you have 90 days in which to file a claim. So if you get the bounce, stay right there and insist that you be given the printed regulation on the subject as well as the necessary forms you must fill out to collect this penalty. This applies, of course, only within the U.S., before or after international flights. European carriers on their own home territory vary dramatically on how they handle such delicate matters. BA and KLM are as thoughtful as U.S. airlines in crisis situations. I would not, however, wish to tussle with Iberia or Alitalia when only their compassion dictates. (Europe, unlike America, has no laws governing bumping offenses.)

AUSTRIA

INCLUDING BUDAPEST

USA: Austrian National Tourist Office, 500 Fifth Ave., Suite 2009–22, New York, NY 10110, Tel. (212) 944–6880; 11601 Wilshire Blvd., Suite 2480, Los Angeles, CA 90025, Tel. (213) 477–3332; 500 North Michigan Ave., Suite 1950, Chicago, IL 60611, Tel. (312) 644–8029; 1300 Post Oak Blvd., Suite 960, Houston, TX 77056, Tel. (713) 850–9999. *CANADA:* Check listings in Montreal, Toronto, and Vancouver.

SPECIAL REMARKS: (1) Routine holiday questions in Vienna are handled by the official Tourist Information Office (Oesterreich Werbung at Margaretenstrasse 1, 1040 Vienna; Tel: 5872000). The knowledgeable and capable comanagers are Dr. Klaus Lukas and Dkfm. Frank Kuebler. (2) There are 9 Provincial Tourist Offices (locally called Landesfremdenverkehrsaemter). (3) Skiing: In the U.S., if you are trying to decide what the conditions are, pick up the "Austrian Snow Phone" and dial (212) 697–8295 around the clock any day of the week for a recorded report on all major resorts. Fishing: Please check "Badgastein" for this rapidly developing freshwater sport. (4) "The Bonus of Budapest" is an enchanting afterthought—appropriately placed at the end of this chapter. Your departure point should be from Vienna, the closest western base to Hungary. Now that Eastern Europe is opening up for more relaxed travel, Vienna assuredly will serve as the springboard for tours, car rentals, flights and other excursion facilities. Ask a local travel agent or your hotel concierge for details.

TELEPHONE: Access code to USA: 001. To phone Austria: 43; time difference (Eastern Daylight) plus 6 hrs.

Austria has it all: Sophistication, natural beauty, excellent food, cheerful people, antiquity, flowers in summer, snows in winter, and prices for every budget. In the capital, Salzburg, and Innsbruck you'll find outlanders who have long savored their heady lures; in smaller centers you will experience a sample of living that has remained relatively undisturbed since the days of Franz Josef.

In winter the ski stations get the big play; in summer, fall, and spring, the cities are aflutter with visitors. Every day of any season music is a staple in the Austrian cultural diet—both the quantity and quality are overwhelming. For skiers, the first weekend in January to Easter is the choice period; Christmas, though cold, is also considered High Season. At this time hoteliers usually book only in fortnights covering the yuletide period and New Year. While Austria traditionally has been known for alpine (downhill) skiing, it now boasts nearly 8000 miles of cross-country trails for Nordic enthusiasts. You may want to dress for Austria's chic resorts or at the music festivals, but in general this is a country where you let down your hair and have fun.

FESTIVALS   The Salzburg Festival, Austria's most famous, is held from the latter part of July to the end of August. (There's another at Easter and yet another in mid-January, but on almost every night of the year you can find a classical concert to attend.) The average program includes 8 operas—by Mozart, Strauss, Verdi and others, plus a world premiere—in 27 performances. Other events: Major orchestra concerts, instrumental recitals, Mozart matinees, serenades, lieder, ballet and sacred music. The focus for the grand performances is the *Festspielhaus,* while virtuosi, duets, and chamber music groups perform in the numerous halls and salons nearby—often several going on simultaneously. Hence, if you can't manage tickets for the main billing, there are superb alternative choices most evenings. *Don't attempt the top concerts or operas, however, without confirmed reservations in advance.* (This holds for both the Easter and Whitsun festivals as well.) Write directly to Salzburger Festspiele, P.O. Box 140, 5010 Salzburg, Tel. (662) 842541 or in the USA you might try Dailey-Thorpe, 315 W. 57th St., NYC 10019, Tel. 307–1555. If you can't find living space (as is probable), write to the Landesreiseburo or the Stadtverkehrsburo in Salzburg, either of which will try to find a private family with an extra pallet. Tickets are sold out a year or more in advance to the grand events; hence, try to have these, too, ahead of time. Scalpers' rates are outrageous, so you may wish to settle for performances in the smaller halls, which also are superb but far lower in cost.

Other most illustrious events are the **Vienna Festival** (mid-May to mid-June; a glory of operas, operettas, concerts, and plays), the **Bregenz Festival** (late July to late Aug.; performances on a gigantic floating stage on Lake Constance), the **Graz Steirischer Herbst Festival** (Oct.; modern music and art exhibits), and the **Schubert Festival** (mid-June for 2 weeks; at the 16th-century Hohenems Palace; concerts plus lectures on the Master himself). Consult the Austrian National Tourist Office for details about these.

TRANSPORTATION   **Austrian Airlines** does a fine job internationally while sweeping the domestic skies through an ally called **Austrian Air Services.** The former offers a splendid Vienna-New York route; it also covers a wide span of Europe and skips out to Japan, the Middle East, and Africa with a very modern

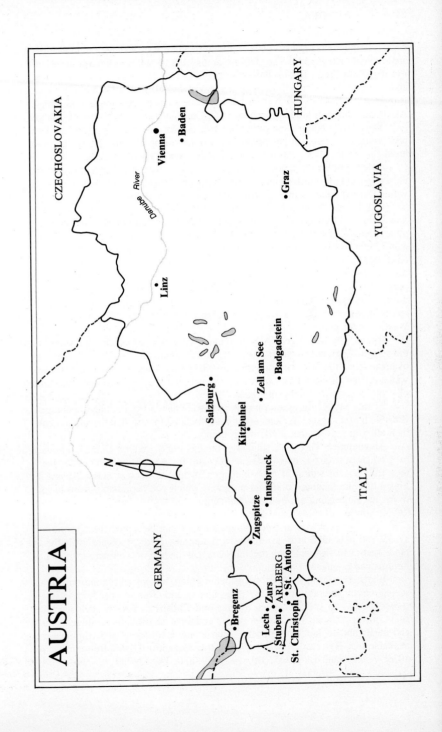

AUSTRIA

fleet. Ground connections by bus and train in and out of Vienna are good (taxis are wickedly expensive). The staff are among the friendliest aloft and the quality of the cuisine is among the highest flying, too. Salzburg Airport is young and is getting more active; nonstop flights between JFK and Vienna offer convenient AUA links to Salzburg. Apart from sales reps in most major U.S. cities, AUA maintains full-grade offices in NYC, Chicago, Los Angeles, and Toronto.

Taxis All modern cars; prices are still fair for midcity romps but, as I've just pointed out, you might prefer some other transport (bus, jitney, or even hired car) rather than a cab for airport shunts. Meters operate on a zone system.

Unless you're desperate, never take a taxi in Salzburg, where meters are the fastest ticking mechanisms I have ever boggled at in my travels. The convoluted traffic patterns (due to the bridges) add to the distances.

Car Rental Walther Erhart, long the most dynamic agent in the capital but now involving himself in the highly personalized specialty market and carriage trade, has volunteered to be a consultant to any reader who has problems in his nation or who may be traveling into Eastern Europe. Phone him at his private number (86–25–15) or write to him at 18 Erlenweg, A-2380 Perchtoldsdorf, Austria. There's a branch in *Salzburg* (10 Dariogasse, tel: 20400), which Walther's personable nephew Fritz runs capably. This one does not, however, have self-drive vehicles. For this, try Hertz or Avis. What it does have, however, is a splendid guide service headed by Pia Starzmann-Erhart who can open any East-West door for you.

Roads The impressive Arlberg Tunnel is useful, especially for skiers to the region. The chute, which is almost 9 miles long, cuts out the arduous haul over the Pass; the price of admission is AS 150 for a normal car. The expressway over the Brenner Pass between Innsbruck and Italy is negotiable any time of year—a boon for winter motorists.

Trains My recent meals on rails in this country invited admirable comparisons with prison grub. Waiters often push the large menu, then the small menu, then tell you gravely that the larder is empty.

About fares: There's a surcharge on EC trains. Senior Citizens (women over 60, men over 65) may obtain an ID Card for AS 200, which entitles them to a full year of riding at 50% reduction in first or second class. Austria is linked into the famous Eurailpass program, which you'll probably want to join if you are railroading a lot on the continent.

If you're outward bound from Vienna, ask about the pickup service from your hotel for both you and your luggage. Cars can be rented through the rail agents and deposited at a dozen Austrian stations. Bikes, too, are available at more than 130 depots—and the rates are cut in half if you arrive by train. Returns can be made at any station.

Boats The Danube offers mainstream entertainment and wondrous sightseeing on the numerous ferries, putt-putters, and even a speedy hovercraft (*schnellboot*) that roars between Vienna and Budapest. Variety includes brief spins on the Danube Canal to nostalgic riverboat shuffles to cabin relaxation and meals aboard fair-size cruisers—with many destinations and combinations available too. Reservations via any good travel agent or DDSG Reisedienst, A-1021, Wien, Handelskai 265, Tel. 1–21750–430; Tx. 134789.

FOOD Wonderful cuisine with a distinctive approach. Each region has its own specialties. Try to work in a sampling of Frittatensuppe (consomme with thinly sliced pancakes in it), Viennese Tafelspitz (boiled beef with a cream and chive mantle plus a side dish of horseradish mixed with applesauce; it has first cousins called Fleischteller and Suppenfleisch, but ask for the first), and Topfenknodel (a sweetish sphere of baked cottage cheese glazed with sugar, wading in a light syrup and plum gravy). While the most elegant restaurants (especially those in hotels) try to sell the idea that they purvey French derivatives of nouvelle cuisine, they can never forsake the inbred adoration for a hardy boiled brisket and a daily dose of Wiener Schnitzel. Sweets are a mainstay of every proper Austrian meal. Try the Imperial Torte from the capital's leading hotel. (The Imperial also will mail one home for you or send them as gifts.) I think its mellow creamy chocolate and moist interior is several notches better on my beltline than the drier dark creations of Sacher.

DRINKS Wines are your best bet. The earlier scandal over sweetening additives led to rigid controls. Prices average $9–23 per bottle and $2–6 for ¼ liter.

Klosterneuburger is perhaps the best white wine. Other dependable and sound labels are Kremser, Durnsteiner, Hohenwarther, and Nussberger. The finest red wine I've experienced is Voslauer; red wines from Baden are most often superb. From the Wachau district along the Danube, Sudbahn and Burgenland pressings win the local medals.

Of the beers, Gosser Brau is a rich brew made in Styria. It's full-bodied and fine; choice of light or dark. Schwechater is tops in Vienna.

Imported potables are relatively expensive. Bourbon and rye are amply abundant. Strictly for nickel-plated gullets, you'll find a local rum, a "club whisky," and a schnapps; also the local plum brandy or slivovitz. Enzian is another brandy, distilled from the roots of the tall curious yellow gentian. Locals seem to worship it, but I find it repugnant. Finally, Bowle is a delicious summer punch made of cognac, white wine, champagne or curacao, and fresh fruits: served from a bowl at perhaps $3.50 per glass.

TIPPING "Trinkgeld" will pop up inevitably during your Austrian journey. It means "money for a drink." Here is a rough guide of the gratuities that you will be expected to give:

Waiter—5% extra (to the man who serves you, not to the headwaiter; in more modest places the Austrian equivalent of 35¢ is enough); bartender—10% of drinks; maid—10 schillings per night; washroom attendant—5 schillings; taxi driver—10% of fare; doorman—10 schillings; porter and bellboy—10–15 schillings.

CITIES AND REGIONS

BADEN (Also called *Baden bei Wien*) The first choice for overnighting would be the **Krainerhuette,** which is not very large but is tasteful and comfortable. This can be followed by the **Parkhotel,** which features a large swimming pool plus health center; the service and cuisine are outstanding. The **Herzoghof** and the **Lotte Papst** are recommended. Another alternative would be the **Clubhotel.**

BADGASTEIN's innkeepers make up some 7000 beds daily in the summer season (cures and medical treatments) and the winter season (skiing), but between mid-October and mid-December, as in most similar resorts, nothing is open. The balconied, 100-room **Parkhotel Bellevue** garners the affluent young and the twinkling old; lodge-style downstairs bar is a social nucleus in winter. The colorful **Alpenhof Bellevue** is a chalet 400 meters above the main installation. Accessible by chair lift from below or a morning's ski from the upper slopes; hot lunches, group barbecues, apres-ski nuzzling, poolside lounging, or rustic overnighting in its 31 bedchambers. The **Elisabethpark** has a thermal swimming pool and an especially attractive a la carte restaurant called Pralatur. The mood is a blend of crystal chandelier and open timber-beamed ceilings, French fussy elegance, and rich, Austrian, hardy decor. **Salzburgerhof** has excellent thermal facilities; so does the **Eurotel.** I prefer the former because it's half the size of the latter; prices are lower too. In the budget category: (1) **Schillerhof,** (2) **Wildbad,** (3) **Sonngastein,** (4) **Eden,** (5) **Pension Stelzhamer,** and (6) **Savoy.**

For dining the Grill of the **Parkhotel Bellevue** is the unchallenged leader. For summer motorists, the **Gruener Baum** is a pleasant outdoor valley haven.

Fishing: Badgastein is the nearest town to 3 nooks that lie south of here and that specialize in superb angling plus Austria's most distracting scenery. The trio—or *Dreier Drill,* as they've come to be known—are (1) *Dollach* in the center (**Hotel Schlosswirt** with every convenience, centuries of history, and excellent cuisine); (2) *Matrei,* to the west (**Hotel Rauter** is larger and also excellent); and (3) *Techendorf am Weissensee,* to the east (the **Sporthotel Alpenhof** is a converted lakeside farmhouse where your appointed hen will provide a personalized egg for your breakfast daily). Prices are laughably low by fancier European standards—*and everything's included!* Write the above hotels for details.

BAD ISCHL Overnighters—if they don't choose the **Kurhotel Bad Ischl** where stays are generally longer—would probably be most comfortable in the **Post.**

Goldenen Schiff and the **Sporthotel** are also good. **Stern** is a solid budget entry.

FELDKIRCH   The **Alpenrose** is a fine spot for pausing; it's tiny, charming, and very Austrian. The **Baeren** is slightly larger while the **Illpark** and **Weisses Kreuz** are much more commercial in concept.

GRAZ   Hotels? (1) **Wiesler,** (2) **Daniel,** (3) **Europa,** (4) **Steirerhof,** (5) **Weitzer** and (6) **Parkhotel.** The city's not very thrilling in my opinion, so you might find country places more diverting.

INNSBRUCK   It is known for its appeal to skiers, although the slopes range far above the town itself. The satellite hamlets in the region (such as *Igls,* included at the end of this hotel text) offer great beauty and color. The city has been a crossroads community for centuries and the small but lovely Old Town is a reflection of this venerable Inn-breeding. A reminder that our ratings differ a bit from the official local judgments. Refer to "About the Stars" for our personal ranking.

☆☆☆ **Europa-Tyrol •** is tops for sophistication; bar in leather and wood; 110 all-fresh bedchambers. Ask to see the gorgeous Barocksaal, usually given over to special events and one of the most graceful salons in the nation.

★★★ **Goldener Adler •** born in 1390, wins a laurel wreath for color, antiquity, and charm. Sleekly rustic upstairs dining salon; superb food here with more tavern-style bites and brews in the vaulted cellar restaurant. A quiet retreat and a good one.

★★★ **Schwarzer Adler •** traces a heritage of more than 4 centuries. Adlerstube with wooden dado, leaded windows, and copperware; Jagerstube for Tyrolean specialties; only 25 rooms with bath or shower, but oozing with character and unique identity.

☆ **Scandic Crown •** is as cool as its arctic name. It provides 382 pillows, some suites, and attractive, warmly inviting dining nooks near the city's Triumphal Arch. It also offers a pool, sauna, and fitness facility.

Innsbruck • housing up to 140 guests, is substantial; the pool and sauna are added assets. The similarly named **Ibis Innsbruck** is more modest in price but good for the value; it's a little bigger in size.

Maximilian • is a recent arrival in the medium-low-priced bracket. All 40 units with bath and shower. Centrally situated on the Marktgraben.

Grauer Baer • specializes in package trippers, who total about 200 souls on a good night. Basically quite satisfactory.

In Igls, a 10-minute drive above Innsbruck.

★★★★ **Sporthotel** • is just the ticket for the luxury sport buffs. Space for 140 pastimers who like chalet-style living under a hotel roof. The food is exceptionally good.

☆☆☆☆ **Schlosshotel Igls,** under the same management, has huge rooms; Tyrolean appointments; pillows for only 32 noggins. Room #36 is perhaps the finest single accommodation in all Austria, in our view; #21 and #25 (one under the conical tower roof) are splendid doubles. The pool and fitness center provide good reason for the expanded dining facilities.

★★★ **Parkhotel Igls,** with a penthouse swimming pool, is another bucolic hillsider. Glorious setting; less costly and more tranquil than the leader; ice rink and 4 ski lifts nearby; about 50 spacious bedrooms, most with balcony and superb mountain comfort.
When hunger strikes, try **Kapeller;** this "Chapel" creates a lovely mood to set before a hungry appetite. **Philippine Welser** is woody, Tyrolean, romantic, and amply rewarding for regional cuisine. **Wildermann,** outside of town in the beguiling settlement of *Lans,* is a cozy, antique, rustic, hillside hideaway where the food is well served in the regional manner. *This* is Austria!

Stiftskeller is controversial but attractive. Food varies.

Stiegelbrau is atmospheric; the cooking is good, but the selections are very limited. Bierstuberl on one side, exclusively for males; nonsegregated dining facilities across the hall, with a relaxed, comfortable, middle-class patronage; rolls and *blatte* (delicious unleavened bread) are offered free.

Weisses Kreuz once played host to Mozart when he performed for the Empress; I've gone back a few times since 1787, and found it much improved.

NOTE · · · If you are staying in this city for at least 3 days (and that's easy to do), you become an automatic member of Club Innsbruck. Ask at your hotel concerning the hospitality program.

REGIONAL TYROLEAN APPAREL: **Lodenbaur** (Brixnerstrasse 4) is the unequivocal choice. Fritz Baur runs this splendid house with keenness and charm. **Lanz** (Wilhelm Greilstrasse) is also fine.

HANDICRAFTS: **Handwerkskunst** (Wilhelm Greilstrasse) is my preference.

SILVER CRYSTAL: **Swarovski,** at **Wattens,** 10 miles east of Innsbruck, is globally famous for its artistic glassware, which includes their own brilliant "zoo" of ornamental animals, pendants, table accessories, chandeliers, and fantastic precision binoculars. (I own a pair of the latter, which are almost indestructible; never have I had such clear vision at sea or in hazy mountain conditions. They are waterproof, but also come with a floating neck strap for hardweather deck work.) The chalet is the factory showcase where you can buy the whole range of inventory and see demonstrations of the art which has made this a great name in crystal since 1895.

KITZBUHEL   Again, a reminder to refer to "About the Stars" for our personal (not the official) rating system.

★★★★ **Zur Tenne** • is an upland haven in "alpine deluxe" motif. Space for about 90 in several contiguous houses; 10 rooms with open fires, rich in *gemutlich* atmosphere; sauna and pool; timber-lined grill. Loads of fun.

★★★ **Tennerhof** • with a similar name to the first midvillage entry, is often regarded as the social hub of wintersport. Its 40 bedrooms are excellent, but so much time is spent in the charming lounges, at various sipping nooks, and in conversation with other snowbunnies and jacks that there's hardly a night for snoozing.

★★★ **Parkhotel** • is an old-timer that has been turned into a sprightly born-again hostess for the '92 season. Accommodations are fresh and comfortable; public areas are inviting. Best of all is its central location.

★★★ **Weisses Rossl** • boasts 40 units and some of the nicest folk in the hills; very well maintained; pleasant atmosphere; tennis court, center-of-town situation. There is a spell of welcome provided by the Hirnsberger and Klena families that gives this house an endearing quality. A completely subjective opinion, but we just like it.

★★ **Goldener Greif** • offers a weensie, heated-water, interior swimming pool, restaurant, grill, and casino; Tyrolean-style, with 55 rooms and 55 baths. The painted facade in regional motif is carried out in the tone of this entire house. Very good indeed.

Reischhof Chalet • is an intimate expanded inn of great charm for about 80 guests. A favorite of many North American skiers.

Alpengolf Lutzenburg • is another wide-bodied chalet. The public rooms feature open timbers; so does the pool. Not expensive, but you'll need your own transportation—whether in wheel form or on skis.

Schloss Lebenberg • an overdone, highly polished castle on a hillock 5 minutes from town, offers fancy-schmanzy comfort, a glass-enclosed swimming pool, condominiums by the score for its ever-expanding following of investment settlers, and fairly steep prices.

Maria Theresia • is a bit closer to the bright lights; it's a viewful chalet-style place, with space for about 200 sporting types.

Jagerwirt • is smaller, contemporary, and attractive, with its Hallali restaurant and its abundance of south-facing private balconies.

KLAGENFURT   occupies a flatland set half a mile back from the wide and beautiful Worthersee, a popular lake that is surrounded by lawns, mountains, cyclists, and promenaders. In the town stops such as the **Carinthia,** the **Sand-wirt,** or the **Dermuth Anna** are certainly adequate, but if we really had our druthers we'd move along the coastal roads to the more lake-oriented villages of Portschach or Velden. (See separate entries.)

LECH   As ski resorts go, this is the funspot of the Arlberg, while *Zurs* is more known for its chic. The ski pass includes a generous 74 lifts plus cableways all over the Arlberg slopes.

   ★★ **Gasthof Post**   is a brightly decorated 3-story chalet; extensive antique collection; substantial amenities; ingratiating atmosphere for up-market sporting types.

   Schneider,   across the covered bridge from the Gasthof Post, is a slick mock-up of rustication; indoor swimming pool; impressive, even dramatically imposing, but somehow too contrived and polished.

   Kristberg   is a tiny house on a tiny knoll; pleasant view; attractive and smashingly successful Egon's Scotch Club with dancing nightly.

   Kristiania,   similar in personality to the Kristberg, is a traveler's reward if you are seeking a pension instead of a hotel atmosphere.

   Krone   is almost in the belfry of the town chapel; still fairly comfortable, but becoming seedier with advancing age; now a bit campy.

   Arlberg   is another one you might want to try. Only 56 rooms but very choice, with an abundance of sport facilities under its roof.

   Berghof   is a cozy corner for medium-budget travelers.

   Goldener Berg   in *Oberlech* is fun for dining in an alpine atmosphere.
   On a sunny day, try the antifreeze at the Ice Bar of the **Tannbergerhof;** a handsome slice of the good life. You also can scorn the thermometer on a sleighride to nearby *Zug* where **Auerhahn** is a snug luncheon spot; **Rote Wand** is more conventional. Meanwhile, your horse will dine from his feedbag waiting to jinglebell back to Lech before dark (or possibly after).

PORTSCHACH AM WORTHERSEE

   ★★ **Parkhotel**   is considered by various observers to be one of the better havens in the nation. The appeal is in its air of refined rusticity and the views of the lake and mountains. It is quietly sited on a 56,200-square-yard promontory, surrounded by the famous flower-beaches of the region and well-tended parks. Tennis courts; enclosed pool, glass lined on one side; health baths; cozy

Weinstube; 25 suites and 150 bedchambers, all with bath, balcony, and unimpaired view.

☆☆ **Schloss Seefels**   is also one of the better stops along this shore. Tasteful appointments; most units with private bath; up-to-date amenities; peppy discotheque; swimming, boating, and sipping done by the waterside.

ST. ANTON AM ARLBERG   is one of Europe's capitals of winter sport. It is not as smart as Zurs or Lech, but it is certainly one of the leading shrines in Europe for serious skiers. Each morning the lift lines are long, but you need not endure this since most Arlberg ski tickets include St. Anton in the package. Nearly all of the villages interconnect. In summer it is a sleepy little hamlet in which most of the hotels that line its single main street snooze cozily. **Sport** is the most lively. I'd categorize it in the newer breed of hostelries. Open year-round, it features the Graf Montfort dining salon, the intimate Supper Club, the tiny Le Gourmet, the Hubertus Klausen, the chummy informal Tavern, and the active Drop In discotheque. The indoor pool has its own rock-bound waterfall and floral colorations. Accommodations are sumptuously alpine. The invitingly painted, Old Worldly **Schwarzer Adler** offers more charm and European flavor. Excellent service and warm-hearted restaurant personnel; some units with working fireplaces; appointments in most areas superb, others lackluster; mood dressy rather than sweater-prone. **Post** is a large rambling structure that has long commanded the approval of traditionalists. The gathering place of the Continental Establishment. **Arlberg** glows with the kindness and caring of its staff. Most hotels offer a pension plan, so outside dining is negligible and hardly worth considering. In any case, these ski hotels maintain their clientele year after year largely on the basis of their proud kitchens.

ST. CHRISTOPH   (also in the Arlberg) is a tiny ski station which links into the same lift system as the other Arlberg towns. Stay at either the **Bellevue** or the **Hospiz. Alpenhof**, which is actually in the nearby settlement of **St. Jakob**, is choice. **Stuben,** in the same ski-haul network, offers the **Hubertushof,** the **Mondschein,** the **Post,** and a sprinkling of nice medium-priced guest houses.

ST. GILGEN   is a beauty spot across the lake from St. Wolfgang. It, too, becomes jammed in summer, but somehow the layout seems to afford more living space than its sainted neighbor. The town, the gardens, and the marine locale form a breathtaking assemblage of colors. For lake views (and you should specify when you reserve), choose either the **Hollweger** or the **Parkhotel Billroth.** After these, in varying degrees of comfort, elect the **Aberseehof, Haus Tirol** or the **Christabauer.**

ST. WOLFGANG   gives its name to the Wolfgangsee, the enchanting lake on whose shore it grew. In summer it is packed, and caravans of buses creep through its narrow lanes at an exasperating pace, but if you can catch it during the fringe seasons or in the autumn when the forest slopes are changing their leafy mantle, then you will be enthralled by its bucolic charm. The waterside **Weissen Rossl** must be one of the oldest buildings in this part of the world—and attractive. If you don't overnight, then at least try to have a drink on its covered wooden terrace or a meal at its famous restaurant. Also pleasant are the **Mirabell** (small and cozy), the **Post** (with its several annexes), and the larger **Schloss Eibenstein.**

SALZBURG

ATTRACTIONS

In addition to the classic attractions such as Mozart's birthplace and the Mozart Museum, do visit the enchanting Salzburg Marionette Theater—probably the best-known company of its kind on the boards today. It recently added advanced holography to its technical achievements. The Salzburg Festspielhaus, like the Vienna State Opera House, ranks at the top in theatrical facilities. This supermodern 7-unit structure contains 2340 seats—none more than 115 feet from the stage. Equally interesting to music-lovers are the Palace Concerts, now scheduled for most of the year. The University is in the center of the Old City and you can visit its various ancient departments. Hike or ride up the Monchsberg above town and wind down through the lanes among castles and forests. There's a cable car, 9 miles out, which zips up 6170 feet of Alp (the Durrnberg) in 8 minutes, for a commendably modest price. While in the region you can visit the Hallein Salt Mine, plus the Giant Ice Caves at Werfen (May to Oct.) If you are interested in loden cloth, the variety is greater here than anywhere else in Europe. Pipe smokers and hunters will revel in collections at the Jagdhof (see below). Need a guide? Call Pia Starzmann-Erhart (20400 or 08651/3885). The family has been helping visitors for 3 generations.

HOTELS

★★★★★ **Goldener Hirsch** ● offers charm and local color and a country-tavern-style that boasts more than 400 years of nubile grace; small, intimate, and delightful. You'll find more creaks and original tones in the older segment; there are now 2 newer wings craftily combining Old Goldener Hirsch-flavored garniture with twentieth-century architecture. The bar and excellent dining room are the gathering places of the luminaries from the music world. Traditionally the city's number one address for cozy comfort and affable hospitality overseen by its able director Count Johannes Walderdorff.

☆☆☆☆☆ **Kobenzl** • 2500 feet above the city on the Judenbergalpe, is tacked nimbly to the clouds—just the ticket if you seek mountain calm. This gorgeously fashioned, spectacularly situated aerie is spotlessly maintained; with heated swimming pool and sauna; wide-angle lodgings; glorious suites overlooking the valley; closed Nov.–March.

☆☆☆ **Osterreichischer Hof** • is striking and very good, but its tone is more hotel-like. The more conventional wanderer might prefer this one to the Goldener Hirsch for in-town living. Glass-front "Panorama" floor with private baths, air conditioning, and river view; each unit in its own distinctive decor; all 4 restaurants with waterside frontage, my favorite corner being the Zirblstube.

☆☆☆ **Sheraton** • provides a woodland address facing romantic Mirabell Park in midcity. Modern Sheratonian fillips such as air conditioning, electric blinds, minibars; TV and in-house movies; 5th floor designated as VIP level; airy suites; 165 rooms; good baths. The handsome dining spread overlooking the gardens was disappointing gastronomically on an earlier try and variable on later samplings, but the bar is lively, chummy, and musical every evening.

Winkler • remains physically colorful, but it has an extremely commercial air possibly pinned to the fact that it lives and breathes for a travel agency.

Mercure • is a relative youngster whose midcity location is an asset. Additional space is welcome here, especially during festival weeks.

Bristol • with elegant public areas, retains its famed hospitality, cordiality, and easy homespun graces. The front can be very noisy. Closed in winter.

★★★ **Schloss Monchstein** • is a splendid, cozy hideaway. It is not expensive for its palatial-though-homey rewards.

Haus Ingeborg • about 10 minutes out, is a 4-century-old cutie that oozes with Tyrolean grace. Very small, very select, and very much to be recommended if you have a car. Open March 1–Oct. 30. **Schlosshotel St. Rupert** is a 55-pillow castle 1½ miles out; lovely gardens; quiet; open Apr.–Oct. **Fondachhof,** an attractive two-century-old suburban villa, has a pool and pleasant dining (for house guests only); for tranquillity lovers.

Pitter • bustles with conventions; it's good for its type. **Auersperg, Stieglbrau, Kasererbrau, Markus Sittikus,** and **Zum Hirschen** are next in line. **Weisse Taube** offers friendly service and a cuisine that is warmly recommended.
Elefant was born in A.D. 1200; it's known for its inviting ground-floor Stube; 40 clean, nice rooms. **Blaue Gans** I rate routine to poor. **Eder** is similar in size and only marginally better.

Pensions

Eschenbach and **Herbert** are two possibilities; nearly all the better ones are slightly out of town so that a car would be useful. The **Airport Hotel** is functional and little else.

Environs

★★★★★ **Schloss Fuschl** • at *Hof* near *Fuschl,* 15 miles due east, is a glorious oasis for the peace-seeking, monied traveler. Marvelous scenic terrace seating 80; impressive Jagerstube; ornate bar; some dishes extremely spare for their rich price tags (the shrimp cocktail gave an impression that prawns must be an endangered species); Winter Garden; marble swimming pool; 9-hole golf course; tennis; automatic bowling alley. Total of 84 rooms and palatial comfort; patrician furnishings; swimming, horseback riding, boating, lake or stream fishing. Two romantic suites and a bungalow nucleus lakeside; 2 simple hillside guest houses (one a long hike). If this Schloss is filled or closed during the mid-April-to-end-Oct. period, drive on to the Jagdhof.

★★ **Jagdhof** • which flanks the entry road to the aristocratic Fuschl estate, is far more modest than the Schloss, with a complement of 50 rooms in 2 buildings, the best being in the annex. Viewful window-lined restaurant plus terrace; outstanding upstairs museum of smoking pipes, guns, and articles of the hunt. Low prices.

★★★ **Schloss Haunsperg** at *Oberalm bei Hallein,* about 15 minutes by car from central Salzburg, offers additional country calm and polished antique elegance, with painted pastel towers, a baroque chapel, belfries, gardens, fine furnishings, and the evergreen hospitality of the Markhof family. Suites and twins available at remarkably low prices; Tel. (06245) 2662; intimate and laden with charm.

Anif is a neighboring village where the rustic **Friesacher** is winning more and more friends, especially to its handsome restaurant; book only in the main building. **Schlosswirt** offers accommodation, but it is more well known as a country-style dining establishment (within a short stroll of the Water Palace).

RESTAURANTS

★★★★★ **Goldener Hirsch** • not only sets the most attractive table, in my view, but without pretensions it provides the classic gastronomy of the region intelligently and with the grace and style of true Salzburg hospitality. The vaults seem to hug the audience into intimate huddles. Attendants wear regional costume (as do all staff in this house); crockery bears the symbol of the hotel (which you can purchase for your own home if you wish). The mood is the quintessence of local color.

★★★ **Zum Mohren** • *Judengasse 9* • is the cellar of a house that was built in 1423 and, as you might have guessed from the address, was formerly in the Jewish quarter. Early Salzburg had canals that served the river and this establishment had been a waterside tavern since the 16th century; now it is well inland, of course. Outstanding dishes include the herring fillets, hare with sweet-and-sour cherries, boiled beef with horseradish sauce, and *backhendl* (a marvelous Austrian fried chicken).

☆☆ **Purzelbaum** • *Zugallistr. 7* • is a cozy magnet for Salzburg's cognoscenti. Informal air with working bar and counter; ice cream-parlor tables; banquettes and bentwood chairs; fresh atmosphere that matches the lightness of the cuisine and the humor of the ambience. (Its name translates as "Somersault.") Not spectacular, but certainly attractive and worthy. An oddity: steak served on an antique flatiron filled with hot coals. PS: Turbot in cream sauce is better.

☆☆ **Alt Salzburg** • behind the Goldener Hirsch wins my vote for elegance among the independents. Arched alleyway entrance flanked by flags of various nations; French bar just inside; twin inner sancta under brick vaults. Continental fare is the chef's calling. Service is variable. Highish tabs.

★★ **Peterskeller** • is the traditional showplace if not the pulsing magnet of tour operators. Never a shrine of gastronomy, its cookery seldom matches the excellence of its wines. Regional dishes only; perfunctory service; dim Old World atmosphere; low price tags; supervision by the savvy Benedictine monks who own it.

Weinrestaurant Moser • features 3 rooms with vaulted ceilings, amiable staff, substantial local selections only.

Cafe Winkler • offers lunch and dinner around the calendar with a view, too. The vista will thrill you more than the chef will.

K & K • is modern, clean, zestless visually, but highly popular. I can't imagine why, because both cuisine and service were a shambles on my several tries.

Cafe Mozart • *Getreidegasse* • is perfect for pastry (56 types), coffees (about a dozen mixtures), snacks, and conversation. It's an upstairs assemblage of several period rooms and nooks, plus an art gallery on the uppermost tier. As a coffee house, here is an institution of peerless merit.

Zum Eulenspiegel • *Hagenauerplatz 2* • in the 15th-century city gatehouse, has 3 floors, sophisticated tavern-type ambience, and hungry tourists 6-deep. The jokes and proverbs on the walls are earthy. Very near, **Hagenauer Stuben** • *in the Mozart Museum* • combines a fine delicatessen with a tiny snackery. It's very handy for rush-rush sightseers.

Festungsrestaurant • *in the Festung, or castle* • and **Stieglkeller** • *Festungsgasse 10* • are more famous for folk dancing (summer only) than for groceries; check with your concierge first, because on some evenings nothing happens; the latter spot, designed vaguely like the inside of a beer barrel, is the only place I've ever found where the customer climbs 5 flights of stairs to get to the cellar. And when the bus tours roll up, you can forget about receiving service of any kind.

Augustiner Brau • *Augustinergasse 4* • is a mammoth, old-fashioned beer hall and chestnut-garden that can handle 2000 merrymakers. Self-service throughout; cold plates and snacks only; opens daily at 3 p.m.; colorful and amusing, despite some oafs in attendance.

☆☆☆ **Eschlbock** • *at Mondsee* • is a hotel by the lakeside where an inventive chef does modern things to Old Austrian recipes. The shrimp hash is an interesting surprise; quail is delicious; desserts are outstanding. A 20-minute excursion from midtown.

When the Salzburg sun sets, there's gambling at the plush **Casino** up in the clouds of the Monchsberg. Handsome furnishings in a handsome building; 1 baccarat and 5 roulette tables; pleasant bar; open from 7 p.m.–2 a.m. (4 a.m. on weekends) except on Christmas Eve and religious holidays; entrance fee of $AS170 (which includes 3 chips with a value of $AS200, a nice bonus). *Take along your passport, or you won't be admitted.*

〰〰〰〰〰〰〰〰〰〰〰〰〰〰〰〰〰〰〰〰〰〰〰〰〰〰〰〰〰〰

SHOPPING

COUNTRY FASHIONS AND SPORTING GOODS: **Sport und Waffen E. Dschulnigg KG** (Griesgasse 8). Dschulnigg has it all. Here is a preserve for the aficionado or the expert hunter, fisherman or archer. Furthermore, the clothing displays offer a stunning wardrobe of loden for both sexes, plus accessories in all colors, as well as handknitted vests and walking jackets in boiled wool. Parents should not miss the exclusive line of apparel for the 4–14 year old set available at the next-door store called **Cosi's by Dschulnigg** (Griesgasse 6).

For strictly regional costumery there are good selections at **Alois Wenger u. Co.** (Getreidegasse 29 and Linzergasse 58), **Lanz** (Schwarzstrasse), and **Madl** (Universitatsplatz 12). The latter specializes in a *haute couture* expression of *Trachten*.

NOTE · · · If you are headed for Vienna, then don't wait to buy these delightful costumes in the capital. Salzburg is *the* place for such garments. The selection is wider, the loden and other materials are top quality, and the prices are correct. Moreover, in Salzburg almost the entire population (children included) wears this handsome garb every day, so you can see for yourself what cuts and colors are in fashion. Vienna, being more metropolitan, dresses itself in conventional business suits and ladies' attire.

CRYSTAL AND PORCELAIN: Sigrist (Griesgasse 13) has been at the head of the table since 1838. To name only a few of the "greats" on display: Meissen, Dresden, Wedgwood, Villeroy & Boch, Lalique, Riedel, Waterford, Christofle, and on and on. In brief, it's a selection of Europe's finest production. **Rasper & Sohne** and **E. Bakalowitz** (Mozartplatz) are both worthy. **J. & L. Lobmeyr** (Schwarzstrasse 20) spotlights Herend of Hungary among others.

GLASS SPECIALIST: Fritz-Reiner Kreis (Sigmund-Haffner-Gasse 14) has handmade ceremonial or table glass that is etched on the premises in designs of lasting tradition—the "Tree of Life" motif is one of the most popular. Schnapps sets, bells, mirrors, marriage and baptism commemoratives are all available. Most initialing can be done in an hour; more complicated work and special orders would have to be shipped.

HANDICRAFTS: Salzburger Heimatwerk (Residenzpl. 9) is right under the Glockenspiel Tower. Here you'll find literally thousands of distinctive craft items—imaginative, fanciful, flattering, or novel.

JEWELRY: Lahrm (Universitatsplatz 5 and 16) is a treasure house. The personable Mr. Lahrm has classic pieces plus antique accessories for regional attire as well as less expensive items that fall into a distinctive costume category. Hearts are a specialty. Next come two **Koppenwallners: Anton** (Klampferergasse 2) and **Paul** (Alter Markt and Universitatsplatz 4). The former focuses on less costly items for *Trachten* (Salzburger dress) while the latter features more conventional styles. **H. von Rautenberg Nachfolger** (Alter Markt 15) is a very worthy alternative with especially beautiful garnet pieces.

LEATHER GOODS: Slezak (am Makartplatz 8 plus a branch in the Sheraton Hotel) has been a leather specialist for more than a century. Gold-embroidered evening bags and belts; all styles, sizes, and types of suitcases; roomy attache and briefcases; the "Geiger" line of jackets and skirts; silk and cotton blouses; gorgeous sweaters at equal to or lower than English or Scottish tariffs; gloves; unusually fetching souvenirs and accessories. It's a paradise from which to mail gifts to the U.S. Mrs. Dorli Gehmacher and her staff will all charm you with their Austrian hospitality. Unrivaled for taste and old-line integrity.

LEDERHOSEN AND LEATHER WEARABLES: Jahn-Markl (Residenzplatz 3) always comes up with top-drawer specialties—and thanks to friendly Erwin Markl, there's a cozy feeling about this ancient little place. The initial outlay for one of his super-fine, ever-chic suits made of suede, deerskin, or chamois might seem costly, but actually here are prime investments because they last for 10 to 12 years *without cleaning!*

REGIONAL CERAMICS: Guglhupf (Franz-Josefs-Kai 5) is where cheerfulness is the name of the game. Here you will find the full range of Gmundner Keramik artisanware from upper Austria—breakfast sets, dinner ensembles, cups, vases, candlesticks—all the gladsome, colorful dollops of springtime that bring such joy to meals and snacks.

SCHRUNS

☆☆☆ **Kurhotel Montafon** Top-class international spa a skip-and-jump from the Swiss and Liechtenstein frontiers; rich and celebrated clientele; medical supervision. ★★★ **Lowen** is a pleasant and fresh alternative choice. Very sporting in atmosphere; stunning glass-bound swimming pool; refined rustic decor with open beams, dried flower arrangements, and handsome textiles.

SEEFELD (1) Klosterbrau, (2) Post (also on the main square), (3) Laerchenhof, and (4) Tuemmlerhof.

SEEFELD (1) **Klosterbrau,** (2) **Post** (also on the main square), (3) **Laerchenhof,** and (4) **Tuemmlerhof.** There are dozens more in this lovely town; most are seasonal and heavily tourist oriented.

VELDEN AM WORTHERSEE (1) **Schloss Velden** (traditionally one of Austria's leading lights), (2) **Europa,** and (3) **Seehotel Hubertushof. Schoenblick** is an attractive smaller house.

VIENNA

ATTRACTIONS

Hofburg • *Winter residence of the Hapsburgs; Michaelerpl. 1 is one entrance of the several that provide access* • The Hofburg is a self-contained city within the Old City of Vienna. It is the site of the luxurious winter palace of the Imperial Family as well as a variety of museums, courtyards, the National Library, the Burgkapelle, the Schweizerhof apartments, the glittering, incomparable stores of the royal family, the Spanish Riding School (see below), and other sights. The architecture in this huge complex ranges from early Gothic to late 19th century.

Schatzkammer • *where the Imperial Treasury has been reconstructed* • Charlemagne's sword as well as a crown made for the Holy Roman Emperor are two of the many highlights of this glittering collection of centuries-old jewelry, royal vestments, and priceless Hapsburg treasures.

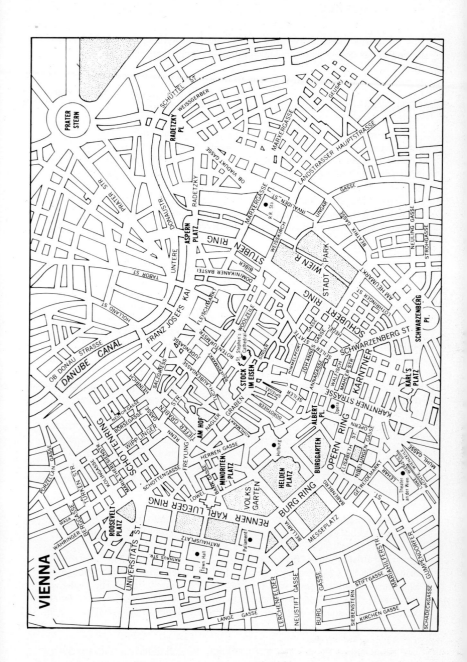

Albertina Museum (Graphische Sammlung) • *Augustinerstr. 1* • The Albertina's huge collection of drawings, prints, and engravings is among the world's finest. Built in 1747 and at one time a royal residence, it opened as a museum in 1822. It is on the outskirts of the Hofburg, near the Staatsoper. The collection, which includes over a million items and begins with the works from the 14th century, features Albrecht Durer's complete etchings.

Stephansdom • *Stephanspl. 1* • The pivotal sightseeing target of midcity, construction of Austria's finest Gothic church began during the first half of the 13th century and has continued into this century. In the North Tower hangs the 20-ton **Pummerin,** the cathedral bell, which you can ride to by elevator.

Spanische Hofreitschule • *Spanish Riding School* • Emperor Karl VI ordered this showcase for the all-white Lipizzaner stallions; today's riders perform precision horsemanship that originated four centuries ago. To attend you can purchase a ticket (at increased rates) from a local travel agent or write as much as 6 months in advance to Spanische Reitschule, Hofburg, Josefspl., A 1010 Wien (this reserves one of the 600 seats or 200 standing-room spots; you pay when you pick up your ticket). If you miss the regular performance, try to see the men and their mounts go through their paces at one of the daily training sessions. The latter do not take place July–Aug, so ask locally what's available.

Uhrenmuseum der Stadt Wien • *Schulhof 2* • Despite its modest size (the building was originally a private home), the Clock Museum contains over 3000 timepieces beginning with a medieval sundial and winding up with space-age chronometers. Between the two extremes are musical clocks, an astronomical piece, and, most charming of all, a group of unusual and intricate performing tick-tocking figurines. Exhibits are arranged chronologically, of course.

Augustinerkirche • Built in the 14th century, this was the parish church of the Imperial Family. A number of Imperial weddings took place here, including Napoleon's proxy marriage in 1810 to Marie Louise, daughter of Emperor Francis I. The adjoining **Chapel of St. George** giddily boasts a collection of urns inside of which are the embalmed hearts of over 50 members of the Hapsburg family.

Ruprechtskirche • *1 Ruprechtpl.* • Believed to date from the 9th century, it's bound to be Vienna's oldest church.

Kunsthistorisches Museum • *Maria Theresien-Pl., 1* • Not surprisingly, many of the art treasures once belonged to the rulers of the Austro-Hungarian Empire. (Nobody suggests who they belonged to prior to that.) The Breughels are among the best and most numerous in the world; Rubens, Durer, Titian, Van Eyck, Velasquez, Vermeer, Holbein, and Rembrandt also jostle for attention on these hallowed walls.

Staatsoper • *Opernring 2* • If a city may be said to have a soul, the Staatsoper is its likely location. Performances tend to be sold out, so to be sure of a seat, reserve tickets at least four weeks in advance of the performance date by writing to Osterreichiscne Bundestheaterverwaltung, Goethegasse 1, A–1010 Wien. Tickets for the Vienna Festival in May are available by mail (if you're lucky) from Wiener Festwochen Bestellburo, Lehargasse 11, A-1060 Vienna.

Karntstrasse 38 • *just behind the Opera* • is where you'll find the main branch of the Vienna Tourist Board.

Rathaus • *Rathauspl., 1* • A key element in Franz Joseph's plans to modernize Vienna, the neo-Gothic structure with some Renaissance-style elements was built in 1872–1883. Its arcaded courtyard is the site of openair concerts during the summer months.

Burgtheater • *Dr. Karl Lueger-Ring, 1* • Founded 200 years ago as the German National Theater, it's located across from the Rathaus.

Sigmund Freud Museum • *Berggasse, 9* • Until 1938 when he and his family fled the Nazis, this was the house where the doctor lived and practiced. (Local wags opine that Freudian couches can never replace the confessionals provided by Vienna's ubiquitous coffee houses.)

Volksoper • *Wahringer Str., 9* • This is *the* theater for the musical whipped cream for which Vienna is renowned, although its repertory also includes heavier fare. It's a diet chiefly of light opera, operettas, and musicals.

Schloss Belvedere • *Prinz-Eugen-Str. 27; entrance also on Rennweg* • Actually consisting of two palaces, it's the home of three museums. In the **Upper Belvedere** you'll find works by Gustav Klimt, Egon Schiele, and Oskar Kokoschka, as well as temporary special exhibits. Across the sculpture garden is the **Lower Belvedere,** for Medieval Austrian Art and another facility for Austrian Baroque. From mid-May through Aug. there is a sound-and-light performance at 8:30 p.m. daily.

Schloss Schonbrunn • *Schonbrunner Schloss-Str., 13* • This 1441-room palace, Vienna's answer to Versailles, was the summer residence of the Hapsburgs. (To get there, catch the U4 subway or #58 tram from the city center.) Originally built in 1696 at the beginning of Vienna's Golden Age, it was extensively modified a century later. The **Imperial Apartments** are open to the public, as are the **Imperial Chapel,** the lovely rococo **theater,** and several **ballrooms.** Surrounding are impeccably groomed baroque gardens that include the 500-acre **Schonbrunn Zoo** with cafes, a beer garden, and romantic pathways. Nearby, the **Gloriette Monument,** a huge stone arch, frames a panoramic view of the countryside with Vienna in the distance.

Museum Moderner Kunst • *Palais Liechtenstein* • is the pacesetter for exciting contemporary works in this highly traditional city, a place where there's almost no middle ground but only well-in and far-out artistic expression. Here you can see the "leading edge" of sculpture today, such as that produced by Benjamin Jakober (one of Europe's brightest new luminaries).

Donauturm • *Danube Tower, Donaupark* • If getting a bird's eye (read "touristic") view of Vienna appeals to you, the best panorama of the city can be had from this 840-foot-high tower. First, take one of the two high-speed elevators to the viewing platform. In clear weather, there is an overview not only of the city and the celebrated Vienna Woods but you may also see the plains of Hungary and the snow-capped Austrian Alps in the distance. Below the observation deck are two revolving restaurants.

Prater • Even if you think you've outgrown amusement parks, the 1325-acre Prater may change your mind. Once an Imperial hunting ground of the Hapsburgs, it was opened to the public in 1766. The most famous ride in the Prater is the **Riesenrad,** the giant Ferris wheel that has remained in operation, except for the war years, since 1897. The apex of the Riesenrad is an excellent perch from which to survey the city. The Prater also has a Lilliput railroad, four beer gardens, a large wooded area with miles of paths and cycling routes, a swimming pool, golf course, and stadium.

HOTELS

Please refer to "About the Stars" for an explanation of our personal rating system, which does not necessarily correspond with the official local rankings.

☆☆☆☆☆ **Imperial,** formerly a noble estate, is the blue-ribbon choice for the client who wants grandeur, suavity, and action with million-$ elegance. This imposing, 160-room, fully air-conditioned hostelry has ultramodern or classicstyle rooms; Royal Suites, with palatial opulence at a palatial rate; many choices of accommodation; splendid baths—some like Florentine jewelboxes. The Cafe, often with music, is popular by day or by night; revamped dining salon where you can sample that lux-ious Imperial Torte (see "Food"). Top of the peerage.

☆☆☆☆☆ **Bristol,** sharing the Imperial administration (CIGA) and with similar tariffs, retains a position equal to the above entry but in a style that speaks more of period decor. Its marvelous Korso (see "Restaurants") is *the* after-theater-and-opera gathering spot in the capital. Graciously traditional throughout; well-appointed, silk-lined bedchambers shine with a special pride. Top-floor Club Rooms come with open fireplaces, knockout vistas, and a hard-and-software complement of executive gadgetry; sauna under a domed tower; viewful terrace. A fine house.

★★★★★ **Sacher** trades on its global reputation for Old Worldliness. Turn-of-the-century furnishings, high ceilings, oil paintings, and statuary abound; modern touches elsewhere have enhanced its efficiency. Its drawbacks, however, are equally significant. In my judgment, most of its accommodations are painfully small for transatlantic travelers with ample luggage; the house policy of not accepting *any* credit cards seems ill-advised; service can be pushy after-opera when the waiters want to leave. Undoubtedly here is an aristocrat—of that there's no question; but whether you are lured by its personality depends upon you.

☆☆☆ **SAS Palais** • is indeed a palace that the Scandinavian airline advanced in a time warp from the 18th century to the 20th. The exterior was maintained intact while inside the trend is toward cool Scandinavian tones, modernity, and practical business facilities for today's execu-culture. Excellent location for shoppers or sightseers.

☆ **Palais Schwarzenberg** • *Schwarzenbergplatz 9* • an island of serenity occupying the right wing of one of Vienna's most beautiful baroque palaces, exudes the feeling that the visitor is ensconced in a provincial mansion. Too bad, then, that many of the nicer old-fashioned features are consistently being replaced with modernity. Garden, park, and plaza setting just off the Ring-strasse, 5 minutes from the central whirl; client capacity now at 75; frequent complaints of overbooking from incensed travelers who even have sent deposits to secure accommodation; intimate hearthside bar; smartly outfitted dining room with superior culinary standards; alfresco meals facing the vast greensward in summer.

☆☆☆ **Intercontinental** • resides in a quiet but not inconvenient situation near the Wienfluss and Stadtpark; Brasserie for quick meals; excellent midday buffet. The Rotisserie and Crystal Bar are poshly outfitted to match the gracious elegance of the lobby and lounges. Between houses that often vie for the same audience, I much prefer this to the frigidity of the Hilton (see below).

☆☆ **Marriott** • appears in midcity wearing vaguely palladian architecture and American inner comforts. The Symphonika restaurant is the most refined performer of the 5 dining and sipping segments; health club and indoor pool; many cheerful suites with lovely views. Functional but uplifting.

☆ **Hilton** • is a white-structured city in itself that offers 620 latchkeys, a quartet of restaurants (Prinz Eugen Grill is overrated in my opinion), shops, and—most convenient of all—the main city air terminal smack under its hangar-wide roof.

☆☆ **Plaza Wien** • Hilton's newest entry, was recently added to the chain-link collection and a fine house it is, too. Being smaller than the original, it also has benefited from a more agreeable personality. It's conveniently sited on the important Ringstrasse (Schottenring 11), offering 223 rooms, lots of suites (some with four-posters), a ''no-smoking'' floor, two restaurants, a breakfast nook, piano bar, and fitness club. The location and communications facilities probably will make it a good choice for business travelers.

★ **Ambassador** • has dual entrances from 2 avenues; twin lobbies; handsome, spacious accommodations with comfortable bathrooms; small dining room (for clients only) with superb cuisine; unusually friendly attention.

★★ **Konig von Ungarn** • is noted for its splendid restaurant in a cozy corner of its interior courtyard. The ancient private house has been restructured with a mandate on tranquil luxury. Space allotments are not vast but the rooms are well thought out, the appointments are traditional and of top quality, and the baths are excellent. As comfortable and as pleasant as any traveler could find for the price.

☆☆ **Europa** • is in more contemporary tone with superb modern furnishings and has a first-rate midcity address in the Neuer Markt.

☆ **President** • is well groomed. Some twins with a 3rd bed; smartly furnished; summer breakfast garden; Nordic dining salon.

Strudlhof • is modern and economically priced.

Astoria's • styling is uninspired, but there's ample space in the bedchambers.

Am Parkring • is on the 11th to 13th floors of a commercial office building. Quiet, viewful units; excellent maintenance; tiny singles with half-bathtubs; small, functional, tasteful doubles; cramped luggage space; Lilliputian balconies on the top 2 floors; demipension is mandatory.

Parkhotel Schonbrunn • facing the palace grounds, only 10 minutes from the center by subway, can take pride in its lobby, lounges, shops, swimming pool, and a pleasant garden wing. And while it takes pride it also takes tours, in caravan waves! Okay but grimly commercial.

Ramada • with space for 500 visitors and very smart looking, is roughly midway between Schonbrunn and midcity. I like Ramadas in Europe (more than in the USA) and this is a good one—*if* you don't mind the outlying location.

Trend • adheres to the standard pattern of clean, narrow-dimensioned, moderately priced accommodations, production-line cuisine, and an outlying situation better suited for self-drive motorists than for taxi-borne thrifties.

Regina • a spacious Old World house that is slightly out of the midcity whirl is smart and most appealing.

The **De France** (with an "executive floor," a bright and cheerful atrium, plus an ambience of the 19th century when it was originally created) and the **Prinz Eugen** (7th and 8th floors rear the best) are members of the same corporation that runs the Parkhotel Schonbrunn. Other notables are the **Erzherzog Rainer,** which emphasizes its dining facilities and extra-attentive service in addition to spruced-up rooms, and the **Am Stephansplatz,** which stands opposite the cathedral—very nice in its own way and graceful. The **Tyrol** is a perked-up cutie, and **Kummer, Royal** (excellent rooftop solarium; kindhearted people; magnificent views from upper quarters), and **Clima** are other pleasant, moderately priced choices. **Atlanta** was given more sparkle, not long ago, and is an inviting small hotel. Our thumbs down for the **Graben;** thumbs up for the apartmentlike **Capricorno,** if you plan to stay for 2 weeks or more. **K & K Maria Theresia** is a reasonably priced entry in the Spittelberg sector.

Vienna Woods? This is about 20 minutes from midtown and wonderfully tranquil. **Schlosshotel Wilhelminenberg** has been dolled up with suites and restyled lounges. Not expensive and very appealing for schlosshoppers.

Pensions?

Top choices in the better districts: **Elite, Arenberg,** and **Schneider.**

RESTAURANTS

☆☆☆☆☆ **Korso** • *Bristol Hotel* • is the nation's capital for after-opera dining. Nothing can touch it for putting a soigne nightcap on the evening! As it is so much the "in" place to be in Vienna, be sure to book ahead *always.* Polished wood interior, beveled glass panels, burnished brass and excellent table settings.

☆☆☆☆☆ **The Three Hussars** • *Zu Den Drei Husaren, Weihburggasse 4, about a block from the Ambassador* • is Vienna's traditional independent leader. Classic atmosphere; topflight international cuisine; reserve in advance. A famous and delicious feature is the mammoth selection of hors d'oeuvres on rolling carts. *Dinner only;* closed mid-July through August.

☆☆☆☆ **Stadtkrug** • *rear* room, across the street from The Three Hussars, offers a grand piano, costumed gypsy musicians, and 16 candlelit tables in Renaissance surroundings. Now serving both lunch and dinner every day of the year; reserve ahead in the Sakristei Room, *ignore the simple entrance segment, and walk straight through.* The above three restaurants feature live music.

☆☆☆☆ **Konig von Ungarn** • is small and select—especially in its finely tuned harmony of Central European specialties. The mood is that way, too.

Kuckuck • *Himmelpfortgasse 15* • is highly regarded for *nouvelle cuisine,* but is that why you came to Vienna? The chef, however, does lean toward Austrian interpretations of this medium.

★★★★ **Sirk** • in Art Deco style, is located in the Bristol Hotel building. I consider it one of the best and most attractive buys in the nation—whether at lunch, snacktime, dinner, or after opera. The ground floor evokes an informal mood, while the upstairs seems more appropriate for lingering romantic exchanges. On both levels the service and cuisine are cosmopolitan and cheering. At its moderate price scale, enthusiastically recommended.

☆☆☆☆ **Belvedere Stockl** • *Prinz-Eugen-Strasse 25* • borders the Belvedere Palace gardens on one side and the busy boulevard on the other. Ocher stucco mansion; 15 tables with a long handsome culinary display as its centerpiece attraction; friendly, sophisticated attention; urbane decor. For the appearance and gastronomy, the tariffs are quite reasonable.

Hilton has its expensive Prinz Eugen Grill—patrician to its damask-clad core. While it features a costly set-price gastronomic menu of some interest, other selections are laughably limited. The "library" segment offers the most appeal.

★★★ **D'Rauchkuchl** • *Schweglerstrasse 37, a short ride from the center* • bills itself as "Vienna's Only Medieval Restaurant"—a cheerful overstatement but not a serious one. The baroque Savoyen Rooms upstairs are copied from ancient castles. And true to form at any self-respecting bastion, the "authentic" bar surrounds a swimming pool. A bit of a hoot, but nice.

★★★ **Wiener Rathauskeller** • *Rathausplatz, in City Hall* • shouldn't be missed for local color. The municipally owned, immense eatery has four distinctively different dining areas, each a gem in its way, which one should examine before being seated; 2 open for lunch as well as post-7:30 dinner. The cookery is certainly not the most delicate in the world, but for a huge restaurant complex of this type, few can top it. Surprisingly reasonable tariffs; first-quality ingredients; service that was perfection—and friendly.

Kervansaray • *Mahlerstrasse 9* • serves doner kebab, yoghurt sour yayla, moussaka, and other Turkish tempters in luxurious surroundings. Upstairs there's a noteworthy seafood restaurant called the ☆☆☆**Hummer Bar,** where "lobster" is only one fruit of the sea. Downstairs is **Do und Co,** which is a crowded delicatessen for fancy lunchtime snacks. A few doors away, **Scampi** is another maritime nook; more cheerful in green and white; cheaper; lots of fun if you are feeling fishy.

Lindenkeller • *on the Rotenturmstrasse in the First District* • is excellent.

Zum Weissen Rauchfangkehrer • *Weihburggasse 4* • is intimate, charming, and a favorite of actors, artists, and journalists. Classic German decor, piano, friendly reception, rough service, decent food for the price. Closed Sunday, all of July and August, and many holidays.

Paulusstuben • *Walfischgasse 7, 1 minute from the opera* • is a midtown transplant of a Grinzing *Heuriger* (see below). Handsome facade; shabbily comfortable interior; friendly but uninspired service; dreary regional dishes.

Gosser Bierklinik • *Steindlg 4* • seats about 350 customers overall in the amusing cellar or in the Biedermeier restaurant. Open every day of the year; no music; reasonable tabs.

Griechenbeisl • *Fleischmarkt 11* • where the Old Taverne atmosphere has been laid on with a trowel, is larger, noisier, and poorly ventilated; it is the granddaddy of Viennese dining establishments.

The Viennese coffee houses, one of Austria's greatest traditions, have experienced a revival lately in spite of the onslaught of the brash, cafe-espresso bars that have crept up from Italy. The **Mozart,** the **Landtmann,** and the **Pruckel** are worthy choices. Artists have always been drawn to **Hawelka** and **Alt Wien.** Incidentally, next to Alt Wien *(Backer Str. 9)* is a funny place where canine reverence is at its finest: **Oswald & Kalb** is a charming family restaurant filled with bozo portraits, and happy wag-tail guests.

Konditoreien (Confection Shops)

★★★★ **Demel** • *Kohlmarkt 14* • has a clientele that have been stuffing themselves since A.D. 1813. The inventory includes aspics, cookies, salads, sandwiches, cold meats, iced juices, chocolate puffs overflowing with Chantilly, and Viennese coffee (black coffee, sugar, and hot milk stirred into a king-size cup, topped by great blobs of whipped cream); a countergirl—also, on occasion, of 1813 vintage—will bring your plate to your tiny table. The service is sweet, but horribly disorganized, especially at peak hours—so go just before noon, if you can. Open every day; ground-floor see-and-be-seen salon plus a parlor upstairs; poor selection on Sundays.

Other outstanding examples are **Lehmann** and **Heiner.**

For a more commercial type of operation, pop in at one of a score of **Aida** shops. All guarantee tiptop freshness that only a volume operation can turn out at such lowdown tariffs.

Wine gardens

Vienna is famous for its *Heuriger*—the "new-wine" or "fresh-wine" gardens. The most celebrated of these establishments are in *Grinzing,* 15 to 25 minutes by taxi. Look for the garland of pine twigs and vine leaves over the door. Try their old-time specialty, Backhendl, which is very young, milk-breaded chicken. Typical, sound examples are **Das Alte Haus** on the main drag called Himmelstrasse at #35 (where we had a delicious meal; go up the small exterior staircase to the timber-and-brick inner sanctum and turn to the right, which is our bid for the snuggest corner), the **Passauerhof,** the **Figlmuller,** and several others on Cobenzlgasse such as the **Altes Presshaus** (#15) and **Weinbottich** (#28). **Hauermandl** (#20) offers a garden at its courtyard entrance, a gypsy wagon on its roof, a wine press, 4 rooms, a Kellerstube composed of a long darkened arch, friendly service, and delicious farmhouse cookery. About a mile down the hill at Pfarrplatz (you'll need a taxi or car), **Franz Mayer** is in a cul de sac sharing nods across the plaza with a charming little chapel. Built around a barnyard close; attractive windowed hall with community tables; convivial

Austrians poised in various stages of ingestion. Very regional and quite good. Locals feel Grinzing is too touristic; many are moving over to *Sievering, Nussdorf,* and *Heiligenstadt* in the 19th district or to the Brunnergasse in *Perchtoldsdorf,* about 30 minutes by taxi. The **Spieelhofer** • *Hochstrasse 75* • is the top winery here. **Schubel-Auer** • *Kahlenbergerstr. 22 (Heiligenstadt-Nussdorf)* • has gained fame for its following of philharmonic musicians who sometimes play on Sunday mornings here. **Zimmermann** • *Mitterwuzer-gasse 20 (Neustift A. W-Salmannsdorf)* • is big, sprawling, and bustling. Also, it's fun. All shut down intermittently, whenever the barrels run out; light buffet and wine only except where noted, with no spirits or beer.

NIGHT LIFE

Moulin Rouge (Walfischgasse 11) is Vienna's most noteworthy; two-tier circular room with excellent viewing potential; B-gals aplenty; strips, magic acts, and similar variety wheezes more-or-less continuously through the evening. If the double-barreled entrance fee doesn't put you into an immediate catatonic state, perhaps your whisky at close to $20 per slug, beer at $12 per mug, or champagne at $350 per jug will. By contrast, you should pay between $5 and $10 per Scotch in most other places, with door charges skittering between zero and $5. **Fledermaus** (Spiegelgasse 2) has a low admission nibble. Long, well-ventilated room; 5 alcoves for intimate sipping; danceable combo; friendly atmosphere; large drinks; cabarets in German at 11 p.m. and 2 a.m., which can be dull if one doesn't understand the language; smooth operation. **Eve** (next to the Astoria Hotel) ranks high. Snug ambience; 2 orchestras; sleek houris eternally disrobing. **Queen Anne** (Johannesg. 12) is the top disco. **Casanova** (Dorotheerg. 6–8) bubbles about its "Erotic Air," aired from 9:30 p.m. to the whee hours nightly. Revue-type shows as perceived from theater seats, fancy boxes, or from the bar. For an entry fee of nearly $20, you can drink or abstain, whichever is desired. **Wurlitzer** (Schwarzenbergerplatz 10) is amusing for jukebox dancing. **Eden Bar** (Liliengasse 2) is *the* perch for chic Viennese night owls. Ho-hum decor; excellent 4-piece combo; no pickups; closed Sundays from May to July and various holidays.

Elegant tastes? The **Reiss Bar,** a few doors off Karntner Strasse on Marco d'Aviano Gasse serves a wide selection of champagne, *sekt, vin mousseux,* and other effervescence in Art Retro surroundings. Many attractive young executives and their bubbly mates clink goblets here.

Gambling Casino? Vienna's **Cercle Wien** is up 1 flight in the Palais Esterhazy (Karntner Strasse). Roulette, chemin de fer, punto banco, and blackjack comprise the play-for-pay; 170 schillings admission, but you are given chips of 200 schillings value. A Diners Club credit card may be used to buy a small stake in chips to get you started. Take your passport.

SHOPPING

SHOPPING HOURS: *Vienna* • Weekdays from 8, 8:30, or 9 a.m. to 6 p.m.; generally no noon closing in midtown; shuttered Sat. at noon or 1 p.m. *Other cities* • same openings; closing hours variable.

BEST AREAS: Midtown is laced with malls for pedestrians only which are lined with benches, transplanted trees, and cheerful lighting patterns. These traffic-free islands of serenity include Karntnerstrasse (the main shopping street with the most chic addresses), Graben, Stephansplatz, Kohlmarkt, and Naglergasse; several more are in the outlying precincts. They are a delight. Along the Mariahilferstrasse are large department stores and more popularly priced shops.

SAVINGS ON PURCHASES: If you spend a total of at least 1000 schillings in any one shop, then you are eligible for a fat VAT rebate. Right now this tax is on three tiers of 10%, 20%, and the sizable 32% (for new cars, boats, and car rentals). These taxes are always added to the net amount of the merchandise so the price tag will show the gross amount, which includes the VAT. This might be confusing to shoppers because, in reality, what you will get back is actually 16.66% (on the 20%) and 24.24% (on the 32%). Sales personnel will explain the mechanism of the Refund Form U-34, which requires a customs stamp *before* checking in your luggage (if flying). There are airport facilities that will grant you your money immediately, but there is an additional tiny service charge deducted. Here, too, customs officials must stamp the papers at the border. You may also mail these documents back in the self-addressed envelopes you are provided with and the store will usually process them within six weeks.

AUCTION: Try to go to the enormously intriguing **Dorotheum Auction** (Dorotheergasse 17) if it's operating while you're there. Full details on this fascinating landmark and how best to handle yourself for the greatest fun and greatest bargains (which are often fantastic) are outlined step by step in our *Shopping Guide.*

CAKES: The **Imperial Hotel,** as mentioned earlier, offers its fabulous **Torte,** which can be purchased at the desk or mailed (in excellent wooden presentation boxes) to any recipient in this fat wide world. It remains fresh and rich for an extraordinary period—but disappears quickly once seen and tasted.

CUTLERY: Deckenbacher & Blumner (Karntnerstr. 21–23 and Mariahilferstrasse 70) takes rightful pride in its stag-handled carving sets, matched sets of knives, and similar items.

DOWN QUILTS: **Gans** (Brandstatte 1) is the nest. There are 4 different stuffings and designs for every boudoir and climate. Easily the most upmarket down in the world.

ENAMEL JEWELRY: **Michaela Frey Team** (Gumpendorferstr. 81) is the master, combining both tradition and uniqueness of outstanding artistic character and high-fashion flair. Prices are reasonable. Here at its headquarters you'll find bracelets, rings, necklaces, brooches, earrings, coordinated silk scarves and decorative shawls for ladies; parents will be thrilled to see the special line for children. Due to the clever blend of color, finish, and mood, everything is in perfect harmony with seasonal trends.

EMBROIDERY: **Zur Schwabischen Jungfrau** (Graben 26) has table linens that exactly match certain patterns of Augarten, Meissen, and Herend china to create a "total" look while dining.

HANDICRAFTS: **Osterreichische Werkstatten** (Karntnerstr. 6) offers a most interesting variety of high-quality wares made by Austrian artisans. **Elfi Muller** (Karntnerstr. 53) is basically a souvenir shop.

JEWELRY: **A.E. Koechert** (Neuer Markt 15) is worth the time of anyone who likes extraordinarily fine brooches, rings, necklaces, and original creations in the renowned Viennese style. Austrian handwork in precious metals and gems not only has its distinctive flavor, but labor costs are so low that only Portugal can offer such comparatively modest price levels in this magic. Continuously since 1814 this landmark was designated by successive Emperors as Crown Jewelers to the Imperial Court. Gorgeously opulent pieces are available to the millionaire trade, but for travelers like us, who haven't much to spend, Koechert also shines with equal brilliance. There's an intangible quality, an ethereal beauty to their pieces, which is impossible for us to describe; all we know is that we love it and that you won't find it elsewhere. Ask for Dr. Dietrich, Wolfgang and Christoph Koechert. A treasure house.

LEATHER GOODS: **Madler,** not connected in any way with the world-renowned Zurich company, (Graben 17 and Mariahilferstrasse 24) carries a sumptuous selection of suitcases, carry-on bags, handbags, briefcases, and scores of stunning, hard-to-find specialty items. The styling has chic and flair; the price range is appealing.

PETIT-POINT: **Maria Stransky** (Hofburgpassage 2) has enjoyed an international esteem for more than 80 years. Situated in Vienna's historic Hofburg (Imperial Palace), great attention is afforded to every customer in explaining the history, creation, and elaboration of this art. The experience of going will be unforgettable for anyone who appreciates this craft. Be sure to ask for Ingrid Vytlacil and let her show you the finest in brooches, pendants, bags, purses, eyeglass cases, and pictures.

PORCELAIN AND GLASS: **J. & L. Lobmeyr** (Karntnerstr. 26) is distinguished for its crystal specialties. There is also a good selection of Herend china from Hungary plus gift articles and other *belles tournures*. They are proud to show you their outstanding museum or to tend to your special needs. **Wiener Porzellanmanufaktur Augarten** (Stock-Im-Eisenplatz 3, Mariahilferstrasse 99, and the Schloss Augarten) has magnificent Spanish Riding School figurines and some knockout dinner settings. **Rasper & Sohne** (Graben 15) has a wide choice of items. **E. Bakalowitz** (Spiegelgasse 3) made its mark designing chandeliers.

REGIONAL CLOTHES: **Loden-Plankl** (Michaelerplatz 6) is one of the oldest for typical Tyrolean suits and sweaters; **Tostmann** (Schottengasse 3a) is highly regarded for its dirndls; **Lanz** (Karntnerstr. 10) is also very good. **Resi Hammerer** (Karntnerstr. 29) is the Loden Queen's palace of fashion when it comes to exciting Austrian design, materials, and sterling quality. While olive tones are basic, the mixes are so cleverly matched that your wardrobe can grow and vary with almost limitless pleasure.

ZELL AM SEE   is in a scenic bowl fed by the snows from the distant Grossglockner, Austria's majestic mountain peak. While the older hotels snuggle at the edge of the lake, some of the later models are several files back or hug the shouldering slopes.

☆☆ **Salzburgerhof**   dominates as an oversized, flower-girt, balconied chalet. Excellent dining in the streetside Burger Stube with its great timbers, leaded glass, tapestried chairs, and candle illumination at night. (Try the trout in herb sauce if they have it.) There's a pool, terraces, gardens, everything you could wish for in a resort hotel.

★ **Tirolerhof**   Who wouldn't be taken by the forthright Tyrolean personality of this aptly named spot? The bleached timbers, the wrought iron, the painted features on the walls, the flowers—even the Roman amphorae—have a capacity to charm.

Katharina, not directly in the center and with its own tonsure of blossoms, a pool, and its parkland setting, tends more toward the modernistic. **Porschehof** is more regional in tone and appealing. **Clima Seehotel,** smack on the lake, is old-fashioned with pockets of renewal; extremely generous in its visual rewards of the water, the sailboats, the landscape, and the gliders soaring above. The buffet is overwhelming in its presentation, savor, abundance, and elan. For economizing with no loss of atmosphere, hardly anything in the neighborhood can touch the **Erlhof.** It is a honey for the flavor of the Alps and for absorbing the sun on the southeastern shore of the lake. What's more, the cookery is outstanding for its category.

The shop of **Isabella Bader** (Anton Wallnerstr. 5) is where this talented designer creates some of the most beautiful dried flower displays ever purloined from Mother Nature. As these items require meticulous work, don't expect them to be inexpensive. Still, some items sell for as little as $15 while the more intricate, large combinations range up to $500.

ZURS AM ARLBERG   This town lives for winter only. The major houses close as the snow vanishes.

☆☆☆☆☆ The **Zurserhof,** merrily rich, is the leading hotel here—and one of the top spots on the European winter-sport circuit. Beautiful appointments in Peasant Baroque; sumptuous wing of suites, all with working fireplaces; a living museum of fine regional furnishings; the hitching post of many international notables.

★★★★ The **Lorunser,** with 70 rooms, offers more sporting *Gemutlichkeit* and a younger clientele. Gracefully outfitted Fitness Center to unkink the muscles and dissuade the calories from lingering on your frame. Its set-meal gastronomy (with options, plus a policy of answering requests for special dishes) is one of the best I've experienced in the Alps. The delightful Jochum team, Herbert and Inge, couldn't be nicer.

☆ The **Alpenrose-Post** comes with its own swimming pool and sauna; 2 bars; tea dancing daily plus nightly revels. Somewhat commercial in tone; nevertheless a handsome haven for highlanders. **Edelweiss** is simple, cozy, and bustling. Its *Stubli,* where you should sample the delicious *Backhendl* (fried chicken, Austrian version), is always jammed.

★ The **Alpenhof,** hill-bound and offering 50 units, is infused with the giant-size grace of the owning Thurnher family. Intimacy is the pivotal word here—with all the comforts of household living, including much of that feeling, too.

THE BONUS OF BUDAPEST

The Hungarian border is only 45 minutes east of the Austrian capital. And to Budapest—one of the most enchanting of medieval cities—the drive (bus or private car) takes only 3½ hours on an excellent highway. If you don't already have it, a visa can be obtained at the frontier (2 photos required, but even a photo booth is available; these rules may be relaxed soon so ask locally); trains are also quick, but you might still need a visa beforehand for rail travel. In Vienna you can obtain one at either the Hungarian Embassy (in two palaces at Bankgasse 4–6) mornings only on Mon. through Fri., or weekdays and Saturday mornings at IBUSZ (Karntnerstr. 26) in midcity. The price is about $10. (I repeat, all of this visa information may have changed by the time of your arrival, so be sure to check just before your departure date.) Air connections are convenient at either of the city's two airports; they are linked by bus shuttles. As mentioned, standard ferries or hovercraft zip along the Danube, adding another dimension of fun to your summer adventure. The comfortable MS *Mozart* makes a 4-day roundtrip with a stop in Bratislava as its Czech-point on the route. Dollars buy a lot of Florints so it's a buyer's market for visitors.

The city extends on either side of the swiftly running Danube with 8 bridges joining the 2 integrated towns of old **Buda** and newer **Pest.** For comfort, it is astonishing to hidebound western visitors that such modernity even exists in

Eastern Europe. The **Hilton,** at the top of Buda, with a magnificent view of the town and river, is joined to the imposing Fisherman's Bastion and to the spellbinding polychromatic Matthias Church, which is a mere 700 years old and in a state of perfect preservation. Unfortunately, reservations for promised riverside accommodations here are not always honored. Nearby, in this former ghetto, are art galleries, an archaeological exhibit dating back to the Roman occupation, a pharmaceutical museum, and a warren of wonderful antique streets devoted to pedestrians only. The modernistic **Duna** (Danube) **Intercontinental** stands tall on the lower Pest side of the river at the valley floor; filled with Westernisms, including East Europe's first squash court. The water-taxi dock here is a handy asset for sightseers. **Hyatt** also has built a stately house that even features glass-clad elevators; **Forum**—with its zesty Viennese coffee *haus*—is yet another ultraslick hotel while **Gellert** remains the doyenne of the dowagers, reflecting an air of traditional elegance. The beer bar here is the top snackery and gossip haven in town. The **Thermal** is a bath hotel of top quality on *Margit Island* (the city is perched on hot water springs). It recently was updated and given a Kosher restaurant from the midcity Hanna establishment. A 163-room **Ramada** hisses and bubbles on the island, too—linked to the Thermal by a tunnel (heated, of course). The air-conditioned **Penta** (15 minutes out of the center) and the **Novotel** (by the Convention hub) are pool-ed, sauna-ed, and comfort-ized as well as being low in cost. **Marriott** and **Sheraton** should be open for your arrival and **Kempinski** of Berlin is already working on a 13-story luxury house that could be the pace-setter for all Eastern efforts in the hotel trade. The **Taverna** provides 224 midcity bedrooms and a heavy concentration of dining and entertainment facilities; twin units run around $55 per night. Tariffs are similar at the renewed turn-of-the-century **Remi Nemzeti.** Prices in any of these are 30–50% less than in Western European hotels of like luxury.

Dining is another surprise. I recently hosted two friends for lunch at a splendid tavern, ordered apricot schnaps first, wine, soup, cevapecici, crepes (palatchinkin and piquant marmalade), coffee—and the bill came to less than $15 for all three, including tip! In most top-level city restaurants, a meal for two will ring up approximately $65, including music and wine.

Restaurants in the hotels mentioned above are fine—even excellent—but perhaps are too sterile and too predictable. Always they are more expensive than the independent dining spots. Most feature gypsy violins, zithers, and a multitude of mustaches and spaniel eyes. **Matyas Pince** plays largely for Eastern groups and is better avoided. **Vadrozsa,** with its rose garden and villa setting, is elegant and deserving. **Gundel**, named for Hungary's top chef in the early 1900s, is of the old school and excellent, with a delightful garden in summer. **Legradi Testverek** is a fancy cellar where the elite meet—and with good reason. **Alabardos** is next, followed by **Fortuna** and **Legradi Brothers.** The latter is traditional, far too expensive for the value, and lacking the refinement it pretends to provide gastronomically. The **Szazeves** ("100-Year-Old Restaurant") is often suggested by tip-hungry concierges, but I doubt it can last another century. **Vigado** (near the Hyatt) serves marvelous creamy lamb soup with tarragon. **Cafe Pierrot** is a piano bar and favorite hangout of the "in" crowd. You can sip goulash or gambol through a gypsy repast at the **Budapest Casino,** high above the city. There's another on board the riverboat *Schonbrunn* moored in front of the Forum Hotel in Pest. It is located atop the Hilton.

As for excursions, take the marvelous ½ hour-drive to the artists' colony of *St. Andrews (Szentendre),* with its pastel cottages and myriad studios. Margit Kovacs **ceramics museum** is a *must.* Have a meal at either the **Golden Dragon** or the wonderfully rough-and-ready **Rab Raby** tavern. The **Regimodi Vendeglo** is also a splendid choice for fish or game; start with the clear pheasant broth. Other nearby touring centers are the town on the Danube Bend called **Esztergom** with the largest cathedral in the nation or *Pannonhalma,* site of a Benedictine college. (Catholicism is thriving in this nation.) At *Eisenstadt* you'll find the **Esterhazy Castle,** where Haydn composed as well as conducted much of his music, and about 15 miles away is **Forchtenstein Castle,** with its colorful uniform and arms collections. If you are looking for a weekend away from Budapest, try *Pecs,* down by the Yugoslav frontier and hugged by the Mecsek range of foothills. It's a hub of numerous grand museums, converted mosques, and cultural interfaces that span eight centuries of exchange. These almost all center around Szechenyi Square, perhaps 3.5 hours from Budapest by car. **Pannonia** is a suitable hotel, followed by **Palatinus.** The more suburban **Hunyor** is lovely and quiet at the end of a day of ardent sightseeing.

Try Budapest and the neighboring prizes for a weekend or for a week. It is possibly the happiest capital in the East and a lot more jovial than many western ones I know.

BELGIUM

SPECIAL REMARKS: (1) To move around cheaply, ask about tourist benefits at the information headquarters. This entitles you to a day of unlimited tram and bus travel plus reductions on some shopping items as well as a free drink or a restaurant bonus. (2) The youth center called "Welcome to Brussels" sponsors an English-speaking guide service so that local citizens can improve their language facilities while promoting good relations with foreigners. Volunteers of all ages. (3) The Directors of Press and Public Relations are Jacques Van Gampelaere (Flanders) and Pierre Coenegrachts (French); they can answer any question or point you in the right direction. Their multilingual staff is one of the finest in Europe. Their counterpart in the U.S. is Ms. Frederique Raeymaekers.

TELEPHONE: Access code to USA: 00. To phone Belgium: 32; time difference (Eastern Daylight) plus 6 hrs.

Within your first hour on Belgian soil you'll confirm that its skies are punctuated by more spires and castle turrets than any other nation you've ever visited. The size of the State of Maryland, here is one of the most densely populated countries in Europe, oozing with a beauty, culture, and elegance that are not seen in thousands of miles of travel elsewhere on Earth's real estate.

The Flemings are the northerners; the Walloons are from Dixie, a nation divided into 2 major linguistic areas—Flanders, where Flemish is used by about 5.6 million, and the Walloon section, where French is the official tongue of a minority of 3.2 million. The bilingual capital is neutral ground, a city of 1 million convivial souls. Yet another idiom exists but it comprises only about

60,000 German voices heard near the eastern frontier in a region called *Ostkantone* (or Eastern County).

As Belgium is so small, you'll very likely see most of it in a brief time span—and much of it will be in bloom if the season is right. Don't think that Holland has a touristic monopoly on blossoms, bulbs, and botany in the Lowlands. The Royal Palace at *Laeken* is a worthy target.

Antwerp, Ghent, and *Bruges,* under an hour from Brussels on the superhighway, draw the most attention outside the capital. To cover a lot of territory fast (which is not recommended, since the greater rewards come from lingering), here's a once-over-lightly itinerary that can be comfortably done in one highly active day: Start from Brussels at 8:30 a.m. Take the expressway straight to Bruges, ignoring Ghent, which you'll be seeing later. Enjoy a 35-minute boat ride on a canal, sightsee where you will, and then amble down either the expressway or Route N-10 (distances about even) to *Ostend* with its salty scenery and modern Kursaal Casino.

If there's time, you might wish to run out to *Knokke,* Belgium's most chichi seaside resort, a few miles along the coast to the north. If not, perhaps you'd be happier to head straight for lunch in *Bruges.* Then climb back on the expressway to *Ghent* for a view of Van Eyck's "Holy Lamb" at the **Cathedral;** follow this with tea at the ramshackle Cour St.-Georges, oldest hotel in the north; the rooms are poor but the dining facilities passable. Those with extra fortitude may want to run out to the **Castle of Laarne** for a peek at its multi-million-dollar silver collection, its tapestries, its furniture, and the spook who haunts its grandiose halls. You should be back in Brussels by dinnertime— dogtired but well pleased with your comprehensive excursion.

The *Ardennes,* a sizable area that stretches south and southwest, to the French and Luxembourg borders, unfolds the most beautiful vistas in the nation. With its rolling hills, lazily gliding waters, dense forests, tidy farms, and classic villages, it is a kaleidoscope of bucolic charm. A special attraction is the **Grottos of Han,** about 2 hours from the capital. The underground streams are interesting, the colors are exquisite, and the rooms are so huge that musical events sometimes are presented in them.

Sound-and-Light *(Son et Lumiere)* spectacles glow from May 1 through September 30 in the courtyards of medieval castles at *Bouillon, La Roche, Ghent,* and *Bruges,* plus a stunning eye-popper several nights each week in the **Grand' Place** of the capital.

The **Carnival** de *Binche* (pronounced "Bahn-ssh"), inaugurated by Maximilian more than 4 centuries ago, is worth a 500-mile detour from any set itinerary, if you happen to be in Europe just before Lent. The pseudo-Peruvian costumes are fantastically colorful—with ostrich-feather headdresses 4 feet tall. On the climax day, 500 participants "dance" the grand parade. *Wear your oldest clothes if you go to this*—blue jeans, if possible—because the crowd will kiss you, hit you painlessly with air-filled skin bags, and throw oranges at you, all simultaneously.

TRANSPORTATION **Airline** Your first glance of Belgium will probably be via Brussels Airport, one of Europe's best, cleanest, and most thoughtfully constructed. It even provides quick rail service to town (less than a tenth of the taxi fare). **Sabena** is fine on intra-European flights. I have not flown transatlan-

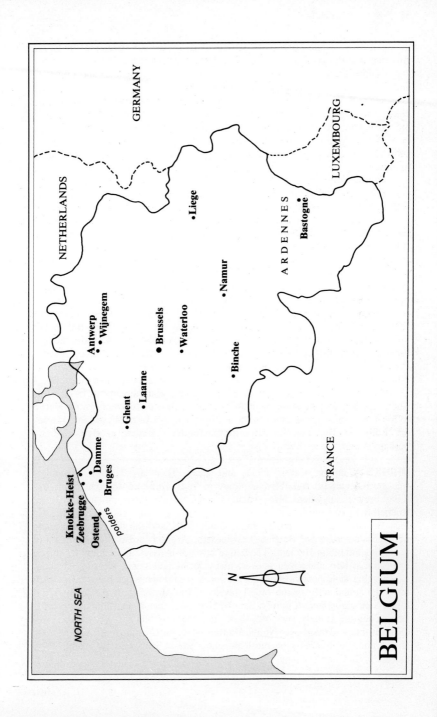

BELGIUM

tic on it for a while so I can't comment on its service standards. In North America it calls on Montreal, Toronto, New York, Atlanta, Boston, and Chicago. Globally, you can carry on with Sabena to Africa (South and Central), and the Easts (Middle and Far).

Taxis Belgian taxi fares are among the highest in the world. Tips are included, *so don't bother with any further voluntary doles,* even though drivers may grumble, whine, or even withhold change.

Metro Possibly the most civilized in the world. With one $8 card, the subway can be used for 10 trips. Buses, metros, and trams stop running at midnight.

Trains Very good.

The 5-day-minimum Tourist Card ("abonnement") is perfect for excursioners. (Five days should be sufficient to cover this little land, but versions of this T-Travel Card now are issued for 16 days, too.) There is also the wider-ranging Benelux Tourrail plan, which covers 3 nations for 10 days of limitless conveyance.

Ferry Connections There's a **Jetfoil** between Ostend and Dover or Folkestone. The 250-passenger **P & O** vessel skims along at close to 50 mph. A larger conventional ferry also plies these routes, but the travel time is longer, of course. Trains meet the ships for swift passage to the capitals.

FOOD If you can pay the price, you'll get fat fast in Belgium. But, never mind, there are vast numbers of good, inexpensive places, too. In its ranking establishments gustatory standards are so high they challenge or rank even better than the leaders in France. The approach to cuisine, too, is similar. Local traditions include beer soup, eels in green sauce, and mussels in many disguises.

The citizenry takes justified pride in the sweep and the scope of its cheeses. There's a bewildering assortment from strong, classic, Munster-school **Herve** to local goat-milk preparations to those from such abbeys as **Westmale, Trappist, Folies de Beguine, La Pave de Bastogne, Fromage de Brussels,** and perhaps 4 or 5 dozen others.

DRINKS Trappist beer is unique and cheap. There are 2 types: "Double" (the normal variety) and "Triple" (hard to find). Both are different from anything brewed anywhere else—vague Coca-Cola overtones; a curiosity. The Rochefort monks produce a 3rd kind from oranges. Other national quaffs (Artois, Haecht, Gueuze-Lambic, Duke, Ginder Ale, and the like) produce many international prizes for Belgian brewmasters. A good ⅓rd of the nation's 189 breweries bubble in Brabant. The native brew of Brussels is Le Lambic; sipped naturally, it will make you pucker; many locals add sugar; we suggest about 328 heaping tablespoons per glass. The locals also down Kriek-Lambic, a cherry beverage found only in the oldest taverns. And speaking of pubs, don't fail to visit an *estaminet,* a purely Belgian invention that is the ultimate in coziness. They are usually very old, dark, and chummy and serve liquids as well as light bites. **Image de Notre Dame,** up a narrow lane off rue Marche aux Herbes, is possibly the most authentic one in Brussels, but many others exist.

CITIES AND REGIONS

ALDEN BIESEN is in Limburg near *Bilzen*. Here you'll find the home of the Teutonic Order as well as one of the most extensive castle neighborhoods north of the Loire Valley. Most have been restored and the visitor is welcome around the calendar. It's an easy excursion target from Brussels or Liege.

ANTWERP

Antwerp is one of the greatest ports on the European continent—yet it's 54 miles from the smell of salt water. The Scheldt River is the answer: 60,000 barges and 20,000 ocean-going ships tie up to the 60 miles of docks every year. In warm weather you can see much of the waterfront by boat. The 6-lane, 2000-foot-long John F. Kennedy Tunnel eases train and car traffic under the river. This city remains the world center for the diamond trade, much of it concerned with cutting and industrial applications. Its heartbeat is Pelikaanstraat, but if you want to observe the entire process from mining exhibits to cutting to setting to, yes, even selling the highly finished product, go to fabulous **Diamond Land** at Appelmansstraat 33-A in the same district or visit the **Provincial Diamond Museum** at Lange Herentalsestraat 31–33. The free tours and browsing are blue-white with fascination. Flemish is the regional language; the **Rubens mansion** is a sightseeing must, along with the **Royal Art Gallery.** "Mad Meg" of the **Mayer van den Bergh Museum** is in a private house that creates a perfect showcase for some of the nation's finest artworks. Also in midcity is the 9th-century-old **Steen Castle** housing the **National Maritime Museum** and the **Plantin Moretus Museum** (patrician house with ancient printing plant); so is the magnificent statue in the Grand Place of the Roman centurion who saved the town, thus providing the legend from which the metropolis took its name. On a religious note, **Our Lady's Cathedral** is only one—and marvelous—example of the 30 Christian churches; there are also 22 synagogues, 16 mosques, and 3 Buddhist temples in town. If you have more time, the **Butchers' Hall** and **Brewers' House** museums are lesser known but contain fascinating collections of art, musical instruments, archaeological finds, and furniture, none of which is related to their guild or trade names. The **Ethnographic Museum** is a lively, fun-filled folkloric trip into the past, even with puppets to spice it up for kids. The **Zoo** includes an aquarium in the gardens, a delphinarium, a unique aviary, and a nocturama. About 5 minutes by car from the center, stroll through the fabulous open-air **Middelheim Park,** a year-round sculpture garden; you can dine at the palace among moats, swans, Rodins, and Moores.

About halfway between Antwerp and the capital is **Fort Breendonk,** a former Nazi concentration camp. It has been preserved intact as a national museum; even the torture chambers are still there.

HOTELS

Please remember that our rankings here do not necessarily jibe with the official local version. See ''About the Stars'' for an explanation.

☆☆☆☆ **Rosier •** is head, shoulders, and feathered cap above all competition as the finest and most exclusive lodging in these precincts. Striking entrance; slightly less striking 1-table and 5-table restaurants, both closing at 11 p.m. for the clients' tranquillity; high tea a joy here.

☆☆ **De Keyser •** in midcity, evokes a clean modern air enhanced by quality appurtenances. Compact but well-preserved, it stokes up enviable cookery in its ovens. Its Old Masters restaurant is ingratiating if you want to dine in formal surroundings. The Paint Box provides more casual atmosphere and lighter selections.

Holiday Inn • about a mile out on the E3 pike near Middelheim Park, greets motorists with several interesting tapestries in its front hall. Airy Wellington restaurant has some of the finest hotel fare in the region and a noteworthy brunch on Sundays; coffee shop; cheaper Campaign Bar; 5 attractive penthouse suites; more than 300 look-alike quarters stacked in a high-rise configuration.

Scandic Crown • features a pool and sauna; overall it's barely passable, if that.

☆☆☆ **Pullman Park •** is out at the convention center, a glittering glass-bound, atrium-design creation in polished glass. It contains 215 rooms, 3 suites, 2 restaurants (Tiffany's for formality and the Parc Relais for ease), the Jockey lounge, Facets for nightlife, and a fitness room and sauna to rinse away those sins. A bright modern gem in the diamond city of Belgium.

Switel • with dreary surroundings, makes a splash with a good-sized swimming pool and a spacious parking lot (important in this traffic-choked anthill). The dining salon is colorful; the cafe served what was perhaps my most repellent ingestion ever on Belgian soil; its bedrooms are substantial but totally lack inspiration.

RESTAURANTS

☆☆☆ **Relais Esterel** • *Tolstraat 70, near Museum of Fine Arts* • serves dinner only, from 6:30 to 2. Tapestried banquettes; 10 handsomely set tables in its main area and a scattering more up a few steps; very expensive. Outstanding specialties of roast goose liver with cabbage and delicate fish stuffed with spinach; comprehensive *cave;* delicious skilletry.

★★★ **'t Fornuis** • *Reyndersstraat 24* • is happily tended by patron-chef Johan Segers, whom you might wish to ask for his suggestions for your day. This small enterprise is extremely cozy in an old-fashioned Antwerp mode with red brick, a beamed ceiling, blending rugs, and distributed candles. Seafood and seasonal preparations are its greatest pride.

★★★ **Sir Anthony Van Dijck** • *Oude Koornmarkt 16* • To enter you must stroll through this "Old Grain Market," a courtyard complex of restored 16th-century buildings called the Vlaaikensgang. Sophisticated rooms; piped classical music softly in background; illumination from a few baby spots and a candle on every table markedly too dim; suave minions. A sound bet but not quite up to the aforementioned institutions in savor.

Manoir • *Everdijstraat 13* • nests in a venerable private home. The decor is split between its two sections, the smaller of which is in charming 17th-century baroque and the other with high ceilings in a vaguely Japanese mode. Luxury French-type dishes are the accents here. It is open every day in the week from 12 to 3 and 6 to 10. Costly and trustworthy.

☆☆ **Vateli** • *Kipdorpvest 50* • offers nouvelle cuisine for moderate outlays. Amenable atmosphere, service, and value.

★★★ **La Perouse** is an affluent and interesting novelty. It's the dining salon of the *Flandria XVI,* which is moored between Sept. 15 and May 15 at the Flandria Co. dock on the Scheldt River. (In summer the boat makes daily tourist-class shuttles between Antwerp and Flushing.) Refitted wooden deck; a la carte ordering only; piano music at night; amusing in sunlight or starlight, but not advised during rain, fog, or storms. Closed Mon. The smaller *Flandria XVII* is used for private parties and charters as well as for warm-weather toots to Rotterdam.

Ciro's • *Britselei in the Palace of Justice area* • is best known for its reasonably priced "Steak Ciro," which is served with chips (french fries) and salad.

Cafes

Den Engel • *Market Sq.* • is a famous old haunt that is often packed with local devotees. It is very plain and the tone is lively. A feature is its De Ton ("Barrel") game in which brass cylinders are tossed at the 12 holes in a board. Its special De Koninck ("The King") beer is dark and delectable.

Quinten Matsys • *Moriaanstraat 17* • is the oldest in the region, with roots that stretch back unbroken to A.D. 1565. "Traditional" says it all.

De Groote Witte Arend • *Reyndersstraat 18* • was an ancient convent. Myriad of rooms; benches in refectory style; open courtyard for sunny sipping; piped classical music always. Selected beers (particularly Trappist types) are available, and so are cheese or pate plates as well as cakes.

Kulminator • *Vleminckveld* • is more of a pub. Here you will find 550 varieties of beer, all of which are served in their proper glasses at the proper temperatures. This establishment is named for a Berlin beer that is served extremely cold in a receptacle smaller than a cognac glass. Snacks are on hand; there is a summer garden behind it. Great fun for aficionados of the malt and the hops.

SHOPPING

Diamonds, diamonds, diamonds! This is where more than 60% of the world's sparklers are cut and polished. You can witness the story graphically at the midtown building called **Diamondland** (Appelmansstraat 33-A) in the heart of the gem district. Craftsmen are at work; there are showrooms and purchasing counters; all will be explained.

ARDENNES   Here is a glorious area which is a 1- to 3-hour's drive south and southwest of Brussels and which incorporates the lion's share of the provinces of Namur, Liege, and Luxembourg (not to be confused with the neighboring Grand Duchy). Here you will enjoy the bucolic serenity of rolling hills dotted with woods and heaths, precipitous narrow valleys and sleepy rivers from the Meuse to smaller serpentine streams and picture-postcard tidy farms.
Liege, its largest city, is industrial. (It is covered alphabetically later on.) *Charleroi, Namur,* and *Arlon,* next down the scale in size, beckon with only mild interest. *Dinant,* about 60 minutes from the national capital, is a very popular resort hub. The Meuse is particularly lovely here; cruise boats are available for short runs. Its preeminent specialties are "Cookee Dinant"—a type of gingerbread that is normally pressed in ancient molds—and copper items, ham, and sausages. *Bastogne* is way down in the Ardennes Forest. On a nearby hill stands the magnificent **Mardasson Monument,** a mammoth 5-pointed star that is dedicated to the American fighting men who were lost in the Battle of the

Bulge. The **War Museum** and the **Bastogne Historical Center** also provide something to see in this otherwise somnolent settlement. If you're lingering or merely hungry, the centuries-old, pink-faced **Lebrun** is just about the only show in town. **Le Borges** could be your alternative choice, located smack on place McAuliffe. All the rest of the centers in this vast area are small towns or villages, some of them charming and some of them apathetic.

Les Ramiers at *Crupet* (perhaps 7 miles via the main highway south and a small road west) is for dedicated students of cuisine only. No bar or lounge, although drinks can be had in benign weather at the bank of a brook; 1 narrow, constricted dining area with 7 tables and the other with 6; sterile atmosphere; costly; closed Mon. evening and Tues.

Hostellerie Val Joli, at the tiny village of *Celles* (about 7 miles almost due west but slightly south of Dinant), sits tranquilly beside a trout stream in a pretty valley; compact lounge and cheerful dining room; total of 10 tables with yellow linens and brown Alpine chairs; antiques nearly everywhere; fish, game, crustacea, and fabulous desserts are the features of Proprietor-Chef M. Ortmans; outstanding wine card.

Hostellerie de la Poste at *Havelange*, 18 miles along the road from Dinant to Liege, is a 13-century-old post house with 12 units with bath.

Hostellerie St. Roch, in *Comblain-la-Tour*, is conveniently reached by train. This felicitous escape hatch is directly on the Ourthe River. Bar with fireplace and mounted roebuck trophies plus lounge with b-i-g overstuffed chairs; 12 tables, lots of flowers, lots of pewter; dominant emphasis on mousses, pates, game, trout, its own smoked ham and fantastic desserts; handful of rooms with attractive old-fashioned furniture, colorful chintz, minibar, small color TV and modern baths with each. This beautiful hideaway is particularly noted for the warmth and charm of M. and Mme. Dernouchamps-Cawet.

Le Sanglier des Ardennes is sandwiched between the main street and the Ourthe river in *Durbuy*, an enchanting spot on the map that bills itself as "the smallest town in the world." (Isn't that a clever ploy to contain urban sprawl?) While this inn is spotlessly clean, it has a very well-used family-type milieu with cluttered decor not to our tastes; saved by its second dining room, which is a terrace overlooking the stream. The cookery is delectable. Its specialties include fresh homemade foie gras, trout pate, wild duck, wild boar, ham, grilled trout fillet on a salad bed and local cheeses; its wine cellar is extraordinary. The doors are closed in January and on every Thursday.

Vivier d'Oies, at *Dorinne* (about a mile from Spontin) offers some of the finest cookery in the Ardennes, especially the sole with lobster sauce and the tender piglet with pepper kernels. Closed Wednesdays and part of June and July.

Zur Post in *Saint-Vith*, 8 miles from the Luxembourg border, is another period coach house. It combines dignity with refinement. There is space for only about 35 clients. While its fare is light and innovative, it is not truly *nouvelle;* M. and Mme. Pankert take special pride in their Coquille St.-Jacques, Ballotine de Sandres of salmon and their variety of game in season.

L'Auberge du Moulin Hideux at *Noirefontaine*, 5 miles from the frontier on the highway to Sedan (France), is a pleasant 13-room hotel with a captivating restaurant. The rose-colored house nestles in a sleepy hollow, offering homey comforts, crackling fires in cold weather, and river views through cottage windows. You'll discover a comfortable glass-lined veranda in the bowers over a brook, fresh furnishings, and a handful of rooms, some with garden access. There's also a tennis court. You'll pay plenty for fine rewards. Don't miss a drive to *Orval's* Abbey, nearby, and the Basilica in the French town of *Avioth*.

BRUGES

Bruges is often labeled the "Venice of the North." In its youth, when it was world-renowned for its immensely prosperous wool and cloth trade and equally as a trading center and port, it boasted a population of nearly 40,000— as big as London or Cologne. But in the 15th and 16th centuries political conflict, the silting of the Zwin estuary that linked the city to the sea, and the rise of nearby Antwerp led to its deterioration into moribundity. Over the past decade it has been restored, with cobblestones, hundreds of old houses have been reconstituted, facades cleaned, trees planted in squares. Large areas have been closed to traffic. And with the plangent celebration from the belfries instead of the roar of traffic, here is convivial transport to the sights and sounds of the Late Middle Ages. The result? Save for Brussels, it is the greatest attracton to visitors in Belgium.

ATTRACTIONS

If you're headed toward this land for Ascension Day, Bruges' globally famous Procession of the Holy Blood shouldn't be missed. The ancient architecture now glows; its intimate, fine museums are superb; be sure to see Memling's work at the Hospital of St. John, the Town Hall, and the Belfry Tower. Noteworthy churches are Notre Dame and the 10th-century St. Saviour. Handmade lace and the wonderful little local pastries are the industries of greatest interest.

Two pint-size but outstandingly pleasant excursions: Take up a seat in one of the small motorboats and laze at random along the canals, which are among the most romantic settings on this planet. The duration is about 30 minutes. Or glide along the canal to *Damme* for about the same time. Because some trips ply the year round while others are limited to High Season, you might wish to inquire at the Bruges Tourist Office for schedules. It's a delightful town through which a tour is highly recommended.

HOTELS

★★★★ **Duc de Bourgogne** ● is a 9-room hostelry that features an internationally acclaimed restaurant. For the utter beauty and enchantment of its canal corner location, nothing can touch it. Be sure to pick your room here. The lobby and the dining areas are lovely. The price tags are tinged with gold.

★★★ **Orangerie** ● also by a sleepy canal, is remade cheerfully from a 16th-century shell containing 18 rooms, tinted leaded glass, open hearts, and open hearths. It is a marvelous blend of antiquity and friendly comfort at reasonable prices. No dining room but there's a majestic salon for breakfast, teas, and chitchat.

★★★ **Pand** ● is a luxurious conversion of a private home into a 24-room hotel. The accent is still on ''home'' like comforts—home, that is, if you were raised in a palace! A splendid retreat.

★★★ **De Snippe** ● offers only 7 rooms, but they are luxurious. Emphasis here is on exceptional gastronomy in a graceful dining salon with its wildlife theme.

★★ **Pullman** ● was developed with disarming flair from the assemblage of several ancient houses; the meld of old and new is cunning; swimming pool, lamplit dining room, bar with medieval weapons, and garden.

'T Bourgoensche Cruyce ● is directly across the canal from the Duc de Bourgogne. While it is generally respected most for its small and charming dining room, its 6 units are compact and comfortable.

★★ **Prinsenhof** ● features select Old World furnishings, architecture, and art. The 16 rooms are pleasantly homespun.
Other solid choices in this cozy and atmospheric category include **De Castillon, Ter Brughe,** and the canalside **Adornes. Biskajer,** near the Van Eyck statue, is small, contemporary, and moderately priced.

★★★ **Die Swaene** ● *Steenhouwersdijk 1* ● converted from a venerable dwelling, has a serene position on a canal. Just inside its entrance is a stuffed swan as its identification. There's a pleasant homey feel to its 28 accommodations, all with double beds; pleasant restaurant. Almost too ornate in its public rooms, but generally fine and worthy as a luxury choice.

Boergoensch Hof ● stands opposite the alley from 'T Boergoensch Cruyce. The mixture of modern and Old World themes is not too successful. Bed and breakfast only.

Oud Huis Amsterdam • *Spiegelrei 3, a handy but residential area of midtown* • A converted home with glass-lined conservatory in front; open patio; intimate feeling that is pleasant if you resist institutional dwelling.

Erasmus • centrally situated at Wollestraat 35, is tranquil, comfortably appointed, with a chipper bar and a two-tiered restaurant. The decor is uplifting. **Egmond** • is close to the Minnewater and Beguinage in a quiet locale with only 9 bedchambers.

Europ • serves breakfast only; it's rather tour-oriented. Adequate amenities; mostly showers rather than full baths; congenial staff. Agreeable for overnighters.

Park • in Zand Square just next to the Pullman, has 61 quarters with bath, radio, and TV on request. The rates are reasonable and the approach is contemporary. A nice cohesive little house that is well run.

Sablon • has 46 units and 30 baths; the main structure dates from 1772. While it has experienced updatings since the 18th century, some parts remain oppressively old-fashioned.

Novotel • in our view, should be reserved for crucial emergencies only; bare surroundings.

RESTAURANTS

See also places that are later listed in neighboring ''Damme and Bruges Vicinity.'' It's a village on the outskirts.

★★★★ **Duc de Bourgogne** • *Huidevettersplein 12* • wins for atmosphere. It is enchanting to the eye, satisfying to the palate, and—as would be expected—costly; a romantic canalside oasis.

★★★ **'T Bourgoensche Cruyce** faces the above establishment from across the canal, enjoying an equally captivating view. The cookery is refined, beautifully served, expensive, and somewhat more regional in concept. Small, so be sure to reserve ahead.

☆☆ **Den Braamberg** • *Pandreitje 11* • is a highly elegant contender. Entrance in black-and-white with banks of blooming geraniums; 8 tables; service table a converted antique bed; open kitchen; attractive and restful bar with part of *cave* to be seen; French cuisine in tandem with local specialties.

't Pandreitje • *opposite Den Braamberg* • is elegant in a more classic frame. Total of 9 tables; copper-lined kitchen in view; nouvelle cuisine with seafood its specialty; closed Sun.

☆☆ **"De Snippe,"** already mentioned under "Hotels," is up-market and very serious. Small and cozy room; comfortably large black-leather chairs; ample menu with fish, crustacea, and game particularly recommendable; excellent skilletry; fabulous cellar. This does not operate on Sun. or before 6 p.m. on Mon.

De Witte Poorte • *Jan Van Eyckplein 6* • is in one of the city's most historic quarters, ancient in mood, but modern in gastronomy. The garden is a blissful part of the showplace. Brick-lined vaults; set menu with choice of 5 wines; total sums close to $60 per person. Closed Sun., Mon. at lunch, and odd times of the year, so be sure to reserve.

Kardinaelshof • *St. Salvatorkerkhof 14* • is the best spot to fish for seafood. Prices are not unreasonable in this carefully converted town house.

De Visscherie • *in the same courtyard as the Duc de Bourgogne* • whomps up a magnificent waterzooi' and other preparations of the denizens of the deep; it's near the Fish Market.

Pannenhuis • *Zandstraat 2* • is a restructured *huis* with a few accommodations and a lot of oohs and aaahs for its fare. It has the plush air of a country estate.

Hof Ter Doest • *Ter Doeststraat, Lissewege* • is sited in a former abbey, a part of a huge complex of barns and farm buildings. Its capacity for 200 has special appeal to conducted tour operators. This one is renowned for its grilled meat cooked on a big fire. Its T-bone is so huge that no opening course is necessary.

BRUSSELS

Home to about a million, Brussels is the center of government, industry, business, and culture. For some time it had been enjoying the wildest construction boom of any capital in Europe—a Low Country that swiftly became an ultra-High-Riser. It has polished its glorious architecture and recently freshened up a splendid heritage that had begun to wilt from earlier neglect. The results are stunning, making it one of the most glittering capitals in captivity. It is also becoming headquarters for virtually every multinational firm of importance needing a base on the Continent. *Art nouveau* has deep-set roots in this city and today's Belgians are wisely focusing appreciative attention on the designs of Victor Horta and his disciples. It boasts an excellent airport, 6 railroad stations, a luxurious *(sic)* music-fed subway, plenty of excellent hotels, gourmet restaurants, movies, and shops. The art—the city itself is a living museum—is shown in some of the finest museums on the continent.

ATTRACTIONS

Grand' Place • Much of the history of Brussels may be traced to this square—in my opinion, the most spellbinding in Europe. A thriving marketplace in the Middle Ages, it now is home to baroque guild houses with golden facades, the King's house, and the Town Hall. If you see it first by daylight, be sure to return at nightfall and vice-versa. Surrounding Grand' Place are narrow cobbled streets that Sunday mornings, welcome visitors to the square's bird and flower markets but, of course, not in winter.

Town Hall • *Grand' Place* • A premier example of 15th-century architecture and the loveliest building in Brussels, the Town Hall is purely Gothic. Topping the spire is a statue of St. Michael, patron saint of the city. A rare collection of tapestries hangs inside.

Maison du Roi • *King's House, Grand' Place* • A bread market, a court, a prison—this has been home to all since its construction in the 13th century. The City Museum is its present tenant. The museum boasts the arts and crafts of Brussels: intricate tapestries and wrought gold. Everything from the wondrous Bruegel's *Bridal Procession* to 500 cornball outfits worn by the everpresent Manneken-Pis.

Maison des Brasseurs • *Brewery Museum, 10 Grand' Place* • Belgian beers have long been famous. This building, once run by the medieval brewer's guild, displays old brewing equipment.

Manneken-Pis • *rue de l'Etuve* • This famous bronze statue of a boy has prompted many stories. One tells of a king who wanted to immortalize his son in the last position he saw him in just before the youngster was accidentally killed.

Palais de la Nation • The senate and the chamber of representatives convene here, just as the Supreme Council of the Duchy did in years past. In 1783 Guimard put the finishing design touches on the classical facades that still stand today.

Palais des Beaux-Arts • *rue Ravenstein* • Built in 1928 and designed by architect Victor Horta, this structure serves as the meeting ground for the cul-

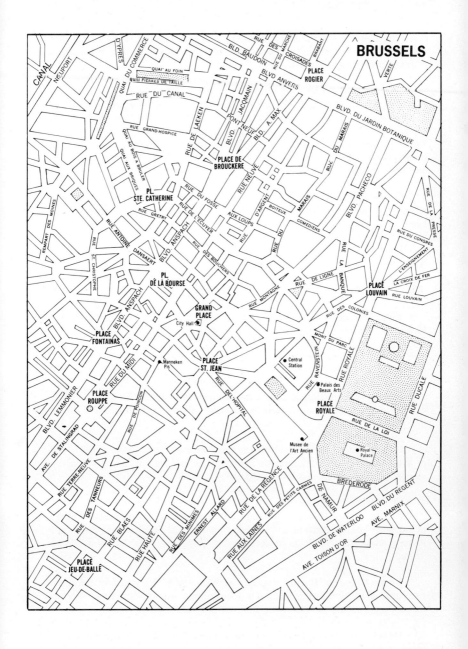

BRUSSELS

CANAL

NEUPORT

D'YPRES

RUE DU COMMERCE

QUAI AU FOIN

QUAI PIERRES DE TAILLE

RUE DU CANAL

BLD. BAUDOIN

RUE DES CROISADES

RUE DU MARCHÉ

BRABANT

PLACE ROGIER

VERTE

BLVD. ANVERS

BLVD. JACQMAIN

PONT NEUF

BLVD. A. MAX

RUE DU MARAIS

BLVD. DU JARDIN BOTANIQUE

QUAI AUX BRIQUES

RUE GRAND-HOSPICE

QUAI AUX BOIS A BRULER

RUE DE LAEKEN

PLACE DE BROUCKERE

PL. STE. CATHERINE

RUE DU FOSSE

RUE NEUVE

AUX LOUPS

RUE D'ARGENT

BOITEUX

BLVD. PACHECO

RUE DE LA PRESSE

REMPART DES MOINES

RUE GRETRY

RUE DE L'ECUYER

COMEDIENS

RUE DU CONGRES

RUE ANTOINE DANSAERT

BLVD. ANSPACH

RUE DES BOUCHERS

RUE DU

L'ENSEIGNEMENT

LA CROIX DE FER

ST CHRISTOPHE

PL. DE LA BOURSE

RUE MONTAGNE

RUE

RUE DE LIGNE

RUE LA BANQUE

PLACE LOUVAIN

RUE LOUVAIN

GRAND PLACE

City Hall

RUE DES COLONIES

BLVD. ANSPACH

PLACE FONTAINAS

Manneken Pis

PLACE ST. JEAN

Central Station

MONT DU PARC

RUE ROYALE

RUE DU MIDI

RUE DE L'HOPITAL

RUE RAVENSTEIN

Palais des Beaux Arts

RUE DUCALE

RUE DE FRANCOIS

PLACE ROUPPE

PLACE ROYALE

BLVD. LEMMONIER

AVE. DE STALINGRAD

Musee de l'Art Ancien

RUE DE LA LOI

Royal Palace

BREDERODE

RUE TERRE-NEUVE

RUE DES TANNEURS

RUE BLAES

RUE HAUTE

RUE DES MINIMES

ERNEST ALLARD

RUE DE LA REGENCE

RUE DES PETITS CARMES

DE NAMUR

BLVD. DU REGENT

AVE. MARNIX

PLACE JEU-DE-BALLE

RUE AUX LAINES

BLVD. DE WATERLOO

AVE. TOISON D'OR

tural life of Brussels. It contains a concert hall (3000 seats), several small theaters, a movie house, a king-size exhibition hall, a restaurant, and the headquarters of many artistic associations.

Museums of Ancient Art and of Modern Art • *place Royale 1* • These two compatriots form certainly one of the world's finest showcases for intelligent viewing of graphic and plastic arts. It penetrates 8 floors *downward* with semicircular lightwells bringing soft reliable natural illumination to cunningly situated galleries. Sculpture especially is revealed in all its purity. Though many international titans are represented, artists are predominantly from the French and Belgian schools.

Grand Sablon • This square is at the center of the antique market. On Sat. all day and Sun. until 1 p.m., browsers and buyers will find books and antiques here.

Petit Sablon • A sprinkling of 48 statues, each representing a medieval trade guild, pattern the formal garden that fills the square. In the center stand the statues of the Counts d'Egmont and de Hornes, two beheaded stalwarts who objected to the Spanish persecution of Protestants.

Tour D'Angle • This tower is part of the twelfth century bulwark that protected Brussels.

Automobile Museum • *at Autoworld in Parc du Cinquantenaire* • Vintage cars glitter by the score—actually 360—some famous, some cute (like a 1903 Olds), some massive. Films offered; also refreshment. Hitler, Roosevelt, Kennedy, and several monarchs were backseat drivers in some of these venerable classics. Other exhibits dedicated to aircraft, military, and art are also are in this park.

Galeries St. Hubert • *rue Marche-aux-Herbes* • Constructed in 1847, this is the oldest arcade in Europe. In the 19th century the arcade served as an elegant promenade, as it still does today.

St. Michael's Cathedral • *place Ste. Gudule* • Begun in the 13th century, it celebrates Belgian Gothic architecture. In the beautiful mausoleums lie Charles of Lorraine and the Archduke Albert and his wife. St. Michael's is Belgium's national cathedral. While most sections are being restored, the choir can be visited.

Toone • *Puppet Museum, Impasse Schuddeveld* • This is one of the finest museums of its kind in Europe, but it is open only around show times. Performances are frequent in the tiny theater; not in English, of course.

David and Alice Van Buuren Museum • *41 ave. Leo Errera,* • Wonderful paintings of the 16th and 20th centuries, lovely gardens and handsome sculptures adorn this 1930s house, much of it dedicated to exemplary art-deco furnishings.

Maison Horta • *Horta Museum, 25 rue Americaine* • Here, followers of architecture may discover the magic of Horta, one of the premier modernists.

HOTELS

Since Brussels attracts armies of expense-accounters, all of the luxury houses cater especially to this group. They charge accordingly. On weekends they are almost empty as businessmen return to their homes. Special rates often are available then.

☆☆☆ **Hilton** • continues to appeal to the international business community. Busy-bee lobby; lunch and/or dining centers (see "Restaurants"); cheerful coffee shop; 24-hour cable, Telex and room service; extensively renewed bed-chambers by Rita Houben, and beauties they are; an executive floor (17th) loaded with gadgets and extras; boutiques; same-day laundry; health club with outstanding sauna; underground parking for 150 cars—and the fees here are appropriately stiff in this traffic-choked district.

★★★ **Amigo** • boasts perhaps the most romantic situation in the city. Step out of its slate-floored lobby and you are in the midst of one of the most breath-taking assemblages of medieval architecture in existence: The Grand' Place. It also offers dignified art-filled salons, a cozy bar, and comfort in rooms of varying size— some with tantalizing spire-tip views. The staff is one of the most concerned and most efficient to be encountered in this nation. If you are a light sleeper, request an inside or upper-floor accommodation.

☆☆☆ **Sheraton** • 30 stories tall, is the Biggest Boy in the Belgian hotel network. Midcity venue; gracious lobby; sumptuous Le Comtes de Flandre restaurant with muraled walls, cleverly planned electric candles, tables a bit close together, and good but not especially outstanding fare; Pavillon Restaurant (really a coffee shop) in Art Deco open 18 hours per day; cocktail lounge; Horizon Club at its crown, with a lovely glass-bound swimming pool plus snack bar, sauna, massage parlor and gymnasium; parking for 1000 cars. Save for the annoyingly cramped baths, there are generous measurements in most of its bed-chambers. This plant is physically a stunner.

★★★ **Royal Windsor** • has, perhaps, even more personality. Bedrooms are in pastel shades with Louis XVI furnishings. There is a darkling cozy richness in its gathering nooks on the ground floor and a gleaming fresh welcome upstairs. Stately exterior topped by a handsome gabled roof; restyled 4 Seasons restaurant; Crocodile discotheque, the top spot in town for wholesome revels; Wellington Pub plus the Waterloo Club for libations and chitchat; quick-service coffee shop. In winter, incidentally, the Friday-through-Sunday rates are lowered considerably and July–August tariffs are about half the high-season tabs.

★★ Mayfair • is discreetly modern and quietly hushed in tone. Breakfast only; bar; limited conference facilities; boutique; hairdresser; parking; 100 nests in timeless ambience. Its facilities and its serenity are felicitous.

Scandic Crown • comes on strong with wham-oh modernity that borders on institutionality. Striking colors are splashed throughout, sometimes very effectively. Lean and linear 10-story edifice; extremely dramatic lobby with more than 1000 long glass "candles" hanging from low ceiling; daringly avant-garde Hugo's Rotisserie for nouvelle cuisine neither cozy nor fetching; Place du Marche cafe; intimate Hugo's Bar. The Maisonnette-type and the Presidential Suite are the largest, while the 320 red-red billets are universally smallish, with low beds, midget baths, and limited storage space. There is talk that this may become a Ramada link by the time of your arrival. If so, you can still go with confidence since this is an excellent chain on the Continent. (See below.)

☆☆☆ **SAS Royal** • the Scandinavian airline giant, now provides 240 smart, fresh units in the Grand' Place vicinity. There's a fine restaurant, a bar with music, a fitness center, and special effects for the executive. In fact, this is where SAS focuses most of its attention—a swiftly growing chain of hotels that pointedly combine luxury and efficiency for business travelers.

Jolly Hotel Atlanta • is a trim enterprise; its latest wing is a splendid attraction, boosting its room count and adding a vast shopping enclave plus a rooftop breakfast oasis. Its level of quality is found only in very few other houses owned by this large Italian chain. Here is a friendly, informal, and unpretentious stop.

★★ Metropole • is a rambling, 500-room old-timer whose time has come back through tasteful and meticulous restoration. If you wish authentic Old-World empire style, this is a hint of a glorious bygone era. Comforts, however, are in tone with today's requirements.

Ramada • vastly better than its confreres in the U.S.A., is improving with age—a happy evolution that's visible in other overseas Ramadas. The exterior, however, remains architecturally boring. Inside there's the Garden Restaurant for light grazing and the Refuge for more serious meals.

Bedford • offers taste and decor that are still quixotically torn twixt modernity and traditionalism. Two restaurants on 2nd floor; garage; exhibitionart gallery; nice bar; immaculately clean.

★★ Pullman • is a period piece with lofty ceilings and ornate Louis XVI accouterments. The Pullman Bar recaptures the earliest Wagon-Lits decor. Except for numerous modernizations, it is reminiscent of a colonial house of yore. Especially recommendable for its antique mood.

Europa Brussels' • facilities boast ample allure and its staff seems to have mastered their work. Enticing Dukes Coffee Shop surrounding a fish pond; elegant Beefeater restaurant ornately decorated with oil portraits on paneled backdrops; snugglesome air-conditioned bedrooms featuring rich textiles, dark-wood furniture, and high-grade fittings and garnishment. There's a health club with sauna, solarium, massage, and jacuzzi. Weighing against these attractions, however, is its location, which is too far from the action for the convenience of shoppers and sightseers.

Albert I • ideally located on the Place Rogier of midcity, was a grand old-timer that lost its pride, but has now been restored carefully in art deco style. Reasonable prices for substantial quality. A period piece reborn.

L'Agenda • provides a cozy atmosphere; carefully maintained; 8-table breakfast room in shades of pink, with no other meals served; 40 pleasant, ample-size bedrooms. I like this congenial little haven.

President Centre and **President Nord** cater largely to business travelers. The former is slightly less cold and spartan than the latter. Only breakfast is available; their rooms are compact and dull. **President World Trade Center,** however, is a beautifully composed congress hub, one of the better examples of its type to be found in any nation. Two attractive restaurants; cheerful lounges; 312 units; discotheque; fitness club.

New Siru, next to the Sheraton, is better for dining in its beautifully executed Le Couvert restaurant than for sleeping in its so-so bedchambers. Its sister operation, **Archimede,** on the *rue* of the same name, provides better accommodation, in my opinion. Still, it's good for the price and the location is first rate. **Arlequin,** near the Grand' Place, is outstanding for the value. The **Alfa Sablon** (60 units at $140 per twin) is another fresh candidate in this ever-growing metropolis.

At the airport you'll find the freshly landed **Sheraton** at the drome's entrance (access and exit totally covered), the **Holiday Inn,** the **Novotel,** the **Mercur,** and the **Sofitel.** Since the inner heart of the city is only 20 minutes away and is so easy and so inexpensive to reach, it seems more logical to pick a town address in one of Europe's most enchanting historical centers.

RESTAURANTS

Because most restaurants are small in capacity and because lunching and dining are characteristically such a serious and extended business with only one seating per meal, reservations in advance are mandatory in all good establishments, including bistros. Most of them push a special aperitif of the house that is usually champagne-based and delicious. Finally, when you think you are fed to the brim, cheeses are likely to be offered in bewildering variety. Below are some of the best of the crop, but the Brussels harvest is truly burgeoning with dozens of newcomers in the rapidly growing fringe districts.

☆☆☆☆☆ **Villa Lorraine** • *ave. du Vivier d'Oie 75* • remains a glory for capital diners with no shortage of capital. Other guidebooks hesitated about its status during a transition period, but I have held steadfast to an opinion that it remains one of the world's finest restaurants. Parkland situation bordering the Bois de la Cambre, about 10 minutes by taxi from the center; converted mansion resplendent with deep-pile carpets, rich brocades, and colossal floral decorations; intimate bar with leaded stained-glass doors leading to an open, bower-shaded terrace; sumptuous, even regal, interior dining room; crackling hearth in winter; captivating garden patio, glass-lined for dining with nature on inclement days. The b-i-g prices match the rewards in every way.

☆☆☆☆☆ **Dupont** • *ave. Vital Riethuisen 46* • also stands tall not only in the Low Countries but in the highest ranks of *haute cuisine* all across the European tablescape. It is a celebration for the hedonistic senses. Mme. Claude Dupont will guide you through the door of this converted town house, which is less than 10 minutes by taxi from the center. Immediate impression of spaciousness and grace in the single salon; Hessian walls that reflect subdued light from shaded sconces; delicate crystalware and cut flowers; deeply comfortable banquettes. Master Chef Claude Dupont inclines his extraordinary talents toward nouvelle cuisine. The freshly poached duck liver on a bed of 3 dainty salads and topped with shaved truffles was super. So was the langouste vinaigrette. The steamed turbot in a light sauce perfumed with leeks is a deep-sea delight. It is shuttered Mon., Tues., and from mid-July to August 22.

☆☆☆ **Comme Chez Soi** • *place Rouppe 23* • unquestionably offers some of the finest gastronomy in the nation. It is just as expensive as Villa Lorraine but has not a fraction of the space, grace, and charm I found at the Villa. *Very* cramped quarters. If you occupy an aisle location (men usually do), you may feel like a tumble-dried shirt by meal's end due to the frenzied bistro-rush traffic of waiters bumping into your chair and leaning over you (with various patches of their anatomies in your face) in order to serve the wall seats. Open glassed-in kitchen; uninteresting porcelain at a time when chefs use this as a showcase for their creations; its in-season mousses of ham, salmon, wood pigeon, snipe, woodcock, and others are celebrated. Many discerning gourmets forgive (or never even notice) its shortcomings, but personally, I'm not among its staunchest disciples—especially at such lofty price tags. This one is closed on Sun. and Mon.

☆☆☆ **Roland de Reu** • *chaussee de Bruxelles 226–228* • offers a unique adventure in anyone's lifetime—plus the warmest and friendliest welcome possible to imagine. This maximum 7-table dining room in this charming private home is totally operated by delightful Maitre de Reu. This one-man-band single-handedly greets his guests at the door, pours their aperitifs, prepares every dish, speaks flawless English, and often sits down briefly to fascinate his clients with his sparkle and fun. During and after the meal he happily ushers clients to his kitchen to watch or to chat.

☆☆☆☆ **L'Ecailler du Palais Royal** • *rue Bodenbroek 18, near the Grand Sablon* • specializes in seafood. Main ground-floor chamber with green plaid walls, brass sconces, sea-tone textiles, and a restful oil painting dominating one side; 12-stool counter dominating the other. Upstairs outfitted with rich woods, swinging saloon doors, hurricane lamps.

☆☆☆☆ **Bruneau** • *ave. Broustin 73* • has at its ground-floor entrance an excellent gourmet shop and on the 2nd and 3rd floors its dining rooms. Gracious Mme. Bruneau coddles the guests, while her husband is in love with his kitchen. Because he detests making the same plate more than several times, he continually invents superb new wonders. A small folder lists from 5 to 12 different seasonal specialties for every month of the year. Closed Tues. night and all Wed. plus a brief period in mid-summer.

★★★ **La Maison du Cygne** • *Grand' Place 9* • remains as good as ever— and as beautiful. When passing in or out, don't forget to rub the arm of the little Everard t'Serclaes statue in the building's facade and make 3 wishes; it has dispensed good luck since A.D. 1320. Head for the little elevator and ride upstairs, where you will find paneled walls, sumptuous banquettes, and a huge rotisserie grill at one end; 3 sectional divisions lend a feeling of intimacy here.

Hilton has 2 restaurants for various needs and times of day or night:
☆☆ **Maison du Boeuf,** is the choice for North American travelers who yearn for a home-style feast. American Hereford roast beef from cart; soft-shelled and Alaskan crabs flown in; steaks also a feature; copious wine card plus array of beers; savory Yankee salads; cheesecake featured; service speedy and perfunctory.

Cafe d'Egmont, also a Hilton enterprise, is gardenlike and popularly priced even if the cookery is uninspired. Its attraction is heavy during all 3 meals as well as at teatime.

☆☆☆☆☆ **Romeyer** • *chaussee de Groenendael 109 in Hoeilaart; there's a shuttle from town* • occupies a charming country house with a garden, ponds, and ducks. The decor is luxurious. If you're feeling extravagant, try the Boudin of lobster, the langouste with little vegetables, the truffles under ashes, the duck au chambertin, the stuffed crayfish, the turbot en croute or the game in season. Habitually the destination of visiting gourmets.

☆☆ **L'Huitriere** • *quai aux Briques 20* • is superb for honest sea fare. Main-floor wood-paneled room with inset tiles and enough coffee grinders to send Messrs. Chase & Sanborn into ecstasies; less inspired but more polished upstairs dining salon for overflow traffic, of which there is usually plenty. Wild fowl, grills, and other terra firma critters are also available, but it would be a pity not to bid for the ocean offerings. Closed Mon.; reserve ahead.

Francois • just a few doors away from L'Huitriere, is an imposing salt-water alternative. The mussels (I counted 20) on an iced platter were a repast in itself. Moreover, the serving of turbot Duglere was so huge that it might have been cut from a whale. The fried shrimp was a little disappointing. Very popular with locals; not too costly.

Rugbyman One and **Rugbyman Two** ● are side-by-siders on this same row of mongers. Both feature maritime wares, but the latter inclines heavily toward lobster (at which it excels).

Jacques ● *quai aux Briques 44* ● which is actually located at the municipal Fish Market, is even more rewarding for saltwater fare. It's very simple, so don't expect much—until you open your mouth. *Then* it's a delight.

☆☆ **La Sirene d'Or** ● *place Sainte-Catherine 1A* ● is nearby at the big Vegetable Market. For its laid-back (nay, almost boudoir) ambience you'll pay more. One scrumptious specialty is bouillabaisse; all of its catch is so fresh that it is sassy.

Scheltema ● *rue des Dominicains 7* ● holds about 60. Long, narrow, unfancy chamber with 3 seating areas; open kitchen at rear; comparatively inexpensive. On Thurs. and Fri. evening, when it's open after 11 p.m., it's a good spot for after the theater. Otherwise great, hulking business executives rub (and bend) elbows at its crowded lunch hour. Superior returns for your money.

L'Oasis ● *place Marie-Jose 9* ● is trying hard to achieve a following. I'm no big fan of its gastronomy, but the park-front setting and mansion structure are alluring. Expensive.

Trente Rue De La Paille ● is both the name and the address of this entry, which is situated in an old house; it is a very good bistro. In its slightly clubby atmosphere are a fireplace and about 12 tables, plus a bar where you can eat. It smells most pleasantly of smoked fish, for they do this freshly to your order. The menu appears on a blackboard. The decor, the young waiters, and the young owners all beam with cheerfulness. Other bistro choices that are fun include **Le Prevot** ● *95 rue Victor Greyson* ● and the fancier **Au Beurre Blanc** ● *2 rue du Faucon.* ● You also might go for the lobster croquettes at **Le Chalet Rose** ● *49 avenue du Bois de la Cambre.*

Leon ● *rue des Dominicains 2* ● might be viewed as the quintessential popular national restaurant—noisy, crowded, but efficient and rewarding at a medium cost. It is probably the best place in the city to savor the Belgians' favorite dish: mussels served any one of 8 ways, but always with a mountain of french fries. Particularly recommended are the *moules au vin blanc* (steamed in a white wine sauce) or *provencales* (with garlic, tomatoes, and herbs, served somewhat like a pizza).

Fruit de ma Passion ● *J-B Meunier 53-A* ● suffers from its boring residential location and uninspired decor. The cookery, however, is invested with talent, sensitivity, and honesty. Veal glace with green lemon and ginger is masterful. Vaguely amateurish, but recommendable.

Cafes

Brussels offers these in abundance, each with its personality. **De Ultieme Hallucinatie** ● *rue Royale 316* ● is Flemish in tone, replete with the full panoply of art nouveau. **Falstaff** • *rue Henri Maus 25* • is near the Stock Exchange, with many of its brokers glowing under the stained-glass windows of Horta. The house drink is half-and-half (white wine and Spumante). **Chez Moeder Lambic** • *rue de Savoie 68* • stocks a huge selection of beers. **Cirio** • *rue de la Bourse 18* • is where you go to read your newspaper. Max Ernst preferred to doodle at **Fleur en Papier Dore** • *rue des Alexiens 53* • which is one of the oldest cafes in town.

NIGHT LIFE

Doing the town in a big way? Better take along at least $150 if you plan to have a whirl—because it will cost plenty.

Show Point (14 place Stephanie) is the leader in after-dark entertainment. Always-fresh decor; better than average floor show featuring plenty of nudity; expensive.

Play-Night (rue Jean Stas 13) is also in the forefront of local cabaret. Main show at midnight.

Brussels Jazz Club (13 Grand' Place), which resides in one of the world's most breathtaking nightscapes, is a magnet for listeners.

Mainly for dancing? **Crocodile** of the Royal Windsor (disco music) offers the most respectable venue. **Le Vaudeville** (15 Gal. de la Reine) is another top-grade nightspot. **Mirano** (chaussee de Louvain 38), with its attractive decor, strongly beckons disciples of Terpsichore. They have mask parties here too. **Le Garage** (16 rue Duquesnoy) is loud, dark, and typical of outsize discos. **Chewing Gum** (place de la Vieille Halle-aux-Bles 25) is said to be the top gay bar. **Capricorne** (rue d'Anderlecht 8) is its counterpart for women.

There are about 20 others if you're manic for the sport. They change in character so quickly as you run down the list, that you'd better ask your hotel hall porter which place suits your needs on the eve of your "big night out."

SHOPPING

SHOPPING HOURS: Everything operates full blast from 9:30–6. On Fri. almost all of the establishments in the center remain open until 8.

BEST AREAS: There are three main districts: (1) lower town around blvd. Adolf Max and rue Neuve, (2) Porte Namur, place Stephanie, and ave. Louise uptown, and (3) the Grand Sablon and the streets radiating from it. Shopping arcades, known as *galeries,* abound. Wares are high here, but so is the quality.

SAVINGS ON PURCHASES: V.A.T. runs anywhere from 19–25%. This is deducted from all purchases that are mailed. However, if you wish to carry the items you must spend a minimum of 5000 B.Fr. in each shop to be eligible for the rebate and show the corresponding invoices. These are stamped by Belgian Customs at border points and sent back to the shops which then may make the refund.

BAKED GOODS: Dandoy (rue au Beurre 31 and rue Charles Buls 14, both just off the Grand' Place) ships molded "speculoos" (crisp, rich spice cookies) worldwide; large individual ones from $4–13. **Wittamer** (Grand Sablon) is tops for its *patisserie*.

BOOKS: Smith and Son (blvd. Adolphe Max) stocks a large selection of hardcover titles and more than 2000 paperbacks. **Librairie des Galeries** (Galerie du Roi 2) has a large and versatile section of art volumes. Concurrently there is always a small exposition of regional painters.

CHOCOLATES: The Belgian stars are **Godiva, Wittamer, Neuhaus, Mary, Leonidas, Nihoul,** and **Corne.** All have several branches scattered through the city. Fun, fanciful, and fabulously fattening, they are almost guaranteed to make their buyers happy.

CRYSTAL AND PORCELAIN: Buss (Marche aux Herbes 84–86) is just at the edge of the Grand' Place. All the "greats" are in stock: Val St. Lambert, Rosenthal, Christofle, Lladro, and many more, with savings running up to 40% of stateside prices. Shipping facilities available. Ask for Mr. Buss. **Art et Selection** (#83 on the same street) also is superb. The mood is a smidgen more elegant but the products are similar.

DEPARTMENT STORES AND SHOPPING ARCADES: Covered galleries that shelter the walker from inclement weather abound. The oldest, built in 1846, is the **Galeries Saint-Hubert** near the Grand' Place. **Rue Neuve** has been closed off as a pedestrian browsing street. **Innovation** is the No. 1 department store. Then there is a huge shopping center called **City II.** (**Marks & Spencer** and **C & A** are popular-level competitors.) At one end of ave. Louise you'll find **City Gardens,** another complex that takes pride in its surrounding flora. Latest entry in this field is the **Sablon Shopping Gardens,** with many antique shops plus three restaurants.

LACE: F. Rubbrecht (Grand' Place 23), sited in a charming building known as the "House of the Angel" since the 16th century, is famous for quality, fair prices, and reliability. It offers a tempting variety of rectangular, round, oval, and bridge tablecloths; place mats with napkins; table centers; roll baskets and covers; guest towels; doilies; aprons; traycloths; coasters; handkerchiefs; wedding veils—and even christening gowns. Antique lace—unique pieces from private collections—is also on display. A selection of some of the most splendid pieces of handcrafted Val-Saint-Lambert Belgian crystal matches beautifully with the lace—each one enhancing the elegance of the other. Also ask to see the unique bronze miniatures from Bermann-Vienna. Young Mr. and Mrs.

Rubbrecht, assisted by their staff, will offer you a friendly welcome. Tops in the nation.

LEATHER: **Delvaux** has been a stalwart in Europe's peerage of this craft for more than a century-and-a-half, but the name hasn't traveled afar like Loewe, Gucci, Hermes, and others in this specialty. Store locations in Brussels: blvd. A. Max. 22, ave. de la Toison d'Or 24, and Galerie de la Reine 31.

OPEN-AIR MARKETS: **Marche-aux-Puces** (or **Vieux Marche,** which we call the Flea Market) can provide plenty of laughs if you're a bargain hunter. *Always* wrangle until your face is purple or puce. This functions daily from 8 a.m. to 1 p.m. at the place du Jeu de Balle. The **Antique Market** teems next to Sablon Church all day Sat. and until 1 p.m. Sun. The tents in which it is held are in the Brussels' official colors of green and red. The merchandise runs from modest to very expensive things, including silver, porcelain, and furniture. Haggle like mad here. The bustling **Food Market** operates on Sun. from 8 a.m. to 1 p.m. near the South Station. It offers a tremendous variety of produce, fruits, flowers, spices, and imports from the Mediterranean (olives, peppers, others). Quite a sight! There's also the **Bird Market** on Sun. and Mon. mornings in the Grand' Place.

Sporting goods: **Maison du Chasseur & Mahillon Reunis** (ave. Louise 413) has the top stock of hunting equipment in the nation, anything from Belgium's fine Brownings to a crossbow to smart field apparel for both sexes—even artwork related to nature.

DAMME AND BRUGES VICINITY During the 15th- and 16th-centuries this bewitching little village was the principal port in Northern Europe for warehousing imported wines and herring, which were then pulled by horses to Bruges—only a skip and a jump away. Damme still maintains a colorful air of charm. Many pilgrims opt to visit it by the 30-minute canal ride.

★★ **De 3 Zilveren Kannen** occupies a lovely, typically regional, 3-story house in which every touch is old, mellow, and warmly Flemish. Bounteous display table at entrance; beamed ceiling; large fireplace with well-designed keep-warm apparatus in center; 9 tables for 30 clients.
The next-door **By Lamme Goedzak** is well regarded locally—except in midwinter when it's closed. Extensive decorative talents have been employed in the restoration of this ancient building and its 14th-century cellars.

☆☆☆ **Bruegel,** ½-mile out of the village, is rated by some gastronomes as the Number One dining place in the district. It occupies a lovely white-brick building that is fronted by a canal in the open countryside. Shuttered on Tues. and Wed.

De Waterput, among the polders, is an informal farmhouse where the chef is likely to feed you *his* choices of his day's cooking. It's a lot of fun, very special, and not expensive. Reserve ahead. **De Lieve,** behind the Town Hall, has a refined kitchen and an abundance of charm. **Gasthof Maerlant,** one of the most antique of dwellings, offers a bewitching view of the market square, a sunny garden, and traditional cookery plus a hint of modern cuisine.

☆☆☆☆ **Weinebrugge,** a few minutes south of Bruges on a residence-lined pike of little scenic interest, is where owner-chef Jacques Galens practices his high-priced magic—but he really needs no practice, because he's a master. The salon, with open timber beams, peeps through French windows at a bit of greenery; there's a vast open hearth dominating one end of the air-conditioned room; the presentation and service are immaculate. Closed Wed. and Thurs. as well as all of Sept.

★★★ **Goedendag** in *Lissewege,* 6½ miles from the hub, occupies a white cottage-like structure on Hoogstraat. Bar at entrance; large open copper grill producing outstanding specialties; eye-appealing food displays; courteous staff; tall tariffs.

Herr Halewyn, on a fetching square in *Walplaats,* is a find for light dishes and snacks. Moderate, low-ceilinged building, intimate with tasteful mixture of the past and the present; outdoor terrace in season; good wine roster; cheese plate, crudities, lamb brochette; closed Mon. and Tues.

GHENT Culture, beauty, and charm abound, and most of the finest edifices are now freshly steam cleaned. Once second only to Paris in terms of continental influence, the city at the join of the Lys and the Scheldt is full of memories. After you've been awed by Van Eyck's splendid *Adoration of the Lamb* at St. Bavon Cathedral there are more than a dozen museums to gather into your collection, a fine botanical exhibit, and merchant- and guildhouses that recall medieval prosperity hereabouts. The hotel situation has improved dramatically in recent times.

HOTELS:

Gravensteen, in the shadow of the Castle of the Counts, is housed in a patrician mansion. It offers private parking, a garden and a *belvedere* from where you can admire the world-famous Ghent towers. All rooms with private bath, radio, TV, mini-bar, and heating with individual control.

Sterling provides about 200 luxury units next to the exhibition hall of Flanders Expo. Mostly for tradesmen types. Very good for its purpose.

Flanders, near the station, is recommended both for business and recreational travelers. Marblesque lobby, smart restaurant, bar, and an "orangerie" where the Sunday brunch develops crusades of followers.

Astoria provides an exceptional position a few minutes from two highways (E17 and E40) and in the neighborhood of the station. Bedchambers are classically furnished. This tot (it has only 15 rooms) takes pride in the service and intimacy it offers.

Himatel, also in the station area, is small and functional; a bar but no restaurant; it has a garage.

Arcade provides good but simple shelter for 250 guests; play area for tots; very central and useful for bargain-seekers.

Ibis is a link in a successful chain of clean, low-cost hostelries. It, too, is in midtown; 50% reduction for children under 12 (that's age, not total).

Novotel is in the very center; not much zest but okay for efficiency and economy.

Europa is clean-lined and modern in tone. Moreover, its canalside situation in a residential district near St.-Pieters Station affords much more peace and quiet than any of the midcity turnstiles; brick and glass exterior; broad window-wrapped lounge with warming Persian carpets; ingratiating colonial restaurant; stained glass counterpointing the turn-of-the-century bar. Definitely recommended when the sojourn isn't too long. **Holiday Inn** is a bit out of the center, beside the turnpike exit from Brussels. Dining is its weakest feature. **Condor,** on the E17 (exit UZ), is useful. There's a free coffee nook on each floor. **Cour St.-Georges** is suggested only for its Old World restaurant. The hotel itself was founded in A.D. 1228—and when you see it you'll believe it. The **Ascona** tries to be modern, but I found it a bit weary from the effort. The **Carlton** is a drive-inn. Not much public space, but passable for pit-stoppers to whom sleep is the main concern.

For mealtiming in the center of town, try **Jan Breydel** • *Jan Breydelstraat* •, **Waterzooi** • *St. Veerleplein 2* •, **Apicius** • *M. Maeterlinckstr. 8* •, **Graslei** • *Graslei 7* • and **De Drabklok** • *Drabstraat 30* • . **Claridge** • *Kon. Maria Hendrikaplein 36* • and, a bit out of town in the direction of Antwerp, **'t Boerenhof** • *Gentstraat 2* • also is a worthy choice. **De Gouden Klok** • *Koning Albertlaan 31* • and **Buikske Vol** • *Kraanlei 17* • are enjoying great esteem from an audience that knows first-rate gastronomy.

Many small and cozy restaurants are cropping up in the historic "Patershol" quarter, near the Castle of the Counts, turning this deteriorated but now gradually renovated district into a gastronomic adventure. **Karel De Stoute** • *Vrouwebroersstraat 5* • is one of the best candidates in this sector.

KNOKKE-HEIST La Reserve is one of the leading resort hotels in the nation. Situated on the shores of a little lake 200 yards from the sea, it directly faces the Casino. Beautiful interior; swimming pool; fitness center and health clinic; general atmosphere tends toward elegance. **Aquilon** wins orchids for the finest independent kitchen in the region. The prices, not incidentally, are at the high-tide level.

LIEGE, close to the German border, is embraced by the Meuse basin, which long ago inspired the masters of Mosan art; today it has become a student center and a springboard to the Ardennes. The legendary FN-Browning small arms plant, plus 20 smaller but fine competitors (obtain entrance to some through the local Tourist Office) headquarter here. It has been an armament hub since the Middle Ages. The panorama from the Cointe is particularly worth enjoying. The **Batte Sunday Market** is *formidable* for hagglers and adventurers; go before noon.

As for hotels, the **Urbis** is in the center offering 78 fresh new rooms.

Holiday Inn caters heavily to conference-goers since it is located so near to the congress hall. You might prefer the **Ramada Inn** (100 air-conditioned rooms; good cookery), which greatly resembles its sister operation in the capital. The 100-chamber **Post House** is a motel with such added attractions as a pool, a grill, and meeting facilities.

The **Couronne,** hard by the station, is continental in tone, but so-so in appeal. The **Cygne d'Argent** also evokes a special European flavor which some travelers enjoy.

★★★ **Le Vieux Liege,** sometimes called Maison Havart (41 quai de la Goffe), muses nostalgically on the banks of the Meuse; reasonably good cookery. Strikingly handsome sixteenth-century structure of brick and cross-hatched timbers; 2 floors with candles, brass chandeliers, flowers, tilework, and copperware; extremely inviting rustic milieu; costly.

☆☆ **Chene Madame,** out of the center (about 10 miles) at *Neuville en Condroz,* is an ideal setting for game in the autumn. Other preparations are blue-ribbon too—in a price range that may make you wonder just who's being hunted.

As Ouhes • *place de Marche 21* • is a luxury bistro serving local specialties plus Lyon-type selections.

La Ripaille • *rue St. Georges* • counts only about a dozen tables at its fresh precincts; local atmosphere and cuisine; sausages, lamb stew, and quail with juniper berries among its features. Advance reservations are mandatory here.

Mame Vicou • *rue de la Wache 9* • is gaining a fame for its refined presentations. A serious kitchen and nice people who run it.

OSTEND, very maritime in feeling, is one of Belgium's most famous seacoast resorts and seafood shrines (one of the very best in the North). It is the summer retreat of thousands of bathers who enjoy its golden sands. On the scenic, speedy superhighway from Brussels, you can stop at Bruges and Ghent, and then breeze up here in practically nothing flat. The Kursaal is among the world's handsomest gambling casinos. Zeebrugge and Knokke-Heist are just up the pike.

For overnighting, everyone now seems to head to the **Andromeda,** which is next to the Casino directly on the sea. Modern and functional; 95 bedchambers; humdrum cuisine; prime for this little port. The **Melinda** now takes second place. Not distinguished but not bad. The restored **Thermae Palace,** a big seafront bath establishment, is city-owned and privately operated. Several other hotels, among them the **Bero,** the **Die Prince, Strand,** and **Prado** as well as the 50-room **Riff** are challengers that provide a cheerful flair, otherwise rare on the coast.

When hunger triggers thoughts of food, try this modest house before seeking out fancier digs: **Belgica** is one of the perhaps 30 harborfront candidates fighting tooth-and-fin for attention. There's no decor to speak of—but oh, my, what delicious things swim out of that tiny little kitchen! The sole is extraordinary and always sea-fresh. **Au Vigneron,** 2 miles out at rue de l'Archiduc in *Mariakerke,* is also small and excellent but expensive. Chateaubriand in Papillote is its greatest pride. Be sure to book ahead of time (Tel. 70.48.16). Favorable comments have arrived about **Le Perigord, Georges V,** and **Prince Charles.**

DENMARK

USA: Danish Tourist Board, 655 3rd Ave., 18th floor, New York, NY 10017, Tel. (212) 949–2333. Scandinavian Tourist Board (Denmark-Sweden), 150 North Michigan Ave., Suite 2110, Chicago, IL 60601, Tel. (312) 726–1120; 8929 Wilshire Blvd., Beverly Hills, CA 90211, Tel. (213) 854–1549. *CANADA:* P.O. Box 115, Sta. N, Toronto, Ont. M8V 3S4, Tel. (416) 823–9620.

SPECIAL REMARKS: (1) For the usual sort of travel guidance, go to the Tourist Information Office, H.C. Andersens Blvd. 22 or telephone (33) 111325 in the capital. The Copenhagen Tourist Association aids travelers by selecting and registering the best of thousands of private homes it has inspected in the capital. Requirements are rigid: cleanliness, comfort, a telephone, and a separate entrance. If you can't get a hotel reservation go to Central Railway Station Kiosk "P." To obtain dwelling space by mail or by phone, be in touch at least 3 days in advance with the following: Hotelbooking Copenhagen, Kiosk P, Central Railway Station, DK–1570, Copenhagen V; Tel: 45–33–122880. (2) SAS offers the very same service at Copenhagen Airport. These are inexpensive, simple, but excellent accommodations. (3) The hard-working Danish Tourist Board has a network of 10 foreign branches. (4) The 139 domestic offices are autonomous and supply information to tourists as well. (5) Students seeking inexpensive shelter should write the **Danmarks Vandrerhjem** (Youth and Family Hostels Association), Vesterbrogade 39, DK–1620 Copenhagen V, for tips. Tourist Information in Copenhagen is a font of aid; so is **Use It** at Radhusstraede 13, DK–1204 Copenhagen K.

TELEPHONE: Access code to USA: 009. To phone Denmark: 45; time difference (Eastern Daylight) plus 6 hrs.

For delight and enchantment, Denmark is totally captivating. There are 3 secrets to this extraordinary charm. First is the beauty of its seascapes and countryside—cool green forests, tranquil sunny fields, crazy thatched cottages in brilliant whites or soft pastels. The rolling terrain has a storybook quality, a gaiety which is taken into Danish homes and even to Danish table settings, from Flora Danica porcelains to ringlets of flowers around candles to tulip-stem glasses to acorn-patterned silverware.

Second is its polish. Denmark is cosmopolitan, taking its pleasures in a carefree, sophisticated, and urbane way.

Third—most important—is its people. Danes have a knack for banter, wit, and graceful language. You can't help feeling happy among them.

TRANSPORTATION **Airline SAS** links together the Scandinavian heavens domestically and then spreads its wings all around the globe. It even has check-in desks at several dozen hotels in Europe, the U.S., and Asia, so you can be rid of your luggage long before you leave for the airport. For Euroclass passengers, some cities in Scandinavia have effected a telephone check-in system, so ask about this convenience. Through alliances with other foreign airlines it is streamlining point-to-point services to and from anywhere. It has pioneered connections recently with Eastern Europe. In the USA, it ties in conveniently with Continental at Newark—an international airport, incidentally, which I much prefer to JFK for quick service to Manhattan. This is part of a developed ''comprehensive traffic system.'' Indeed it is, since SAS provides 700 flights a day to 82 foreign destinations linked to 1400 departures daily to 130 US cities! Now *all three* Scandinavian capitals are served by nonstop daily departures via Newark. While it has almost created an airborne sainthood for business-class travelers, it also blesses ordinary souls with extraordinary service. And look, too, for the advanced self-service automated ticket dispensers that are appearing throughout the system. The SAS concept is simply to iron the kinks out of travel. If this means getting you to the airport by posh limousine or by hovercraft, or even to reduce your hoofing with autowalks to the ramps, SAS will seek to render those mercies. It runs its own hotels, outfits sleek lounges with pampering amenities, and has dramatically refashioned Copenhagen Airport—with the addition of gateway shopping that vies with the finest establishments of this sort on the continent. Tariffs on perfume, spirits, tobacco, and cosmetics are among the lowest in Europe; other merchandise such as silver, fur, jewelry, and foodstuffs are bargains too. In the Nordic skies, SAS is not too interested in your tax-free cigarette purchases. Save those smokes till you land since airborne puffing is prohibited. (Finnair also doesn't permit smoking aloft.)

Taxis Better than they were, but still not plentiful when it rains or at theater time. Usually you must get them by telephone (01-353535 in Copenhagen); your hotel porter, or anyone in the store or restaurant you are in will do it for you.

A taxi ride is pretty costly, but it includes an automatic full tip.

Trains and Ferries Pride of the Danes are the *Lyntog,* crack trains that fan out from Copenhagen to the major cities. The *Englaenderen* (''Englishman'') boat special, fastest and best of all, runs from the capital to Esbjerg (port for England) and back. Intercity expresses lace up the spaces between Jutland, Funen, and the capital every hour. Incidentally, the overnight ferry between Esbjerg and the British coast is extremely comfortable.

The ''Bird Line'' project—called ''Bee Line'' by locals—is the rail-and-

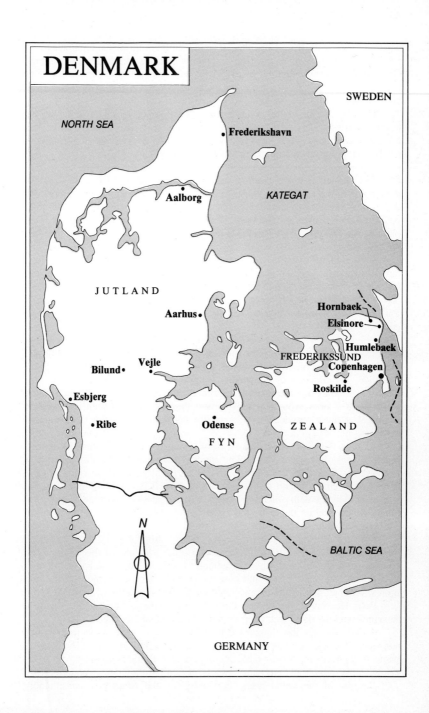

DENMARK

SWEDEN

NORTH SEA

• Frederikshavn

KATEGAT

• Aalborg

JUTLAND

Aarhus •

Hornbaek

Elsinore •

Humlebaek •

Bilund • Vejle •

FREDERIKSSUND

Copenhagen

• Esbjerg

Roskilde •

• Ribe

Odense •

Z E A L A N D

F Y N

N

BALTIC SEA

GERMANY

superhighway seam from Copenhagen to the southern tip of the archipelago. A train-and-car-ferry handles the 1-hour, 11-mile gusset between Denmark and the German island of Fehmern. Smart drivers get advance reservations for their autos, giving them priority when the pickaback train ferries are loaded. From here, a bridge joins the mainland—and you're off running!

The 500 islands of this maritime nation are linked by clean, efficient, attractive ferries (many with space for cars). You can also ride the rails, bus routes, or ferry lanes at reduced prices, so be sure to ask your travel agent about the Danish programs that apply to your needs or budget.

FOOD Though costly enough to induce lockjaw just by looking at a menu, the cuisine in the land of the Danes is most often incomparable. One reason for this is that the Danish larder includes chiefly expensive ingredients. In other countries where pasta, ground meat, or cheaper seafood can fill a void for small outlays, the Danes—as all Nordics—retain their love for salmon, tiny shrimps, herring, game, and similar luxury delicacies. Except for outdoor foodstands and a growing number of ethnic restaurants, you can seldom eat at bargain levels, but you may find yourself swallowing less at each sitting. (That goes for drinking too.) Copenhagen establishments are distinctive as a group and just as memorable as individual beauty spots. Out of the capital, try a "kro," not a norseland fowl but their word for tavern, and far more intimate than the ones found in other nations.

DRINKS Danes are among the greatest beer drinkers on earth. Carlsberg and Tuborg, though merged commercially, continue to produce their own delightful formulae. The products of the smaller Wiibroe Brewery up in Elsinore are also fine. If you don't like the stronger "Export" (Gold or Silver Cap) grade, there are at least 7 or 8 types to choose from; the dry, pale "Green" Tuborg or "Hof" Carlsberg (never exported) and the Carlsberg bock-style are perennial favorites.

Akvavit is the national "hard" drink. King of akvavits is the "Aalborg" brand. It looks like water, smells like caraway seeds, and tastes like cleanliness itself; it also kicks like a broadside of 16-inch naval guns. It's terrific. Drink it *ice-cold* and chase it with beer, as the Danes do. It is more common to see it sipped at midday with *smorrebrod* (open-faced sandwiches) than in the evenings, when wine is frequently the beverage to serve with cooked foods and in a mood of continental formality.

Ever try Greenland Sermeq Vodka? Every drop of water in it has been brought to the distillery from the super-pure inland ice cap of this island to be blended with alcohol and other ingredients. Bestle's Greenland Kwan Akvavit incorporates the same water and curative herbs to produce a more gentle and mild savor than that of the caraway and cumin that are normally employed.

Peter Heering is marvelous. On only one of the country's 500 islands—Zealand—can the dark, rich cherries with their special flavor be found.

A dark ultra-mellow liqueur has been produced for generations from choice sun-ripened black currants infused with fine West Indian rums. The generic name is Solbaerrom, a delectable accompaniment to cheese courses, hot pancakes, apple dumplings, and other sweets. Again, chilling does wonders for it.

Because of the brutal taxes, bottled spirits and wines cost considerably more than we pay at home. At bars, the prices alone are enough to produce a mile-wide hangover.

Skal This is one of the friendliest, most gracious national customs in the world. In Denmark and in all Scandinavia it is faithfully followed.

It's a toast, of course—and the rules are rigid. Here's what you do: Wait until somebody gives the signal. Then raise your glass, look the recipient in the eye, nod, and say "Skal" (pronounced "skowl"). Drink bottoms up, never permitting your eyes to waver from the eyes of the recipient. When you finish, raise your glass again and bow slightly; only then can your fixed gaze be lowered.

If you are host, you must "Skal" each of your guests individually at some point during the meal; a guest may "Skal" anyone at any time at any part of the table, with 2 exceptions—the hostess (throughout Scandinavia) and the host (Norway and Sweden). In Denmark you may salute the host with this gesture, because the Danes are less formal than their Nordic brothers, but it is horribly bad manners everywhere to salute the lady. If the party were a large one, she'd be drunk in 10 minutes.

TIPPING The trend is moving away from this custom since so many Scandinavians feel that handouts are demeaning to the recipient. In restaurants the tip is automatically extracted. In dining places any *small* gratuity is entirely at your option, but is generally given *only* if the service has been exceptionally attentive. The same applies for the concierge, floor waiter, and maid. Taxi drivers are *not* tipped.

CITIES AND REGIONS

AALBORG The old district dates back a thousand years and certainly merits a day of exploration. Evidence of its origins are the 700-or-so wraiths who haunt the nearby Viking burial ground at *Lindholm*. The Monastery goes back to the early 15th century, but if you have transportation it might be more fun to visit the log cabin built by Danish-Americans in 1912 at Rebild Forest, or take binoculars and scan the **Lille Vildmose,** a great savanah that is one of the last homelands for the vanishing black stork. For modern art, the collection at **Nordjyllands Kunstmuseum** is noteworthy. On a recent visit the town was about to open a **Shipping and Naval Museum** at the west flank of the port. It should be interesting.

☆☆ **Phoenix** ● is one of Jutland's outstanding hotels. It has been in continuous operation for more than a century in a building that predates the American Revolution. Colorfully executed and carefully maintained; recently expanded to 180 rooms with bath; delightful English pub called the Brigaderen; radiant heating—and similar reception.

Slotshotellet • on the waterfront, is modern; good for families. (''Slot,'' incidentally, means ''castle'' in Danish and not what Nevadans might suppose.)

Scandic • a bit outside of the center, is better for motorists.

Hvide Hus • in Kilde Park has grown with dignity. Third-floor outdoor heated swimming pool; sauna; shops; bar with open fireplace; snack center plus panoramic penthouse grill; 202 rooms in efficiency style, each with private balcony and refrigerator.

Limfjordshotellet • by the harbor, is a medium-priced 180-room-and-bath contender in contemporary style.

Ansgar • also in midtown, is well outfitted. Good for the mid-range budget.

Chagall • yet another in midcity, offers fresh cheerful surroundings. The mood is uplifting.

Scheelsminde • is a charming motel in an old country house, renowned for its first-rate cuisine.

Hafnia and **Park •** are traditional with moderate price tags. The latter has been extensively perked up and expanded in a pleasant way.

For your first meal try the **Faklen** (Jomfru Anegade 21). The building is 300 years old. Cheerful interior; cunningly illuminated cross-hatched beam ceiling; low, tasteful center partition topped by colorful plants; tartan wall-to-wall carpeting; the waiters sport kilts; candles on every table; 40-place banquet room. **Fyrtojet,** next door, in rustic style, offers well-prepared food at popular prices. This entire street of antique houses is devoted to dining, snacking, and sipping. **Cafeen** and **Dufy** are Gallic in tone. **Penny Lane** is good for fish. **Jensens Bofhus** (C. W. Obels Plads) is a charming 2-story restaurant in an old merchant's house. For snacks, the handsome 6-story **Duus Vinkjaelder,** a splendid Renaissance house, should soothe light appetites agreeably. **Regensen** is sound and inexpensive. In summer, try the **Zoo Restaurant** as a lovely grazing land.

For revels after gloaming, the **Dancing Palace** spells romance for many pairs of local citizens. Also popular are the **Gaslight** and the **Disco World.**

AARHUS, Denmark's second hub, is ¼ Copenhagen's size. A vacation city, a university city, it boasts a unique open-air museum—the **Old Town** was rebuilt with original medieval bricks and timber. The **Concert Hall** is one of the most active in the North. The **Fire Protection Museum** may sound dull, but wait until you boggle over those 60 or more fire engines, some of them manual or horsedrawn and dating back to 1850. Open April to late Oct., but closed Mondays. Another attraction is the **Moesgard,** containing prehistoric artifacts;

nod "hello" to the **Grauballe Man,** a 2000-year-old resident of the region and still a sparkling conversationalist. The town is as green as an Irish instep, swept by bracelets of sandy beach and punctuated with tall leafy forests. The harbor has perked up commendably in recent times.

☆☆☆ **Royal** • in a period building and very handsome, has refashioned itself smartly and added a fine little casino. Traditional, fresh, and temptingly supplied with good restaurants and cozy corners.

★★★ **Marselis** • also wins a generous supply of laurels. Outskirts situation in a wooded grove at the lap of the sea; new swimming pool and fitness center; attractive ceramic art inset along walls and corridors; waterside restaurant with piano melodies counterpointing the beat of the waves; simple but comfortable units with a nautical view through full-length windows. If peace is your motive, look no farther.

Atlantic • smack in the middle of the busy port, is another high-tide contender. Many doubles with balcony. The ferryboat landing is practically at its doorstep where ships embark for Kalundborg, the rail link to Copenhagen.

Ritz • has become increasingly ritzy and is now recommendable for upper-medium budgets. The dining room and the bedchambers are dressed up in a pleasant fashion.

Ansgar • is more of a family retreat without any special froufrou but with substantial comfort and solid value for your kroner.

Scandic • is rather young and button-bright. It's on the outer ring road but still only a 10-minute drive to town. Prices are upper-middle bracket.

When hunger strikes, your first inclination should lead you to your hotel dining room—especially if you are booked in any of the above-mentioned leaders. Among the independents you will find a refined crystal-chandelier sort of atmosphere and reasonable international cuisine at **De 4 Arstider.** The **Cafe Mahler** features intimacy with its French cuisine. **Barberen** is an inexpensive little shaver incorporating the decor of an antique barbershop, while **Kellers Gaard** occupies an old grocery store at Radhuspladsen—and a handsome building it is. **Fiskehuset Marstrandsborg** is fun, fresh, and ideal for deepsea critters. Locals praise the **Windsor Pub** in the Hotel Windsor; it is a sizzling steak restaurant. On the outskirts, **Gammel Abyhoj** is sited majestically in a vast private park. The table is international; reserve before driving out. For night life, **Glazzhuset,** in the center at Clemensborg Stroget, is an animated jazz cafe with live music.

ANS is a village 20 minutes southwest of *Viborg* and 15 minutes north of *Silkeborg.*

★★★★ **Kongensbro Kro** nestles cozily just off the highway intersection, down by the edge of a lovely lake that sparkles about 2 miles southeast of town. Old-style inn restored in the Danish tradition by the proprietary family; forest-green dining room with excellent skillet skills; cellar-cited tiny pub and TV nook; 17 bedchambers. If you're in the region, make an effort to search out this little gem.

COPENHAGEN

The 800-year-old city *is* metropolitan Denmark. Pronounce it to rhyme with "Haig" not "jog;" the latter is strictly the German way. More than ¼ of the 5 million national population live and work here. Government, industry, the international airport, the best hotels, restaurants, shops, and amusements are all here. So is one of the finest zoos in Europe. So, too, is the princess of the harbor, the Little Mermaid.

One of the quickest routes to reward is an orientation stroll through mid-city, down the famous pedestrian mall for shoppers known as Stroget. There's a spur off to the Latin Quarter on Kobmagergade where university students have gathered since the 17th century. Then take a browse along the beautifully restored Pistol Street (about halfway down from Town Hall Square), pass the canals of the old fishmarket, to the former red-light district of Nyhavn (now tamed and even becoming fashionable). The entire circuit will take under an hour, but you'll surely wish to pause along the way.

The **Copenhagen Card** is your passport to the city's wonders: free admission to 45 museums, castles, the zoo, aquarium, unlimited travel on local buses and trains, and a 25% discount on ferry crossings to Sweden. It's inexpensive, the price depending on the 1- to 3-day duration (children half fee). Obtainable at rail stations, travel bureaus, or at Danvisit in the same building as the Tourist Information Office, 22 H. C. Andersens Blvd. If you intend to do even minimal sightseeing, it will represent a great saving.

ATTRACTIONS

Tivoli ● Of the attractions in Copenhagen, Tivoli, which is approaching 150 years old, should be your priority stop. It's incomparable: Central Park, the Botanical Gardens, the Atlantic City boardwalk, the Flower Show, and a tiny European-style Disneyland rolled into one. The setting and atmosphere are wonderful; the location is smack in the center of Copenhagen. Admission of about 30 DK; prices are halved for children. You can hear a 54-piece symphony

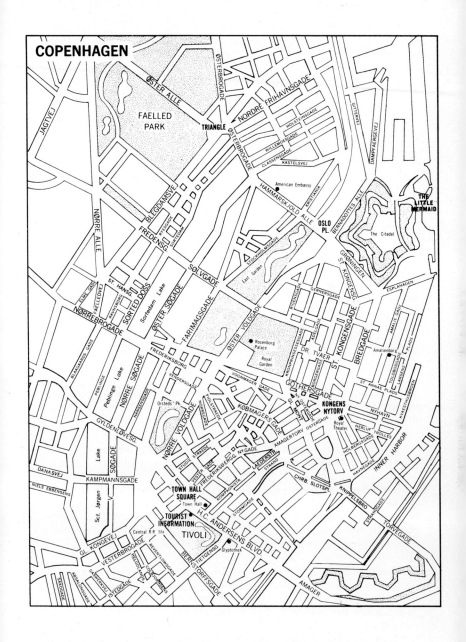

COPENHAGEN

FAELLED PARK

ØSTER ALLE

JAGTVEJ

NORRE ALLE

ØSTERBROGADE

NORDRE FRIHAVNSGADE

HOLSTEINSGADE

WILLEMOESGADE

CLASSENSGADE

KASTELSVEJ

TRIANGLE

American Embassy

HAMMARSKJOLD ALLE

KRISTIANIA

GITTENVEJ

DAMPFAERGEVEJ

THE LITTLE MERMAID

OSLO PL.

BERNADOTTES ALLE

The Citadel

GRØNINGEN

ST. KONGENS

ESPLANADEN

BLEGDAMSVEJ

FREDENSG.

SOLVGADE

RYESGADE

SORTEDAM

STOCKHOLMSGADE

East Garden

GERNERSGADE

AMALIE GADE

ST. HANS G.

FAELLEDVEJ

RAVNSBORG

SORTED DOSS.

ØSTER SØGADE

FARIMAGSGADE

ØSTER VOLDGADE

Sortedam Lake

NØRREBROGADE

ELMEGADE

BLAAGAARDS GADE

NØRRE SØGADE

FREDERIKSBORG

VENDERSGADE

Peblinge Loke

Orsteds Pk.

GYLDENLOVESG.

SØGADE

Lake

DANASVEJ

NIELS EBBENSENS

Sct. Jørgen

KAMPMANNSGADE

KONGEVEJ

GL.

VESTERBROGADE

Central R.R. Sta.

TIVOLI

TOURIST INFORMATION

TOWN HALL SQUARE

Town Hall

H.C. ANDERSENS BLVD.

BERNSTORFFSGADE

HELGOLANDSGADE

COLBJORNSENS

REVENTLOWSGADE

ABSALONSGADE

SAXOGADE

VESTERVLI

ISTEDGADE

TIETGENSG

Glyptothek

STENOSGADE

Rosenborg Palace

Royal Garden

KRONPRINSESSEGADE

ROSENBORGGADE

DR. TVAER

ST. KONGENSGADE

ADELGADE

BORGERGADE

GOTHERSGADE

VOGNMAGER

GADE

KØBMAGERGADE

KRYSTALGADE

NØRRE VOLDGADE

NØRREGADE

TOLDBODGADE

BREDGADE

Amalienborg

AMALIE GADE

LARSENSG.

ST. ANNAE PLADS

KONGENS NYTORV

NYHAVN

Royal Theater

HERLUF TROLLES

HOLBERGSGADE

HAVNEGADE

KVAESTHUSBROEN

INNER HARBOR

AMAGERTORV

ØSTERGADE

GL. MONT

KOMPAGNISTR.

STUDIE STRAEDE

VESTER GADE

FREDERIKSBERG

NY GADE

LAEDERSTR

STRAND

CHRB. SLOTSPL.

STORMGADE

KNIPPELSBRO

OSTERGADE

TORVEGADE

STRANDGADE

AMAGER

orchestra and some of Europe's greatest soloists in the stunning Concert Hall. At midnight on Wed., Fri., Sat., and Sun. evenings there are marvelous fireworks. Visiting Copenhagen without seeing Tivoli is like visiting Manhattan without seeing the Statue of Liberty and Lincoln Center. It's open from late April through mid-Sept.

Radhuset • *City Hall, Radhuspladsen* • Built in 1905, this fine building is the administrative center of Copenhagen, and houses the unique astronomical clock, **Jens Olsen's Verdensur** (Jens Olsen's World Clock). You may also want to climb the City Hall Tower that reaches 346 feet.

Christiansborg Slot • *Seat of Government, Christiansborg Slotsplads* • The Royal reception, conference, and Parliament chambers are here, as are the ruins of Bishop Absalon's fort, built around A.D. 1167. Guided tours in English are available daily except Mondays.

Nationalmuseet • *National Museum, 12 Frederiksholms Kanal* • Here are vast collections illustrative of Denmark's antiquity—from the Ice Age to the Vikings. Also included are Romanesque and Gothic church interiors, European coins and medals, and primitive ethnographic artifacts from various cultures. **Note:** Most museums close on Mondays.

Ny Carlsberg Glyptotek • *New Carlsberg Museum, Dantes Plads* • Just behind Tivoli, the museum offers a fine collection of 19th-century French and Danish works, as well as Egyptian, Greek, Etruscan, and Roman art.

Tojhusmuseet • *Royal Arsenal Museum, 3 Tojhusgade* • Weapons and uniforms from all over the world are included in this huge collection. The beautiful edifice was constructed in 1600 by Christian IV.

Holmens Kirke • *Holmen's Church, Holmens Kanal* • Built in 1619, this is the church used by the Royal House and Navy.

Amalienborg • *Queen's Palace* • The official residence of the Royal family was built in 1750. When the queen is at home you can see the changing of the guard daily at 12 p.m., before which the bearskin-capped royal life guardsmen make their traditional 30-minute march from the Rosenborg Castle barracks. Following the guards along this march is an old city custom.

Kunstindustrimuseet • *Museum of Decorative Art, 68 Bredgade* • One of Copenhagen's premier charms is this fine collection of European and Oriental handicrafts, which is set in the typically ornate style of the rococo period. The garden, which was laid out in 1757, is beautiful too.

Kastellet • *The Citadel, at the Langelinie* • This 300-year-old military fortress is a definite must on your tour of the city. The Citadel, which covers approximately 50 acres, was originally built in 1629. The old guardhouses still stand inside the magnificent Zealand and Norwegian gates. Also, don't miss the

Gefion fountain, which dramatically depicts a bronze goddess charioteering four mist-snorting oxen.

Den lille Havfrue • *The Little Mermaid, Langelinie* • This charming statue, which reclines on a rock at the harbor shore near the Kastellet, has come to symbolize Copenhagen. It was placed in 1913, the work of Danish sculptor Edvard Erikson.

Legetojsmuseet • *Toy Museum, 13 Valkendorfsgade* • This is certainly an amusing treat for adults and children alike. The fine collection includes toys from 1840 to 1930, with extraordinary model trains, tin soldiers, and a colorful variety of mechanical toys.

Rundetarn • *Round Tower, Kobmagergade* • This spectacular spiral tower was erected by Christian IV in 1642 and reaches 120 feet. You can still climb the 687-foot spiral walk to the observatory.

Tycho Brahe Planetarium • *Gl. Kongevejio* • This is a more modern form of observatory, well landscaped into a lakeside setting. Performances hourly every day from lunchtime until evening. Exciting space exhibits plus a wondrous Omnixmax film dome. Restaurant facilities are available.

Musikhistorisk Museum • *Museum of Musical History, 32–34 Abenra* • Musicians and music lovers alike will enjoy this nice collection of historical musical instruments.

Botanisk Have • *Botanical Gardens, 130 Gothersgade* • A relaxing place to stroll along and view a fine variety of tropical and subtropical plants.

Rosenborg Slot • *Rosenborg Castle, 4A Oster Voldgade* • This majestic Renaissance castle was built in the 30 years between 1603 and 1633 by Christian IV. Its lavish interior contains the treasures of the Danish Monarchy from the 15th to the 19th centuries, including the striking crown jewels.

Statens Museum for Kunst • *Royal Museum of Fine Arts, Solvgade* • This should be considered a major point of interest for art loving tourists. It includes a comprehensive representation of Denmark's greatest artists, plus a fine assortment of European paintings and sculptures.

Excursions

Frilandsmuseet • *Open-Air Museum, Kongevejen 100, Sorgenfri, Kgs. Lyngby* • This wonderful museum, set in a beautiful pastoral countryside north of Copenhagen, represents the history of Danish rural life. Danish farmhouses of all styles and from all regions have been dismantled and reconstructed here, as have their respective typical environs. Chickens strut around thatch-roofed barns and in summer you can watch sheep being sheared and a variety of other bucolic crafts. There is a modern restaurant, but these are the perfect surroundings for a picnic, and tables are provided. In winter the park opens only on Sundays.

Kronborg Castle • *Hamlet's Castle at Helsingor* • Forty-five minutes north of Copenhagen by train stands Hamlet's famous castle. It's an imposing Renaissance structure, with a fine banquet hall and chapel.

Frederiksborg Castle • *Hillerod* • About a 40-minute train ride outside Copenhagen lies the beautifully situated town of Hillerod, and there the spectacular Frederiksborg Castle. It was built between 1602 and 1620, and it sits just above its own magnificent lake. Inside the castle you'll find Denmark's National History Museum, which offers a grand collection of paintings, portraits, Danish furniture, and art treasures. There is boating on the castle lake, and the enchanting castle park is an ideal picnic spot.

Louisiana Modern Art Museum • *Humlebaek, 13 Gammel Strandvej* • Unquestionably Denmark's most important modern art collection, Louisiana is delightfully situated overlooking the coast about 35 kilometers north of Copenhagen. If you're on your way to Helsingor to see the Kronborg Castle, stop in for a look at this lovely museum.

Canal Tours of Copenhagen • *Canal Sightseeing Tour* • You can enjoy the waterways of Copenhagen by either a guided or unguided boat tour. Tours concentrate on the smaller canals as well as greater harbor tours. Boats leave at frequent intervals (summer only) from Gammel Strand, Kongens Nytorv at Nyhavn, and from Christianshavn. For full information telephone (01) 13 31 05.

Hydrofoils • These speedy boats whisk commuters or sightseers between Copenhagen and Malmo, Sweden, in 35 minutes. Departures are hourly from the **Flyvebadene** pier at Havnegade 49 in the Nyhavn district near midcity. See two countries for the price of one—and don't forget your passport, though I've never been asked to show mine.

HOTELS

Wickedly expensive in this capital. Summer is low season, so possibly you can negotiate a better price this time of year.

☆☆☆☆ **d'Angleterre** • a monument for more than 2 centuries, continues in a leadership capacity for luxury living in the heart of this refined city. Here's a benchmark example of sophistication and taste. Most bedrooms already are superb and the more impressive late refashioning includes a brasserie with a colossal art-deco clock as its focal point on the parkside, brightened lounges, and a petit dining salon. The Palm Garden features entertainment in summer.

The hospitality quotient, as evinced by some staffers, seems below the expected level you anticipate when you first view the sumptuous appointments.

★★★★ **Plaza** • leans to classic traditionalism. The bar, in the form of a serene English private library, is the most gracious public room you are likely to see in the nation. Adjoining is the beguiling Flora Danica salon for light lunches and cocktails. In this old building architectural obstacles make the construction of any large suites almost impossible.

☆☆ **Royal** • in midcity opposite Tivoli, is a statement in Danish mid-fifties modernity. The registration procedure at a pod of electronic modules is a stab at efficiency that works very well but is bereft of human warmth. Spacious lobby; heavily patronized sauna and massage facilities; 120-car garage; a business-traveler's office that seems to appeal to commercial types. The Summit restaurant offers one of the best vistas of the capital, along with high-style cuisine. Both this one and the next are hitched to SAS, which performs a prescribed service with flying colors.

☆☆ **Scandinavia** • is almost twice the size of its Royal stepsister, equally as streamlined, and with a similar tilt toward the business traveler and groupies. Somewhat outlying off-bridgehead location, a pleasant but longish stroll (or free shuttle) to Tivoli Gardens; trim lobby with area for well-presented light bites; health center with saunas, gymnasium, indoor pool, and expert supervision. The candlelit cellar nook called After 8 often features live music but the record collection from the Early Wax era to the present is a rare treat.

★★★★ **Kong Frederik** • is in two segments, the original part having more decorative flair. Good location just off Town Hall square; charming lobby and hearth-warmed King's Gallery lined with paintings of all 9 Frederiks; Queen's Grill; Queen's Pub for informal revels; blissful Roof Garden plus Queens Garden restaurant (now roofed). Appealing but often crowded dimensions with inadequate storage space for luggage and rather dim (but cozy) illumination; 5 suites are directly off the penthouse terrace. Here's an excellent value for your kroner in this high-price-hotel nation.

Palace • with its excellent midcity location, is a glorious monument—to opportunity missed.

★★ **Sophie Amalie** • at harborside, is all dressed up in bright rig. There's a grill at ground level; sauna; little coffee shop at split level. The revamping has brought distinctive flair to this Danish lady.

★★ **Sheraton** • with a full-blown international mien, boasts wall-to-wall carpeting, clever illumination, and a bold textile sculpture that warms its lobby; pleasant bar adjoining. The King's Court restaurant is indeed inviting; the Felix Brasserie, with manneristic Art Retro decor; active fitness center. Generally fine and even improving.

★★★ **Neptun** • is a zesty little package of taste in one of the best districts of the capital. Skt. Annae Plads. One of its most appealing aspects is the reasonableness of its prices for the allures offered. Smart white entrance in Palladian style; homey salon with malacca chairs and Kelim carpets; fresh-faced breakfast room with hardy Danish fare; modernistic but not aggressive furnishings in its 66 bedrooms; a few suites cheered with potted plants and exceptional decorative features. As with many Danish hostelries, the bathrooms are poorly executed. This one has flair.

★★★ **71 Nyhavn** • bristles with personality. It is a converted "New Harbor" warehouse hard by the docks—an especially desirable mooring for saltier voyagers. The timber-and-stucco interior is the ubiquitous servant of its 1804 construction. Friendly staff; attractive candle-lit restaurant with appetizing sea fare; 15-seat bar off lobby; no tubs (only showers) in its grim, cramped baths. Adequate space is a problem here.

☆ **Alexandra** • is a cheery corner house in midtown. Bath and showers in every unit; only breakfasts are served; lounge in an equestrian theme; it is closed December to March as an economy move. Best perches are the spacious 3-window corner doubles; there's a handy garage next door.

★★ **Copenhagen Admiral** • in the bracing dock area overlooking the ferry passage, is a mini-giant of 366 rooms or so-called "suites." A clever blend of rural atmosphere of the 1780s with Danish design of the 1980s incorporating massive, blond, 200-year-old logs in partitions, in panels, on the ceilings, and even in "trees" in some of the bedchambers. Economizers seem to like it, perhaps because its rates are substantially under those of the competition.

☆ **SAS Falconer** • ("Three Falcons") recently underwent a refreshing renovation program. Tasteful lobby; intimate dining facilities with superb cuisine at decent tariffs; charming bar; superior service; big, big windows; bank; hairdresser; florist; art gallery; a welcome parking lot directly in front for harried motorists.

Imperial • has a bustling, commercial feel to its rather severe lobby. Units small and starkly furnished; singles uncomfortable for travelers with transatlantic luggage.

Richmond • has a free interchange breakfast plan with Mercur. The extra fillip here is La Cocotte, which is one of the finest French restaurants in the city—and, not incidentally, possibly the most expensive. The excellent local version of smorgasbord in another sector continues to be offered from noon to 2 p.m.

Vestersohus • a favorite of many of our Embassy staffers, occupies a lovely old house on the lake. Breakfast-only in 2 small waterside dining rooms; most quarters sizable, with ample closet space; 50 twins or convertibles and 30 singles, only about half of which have private plumbing; 6 apartments, some with fully equipped kitchen-dining area, of which #21 is the choicest; tariffs 20% lower in winter; especially good for families and long stays.

Opera • debuts behind the Royal Theatre; Den Kongelige restaurant on the ground floor; very costly tariffs for the best stalls in the house. **Ascot** serves breakfast only; it is agreeably fresh. **Sara Hotel Dan** resides just 10 minutes by foot from the airport. The total renovation is a badge it wears proudly. The chain that runs it is one of the finest in the north. Other airport candidates include the SAS-sponsored and nicely refitted, as well as expanded, **Globetrotter** and the **Bel Air**. They share a similar transient personality. The **Grand** became grander a few years ago; it was extended, given a fresh facade in Danish colors (white and red), added marble baths throughout, plugged in TV, video, and minibars, and is generally looking spiffy today. **Mercur** and **Astoria** were restyled in fetching ways. Both are in midcity. The latter offers an attractive snack center and a reasonably priced *smorrebrod*.

RESTAURANTS

☆☆☆☆ **L'Alsace** • *Pistolstraede, through the passageway next to Bee Cee on the Pedestrian Mall* • dominates the Old Quarter. You'll discover an utterly charming ambience with brick walls, benches, prints, an open kitchen, an oyster bar to wet (and whet) your appetite, and a dining terrace in a lovely sequestered courtyard. There's a highly refined menu with reasonable prices; trout and other freshwater fish a specialty; 48 tables inside and 25 outside; good wine list; friendly and informal staff; open from 11:30 a.m. to 10:30 p.m.

In the same nooklike complex several other fattening possibilities exist: The **Bee Cee Cafe** • *Ostergade 24* • is a delightful money-saver where the accents are on salads, snacks, cheese, and wines. In the same vicinity of Pistolstraede there is a seam-splitter called **Kransekagehuset,** which specializes in (of course) kransekage, the tooth-destroying almond marzipan that the Danes love; other pastries along with tea, coffee, and chocolate are available, plus an outside apron for summer pastimes. The house motto, not incidentally, is "It should be worth the calories." (It is.) Then, if you stroll through City Passage, look for **Cafe Bernikow** with its darkly alluring turn-of-the-century furnishings, paintings, and snugglesome wine-bar atmosphere. Otherwise, there is the nearby **Greens** • *Gronnegade 12–14* • in the same district, which contributes hoedowns on crisp vegetarian greenery and health foods.

☆☆☆ **Kong Hans Kaelder** • *16th-century cellar near Magasin du Nord on the Vingardsstraede* • In dramatic—almost flamboyant—contrast to the quiet-spoken L'Alsace, the open kitchen of this strikingly effective establishment splits its center. The front has a counter with 14 high seats inside the entrance where 9 less costly selections are offered. The rear, under an all-white geometrically aligned 4-arched ceiling, has 8 tables at lunch and 15 at dinner. To the extreme rear is a lovely 2-arched candlelit lounge with a small bar and d-e-e-p cushioned sofas. Closed July 15–Aug. 15 and Sun.

☆☆☆ **Leonore Christine** • *Nyhaven 9* • With its entry covered by a blue-and-white awning, this gracious antique house overlooks the ancient ships in the midcity canal. Floor-to-ceiling windows allow for peaceful viewing of the maritime scene; flowered plates, bentwood chairs, and candles in porcelain holders for intimate illumination. The menu (with a daily selection for lunch and dinner) is presented beside your table on a music stand, a touch which some might feel is too precious although it suits the sophisticated atmosphere very properly. Excellent but limited gastronomy; extremely pleasant. By all means, adjourn for a moment to go to the restroom, which you can reach by passing through one of the most typically attractive private salons in the north. Closed Sun.

☆☆ **Cafe Lumskebugten** • *Esplanaden 21* • This resident of the picturesque harbor area occupies a long white, window-lined wooden structure that is a charming period piece of Danish architecture. Because of its construction the few tables inside are in a row along its entire frontage. Decor consists of sailing ship models and pictures of the nation's royalty and other well-known personalities. The menu features approximately 20 classic dishes of the country. Very reasonable and attractive in a homespun way. Closed Sun.

☆☆ **Les Etoiles et une Rose** • *Dronningens Tvaergade 43* • Here's a curious but pleasant blend of French elegance and Danish simplicity, both in the decor as well as in the gastronomy. Off-white curtains and light cane furnishings; Mediterranean notions from the kitchen presented in a lovely nordic fashion. An enjoyable wine option of several vintages served by the glass to match your various dining choices. Fresh and charming.

★★★★ **Sct. Gertruds Kloster** • *Hauser Plads 32* • One of the most talked-about restaurants in the city—and most of the chat is favorable. Location in a tranquil little square; library bar with Chesterfield sofas, brass lamps, and marine prints; vast network of cellars (in a restored monastery) illuminated by more than 1200 candles—and *no electric lighting anywhere;* mirthful yard-long instruction sheet issued with your cocktail to guide you to and from your table. While the surroundings are highly engaging I found the cuisine and prices too low and too high respectively. If you care more for atmosphere than for gastronomy, you'll probably enjoy it.

☆☆ **Kongens Have** • *Kronprinsessegade 13* • A budget treat at lunchtime on a sunny day—or even for dinner when the weather is balmy. Within its dull building, which looks shabby but is not, there are 16 tables. Virtually its sole enticing attraction is the open-air garden to the rear that accommodates 50 different parties. Local-style comestibles are dished or glassed up from 11 a.m.– 11 p.m. every day.

☆ **Egoisten** • *in the little Hovedvagtsgade street* • A reliable entry that merits the attention and respect of cognoscenti. Its fittings, its tiny bar, its 10 tables and its atmosphere could scarcely be more cozy in the way that can only be found in this northern land. While the choices are limited, each dish is prepared and presented with a flair. A rewarding find on the upper-medium budget scale.

A Hereford Beefstouw • *2 branches; Vesterbrogade 3 and Abenra* • this enterprise specializes in juicy, marble-textured Hereford steaks. No-nonsense ambience; clever use of acrylic lighting; a few modern paintings to add splashes of color; open Mon. through Fri. from 11:30 a.m.–10 p.m.; closed weekends at lunchtime. The cost of a T-bone is about $14; by Continental standards the quality is excellent.

Bof & Ost • *"Beef & Cheese,"* *Grabrodretorv 13* • Pleasant cellar on a pretty square; 3 connecting rooms with low ceilings, whitewashed walls, and scrubbed birch tables; extremely popular as a neighborhood drop-in spot for an unelaborate meal or simply cheese and wine. Here is a friendly elbow-to-elbow atmosphere. Closed Sun. **Peder Oxe** is next door to Bof & Ost, in an 18th-century building. Same management; spotlight on a mix-it-yourself salad bar; meats also on call; spacious and fun.

★★★ **Paustian** • *Kalkbraenderikaj 2* • is out at the northern docks, an architectural creation of Jom Utzon (who created the Sydney Opera House). High, wide, and handsome, it also contains a sales exhibition center for Danish and other European household design. The dining room is white, window-lined, and restful. The food—all Danish—is delightful. A 5-minute taxi ride from midcity.

Gilleleje • *Nyhavn 10* • is alluringly inviting with its 13 tables, Iranian and African heads, skins and weapons, wooden beaded screens, highly varnished dark tables, and plants. Rather expensive; open for lunch and dinner straight through from Monday through Saturday; closed Sundays and holidays.

★ **Cafe Victor** • *Ny Ostergade 8* • is very popular with young people, intellectuals, and avid conversationalists. It is in the colorful Pistolstreet district. The food is reasonable, the surroundings are mirrored or window-lined, the pace is lively. Here's *the* scene in Copenhagen.

Krogs Fiskerestaurant • *Gammel Strand 38* • This purveyor of splendid seafare faces the docks across the street from where the nation's most famous fisherwomen used to peddle their wares. Specialties are lobster salad and filet of sole steamed in white wine. Tourists seem to gravitate here. Closed Sun.

Fiskekaelderen • *Ved Stranden 18* • is known to settled Copenhageners who settle into the wooden booths and intimate cellar mood. The building dates from the 1700s.

Den Sorte Ravn • *Nyhavn 14* • I'd place this down the scale from the two above leaders. Cellar (again); only 12 tables; low ceiling and red brick floor; open kitchen; no attempt at special eye-catchers except small, appetizing cheese display at entrance; good food and very friendly people. Not cheap.

Tivoli Gardens (May to mid-Sept.) has a number of first-class restaurants out of its total complement of 25. Leading the pack is the Divan I.

☆☆ **Divan I** ● When the sun or stars are shining, the air is balmy, and the crowds are reasonable in size, it is heavenly to unkink on its sylvan terrace while lingering over its costly but appetizingly sophisticated fare.

☆ **Divan II** ● is also deluxe but not quite as tempting.

Belle Terasse seemed pretentious and overpriced, but you might disagree; and **Perlen** is a bit more moderate. Somewhat lower in cost are the **Groften,** perhaps the most Danish of all in personality, and the **Balkonen,** which is a chintzy all-you-can-eat buffet with carvery option plus a la carte, with mediocre vittles in an indoor-outdoor combination.

Due to severely increasing labor problems, *lunch-only* restaurants have now burgeoned into a substantial separate category. Most of these small oases, normally family-run, are open only from 11 a.m.–2 p.m. or sometimes 4 p.m. from Mon. through Fri. All are blessedly inexpensive; the majority offer light dishes in the traditional Danish style.

Sankt Annae ● *Sankt Annae Plads 12* ● Everything you eat, save for the salt and pepper but including the mustard, is homemade. While the accent is essentially on open sandwiches, 2 or 3 warm dishes are featured daily. There are 11 well-lit tables with roses on each. The aura is homey, the food is good, the prices are right, and it is so popular among businessmen that advance reservations are recommended. Closed Sat. and Sun.

Ida Davidsen ● *St. Kongensgade 70* ● In this one you will find 10 to 15 warm choices in addition to its sandwiches. The normal hours are from 10 to 4. Closed Sat. and Sun.

Kongens Kaelder ● *"King's Cellar," Gothersgade 87* ● You'll find 3 small rooms in a charming old basement; the tables with candles and the plants add to its atmosphere. Read the slate menu on one wall, stroll through its very modern kitchen to look over its dishes, and then order at your table.

Ostehjornet ● *St. Kongensgade 56* ● Located above a cheese shop. The light bites are exceptional. Closed Sun.

Slotskaelderen ● facing the fish market, has been nicknamed "Hos Gitte Kik" for possibly 100 years. Prime ministers and other illustrious figures have often frequented this most famous establishment in its genre. Tavern atmosphere and simple; nevertheless, a treat. Closed July; Sat. and Sun.

Among *hotels,* my first choice is the **Plaza,** which boasts the lovely **Flora Danica** and the invitingly sumptuous **Library Bar.** For truly breathtaking views go to the **Top of the Town** in the **SAS Scandinavia.** La Cocotte, an independent enterprise in the **Richmond,** is superb for French cuisine at stratospheric prices. (Don't confuse this one with the fine lobster house in the *Citadel;* the names are similar: **Glasis La Cachotte.** It cooks modern cuisine as well.) **Saison** in the **Osterport** features Scandinavian fare—and tops it is, even if the location in a train depot is eccentric. The **Queen's Grill** of the **Kong Frederik** is a charmer for intimacy, while the penthouse of the **Scandinavia** is a wow for panorama. **Le Restaurant** of the **d'Angleterre** is too confining for my taste, and the service in the **Brasserie** is either too brassy or doesn't exist.

Ferry tale? Try the restored **Faergen Sjaelland** at its mooring at Kajplads 114. Chef Ole Petersen runs a tight galley.

If you're making the North Zealand "castle" excursion, there are several stops for your noon meal.

★★★★ **Sollerod Kro** ● remains my annual favorite; enchanting, expensive, in the village of Sollerod (about 25 minutes out of the capital toward Elsinore). Cream-colored 17th-century stucco building; thatched roof: a quiet rockbound pond and a tiny church in front; cottage windows and painted doors; a lovely presentation of food that perfectly matches the fairy-tale surroundings. *Always reserve in advance.*

★★★ **Den Gule Cottage** ● is a yellow 2-room, thatch-roofed, stucco-and-timber dwelling in a romantic park facing the Swedish shore from *Klampenborg* (15 minutes by train from Westerport Station in central Copenhagen; $2 fare; only a 3-minute stroll from the stop to Strandvejen 506; Tel. 01–640691 to reserve). Sea or lawn views; colossal flower displays; small select menu. My seafood mousse and roast beef were above average and not costly. If the day is fair, ask about the horse-and-carriage rides through the woods; these trot off from nearby stables. On long summer twilight evenings this is a haven of dreams.

Store-Kro, near *Fredensborg,* features a large, semipaneled, gold-pillared room in smooth but coldish international rather than Danish decor. The **Marienlyst** at *Elsinore* is suave and international. Then there's **H. C. Andersen Huset** at *Asserbo,* 24 miles from Copenhagen. While it boasts 150 years in age, it still exudes Mr. Andersen's youthful spirit. **Bregnerod Kro** is another charmer within short commuting distance in the direction of Hillerod. Its red roadside building, with 2 freshly thatched roofs, has offered food and/or lodging to the hungry and/or the weary for more than 3 centuries. The cuisine is good but not spectacular, because it dishes up simple country fare—just that.

NIGHT LIFE

Copenhagen of yore was a naughty town. Porn purveying today, however, is minimal, pick-up palaces have almost vanished in the fearful shadow of AIDS, gay haunts are almost vacant, and the former red-light district is developing gradually into a silk-stocking zone. Hotels now serve as the gathering spots for respectable conviviality and bar lounging. Door charges at the remaining few cabaret or club-type bars cost $6 to $11, depending on the night of the week.

Hard beverages—as everywhere in Scandinavia—are thumpingly expensive. Champagne? Say "gulp" right now and save a small fortune.

Daddy's is in the cellar of the giant Palads Cinema complex (with 19 theaters) on Axeltorv. The neonostalgic theme locks onto the Marilyn Monroe and Chuck Berry era, with live music several times each week.

Annabel's at Lille Kongensgade 16 leads the disco parade every night from ten to dawn.

Tordenskiold is a worthy alternate; it's centrally sited on Kongens Nytorv and harks back to times of maritime prowess in the Hansa.

Vin & Olgod at Gammeltorv near the site of the Old Town Hall (A.D. 1200), throbs with very special, very Danish zest. Capacity for 400 merrymakers on 3 different levels; separate segments successively devoted to an English pub, a Portuguese bodega, a ratskeller, a grillrotisserie, and a whopping Main Hall. Emphasis on drinking, snacking, and musical revelry; more frolicking by adults than by teen types; oompah band; songbooks at each place setting; locked-arms singing; "dancing" on the benches whenever the spirit moves. Low prices; active from 8 p.m.–2 a.m. but never on Sunday. Heaps of hilarity for the fancy-free of all ages. Highly recommended for its delightful, authentic Copenhagen color.

In Tivoli Gardens, **Dansetten** is the leading light.

Kakadu ("Cockatoo") is peopled by businessmen in 3-button gray flannels and business girls in no-button gowns. **Fellini** in the Royal Hotel puts on a dazzling show. **After 8,** previously mentioned, is for whispering sweet nothings in the Scandinavia Hotel. The Sheraton piano bar in the **King's Court** specializes in champagne with its blue notes.

Wonderbar is well-known for unattached girls in search of companionship. Intimate and cheerful, with pleasant salon furnishings and almost prudishly decorous atmosphere; open until 5 a.m. and occasionally absolutely dead.

On a one-to-one basis, the capital has scores of **escort services** for lonely gents. Any issue of *Copenhagen This Week* lists many with phone numbers and details; some even accept credit cards.

Woodstock is great fun for the sounds of the sixties; opens at 9 p.m. and closes late. **Jazzhouse Montmartre,** as the name hints, is a modern jazz parlor. Open Tues., Wed., and Thurs. from 8 p.m.–2 a.m.; Fri. and Sat. from 9 p.m.–4 a.m. Closed Sun. and Mon. Some of the top names in notes appear on its bandstand. **Trocadero** shouldn't be recommended to anybody with less than the consolidated toughness of the National Hockey League. For music buffs, **La Fontaine** (swing and contemporary bars) and **De Tre Musketerer** (New Orleans beats) are the current hot spots, featuring some of the best itinerant U.S. and continental combos.

On The Rox is one of the leading discos; the kitchen team works until 3 a.m. **Cafe Sommersko,** on Kronprinsensgade, is the public gathering place of the local young people, mainly students. If you are absolutely tireless, try the new **Scala** opposite the main gates of Tivoli. It is loaded with discos, more than a dozen restaurants, and 5 movie houses.

You'll have kegs of fun in Copenhagen. It's known far and wide as the "Paris of the North"—but that's wrong. For our money, that's as unfair as calling Paris the "Copenhagen of the South."

SHOPPING

SHOPPING HOURS: Weekdays generally 10 a.m.–6 p.m., no noon closings; Sat. 10 a.m. to 1 or 2 p.m. (except on the first Sat. of every month when they don't close till 5 p.m.). Many stay open until 7 p.m. on Fri.; department stores pull down their shades at 8 p.m. on Fri.

BEST AREAS: Stroget is a pedestrian street ¾ of a mile long. It links the Radhuspladsen and Kongens Nytorv. Down its length are five streets: Frederiksberggade, Nygade, Vimmelskaftet, Amagertorv and Ostergade. Parallel to the Stroget on one side are Farvergade, Kompagnistraede, and Laederstraede—and on the other, the Latin Quarter around the University. Nearby Fiolstraede and Kobmagerade are where locals often stroll. PS: See our postscript further along on **Copenhagen Airport's** duty-free shopping center.

SAVINGS ON PURCHASES: Scores of Americans consider that Denmark offers the most appealing shopping on the Continent. The 18.03% "MOMS" tax is effective on a national scale only *within* the country. Exported merchandise is granted a significant deduction. Therefore, make arrangements to ship your major purchases direct to your home or, for pickups by you, direct to the airport or other Danish point of exit. Then, too, goods can be carried out with your luggage (new regulations allow everyone not residing in E.E.C. nations to take as many articles as desired provided the *total* amount purchased in each store is worth 600 Dkr. or over), but be sure to consult with your merchant as to how to obtain your tax rebate and find out about the immediate reimbursement plan for airline passengers.

BOOKS: Denmark is one of the handiest countries in which to restock your supplies of stateside books and magazines. **Boghallen** (Town Hall Square), **G.E.C. Gad** (Pedestrian Mall), and **Arnold Busck** (Kobmagergade) offer the most versatile volumes in our language.

BOUTIQUE: Bee Cee (Ostergade 24 and Copenhagen Airport) stands for the ubiquitous Birger Christensen—and by now you should know that his name hallmarks q-u-a-l-i-t-y. The spirit throughout is so winning that the chic buyer of any age finds it irresistibly a la mode. Here are selected eye-arresting sportswear, casual clothes, accessories and other temptations. Manageress Sally Teller and her staff are experts in the rapidly changing fashion game.

CLOTHING: Brodrene Andersen (Ostergade 7–9) has been a stitch in time for well over a century in stylishly attiring the Establishment fraternity—including, we might add, the Royal Danish Court since its more recent princes were in knee pants. Andersen's richly conservative paneled interior exudes masculine character—and so does its debonair clothing. General manager Jorgen Nexoe-Larsen (3rd generation), your impeccable host, opens a sesame of sartorial treasures—names such as Zegna, Cerruti, Gant, Hugo Boss, Rene Lezard, Kenzo, Seventy, and Chester Barrie plus a Pringle Shop, Danish sweaters and cardigans, and 100% hand-tailored outfits. Also you will find a well-stocked women's department where there are troves of lovely sweaters, skirts, and slacks. In addition to Director Nexoe-Larsen there are Mrs. Brandt in the Ladies' Department and Mr. Gullov, who are ready to solve your problems. Far-and-away the leader.

FURS: More high-grade mink is raised in Denmark than in any other foreign land—and the quality and savings are unbeatable. By far the most eye-gleaming assortment, in our opinion, can be found at the century-old house of **Birger Christensen** (Ostergade 38, and Copenhagen Airport), Purveyors By Appointment to no less than 3 Royal Courts and to most of the important foreign embassies. They not only offer a reservoir of the largest stocks and widest choices in Europe—but these are sophisticatedly understated and *different*. The inventory is umbrellaed to cover all ages and budgets. The feature here is their world-famous Danish mink in a color galaxy of 20 mutations; there is also a large line of modestly priced Fun Furs. The alert and charming Birger Christensen has outlets in U.S. and Canadian centers, one in Tokyo, and his own store in Paris. As the only major house in the world to create new collections twice yearly, its fashion shows continue to be smash successes throughout the world. Ask for this instantly likable dynamo in person.

GLASSWARE: The nation's only producer is **Holmegaard** (Ostergade 15), which since 1825 has triumphantly combined craftsmanship with excitingly different ideas. Dozens of free brochures; a glittering wonderland. **Skandinavisk Glas** (Ny Ostergade 3), projects a wider attraction because of its greater versatility.

HANDICRAFTS: **Haandarbejdets Fremme** (Vimmelskaftet 38) is the fascinating headquarters of the Danish Handcraft Guild, under the patronage of Queen Ingrid. It houses many of the patterns which her daughter, the reigning Queen Margarethe, another royal needlewoman, has fashioned. One segment is devoted to the imaginative apparel created by Denmark's most talented designers. The other contains a world of artistry that is manifest in knitting, embroidery, carving, pottery, jewelry, weaving, and other textiles. Not only are these treasures available for purchase in their finished form, but scores of do-it-yourself packages are available. The startlingly low prices and the portability of such gorgeous flat-packing inventories, make this a trove for gift items that can be carried away on impulse.

HI-FI EQUIPMENT: **Bang & Olufsen Center** (on the Stroget at Ostergade 3–5) is the design king of this specialty, the creator of the fabulous super-thin line of sophisticated stereo turntables and sound terminals that seem as natural on display in a Museum of Modern Art as they are in a fine home. Erling Christensen will show you everything and explain how you can own the very best while realizing major savings in purchasing.

HOME FURNISHINGS: Illums Bolighus (Amagertorv 10, with "Mini-Illums" at Tivoli—the latter open late on Sat. and all of Sun.) translates as "Home House." This Center of Modern Design is the closest we've ever found to being *the* dream shop of any American host or hostess. Graceful Danish furniture galore; the nation's longest shelves of porcelain, stoneware, and faience; Gastronomic Boutique; restaurant; art gallery; the famous Wooden Articles Department; Arts and Crafts Department.

PIPES: W. O. Larsen (Amagertorv 9) is not only one of the outstanding establishments in Europe for pipes and blended tobaccos, it also is one of the world's most fascinating centers for viewing the history of smoking. Even if you don't smoke you can pass an hour of riveting interest admiring the assemblage of rare briars, bone, porcelain, and clay pipes which have been collected from all over the globe, including a unique American Indian peace pipe. Each one of the Larsen masterpieces is handcrafted with its own meticulously fashioned stem. The 128-year-old firm has been in the same family from father to son through 4 generations and the fifth is already extremely active in the business.

PORCELAIN: Celebrated **Bing & Grondahl** (Amagertorv 6), is the pioneer who revolutionized the industry by achieving the final historic breakthrough of the *under*glaze decoration techniques which are amazingly resistant to all kinds of soaps, detergents, and acids. It is impossible to put into words the magic which, in their consummate artistry, they have conveyed to their soaring birds, swimming fishes, friendly dogs, and sweet children in Hans Christian Andersen figurines, alluring dinnerware, and gorgeous porcelain lamps.

Royal Copenhagen, at the same address, is also venerable, highly distinguished, and universally respected. **Frosig** (Norrebrogade 9) is a small, crowded center for "seconds" of all leading producers. Please get all of your porcelain while you're on Danish soil, because the markup in North America for exactly the same items is staggering.

SHOPPING AND LEISURE CENTER: Scala (Axeltorv, opposite the fabled Tivoli) is a fresh approach to marketing. Its five floors are crammed with a cinema complex, fitness club, ethnic restaurants galore *and* all sorts of stores. There's even a stage for frequent live music shows. Open 9 a.m.–2 a.m. It really hums.

SILVER: My leading choice is **Hans Hansen Silver** (Amagertorv 16), which I regard as the most intimately tasteful silver store in all of Denmark. The design and craftsmanship in this 3rd-generation landmark are perfection, combining the skills of revered masters with the dynamic forms of the sculptor's art. Proprietor Moller Larsen will be your mentor.

SWEATERS: Sweater Market (15 Frederiksberggade) is an absolute explosion of magnificent wool. On any given day these premises count close to 20,000 items on inventory. A dazzling array of these come in patterns that are original Scandinavian designs. One specialty is the super-soft weaving that has literally put Iceland on the fashion map: snow-smooth Icelandic jackets, coats, scarves, mittens, and hats—both knitted and brushed—that make anyone yearn for the recurrence of an Ice Age. The prices on goods shipped home for you will be at export levels exclusive of Danish taxes. Moreover, the tab will include handling, postage by surface mail, and insurance.

WATCHES: **Ole Mathiesen** (Ostergade 8). It is startling to discover that Swiss watches can be found in Denmark for the same or even lower prices than those in Geneva, Lucerne, or Zurich. And what better place to go shopping for one than in the ingratiating company of Ole Mathiesen himself, the proprietor of this distinguished shop and the designer of the superb wristwatch series that bears his own name? While almost any major brand is obtainable here, the house specializes in Patek Philippe, Audemars Piguet, International Watch Company, Cartier, Paris, and Ebel. Here is a boutique where the timepiece is pre-eminent and the time allotted to each client doesn't matter a tick. A splendid and super-friendly address where time and money are both well spent.

PS: If you've forgotten anything, then be sure to remember **Copenhagen Airport** and the reinvigorated transit hall shopping center open daily from 7 a.m.–10 p.m. It's a duty-free playground offering some of the most dizzying bargains in Europe today. Try to check in an hour or so earlier than usual, because everything that has tempted you in the city by the great Danish merchandisers is on display here—and at rates that will delight you.

ESBJERG is best known as the ferry port for England; the harbor itself—Denmark's largest and the world's third biggest fishing port—is quite engaging for salty types. Friends of nature will admire its Fishing and Maritime Museum with its Saltwater Aquarium and the large open-air Seal Basin. **Esbjerg Museum** focuses its scholarly attention on the development of the town as well as on Iron Age legacies, while the **Kunstpavillon** concentrates on Danish art. Students of architecture and interior design shouldn't miss the curious **Saedden Church,** a strange brick structure illuminated inside by 804 suspended lightbulbs. The **Skt. Nicolaj Church** is the inspiration of Spreckelsen, the Danish architect who designed the new triumphal arch in Paris. At the **Britannia** the facilities are modern, the cookery is delicious (especially the finny fare), and the prices are right. Also good is the viewful **Olympic** with some eye-popping panoramas of the harbor. If these two are booked solid, you would probably find reasonable shelter at the **Guldager Kro;** the **Ansgar** also provides notable value. The **Hjerting** is ideal for seaside surfing and golf. The **Hermitage West,** within its own park, is modern and motel-ish.

FYN

Svendborg, in *Svendborg,* is well regarded. Appetizing food and friendly service; dinner music; with 60 rooms and 60 baths; very pleasant indeed. Another charmer is the well-regarded summer only **Christiansminde.**

★★★ **Hesselet**—to me, one of the most charming isles of enchantment in the nation. Don't miss at least a meal, a sip, or a snooze at this waterside worthy in *Nyborg.* Two levels, trimly composed of wood, brick, and glass; forested tonsure with an apron of green reaching to the sea; golf course within chipping distance; sauna; sedate library plus a "garden room" for tranquil hours. Accommodations sumptuously outfitted with grass-woven wall coverings or textiles, divans, easy chairs, and Oriental artworks. The doubles are nice, but the suites are exquisite.

Steensgaard Herregaards Pension at *Millinge* was begun in the 14th century and completed as a manor house in the 17th (which gives you some idea of the labor problems in Denmark). Locals utter words of praise for this one. Also see **Odense.**

JUTLAND PENINSULA From the German border working north, here is a selection of fair-to-good candidates: In the *Krusaa* area, the **Am Granze** and the **Europa,** both on the German side, are functional. Even the **Krusaagaard** and the tiny **Holdbi Kro,** on Danish soil, are more affluent in human warmth than these 2. The latter was perked up. At *Abenra,* the low and linear **White House** is a worthy fjord-stop; it is whiter than its namesake at 1600 Pennsylvania Ave. A couple of miles south of *Haderslev,* the **Syd** should be considered utilitarian at best. In *Kolding* (where you should visit the ancient **Koldinghus Castle** and the **Museum**), the **Saxildhus** is attractive and immaculate. Excellent restaurant. Worthy on every count. Equally good are the new modernistic **Scanticon Kolding** and the sparkling **Hotel Kolding,** in midtown, with its chummy Bacchus Bistro. Solid comfort and good value. Motorists will probably find the **Tre Roser,** in the city's park, an excellent traveler's rest. Boasting a pool, paths, woods, and ponds, the kids will probably never get to bed. While in this town, please don't miss the **Geografiske Have,** a botanical wonderland with specimens from the seedbeds of the globe. Just outside *Vejle,* on the brow of a hill overlooking the fjord and forests, the **Munkebjerg** is one of the best and most reasonably priced first-line hotels in the region. This former monastic site is now a modernistic linear retreat for the laity. Rough-brick and wood-lined corridors; window-girt dining room with so-so cuisine; fireside lounges; dancing to live music; golf, tennis, billiards, and swimming pool; sauna; hairdresser; comfortable modern-provincial bedchambers, all facing the pines. In the town itself, the 11-story, austere **Scandic Australia** presents a first-rate chef, adequate accommodations, and the Kangaroo Pub. One-half mile from *Skanderborg,* the slick-rustic **Skanderborghus** provides a beautiful woodland-and-lake view. It has 47 small rooms, most with toilet plus bath or shower. (Numbers 22, 23, 122, and 123 are corner units with more space.) Connected restaurant-lounge-bar wing as an independent entity, to preserve a modicum of quiet for sleeping guests (sit at the far end for the best vista); excellent cuisine, presentation, and service; sauna; fishing privileges. Inexpensive and mightily gratifying for a weekend, a week, or an era. In ancient and scenic *Ebeltoft,* northeast of Aarhus off the prime north–south artery, you'll find the seaside **Strand.** In *Randers,* the **Randers** calls itself the "Leaping Salmon Hotel"—and it's a good catch for the provinces. The 88-room-and-bath **Scandic Kongens Ege** ("Royal Oaks") resides in a 16-acre park at the town's edge. Bellevue Restaurant for dinner, a charming tartanesque lunch salon, a hunter's lounge, a discotheque, plus the Fireside Bar and the King's Corner nightclub—and a sauna to sweat it all off. At the *Rebild Bakker* turnoff 16 miles south of Aalborg, the **Rold Stor-Kro** is a laudable entry. Lovely situation on the fringe of Denmark's largest forest, on the heather of which the Danish-American July 4th celebrations take place annually. Sprawling sun terrace; 2-tier restaurant with oversize windows; snug downstairs bar with TV; children's playroom; extraordinary wine cellar. All accommodations, most of them with bath and shower, face the wood; a few so-called cabin rooms with double-decker beds; the color and eye-appeal of the public quarters are not carried into the sleeping sections. The **Hanstholm** takes its name from its headland setting on the lighthouse cape about 70 miles west of *Aalborg* and 15 miles north of *Thisted*. Perched on a lime rock 125 feet above the North Sea; nearby harbor entrance, Denmark's only year-round ice-free port; game preserve, beach, swimming pool, sauna, and wilderness all in your hip pocket. Long, brick, motel-like structure; lots of wood and warming touches; peaceful views of the dunes; excellent table. Very restful. **Madsens** at *Bjerringbro* (south of *Viborg*) is a worthy haven in midtown. At *Nykobing Mors,* the **Sallingsund Faergekro** is a cozy mooring whose name means the "Ferry Inn"—and so it is.

Other possibilities? At *Billund,* the **Vis-a-Vis** is a very pleasant entry across from the toy town of Legoland (which is a *must* if you are traveling with children). At *Frederikshavn* there's a thatch-roofed charmer in the **Svalereden** for weekend smorrebrods; this rural delight is a couple of miles south of town. The **Frederikshavn** offers a subtropical atmosphere for watersport; designed chiefly for nordics who wish to spook the winter demons away.

ODENSE   This third city of Denmark is Hans Christian Andersen's hometown where the museum is a must for sightseers; his top hat, his manuscripts, and his trunk, lovingly preserved, rate as high with local burghers as the Holy Grail. His childhood home is another aspect of this literary lore. There's a festival of Andersen plays and fairy-tale reenactments every summer at **Funen Village**—held in the open air. This compound contains farm-houses, mills and numerous exhibits of rural life. Kids of all ages build up a head of excitement at the town's **Railway Museum.** Nearby are flower and bird parks, a terrarium, and beaches well served with ice water. A river cruise is a nice feature in summer. In this major port, rich in industry, you'll also find King Canute's famous monument in the Cathedral which bears his name and the A.D. 1090 crypt which contains the remains of some of Denmark's greatest kings. The town itself has moved into its second millennium.

Among its hotels, **H.C. Andersen** tops the list. There's a well-regarded dining room in traditional tones. **Grand** (part of the **Sara** chain) would be the next choice. Fine restaurant, popular bar, and cabaret dancing nightly in season. **Windsor** has an intimate demeanor and can be recommended. In this upper level the **Plaza** is good, but the new **Scandic** is about half the price. **Motel Brasilia,** at the outskirts on the road to Middelfart, is a charmer. Extra-pleasant surroundings enhanced by ducks and swans as your neighbors; attractive restaurant called the Blommenslyst Kro; #37, a quiet gardenside suite with a refrigerator and a little sitting room. **Motel Odense,** on the Nyborg pike (E-20 and Route 9), is a half-timber farmhouse that is more alluring on the outside than in. Sleeping setup with toe-to-toe bed arrangement; linoleum floors and throw rugs; splash-all showers. The fresh, young **Motel Naesbylund Kro,** the **Motel Munkeris,** and the **Ansgar Missionshotel** are fair bets.

In this town you can eat reasonably well at the dining room of the **Grand.**

Among the independents, the **Under Lindetraeet,** opposite the H.C.A. Museum, is perhaps the most distinguished—with corresponding high prices for superior food and service. The **Old Inn** ("Den Gamle Kro" of 1683) boasts a covered garden in summer; it has an interesting atmosphere and excellent fare. An ancient cellar has been tricked out as a cocktail lounge and coffee nook for post-gustatory sipping; it works in tandem with the modern **City Hotel.** Both the **Marie Louise** and the **Zander** are refined and good for value. **Rode7, Franck A,** and the **Raedhuskaelderen** are all solid medium-budget choices with charm. Out at Funen Village (2 miles), the **Sortebro Kro** is an ancient inn and a national trust; it fairly oozes Danish flavor from every beam and ladle.

RIBE   This is Denmark's oldest town, and it's a charmer with its tilting houses and cobbled ways. There are more than 100 buildings that are National Trusts. For overnighting my choice remains the **Dagmar.** Its dining room is a grace note of Old World harmony. Now all bedchambers have been given a dash of New World convenience. After this would come the tiny **Weis Stue.**

ROSKILDE   This town, only 20 miles west of the capital, also is one of the oldest in Denmark, its **Cathedral** containing the dust of 38 monarchs! Don't miss the fleet of 5 reconstructed vessels in the **Viking Ship Museum,** 11th-century boats sunk in the fjord to protect the town from attack. **Svogerslev Kro,** 2 miles from the center on Route 155, is a 250-year-old thatched-roof tavern; **Club 42** fairly brims with antiquity and charm, too; **Palae Cafeen** is for more conventional dining. Something that you may find fascinating is the **Lejre Research Center,** 7 miles west of town, where Iron Age houses have been reconstructed and where in summer people live almost exactly as prehistoric families existed in early times.

ENGLAND

INCLUDING THE COTSWOLDS, LAKE DISTRICT, AND WALES

> **USA:** British Tourist Authority, 40 W. 57th St., New York, NY 10019, Tel. (212) 581–4700; **CANADA:** 94 Cumberland St., Suite 600, Toronto, Ontario M5R, Tel. (416) 925–6326.

> **SPECIAL REMARKS:** If you pop over to Victoria Station, Forecourt, 12 Regent St. off Piccadilly Circus, Selfridges or Harrods, or the *Heathrow Travel Centre,* you'll find a veritable font of courtesy and assistance from the BTA. To get you started, ask here about money-saving tourist tickets and discount cards. They cover almost everything that moves or has stayed put for the past thousand years.

> **TELEPHONE:** Access code to USA: 0101; USA Direct 0800–89–0011 (a special AT&T service). To phone England: 44; time difference (Eastern Daylight) plus 5 hrs.

England's 55 million people find things pretty crowded on their 93,000 square miles. Add to that the fact that its capital has become the traveling world's favorite city and you've got a bubbling stew of humanity, possibly the most gregarious, and international hub in the West. But do try to see more than the burgeoning metropoli. Rivers and streams abound—and throughout the land there are bounteous gardens and glens. The coastline is hospitable, full of inlets into which big ships can travel. Go to the moors, the heaths, the dales, and lakes, the hamlets. Run out to Cambridge or Oxford for an excursion (but avoid the latter on the first Mon. and Tues. of Sept., when the annual St. Giles' Fair turns it into a shambles). Try the Shakespeare country in Warwickshire; try Canterbury in Kent, one of the ecclesiastical matrices of civilization, or Rye and Dorking for simple village charm; try Winchester, the former capital of the realm,

for a permeation of history harking back to the Knights of the Round Table; try the 35-mile-square Lake District, a miniature Switzerland in Cumbria; try the cathedrals and serene stone villages of Gloucestershire; try rugged Cornwall, the Hardy country of Dorset and Wiltshire, Raleigh's Devon, the castles of Snowdonia, the poetic Cotswolds, the Derbyshire peaks, the Yorkshire moors, the Scottish Highlands, the hot springs of Harrogate, the unbelievably broad beaches of Southport, the renowned antiquities in the valleys of the Usk and the Wye. Around every bend in the road you'll find an ever-changing landscape, with customs, dialects, ways of life new to you, but as old to the culture as Chaucer and Malory. Look for the real England at the roots of her grass.

The single event that everyone tries to witness is the **Changing of the Guard** ceremony that takes place daily in summer (every other day in winter, weather permitting) at Buckingham Palace. If you're *really* hooked, then you also should catch the Horse Guards at Whitehall. You'll probably not want to miss **Windsor Castle** either . . . and the **Tower of London.** (See under "London" for both.)

Possibly the greatest provincial attractions to travelers are the more than 1000 **castles, homes, and gardens** that have been opened to the public, on payment of a modest fee. The National Trust, a nonofficial, nonprofit body, now owns 260. Of the grand total, 40 are "Great Houses"; the balance consists of stately mansions, country manors, abbeys, and sentimental shrines such as Rudyard Kipling's former residence. Most popular and most outstanding is Woburn Abbey and Zoo Park (42 miles from London, 54 miles from Stratford-upon-Avon) belonging to The Duke of Bedford Trust; 1.5 million guests per year "oh" and "ah" at the 3000 deer, the safariland of African animals, the multimillion-dollar art collection, 3000 acres of enchanting parkland, the model village, the cable car system, the exhibition of 17,000 toy soldiers, the Zoo restaurant, and the splendid antique furnishings. (For a dining "event" here rather than simple nutrition, order a table at the exclusive Paris House.) High in popularity is Chatsworth (on the River Derwent 33 miles southeast of Manchester), which is renowned for its magnificent gardens with water effects. The Duke of Norfolk's Arundel Castle (near Brighton), the Duke of Marlborough's Blenheim Palace (8 miles north of Oxford), where Sir Winston Churchill was born, Beaulieu Abbey and Palace House, with a fine vintage-automobile museum (14 miles from Southampton), and the Marquess of Bath's Longleat where 50 African lions roam the ancestral park (24 miles from Bristol) are also favorite tourist targets. Lord Astor's Cliveden is now a deluxe hotel that also can be viewed by the public 2 days per week. The later home of Sir Winston, Chartwell (2 miles from Westerham, in Kent), is a beloved monument to recent history. It maintains the flavor of the period between the wars—the happiest years of the great statesman's life. Queen Elizabeth joined the peerage by opening her 274-room Sandringham House in Norfolk to the public (except from July 21 to Aug. 9, when she is in the residence). Be sure to check whether the day of your visit coincides with the variable schedule at the mansion. If you are seriously interested in touring this circuit, the oversize, exhaustively detailed annual *Historic Houses Castles & Gardens In Great Britain and Ireland* (ABC Historic Publications, London Road, Dunstable, Bedfordshire, England) is an absolutely invaluable aid. Then, if you intend to visit the great estates and magnificent gardens of this nation, be sure to join the **National Trust;** subscription is so low in cost that in a couple of days you will begin to realize significant savings over the individual admission charges (which usually range between $7 and $9 per entry). Its U.S. affiliate is **The Royal Oak Foundation** (41 E. 72nd St., NYC), a publilc charity, which means your membership is tax-deductible. (Thc National Trust fee is not.) There are other benefits, too, so write Director Arthur Prager for details. Avid sightseers can literally save hundreds of dollars over an extended vacation—and the rewards are spellbinding.

    Canal and river cruising has undergone a renaissance among U.S. visitors. **Inland Waterway Holiday Cruises** (Preston Brook, Runcorn, Cheshire) and **Inland Cruising Co.** (The Marina, Braunston, Daventry, Northamptonshire) churn up a wide variety of excursions along much of the country's canal network from midspring to midautumn. Here is about the ultimate in leisurely touring between London and Manchester. Rates are by the week; see your travel agent for bookings, but be sure to nail them down early. A briefer foray can be had aboard the *Fair Lady* of Camden Lock, Chalk Farm Road, Camden Town. For a more sybaritic approach involving a longer, live-aboard-dine-about experience that combines luxury, enlightenment, and gastronomy, please refer back to the introduction; there's a report on the barges of delight to be had via the **Floating Through Europe** cruises; these include British and Continental ports of call. For additional inexpensive communing with the H_2O of Britain's canals, write to **UK Waterway Holidays** about piloted boats or their self-skipper program. In England it's at Penn Place, Rickmansworth, Hertfordshire WD3 1EU. The color brochure lays out numerous voyages, all prices, and engaging highlights.

    Sound and Light spectacles are presented at the Tower of London, Buxton, Canterbury, Carrickfergus Castle, Dover Castle, Eltham Palace, Kenilworth Castle, Greenwich, Cardiff Castle, Gloucester Cathedral, Southwark Cathedral, Ragley Hall, York Minster, and Norwich Cathedral in Norfolk, and Greys Court in Henley-on-Thames; there's also one aboard the H.M.S. *Victory* in Portsmouth (while here don't miss the Tudor warship *Mary Rose,* lately recovered from the deep), plus others at Pembroke and Stirling Castles; at Winchester, Worcester, and Durham Cathedrals; at Bury St. Edmunds, Hampton Court Palace, Rochester, St. Paul's and Lichfield Cathedrals, and Sherborne and Tewkesbury Abbeys. Consult your nearest British Tourist Authority for last-minute information on the whens and wheres.

    The **Chichester Drama Festival** presents stellar performers in an interesting Greek-Elizabethan playhouse. The theater, situated in a 43-acre park, is 62 miles southwest of London. In summer, special trains will whisk you back to Victoria Station by midnight; schedules also geared for matinees; express buses also make the journey; for details consult your hall porter. Tickets are low in cost compared to U.S. levels; those who hunger for more than the arts may dine at the Theatre Restaurant. The precurtain smorgasbord is said to be excellent.

TRANSPORTATION   **Airline** British Airways is the colossus that spans the globe—164 cities in 76 countries!—and dominates the domestic skies. Concorde is its proudest zipper over the Atlantic with twice-daily flights in each direction between London and New York plus 3 calls per week to Miami and

Washington. In Europe BA covers a lot of ground and does its travel tasks extremely well. Cabin crews are cheerful, wonderfully attentive, and smartly groomed. Overall, the entire BA network is splendid today.

The gateway is served by 4 airports: London (Heathrow) Airport plus ever-expanding Gatwick (a fine recently opened North Terminal for long and short BA hauls); use bus or the train's excellent speedy connections to town; Luton (charters), and the London City Stolport (more for business hops; specialized; see below). Heathrow itself is divided into Terminal 1 (British, Irish, European, and a few North American flights), 2 (European airlines), 3 (mainly intercontinental), and 4 (BA's main hub for long-haul passengers as well as those going to Paris and Amsterdam). Buses to town are frequent and go to various points in the city. Incidentally, there's a subway link (carry your own luggage) between Heathrow and Piccadilly Circus (under an hour) with trains leaving to and fro every 4 minutes during peak periods. Grocery-style baggage carts are available at Heathrow free of charge; alas, porters have become obsolete. Stansted's Stolport is chiefly for national and nearby European connections. It's in the City's East End; the name is derived from STOL, aviation parlance that stands for Short Take Off and Landing—planes that need runways of only 2500 feet in length. You may find this handier if you are destined for Paris, Amsterdam, Brussels, Dusseldorf, or Rotterdam. A new express rail link (every half hour) has just been hitched to Liverpool St. Station connecting with the Victoria subway line via Tottenham Hale terminus. Incidentally, since BA is such a volume purchaser of bed nights, restaurant reservations, and theater tickets, you can use the airline itself for these services and benefit from discounts.

BA in a link-up with United Airlines now offers through check-in conveniences to almost 400 destinations worldwide. What a blessing it is to enjoy such seamless service.

Taxis In my view, they're the finest, most comfortable, best-designed taxis in the world. The classic version, however, is being challenged by the gradual introduction of a sleeker style called the Metrocab, operated chiefly by "mushers" (owner-drivers). While it would take almost a decade to fully replace the older cabs, a chorus of harrumphs is already being heard across the land. It's a hollow bruit in my opinion because, if anything, the new hacks are better than the traditional FX4 models. An average trip in the center of the city runs around $5. For each additional rider above one person, there's an extra charge.

If you're traveling between the capital and Heathrow Airport and choose not to utilize the bus (about £2.50) or subway shuttle (£1.50), legislation now limits the hop to whatever is shown on the meter (it should average about £20). And, finally, law permits sharing a cab with other occupants—as many as 4 if you can find 'em.

Trains Because Britain invented railways, it has a station for every 5 miles of line. Comfortable, air-conditioned InterCity trains are usually fine. In this group are the rockets that can hit 125 mph. Should you want to travel overnight, the BR sleeper network is extensive and excellent.

If you plan to do a lot of moving around in the U.K., the BritRail Pass can save you hundreds of dollars over the vacation tracks. They have also hitched their wagons to the French rail service (with the BritFrance Rail Pass) so continental coverage can be combined. Go to BritRail Travel International Offices in New York, Vancouver, or Toronto for details. Remember that these are *only* for sale in North America. There's also a special BritRail Youth Pass that's even cheaper than the standard version; you've got to be between 16 and 25 to qualify. A Senior Citizen program as well as a Children's reduction span the extremes of the age scale. Again, pick it up *before* you leave.

The "open-plan saloon carriage" is most common, although a few "compartment" type coaches are still in use. First-class and standard-class designations remain, with smoking and nonsmoking sections. Seats are bookable in advance on all long-distance trains; my recommendation is that you make a reservation for trunk routes, such as London-Edinburgh.

Car Rentals There are all the standard giants, of course, but we've had exceptional service from a company called **British Car Rental,** which has depots in about 100 locations in the UK. Part ownership is by The Rover Group, so the vehicles are from that car maker. You can order one toll-free in the USA (Tel: 1–800–448–3936) or in Britain by phoning 0203–633400 (Fax 0203–520681).

NOTE · · · Crossing to Ireland on the "Sealink" network makes rail, ship, or car connections pleasant, convenient, and economical. It hooks into numerous U.K. destinations as well as into continental gateways. I prefer this line to all others, but if you are in a special hurry, the swift Hoverspeed ships link the two banks of the channel in one third the time. Ports are Dover, Calais, and Boulogne.

Brittany Ferries offers a 24-hour car-ferry spin between Plymouth and Santander (Spain). While it eliminates your weary wheel hours, it does not save much time or money for Iberia-bound voyagers—and it denies motorists the pleasures of the French countryside and adventures in Gallic cuisine.

The "Motorail" trains are available on certain longer journeys. Accommodation is very limited; book well ahead. Winter and summer schedules as well as departure points vary, so be sure to check carefully.

A helpmate for the rod-riding wayfarer is BR's timetable, obtainable at bookshops or station kiosks.

FOOD Almost every ethnic expression of gastronomy is represented. In general, the quality is high and some places you can even find English cooking. (London is going through an aberrant phase now that you will read about below.) The fine restaurants offer delectable food which today rivals the best kitchens on the Continent. After suffering years of scorn for their table, you'll find today's Englishman decidedly chauvinistic about his British fare and especially about the divinity of homegrown lamb, beef, and products from the dairy. London, of course, with its overwhelming influx of world travelers, is strikingly influenced by international trends in the culinary arts while country pubs and remoter establishments retain more stick-to-the-ribs choices and stick-to-tradition attitudes. Among the constellation of fashionable stops there is a tendency among chefs to confuse richness with excellence; a surfeit of cream seems to find its unwheyward way into nearly every whip or fold from the kitchen.

In the capital—as billings continue to skyrocket in the smart and swanky establishments—a reaction among yuppies is evolving that sends them to some of the ugliest "in" spots to be seen this side of a cafe by the steel factory.

Decor is not only minimal, it is purposely hideous. The worse it becomes, the more rapturous become the Hoo-rah Henrys (clad in pinstripe suit jackets over jeans) and their Sloane Rangers. Moreover, this ardent audience of inexperienced "Foodies" is now paying only marginally less for indifferent bistro cooking than they would for top-grade gastronomy in a beautifully decorated and comfortable salon.

While English nutrients are both inventive (historically) and very, very pleasing, chefs, in my opinion, have not sufficiently exploited their own British treasury of recipes. Instead, they are cribbing more and more from French themes. As you read the London restaurant section further along, you'll be startled to see how many of the capital's shrines of gastronomy have French names and Gallic-based preparations. Good it is, but a pity, too, because the British larder is bursting with unnoticed opportunity. The blame (or credit) for this might rest on the shoulders of the famous Roux family (Gavroche and a host of other restaurants) who have trained cooks in their French heritage and generously set up many promising young talents in their own establishments. While this influence now has almost reached cult proportions, I, personally, regret observing the suppression of purely British culinary efforts.

Certain items have always been good: Roasts, grills, salmon, Yorkshire ham, Stilton cheese (a favorite for 250 years), and bacon. One of the most controversial events since the Reformation has been a manufactured cheese called Lymeswold—the Brits having so few varieties, this one provoked headlines up and down the land when it appeared a few years ago. The texture is creamier than the usual hard types. A tip on salmon: so much of it is ranched today that the better grade with its firmer flesh is usually designated on menus as "wild." Ask if you have doubts.

Meal hours are fixed. Breakfast used to be heavy, but now it is comparatively light; lunch is substantial; tea, at 4:30 p.m., is a sacred ritual in every walk of life; dinner, eightish or later, is the biggest repast of all.

NOTE · · · English oysters are expensive but superb. Imperials (available all of the "R" months) are considered the finest; the larger Colchesters (Sept. to March) are also exquisite. Don't miss them if you're a bivalve fan.

In case you're as baffled by the difference between these so-typical lookalikes, steak-and-kidney *pie* is made with pastry crust, while steak-and-kidney *pudding* ("pud" to the locals) is made with a suet dumpling top which is indigestibly deelishus.

DRINKS Please refer to our "Drinks" report in the "London" section further along.

TIPPING Railway porters (an endangered species, so you're not too likely to find one) get 50 pence per bag. At Heathrow Airport porters no longer exist so a baggage cart will be your little red wagon in most instances. If you need special aid, Skycap service costs £5. Taxi drivers get 15%, or a minimum of 30 pence. The hotel service charge is included in your bill, but you may wish to give 50 pence to £1 a day extra to the hall porter and your chambermaid; bellboys, door-keepers, bartenders, and others who give you special attention receive separate consideration, perhaps 50 pence maximum per favor. In restaurants, the custom had been to leave about 10% of the bill, but in medium-price establishments diners are reducing this to 5% or even a token gesture. In very expensive places ask if service is included. (It usually is.)

SPECIAL FACILITIES FOR CHILDREN   The British Tourist Authority suggests **Childminders** (67 Marlebone High St.). Others include **Universal Aunts** (36 Walpole St.), **Visitors Welcome** (17 Radley Mews), and **Junior Jaunts** (4A William St.). Nanny's rates usually are calculated by the hour and vary according to time of day. **The House on the Hill** (33 Hoop Lane, N.W. 11) and **Walton Day Nursery** (239 Knightsbridge) will take care of toddlers all day long, and the latter by the week. Outside London, **Norland Nursery Training College** (Hungerford, *Berkshire*) will board small fry, and **Holiday Parents** (Petersfield, *Hampshire*) will place them in English homes (temporarily!).

OVERNIGHT IN A CASTLE OR A COUNTRY HOUSE   You might query an organization called **Country Homes & Castles** in Great Britain, which lists more than 100 addresses (mostly fine estates rather than historic fortresses). For the photo-filled brochure write to R & I Tours Ltd., 118 Cromwell Rd., London S.W.7. This year, many more have been added to this chapter. Since most are in remote, unknown villages or stand alone in a glen or upon a blasted heath, I've tried to group them near to centers that are on the tourist's circuit. Hence, you may have to scratch around a bit to locate them but they are well worth the scratch.

PRIVATE HOUSES   Bored with hotels? How about a mansion, a mill house, a cottage, or a castle? **Blandings** produces a color brochure with dozens of house-and-garden choices. Details on accommodation, staff, vehicles, pets, plus fishing and game rights are included. A major country estate rents in the £2000 per week range but the options are so varied and numerous that you should ask for the publicity. Try Blandings, 225 Ebury St., London SW1W 8UT, Tel. 8235585, Fax 8248592, Tx. 947093, Agency 9. Here's an excellent way to bide a while in an English home or enjoy the rich tranquillity of British rural life.

If you want to be chiefly in the southeast, write to Ginny Rhodes, **Country Style,** Sparr Farm, Wisborough Green, W. Sussex RH 140AA. They can put on anything from a castle tour to a picnic.

Incidentally, if you wish to further your European homelife, one superb company in London offers villas with pools and lovely gardens in a number of Mediterranean countries. Go to **CV Travel** at 43 Cadogan St., Chelsea, London S.W.3 2PR. Proprietor Richard Cookson is the definition of kindness and helpfulness (tel. 5810851). The color-photo brochure of the various properties is a knockout for sunlit temptations.

CITIES AND REGIONS

ASTON CLINTON is a charming center in Buckinghamshire with one especially fine stop for diners or overnighters. It is composed of a converted complex of stables, malt-houses and a brewery.

This is also one of the best areas possible for excursions. Very nearby you will find the wonderful **Buckinghamshire County Museum** (check the opening since its refurbishing program), **Claydon House,** with its links to Florence Nightingale, **Mentmore** and **Hughenden Manor** near **High Wycombe,** where Disraeli lived until his death. The Rothschild family also had strong connections in the area. **Ascott House** contains superb examples of the family's French and Chippendale furnishings. But most spectacular of all is **Waddesdon Manor.** Okay, so the outside is hideous. Inside, the collection of porcelains, oils, and furniture is more luxurious than those items belonging to the monarchs of Europe who, incidentally, were so often creditors to Ferdinand Rothschild's banks. This destination alone could occupy several days of viewing. Railroad buffs will find delight in *Quainton,* a center for vintage trains of the steam era.

☆☆☆☆ **Bell** chimes on both sides of the A-41 London–Oxford trunk road. Restaurant-*cum*-inn, complete with courtyard on one flank; captivating, seasonally toned dining salon with separate bar; ambitious cuisine that shuns *nouvelle* intrusions. Many doubles have been beautified and expanded into junior suites—the taste exquisite and the maintenance perfect. The phone number is (Aylesbury) 630252. Energetic Michael Harris, whose courage and skills everyone admires, has a mind-set for hospitality. I must confess my hopeless prejudice for the Harris clan and their wonderful house.

BATH This ancient city of Roman frolic is rapidly becoming second only to London in importance for the vacationer to Great Britain. Not only is it beautiful in the purity of its architecture, but it offers sophistication, comfort, and some of the best cuisine outside of the capital. Attractions in town include the **Roman Baths, Assembly Rooms,** and a **Costume Museum;** the **Abbey Church** and the **Old Church** are staples, and you'll probably like **Lilliput Alley;** all are big draws throughout the year, as is the **Theatre Royal,** which offers excellent London programs. Shopping along the well-planned pedestrian malls can be far more convenient than London's congestion with almost the same variety in quality goods. Strangely enough, one of the best collections of Americana likely to be found outside the continental U.S. is at Bath's **American Museum!** (How is *that* for bringing coals back to Newcastle?) The marvelous assemblage includes excellent quilts in patchwork, album, sawtooth, and other classic patterns, hooked rugs, pewter, Indian items—everything from Shaker simplicity to the ornate glass of Louis Comfort Tiffany. Additionally there is a store for souvenirs and a tearoom for snacks.

☆☆☆☆ **Hunstrete House** • is one of the most tastefully outfitted and purely beautiful mansions to be found anywhere in the British Isles. Only a few minutes out of town, surrounded by meadows with free-ranging deer, the estate has roots dating to the 10th century. The exquisite antique furnishings, the artwork, the textiles, the cheerful mien enhanced by flowers are captivating. A tennis court and pool are in their own sector to ensure peacefulness. The gastronomy is both honest and luxurious; it's served in a graceful, window-lined salon facing a fountained patio.

★★★ **The Priory** • affords the visitor with a city address in a country venue. It stands at the edge of the town inside its own walled garden where there's also a pool, terrace and furniture for relaxing outdoors. Rooms are not always the largest; dining in the manorly restaurant or in the cheery Orangery. Only 21 units, which makes for an intimate, clublike atmosphere.

★★★★ **Ston Easton Park** • is a Palladian mansion of majestic proportions on a 200-acre expanse of Somerset terrain—the house itself being far more imposing than the surrounding countryside. It is one of the exceptional manifestations of West Country architecture with high ceilings, broad windows, gorgeous moldings, and the trappings of elegance that can never be recaptured in the present era. It is purely a period piece of the highest caliber. The kitchen work is a meld of English traditional country fare and French delicacy. An indication of its clientele is suggested by the glittering assemblage of Rolls-Royces in front and the occasional private helicopter on the nearby landing pad.

★★★ **Royal Crescent** • *in the town of Bath* • is located within the famous 18th-century crescent of buildings that overlooks the vale. Historically it is unique, one of the few public hotels to occupy such important premises. Elegant public rooms but disappointing dining facilities; expanded accommodations; majority of the units with fireplaces; maintenance standards lower than what I would have expected for such a patrician establishment.

☆☆☆☆ **Bishopstrow House** • *southwest of Bath* • lies in the captivating Wessex Downs, but well within the realm of activities that define this area and its attractions. (See "Warminster.")

☆ **Francis** • with a washed facade and busy lounges, offers 94 rooms, all with private plumbing; clean and pleasant; friendly staff; spectacularly accoutered restaurant with cuisine that pales by comparison. Since the front faces a lovely park, but also borders a noisy street, light sleepers should bid for the back of the house.

★★ **Homewood Park** • overlooks the vale of Limpley Stoke. It is 5 miles south of Bath adjoining 13th-century Hinton Priory, an attractive ruin. One of the best Victorian-style addresses in Britain. Ask about its new sister hotel in Bath itself.

☆ **Lansdown Grove** • high in the city, is tranquil; it sets a fair table, too. **Royal York** is getting a bit fusty. The **Cliffe,** 5 miles out on A-36, is a stone-shelled sweetie; a wonderful site in a quiet valley; 8 bedrooms and baths; careful supervision. **Hole-in-Wall** has been adequate (but not more) for both shelter and cookery; dishes lean toward Italian persuasions. Other local choices *for dining only* include the colorful **Popjoys, Sweeney Todds,** and a 600-year-old pub called **The George** (10 minutes out) with Hanging Judge Jeffries's gallows and medieval prison tack.

Limpley Stoke • *in the village of Limpley Stoke* • is nice but sleepy; the cookery is also pretty good by suburban standards.

Northey Arms • on the A-4, is chiefly a pub, but its duet of bedchambers are charmers.

☆ **Bell House** • *at nearby Sutton Benger (outside Chippenham)* • offers a cozy complement of 17 rooms, half with private facilities and many with balconies; each bed with its own rolling table for pajama breakfasts; superior comfort; book away from the roadside for serious snoozing; not scenic in its locale, but an excellent rural headquarters for touring Wiltshire and Somerset.

★★★★ **Manor House** • at the neighboring Dr. Doolittle village of *Castle Combe,* is a spellbinder for the setting but only satisfactory for its innkeeping. The hamlet, incidentally, once was voted the prettiest habitat in all of England, even though it's virtually trampled by rubbernecks on Sundays and holidays. Lovely apron of grass edging a stream and murmuring fall, surrounding forests, tiers of flowers; antique shop plus furnishings inside the hotel marked for sale to visitors; adequate accommodations, with the best views from #4 or #2; Garden Wing not up to the original edifice.

★★ **Castle** • on the town square, is also attractive. Lounge ceiling beams so low that one timber is inscribed "Duck—or grouse!" The food here is varied, but the living space is more limited than in the Manor House.

Cliveden • mentioned previously as an excursion target, also is now a hotel, with rates dancing from just plain shocking to neck-snapping for the grandest Nancy Astor suite. Clearly, for such tariffs one would expect imperial treatment—or probably shares in the estate. (When the Sunday and Tuesday bus tours roll in, guests are separated from gawkers by only a velvet rope.) Alas, one has to ask is this game worth the candle? Its broad windows in the exquisite dining room and library overlook expansive, well-tended gardens and Berkshire landscape. If space permits (and that could be frequent at such rates) non-residents may dine here at close to $85 per setting. Indeed, the site *is* majestic. Should you be tempted to such extravagance look for Taplow on the map or phone Burnham 68561—*after* you've consulted your accountant!

BLANCHLAND

★★ **Lord Crewe Arms** • will happily haunt you. This 12th century inn, in a ghost village of Durham, is ch-ch-ch-charming.

BRISTOL has a busy, salty atmosphere and a burgeoning art center; the **Glass Museum** is outstanding; this industry has long been the city's pride. Unless business compels you to be here, nearby Bath is far more attractive for the vacationer. If you must, then lay your head down on **St. Vincent's Roeks** (hotel on Sion Hill), the **Grand,** or the **Hilton.** The **Holiday Inn** is in midcity edging a motorway. Okay, but hardly inspiring.

For mealtiming, my first choice would be the **Edwards,** followed by **John Harvey's.** Less fancy but enjoyable are **Jameson's** and **Bistro 21.**

☆☆ **Thornbury Castle** • *out at Thornbury* • is a 16th-century structure in its own compound. Ten lovely bedchambers have been tucked into the turrets overlooking a marvelous courtyard garden. When dining, order French rather than homebred wine, which cloys.

CAMBRIDGE is, of course, one of the oldest college towns in England and in terms of aesthetics it is far more attractive than highly urbanized Oxford. **Saint Benet's Church,** which was the sire of **Corpus Christi,** dates back to the 11th century. The **Old Court** (indeed, the most ancient in Cambridge) is amply worth your viewing time. Ask the warden to show you this college plus, perhaps, a look into the sacrosanct dining hall with its brass chandeliers, portraits of scholastic masters, and lavish paneling. Across the lane is **King's College** and its grandiose **Chapel** where Evensong can be heard during the school terms from October to early June. After a stroll through the campus and the interweaving town, take a punt (a shallow-draft boat) along what are called **"The Backs"** where the river runs behind the university buildings.

While Cambridge has achieved prestige in almost every art and science, it has flunked disgracefully in its innkeeping. The **Cambridgeshire Moat House** scores with 100 units plus 18 golf holes. It's touted as a "leisure hotel." **Garden House** and **Post House** trade heavily with groups. **University Arms** is passable. For lunch or dinner, pick the up-market and rather Gallic **Midsummer House.** More modest are the **Angeline** and pubs called **The Free Press** and **Cambridge Blue.**

CANTERBURY is the home of the mother church for Anglicans globally, the **Cathedral** being the site of Thomas Becket's murder. You also must see **St. Augustine's Abbey, The Weavers,** and other ancient houses. ★ **Slatters** tells the best tale of all for an overnight pilgrimage. French Restaurant; full carpeting; small bedchambers. Clean and worthy and well located for sightseeing in the Cathedral area. The ☆☆ **Chaucer,** with more rooms, is comfortable. The carefully refurbished **County** dates back to the 1500s, but the amenities of today are ample. You might also try the cozy **Howfield Manor.** If you are prone to dine away from your hotel, try **George's Brasserie** or **Sully's.**

CARLISLE The **Crown and Mitre** reigns supreme at this key hub on the road to Scotland. Coffee shop for light bites; cranberry-colored Belowstairs Restaurant accurately named and adequately provisioned; Edwardian Peace & Plenty Pub; Jonesian Railway Tavern. The front singles were minuscule; others, however, were spaciously sized and flairfully outfitted. **Crest** is clean and fresh; a bit more costly too.

★★ **Farlam Hall** • *near Brampton, 9 miles from Carlisle* • is nestled in 4½ acres of walled gardens. Distinguished dining salon facing a pond and meadows; superior English traditional furnishings in its 11 rooms, all with bath. A nice piece of Cumbria run by ingratiating people for surprisingly low tariffs. Odd closing times in winter so be sure to reserve ahead.

CHAGFORD Here's a touchstone edging the great fastness of Dartmoor, a wild and beautiful morsel of central Devon.

☆☆☆ **Gidleigh Park,** a remote mock-Tudor country house sited inside a national preserve, has brought fame to the region. Forest surroundings with a small river in front; oak paneling; abundant flowers; croquet lawn (plus) tennis; color TV; some balconies; fires in cozy hearths; noteworthy cuisine plus a *cave* of astonishing variety, many bottlings from California. The wine list is not simply a catalog but an intelligently composed description of pressings and their value relative to similar vintages—the most helpful table guide I've ever seen by an oenophile and hotelier. Since it is so far from any other shelter, be sure to phone or book in advance (Tel: 06473-2367 or 2225).
Overflow guests sometimes are happy at the ☆ **Mill End.** ☆ **Torr House** is another pleasant choice as are ☆ **Easton Court** and ☆ **Teignworth,** all small and hospitable guest houses and all within a 3-mile radius.
The ★ **Three Crowns,** with a thatched roof, is in the comely village of Chagford.

☆ **The Globe,** an 18th-century coaching house, features large bedrooms and menus consisting typically of such dishes as mussels in white wine, venison, and game pie, raspberry gallette with clotted cream and local cheese. Prices in these Chagford digs will be at least 50% under those at Gidleigh. And very nice they are for modest country living.

CHESTER is an engaging town for fans of architecture. The timber-and-stucco houses, covered walks, and balconies are a living national trust. The graciously imposing **Grosvenor** wins the hospitality honors. Smart public rooms; rich leather-padded Arkle Bar; coolish dining salon; 87 comfortable, fully carpeted bedchambers. A giant multilevel garage is available for parking immediately behind the hotel. The **Blossoms** is a sound alternative choice. Entrance on the sidestreet facade; downstairs Buttery and coffee shop; public rooms pleasant; bedchambers inclined toward motelish motivations. The **Post House** has been spiffed up. Both the **Washington** and the **Westminster** have been modernized in this era; both are small, near the station, have ingratiating bars, and are good bets for budgeteers. For nutrition, try **Pippas** (nice but small), **Jade Cantonese** (Chinese),

Mollington Banastre (a country house), **Parker's,** and the **Schooner Inn; the Snooty Fox** is okay for snacks.

COTSWOLDS

To view its treasures properly an automobile is a necessity. Although the majority of its most intimate corners can be absorbed within 2 or 3 days, lingering for a week brings rich rewards—especially in spring, summer, or autumn.

Broadway is perhaps the most logical springboard from which to plunge. It is only 15 miles from Stratford-upon-Avon, 25 miles or so from Warwick Castle, Kenilworth Castle, Banbury and its cross, Sulgrave Manor (ancestral home of George Washington, where you'll find the original Stars and Stripes), the Duke of Marlborough's Blenheim Palace where Winston Churchill was born, Worcester with its cathedral and its porcelain works, and a host of closer storybook hamlets with poetic names such as Upper and Lower Slaughter, Bourton-on-the-Water (the "Venice of the Cotswolds"), Moreton-in-Marsh, Stow-on-the-Wold, Chipping Campden, and many more. Here you can linger among honey-colored stone dwellings, ponds and streams, or antique hunt in the townlets.

☆☆☆☆☆ **Buckland Manor** • *a mile from Broadway (on A-46)* • is set on a hillside where horses graze and tall beeches are silhouetted against some of Britain's loveliest skies. The mounts are available to guests; there's tennis, a pool, croquet, a putting green, and gracious gardens on the estate; golf is nearby. While the manor dates to the 13th century, its 11 bedchambers and public rooms offer every contemporary comfort in traditional tones: polished oak furnishings, deep-pile carpets, candles, flowers on almost every surface, leaded windows, rich textiles, open fires and wide-open, nonstop smiles from Host-Proprietors Adrienne and Barry Berman. Dining is as masterful for its flavor as it is for its presentation. Since Broadway, like other Cotswold hamlets, can be bustling from daytime tourism, here is the perfectly peaceful answer for enjoying the best of both wolds.

★★★★ **Lygon Arms,** standing directly in the center of Broadway for more than 6 centuries, is an inn with strong commercial tendencies since it has expanded well beyond its original structure. This ancient-and-modern hostelry (now under the London Savoy aegis) is usually a pleasure. In its way, the 20th-century wing is every bit as appealing as is the very room where Cromwell courted the sandman. In winter, special-interest weekends perk up the local activities.

★★ **Broadway** • half-timbered and stone, across the main pike, is more modest. Lower rates; amiable family atmosphere; handsome 2-story lounge and adjoining gardens.

☆☆☆ **Dormy House** • *on the forested escarpment above Evesham Vale* • perhaps 5 minutes by car from Broadway. There's a cozy blend of Cotswold stone, fires in hearths, tall trees, good cuisine, and ample comfort in its 50 bedchambers. A nice flavor of country life.

Collin House • is recommended by world travelers who certainly know the inns-and-outs of country life. It's a 16th-century home with inglenook, log fires, mullioned windows, 8 acres of park and gardens, plus the hospitality of Judith and John Mills.

For dining, the **Hunter's Lodge** is substantial; among the hotels, **Buckland Manor** and **Dormy House** set nice tables. Shoppers should not miss a visit to **Keil** for antiques (some say he has a better collection than the Victoria and Albert Museum in London) or **Heyworth,** where the stylish woolens and cashmeres dramatically undercut U.S. prices for top quality. Both are on the main (and only) street.

At *Banbury,* **Whately Hall** bounds away with local thunder; its downstairs dining room is a special hallmark of pride, as is the brick bar room. The building has hosted Benjamin Franklin. Please note that this bustling center is not as quiet as most of the other hideaways. Take an excursion (2 miles) to the storybook walled-and-moated **Broughton Castle.** *Moreton-in-Marsh* boasts the chef-blessed **Manor House** and the slightly commercial **White Hart.** Both delight the souls of antique hunters. *Stow-on-the-Wold*'s bid is the **Unicorn,** but the cuisine is abysmal, in my opinion. **Wyck Hill House** might be better now. *Bibury* provides the **Swan** for country living and perhaps some trout casting from the banks of the Coln. **Bibury Court** is fair. *Tetbury* offers ☆☆☆ **Calcot Manor** in a colony of stone farm buildings; dining is superb; the Balls are gracious hosts. *Burford,* especially captivating for its harmonious stone dwellings, tucks the **Lamb Inn** into a cozy corner of the townlet. This home lives for teatime. *Chipping Campden* offers **Cotswold House** in the market square and the **Kings Arms.** I'm hearing favorable comments on **Charingworth House,** too, but I haven't tried it personally. The village is appealing. Nearby *Sutton Benger* and *Castle Combe,* on the Cotswold fringes, are covered earlier under "Bath." At *Cleeve Hill,* near Cheltenham, the **Malvern View** is recommended for golfers, who'll find the links and the Severn Valley a perfect 2 for tee. Not far away at *Southam,* the **Dela Bere** is so colorful and visually appealing that its popularity is becoming a detraction. At *Bourton-on-the-Water* the **Old New Inn** plunks all 24 of its bedchambers on the ground floor. It also is a target for its amusing model village. *Upper Slaughter* is rewarded handsomely by **Lords of the Manor.** (See "Warwick" for **Mallory Court.**)

Don't expect (thank heaven!) Statler-style concepts in any of these hostelries. They are all inns. Most of them date back to the middle-15th century and are operated by good-hearted people who think that you've come to *see* how they live, not *change* how they live. The cookery has improved to the point of excellence in most cases and only passing-fare in others. But even when it is only fair, it will still be interesting. One thing is certain: from the *Forest-of-Dean* to *Shipton-under-Wychwood* and from *White Ladies Aston* to *Tintern Abbey,* you'll be enchanted by this uniquely colorful loop in the British skein.

COVENTRY   is the home of Jaguar cars and the Lady Godiva legend. There's a bombed-out shell of a 5-century-old cathedral, an adjoining new one in rose-gray sandstone, a treasure house of 20th-century craftsmanship, and many remnants of medieval times. The **Leofric** is one choice for overnighting, and the' modern **deVere** is another. Basically it's an industrial hub.

DEDHAM

☆☆☆☆ **Maison Talbooth** • resides on a verdant slope among rolling Essex hillsides. In the Colchester region, this small hotel on the Stratford Rd. has 10 sumptuous Victorian suites that look out onto 3 acres of beautifully maintained garden.

★★★★ **Le Talbooth** • under the same care as Maison Talbooth, is a half-mile away from its sister. An ingratiating half-timbered house, this converted mansion dates back to A.D. 1500. Two of its rustic dining rooms peep through leaded windows onto the romantically reflecting Stour River. While art followers will recognize the house from Constable's painting "Dedham Vale," New Englanders will probably be fascinated with this site and the church in Dedham itself, which has Colonial connections.

The same team operates an amusing restaurant down the road called **The Pier** at nearby *Harwich*. Decoratively, it was copied from an American counterpart in Boston, a sprawling maritime edifice that overlooks the salty pilot-boat harbor of one of England's major ports. I am not very fond of the **Dedham Vale Hotel** or its fussy **Terrace Restaurant.**

EAST GRINSTEAD

★★★★★ **Gravetye Manor** • *West Sussex* • This authentic Elizabethan stone mansion from 1598—now expanded with new suites but in the traditional style—is surrounded by an enchanted realm conceived and created by England's pioneer landscape gardener William Robinson. It has the advantage of being in a thousand acres of forestry commission land—as well as enjoying the blessing of Peter and Sue Herbert as hosting proprietors, two radiant and genteel professionals who tend to their guests, their splendid gastronomy, their exceptional wines and their clients' comforts as ardently as they tend their immaculate grounds. As one of Britain's premier estates, you can expect prices that approach London levels, but few places on this planet can provide such generous slices of English country life at its finest.

In this area of Sussex and neighboring Kent, request the staff to point you in the directions of the scores of historic and noteworthy sightseeing targets. For starters, take the following longish one-day loop and roll home wobble-kneed but inspired: Off first to **Wakehurst Place,** only about 10 minutes by car from Gravetye. This combines both informal and formal English gardens, the lake area being the gem in the center of the setting; coffee is available in the handsome stone house. Then to captivating **Hever Castle & Gardens** (perhaps 30 minutes away), home of Anne Boleyn long before the American Astors took over and restored it. Antiquity here has been meticulously maintained. Have a trencherman's pub-lunch in the **Castle Inn** in the 9th-century village of *Chiddingstone* where the hamlet will be inspiring even if the food is not. Ingestion done, ramble on to **Leeds Castle,** which is thoroughly rewarding despite its galloping case of commercialization. And, finally, turn homewards via **Sissinghurst** with its blissful English gardens, the Tudor and Elizabethan castle, and a bustling little gift shop cascading with attractive inexpensive souvenirs. This area is as thick as a Christmas pudding with richly rewarding sightseeing candidates—from pre-Hastings times to Churchill's **Chartwell**—so study a map and chart well your own path to the highlights that interest you most.

HARROGATE

☆☆☆ **Majestic**—for position and comfort. While the public rooms and many premium quarters have been refreshed handsomely, my inside bedchamber seemed to face more tubing than might have been seen at an Apollo launching pad.

☆☆☆ **Old Swan,** hatched in 1679, is fun for antiquarians. Ancient bar; skylighted Bramham dining room; total of 140 units and 90 baths; 3 suites; book only the newer rooms here.

★ **Crown** follows the Old Swan; the public rooms are very attractive; bedchambers are routine.

☆ **Pool Court** • *Pool-in-Wharfedale* • is a worthy hideaway in West Yorkshire. The hospitality is noteworthy.

★★★ **Devonshire Arms** • *at Bolton Abbey* • lies 15 miles across the Yorkshire dales through some of the most glorious countryside in Albion—a lovely daylight excursion for an overnight in the country. Charming inn with a dozen sleeping quarters and hardly any private plumbing; delicious food and excellent service; cozy dining room overlooking the glistening Wharfe River; friendly rustic atmosphere that any open-hearted traveler would adore for its simple good cheer. After lunch, walk through the back gate and across the meadow to the riverbank; turn left and stroll a ½-mile up to the beautiful ruins of the abbey itself; then return along the highway, where glimpses of the hills and bright water peep through openings in the moss-gathered graystone walls.

IPSWICH This is the nearest center to ☆☆☆☆ **Hintlesham Hall,** a fabulous country house providing superb comfort, magnificent views of East Anglian countryside, and (if you are so inclined) excellent bird shooting in season. The obverse of the estate is in stately Georgian while the reverse-side architecture is in ingratiating Queen Anne style. Some units majestic and vast; others more intimate and with open-beam ceilings; still others (the least expensive) in more conventional decor. Cuisine derived chiefly from the estate and commendable for presentation and flavor. There is much to see in the region so 3 or 4 days would not be overdoing it.

LACOCK   Here is *Wiltshire's* best preserved time capsule, a National Trust Village of the Middle Ages entirely built of local stone, lichened brick, mossy rooftiles, and ancient timbers. The snug cottages tilt with perilous amity toward each other over flowered lanes. Chimneys and gables punctuate the skyline. The **Abbey** is supplied with instruction "fans" that describe in detail far more than you'll ever remember; you carry them and read as you walk; there's even a copy of the Magna Carta for close study. Most important, of course, is the fact that the Abbey is also the former home of William Henry Fox Talbot, a pioneer of film invention and photography; his story is told in this living museum.

★★★★ **The Sign of the Angel ●** is the heart of the matter if you are searching for antiquity: only a few bedchambers but a marvelously intimate hearthside pub of 5 tables and a promising wine cradle above the mantel. Honest English fare with one grill available per mealtime. The potted crab, salmon mousse, and roast pork were splendid. Rates run about $75 per night per couple, the most expensive in the hamlet. (Indeed, its name came not from heaven but from an "angel" or gold coin of the era.)

★ **King John's Hunting Lodge ●** boasts a mere 2 rooms, one of them with a four-poster.

★ **Carpenter's Arms ●** in Wiltshire stone, is twice as large. **The Red Lion** is proud of its accommodation with a half-tester (not a member of the staff, but a bed with 2 posts instead of 4). **The Old Rectory** is the final choice except for the private houses, which rent twin units for about $30. You can inquire about the latter at the National Trust House on the main street where you can also find excellent souvenirs and gift items of regional flavor.

LAKE DISTRICT

This is the romantic area in the far north of England, just south of the Scottish frontier. The sylvan hills and lush dales reside within the Cumbrian borders. Rain is common, but coziness and exquisite beauty are guaranteed. The region is a virtual trove of links to the English literature of Wordsworth, Tennyson, Scott, Stevenson, and other titans. The best way to see it is by automobile, stopping 2 or 3 days in the major resorts. There are lake boat rides to be had at most docks and windsurfers and skiffs for rent nearly everywhere. There's pony trekking at *Troutbeck,* gardens galore in the National Trust or otherwise, fascinating **Dove** cottage and less interesting **Rydal Mount** (the former was the poet's residence during his prime time; the latter was Wordsworth's home in his later years), the **Model Railroad Museum** at *Askham,* and the **Century Theatre** at *Keswick.* But my favorite of favorites—and, I confess, I'm bonkers for ships—is *Windermere*'s delightful **Steamboat Museum.** Here the meticulously restored vessels nibble at the lake's edge under roofed-over piers. *Dolly* (born in 1850), as one fine example, is *the oldest mechanically powered boat in the world*—and a sweet one at that. Apart from the many timbered dowagers on show and the absorbing interior exhibits, you can enjoy an inexpensive 45-minute ride on one of these stately, silently chuffing old-timers with a wizened smiling skipper whose wife will make you a cup of tea straight out of the ship's polished copper boiler. And with it all, you glide through scenery immortalized by the English Romantic poets and captured forever on canvas by Constable and Turner.

As for hotels, several are outstanding by standards anywhere.

☆☆☆☆ **Sharrow Bay** • *on the quiet far side of **Ullswater Lake,** just beyond **Pooley Bridge** •* commanding sweeping vistas of water and hillscape that resemble the best of the Scottish highlands. Sleep is divided between the main Country House and neighboring outbuildings, all rather limited in the space of the accommodations but nevertheless comfortable if not somewhat prissy. In fact, throughout the various parts, a prodigious sneeze in the many porcelain-filled precincts could cause a crockery disaster of national significance. Dining rooms (smoking and non) are in the main house with the cocktail hour and meal established at a set time. The delicate and variegated gastronomy is world famous—as prolific as that ordained for a 16th-century monarch's feast. Proprietors Francis Coulson and Brian Sack are the souls of professional skill and hospitality. A high spot among the fells.

☆☆☆☆ **Miller Howe** • *on a hillock above the somewhat busier **Lake Windermere** •* (There are more than 20,000 boats registered on the small body of water!) In the local dialect "Howe" is similar to the French "chez"—and a lovely home it is with its excellent antique furnishings, paintings, prints, and scenes of early lakeside life. Almost half of its 13 rooms face the greensward and waterfront, some with private balcony. Chef-Patron John Tovey produces cuisine that rates among the finest in the land. An oasis of gentility, taste, and calm.

☆☆☆ **Leeming** • *on a hill overlooking the water at the far end of **Ullswater** •* is one of the biggest catches in any of the lakes. Its front apron slopes down to a forest of cypress, fir, and pine trees; exquisite, refined regency dining room with French blue ceiling and gilt trim; viewful lounges with open fires for cooler days; elegant public rooms; 17 bedchambers, most with private bath; no telephones, but a call system and radio in each unit. Highly recommended.

Howtown • *on the same lake beyond **Sharrow Bay** •* is lodge style, designed mainly for long-staying visitors. Dark woody bar; dining room with hearth, oils, and pewter plates; lots of horse brass, copper, stuffed foxes, antlers, and other hunt thematics. No private baths for its 16 units; a pair of 2-bedroom cottages for self-catering; reasonable rates. A 4-night hitch is par.

★★ **Michael's Nook Country House** • *in Grasmere* • is something rather special in the region. Reservations are an absolute must, and to be privileged to ingest even a morsel in its refined sanctum sanctorum you had better be a resident guest or reserve at least a meal in advance; stragglers are decidedly unwanted here. The 10 rooms are pleasant and rich with touches of Victoriana, especially the baths, which are studies in polished brass and nickel. A pompous period piece that is beautifully maintained but of dubious value to well-meaning travelers who might not be greeted warmly here.

☆ **Wordsworth** • is very nice in a more commercial way.

At a more plebeian level, the **Swan** is a comfortable sort of old-shoe hostelry with 35 bedchambers and 11 private baths. Its management by the Trust Houses Forte organization assures travelers of reasonable shelter. Next comes the **Prince of Wales,** garbed in regency accoutrements, followed by the **Red Lion,** which provides dens of no particular distinction.

★ **Pheasant Inn** • *at Bassenthwaite Lake near Cockermouth* • is a low-beamed-and-stucco white building on highway A–66. Don't miss a meal or a drink at this unbelievably ancient place. The bar is deep brown with antiquity; the dining room is a handsome tavern with open timbers; the rooms are spare but satisfactory for short stays.

Armathwaite Hall • *in Keswick* • is one of the most imposing sylvan retreats in the entire Lake District, but complaints have been rampant of late. Venerable estate 7½ miles out of town, at the north end of Bassenthwaite Lake; beautiful green apron sloping to the water's edge; L-shape castle; baronial furnishings; closed Nov. to April. A pity that this one seems to be slipping.

Castle Inn • personally run year-rounder, is also up at the Keswick end of the lake. Crossroads situation; clean, attractive appointments; modest rates. For motorists in search of a cozy 1-night hitching post.

☆☆☆ **Lodore Swiss** • *on the outskirts across the road from Bassenthwaite Lake* • generates a younger, more sprightly aura. Building in gray Borrowdale stone; heated swimming pool; 2 saunas; 2 gyms; sun lounge; masseuse; tennis court; dancing twice weekly; nursery with resident nanny. Fresh, well-appointed public rooms; cheerful bar; waterfront dining salon; La Cascade Grill; 73 comfortable accommodations and 65 baths.

Keswick is smack-dab beside the old station. Lovely manicured garden; 75 bedchambers in a mansion that is again seeing better days.

Royal Oak stays open year-round. Careful maintenance; basic but pleasant enough especially in its newer nests. The **Skiddaw** will save you money. The **George** reeks with antiquity, among other things; nice people, however. The

Derwentwater has an excellent position but an invasion of bus tours spoils its peace. The **Scafell** attracts many climbers; adequate comfort.

★★★ **Belsfeld** • sprawls scenically over the side of a gardened knoll in *Windermere*. Most of its 85 accommodations boast baths, radios, pants presses, and other amenities. There's also an indoor pool. Unquestionably the leader.

Old England • *also in Windermere* • has slipped largely because of its convention trafficking. Nice terrace above the water overlooking the small-boat docks; mixture of Victorian and Flash Gordon appointments; modern lakefront wing bringing capacity up to the 100 mark, the latest of which are the best.

The **Hydro** is big and rambling, but some regency touchups have helped; it specializes in group traffic. **St. Martin's,** across from Old England, is a tiny, clean economy stop.

★★★★★ **Langdale Chase Hotel** • *in Ambleside* • is a midget's skip from Windermere and one of the most panoramic vantage points in the Lake District. Stubbornly Victorian in its old-fashioned atmosphere; enough wood carvings to have kept 100 whittlers busy for 20 years; buckle-bending teas for hikers' appetites; 36 rooms and 20 baths; the Boathouse, the prime buy, is closed Dec. 8 to Feb. 1. We like the garden and the kindness, but some pilgrims may find the decor as overpowering as a 3-week holiday in Hagia Sophia. Otherwise warmly recommended.

The sprawling **Salutation** is 2nd (many package tours) in Ambleside; it is stalked closely by the **White Lion. Low Wood,** on the outskirts, is a fair bet for budgeteers; it has 141 bedchambers; bid for the newest ones.

LONDON

ATTRACTIONS

Dial 730–3488 and an official service will give you full details on hours and locations of important London sightseeing events, art exhibitions, and theatrical performances. Note that London has two new area codes for telephones—44–71 for the center of the city, and 44–81 for the outlying areas. (It's an amusing commentary on snobbism to discover that many individuals feel it is "fashionable" to have a "71" prefix; so, noting this foible, the telephone company sells an "81"-to-"71" supplemental relay. Hence, you can never be completely sure the person you've phoned is located where he or she is believed to be.)

City of London

The City of London is the small part of today's greater London which was originally founded by the Romans. The City, as it is commonly called, is now synonymous with London's commercial and financial district. And with its own police force and roughly 6000 permanent residents, it is something of a private town within a big city.

Tower of London • *Tower Hill* • William the Conqueror built this world-renowned fortress in the 11th century. Within its sturdy walls are the Crown Jewels, the chapel of St. Peter's, Sir Walter Raleigh's prison cell for 12 years, the death ground of the tragic Little Princes, and the execution row on which Anne Boleyn, Lady Jane Grey, and numerous other political victims met their fate. While in this district, don't miss a stroll around; **St. Katharine's Docks** with its Thames barges snug at the piers is fun for seafarers.

Chapels Royal • The sublimity of these little chapels is one of London's best kept secrets. The reason? Unless the tourist dresses conservatively and is mannerly, he or she is not wanted by the vicars and congregations. Also, cameras are banned. Sequestered in many of London's most famous buildings, some of these chapels date back to the 11th and 12th centuries. Should you wish to attend, you'll find a listing of the locations and hours in Saturday's better-grade London newspapers.

St. Paul's Cathedral • *St. Paul's Churchyard* • This magnificent cathedral crowns Ludgate Hill (and London's landscape) as Sir Christopher Wren's finest architectural feat. Most wanderers prefer the brilliant dome to the chilly nave (usually a trend in human relations, too). Wren, Wellington, and Nelson are among the greats who are buried in the Crypt. There is a small admission charge to the crypt and 3 galleries. Don't miss the "Whispering Gallery"!

Guildhall • *Off Gresham Street* • Near St. Paul's Cathedral, this majestic 15th-century hall has long been used for ceremonial occasions. It now houses a beautiful library and art gallery.

Barbican Centre for Arts and Conferences • This is London's costly arts complex—a project which ran 10 times over budget and was finally hatched for $285 million! The London Symphony and Royal Shakespeare Theatre now call it home. There are galleries, exhibition halls, a library, 2 restaurants, conference rooms, 3 cinemas, an artificial lake, and even a rooftop greenhouse aflutter with full-grown trees. The **Museum of London** also was set up here with its artifacts dating to the time of Roman occupation; its Fountains garden restaurant serves breakfast and lunch, plus afternoon tea.

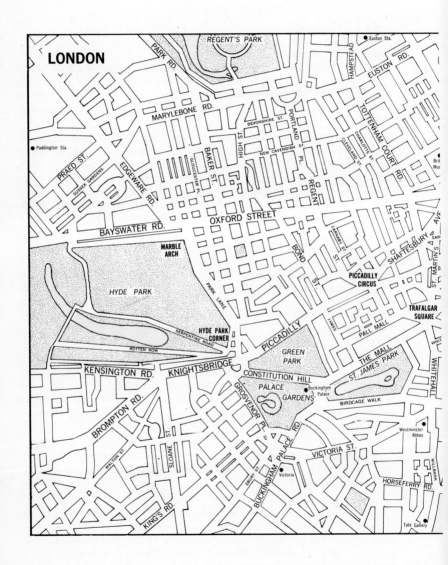

Old Bailey • Famed Old Bailey dispenses English criminal justice in open session. It is the fount of much of America's jurisprudence. Worth a visit if you're a barracks lawyer, a veteran juror, or just plain snoopy about other people's malfeasances.

Dr. Johnson's House • *17 Gough Square* • This is where Johnson lived while writing his *Dictionary*. A small museum now houses his relics and contemporary portraits.

West End

Covent Garden • For more than 3 centuries Covent Garden was London's central market for produce and flowers. Now its delightfully airy structures house 49 quaint shops. You'll also find many cafes and restaurants here.

St. James's

Buckingham Palace • *Buckingham Palace Rd.* • This is the official royal residence of Queen Elizabeth II, and the royal flag flies above the roof when the queen is at home. Although the palace is not open to visitors, you shouldn't miss the famed Changing of the Guard ceremony that takes place daily at 11:30 a.m. from April to early August and every other day in winter (weather permitting).

St. James's Palace • *Pall Mall* • Built by Henry VIII, this lavish structure still serves as an official royal residence. The palace itself is closed to the public, but the lovely courtyards are open.

National Gallery • *Trafalgar Square* • This distinguished institution displays priceless works by artists of every major European school: El Greco, Gainsborough, Holbein, Da Vinci, Michelangelo, Rubens, and Titian are only a few examples.

National Portrait Gallery • *2 St. Martin's Place* • Portraits of just about every famous English person in history are in this fascinating gallery, which stands just behind the National Gallery.

Westminster

The Houses of Parliament • *Parliament Square* • The Houses of Commons and Lords are located here, the seat of English government. Look to the towers to see if they are in session; a flag by day and a light by night (above Big Ben) are the signals. To witness a debate from the Strangers' Galleries of either House, wait at St. Stephen's Entrance for admission. When in session: Commons Mon.–Thurs. 2:30 p.m.–10 p.m. and 9:30 a.m.–3 p.m. on Fri.; Lords Tues. and Wed. and occasionally Mon. from 2:40 p.m., Thursdays from 3 p.m., and some Fridays from 11 a.m. (The above closing times are not accurate because debate could continue through the night.)

Westminster Abbey • *Broad Sanctuary* • This glorious Gothic church is now past the 9th-century mark. Within its marble floors and crypts rest so many historical figures that it is perhaps the English-speaking world's most famous shrine. It is open daily.

Westminster Cathedral • *Francis St.* • This church is a splendid example of the early Byzantine style.

Tate Gallery • *Millbank* • A fine gallery that excites young moderns more than it does traditionalists. Its collection of English painters from the 17th to the 20th centuries is supplemented by Continentals (Seurat, Van Gogh, Rouault, Picasso, Chagall, Renoir, and Braque), as well as by an assortment of Americans (Pollack and de Kooning, among others). The neighboring **Clore Gallery** has taken over and augmented the Turners—about 300 oils and a feast of 19,000 watercolors and drawings that appear in ever-changing cycles.

Imperial War Museum • *Lambeth Rd.* • Anything that went "boom" since 1914 is represented in British dimensions here. It is a fond and heroic repository of many of England's finest hours.

Bloomsbury

A delightful district so often given to song, it contains several pretty squares including Bloomsbury, Russell, and Bedford. The area was the home of many famous literati, most notably Virginia Woolf, D. H. Lawrence, and E. M. Forster. Also within its bounds are the University of London and the British Museum.

Sir John Soane's Museum • *13 Lincolns Inn Fields* • Perhaps a bit more for the specialist, Soane's collection includes paintings, drawings, and antiques. Most noteworthy are Hogarth's "Election" and "The Rake's Progress," as well as original Piranesi drawings.

British Museum • *Great Russell St.* • This extraordinary edifice is so massive that it challenges any first-timer to spend at least 3 or 4 days among its fabulous archaeological, historical, and literary wealth. Those in a hurry usually beeline for the Elgin Marbles, the Rosetta Stone, the Magna Carta, and the Egyptian Sphinxes; the reading room that spawned part of Karl Marx's utopian works is also popular for a peek. Open from 10 a.m. to 5 p.m. on weekdays and from 2:30 p.m. to 6 p.m. on Sun.

Dickens' House • *48 Doughty St.* • Dickens lived here only two years (from 1837 to 1839), but many of the great writer's relics flavor this charming terraced house.

Jewish Museum • *Upper Woburn Place* • A handsome and impressive collection of Jewish ritual objects and antiques.

Knightsbridge

Victoria and Albert Museum • *Cromwell Rd.* • Founded (at another site) during the 1851 Exhibition, the museum offers a melange of works from various periods and from many cultures. The English period rooms are perhaps the best feature, but splendid collections of armor, ceramics, paintings, and metalwork are also worthwhile.

Science Museum • *Exhibition Rd.* • A vast and interesting collection illustrating the history of science and its effect on industry.

Natural History Museum • *Cromwell Rd.* • Built in 1881, the vast halls contain spooks from zoology, entomology, paleontology, and botany.

Hyde Park • You may graze over 363 well-groomed acres that are a constant delight to natives and visitors alike. The renowned Speakers' Corner, near Marble Arch, is the Mad Hatter merry-go-round for debaters who are permitted to blow off steam on any subject short of obscenity (not unknown). Fanatics from all over the world rant, rave, and spout their philosophies here on Sunday. Bring a lunch or stop for a bite at the nearby park food kiosk.

Kensington

Kensington Palace • *Kensington Gardens* • William III converted this charming building into a palace in 1689. Its exterior was redesigned by Wren.
Kensington Palace Gardens is a street lined with some of the fanciest mansions of the 19th century. Many were designed in the grand Italianate style by the famous architect of that era, Pennethorne.

Around Town

Theater • London has 50-plus theaters that display perhaps the greatest talent and variety in the world. You'll find a wide range in ticket prices (well below Broadway levels), and seats are usually (though not always) plentiful; most box offices open at 10 a.m., and it is cheaper to buy tickets there rather than through an agent. The modern **Royal National Theatre** (South Bank) is a sensation. It contains the 900-seat Lyttelton, the 1150-seat Olivier, and the small, experimental Cottesloe theaters beneath one roof. The historic **Old Vic** has fresh makeup, too.

Tea at the Ritz • Posh? Indeed. But since so many tourists in jogging shoes (read ''Americans'') have been popping in for a cuppa and destroying the proper English atmosphere, it is now restricted to hotel guests only—or so they say. If you are in conservative attire you might try it anyway. For a glimpse of the stately London of yore, I suggest that you book in advance (for 3:30 and 4:45 p.m.) and then go to the spacious, gracious, changeless ground-floor lounge of this old-fashioned landmark. Its assorted finger sandwiches are excellent. Men should wear jackets and ties. If this one is blocked, the Chinoiserie of the

Hyatt Carlton Tower is always pouring in a most democratic fashion. The **Savoy** is also a traditional choice.

Mudlarking • The Thames provides other pastimes for those with boots—scavenging for treasure! If you've got Wellingtons, low tide is the time to burrow (especially at inward curves) for coins, battle relics, marine artifacts, and whatnots from the ages. Best locations are on the south bank near the Tower Bridge and downstream of Vauxhall, Blackfriars, and Kew bridges. The Port Authority (Tel. 03752–3444) can tell you the times of ebb and flow.

Markets • For antique hunters, the outdoor stalls on Portobello Road are a Saturday walk. That's also the best time to visit Camden Passage in the suburb of Islington. Friday mornings are the most rewarding time to browse through the New Caledonian Market. Fulham and King's Road, Chelsea, are for those who can afford sentimentality in the more expensive bracket; Beauchamp Place, just off Knightsbridge, is for zillionaires; Kensington Church Street and Notting Hill Gate remain popularly priced playgrounds.

Walking Tours • In *Time Out* magazine or at one of London's many information bureaus you will find lists of tour companies that offer a wide variety of specialized walking tours. Trained guides will show you, for example, Shakespeare's London, or that of Dickens.

Boat Tours • "Jason's Trip" is a fine midtown canal cruise from Argonaut Gallery (60 Blomfield Rd. Tel. 286–3428 or 9869) to the Camden Town locks. You will glide through Regent's Park, its world-famous Zoological Gardens, and other points, in a 90-minute loop. Book well in advance, get a confirmation that your boat will sail, and hope for good weather. As an alternate, you can sail from Westminster Pier upstream to Kew, Richmond, and Hampton Court in almost 4 hours (each way; summer only). If the ride up covers more water than you care for, your ticket also will enable you to ride the train home. The same company (Thames Launches and Thames Motor Boat Co.) operates evening cruises with launchings at 7:30 p.m.; there's a regular daily trip to Tower Bridge and Greenwich. The *Zoo Water Bus* departs hourly between 10 a.m. and 5 p.m. in summer from Little Venice; the combined fare and entry to the zoo is about $10. The *Jennie Wren* plys between Camden Town and Little Venice; similar low rates and good value.

Thames Flood Barrier • Today's newest tours actually cruise right through the colossal barricades, providing you with an eyeful encounter with the engineering forces that may one day save London from seaborne extinction. Departures at 11:15 a.m. and 1:30 p.m. from Westminster Pier; duration about 3 hours; an engaging bit of guidance as to the haunts of Dickens, Nelson, and other habitues of England's primary waterway. One of the world's modern wonders—and you can almost touch it!

Excursions

Greenwich • This lovely historical borough lies alongside the Thames (some 50 min. from London by boat) and has long been associated with British sea power and everything nautical. Board the boat, which leaves every 20 minutes, at Westminster Pier. Once in Greenwich, you can board and inspect the original *Cutty Sark* (in drydock), visit the *Gypsy Moth,* idle through the charming streets— and if you've packed a picnic, take your lunch to the beautiful 200-acre **Greenwich Park.** Or you can straddle the **Greenwich Meridian** which bisects the path a few yards north of the gates to the 17th-century **Old Royal Observatory.** After lunch, take in the **National Maritime Museum,** which boasts excellent exhibits showing Britain's great nautical past.

Kew Gardens • These are the Royal Botanical Gardens, and they offer an exhilarating array of many thousands of plants and trees. While the emphasis is on research and experimentation, the serene walks that cover the grounds make for peaceful, relaxing walks for visitors.

Hampton Court • *E. Molesey, Surrey* • suffered a fire not long ago, but it remains a marvelous sightseeing attraction even in its current state. The magnificent palace stands beside the Thames in the southwest corner of greater London. Originally undertaken for Cardinal Wolsey in 1515, it was later taken over and added to by Henry VIII. In addition to the gardens, which are widely considered some of the best in the world, there is an "Orangery," lovely courtyards, and a popular hedge maze. Inside, enjoy sumptuous state rooms, a picture gallery, Tudor kitchens, and the original tennis court!

Windsor Castle • It's on all the tour routes, of course, and a *must* for first-time visitors. The monarchs of Britain have called it home ever since William began his conquering. The Round Tower and St. George's Chapel (where the Knights of the Garter are installed) are two of the magnets within. There are Royalty and Empire exhibitions by Madame Tussaud, the quiet Valley Gardens nearby or at Savill, and beasties at Windsor Safari Park. When you are feeling faint from too much sightseeing take refreshment at the **Horse & Groom,** opposite the fortress entrance, where publicans Diana and Tony Stevens are especially hospitable to colonialists. It's about an hour's drive back to London.

Glyndebourne • *Sussex* • is a music festival that may teach you to dress up in smoking attire or other finery, consume a picnic in exquisite discomfort, and plod around in the rain while absorbing culture and water in equal amounts through evening pumps. Though the hall and lounges are indoors, many Brits defy the elements and take their mealtime break outside. If you can obtain (wickedly difficult) tickets, you may wish to linger on or dry out at **Horsted Place,** a stately country house where you can be suite-treated for $340 per night. Another private estate (about half of Horsted's prices) is **Stone House** at neighboring *Rushlake Green;* book pronto (Tel. 0435–830553) because it has only 6 rooms.

HOTELS

Because of the variety of hotels in the capital, it is not appropriate to rank the Old Guard with the Avant-Garde. The ratings, therefore, have been divided into "Traditional," "Contemporary," and "Assorted" brackets. The candidates surrounding Heathrow Airport and in outlying districts are covered separately toward the end of this section.

TRADITIONAL HOTELS

☆☆☆☆☆ **Berkeley** • Pronounced "Barkley," this landmark resides on a lovely site edging Hyde Park in the fashionable Belgravia district. At hand are such features as the wood-paneled restaurant in brown hues with chintz-shaded lamps on tables and soft intimate tones; the historic Buttery linked to Le Perroquet bar with buffet lunch and Mediterranean (fish/pasta) dishes at night; the gorgeous penthouse pool with sliding roof, refreshment facilities, and sauna—a galaxy. There are 27 suites and 160 knockout doubles; the flawless demisuites among the latter group are favorites in the house. A beautiful oasis ably managed by Director Stefano Sebastiani.

☆☆☆☆☆ **Claridge's** • Finding space will be the problem since it is inhabited by client legacies that go back to the time of the Picts. Time, in fact, has been taught to stand still here; even renewals carefully maintain a dated character. General Manager Ronald Jones is mixing in spice and vitality without altering its mandate on traditional values. Entrance rebuilt in the style of 1932 with dazzling Art Deco fillips; restaurant given its original grace and nobility; softspoken piano or string ensemble music at times in the lounge; numerous rooms renewed and air-conditioned; staff on full alert all the time. Excellent.

☆☆☆☆☆ **Connaught** • This spell-weaving old-timer couldn't be a more felicitous choice for the traveler in search of comfort and tranquillity in the homespun way—provided, of course, that you live in a palatially homespun mansion. If you desire a spacious room, flawless service, a superior restaurant and grill, a faintly English-Manor-House atmosphere and quiet British gentility that is nearly Edwardian in tone, here is surely the place for you. Kindly, mannerly, attentive staff. The cuisine in the Grill vies with the most exalted in the capital. Book l-o-n-g in advance.

☆☆☆☆☆ **Dorchester** • This Park Lane institution has recently emerged from a lengthy renovation that preserved the famous Dorchester traditions but added freshness and vitality to virtually every cranny. A new wrinkle is the Oriental (Cantonese) restaurant to supplement the Grill, Terrace Penthouse, Pavilion, and bar. A sultan owns it, and he's dedicated a fortune and more than two years to its improvement. The results are dazzling. In other words, it's the same grand old Dorchester.

★★★★ **Savoy** • There is a personality and history in this landmark that can't be found elsewhere. Minibar in every accommodation but personal service always available; color TV and cable TV throughout; vast majority of abodes exceptionally spacious. You might enjoy the Thames Foyer with its atmospheric period mirrors and the teas and pretheater light bites at such reasonable prices; a mezzanine snackery over the front entry. These are augmented by the River Restaurant for luncheon and dinner. Savoy Grill (harp music; 6 p.m. service for theatergoers) with traditional food reinterpreted for modern tastes. An English classic.

★★★★ **May Fair Intercontinental** • A total renaissance recently overtook this house, leaving it with a new persona. Beginning with its white marble-clad entrance, it moves to a stunning wood and polished-stone reception, then to the handsome Chateaubriand restaurant and the off-lobby bar. All bedchambers have been sedately restyled in English and French motifs; throwaway card keys have been employed; there's color TV plus free in-house movies; baths in pink Portuguese marble; hairdryers; large beds; many fine suites. It provides an air of quality that puts this well-situated house in the top rank.

☆☆☆☆ **Stafford** • is a converted manse tucked away in a little mews. It sparkles with a distinctive personality that evokes the flavor of England. Handy location that is quiet, though the house is merely 100 yards from Piccadilly; private-homelike lounge; bustling dining salon; graceful bar (from which, it is vowed, the first martini was exported to the Colonies); 65 ample-size units, all with bath; not for bargain hunters. Definitely for the discriminating.

☆☆☆☆ **Dukes** • This 1908 model has been fitted out to recapture the gas-light-era clatter of horseless carriages over its cobblestone court. Wrought-iron entrance; clubby brown and green lobby; tiny bar; St. James's restaurant. Total of 52 tiny fiefs (29 named for illustrious duchies), some of which are in a separate enclave; soft, earth-tone carpeting; bath, telephone, TV, 3-channel radio; suites with fireplaces and fully equipped kitchens. The staff not only will try to address you by name, milord, but will stock your castle with fresh flowers, a salver of fruit, and warmed copy of the *Times*.

★★★ **Ritz** • Grandly conceived main floor with pillared corridors, chandeliered lobby, palm-court lounge for tea-timing, and huge, column-lined rotunda dining salon displaying gilded garlands of laurel; many upstairs rooms equally sumptuous and spacious; quite a few routine singles have been joined to form deluxe twins featuring Louis XVI marble fireplaces. Cuisine, on my several tries, was not one of its strong points. Below the ground level, an independently run casino in formal attire gambols along. Manager Terry Holmes has given a ritzy new sparkle and flair back to this stately dowager and in return he'll ask about $400 per twosome per night.

☆☆☆ **Park Lane** • This old-timer is becoming more vigorous with age. I'm especially fond of the elegant, wood-lined and mirrored Bracewells restaurant; a gleaming silver bell reveals a staple of the house: roast beef and Yorkshire pudding; the dressed crab also was superb. A few steps below Bracewells you'll find an inviting palm-dotted bar with more foliage in the Garden Room restaurant. Air-conditioned suites, many facing the park and some with Jacuzzi-fed baths; harmonious colors in bedrooms, all with double-glaze windows, color TV, and frigobar. Overall, a handsome renaissance.

★★★★ **Hyde Park** • A stunning example of Victorian expression. Park Room overlooking the greenery, with live piano music; darkly woody Grill; now just a century old, it is very well maintained from marble to carpets to panels to crystal chandeliers. Its masterful General Manager Paolo Biscioni, known globally for piloting Rome's Grand Hotel so, well, *grandly,* is performing his usual wonders now in London. Two big pluses are the spaciousness and its splendid location in the epicenter of the Knightsbridge shopping bonanza.

Langham Hilton • first a hotel in 1865, has just reopened after several changes of career over the past century. Restoration of the noble Edwardian structure cost about £85 million, but the revision has maintained the space and grace concepts of its era chiefly in the public rooms. The bedchambers (410 units including 50 suites) are largely contemporary and hardly inspired. Let's wait a season to see how it shapes up before rendering a star ranking.

★★★★★ **Halcyon** • This represents the most dramatic incursion of British country hotels coming to London—well, *almost* to London. Holland Park is one of the capital's fashionable residential neighborhoods, but excellent subway connections put you within 15 minutes of the shopping and theater districts. The decor is stunning, all of it assembled by the talented American Barbara Thornhill. The lounge overlooks a tree-lined street; there's a hearth, a grandfather clock, oil paintings, and rich, brocaded antique chairs. Rooms reflect the sumptuous splendor of the Belle Epoque with emphasis on luxurious textiles, cushions by the dozens, flowers on every surface, and an abundance of riches throughout its 44 rooms and suites, many with 4-posters, all air-conditioned and some with Jacuzzis. The 6 categories of accommodation begin at close to £100 and range up to the £350 Halcyon Suite, with its own conservatory and view onto the park and tennis grounds. Downstairs the intimate lounge and adjoining Kingfisher restaurant are the "in" hideaways for the most distinguished members of the theatrical community. The quality of the cuisine befits the exquisiteness of the salon and patio. Something unique for London that I applaud for that very special traveler of discernment.

P.S. In the thrall of success of such small, expensive, and personalized hotels, London has produced quite a few more deluxe tykes of this ilk. Noteworthy are **Draycott,** with 2-dozen rooms, posh appointments (but no restaurant), and a residential locale at 24 Cadogan Gardens. One that's nearby called **11 Cadogan Gardens** became known for its sound value and homey atmosphere; it has gone *raahthah fahncy,* especially with its rates. **Fenja** at 69 Cadogan Gardens is a little gem, one of my favorites. Beautiful and luxurious is **Pelham** (15 Cromwell Place); it has a restaurant. **Beaufort** (33 Beaufort Gardens) is a Victorian stalwart almost in the shadow of Harrods.

☆☆☆ **Egerton House** • is also near Harrods' doorstep in Knightsbridge. Some of its 30 rooms come with four-poster beds and all have marble baths, satellite TV, and rich, heavily textiled fittings; many face the garden. There's a charming breakfast salon; tea can be taken in the study. Just right for gracious city dwelling.

☆☆ **Grosvenor House** • Big, commercial, group-conscious, and, as one might expect, lacking in personal attention. Attractive 90 Park Lane dining salon with entrance lounge, soft-spoken homelike appointments and firelit hearth; excellent food too. Breakfast Pavilion for light meals; poorly done Pasta Shop with routine Italian cookery; a magnificent swimming pool; Crown Club executive floor.

☆☆ **Brown's** • Since 1837 this has been one of the most famous hostelries in the British Empire, a staunch guardian of properly maintained traditionalism. Lobby and public quarters freshened; shortage of staff; mazelike corridors, a result of linking 11 townhouses together to create this composite; older units beautified; 142 rooms and 5 suites; Dover St. chambers quieter during the early morning hours than are those facing Albemarle St.; an overall feeling of slow-motion activity among antebellum furnishings.

☆☆ **Dorset Square** • is composed of a pair of Georgian houses near Regent's Park; the location and the hotel share the same name. Polished antiques, half-tester beds, and blossoms everywhere bespeak the distinctive personality of this cozy 30-room retreat.

☆☆ **Cadogan** • Here's a well-situated address in Knightsbridge where Oscar Wilde courted Lillie Langtry and where the management had the notorious playwright arrested and turfed into Reading Gaol. An air of pristine traditionalism pervades this stately house, harking to Edwardian allures and lore yet boasting an abundance of 20th-century comforts. A fireside ambience, at once intimate, appealing, and, well, arresting.

CONTEMPORARY HOTELS

☆☆☆☆☆ **Inn on the Park** • Its richly appointed lobby has wood paneling, crystal illumination, sandy-beige marble flooring, and a table where guests sit, rather than stand, to register. Secluded enclave of shops; mezzanine dining complex composed of the window-lined Four Seasons Restaurant with its own lounge plus the Queen Anne–style Lanes for lunch and theatergoers, also with a bar; cuisine in both of international prominence. Cleverly engineered "Conservatory Rooms" on second floor; tasteful furnishings; TVs set into stately highboys; marblesque baths. Its 27 suites vary in motif and mood while their prices are universally stratospheric.

☆☆☆☆☆ **Athenaeum** • In some ways this patrician hotel is a smaller (100-room) version of the above entry—a sort of Innlet on the Park, which is kept in a high state of polish by Manager Nicolas Rettie. Many suites and doubles glisten with spring, summer, and autumn decor; some have leather-top desks; tweedy carpets; complimentary videos; high-power showers; linen sheets; even jogging suits and maps are available. The Sunday brunch is worth a trip to London. If more spacious living is your bidding, the **Athenaeum Apartments** that adjoin—and which are equally tasteful—provide excellent value. The comfort is ample and the savings realized by having your own kitchen can add e-l-a-s-t-i-c to your London budget. Maid service Mon. to Fri.; all hotel facilities available to residents; direct-dial phones; excellent for week-long or lengthier visits. Overall, this house's flexibility and appeal make it very special indeed.

☆☆☆☆☆ **Hyatt Carlton Tower** • Always a major contender, this one seems to improve steadily. Splendid business center, health club, and overall modernizations. The famous Rib Room on the ground floor is rich with wood paneling and fine paintings; an Oyster Bar is another pearl. The Chelsea Room (one of my favorites in the capital) remains sedate and in the finest tradition of international *haute cuisine.* Bedroom themes employ muted colors in a sundae of beige, peach, blue, pistachio, and other flattering hues. With all this massive revamping, the dignity and Chippendale mood have not been diminished. If anything, the house generally has added good taste to almost every corner.

☆☆☆☆ **Capital** • This house's restaurant has generated a mighty following of culinary loyalists—and if you have a taste for aesthetics it can also satisfy *that* hunger. No real lobby to speak of—merely a hall porter's desk and reception counter; cozy-corner bar plus a pair of intimate lounges; vaguely French bedchamber decor, but with Ralph Lauren fabrics; compact baths. If you are staying a week or longer, ask about the savings to be had in the apartment wing. There are no historic or sylvan vistas from any of its 60 windows. Proprietor David Levin devotes every erg to his discerning clientele. Warmly recommended for its superb location, friendly staff, and fine management.

Churchill • Its gigantic lobby is an immediate indicator of this era in mass-minded hotellerie; you'll be instantly struck by the fact that as many as 1000 souls can live here at the same time. Here's a Winnie that went Phoo, as far as I'm concerned.

★★★★ **Blakes** • Here is the exact opposite—a small *intime* Victorian hideaway (but only in structure) on two sides of a residential street that caters chiefly to the With-It crowd, fashionable communications executives, stunning top-line models, and youthful up-market travelers who shun the conventional. The novel approach features a Pacific-island lobby covered by a colossal garden parasol and dotted with wicker furnishings which are more decorative than comfortable. There's a Retro-deco downstairs restaurant-cum-bar, a spotlit lounge, a sauna, and a host of smiling staff members, often in jeans; across the lane are the "Bosies" and "Benzies" annexes with additional accretions now linked in. No two nests are alike. Its tiny baths are often whacky in layout but charming in presentation. Sometimes adequate space is at a premium, but overall there is such an air of fetching, luxurious Bohemianism at every turn that most adventurous wanderers will forgive the occasional bruised elbow or overflowing closet. Bizarre, but excitingly fresh for those who dare to be different.

☆☆☆ **Intercontinental** • This one—don't confuse it with the previously mentioned May Fair Intercontinental—resides in the same convenient hotel cluster as the Hilton, the Inn on the Park, and other top-line contemporary stalwarts. The coolness of its entrance and lobby belies the easy grace, the rich colorations, and the luxurious comfort provided by its bedchambers. Softly elegant Le Souffle restaurant; coffee house for uninspired yet costly snacks and buffet breakfast; viewful 7th-floor discotheque in Art Retro for sipping and dancing; sauna and cool-off pool; select boutiques with price tags that may send you reeling; underground parking. The better, costlier units face Hyde Park (with the dual-glaze windows shut, they are quiet); extra-light sleepers may opt for a vistaless courtside address.

☆☆☆ **London Marriott** • This American import resides (appropriately) opposite the U.S. Embassy and within walking distance of major shopping tenderloins. Energetic Manager Henry Davies has performed a masterful task in making a well-appointed and comfortable house into an even more luxurious address. The Diplomat restaurant, in 2 tiers, is a gracious corner of London. There's the chipper and classy Regent Lounge with 24-hour service—one of the most elegant round-the-clock operations I have seen anywhere. As for accommodation, the king rooms are best for size because most normal doubles appear somewhat restricted in their dimensions.

★★★★ **Montcalm** • If you have a passion for brown, here is your own true love. Sand, beige, sable, fawn, sorrel, umber, cocoa, chestnut—you'll find them all within these precincts. Most of the ground-floor walls are upholstered in suede; furnishings are in leather; even the elevator has kidding around it; baths are carpeted. Suites feature spiral staircases and attractive 1½-story windows; ordinary twins are not spacious, but they are passable if your stay isn't a long one. The cuisine is artfully conceived in a primarily occidental fashion even though the hotel is owned by the Nikko interests and Japan Air Lines. The staff couldn't be nicer; the service is gracious.

☆☆☆ **Sheraton Park Tower** • Cylindrical, 18-story, concrete-and-glass building affording all-around views of Knightsbridge; penthouse top-of-the-mark suites; wide bay windows; impressive travertine lobby enriched with wood, modern tapestries, orange textiled furniture, metal sculpture, and cunning illumination; inviting bar adjoining; casino; spring-daubed Le Cafe Jardin coffee shop in dusty rose and grass green; underground garage. A novel structure that's very well situated.

☆☆ **Westbury** • This house is better in its public sectors than it is in its limited-size bedchambers. Cheerful color schemes lend an eye-expanding illusion; the baths remain bruisingly narrow-sided. It is convenient for shopping and theater going.

☆☆ **Hilton on Park Lane** • This entry should not be confused with its lower-cost Kensington cousin (see below). Impressive mahogany and marble lobby; English-toned restaurant; several bars, plus the sip-and-dance nightclub as well as Trader Vic's in the basement; health center; underground parking;

every unit with radio and TV plus full-length movies via videocassette; one Y-shape wing houses studio-style accommodations only. There are 6 viewful executive floors with private lounge for complimentary breakfast and cocktails—at an overall premium cost, of course.

☆☆ **Londonderry** ● In the high-rent cluster bound by the Hilton, the Intercontinental, and the Inn on the Park, this smaller house shines with luster. There is so much polish and starch—receptionists wear tailcoats and *boutonnieres*—that they crinkle when they walk. Gleaming marble lounges; delightful *intime* cocktail bar; dignified Ile de France restaurant; smallish bedrooms; fully air conditioned. Recommended for its location and its snap, crackle, and English pop.

Royal Garden ● This 500-room, T-shape giant overlooks Kensington Gardens and Hyde Park. Much of its physical plant is well designed, comfortable, and appealing to the eye. During all of my various visits, tour groups have been homing in like swallows returning to you-know-where. Personally, I have always had fine service here—and I've always booked in incognito—but travelers sometimes complain of staff indifference. The rates are reasonable.

Gloucester ● The spatial concepts are so cleverly executed here that the untrained observer could scarcely guess that a thousand souls are sharing this address. Fresh lobby arcade rising to a mezzanine level; clubby grill; Hunter's Lodge restaurant; sumptuous lounge; Le Chateau wine bar (upstairs portion with tables; cellar section with counter libations), a very popular fad in present-day London; sauna; hairdressing facilities for men and women. The accommodations, though extremely well equipped, seemed rather spare in dimensions.

Royal Lancaster ● The lobby boasts Hal's Bar; the Beefeater Restaurant has springlike tones to complement the branch-top vistas from its wide windows; the Mediterranean Cafe features a lovely centerpiece ceramic tree; the Pub glows with burgundy undertones. The viewful premium bedrooms come with grass-fiber wall coverings, raw-silk spreads and terrific music-news-and-TV consoles.

☆☆ **Holiday Inn Mayfair** ● is set only a block from Piccadilly Circus. Clean-lined marble-and-wood reception and foyer; costly and suave white-and-gold Louis XV restaurant; adjoining cocktail area; convenient underground parking. Most bedrooms are expansively proportioned (ask for a large unit).

☆ **Portman Intercontinental** ● Sunday Brunch in a New Orleans jazzy mood at the Truffles restaurant is part of this dynamic milieu. Otherwise the cuisine is in the modern French style. There are also a pub and a cleverly cooked-up bakery, which add to the gustation and fun hereabouts. British Airways maintains an office too; theater ticket desk; jeweler; news kiosk; car park. Accommodations in 2 towers. A rewarding value.

☆ **Selfridge** • If shopping is your bag, then here you are—and here you may stay. This one is tucked right into the middle of Selfridge's—the famous department store. Handsome wood, glass, and burnished-metal entry and foyer; paneled lounge; cobble-paved Fletcher's Restaurant with a vendor's barrow of garden produce to tempt incomers; charming oaken Stoves Bar recalling the days of Dickens; chipper Victorian Picnic Basket coffee shop open from 7 a.m. to 1 a.m. Its 330 units feature room-wide windows that provide an impression of space when, in fact, little exists. Fitted Empire furniture enhances the clever maximizing of minimum dimensions.

★ **Portobello** • This 20-room, 5-suite sweetie is just plain fun. A handsome pair of Victorian homes have been joined in harmonious wedlock by Tim and Cathy Herring, an affable, young, and talented couple. Palms abound, cheer pervades, and good taste is in evidence down to the smallest detail. Its main drawback is in the miniature baths.

Forum • This jumbo is zooming toward success not only because of the jet thrust from its airline sponsors, but because it is a model of what keen administration, smart budgeting, and shrewd architecture can do. While the bedrooms are cramped (the brochure is a triumphant illustration of what a wide-angle lens can do for a microscopic subject), the prices are at bedrock level for these cheerful surroundings.

★ **Cavendish** • Here is a 255-unit, first-class (not deluxe) midtowner that bears a striking resemblance to our own Pan American Building on Park Avenue in Manhattan. Attractive public rooms including the 24-hour Ribblesdale Restaurant, dark-tone Sub Rosa Bar (named after the original Cavendish's famed Rosa Lewis), and mezzanine lounge-bar. All bedchambers with tiny baths, bedside radio and TV controls; limited luggage space; building-wide fresh-air ventilation; round-the-clock laundry at standard town prices (a considerable saving); only continental breakfast or snacks served in the rooms. Ask for rooms ending in "21." Its simple, clean-lined efficiency is almost Scandinavian in tone.

Holiday Inn Marble Arch • Since this house is more conveniently sited than its crosstown counterpart (see below), its designers opted for fewer frills as inducement to register; the accent is therefore on functional simplicity.

★ **Lowndes** • Structurally and decoratively here is one of the more attractive small hotels in London—with the added advantage of having one of the best addresses in the embassy neighborhood of Belgravia. The traditional Adam style predominates—a signature of its elegant heritage, which is now trending toward popular mass appeal. Good value £ for £.

Holiday Inn Swiss Cottage • Named for the neighborhood, it's a 10-minute subway ride from Piccadilly. Architecture and decor? Arabesque, with persistent use of arches, vaulting, tiles, and carpets. Henry VIII Restaurant, overlooking a garden; King Henry Bar, studded with director's chairs and potted palmery; indoor pool; soft-drink and free-ice machines stationed like stoic sentinels on each floor. All 300 chambers duel with the din on 2 main arteries; all sport goatee-sized balconettes. The slightly lower tabs here, versus those of its downtown cousin, can be nullified with the flick of a taxi flag.

★ **Howard** • From its perch on the Strand, this deluxe rehash of an older hostelry overlooks the Thames. Elegant 18th-century decor; 150 bedrooms; penthouse suites; Quai d'Or French restaurant with Temple Bar adjoining; terraced apron of gardens.

Kennedy • It is convenient to Euston Station, but huddled neglectedly in a metropolitan backwater that I doubt many travelers will like. Okay for its moderate tabs, however.

Imperial • Entrance cupped in a fountain court; s-p-a-a-a-a-c-i-o-u-s lobby pointing clients to cubicles in 3 wings; mass-production dining room; achingly tiny bedchambers and unbelievably cramped baths. No, thanks.

President • This 7-story candidate has gold and brown carpeting, fresh wallpaper, and lively curtains; dining room with saw-toothed counter available. The service kills it, however.

Bedford • Here's what might be dubbed a 180-room vice president. Same pattern of its busy-busy carpet; similarly conceived lounge and dining room, but pleasant garden adjoins; minuscule bathrooms with separate toilet; closets much too small. Routine.

Washington • As an example of mass-production hotel technique, 60% enlarged by a streamlined wing, this one doesn't come off for us. Neither does the staff, who seemed to prefer being elsewhere.

Bloomsbury Crest • Here's a lackluster commercial pod that occupies part of an office building near Russell Square. In my judgment, this dreary number wouldn't be fun for holidaymakers. Its sister operation, the **Regent Crest** near Regent's Park, peeps from its garden with 350 rooms—each cross-pollinated to resemble the original plant.

★ **Hilton International Kensington** • *way out on Holland Park Ave., near Shepherd's Bush* • is offered to Hiltonians at nearly ⅓ off the deluxe rates of the Park Lane entry. While it is handsomely decorated in richly textured materials, the location is unfortunate because today's taxi fares can push daily expenditures up to top-line levels. If, however, you don't mind using public transport, the subway (tube) and bus stops are practically at your doorstep. Buff brick facade; Nipponese restaurant; periodic medieval feasts in the Tudor Tavern; individually adjustable thermostats in all units; likewise refrigerator/bar and color TV. Very well presented; here's a concept that we laud.
   Novotel has bunk space for 1300 far out on Talgarth Road. You might hope you are not one of the innmates. The 826-bedchamber **Tower** on St. Katharine's Way reflects all of the charm of the World Trade Center it was meant to complement. Finally, the economy-priced **London Metropole,** on Edgware Road near Marble Arch, counts a mere 555 accommodations. The

entrance is so awkward for motorists that they would find it much easier to drive only to the back portals. I like the efforts made here to stoke up decorative warmth in the public rooms. The sleepers, however, remain little more than body-size cubicles. The **Royal National,** with its 556 units, functions chiefly for tours. Reasonable prices; reasonable rewards.

ASSORTED HOTELS

Here is a grab bag that I won't even attempt to classify. Some of its entries are big, some tiny, some new, some with a sprinkling of modernizations, some ancient and flavorful, some downright decrepit. Because of these myriad variables and the added factor of personal taste that would make one house appealing to one traveler and absolutely hideous to another, we will only describe them briefly and let you be the judge.

L'Hotel ● *28 Basil St., S.W. 3* ● nudges shoulders with its posher brother, the Capital (see earlier), sharing the same expert management of Proprietor David Levin. Prices, however, are significantly below Capitalist levels while taste and space considerations in bedrooms are nearly the same. Furnishings lean to American Colonial; fabric walls; 4 units with gas-burning fireplaces; direct-dial phone; TV-clock consoles; every amenity is here. There's also Le Metro, a splendid wine bar downstairs with snacks available.

Le Meridien Piccadilly ● With a name that hints at its French connection this landmark, first born in 1908, is born-again with all the opulence common to the turn of the century. Above the entrance, on a pillowed terrace, you will discover a conservatory with brasserie. The Oak Room features the Burgundian masterwork of Chef Michel Lorain as well as English cookery. There's a music room, a nightclub, a glittering array of architectural trinkets from the Age of Elegance and—oh, yes—even some bedrooms. The last combine traditional English stylizations with up-to-date accoutrements. There's a health club, too, plus golfing opportunities at Richmond Park (½-hour drive—by limo, not One Wood).

Chesterfield ● This comprises the union of 2 old houses, incorporating charm, varilevel stair climbing, nice rooms, a Buttery spread with reasonable food buys, and a restaurant that glows with a Regency tradition. Very central.

Dolphin Square ● Here's an exceptional value. A total of 1050 privately leased units are contained in a quadrangle of houses, each named after a British naval personage. Rodney House is the operative nexus and the site for 150 transient accommodations, available by the day, week, or month. Quiet, convenient location; hall porter, reception, key and cashier counters; extraordinarily well planned and executed all-purpose shopping arcade; overlooking the heated indoor pool is a pleasant, popular-price restaurant open from 7:30 a.m. to midnight; 2 bars; 8 squash courts; Finnish log saunas; 350-car underground garage; attractive gardens; 26 automatic elevators. One-, 2-, 3-room apartments; 30 so-called Guest Rooms for economizing voyagers (public toilets and tubs). Tabs very low for the market; discounts usually given for stays of a week or more; most accommodations with fully equipped kitchenettes; TV installed upon request for a small additional charge; free maid service 6 days per week.

The Chelsea ● This 220-unit midtowner features a swimming pool in its courtyard overlooked by the Bohemian Bar and the romantic Papillon Restaurant. All public sectors are attractive. Very convenient.

Wilbraham ● This neighbor of the above is older in style but fresh in appearance. Varying assortment of 62 rooms, 34 with bath; substantial and nice as a London townhouse. Prices are surprisingly low for the reward but reception staff are sometimes brusque—possibly a result of too much success.

White House ● This former apartment-style abode overlooking Regents Park was transformed into a medium-budget hotel. Circular lobby marblesque and carpeted; dining salon featuring an "Executive Menu" plus other choices; Wine Press in *auberge* style for sipping as well as for club breakfasts.

St. George's ● Somewhat remote situation, but easily (and economically) within reach of the visceral midsections of the city; split-personality building shared with B.B.C. headquarters; ground-floor entrance; 14th-story lobby; adjoining panoramic Octave Restaurant; bar-lounge combination; all units with truly spectacular townscape vistas through huge full-wall windows. The accommodation I'm crazy about is the so-called Bed-Sitting Room, which is enormous and plushly outfitted. Recommended in its upper-medium category.

Elizabetta ● Bustling, relatively far-out location; boxy, 7-tiered exterior; silver slipper-sized bar-lounge; miniaturized restaurant with Middle Eastern cuisine. A grave disappointment to us.

Kensington Palace ● This house offers a better than average share of appeal. Lobby tasteful and air-conditioned; coffee shop bubbling from 7 a.m. to 12:30 a.m.; good maintenance; heavy business from conducted tours. Only a few of its accommodations in dismal studio motif; conventional twins much better by comparison.

Ramada ● Edwardian touches, molded ceilings, and Italian marble. The Carvers' Table is a cut above average for hotel dining, too. Rooms well outfitted but not too spacious; convenient for those in the fashion and textile trades since Oxford St. is only 50 yards away.

Royal Trafalgar ● This 110-box bastion is excellently positioned for addicted sightseers—but that's about that, as far as we're concerned. Tiny lobby where I saw throngs almost as dense as Attila's troops; Angus Steak House concession plus Battle of Trafalgar Pub. All rooms seem to have been thoughtfully proportioned so that guests can reach almost anything from dead center; all come with bath, radio, TV, and round-the-clock service.

Leinster Towers ● a community of several former houses, offers 165 accommodations under one roof. Hodgepodge interior; all units with weensie private baths and more than half with cooking facilities; possibly the narrowest beds this side of Fort Bragg.

Strand Palace, Regent Palace • are in a chrome steel, imitation leather motif. Chillingly sterile a few moons back but their Trusthouse Forte masters are successfully pumping color and life into this pair.

Norfolk retains its splendid 19th-century mien; cheery brasserie and darkly handsome winery plus a rich atmosphere in its English Tavern; well-appointed bedrooms. **St. James Court** is an expensive renovation in exclusive Buckingham Gate. Public rooms and restaurants (beautiful Auberge de Provence, Mediterranee, and the Szechuan Inn of Happiness) very appealing, but bedchambers cool and zestless. Ownership by the Taj Group of India attracts many upper-echelon Asiatics as clientele. **Basil Street,** in London's prized shopping district, is an enchanting meld of Edwardian and Georgian motifs; a lovely period piece of innkeeping with many fine antiques.

Cumberland is a frenetic colony that's undergone extensive revamping; commercial, but very good value; Coffee Shop excellent as are the Dukes Bar and the Japanese restaurant. **Abbey Court** (20 Pembridge Gardens W2) and **Stone House** (16 Sydney St. S.W.3) are two nooks—22 units in the first and only 3 in the latter—that are homelike and highly personalized. Prices are low but rewards are ample if you are anti-hotel in nature. **Swallow International** has a cavernous marble lobby; Cavalier Room and Cromwell Coffee Shop for pack'em-stack'em feedings; Stuart Bar, a dim water hole. No thanks. **Post House** is larger but lackluster. **Embassy** blends modernisms with period themes in a happy meld of 2 distinct ideas. The medium tariffs and the all-out effort of the staff are big pluses. **London Ryan** is strictly an overnight stop. The **Averard** is slipping, in my opinion. **Mt. Royal** is a commercial colossus offering excellent amenities but not an overabundance of flair; groupy but reasonable in price. The **Londoner** is less frenetic but just as mercantile. It seemed very expensive for the value.

Belgravia Sheraton • provides shophounds with excellent fields for the chase. Sit-down check-in plus a glass of pink champagne; special, thoughtful touches for women guests; expanded atrium lounges; glass also covering the restaurant and lightened with mirrors and painted wallpaper; 9 studio suites; refashioned doubles, all with in-house video and color TV. A warm clublike reformation.

Hyde Park Towers • gave its 108 rooms a facelift. Restaurant with dancing; coffee shop; commercial but sound.

Park Plaza • opposite Hyde Park, is an amiable bet for families, provided the children are carefully watched whenever they cross traffic-clogged Bayswater Road.

Mandeville • is a 163-room warren which might bring to your mind a run for captive conducted-tour rabbits; La Cocotte restaurant, cocktail bar, Boswell's Pub, and Orangery coffee shop. **Royal Westminster** is close to Buckingham Palace. Utilitarian bedrooms; brick-lined, beamed-ceiling Thatcher's *(sic)* Restaurant with prime vittles.

HEATHROW AIRPORT

Sheraton Skyline • is suavely luxurious. Large, tropical-lush, central Carib Patio featuring a fine pool, and a popular, b-i-g Sunday buffet-brunch from 11:00–2:00; Diamond Lil's reincarnated Gold Rush Saloon with honky-tonk ivories and bouncing banjos; Colony Room an Edwardian dine-and-dancer; never-say-dry Cafe Jardin; excellent maintenance throughout; expensive.

Heathrow Penta • is a sprawling, 4-level structure. Sweeping lobby-lounge; expansive polar-frosted Rib Room; The Flying Machine and Sir Francis Drake bars with respective aero-nautical gimmickry; coffee shop; discotheque; indoor pool, bar, and sauna bordered by flowers and fountains. All of its soundproofed chambers provide vivid hues, TV, and air conditioning.

Holiday Inn • architecturally is splayed like a 3-bladed prop; its sister ship is 10 miles away at Slough. Blue Ribbon feedery revving till 2 a.m.; hearty Beefeater Bar; Satellite Coffee Shop; health center embracing pool, sauna, mas-sagery, gym, and tennis courts; golf links. All 300 units sport smallish but practical baths and showers, the standard entertainment package, floor-to-ceiling panes, and annoying open wardrobes; kids under 12 ride on their parents' ticket.

Sheraton-Heathrow • resides on a mile-distant pasture that overlooks an unsightly factory. Low-profile concrete building; cockpit-size lobby in Star Wars Gothic; raised bar; Cranford Restaurant for seafood and grills. The Footlights nightery, staged as a Victorian pub, also offers vittles. In-'n-out swimmery plus steam room; poolside snacks; frequent bus connection to Knightsbridge.

Excelsior • is still superior for its purpose and still richly priced for its league. Its coffee shop, pub-style Tavern Bar, brick-bound sunken Rotisserie, and posh Draitone Manor restaurant are further pluses on its manifest. Adjoin-ing this, there's the 8-table "Library" with crystal glasses, superb cookery, and genuine bookery.

Edwardian International • has 460 rooms, including 9 suites, all with bath, telephone and TV; facilities nearly always open, with restaurant on 24-hour and snack bar on 20-hour basis; heated, floodlit, open-air pool; shopping arcade; flight transportation provided to terminus. The efficient, amiable service standards are a blessing.

Ariel • is a 184-room, doughnut-shaped structure. Soundproofed, air-con-ditioned bedrooms; showers in each bath; TV and radio; free transportation to and from the airport; a specialty restaurant functioning night and day.

Post House • is practically a self-service sanctuary. Imposing 10-tier house posted on 15 acres; vast lobby bordering on the brash; supermarket carts for transporting your own baggage. Great Britain Grill, Buttery, and Bar all in tribute to I. K. Brunel, the 19th-century marine wizard; pool, bank, boutiques, and news kiosk rounding out the public precincts. All cubbies are standardly furnished and are available in 8 color schemes; a continental breakfast will be left *outside* your door; offspring under 16 slumber gratis if they share the parental billet.

Crest ● is the cheapest of the lot. Simple reception; Globetrotter Bar only 800 feet from a runway; lusterless Silver Table restaurant. Lookalike sleepers with radios, phones, adjustable air cooling and reportedly the only triple-glaze panes in or around London.

IBIS ● is a link in a European economy chain. Nearly 250 rooms with doubles about £30 and singles in the £25 range.

At **Gatwick Airport,** choose either of the two **Copthornes.** Both are pleasant and, alas, expensive. The 586-unit **Hilton** is up to the usual Hilton International standards; it's only a 5-minute walk from the terminal. This luxury entry offers a pool, squash courts, and sauna. **Crest** is also a good choice for a modern hotel.

If you're ever stuck for a place to stay, bookings can be made at the Victoria Station Tourist Information Centre (forecourt) or the Heathrow Tourist Information Centre.

RESTAURANTS

In London, Mayfair is chichi and costly; Soho and Chelsea are more theatrical and bohemian in flavor, although the tabs can run plenty high here too. *Most* major independent restaurants and hotel grillrooms (not hotel dining rooms) are shut tight on Sundays. It is *always* wise to make advance reservations in London, regardless of the place or hour. Refer back to the "Food" section for dining trends in the capital.

Fashionable Dining

☆☆☆☆☆ **Tante Claire** ● *68 Royal Hospital Rd.* ● This Gallic "auntie" is one of the most expensive redoubts of London Town, but we feel high ambition should be amply rewarded. Although expanded enough to provide comfort, Proprietor-Chef Koffmann prefers to play to a small and discerning audience. Indeed, his style of gastronomy is so thoughtfully planned and individually composed that he is necessarily restricted in his offerings. Perhaps more than any other *cuisinier* functioning in the capital today, his preparations represent an "instantaneous" selection of what is best on the morning market and the cultivation of a full meal around those selected items. A modern, softspoken mood prevails.

☆☆☆☆ **Waltons of Walton Street** ● *121 Walton St.* ● Continues to be the choice of the Rolls-Ferrari set and foreign high society. The cuisine is judiciously innovative. Georgian windows overlook the quiet street; a dark inner nook is available for more intimacy (better after theater). On various visits, I've sampled such inventive creations as a lightly whipped camembert mousse, roasted lobster with coriander and ginger, sauteed Scotch beef with marrow and pine kernels, a salad of yogurt, mushroom, and celeriac, and a white-and-dark chocolate slice with coconut flavoring. The wines disclose their patrician bearing—and are priced accordingly. Some of its additional attributes include Sunday opening as well as special fixed price options for after-theater supper and a very reasonable meal at midday.

☆☆☆☆ **Chez Nico** ● *35 Great Portland St. W.1* ● named for Nico Ladenis, left his original digs (now Cavaliers) and after an airing in Berkshire, which he sold, he opened this splendid third act. And for an encore, he reopened **Very Simply Nico** at 48a Rochester Row S.W.1 and renamed it **More Simply Nico.** Try to catch his act wherever he may be playing. Nico is a genius who sometimes can cast himself as a brat when the customer doesn't suit his fancy. Nevertheless, temperament can produce fine victuallers and here's a case in point.

☆☆☆☆ **Le Gavroche** ● *43 Upper Brook St.* ● In the earlier years of its fame this entry had failed to garner my personal enthusiasm, but it seems to have shifted gears and now approaches gastronomy with less ornament and with dedicated honesty. However good the food, I still find it difficult to swallow the absurd prices. A few bistro dishes are exceptions but these are not why you came. The atmosphere is sophisticated and sedate. Waiters are often aloof.

☆☆☆☆ **Rue St. Jacques** ● *5 Charlotte St.* ● is another in the modish all-Gaul tradition, even though talented Chef Gunther Schlender has Teutonic roots. Try his armagnac-scented lobster mousse—a masterpiece of modern gastronomy; juniper-flavored guinea hen is also a favorite of mine here. The mirrors, posh decor, and intimacy evoke the sensation of grand *richesse,* though an evening here will cost about half of that at Le Gavroche.

Interlude ● *7 Bow St.* ● It was sold, chefs moved in and out frequently, and its fad value is fading while the quality of gustation follows suit, in my opinion. Still, it's one to watch if they ever get the right combination.

☆☆☆☆ **Ciboure** ● *21 Eccleston St., S.W.1* ● There's a cheery greeting from the flowered windowboxes at its entrance. The hospitality is carried inside with a foyer bar and 3 tables, plus more further in; pale yellow walls; black and white contrasts; fresh gray or white tops over striped undercloths on well-dressed tables. The rosette of lamb with apricots and mint is a delight; so is the turbot with green peppers, and orange. If you've failed to reserve and can't get in, **Ken Lo's Memories of China** is just across the lane and is an excellent Oriental choice. (The master chef from China has a similar but wonderfully viewful branch at Chelsea Harbour, the latest redoubt of the ''in'' set.)

☆☆ **L'Arlequin** ● *123 Queenstown Rd.* ● The food is superb. The people—Chef Delteil and his wife—are warmhearted. And now that it has stretched out into the adjoining masonry, it is marginally more comfortable. When you taste the thinly sliced duck and other preparations, however, you may be able to forgive any space limitations. Try also the chubby scallop-fed ravioli should any doubts linger. Luscious!

Clarke's • *124 Kensington Church St.* • Everybody is talking about this eccentric. It features home cooking for people who hate to eat at home. The $46 menu is not only set, it is hammered in stone: *one* choice of first course only; the same for the main dish and sweet. In my case, the "choices" for two of the plates were simply not items I cared for and, hence, I felt like a spoilsport for leaving so much on my platter. The quality and presentation, however, were exceptional. Plain room with blanched wooden floor, modern paintings, and a hostess who is the soul of hospitality. Nevertheless, you gits what you gits and that's that, buster. On this same street (which is becoming a gastronomic district) there are two restaurants I much prefer: **Kensington Place** (just up the lane at #201), where the decor is awful but the cookery is splendid, and **Boyd's** (across the street at #135), where the conservatory atmosphere is pleasant, the people are cheerful, and the dishes are delightful.

Bibendum • *81 Fulham Rd. S.W.3* • is breathlessly sought after by the young and fashionable, taking perhaps 2 weeks to secure an evening table (lunch is easier). While the bistro cookery (hardly cuisine) is flavorful, I feel foolish paying $50 for fish-and-chips (fried plaice and french fries), which costs $2 at street stands (admittedly not as refined). Very chic, rather wan decoratively, and oh-so-de rigueur.

Alastair Little • *49 Frith St. W.1* • is even more of a not-so-*beau-geste* and it, too, is dazzling to those Little-known disciples for whom fad is fonder than fact. The ugly, hideous, almost frightening illumination has to be seen to be truly believed; then come cheap chipped plastic tables, paper napkins, bus station cutlery and tableware, a bathroom downstairs in the next building, crudely presented food by ill-kempt and sloppily groomed minions, and flavors that kitchen trainees might revere but experienced diners can live without. Ah, where's the finesse of yesteryear, Alastair?

☆☆ **Sutherlands** • *45 Lexington St. W.1* • is less minimal in its bid for otiose style; hence, a touch of grace to greet the eye and smart personnel to offer a decent reception. The long salon has a spacious air so that business types (or better yet, romancers) can speak privately. Chef Hollihead manifests a legacy of careful tutorage under master *cuisiniers*. His combinations of ingredients are vivid in flavor and not silly simply to be innovative. There's a sense of intelligence and responsibility. Moreover, it just tastes good.

★★★ **Le Caprice** • *Arlington St. S.W.1* • Here is a reincarnation of what was once London's most fashionable establishment. Models, design leaders, and theater personalities are always propped at the counter or at its lively tables. Cuisine is chiefly brasserie style, unpretentious and damned good. Main courses run from $9 to $13; not bad for being on the cutting edge of the city's sophisto-category. P.S. The Sunday brunch is a wow. If you like this mood, you'll also enjoy lunch (only) at **L'Express** ● *16 Sloane St.* ● below a boutique. Bagel and lox for (gulp) £10; chicken tika at £8. Ample food but ample prices too. Very, very noisy with happy sounds. **Joe's Cafe** ● *126 Draycott Ave.* ● is a brother operation that opens at night as well as noontime.

☆☆☆ **Hilaire** ● *68 Old Brompton Rd.* ● still attracts South Kensington's disciples of the newest of *nouvelle*-isms from the hardworking kitchen. At $75-or-so for two, the value certainly is here when it comes to such labor-intensive comestibles. The set lunch is a good buy, but wines are lofty in price.

☆ **Cecconi's** ● *5A Burlington Gardens W.1* ● The address is one of London's best. Trellis-back chairs with French-blue cushions; fresh-cut flowers; filmy curtained windows along 2 entire lengths of the salon. Elegant simplicity is the keynote, sung to the tune of very small portions of fine Italian cuisine. If the prices don't disturb you here, then certainly nothing else should. **Santini** (29 Ebury St.) seeks this same up-market Italian following, but its cold mood and frigid staff can't bring it off, in my opinion. Food's okay but spare.

★★ **Eleven Park Walk** ● *S.W.10* ● purloined its straightforward moniker from its swanky address—and a *very* chi-chi spot it is. The house is abubble with charming young things in the latest fashions, all escorted by a bedizened host of admiring suitors. It is clearly the haunt for second-magnitude stars, dressed-to-the-nines models, and denizens of the couture cult. It glitters with mirrors on 2 sides, broadening the outlook and providing the perfect backdrop for such overt narcissism. Cookery leans toward the north-Italian preparations.

Orso's ● *27 Wellington St. W.C.2* ● is more straightforward, telling you like it is for Italian cookery. Journalists, editors, and publishers are usually at this Covent Garden site at lunch while theater personalities dominate at night.

l'Incontro ● *87 Pimlico Rd. S.W.3* ● is the rage for chic ladies at noontime. Chiefly seafood of Venetian style and very light. The black and white decor is spare but fresh.

★★★ **Menage a Trois** ● *15 Beauchamp Place S.W.3* ● The formula is both peculiar and spectacularly successful: *only* cold or hot starters are served plus desserts. I was dazzled by quail in a deep-fried pastry parcel and then thought I could manage turbot stuffed with crayfish. It was too much, but still I sampled cheese in a puff basket. All were delicious, interesting, and tailored for diets that do not wish to plough through conventional courses in an order that has been prescribed since dining rituals were first established. Downstairs location; windows peering at passing patellas on the street outside; white brick walls; 3 alcoves plus a niche for a jovial piano player. Hardly cheap—and that's just for starters—but different·and very, very good.

★★★ **Lindsay House** ● *21 Romilly St.* ● is in the nucleus of the theater district with both pre- and after-performance sittings. The talented Malcolm Livingston (see below) put it all together—and a beauty it is. Ground floor reception and lounge in salon style. Upstairs dining room with antique mirror over the stately hearth; pleated wall textiles and curtains; fine oil paintings. My traditional Southdown duck in spices was superb; veal and watercress also is excellent, but do leave space for the ambrosial summer pudding.

★★ **The Greenhouse** • *27a Hays Mews* • Situated a half-story below ground, white walls plus lazy ceiling fans, candles, and fresh flowers on the tables. Friendly professional reception with no haughty pretense; great variety in the menu. As with so many appealing places, it's the full experience that counts—and this one rates mighty high by that measure.

★★ **The English House** • *3 Milner St.* • This one is a cousin to the above Lindsay House and is similarly appealing. Emphasis is on ornate presentation. Indeed the house itself is a Victorian masterpiece. Ground-floor dining; a tier above for drinks and conversation; wonderful private salon above that. To some the decor may be stiffling, but it is a carefully groomed monument to a rich, bygone era.

★★ **English Garden** • *10 Lincoln St., near Sloane Sq.* • sprouted from the Milner St. concept and is directed by Malcolm Livingston, the genius who started Walton's. This one reveals a bit less frill and finesse but its atmosphere is more animated. Main restaurant in light restful tones enhanced by lots of glass. Upper salon for more private gatherings. A fashionable spot and not terribly expensive.

☆☆ **Eatons** • *49 Elizabeth St., off Ebury St.* • A mere 12 tables in 2 cozy adjoining rooms; beige Hessian walls; attractive art; white timber beams. Its modest menu and wine list (the house red is quite nice and reasonably priced) belie the splendid quality produced in the kitchen. Some selections to try: the melon with shrimp and avocado, the salmon blinis, the curry chicken pancakes, the veal scallop, the pork with red cabbage in a pastry shell. For such reliable quality, tariffs are surprisingly reasonable. Closed Sun.; dinner only served on Sat.

★★ **Frederick's** • *in Camden Passage* • Two unusually attractive dining levels, with the upper one displaying a variety of wines; lower segment, down a few steps, fronted by tall wide windows overlooking a garden patio. Popular and worthy.

☆☆☆ **Boulestin** • *1A Henrietta St.* • offers an elegant salon with gleaming old chandeliers and cunning illumination; a constant parade of inventive dishes from imaginative chef Kevin Kennedy; meticulous attention from staffers; very well regarded—and with good reason.

Turner's • *87 Walton St.* • is in the city's prime restaurant district and Brian Turner has one of the top names in gastronomy. Then why weren't several tries at the tables very rewarding? The frontage of blue enameled cottage windows is appealing; the interior is fresh; Mr. Turner is hospitable, but the pudding was not proof of his exalted reputation.

La Croisette • *168 Ifield Rd.* • recalls a Riviera mood, contrived as it is with service personnel in oystermen's sweatshirts, iced seafood displays, and artwork of the Cote d'Azur. I thought the entrance tatty; it led down a chipped and scruffy spiral staircase to a miserably ventilated arched cellar. Extremely cordial reception; immediate offer of an *aperitif,* gratis; abundant and superior set meal, plus rather expensive wines. Closed Mon. and lunch time, except on Sun.

Le Suquet • *around the corner from Walton's on Draycott Ave.* • This one, operated by the La Croisette people, is done with open beams, stucco walls, bottle-glass windows, tiny flower bouquets and candlesticks on dark blue cloths; the floors are tiled, the chairs small, the atmosphere Provencal. Waiters in blue sweaters serve better wares, in my opinion, than their colleagues at the alma mater.

Quai St. Pierre • *Stratford Rd.* • is another member of the La Croisette sisterhood. More Old World in style; busy and upbeat; brightly illuminated. Different and deserving of attention.

Inigo Jones • *14 Garrick St.* • is tucked away in a former mission house in the heart of the theatrical district. It's so expensive nowdays that unless you've got to go, you need not bother. First courses about £9; main dish around £20; cheese £6. The menu *suggests* a 15% tip, which is then automatically tacked onto your bill. How's *that* for the power of suggestion?

Medium-priced Dining

☆☆☆ **Harveys** • *2 Bellevue Rd., S.W. 17* • is in a grim area south of the river, but Chef Marco White is changing the local ecology. Fresh lighthearted vernal decor; highly inventive dishes with set menus from $25 to $45 at lunch and a bit more at dinner. An astounding value that brings new adventure to the table.

☆☆☆ **L'Etoile** • *30 Charlotte St.* • started off nobly when this century was in diapers. How it continues to get better, I'll never understand—but it does. The French-based cuisine is, in fact, more delicate than that of some of the biggest names in Paris. The wines are exquisite and treated with grace and solemnity. Highly skilled waiters in swallowtail coats; yellow walls ending at a ruby border; red figured carpet. The same clientele keeps coming back delightful year after delightful decade.

★★ **Green's** • *opposite the Cavendish Hotel at 36 Duke St.* • evokes the atmosphere of a private club without any of the stuffy associations common to this English institution. Old World mood in a fresh setting; splendid reception and service; cheerful cocktail bar and champagne lounge; polished darkwood counter and banquettes; numerous Spy prints for decor; handsome paintings. The menu is extensive and praiseworthy for its dedication to British selections. Especially appealing are the dressed crab, grouse, and pheasant (in season). Both the toping and the dining segments are highly recommended.

Luigi's • *Tavistock St.* • is recommended especially as an after-the-final-curtain entry. Reservations a *must;* bid for more ingratiating upstairs perches.

Borgo San Frediano • *62 Fulham Rd.* • is honest, fun and good. Wonderful *antipasto* table at entrance; house wines excellent; palsy greeting and smiling, rushed service. A spot to enjoy—at about $22 per maw. **Sale e Pepe** (9 Pavilion Rd.) and **Montpeliano** (13 Montpelier St.) are so boisterous, and the latter is so snobby, that I can easily make it through this life and the next without 'em.

Jams • *42 Albemarle St. W.1* • has a window-fronted ground floor plus a cellar between which flit outlandish waiters in modish rags. Yuppies yup it up here on red pepper pancakes with smoked salmon and red caviar (the *only* red in their lives), goat cheese on warmed greens, and other queer creations. Pretense? You've got it.

English Traditional Dining

☆☆ **Simpson's-in-the-Strand** • *100 Strand* • around the corner from the Savoy, still lives up to its long and distinguished reputation. Men's Bar in cellar and venerable, paneled, ground-floor restaurant (ladies admitted to latter only Sats.); rich, decorous, comfortable main restaurant up 1 flight (ladies always welcome). Closed Sun.; mandatory to reserve in advance for lunch; it's custom to tip your carver. Two oddities: (1) gentlemen are requested not to smoke their pipes in the dining room, and (2) tea is available but politely discouraged here (Simpson's avows it's for teatime *only*—an hour when its portals are shut).

☆☆ **Rules** • *35 Maiden Lane* • also a short hike from the Savoy Hotel, presents a charming Edwardian impression of seediness. Creaky, rippled floors; dimensions cramped; friendly welcome. Game, pies, mutton chops, the hearty fare (and feel!) of Old England.

Wilton's • *55 Jermyn St.* • a turn-of-the-century period piece, appeals to well-heeled Edwardian traditionalists. Although roast beef is *not* the main attraction, it is always available and nearly always excellent. For decades this busy bistro has been famed for its piscatorial splendors, which retain the highest quality. The Oyster Bar is a pleasant voyage into the past; then sail home with savouries (such as welsh rarebit) or Old English puds (sample a syllabub).

George and Vulture • *3 Castle Court* • is a 2-story, open-grill rough-and-ready chophouse, with ancient, friendly waiters and a near-medieval setting; it claims title as the oldest tavern in existence, founded in A.D. 1175. Open for lunch only, Mon. through Fri.; go before 1 p.m. or after 1:45 p.m., because its regular stockbroker clientele keeps it jammed. Medium prices for no-nonsense cookery; more British than the British; you may have to share a table. Not spectacular, but veddy, veddy Plantagenet.

Seafood

☆☆☆☆ **Poissonnerie de l'Avenue** • *82 Sloane Ave., S.W. 7* • certainly must rate as one of the unsung maritime kings in Europe—and with prices so reasonable that you'll be happily surprised. A clublike nookery that grew over 2 oak-paneled floors; rouge carpets; chummy counter service plus numerous tables; specialties chalked onto a blackboard; big, varied menu; beautiful presentation; outstanding quality. Top recommendation, but getting a seat will be a problem. Lunchtime is easier than evening.

Scott's • *20 Mount St.* • is decked out with raspberry-damask wall coverings, marble columns, Spy prints on white brick, bas-relief panels, and crystal chandeliers. While it remains one of London's leading establishments, readers have complained lately; perhaps at such high tariffs they expect perfection.

★★ **Sheeky's** • *29-31 St. Martin's Court* • is for the broad-minded. Steamed or grilled seafood only (an oddball lease prohibits frying the fish). Old creaky atmosphere that I love; worn wooden floors; chummy service by waitresses in dental-assistant gowns. The steamed turbot is sinfully delicious; so is the grilled sole. Smack in the theatrical district so very useful to pre-show diners; also serving until 10:45 p.m. A 10-strike for no-frills sea fare.

Wheeler's • *19 Old Compton St.* • is the original link in the chain that includes **Vendome** and numerous others. I feel it is stale and needs revitalizing. **The Ivy** • *1 West St.* • was taken over by the Caprice interests and is now one of the best pre- and after-theater establishments in the Covent Garden district.

Manzi's • *corner Lisle and Leicester Sts., W.C.2* • is the oldest maritime den in London; reasonable tabs; grilled sole the specialty; unusually rewarding and money-saving.

Bentley's • *11 Swallow St.* • swims in as a firmly fleshed midtown wiggler. Busy ground-floor bar and oyster counter; one-room upstairs restaurant with azalea-red walls hung with paintings; unwatchful disattention by frumpy waitresses; rush-rush atmosphere. Cookery that is almost *too* simple (some would say "bland"); reasonable-to-rich prices.

Hotel Dining

☆☆☆☆☆ **Capital** • capitalizes on a well-deserved reputation for distinguished continental fare. The styling is another fillip of gracious swank and Louis XIV comforts. Few tables, so reserve ahead; small adjoining lounge for studying the tempting menu over an *aperitif.*

☆☆☆ **Halcyon** • offers its very springlike Kingfishers restaurant and inviting bar, opening onto a patio. It has quickly caught on with theatrical luminaries. Dishes are inventive, pique your imagination, and seldom let you down; wines are costly. A different experience.

☆☆ **Connaught Grill** • has been a fixture on the London scene for decades. It is traditional and reliable, but not exciting gastronomically. Sunday lunch in the dining room is an institution.

☆☆ **Savoy Grill** • also is a London staple, but the decor is cold. One of the fun snack spots in town is **The Upstairs,** overlooking the hotel entrance. Executive Chef Anton Edelmann wins praise from this book any mealtime.

★★ **The Buttery** • in the Berkeley is the nexus for an excellent buffet at midday with the accent on pasta and Mediterranean fish preparations at night. (More properly, these relate to the Adriatic, since so many recipes are Venetian.) This is an historic room that was taken almost intact from the older hotel in another part of London.

☆☆☆ **Claridge's** • has been given a shot of adrenaline, plus better lighting, and the chipper little cosmos known as the Causerie for buffet choices.

☆☆ **Ninety Park Lane** • is a delight in many ways. The aesthetics are superb; gastronomy varies; wine prices are thunderous. There's a sure command of comfort here.

Hyatt Carlton Tower's Rib Room • retains its mandate on beefeaters, but now is far more attractive than it was during the height of its popularity in the seventies.

☆☆☆ **Chelsea Room** • is also in the Carlton. Personally, I had always found it worlds better than its more famous companion. The staff attention is perfect; the crystal wall panels glisten as does the glassware on the tables; wide windows overlook the lovely park. Distinguished, but relatively unsung for such outstanding culinary performance.

☆☆☆☆ **Inn on the Park's** • parking places are mentioned under "Hotels"; chic and top quality.

★★★ **Meridien** • The Oak Room offers both English and Continental cuisine. It's a very handsome place, too, with a stellar chef.

Hilton • Conventional dining is available, but most people know it for the **Trader Vic's** polynesian hutch.

☆☆ **Intercontinental's Le Souffle** • offers a soignee effect evoked by an interior room (no windows) in rouge and black. Prices are as stunning as the surroundings. And the souffles live up to the promise.

Ritz • boasts one of the most gorgeous rotundas in Europe; the gastronomy has been noteworthy at times, but on a recent trial it varied between ho and hum. Director Terry Holmes undoubtedly will be giving this aspect full attention.

Dining Adventures?

Justin de Blank • *54 Duke St., W.1* • is a sort of do-it-yourself delicatessen for the celebrity set. This *is* the scene for take-it-home Londoners, tourists who are closet snackers back at their hotel rooms, and drop-ins. Cute and costly. You can also lunch on this master's recipes at **The General Trading Company** (144 Sloane St., Sloane Sq.) in between shopping.

☆☆ **Les 3 Plats** • *4 Sydney St. S.W.3* • and **Garvers** • *61–63 Lower Sloane St. S.W.1* • are attractive moderately priced creations of the famous Roux entrepreneurs. They have successfully brought down costs for high-grade cookery and served it in fresh appetizing surroundings. At the first I've tried lotte on a bed of spinach, boudin, and casoulette; all superb. The salmon mousse and duck in country sauce at the latter were also delectable. The first is cheerful and provincial while the second is sleek and contemporary.

Kosher Cookery?

Bloom's • *90 Whitechapel High St.* • is a no-nonsense ethnic paradise. Takeout order section and standup counters near the entrance where legions of ravenous lunchtime *landsleit* celebrate the glories of pastrami, corned beef, roast beef, chopped liver, tongue, and other inspired deli-cacies; table area with napery as white as a bar mitzvah boy's collar also jammed with midday mavens munching blintzes, gefilte fish, kreplach, and other traditional tempters.

The Widow Applebaum's • *46 S. Molton St.* • is a snack and sandwich noshery on a midtown pedestrian mall. (Remember that "corned beef" becomes "salt beef" in the land of the Picts.)

East Indian Curries?

☆☆☆ **Red Fort** • *77 Dean St. W.1* • Cool, but still exotic with dishes not often experienced in the west and from remote regions of India: Goa-style fish is one example.

☆☆☆ **Last Days of the Raj** • *22 Drury Lane* • Can you imagine Indian *nouvelle cuisine?* Here it is—light and lovely.

☆ **Shezan** • *16–22 Cheval Place* • a short walk from Harrods, is more traditional and quite costly. Ground floor entry; uninspired lower level with tile floor; brown and beige walls in brick or with textile covering; leather chairs. Excellent service.

Bombay Brasserie • *140 Gloucester Rd.* • weaves a spell of elegance while producing many delicious specialties. Try the vegetarian highlights.

Veeraswamy's • *99–101 Regent St., with entrance on Swallow St.* • is larger than Jamshid and more famous; residents often are cynical about this colorfully decorative old-timer, but year after year I find it provides top value. An Indian friend opined to us, "It suffers from having been the first of its kind in London."

Gaylord • *79 Mortimer St.* • possibly the plushiest exponent of tandoori cookery. This is an overnight marinade of chicken and kebabs baked in a special Indian oven (the "tandoori") and followed by the curry course.

Italian?

Quite a few already have been noted in the foregoing sections, but you might wish to add **La Lupa** • *23 Connaught St.* • and **Trattoria dei Pescatori** • *57 Charlotte St.* • to your list.

Chinese Food?

Tiger Lee • *251 Old Brompton Rd.* • has been, from time to time, one of the most talked about Chinese kitchens in Europe. I still find it distasteful in many respects—from pushy, hard-sell waiters to boring modernistic decor to undistinguished platters at head-thumping tabs (only the host receives the menu with the prices) to myriad mistakes in ordering and billing—which may or may not be intentional. Who needs it?

Zen • *Chelsea Cloisters on Sloane Ave. S.W.3, 20 Queen St., and 83 Hampstead High St.* • has developed a following at these three locations. I've tried only the first and that was splendid. Quite fashionable too.

Ken Lo's Memories of China • *67–69 Ebury St., plus the scenic latecomer at Chelsea Harbour* • and **Poons** • *King St., in Covent Garden, and not the hole-in-the-Chinese-Wall in Soho that also is called Poon's* • are recommendable chopstick stops; both are for the up-market trade. Decor smart and refined—like the clientele.

Tai Pan • *8 Egerton Garden Mews, S.W. 3* • pans out Hunan, Peking, and Szechuan cuisine. Downstairs site; carved wood dragon-motif buttresses; several intimate booths with slated wood benches overlooking other tables; open daily for lunch and dinner; happy, attentive staff; over 80 available dishes.

Lee Ho Fook • *15–16 Gerrard St.* • has a split personality; it is divided into 2 segments. Though the fancy address wins most of the attention, I've always much preferred the modest and cheaper family nookery just around the corner at 41–43 Wardour St. Look into both, and take your choice.

Good Friends • *139 Salmon Lane, E.14* • is an old-timer in Soho. Cantonese dishes at reasonable tariffs. Dull, no-nonsense ambience; on Sun., popular with Chinese Embassy personnel.

Gallery Rendezvous • *55 Beak St., W.1* • despite its unlikely name, specializes in northern fare; it is one of my favorites, as is the same-ownership **Dumpling Inn** • *15A Gerrard St.* • although the staff in the latter seemed to think it was bestowing a favor by serving mere mortals. (**Soho Rendezvous** and **Ley On's** are other members of this tong.)

Mr. Chow • *151 Knightsbridge* • remains a pacesetter for London's trendy set. I'm not a part of this trend and while I have enjoyed the cookery both here and at its Manhattan precincts, the service in both places has been as low as the prices were high.

Japanese?

Saga • *43 S. Molton St.* • offers a tavern atmosphere with open beams and booths; tables up front and cooking counter farther back; attractively costumed waitresses. The raw fish (very expensive) platter and tempura were excellent.

Masako • *St. Christopher's Place* • is in a charming mews amid antique shops and boutiques. Cork walls divided by black enamel beams; red carpets; small stage surrounded by bamboo; excellent sukiyaki, tempura, and many more Nipponese creations. Others in this group include **Sushi-Masa, Nanten, Ginnan, Nankin,** and **Hiroko** of the Kensington Hilton.

Tea Dancing?

The Waldorf Hotel • *Aldwych, W.C.2* • does a step backward in time each Friday and Sunday from 3:30 to 6:30 p.m. in the Palm Court. It takes some doing to distinguish the performers from the clients. A more down-market version of *the dansant* occurs daily at **Cafe de Paris** • *3 Coventry St., W.1* • beginning at 3 p.m. Both can be fun in their manneristic manners, but the tea and nibbles are better at the Waldorf.

NOTE · · · Covent Garden, the central London complex that features its renowned Opera House, today blossoms with scores of restaurants and shops. The fun here is plucking just the flower that suits your mood. **Chelsea Harbour** is the hottest spot in the burgeoning docklands. The central building is in Sing Sing architecture, containing several eateries: the previously noted **Ken Lo's, Deals** (a noisy tavern with California-style cookery), **Chantegrill** (steakhouse with a salad table and heaps of flowers), and the **Waterfront** (oyster bar plus many Italian choices). Take a stroll in the marina afterward.

DRINKS

Plus Pubs and Wine Bars

The celebrated Public House—"pub," for short—traditionally has been the heartbeat of England. On one side you'll find the Public Bar—plain, utilitarian, for drinkers who want no nonsense. On the other side, with a separate entrance, is the Saloon Bar—better decorated, more comfortable, the one you'll probably head for. Prices are usually a trifle higher in the latter. Then, of course, there are 3 styles of classic pubs: City Tavern (spirits and wine featured above draught beers), Gin Palace (typically Victorian if authentic), and Alehouse (plain, ancient, and historic).

As for what to order, there are 3 major British brews: Mild ale ("mild"), a medium-sweet, medium-brown, inexpensive choice which is becoming more rare in central London; bitter beer ("bitter"), a pale brown, heavier variety; and Burton ("old"), which is deep brown, quite sweet, and richest of all. Burton is available September and June only.

Beer, gin, rum, and liqueurs are plentiful and good; Scotch is costly (it's weaker than that which reaches the U.S.). You'll pay £1 for a "small" (Understatement of the Year) and perhaps £2 for a "large' (junior-size) portion in today's London.

English wine? Local viticulture gradually is coming to harvest—a very slow process if you consider that the Romans, the Normans, and the British of the Middle Ages had vines growing all over London. Today, Harrods carries a sampling of the 140 products from England's commercial vineyards. Some of the more notable names include Beaulieu, Felsted, Pilton Manor, Hambledon, Kelsale, Hascombe, Cavendish Manor, Lamberhurst, and Chilsdown. I doubt that you'll become addicted.

NOTE · · · *Don't drive a car if you have consumed even as little as 2 pints of beer!!* Under the mercilessly stringent provisions of the Road Safety Act, the vehicle operator doesn't have to be drunk to face huge fines, 4 months in the pokey (or both), and loss of his or her license for one year. Suspects are required to take a roadside "Breathalyser" test. There is no recourse for either resident or visitor. The police are tough, too.

Characteristic Pubs

Cockney Pride • *Jermyn St.* • Large cellar room festooned with cornball Victorianisms; old-fashioned horseshoe bar offering such Olde Englande standards as faggots (mincemeat-and-peas pudding), toad-in-the-hole (sausages in batter pudding), shepherd's pie, and many more historic tidbits—all priced at a pittance. Waiters in fancy vests and bowlers; waitresses in long Gay Nineties gowns; player piano tinkling in the background.

Red Lion • *48 Parliament St.* • is a favorite with students from Guys Hospital. The Public Bar is on Parliament Street, the Saloon Bar on Derby Gate. Downstairs is best; no darts; ladies welcome.

Antelope • *Eaton Terrace* • is a gem—not too moldy, not too chichi, a gentle introduction to the science of pubbery. Prices higher than average, but *still* low; excellent for a plain, cheerful dinner.

Prospect of Whitby • *57 Wapping Wall* • like the Cheshire Cheese (where you should be sure to sit at Samuel Johnson's table) and the George and Vulture, is a tavern drawing huge numbers of tourists rather than a true pub. It once installed a Hawaiian band and a singer—to me, the ultimate abomination in these ancient English surroundings. Hangout of students who are sometimes rowdy. Dock area; rambling, helter-skelter building raised in 1520; Pepys Room for dining; stuffed alligator, human skull, and other oddities suspended over bar. Closed Sun. (**Dirty Dick's** and **The George** also attract droves of rubber-neckers.)

Sherlock Holmes Tavern • *Northumberland St.* • is a so-called museum tavern. On the ground floor, you'll find the main bar, a scattering of tables, and, as wall decorations, a fascinating collection of "memorabilia" from his most famous "cases" (a plaster mold of a "paw print" of the hound of the Baskervilles, Detective Lestrade's "handcuffs," the "code" used in the story of the dancing men, etc.); to the side there's a painfully plain little nook for the earnest toper. Upstairs is the grill, with tapestried wall coverings and white banquettes; to the rear of this section is a glassed-off montage of the famous fictional sitting room shared by the great sleuth and Dr. Watson at "221-B Baker St." Food adequate for pub (not restaurant) level.

Dickens Inn • *St. Katharine's Docks, near the Tower of London* • The quay area stirs merrily with life aboard several Thames barges and scores of recreation boats. The restaurant is located upstairs in an ancient warehouse that was moved on wheels to this colorful site. The neighboring **Beefeater** is chiefly for dining and a touristic type of cabaret evening.

The **Buccaneer** • *Leicester Square* • is an imposing example of its name-sake. There's a galleon theme floating on a Polynesian undercurrent.

Not enough? Then try these: For visual appeal the **Admiral Codrington** • *Mossop St.* • for filmmakers, the **Intrepid Fox** • *Wardour St.* • for doctors, the **Crown** • *in Chelsea* • for rowing enthusiasts, **The Dove** • *Upper Mall* • for old-time smugglers, **Anchor** • *Bankside, Southwash* • for world travelers, the **Fitzroy** • *Charlotte St.* • for cinema types, **The Victoria** • *10 Strathearn Pl.* • for experimental theater, **The King's Head** • *the back room at 115 Upper St. in the antique district of Islington* • for Egyptologists, the **Museum Tavern** • *Great Russell St.* • for Members of Parliament, the **St. Stephen's Tavern** • *just a skip from Westminster* • (listen for the bell—a signal that a vote is about to be taken in the Commons).

Wine Bars

Doubtless these are beginning to supplant the pubs. These colorful oases serve quiches, goulash, cold meats, pates, and cheeses, generally in the range of £2 per platter or less. An overwhelming variety of fair-quality wine is on hand for prices which vary with the quantity you order (pitcher or individual glass); fortified pressings are also on tap. In most cases they function from 11:30 a.m. till 3 p.m., and 5:30 p.m. till 11 p.m.; some remain open later and on Sun.; the hours are extremely variable. Although tipping is not expected in pubs, it is definitely required in wine bars, especially when food is consumed; 10% is considered reasonable.

Le Metro • *28 Basil St.* • the most talked about conversation pit in London, is downstairs in **L'Hotel.** A wine bar with super food that is supervised by the Capital chef. Top-grade vintages are available by the glass.

Ebury • *139 Ebury St. S.W.1* • occupies the ground floor of a converted early Victorian house with walls of dark green wash and cream paint. The salads are excellent. One nice feature: tables can be reserved.

Downs • *5 Down St. W.1* • operates on 2 floors joined by a central spiral staircase. Large bar upstairs with stools; downstairs food counter with inviting display of meats. Candlelit and intimate; convenient to residents of Park Lane and Piccadilly hotels.

Ruby's • *28 Sussex Place, W.2* • resides in a quiet backwater opposite the Victoria Tavern—but that's the only thing quiet about it, because as the shades of evening are lowered, its 3 floors are jammed with eager conversationalists.

Mother Bunch's • *under the Arches F and G in Old Sealcoal Lane, (E.C.4) behind Ludgate Circus* • The Dickensian flavor is strong; cuisine varies from the simple to the truly luxurious.

Wine Bar • *Villiers St.* • quite literally *is* a hole-in-the-wall. I like its food and its kookiness.

Russkies • *6 Wellington Terrace, Bayswater Road, W.2* • is a long cellar combining both Victorian and modern elements.

Slatters • *3 Panton St., Haymarket, S.W.1* • is a standby for the theater crowd, possibly because of the unusually friendly service. **Motcomb's** • *26 Motcomb St., S.W.1* • is the sovereign of the fashionable Belgravia district. Thick wall-to-wall carpeting and banquette seating add to the feeling of poshness upstairs. Go to **Swifts** • *93–97 Pelham St., S.W. 7* • if you are looking for scrubbed wooden floors, an authentic oak bar, an inviting gallery, and seafood specialties.

Cork & Bottle • *44–46 Cranbourn St., W.C.2* • is reached through a garden gate and composed of 2 adjoining cellars. Its New Zealand owner strives to add adventure to the cookery. A good candidate for a pretheater nip.

Penny's Place • *6 King St., Covent Garden, W.C.2* • is colorful mainly because of its location. **Blake's,** in the same neighborhood, is appealing to the eye and handy for theatergoers, but my several samplings of the food were grim news for the taste buds. **Bailey's** • *41 North Audley St., W.1* • is strongly influenced by its proximity to the U.S. Embassy.

Crawfords • *10–12 Crawford St., W.1* • is a candlelit hideaway with soft popular music in the early evening followed by entertainment later on. Half of the premises comprise a restaurant in which tables may be reserved.

The Loose Box • *7 Cheval Place, S.W.7* • is popular with young people who don't seem to be bothered by un-loosened pursestrings. Costly.

Fino's Wine Cellar ● *123 Mount St., W.1* ● is approached by a steep staircase beneath its stained glass and wooden canopy. The bar is long and narrow, with small recesses for those who may collapse in obscurity. Very "in" with the advertising world.

The Loose Rein ● *221 Kings Road, S.W.3* ● is a modern spacious basement beneath a wine emporium.

COUNTRY DINING NEAR LONDON

All of the following are easy excursions on a sunny day.

☆☆☆☆☆ **L'Ortolan ●** *on Church Lane in the village of Shinfield (near Reading)* ● remains a national asset to gastronomy and certainly it stands proudly against any offerings on the Continent too. Elegant country house and garden; bar lounge just off entrance; lawn tables for sunny days; inner salons plus an airy, charming conservatory. John Burton-Race is a young genius whose gifts are revealed in the composition, the exquisite presentation, and the harmonious yet complex evocations of his kitchen. As he is continually experimenting, the dishes change with frequency. His amiable French wife Christine can help you decide on a cascade of jewel-like combinations from his modern masterworks. Cold stoves Sunday evenings and all Mondays; best to phone for a table (0734) 883783. Watch this one for stellar recognition.

★★★★★ **Gravetye Manor ●** Refer to "East Grinstead," where it is *not,* but where it is *near.* To get there, take A-22 (the Eastbourne Road); about 7 miles past Godstone, at the crossroads, turn right on B-2028 to Turner's Hill. *Advance reservations advised;* if you get lost, phone 0342–810567 and a St. Bernard with a packed hamper will be promptly dispatched.

The Compleat Angler ● at *Marlow, Buckinghamshire* (31 miles) with riverside or garden-front bedrooms and private baths. This inn—with its famous but not terribly inspired Valaison restaurant and cheerful bar—which sits beside a peaceful view on the Thames, reaches a pinnacle of pastoral beauty. My repeat try at the tables was dismal, however.

★ **Ye Olde Bell,** *Hurley* ● *Berkshire* (32 miles; about ½-hour beyond Northold on M-4), dates from A.D. 1135; for overnighters, 25 rooms. It's oozing with lazy charm; sound but not top-London-class fare at top London-class prices; limited selections.

Berkshire

☆☆☆☆ **Waterside Inn ●** *Bray* (31 miles) is an evergreen veteran, a training ground for great young chefs and a frequent shrine for gourmets. A recent sampling proved to be superb, but there have been less glorious moments. The experience of going is enchanting—and the food can be too. Reserve ahead.

The Great House and **French Horn** • both in *Sonning-on-Thames* (36 miles), a captivating rural village; in the former you may enjoy country roast beef while watching the boats skim past, and in the latter (more costly), across the bridge, you'll find an even better river view, but the specialties are more continental.

King's Head • at *Little Marlow* (5 miles from Maidenhead) is still another worthy destination on a clear day. The **Little Angel** in *Remenham* (36 miles) is a cozy and genial retreat across the bridge from Henley; solid, unelaborate cookery; nice clientele. **Skindle's Hotel,** *Maidenhead* (27 miles), once the pick of the area, has skidded in my view. No longer recommended.

★★★ **Bel and The Dragon** • has resided in *Cookham Village* since the reign of Henry V, early in the 15th-century. It is constructed of wattle and daub, with plenty of open beams, signets of age, and cozy warmth. Swiss ownership and management; fair cuisine; medium prices. "Bel," incidentally, is derived from the name of a Babylonian idol. Even if you don't dine here, do stop for a drink in the bar and look around.

Bedfordshire

★★★ **Paris House** • (42 miles) is located beautifully inside famous **Woburn Park,** already mentioned in the introduction to this chapter. Distinguished cuisine in a stately setting. Closed Mon.; also Sun. eves in winter.

Hertfordshire

The Marquee • at *Hertford,* halfway 'twixt London and Cambridge, is a beloved proponent of English dishes. Witness: Moneybags of Apple and Pear (order first or there won't be any left) or Trinity College's Burn't Cream; Rack of Southdown Lamb in Pastry; Choux Swans with trout filling—the list is devastating. Also many prime international specialties. Two dining salons: upstairs romantic, downstairs plush, with owner Norman Swallow dashing between the two.

Surrey

Mayflower Hotel • *Cobham* (19 miles), is a plushy oasis for the Hungry Man; also nice here is the **Talbot,** which boasts ownership of Nelson's chair. **Whyte Harte** • *Bletchingley* (22 miles), a 14th-century inn with old beams, open fireplaces, and better-than-routine vittles supervised by C. H. Mathews. The **Old Bell** • *Oxted* (22 miles), another inn of the same vintage without quite the flavor of the Whyte Harte, but very pleasant all the same. **Onslow Arms** • *West Clandon* near Guildford (about 30 miles), an A.D. 1623 roadside hostelry thick with atmosphere, and mellow with its Free House varieties of beer, ale, and porter. **Great Fosters,** *Egham* (18 miles) features unique 4-centuries-old gardens and 23 guest rooms for lovers of antiquities and service.

Sussex

The Maltravers • *Arundel* (58 miles) is in the forefront with its gastronomic delights, its furnishings of rare antiques and fine paintings, and its unusual policy, for rural establishments, of staying open until 11 p.m. or after; closed Mon.; as good as ever.

NIGHT LIFE

London's nightscape—as in Paris, New York, Hamburg, and a host of other cities where the moon is better known than the sun—*is one of the fastest-changing in the world.* Entertainment establishments rise and fall so swiftly that even the most up-tonight tip sheets have difficulty keeping *au courant.* If you are looking for something special, ask the night hall porter at your hotel.

The expensive **Royal Roof** of the Royal Garden Hotel gracefully combines sophistication and well-trained staffers with a fine flair for theatrics. Beautiful presentation of The Royal Strings, a harmonic blend of 7 violins, a guitar, and an accordion that plays en masse for several numbers, then the musicians individually stroll among the diners while maintaining perfect melodic unison; 20-minute performances at 11 p.m. and midnight.

Tiberio (22 Queen St.) offers most of its glitter in the celebs who attend. Piano tunes during dinner; live quartet for dancing. Kitchen work chiefly Italian.

Elysee (13 Percy St.) is a haven that effuses a Hellenic charm all its own. The decor is routine, but when the crowd is right it's delightfully lively. Big Greek patronage—and what people are merrier? Ground floor with 15 tables, a small bar and dance floor, 3 to 4 musicians (*bouzouki* and accordion). Summer roof garden for nearly 100 midday or evening munchers, some of whom spontaneously leap up to provide impromptu entertainment; hours noon to 3 p.m. and 6:30 p.m. to 3 a.m.

Among the hotels, the **Savoy,** the **Inn on the Park** (Vintage Room only), the **Hilton,** and **Grosvenor House** all offer the Light Fantastic in their restaurants (separate from their grills); **Claridge's** doesn't believe in all that jazz.

Private and chic?

Ask friends to squeeze you in to **Groucho's, Ormond's, Regine's** (only a stagger from veteran **Annabel's**), **Stringfellows,** or **Tramps.** All of these are in the forefront of tonight's London cafe society scene. You'll need local sponsorship and perhaps about $400 if you wish to join. (Temporary membership is less if they permit it.)

Gambling?

Almost everything goes except pitch-and-toss—a game played by miners that all too quickly can involve staggering sums. British casinos have few slot machines (fruit machines, in local parlance); the fancier clubs scorn them. Horses, dogs, football, the gender of an expected royal heir—just name it, and somebody will snap up your wager, but usually in one of England's 2000 licensed betting offices. Better bring cash or traveler's checks, not personal checks, if you plan to play. Some houses are stricter than others about this. Stringent laws now require visitors to register in advance at the clubs where they wish to gamble.

NOTE · · · *Pick your place carefully, especially if you roll 'em high!*

Meal and spirits services follow the more lenient rules governing pubs; no alcohol is libated at the gaming tables; hours also can vary with the neighborhood, so it would be wise to check first if you wish to imbide at gaming tables.

The **Victoria** (150–162 Edgware Rd., W.2), possibly the largest contender in the British Isles *or* Europe, might be termed a "gambling factory." Production-belt operation that woos "mass" (*vs.* "class") patronage; 1st floor featuring blackjack, roulette (London's wheels have only one zero, not two), and chemin de fer; 2nd level offering gin rummy and *kaluki* (13-card rummy); 2 slot machines; restaurant service from lunch to breakfast. Only this house and the **Sportsman** (Tottenham Ct. Rd.) offer craps in London (with slightly more favorable odds than in the U.S.).

The **Clermont Club** (44 Berkeley Sq.)—with 85% of its 5000 disciples from overseas—is known to be chic. The stakes are high and the membership is ultraexclusive.

Rendezvous (Hilton) lures many Middle Easterners.

Historic and famous **Crockford's** (30 Curzon St.) is operated by Curzon House. It's a staple.

Other choices in this group include the **Charlie Chester Casino** at 12 Archer St. (functioning noon to you-name-it, with roulette, blackjack, and Las Vegas dice); and the **Golden Nugget** at 22 Shaftesbury Ave. (6 types of play). None of these measures up to the establishments listed above. Still other boxcar candidates include a casino in the **Sheraton Park Tower;** one operates in the cellar of the **Ritz** (refer back to "Hotels"), where the French Salon features blackjack, American roulette, and punto banco; the **Sportsman** (3 Tottenham Ct. Rd., W.1).

Discotheques?

These, of course, are among the most perishable of all institutions in the entertainment field. They pop up quickly (generally with insufficient investment capital), stay "in" for a short lifetime, and fold up when the "chic" crowd takes its fickle fancies elsewhere.

Shaftesbury's seems to be the focal point tonight. A modest fee is charged to enter (higher on weekends), but whatever the fee, it will be long remembered back in Duluth. Food and beverages stretch the imagination for exotica. **Burlesque** (14 Bruton Place) appears to be an evergreen winner after sunset. With its combo-notion of recorded and live music, it can also be the noisiest. Friday nights come on the jammiest; prices are average. **Gullivers** (11 Down St., W.1) is more upbeat than its address might suggest. **Studio Valbonne** (62 Kingly St.), with excellent music for dancers, is averred to stage topless waitresses around a swimming pool. **Miranda,** across the street, is popular at lunchtime with well-groomed gents from the financial district. **Speakeasy** (48 Margaret St.) speaks boldly. **Hippodrome, Le Palais,** and **Curzon** also seem to hang in there as stalwarts. Next comes the **Saddle Room** (1-A Hamilton Mews). Gussied-up tack stall; rustic paneling; main dance floor plus upper tier; running strong from 10 p.m. to 4 a.m.; better than it was. **Lulu's** (9 Young St.) is aptly sited; very "with it."

SHOPPING

SHOPPING HOURS: London, in general, 9 a.m.–5:30 p.m.; large department stores as well as other shops open on a specific weeknight (Thurs. on Oxford St., Regent St., Bond St., Kensington High St.; Wed. in Knightsbridge and on King's Rd. and Sloane Sq.); smaller shops in Chelsea, Soho, and similar districts close at 1 p.m. on Thurs., but usually operate all day Sat.; Covent Garden shops open from 10 a.m. until 8 p.m. Mon. through Sat. A High Court ruling last year has given merchants the right to remain open on Sun. However, it is advisable to check before setting out.

BEST AREAS: London can be divided roughly into seven main zones: (1) Oxford St. (big department stores, chain operations, and boutiques), (2) Regent St. (more department stores and specialty shops), (3) Bond St. (high fashion, jewelry, and exclusive luxury items, (4) Kensington High St. (boutiques, chain stores, antiques), (5) King's Road, Sloane Sq., and Fulham Rd. (youthful fashions, oddments, and "in" articles), (6) Knightsbridge (Harrods and Harvey Nichols the two most exclusive department stores, other top name shops and fashionable boutiques) (7) Covent Garden (a potpourri).

SAVINGS ON PURCHASES: Most goods may be purchased by *overseas visitors* without the 17.5% VAT tax, of which you get back 14.89% of the retail price. There are, however, additional charges to be considered too. (See below.) Stores are not required to operate this scheme and those that do usually require a minimum to be spent.

NOTE · · · Tourist Tax Free Shopping is a streamlined refund service subscribed to by over 12,000 shops in Britain. Participating merchants display the "Tax Free for Tourists" red, white, and blue sticker. Vouchers have been simplified and can be issued for as little as £50, but the big department stores require that you spend anywhere from £75–150. They also tack on a handling charge for doing the paperwork. (This could change but the store will advise you.) Once stamped by Customs all the forms can be returned in *one* envelope to the appropriate company and the refund is made quickly by *one* check to the purchaser's home address in his own currency, or the payment can be reflected on a credit card account. Remember that a small administration charge has been deducted when the store has filled in the voucher.

ANTIQUES, CHINA, GLASS, AND GIFTS: The General Trading Company (Mayfair) Ltd. (144 Sloane St., Sloane Square, 10 Argyle St., *Bath,* and 2–4 Dyer St., *Cirencester*) occupies elegant headquarters in 4 gracious, spacious, serene, Edwardian mansions. In antiques, English period pieces, prints, pewter, china, and *objets d'art* are the specialties. Also on parade are comprehensive displays of modern bone china and fine table glass in quantities; a big and versatile gift department of handicrafts, leather work, porcelain cachepots, picnic accessories; a garden department; a soft furnishings department with imaginative and tasteful fabrics for contemporary or period decoration. Safe shipment is guaranteed to any place on the globe.

BOOKS: As most travelers know, **Foyle** (113–119 Charing Cross Road) is probably the world's biggest bookshop with an inventory of 4-million volumes. While there, we'd suggest that you inquire about the famous monthly Literary Luncheons at the Dorchester, which no U.S. booklover should *think* of missing. Wonderful!

BURBERRYS RAINWEAR AND APPAREL: Since Thomas Burberry invented his celebrated waterproof cloth around 1856, **Burberrys** (18 Haymarket and 165 Regent St.) has become a familiar name to literally millions of shoppers from Tampa to Tokyo. Here are probably the world's finest weatherproofs under the sun (*and* clouds!). Because the "Burberry Look" has developed into such a highly fashionable rage, you'll find the crowning glories of all: trench coats and overcoats lined in that unmistakable, instantly identifiable Burberrys's check, plus a vast assortment of supremely chic Burberrys's luggage and umbrellas, a complete floor for ladies' topcoats, as well as a distinguished selection of casuals and knitwear and a forest of tweeds, beautifully soft cashmeres, and camelhairs. You should request details about the personalized monogrammed label. Now you'll find sunglasses, wristwatches, food, and toweling with their own special stamp. At Haymarket ask for Mr. Jordan; at Regent St., Mr. Auld will be your special mentor. These gentlemen understand North American tastes and will go all out to be helpful (as will all the Burberrys sales staff).

CHINA: Chinacraft has been the peerless leader for four decades. What inventory they carry! Furthermore, they have taken over London. A few addresses: 556 Oxford St., 7/11 Burlington Arcade, 130 New Bond St., 198 Regent St. **The Reject China Shops** (134 Regent St. and Beauchamp Place) don't only specialize in "rejections." The word only indicates that the prices for fine pieces are dramatically low, made possible through the enormous sales volume of this merchandiser. Both are tops in their individual categories.

DEPARTMENT STORES: Harrods, Marks & Spencer, Peter Jones, Selfridges, John Lewis, Peter Robinson, House of Fraser (Oxford St. and Kensington), **Dickins & Jones, Harvey Nichols & Co.**

ENGLISH LIFESTYLES: Mulberry (11/12 Gees Court, St. Christopher's Place) offers the mood of Britain in clothing, accessories, leather, rainwear and casual togs for both sexes. The quality and selectivity are phenomenal. One of the best stops in all of England to enjoy this microcosm of distinctive dress.

ENAMELS, PORCELAINS, and ANTIQUES: At **Halcyon Days** (14 Brook St., Mayfair, W.1, and 4 Royal Exchange, Cornhill, E.C.3) the 18th-century art of English enameling flourishes once more. Thanks to the efforts of Susan Benjamin, the owner, this revived Georgian craft offers a vast range of exquisitely tasteful collectables. For each Christmas, Valentine's Day, and Mother's Day a box is introduced with a new design; there is also a Year Box suitable to commemorate a special event on your calendar; egg-shaped boxes with zodiacal signs are popular; museum selections, venerable institutions and historical occasions are represented (often in limited editions); themes refer to music, sports, animals, flowers, heraldry, and many other topics. Twelve dainty thimbles with a blossom and quotation for each month can be purchased singly or with a display stand for the whole set. Boxes carry messages such as ''Thank you,'' ''Happy Birthday,'' and ''With our love,'' to mention just a few. Unique designs on a commission basis may be obtained as well.

FOOD DELICACIES: Fortnum & Mason (Piccadilly) is the only store we know where the clerk who fetches your can of tomato soup wears a cutaway coat and striped pants. Its downstairs restaurant for light lunches is popular and good. There are splendid Food Halls in Harrods and Selfridges department stores.

FOOTWEAR: Church & Co. (58 Burlington Arcade) is a classic and the quality hasn't varied in a century, though the styles have. **Alan McAfee** (5 Cork St.) has been the choice of discerning men worldwide for many years too.

GOLDEN JEWELRY: Lalaounis (*174 New Bond St.*) is the established name in this Greek and Byzantine field. Happily, you don't have to travel all the way out to Athens to see it and buy it. What a glorious collection.

HATS: Continuously since 1759, there has existed only one top-ranking center in the western world—**James Lock & Co. Ltd.** (6 St. James's St.). The lid of this prize package is the hat—every conceivable male headgear. Be sure to ask for the ever-cordial Mr. Brine.

IRISH SPECIALTIES: The Irish Shop (11 Duke St.). If you're not visiting the Emerald Isle, this house offers its specialties right in the heart of London.

JEWELRY: Garrard (112 Regent St.) began business in 1735 and has been serving English sovereigns and subjects with equal dedication ever since. Prices cover such a range that you might shop for a monarch's crown or a nephew's frivolity as the mood strikes.

MEDITERRANEAN MOODS: Casa Pupo (56 Pimlico Rd.) stocks joyful ceramics, table decorations, wicker accessories and the fun elements of Europe's Latin climes. Very uplifting in any household.

MEN'S TAILOR: Chester Barrie (32 Savile Row), **Scherer & Nilsson** (33 Old Burlington St.), and **Benson Perry & Whitley** (9 Cork St.) are all houses of fine repute.

PERFUMES AND TOILETRIES: **House of Floris** (89 Jermyn St.) To cross the threshold here is to take a fascinating step into this empire's history. A family institution founded in 1730 and Perfumers to H.M. The Queen, it remains irresistibly alluring with its heavenly arrays of exquisite flower fragrances set in an unhurried atmosphere of elegance. One of its latest ambrosias for ladies is "Zinnia," a blend of summer flowers enriched with rose, violet and iris, and hints of spice. There are 18 classics such as Florissa, Lily of the Valley, Red Rose, and Stephanotis, plus scents for the home and potpourris. You'll receive a 10% discount on all mail orders. Ask for the comprehensive free catalog.

SADDLER: **W. & H. Gidden Ltd.** (15d New Clifford St., Bond St.), established in 1806, is 7th heaven for the equestrian.

SHIRTMAKERS: **Hilditch & Key** seems to command the best properties on Jermyn St.—at #s 73, 37, and 87 (as well as at Harrods)—the traditional lane for such specialty attire. And today women also can take advantage of their historic talents. **Turnbull & Asser,** a few doors away, has a choice of materials that is full of verve.

SHOTGUNS: **Purdey** (57–58 S. Audley St.)—but only if your banker calls you "Mr. Niarchos," because that storied "pair of Purdeys" will set you back at least $16,000. **Holland & Holland** (13 Bruton St.), also remarkable, comes next on the ladder.

SILVER AND JEWELRY: **Mappin & Webb** (170 Regent St.) is the first in this traditional prestige industry. The sterling is glorious, but the Mappin Plate (at one-fifth the price) is also superb. It contains many of the sterling designs and comes with a lifetime guarantee.

SPORTING EQUIPMENT AND SPORTSWEAR: If you were an Abercrombie & Fitch fan, you'll revel in the overseas twin, **Lillywhites** (Piccadilly Circus), the best known and most exciting center of its type abroad.

STATIONER: **Frank Smythson Ltd.** (54 Bond St.), which holds the Royal Warrant of Stationers to Her Majesty the Queen, is a delight.

LUDLOW **Feathers** fluffs up a half-timbered facade, a bevy of bedchambers dripping with Shopshire history and an oak-and-brick restaurant that should take you back to 1565 faster than the Shrewsbury Stage.

LUTON Charter airline flights often land or start from here. If you are stuck, the 151-room **Strathmore** is a fair choice for clean, modern accommodation.

MIDHURST This medieval hamlet, similar to Rye, is proud of its twin-winged A.D. 1430 and A.D. 1650 **Spread Eagle.** White Tudor facade; skylit entrance; beamed dining room with copper-clad hearth and talon-to-talon tables affording fine views of the courtyard. Trio of bars including the vaulted Coal Hole; a dart room; heavily timbered hunting theme lounge; the Cromwell nook, where The Protector hanged his adversaries. The 20-chamber **Angel** might be heaven for those seeking a more central location, more informality, less deliberate charm, and less pretension than its more famous opponent.

MELTON MOWBRAY   **Stapleford Park** is near *Leicester* and *Oakham* (see below). The estate gained fame for its thunderous rates, its palsy publicity hype, and its decorative daring, which employed numerous talents to take respective creative cracks at individual "Signature" bedrooms. Uniquely flamboyant concept, not at all cohesive, and an outright challenge to British Establishment mores. But why not take a new course since the lord of this manorism is Bob Payton, a fast-food mogul from Chicago? His Payton Place has American dash plus a mixture of European panache.

NEWBRIDGE   The **Rose Revived** is a favorite stop in Oxfordshire, a sweet inn at the junction of the Thames and the Windrush. The kitchen's good, too.

NEWCASTLE   The **Gosforth Park,** overlooking the racecourse, romps over the finish line by at least several lengths. Handsome Brandling Grill; adjoining Silver Ring Bar; fitness center and wonderful sport and leisure facilities, plus barber and beauty salons, a sauna, boutiques, and a riding school. The **Royal Station** in midcity offers solid comfort in rather dull surroundings. The **County,** in the Gosforth stable, is a mod-lined shoo-in for its moderate stakes. Its elegant paneled dining salon is especially attractive at night. The 8-story **Swallow** is close on its heels. **Gateshead Swallow,** at **Gateshead,** is more of the same. There's a young challenger in the 151-unit **Holiday Inn.** Newcastle is nearly always jammed with business travelers and conventioneers. Be sure your booking is confirmed before arrival. Dining? Much of it is done in the hotel restaurants.

NEW MILTON

☆☆☆☆ **Chewton Glen,**   a stately Georgian mansion growing within a sea of flowers 90 miles southwest of London, is one of the most glorious inns in England. Red brick edifice sprinkled with green shutters; convenient and attractive parking entry; homey lobby; thickly carpeted, book-lined Sun Lounge; Marryat Restaurant with justifiably renowned fare; Garden Room dinery, cocktail bar, 2 indoor tennis courts; leisure club; indoor-outdoor swimming pool; small golf facility. Main house expanded gracefully on garden side; independent wing reached by a covered walkway just the ticket for romantic types. There are color TVs throughout the house and many additional sparklers that heighten the luster of this gem. Proprietor Martin Skan and his cheerful aide Brigitte Stuart are working wonders here—virtual perfection at expensive tariffs that merit every single pence. (Incidentally, if you are making your way between Southampton and London, here is a gracious alternative to England's dismal port city.) For your booking convenience, The Glen has strung up a direct telephone reservation line on the 800 system: 1–800–344–5087. A bell-ringer it is!

NORWICH   a lovely town of Saxon and Norman heritage. It is said that there are more churches here per capita than anywhere in Europe. True or not, it's a challenging statistic. Start, of course, with the **Cathedral** (begun in 1069) or you may never finish. Take in **Elm Street** and bunk for the night at the easygoing **Hotel Nelson.** For a residential experience you might prefer private homes in the district listed as **Wolsey Lodges,** which originated in East Anglia. The local Tourist Board can fill you in.

NOTTINGHAM   The **Forte, Victoria, Royal Moat House,** or the **Strathdon** provide a fine, varied choice of hotels in the center, close to Nottingham Castle and the "Tales of Robin Hood," which explores the exploits of the affable outlaw. The **Cotswold** is one of the better bed-and-breakfast choices. Sherwood Forest is just down the road apiece.

OAKHAM   This is the heartland of the British hunt—rolling hills, Rutland Water (a lovely lake), and nonstop communion with the totally bewitching natural environment. In the town you'll find the **Buttercross** (a covered market), the ominous **Stocks,** and an engaging museum of old farm implements. **Oakham Castle** features a pedigree harking to the 12th century. The **Great Hall** is merely a shell of secular architecture, but peculiar in that every peer who has passed through the parish has always left a horseshoe—some gilded, some colossal in size, some beautifully fashioned—to decorate its walls as a gesture of good fortune.

★★★★★ **Hambleton Hall** • is another such gesture, very much in the 20th century but carefully nurtured in manoristic grace by its enthusiastic proprietors, Stefa and Tim Hart. Their 15 rooms are as fine as any tasteful traveler could desire; so is the notable cuisine in Franglais style; and so is the friendly greeting of the credo carved above its portal: *Fay ce que voudras* ("Do as you please"). **Whipper Inn** • in the center, comes with fine credentials for an intimate hideaway. Personally, I haven't stayed here, but I know the people behind it are dedicated and tasteful.

Nearby is *Stamford* with its **Browne's Hospital,** continuously in service (even today as an alm's house) since 1473. You can visit it. For lingering, there is:

★ **The George** • is an historic Stamford inn used by highwaymen of yore and is still in tune with travelers' needs.

★ **Ye Old Barn** • *in a mews* • is for snacks, and **Scotgate** is for ploughman's fare in a Victorian setting.

As an excursion, I recommend Henry Cecil's **Burghley House,** a marvelously silly Elizabethan palace—still inhabited by the Exeters—with minarets, spires, porcelains, portraits, and the tidy landscaping of Capability Brown. Best of all, it is only a 15-minute return by car to Hambleton Hall.

OXFORD   is a traffic choked center mixing higher education with higher blood-pressure readings for motorists. Strangely, the dwelling space hereabouts—not unlike its scholastic colleague, Cambridge—earns poor marks. **Linton Lodge** would be the choice for comfort and fellowship. Next would probably be the **Randolph.** Continual modernizations; dining room plus Ox-in-the-Cellar Buttery; some up-to-date units in plain but passable taste; many Gothic touches; next-door garage. For budgeteers, the **Tackley,** on High Street, is old-fashioned but sparkling; **Isis** on Iffley Road, a former hotel, is a guest house today; **Old Parsonage** oozes atmosphere from its stone walls and leaded windows. At mealtime pub crawlers generally enjoy **The Bear,** the **Turf Tavern** or **The Perch.** For a more refined atmosphere ☆☆ **15 North Parade** is a rewarding choice with modern cuisine and prices that rise to the occasion. It's good value, though, and hostess Georgina Wood is a bright entrepreneur. The antique photos are diverting.

At *Great Milton,* not far away, ☆☆☆ **Le Manoir Aux Quat' Saisons,** a 3-story red-roofed edifice of yellow stone, is attracting ample attention to its 27 acres, 10 bedrooms, and stellar gastronomy. There's tennis and an outdoor pool. Best of all, there's the peace and refinement of an English country lifestyle in tiptop form. Personally, I prefer the accommodations to the cuisine. In Oxford, the same enterprising proprietor, Raymond Blanc, has his **Le Petit Blanc** at 61a Banbury Rd. Light and all-Gaul in concept.

RYE is a bewitching, stone-girt seacoaster that rises above a vast marshland.

★★★ **Mermaid** • is feudalism fused with modern provincial comfort. Long stucco-and-timber ivy-clad building topped with chimney pots; oaken dining den; Dr. Syn's Chamber paneled and branched with aphorisms from the Bard of Avon; Giant's Fireplace Bar (look up the flue, which was once used by smugglers); tranquil courtyard. Twenty-five of the 29 accommodations come fully plumbed; all tend toward the diminutive but are jam-packed with Elizabethan emollients such as 4-poster beds and brassy lamps.

SALISBURY The **White Hart** provides the greatest comfort for your pounds provided you receive one of the larger and quieter kips. (Ask to be shown a room.) Woody highlights in bedroom decor; good baths; 25-unit annex. You'll be charmed by the original parking lot sign that lists the prices for feeding the horses and washing the carriages. The **Red Lion,** which dates back to the 17th century, comes up with a handsome antique dining room, full carpeting, a later wing in which the rooms are smaller than the older ones. Total of 50 units and 30 baths; very nice staff; enjoyable if you're unapprehensive of beamed ceilings and floors that sag with your footsteps. The **Rose & Crown** is a pleasant country town house; its site by the river is peaceful. The **Old Bell,** in the center, is a solid choice in the medium-price category. **King's Arms,** also old-fashioned, has a Tudor facade and a matching interior. The **County Hotel** compiles a curious set of statistics: 32 rooms, just a few private baths, 3 restaurants, and 7—yes, 7—bars. A tiny hostelry called the **Cathedral** is okay but not much more. If you prefer the suburbs, why not drive 8 miles farther to the sweet little **Antrobus Arms** at *Amesbury* (near Stonehenge)? Reasonably comfortable inn; inviting bar; fine restaurant. All 18 bathed accommodations are named for regions; bid for "North Devon," a *grand-lit* double; it was delightful.

SOUTHAMPTON   For Americans, the *Mayflower* voyage is strong reason to visit this Pilgrim's memorial. **Ocean Village** is a thriving marina with a shopping and snack pavilion; other waterfront pastimes abound for salty types. Medieval walls house museums connected with local history. (Henry V pushed off for Agincourt via the West Gate.) Accommodations at the **Polygon** or the **Park** (both on Cumberland Place), the **Post House** (close to Mayflower Park), the **Dolphin,** or the **Moat House** (a bit out on Highfield Lane). For a colorful snort, look in on the historic **Red Lion** or **Duke of Wellington** pubs. **La Brasserie** is one of the top restaurant choices. More luxurious digs can be found at the **Wessex** in *Winchester* (13 miles) or at the beautiful **Chewton Glen** at *New Milton* (18 miles).

STRATFORD-UPON-AVON   There's much to see: Shakespeare's birthplace, Anne Hathaway's Cottage, The New Place, John Harvard's House, Knott Garden, Hall's Croft, and an Antique Car Museum. Nearby are Warwick Castle, Kenilworth, Mary Arden's House, and the enchanted rovings through the Cotswolds (see separate section). The town groans with so many tourist groups that it is difficult today to find a trace of intimate dwelling space anywhere within the immediate limits. Arrange your tickets for the **Royal Shakespeare Theatre** well in advance. If you haven't done it in London possibly you'll have luck here at the Tourist Office, 1 High St.; or try at the theater; dining is not bad at the Box Tree salon in the theater itself. The Royal Shakespeare Company has the 450-seat **Swan,** an auditorium within the shell of the Memorial Theatre, which burned in 1926. It is dedicated to 16th- and 17th-century drama influenced by W.S. Incidentally, April 23 is the Bard's birthday—and does this hamlet celebrate! (Excuse the pun, please.) You might also enjoy the **Arms and Armour Museum,** the **Antique Arcade,** the **Antique Market,** and other engaging browsing along Sheep and Ely Streets.

  The 260-chamber **Moat House** hunkers discordantly upon 4 acres of carefully Tudored riverside garden. Long, low structure; Warwick Grill of no special distinction; octagonal Actor's Bar; ballroom; parking area. Rooms reasonably proportioned; each offers an individually controlled thermostat, a radio, taped melodies, and a direct-dial phone. The venerable **Welcombe,** on Warwick Road, an inconvenient 3 miles outside the town but soothingly quiet, is the best-known luxury house in the region. Sprawling park surroundings with 18-hole golf course; originally constructed so there would be 1 window for every day of the year (there may be as many chimneys, too). Because of its remoteness, readers have complained of difficulties in securing theater tickets from the busy marketplaces in town. In the center you'll find the **Shakespeare** with its charming Tudor architecture replete with gables, open timbers, leaded windows, and hanging flowerpots; gimmicky names for the bar ("Measure For Measure"), the dining room ("As You Like It"), and the bedchambers—all of which bear the title of a play, a poem, or one of the Bard's characters (we can't tell if the bridal suite is "Romeo and Juliet," "A Lover's Complaint," "Much Ado About Nothing," or "Love's Labour's Lost"). **Swan's Nest** is generally modern; comfort in abundance; above-average kitchen. **Alveston Manor** has been slipping. Fine old main building which contains only the smallest fraction of the complement (and which often is chilly in winter); 100 rooms in Charlecote and Warrick wings with simple, almost raw, billets. The **Falcon** is a timber-and-stucco house that reflects the general antiquity of the town; basically sound; reputedly superior cuisine. **Stratford House** is a Georgian house about 100 paces from the Royal Shakespeare Theatre and near the Avon. Bed and breakfast at reasonable tariffs. The Tudor-style **White Swan** has 60 pleasant rooms and few private baths. **Ettington Park,** in 42 acres of woodland near Alderminster (south of town), is a somewhat spooky Victorian Gothic holdover from the mid-19th century. Grand in concept, but the lovely mood sometimes is eroded when groups move in. Information about boarding houses or the local youth hostels can be garnered from the previously mentioned Tourist Office.

Many first-timers blindly insist on residing in Stratford while attending the Shakespeare performances or touring the countryside. Seasoned wayfarers with their own transportation more shrewdly avoid the crush of this touristic hub by finding the true Arcadian solace of rural England in the neighboring Cotswolds. (See the separate villages and listing under ''Cotswolds.'') The distances are short and cover some of the most inspiring landscape under Merlin's wand.

Dining possibilities are extensive in Stratford. Here's how we rate the ones we sampled:

★★ **Giovanni's •** has a refined continental tone; bar with stools and leather Chesterfield chairs; restaurant with cassis-hue walls and sconces; good quality for average prices.

★★ **Marlowe's •** can be reached via a narrow midtown alley and up a flight of steps; private house of timber and stucco; entry bar; 2 richly antiquated dining salons; brass chandeliers, plus candles and an open hearth.

★ **The Dirty Duck •** is a spoof—so named by the proprietor of this outstanding drop-in spot as a parody on the neighboring White Swan. A favorite haunt of thespians.

The Beefeater • comes next, and then **Mayflower** (this Chinese restaurant overlooks Harvard House through wide windows; simple large room; poor service but very digestible cookery—if you're not from Yale, that is.) The upstairs restaurant of the **Shakespeare Theatre** offers a steak dinner for about $14. Be sure to book your table in advance.

SUNNINGHILL's Royal Berkshire ascended to its throne smartly; a Queen Anne mansion with 5-star standards and tariffs to match. Total of 52 sumptuous chambers, all with color TV and refrigerators; Olympian gamut of sports facilities on its 15 manicured acres. Excellent, according to reports.

TAUNTON

★★★ **Castle Hotel •** has been a Somerset landmark since A.D. 1300 though its roots go back 6 centuries earlier. A Norman fortress stood here; there's a historic lounge with parchment tones, antlers, and shields; a later one in oak; Bow Suite is exceptional; some doubles with gothic windows overlooking the castle green; superior cuisine, among one of the finer kitchens of all Britain. For sightseeing, the **Military Museum** is engaging.

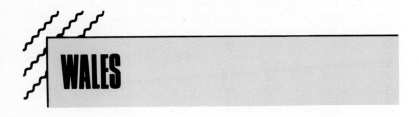

WALES

Distances are lengthy in this remote region—a country within a country— and since town names are so obscure to foreign ears, all Welsh selections are collected under this single heading for the convenience of motorists. If you range as far as these western hills and littorals, several stops are outstanding, but be sure to consult a detailed map of the area in order to find them.

★★★★★ **Bodysgallen** (pronounced "Bodess-gathlin") • *near Llandudno (spoken as "Lan-did-no" in Gwynedd* • not too far from the Holyhead ferry terminus for Ireland and in sight of the imposing and valiant **Conwy Castle.** Lovely and noble, it easily ranks among the finest country homes of Britain— with great hearths, 17th-century paneling, a fabulous Knot garden and rockery surrounded by boxwood hedges, and period bedrooms in the main house or in an adjoining colony of charming private suites. It is far to go, but in my view, worth almost any detour to enjoy such a unique travel experience. Be sure to book ahead (Tel: 0492–84466).

Plas Bodegroes • *Pwllheli, Gwynedd* • also is in the north and west of Port Meirion; it's really a restaurant with rooms. It's a comfy Georgian house without pretense, better known for its table than for its accommodations. A fine base for walkers and nature buffs. The **Portmerion** is a caprice of Mediterranean inspiration. It has a good bloodline and an enchanting situation.

Bodawen Country House • *Porthmadog, also in Gwynedd, North Wales* • is a 10-room home almost in the shadow of Mt. Snowdon and only 5 miles from the impressive Aberglaslyn Gorge. Go here for nature loving, peaceful walks, and appealing, wholesome mealtimes at Peaches (its delightful restaurant). ☆**Cawdor Arms** at *Llandeilo* in Dyfed (Tel. Llandeilo 0558/823500) is as well known for its generous Welsh breakfasts as it is for its homespun Georgian comforts. At famous *Cardiff,* the **Park** is recommendable. The **Holiday Inn** is a prediction-come-true. **Celtic Manor,** outskirting *Newport,* provides ingratiating shelter and a bonus of two restaurants. Slightly north is **Cwrt Bleddyn,** near *USK.* It's an old gabled house with contemporary comforts. West of Cardiff, near *Bridgend,* the stately Victorian **Coed-y-Mwstwr** resides in a 17-acre park. Tennis and golf (9 holes) available. South of Cardiff, close to *Barry,* there's the noble **Egerton Grey Country House,** which is a gracious trip into antiquity. The cookery is wonderfully regional—with just a pinch more.

Bontddu Hall resides near *Dolgellau,* south of the nostalgic *Ffestiniog Railway,* a favorite of steam-era chuffing buffs. In the *Tywyn* area, I like the **Minffordd** in *Talyllyn.* **Warpool Court** takes command at *St. David's.* **The Mill** is the best of the grist from *Glynhir* in West Wales. **Ruthin Castle,** at *Ruthin,* not on the sea, is a comfortized fortress which, alas, specializes in medieval banquets every night except Sunday. The waitresses are in costume; there's folk singing and clog dancing; there's cuisine done in the manner of the Middle Ages; there are tour groups almost scaling the turrets. Surprisingly high living standards, but not too rewarding after the novelty has worn off and the Clwyd Valley sights have been seen. Friends report pleasant tidings for **Porth Tocyn,** a country house hotel of high standards at *Abersoch* on the Lleyn peninsula; seafood dishes are the chef's specialty. For more rooms-with-a-view the **Cliff Hotel,** linked to the links at *Gwbert* (near Cardigan) is tops. In the *Gwent* region, there is the **King's Head** at *Monmouth.* There's also the distinguished **Llansantffraed Court,** above Raglan at *Abergavenny;* 21 rooms and beautiful surroundings. In *Pembroke,* the **Underdown Country House** comes well recommended for sylvan, easygoing pastimes; I haven't been there personally, however. With few hotels for miles in any direction, be sure to wander with an easy itinerary and firm reservations.

Obviously you'll find scores and scores more. These represent a broadly comprehensive, hand-picked assemblage of the better ones in some of the most scenic locales. There are castles everywhere, hundreds of guest homes, comfortable farmhouse accommodations, and miles to wander—at prices that are much lower than in central England. (The season is predictably shorter at coastal resorts, but further inland most places stay open year round.) Half of the fun is in digging up little inns for yourself, to discover that farmers have gathered in the bar for an informal singsong and a few braces of stout. If you wish for other targets write to the **Wales Tourist Board** (you'd tickle their patriotic hearts if you addressed it as the **Bwrdd Croeso Cymru)** at P.O. Box 1, Cardiff, CF1 2XN, Wales.

WARMINSTER

☆☆☆☆☆ **Bishopstrow House** stands in its own glorious parkland with almost as many flowers inside the handsome Georgian mansion as outside, the softspoken Wylye whirling gently below its grassy slope. The Wessex conviction for melding home and garden unites antiques, a conservatory, fireplaces, and sumptuous furnishings with views of rolling Wiltshire panorama. Bedrooms with individual decor, color TV, books, fine carpets, and artwork. The palladian indoor pool and tennis court are added incentives for lingering. This region is flourishing with sightseeing targets. **Longleat House** is famous but becoming infamous rapidly as commercialism creeps over its ancient walls. Kids, however, will probably go ape/lion/and/or aardvark for the animal-filled Safari Park on the grounds. **Stonehenge** is 30 minutes away. The lakefront **Stourhead House** and gardens are marvelous; so is **Wilton House** with rooms by Inigo Jones, noteworthy paintings, and some of Mother Nature's brightest ornaments.

☆☆ **Beechfield House** • *at Beanacre, about 15 minutes from Warminster* • is an elegant example of Victorian stonework and modern life-styles. Authentic architecture and accoutrements; attractive grounds; heated swimming pool; fishing on the Avon—a 300-yard flycast away (the footpath leads to Lacock; see separate entry); also close to Bowood (illustrating the skills of Robert Adams and Capability Brown) and within 20 minutes of Bath. Less costly than Bishopstrow House and quite a bit less luxurious.

WARWICK The **Castle** • possibly England's finest, is the first drawing card for most visitors; it can easily occupy a full day with its towers, dungeons, state apartments, and parks—even a picnic ground. Apart from the medieval aspects, it now features a compelling wax museum of more recent figures in British history who are portrayed in the settings of the private apartments. It sounds corny, but it is so well done that you can't help being fascinated. Opposite the Castle gate is an **Elizabethan model village** with replicas of major estates in the area. If there's time, try not to miss the **Lord Leycester Hospital**—not as a patient, but for cultural purposes.

The **Lord Leycester** offers a tartan Grill, a masculine wood-lined bar, damask-clad corridors, 45 comfortable, fully carpeted rooms, and 6 private baths; its best doubles with plumbing aren't at all expensive, if you can hook one. Not bad. The **Warwick Arms** comes up with passable accommodations. **Saxon Mill,** 10 minutes along Kenilworth Road, is for dining rather than for overnighting; poor and cocky service; food that edges on being overpriced; impressive, however, as a place to see. **Spencer's West Gate Arms** turns on eye appeal and high quality cuisine for its distinguished following. **De Monfort** is modern in concept, if not downright chilly in tone. Look for it in neighboring *Kenilworth,* a short spin from town.

★★★★★ **Mallory Court** • sits placidly in 10 charming acres of rolling countryside on Harbury Lane, at *Tachbrook Mallory* (Leamington Spa) about 2 miles from Warwick. Allan Holland masterminds the French cuisine (some of it nouvelle) that appears in the oaken dining salon; bedrooms are spacious and individually distinctive; service is Mallory Courtly. A winning base for Cotswold rovings or for visitors who enjoy Stratford-Upon-Avon from a little bit afar.

WELLS The **Cathedral,** of course, is the focal point, along with the adjoining **Bishop's Palace.** The restoration and preservation techniques currently in progress are as engaging as the mood of Middle Age charm; organ recitals often given.

The elfin, 10-room, 5-bath **Crown** takes the throne, but it could easily be unseated by a stalwart sovereign if one were to march in. Legend has it that William Penn once gave a speech standing at one of its windows. The **Star** shines brightest in its Tudor dining room, Grill, and friendly lounges; 22 chambers; few private baths; kindly staff; worthy if you don't hanker for your own plumbing. **Gate House,** the oldest hostelry in this ancient town, is built right into the cathedral walls; the situation is handy for clerics, but it offers only basic amenities. The **Swan** seems Routine Antiquity; somewhat molted when compared with the smarter chicks of similar vintage.

WINCHESTER The modern-lined, 91-room **Wessex,** built over a Roman well, is the pacesetter. Situated across the lawn from the world-famous cathedral; twentieth-century architecture which does not clash, odd as it might seem, with the moss-raked edifice; sound restaurant overlooking the hallowed resting places of some of Albion's greatest personages; cozy Buttery for late-hour snacks; well-appointed rooms. A satisfactory meal may be had here, at the more atmospheric **Elizabethan,** or at the **Royal Hotel.** Just west of town (look for *Sparsholt*) the 17th-century ★★ **Lainston House** is outstanding for accommodation and stately mansionhood, but management has an amateurish cast to it. When and if it mellows this could be one of the truly prestige addresses of Britain.

WOODSTOCK

☆☆☆ **The Feathers** ● with 15 smallish rooms and a grand following for its excellent gastronomy, is now the talk of the town. Tiny lounges; gardenside bar; clean, fresh atmosphere and willing personalized service at big city prices.

The 750-year-old ★★**Bear** ● a short lope from Oxford, rears up as the 4th-oldest inn in Albion. Its 3 structures face the town market, the most ancient comprising a thickly beamed and happily hearthed lounge-bar, a taper-lit dining room further brightened by flowers and mellowed by pewter and brass, and a tally-ho cocktail nook.

★ **Woodstock Arms** ● is a fine low-cost stop with plenty of color. At lunch, you might enjoy the self-help open table (about $6) at the stone-and-timber **Star,** right on the main lane with the above hotels. The bar is clad with chamber pots; apart from the questionable expression of poor taste, the food is good.

WORCESTER Here the overnight pick is **Fownes;** next come **Ye Olde Talbot,** and the **Giffard** followed by the **Star.** The **Raven** is okay in nearby *Droitwich*—and boasts 18 singles and 30 doubles, 40 of which have small baths. English dishes; fair tariffs that include breakfast.

YORK Many visitors are drawn here to view **York Minster,** restored after catastrophic fire damage from a lightning strike. On the outskirts ★★★★★**Middlethorpe Hall,** in 26 acres of park, is one of England's finest Queen Anne hotel-homes. Top-rank British cuisine by a chef who has trained with the best kitchen masters in France and England; 3 separate dining salons for greater intimacy. Splendid atmosphere combined with ingratiating hospitality. **Royal Station,** the **Chase,** and the **Post** are only fair. Over in West Yorkshire, not far from *Leeds,* **Pool Court,** sited at *Pool-in-Warfedale,* is sometimes promoted as "a restaurant with rooms." Of the latter: Only 4, and they are in love with the garden scenery. Of the former: Don't miss it if you are near the Harrogate-Bradford-Leeds triangle. A fine Georgian redoubt.

FINLAND

INCLUDING LAPLAND

> **USA:** Finnish Tourist Board, 655 Third Ave., New York, NY 10017, Tel. (212) 949–2333

SPECIAL REMARKS: (1) Once you've arrived, **Finland Travel Bureau,** Kaivokatu 10, Helsinki, is the master organization. (2) There's an extensive network of offices throughout Europe where you can find additional aid. Check **Finnish Tourist Board** listings in London, Paris, Copenhagen, Oslo, Stockholm, Amsterdam, Zurich, Hamburg, Milan, Madrid, and Munich. Once you arrive, the Helsinki source is at Unioninkatu 26. (3) There's a live-wire staff at the **City Tourist Office** in the capital (Pohjoisesplanadi 19) who can be of enormous on-the-scene assistance. (4) Most municipalities provide their own information facilities. Ask everywhere for the **City Tourist Office.**

> **TELEPHONE:** Access code to USA: 990; to phone Finland: 358; time difference (Eastern Daylight) plus 6 hrs.

This most northerly Republic in the world is called *Suomi* by its residents. It sprawls over an area that would hold 16 New Jerseys. A large gelid chunk of the nation lies above the Arctic Circle. Nearly 200,000 islands and a like number of lakes give Finland's map the strikingly beautiful zigzag venation of blue and white—apt colors for the national banner. Most of the terrain is low-lying; some regions are a broken jumble of fir-coated hillocks, fells, ridges, and hollows, while others are monotonously flat for seemingly endless miles. Happily, some of its most enchanting scenery is in the surroundings of its gateway and capital, Helsinki.

Finland has a population of almost 5 million and while Lapland is a huge

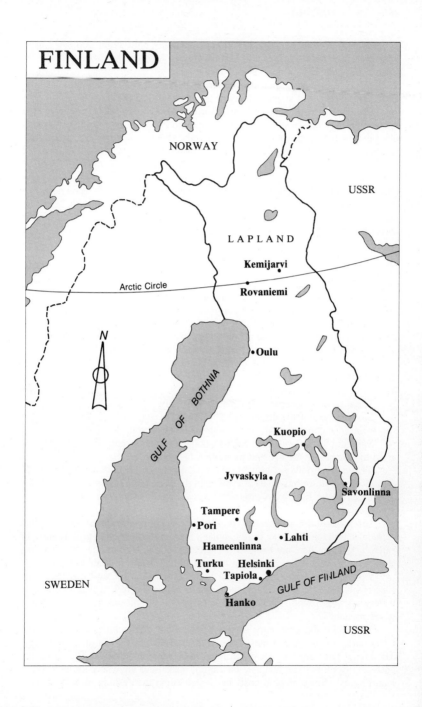

FINLAND

NORWAY

USSR

LAPLAND

Kemijarvi

Arctic Circle

Rovaniemi

N

Oulu

GULF OF BOTHNIA

Kuopio

Jyvaskyla

Savonlinna

Tampere

Pori

Lahti

Hameenlinna

Turku

Helsinki

Tapiola

SWEDEN

GULF OF FINLAND

Hanko

USSR

geographical portion of the Finnish map, it counts only about 200,000 Lapps who hang out their wash on the Arctic Circle. Most of her 10 cities and 84 towns cling to her coasts. Forestry is the basis of her economy, with wood-working as a derivative industry; seafaring is her lifeline. Agriculture, metals, and shipbuilding split a large chunk of the occupational pie.

The Gulf Stream is so benign that in the lower and middle reaches of the nation you may dress as you would for an Ohio February or a northern Califor-nia July. In the south there is snow for only about 5 months; in Lapland this stretches to 7 months. In Helsinki your midsummer days will last 19 hours. At Utsjoki, on the northern tip of Lapland, there is continuous daylight for 73 days.

TRANSPORTATION Airline If you want to see a lot of this lake-laced nation of great distances and few roads, **Finnair** will be your flying carpet to 22 of the country's destinations. Ask about the **Holiday Ticket** (15 days of unlimited travel for about $300); there are also the **Finland for Visitors,** the **Adventure Holidays,** and several other programs, which are crafted to the whims of curi-ous outlanders. Finnair is a lifeline to many areas and it does its job with grace and skill; its entire service area is now broader through teamwork with neigh-boring SAS. Over the Atlantic (NY-Seattle-Los Angeles), it is satisfactory, too, but its real strength is in answering the very special needs of this vast northerly clime. Few airlines I've used display such a sense of caring. Ground services are especially well thought out. If you fly into or out of the capital, the bus connections are quick, frequent, and clean; terminals are at the midcity station or at the Intercontinental Hotel; much cheaper than taxi fares.

Taxis Costly, even for short runs. From 6 p.m.–10 p.m. there is an eve-ning supplement of 6 FM; then from 10 p.m. to 6 a.m. the night rate is boosted by 12 FM over the daytime fare.

Three passengers cost more than 2—but only a trifling sum.

Since so few of the drivers speak English, *be sure* to have handy a written slip from your concierge which bears the address of your destination.

Smoking is prohibited on Finnish domestic flights, part of a national pro-gram to discourage the use and promotion of tobacco.

Trains The railways offer the Finnrail Pass, which provides 8, 15, or 22 days of travel (train-bus-boat) at astonishingly reasonable prices. Finland also is a member of the Eurailpass program—a real benefit when such great distances are involved.

International Car Ferries The ships are modern with dining facilities that include sumptuous Nordic buffet tables, conventional meals, grill rooms, or cafeterias. Then there are bars, discos, saunas, pools, barbers, hairdressers, and children's salons. Pullman seats in lounges or cabins are available.

On the most important Helsinki-Stockholm loop, the well-managed Silja Line (with the *Silja Serenade* as the flagship) parades a superb fleet through the waterways year round. They also offer cruises to Turku, past thousands of tiny wooded islands.

In general the new ships of the Viking Line offer similar amenities. The *Cinderella, Mariella,* and the *Olympia* are trendsetters for size and modernity. The higher fares are for outside or upper-deck accommodations. The remainder cost less. Bookings can be made on both of these lines anywhere through Amer-ican Express. Since alcohol costs much less afloat than ashore in both of these nordic lands, drinking parties are often the motivating cause for these heady voyages.

On the Helsinki-Travemunde passage to and from Germany, the swift and rather costly **Finnjet**—at 31 knots, the fastest passenger ship in the world—cuts this crossing from the former 2½-day run to 22½ hours. Departures are made every second day.

Cars As a safety measure, cars are now required to drive with headlights on in suburban areas *at all times*. All safety belts should be buckled. Strollers must wear reflectors (noses don't count) if they walk along roads at night.

FOOD In a land of lakes and seas, fish are abundant, but so are fowl, game, and meat. The Finns are inventive mixmasters.

Among the 2 most popular favorites are an historic concoction amusingly named Jansson's Temptation (a gooey casserole of potatoes, anchovies, onions, cream, and herbs) and Russian-originated vorschmack (a seemingly outlandish but delicious conglomerate of lamb, herring, mashed potato, cucumber, beet root, sour cream, and garlic).

Try not to miss that glorious midsummer gustatory treat called rapuja (the minisize freshwater crayfish which the Swedes know as kraftor).

The Finnish interpretation of smorgasbord is called voileipapoyta. The traditional festive version for such everyday fare is called pitopoyta. Try specialties such as sillisalaatti (herring salad), smoked poronliha (reindeer), kesakeitto (fresh vegetable soup with milk), sauna sausages (munched after *you* bake in the baths), or such "normally" hot dishes as kalakukko (fish and pork pie with salt-baked potatoes), karjalanpiirakat (piping-hot Karelian pastries), maksalaatikko (liver pudding), lanttulaatikko (turnip casserole), punajuuri salaattia (beetroot salad), and paistetut sienet (fried wild mushrooms). The hungry citizenry here normally wash these down with milk or piima (buttermilk) or kalja (non-alcoholic beer). Wild game? The most popular candidates include grouse, wild duck, ptarmigan (when roasted it's called riekkopaisti), venison, smoked bear, and a curiosity of the Far North, reindeer tongue (poron kieli).

For the perfect finish to your local repast, there are scads of luscious fruit soups made from the wild or cultivated berries of Finland—the lingonberry, cloudberry, brambleberry, bilberry (similar to our huckleberry), and others. These taste gems also garnish pancakes or bejewel the savorful pastries of the nation. If you are trying to budget, better avoid cloudberries (*multer* berry); they are rare at any time, soft, perishable, but exquisitely delicious with sugar and cream.

The Finns nourish their bodies while stoking their high spirits, since the majority of Suomi dining spots are what would constitute nightclubs in most other lands. If you have your main meal at midday—and merely nibble and tipple before midnight at places which cater to revelers—your savings will be surprisingly high. Although some offer dancing as early as noon, the more usual opening time is 4:30, with a pause from 7 p.m.–8 p.m.

DRINKS The Finns, as a group, are just about the wettest Wets or the dryest Drys going. The polite 2-sherry or 1-whisky sipper is practically unknown, except among the ladies.

Prohibition was tried and abolished. In its place, the State formed the alcohol monopoly (with 27 branches in the capital alone) to centralize control of all intoxicating beverages and to hard-sell the advantages of beer and wine. Its stocks are large and well chosen; its prices range from steep to outlandish—income from the monopoly accounts for 9% of Finland's total budget! If you like your weekend tipple, remember that these are open on most weekdays from 10 a.m.–5 p.m., an hour later on Fri., plus 9 a.m.–2 p.m. on Sat. in winter; from May 1 to Sept. 30 there is no Sat. operation.

Authorized hotels and restaurants serve liquor from 11 a.m.–1 a.m. Room service in hotels stops earlier. For teetotalers there are a sizable number of dry hotels, spearheaded by the powerful YMCA chain.

Though soberingly expensive, whisky is popular among the more cosmopolitan inhabitants. Finns drank more cognac than citizens of any other nation until the price more than doubled in one thundering jolt.

Two national liqueurs of consequence present themselves to the connoisseur. Lakka, made from Arctic cloudberries and Mesimarja, distilled from the rare Artic brambleberry that forms its essence. Costly but delicious. *Don't miss them*—but make certain you get them *well chilled!*

Finland boasts 12 major breweries. Helsinki's kingpin is Koff; Turku's Aura is a leading light; Lahti glows with Mallasjuoma.

Only 3 types of beer are vatted. Pilsner, the lightest, guarantees less than 2.2% alcohol; it is often called by the Swedish name, Latol, and tastes like frog soup; it is also so flat that the froth disappears before the rim of the glass approaches your lips. The most popular choice, "3rd Class" (so named from a taxation gimmick), goes for about the same as its Milwaukee cousins. Strongest is "A" ("Atomic"), the export variety.

NOTE · · · Finnish toasts? *Skol* is the most common; *Hei* ("Hey") is the most friendly, relaxed, and familiar; *Kippis* is the one usually taught to foreigners.

TIPPING   Almost none.

Zero for taxi drivers. Curiously, cloakroom attendants pull down a big 5 FM for just checking your hat and coat. Hotel baggage porters earn 1 FM for every piece they tote. A doorman usually gets 2–3 FM.

CITIES AND REGIONS

AULANKO,   3 miles from Sibelius' birthplace of Hameenlinna, is the most glittering sapphire in the bracelet of western lakes. This is a lodestar for the holiday-minded—accessible by car (slightly over an hour on the highway from Helsinki), by train, or by the Silver Line water coach that glides between Hameenlinna and Tampere. The **Hotel Aulanko** boasts private baths, a so-so restaurant for 700 clients, a bar, 3 saunas, and a resident orchestra. The **Youth Hostel** at Lake Aulangonjarvi affords more modest shelter for the overflow summer throngs. To gild the lily, there's a daily lake cruise for the restless—restaurant aboard—which touches other nearby beauty ports. If you are making a Sibelius pilgrimage, the composer's recently renovated house, **Ainola** (named for his wife), is located just outside *Jarvenpaa* and roughly in the same highway direction from Helsinki. The couple are buried in the garden of this spot they loved so dearly.

HANKO, a sleepy seacoast town, draws the elite to savor its southern summer charms. For overnighters it offers the delightful little **Regatta Hotel** with its own swimming pool.

HELSINKI

Pronounced HELL-sinki, not Hell-SINKI, the city is still Helsingfors to the founding Swedes. This capital, at the same latitude as Oslo and Leningrad, is the main port, the center for slightly more than a ½ million toilers.

Its peninsula, flecked by a lovely archipelago, is surrounded on 3 sides by the sea. Architecturally, it's a mishmash of Empire, New York Public Library, Byzantine, and the futuristic fantasies of Aalto, Rewell, and the Sirens. If you have a special cultural itch, Helsinki probably can scratch it. Within the environs is the grand sum of 66 museums! But for me, the most rewarding summer orientation circuit is a morning or afternoon cruise around the gleaming Helsinki archipelago. (In my opinion, the "Eastern" loop is best.)

ATTRACTIONS

Helsinki Card • Before you even begin, purchase one of these at the City Tourist Office, travel agencies, or at many other sources in town. For a sightseer, it is a gilt-edge investment, providing discounted (or free) transportation, museum entry, gifts, saunas, hairdressing, tours, theater, opera, and a list too long to describe here.

Temppeliaukio • *Its name is also its address* • Here is a modern wonder of church architecture, built into rugged, undressed rock and capped with shimmering copper. It must always remain unique in concept, if not in execution.

Kauppatori • *Market Square* • Located along the waterfront of South Harbor at the end of the tree-lined Esplanade, this popular square filled with colorful stalls is one of the best places to experience the rhythms of life in Helsinki. Each morning (except Sun.) the square is the scene of an open-air market that sells everything from fresh produce, fish, flowers, and snacks to handmade baskets. The **Evening Market** pipes from 3:30 to 8 p.m. (May 15 to late Aug.); emphasis is on craft items from such faraway places as Lappish villages in the North Calotte. Behind the square you can see onion-domed **Uspenski Cathedral,** a Greek-Orthodox house of worship. Just along the edge of the market is the **Presidential Palace.**

Fountain of Havis Amanda • The statue of a sea nymph, sculpted by Ville Vallgren, has come to be a symbol of Helsinki rising from the waters. It is a good vantage point from which to watch the lively doings in the market.

Kansallismuseo • *Mannerheimintie 34* • The museum was designed in 1910 by the architects Gesellius, Lindgren, and Saarinen. Its focus is archaeological, ethnological, and historical, and the vast collections include prehistoric artifacts from Scandinavia and Russia, in addition to Lapp, Finnish, and Ugric folk art, textiles, household items, and regional costumes.

Sibelius Monument • *Sibelius Park* • Jean Sibelius is honored here graphically, but the composer's bittersweet music is frequently presented at the waterside **Finlandia Hall,** an opus by Alvar Aalto, with stark, but graceful lines. The former, a large tubular sculpture by Eila Hiltunen, is attractive by day and at night when it is illuminated by floodlights.

Seurasaari Island • You needn't hop a boat to reach Seurasaari with its open-air museum of rural Finland because this island is linked to the mainland by a footbridge. The open-air museum has eight authentic 17th-century farmhouses, a 17th-century wooden church (where you can attend Sunday services in summer), and an 18th-century manor house, all from different parts of the country. There is also a windmill, a village store, and a "savusauna" (smoke sauna). In summer, visitors can enjoy folk dancing and folk concerts as well as swimming. Meals are available at the museum restaurant.

Suomenlinna • *Finland's Fortress* • At the mouth of South Harbor are a cluster of rocky fortified islands, the largest of which is Suomenlinna with Sveaborg Fortress. A 15-minute ferry ride from Market Square, the island is a popular getaway spot for visits to the fortifications and its parks and interesting pathways. In summer you can swim at the beach and enjoy a bite to eat at Walhalla, a restaurant in one of the old forts.

Linnanmaki Amusement Park • Often likened to Copenhagen's Tivoli Gardens, Linnanmaki is a favorite place for merrymakers throughout the warm months. Here you will find lots to interest young folk plus a myriad of ways to please the palate and quench the thirst of grownups who come to spend a leisurely few hours in the open air.

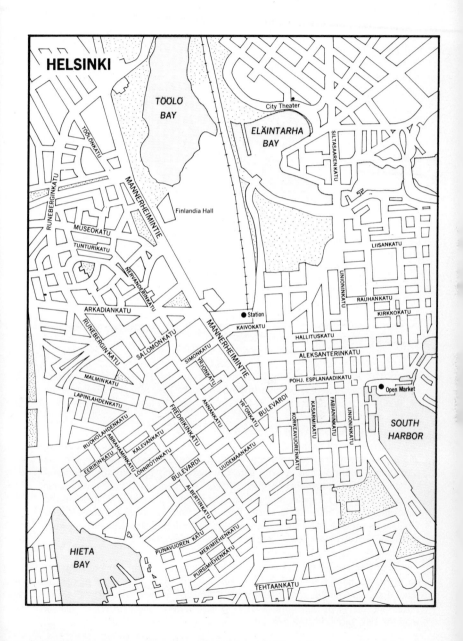

HELSINKI

TÖÖLÖ
BAY

City Theater

ELÄINTARHA
BAY

SILTASAARENKATU

TÖÖLÖNKATU

MANNERHEIMINTIE

RUNEBERGINKATU

Finlandia Hall

MUSEOKATU

TUNTURIKATU

LIISANKATU

NERVANDERINKATU

UNIONINKATU

RAUHANKATU

ARKADIANKATU

KIRKKOKATU

RUNEBERGIN KATU

SALOMONKATU

● Station

KAIVOKATU

HALLITUSKATU

ALEKSANTERINKATU

MALMINKATU

SIMONKATU

YRJÖNKATU

MANNERHEIMINTIE

POHJ. ESPLANAADIKATU

LAPINLAHDENKATU

FREDRIKINKATU

ANNANKATU

YRJÖNKATU

BULEVARDI

● Open Market

KASARMIKATU

FABIANINKATU

UNIONINKATU

KORKEAVUORENKATU

RUOHOLAHDENKATU

EERIKINKATU

ABRAHAMINKATU

KALEVANKATU

LÖNNROTINKATU

UUDENMAANKATU

SOUTH
HARBOR

BULEVARDI

ALBERTINKATU

HIETA
BAY

PUNAVUOREN KATU

MERIMIEHENKATU

PURSIMIEHENKATU

TEHTAANKATU

Bus and Tram Tours • If you wish to begin your stay in Helsinki with an overview of its major sights and landmarks, the city-owned STA bus company offers a 1½-hour tour with commentary in English. These originate at Asema-aukio (Tel. 90–585–166); pickup at your hotel is also available. The Ageba organization (Passenger Pavilion, South Harbor; Tel. 90–669–193) arranges 2- to 3-hour city tours from different departure points. If you prefer a more independent swing through town, tram #3 threads its way past most of the touristic highlights.

Boat Tours • Known as the "Daughter of the Baltic," Helsinki is bounded on three sides by water and is surrounded by numerous islands. To get real feeling for the city, take to the waves. In summer only, motorboat excursions depart from Hakaniemi Square and Market Square. Some tours will set you off at Suomenlinna or Korkeasaari. If you take the pleasurable 1½-hour circuit, I'd recommend the "Eastern" loop, filled with lakes, canals, lovely houses, birches, willows, silvery coves, harbors, an icebreaker depot, and even a chug past the zoo.

Silverline Tour • This 3-day adventure covers the rich south of the nation. Departures are frequent from early June through late Aug., and the reasonable price includes transportation, transfers, sightseeing, hotels, meals, English-speaking guides, entrance fees, and tips.

HOTELS

If you haven't got a confirmed reservation, the **Hotellikeskus** ("Hotel Booking Center") *might* be able to bail you out. This office is in a separate building near the Helsinki Railway Station and the telephone is 171133.

☆☆☆ **Intercontinental** • facing a sylvan park, conveniently backs on the city airline terminal, opposite the Congress House. Ten-story plant with nearly 555 rooms; lobby and lounges richly outfitted in polished wood and comfortable furnishings; rooftop Club A with dance orchestra and bar plus the wonderful Galateia seafood restaurant; excellent saunas and glass-lined pool at the same altitude; Brasserie for pleasant and relatively inexpensive nibbling; standardized bedchambers plus wide-angle suites; one entire floor set aside for nonsmokers. Don't confuse this one with the brand-new **Strand Intercontinental,** a luxury candidate that is now greeting guests at John Stenberginranta 6.

☆☆☆ **Hesperia** • is the next-door neighbor to the original Intercontinental on Mannerheimintie, and is similar in amenities if not slightly more modern in tone. Excellent public rooms including a French- as well as a Russian-style restaurant; plenty of night life; a pool, saunas, barber, and hairdresser. Cooler than the IHC in mood, but certainly worthy.

☆☆ **Ramada President** • comes with high-quality credentials. Midtown site; modern decor throughout; restaurant; coffee shop; bar; pool; sauna; nightclub.

☆☆ **Merihotelli Cumulus** • at seaside, is a fairly long run from midtown, adding to the outlay by gadabout sightseers. Grill-bar and 300-seat restaurant with green plants galore and a fine panorama; waterfront terrace; nightclub in basement; rooftop saunas with plate-glass windows; the best units facing the harbor.

★ **Arctia Marski** • is in the forefront of the 14 Arctia hotels or restaurants in the nation. Main bar in lobby corner; copper-ceilinged dining room; window-fronted restaurant up one flight. There are the cellar-sited Fizz nightspot and the Kellari eatery. A busy hive after dark.

☆ **Palace** • provides a magnificent harbor setting with a lovely sweep of the city and archipelago. Small, unimpressive ground-floor lobby; La Vista— and what a *vista!*—Italian-style restaurant up one flight; luxurious, popular 10th-floor dining room and the little American Bar; saunas; charming Finnish-style decor on 9th floor. An excellent mooring.

☆ **Vaakuna** • is enjoying continuing success and seemingly endless physical revisions. Grill open until midnight; attractive smorgasbord available; penthouse bar and snackery; Scotch Bar; 2 saunas; dark-wood singles; grandly modern Presidential Suite; good baths.

Klaus Kurki • is a turn-of-the-century re-creation in midtown with a cool Finnish entry and a warm French heartland. Cozy booths in the restaurant; wine and beer cellar; polished wood and brass; bedrooms usually snug but invitingly outfitted.

Helsinki, in midcity, is moderate in price, tour-oriented in mood, and okay as shelter, but far from inspiring.

Olympia, 10-minute haul from the center, shares the building with the Sport Palace. Pleasant 308-seat dance-restaurant enlivened by multicolored umbrellas hanging from the ceiling; self-service grill in basement; pool and sauna; bowling alley; lone concrete tennis court; overcrowded, undersized lobby.

Ursula is close to the **Merihotelli,** but without the same glorious waterfront view. Peiping style avant-garde lobby; clinical breakfast room; bedchambers that fairly sparkle with cleanliness and flair.

Torni, an old-timer, has been converted from a wretched relic to a United Nations of innkeeping. Now it includes a Balkan corner, an Irish pub, an American bar, a French snuggery, and a Spanish grill. Its appeal is catholic, though Roman it's not.

Although none of the following wins orchids for excellence, here's the way I'd rate the rest of the pack: **Seurahuone** (retaining its old style), **Hospiz (YMCA), Academica, Satakuntatalo,** and, out of town, the **Dipoli** at *Otaniemi.* You can find basic short-term shelter at flyways' **Rantasipi Airport,** the

Park, or the **Metrocity.** The **Pasila** is of recent vintage, so you might like it for that reason alone.

★★★ **Torppa** • (frequently lengthened to Kalastajatorppa) forms the nidus of what is probably the most imposing and impressive hotel-restaurant complex in Finland. It is 3 miles from midcity—a 15-minute ride by tram #4 to the end of the line—overlooking a fetchingly serene sea inlet. The original structure is the gloriously beautiful Kalastajatorppa ("Fisherman's Hut"). Disappointingly small, garish-modern lobby; amiable little sunken bar adjoining; cheerful breakfast-cafe room to rear; long hike to the Round Room for dining and dancing and the Red Room nightclub; 2 pools; 4 saunas; gym, hairdresser, and barber. Massive Presidential Suite (Ronald Reagan overnighted here on his zip to the Moscow summit); 9 smaller suites; most bedchambers facing the water, some in the "old" hostelry; all singles front the woods.

☆☆ **Rivoli Jardin** • is considered separately because it specializes in singles accommodation for the business traveler chiefly. Excellent comfort and decor; no restaurant since it is thought that this type of client is not the sit-in sort.

RESTAURANTS

Independent Restaurants Without Dancing

☆☆☆☆ **Konig** • *Mikonkatu 4, just off the Esplanade, 5 minutes' stroll from the Hotel Marski* • in strikingly attractive and tasteful contemporary garb, is what used to be a favorite haven of Sibelius and ranking artists of the turn-of-the-century. Charming bar down one flight; excellent cuisine for its gastronomic following. Try the pheasant Titania if in season.

★★★ **Havis Amanda** • *Unioninkatu 23* • is widely rated as a contender for the ranking fish and seafood restaurant in the capital. This cellar boasts an ingratiating deluxe tavern ambience. Its prize freshwares are in a counter display at the entrance.

☆☆ **Bellevue** • *Rahapajankatu 3* • is about a 5-minute walk from the port, in a house of the 1920s. Russian cooking with delicious borscht, but poor piroshki. Try the fried salmon with creamed mushrooms. Service is not too exaggerated even if the bills are. Another Slavic choice might be the **Alexander Nevski** (Pohjoises plandadi 17).

☆☆ **Savoy** • *Etelaesplanadi 14* • an aeric atop a midtown office building, offers a sophisticated atmosphere highlighted with stress-form plywood furniture designed by Alvar Aalto; white-brick and timber surroundings; brass lamps over flower settings; international cookery intertwined with local fare. We especially liked the forsmak (minced lamb and herring, served at lunchtime only with a potato baked in salt—but *don't* eat the jacket!).

★★★★ **Walhalla** • *on the island of Suomenlinna* • is built into the fortress itself. Take the ferry (summer only) and then walk the 800 yards among the ramparts along a marked path; fair weather is advised. Brick walls 10-feet thick; pale, polished wood floors; colorful linens and handsome glassware. The Finnish buffet is one of the finest in the Nordic lands and very reasonable for such a spectacular all-you-can-eat repast; a la carte choices are also tempting; the beetroot schnitzel is unusual and thoughtful for dieters or vegetarians. A scenic worthwhile excursion to occupy about 3 hours pier-to-pier and back again.

NJK • *Valkosaari* • and **Sarkanlinna** • *Sarkka* • are both yacht clubs on islands; both summer only; phone first.

Piekka • *Mannerheimintie 68* • whomps up regional cookery. Anyone for bear steak?

No Name • *Toolontorinkatu 2* • awarded itself the enigmatic moniker it has—or hasn't. It used to be Motti, the city's fashion leader for gastronomy and style. The impish thrust toward titular mystery is carried into the kitchen as well as into the atmosphere. This one's on you, I fear.

Restaurants with Dancing at Night

☆ **Kappeli** • *Chapel* • is a culinary monument near the sea end of the Esplanade, sited on the park which centers this apex boulevard of the city. In summer, a bandstand, opposite, tootles with military airs. Pleasantly subdued main establishment in long, high-ceilinged room with windows top to bottom on 3 sides; sizable, lovely open terrace for warm-weather consumers; separate cafe adjoining; Taverna in cellar with lower prices; table d'hote and a la carte menus at high tariffs. If there is a single landmark restaurant in the nation which virtually every Finn knows, here it is.

Kalastajatorppa • *Fisherman's Hut* • mentioned previously, is next in national and international fame. Though the epitome of spaciousness and graciousness, the gastronomy is easily forgotten.

Adlon • *Fabianinkatu 14* • affects a phonied up medieval mien, a red-brick courtyard, and fake little semicircular balconies around its upper periphery. Through another door is the principal hall in 1920-ish decor. Lunch in the attractive bar Mon. through Fri.; open until 3 a.m. A show plus dancing.

Casino • *Kulosaari, a 15-minute taxi ride from the center* • is presented on the rocks. Magnificent seascape view; rollicking summer bounce. Better order a table in advance; occasional shows.

Inexpensive Dining

Chez Marius • *Mikonkatu 1* • is so tiny that one Finnish wag quipped, "There's no room for dancing. The idea here is to keep breathing." French cuisine tenderly administered by M. Marius Raichi, formerly of the local film industry and an Oscar-winning personality. Licensed to serve beer and wine; *lunch only!!!* Reserve in advance.

Fen Kuan • *Eerikinkatu 14* • offers such startling Finno-Ugric delights as nasi goreng and sukiyaki. Not the Oriental recipes to which we Occidentals are accustomed, but nevertheless a sweet-and-sour treat in this northerly clime.

Happy Days • *Pohjoisesplanadi 2* • faces the Esplanade with 4 separate restaurants and terraces. Popular for value, companionship, and pleasant scenery.

SHOPPING

The Finnish eye for form and flair for originality are so exciting that in many creative fields the Finns surpass their northern neighbors.

SHOPPING HOURS: Weekdays 9 a.m. to 6 p.m., except 8 p.m. for department stores on Mon. and Fri.; Sat. 9 a.m. to 2 p.m. Holiday eves have Sat. closing times.

BEST AREAS: Esplanade Blvd. is lined with many fashionable boutiques and shops. The **Senaatin-Tori Center** features scores of shops and snackeries under one roof. It's on the Senate Square.

SAVINGS ON PURCHASES: Foreign residents can benefit from the 11% tax write-off for purchases over 150 FM—even if you buy with credit cards.

BATHWEAR AND SAUNA ITEMS: Within the charming premises at Aleksanterinkatu 28, the **Sauna Soppi-Shop** has the biggest collection of sauna-related articles we have ever seen—even including the hot boxes themselves. Its colorful and very fetching ancillary line, which can also be used in the home, at the pool, or on the beach, provides much greater interest to the average visitor; ask for Laila Iharvaara.

CRYSTAL, PORCELAIN, AND CERAMICS: In its handsome showroom at Pohjoisesplanadi 25, is the **Arabia Nuutajarvi Center.** The former contributes the porcelain and ceramics and the latter the glass. In flair and elegance, it is in the Very First Rank. The factory is at Hameentie 135 (accessible by bus) and there you can visit the museum, Exhibition Gallery, and net a few bargains in seconds.

DEPARTMENT STORE: World-famous **Stockmann** (Aleksanterinkatu 52B) is Finland's largest retail operation—a northern Saks-Magnin's-Macy's rolled into one. This landmark, with branches in *Tampere, Tapiola,* and *Turku,* for more than a century has been a national institution. If you're in a rush you can centralize all of your marketing here, with an English-speaking guide to help you. Its Finnish arts and crafts are especially fine.

FASHION: Widely heralded **Marimekko** can be found at **Vintti** (Keskuskatu 3) and **Marimekko** (Pohjoisesplanadi 31).

JEWELRY: Galerie Bjorn Weckstrom (Unioninkatu 30) will make you flip when you see the gloriously conceived and crafted creations. The distinctive style of its Lapponia Collection for men and women combines thousands of years of jewelers' art with the stunningly original, world-famous designs of Bjorn Weckstrom, whose sculptures are also on display. For Arctic gems, **Kaunis Koru Oy** (Senaatin-Tori Center) has unusual and distinguished stocks; competitive prices; spectrolites and other semiprecious stones mined above the Arctic Circle; wide range from inexpensive to fairly costly. **Kalevala Koru** (Unioninkatu 25) specializes in reproductions of ancient Finnish designs in silver and bronze plus a sizable handicrafts section with door chimes, rugs, sweaters, and additional lures.

OPEN-AIR MARKET: From 7 a.m. to 2 p.m., (plus evening hours) the wonderful **Kauppatori Market Square** at the harbor bristles and bustles with stalls and throngs. You'll find flowers, vegetables, fish, wearing apparel including marvelous fur hats, small articles of furniture, paintings—just name it or spot it, and it's yours. Go early to savor the best of its delightful color.

WEAVING: Vuokko (Pohjoisesplanadi 25) offers textiles in natural fibers designed by Eskolin-Nurmesniemi for dresses, skirts, and decorating use.

JYVASKYLA is the northern harbor for the boat ride up the lake from Lahti. Many structures of this unusually eye-appealing town were blueprinted by the celebrated Professor Alvar Aalto.

If you wish to linger, the **Rantasipi Laajavuori Hotel** has its limitations— the scenery not being one of them. (This chain specializes in choice vistas.) The young **Cumulus,** part of a cooperative group, has ordinary, clean, middle-quality standards throughout. Summer-only hostelries include the 84-room **Laajavuoren Kesahotelli** and the 272-unit **Rentukka.** All others here are small, simple, and Spartan.

KEMIJARVI is proud of the 60-room **Suomu,** which boasts a dining room with the Arctic Circle running right through its middle. Handmade furnishings; facilities for winter and summer sports; an architectural duplicate of a herdsman's hut.

KUOPIO is the touristic capital of the Eastern Lake District. Here is the jumping-off point for the renowned lake excursions. Dominating the settlement is a big hill that is crowned by a tower with a revolving restaurant. Try to visit this center, if you can, in the January Market Days. (The stands in Market Place function year-round on weekdays and are fun for visiting, too.) The curious, unique, and legendary Greek Orthodox church and monastery near Kuopio (its museum is in the city proper) is worth a special journey—especially in summer when you can do it by boat.

The region has sparse pickings for the pampered. The **Cumulus** is tops, followed by the **Atlas**. The **Puijonsarvi** is commercial and routine. The **Kalla** and the **Kaupunginhotelli** are lower-ranking also-rans. The **Iso-Valkeinen** is situated just outside the town. The **Rauhalahti Hotel** is 4 miles from the center on Lake Kallavesi. All are in the medium-price range.

LAHTI, a 65-mile inland ride from the capital, was a market crossroads for hundreds of years. One of its key attractions is the twice-daily hydrofoil service up the lake to Jyvaskyla. The one-way ride takes 3 hours, and it is so lovely in good weather that it shouldn't be missed.

Among its shelters, the town offers the much improved **Seurahuone,** on its main street. Pleasant restaurant with both student waiters and old pros; 120 rooms; worthy. **Ascot, Musta Kissa,** and **Lahti** are my next picks.

LAPLAND To have a taste of this pristine wilderness, where reindeer stroll nonchalantly beside the roadway, fly Finnair's jet to **Ivalo,** the only airport I've seen with a fireplace in the hall. Rent a car and drive to **Riekonkieppi,** a nearby complex of splendid cabins, some with their own hearth, sauna, and kitchen (Tel. 9697–81711). You can pan for gold, view a Lapp village, see a bear's cave, shop for wolf hides, and experience the haunting solitude of the pure northern fastness. Or you can bid for a **North Cape Tour.** This flies you from Helsinki to Rovaniemi (Lapland's gateway where the airport's welcoming sign is spelled out in antlers). Next you climb aboard a motor coach to strike out almost due north for Enontekio. From here you proceed still farther north to Alta and finally to Ultima Thule—Hammerfest, Norway, the most northerly city in the world. After overnights here and at remote Inari, you are driven back to Rovaniemi, bedded down in the Polar Hotel, and flown back to Helsinki the following morning. At *Inari* (25 miles from Ivalo) there's a fascinating Lapp settlement museum called **Saamelaismuseo** (June to Sept.). In rugged cottages are Lappish costumes, utensils, music, religious items, and manifestations of daily activity—oddities such as stuffing shoes with hay (for warmth; more efficient than socks) to crime and frontier punishment. Finnair's **Midnight Sun Flight,** which lasts a night and a day, leaves Helsinki every day throughout June, visiting Rovaniemi on the Arctic Circle. Boating types often rent a vessel in Turku and sail around the archipelago to absorb some of the greatest beauty the North can offer.

For winter sportsmen, the facilities in Lapland are made-to-measure for rawboned pioneers of new slopes and resorts. *Rukatunturi,* a herringbone below the Arctic Circle in eastern Finland, boasts a slalom track, 3 lifts, lights on downhill runs, and the longest jumps in Scandinavia. For experts. *Pallastunturi,* mostly for beginners, provides a special Christmas program, including a gift from Old St. Nick—free skiing instructions. The Finnish Travel Association can fill you in.

ROVANIEMI, less than 10 miles below the Arctic Circle, is known as the official gateway to Lapland. Still, it's a long way south of the main ranges and camping sites of the Lapps and their reindeer herds. The 350-room **Pohjanhovi** ("Nordic Court") with its river-side site and savory cookery is the leader. The internationally famous **Polar Hotel** is more in the town center; it's sleeker than you'd think for such a faraway place. **City Hotel** boasts a sauna on its top floor; very reasonable prices for rooms. **Ounasvaara** rolls out a jumbo-size restaurant and 39 pedestrian accommodations. (Sportsmen, incidentally, might be interested in the Polar's 10-person, log-lined **Bear's Den,** a guest lodge 18 miles north on the shores of *Karhujarvi,* which translates as "Bear Lake.") Refer also to "Lapland."

TAMPERE, 109 miles northwest of Helsinki and encompassed by lakes, is 2nd in size. It's proud of a 1000-seat outdoor auditorium which revolves somewhat less rapidly than a merry-go-round in season only.

Ilves, a modern high-rise with plenty of zest and nordic style, would be my first choice among hotels. **Rosendal,** pretty good for shelter, is also noteworthy for its restaurant.

The **Arctia Rosendal,** not far from the Summer Theater is geared for the congress rather than the individual trade. **Tammer,** in town, sports an English colonial ambience. **Cumulus** is satisfactory. **Kaupunginhotelli** has small rooms; not exciting but clean and adequate. **Victoria** is quite a substantial medium-bracket entry. The **Tampere** is run by the Arctic group and is substantial.

TURKU, a skip and a jump due west of Helsinki, is Finland's cultural center, its oldest city (it was the Finnish capital for 6 centuries), original seat of its tradition-rich A.D. 1640 university, home of its 13th century Cathedral, 9 museums, 3 summer theaters, 2 concert halls, and an important passenger port for Sweden. Shipbuilding, foodstuffs, and ceramics lead its commerce. The Handicraft Museum, one of the few building complexes to survive the great fire of 1827, is especially worth visiting.

The **Marina Palace,** standing on the western bank of the Aura River in the center of the city, is one of the best hotels in the nation, with unusually high standards of quality. Handsome pool and 4 saunas; open-air Sunmarina Restaurant in summer. **Ikituuri** is iki from too many tuuris. **Seurahuone/Societetshuset** has a split Finnish-Swedish official name which in local English nomenclature is "Sausage House." Delightfully cozy bar; excellent cookery with special accent on seafood; thoughtful, warm service. From sausages to—the historic **Hamburger Bors.** You might relish the refurbishing. The tasteless, unattractive **Turku** is a pale turkey bustling with conducted tours. The **Rantasipi Ruissalo** is a clean-lined, fresh-faced sea-sider which to me resembles a block of studio apartments. **Domus,** a student dormitory in winter that becomes a 70-room hotel in summer, could scarcely be more basic—but *what* a bargain!

FRANCE

USA: French Government Tourist Office, 610 Fifth Ave., New York, NY 10020, Tel. (212) 757–1125; Public Info. Div. at 628 Fifth Ave.; 645 N. Michigan Ave., Chicago, IL, Tel. (312) 337–6301; 2305 Cedar Springs Rd., Dallas, TX 75201, Tel. (214) 720–4010; 9454 Wilshire Blvd., Beverly Hills, CA 90212, (213) 272–2661; **CANADA:** 1 Dundas St. West, Toronto M5G 1Z3, Tel. (416) 593–4723; 1981 Ave. McGill College, H3A 2W9 Montreal, Tel. (514) 288–4264. But, instead of dealing with all of the above phone numbers, I suggest you ring *France-on-Call* (1–900–990–0040 at 50¢ per minute) and get the scoop from the information bank set up by the Fench Government Tourist Office.

SPECIAL REMARKS: (1) The City of Paris has its own Information Bureau (127 ave. Champs-Elysees) linked by telex to similar centers in other French hubs. At your service are an exchange office, accredited representatives of touring agencies, and hotel reservations facilities. (2) Additional locations for aid in Paris are at the Palais de Congres, Invalides, Gare du Nord, Gare de l'Est, and Gare de Lyon. (3) France no longer requires visas for visiting Americans. Though respectful as a diplomatic fillip, this does not imply any warmer public greeting or provoke any wider smiles, especially in the larger centers. Nevertheless, "officially" the nation is trying hard to offer hospitality. One fine effort is the *Welcome* program via some 1000 centers across France. The toll-free phone link is 05-201-202. The service is in English, too, with scores of tips on what to see and do throughout hundreds of regions in all Gaul.

ENGLAND

ENGLISH CHANNEL

Calais

BELGIUM   GERMANY

Le Havre
Rouen
Deauville   Trouville
NORMANDY   Seine R.
Reims
Paris
Barbizon
Chartres   Fontainbleau
Strasbourg
Colmar

BRITTANY

Loire River

CHATEAUX
COUNTRY

Dijon
Chagny
SWITZER-
LAND

ATLANTIC
OCEAN

Perouges   Chamonix
Lyon
Angouleme   Courchevel
Grenoble
Bordeaux
ITALY

Avignon
Nimes   Aix-en-   Nice
Arles   Provence
Biarritz   Cannes   French
St. Jean-de-Luz   Carcassonne   Riviera
Lourdes   Marseille   Antibes
St. Tropez

MEDITERRANEAN SEA

SPAIN

N

FRANCE

> **TELEPHONE:** Access code to USA: 19 (dial tone), USA Direct: 19 (dial tone) 0011 (a special AT&T service). To phone France: 33; time difference (Eastern Daylight) plus 6 hrs.

For more than 13 centuries the Gallic influence has been manifest throughout the civilized world. Every tick of that clock is revealed in some beautiful, historic, or interesting way in today's France.

You can live in abbeys where the vaults date back a thousand years, dine where Benedictine monks maintained our cultural heritage through the Dark Ages, dance in cellars where the *renaissance* itself was born. The country is so ancient, the history so rich, and the sights so resplendent, that every corner beckons the tourist to follow his special interests or whims. Naturally, Paris is the heartbeat, but very nearby are the playgrounds of France's royalty—the Loire Valley with scores of splendid chateaux to be visited, and even closer are the elegant palaces of Versailles, Fontainebleau, Saint Germain, plus the gracious estates that border the Marne and St. Cloud. The haunting forests of Barbizon also lie within a short drive of the capital.

Farther afield but still within easy reach of the City of Light, are the tranquil shores of Brittany and the snug half-timbered clusters of houses in Normandy. Mont St.-Michel towers above the lonely sands while not far away at Giverny, Monet's willows and lily ponds create a mood of pastoral springtime.

The great wine districts of Bordeaux, Champagne, Burgundy, Alsace, and the Rhone Valley are thick with sites and scenery, plus some of the finest cuisine in the world. Up to the Alps or along the Pyrenees and down to the sun-burnished flowered hills of Provence, there are weeks of vacations to be taken. The highest peak in Europe is Mont Blanc. The bluest sea is at the doorstep of the French Riviera. You've got 13 centuries to cover, so get going. *Allez!*

TRANSPORTATION **Airline Air France** not only covers the home territory, but it spans the globe, bringing French refinement and finesse to scores of destinations. U.S. gateways (including New York, Boston, Newark, Washington, Chicago, Houston, Miami, Los Angeles, San Francisco, and Anchorage) lead to Charles de Gaulle Airport Terminal II. Out of New York you can fly directly to Lyons year-round and there's a nonstop Riviera run between New York and Nice. From Newark you may wing off to Orly. Rail and bus get you to central Paris in 40 minutes or to Orly in under an hour. (If you are connecting with a flight from the other airport, ask for the free bus transport voucher due you.) If you are popping over to London, there's a convenient link to the near-town "Stolport" (called City Airport) from CDG II; one hour and no fuss. AF is one of my favorite carriers. High-budget travelers, of course, can soar with Concorde across the Atlantic in a jiffy or relax in the sumptuous first-class seats that adorn the widebody fleet. (Confession: As much as I like Concorde—and that's a lot—I would prefer first-class trans-Atlantic passage in an AF widebody jet.) Le Club class is the upgraded business nomination: separate cabin, new wider seats (now 7 instead of 8 across), and private restrooms on 747s. If you plan to fly within the nation, ask your travel agent or Air France stateside about the Air-Inter discounts for domestic travel. The savings are truly impressive.

Taxis At night, when it rains, during meal hours, and at the peak of the rush, Paris' 14,500 taxis are as elusive as ever. From the discovery of the internal combustion engine until a few years ago, cabbies just plain quit as soon as the clock struck lunch or dinner. But now, legally at least, they're supposed to take *you* where you want to go, instead of only in the direction of their garage, mistress, or home. Unhappily, the brutes usually won't, and few additional vehicles seem to be available during these key periods.

Fares are based on tiers. The meter should read "libre" until the flag is lowered. In midcity on weekdays and Saturday (except at night) the "A" designation should be visible; "B" (more expensive) is for suburban hauls such as to the airport (around $30 compared to $6 by bus); "C" is the most costly holiday and night rate. The driver is supposed to change the meter to a new level as you pass into the suburban zone, usually the *peripherique* or ring road.

NOTE · · · Stay away from large, luxurious taxis without meters that roam the gin-mill areas at night. Drivers purposely avoid quoting a price or indicating a fee, but when you arrive at your destination, you'll know you've been taken for a ride. Costs are outrageous.

Don't be startled by the shaggy companion riding beside your driver. Many cabbies, especially women, enjoy the fellowship and protection of dogs to discourage wheelborne criminality. Don't reach out to pet the pooch; I did once and almost became a southpaw.

Trains The French National Railroads (SNCF) are among the best and the fastest in the world. Don't forget to have your ticket *compostes* on the quay; if not, you might get fined. Regular routings include 125 mph cannonballing along numerous strips of trackage. They link Lyon and Paris with a 168 mph zipper switch in Geneva and the Savoy region at slightly slower speeds, and add on their extra-comfortable "Corail" service to major French destinations. TGV, for *Train a Grande Vitesse,* was the pioneer of swift rail travel and now a new generation has been born with the TGV *Atlantique,* which offers a commercial speed of 186 mph (Brittany, Loire Valley, and Bordeaux); it hit 320 mph on a test run not long ago! So who needs Concorde?

If you plan much train travel, take advantage of the Eurailpass, which we've earlier described in detail. SNCF also offers a very innovative and flexible **Rail-and-Drive** combo plus the well-established and money-stretching **France Railpass** scheme, so be sure to check with your travel agent. The savings don't stop with the transport alone, but extend to the attractions you'll want to visit en route.

Barges Some are exceptional. *The Princess* has been called "the floating chateau" and at more than $40,000 for 9 nights, you might appreciate that bruited charge for 5 staterooms! The *Normandie,* with 53 cabins for 106 passengers, is a more reasonable $1000 per person for 6 nights on the Seine. Both can vastly broaden your perspective of French history, Gallic cuisine, and life along Europe's most scenic waterways. Your travel agent can provide details.

FOOD It's the *dernier-cri,* of course. Within the nation there are regional styles as well as modish food fashions. Nouvelle cuisine is not so nouvelle anymore. It is being supplanted by *libre, moderne, instantane, marche, personnalisee, actuelle, courante,* and a shopping basket full of other terms suggesting yet another twist in the historic French gastronomic trail. Nevertheless, around almost every bend in that lane, you will find pleasure. You may also discover today a return to older conventions in cooking. And to dump carloads of cholesterol back into your blood vessels, many-a-chef is specializing in tasty *abats,* the richest visceral innards of the animal kingdom.

If you are touring, country hotels usually charge extra for breakfast; a simple coffee and bread will add $8 to $13 to your bill (per person!). If this rapacity galls you, take your first meal in a village cafe and save $6 or so per appetite. Then be sure that the hotelier has not "automatically" tagged breakfast onto your overnight bill.

You'll witness the continuing popularity of the *bistro.* Here the chefs reduce the number of selections to only a few well-prepared specialties, feature fixed menus, offer spectacular trays of rillettes, terrines, and other garniture for nibbling, and all at a price that you'd pay for only an appetizer in one of the 3-star establishments. A few gastronomic snobs may sniff scornfully at this trend (going like wild*feu* today in Paris), but we'll bet you a *feuillete de homard* that you'll find some of France's most rabid critics waiting patiently in a long line to gain entry to a bistro when they can't justify writing off a more costly meal on their expense accounts (which are now severely limited by government edict).

Every kitchen sorcerer and saucerer's apprentice undercooks at least a few showcase dishes and even serves some viands raw, only mellowed in natural impact by marinades. Strange invaders from the realms of botany and zoology are appearing on the fashionably large plates (about 2½ inches greater in diameter than customary dinner service), while piscatorial preparations now are being ladled into wide shallow bowls. The trend is to have *everything* created and displayed by the chef, with virtually no emphasis on the theatrical flambe flourishes by tableside maitres. Kitchen kings scour and scout roadside weed patches in quest of fresh savory ingredients for new stews and soups; flour for sauces is never used; specialties of the 15th century are being resurrected; and the alternation in color of items on today's platters is almost as imperative as the gustation itself.

Americans, not incidentally, are becoming *objets* of scorn at scores of top French restaurants. The reason is that many have phoned or written from the U.S.A. to reserve tables for the date of their visit. Out of several affirmative replies they accept only one, but fail to notify the other restaurateurs that they are not arriving. Since most establishments are small such behavior can result in significant losses. Hence, infuriated chefs are instructing their staffs to ignore entreaties from no-show Yanks in favor of Europeans, who more frequently honor their requests for tablespace. Retribution awaits at the nearest hamburger stand—and the punishment certainly fits the crime.

DRINKS Each region proudly offers its own distinctive wine. If you're not particular (or if you're a tried-and-true traveler), much of the time you'll stick to *vin ordinaire,* the routine carafe table wine. It's eminently satisfactory.

Broadly speaking, it's *red* with meat or game, *white* with fish, fowl, oysters, or hors d'oeuvres. If the meat is heavy, gamy, or spicy, Burgundy is usually chosen over Bordeaux. Nowadays, if the Burgundy is a light one or if

Top Vintages at a Glance

Alsatian	78	79	81	82	83	85	88	
Bordeaux (white)	81	82	83	85	86	87	88	
(red)	76	78	79	81	82	83	85	86 88
Burgundy (white)	81	82	83	84	85	86	88	
(red)	78	79	81	83	85	86	88	
Champagne	79	81	82	83	85			
Cotes-du-Rhone	78	79	82	83	85	88		
Loire:								
Muscadet	82	85	87	88				
Anjou	85	86	87	88				
Pouilly-Sancerre	85	86	87	88				

you are dining in a warm region such as the Riviera in summer, the house often serves this red wine chilled. Personally, I find it a bit put on, but each to his own *gout*.

Champagne is the only type correctly served through all courses of a meal. In scores of restaurants, the house aperitif today often is based on champagne, with an additive such as *cassis* or *framboise* to freshen the flavor—a jovial advance over the older *kir* (chilled light white wine and cassis). For your champagnes, look for a dated bottle, because that is the signal from the producer that it is worthy of being identified by year.

Cramant de Mumm is an elixir of great delicacy and rarity, so small in supply that it is sold or given as gifts only to pet restaurant proprietors of this topflight vintner. Halfway between a "full" and a "still" champagne in effervescence, it offers the connoisseur a lovely bouquet and just enough bubbles to add its very distinguishable tang and zest.

Among the lower-price red wines, Beaujolais is usually an excellent bet. It should be ordered young. Get either Brouilly, Moulin-a-Vent, Julienas, Morgon, or Fleurie (the sub-names on the label) if you can. Other standbys in this range are Bordeaux varieties of St.-Julien, St.-Emilion, Medoc, Pomerol, and St.-Estephe.

Among inexpensive white wines, Chablis is very tricky, due to minuscule supplies of sound types. If you like your whites dry, Pouilly Blanc Fume, Pouilly-Fuisse or Muscadet should do the trick without breaking the bank. What passes for genuine Chavignol in many places today is horrid. But Traminer, from Alsace, still has an affinity for a good filet of sole.

Order Vouvray or *vin mousseux* (sparkling wine) if you want to save money. Though cheaper than champagne, they have attractive similarities. Reason: The champagne name and the *methode champenoise* refer (under E.E.C. regulations) only to the Champagne region, and these varieties originate outside the legal district.

Traditionally, a good buy always has been cognac. Delamain and Bisquit are softer mellow types that are not very expensive; with age the prices can soar. Armagnac is similar but a bit harder; it seems to be enjoying a fashion upswing nowadays. The people of Normandy are weaned on Calvados, a pungent applejack that can do wondrous things when it's old and warmed. True-blue Normands claim that if sipped between courses it "reams a hole in the belly to make room for more food." As for cordials, there are scores, most of which you probably already know.

Most of the homegrown beer is frightful—bitter, watery, with an aftertaste of liver-fed pollywogs—but you'll see a lot of it because it's cheap. Fortunately, some Alsatian types ably contradict this statement. Always ask for "bee-air," because "beer" to the French waiter means "Byrrh," a popular red vermouth-type aperitif. Imported brews abound everywhere.

TIPPING   Every human being who serves you will proffer a hand with stunning rapidity. At the movies, if you don't tip, the usherette will probably flash her light into your eyes until you do.

Hotels add up to 30% in service charges and taxes, depending on class and location. "Restaurants de Tourisme"—most of the better-known places fall into this official category—automatically take a 15% service bite; you are expected to add another 5% to 7% for the waiter. Give the checkroom attendant 1 franc, the washroom attendant 1 franc, and the wine steward (if you use him) 5 francs. Taxi drivers get 10–15%; hotel doormen (when calling a taxi) get about the same, ordinarily, and more if they go out in the rain to capture your vehicle.

CITIES AND REGIONS

AIX-EN-PROVENCE   While Cezanne was born and worked here, little beyond his studio and his parents' home remains. The mountain he painted so often, Sainte-Victoire, is something you will recognize. Hotels: (1) **Mercure Paul Cezanne** (tucked into a quiet nook of the mid-city district; lovely paintings in lobby; intimate in concept and not many accommodations, so be sure to book in advance), (2) **Hotel du Roi Rene** (good physical plant; grand in approach, but a bit frayed in presentation; nice staff; if you drive, empty your car of all valuables for the night if it is parked out front), (3) **Augustins** (without restaurant). Our top choice for dining would be **Clos de la Violette** (wonderful in the summer when the garden is in flower and you can dine outdoors; more luxurious than the prices would indicate).

ALBI   **Hostellerie Saint-Antoine** seems tops in town. Out of the city, the same administration runs the rustically posh **La Reserve,** which is a polished Tarnside gem.

ANGOULEME   This is in the midst of the cognac district, so if you are touring why not stay in a house where the elixir is made: ☆☆☆ **Hostellerie du Maine Brun,** about 5 miles outside of the town? A delicious white cognac is distilled here. One of the most exquisite experiences a traveler could enjoy is a summer dinner on the outdoor terrace beside its brook, a great forest of trees and acres of sunflowers between you and the golden gloaming. Not incidentally, the meal may be a landmark in your gastronomic experience too. Adequate-to-good accommodation; gracious host-patron and cheerful minions; deer in its private park; a pool; a handsome bar and dining room—but don't miss sundown! My second choice in the region would be the streamside ★★★ **Moulin du Roc** at *Champagnac-de-Belair.* If you can swallow the haughty drift from staffers, you might delight in the sylvan setting and even relish the fine cuisine of the modern mode.

ARLES   **Jules Cesar** is the best of an inferior lot but the cuisine is good. Although barny and quite cool it is adequate. The 70-room **Mercure** is cool in spirit but okay for comfort. Then, the **D'Arlatan** is often regarded as the nearest competitor, followed by the **Calendal.** For dining the **Marques** in the Jules Cesar is excellent, but **L'Olivier** has more visual charm. Both are reasonable in price.

AUCH   First, see the Cathedral with its magnificent carvings backing the altar. Then plan a meal at the hotel here.

   ☆☆☆ **Hotel de France** (in Gascogne). It is especially noted for its cuisine, which is masterminded by Chef Andre Daguin—and which is worth a special detour.

AUTUN   It looks as if it were designed as a cover for a book of fairy tales. It was founded by Augustus in 15 BC so many of its charms are Roman. The archaeology, the Christian relics, and the modern comforts conspire to provide great appeal. **Hotel des Ursulines** with 30 rooms and a commendable restaurant is your best bet for a pause in this heartland of Burgundy. Slightly north at *Arnay-le-Duc,* **Chez Camille** is another lovely choice. Monique and Armand Poinsot are the essence of hospitality. His cooking skills are esteemed locally and his tabs are very reasonable. A charming nook for repose and restauration.

AVIGNON   This rampart-ringed "City of the Popes" is wonderful for sightseers and convenient for strollers. The Palais des Papes is the focal point; see also the Petit Palais and the gardens atop the panoramic heights. At neighboring *Villeneuve-les-Avignon,* visit **La Chartreuse,** now an art center but since early church history a home for the highest princes of the clergy. Hotels (1) ★★★★ **Le Prieure** (a small and not too costly rural gem, at Villeneuve-les-Avignon; superb kitchen that follows the seasons and changes menu daily; kind reception by Marie-France Mille; closed Dec. to mid-Feb.), (2) **La Magnaneraie** (in the same village; built around a courtyard), (3) **Europe** (in town and dating from 1580, but fully modernized to current standards; recommendable kitchen; one of the best value-for-money stops in southern France with grace, comfort, and beauty at every turn), (4) **Mercure Palais des Papes** (also in the center; modern building but somewhat institutional), (5) **La Mirande** (a near neighbor, new and luxury category), (6) **Novotel,** and (7) **Ibis** (both the latter on the outskirts and chiefly for motorists). At mealtimes try (1) **Hiely,** (2) **Brunel,** (3) **Auberge de France.** At *Noves* (7 miles out): **Auberge de Noves.** At *Les Angles* (2 miles): **Ermitage-Meissonnier.**

BARBIZON   Here, along with nearby Fontainebleau (see later), is one of the few short excursion points from Paris. Stevenson wrote his *Forest Notes* here; Millet, Rousseau, and other Barbizons had their studios in the village or regularly visited the fantasy woodlands. The paths among the pines and peculiar, haunting rock formations are enchanting, so don't fail to wear your walking shoes.

☆☆☆ **Hotellerie du Bas-Breau** • is a fine old timber and stucco structure on the main street where the food is expensive but good, and the comfort is ample; service, however, can be spotty.

Auberge de la Dague • is more attractive on the outside than in the interior; rates, however, are reasonable.

★ **Hostellerie de la Cle d'Or** • is more well known as a restaurant than for its 15 rooms. But both aspects are appealing and recommendable. Often the first choice of well-traveled French.

BEAUNE   Be sure to visit one of the Burgundian wine cellars that are in the town or at the famous chateaux that dot the neighboring countryside. For overnighting, it's the smart 50-room **Le Cep** with its striking restaurant. The **Belle Epoque** and **Henry II** do not offer dining facilities, but their accommodation is satisfactory. The **Central** is more modest but more than adequate. In *Nuits-Saint-Georges* the **Domaine Comtesse Michel de Loisy** is simply a bed-and-breakfast haven, but what a tasteful one! The rooms are filled with fine antiques, there are occasional wine tastings and gala dinners, plus the enduring hospitality of the countess herself. Rates begin at 450 FF; phone her at 80–610272 or Telex 351653 Loisy. In this area there are scores more; most give their all to tour groups. For independent dining, try the charm-laden 17th-century **Auberge St. Vincent,** opposite the Hospices, or the **Morillon** at 31 rue Maufoux. In nearby *Levernois* you can stay and dine very well at the **Hostellerie** operated by one of France's top chefs. Then up toward *Nuits-St.-Georges* there are two wonderful stops: **Chateau de Gilly** just outside of *Vougeot* and the more modest **Chateau de la Berchere** at *Boncourt le Bois.* Gilly—and lovely it is—closes Jan. to mid-March.

BIARRITZ

☆☆☆☆ **Palais** • is under municipal ownership. With 140 bedrooms, it also offers a stunning swimming pool, complete with chic cabanas and all luxuries; sumptuous and lethally expensive.

☆☆ **Regina et Golf** ● lies between the golf course and the sea. A good find, although it's closed Oct. through May.

☆☆ **Miramar** ● is in a midtown situation. It's the only major hostelry open all year. Big on fitness (especially seawater magic called *thalasso thera-pie*), health, sports facilities, it also offers a nightclub; pleasant 3-tiered building with sea orientation; not dazzling, but noted for its kind and efficient adminis-tration.

These will be followed by the **Plaza,** the beachfront **Windsor,** and the **Ocean.**

For saving money, I'd choose the intimate **Palacito** or the **Etche Gorria.** Still cheaper are the pension-style **Central, Monguillot,** and **Port Vieux.** Most of the aforementioned are open in summer only; most insist on full pension.

☆☆ **Cafe de Paris** ● is the top dining establishment in the city. You'll enter through an aviary, with a hearth on one side and the Atlantic on the other; friendly but forgetful service; closed in Feb.; expensive; father-and-son Pierre and Robert LaPorte alternate between managing this house and the Relais de Parme at the airport.

☆☆ **L'Operne** ● has a glorious command of the coast from its window tables; the seafood is outstanding.

★ **Galion** ● also has a viewful setting, a fine garden, and excellent marine fare.

★★★★ **Chateau de Brindos** ● is in a wonderful waterside setting in its own parkland; nouvelle cuisine that vies with anything in the district; charming rooms, too, for overnighting.

☆☆☆☆☆ **Les Pres d'Eugenie** ● is down the pike, vaguely north of Pau (about 25 miles), in the department of Landes. Here, the noted monarch of modern chefs, Michel Guerard, practices his alchemy at *Eugenie-les-Bains.* For low-caloried masterworks here indeed is a dining shrine. Always reserve in advance, especially if you plan to overnight in the 40-room establishment; closed winters; ovens begin stoking in April. A marvel of inventive new techniques known universally as *Cuisine Minceur* ("the cuisine of slimness").

BORDEAUX The **Sofitel Aquitania,** looking onto a lake and with its own pool, is sleekly commercial and modern; 212 air-conditioned units; cool but good. It is handy to the city's Exposition Hall. The **Mercure** has a dollop of personality, but not much. Otherwise, try the **Normandie,** although it offers no dining room; the **Alliance** is reasonable but not inspiring; the **Majestic** and **Atlantic** are so-so; and the **Terminus. Novotel** and **Ibis** are inexpensive, clean, and spiritless. Over at neighboring *Pauillac,* you might prefer the cozy and inviting **Chateau Cordeillan-Bages,** which is into the heartland of the vine-yards (tel. 5659–2424). If you are looking to avoid city life, here's your an-swer.

Restaurants:

☆☆☆ **Chapon Fin** • has its charms, if you don't mind the cavelike effects or the artificial sky; its famous table is traditional as well as inventive.

☆☆☆ **Saint-James** • offers more of nouvelle cuisine; Jean-Marie Amat, who cares for this sanctuary also runs the excellent but cheaper **Le Bistrot de Bordeaux;** Amat's sister operates the cozy **Vieux Bordeaux.**

☆☆ **Reserve** • is 5 miles out at L'Alouette. It is worth the journey, but reserve ahead because it is popular.

☆☆ **La Chamade** • comes next; try the salad of sole with leeks and you may rate it tops.

★ **Dubern** • is one of the most atmospheric houses in the area; the kitchen has come back dramatically lately.

☆☆ **Le Rouzic** • is good bistro dining, but only if you're feeling expansive and expensive.

La Tupina • is more of a budget bistro.

BOURG-EN-BRESSE   The most hospitable nests are at **Le Logis de Brou,** which is near to the beautiful medieval church and adjoining antique buildings. **Du Prieure** was opened recently by the former proprietresses of Le Logis. It has 14 rooms and the ladies' traditional hospitality. But, what you really want to do in this town is dine.

☆ **Auberge Bressane** • is across from the magnificent 16th-century Eglise de Brou, which you should visit by day; excellent Quenelles or chicken in cream sauce with rice; frogs legs okay; substantial meal for 2 about $55 with wine.

Chalet de Brou • 15½-miles out in the village of *Brou,* opposite the church; an economy stop.
Also see comments listed under "Perouges."

CAHORS   The lovely ★★★ **Chateau de Mercues** stands almost half-a-mile above the Dordogne vale, splendid for viewing and for pausing. The cuisine is recommendable too. It's expensive, but everlastingly memorable.

CALAIS   (1) **Meurice** (good kitchen, but rooms basic), (2) **Sauvage** (also basic). Skip the rest. In fact, if you want to skip the entire country, Calais is the ferrypoint for the world's largest commercial hovercraft (belonging to the **Hoverspeed** company), which zips in triangles between here, Boulogne, and Dover. Also see "Montreuil-sur-Mer."
   This is not to imply that you should leave the area without browsing around. The Pas de Calais area is rich in history. Here are a few excursion points: *Boulogne* (Caesar, Claudius, Charlemagne, Napoleon, and Hitler all contem-

plated English invasions from here; the antiquities and the Sea Center are excellent); *Arras* (a Flemish touch in France); *St. Omer* (see Notre Dame and watch postmen delivering mail in a rowboat); *Sangatte* (the Continental terminus of the Channel Tunnel, with working models and video shows at the Exhibition Center).

CARCASSONNE   Its sites are greater than its comforts. But in a day you can visit the ramparts, main gates, and Comtal Castle. If you stay longer, be sure to go to the museum for its excellent oils and see St. Nazaire, which dates back to the 11th century (the windows are gems). Ecclesiastical architecture is the chief reason for going—and it is rich in that. Hotels: (1) **Cite** (interestingly situated in the Old City, high above the "new"; excellent, thoughtful service; ample comfort; open Apr. to Sept. only; the leader), (2) **Terminus** (antebellum and clean; passable but not distinguished), (3) **Montsegur,** (4) **Domaine d'Auriac.** For dining, try (1) **Logis de Trencavel,** (2) **Auberge Pont Levis,** or (3) **La Cremade.**

CASTILLON DU GARD   This is near *Remoulins* in Provence.

★★★ **Le Vieux Castillon** • offers only 23 bedrooms. It is reconstructed from medieval, meridional houses very close to Pont du Gard (under 2 miles) and 15 miles from Avignon. It is about as *"vieux"* as the ink on this page, even though the hamlet and its hostelry are being heavily promoted as antiquity itself. For such instant history, I'd prefer a motel on the A-6.

CHAGNY

☆☆☆☆☆ **Lameloise** • is a small modest hotel in the center of this hamlet with a far-from-modest restaurant. The house reflects Burgundian tastes, with open-beam ceilings, magnificent tapestries, wrought-ironwork, arches, vaults, and rich furnishings. The $140 gourmet menu for 2 people is vast. My $45 repast for one was more than ample for an ordinary appetite. Delicious brochet, slices of duck with grapes, and Bresse chicken; outstanding cheese trolley—and those desserts! They are fabulous—especially the feuillete with fraises. If you stay overnight, ask to see the room first, since some are grand and others grim. Just a bit north at *Puligny-Montrachet,* **Le Montrachet** is an inviting house in the famous village square; a beautiful Burgundian dining salon and a handful of accommodations.

CHAMONIX   (1) **Croix Blanche** has a midvillage situation that can be noisy; main dining room with copper-and-iron hood drawing sparks up the chimney; "modern" rooms with beds lower than your ski bottoms; "traditional" accommodations better; all units with baths; 4-season operation; nice staff; recommended, (2) **Mont-Blanc** offers a charming split-level round-the-hearth dining room called the Matafan; gardenside terrace bar; tennis court; pine-lined bedchambers; attentive direction; a favorite with North Americans, with good reason, (3) **Auberge du Bois Prin** is very atmospheric, (4) **La Sapiniere.** New (and untested by us) is **Les Aiglons,** which blends modernisms in design with traditional mountain hotel concepts. Extensive sport and health facilities; viewful suites and standard twins; well-equipped accommodations. We look forward to seeing this promising sporty candidate. Down the line in attractiveness come **Albert 1st** and **Hermitage-Paccard**. **Au Bon Coin** is a dainty little corner with lots of heart plus soothing tabs. If none of these suits your taste, there are approximately 100 others on the immediate and nearby slopes. For cuisine, try (1) **Le Royal** in the Casino; Park Avenue living-room ambience; glass-enclosed view of illuminated garden; elegant, (2) **Lion d'Or**, (3) **La Tartifle**, (4) **Le Choucas** for snacks, (5) **Le Creperie** for crepes of all types. The best hotel dining is at the **Albert 1st**.

COLMAR   Culturally, visitors come to see the famous altarpiece of Issenheim, the Old Town, and the Museum of Unterlinden, but gastronomically much is happening about 20 minutes up the pike at *Illhaeusern,* which has also put the area on the culinary map.

☆☆☆☆☆ **Auberge de l'Ill** ● on the banks of the Haut-Rhin, is one of the top stops in the nation. Spectacular turbot souffle with lobster sauce, noisettes de Chevreuil, and ice cream; perfect attention from an alert corps of captains and waiters. Closed July 1–7, February, Mon. evening, and Tues. Summary: superb for country dining!

In Colmar itself, the gastronomy also deserves attention, especially at the highly acclaimed **Schillinger** (try the duck in lemon sauce) or the **Fer Rouge** (salmon topped with seasonal vegetables); the much less expensive **Maison des Tetes** provides satisfactory fare.

CONDRIEU   is basically a convenient highway junction near Lyon for north-south routes as well as east to Switzerland.

☆☆☆☆ **Hotellerie Beau Rivage** ● is a captivating tie-up right on the Rhone, despite the rather industrial aspect of the river at this point. Waterfront terrace; splendid restaurant (try the quenelles de brochet, the trout, or the marmite du pecheur); cordial service. If it's available, book room #35, with renaissance furnishings and about an acre of space. Lovely in every regard and still one of my favorite crossroad stops in France.

COURCHEVEL 1850   (The numerals indicate the altitude in meters.) Indisputably, this is France's kingdom of winter sport. The natural panoramas in the 3 contiguous valleys (Courchevel, Meribel, Thorens) form a tableau that is breathtaking by any alpine measure—with skiing opportunities that are thrilling and almost endless; moreover, there are no waiting lines and the runs are perfectly maintained. Until Olympic fever struck, the charm of nature hereabouts was horribly despoiled by some of the ugliest architecture in the nation. Disciples excused this by saying that the town (created in tiers of elevation) was "purpose built" as a ski resort—as if having a singular mission provided a license to erect grim, spiritless layers of concrete streaked with neon and tinseled with aluminum extrusions. Much of this is being relieved through the greater use of timber cosmetics. Blockhouses are being clad with rustic stonework and pitched roofs take on an alpine aspect. In any case, whatever may be left over of the visual pollution might be forgotten when you consider that there are nearly 400 miles of glorious ski runs and approximately 800 instructors in the neighborhood.

Among hotels, **Le Byblos Des Neiges** is dramatically the most expensive, excellent for situation, and startling in its flamboyance. The keynote is its massive use of wood for interior support and cunning plate glass positioning to capture the natural views. The pool, sauna, gym, bars, and dining are noteworthy, part and parcel of the services of most top hostelries in town. The **Des Neiges** is less eye-popping and, in my view, gains by the more understated grace. The expanded **Bellecote** (also located directly on the ski slopes) takes the form of a wooden chalet that evokes a welcoming rustic tone. Walls are thin and its short narrow bathtubs were never designed for long legs and sport-weary hips. The pool, however, is ample in size if you need to stretch out and now they have cleverly added a few individual chalets in the garden for more luxury-minded guests. **Annapurna,** well designed, resides high among the best runs of this particular mountain. **Le Lana,** also in the expensive group, offers a lobby with a golden Buddha altarpiece, a plaster blackamoor, tropical plants, and artificial fur-covered pillars: *Chacun a son gout!* **Pralong 2000,** ultramodernistic, is more than satisfactory if skiing is your motive for staying in Courchevel. **Pomme de Pin** offers rooms that are relatively inexpensive, but it is better known for the sparkling and costly gastronomy in its Batteau Ivre restaurant. Among other lower-cost choices, the **Courcheniege** is beautifully situated. **Kilimandjaro** gains from its intimate, friendly family direction; they set an excellent table. It is one of the best values of all even if the building looks dismal. Among restaurants, the ☆☆☆☆ **Batteau Ivre** is easily the finest in the town, in my opinion. You couldn't pay me to go to the **Chabichou** after being sickened by food (and rude service) at its summer digs in St. Tropez. The Trop troop moves up here for its haughty brand of winter sport. Another chum writes to tell me that his tummy recently did a French revolution in the Courchevel restaurant. I can live without it, if you'll permit the turn of phrase. **La Bergerie** is so costly that you may feel you've been hit by an avalanche when bill-time comes. Ventilation is miserable; service is oh-so-snobbish; music is loud; the style of chic is expensive informality.

Most hotels require full- or half-pension. Some offer meal vouchers to huts sprinkled over the mountain ranges, so be sure to ask if you don't wish to be force-fed every morsel at your living address. For snacks, the midvillage pizzerias usually offer crepes in a Franco-Italo effort to please every palate. *Le hot dog* also makes a frequent appearance along the main drag.

DEAUVILLE and **TROUVILLE**   are tete-a-tete resorts linked by a bridge over the Touques River. The former, more patrician, offers all the accouterments of High-Life leisure—yachting, racing, polo, golf, aero-clubbiness, gambling, curling (the outdoor variety, too), a covered pool for year-round dipping, a wide flower-lined beach, and a budget that headlines some of the world's greatest entertainers. After dark the dazzling white Casino is now open year-round; it contains Regine's, a link in the posh nightclub chain. Trouville is less opulent, with more of a busy-port personality. Parisians, who can make the drive in about 3 hours, crowd both in increasing numbers. (See also ''Normandy,'' near the end of this chapter.)

☆☆☆☆☆ **Normandy** • is once again one of France's finest hotels following a timely and dedicated renovation of its bedrooms. Fronted by tennis courts and sea; Grand Siecle architecture; covered and heated pool; special diet program if desired. Stratospheric rates. Open all year.

☆☆☆☆ **Royal** • is also excellent in a traditional fashion; graceful for mood and superb for comfort.

☆☆☆☆ **Golf** • has a 1st-rate view and extra-good cuisine; it's popular with golfers and the older generation.

Our choices next in line are **Altea** and **La Fresnave**.

Now let's take a look at the local dining spots: (1) The **Casino** can boast the Cafe de la Boule, Banco, and Dolce Vita for varying moods. (2) **Ciro's** on the beach promenade for lunch and dinner any day or night year-round. Both have the Casino supervision. The latter is a glass-faced beachfront haven for delectable seafood specialties. Among independents, I'm awfully fond of the ★★ **Spinnaker,** a charmer. Finally, be sure to slip on your espadrilles and hike out to the little restaurants along the Touques River for the petite and delicious *crevettes grises*—the best shrimps in all Gaul.

☆☆☆ **Ferme St.-Simeon** • is in *Honfleur,* about 9 miles from Deauville. It is yet another fine possibility. *Very* expensive.

See also "Normandy Beachheads," further along.

FONTAINEBLEAU   As an excursion point from Paris, this royal enclave (with Versailles) tops the list. Less than an hour from the bright lights, it is also a delightful site for weekending and sharing the beauty that so many French regents enjoyed since the Middle Ages. Few travelers realize it, but the region offers its own Chateaux Country, with the magnificent, perfectly preserved **Vaux le Vicomte** as one of the most impressive estates in all of France only 12 miles away. (Be sure to check opening dates and times.) In contrast to pomp, there are the forest paths of romantic **Barbizon** (previously described) only a few minutes along the highway. If you wish to linger, **L'Aigle Noir** faces the gates to the palace grounds. It offers alfresco dining in summer, a splendid salon for inclement days, very handsome bedchambers, some with open timbers and textiled walls. If you are coming only for the day, dine here rather than at **Chez Arrighi,** where we had a ghastly bout with the vittles. **Legris et Parc** is a less costly hotel choice with ample comfort and a gracious garden setting. Try not to miss the quiet majesty of Fontainebleau and the fringe benefits of the neighboring hamlets.

JOIGNY   A lot of inland voyagers begin their canal explorations at this staging point.

☆☆☆☆ **A La Cote St. Jacques** • is a small hotel with a splendid restaurant. Try the supreme de bar with sea urchins, the fruit de mer with zucchini flowers in a light cream sauce, or the delicate pigeon salad. Bid for a room in the Yonne-side annex; pool and boat landing-charter boats available across the river at Joinville for canal trips.

LAGUIOLE   What? Never heard of it? It's in the Tarn Gorge on the N9 north of Montpellier. And it's been put on the map by Michel Bras, a young genius who is being visited (and praised) by chefs from all over the civilized table. His restaurant (with a handful of rooms) is called ☆☆☆☆ **Lou Mazuc.** Here's a cooking talent comparable with Freddy Girardet (of Crissier) when he began about a dozen years ago. Watch him—and make the detour if you can.

LES BAUX   Baumaniere crowns a rugged, rock-tortured valley less than 2 hours northwest of Marseille. The main building has 10 almost shabby and depressing (to me) regional-style rooms; there's an adjoining annex with a few more, as well as the Cabro d'Or ½ mile down the slope, with its own dining room and extra-tranquil privacy. Accommodations in the former cost almost double the tariffs of the latter. Fine cuisine traditionally had been the reason for going, but I would no longer make a special detour. **La Riboto de Taven** is moving up quickly as a noteworthy kitchen. The oysters in their special pastry and sauce are majestic. And here comes **Mas d'Aigret,** which is currently receiving lots of acclaim. The gardens, terraces, and several salons are appealing, but there are only about a dozen rooms, so you'd better be sure to reserve. (P.S.: For golfers, the hotel has composed a program of play at courses nearby.)

LIGNY   is of use if you are traveling north on the A2 toward Brussels or Lille, about 100 miles above Paris. The **Chateau de Ligny** • *Ligny en cis Haucourt* • is an inviting but rather worn stopover begun in the 13th century and finished in the 17th. It's more of a hunting retreat or a squire's redoubt rather than a vast, imposing palace. The people are awfully nice here. Reserve ahead due to its remoteness; Tel: (27) 85 85 84.

LYON,   the nation's second city, resides at the junction of 2 rivers (Rhone and Saone) and 2 worlds (central and northern Europe). This apex between the Alps and Burgundy contains an alive, thriving, and vitally stimulating city. Satolas Airport this year will double its capacity to 8 million, providing many new services for traffic to and from the Winter Olympics. The high-speed TGV trains link Lyon to 18 other centers. Renowned for its silks and its stupendous dining establishments; chocoholics swoon to the rich handmade creations of Bernachon, often praised as the finest chocolatier on this globe; dazzling Roman antiquities, chateaux, cultural attractions that include the fine **Gallo-Roman Museum** and the **Amphitheatre des Trois Gauls,** where the first Christians may have been martyred in the 2nd century. **Excavations** date Latin inhabitance well before 15 B.C. when it was called *Lugdunum.* It has its own ballet center, symphony, and busy theatrical season.

    Cour des Loges, in the Old Town, is a modern adaptation of a Renaissance monastic structure. Today's "cells" are lovely suites and bedchambers assembled under a glass atrium; indoor pool, sauna, and terraced gardens. Restaurant and *tapas* bar for snacks. Lots of charm.

    Sofitel offers 200 bedrooms, a superb panoramic restaurant called Les Trois Domes at rooftop level, and 2 bars that are enjoyable. **Pullman Part-Dieu,** in a tower that forms part of one of Europe's largest shopping centers, is architecturally exciting but not as comfortable as the Sofitel. A Moroccan-style lobby rises through 8 floors of hanging gardens cascading from loggias; the blue and teal l'Arc en Ciel restaurant overlooks the city and the Rhone; bedrooms are plainly modern but adequate. **La Maison de la Tour** comes warmly recommended by savvy travelers, but I haven't tried it personally. After these, there are the **Grand Hotel Concorde** and the **Beaux-Arts** (no restaurant). Another **Sofitel** is far out near the airport; and a **Novotel** (okay for motorists) is located on the *autoroute* approach from Geneva.

☆☆☆☆ **Paul Bocuse ●** one of the acknowledged giants of French cuisine, plies his famous trade in a sprawling converted house on the banks of the Saone about 15 minutes by car from Lyon. Entrance via a small garden and a patio displaying a colossal caldron; further access beside glass panels with a view of the kitchen; 2 interior salons, one facing the river; brick-red ceiling with open timbers; tile floor (cold in winter); candelabra, cut flowers, and plants dotting the rooms. The original restaurant, which is now used for overflow traffic, is the more majestic. There is nothing timid about the maestro's flavorings. His are deliberate culinary statements—without the remoteness or subtleties that are often so faint as to invite puzzled glances from diners who pretend to recognize the savorings. Garlic appears boldly; so does pepper. The chicken in *chemise* (a specialty) nests in a football-size membrane, a masterpiece of presentation. There is an uneasy mood of commercialism that the sensitive guest might resent: Paul Bocuse postcards, dishes, cookbooks, chocolates, luggage, and automobile stickers (declaring ''This is the emblem gourmets will know.'')—all of which cause the reflective diner to wonder about his role in this smoothly orchestrated promotional scheme.

After this stellar restaurant, you also would not be unhappy at the wonderfully classic and masterful ☆☆☆☆ **Orsi,** the posh and candle-lit ★★★ **Nandron,** the **Fedora, Les Fantasques,** or the delightful ★★ **Mere Brazier.** In addition, I have had good luck in the popular **Leon de Lyon** as well as the smaller **Bourillot. The Auberge de Fond-Rose** is also good, but its fashionably modern cuisine is expensive. For less costly wares, try a Rose by another name: **Chez Rose,** a family-run stop for locals who enjoy well prepared food and little pretense.

For luxury, beauty, rest, and nutrients, you might try **Le Chateau** at *Faverges de la Tour (Isere),* east of Lyon on the N-75. Take the La-Tour-du-Pin exit from the A-43 motorway to Geneva. This is a sumptuous redoubt of 40 rooms (the best ones in the castle itself). Pool, tennis, gym, and a 9-hole golf course. A breathtaking rural gem.

MARSEILLE, the oldest city of France, dates back to Grecian times, when it was called ''Massalia.'' It's the chief port, with heavy Italian influence, routine hotels, superb restaurants, Chateau d'If (Monte Cristo's famous island prison, an interesting 30-minute boat ride away), practically no major monuments except l'Abbaye de St. Victor or the Basilica of Notre-Dame de la Garde, plenty of color, new construction, a frenetic atmosphere. First, take a drive along the scenic **JFK Corniche,** which finally leads to the municipal beaches. Be sure to visit the **Vieux Port** for salty flavors and perhaps sip a glass of Tavel in the smart **Place Thiars** or the zesy **Cours Julien.** Be a bit careful where you wander in this toddling town of sailors, immigrants, and transients.

Hotels are nothing special here. **Sofitel Vieux Port** probably leads the parade, followed by either the **Mercure** or the **Pullman Beauvau** (without dining room). **Residence Le Petit Nice** is a very lovely hideaway on the Corniche; the food is exceptional. Then I'd rank them this way: (1) **Novotel,** (2) **Concorde-Palm Beach,** (3) **Bompard,** (4) **Rome et St.-Pierre,** (5) **Castellane.**

This city is almost universally conceded to be France's foremost seafood center. **Calypso** (3 rue Catalans) banks on the Atlantic for its wares. Expect to spend about $90 per appetite. Delicious. **Jambon de Parme** (67 rue La Palud) offers exceptionally fine fare at similar prices. **Au Pescadou,** inland at place Castellane, will give you the greatest shellshock of your culinary lifetime. You'll count no less than 50 types and grades of crustaceans at the market-stall entrance; just point your pinkie at any one of them, and it will be yours. Almost anything that swims, frolics, or creeps in the Mediterranean is here. Noisy; rough service; ghastly decor—but, my, what a piscatorial paradise! **Maurice Brun** (18 quai de Rive-Neuve) has been highly recommended, as are **Fonfon** (140 Vallon des Auffes) and **Peron** (56 Corniche JFK). **Le Petit Nice** (in the same corniche district) is one of the more bewitching stops on the coast, and the gastronomy is scintillating. You can also stay in one of its 15 rooms. Superb—and costly.

MEGEVE It's a sunny ski center, just a few miles from the more challenging slopes of Chamonix. Choice of more than 100 establishments with over 2000 accommodations from Christmas to Easter and July through August. Our rankings now stack up this way: (1) **Chalet Mont d'Arbois,** (2) **Fer a Cheval,** (3) **Coin du Feu,** (4) **Loges du Mont Blanc,** or the equally expensive (5) **Parc des Loges.**

When it's time to tie on the napkin, the last two hotels have the top dining along with Les **Fermes de Marie**—and most mealtimes are passed in your hotel.

MIONNAY This crossroad not far from Lyon, certainly is one of France's more unprepossessing corners. But . . .

☆☆☆ **Alain Chapel •** provides surprisingly cosmopolitan accommodation and outstanding gastronomy though its namesake chef-patron is no longer with us. The 12-room hostelry is hard by the pike, but it is an oasis of exquisite beauty. Roofed entry gate to a small inner court; summer garden with geometric pool; rather formal dining room with sconce lighting, floral sprays, gleaming crystal, and pale yellow tones. Refined accommodations; subtle gilded wallpaper; 15th-century-style doors; full carpeting; the atmosphere of a fine home. The cuisine is celebrated for its inventiveness and luster. All in all, an experience that is elegant, hedonistic, and related in no way at all to its unfortunate existence in modest Mionnay. Closed Mon. and from Jan. 10 to Feb. 10.

MONTREUIL-SUR-MER Here's a convenient ferry point and rest stop for crossings to Dover and other British ports. ★★ **Chateau de Montreuil** is a delight for comfort, beauty, and cuisine: a romantic ocher house in its own garden across from the ancient citadel. (In bygone centuries the sea came up to the town's fringe.) The Germains are excellent hosts; try his Mousseline d'huitres or St. Pierre fish; some preparations clearly designed for frequent English traffic.

MULHOUSE The town's not much, but it boasts possibly the finest sportscar museum in the world with more than 120 Bugattis and racing *marques* of great rarity, all given gemstone treatment by the French government. For automobile buffs here is Mecca on Wheels. If you overnight, the **Parc** is the name to remember, possibly followed by the larger, more austere **Altea.** None of the other major stops has dining facilities. The Parc offers fine cuisine in lovely gardenside surroundings. The **Poste** is tops among the independents.

NANS-LES-PINS This is a lovely corner of Provence and convenient for viewing the ancient site of *St. Maximin* (east of Avignon). ★★★★ **Domaine de Chateauneuf** is a gracious manor edging the Sainte-Baume golf course. Wonderful gardens; excellent cuisine; very nice people. One of the most restful country houses I've found.

NANTUA **Hotel de France** (in midtown; traditional and cozy; nice people in Yvette and Paul Pauchard; abundant menu by talented young chef Dominique Fugier; don't order house wine, Roussette de Seyssel, as it is green and severe).

NIMES **Imperator** is the first choice. **L'Orangerie** is about half the size and with double the personality. The **Novotel** is a reasonable money-saver. About 5 miles away, in *Garons,* the **Alexandre** offers only 5 bedchambers in modern dress, yet the cuisine carries on the finest traditions of *la belle France.* It is sited near the airport, but the birds don't fly by night. Closed Aug. 30 until Sept. 15. At the "Ouest" junction of the Paris-Lyon *autoroute,* the **Sofitel,** the **Novotel,** and the **Mercure** all cluster together in a motorists' village. We stayed in the first with its pleasant grill, swimming pool, bar, and amply comfortable bedchambers.

PARIS

ATTRACTIONS

Tour Eiffel There are three platforms from which to see the city. From the third level, which you can reach only by elevator, you can—rarely—see up to 40 miles in every direction. You can also take a stairway still higher. (Refer to *Jules Verne* under "Restaurants.") After-dark illumination makes it more beautiful than ever.

Champs-Elysees

Arc de Triomphe • *place Charles-de-Gaulle* • Situated in the middle of place Charles-DeGaulle (formerly l'Etoile), this is the beefiest triumphal arch in existence, standing above the tomb of the Unknown Soldier. Time is taking a toll, however, so don't be surprised to see scaffolding at its skirts. The top offers another *belle vue* of Paris.

Musee Jacquemart-Andre • *158 blvd. Haussmann* • Less daunting than the next entry, which is an art megalopolis, this mansion house will occupy a morning for a study of the Italian 18th-century paintings, some fine ones by Tiepolo, and excellent contributions by Rembrandt.

Louvre Museum • *place du Carrousel* • You can now enter via the controversial (and usually dirty) glass pyramid designed by I. M. Pei, which stands seven stories over the subterranean Welcome Center; this is bang in the middle of the Cour Napoleon and—like it or not—it's something to see since everyone in France has an opinion of it. In my view, it so dominates the classic French architecture that it destroys the nobility and calm of the former esplanade. Further renovations and expansions will continue in coming years. The *massif* began as the residence of Francois I, and as buildings were added and remodeled, remained a royal residence until the Court relocated at Versailles in 1682. At the **Cour Carree** site a dungeon conceived by Philippe Auguste in the 12th century is a change of pace from gallery hopping.

Musee d'Orsay • *formerly the Gare d'Orsay* • is the lovingly recaptured architecture of the nation's most splendid rail station, an administrative extension of the Louvre, and now home for one of the grandest collections of the frenzied period—1850 to 1910—in this remarkable art cauldron: 1500 pieces of sculpture, 2300 paintings, 13,000 photographs, art objects and furnishings in the thousands. Orsay not only received the finest treasures of the **Jeu de Paume** (by the Tuileries, freshly renovated and dedicated to contemporary art), it also became heir to heretofore unseen assemblages in the Louvre's vaults and hitherto unsung beauty from a multitude of state sources. In short, it is a landmark restored for the preservation of landmark aesthetics.

Jardin des Tuileries • A sizable part of the Tuileries was laid out in 1664 by Le Notre, whose work remained a private park for the royal family. It had become rather neglected, but once the updatings at the Louvre were completed, the contractors started redesigning the gardens in the original style of Louis XIV. Spring is best, of course.

Montmartre

Many foreigners believe that Montmartre is the *real* Paris; built on a steep hill, the neighborhood is known for its quaint cobblestone streets and artists' haunts.

Old houses stand along narrow streets and lovely squares, of which place du Tertre is one of the most picturesque. Don't be surprised, though, if the area now seems a bit honky-tonk.

Sacre-Coeur • This oft-painted tall, white Romanesque-Byzantine church is visible from most of Paris. The view from the dome is the stuff of eagles.

Les Invalides

Invalides • A vast complex, now including a museum and two churches, has functioned as lodgings and a hospital for wounded military veterans ever since 1670. Hence, its name. Above the gray edifice shines the gold-leaf dome designed by Mansart. Beneath is the tomb of Napoleon.

Rodin Museum • *77 rue de Varenne* • One of the loveliest small museums of Paris. On display inside and arranged outdoors are originals or casts of the complete works of August Rodin.

Musee des Thermes et de l'Hotel de Cluny • *Cluny Museum, entrance 6 place Paul-Painleve, off Blvd. St.-Michel* • In this historic tandem you'll discover side-by-side buildings. One, the Palace of Thermes, was built upon 3rd-century Gallo-Roman baths; the other, a comprehensive collection of medieval and Renaissance art and artifacts, featuring a notable display of tapestries that includes the well-known series *Lady with the Unicorn.*

Le Jardin de Luxembourg • This is really the backyard of the Palais du Luxembourg (rue de Vaugirard), now the Senate. Romantic for strolling.

Latin Quarter

It's been a center of learning since Peter Abelard and his students left the Church-run school on the Ile de la Cite to continue their studies on the Left Bank of the Seine. "Latin" derives from the fact that Latin was the language of instruction until 1789, and both students and teachers spoke it in their daily lives.

The Sorbonne • *rue des Ecoles* • Founded in 1353 to teach theology to a small number of impoverished students, today the Sorbonne is one of the liberal arts colleges in the University of Paris. The buildings in this complex were built under the aegis of Cardinal Richelieu in 1624–1642. The Cardinal's tomb is in the south transept of the Church of the Sorbonne.

Pantheon • *Place du Pantheon* • At the summit of Mount St. Genevieve, the shrine contains the tombs of Victor Hugo, Voltaire, Rousseau, Emile Zola, and heroes of liberty.

Ile de la Cite

This ancient matrix was called Lutece by the Celtic-speaking Gauls who established a village here. The largest building now on this island is the **Palais du Justice** where you can visit the 14th-century dungeon.

Notre Dame Cathedral • It's been a top draw for travelers since 1163. You can mount the towers to see the bells and timidly step outside on the roof platform for a peep at the cathedral roof with its gargoyles, the Ile St. Louis below, the Seine and its bridges. You also can visit the Gallo-Roman crypt and see remains of medieval Paris.

Les Halles

Until recently Les Halles was the central wholesale market of Paris where workers' cafes specialized in delicious onion soup and accordian music. In 1971 the market was transferred, leaving a vast hole that has since been filled with the Forum des Halles, a multilevel underground garage-shopping center with cafes, boutiques, a bookstore, bakeries, and other shops. Unfortunately, the architecture is uninspired, it did not draw the taste levels predicted, and it is becoming downright seedy.

Georges Pompidou Center of Art and Culture ("Beaubourg") • *between rue St.-Martin and rue du Renard and also fronting Le Marais* • Completed in 1977, this is possibly the most hideous structure ever to be dedicated to the preservation and exhibition of beauty. Unhappily it will probably stand as an everlasting hymn to modern intestinology—architecture so repugnant to me that it defames France's historic role as an arbiter of taste and erudition. The building notwithstanding, its collections, presentations, and quirky tricks of holding a mirror up to life bring a fresh, bright, and idiosyncratic touch to art appreciation. The open space out in front of the Pompidou Center is the site of impromptu performances—music, mime, magic—and there are some pleasant cafes in its multiform shadow; the snack bar within is as unappetizing to my taste as the edifice which houses it. Inside are galleries for temporary art exhibits, a large performance space, and, on the third through fifth floors the home of the **Musee National d'Art Moderne** (Museum of Modern Art), which includes ragtag environmental pieces among its contemporary paintings, mobiles, and sculpture. You may wish to visit Brancusi's Atelier, an atmospheric reproduction of the sculptor's studio.

Le Marais • *Marais District* • A quarter brimming with proud 16th-, 17th-, and 18th-century private mansions. Untouched by commercialism, it is one of the most interesting parts of the Right Bank for strolling.

Picasso Museum • *5 rue de Thorigny* • Located in the Hotel Sale (Aubert de Fontenay), this handsome palace of the late-17th century contains several thousand works of art—not all of them by the Spanish artist, but many splendid pieces collected by or given to Picasso by other masters of his time. A Van Dongen, as one example, is the finest I've ever seen by this Dutchman.

Place des Vosges • Completed during the reign of Henri IV, this was once a meeting place of aristocrats. Mme. de Sevigne was born at No. 1; Victor Hugo lived at No. 6; and Cardinal Richelieu resided at No. 21. Still not enough for a bridge party.

Musee Victor Hugo • *6 place des Vosges* • These rooms in the house where Hugo courted his muse are furnished as they were during the poet's lifetime.

Place de la Bastille • Now a major traffic intersection, this is where the infamous Bastille Prison stood. If you feel like risking your own life to taxis, buses, and cars whizzing by, you can pace off the outline of the edifice by following the white periphery painted on the street surface. The July Column a its center commemorates Parisians killed during the July Revolution. The view from the top of the column is excellent in good weather. **Opera de la Bastille,** a political football in its inaugural months, is settling in and adding to the city's musical life.

Around Town

Jardin d'Acclimatation • *amusement park* • Tucked away in a far corner of the Bois de Boulogne is this modest-size park within a park with rides, marionette shows, a riding school, and a minicar racing track.

Markets • Paris is famous not only for its chic boutiques but also for its colorful and varied outdoor and arcade markets. **Bird Markets** • *On Sun. at place Louis-Lepine on the Ile de la Cite and every day at Quai de la Megisserie.* **Flower Markets** • *Every day at place Louis-Lepine (except Sun.), Place des Ternes (except Mon.), and next to the Church of the Madeleine (except Mon.).* **Flea Market** • *At Porte de Clignancort, from Sat. through Mon.* • there are stalls and displays with everything from secondhand Levis to antique coins— some values if you have the patience to hunt them down. **Stamp Market** • *Corner of ave. Gabriel and ave. Marigny (Thurs. afternoon, Sun., holidays).* **Food Markets** • For sightseeing with vitality, some of the best areas are *rue Mouffetard* and *rue des Belle-Feuilles* for produce, *rue Cler* for sausage, hams, and cheese, *rue Poncelet* for similar wares. **Covered Markets** • include *Passy, St. Quintin,* and the ancient *Chateau d'Eau.*

Boat Tours • The **Bateaux Mouches** fleet (Pont de l'Alma; Tel.: 4255–96–10) includes *La Patache* (theater, TV, 800 capacity, the *Galiote* (theater, dance floor, same general facilities), the *Jean-Sebastien Mouche* (flagship with 300-place restaurant), *Le Coche d'Eau* (self-service restaurant), and the *Parisien* (the best cookery of the five). You have your choice of 2½- or 1¼-hour rides; frequent departures from morning through evening; full of kids before noon, businessmen at lunchtime, tourist mobs in midafternoon, romantics at 5 p.m., and international celebrities after dark; boarding tickets range from around $2.50 to $7. Meals are served on 12:30 p.m. and 8:30 p.m. voyages. **Vedettes Paris-Tour Eiffel** (Port de la Bourdonnais; Tel.: 4705–50–00) operate small rivercraft at 20-minute intervals from the wharf near the Eiffel Tower. The usual tour lasts 90 minutes, but there's also a 5-hour circuit that incorporates lunch or dinner at the restaurant in the Eiffel Tower. This one and the **Vedettes du Pont-Neuf** (Pont Neuf; Tel.: 4633–98–38) did not seem (to me) as good for visibility nor were they as comfortable as the *Bateaux Mouches,* but they are pleasant all the same. **Bat-O-Bus** is a floating taxi service on the Seine. Look for signs along the riverbank. Each hop costs roughly $5 and in itself is a scenic alternative to the *mouches*.

Helicopter Ride • Four-place choppers that make 30-minute rounds above town can be booked through Societe Helisab, Auberge de l'helisation, Chalon Moulineux, 91740 Pussay (Tel.: 4495–43–79).

Rambles in Paris • These are popular walking tours covering the maximum of interesting places with the minimum of pedestrian effort. On each day of the week, a different quarter is explored. Strollers meet at the starting point for the day. (Tel.: 4535–24–05.)

Bus Tours • If you are in Paris for only a couple of days or want to orient yourself before striking out on your own, bus companies offer trips around the capital with commentary in several languages. Depending on your interest, you can choose tours covering historic sights, "modern" Paris, and/or Paris by night when many important landmarks are illuminated. Try SNCF (the Paris bus company), 16 blvd. des Capucines (Tel.: 4742–00–26), Cityrama (Tel.: 4360–30–14), or Paris Vision (Tel.: 4269–14–89).

Excursions

Barbizon • On the edge of Fontainebleau, you'll find wonderful forests depicted by artists who gave this name to their school of painting. Here are the homes of Robert Louis Stevenson, Theodore Rousseau, and Aime Millet, whose workshop you can visit. (See separate listing.)

Vaux-le-Vicomte • At *Vaux,* halfway between Fontainebleau and Vincennes, this great chateau employed many of the artists who were later to build, decorate, and landscape the grandeurs of Louis XIV at Versailles, Trianon, and Marly. Here is the evergreen genius of Le Notre, Le Brun, and Le Vau on perpetual show as commissioned by the royal treasurer, Nicolas Fouquet, who ended his life not in the splendor of his creation but in prison. It is not on the usual touristic circuits, but Vaux is not to be missed by any true Francophile.

Saint-Cloud • On a hill above the left bank of the Seine, Saint-Cloud is known for its park designed by Le Notre from which there is an especially good view of Paris. It's a good spot to tour on bikes, which can be rented.

St.-Denis • The burial place of French royalty, the Cathedral of St.-Denis (begun in 1137) is a museum of French sculpture because of all the tombstones here.

Chartres • Set on a hill above the Eure River, Chartres draws migrations of visitors to view its cathedral, an architectural poem built in 1195–1220, with spectacular stained-glass windows and statuary.

Reims • The Cathedral (constructed 1211–1294) is a marvel of the Gothic style. It has abundant sculpture and six stained-glass windows by Chagall that replaced some of the many destroyed in World War II.

St.-Germain-en-Laye • An excursion to St.-Germain-en-Laye, a summer residence of French royalty, is one of the loveliest daytrips outside of Paris. (It's the last stop on the Paris Metro, about 25 minutes from midcity.) After walking through the cool forest and along the mile-long terrace above the Seine there's still the 16th-century chateau with the **Museum of National Antiquities.**

Versailles • In 1682 the French king and his Court left Paris for Versailles, where they lived in untold splendor until forced to vacate in 1789. Royalty is long gone, but the magnificence of this national treasure has been preserved. The gardens were laid out by Le Notre. You may look into the **Royal Apartments** and see your lovely self many times over in the **Hall of Mirrors;** 85 rooms have been newly restored and opened to view after 7 years of meticulous renovation; 2 floors display 16th- and 17th-century paintings. Opening times have been extended (until Sept., 9 a.m.–7 p.m.); gardens from 7 a.m. to dusk; closed Mon. Set away from the chateau are the Grand Trianon and the Petit Trianon.

HOTELS

All hostelries considered to be worthy of receiving outlanders are classed as *Hotels de Tourisme.* These are broken down into 5 categories: deluxe, 4-star, 3-star, 2-star, and 1-star. The same applies to the *Relais de Tourisme* (suburban stops) and *Motels de Tourisme* (on major highways). Price controls cover only the lowest 3 groups.

The previously mentioned **City of Paris Tourist Information Bureau,** at 127 avenue Champs Elysees, will spring to your rescue in emergencies by finding you a room within a 60-mile radius of Cannes, Nice, Marseille, Reims, Lourdes, Strasbourg, Tours, Rouen, Lyon, Vichy, Dijon, Aix-les-Baines, or (of course) the capital. Reservations guaranteed for one night only (this avoids competition with travel agencies); direct connection with Paris Welcome Information Offices at main railway stations, with Hostesses of Paris on tap; Telex network, currency exchange, and similar services; open at 9 a.m. to midnight including Sun. Small fees. Passengers arriving at Charles de Gaulle Airport without a room reservation can waltz right over to a push-button computer that indicates the availability of space in more than 300 Paris hotels. There's also a telephone link for booking your pillow, plus photos, prices, addresses, and all required details. Look for it in Aerogare #1 near the Aeroport de Paris Information Counter. Tip: The months that Paris is most crowded are March and October. A hotel reservation in advance is well advised since trade shows occupy so much of the space even years before the annual fairs.

All French Government Tourist Offices have definitive lists of Gallic stopping places everywhere, free of charge. A splendid bet for the less well-heeled vacationer is the *Logis de France Guide*—a roundup of more than 4000 clean, modest country and resort hotels, hand-picked by the **Federation Nationale des Logis de France;** it's available at this organization's Paris headquarters, 25 rue Jean Mermoz. For more opulent tastes, the **Relais et Chateaux** (also nonprofit) offers a superb compilation of leading French or foreign-owned rural oases—chateaux, manor houses, converted monasteries, and the like—all with well-known restaurants (a few entries are for dining only). Although a handful are substandard, the majority offer dependable quality. For details drop by the information office at the Crillon Hotel on Place de la Concorde.

Prefer an apartment? The 161 real estaters who formed the **Federation Nationale des Agents Immobiliers** (163 rue St.-Honore, Paris 1) are girded to attack all the formalities and then plunk you into a chalet, villa or most any other sort of dwelling you select. Another organization called **Flatotel** (14 rue du Theatre and Porte de Versailles) deals out apartments of various sizes in these two Parisian sites.

A farmhouse? Write to **Gites de France** which can send you prices, locations, and other particulars on renting an abode in rural Gaul. While I haven't hoed this row, friends who have say it is an enriching, low-cost experience for the adventurous. Address: 34 Godot de Mauroy, 75009 Paris.

☆☆☆☆☆ **Plaza-Athenee** • for decades has catered with conspicuous success to inconspicuously wealthy travelers, people who have wanted the best in fashionable and reasonably quiet surroundings. Very First Rank cuisine at the Regence, a gastronomic shrine where the lobster souffle has almost become a minor deity; the Relais, directed by Werner Kuchler, is known globally for its predominance as the social and fashion hub of Tout Paris, a happy, spirited place that functions from lunch through tea time and dinner. Chef Claude Barnier is the master of all the kitchens. While the courtyard restaurant has now been tailored for year-round operation, its vivid blooms, pools, bridge, freeflying songbirds, gay red parasols, and polka-dotted tablecloths create the impression of Eternal Spring. Every room offers a good bath, an excellently stocked refrigerator, color television, 4-channel piped music, and news broadcasts in English; the penthouse is composed of 4 supersuites. Cheers to Franco Cozzo and his fine staff for their performance!

☆☆☆☆☆ **Ritz** • lives up to every star in its rating. Much of the thanks go to master hotelier Frank Klein. All extra-gracious accommodations have air conditioning, color television, in-house video, minibar, marble baths with telephone and a host of fresh amenities. Suites include those dedicated to the memories of Coco Chanel, Marcel Proust (who himself could probably never afford to stay in one), and the Duke of Windsor, as well as some Imperial spreads proudly ornamented with authentic 18th-century garniture. The Espadon Grill offers a bar as well as the summer and winter terraces, overlorded by Chef Guy Legay, formerly of Le Doyen. The Hemingway Bar also benefited from the editing process. The Health Club is absolutely peerless. If you are willing to pay the ritzy price, here, unquestionably, is one of the most elegant addresses in France today.

☆☆☆☆☆ **Meurice** • also is magnificent. Direction in the capable hands of Philippe Roche, with day-to-day operations supervised by Manager Dominique Borri, a highly professional team. There are full air conditioning, the blissfully comfortable restaurant on the Rivoli rue, and beautifully updated rooms and suites. Impressive crystals, bronzes, gold leaf, marble, and textiles of museum quality incorporated into the noble, high-ceilinged salons, the proportions of which put this house in a peerage with the great palaces of Europe. The 18th-century stylization extends from the portals through the modern adaptations of the corridors and into the gracious, wide-angled accommodations. Most of the baths are in marble; twins all boast separate showers; all face the park. Unquestionably an aristocrat.

☆☆☆☆☆ **Crillon** • is a full-fledged member of Paris's elite group, appealing nowadays not just to diplomats but to jet-setters and the upward-moving young. Smart entrance with a swanky boutique of Crillon items; courtyard used for summer dining; marvelous Concorde-facing Les Ambassadeurs restaurant, a study in decorative magnificence; chef Christian Constant (formerly of Grand Vefour) supervises what is rated as among the very top cuisines in Europe. Wood-lined elevators; 3-cabin Telex room; corridors are decked in rich attire; all public areas given the splendor of its 1909 inauguration. There's a new sauna and fitness center. While the bedchambers are chipper, bright, and well equipped, they maintain the traditional tone; a trio of grandiose pillar-front suites on the Concorde; 4 duplexes with penthouse views; all baths have been revivified, most of them with thermal taps in tubs and showers, and many in marble; frigobars are in every unit as are color televisions. Skillful direction by Herve Houdre, formerly of New York. Regal it is and at royal price tags.

☆☆☆☆☆ **Bristol** • always posh, has, astonishingly, grown even *more* luxurious. There is a 28-room wing capped by a covered swimming pool with a wooden deck and a maritime motif that can be opened in summer for viewing the rooftops of Paris. There's a grill on the ground floor, a bar and in-house boutiques; a captivating garden spread over the garage and surrounded by a colonnade of the former cloister; a "Residence" has been created for longer-staying guests. Rich Gobelin tapestries and splendid paintings; stunning oval dining room; refreshments served in the lounges by 18th-century-clothes-clad butlers; air conditioning, television, and radio; beauty parlor, barber shop, masseur, and many other services.

☆☆☆☆☆ **George V** • is a stronghold of traditional French values to suit affluent international tastes. It is brighter and fresher than ever too. A stroke of architectural genius is manifest in the exquisite floral garden that has been placed behind lobby glass, providing a sensation of springtime even on the darkest days of winter. Extensive renovations, including Le Grill (open late), which offers live music after 7 p.m. and a brasserie mood for the luxury trade. The bar features modern crystal chandeliers, matching sconces, and comfortable booths. The President Suite has to reach a bit these days to find a President worthy of it; it is nothing short of awesome. My favorite doubles overlook the tranquil

Marble Court. The artwork alone in this landmark was recently reckoned (by Sotheby's) to be worth $6 million.

☆☆☆☆ **Intercontinental** • can also boast about its central location embracing the original and lovely Garden Court. There's the canopied Terrasse Fleurie on one side overlooking a central pond for seasonal outdoor dining; its adjoining lobby is strikingly attractive. Le Bistro for lighter biting and libations to music (piped from noon until a pianist comes on from 9 p.m. to 2 a.m.); Bar Rivoli with an after-gloaming harpist; coffee shop. Full air conditioning; double-pane windows for silent-nighting; ample space in rooms with soft-view hues in blue, gray, green, or burnt orange; wall-to-wall carpeting; first floor refashioned; some spectacular suites and a host of junior suites that are as cheerful as spring.

☆☆☆☆ **Prince de Galles** • ("Prince of Wales"), cheek-by-jowl with the George V, has long been a cordial, attractive, and comfortable haven. Huge sums of money were pumped into it by its U.S. Marriott owners to provide even further decorative zest. Traditional units have been freshened; there's color television throughout; the off-lobby English bar is warmly inviting; hairdressing facilities for men and women. Most baths with twin washbasins and wallpapered ceilings; corridors particularly fresh, cheerful, and colorful; outstanding gastronomy; terrace dining in summer.

☆☆☆ **Paris Hilton** • with the Eiffel Tower standing in its background on the Left Bank, requires a hop for every midtown errand, shopping jag, or sightseeing jaunt; marvelous vista from Seine-side rooms; dreary claustrophobic view from rear windows, overlooking the Atomic Energy Commission complex; furnishings improved; Toit de Paris supper club handsomely styled. La Terrasse with vittles from 7 a.m. to 11 p.m. Convenient 300-car underground garage; 6 refreshment centers of varied Hiltonian interest.

☆☆☆ **Lancaster** • is the French outpost of London's Savoy group. Much has been done in public sancta to upgrade the tone; it certainly does provide the wayfarer with old-fashioned *personalized* attention. Most of the rooms are satisfactory but comparatively small in their dimensions; no two of them are outfitted alike. Many business executives appear regularly at lunchtime. The location is handy to the Etoile and the Champs-Elysees.

☆☆☆ **Tremoille** • is a kid-sister of the neighboring Plaza Athenee, whose dining and other facilities clients here may use. It is a convenient arrangement that combines lower tariffs with extraordinary comfort and abundant luxury. You'll discover generous space, highlights of Maytime from the decorators, and graceful traditionalism throughout. A fire crackles in the hearth in winter; a bar with intricately carved panels nods invitingly; a small adjoining restaurant is available for grills and snacks. Look at units ending in #s 2, 3, 9, 10, and 12. Quiet, elegant, and highly recommended.

☆☆☆ **Royal Monceau** • continues to enjoy a place of respect in midcity and as a hotel linked to the fine CIGA chain. Lobby festooned with the graceful dignity to match its stately facade; corridors continue the motif of the 1930s; seventh floor renewed and given duplex garden suites; pool and fitness center plus sauna. Le Jardin and the Italian Carpaccio restaurants; carefully prepared cuisine that is not exactly for the budgeteer, kindhearted reception, and cordial attention by a well-trained staff.

☆☆ **Meridien** ● with over 1000 latchkeys, is really more of a hotel-city than an inn in the traditional sense. Its lobby, only slightly smaller than the state of Delaware, is dominated by thickets of easy chairs and illuminated by a tubular forest of suspended lamps; a gelid stainless-steel bar plus cool courtside Clos Longchamps restaurant, which is one of the city's best. Colorful Arlequin Rotisserie beautifully restyled; Japanese Yamoto corner; cellar-cited circular cafe; nightclub—well, you name it and it's probably there. The lookalike bedchambers feature one flank clad in the same carpeting that cloaks the floor; their other facilities include semifitted furniture, radio console and TV, refrigerated bars, baths with space-age tubs and cleverly designed glass splash-plates for showers. Basically sound, but with a chillfactor associated purely with the twentieth century.

☆☆ **Pullman Saint-Jacques** ● is another Orwellian creation—this one with a mere 812 accommodations. It is handy to the major train stations and the route to Orly Airport (shuttle every ¼-hour), and not too far from Montparnasse. Impressive cubistic facade; 15 floors of windows angled port and starboard; airy blue-and-white lobby with greenery, a fountain, and drilled steel columns; once again the full panoply of restaurants; pentagonal bedchambers in orange, blue, or brown tones; sparrow-size baths with marble-top basins and dip-your-toe tubs.

☆☆ **Concorde-Lafayette** ● connects with the Paris Convention Hall. Its first 2 dozen tiers cater exclusively to groups, with no room service available. The next 8 levels stack up for independent bookings; these come with coral textiles, matched furnishings, brown carpets, and dimensions that seem a shade smaller than those of the above entry. Comfort standards, however, are about the same. Its crowning joy is the panoramic penthouse restaurant and bar.

☆ **Grand** ● *21 rue Scribe* ● despite its convenient central address, seems well on the way to achieving its goal as a convention hotel. Nevertheless, it provides a lot for your francs, including some of the lowest priced suites in the city. Rooms in 5 color schemes; air conditioning; marble baths; in-house films on TV. The exterior brightened with glass and burnished metal. Lively bar and Cafe de la Paix, the fresh open-plan restaurant for quick meals, a refashioned terrace, and much more sparkle.

★★★ **L'Hotel** ● *13 rue des Beaux-Arts, on the Left Bank* ● is dramatically unorthodox: a transformation of the seedy, moldy, 30-room, 3-bath Hotel Alsace—its only pale distinction that Oscar Wilde died there—into a luxury-class operation of 2 suites, 25 rooms, and 27 baths. To the rear of its lobbyette is a greenhouse-style terrace restaurant with a tiny fountain, 2 caged monkeys, parrots, drawable curtains under its light-well ceiling, and a mass of vines. The bedrooms, each different and some air-conditioned, are all decorated in exquisite taste. The cellar-to-roof drawback here is that all of its dimensions have been telescoped into such super-compactness, including luggage space, that any large-framed guest would find this doll's house (more Ibsen than Wilde) uncomfortably cramped.

☆ **l'Abbaye St. Germain** • *10 rue Cassette* • formerly a convent and later a student dormitory. Interior patio plus garden, with birds aflutter; Art Deco lounge; some of its 45 units overlooking the garden; a few with private terrace entry and breakfast balcony; bath and shower for each accommodation; soft lighting, nice carpeting, colors tending toward teals and browns; no restaurant; intimacy is its chief commodity. The rates are very reasonable for the personalized rewards.

★★ **Chateau Frontenac** • *just off the Champs-Elysees* • is attractive to the eye, and is very much on an improvement cycle. The lobby, luxurious new dining room, and some suites are especially appealing. Desk staff are helpful.

☆ **Le Warwick** • *nudging the Champs-Elysees from rue de Berri* • is delightful; good taste is in ample supply. The astute management can be proud of the compliments this young house already has generated. Dining in La Couronne restaurant also is receiving attention in Parisian gastronomic circles.

★★★ **Raphael** • *2 blocks from the Arc de Triomphe* • exudes understated grace and dignity. Its salons are filled with beautiful oil paintings and its bedrooms evoke the grandeur of a manor. **Majestic** • *nearby at 29 rue Dumont d'Urville* • is under the same management, but as a town house it is more modest. No restaurant, but breakfast room; some kitchenettes; beguiling penthouse.

★★★ **San Regis** • *nearby, at 12 rue Jean Goujon* • is small, cheerful, and increasingly up-market (roughly $300 per twin). Lots of light plants and decorator touches; deep-seat comfort; mix of antiques and modernity. Ten posh, fresh-faced suites. Lovely but $$$!

☆ **Cambon** • on the *rue* of the same name, is handy to the major sights and is in the heart of the fashion district. Modern fresh ambience; especially attractive attic rooms. Hospitable manageress who welcomes American guests.

☆ **Lotti** • provides a pleasant bar and grill adjoining the small restaurant; revamped completely but maintaining its traditional tone; some garret-style accommodations. An intimate type of house with many antiques but full modern amenities such as air conditioning.

☆ **Brighton** • brightens its enviable site on the convenient rue de Rivoli. Traditional rooms with full carpeting, French windows, brass beds, and good illumination; superb maintenance; ample comfort and coziness; #410 an excellent 3-bed corner accommodation; back units quiet. No restaurant, but a spread for breakfast; nice personnel who truly seem to care. It is just what a small, medium-priced hostelry should be.

★ **Napoleon** • *near the Etoile* • provides a modernized Regency manner. Looking up (as Bonaparte might) and very well sited. Its restaurant is highly respected generally, but especially (of all things) for its sauerkraut!

Hotel France et Choiseul • *across from place Vendome* • is making the most of its near-perfect address. Louis XVI Emperatrice-style foyer, muraled walls of the main salon, and courtyard—all ''protected'' by the French National Art Commission. Upstairs its 135 rooms are pretty standard.

Westminster • has been restyled in traditional tones but with American efficiency and comfort standards. Pastel color schemes run counterpoint to marble-top fireplaces; Louis XIV antiques resist the chill of full air conditioning; soft hues grace the Chenets cocktail lounge and Le Celadon restaurant; bedchambers with in-house music and color TV, all face the courtyard or *rue de la Paix*. A splendid revolution of a former abbey.

Sofitel de Paris • *across the rue from the Parc des Expositions* • the address should give you a pretty fair idea of its fair-minded function.

Nikko • *southwest of the Eiffel Tower on the shore of the Seine* • impresses me only by its size.

Victoria Palace • occupies a silent setting. Friendly reception; equally ingratiating staff; dining room with quality cooking; streetside bar; 3 lounges; well maintained. A solid value for the money.

Grand Hotel Littre • is physically linked to the Victoria Palace. Charming bar; 3-tier lobby; TV room; 2 small but comfortable lounges; sparkling dining room to brighten the visitor's welcome; good cuisine, too. All 4 suites and 120 rooms come with adequately spacious private baths. The decor is restful and practical; try to reserve on the courtyard for sun and tranquillity.

★★ **Bretonnerie** • *near Pompidou Center in the Marais* • is a delightful period piece of the 17th century, with open beams, rich textiles, and cozy mansion-house architectural features. Write well in advance for reservations because its personality is becoming known and appreciated.

Normandy • Ask to see an accommodation (especially the ''07'' series) before booking if you can.

Royal Hotel • *near the Etoile* • Tranquil; midget lobby; side-street locations the quietest, despite double windows on the avenue side; everything spotless. All accommodations stayed in or inspected over the years, while small and costly for the category, have looked pert and have smelled as fresh as a mountain pine grove.

Vernet • *a 2-minute stroll from the Etoile* • quiet side-street harbor in the *coeur* of Paris; friendly family atmosphere; bar and pleasant restaurant; 63 Gallic bedchambers; only 2 without private bath.

Hotel de Castiglione • has a clean, rather commercial lobby; appetizing dining room and handsome tartanesque bar up 1 flight; 110 units, most with private baths. Comfortable.

Lido • well-scrubbed and polished, offers many thoughtful minutiae. Fairly tranquil considering its proximity to place de la Madeleine; bright, modern lobby; no restaurant; large bedrooms. Aim high for *les toits de Paris* view.

Meridien Montparnasse • *on the Left Bank, one block from the Montparnasse Railway Station and just above the subway stop* • Plastic galore in the lobby but more warmth upstairs; every convention facility imaginable. Surprisingly for such a vast hostelry, the service is good.

Holiday Inn • *on place de la Republique* • introduced 350 rooms at what was the site of the 1866-vintage Moderne Hotel. The original facade remains, but the inside has been totally *moderne*-ized.

Madeleine-Palace • *8 rue Cambon* • has a total of 116 spiritless accommodations and 110 baths or showers; King Charles Restaurant.

Madeleine-Plaza • *directly on the place de la Madeleine* • has peapod rooms that glisten. Top floor the most tranquil in this traffic-choked zone; 18 units perhaps a few centimeters more spacious. Especially warm greeting for readers of this book from the receptionist.

Hotel de Castille has come up in the world of innkeeping; so have its prices; quite worthy nowadays. The **Terminus St.-Lazare-Concorde** I regard with all the affection I might reserve for a giant bus station. **Ambassador** is improving. The venerable **California** is dressed not for leisure but in Louis XVI style; self-dial phones plus TV, radio, and minibar.

Hotel de l'Universite • *near St.-Germain-des-Pres* • offers ample flair. Handsome wrought iron staircase; 12th-century bar; 20th-century Club 22 for snacks; wooden beams, vaults, marble, textiles, and stucco blending into a tasteful composite in which no 2 units are the same. Simple furnishings; reasonable prices that vary with the particular accommodation; again, no restaurant. Left Banker that is worth the investment. The **Cecilia** is a friendly but unostentatious port for voyaging families. Exceptionally sympathetic house without fancy frills.

Bradford • *a 5-minute hike from the Champs-Elysees* • in a quiet backwater, is best for location, but otherwise not terribly inspired.

Scribe • was a grand old place that has been restored with tons of synthetic material. Modernization has detracted from the stately atmosphere. The lobby, however, features black marble pilasters and a glittering chandelier.

Vendome • boasting a situation similar to the Ritz, has been moving ahead manfully. Empire decor plus brass bedsteads; oldish corridors; ample space provided; smilingly helpful staff. We like its slipper-style comfort.

Madison • *opposite the St.-Germain-des-Pres church* • is tops in its vicinity. Fresh lobby; front units nicest and largest.

Alexander • *conveniently sited on fashionable ave. Victor Hugo* • is a charmer, but it is so well known now that you must book almost a month ahead. Reserve on the rear for quiet; no air conditioning; no restaurant but still very tasteful.
    Edouard VII • *ave. de l'Opera* • has 90 old but adequate rooms, 80 baths, steel beds, an abundance of stained-glass windows in the upstairs halls, and a bustling impersonal mien; not special. **Lutetia,** one of the few big hotels on the Left Bank, is favored by French senators from the provinces. Some love it, while others don't appreciate its dated mien. Personally, I enjoy it, especially for dining. The **Le Paris** restaurant, masterminded by Jacky Freon and now outfitted in Sonia Rykiel raiments (the restaurant, not Jack), is one of the most revered gastronomic shrines in the capital today. Very rich in price and decor. The **Saint-Simon,** also on this *rive*, is chiefly for tranquillity seekers. Family-run pension atmosphere in which no meals are served; no concierge; no elevator; small cellar bar; pleasant for that specialized client who seeks its milieu. **Chomel** • *a Left Banker, too* • is an extremely well-run small hotel with a fresh homespun air. **Grand Hotel du Mont-Blanc** • *near Notre-Dame* • seems haphazard and far from Grand. **Astor** (breakfast only) and **Mapotel Pont Royal** are average. The latter is enhanced by Les Antiquaires restaurant. The **Montalembert,** its neighbor, is similar in price but better in *quid pro quo*. Its 65 units with bath or shower recently were refashioned with verve. Much improved and well managed today. **Cayre,** with a fresh façade and entrance, is coming up, too. Now okay for the outlay. **London Palace** • *on tree-shaded blvd. des Italiens* • is convenient to the Opera, the Louvre, and excellent shopping zones. A good buy, especially during the July–Aug. discount period. **Mercure** offers 190 latchkeys at Montparnasse. **Aramis** • *between Montparnasse and the Luxembourg Gardens* • with only 42 rooms, is cozier. **Richmond** • *in the 9th arrondisement* • is for shelter-seekers only. **Vermont** is even more simple, with no lobby or lounge, meager plumbing facilities, and small sleeping cells. For unfinicky pilgrims only. In the same category and equally inhabitable are the finely honed 23-room-and-bath **Massena,** the cozy **Tronchet** with 2 atelier units under the eaves, and the **Regent's;** with a pleasant patio; each has distinctive color and charm as well as its particular drawback, but in all 3 your happiness depends on which bedroom you draw. The **Regina** is old, comfy, and clean; here's another candidate for wanderers with large broods. I've not yet seen Pierre Cardin's **La Residence Maxim's,** which recently opened at 42 av. Gabriel in the 8th arrondissement; it boasts 39 suites and prices that are said to be *formidable*.

Apartments?

    Elysees Concorde has about 200 of them in the center of the city—all dimensions and all prices for long-term visitors. Get in touch at 9 rue Royale; Tel. 4265–1199; Telex 640793F.
    Relais Carre d'Or is composed entirely of suites ("apartments" in European terminology); there are 23 of varying sizes. The location is good (46 av.

George V), next to Fouquet's and just off the Champs-Elysees (Tel. 4070–0505)

Environs

Orly Hilton   is 20 to 30 minutes from the heart of the city (take a bus to economize), directly across the street from the main terminal building. Modern sawtooth exterior with double windows, soundproofed ceilings and walls, and 100% air conditioning; a beauty parlor and barbershop, plus other commercial niches; cunning series of vitrinelike ponds and gardens leading to a separate zone containing (1) The cheerful coffee shop with light dishes (open 6:30 a.m. to 11 p.m. daily), (2) L'Atelier Bar (12-seat counter; tiny dance floor), and (3) La Louisiane Restaurant, an appealingly romantic touch of creole culture and cuisine. Free hotel-terminal shuttle service is offered.

Novotel   overlooks the freeway at a median point between the city and Orly Airport, 15 minutes by the Metro to the hub of the urban action. Its highrise neighborhood is unattractive; bleak, stark efficiency is its bag.

Orly P.L.M., the airess of its landed big-city sister, makes few pretensions toward luxury. The **Air Hotel** makes none. The **Frantel,** looking through lozenge-shape windows upon a roadside heath, is for the fogbound only; listed here merely as a convenience, not as a recommendation. **Holiday-Inn**-vaded the nearby industrial suburb of Rungis with 180 chambers and opened another 90-room unit at Porte de Versailles.

Curiously, the mammoth Charles de Gaulle Airport at *Roissy* (a hell-and-gone ride of almost an hour's duration for unfortunate passengers who must transfer en route) has a trio of routine hotels for the weary—the 352-room **Sofitel,** which is as heartless and dreary as a military barrack, the even less flossy 250-unit **Holiday Inn,** and the 360-room **Arcade Roissy.** The last is for budget flyers with good basic accommodations, but with air conditioning that seems to go off when you need it most.

~~~~~~

RESTAURANTS

Expensive

☆☆☆☆☆ **Robuchon** • *32 rue de Longchamp* • is named for its *chef-patron,* probably as well known in Paris as the president of the republic. Decoratively both fresh and exotic; palm fronds trace delicate patterns on softly illuminated rose-toned walls; similar artistry appears in the creative motifs employed for arrangement of food. The raviolis de langoustine au chou has given new meaning to simple ravioli; in fact, the dough was more like the dumplings in wonton soup (now copied by almost every chef in Europe, but rarely with such skill). Still following a delicious theme, his risotto de veau aux truffes raises the North Italian concept to magnificent new heights. Though this house has become a classic, the thinking is still modern.

☆☆☆☆☆ **Ambroisie** ● *9 place des Vosges* ● is one more up-front contender. French decorative motifs spread tastefully over a duet of rooms; seating for roughly 40; set lunch about $55 and superb, also a la carte. Chef Pacaud is among the champions of modern light-touch cuisine. His most celebrated dishes include mousse de poivrons rouges and his delicate treatment of that once-scorned denizen of the deep, ray fish; the crab ravioli or saffroned butter-bathed scallops are in the mainstream of today's gastronomy; his pastries are in the Cartier class. Closes Sun. and Mon. at lunchtime.

☆☆☆☆☆ **Apicius** ● *122 ave. Villiers* ● is the skyrocket carrying Chef Vigato into the culinary welkin—along with his radiant and hospitable Madeleine. Here is something of an iconoclast to cookery, a master who remembers wholesome flavors of homestyle food and who reinvests these dishes with beauty and delicacy. There's even a hint of bistro selections in the ingredients (trotters, for instance), but his treatment redefines such humble wares. To end it all, try a chocolate preparation; they redefine the flavor. Of the 3 linked salons, I prefer the long front window-lined room with its airy modern tones. Go now because soon it will be impossible to get in.

☆☆☆☆☆ **Taillevent** ● *15 rue Lamennais* ● has long, long continued to radiate its glories. The *cave* is fantastic; the wine list carries more than 500 choices, with 260-thousand bottles to back it up. All details of creation and presentation shared by Proprietor Jean-Claude Vrinat and Chef Deligne. Excellent kitchen, though it is minuscule; friendly reception; convenient location near Champs-Elysees; high tariffs; closed Sun.; *always* phone beforehand for your table. And, if you can, book here at night.

☆☆☆☆☆ **Laurent** ● *41 ave. Gabriel* ● can provide one of the most refined and altogether entertaining dining experiences in the capital. From the moment you are received with dignity and warmth in its rotunda to the final bow when you are escorted to its elegant portals, everything-but-everything reflects the finesse of *La Belle France*. There are crystal chandeliers, a massive floral centerpiece in its circular dining saloon, silver candelabras, and every table with its own flower selections trimmed to perfection; marble pillars glow warmly in the soft light; spacious windows overlook illuminated shrubbery in the surrounding park; discreet live piano music tinkles continuously. In summer the outside terrace is the stuff of pure romance.

★★★★★ **Jules Verne** occupies an upper tier in the Eiffel Tower, so glorious for its panorama that it is a wonder that the chef should even bother to boil an egg. He does considerably more than that, however. Here's *haute* cuisine both in deed and in pun. Jaded Parisians used to snub you as a *touriste* at the very mention of the place, but now they are standing in long lines waiting for a table. (Actually, it is often booked weeks in advance, so try early.) The interior decor matches the mechanical structural motif of this spectacular aerie. The puff pastry with sea snails and leeks was splendid; so was the duck pate with pistachio; desserts are evocations of pure art—all beautifully served in a breathtaking setting. Prices, surprisingly, are not sky-high. Take the exclusive private elevator, not the spectator one. (Tel. 45556144.)

☆☆☆☆☆ **Rostang** • *10 rue Gustave-Flaubert* • is one of the brightest lights on the Paris culinary horizon—it is also one of the more attractive *intime* heavens in the city. One salon with a view to the chef and the busy kitchen— diverting, possibly appetizing, or gimmicky, depending on your own *vu*-point. Lace curtains mantle the arched windows; brown carpets and textiled walls lend softness to the room; burnt orange colorings yield warmth; quiet music ripples the air. Our sampling of the fresh duck liver in a warm *brioche,* the petits chevres et St. Marcellin, the feuillete de coquilles St. Jacques, and the sparkling choice of jewel-like desserts were memorable gems from the kitchen. If everyday food and lower prices are more to your liking, Rostang offers the simpler **Bistrot d'a Cote** next door and yet another by the same name at 16 ave. de Villiers.

☆☆☆☆ **Alain Senderens-Lucas Carton** • *place de la Madeleine* • remains one of Paris' stylish restaurants and easily one of the most expensive. The house itself (the former home of Lucas-Carton) is a venerable landmark with decor that goes back to the turn of the century. Proprietor-chef Alain Senderens still stirs the magic of his craft. Upstairs there's a private club for residents or frequent visitors to Paris. Membership here is more cherished than enrollment in the Legion d'Honneur. Closed Sat., Sun., and holidays.

☆☆☆☆ **Guy Savoy** • *18 rue Troyon* • is in the forefront of imaginative cuisine. I'm delighted by his Lotte confites and house-made Napoleons; the lobster is splendid too. But the prices? With wine each diner could easily digest $130 worth of organic matter. If you can swallow that, it's money well spent. Closed Sat. and Sun. and early Jan. At #13 on the same *rue,* G-S runs **Le Bistro de L'Etoile,** which, of course, is simpler and cheaper. Then at 75 ave. Niel he has the newer **Le Bistrot de l'Etoile-Niel,** which is an able protagonist of *cuisine bourgeoise.* All 3 can be enthusiastically recommended, but in their respective categories, of course.

☆☆☆☆☆ **Vivarois** • *192 ave. Victor-Hugo* • is a study in modernity that some like and some don't. Its working proprietors are M. and Mme. Claude Peyrot; certainly he is a virtuoso, a grand master of gastronomic genius. Pastel-yellow or sage clothed tables too close together; charcoal-hued banquettes; white Knoll chairs with cushions; beautiful, gleaming, superefficient kitchen. You might hope that le loup Farci de quenelle de brochet is on the menu. They are closed Sat. and Sun. and normally from July 15 to Sept. 10.

☆☆☆ **Beauvilliers** • *52 rue Lamarck* • is enchanting, especially for its terrace. There's a mood of luxury, but the cuisine is not complicated, with such offerings as grilled turbot, fine roasts, and cassoulettes. The atmosphere will be your main course.

☆☆☆ **Lasserre** • *17 ave. Franklin-D.-Roosevelt* • has been on the scene
for many a year, grew weary for a spell, and is now in good form again.
Sumptuous decor brightened by flowers, greens, and a sliding roof that opens
at the touch of a button to admit sunlight or moonbeams; gold-rimmed service
plates, silver-necked carafes, antique silver vases—all polished, including the
greeting. Closed Sun. and the last 3 weeks of Aug.; always nail down your
table ahead of time.

☆☆☆ **Chiberta** • *3 rue Arsene-Houssaye* • is fresh and gaily attractive.
Jean Michel Bedier is continuing the sorcery he formerly conjured up at the old
Garin and at Le Camelia in Bougival. Inventive dishes with a distinct inclination
toward the ''new school'' of French cooking; expensive and worthy.

★★★★★ **Tour d'Argent** • *15 quai de la Tournelle* • remains a landmark
and an evergreen attraction for Americans and other outlanders, who comprise
so much of its clientele. The penthouse views of the Seine and Notre Dame are
the chief reasons for going. Opposite the entrance is Comptoirs de la Tour, a
smart boutique where you can purchase the restaurant's wares for supercharged
prices. A Parisian fixture and a costly one, especially after dark.

☆☆☆ **Faugeron** • *52 rue de Longchamp* • offers splendid, glittering surroundings highlighted by chandeliers and softened by mellow velvet wall coverings; a thing-of-tomorrow kitchen, even supplied with a bridge from which
the chef can observe his crew; spacious floor plan; cuisine that employs the
grand as well as the modest in terms of ingredients, e.g., goat cheese, whiting,
milt, or calf's liver. Closed Sat. and Sun.

☆☆☆☆ **Grand Vefour** • *17 rue de Beaujolais* • has undergone a renovation of both its cuisine as well as its salon. The chef has come from one of the
city's most select spots (Jacques Cagna; see below) as well as the first maitre;
the sommelier is from the Tour d'Argent. The lush decor is a pinch less than
baroque; refreshed murals from Napoleonic times; gilded woodwork; comfortable banquettes; fine old bas-relief ceilings; interior orientation that might dis-
may claustrophobes. Here is an exalted house that the owning Taittinger
champagne (and Crillon) family has restored to greater glory.

☆☆☆ **Jacques Cagna** • *14 rue des Grands-Augustins* • has long been one
of my favorite private corners of France, occupying one of the oldest buildings
in Paris. The main dining circle is up one flight to a quadrant surrounding the
stairwell in which hangs a giant porcelain chandelier with frosted flowered reflectors. Heavy antique timbers; wooden floors; small attentive staff. The turbot
Farci and the ray in mustard sauce were splendid examples of melding delicious
light flavors with color choices. If you top your meal with a reine de Saba (a
devastatingly delicious chocolate fudgelike cake with English light custard) you
might expire from ecstasy and immediately rise to the 7th tier of heaven. Less
costly than the big-name houses, but very pleasing gastronomically.

☆☆☆ **Lamazere** • *23 rue de Ponthieu, close to the Champs-Elysees* •
remains among the most expensive dining establishments in the city. Owner

Lamazere is in love with truffles, foie gras, and cassoulets. While at least 50 other dishes are always on his card, these are the highest triumphs of his extremely high cuisine. I found the decor pretentious, the attention urbane, the tariffs astronomical, and the quality above average.

Ledoyen • *carre des Champs-Elysees* • occupies a position in the sophisticated Parisian whirl of cost-is-no-limit patronage. Now that Regine, the doyenne of discotheques, is at the turntable, the luxury is even more superheated. Marvelous park setting (convenient for motorists) and handsome entrance; large plate-glass windows; sumptuous sink-in armchairs. Big shots love the phone link to the tables and the fax facility.

☆☆☆☆ **Le Duc** • *243 boulevard Raspail* • something special for fish eaters. Its maritime mood is fashioned of 15 flower-decked tables, varnished bulkheads, prints of old ships, brass lamps in gimbals, and hints of its Mediterranean origins. The iced shellfish platter was so overwhelming in amplitude, arrangement, and variety that it almost constituted a graduate course in oceanography. This should have served as a generous meal by itself. The service was skilled but busy, the atmosphere was talkative, and the billings are blue-ribbon.

★★ **Maxim's** • is a venerable landmark, one of the world's most glittering showcases of haute couture and celebrated countenances. If you go for that mood, you'll probably like it.

☆☆☆ **Paul et France** • *27 ave. Niel* • is the ambitious realm of Chef Romano, who is bringing many "insider" Parisians to his doorstep. Everything works perfectly. You can be one-up on your chums by "discovering" this one.

☆☆☆ **Au Trou Gascon** • *40 rue Taine* • is guided by talented Chef Dutournier whose *ravioli de foie gras* has set Parisian tongues wagging. He can perform the same tricks with several other dishes. Splendid. ☆☆☆ **Carre des Feuillants** • *14 rue Castiglione* • is also under Dutournier supervision and it is newer. A trio of rooms plus a large open kitchen and grill.

☆ **L'Arpege** • *84 rue Varenne* • is well regarded locally and indeed some dishes are splendid; others are bizarre. First courses seem more interesting than main choices and sweets are the weak link in the food chain—although some Passard disciples rant that I'm dead wrong on the latter judgment. If you ask pointedly about the ingredients, you may have an interesting experience. Otherwise, the droll mixing of flavors may be too far out to enjoy. Haughty service standards, but quality and prices are high. (Nobody seems to disagree with that final comment.)

Olympe • *8 rue Nicolas-Charlet* • functions for dinner only. Delicious lobster in herbs. Many worshipful followers, especially in the fashion world; if you can manage a reservation, you won't be disappointed.

★★★★ **Le Train Bleu** • *Gare de Lyon* • began life as Le Buffet in 1901, changed its name, and is still one of the dining delights of contemporary as well as nostalgic Paris. Although the sumptuous salons overlook the comings and goings of trains, from this point on its resemblance to any other station restaurant in the world is totally absent. The staircase is a gracious wonder; huge chandeliers hang from gold-leafed ceilings; walls are decorated with carvings; superb woodwork and brassware are abundant.

Le Relais Paris-Est • *Gare de l'Est* • tries to do a similar thing, but I think it comes off the rails. Costly, too.

☆☆☆ **La Maree** • *1 rue Daru* • makes the stylish inner circle—and it is gaining ground steadily with disciples of seafood. Animated atmosphere created by a chic clientele; soft glow provided by chapel-glass stained panels and Edwardian globe fixtures on mirrored scones; split-level construction (I prefer the sunken zone nearer the front); ruby-hue velvet banquettes; fresh flowers on tables; enormous broadside menu; service improved. The prices are in line with its quality.

La Cagouille • *12 place Brancusi* • is a specialist in fish—and prepared in many different ways by Chef-Patron Allemandou. Not fancy, but very sincere in all regards.

MODERATE

★★ **L'Avant Seine** • *1 rond-point Rhin-et-Danube* • is one of the best buys for quality to be found, but it is not directly in the center. (Take the metro with the blue light to the last stop, Bourlogne Porte St. Cloud; it is facing the exit.) Attractive mirrored ceiling, cottage windows, carpets, soft ambience. Perfect service and a noteworthy performance in every respect. Worth the money and the trip, but never on Sundays.

★★ **St. Moritz** • *a few steps off the Etoile, adjoining the Royal Hotel* • is a handsome contender. Sleek interior highlighted by pale wooden coffers inset with wall plates; colorful, well-appointed decor; cuisine substantial, but not in the grand category; the fruits de mer (seafood) platter a good catch; closed Sun. and all of Aug.

☆ **Coconnas** • *2 bis place des Vosges* • is agreeably situated in an ancient flower market which Henri IV later converted into his personal pavilion. Long, narrow room with 20 wooden tables; simple decor; immaculately clean; special attention to pates, a dish called Merlan en colere (''a whiting biting his own tail'') and poule au pot; becoming more and more expensive, unfortunately. Closed Tues.

☆☆ **Comby** • *116 blvd. Pereire* • is well run by a veteran chef who has been on the cutting edge of all the modern gustatory trends. Now he is on his own and moving back to traditional French conventions. My roasted partridge and gratin of fruit were superb. The decor is also traditional. Closed weekends and part of July.

★★ **Fermette Marbeuf** • *5 rue Marbeuf* • is located on one of the most central corners of Paris, up a few steps into an ersatz Eden of flowers and artificial garden. There's an artifice in the food, too, but the contrivance is delightful. Patron Jean Laurent is an alchemist of outstanding skill.

Pierre du Palais Royale • *10 rue Richelieu* • is a marvel for foie gras, but then you'll probably be captivated by dozens of creations by Nicole, Daniel Dez, and the talented crew. These friendly people have been in the front line of Paris cuisine since before the invention of the goose.

Chez Benoit • *20 rue St. Martin* • plays its poor little heart out for the ultrapampered Nescafe Society of Paris. Slum-district location that the fad followers find irresistibly with-it (now practical however, for visitors to Pompidou Center); drab rooms; no decor; passable cookery if you have the house salad and navarin of lamb; plenty of smoke. Expensive it is, that's a truth.

☆☆ **Hubert** • *25 rue de Richelieu* • is fancy but not overpriced. Mock skylight decor, pleated curtains, flowers and candles on all tables. Very careful classic French cuisine.

☆☆ **La Boule d'Or** • *13 blvd. La Tour-Maubourg* • is the answer to hearty appetites. Each table is swaybacked with nibbling items just to hold you over until the real feed began: pickles, rolls, and chunks of farmhouse butter the size of the Arc de Triomphe and an enormous rillette portion containing at least a pound of meat—merely a starter! Tete de veau ravigote and canon d'agneau aux aubergines are designed to quell the hunger pangs of Olympic decathlon champions (I've seldom seen a male in the place who weighed less than 200 lbs.!); desserts from cabbage-size pears in nests of cream and pastry, to towering souffles, to shells of sweets so tempting that ladies' corsets split asunder at the sight of a passing tray.

☆☆ **Joseph** • *56 rue Pierre-Charron* • is peopled by top French executives and a smart lunch crowd. It is also handy for travelers who stay in either the George V or Prince de Galles hotels. Friendly atmosphere; routine prices; closed Sun.

☆ **Quai d'Orsay** • *Left Bank, near rue Fabert* • claims many happy disciples. The elbow-to-elbow bistro character is so popular—especially with a young assemblage of chatterers—that bookings must be made a day ahead. The stuffed neck of duck is the stuff of dreams—perhaps not for the *canard*.

★★ **Cafe de la Paix** • *12 blvd. Capucines* • When this Paris landmark was reopened a while back it remained in the former 19th-century style. The restoration satisfies any nostalgic Francophile.

Duquesnoy • *30 rue Bernardins* • is one I haven't tried personally, but friends in Paris hold it in great esteem. Grown men swoon over the turtle-and-lobster ravioli, or so it's said.

Hotel Dining

Space prohibits a special rundown, so please refer back to the "Hotels" section where there is some description of the more noteworthy tables. In brief, here is a star rating for the 9 leading houses (all are expensive):

☆☆☆☆☆ **Plaza Athenee**   ☆☆☆☆ **Meurice**
☆☆☆☆☆ **Crillon**   ☆☆☆☆ **Royal Monceau**
☆☆☆☆☆ **Bristol**   ☆☆☆ **Lutetia**
☆☆☆☆☆ **Ritz**   ☆☆☆ **Intercontinental**
☆☆☆☆ **George V**   ☆☆☆ **Prince de Galles**

Bistros

These remain the rage in Paris due to high quality and the reasonable values they offer. Selection is almost always limited to a few well-prepared dishes—and 99% of the time in the traditional style of cooking. The decor borrows extensively from the Belle Epoque, with forests of curlicue wood, panels of leaded stained glass, morning-glory lamps, smoked mirrors, bentwood chairs, marble-topped wrought-iron tables, and other beautifully rendered facsimiles of the era.

Bistro de Paris • *33 rue Lille* • is evocative of Paris at the turn of the century. It has continuously attracted attention as one of the finest in the city. A full meal might cost $50. Closed weekends and holidays.

Bistro d'Hubert • *36 place March e St.-Honore* • is known for its vodka-spiked turbot which, naturally, puts the price up a bit. Many choices, however, are less costly and excellent.

La Coquille • *6 rue Debarcadere* • is the pride of Chef Laudecker, who cooks up the namesake dish (scallops) in their shells. Somewhat different from other bistros, this one features game in season. Closed Sun., Mon., and festivals.

Le Roi du Pot-au-Feu • *34 rue Vignon* • is in one of the highest rent districts of central Paris, but its chowder sells for only about $8 per bowl. Amusing decor composed of cartoons, a well-used piano, and as might be expected, a busy zinc bar. You'd have difficulty spending as much as $17 for the specialty and wine.

Au Petit Fer a Cheval • *30 rue Vieille du Temple* • is important because of its situation in the Marais near the Georges-Pompidou Art Center, otherwise known as the Beaubourg—a very useful address when you are visiting the museum. If you arrive in tandem, sit at the table with the antique Metro benches.

Gerard • *4 rue du Mail* • serves a wonderful salad for $4.50, and a buckle-bending pot-au-feu for about $9. For approximately the same price, the beef filet is an excellent buy. This one functions until 11 p.m. You wouldn't be disappointed if you mistakenly turned up at **Gerard et Nicole** • *6 av. Jean Moulin* • which is no relation. Still, the mood is homespun and the *magret* (duck breast) is worth a detour.

Le Cameleon • *6 rue de Chevreuse* • is in Montparnasse. Chef Raymond, father of the above Gerard, is an honest man who converted from butchering to cooking. His talents are myriad but kept simple on purpose. He excels at salads and meats at very good prices.

Le Singe Pelerin • *15 rue Montmartre* • occupies a site near historic Les Halles. The ceramic murals are noteworthy; the atmosphere is genuine; cuisine in the former fashion of Les Halles—hearty in winter and fresh in summer.
     The fresh and contemporary **Le Bistro de la Gare** • *73 Champs-Elysees* • the neighboring **L'Assiette au Boeuf, Bistro de la Gare** • *59 blvd. du Montparnasse* • and the chain called **Bistro Romain.** A meal at these can be had for from $17 to $30. If I have any criticism to make it is that the main dish often is not up to the exceptional attractiveness and taste of the first course or the spectacular desserts. Nevertheless, the experience is one of significant reward for the outlay. **L'Assiette** • *181 rue du Chateau* • should not be confused with the one above of similar name. This is more of an individual spot less given to organizational concepts. **Le Gros Minet** • *1 rue des Prouvaires* • is another interesting and authentic candidate located near the garden and esplanade that was Les Halles. Tile floor; zinc counter; ground-floor room plus another small segment through the kitchen and up a narrow spiral staircase over the pantry. Ask the kind proprietor to show you his *cave,* which dates back to 1660. For around $18 you will be regaled with enormous pans and casseroles of terrine, rillette, and salad; then the set meal includes a flank steak (*onglet*) with sauteed onions or several other choices of entree.

Pied de Cochon • *6 rue Coquilliere* • seems to have drawn every tourist since Pepin the Short. While the entire district surrounding Les Halles was rebuilt in a tawdry 21st-century movie-set motif, people still are driven here as if by inertia. The plateau de fruits de mer is worthwhile.

Au Cochon d'Or • *31 rue du Jour* • is in the same district; sadly, this classic house seems to be in decline under its new management. Pity.

Les Gourmets des Ternes • *87 blvd. Courcelles, near the Etoile* • is a place no beefeater should miss, for steaks. While the menu lists a stampede of meats, don't fail to have the house's enormous special cut, which is so tender that I almost guarantee it will bring tears to the eyes of any dedicated carnivore. The one room is divided into 2 segments by arches and pillars; it is girdled by smoky mirrors; paper "tablecloths" complete the tone. This one is more expensive than the others, but well worth the effort.

Chope d'Orsay • *10 rue du Bac* • is where busy, cordial matrons serve up artistic platters to their loyal clientele at a dozen small tables. The salon's ceiling and walls are cloaked in a rich textile; copper skillets blend with old furnishings for warmth; lace curtains drape the streetside windows. The terrine of smoked sturgeon and salmon appears as a delicate pink and white banner; medallions of scallops in saffron were as lovely to the eye as they were to the palate; and the baba au rhum for dessert was a totally sinful escapade. The wine selection is small and not noteworthy, but perhaps this is effected in the interest of economy. An abundant feast will nudge the $40 mark—yet it will be memorable.

Chez Josephine • *117 rue du Cherche-Midi* • couldn't be more typical as a middle-class bistro. Don't expect plush seats or fancy service. The well-known skillets are mastered by chef Jean Dumonet, who is beloved for his truffled andouillettes, his ballottines, his sweetbreads with morels, and his rabbit in mustard sauce—all for reasonable sums.

INEXPENSIVE

Stefany • *5 ave. de Ternes* • is a breath of springtime—as fresh and as uplifting as its artistic color-splashed menu. Long room divided into segments, cheerful touches of pink, green and moss tones with blond wood, plants and bright flowers. Small selection of dishes but very nice and beautifully presented, all inclined toward the modern style; main courses in the $8 range; outstanding wine list. Aesthetically and gastronomically a treat.

Chez Maitre Paul • *corner of rue M.-le-Prince and rue Casimir Delavigne* • is a honey of a little place for economy trippers. The Man Himself does all the cooking, and he features a wine called Bourgueil from his own vineyard in Touraine. Try his smoked sausage for a country treat. Always full— so reserve in advance. Closed Tue.

Au Pactole • *44 blvd. St.-Germain* • draws many businessmen at lunchtime and families in the evening. Enclosed sidewalk terrace; 7-table interior sanctum with gold wallpaper, oil paintings, and flowers. The set menus are the star attractions here—a 4-course one and a 5-plate spread with more selections available.

Au Petit Riche • *125 rue le Peletier* • turns back the mechanism of timelessness to before this century began. If you've got a kink for globes, polished wood, and the decor of saloons in ships that were retired long, long ago, then you may worship this artifact which is run by Christian Lameloise, son of the titan who put the hamlet of Chagny on the French gastronomic map. Go early; on our first attempt they would not serve us at the wicked hour of 9:15 p.m. Closed Aug. as well as Sun. and holidays.

Chez Andre • *53 blvd. St.-Marcel* • holds a special attraction for journalists and exquisite mannequins from the couturier precincts that it flanks. Paper "tablecloths"; noisy room with old-fashioned partitions; busy enough to encourage early or late arrival by the wisest diners; no reservations taken.

Le Berthoud • *1 rue Valette* • is a splendid stop for rubbing the nap off the elbows. It's more engaging than a barrel full of people—and that's just how you'll feel when coffee time rolls around. Fascinating, inexpensive egg dishes bobbling in pools of melted butter or cream or both; Moujik (Russian tasties); heaps of salad; wee sausages to lion-share steaks for moderate outlays; calories-be-damned desserts. If you enjoy humanity at close quarters, you might relish this community plate.

Bar de Theatre • *catercorner to the Plaza-Athenee* • is a noon and after-theater gossip-and-groceries hangout for young dress designers, high-fashion salesgirls, and models who haven't quite reached the pinnacle. Tiny tables for these tiny appetites; passable fare; fast service; very reasonable tariffs.

Au Beaujolais • *19 quai de la Tournelle across from the famous Tour d'Argent* • is ultramodest. Meats hanging from the ceiling; butchers' aprons hanging from the shirt-sleeved waiters; happy bellies hanging from some of the best-fed clients in Paris. About as atmospheric as a pilot's ready room; tantalizing menu; always reserve in advance. Closed Mon. and in Aug.

Chez Rene • *around the corner at 14 blvd. St.-Germain* • has the same sort of personality but is even noisier (if such a thing is possible) than Au Beaujolais; same prices; similar but less refined cookery. You can stuff yourself for about $23, except on Sun. Bring earplugs.

Chez Marius • *30 rue des Fosses-St.-Bernard* • run by Jacques Chalvet, surges with energy. Two floors which are as simple as π; mouth-melting coq au vin; juicy grills. Parisian gourmets who can afford much more often dine here.

Chez Edgard • *4 rue Marbeuf* • is a midtowner that is a lower cost version of Lucas-Carton. Very big with middle-class French families and seekers of value.

La Pomme Soufflee • *37 bis rue Ponthieu* • is designed in the shape of a lollipop, with tables along the stem and a jam-up of noisy diners in the "pop" division. Light bites and quick service are the specialties of this busy beehive. Fair, but distressingly cacophonous.

Le Boccador • *7 rue Boccador, near the Plaza-Athenee* • maintains its mandate on excellence. The prices are much lower than you would suppose from looking at the place, the neighborhood, and the culinary presentation.

Outdoor restaurants

★★★★ **Pre Catelan** • *in the Bois de Boulogne* • when one of its all-too-frequent business conventions, wedding receptions, or group functions is not overrunning the premises this is one of the most attractive places for a summer lunch or dinner. Because this landmark now caters almost primarily to this patronage, it has lost much of its charm for the independent pilgrim. The cuisine—some of it in the new style—can be interesting since such care is taken with it. Chef Gaston Lenotre also operates the softly yellow-and-blue **Pavillon**

Elysee (in the garden of the same name). On an early sampling, I preferred the cooking at his newer establishment.

★★★ **La Grand Cascade** • is a woodland alternate in the Bois and was once the hunting lodge of Napoleon III. It is slightly less costly than Pre Catalan. This smart house always has a tempting selection of piscatorial preparations. (It runs a seafood restaurant in town, too.) Serious, scenic, and salubrious.

★★★ **Auberge du Vert-Galant** • *42 quai des Orfevres, Ile de la Cite* • sits on the bank of the ancient island in the Seine and offers a memorable panorama of the river and the Left Bank. Firmly sustained by lawyers, because it is just a tort's throw from the Palais de Justice. Adequate but not spectacular kitchen; high but not exorbitant fees; when the weather is right, not a plaintiff to be found.

☆☆ **Le Chalut** • *94 blvd. Batignolles* • specializes in fish. Its decor could not be more unattractive and less inspired if it had been designed by a haddock. Enormous menu; meals in the high–medium range. Pack-jammed, especially on Fri; closed from May 30 to Sept. 1.

☆☆ **Prunier** • *9 rue Duphot* • has lured back a Parisian following that had abandoned it during its sinking spells. The careful attention to restoring tradition and adding new zest to the cookery is paying off in gustatory dividends. Closed Mon. Also for seafare **Fouquet's** • *99 Champs Elysees* • is another old timer that is making a spirited comeback. Scallops a la nage are delicious; open Sundays, too. There are also two newer branches: **Bastille** (in the Opera) and **Defense** (in the CNIT complex). **Villars Palace** • *8 rue Descartes* • is the fish fancier's fad as of this instant. I thought it was overrated in the extreme. Also operative on Sundays—a rare catch in Paris.

Cheese

Ferme Saint-Hubert • *21 rue Vignon* • is a twinsome with one part serving marvelous cheese dishes, both hot and cold, and the other segment dedicated to purveying a seemingly endless inventory of packaged *fromage*. The alchemy is perfect for shopper or snacker.

Kosher

(1) **Le Sportif** • *24 rue Vieille-du-Temple* • (2) **Eden** • *36 boulevard Bonne-Nouvelle* • (3) **Falmbaum** • *37 rue Faubourg-Monmartre* • closed Jan. to Apr., and (4) **Henri** • *9 passage Basfoi* • For a nosh of gefilte fish (or maybe a corned beef sandwich), try the **Goldenberg Delicatessen** • *7 rue des Rosiers, not far from place des Vosges, or its branch at 69 avenue de Wagram* • which stays open 7 days a week from 8 a.m. to midnight. Oy-vay, is *that* good!

Chinese

Dave ● *39 rue St. Roch* ● is in the first district and in the first line of "insider" spots for oriental buffs. Here's where you'll find the Ben Jakobers of the sculpture world, the top fashion photographers of the moment, and the painters who count right now and tomorrow. It's easy to understand when good taste is universal.

NIGHT LIFE

"Revues" are the big draw for bus groups. They pay a small sum for a tribe of 50-or-so spectators, but if you go individually you'll probably be asked to shell out around $60 per noggin. The bruit includes "50 girls—FIFTY!" plus a quiverful of exclamation points. Most refuse to serve anything but champagne at $35 to $100 per bottle at the tables; if you do manage to ransom a Scotch and soda here, it might fizz in for around $15 per cup. Such beverages on a drink-by-drink basis, however, normally can be had only if you stand at the bar. All the big ones are out for the indiscriminate spender who won't bother to check the bill or for the tour-package gawker who is given a prepaid *flute* of bubbly and then promptly forgotten.

The **Lido** (116 bis Champs-Elysees) stages what is probably the most elaborate spectacle in Europe today—imaginative, grand, dynamic. It stuns the customers with its ensemble of at least 50 dancers, showgirls, seminudes, and headline international acts. In the spacious 1200-seat venue located in the Normandie Cinema Building, the theater-restaurant affords all customers an adequate view of the stage; the slope-away design terminates at a ringside tier that sinks to navel level. Fantasy effects have been introduced by extending mechanical equipment out over the audience—all subtle, surprising, tasteful, a socko hit! Shows at 10:30 and 12:30, so if you want to dine here, too, around 9 p.m. is the best time to go. A microcosm of the Lido world can be found at the smaller and less costly **Carbaret des Champs-Elysees** nearby.

Up at Montmartre, the renowned **Moulin Rouge,** sketched by Toulouse-Lautrec and later known for its can-can, is a sister to the Lido. Although the tariffs are just about the same, it is purposely geared to a lower category. Huge, tiered, theaterlike hall; bar atop the pyramid; brightly illuminated lavish show with some seminudes. Again the TV "spectacular," with enough feathers and chiffon to bury the Gare du Nord.

The **Crazy Horse Saloon** (12 avenue George V), revamped, comfortable, and nearly doubled in size, but still with a full stock of sex symbols, continues to draw masses of U.S. tourists. Contrived, occasionally salacious, sometimes entirely nude striptease, cleverly aided by projected images; thunderously loud musical assists; rapid, knock-'em-back service; your 1st drink at the bar will pour for close to $20; if you are seated at a table the cost will be about $65 for your patch of upholstery and 2 drinks; it is open every night year-round. Perhaps I'm being stuffy or miserly, but at these prices, for what is there, I always have the feeling of being suckered. If you go, watch your billings and check your change (especially the folding money).

Le Lapin Agile (in Montmartre on rue St. Vincent) will help stoke up the nostalgia for the earliest Americans in Paris. Jazz is also coming back with a renewed beat to Saint-Germains-des-Pres, the Left Bank venue of yore. Check first to learn who's playing at the fanciful **Le Bilboquet,** at the *art*fully nouveau **Montana** or at the sleek **Latitudes,** all riffing near to each other on the nocturnally historic rue St.-Benoit. I'm fond of the rough and sweaty **L'Eustache** (37 rue Berger) which on several tries recalled early times on the jazz circuit. More cosmopolitan is the adult-oriented **Lionel Hampton Club** in the rather sedate Meridien Hotel.

For the revue type of attraction, the **Folies Bergeres,** with its 40 tableaux displaying 1600 costumes, is the most glamorous. (As with all shows in its century-plus history, the title of the latest production contains 13 letters.) **Casino de Paris** is runner-up is in this category, but it's a pretty slow track. **Paradis Latin** (28 rue de Cardinal Lemoine) enjoys a certain fame. Jean-Marie Riviere runs a good show and a tasteful one.

For clubs with a dress-up air, **Le Palace 999** (8 rue Faubourg Montmartre) seems niftyest in the post-midnight circuit. There's a winter garden with ruby velour sofas, 4 dance areas, lounges, and **Le Privilege** cellar restaurant with sometime jazz groups and piano music. **Le Garage** (41 rue Washington) is more like an elegant pit stop with suspended foliage and garden chairs. **La Piscine** (32 rue Tilsitt) is a turned-on, vibrant, youthful splash in the town plan. **Atmosphere** (45 rue Francois 1er) and **Apocalypse** (40 rue du Colisee) are also freshets that I prefer to such old after-guard warhorses as **Regine's** (49 rue de Ponthieu) and **Castel's** (15 rue Princess) The last two trade too heavily in nabobery to suit my after-dark tastes.

Le Milliardaire (68 rue Pierre Charron) offers a parade of sexy-looking women and oily muscular male escorts on a tiny stage between 10:30 p.m. and 12:30 a.m. nightly. There's a nuzzling atmosphere; numerous darkened nooks occupied by "clients" and B-girls with a marathon state of thirst. Provocative but expensive.

The tariffs at **Chez Raspoutine** (58 rue de Bassano), yet another Folies' folly, are OUTRAGEOUS. Nevertheless, the show and food are appealing. **Monseigneur** (94 rue d'Amsterdam) offers high-life violin serenades to the tunc of very high prices. You can also find gypsy strings and the Hungarian spirit at **Paprika** (14 rue Chauchat), especially after midnight; here's fodder as spicy as the name. **Alcazar** (62 rue Mazarine) offers a gay-oriented evening to its followers. Turn-of-the-century atmosphere; singing, jesting waiters; kooky diversions plus a zesty parade of entertainment. **Coupe-Choux** • *rue Lanneau* • is a gathering spot for Left Bank theatrical types; so is **Espace Cardin** • *av. Gabriel* • which draws intellectuals to its precincts on the other *rive;* go late to both if you want to be with the "in" crowd. **Michou** • *80 rue des Martyrs* • does a similar thing in its own more modest way. **Etoile de Moscou** • *6 rue Arsene-Houssaye, near the Etoile* • is a semicircular family-type club with loud singers.

A continuing passion in the capital is punk rock and the leading purveyor of the moment is **La Scala,** occupying a mirrored 3-story cavern in what used to be the Magasin du Louvre (entrance on rue de Rivoli). The decibel level (except in one quiet bar) easily could dwarf mortar practice at Parris Island. Admission is a big fat $20 including one drink and $8 for subsequent quaffs.

SHOPPING

SHOPPING HOURS: Most of the deluxe establishments stay open Sat. but are closed Sun. and perhaps Mon. mornings. Hairdressers, however, function on Mon. Food stores operate all day Sat.; some of them do business on Sun. mornings, too, but many are closed Mon. Department stores are busy every day except Sun., with hours from 10 a.m.–7 p.m. Boutiques and specialty shops generally open at 10–10:30 a.m. and lock up around 6:30–7 p.m. Many no longer shutter during the lunch hours, particularly those in areas heavily traveled by tourists (Champs Elysees, Faubourg Saint-Honore, St.-Germain-des-Pres, place des Victoires). If you find a very small shop darkened during normal business hours usually there will be a sign taped on the door that reads, "be back in ten minutes" which suggests that the owner is also the salesperson.

BEST AREAS: Right Bank: Faubourg Saint-Honore (boutiques, haute couture, galleries), ave. Matignon (galleries), rue de Rivoli, place des Victoires (boutiques), ave. Montaigne, ave. George V, and ave. Francois 1er (haute couture), place Vendome (jewelry), Champs Elysees (the full gammut—including automobile showrooms), Opera district (department stores), rue de Paradis (crystal and china), Marais (fashion boutiques). Left Bank: rue de Seine, rue Bonaparte, and rue de Bac (galleries), St.-Germain-des-Pres, rue des Saints-Peres, and rue de Grenelle (boutiques).

SAVINGS ON PURCHASES: It's important to know that you're entitled to a 13% to 22% TVA (*Taxe de Valeur Ajoutee)* refund for items you buy over a certain minimum price. Always ask the salesperson to guide you because this costs the store absolutely nothing except, perhaps, a little lost time. Request a *Fiche de Douane* and be sure to carry your passport as proof of nonresidence. The form *must* be shown to the French Customs officials and validated at your point of departure, so keep it handy. This may come back to you through the mails to your home, or via a refund to your credit-card account. Be sure to pack the items for which you are claiming a refund near the top of your luggage or in some convenient place where Customs may verify them should they wish. For all of the details on this bonanza you might like to consult *Fielding's Selective Shopping Guide to Europe,* which describes the process in greater detail.

NOTE · · · The **Airport Shops** in the International Zone at Orly, Charles de Gaulle, and Nice? Watch out! Although you might be assured to the contrary, we would bet our shoes that very few items of their merchandise are tax-free.

ANTIQUES CENTER: **Le Louvre des Antiquaires** (2 Place du Palais-Royal) is a huge 3-story complex dedicated to the purchase and sale of antiques. This site houses 250 different shops representing many different specialties, plus cafes, restaurants, and exhibition halls. It is open from 11 a.m.–7 p.m. from Tues. to Sun.

ARCHITECTURE IN MINIATURE: **Galerie Architecture Miniature Gault** (206 rue de Rivoli and up in Montmartre at 5 bis rue Norvins) is a playland of marvelous ceramic houses, churches, and buildings from Europe's most attractive regions. These make splendid home decorations and collector items of surprisingly low cost. Each creation carries a certificate of authenticity. A great shop with a grand exposition.

ART GALLERIES: Literally hundreds. Serious devotees should first pick up a current copy of *l'Officiel des Galeries* (15 rue de Temple), the definitive source of information about which painters and sculptors are being shown where in the whole nation.

AUCTIONS: The **Nouveau Drouot** (9 rue Drouot) is the top center of this traditionally regulated industry. (Private auctions are forbidden in France.) Flee to the Secretariat for English-speaking assistance. Inspection of articles from 11 a.m.–6 p.m. on the day before the auction, or from 11 a.m.–noon on the day the hammer falls; mixed sales held Mon., Wed., Fri. from 2 p.m.–6 p.m., closed Sun. and all of Aug.

BOOKS: **Galignani Library** (224 rue de Rivoli) has an incontestable claim as the oldest foreign bookstore on the continent. And you'll find one of the widest choices of English-language books to be found anywhere in Europe. They are especially strong in Fine Arts. Go to **W.H. Smith & Son** (248 rue de Rivoli) for your thrillers and magazines. If you still can't find it, **Brentano's** (37 ave. de l'Opera) and **Nouveau Quartier Latin** (78 blvd. St. Michel) are additional candidates. And, of course, there's the fun of browsing for second-hand volumes at the stalls along the Left Bank.

BOUTIQUES: The hottest areas for fashion—both classic and contemporary—are now the rue Faubourg Saint-Honore, the place des Victoires, St.-Germain-des-Pres, rue des Saints-Peres and rue de Grenelle. The last three are on the Left Bank.

On the rue Faubourg Saint-Honore, names to remember are Sonia Rykiel, Christian Lacroix, Ungaro, YSL, Gucci, Gianni Versace, Daniel Hechter, and the stellar labels you see every day in the fashion magazines.

Place des Victoires is a fashion mecca. **Mercadal et Fils** (see "Footwear") is a great name in the district as are **Kenzo** and, for men, **Cacharel.** This is really the big news area of Paris today.

Other Left Bank hot shots are **YSL** and **Michel Klein;** the rue des Saints-Peres includes **Angelo Tarlazzi, Maud Frizon,** and **Sabbia Rosa** for lingerie.

In addition, the French institution of **Lubin** (64 Faubourg-St. Honore) features $10 to *haute elegance* gift items. **Line Vautrin** (3 rue de l'Universite) and **Burma** (16 rue de la Paix plus 2 branches) feature an assortment of costume jewelry and trinkets.

BAKERY PRODUCTS: **Poilane** (8 rue du Cherche-Midi) established the state of the art of breadmaking a century ago. It has been producing apple tarts, butter cookies, and glorious munchables ever since. For classic French patisserie, don't miss a visit and a sackful of Poilane goodies.

CHEESE: **La Ferme Saint Hubert** (21 rue Vignon) is the whey to anyone's gastronomic heart. There are no fewer than 180 varieties on display!

CHINA AND ACCESSORIES: **Villeroy Boch Creation** (21 rue Royale) is the Parisian showcase of the Luxembourg masters who have enchanted European households for well over two centuries. Here you'll find collections such as *Basket, Siena, Naif, Amapola,* and many more. Splendid choices from an historic manufacturer.

DEPARTMENT STORES: **Au Printemps, Trois Quartiers, and Galeries Lafayette** are the leaders. They are so close together that you won't need a taxi to cover them all. **Au Printemps-Nation,** a 5-story branch, is also open on Paris' eastern edge. **Bon Marche** on the Left Bank is the biggest and cheapest.

FAIENCE: **Quimper Faience** (84 rue St. Martin) derives from its Brittany base, where you should also visit its factory outlet if you travel in western France. In the capital you'll see breakfast-lunch-and-dinner sets, decorative plates, and colorful gift items made world famous by the Breton potters.

FOOTWEAR (LADIES): **Mercadal et Fils** (3 place des Victoires) is one of the most "in" names in Paris. Others that might fit the bill include **Andre Pfister** (4 rue Cambon), **Cedric** (11 rue du Faubourg Saint-Honore), and **Charles Jourdan** (12 rue du Faubourg Saint-Honore).

GLOVES AND SCARVES: **Denise Francelle** (244 rue de Rivoli) has been our favorite for eons—and she gets better every year. There is room for exactly 5½ customers, and it's always crowded—but her selection is so smart and her prices are so sensible that her vast international clientele couldn't care less. She must have a colossal storage room because in gloves alone she carries all sizes of about 400 different models in each of the popular colors. You'll find styles for every mood. In addition to scarves, two of her popular specialties are handmade beaded gloves and umbrellas. Problem-solving dividend, even when you're back in the States: For a nominal postage fee, Madame will airmail one pair of gloves per box to your Christmas or special occasion designee. And what a sensation they cause when they arrive from Denise Francelle of Paris! Ask for Mlle. Edith.

GREEK GOLD JEWELRY: **Lalaounis** (364 rue St. Honore, near Place Vendome) is the preeminent creator in this distinctive medium. Lucky Parisians now have a showcase of these works. (See "Athens.")

GOURMET FOODS, LIQUORS, GIFTS: **Hediard** (21 place de la Madeleine) is where Paris' most knowing and known pinkies point at the gems of taste. If you want to take home a present to a discerning gastronome get in line quickly.

HAUTE COUTURE: The tariffs in most of the major houses—**Cardin, Chanel, Dior, Givenchy, Gres, Lacroix, Lanvin, Laroche, Patou Ricci, Saint Laurent, Scherrer,** and **Ungaro** among them—start in the $6,500! range. If you're smart and sharp-eyed, from seeing the collections you can approximate the latest couture look in ready-to-wears at these original establishment's boutiques (or many lesser ones) at less than half the original prices. If you want to attend some showings, merely call the reception desks at the places desired and invitations should come by return mail. When you arrive, a saleswoman will hand you a program and escort you to your seat. If you're determined to buy on the spot, circle the number of the item on the card. But those tariffs—ouch!

LINGERIE: **Cordelia** (21 rue Cambon) features many items from the Dior line. The female member of this writing team thinks of them as "delicious." The male member of this writing team thinks of them—often.

PERFUME: This remains the No. 1 bargain in France, which as a nation maintains a firm grip as *parfumeur* to the world. By a wide margin more famous scents are produced in France than in any other land, a fact which puts this industry among the top seven export items of the country. As a nonresident you're entitled up to a 40% saving on perfume purchases—obviously a great way to save money!

ASSORTED FRAGRANCES: **Sagil** (242 rue de Rivoli) not only has one of the best locations in Paris, but its inventory of scents is like the Library of Congress for perfumes. Go here for the classics or be challenged by the daunting collection of important new products. Lots of gift items too.

SILK FLOWERS: **Trousselier** (73 blvd Hausmann) wears the crown as the finest creator of handcrafted artificial flowers in silk anywhere in the world. When we asked how many species they could duplicate, we were told "every one nature produces."

PEROUGES (Cite) If you are in the Lyon district, please reward yourself with a visit to this historic enclave with roots going back to 1167. As it developed, a small medieval hamlet appeared and has been kept in exquisite preserve by its proud residents, by archeologists, and by artists who love it. It takes about a day to absorb the quiet wonders of the village and if you can plan to be here on a weekday I think you will appreciate it more than when the French are here en masse on all Saturdays and Sundays.

★★★★★ **Hostellerie du Vieux Perouges** ● is operated by Monsieur and Madame George Thibaut. Except for providing obvious comforts, the rooms are unchanged in appearance since the Middle Ages, containing the furniture, pewter, textiles, and accouterments of the period. Across the cobbled courtyard, the restaurant provides an enchanting journey back in time. In cool months, a vast hearth crackles merrily; waitresses in costumes of the era present parchment menus; a giant scroll is your wine list. The cuisine reflects Bressan tastes, and delicious it is. Costly by country standards but low compared to city living. If crowds have not overrun this little morsel of paradise, you will have one of the outstanding experiences of your travel days and nights here. Highly recommended, especially in spring and autumn.

PESSAC-L'ALOUETTE   **La Reserve** (one of the more rewarding residential pauses in the Bordeaux region). It's a pleasant alternative to Bordeaux city living, in the center of the wine district and near the beaches of coast of Aquitaine.

REIMS   Squalid for a city its size and for marketplace of the luxury champagne commerce. If you are not looking strictly for hotel-style shelter, the ☆☆☆☆☆ **Chateau Les Crayeres** offers 16 accommodations, an estate setting, 18th-century appointments, and gastronomy overseen by chef Gerard Boyer (see below). The Pommery-Lanson champagne barons now allow it to be used by the public. Otherwise, the picture looks like this: (1) ☆☆ **Altea Champagne,** with a pleasant restaurant called Les Ombrages, (2) **Les Templiers,** quite fashionable and *mais oui,* expensive, (3) **De La Paix** (with a swimming pool), (4) **Le Bristol** (satisfactory *if* you draw one of its colorful rooms; clean and reasonably priced; nice people; no dining salon), (5) **Grand Hotel du Nord** (so designed that some of the shower stalls are smack by your pillow), (6) **Continental** (enough globes in its restaurant to recall the Shade of Edward II; otherwise, cold and Shade-less). The 2-story, chilly **Novotel** (2½ miles out) is motelish in feeling. All 125 units set up for 3 people; coin-operated photostat machine in the lobby (why?); shopping center across the pike; grill room surrounding the bar; an air of boredom surrounding everything else. **Royal Champagne** (20 minutes toward Epernay, at *Champillon*) is a fine and quiet alternative. About 10 km from *Epernay,* at the village of *Vinay,* **La Briqueterie** is a charmer. At nearby *Fere-en-Tardenois,* the **Hostellerie du Chateau** is a back-country beauty gobbled up by Japanese interests and turned into a sporting complex. Ask locally if you have a yen.
   For your nutrients, try them in the following order.

   ☆☆☆☆☆ **Boyer** • which is among the most esteemed kitchens in all Gaul.

   ★★ **Le Chardonnay** • which used to be a Boyer property but is now owned by Jacques Lange, is cheaper and simpler, but still very good.

   ★★ Le Florence • has especially good chicken in champagne sauce and gratin du sole.
   Le Continental • opposite the rail station, is good in the moderate-price category.
   At *Montchenot* (6 miles) ★★ **Auberge du Grand Cerf** • is recommendable for serious dining.
   At *Tinqueux* tuck in your napkin at **L'Aissiette Champenoise.**

ROANNE has been made famous in this century by the cooks at one great establishment; many claim it is the finest anywhere.

☆☆☆☆☆ **Troisgros ●** offers incredible scallope de saumon; try it, or if that's out of season, poisson St.-Pierre a l'oseille; both are culinary masterworks. It offers a few rooms, but the focus here is on the gastronomy served up in its deceptively simple paneled salon dotted by nondescript oils and an illuminated mural of a chef in action.

ROCHEGUDE gives its name to a hotel chateau that sits among vineyards just north of *Orange.* The origins go back to Roman occupations; lovingly maintained architecture; pool; fair cuisine; haughty attitudes. Unique as a pause (but not more) in Provence.

ROUEN Also see "Normany Beachheads" at the end of this chapter. It's a town of hundreds of medieval timber-frame houses, churches painted by Monet, a marketplace where Joan of Arc was burned, and a recently discovered School of the Jews. The **Rouen Cathedral** was razed by fire and only rebuilt in 1201; it took 3 centuries to finish it (in case you were thinking that construction takes a long time today). The **Great (?) Clock** ("Gros Horloge") has but one hand; still you should see it and the **Belfry. St Owen** features the nation's grandest organ; **St Maclou** is unique for its flamboyant style. There's an extensive regionally oriented **Ceramics Museum;** I enjoyed **Le Secq des Tournelles** for its wrought iron. Hotels: (1) **Dieppe** (with superb dining; try the Canard a la Rouennaise), (2) **Pullman,** or (3) **Altea** (new and agreeable). For dining, **Gill,** near the cathedral, is twice blessed: (1) for the ravioli of langoustines and (2) for the swirl of fresh fish from which to choose. **Bertrand Warin ●** *9 rue de la Pie* ● is a converted Norman residence with a bit more decorative flair, inventive cookery, and rather lofty price tags. **La Couronne** has a fine table and is noted as the oldest auberge in Normandy. **Les P'Tits Parapluies** is said to be good, too, but I don't know it personally. For snacks, sweets, and teas, **La Tarterie** ● *28 pl. de Carmes* ● fills the bill.

STRASBOURG (1) **Hilton** (Maison du Boeuf restaurant—which also sneaks in some delicious fish dishes; a bar, health club and sauna, beauty salon and barber shop, plus 247 rooms—8 units for nonsmokers only—in a 7-story edifice), (2) **Terminus-Gruber** (colors that will either delight or fell you; each floor in another hue-and-cry scheme; richly attractive Cour de Rosemont dining room, plus a second restaurant with less charm; very good for avant-garde travelers who like those decorator shades), (3) **Des Rohan** (near Cathedral; small and tasteful at reasonable prices), (4) **Mercure** (also near the Cathedral; new with 98 rooms; a link in an extensive chain of medium priced hotels), (5) **Sofitel** (modernistic structure, suggestive of a better-grade Statler; coolish bar and Saint Pierre restaurant with an inventive menu; indoor-outdoor patio; underground carpark; 180 rooms, all with bath, radio, telephone, and pastel bed linens; pay-as-you-chill air conditioning; pleasant, but you might as well be lodging in any up-to-date hotel anywhere in the world), (6) **Grand** (latest units smaller and more expensive than more comfortable traditional ones; no restaurant; fair value without oomph), (7) **Holiday Inn** (La Louisiane restaurant its best feature), (8) **Nouvel Maison Rouge,** (9) **Monopole-Metropole** (inviting hunting-lodge dining room its most worthy feature; kindly staff; most bedrooms now halfheartedly renovated, but many remain with makeshift baths and shift-less space). Among the city's independent restaurants, here's the rundown: (1) **Au Crocodile,** (2) **Buerehiesel,** (3) **Valentin Sorg,** and (4) **Maison Kammerzell.**

SAULIEU   just north of *Beaune* in the fields of Burgundy, is famous for ☆☆☆☆☆ **La Cote d'Or,** the luxury inn and restaurant inspired by personable Bernard Loiseau, the smiling, avuncular chef who cooks like an angel. He also charges like the devil but the experience is worth it.

SEYSSEL   It's a town on the Upper Rhone and the ☆☆☆ **Rotisserie du Fier** is the reason for going. Beautifully situated beside the Fier tributary; lovely room with elm paneling; marvelous cuisine by young Chef Pierre Michaud; kind hostessing by Jacqueline. The low prices are astonishing.

TALLOIRES

☆☆☆ **Auberge du Pere Bise** ● is an outstanding parkside and lakefront inn. A while back the cooking was in a funk; then it closed for four months to get its act back together and to refreshen the interior. Despite the temporary dip it still draws gourmets from all over the Planet Earth. My recent sampling at the tables was very, very rewarding—also very, very expensive. Nevertheless, this house is revealing an upward vector once again; mid-winter closing and spring closing; check before going.

THOISSEY

☆☆☆☆ **Chapon Fin** ● is more alluring for its tables than for its sheltering arms with 28 rooms. The *St.-Jacques maison,* or the gratin of crawfish (also grenouilles), or the poularde a la creme aux morilles are reason enough to make a 100-mile detour.

TOURNUS   With Roman remains, a clock tower, crumbling fortifications, and an abbey within sight of the Saone, here is a captivating stop in view of the Macon Slopes. **Hotel de Greuze** offers austere refinement and neck-snapping prices; the adjoining **Greuze** restaurant—an independent entity—equals it in stunning tariffs, but the cuisine struck me as crude and graceless in its presentation. Across the street, **Le Terminus** offers reasonable comfort and a fine homespun meal at a fraction of the **Greuze** rates. The modest but nice **St. Philibert,** next door, comes in at one-fifth the luxury tabs. The town is convenient for motorists, just off the *autoroute* between Lyon and Paris.

VALENCE

☆☆☆☆☆ **Pic** ● is just south of *Vienne* (see below). It's a world-famous restaurant, where the management also offers a few bedrooms for those who linger. Lovely shaded garden in summer; be sure to reserve ahead because it closes in Aug., school holidays, as well as Sun. evenings and Wed. Expensive.

Then, a bit outside of *St.-Romain-de-Lerps* (west of the A7, exit Valence Nord or Sud), there's the impressive stone **Chateau du Besset,** set in a vast park and glowing in elegant 15th-century style. You'll find a pool, tennis, terraces, cuisine of grand repute, and celestial tranquillity.

VEZELAY   is in Burgundy, about 2½ hours southeast of Paris.

La Poste et Lion d'Or • is a charmer. So is **Le Pontot,** with 10 bedrooms in a towered medieval structure of the Old Town.

☆☆☆☆☆ **l'Esperance** • at *St.-Pere-sous Vezelay* wins the orchids due to the skilled cooking of Chef Marc Meneau, one of the "greats" in today's French firmament of gastronomy. His style tends to lightness, simplicity, and sophistication; it is also greatly reliant upon seasonal products. This inn and restaurant is at the base of the Roman Ste. Madeleine Basilica. Dining in the glass-covered conservatory is a reverie that melds well with food and service. Madame Meneau is a charming hostess; their hunting dog will offer a warm wagtail welcome from table to table. A meal for two with a moderate burgundy will cost about $300. At *Lugny,* nearby, the Audan family run the historic and captivating 10-room **Chateau de Vauct.** Certainly worth a try.

VIENNE

☆☆☆ **Pyramide** • was once rated as the world's finest. It has been attacked rather brutally in the press. And defended loudly in response by loyal clients. The turbot in champagne is internationally celebrated. Closed Nov. 1 to Dec. 1, Mon. nights and all day Tue.

VONNAS

☆☆☆☆☆ **Chez La Mere Blanc** (a.k.a. **Georges Blanc**) • has been in the Blanc family for 4 generations, and once you see it, you might apply for adoption. Though it offers excellent comfort in its 7 suites and 27 bedchambers— and at prices that are easy to swallow—most of its fame centers on the dining room: stone floor panels, open-timbered ceiling, tapestries, oil paintings, fresh flowers, candle illumination, and a menu that maintains the glory of Ain, where it resides (not far from Macon). There are two fixed price menus plus a la carte—outstanding value.

FRENCH RIVIERA

SEE SEPARATE CHAPTER ON MONACO

For years tourists have been fed on the belief that the Riviera is a shallow, sybaritic waist-land and cultural wasteland. Nothing could be further from the current truth. Apart from a rich history involving the entire Mediterranean population and dating back through antiquity, the Cote d'Azur today is a dazzling showcase for graphic and plastic arts. Running from A-to-V, *Antibes* offers the Chateau Grimaldi containing one of the best Picasso collections in the nation. *Biot* boasts a breathtaking hillside museum of Fernand Leger—with such well-preserved colors that you are unlikely to find similar quality elsewhere. *Cagnes-sur-Mer* is not only the preserve and former domain of Renoir, but it's also host to the Museum of Modern Mediterranean Art. *St. Jean-Cap Ferrat* is bristling with impressionist work in its Ile-de-France Museum; the Renoirs, Monets, and Sisleys are outstanding. While *Gourdon* displays naive painting, *Menton* displays the work of Jean Cocteau both in the museum as well as in the town hall. *Nice* is jammed with treasures ranging from Chagall to Matisse to Degas to Signac to Rodin plus a cavalcade of other titans. *St. Paul de Vence* presents a stupefying indoor-outdoor collection at the Maeght Foundation. *St. Tropez,* long a rendezvous of painters, has collected its finest children within the l'Annonciade Museum. At *Vallauris,* Picasso's "War and Peace" adorns a chapel and a special museum for Alberto Magnelli also resides in this town. *Vence* has warm links with Matisse—demonstrated at the famous Chapelle du Rosaire, while another chapel (St. Pierre at *Villefranche*) evokes the clear light and coastal disposition of Cocteau. This is only a sampler because the list of masters and masterworks is too vast to include here.

Information Centers Try either the **Services du Tourisme de la ville de Cannes,** at the Palais des Festivals (on the Croisette), or the **Welcome Information Service** branches in Nice and Cannes. The first offers an Information Desk, an English-speaking staff (including hostesses who have lived in the States), a greeting service (at that hideous Maritime Station, at the rail terminals, and on the autoroute), cruise ship, and other aids. It keeps 2 women in touch with all hotels and pensions to find space for new arrivals. It's open every day until midnight during this rush season. The 2nd comes up with the same type of aid, plus a helping hand to locate immediate hotel accommodations for stranded travelers. It is connected by Telex to 12 companion bureaus in major cities. Both have absolutely nothing to sell; their only aim is to assist you so that you'll get the best possible impression of the Cote d'Azur.

ANTIBES   is on the main Nice-Cannes line. Nearby there is probably the most famous independent dining establishment of the Cote d'Azur—

★★★★ **La Bonne Auberge** • Today (or tonight) the food is superb, but when the prices come as high as they do down on this coast, some readers will balk if only for that reason. Nevertheless, Chef Rostang deserves the praise he wins continually; try his lobster soup with delightful raviolis or the *loup,* a fish from the Mediterranean. The ambience remains delightful and luxurious.

★ **Les Vieux Murs** • occupies a site on a cannon point of the ancient seagirt ramparts. Lovely antique setting as permanent as time itself; stucco walls; arched ceilings; colorful regional interior. Fish soup and grilled fish are the better bets. As a simple but viewful perch, it is appealing—especially on the summer terrace.

☆☆ **L'Oursin** • (rue de la Republique) is also a winner. Fresh, fresh shellfish during the R-months; a good catch. Book ahead to be safe.

The coastal hamlet offers a caravansary of attractions in its eye-popping **La Siesta.** This amusement center (plus a casino), 7 miles from Cannes and 12 miles from Nice, adjoins the highway bridge over the Brague River. Also diverting is **Marineland** with its assemblage of aquatic residents who perform a couple of times each day (year round) and once a night in July and Aug.; you'd better check locally for the exact times. All the splashing takes place at the intersection of RN 7 and the route to Biot.

The **Automobile Museum,** on the *peage* halfway between Cannes and Nice, is a splendid ultramodern building with dazzlers such as Voisin, Panhard et Levassor, Delage, Rosengart, Bugatti, Ferrari, Rolls, and a glamorous 1925 Hispano Suiza on display.

For lodgings try the **Royal** first, followed by the tiny **Josse.**

BEAULIEU

☆☆☆☆☆ **La Reserve** • as fresh as a Mediterranean dawn, evokes an atmosphere of intimacy, luxury, and elegance. Beguiling lobby; lounge recalling the best reception room in Rome's Farnese Palace; richly appointed bar; beautiful summer patio for alfresco dining when the wind is low; dining salon segmented into 3 parts, with the center portion the private domain of Reserve residents; many balconies; 5 suites and 54 rooms in exquisite taste; Chef Joel Garault supervising masterful cooking based on the season's whims; delicate Limoges picking up the house color scheme; fully air-conditioned; Telex and Fax. The large pool (heated) area, extending into the bay, incorporates a sun-restaurant, 3 saunas, a massage room, detension hydrotherapy with high-pressure hose, 38 dressing rooms, a bar, and an inside restaurant; this complex is also reserved for the exclusive use of hotel guests. Director Henri Maria maintains a standard that renders this house the virtually unchallenged jewel of the coast. Closed Dec.

☆☆☆ **Metropole** • situated in a 2½-acre, flower-girted park directly bordering the surf, is proud of its revisions, although they are not as sumptuous as those of the neighboring La Reserve. Professional guidance by veteran manager Badrutt whose experience is your guarantee of holiday satisfaction. Heated pool, barette, and seaside summer restaurant on a terrace above its rock "beach"; quiet ambience; traditional furnishings; sumptuous lounges; air conditioning. Very pleasant indeed.

BIOT A tiny hilltown has been brought fame and prosperity due to the **Fernand Leger Museum,** which is located on its outskirts—a monument that merits all the attention it has attained worldwide; the collection is extraordinary and the museum has been newly expanded to accommodate the treasury of items. It is rare to see so many of the master's excellent ceramics under one roof as well as carpets, paintings, sketches, reliefs, and even wire sculpture. If you have only observed Leger's two-dimensional art, this is a dramatic revelation of his wider visions. The building is airy and well lighted, the front adorned with a vast mosaic across its entire facade. The hamlet is a medieval twist of antiquity with arcaded walls, a belltower, and some of the most tourist-spoiled citizens in Provence—an honor that takes some doing to achieve. Especially given to this regional hauteur are the self-satisfied restaurateurs who turn away (gracelessly) more customers than they feed. **Jarrier** is the most expensive and the best, in my opinion. It is a pleasant auberge laboring under stone vaults and a reputation that exceeds its capacity to serve. **Les Terraillers,** another rocky grotto, is also recommendable—if you can get in. The **Poste** is acceptable for light refreshment. **Les Arcades,** in midvillage, seemed rather grotty, with uninspired fodder. If you arrive later than 2 p.m., you can forget any hope of dining in a decent place. In fact, it might be better to avoid a meal altogether in this popular center and take your nutrients down on the coast where there is a greater selection. Biot's penalty is its great charm.

CANNES

Normally about 25 minutes from Nice via the autoroute, Cannes is so popular in High Season that it can be uncomfortably overcrowded. There's a magnificent second yacht harbor, called Port Canto, at the eastern extremity of the bay, with 450-car parking lot adjoining; it's connected to a second car park west of these piers by a free bus shuttle service. This auxiliary nautical port-of-sport boasts a clubhouse, heated pool, exhibition hall, card rooms, and bowling facilities—the works. Take a stroll along the Croisette, the main boulevard that separates the beach from the more lush hotels. Overlooking the city and illuminated at night is the 10th-century Castrum Canois with the Museum of Mediterranean Civilization in its dungeon. Smack in the center of town is the original yacht basin, crowded by the Maritime Station; big ships must be reached by lighter, however, because of the harbor's relatively narrow and shallow conformation. Boats run frequently to the Lerins, where the fifth-century Monastery of the Cistercians was St. Patrick's starting point for evangelizing Europe; it is open to women visitors, too. At the Royal Fort on Ile Ste-Marguerite you might like to visit the cell that has inspired stories, plays, and movies by the ream— once occupied, they say, by the man in the Iron Mask. The beaches surrounding Cannes (summer bathing only) are the best east of St.-Tropez now that tankers have been rerouted to avoid oil spills. (Helicopters resolutely police the coast to shoo the ships away.) The Palais des Festivals is functional again. There are 3 casinos—the Municipal house (Nov. 1 to May 31), the Palm Beach (June 1 to Oct. 31; a beauty), and the Casino des Fleurs (all year). The town has unveiled a $100-million hub for meetings, receptions, TV, theater, and congresses. Then you'll find a Sports Palace; an active polo green; 3 golf courses; an annual Film Festival, automobile *Rallye,* and other events; Super-Cannes, with its spectacular vista; a spate of luxurious hotels; a collection of villas unequaled in France; a continuous parade of suntanned celebrities; a busy sidewalk trade in sex (of any inclination); and a gala almost every night. Much more lively and fashionable than metropolitan Nice.

HOTELS

☆☆☆☆ **Gray d'Albion** ● offers such dash, panache, and tasteful razzle-dazzle that it easily takes the lead for interior sparkle. Glittering use of polished marbles, high-sheen woodwork, bronze, and mirrors; extremely comfortable furnishings; excellent location with balconies surrounding the white edifice of 200 bedchambers. Le Royal Gray is the most prestigious of its 3 superb restaurants; discotheque and piano-bar called Le Jane's; private beach; full air conditioning. This resurrected old-timer is a study in living art nouveau.

Carlton ● now under Japanese ownership, may be in for some revision soon. Let's suspend judgment for the nonce. Personally, my favorite haven here would be in the west wing because of the quiet, the lovely foliage, and the breathtaking vista of the Riviera sunsets.

☆☆☆ **Grand** ● provides a set-back garden situation; it was erected by master hotelier Paul Augier of the Negresco interests in Nice. Ultramodern L-shape structure with all-glass fronts for every accommodation; 90 rooms with seaview terraces; 300 studios and apartments available for long-term rentals. The bar, snack foyer, and public quarters are a mushroom patch of Saarinen chairs and white-top tables; the cozy little grill is best after dusk. The penthouse has an exotic cluster of 10 demisuites with curtains that separate the beds from the sitting areas; these are absolutely enchanting in 21st-century stylizations. The "normal" sleeping chambers have ersatz-leather furnishings, low beds, silk wa-

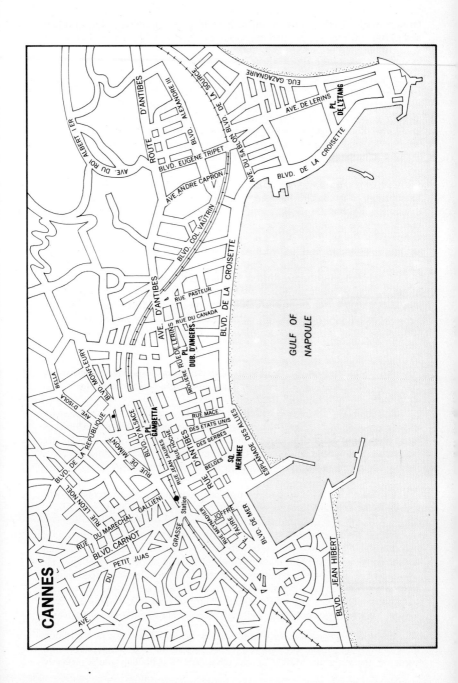

termark wall coverings and dominant hues of mustard, salmon, lagoon blue, and Formica white; garage, parking space, sun lounge, and private beach are at your command. Very good indeed.

☆☆☆ **Majestic** • presents an elegant high-ceiling, marble-clad lobby and reception area; a stylish dining salon, with garden terrace; a grill in modern coolish tones; an ill-kempt patio offering a crescent-shape, heated seawater swimming pool in the palm grove (meal service on its aprons); a beauty parlor and barbershop; an underground parking station. Upstairs, the units are outfitted with sumptuous creature comforts and costly engineering details. Book your room only in the revitalized quarters.

☆☆☆ **Martinez** • is one of France's largest resort havens. It even offers 7 tennis courts at its seaside doorstep. Central situation; better lobby and entrance; extensive renovation of all 405 rooms and 15 suites; snack corner for light bites; outdoor terrace restaurant beside a handsome cascading swimming pool; award-winning La Palme d'Or interior dining salon; very pleasant L'Amiral bar extending to Croisette. Private beach with restaurant, circular bar, water skiing.

☆ **Novotel Montfleury** • offers 235 air-conditioned rooms, 3 restaurants, a bar, 10 tennis courts, 2 heated pools, and an ice-skating rink within the 9-acre hillside estate. Rates are not steep; comforts are abundant; vistas are among the most beautiful on this Azure Coast; closed Feb. to early March. Not in the town itself so its remoteness may be an asset or a debit depending on your desires.

☆ **Le Fouquet's** • with a mere 10 rooms, has no restaurant but plenty of crisp, neat elegance; it gives the impression of being a deluxe gemstone.

☆ **Victoria** • is winsome but costly. Gracious overall decor introduced by its English-style lobby; wood-toned bar; captivating garden with a small swimming pool; front units with terraces and striped awnings; flowered carpets; silk bedspreads and padded headboards; baths with basins in alcoves; radio and electrically controlled shutters; no restaurant. It has style, however.

Cristal • from what I observed in a late construction stage, probably will live up to the favorable local expectations. Space for about 100 guests.

Sofitel-Mediterranee • at the edge of the Old Port and a public beach, is becoming and cheerful with its bowers of flowers and plants; pool and sun terrace on the roof. Viewful maritime lounge; amiable outdoor terrace; gay yellow-and-white La Louisiane Restaurant; partially air-conditioned; piped music. Its upstairs has also been refashioned; accommodations are now ample in size, with fresh furnishings and bright ambience; try to book #312. This corner is very noisy, of course, but so is practically every other bayside site in Cannes.

Good accommodations in Cannes at low prices? These are rare birds on these high-flying shores. Perhaps you'll have luck at the **Belle Plage,** about 150 yards off the Plage du Midi (Cannes' other beach). Although you'll probably be asked for a demipension arrangement, you may be able to wrangle a bed-and-breakfast rate if you talk fast. The **Solhotel,** in the same neighborhood, is popular. Otherwise, there's the value-packed **Villa Palma,** near the Martinez, and the downtown **Athenee** in a nice plant.

RESTAURANTS

☆☆☆☆ **Royal Gray** • *in the Hotel Gray d'Albion* • is modernistic and superb in a sophisticated tone.

☆☆☆ **Palme d'Or** • *in the Martinez* • is very close in quality, but I prefer the atmosphere more in the former.

☆☆ **Le Festival** • *55 blvd. Croisette, opposite Palais des Festivals* • is run by former Parisian interests with chef Claude Rocher, previously of the capital's Plaza-Athenee, at the stoves. Gay colors; fresh decor; animated, high-decibel atmosphere; choice of sidewalk or interior placement. If the sun is shining, enjoy a lazy noonday meal in the open section.

☆☆ **La Poele d'Or** • *23 rue des Etats-Unis* • insists on getting better and better. Don't be put off by its decor, which is as plain as an old *soulier.* About a dozen tables; noted for its mousseline of trout and the Bresse checken in a creamed morille sauce (mushrooms of a very special sort); platters prepared by Proprietor-chef Chartier, a master of the kitchen who is destined for greater fame. Reasonable prices for splendid gastronomy.

Gaston et Gastounette • *6 quai St.-Pierre* • ranges from excellent to dreary, depending on how you hit it. Travelers have complained of being given the a la carte menu and having to demand the fixed-price card; others squawk about waiters who are marvels at addition (they seem to keep adding, ADDING, and A-D-D-D-D-D-D-I-N-G). You might want to check your bill carefully here. Variable.

In the vicinity of the station, try either **Au Bec Fin** or **Bougourne.** Both are moderately priced and have respectable wares.

At lunchtime in summer, the lounger's ritual is to shake off the sand and take a meal (in bathing attire) at any of the 34 strand restaurants that line the seaside of La Croisette. Tops for cuisine and fashion is Ulrica's **Ondine,** which, some opine, can become a bit gay (hardly unique on this coast); November closure, but it reopens in December. **Maschou** is more of the same and is equally good for relaxed ingestion. The **Carlton** beach usually plays it pretty straight. The cookery is reliable, too. All offer a special flavor of lifestyle that is quintessentially Canoise—parasols, bare feet, and bared souls.

Night Life The **Municipal Casino,** fully renewed, should be open for your play. (Ask about it locally.) In summer the action is at the **Palm Beach. Ragtime** is suitable as a diner with music. **Entrecote** slices the same way. **Bosa**

264 · · · FRANCE

Nova offers dinner music and nutrients, but the sounds are Brazilian. **Des Fleurs** blossoms year round, while **La Siesta** snoozes all but July and Aug. **La Chunga** features guitar pickin's from the *pampas;* saddles and tack for decor; high-stirrup society roundup on busy nights; not too expensive, and chic. **CanCan** is a discotheque as is **Club 10; Gay Boys** has a boy-oh-boy show while **Duboys d'Angers** is more of a diner and piano bar. **Akou-Akou** features an exotic atmosphere. No place here is for timid types. The casinos are often best for conventional entertainment.

CAP D'ANTIBES

☆☆☆☆☆ **Hotel du Cap •** is a baronial, Second-Empire-style structure that counts among its guests the wealthiest travelers in the world. Exquisite rooms; full air conditioning; the staff-client ratio is an almost unheard of 3 to 1. Open from Easter to late Sept. only. The Two Fountains annex is cheaper, but views are more limited.

☆☆☆☆☆ **Eden Roc •** the hotel restaurant, is also open from Easter to late Sept. It is by the sea, about 200 yards down the slope from the residence. Outsiders may dine here, but be sure to reserve ahead.

If you are in town only to see the **Antibes Museum,** with its Picasso exhibit (the artist lived in the chateau), then the seaview **Bacon** (also known as **Chez Victor**) is fine for bouillabaise. It's a short stroll from the chapel, belfry, and jumble of houses.

CAP MARTIN The sea-level **Victoria** rules the ripples in a modest pond. Lobby plus main-floor bar, but no restaurant; 32 units with good private bath; 22 with balcony; classical decor highlighted by silks and brocaded walls. The **Alexandra,** with Le Sporting nightclub directly in front, is less prepossessing. Never exposed to the sun—a crucial drawback to most holidaymakers; all units with small loggias; fully air conditioned and carpeted. **Le Pirate** is the liveliest dinner mooring in the vicinity. It is executed in phony gypsy-encampment style with a roaring fire, flamenco dancers, bare-chested waiters, and gimmickry galore. Photos of many celebrities line its walls. Rickety structure resembling a gussied-up nest of packing cases; prices bordering on outrageous; lunch starting at 1 p.m. and dinner from 9 p.m. onward.

EZE BORD DE MER This is the seaside sister of the next village. (In antiquity, to avoid piracy, inhabitants retreated when danger hove into view.)

☆☆☆ **Le Cap Estel •** is a converted princely home on a lovely promontory, its pool just above the sea's edge; 35 suites; 10 rooms. Closed Nov. to Feb. A dream spot relatively free of bluebeards.

EZE VILLAGE This most scenic hamlet is nailed to the mountain along the Middle Corniche halfway between Nice and Monaco. It is noteworthy not only for its rich panoramas and stone-lined lanes, but for a pair of incomparable hotel-restaurants.

★★★★★ **Chevre d'Or** • is probably the most impressive (but not necessarily the most expensive) establishment that clings to a Riviera cliff. Almost incidentally, the food—now modernized—happens to be very fine, indeed. Nothing really matters here except the craggy earth, the cobalt Mediterranean, and the cornflower or black velvet sky. You'll probably pay scant attention to your plate, but if you do, you should find it pleasing in the extreme. The restaurant has been redecorated, the terrace given a retractable roof, and the parking area expanded. A few rooms, a pool, a garden, and kind personnel complete the picture—and a lovely one it is!

★★★ **Le Chateau Eza** • is at the end of the same footpath where the cliffwalk terminates in a botanical garden. This converted private home of a nobleman now has a handful of accommodations, 2 tiers for outdoor dining, and an indoor salon; warm welcome by Danielle Le Stanc, whose husband Dominque has given a deserved fame to the house gastronomy. If you are a daytime visitor, it is an excellent stop for a light lunch. A rock-bound eagle's nest of great comfort and beauty.

GOLFE JUAN   **Beau Soleil** would be my first choice of hotels.

☆☆☆ **Chez Tetou** • is indisputably outstanding for finny fare. Alfresco terrace with 9 tables; enclosed terrace with about 16 tables; main room unadorned; scrubbed wood tables. Dozen-item seafood menu, with the sole meuniere and the bouillabaise especially enjoyable but rather expensive. Friendly, informal atmosphere; open day and night in summer, but only at noon in winter.

HAUTS DE CAGNES,   in the walled city above Cros-de-Cagnes, has narrow, hilly streets, but they are worth the scramble.

★★★★ **Le Cagnard** • is a little charmer that commands a splendid view of the valley and a glimpse of the sea. Twelve small and tastefully but simply decorated rooms, all with bath, are available for overnighters.

JUAN-LES-PINS   and Cap d'Antibes are on the opposite sides of an oyster-shaped peninsula—geographically close, but socially so far apart they barely nod to each other. The former is a vast vacation center on the popular level, with its own Jazz Festival in July. The latter is a more sheltered retreat that caters to the rich. Commodores will now find a better yacht basin than ever before. A 5-star attraction is the Chateau Grimaldi, the reconstructed medieval fortress filled with Picassos—a *must* for every sightseer. Since parking is difficult here, you'd be wise to leave the car below and to hike to its portals on foot. Perhaps even more interesting is the Escoffier Museum, a few miles inland at *Villeneuve-Loubet.* This shrine to one of France's master chefs also is used as a center of culinary education, technology, research, and historical reference dating back to the 14th century.

★★★ **Belles Rives** • open from Apr. to Oct., is proudest of its seaside situation, its charming beach restaurant with a fabulous built-in vista, and its boating facilities for waterskiing or sailing. Splendid terrace; furnishings colorful and attractive; repainted halls; immaculate mien. Its rooms have been pepped up and it is a formidable contender.

☆☆☆ **Juana** ● is appealing, too; the pleasant terrace garden in front is tempting for lunching or dining. Hard work that shows happy results. The little **Astoria** stays open all year. Of its 53 rooms, 32 come with bath, 21 come with shower, and only 5 lack balcony. A coffee shop and bar are operative; the use of a nearby private beach is part of your package.

LA NAPOULE, west of Cannes, is the proud owner of the beautiful and interesting **Chateau de la Napoule Art Foundation.** Two galleries with capacity of up to 100 paintings; courtyard recitals during the summer; chamber music concerts and small theatrical performances from time to time.

LA NAPOULE-PLAGE, 5 miles west of Cannes.

Ermitage du Riou ● swimming and golf; seafront construction has given this one a backseat location. All rooms are large and comfortable; those on the rear, overlooking the river, are less noisy.

Royal ● offers 200 rooms; nice restaurants and two bars, tennis, a pool, and many other leisure items are included in the overview.

La Brocherie II ● at the boat basin, sails in with a lovely vista, failing skilletry, and yachtsman prices.

MENTON, east of the Monaco enclave, is very seasonal and most of its leading hotels do not even feature restaurants. While the **Aiglon** has one, the **Princess et Richmond,** the **Chambord,** and the **Europe** do not. The **Viking,** down a notch in price and quality, has 34 units with bath, 20 with their own cooking facilities. Handsome sweep of the Italian Riviera, the mountain, and Cap Martin from its cost-accounted dining salon. The **Prince de Galles** has 65 bedrooms; homey feeling, with down-to-earth comforts.

MIRAMAR-ESTEREL

★★★★ **St.-Christophe** ● lies on its Red-Roc Beach. Same ownership as Paris' San Regis; 5-tier building with 5 front locations per floor; all rooms with terrace; nice pool; Easter to Oct. only. Tranquil isolation.

MOUGINS (a short ride up from Golfe Juan) does not have many hotels, but ★★★ **Le Mas Candille** beckons with rustic innlike charm. Rooms vary; some with balcony, some opening to garden patios; open beams and hearths; pool; attractive restaurant. My choice for the area.

☆☆☆ **Le Moulin de Mougins** ● is the home of stellar chef Roger Verge, who is capable of producing cuisine and price tags that are highborn and patrician—attitudes that equally apply to guests and to the way they are welcomed. This one is set beside a running stream in the valley below the village. It is composed of a loosely linked bracelet of dining niches, the most desirable being the glass-fronted veranda, which is usually booked by favored customers. The atmosphere of the entire establishment is charmingly esthetic. Tariffs run from wincing to twitching to paralyzing.

☆☆ l'Amandier • where Mme. Verge oversees the skillets, is in the upper town over a small shop where Verge wares are sold almost as souvenirs. White-washed low arches; olive press; stunning floral displays on 2 tiers; menu at $25; inexpensive wines. My bisquit de loup, warm langostine, and lamb were de-lightful. Good value.

Le Bistro • pans out local specialties in a grotto; charm-laden and easy to take at $20 per menu. Also in this same area surrounding the village plaza, La Salle-A-Manger produces a substantial meal for $18 and a plat du jour for $10. Aux Trois Etages is a winsome nest of tables, parasols, and awnings; ideal for lingering at reasonable cost. La Piscine, next door, is attractive, but my meal was disappointing. Feu Follet is cheerful for summerizations. Hotel de France can be pleasant, too, but prices are slightly higher.

☆☆ Le Relais a Mougins • is super-dupervised by Andre Surmain, who first made his fame at Lutece in New York; he's an earnest, controversial, and hard-driving patron who has given this venue some competitive clout. The set menu at lunch has got to be one of the best buys on the coast; the hilltown setting is a delight. Happily, the center has been closed to car traffic, but park-ing lots dot the perimeter of the main sector.

NICE

It's the biggest city on the Cote d'Azur, but you'll probably stay along the shoreline, where most of the tourist activity occurs. It also is convenient to reach since Air France now offers nonstop flights to and from the U.S.A. Nice offers acolytes a race track, an opera house, the nearby Matisse Museum, the Museum of Naive Art, plus 14 other museums, nightclubs, tennis, speedboat-ing, waterskiing, and scores of hotels and restaurants. The Promenade des An-glais, extending for miles along the sparkling waterfront, is wonderful for strollers; so is the Flower Market (1–5 p.m.) on a handsome pedestrian mall. You'll see the Convention and Exposition Hall, the esplanade flanking the Paillon River, a fascinating Museum of Shells (many alive), the Chagall Museum, and a slew of municipal parking spreads. The beaches are sand over pebbles and not too wide; jammed in summer and empty all winter. King Carnival will be burned again this spring on the day before Ash Wednesday, in a spectacle rivaling our own Mardi Gras and dating back more than a century.

HOTELS

☆☆☆☆☆ **Negresco** • remains among the most distinguished and interest-ing hotels in the leisure world. Le Chantecler, famed for its gastronomy, is one of the most elegant clusters for dining anywhere on the entire coast; surpris-ingly, it is not expensive for the noteworthy pleasure it provides. The Salon Royal now gleams in 24-karat gold highlights; it is becoming a gallery of period furniture, sculpture, and paintings. Revampings recently completed by Manager Michael Palmer; epoch textiles incorporated into accommodations and many baldachines added to the upholstered beds; marble baths with built-in hydro-therapy; air conditioning, music consoles, TV, and minibars; large, handsome, lively bar; French renaissance uniforms for key staffers, including knee breeches for the elevator operators; first-rate concierge in veteran Jean Chodzko. Open year round.

☆☆ **Beach Regency** • is not in midcity but half way along the sea route to the airport. It's well done in contemporary fashion, but not the most conve-nient address if you want to stroll to the center.

★★ **Westminster Concorde** • is in one of the best positions in town. There's a happy feeling of traditions preserved here. Very recommendable as a sea-fronter.

☆☆ **Beau Rivage** • with a fresh face from the 19th century, struts along the fashionable seaside Promenade-des-Anglais with postmodernistic style. (Matisse just might recognize the hotel he lodged in and painted in 1917.) Pri-vate beach plus waterfront bistro; excellent dining salon mastered by Chef Jean Retureau, a practitioner of the Mediterranean school of cooking; 120 bedcham-bers in trendy decor.

★★ **West-End** • beautifully situated with one side to the sea and another facing a lovely garden, has employed its share of carpenters, plasterers, and painters over the past half-dozen years. Most bedsteads with carved wooden frames; #417 is an exceptionally nice twin; #419 is a commodious triple; units glancing sidewise at the garden or the sea are tranquil and viewful; the back is quiet but bereft of scenery. Considerably more agreeable; a good value in the medium stratum.

Meridien • also on the shoreline, is a quick-frozen, group-oriented insti-tution with heartless sleeping accommodation. **Elysee Palace** is a youthful 150-room entry in midcity that offers sea views, a rooftop pool, fitness center and an abundance of facilities for business travelers. In even lower categories, I'd prefer to stay in the **Mercure,** the **Bedford,** the **Busby,** or in the older **Conti-nental Messena,** which has now been refashioned into a very stylish modern house with ample comfort and reasonable prices.

☆ **Plaza** • restyled and air conditioned, features a waterfall in the lounge, off-lobby bar, bedchambers ending with "12" with views of the Albert Ier Gardens and the sea. The comfort and appurtenances of its 12 suites and 160 nests, all with private bath, vary sharply.

☆ **Sofitel-Splendid** • also occupies a town site rather than a beach location. Rooftop swimming (the only pool in the city reserved exclusively for its hotel clients); kiddies' pool and cascade; solarium and sauna; no restaurant, but handsome grill-bar (thus no forced-feeding policy); 40-car garage, barbershop, beauty parlor, bank, and travel agency. Bless 'em, every one!

Park • greets callers with a street-level complex that includes 6 airline desks. Garage to ease midtown parking; garishly dramatic lobby with fireplace, a fountain, and flickering gaslights as eternal lighting; bar; breakfast room now doubling as conference room. Top-floor sleepers under its mansard roof the best bet; others a cocktail of good, fair, and poor.

Georges • is almost unbelievably sumptuous for its modest category and bargain-basement costs. Tiny, spotless structure on the hard-to-find rue Henri-Cordier (a few doors from the Ecole Hoteliere); all units with private bath; high-level appointments, including picture windows, chandeliers, crystal sconces, satin spreads, and good furnishings; no restaurant; small lounge.

~~~~~~

RESTAURANTS

☆☆☆☆☆ **Le Chantecler** • is *the* pride and *your* joy at the spectacular Negresco (see "Hotels").

☆☆☆☆☆ **Jacques Maximin** • *4 rue St. Guitry* • is one of the great chefs on this coast who first gained his fame at the above hotel. Now he performs in a converted theater. The opulence almost out-dazzles the gastronomy. If you enjoy expensive, 4-hour, multi-course meals of noteworthy preparation, here's your spot.

★★ **Ane Rouge** • which means "Red Donkey," offers a splendid view of the harbor from a busy streetside perch. It finally has made a serious comeback and is worth a visit. This is totally different from the above pair.

Chez Don Camillo • *5 rue des Ponchettes* • is serene and comfortable; it has placed its 8 round tables so thoughtfully that no one can overhear your private whispers. Smiling welcome and attention; limited menu featuring Italian specialities; veal, veal, and more veal its pride.

Aux Gourmets • *12 rue Dante* • is mastered by Albert Collison, who learned from the best. Classic French dishes rather than emphasis on the newest style of cooking.

Taverne du Chateau • *Old Town* • is a splendid choice for Nicoise specialties. Best of all, the prices are realistic and not inflated by the usual coastal influence.

☆☆☆ **Rotisserie de St. Pancrace** • is located about 15 minutes above Nice, by car, atop a mountain ridge. Dining under the trees is a sylvan gift; the royale de poissons, sweetbreads en croute, and duck with morilles must have been handed down by the gods themselves.

ROQUEBRUNE

★★★★★ **Vista Palace** • with 76 rooms and suites, provides one of the most breathtaking views this side of a NASA space capsule. From one flank you can look down practically every chimney in Monte-Carlo; from the other you can see the blue-mist haze of the Italian Riviera. To enhance the panorama, almost every inch of seafront wall space is plate glass—in public rooms as well as in bedchambers. Some complaints, in fact, have trickled in that the eye-filling restaurant charges ''50% for the menu and 50% for the sights''—a bargain, even if it served grubworms and seaweed (which it doesn't). Quality furnishings; pool agurgle for summertime splashers. Tip-top—so you'll have to drive to the upper tier of the Grande Corniche to find it.

Au Grand Inquisiteur • is situated on a hillside lane in this lovely 10th-century village, most of which must be penetrated on foot through dipping, soaring, crazily winding footpaths between its buildings. Although this one is billed as an inn, its main function is obviously that of a restaurant. Even if its cuisine should prove indifferent, the fortress-hamlet itself would be worth the excursion.

ST.-JEAN-CAP-FERRAT

☆☆☆☆ **La Voile d'Or** • *''The Golden Sail''* • is similar architectually to La Reserve, around the bay at Beaulieu—the work of the same designer. Total of 50 rooms, each with a distinctive decorative theme; bid for a portside unit only if you're feeling affluent; superb marble baths; full air conditioning and soundproofing; excellent waterfront restaurant nuzzling the yacht harbor; excellent beach; pool on a raised garden platform; oodles of beauteous terraces. Director Jean Lorenzi is a master of his skillful trade.

☆☆ **Grand** • is grander than ever these days. Air conditioning; swimming pool; cable car strung to whisk guests from the hotel to the H$_2$O; first-rank comfort; splendid honeymoon suite. The Sun Beach Club incorporates watersports, tennis, and volleyball. A commendable resurgence of spirit and hedonism.

ST.-PAUL-DE-VENCE is the proud custodian of the Maeght Foundation, an art museum-cum-park which alone is worth a transatlantic journey. If you are anywhere on this coast do make an effort to experience this celebration of the senses. It is high on the mountain flank and you can easily occupy a full day viewing the modernistic paintings, mobiles, and sculptures.

★★★ **Colombe d'Or** • *"Golden Dove"* • A greeting at the gate is provided by the stately dove sculpted by the dynamic artist, Ben Jakober, one of the hottest creators in today's Europe. (Ask them to pack one for you to take home in your luggage.) You'll find a warm reception, relaxed patio dining under parasols when the sun is shining, an interior cluster of cozy rooms reflecting slick rusticity, an outstanding collection of paintings, a fine swimming pool, and a magnetic physical allure. The selection is ample; though the food is served atop a lovely mountain peak it still falls short of haute cuisine; nevertheless, the experience will be a delight.

Henry, a short jaunt farther along the walking lane, serves its vittles at a tiny chapel with an adjoining shaded terrace overlooking the gorge. Handsome, worthy for casual meals, and more peaceful than Colombe d'Or. In *Vence* itself, there's the little Hostellerie Lion d'Or which enlarged its name to **Hostellerie et Auberge des Seigneurs et du Lion d'Or** when it remodeled the upstairs to provide its handful of rooms with baths. Its view is nil—but I liked its simple milieu and fare.

★★★ **Le Chateau du Domaine St. Martin** • *in Vence* • commands an eagle's-eye sweep of the countryside. The lobby is Old World in flavor, employing needlepoint, cretonne, and brocade. Heart-shaped bicarbonatized swimming pool (possibly for indigestion sufferers); well-tended sylvan grounds; tower accommodations for the steady-in-balance; some rooms agreeable; others not so hot. The restaurant-dining room, with 3 sides of glass opening to its stupendous vista, is the main attraction. Its ambience is lovely; its cookery and service standards are on par with the finest in the land. Here's a stunning project on a stunning site.

☆ **Mas d'Artigny** • is near the access road to Nice Airport, up in the neighboring mountain range. Much heralded, air-conditioned, and possibly overblown, this haven is a sister operation to the Chateau d'Artigny in the Loire Valley at Montbazon. It's a gilt-edged dreamland, too, for romantic types who enjoy being in luxury while off the beaten pathways of the coastal mash. Suites with individual swimming pools and private entrances from your own garden; main pool and terrace on a tier below the lackluster dining salon and lounges; service as lazy as the climate inspires; tennis and 16 acres of hillside for strolling.

ST.-RAPHAEL's Excelsior, with about 50 rooms, is pleasant enough. The **Hotel au Golf de Vallescure,** 6 miles out, emits a beckoning glow. This is easily my first choice if transportation is available.

ST.-TROPEZ In season it crawls—especially on weekends. But why not, since it boasts what are probably the finest beaches of the province? Climax for regatta fans is the **Nioulargue** in late Sept. or early Oct. At *Port Grimaud*, 3 miles to the southeast, a more residential colony of sun seekers has set up aweigh of life. Topless sunning is legally indulged in especially on the Tahiti or Salins beaches, but an anything-goes-off attitude exists nearly everywhere despite a recent effort by gimlet-eyed police to levy fines on bottomless baskers of both sexes. Moorea is a beckoning strip (of sand and more) and so is Voile Rouge, while "55" is a bit more straitlaced as beaches go.

For residing, easily the most luxurious stop in the area is the sumptuous ★★★★★ **Domaine de Belieu,** not in the busy townlet itself but in the hills 3 miles distant near the intersection of *Gassin* and *Ramatuelle.* Only 12 spectacular rooms, exotic pool area, and a park planted for a Tuscan prince; romantic garden illumination for summer dining alfresco or in the richly ornate salon; antiques, oils, and heirloom furnishings. An utterly refined atmosphere where seclusion is assured. Prices range from $400 to $800 per night; the gourmet menu is roughly $100 per person. Patrician, in every sense.

★★★★ **Le Byblos** • slightly below the Citadel, with a distant view of the harbor, is one of the resort's flashiest bidders. Irregular configuration suggesting a casbah mystique; swimming pool in a palm court; care-less haughty service personnel in its independent restaurant and cookery you can live without; decorative highlights featuring paisley brocades, rich mosaics, and hammered brass; numerous raw stone walls and open beams; some split-level suites; baths with brick tiles and wooden panels. The cramped dimensions of some of the accommodations might present a vexing problem to the long-term visitor; early-to-bedders howl that the swingers frolic too noisily under the dome of night. For those who can afford its wincingly high tariffs, here's a fascinating—perhaps too overwhelming—layout.

☆☆☆☆ **La Pinede** • is a popular, costly but ingratiating San-Trop hideaway. One wing consists of a glass-fronted dining flank and bar plus sleeping facilities, each of the last boasting its own crescent-shape terrace, alcove beds and rheostat illumination. At water's edge is a tiny 4-cell tower that many silver-screened cupcakes have used as a retreat; surrounding this is a small private beach. This one seems more tranquil than Byblos.

★★★ **Mas de Chastelas** • is a softspoken retreat in the hills with 21 rooms, 10 suites, a pool, and 4 tennis courts. Very nice people; good value; attractive as a redoubt.

L'Ermitage • next to the Byblos, offers the disadvantage of remoteness balanced by a quieter mien than its good-time neighbor. Merely 32 units, many with baths and showers that share the bedroom with you; lots of kooky charm that can be fun for the open-minded.

Lou Troupelen is passable, but I'm not so fond of its situation. **Tahiti,** at the site of the same name, seemed replete with bare-breasted gals sans sunsuits and beefcake bruisers. Hardly a discriminating oasis, for the timid. **Le Baou** offers a marvelous hillside view, but the ill-bred staff and tacky appointments put me off completely. **Giraglia** in *Port Grimaud* is moored in a quiet anchorage where no automotive traffic is permitted beyond the gates of this private

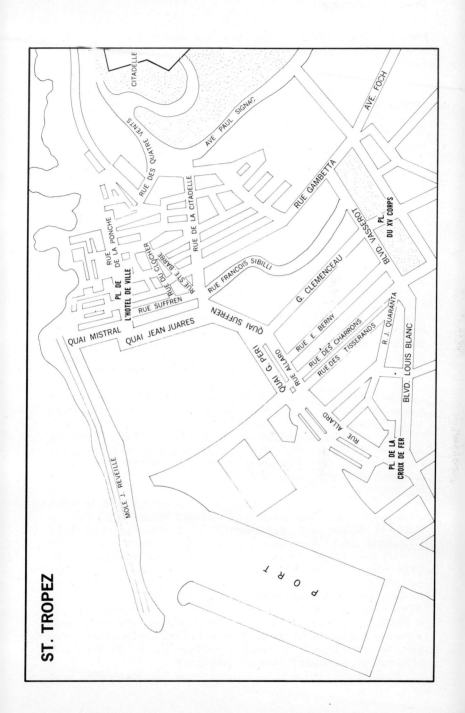

ST. TROPEZ

canal-laced village. Wood-on-stucco construction; maritime decor; tacky undertones but generally amusing in concept and presentation. A bonanza for boating buffs who are seekers of the bizarre.

☆☆☆☆☆ **Le Richemond Golf** ● 2 minutes by car from Port Grimaud, is inspired by the Armleader dynasty of Geneva, one of the most elegant hotels in Europe. It's a traditional, old-style edifice reformed with a cost-be-damned attitude. The result is majestic. Golf and beach clubs; spacious grounds and accommodations; surely one of the pace-setters on this entire stretch of coast.

Pizzeria Romana ● if you are looking for a dining spot, is not quite what it appears. Don't let the name fool you because the menu is much more ambitious than its handle implies. Not only is it good, but *everybody* knows it and *everybody* goes.

Les Mouscardins ● commands a panoramic situation at end of the port quay. It's busy, bustling, attractive, but not fancy, and expensive. Closed mid-Oct. to Feb. 1.

Auberge des Maures ● *4 rue des Lices* ● also costly; shuttered Nov. to mid-Dec. This one tries to create the atmosphere of a gypsy pad, and it does so in an amusing way. The walls are decked with cast-off items and sentimental knickknacks; the dimensions (except for the portions, which are huge) are cozy; the waitresses are tricked out in regional costumes. Outside there's a dawdle-and-dine, arbor-covered patio that is attractive in season. It evokes a sense of comin'-through-the-wry.

Chabichou ● *in Byblos but independently operated* ● is the last word in pretense; a vanity so fierce that the attitude sickened me almost as much as the food—but not quite.
For casual dining or drinking, there are several resorty hangouts along the waterfront. Each features an awning-covered apron partially exposed to the sun, the stars, and the stares of the passing parade; back of this sits a more interior "exterior" patio; finally comes the inner sanctum itself—a tiny culinary enclave big enough for perhaps 3 tables, a small-boned waiter, and the inevitable bowl of fruit. **L'Escale,** now somewhat down-in-the-mouth, used to be the harbor master, with a prix fixe docking fee; **Le Girelier** specializes in simple fish plates and matching tariffs; **La Rascasse** isn't bad; neither are **Tante Marie, L'Equipage,** and **L'Adventure.** For drinking only, **Senequier** (where a coffee will sock you for $4) hosts some of the tightest-hipped gals' slacks on the coast. Deep lounge chairs for loafing from sunup to moonrise—or the reverse. The *only* place to go if you have 14 or 15 hours to kill, plus a cast-iron liver. As for the rest, **La Belle Isnarde** ● *40 bis rue Allard* ● is typical of the less-costly digs in town, while those who don't mind the taxi fare sometimes venture up to **Feniere,** a garden restaurant near the Citadel, or out to suburban *Grimaud,* where **Les Santons** is costly but probably the best restaurant in the area (in the hill town, not in the waterside community of Port Grimaud). Try the suburbs of *Ramatuelle, La Bonne Fontaine,* or *Gassin* too.
Down on this coast night life becomes formal when the customer wears

shoes. **Papagayo,** with orchestra from June to Sept. and stereo in the fringe weeks, has routine decor and no show. On a busy night here, you'll find more shaggy heads than at a conference of Kalahari tribesmen. **Club 55** is the fashion center of the instant. **Esquinade** is a noisy cluster of 3 cellars; records only. **Woom-Woom** if it's still boom-booming can be fun in season. **Les Caves du Roy** has turned on the charm and tuned up an orchestra. **Le Gorille** is still the stop for that predawn breakfast and early-morning-cap. If these don't fill the bill, try **Cafe de Paris,** a summer meeting place of the famous.

On the same road, you'll find **Les Collettes,** where Auguste Renoir did his painting from 1908 until his death in 1919. It is now a museum.

P.S. If you hop over to the isle of *Porquerolles,* which is made for dreamers, repose or dine at the charming **Mas de Langoustier,** on a slope of pine forest overlooking a paradise of 2 turquoise coves bobbing with splendid yachts.

VILLEFRANCHE-SUR-MER has the **Versailles.** In a topsy-turvy arrangement, the lobby, restaurant, and bar are at road level; an elevator drops you down to your accommodations. About 50 small, functional rooms, all with bath, radio, and individual balcony; small sun terrace with excellent view of the passing hubcaps.

Among its restaurants, **La Mere Germaine** is pleasing many palates of distinction. Alfresco terrace-dining for 100 in season is vexingly rushed, however. Next come **La Fregate** and **Le Campanette.** At *Villefranche* on the *haut corniche,* **La Ferme St. Michel** • *in the St. Michel quarter* • offers unlimited servings of both solids *and* liquids for a set price. So set your belt at its widest notch for this girthbuster.

CHATEAUX COUNTRY

Renaissance France flourished at the peak of its elegance in this region. Because of its serene beauties and proximity to Paris, kings, courtiers, and courtesans relaxed here in dazzling luxury. Strongholds were built, aristocracy thrived, and culture was unfettered. To this day, linguistic scholars point out, the nation's purest tongue is spoken in the Loire Valley.

The tumbrels of the Reign of Terror swept away the actors of this historic drama, but little of their glorious handwork was despoiled. Still preserved are roughly 50 great castles or mansions.

From June to end-Sept. 6 chateaux are further embellished with *Son et Lumiere* ("Sound and Light") programs. At least 2 dozen others are floodlit nightly or on weekends for nocturnal excursionists. However, the presentations (except at Chenonceaux and at Blois) are given in French. A **Pass Touraine** (see below) is invaluable for you if you plan to visit a lot of the chateaux or remain in the area for several days.

Your key base should be *Tours* or its vicinity, because this central point is less than 25 miles from most of the principal chateaux.

My candidates for the 4 most interesting structures in this cluster are Chenonceaux, Amboise, Azay-le-Rideau, and Villandry. Cheverny (see below) is in a special category.

Chenonceaux, a breathtakingly graceful castle, straddles the Cher River. Beautiful formal gardens extend from its sides. Within the trussed-arch building are tapestries and other seventeenth-century treasures. Although finishing touches weren't applied until 1634, Diane de Poitiers, beloved mistress of Henri II, occupied it nearly 100 years earlier. Many North Americans vote this one as their favorite.

Amboise, the burial place of Leonardo da Vinci, is smaller and less spectacular—but hardly less rewarding. At this writing, it offers a spectacle called "The Cradle of the Renaissance," which draws upon music from the fifteenth and sixteenth centuries. Here you may also visit the illuminated terraces, the chapel, and the gardens. While in Amboise don't miss the fascinating **Chateau du Clos-Luce** (50 yards from the castle at the end of rue Victor Hugo). This is where Leonardo lived the final years of his life, a renaissance manor filled with the inventiveness and grace of the era's greatest genius. **Azay-le-Rideau,** charmingly sited over the Indre River and surrounded by groves, is now a Fine Arts Museum; from the French point of view, this one is possibly the most dramatic of all. The evening Sound & Light show is replete with torchlights on the lake, costumed ladies and pages; you walk and stand for 75 minutes as you are guided around the periphery. **Villandry** is noted for its magnificent 3-tier gardens, as well as for its history; the top level has a 7500-square-yard lake, the middle level formal horticulture, and the bottom level a grandly conceived layout of vegetables!

Cheverny, tucked away at *Loir-et-Cher,* is one of the most perfectly conceived and best preserved edifices in the region. It is thriving as an occupied homestead under the aegis of the Marquis de Vibraye. Only ½-dozen rooms open to the public, but these are exquisite; fabulous Hunting Museum dating back through centuries of royal hunts. Don't miss this imposing beauty with its tonsure of precisely maintained gardens and parkland.

Others of note include **Chambord** (largest; 40 miles north of Tours), **Langeais** (privately owned and lived in; another with a beautifully preserved interior; no Sound and Light; 15 miles), and **Loches** (so medieval that it's an Olympus for antiquarians and a bore to travelers with no architectural interests; 30 miles south of Tours). The last is atop the village of the same name, commanding a fabulous view from the long walls; Joan of Arc captured this one as well as Chinon. One of the most exciting from the theatrical point of view is **Chateau du Lude** (32 miles), with a pageant—in season—of 350 characters in costume, prancing horses, boats, dancers, and singers; fireworks on Fri., Sat., and for festive nights. The oration is in French, *bien sur!* **Beauregard,** between Blois and Cheverny, once belonged to Francis I, and the taste and refinement are clearly in evidence; very little was changed since the time of its 16th- and 17th-century occupants.

From Tours you can visit **Chenonceaux** (19 miles) and **Amboise** (16 miles) in one evening. Buses leave the below-mentioned Tourist Office at 8:15 or 9 p.m. and return at midnight; the all-inclusive excursion is around $14 per person. Scads of additional bus departures to your choice of other chateaux are available both daytimes and evenings at the Tours railway station; costs vary from $3 to $7, plus entrance fees.

Saumur is on the western extremity of the district, a long drive unless you are heading in that direction, but well worth the time to see it. It was a fighting castle, as its purchase above the river and the fortifications will tell you at a glance.

Spot and floodlighting are employed on various occasions at chateaux in the following places: Ainay-le-Vieil; Bourges (the Mansion of Jacques-Coeur and the Cathedral of St.-Etienne here), Chateaubriant; Chateauneuf-sur-Loire; Culan; La Ferte-St.-Aubin; Fontevrault; Gien; Nantes; Sully-sur-Loire; Tours (with musical program); Valencay.

The chateaux that must be seen by daylight are Beauregard, Chaumont (fabulous stables for equine buffs), Cheverny, Chinon, Cinq-Mars-la-Pile, Langeais, Lavardin, Luynes, Menars, Meung-sur-Loire, Montgeoffroy, Moncontour, Montoire, Montreuil-Bellay, Montsoreau, Ponce, Romorantin, St-Aignan-sur-Cher, Saumur, Talcy, Usse (inspiration for "The Sleeping Beauty"), Vaux-le-Vicomte, Villandry. I haven't seen the "new" Courtanvaux, the castle of the Duke of Fezensac, scion of the oldest family in France. This 500-year-old, 112-room estate is at Besse-sur-Braye, between Tours and Le Mans.

At *Angers,* the tapestries of the Apocalypse are on view at the **Hopital St. Jean.** The chateau is a fine example of feudal architecture of the 13th century. Then take in the 11th-century **Abbaye de Fontevraud,** where several Plantagenet monarchs are at rest. The hamlet of *St. Laurent de la Plaine* reveals the handicrafts, tools, and methods of work employed in medieval times. All this can be absorbed in a day or less by car since driving time is short.

A novel twist is **Les Off-Beat Tours,** which provides a chauffeur-guide to help you explore private chateaux and aristocratic estates of the region. These people know the district so well that you can construct your own days of adventure based upon your particular interests; they put it all together. They are so versatile that they can even do the usual. Write to Philippe Jauneaud for the splendid color brochure; Privileges de France, 37390 Mettray (near Tours); Tel. (33) 47–418000; Telex 751585. A patrician service.

Balloon rides? During four days of attempting to engage an ascent through the Bombard organization, the young English administrators bombed out in the administration so miserably that the effort was futile. Many finally make it, however. Other companies may suffer fewer inflation problems. Overall for an overall viewing experience, it's probably worth the puffed-up price.

Period Shopping? Mailfert-Amos (26 rue Notre-Dame di Recouvrance in *Orleans*) is unique. If you seek an extraordinary example of 18th-century furniture replicated for your home or office, these skilled classical artisans will fashion it for you with absolute fidelity in the finest materials and in the original French techniques. Such patience, scholarship, and devotion scarcely exist elsewhere, so should you care about craftsmanship of bygone ages and wish to own some, don't fail to visit this showroom from Tues. through Sat.

One *must* stop for newcomers—the earlier, the better!—is the Tours Tourist Office at Place du M.-Leclerc, an ultramodern, facility. It is linked by Telex to Cannes, Nice, Paris, and 11 other centers, in case your later reservations have gone awry; it will change your money when the banks are closed (Sun.,

Mon., and after 6 p.m.); it provides brochures and regional information. Hours: 8:30–12:30 and 1:30–9 p.m.; Sun. and holidays 10–12:30 and 3–6 p.m. You can also pick up the money-saving **Pass Touraine** here.

HOTELS

☆☆☆☆ **Domaine des Hauts de Loire** ● *Onzain* ● is a bit distant in the upper Loire, but handy to Blois, Chambord, Chaumont and Orleans on the way north to Paris. Magnificent wooded estate with lawns and pond in front; superb antiques in gracious settings; timbered ceiling in its open-hearth dining salon; new wing also appealing and quite a bit cheaper than the original building; tennis and swimming. The peace beneath the stately trees and among the ivied walls is priceless. The Bonnigals are winning hosts here.

★★★★ **Chateau de Marcay** ● set in an enchanting estate dating back to the 15th century, is only a few minutes from *Chinon* by car in what is known as the Rabelais district. The lounges are intimate and sumptuous, with brass chandeliers, painted beams, rich textiles, and oil paintings; the dining salon is a masterpiece of refined rusticity, featuring a handsome hearth, thick timbers, exquisite table settings, and outstanding cuisine. Lovely pool; small but attractive bar; recently added wing and improved accommodations in the main segment. Manager Ponsard is doing a masterful job very well here; he's also a good friend to traveling Americans.

★★★★ **Chateau d'Artigny** ● stands watch over the Indre Valley on National Highway No. 10 in *Montbazon* ● *7 miles from Tours* ● Here you'll find a 20th-century entry conceived in pure 18th-century style. The site, once the palace of the King's Treasurer, was razed in 1769 and rebuilt over 2 decades beginning in 1912 by the perfumer Francois Coty, who lavished so much money on his pet avocation that he even installed cold-vaults so that visiting ladies could safely store their furs! Grand entrance hall leading to stately lounges; richly carved library; next-door chapel with 4 exceptionally cozy duplex apartments. Total of 56 extra-spacious bedchambers; #5, on the river, is fit for royalty (many chiefs-of-state stop here); #31 features a bath that was the former pastry kitchen, and it's one of the nicest on the garden side; don't let them shunt you over to the so-called "pavilion," a down-the-road annex used for overflow bus groups or late arrivals. Silken putting green; tennis; lawns and paths for walking; fair cuisine; superb maintenance.

☆☆ **Domaine de Beauvois** ● *at Luynes 9 miles west of Tours* ● is also owned by the d'Artigny musketeers. Structurally and decoratively it, too, is an architectural paradise—a manor of both the 15th and 18th centuries. There is more coziness here, but then perhaps you're looking for grandeur. I also noted more careful service and superior cookery here in comparison with the alma mater. The pool is vast; it faces a lake in the woodland vale; smiling, well-trained staff.

Chateau de Beaulieu • *at* ***Joue-les-Tours*** • is more modest. Enormous grounds and homey surroundings in a garden setting; swimming pool; tennis courts; alfresco terrace for summer dining; open every day the calendar round. *Beau* it is.

☆☆☆ **Le Choiseul** • *at* ***Amboise*** *15 miles from Tours* • has been brought back to life through generous injections of francs and love. Excellent bedchambers. Service standards dragged down by earnest young incompetents who may mature with seasoning. The dining room, with its captivating view of the river, is especially recommendable for long, lingering summer sunsets. (Try to ignore the trailer park across the Loire.) It is pleasant to be this close to a town of such exquisite cultural worth, the choice of Francis I and Leonardo da Vinci.

☆☆ **Le Domaine da la Tortiniere** • *near* ***Montbazon;*** *turn left 1 mile toward Tours* • is a century-old mansion astride a hill in a sylvan private park. The terrace, shaded by red umbrellas, overlooks the peacefully winding Indre River. The cuisine, once superb, is now only good.

☆ **Bon Laboureur et du Chateau** • *at* ***Chenonceaux*** • is a knockout for gustation, but merely functional for overnighting. The tariffs are quite reasonable, too.

Chateau de la Jailliere • *Angers is 20 miles east of it; in its own park* • is hosted by the personable and astute Countess d'Anthenaise, who knows this district of ***Varades*** perfectly and can guide you to the best sites. Look for **La Chapelle St. Sauveur.** The elegance of her home befits such a noblewoman, but the prices are remarkably low. Summer months only.

Next in preference—for geographic reasons *only*—come the hotels of ***Tours.*** In general, they're a cheerless, scruffy lot, considering this city's importance as a sightseeing mecca.

Jean Bardet's Parc de Belmont • with only a handful of rooms, is probably your best bet and the restaurant is noteworthy. Its on rue Groison. The site, just off the busy highway, murders any semblance of tranquillity, but it is convenient for the caravans of buses that roll in here to disgorge the thongs who arrive in migratory proportions.

Alliance • also is praiseworthy; a large house overlooking a formal garden and pool; you'll find its 5-story hulk on avenue Grammont.

De Groison • is a charming fragment of 18th-century living in 20th-century comfort.

Univers • offers 91 pleasant units with bath; #232 spacious and quiet; top-rate singles seemed cruelly expensive for the value; minimum cells are available, however.

Central • is a recently revitalized vintage landmark. Still no restaurant; almost spotless housekeeping; 45 rooms, mile-high ceilings; simple but agreeable sleeping quarters. Improved to the point where the French would call it "a proper place."

Bordeaux has been modernized; cheerful interior with matching staff; a good budget choice. The 139-room **Arcade,** near the station, is of recent vintage and inexpensive. The **Foch,** with 14 rooms and 2 private baths, is a value for budgeteers. So is **Criden,** but it's a bit more costly.

Other stopping places in the Chateaux Country or Loire region, some good and some poor, are as follows:

Angers: **Boule d'Or, Croix de Guerre, Anjou.**
Blois: **Medicis** (4 miles out, at St.-Denis).
Chambord: **St.-Michel.**
Charite-sur-Loire: **Le Grand Monarque.**
Chinon: **Cheops, France, Boule d'Or.**
Gien: **Rivage.**
Loches: **France, Tour St.-Antoine, Georges Sand.**
Orleans: **Arc, Cedres, Sofitel, Arcades.**
Romorantin: **Lion d'Or.**
Saumur: **Budan, Roi Rene, Hostellerie du Prieure.**
Valencay: **Espagne.**
Vendome: **Vendome, Capricorne.**

RESTAURANTS

☆☆☆☆ **La Chanceliere** • *1 place des Marronniers in* **Montbazon** • is easily one of the regional "greats"—although in size it is quite small. Refined town house with vast bouquets of flowers; beige enamel painted open beams; tan velour wall covering; marble floors; sparkling tableware, with cuisine that also is radiant. *Menu de degustation* at 300 francs; most a la carte dishes from 90–140 FF. A delight.

For chateau dining, the previously mentioned **Domaine des Hauts de Loire** and **Marcay** would be the picks among the thoroughbreds. **Le Choiseul,** at *Amboise,* and **Domaine de Beauvois,** at *Luynes,* are tiptop, too, followed by **d'Artigny** for its aristocratic bearing.

In *Tours,* the **Rotisserie Tourangelle** • *23 rue Commerce* • has a leisurely, old-fashioned air, shy but eager-to-please personnel, and praiseworthy cookery, **Bure** • *street floor of Hotel Mondial* • is adequate but routine. **La Trattoria** is fair if you seek a change-of-pasta.

Don't forget the previously mentioned **Bon Laboureur et du Chateau at Chenonceaux,** which is a rustic dream spot with heavenly cuisine. At *Amboise,* the little **Auberge du Mail,** behind the river dike and beyond the center of town, offers less costly menus. Sweet postage-stamp-size patio with 9 red-clothed tables under a grape arbor; plain, clean, no-nonsense interior; Gallic family management. Not plushy but substantial. The riverside **Bellevue** served a very decent and inexpensive tourist lunch which I enjoyed. The nearby, more-attractive **Lion d'Or** is very appealing if you are not expecting gourmet-level cuisine.

The **Chateau de Pray** • *1½ miles up the river* • is a hillside mansion with a spacious front terrace offering a fine view of the Loire. Sixteen rooms in pseudo-Renaissance motif; deluxe food and prices; numerous readers have complained about tabs coming up higher than they bargained for, so be sure to check your bill before payment; closed Jan. 5 through Feb. 10. Elegant and pleasant.

In *Langeais,* the **Duchesse Anne** has a beguiling garden in which a cote of snow-white doves will puff up and preen at the first sight of a paying client; their fantails are so disciplined that we have dark suspicions of managerial sorcery. About 50 tables outside, 20 more in the modern dining room, and large windows between the sites. Savory vittles and engaging atmosphere; see-for-yourself kitchen, where the white caps are in constant flurry. Definitely worth a try. The **Hotel Hosten,** almost directly across the street, has a less attractive patio adjoining its Charles VIII bar. Piquant; hospitable attention from the owners; coming up steadily.

In *Guecelard,* 10 miles south of Le Mans on Route N-23, **La Botte d'Asperges** is a slender, long-fronted pit stop with a tiny front terrace that provides a panorama of passing cars and trucks and the **Boucherie Charcuterie** across the highway. In the rear, however, there's a sleepy little garden with even sleepier goldfish, where you may drowse over your Noix de Veau.

If you plan a visit to the previously mentioned Chateau de Cheverny, you can stoke up at the **Hotel des Trois Marchands.** It is in the heart of the toy village, edging on the church square.

Other alternatives of varying magnitude are:

Angers: **Le Vert d'Eau** (closed Fri.), **Hostellerie Chateau** (6 miles).
Bracieux: **Le Relais.**
Chartre-sur-le-Loir: **France.**
Chateau-la-Valliere: **Ecu.**
Chaumont-sur-Loire: **Hostellerie du Chateau.**
Les Bezards: **Auberge des Templiers.**
Montoire-sur-le-Loir: **Cheval Rouge.**
Orleans: **Auberge St.-Jacques, Auberge de la Montespan, Jeanne-d'Arc, Aux Canotiers.**
Poitiers: The people here are spoiled rotten, in my opinion, by the migrations of tourists who sate their gluttonous coffers with money. Though old-fashioned, the **Hotel France** was the *only* place where I was greeted

with courtesy and where any effort was made. For this alone I was grateful.

BRITTANY

Blue is the color. The sea, the dress, the ships. Never mind that the northern littoral with its craggy cliff-bound ports is called *Emerald Coast,* where the scenic ramparts of St. Malo and Dinard reside. Never mind that the great thumb of France that is shoved into the Atlantic is called the *Granite Rose Coast,* which runs to the extremity of Brest. And never mind that the interior, with its early Christian Calvaries and its druid megaliths dating back into the pagan myths of 50,000 years ago is today devoted to whatever agriculture can be scratched from the gray stony soil. The tone of the air itself has its roots in the azure of the sky and the sea that surrounds this distinctive peninsula.

To see it properly you will need at least a week and a car. A bicycle is another possibility if your resolve is strong—and so are your legs. If you are planning to incorporate the neighboring province of Normandy into your itinerary it would be better to concentrate on southern Brittany primarily. Roadways are improving, but distances are deceptively long and time-consuming during the summer months. In winter the pikes are empty except for trucks bearing the maritime cargo. Clearly it is a harsh and inhospitable land when the chill winds blow.

Your greatest rewards, apart from breathtaking views such as those at France's most westerly point, *Pointe du Raz,* will probably be enjoyed in the region between *Baule*'s splendid white beaches and *Quimper,* known for its ceramics and faiences. If you are not a beachcomber, then you can probably live without La Baule. My choice would be to headquarter somewhere in the region of *Concarneau* and make excursions along either shank of the coast. Concarneau itself is an amazing tidal creation. To protect themselves from the sea, early residents constructed a fortification known as **La Ville Close,** which is as picturesque as anything in the annals of Kodak history. The stone houses lying in the narrow lanes and arches peep out across the water to the modern city. There is an excellent **Fishing Museum,** an adjoining Aquarium, boutiques and cafes by the dozen. On the fringes of the Close the hundreds of fishing boats (blue, of course) discharge their riches every day and contribute mightily to the local entertainment. (Incidentally, if you are *deeply* interested in the deep, the seaport of *Brest* now has its **Oceanopolis,** a new marine museum worthy of the most dedicated scholars.)

About a half hour to the south is the landmark village of *Pont-Aven,* made famous by Gauguin and a coterie of the most important artists of his time who chose this as their base while on painting sojourns. As a step back into their heyday of its mainstream culture, the village is alive with galleries, there's a splendid museum with expositions that change every 3 months (based on the scores of painters who worked here and achieved international fame); streets are jammed with sightseers, Breton cookie munchers, cider sippers, and gawkers of every stripe. It is being intensively punished by its popularity and the essential charm (found especially around the bridge that gives its name to the town). The artistic calling is potent; the rivulet is gloriously pristine with its long green beards of algae waving in the currents; the air is throbbing with creative zest. Alas, there is only one hotel in town and that is *not* to be recommended. The boarding houses (by the dozens) are similarly uninspired. But as a site for a day-call it is irresistible.

Quimper offers the only metropolitan atmosphere in the region. Architecturally it is intriguing. Half-timber houses along the *rue du Salle* overhang the lane. There is a medieval character to the shops of the *rue des Boucheries* and *rue du Gueodet*. And an excitement in the **Covered Market.** It will forever remain in your memory if you have a snack at one of the outdoor spreads on the *place au Beurre,* in the center of the Old Quarter. The lace and bonnets so common to this region are on sale in this little plaza as well as the music (on tape or disc) that incorporates Celtic origins. Shoppers will surely want to take advantage of a visit to the *Quimper Faience* factory. If the day is fine, don't miss an opportunity to walk along the river, which runs to the fringes of the great **Cathedral.** Only about 40 feet across, it is spanned by dozens of ornate iron footbridges that are festooned with geraniums; the trail leads to the fortification walls and the gardens within.

Further north (about 15 minutes from Quimper) is the enchanted hamlet of **Locronan.** It was of vital importance to the world economy because of its manufacture of sailcloth and textiles. The stone buildings and the lovely 15th-century Gothic church are in excellent preserve as a result of the misfortune of its citizens in early times. Prosperity faded here so rapidly that the town never had an opportunity to build beyond its original limits; moreover, the inhabitants could not afford to expand or even improve the existing edifices. As a consequence, it sat still in a time warp for nearly half a millennium. The air is filled with the aroma of grilling *crepes* from the street stands. The gardens cascade with gigantic hydrangeas. And the money-plated artisans don't miss a trick in luring tourists into their ateliers.

Running east to **Vannes,** apart from the aquarium, a devoted following of students of magalithic lore appear every summer to indulge their scholarship. This spot has a remarkable atraction for such pastimes.

The fishing port of **Douarnenez** (4 miles from Locronan) cheerfully reveals its affinity for old sailing vessels. It is a reasonable stopping place for lunch while touring the area. Try the Beau Crab at **La Cotriade** (46 rue Anatole-France). There are more exclusive dining spots in town, but this is so honest and pleasantly run by a harmonious family group that I found it the most enjoyable of all. Fronting the Old Port, **La Chasse Maree** would be the choice for the land and sea panoramas. For overnighting, my first choice in this region would be the **Manoir du Stang** at *La Foret-Fouesnant.* It is a lovely stone palace of the 16th century overlooking a lake, flower-filled gardens, and rich meadows. The 26 rooms are excellent for comfort; there is a superb viewful dining salon with cottage windows; the lounge is baronial. A novel touch is the service staff dressed crisply in Breton costume. Open May to Sept. only. **Cha-**

teau de Kernuz at *Pont-l'Abbe* is a contemporary of the previous entry; it features its own fortifications and an ancient chapel. There are beaches nearby plus opportunities for tennis and riding in the vicinity. **La Belle Etoile** lies at the sandy shore of *Cabellou Plage,* a resort extension of the main maritime port but quiet and calculated for enjoyment. It is a mock lighthouse tower that grew into a coastal hotel of distinguished quality. The rooms are substantial, and public sectors contain a number of fine antiques. Best of all, the staff and management are among the most cordial and hospitable to be found anywhere in the province. **Manoir de Kertalg** at *Moelan-sur-Mer* is not really on the *mer* but resides within a vast and beautiful forest. The walks, the fishing, and the silence are ideal for peace-seeking travelers. Also nearby and worth considering is **Les Moulins du Duc;** at *Hennebont,* the **Chateau de Locguenole** is recommendable. On the beach of *La Baule,* the **Hermitage** is the hotel of choice, followed by the **Castel Marie-Louise** and the park-sited **Royal. L'Espadon** is viewful and attractive at mealtimes. *Questembert* is noted for the restaurant **Le Bretagne,** where the oysters steamed in estragon are the food of gods. *Pont-Aven* is famous for its **Rosmadec,** which sits primly by a moss-dotted stream somewhat away from the hurly-burly of the tourist-trodden town. The prices are deluxe and so is the exquisite cuisine. A gourmet's delight for all of the senses. Closed Wed. If you hunger only for a local specialty such as ham and white beans, try **Le Taupiniere,** just outside of the village. **La Ferme du Letty** at *Benodet* is a converted white farmhouse on the outskirts of town. There are 2 rooms; a fireplace in the rock wall; very well regarded by locals and always busy except on Wed. (all day) and Thurs. lunchtime, when it is inoperative. The souffle of salmon is not what you would expect. Instead of flaked fish, the chef chooses a generous morsel such as the heart of the salmon steak and surrounds that with a souffle jacket, all bathed in a succulent butter sauce. Oooo-lala!

If you prefer the north coast, the high-speed TGV zips from Paris to the proud city of *Rennes* in 2 hours. Then take excursions to *Saint-Malo* and westward across the rugged cliffs to *Roscoff.* The scenery and sea-scapes can occupy days of touring.

The once sovereign realm of Brittany is designed for leisure and for rambling. To enjoy it best will take time, so I suggest basing at one of the above retreats and striking out on your own each day for new discoveries at the pace you select.

NORMANDY

Though it lies adjacent to Brittany's eastern flank, the province of Normandy is quite different in personality. Its character is softer. Its soil is richer. Its prosperity noticeably greater. Culturally, it is one of the most rewarding regions on either side of the English channel. Ironically, this French embankment is the focal point today of all of the fighting that ended in 1066 at Hastings on the British side. The interface for the titanic bicultural squabbling can be witnessed at the intriguing **Museum of Bayeux,** which houses the tapestry (actually an embroidery) known as the **Mathilde Frieze.** Here undoubtedly is one of the world's finer monuments to self-education, because if you devote as little as 3 hours to this establishment, the marvelous explanatory displays and the visual aids, you will come away with an intimate knowledge of how two cultures developed from the 11th century onward. After a tour of the detailed graphical reconstruction of the frieze you arrive at a theater that shows a film further delineating the battles of William the Conqueror, finally to arrive at the tapestry itself—beautifully illuminated; you are further assisted with portable audio equipment.

By this time you have become toally immersed in the ecclesiastical styles, the architecture, and the geography of the region. It is time to move on to nearby *Caen,* with its monumental and classic Norman **St. Stephen's Abbey** *(Abbaye aux Hommes)* begun in 1064 and the **Abbaye aux Dames,** which is nearby. William the Conqueror is buried in the Choir of the former church. There's a **Peace Museum** here called **Memorial,** which is dedicated to understanding factors that brought on World War II.

Of course, one of the lasting moments in travel is a visit to the thousand-year-old *Mont St. Michel,* an intellectual and spiritual center standing on a pinnacle of land (which becomes an island at times) and is still utilized as a Benedictine abbey. The 6 monks who continue to live here offer mass daily at 12:15 p.m. Despite the crowding from bus-package groupies, it is one of the most inspiring sites in Europe. Tours begin every half hour; the cost is 32 francs; duration is one hour in English and European languages.

For excursions in the region there is the redolent **Route du Fromage,** which takes you into the country of *Auge* and to farms where the wonderful products of Livarot, Pont L'Eveque, Pave d'Auge, and of course, Camembert are born and bred. You can visit a museum on this craft at *Virnantiers.* Additionally, there is a **Route du Cidre,** which, naturally, refers to the apple juice pressed from local orchards and developed into cider—some of it resulting in the dynamic and beautiful Calvados of international fame. It is opined that a Spanish warship was destroyed along this coast and when it washed ashore the transom bearing its name on the stern had been damaged so that the first and last letters were missing. What remained over the decades were only the letters "alvado" and the locals added a "c" to the beginning and an "s" to the end when, in fact, the ship's correct denomination was "Salvador."

Somewhat further afield, you might like to take the scenic trip through the **Route de la Suisse Normande,** which is south of Caen and moves through harmonious rolling country with interesting chapels and chateaux dotting the circuit. High points will be the **Manor** at *Clecy,* the **Saint-Roch Chapel** at *Pont d'Ouilly,* the beautiful Choir of the **Church of Saint-Martin** at *Conde-sur-Noireau;* the **Chateau de Pontecoulant** is a museum with furnishings and art objects. While in the district, see the chapels of **Saint-Benin** and **Saint-Joseph,** as well as the facade of the 13th-century church in *Thury-Harcourt.*

In quiet salt breezes blowing softly over St.-Laurent-sur-Mer, you can stand beside the magnificent polychrome plaque that marks the spot where the first wave of U.S. troops doggedly fought their way up the sand banks to achieve what was to become the most planet-shaking mass military movement in the annals of mankind. Below lies the full sweep of Omaha Beach and the sun-twinkled waters of the Channel. To the rear is a beautiful chapel, an impressive *rondure* with the names of the fallen, and a reception center for pilgrims. To your flank stretches the immaculate greensward and tidy white gravemarkers stretching over acres of Norman soil.

If you're motoring, strike out first for ***Arromanches-les-Bains*** (roughly 38 miles from Deauville), strategic center of the British zone of attack and site of the only remaining "Mulberry" artificial harbor. The string of containers deliberately sunk to form the breakwater has been raised, but the mammoth concrete pierheads and a large stranded landing craft remain in its sands. A highway with telescopes, charts, and listening devices enhances the historic site. Visit the fascinating Musee du Debarquement (loosely translated as "Invasion Museum"), where battle memorabilia and autographed photos of the commanders are on display, where movies of the fighting taken by combat cameramen are shown frequently during the day, and where an ingenious diorama reconstructs the action on a grand scale.

Then move along to the previously described memorial and cemetery at Omaha Beach in ***St.-Laurent-sur-Mer*** (perhaps 7 miles). From this U.S. fountainhead, take the several-hundred-yard skip to the seaward road marked St.-Laurent-sur-Mer (par la Cote). This detour, about 1½ miles long, permits you to drive directly along Omaha for a snail's eye view. At the north end you may inspect a small complex of Nazi pillboxes.

The most dramatic terrain of all is Pointe du Hoc (7 miles from central Omaha), where Colonel Rudder's American Rangers stormed its cliff, seized and held its German fortifications for 48 hours in which all but 14 of these heroes were killed or wounded—to find later that they had attacked the wrong promontory!

Utah Beach, about 20 miles farther along, holds little of sightseeing interest today—unless, of course there are personal reasons for visiting it.

Rouen is covered separately in an earlier listing.

Hotels and restaurants in Normandy are generally simple and 2nd line. *Audrieu* is proud (rightfully) of its **Chateau d'Audrieu** in the tranquil gardens that produce much of its home-grown food. The table is exceptional and the hosting family who own this exquisite landmark are the soul of kindness. Comforts are superb, but prices are reasonable for the deluxe rewards. Very peaceful and floral; swimming pool. *Caen***'s Novotel,** on the outskirts, is tranquilly sited and convenient for motorists who come to view the battle grounds. Outdoor pool for relaxing. **Relais des Gourmets** has only a couple of dozen bedrooms, but the kitchen is one of the best around. **Malherbe,** in the center but overlooking a wide prairie, next. The modest **Moderne** offers dining facilities; it is a suitable alternate during this hiatus. The **Metropole** and **Royal** come up with breakfast only. For independent dining, **Alcide,** an ivy-covered modern bower, served me a delicate lunch. Slightly east at *Bavent,* the **Hostellerie du Moulin du Pre** is a sip of cider country. Simple and fine for food and rest. If you are saving *Mont-St.-Michel* as a meal stop be sure to pause at the famous **Mere Poulard,** which is known globally for its omelets. Other dishes also deserve praise as well. Be sure to reserve ahead for a table or for a room. Closed from

Oct. to Apr. Here are two others you may want to try: **Du Gueschlin** and **Terrasses,** both very simple and both seasonal (open Apr. 1 to late Oct.) Tourists galore. In winter the 21-room **Mouton Blanc** is almost the only show in town; my hardy and well-cooked fixed-meal consisted of 6 Portuguese oysters, a huge omelet, leg of lamb, beans, potatoes, and apple tart. You may not wish to overnight here (or even in the approach-road hostelries) because it's so noisy and so glutted with excursionists in season that much of the beauty is diminished. You'll also have to climb by foot to your destination, because no cars are permitted on its narrow steep streets. Be sure not to wander off the causeway over the shoal, especially if you're traveling with children; the tides rise so fast that the sands can be dangerous. At lovely *Honfleur,* the **Ferme Saint Simeon** has vivid memories of the Impressionists who painted along this coast. It a charming base and excellent even as a meal stop. Nearby *Avranches* has the 30-room **Croix d'Or** in the rustic style of the region. Then there's the little **Auberge St.-Michel,** opposite the statue of General George Patton. **Bellevue,** across from the Auberge St.-Michel, is another possible bet in the modest-shelter category. To the northeast, the **Verte Campagne** at *Trelly* offers sink-in comfort in rustic, innlike surroundings. The cuisine is noteworthy too. In *Vire,* the **Cheval Blanc,** fronted by a garden Plaza, is the pacesetter, both for its comfort and for its table. In *Bayeux,* the **Lion d'Or** is adequate. *Lisieux?* **Esperance** is a solid bet (100 rooms) and the restaurant is well regarded. The **Place** is about a third the size and is more expensive; no dining room. For dining, try the excellent and attractive **Ferme du Roy** on the road to Deauville. *Balleroy* is puffed up with pride over its 17th-century **Chateau Balleroy,** a ballooning hub created by Malcolm Forbes, a hot-air specialist from way back, an American legend in publishing, a tastemaker, philanthropist, and art collector of international repute. It is not for overnighting, but do try to include it in your sightseeing.

If you are motoring, don't miss **Giverny,** where the home, studio, and gardens of Claude Monet are open for public viewing. Here are the willows, the flora, the Japanese bridge, and the lily ponds that the great impressionist caught in so many reflective moods. From Paris's Gare St. Lazare you can take a train to Vernon ($15 round trip), then walk or taxi the 1-mile route to Monet's house, passing many of the scenes he preserved on canvas. Open April 1 to Nov. 1, 10 a.m. to noon and 2 to 6 p.m., daily except Mondays. If you stay over, try the simple but nice **Les Trois Saint Pierre,** with its associated **Auberge les Cannisses;** they are across the Seine at a village called *le Goulet.* A car will be necessary.

GERMANY

INCLUDING THE "ROMANTIC ROAD"

USA: German National Tourist Office, 747 Third Ave., New York, NY 10017, Tel. (212) 308–3300; 444 South Flower St., Suite 2230, Los Angeles, CA 90071, Tel. (213) 688–7332; **CANADA:** 175 Bloor St. E., N. Tower, Suite 604 Toronto, Tel. (416) 968–1570.

SPECIAL REMARKS: "Reunification" is the cry—whether in political fact or only as a dream becoming reality. Hence, much of what you find in this freshly updated chapter could be slightly different by the time its ink is dry. Always ask locally—especially in east-west frontier regions— about changes that may affect your travel plans. The Berlin area is the most fluid of all since the Wall came tumbling down. Now for a few specifics. (1) **Lufthansa,** the German national airline and not to be doubted for its cleverness, cooperates throughout the world with the German National Tourist Board, so look for their listing in your phone directory. (2) In Germany the **German National Tourist Board** is located at Beethovenstrasse 69 in Frankfurt. It publishes color-illustrated booklets in English covering every region of the Federal Republic. It can also provide a list of all subordinate offices throughout the nation. (3) The **German Travel Association** links in with numerous information centers throughout the country. Their offices are recognizable by a red plaque with a white *i*. (3) At least 50 feudal palaces and castles have been converted into hotels all over the nation. These can be enjoyed either individually or through reasonably priced motoring packages to several. For details write to **Gast im Schloss,** Geschaftsstelle, Vor der Burg, Postfach D-3526, Trendelburg 1, Germany.

> **TELEPHONE:** Access code to USA: 001. To phone Germany: 49; time difference (Eastern Daylight) plus 6 hrs.

This year's visitor to Germany will find every conceivable amenity—luxurious as well as clean bargain-price hotels, delicious food, an unrivaled transportation network, and all the pleasures or comforts of meticulously organized tourist facilities. Nationwide prosperity also enhances the mood of hospitality.

SIGHTSEEING Aside from political factors, Berlin is one of the most interesting and rewarding single tourist targets in Germany. More on this further along. Otherwise, in order of popularity, here are the sights that command most attention from newcomers:

Rhine excursions. The traditional pastimes afloat (both day excursions and several nights) include the Cologne–Mainz runs. (For a shorter time afloat the Koblenz-Mainz leg is a charmer, too.) Comfortable, modern steamers of the "White Fleet" offer interesting programs such as "Rhenish Afternoons," evenings with music and dancing, festival cruises for children, and the like. The majority ply the currents between Basel and Rotterdam (4 days, or 5 in the upstream direction). You can nip off a day doing the Basel–Nijmegan termini or the Strasbourg–Amsterdam route. Ships are modern and quite large for riverboating. If you're making a solo journey, expect to share your cabin with someone (of the same gender, fortunately or unfortunately). There's also the *Rheinpfeil*, a 64-passenger hydrofoil that cruises at 37 mph. Most sailings (or those also linked into the Moselle) are scheduled between March and October, but more runs are being stitched into the winter pattern every year. In some cases (day trips only), part of the way may be covered by rail on a combined arrangement.

If you start from Cologne, you may find it much, much wiser to debark at Rudesheim or Assmannshausen. Low water levels in summer often delay dockings at the Wiesbaden or Mainz terminals as much as 3 hours.

Bavarian castles, particularly Neuschwanstein, Herrenchiemsee, Linderhof, and the Residence Palace at Wurzburg. (Check the German Federal Railways about its combined rail-bus tours during weekends in summer.) From Munich there's an easy low-cost excursion to the Cloister of **Andechs**—first by subway to Herrsching am Ammersee, then from the exit by bus to your destination. It's a baroque joy!

Churches and **cathedrals** are eternal attractions. The granddaddys are at Ulm, Wurzburg, Munich, Freiburg, Mainz, Worms, Speyer, Cologne, Bremen, Marburg, Limburg, Regensburg, Treves, and Aachen.

The **Neckar Valley** and **Heidelberg.**

The **Hag** development and "Bottcherstrasse" in Bremen.

The **medieval castles** along the Moselle (especially beautiful for driving or for delightful loafing aboard one of the tiny steamers). The Rhine, Danube, Ahr, Lahn, Main, and Weser are also studded with ancient fortresses.

Excellent **bus tours** cover many of the nation's most scenic regions such as Garmisch-Partenkirchen, Mittenwald, Bad Tolz, Tubingen, Oberammergau, Rosenheim, Baden-Baden, and many forested, lake, and alpine climes. They offer wonderfully low rates, modern equipment and magnificent scenery. The **"Romantic Road"** tours (see later) between Wurzburg and Fussen in the Allgau Alps (also summer only) and the **"Castle Road"** tours from Mannheim via Heidelberg and Rothenberg to Nurnberg are outstanding, too.

The **motorboat rides** on the Neckar between Heidelberg and Neckarsteinach, on the Moselle between Coblenz and Cochem, or Trier (summer only) and other points, and on the Danube between Passau and Linz. Since I'm kind of boathooked anyway, I like the slaphappy *platten* (flat-bottom barges) rides on Salzach, an Inn tributary, and on the Isar (where rafts are employed).

Bayerischer Wald, a 30,000-acre national park nestling along the Czech border near Regen. This first legally designated wilderness in Germany abounds with wolf, lynx, otter, red deer, bear, beaver, alpine marmot, and 2 rare species of owl (Ural and pygmy). Some captive fauna is available to lazy shutterbugs.

Hitler's Eagle's Nest, atop Mt. Kehlstein far above the valley town of Berchtesgaden and owned by the State of Bavaria, receives hordes of tourists. If you make the trek, it will be for the view alone (when it's a clear day, and often it isn't) because there are no significant buildings or artifacts. Take the special bus up the safe but hair-raising mountain road to a point 450 feet from the summit. Then ride the brass-plated elevator through solid rock up to the peak, which if it isn't in a cloud, will provide an Alpine panorama that should leave you breathless. There are crowded dining facilities (chiefly *wurst* and beer) both at the top and at the lower bus terminal. Naturally Berchtesgaden offers a plethora of snack bars, restaurants, and inns. Count on at least 3 hours for a full visit. Other Hochland flings? Downhill hikers will be pleased to know that scores and scores of funiculars and teleferics are available as conveyance to almost any pinnacle in the land; in winter skiers use them and in the summer most function as lifts so that you can lunch on the heights and easily walk down to the valleys or lower stations.

Son et Lumiere ("Sound and Light") or similar spectacles are available at some historic sites. One outstanding example is at Schloss Herrenchiemsee, a copy of Versailles Palace on an island in the Chiemsee, about 46 miles down the fast autobahn from Munich. The castle is fully furnished with its original treasures and illuminated by more than 4000 wax candles; chamber music is played; the pools and gardens are on show, but Mad King Louis' (Ludwig II of Bavaria, whose eccentricities were taken for madness by locals) pornographic pictures are not. Every Saturday evening from May to September; book in advance in American Express, Munich, or you won't get in; arrive before 5:30 p.m., after which the palace tours end for the day; no photography permitted.

On a completely different note is the museum in the crematory of **Dachau** concentration camp, a 45-minute subway and bus ride from Munich, where at least 30,000 human beings were cremated. Surviving inmates representing 21 nations established this monument to atrocity. Documents, orders, and photographs relating to the torture and extermination of prisoners are displayed. Closed Mon.

Finally there's the **Richard Wagner Festival** at Bayreuth during July and August, the **Munich Opera Festival** during the same period, concerts by the Berlin Philharmonic Orchestra the calendar round and more folk festivals, home festivals, jubilees, fairs, religious events, expositions, congresses, and conventions than anyone can attend. Ask the German National Tourist Association or your nearest German National Tourist Office (New York, Los Angeles, Montreal) for their excellent programs of these topical events. If you write for tickets, do so by late November; after that, it's often a gamble.

NOTE · · · Weather forecasts, road conditions, and information on Germany and its people are broadcast in English and 7 other languages during the tourist season over the South German Radio Station in Stuttgart. They are beamed during the musical program from 10 a.m.–10:45 a.m.

Note for hobbyists, efficiency experts, and industrial spies: Germany's **"Open House"** program flings wide the doors of hundreds of the nation's factories and workshops. The German National Tourist Information Office in New York or Toronto will provide a long list of the names and addresses of these hospitable companies or ateliers.

TRANSPORTATION **Airline Lufthansa** is a sound carrier over the Atlantic; its attention to the business traveler is above average; cuisine often has a regional character that I admire. The East, Midwest, and West are now connected by airbridges to German gateways. Frankfurt Airport links into the Intercity rail network with frequent departures to all European destinations. The S-Bahn (Interurban) trains leave every 10 minutes during business hours for midcity; the ride takes 10 minutes too. At Central Station a great variety of rail possibilities afford further choices. The flying is usually first rate even when the weather is so frightful a Valkyrie wouldn't take off. But if it is raining ask to utilize an umbrella from Lufthansa for ground use. Premium and Business Class receive other thoughtful treats and treatment along the airways.

Taxis In the larger cities, taxis are fairly plentiful. Lots of new ones, because competition is tough. They're cheap when compared, for example, with the Swiss or Belgian brotherhood.

Trains The German Federal Railways surpass almost any other system in Europe today. There's a money-saving German Rail Pass (Flexipass) for unlimited travel *all over united Germany;* it is valid for one month and comes in 5-, 10-, or 15-day (non-consecutive) packages that are very convenient. (Valid also for bus along the *Romantic Road,* the *Castle Road,* or on the Rhine for day trips. You also receive free admission to the Museum of Transport in Nuremburg.) A Youth Pass is another useful fillip; all can be purchased via airlines, which can incorporate the fare into the overall ticketing. Other plans include a rental car or even a bike if you want to explore beyond the national trackage. All Intercity services carry first *and* second class; even better, they now run every hour in a similar fashion to subway passage. New networks link 40 cities on rapid transport to the major international gateway at Frankfurt Airport. Trains are punctual, clean, and comfortable, and feature nonsmoking sections similar to those on Lufthansa airliners. DB (for "Deutsche Bundesbahn") sleepers offer individually adjustable air conditioning, broad beds with foam-rubber mattresses, quilts, folding walls, electric razor outlets, shower-baths, and many other innovations; light-bite rolling "bistros" and DB diners are efficient and reasonably priced; Intercity electric locomotives can average 135 mph on certain runs. The color scheme for DB is red for locomotives, red and gray for Intercity coaches, blue and gray for express coaches, and green and gray for local haulage. The *Komet* is an express sleeper covering the dreamlands between Hamburg and Basel; in season some cars will give you a wake-up call in Chur or Brig (East and West Switzerland, respectively). "Bunk cars" *(Liegewagen)* are available to budgeteers on many intra-German and some international night runs. They're sort of "Economy Pullmans," with no curtains and 3 decks of 6 bunks per compartment; the passenger sleeps (if he can) in his clothes. Far, far better than sitting up. You also can enjoy overnight baggage delivery to your destination, so ask as you check in.

Almost all German trackage and switches have undergone the so-called seamless-welding process; the rhythmic clickety-clack of the wheels is a nostalgic memory nearly everywhere.

NOTE · · · On medium-short hauls, the better trains are now beating the airliners' time—airport-to-city coverage considered.

All fast Intercity trains offer coin telephone service en route.

Luggage problems? Get rid of your heavy pieces by registering them through to your destination; fees are in the flea-bite class. Since all of Germany (including W. Berlin) offers this service, you can forward your possessions direct to your lodgings; it costs only a little more than the railway shipping charge.

Buses Most long-haul buses, particularly in sightseeing districts, are modern—and gentle to the area in contact with the seat. Many offer adjustable chairs, nonsmoking zones, public-address system, lavatories, radio loudspeakers, and huge windows for maximum visibility. The German Federal Railways runs the show so inquire there; private bus tour companies are another matter.

ADAC and AvD, the 2 most important German automobile clubs, offer tour information in most cities. In the ports of Hamburg and Bremerhaven, and at a number of key frontier crossings, they and the German Tourist Association have set up special bureaus to help foreign visitors plan their trips. No charge. There's also a free motorists' aid service for outlanders stranded on the autobahns. Just flag down a red or yellow patrol car or get to one of the telephones set 7 miles apart throughout the network. In the Alps, the ADAC rents snow chains to winter trippers; your small deposit is refunded when you return 'em. Postscript for families: Children under 12 must ride in the back seat, but an exception is made if there is an overflow of offspring.

Car rentals. All the multinationals are everywhere, of course, but I favor **Sixt-Budget,** which offers modest-to-luxury cars—even sports versions—at rates that are guaranteed on a dollar basis—quite reassuring in such times of currency fluctuation. Headquarters: Dr. Carl-von-Linde Strasse, 8023 Munich-Pullach; Tel. (089) 79107-1. Tx. 522 733 Sixt d. Regina Sixt is a legendary friend of the foreign motorist.

FOOD In taverns, cafes, and beer halls or wine gardens—not deluxe establishments—national custom dictates that tables be shared by 2 or more parties if the place is crowded. Quite often you might find yourself sitting with strangers—fortunately, most of the time in a courteous but remote "please pass the salt" relationships rather than one of compulsory small talk and yak-yak.

Contrary to legend, German cooking is often light, delicate, and highly inventive. This nation is becoming a fashion leader in gastronomy, even though a lot of the daring ideas were born in France. In the eastern provinces it will naturally take a while for the culinary advances of the west to seep in. Even so, the east offers platters of its own exotica at the table.

NOTE · · · If in doubt about a good place to eat in a strange town, head for the nearest *Ratskeller*. The word means "council cellar" and it's the place (usually the cellar of the town hall) where in the Middle Ages municipal officials received guests. There is one in most communities; part of the *Ratskeller* is known as the *Ratstrinkstube* (council drinking room). The tradition of quality is stoutly upheld in most of these.

DRINKS Most connoisseurs (if they weren't born in Burgundy, Bordeaux, or Champagne) agree that Germany makes the finest white wines of the world. With typically Teutonic attention to detail, every bottle of character bears its full pedigree on the label—type, year, district, grower, shipper, and often even the condition of the grape at the picking. There are eleven wine-growing regions in Germany: Ahr, Mosel-Saar-Ruwer, Mittelrhein, Rheingau, Nahe, Rheinhessen, Rheinpfalz, Hessische Bergstrasse, Franken, Wurttemberg, and Baden. Then there are six (ascending) tiers of ripeness: Kabinett, Spatlese, Auslese, Beerenauslese, Eiswein, and, finally, the princely Trockenbeerenauslese. "Riesling" is a generic term for any wine of the Riesling grape, as opposed to the Sylvan grape. Moselle, Rhine, Ahr, Franconia, Palatinate, and others are named for their specific districts or valleys, although technically they could be called Rieslings. Steinwein is harsh and rough; most visitors prefer others. Hock, derived from "Hochheimer," is erroneously used by many British drinkers as a blanket appellation for all Rhines and similar types; the vineyards for this are actually on the north bank of the Main.

Liebfraumilch remains an ever popular choice but, practically speaking, there are 2 good bottles of this for 10 bad ones, because this banner covers *all* of the output of the Rheinhessen region. Ask for Oppenheimer Schlossberg, Nierstein-er Domthal, or Nackenheimer Rotenberg for delicious examples, and forget about most others.

All sugarless types (often Moselle, Ruwer, Saar) are best when young— the wine, that is.

If you're a zillionaire, "Beerenauslese" and "Trockenbeerenauslese" are the topmost rungs of wine quality (see below); they're so difficult to produce and so limited in supply that you'll pay from $60 to $180 per bottle at any fine restaurant (a 1921 vintage brings about $400!). They're categories, not brand names.

If you're a plain millionaire, Schloss Johannisberger is the finest "regular" wine in the land; the best years run up to perhaps $120. Other winners, not as expensive, are Deidesheimer Kieselberg Riesling Auslese, Bernkasteler Doctor, and Piesporter Lay. In the medium range, one of my picks would be Jesuitengarten Riesling Auslese, a Palatinate variety available at about $4 per 3-glass-carafe.

But don't be dazzled or intimidated by those important-sounding names, because the government uncorked 4 general classifications for every drop of nectar produced in the country and set official testing numbers for both of the top grades. The categories are: Table wines ("Tafelwein") for the lowliest entries; Landwein, from 15 specific regions, providing fine everyday pressings with distinctive characters; Quality wines ("Qualitatswein") for the middlebung brands; and Quality wines with Award ("Qualitatswein mit Pradikat") for the choicest crushings.

German "champagne," called "Sekt," is frequently sparkling Rhine or Moselle wine. Remarkable strides have been made in recent years to improve its quality. Today, selected labels of the *brut* types have an urbane and noble character. Mumm Dry (no relative of the French brand of the same name) is an excellent candidate for your white; Henkell Rose is a delightful pink nectar. (The Henkell cellars in Wiesbaden produce much of their Sekt from French wines, incidentally. This house is famous and excellent.) Many other so-called German champagnes are still cloyingly sweet, less bubbly than their French originals, and repulsive to the knowledgeable international palate.

German beer is as appetizing as ever—and it's about $1.25 per large mug in the average place. There are Helles or Export or simply Ex (light), Pilsner or Pils (light in color but stronger), Dunkles (dark), Weisse (extra light), served in Bavaria chiefly but available elsewhere, the different Berliner Weisse (Berlin wheat-malt specialty, which is light and lemony). The Bockbier season is January to March; this dark, rich beer is one of the most delicious of all. Bestknown brews are those of Munich, Frankfurt, Dortmund, Donaueschingen (Fuerstenberg), Nurnberg (Siechen, Tucher), Wurzburg, and Kulmbach. (The last is famous for being frozen into an iceblock that packs a 9% alcoholic punch after the solidification!) As a curiosity, you might like to try a stein of Weihenstephan. This brewery, in Freising, has been running continuously for almost a thousand years; the yeast in your potion first saw the light of day in the eleventh century.

TIPPING   In all German hotels there is an automatic service charge of 10% to 15% of the price of the room. Now it is usually lumped into your overall bill rather than itemized separately. For meal service in hotels and restaurants the service bite is 10% to 15%; it need not be noted on the overall billing. For drinks most anywhere a separate tax (*Getrankesteuer*) is levied, but it does not often appear on your tab; generally this is 10%, but in Munich and Stuttgart it is 20%; you're still expected to shell out something for the bartender, however.

CITIES AND REGIONS

AACHEN,   also called *Aix-la-Chapelle,* is known as the city of Charlemagne—and splendid it is! Developing gracefully over 2000 years, it resides almost at the union of Belgium, Holland, and Germany, flanked by the Eifel range and the Ardennes. For sightseeing it is one of the most convenient cities in Europe. The **Cathedral** (Dom) and the **Rathaus** are its focal points and they exist almost back-to-back overlooking the open market and beneath the medieval galleries of the church. The former—magnificently ornate—contains the burial place of the mighty conqueror while the latter is built upon the foundations of Charlemagne's palace. The church **Treasury,** which you may visit, houses one of the richest ecclesiastical collections north of Rome. Children should head straight for the **Puppet Fountain** in the market, which is composed of brass articulated dolls; kids can molest these toys relentlessly but never break them. For dining, the **Rathaus** offers a ground-level restaurant under stout brick vaults. Traditional dishes of the region include Ardennes ham, herring from the neighboring fish market, pork schnitzel, *eisbein* and heavy malty beer. Another choice would be the **Post Cafe,** also within this complex, and the oldest tavern in Aachen (possibly in Europe). More classical repasts are served at the majestic **Gala** (Monheimsallee 44), which, naturally, comes at a higher price level. Best overnighting in the **Quellenhof,** followed by the intimate **Krott. Regence** is fresh but living space is limited. **Novotel** is inexpensive, clean and institutional. **Schlosshotel Friesenrath** is appealing, but it's 6 miles from the center. **Relais Konigsberg** is also suburban; it's moderately priced and homelike.

ASSMANNHAUSEN   This is a convenient cruise stop if you're bound down the *east* bank of the Rhine.

★★★★ **Krone Hotel-Restaurant** ● (21 miles from Wiesbaden and 42 miles from Frankfurt am Main) is an enchanting choice for lunch when sunbeams are dancing on the river. Terrace-dining on the warmer days, under a grapevine "roof"; long, darkly ingratiating paneling, inside salon with low ceilings and ancient spirits; quite expensive; red-wine specialities are Assmannshausener and a sparkling burgundy-type called Schaumender Special Roter Cuvee; open mid-March to mid-Nov.

BADEN-BADEN   This most historic of all spas is famous for its Lichtentaler Allee, Roman baths and thermal ablutions at Caracalla Therme. The 3-story Congress Hall, with its main-floor restaurant and flowering terrace, is at nearby Augustaplatz; the more youthful, jazzed-up casino with a recreational wing, spa gardens, racetrack, and other enticements, is drawing funloving vacationers. Its "Grand Week" of big-time horse racing (late Aug. to early Sept.) is internationally known.

☆☆☆☆☆ **Brenner's Park** ● a classic in the hotel world, occupies a rhapsodic location in a sylvan grove with a terraced stream and fountain exchanging sweet babblings; fast and friendly service; lounge music nightly. There's a breathtakingly attractive, Roman indoor swimming pool with a view of the park, a party room, and—but of course—a beauty parlor. In a lighter mood, there is the summer-only adjoining Villa Stephanie with its own dining salon and 20 superb rooms, including 4 extra-comfortable suites. Among Europe's finest and most costly addresses.

☆☆☆☆ **Europaischer Hof** • has been totally renovated with many new features added. It's a zesty popular mix, yet still quite expensive. Just a toss of the dice from the Casino; charming streamside dining room; candlelight dining on weekends; bar with piano lilts until after midnight. Many suites were created out of smaller accommodations. Alive and thriving, perhaps even too animated if you like the stiffer—let's say sedate—Brenner style.

★★★ **Badischer Hof** • is built as a 4-story atrium; glass-lined garden-front swimming pool; fresh, beige-toned reception; 90 attractive modern bedrooms; all units with bath and most equipped with thermal water taps. Sound, but you pay a hefty premium for that special H_2O.

★★ **Bad-Hotel Zum Hirsch** • has been taken over by one of Germany's larger chains. Busy location; part of its triangular structure spans a street that cuts an isosceles swath through the courtyard. Inviting reception area, restaurant, bar, and elevator; comfortable connecting annex. Many of its accommodations have private balconies and thermal water taps; some units with original oil paintings.

Atlantic • on the Oos River (well, rivulet) offers a lovely terrace for afternoon tea; all units with balconies and a disappointing fustiness.

★★★★ **Fairway** • is a linkside, chalet-style first-class haven, especially for golfing buffs. Magnificent hill-bound, timber-lined course; private swimming pool and tennis courts; breakfast terrace. Ideal for the Sporting Set.

Golf Hotel • is a sprawling, gabled, and gaunt example of typical old-fashioned resort innkeeping; the later wing is somewhat ameliorative; the indoor swimmery with jet stream, sauna, massage, plus solarium segments, and added private baths (bringing the count up to 100%), has somewhat thawed its cool overall demeanor. About 2½ miles from the center of Baden-Baden.

Sophien Park • now under new management, has been fully reshaped. Good value and fresh.

☆☆☆☆☆ **Schlosshotel Buhlerhohe** • is a splendid country retreat up on the Black Forest High Road (Schwarzwaldhochstrasse) and almost 2500 feet above Baden-Baden with enchanting views of the Rhine Valley. It is a luxurious restoration of a great estate by Grundig funding and the highlife genius of Director Wolfgang Rattmann (formerly of the Ritz in Paris). Rose-toned structure with courtyards, towers, gables, terraces, and fountains; grandeur everywhere, including at the table; beauty and health facilities. The nearest town is *Buhl* (Tel. 07226/55100; Fax 07226/55777). Elegance in historic proportions.

Dining

☆☆☆☆☆ **Brenner's Park Hotel** • is classified (quite properly) in the nation's highest gastronomic category. Richly elegant decor, not overstressed, in off-white, crystal, and gold; red and flaxen carpeting; flowers in silver vases;

bucolic vistas from dining room or gardenside summer terrace; service that anticipates your slightest whim.

Casino Restaurant ● has been given a beauty treatment and is far more appealing than previously. You'll also find within the complex the **Boulevard Terrace,** the attractive **Paddock Bar,** and downstairs is the Club Tavern disco-restaurant.

☆☆☆ **Zum Alde Gott** ● (Wein Strasse 10) offers delicate gastronomy that could be construed as a Germanic nouvelle cuisine. Very agreeable.

The **Baden Wine Cellar** is pleasant for a sip and snack. The **Mandarin,** with both Cantonese and Peking perkings, pans out only fair Oriental fare. I suspect the chef was born a little west of the Yangtze—somewhere between Karlsruhe and Pforzheim, for example.

Pospisils ● has a fine name locally, out at the *Oos* suburb, but I've never swallowed more than its syllables.

★★★ **Post Hotel** ● In nearby *Herrenalb,* it occupies a former 12th-century monastery; Klosterschanke Grill, with beamed braces in stone and stucco walls or arches; flowers and candles on each table; the bread is served in 2-foot-long baskets. The smoked trout with whipped horseradish sauce and saddle of venison washed down by local wine was a deliciously memorable repast. Exceptionally friendly staff and management.

Schloss Neuweier ● turns on a reasonably good kitchen in an atmosphere of antiquity. The outlay can be moderate.

Wald Hotel Fischkultur ● at *Oberbeuern* is really a trout ranch, so you can guess at the specialty.

When the sun is glowing, try to sample the unique flavor of the Black Forest. Ride out to nearby villages in the vineyard country—preferably by any route other than the autobahn. Hamlets such as *Varnhalt* (**Hotel Katzenberger**'s Adler), *Umweg* (**Boxbeutel**), and *Neuweier* (**Schloss, Lamm,** or **Rebenhof**) are just a few of the many oases within a 10-mile radius of Baden-Baden. Or you could enjoy a longer excursion down to *Hinterzarten*'s captivating **Hotel Adler** (see later). Here you will savor the peace, the silence, the majesty, and the pastoral loveliness of the romantic *Schwarzwald*.

BERCHTESGADEN Though the valley drive to arrive here is one of the most breathtaking routes anywhere in Europe, travelers usually pause only briefly. If you wander in, the **Geiger** is the most noteworthy for overnighting and for dining. The **Fischer** is also agreeable. There are scores of guesthouses and *garni* hotels for moneysaving buys. My personal choice, however, would be outside of town at the chalet-style **Alpenhotel Denninglehen,** run by hospitable Eva and Hermann Konig. Aesthetically, it's a charmer and if you are a beauty-and-fitness buff, it offers ample services and facilities for recapturing agilities. The exact address is Berchtesgaden/Oberau. Of course, you'll want to visit Hitler's **Eagle's Nest** atop the looming Mt. Kehlstein. (Refer back to "Attractions.'') The Nazi Chief's alpine redoubt at nearby *Obersalzberg* (on a slope above Berchtesgaden) has been totally demolished in a postwar effort to remove all memory of the *Fuhrer*.

BERLIN

Finally, it is one! No longer a divided city. Rebuilding in the eastern portion is feverish now that all 23 districts are united to form one single city of 3.2 million Berliners.

East of the remnants of the Wall, there are approximately 130,000 apartments. State-operated stores that used to line the main boulevard are now being converted to private commerce. A handful of skyscraping hotels have appeared, and monetary union has been effected. The hotels are drab if they are the ones traditionally designated for visitors from Soviet states, but eye-popping in modernity and luxury for Western guests at the **Grand, Palast,** or **Metropol.** (Lesser choices include the **Stadt Berlin, Berolina,** and **Unter den Linden.**) In any case the interface between the two segments is becoming less distinct as peoples from both former Berlins become as one. In what used to be the West there's always light, action, and fun. It's not yet the case in the East, where prosperity still lags four decades behind. Be sure to see both segments. No travel documents are required, passage is uninhibited at any time of the day or night, and one currency is utilized everywhere.

Town Transport, Taxis, and Car Rentals Throughout the united metropolis and suburbs there are miles of subways (U-bahn) and elevated rails (S-bahn) that cover all the districts you'll need. Buses operate, too, plus double-deckers that run all night. Tourist tickets are sold at bargain rates. The city is well accommodated by a 6000-taxi fleet; ½ of them are linked to a central exchange by radio-telephone. When the city was isolated, it was pointless to rent a car since travel was so limited. Today hotels, the airport, and travel agencies represent the multinational services plus local rental vehicles, which often are cheaper.

Tours Excursions are 4 hours long. They originate from the intersection of Kurfurstendamm and Uhlandstrasse; from Kurfurstendamm and Joachimstalerstr.; from the Kaiser-Wilhelm Memorial Church; and from the corner of Meinekestrasse at the Kurfurstendamm. They include so much of East and West Berlin history that I would recommend that any first-time visitor book a tour as soon as possible in your visit.

Surroundings? I experienced a 6-hour spin to neighboring Potsdam by motor coach. It was composed of a shuffle through Frederik the Great's crumbling Sanssouci Castle (you don enormous felt slippers so that your shoes won't mar the flooring) and a whisk through the Tudor-style Cecilienhof Mansion (where the Potsdam Agreement was signed in 1945). Dresden, Meissen, and Leipzig also can be absorbed on a 2-day swing. A rewarding day-long outing in spring,

summer, or autumn is to Spreewald, where Mother Nature is in her most resplendent attire. All, incidentally, are relatively inexpensive.

Travel Information The **Berlin Tourist Office** (Europa Center) maintains
branches at key points to dispense advice, brochures, and every type of assistance to any voyager. Some of the localities include Alexanderplatz (near the
TV tower), the Hauptbahnhof (Oskreuz), Lichtenberg, near the Brandenburg
Gate, Checkpoint Dreilinden, and at Tegel.

ATTRACTIONS

Funkturm • *Berlin Radio Tower, Messedamm* • Built in 1924 for the Third
German Broadcasting Exhibition, this 453-foot steel-latticed tower is an excellent point from which to get a bird's-eye view of the city. An elevator will take
you to the observation deck at 410 feet, or you may dine at the restaurant at the
180-foot level.

The Wall • It used to wind a path of nearly 100 miles around Greater
Berlin, but now only a few remnants remain. Ask locally if you care to see
some fragment of the hated divide.

Brandenburg Gate • *Unter den Linden* • Situated on East German soil and
now unblocked by the Wall, this striking set of columns, crowned by a beautiful
beaten-copper quadriga, again represents the western entrance to the city. It is
more than 2000 years old.

Reichstag • *Parliament Building, Platz der Republic* • Built between 1884
and 1894 in the Italian High Renaissance style, this elaborate building has
undergone much reconstruction since having been burned in 1933 and bombed
during the war. Originally intended as the official seat of the German parliament, it is still used for various political conclaves and may serve the public in
a more important fashion if Berlin again becomes the capital of Germany. It is
situated a short distance north of the Brandenburg Gate. Also, the Reichstag
houses a collection of artifacts illustrative of Germany's recent history.

Tiergarten • One of the city's most beautiful and extensive public parks,
the 412-acre Tiergarten stretches 1¾ miles west from the Brandenburg Gate,
and has a dazzling array of large trees, broad lawns and walks, colorful flower
displays and lakes. The park is a perfect spot for a picnic or simple relaxation.
Also here you'll find the relocated **Museum of Applied Arts** next to the Philharmonie.

Zoo • *Hardenbergplatz 8* • Located at the southwestern tip of the Tiergarten in the heart of the city, this 74-acre zoo was Germany's first, having been
laid out in 1841. It is still said to contain more species than any other zoo in
the world. Last time I counted there were in excess of 13,000 critters.

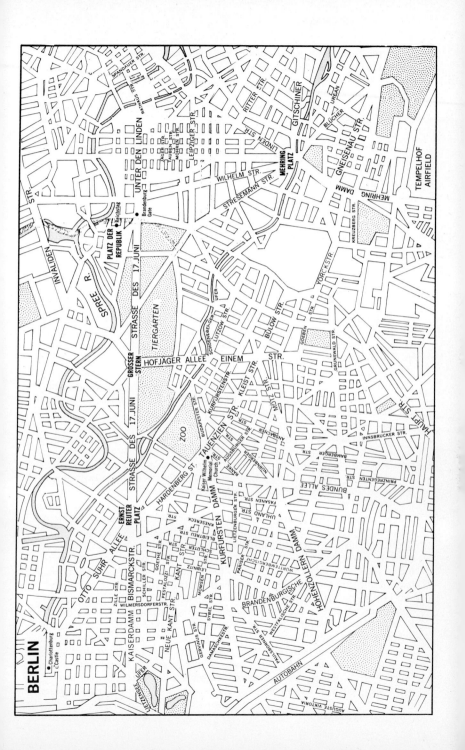

Aquarium • *Budapester Strasse 32* • Right next to the zoo is the Berlin Aquarium, which has the largest and most comprehensive collection of aquatic animals in the world. Over 250 tanks display an amazing variety of fish. Also housed in the building is a Department of Reptiles and Amphibians, with lizards, snakes, frogs, alligators and crocodiles, as well as the Insectarium, with all kinds of insects.

Kaiser Wilhelm Gedachtniskirche • *Kaiser Wilhelm Memorial Church, Breitscheidplatz* • It's the city's most poignant ruin. Some new parts have been added, such as its modernistic hexagonal bell tower and church. The old, partially destroyed west tower is one of the nation's best-known landmarks. Between the church and the Europa Center you'll find the Globe, a glorious modern fountain and an important meeting point in midtown.

National Galerie • *Potsdamer Strasse 50* • Housed in a lovely modern building in part of the city's cultural center, this is an excellent collection of 19th- and 20th-century paintings and sculptures. Temporary modern art exhibitions are frequent. Also, jazz concerts are held in the museum's sculpture garden throughout the summer season.

Philharmonie • *Matthaikirchplatz* • A few blocks away from the National Galerie on the southern edge of the Tiergarten stands this unusual piece of modern architecture—the home of the world-renowned Berlin Philharmonic Orchestra. The futuristic structure was completed in 1963; it seats 2200. Next door is a new chamber music hall from the same design studio of Hans Scharoun.
For opera, there's the **Deutsche Oper** (34–37 Bismarckstrasse), the small and marvelously classic East Berlin **Deutsche Staatsoper** (unter den Linden) and the **Komische Oper** (55 Behrensstrasse).

War Memorial • *Stauffenberg Strasse 14* • This building was headquarters of the German Armed Forces' Supreme Command through World War II, but now houses a memorial to the German officers who were shot for being part of the anti-Hitler uprising of July 20, 1944. The building's courtyard is filled with impressive statues and commemorative plaques.

Schloss Charlottenburg • *Charlottenburg Palace and Museums, Luisenplatz* • This palace is the finest example of royal Prussian architecture in West Berlin. Originally a relatively small country house in 1695, the huge palace that eventually evolved took over a century to complete. The historic **royal apartments** offer an exciting array of styles from over 200 years ranging from Baroque to Biedermeier. The beautiful **palace park,** behind the building, is intricately laid out in the baroque style, with finely clipped hedges and "embroidery" flowerbeds. A cafe overlooks the orangery. Also situated in and around the Palace are four of Berlin's most important museums. The **Prehistoric Museum** is housed in the palace itself. It includes archaeological objects from the early Middle Ages back to prehistoric times. Across the street from the palace stands the **Egyptian Museum.** Although many of the museum's pieces were lost in World War II, the present collection comprehensively illustrates the development of Egyptian art and culture. Also here is the 3000-year-old bust of Queen

Nefertiti. Next door to the Egyptian Museum is the **Museum of Antiquities and Treasury.** Originating in 1830, the collection has grown to become one of the most important in Europe. The concentration is on small European, Greek, and Roman art objects, such as gold and silver works, small bronzes, vases, cameos, gems, and glass.

Museum Center in Dahlem • *Arnimallee 23–27* • In the fashionable southwest district of the city known as Dahlem stands this vast complex of state museums. The Dahlem museums were the only museums in Berlin to escape damage in the war, and their various collections have subsequently been left to grow at a swift rate. At present the complex includes the following separate museums: the **Painting Gallery,** which exhibits a wonderfully balanced collection ranging from panel-paintings of the 13th century to the great masterworks of Europe through the late 18th century; the **Sculpture Department,** with a fine assemblage covering the 3rd through the 18th centuries; the **Museum of Islamic and Indian Art,** which is the only such collection in Germany; the **Ethnographic Museum,** with comprehensive collections devoted to Africa, the South Seas, and the Americas, which in Europe is only equalled by the ethnographic department in the British Museum; and the **Cabinet of Prints and Engravings.**

Pergamon Museum • *1–3 Bodestasse* • is an overwhelming arts project. It is in what was the east and used to be the prime attraction for visitors from the west. It is vast, somewhat neglected, and contains many of the greatest treasures of the ancient world. Don't fail to see it. A tour will take a full day.

Bauhaus Archiv-Museum • *Bauhaus Archive Museum* • Here is an interesting and eclectic collection of the products of this famous school from the 1920s and 30s. Furniture, architecture, textiles, paintings, graphics, and housewares are among the represented arts.

Olympiastadion • *Olympic Stadium, Olympischer Platz* • Built for the 11th Olympic Games in 1936, this grand oval has room for 75,000 spectators.

Boat Tours • A boat ride on one of the many lakes or rivers in the huge forest areas outside the city center to the west is a pleasant alternative to a bus tour. Most visitors are unaware of these expansive forests and waterways, so you'll be more likely to spend this time with a high concentration of native Berliners. Over 70 boats a day ply the waters of the Havel River, Tegeler See, and Wannsee, and they stop at all the best places. You can even glide over to Potsdam by boat. The biggest of many shiplines is Stern and Kreisschiffahrt, Sachtleben Strasse 60 (Telephone: 803–8750 or 810–0040).

Excursions

Grunewald • *Green Forest* • The Grunewald has restaurants, the 430-foot **Grunewald observation tower,** a 450-year-old royal hunting lodge recast as an **art and hunting museum,** and miles of lakeside vistas and enchanting walks. Perched on a 250-foot hill, the tower offers a magnificent view of the Havel and Wannsee. The lodge has a beautiful spiral staircase, a scattering of Old Dutch masters, and during the season, an idyllic series of courtyard concerts.

Pfaueninsel • *Peacock Island* • This is a fascinating seahorse-shaped islet in the Havel, with the ruins of an **Italian castle** (a pseudorelic, since the romantics built it that way on purpose), groves of California pines, vividly-colored Asian ginkgos, and majestic Lebanese cedars. Also there's a dairy, a hunter's shelter, a memorial to Queen Louise, and dozens of strutting peacocks. Take the S-Bahn to Wannsee Station, and stroll the beautiful footpath through the woods from Konigstrasse.

Tegel Schloss and See • *Tegel Castle and Lake* • This charming estate and its mirror-smooth lake are easily accessible. About 40 minutes outside the city by U-Bahn, this colorful and historic forest inn is the city's oldest, dating from 1550. You may tour the buildings (summer only) or go down to the docks to be ferried out to one of the many rock-and-grass islands. Several interesting lakeside restaurants are also a plus.

HOTELS

Berlin's chambermaids fluff up perhaps 35,000 pillows. Still, it is so popular you should prebook your space in High Season; in winter many hoteliers will offer a 20% discount. Groups and congresses dominate the mood and treatment. When you check in, in all but a few of the top-line hostelries no one from reception will show you to your room. Generally the quality is adequate; some hew the narrowest line possible when it comes to living space. A common wheeze has it that a pitifully crippled Muncherner was seen one morning by his friend, hobbling along the Kurfurstendamm. *"Gott im Himmel!"* cried the Berliner. "What happened to you? Were you hit by a freight train?" "No," replied the friend from Munich, "I just spent a night in your most modern hotel." Calling them "cramped" would be akin to dismissing the Himalayas as "tall."

☆☆☆☆☆ **Bristol Kempinski** • remains one of Europe's tip-top hotels—an institution with historic roots. Restaurant in impressive Berlin style; air cooling, which usually is enough on all but the muggiest days; all baths marble; fresh carpets and furniture, double-glaze windows plus a fortune in behind-the-scene updatings. Superb public areas; outstanding grill; fun-filled bar with dancing; sparkling, oh-zoned jetstream pool and sauna; flawless service.

Intercontinental • with a glass pyramid in its forecourt, undertook an expansion spree a while back that gave it more rooms but not significantly bigger ones. In the process, several restaurants (Hugenotten is tops), a Bierkeller, pool, sauna, 50 suites, and a shopping arcade materialized, the newer wing being my choice for overnighting. It's vast, functional, and performs its duty without a trace of intimacy.

Grand Esplanade • fresh from the builders, offers a mighty presence with space bank for 800 overnighters, Harry's Bar, Orangerie dining orchard, Eck-Kneipe for snacks, pool, solarium, and fitness center. V-shaped construction; modernistic furnishings suggesting that this might be an office in which you also may sleep; coolish overall.

Steigenberger • is another whopper built for wholesale sleeping. Also within are the Park restaurant and the Berliner Stube, 2 bars, a piano lounge, 10 shops, a swimming pool in Japanese garden, and basement parking; living units have bath, color TV, radio, and minibar. Excellent concierge as well as other key service personnel. Residing in midcity, it is a strong contender for the first-class (not deluxe) traveler. Some efforts by this chain are excellent, while others are blatantly commercial.

★★★ **Palace** • sited conveniently in the Europa Center, is rich in decor. Spacious, elegant lobby; adjoining dark-hued bar combining English Establishment with Erstwhile Empire; numerous vitrines recalling images of The Old Curiosity Shop; woody ground-floor grill with open rotisserie; restaurant up one flight to a soft green and blue haven; easy access to the nearby public pool and other thermic therapies.

★★★ **Ambassador** • offers beautiful public rooms, perhaps the most alluring in the metropolis; entrance lounge with spherical copper hearth; captivating canopied dining quarter with deftly prepared but comparatively high-priced culinations; popular bar and grill with quiet patio, flowered chairs, and garden setting; terrace-rimmed coffee shop for nibblers; modern penthouse swimming pool with slide-away roof, plus adjoining sauna, massage parlors, and solarium; beauty salon; eye-catching murals in corridors; woody tones throughout; TV with every latchkey. Somewhat expensive, but not unreasonable considering the rewards in color, flair, comfort, and service.

★★ **Savoy** • is an excellent buy for traditionalists. L-A-R-G-E rooms, all with bath and shower and most with twin basins; doubles ending in ''10'' particularly worthy; casual-style restaurant and bar with snacks available; courteous concierge and reception staffs. Very good indeed for Old-World seekers.

☆☆ **Schweizerhof** • struts an imposing stance across the street from the Intercontinental with which it shares top management. It is always jammed with conventioneers and commercial wayfarers; newer wing for 350 more occupants, plus the Old Marketplace restaurant with cobblestones, streetlamps, and fountain, Le Mascaron nightspot and bar, a banquet hall, and its very own swimming pool. Handsome lobby; spacious corner-sited breakfast garden; wood-shingled salon; chalet-style grill with adjoining 3-table Schutzenstubli and the Zunftstube extension; Wappen Bar with Swiss heraldry; 2 garages; 100% air-chilled; full range of contemporary trappings from Naugahyde furniture to multichannel radios.

Berlin • rates well as a value stop. Choose the newer sector here. Superb grill; breakfast feast table comprising eggs, herrings, 2 hot meats, cereals, yogurts, ordinary and exotic fruits, salads, juices, breads, and a parade of additional slimmers. They believe in starting you off properly each morning.

Excelsior • modern and sleek, is within walking distance of the center; in its fresh shell are several dining areas (including the colorful Peacock with a 25-foot-long breakfast buffet) plus banquet and conference facilities. The accommodations are simple, clean, narrow, and contemporary.

Queen's Crest • resides 3 stops by U-Bahn from the main part of town. It is inclined toward motelishness.

Penta • offers 425 air-conditioned units with minibar, TV and radio, plus a *bierstube,* a cocktail lounge, restaurants, and boutiques. This chain, linked together through the cooperation of several airlines, delivers outstanding value, flair, and comfort for the moderate billings.

Sylter Hof • provides an overall feeling of Frenchiness rather than Germanic qualities. White, clean-lined restaurant; posh Casino Bar; corridors with handsome bas-relief panels, heavy draperies, and mirrors; colored towels furled in pea-pod-size bathrooms; sleek appointments that are beginning to show some wear.

Seehof • has a blue and white checkerboard facade; enchanting situation with restaurant, lamplit terrace, bar, and covered, glass-lined swimming pool all oriented toward the lovely Lietzensee (town lake). It is so thoroughly winning in so many, many ways that one wonders how the designer possibly could have sketched its accommodations in such ridiculously paltry dimensions.

Hamburg • greets you with a canopied entrance; large blue-carpeted lounge; nice copper-tone bar; fresh dining salon; quick-meal corner; flowers everywhere for brighteners. Its units also were planned for small-boned trippers.

Stoessensee • beside its namesake lake bordering Grunewald's greenery, comes up with 2-score functional but uninspired abodes. Watersports (lake or covered pool), tennis, and sauna close by; adjoining supermarket; spartan lobby; midget bar; limp restaurant-cum-clubroom; somber, linoleum-lined corridors. All units are decorated in the Middle Mundane; #1001, for example, provides orange walls, a beige carpet, tartan chairs and sofa, an indestructible table, a minikitchenette, and an alcove sleeping nook. Minimum stay 2 weeks; 40% discount applied to a month or more; bus #94 routed to the doin's.

After the above, our choices would run as follows: **Curator** (new and close to the Kurfurstendamm), **Ibis** (non-central situation near the bus terminus, but handy to the international exhibitions at the Funkturm and new ICC), **Bremen** (above a filling-station complex, useful midcity site; penthouse breakfast room with open terrace for snacks; no bar or restaurant; 44 of its 48 units earmarked as singles), **Am Zoo, Am Studio** (a study in miniaturism; clean as a surgeon's pinkie; low rates; conscientious management), **Steglitz International** (in an of-

fice and shopping complex; 2 restaurants, bar, sauna, fitness room; modern units
with radio and color TV), **President** (behind the Sylterhof in an area of urban
growth; supermodernistic in structure and efficiency), **Arosa** (appealing, but
surely one of the narrowest-gauge hostelries I've ever inspected), **Hervis** (a 10-
minute stroll from Checkpoint Charlie; ample lebensraum; very kind staff), **Plaza**
(140 rooms, all with bath or showers; low tabs in Low Seasons; all in all, pretty
slim pickin's). **Savigny** (routine), **Lichtburg** or its sister the **Franke** (substantial but commercial).

★★ **Gehrhus** • is in a special category, occupying a suburban site about
20 minutes out in the Grunewald district. Here's a castle structure (it's called a
schloss-hotel) that was brightened up and touched up in a most ingratiating way,
revealing the best of its aristocratic origins.

In what was East Berlin, I've already mentioned in the introduction the
handful of hotels that are attractive. More are being built, but for a few more
seasons I believe most visitors would prefer to reside in the western flank of the
city.

RESTAURANTS

☆☆☆ **Alt Luxemburg** • *Pestalozzistr. 70* • attracts serious gourmets for
the presentation and flavor of its modern-style gastronomy. In fact, the tilt here
is more toward French than Luxembourgoise. Very able chef in the international
mold. Attractive setting and stunning prices. Best to reserve well in advance.

☆☆☆ **Florian** • *52 Grolmanstrasse* • draws many from the theatrical set
to its elegant tables near the Savignyplatz. Try the fish in a light mustard topping for a lighter dish or the duck for traditional German flavors.

★★★ **Big Window** • *49 Joachim-Friedrich Str.* • is modest in concept as
well as in price. It is known only by the Berlin cognoscenti (Tel. 892 58 36);
be sure to reserve in advance. The whole shebang is only about 10 yards deep
with tables on either side of a center aisle, kitch on the walls, and wonders from
the kitchen. The affable proprietor, Ivan, will explain (in English) his native
Armenian specialties as well as his own adaptations of them. But please take
our word for it and try the spareribs followed by his Lule Kebab with Lavasch.
The latter is composed of seasoned strips of marinated meat grilled inside a
large crepe. Tear off a morsel of the bread, enfold a nibble of lamb, sprinkle
on the dust of dried levantine berries, and prepare your taste buds for a culinary
treat that you will long remember.

☆☆☆☆ **Rockendorf's** • *1 Dusterhaupt Str.* • has an outskirts location but
a very "in" position among cost-is-no-object diners who don't mind the romp
almost out to Tegel in order to enjoy its blue-ribbon modernistic gastronomy.

Appropriate to its agrestic location and mood, the wild duck is a favorite, although it is lightened of its traditional presentation with overtures to contemporary fashion in high-style cookery. Berry-soaked venison is also superb in season. Prices are pretty fancy, too. If you go, be sure to reserve.

☆☆☆ **An der Rehwiese** • *Matterhornstr. 101* • is not Swiss (as is the next entry) despite its address. The cooking is contemporary, light, and very fine as today's interpretation of German cuisine. In season, try the river salmon with broccoli; masterful. Be sure to reserve ahead.

★★ **Tessiner Stuben** • *Bleibreustr. 33* • and the **Chalet Suisse** • *Im Jagen 5* • both evoke, of course, the muses of Helvetia. Decoratively, too, the inspiration is reinforced by rough stucco walls, wrought iron, copper pots, garlic garlands, and other touches of Alpine lore.

☆☆☆ **Zlata Praha** • one of this reporter's beloved Czech-Points, wins the esteem of Berliners. Two simple chambers; overworked waiters in trim waistcoats and velvet cummerbunds; little English spoken. Slovakian specialties, including Prague ham in a pastry shell, pussta hirtenfleisch (shepherd's meat with dumplings), and rumpsteak lesco (pronounced "laycho") with hot peppers; fascinating sirner paska dessert (a cheese loaf with a chilled tutti-frutti complex). Try—if you dare—the ultra bitter Pilsner Urquell beer, which takes 10 to 15 minutes to draw from the tap (the Slavic toast is "na zdravi").

Ponte Vecchio • *Spielhagenstr. 3* • is worth knowing about for a change of gastronomic pace, Italian style. Everyone seems to agree that it is top of the Latin list. The chef inclines more toward Tuscan dishes.

☆☆ **Conti-Fischstuben** • in the Ambassador Hotel, is a prime catch for seafood anglers. The decor is thick on marine lore; a sampling might cost $65 per angler, with wine.
Churrasco, an Argentinian harnessmate of similar *ranchos* in Frankfurt, Munich, Hamburg, and Bremen. The multitude of restaurants in the **I-Punkt** building, also called **Europa Center?** Punkt, in our opinion. **Holland-Stubl** cooks up nutrients drawn from the traditional Dutch and Indonesian tables. **Fofi's** (Fasanenstr.) gained a degree of fame when Michael Dukakis popped in.

Hardy Wine Restaurant • is a veteran from yesteryear. Limited menu but unlimited grape larder; enchanting turn-of-the century atmosphere; go late when it zings. This one can be fun if you are with a German-speaking group.

Le Bou Bou • rates as a full-scale booboo, in my opinion. It tries to recall an earlier era with modern affectations. I found slaphappy service and larrikin attitudes.

☆☆☆ **Kempinski's** • grill often dishes out some mighty savory viands (especially those sauteed *scampi*). In the hotel dining room do yourself a favor by ordering the kalbfleischrollchen (tender veal niblets bathed in a Boursin cheese and whipped-spinach sauce). Incidentally, Kempinski's **"Funkturm"** is Berlin's answer to the Eiffel Tower restaurant of Paris; about 150 feet up a steel structure by elevator; magnificent view; definitely worth a visit by everyone, if only for tea or a snack.

Palais am Funkturm • in the Fair Grounds is mass-production service in a cavernous exhibition hall.

Berlin Hotel's • grill has a mighty reputation locally. Sometimes it is indeed splendid, but on other occasions I've found the service so totally bumbling as to be downright comic. The food, however, is above average always. **Four Seasons** • in the same hotel, is cheaper, less presumptuous, worse gastronomically.

Huthmacher • proffers big restaurant upstairs with agreeable decor, and bakery-coffee shop downstairs; piano and violin at teatime.

Heinz Holl • (for steaks) hits the steer's eye; flavorful filets on a wooden platter; chummy ambience; only 6 tables; candles in hurricane lamps; sand-colored banquettes. Your waitress will serve you with taurine grace.

Wannsee-Terrassen • is lakeside in the Wannsee District (25 minutes and about 28 DM each way by taxi from the center, or 2.50 DM by S-Bahn); heavenly, open, 3-tiered terrace on a hill, lovely panorama, and mediocre cookery at modest prices; don't miss it, despite its poor kitchen, if the weather is fair. You can have a swim at a sandy beach here, too.

Weinstuben? **Habel,** near Am Roseneck is the choice, with **Kurpfalz** (Wilmersdorfer Str. 93) second.
Cafes? The **Kempinski,** on the boulevard side, takes the honors; excellent for snacks. **Kranzler** (begun in 1834 by an Austrian baker) is very good; from its perch you can command an excellent view of the Kurfurstendamm and Joachimstaler Strasse. **Das Cafehaus-Moehring** • *Kurfurstendamm 234* • perks brightly in an attractive building dating back to 1901. Large pillared room with moss-green bankettes, brass sconces, and paisley walls; back sector with greenery and more tables; delightfully robust shelves of pastries where you can feel your girth expanding as you merely shop for a goody. On the same street at #184 **Bovril** is a converted house with excellent food and a friendly mood.

NIGHT LIFE

A plethora. There are about 220 honest-to-no-goodness nighteries in the heart of the city alone. At **Ku'dorf** • *15 Joachimstaler* • there are two dozen taverns offering almost every brand of German beer. **Sperlingsgasse** is more of the same, where the mood is equally jovial. Counting bars and hideaways in the outlying suburbia, approximately 500 clubs operate, catering to every need, whim, or kink. The entrance fees or cover charges hover between $2.50 and $8, roughly paralleling the cost of a scotch-and soda. As in most after-dark dens, beer is cheap and champagne is hell on the budget.

Among the In Set disco-hubs, the innermost clique gather at **Annabel's,** unrelated to the London shrine of nightlife that bears the same name. Cosmopolitan crowd; modish music; reasonable prices. Maybe you can pry your way in if it is not a busy status-Saturday night. **VIP** is gaining ground with young people who are VIPs only to themselves. **Metropol,** if you don't hanker for intimacy, is your spot—with a mere 43,000 square feet of floor space on which to strut your stuff. The footage is the *only* thing square about it, since it swings with about the same wild abandon as Gotham's Studio 54. You'll find a restaurant, movie, music hall, and theater all at the same Nollendorfplatz spread. Disco doin's from Wed. through Sat. days; special features on other nights.

Among discos for the young and/or animated, try the **Beehive,** stainless-steel **Ca Chauffe, Milch Bar, Orpheus,** or **Kumpelnest 3000.**

Keese features the "Ball Paradox." Ladies of the house phone male guests at their tables and invite them to dance—a scene straight out of *Cabaret.* **Dollywood** is the SRO gayest blade in town. While the show reflects gay preferences, the audience is drawn from the general public. **La Belle Epoque Travestie** and **La Vie En Rose** are other go-ahead nightspots for fringe benefits of this variety. **Chez Nous** has 2 elaborately decorated rooms with quilted and draped walls and ceilings in the style of what might be called Louis XIV½. You'll find fancy candelabra, a gold grand piano, a bar, and—incongruously—a bright honky-tonk jukebox not quite concealed between the 2 ornate sancta. There's also quite an assortment of companionship available or just on show. **Kleist Casino** (fondly labeled "K.C.") also is clad in the gayest of moods. Incidentally, there are about 55 homosexual clubs in this city.

Big Eden (Kurfurstendamm at Knesebeckstrasse, and not the same as the next spot) is chiefly for kids; inexpensive; huge dimensions; a 400-speaker stereo unit. **New Eden** (different building) offers a glass-lined sidewalk cafe and a spacious interior with ultradim illumination and iron-lung ventilation; 2 midget bars; ear-rending music; intermittent melodies by a 5-piece combo. **Coupe 77** remains one of my favorite local watering places. Interior designed as an antique railroad coach; brass lamps, polished woods, quilted leather benches; disc music only; inexpensive drinks. **Big Apple** is a center for punks and mods; hot music, Cokes, beer.

Berlin has a pair of **casinos** *(Spielbank)* now. The newest is atop the **Hotel Stadt Berlin** in Alexanderplatz. The older player is in the Europa Center rolling from 3 p.m.–5 a.m. Roulette and blackjack are available, too.

Porn? Stay away from the live shows as they are often sham acts. Film theaters—myriad in number, vast in choice—charge from 6–10 DM for about as much pepper as you can take—and are *they* hot stuff. Wow!

The most popular rendezvous for prostitutes is now the midriff of Kurfurstendamm, near Lehniner Platz and Uhlandstrasse. It is most heavily patronized from 11:30 p.m. onward. Mobilized *Madchens* usually cruise along Strasse des 17 Juni. While the standard fee is about 50 marks, the unknowing visitor is often persuaded to part with a higher figure. In general, the caliber of this group is brassy, coarse, and very, very tough. Other pickups may be found in such places as the **Scotch 13, La Strada,** and **Mambo.** Striptease shows in all; clip practices prevailing and often perilous for visitors; B-gals housebound until dawn's early light, but freelancers usually available right now.

SHOPPING

The prices of most commodities in West Berlin now correspond with those in the rest of Free Germany. In porcelains, **Staatliche Porzellan-Manufaktur Berlin** carries the most interesting specialties; its dinner sets are beautiful; go to the factory (Wegelystrasse 1) or salesroom (Kurfurstendamm 26a); 25% to 50% off on 2nd and 3rd qualities at the factory only. Optical goods? **Sohnges** now has branches at Kurfurstendamm 139 and 210, and Reichsstrasse 83. For department-store buying, it's a toss-up between Kurfurstendamm's youthful **Wertheim** and the more traditional **KaDeWe** ("Kaufhaus des Westens"); if you pick the latter, don't miss walking up (not riding up!) at least 3 floors; a local institution. For cutlery, **J. A. Henckels** (see "Frankfurt") offers a branch at Kurfurstendamm 33 and another at Schlosstr. 100. For antiques Keithstrasse is the street, with 12 or 14 shops nearly in a row. For books, **Marga Schoeller Bucherstube** (Knesebeckstrasse 12) and **Kiepert** (Hardenbergstrasse 4-5) are attractive and versatile; you'll find scores of new U.S. titles and reprints.

BONN recently celebrated its 2000th birthday. (For the occasion, incidentally, it created an "Eau de Bonn" to rival the scent of Cologne.) It boasts Poppelsdorf Palace, the Rhenish Land Museum, the versatile Zoological Research Institute and Museum, a garden designed just for the blind, and Beethoven as its most famous son—but midtown is a rat race. A frenetic and impersonal atmosphere pervades it. An incredible number of cars jam its streets en route to other destinations; 36 times per day, 3 railway crossings halt traffic for an average of 20 minutes each hour. (To relieve this maddening congestion a *2nd* bridge across the Rhine was built); 36,000 vehicles per day funnel through and clog the Koblenzer Gate along the main north-south link between Cologne and Coblenz. And if this isn't enough, rain falls on its unfortunate inhabitants 162 days per year! Acknowledging that some visitors may want (or have) to stay here, the Steigenberger hotel chain (Frankfurter Hof and a peck of others) operates a sleeping factory in the aggressively ugly City Center—a crassful, classless urban subdivision that reflects far more haste than taste. Although the massive **Steigenberger** functions as an efficient institution, it performs with so little inspiration that it remains a letdown. Passably interesting vista from the 18th-floor Ambassador Restaurant (where the window tables are usually reserved for diplomats); adjoining bar and neighboring swimming pool; Atrium Coffee Shop a tepid and listless decorative blend; a megalopolis of boutiques, kiosks, and service facilities skirting the ground level. Spacious studio singles—a trademark of German hostelries where the solitary executive roams interminably in homeless tangents; light, well-furnished, mod-school doubles, especially roomy in the corner accommodations; the twins ending in "23" are best. While nothing is overtly offensive here, my own impression is one of consuming boredom. The **Pullman Konigshof,** more traditional in tone, shoulders the riverbank. Adequate shelter and no more. The midtown **Schlosspark** is small and clean; it boasts a swimming pool that might be described in the same way. In the diplomatic enclave of *Bad Godesberg,* a mile or so along ''Embassy Row,'' the **Rheinhotel Dreesen** has a beautiful riverscape command but a lead-heavy air. **Rheinland** offers 50 bedrooms with private bath; another routine hatrack. The **Parkhotel Zum Kurfursten,** at *Frankenthal* on the Bonn–Strasbourg highway, got high but well-spent marks from an Austrian reader who raves about its ''food, service, and exceptional standards.'' For additional Bonn-*mots,* refer to nearby Cologne—a sweeter bonbon any day or night.

For dining try the nicely old-fashioned **Wirthaus St., Michael Halbedel's,** or the outlying and costly **Le Marron.**

BREMEN, a seaport of the Hanseatic period, is also known for its musical associations. The Market Place is surrounded by buildings that are eight centuries old. Be sure to visit Bottcherstrasse and the Schnoor for antiquity, inns, galleries, and boutiques.

☆☆☆☆ **Park** • (if you've got wheels and want to drive to your hotel) is majestically situated on 500 acres of Hanseatic real estate, fronted by a small lake and backed by a prairie-size lawn. Just 5 minutes from the station, but celestially quiet; 100 rooms and a trio of suites on the Paul Bunyan scale; dancing nightly in the Halali Bar; jog-togs or bikes available for fitness types; the thinking is so lavish there's even a special alfresco ''Hund Bar'' to furnish tidbits to your dogs. Unquestionably the leader, and a beautiful one.

Plaza • is a modernistic product from Canadian Pacific. Vast silo-style lobby; generally cool decor; quality bedroom textiles.

Crest • probably offers the next most comfort. The drawback here, however, is that it is out of the city heartbeat, so once again a car would be required.

Mercure-Columbus • in a century-old shell, offers an appealing lobby plus a few annual updatings; 170 tiny units with 110 baths; 2 restaurants and bar; it's mood is commercial.

Zur Post • darker than its neighbor, is adequate but nothing more.

Restaurants:

★★ **Essig Haus** • with its venerable Hanseatic woodwork is liked by many; ownership by the Parkhotel. Not as expensive as one would think.

★★ **Schnoor 2** • which takes its name from its address, is extremely well regarded; 400-year-old gabled house in snazzy rustic tones; certainly tops in eye appeal, with cookery just a chef's pinch less savory than Essig Haus.

★ **Beck's** • beer-sponsored, is a colorful multistory house in the Schnoor district and has several sectors with varying themes. The meals are honest for the very modest outlay.

Grashoff's Bistro • is very refined, rather expensive, and recommendable if you don't care whether you're in Germany or France.

★ **Ratskeller** • is a historic site for a peek and a nibble. It's where the Faust legend is said to have been originated centuries ago.

Alt-Bremen • recalling the city from 1750 to 1850, sounds touristy, but it is really fun.

COCHEM **Alte Thorschenke** is a sweet little 14th-century inn by the river with an excellent wine restaurant. Many four-poster beds available, including ones occupied by Maria Theresia, Napoleon, and Goethe. The same interests run the **Park Von Landenberg,** next to the castle where much of the local wine is produced. **Germania** offers a grander atmosphere and the **Brixiade** is more modernistic. Pick your room carefully in this town if you are a light sleeper. Road traffic can raise a horrendous din.

COLOGNE's modern midtown towers contrast dramatically with its beautifully preserved Cathedral, a magnificent structure, the largest Gothic building in the world. I'd venture that one can't appreciate the colossal size and the detailed craftsmanship of the stonework without making the climb (20 minutes, 509 steps) up to the topmost belfry. The views alone are spellbinding, even if your tongue hangs to ground level. Just recently a dozen romanesque churches, which had been closed for preservation, have been restored and opened to the public. (St. Pantaleon, with its 10th-century cloister, is the oldest in Germany.) The massive unveiling suddenly makes Cologne one of Europe's most important centers of medieval architecture and ecclesiastical art. The big draws otherwise are the radically daring Museum Ludwig, the associated Wallraf-Richartz collection, the theater-opera house, the playhouse, the Roman Germanic Museum surrounding the Dionysos Mosaic, plus a splendid gem display, and Phantasialand, the local answer to the Disney realms.

☆☆☆ **Excelsior Ernst** • is the city's foremost address for overnighting; it faces the Cathedral square. Continual updating campaigns; appealing polished-wood, oh-so-richly elegant Hanse Stuben grill, one of the nicest rooms in all Germany; lobby also in Hanseatic tones; every bedchamber sparkling. Antebellum decor; cozy twins and nice apartments; very smoothly managed.

☆☆☆ **Intercontinental** • has established itself as the local leader for modernists. It is certainly the choice, too, for anyone hoping to avoid the carnival atmosphere at the fringes of the Cathedral—skaters, sidewalk painters, saxophone soloists as well as busloads of sandal-clad gawkers. Moreover, if you are a shopper, this is the prime district for such pastimes. Wood-pillared lobby glowing with globe lamps and cushy accoutrements; savvy front-desk team; ground-floor Brasserie and Interview Imbibery dispensing succulent Thuringer sausage and potent martinis, respectively and respectfully; vistaful rooftop Belvedere Restaurant and Bar with terpsichore on tap; pool, solarium, sun terrace, and sizzling sauna; bevy of boutiques; subterranean parking quarters. Recommendable.

☆☆☆ **Dom** • remains one of the better traditional hostelries in the region and it is professionally maintained. Modernized baths; color TV and English video. In this traffic-occluded town, its 650-car underground garage, with direct entry to the hotel, comes as a blessing to anyone on wheels. Cheery restaurant; pleasant summer terrace; spacious accommodations. Excellent location if you hanker to be tete-a-tete to the Cathedral clamor.

Holiday Inn Crowne Plaza • is a block of 300 tiny bedchambers, a pair of restaurants and bars, a swimming pool, and ample parking space. Fresh, clean and adequate.

Maritim • is also a youngster, and in many ways I prefer it to the above candidate.

Hyatt Regency • is over on the east Rhine bank, next to the exhibition center. Dramatic modern architecture employing Hyatt "fixtures" such as a splendid glass atrium, cascades, green foliage, and grand space concepts in public areas. Bedrooms are spare in amplitude. Pool and fitness complex. Very good for its congressional purposes.

☆ **Ramada Renaissance** • recently debuted with 250 units, a gastronomic restaurant (their foreign chefs are often excellent), a pool, and fitness facilities. The lounges are fresh and contemporary; bedrooms are well outfitted.

Restaurants

☆☆☆ **Excelsior Ernst's Hanse Stuben** • is easily my choice as the most elegant hotel restaurant. The cuisine more than matches the glorious setting.

★★★★ **Chez Alex** • not only is outstanding for its French-style cooking, it is also highly attractive. You'll probably like it as a change of pace from German vittles.

☆☆ **Bei Rino** • serves a mouth-melting turbot with rose-pepper, the spice that was the rage in French kitchens almost a decade ago. Whether *vieille cuisine* or *nouvelle,* it's still a *bon marche.*

★ **Die Bastei** • is touristic and possibly a bit naughty. There's a charge for tapwater ($2) and rather shocking surprises if you stray from the menu with its listed prices. Elevated, glassed-in building jutting out almost into the waters of the Rhine; split-level dining; tea music through the gloaming, dinner chords from 7:30 p.m.–10 p.m., and dance melodies thereafter.

Weinhaus im Walfisch • the choice of many U.S. service families, offers 2 floors and tavernish, 2-fisted cookery. Built in 1750, it has been a restaurant continuously since 1837.

For local color, the **Fruh** (to the rear of the Dom-Hotel) or the **Paffgen** couldn't be more characteristic; waiters in dark-blue shirts; no tablecloths, no fripperies; crowded with *Herren* and *Hausfrauen* drinking special Cologne beer, and gossiping like mad; go to either for a sausage, a beer, and to watch the locals unwind. **Alt Koln,** next to the Excelsior Ernst, slaps on Old Cologne in 4711 predictable ways. Aromatic of spit-roasted bantams; fun if your tastes run to corny. At all costs avoid the local *Kolscher Kaviar,* not to be confused with sturgeon eggs. This preparation is heavier than a shotput—a thick, tough red sausage laced with fat and garnished with raw onion. A real yuk if I ever had one.

Cafe Reichard • possibly occupies the most coveted piece of real estate in the Federal Republic, with a glass-sheathed terrace for Cathedral vistas plus a handsome inner salon. As for the food, I think it would be best if you could forget it. Go for the view and feel charity for the chef.

East of midtown in the *Merheim* district, the **Goldener Pflug** is as attractive to the eye as it is to the palate. The turbot is delicate and reasonably priced, but the lobster is outlandish for North American diners used to New England billings. An all-out repast for two can easily dent $350.

CONSTANCE This ancient city of religious, military, and political importance since before the 10th century takes its name from the lake at its doorstep (which Germans call the Bodensee). A Roman fort stood at the lake's spillway into the Rhine. After a brief walk along its bridge and through the Old Town, you will have absorbed its better part—a foray which should take less than an hour. The **Insel,** with roots going back to the 13th century as a Dominican cloister, is the best hotel, but it certainly is no rave. Just a short drive down the pike is *Lindau,* which is far more attractive. Sightseeing here should include a browse through the town and a look at the port with its lighthouse and towering entry pillar. Then stroll to the nearby Rathaus; be sure to see both sides, one with a covered staircase and the other without. Surrounding the center are numerous inns, shops with cheveroned shutters, fish terraces, and the usual plethora of tour buses in high season. The **Bayerischer Hof** is the leading luxury hotel and the **Walliser Stube** is the outstanding restaurant in the area.

What draws most travelers to the lake is the romantic garden on the island of *Mainau,* which can be reached by car, by foot, and by lakeboat. The natural paradise occupies more than 100 acres of ever-changing pageantry—600,000 new bulbs every autumn, 200,000 pansies and primroses, 200 manifestations of dahlias, hyacinths, daffodils, palms, bananas, and an exotic array of unexpected subtropical plants. Viewers will discover more than 30,000 rose bushes of 1200 varieties! There are marvelously whimsical (and colossal) flower sculptures, innovative creations that awe adults and tickle children. Crowning the crest of the terraced park is the baroque castle occupied by the Bernadotte family. Dining and snacking facilities are available, so plan a long day here. In any season this is a *must.*

Psst . . . My German chums won't like to hear it, but by far the best accommodation in the region is on the Swiss side of the lake at the little fairy-tale village of *Gottlieben,* where the ★★★★★ **Drachenburg** and ★★★★ **Waaghaus** are among the most enchanting inns I have ever seen in my travels. More modest accommodation can be found in the nearby hamlet of *Ermatingen,* also on the inner estuary.

DUSSELDORF   is Germany's center of haute couture; beautiful clothes (on beautiful mannequins). It is also one of the world's more expensive cities. The airport offers a rail spur to midtown, and this melds conveniently into the continent's express Intercity system of trains. The main street, called "Ko," runs along a lovely waterway; many hotels; good restaurants, Benrath Castle, scads of churches and art galleries, a revolving 540-foot tower (Rheinturm) that is part of an intricate geophysical clock system, a modern 4-story apartment-style bordello with 228 "tenants" and 8000 "visitors" a day, cosmopolitan citizens, and handsome environs, one of which includes the Minidomm, elf-size scale-downs of world-famous architectural wonders from Gothic cathedrals to Kennedy Airport (open daily from 9 a.m.–11 p.m.; between Dusseldorf and Mulheim). While the Kunst (Art) Museum is noteworthy, those with specialized tastes might enjoy the fabulous glass exhibition next door (at Ehrenhof 1); the range runs from antiquity through Tiffany to contemporary pieces by Steuben, Kosta, and other greats.

☆☆☆☆ **Breidenbacher Hof** • is a classic that has been lavishly outfitted in sparkling attire. This one, from cellar to roof, is a little jewel. For traditionalists—as opposed to modernists, nothing in the city proper can beat it. Elegant reception and lobby salon with select exotica from the orient for highlights; bar-lounge with wood paneling, black leather, and pastoral paintings; marvelous, cozy Eck ("corner") with imaginative selections on a small menu. Fine concierge and staff; grill-lounge with cognac walls and fine Italian mahogany furniture; quartet of gorgeous suites; many little touches so many houses lack.

☆☆☆ **Park-Hotel** • also has been beautified. The lobby, lounges, and especially the suites, are exceptional today with many more renewals each season; superb gourmet-level dining room enriched with wood carvings; Etoile Bar. All bedrooms with quality furnishings, full carpeting, and good baths; streetside units soundproofed. Director Robert Schaller has done wonders here; eminently satisfactory.

☆ **Savoy** • is first-class rather than deluxe. Restaurant with adjoining bar; all 130 units on the small side except for a few corner doubles with wraparound windows and ample space. The swimming pool, sauna, and garage are added pluses for a midcity hotel.

Esplanade • is in the same category and under the Savoy banner. Quieter situation; similar to the Savoy in most aspects; heated indoor swimming pool available to guests at no extra charge (a privilege shared by the next-door **Atlantik,** which is lower priced and might be a worthy bet for budgeteers); sauna (supplement added); woody restaurant-cum-grill; grandmotherly breakfast quarter.

Borsen • a breakfast-only hostelry, is in the same chain as the Savoy; it employs the same decorator, but it is simpler.

Eden • flowers with 90 small but fresh-faced pods, and 70 private baths. Many visitors are especially fond of #264, a corner double with rococollaborations.

Uebachs • attracts an older clientele of loyal wayfarers. You'll probably like its overall feeling of cleanliness and puffy-pillow snap.

☆☆ **Hilton's** • 12-story, 383-room, fully air-conditioned outskirter resides adjacent to the Congress Hall. Expansive off-lobby shopping gallery; sauna; health center; beauty parlor; swimming pool; thumpingly expensive turn-of-the-century San Francisco Restaurant; coffee shop; 1890 Night Club in burgundy velvet, costumed hostesses; inviting Dussel Bar for quiet libations; bedchambers poured from the familiar cookie mold; typically narrowlined baths. A carnival tone but passable.

☆☆ **Intercontinental** • in the same district, refashioned its public rooms in a handsome way, adding, in the process, a facsimile of Paris's animated Cafe de la Paix. Pool and fitness center; penthouse restaurant and bar, where the cost is also skyhigh; expensively outfitted accommodations; more space than is at the Hilton, but not employed to its best advantage.

Nikko • is typical of Japanese exports: fine modernist quality and reliable comfort. Naturally, it is dominated by a heavy oriental trade, since Dusseldorf is the center of Japanese commerce in Germany.

Ramada Renaissance • resides across the river from the city on the airport approach. Taverny public rooms; English country-life feeling which provides a dark nesting quality; rather compact complement of 250 units; upper-medium price range. I like the pool, the availability of smoking and nonsmoking accommodations and the special executive floor with its Renaissance Club. I don't like some of its glitzy decor.

Rheinpark Plaza • is across the river and into the settlement of Neuss. The hotel's perfectly adequate, but no Neuss is good news for anyone seeking a midcity locale.

Penta • is cool and institutional. Its leading features include the restaurant and bar as well as the pool and sauna.

Holiday Inn • is in midtown, has a pool, a darkly handsome dining room, a well-conceived soup'n'snack center and minuscule bedchambers. Prices are reasonable and the staff is unusually cordial and attentive.

Schloss Hotel Hugenpoet • a 25-minute ride along the pike to Essen, dates back to before the 15th century. Local citizens venture here for weekend repasts, wedding parties, and strolls around its historic frog ponds. Only 25 antique rooms, most with private bath; #28, a single, featuring a 300-year-old bed; #27, the bridal chamber, boasting newer springs and a softer mattress (thank heavens!); spooky corridors. Excellent food in the ancient castle dining hall.

For dining, **Victorian** is delightfully imaginative in cuisine (German) and great fun decoratively. The Eck in the **Breidenbacher Hof** would be my choice for any daytime meal, while the grill is nicer for evening. The **Hilton's** San Francisco Room is a good show at a lofty price. The neighboring **Intercontinental** leans to continental cuisine at its penthouse restaurant. Again, costly for the rewards. Among the independents, the prize easily goes to the wickedly cost-be-damned **Orangerie** • *Bilkerstr. 30 (even though it's costly, read no meaning in that address)* • with red textile walls, candle sconces, mirrored coach lamps, and orchard color intonations. Only the host receives the prices on his menu, so if you notice a transfixed glaze on his eyes and the beginnings of paralysis setting in, you'll know why. Perfect service; superb French cuisine; very stylish, but oh those tabs! **Im Schiffchen** • *Kaiserwerth Markt* • is French in gastronomy, astronomical in cost, splendid in performance, and Victorian in style while **Zum Schiffchen** • *Hafenstr. 5* • is a 360-year-old tavern in the former Rhine port; the regional dishes are as solid as its reputation. **Daitokai** is the leading Japanese entry. The **Rheinturm** (tower) restaurant, which revolves, is awful for ingestion; go *only* for the view. **Brand's Jupp** • *Kalkstr. 49* • a bit out of the center, is excellent and not expensive for fine German cookery.

ETTLINGEN

☆☆☆☆ **Erbprinz** • is handsomely sophisticated and worthy as a lunch stop or for overnight on the route between Frankfurt and Munich. This is one of the nation's legendary gastronomic shrines. Some modern concepts have been employed, but largely fine traditions are followed here.

FRANKFURT AM MAIN

It would be difficult to name a city in the Western Hemisphere that has sprung up more gracefully or more rapidly than this energy-charged metropolis. Its gleaming skyscrapers of glass and polished metal counterpoint with lovingly restored antiquity. Locals are properly proud of the beauty of the Romer, the central quarter that links modern Frankfurters to ancient Romans. This area is pulsing with intimate cafes and snack bars. Then, it's fun sipping *appelwoi* (apple wine) in the colorful taverns of Sachsenhausen, the more playful part of town. (Playful, too, is the language, which now labels the high-rise sector of Germany's big apple as "Mainhattan.") You can even board the Ebbelwei Ex-

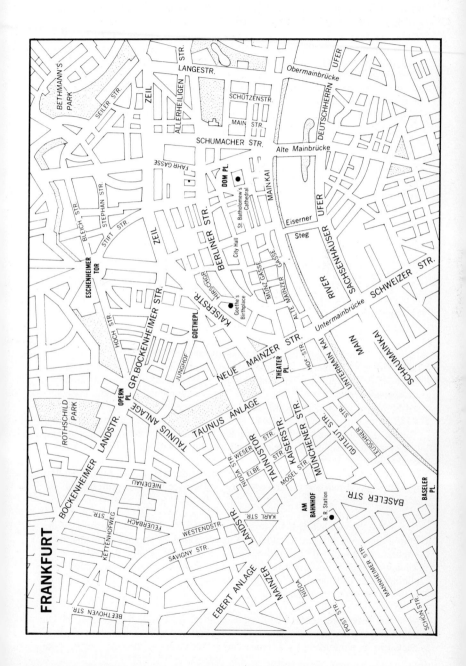

press, a streetcar named for the beverage (served with a free pretzel) and chug around the city's sights. It is unquestionably the transportation hub, the banking center, the leading Trade Fair center, and the home of one of Europe's busiest jumbo jetports (now with a superb rail linkage into the Intercity pan-European network). There are 11 variegated and conveniently sized museums on the Main River bank; interesting ones so far focus on film, architecture, sculpture, folk art, communications, ethnology, crafts, and Jewish culture. This proud assemblage won a recent annual **Temple Fielding Travel Award** for bringing more cultural life to the inner city. One dazzler is a rotating restaurant perched 332 feet up the world's tallest silo. Another is its 1085-foot TV tower, the highest building in the Federal Republic. The Rhine Main airport terminus is replete with the latest facilities and trimmings. Escalators convey passengers to platforms for trains which whisk them to the Central Station in 11 minutes. Incidentally, two dozen local taxi drivers have been licensed as official guides; tours cost roughly $65.

HOTELS

Be *sure,* especially during times of the trade fairs and congresses, to have written or telexed confirmation for your accommodation.

☆☆☆☆☆ **Frankfurter Hof** ● is easily one of Europe's finest. And, believe it or not, it improves almost daily under the expert guidance of General Manager Bernd Ludwig. His connoisseur's attention to wine and gastronomy are special credits to this establishment. Many new rooms, a splendid Presidential Suite (the ultimate in security) and two fresh deluxe spreads. I am partial to #128, a beauty in Art Deco style. Old Frankfurt cellar restaurant (called the "Stubb") with vaulted ceilings. Charming Restaurant Francais in Empire II and rich emerald tones; spacious wicker-and-wood grill with iron firebacks; Aperitif Bar, with squat leather easy chairs; totally renewed Lipizzaner Bar; cuisine in every segment distinctive and rewarding. Bedchambers now with hush-the-traffic windows; good parking facilities; color TV. Service attitudes professional and cordial yet often rushed.

☆☆☆ **Hessischer Hof** ● is smaller, more sedate, and less colorful than the Frankfurter Hof. Mixture of older and newer rooms in varying segments; thoroughfare situation, with extra-ply windows to shut out the noises. Cellar bar for romantic couples; zestless dining room; tiny summer cafe; winter garden with sliding roof; bedchambers roomy and uncozy, with ample closet space; large baths. Now quite recommendable.

☆☆ **Intercontinental** ● commands an ideal site beside the Main River. On an adjoining plot, there's a newer 20-floor, 300-unit annex; this addition—connected to its alma mater by a tunnel and an escalator—jostles the overall room count up to more than 800 accommodations with exactly the same narrow dimensions and routine decor; it includes a swimming pool. The Rotisserie, with French cuisine, is richly garbed in wood and brocade. The ground-level bar and breakfast room are amiable. Mirrored white and off-white Brasserie. An institution, but a good one.

Arabella Grand • offers a splendid new shelter for luxury pilgrims. It contains 378 bedrooms and the noteworthy restaurant called the Premiere. I'd prefer to wait another season or so before giving it a star ranking, but it does look promising.

★★ **Gravenbruch Kempinski** • today is a 350-room hostelry. Two-story pavilions, tennis courts, and swimming pools. A tavern, grill, and the excellent Gourmet are all worthy; bedchambers vary widely in style, but most are outfitted with traditional English furnishings. One mild disadvantage is that it is located 15 minutes from the heart of the city—a short hop from the airport and only a few seconds off the north-south autobahn intersection called Frankfurter Kreuz (a handy pull-off for motorists). Pleasant man-made lakeside site; ground-floor units with direct access to the gardens; 2nd-floor duos with balconies.

Plaza • is located across from the Messe (fair grounds); hence, it is a major asset to exhibitors. Canadian Pacific is the host and occasional North American touches are manifest. Warm color choices of browns, yellows, and orange. Inviting Backerei for odd-hour snacks; additional dining areas more elegant in tone. Ask for a bedchamber facing the lake.

☆☆ **Park** • greets guests with a handsome entrance; the superb La Truffe dining room ideal for business tete-a-tetes; superior service standards; glass-and-stone wing in linear form but older "tower" protected as a national trust. Agreeable, but not luxurious and now engaged in an expansion program.

☆☆ **Savoy** • is bright with lots of hospitality fixin's: Sauna, pool, open grill, attractive bar, nightclub, and restaurant. A lot has been done to give this house dignity and presence; very sound, even if the living space is limited.

Airport Hotel • (a Steigenberger link) offers an older wing plus a newer Executive Tower. The emphasis is on the business and conference trade. The 10-story, Y-shape structure jets in with a full bath count, air conditioning, soundproofing, a large pool under a glass dome for all-season splashing, a sauna, a nightclub, a coffee shop, and a country-club grill plus a conventional restaurant. Exceptionally well done for its particular type.

Sheraton • is even closer to the terminal than the Airport Hotel—it is linked to it by a pedestrian bridge. There are a pool, a sauna, 3 restaurants, the Red Baron nightery, parking for 7000 cars, a subway station beneath you (11 minutes to town) and a first-rate concierge in dynamic Mr. Hofer. Cool, big, but efficient.

A 312-room **Crest** station is here as well as 2 **Holiday Inns** (the Frankfurt entry is pathetic, but even it is better than the one out in the boonies of Sulzbach; these have got to be emergency stops only); America has exported a **Ramada Caravelle** to the airport district; there's an inexpensive, clean **Novotel** in the same region; and a reasonably nice commercial house called the **Arabella** resides in the industrial suburb of *Niederrad.*

National • is peaceful and well-run; Manager Dirk Roggen-Kamper is a concerned host. Many fine antiques; ample space; bedchambers modernized in a thoughtful way; most suitable for the maturer wayfarer.

The **Hamburger Hof** and the **Savigny** are not special. The ever-expanding **Excelsior-Monopol** is hard by the station and chugging along at a sprightly clip; its carloads of improvements show. **Continental** is pretty good in a traditional mood. The **Wiesbaden** is fair in a modest way. The **Queens,** with 279 rooms out in Stadtwald (10 minutes), is spending a bundle on updatings and the latest renewals have been in the restaurants.

The little **Hotel am Zoo** (across from the Zoo garden) is clean, bright, and okay for small-boned travelers; somewhat expensive. **Wurttemberger Hof,** with 16 added singles and baths, is less costly, but less comfortable; students might find it acceptable for the price, however. **Diana** is a cozy nest. The **Westend** and the **Hubner** also are pleasant tykes. The **Luxor** and the **Jaguar** are contenders in second-class; the latter seems to have more spring to its gait. The **Westfalinger Hof** is chiefly for the merchant trade; the back rooms are quieter. The **Rex** and **Gloria,** also in this category, are commercial, commercial—oo-la-la, are they commercial.

★★★★★ **Schlosshotel Kronberg** • is a knockout on the Carriage Trade Circuit. It's 10 miles (about 25 minutes) from the center of Frankfurt at *Kronberg,* seat of the Hesse Empire and the baronial—nay, princely—headquarters of the proprietor, the Prince of Hesse. (His ancestors once conquered Frankfurt.) Avoid the top floor if you hanker for antiquity. It's great for limousine motorists and golfers. This original Tudor castle of Empress Friedrich III, the eldest daughter of Queen Victoria, still retains its grand terrace, its priceless tapestries, its art masterpieces (Titian and Holbein paintings in the dining room), and its beautiful furnishings which so deftly have been combined with up-to-the-minute amenities. Strange as it may seem, prices are lower here than at the top-line institutional hotels in the city, offsetting to a degree the cost of taxi links to town. Exquisite—a heritage preserved.

Viktoria • is much less expensive—perhaps for those seeking a Kronberg address but simpler shelter. Total of 30 starkly modern, unadorned bedchambers; golfing privileges, so duffers can dig their divots with the Kronberg Klan.

Kurhotel Sonnenhof • is at nearby **Konigstein,** a fine home with a swimming pool, large viewful lounges, and traditional furnishings both in the main house and in the newer wing. Of its 2 excellent restaurants, I'm fondest of one with cream-colored wood panels inset with Delft platters, pewterware, and chandeliers suspended from a coffered ceiling. Prices are moderate considering the rewards of space and tranquillity. Perfect for families with a car.

RESTAURANTS

★★★★ **Bruckenkeller** • *Schutzenstrasse 6* • for color and atmosphere mellowed by centuries of time, dozens of candles, and the music of accordion, guitar, and violin. Every stop on the console has been pulled to romanticize this medieval-type cellar with its fine arched ceilings; large, elaborately carved wine barrel; harried service of good-but-not-great food. An entertaining evening and an enriching experience for 2 might total $150—and it would be worth every pfennig.

Klaane Sachsehauser • *Neuer Wall 11* • is great sport—at a quarter or so of the above prices. Our party delighted in the Schneegestober (''snow flurry'') of camembert-like cheese mixed with chopped onion, and the rippchen, a smoked pork chop. It's across the river, in the old quarter of Sachsenhausen where **apple wine taverns** offer their special flavor and revelry. Start with this one, then follow the custom and roam from one to another, taking small dishes at each. Community tables; singing as the mood commands; lots of laughter and jovial fraternizing. But more on this further along. (I've included this one here just to tease your appetite with the unconventional.)

★★ **Borsenkeller** • *across from the stock market (''borse'')* • could be considered Frankfurt's nearest equivalent of a *rathauskeller,* as local food writers boast—and with justifiable pride. Low brick arches, cleverly partitioned sectors, soft lighting, cordial and genteel service of regional preparations. Worth a visit. A meal and drink cost around $30.

La Galleria • *in the BFG Building at Theater Platz 2* • is dark, woody, and very agreeable once you are inside. Having been a Swiss restaurant, it has gone south and become Italian. It's the tops in town, too, for my DMs.

☆ **Erno's Bistro** • *Liebigstr. 15* • is a highly appreciated French contender with gastronomic tendencies toward nouvelle cuisine.

☆☆ **Le Midi** • *on the same lane in a private house at #47* • greets you with a glass Victorian canopy leading to the door. Simple L-shape room with a homespun mien. Ambitious chef who cooks in the modern fashion.

☆☆☆ **Humperdinck** • *Gruneburgweg 95* • named for the composer, also composes masterful gastronomy, but chiefly in the Franco-Itallo mood. Cream-crackle walls and crystal sconces; blue upholstery; gilt trim. The turbot and the lamb on a bed of beets are excellent, as are the warmed salads. The prices are designed for lofty expense accounts.

Perhaps the best nutrients (and values) in this city today can be digested in hotel dining rooms; I have always found them consistent, at least—and that, in itself, is something.

★★★ **Frankfurt Stubb** • in the cellar of the **Frankfurter Hof** will provide a well-prepared novelty. Vitrines in white stucco walls displaying artifacts; each corner different in personality, yet melding nicely into a harmonious whole. Friendly reception by a smiling hostess in period attire; open kitchen where only a portion of the dishes are prepared; ambience of congenial vitality rather than stuporous dignity. The cookery is not to be confused with that of sophisticated gustatory shrines; it is almost cottage fare in its straightforward hardiness, and it is good. Several of the hostesses speak English. This one is a highlight for the city and a "must" for any venturesome visitor.

☆☆☆☆☆ **Restaurant Francais** • for international cuisine and the he-man Grill (Maine lobsters flown in regularly) are at the **Frankfurter Hof** too. You might also wish to snack at the comfortable Aperitif Bar; delicious.

★★ **Intercontinental Hotel** • provides perhaps the city's richest mood in its lovely, river-view Rotisserie—a delight to the aesthetic senses. For light bites and sipping, try the Brasserie, the Wine Room, and the Oyster Bar. Its Sunday buffet has almost become a ritual among Frankfurters.

☆☆☆ **Gravenbruch** • outside of town, is a delight; its outstanding Gourmet room has been injected with vigor by its Kempinski masters.

☆☆☆ **Parkhotel** • boasts a good kitchen and a captivating terrace for dining; La Truffe is one of the top choices in the city for bankers; the hors d'oeuvres merit a blue ribbon.

★★★★ **Henninger**'s • rotating **Frankfurter Museums-Stubb** mounted on a 396-foot-high circular structure is a special spot if you're not acrophobic. You may sit while 360° of landscape passes before your eyes in the course of an hour. It's in the Sachsenhausen Borough, across the Main. Go for the view, not the cuisine. If you don't mind dining in a slow-motion centrifuge, you'll probably be awed by this impressive turn of events.

Zum Storchen • *facing the Dom* • is one of the choice stops for quality German fare. Not expensive, either.

Faust • below the Opera, is colorful but gastronomically unexciting—or worse.

Apfelweinstuben (Apple wine rooms).

Grauer Bock • *on the other side of the river* • is another neighborhood tavern to end neighborhood taverns: Wooden tables, grimy floors, smoky walls, pretzel vendors, great color and animation; hot dogs, sauerkraut, beer, sandwiches, and a redoubtable affair called "Handkas mit Musik"—"Handkas" being the cheese, with vinegar, oil, paprika, onions, and kummel combined on top to make the "Musik."

Gemaltes Haus ("Painted House") and **Dauth-Schneider** are other examples of this school.

Schwarzen Stern • *Romerberg, facing the plaza* • presents an ornate medieval facade that is immediately inviting. Basic regional cookery for about $18 per feed.

Cafe Hauptwache • is good for light refreshments; it has a modern production-line restaurant facing the esplanade on its lower floor and a coffee and pastry parlor at ground level. Go to the latter for extraheavy calories and a peek at the painted figures on the walls.

★★★★★ **Schlosshotel Kronberg** • (see "Hotels") is worth a stop if the sun is shining and transportation is at hand; the best luncheon expedition one can make in the area is the drive to this former castle of Empress Friedrich III— Gorgeous 200-foot open terrace for dining; expensive; so relaxing it's a *must* for anyone who can do it. The taxi price, unhappily, is robbery. Open all year.

★★★ **Gutsschanke Neuhof** • is more rustic but also highly appealing— and far cheaper than the Schlosshotel. It's about 20 minutes out at the settlement of *Neuhof*. Self-contained farming village at work continuously since 1499; locally harvested and husbanded flora and fauna; packaged products sold at the Alte Backstube outbuilding (sausages, dairy goods, sweets, nuts, wines, plus some touristy craft items). Restaurant in the handsome half-timber manor house; 2 floors of compartmentalized dining rooms; outdoor terrace for summer daydreaming; warm, cozy atmosphere; flowers on every table; attentive waiters in cranberry waistcoats. Book ahead.

NIGHT LIFE

which has been adopted universally throughout Germany), so take it from there as to what you can expect in the rougher districts. For fun and sophistication, **St. John's Inn** would evoke almost any intimate confession. It's a pub-style hermitage canonized for candlelight worshipers; horseshoe bar with built-in piano; low cocktail tables with dwarf-size captain's chairs. Waitresses in tartans; white-painted brick wall; woody touches; fireplace crackling during cold months; St. John himself, a topnotch showman, takes to the mike, cues the piano, and belts out tuneful swing-songs at ½-hour intervals. Delicious snacks and light meals are available at reasonable tithings. **Jimmy's Bar,** downstairs in the Hessischer

Hof Hotel, is another pleasant dew-drop-inn for liquids and chitchat. **Pik Dame** specializes in lesbian acts. Skip the next-door **Riz.** For jazz, the **Kneipe** (near the Frankfurter Hof) does it best; some great sounds are created here. Then come the narrow little **Jazzhaus** and the neighboring **Jazz Keller**—all of them in midcity. For pickups, the **Cafe Express** turns on the steam at its central Kaiserstrasse address. **Sex Theatre** specializes in raw, no-nonsense overdoses of the same. **Dr. Muller's,** with several midtown sites, purveys porn to the masses.

SHOPPING

SHOPPING HOURS: A Federal law now standardizes them throughout the country: 9 a.m.–6:30 p.m. on weekdays; Sat., 9 a.m.–2 p.m. except to 6 p.m. on the first Sat. of every month.

BEST AREAS: Kaiserstrasse, Steinweg, and Goethestrasse are the toniest shopping streets. The larger department stores are on Rossmarkt and Zeil. Secondhand antiques shops flank Braubachstrasse and Fahrgasse. When you're hungry walk along the aptly named "Fressgasse" or *Gourmand Alley*. Ladengalerie am Theater is a shopping complex in the BFG building. The Romer (City Hall Square) has been revived.

CAMERAS AND OPTICAL DEVICES: Foto Hobby (Rossmarkt 23) is an excellent Leica agency, possibly the finest and most complete in Europe for this proud name. They even carry antique models, used equipment, and other brands too. Ask Mr. Uhl or Mr. Titsch-Rivero to guide you in this complex field.

CUTLERY: J. A. Henckels, now in 7 more German hubs, plus others outside the country is one of the first places you'll want to visit. Almost no one disputes that the pert "Twins," trademark and colophon of this giant since 1731, symbolize the world's finest cutlery, bar none.

ROSENTHAL: Studio Haus Gilbert (Friedenstrasse 10, next to Frankfurter Hof Hotel) is the local magnet for this most famous of German china.

FREIBURG The **Colombi** offers 7 floors of comfortable modernity and better than average cookery. **Park Hotel Post** is reasonable for economizing. Try the **Kornhauskeller** for exceptional traditional cuisine.

GARMISCH-PARTENKIRCHEN is an Alpine resort with strong tourist appeal and backup facilities sprouting everywhere—so much so, in fact, that a lot of its charm is swiftly vanishing. The U.S. military colony is so ingrained into this locality that the rich Teutonic flavor of yore is almost lost. Magnificent panorama of the German and Austrian Alps; bracing climate; restyled casino; winter sports galore, with ski runs and lifts, bobsledding, cable cars, a glass-lined public swimming pool, and much more. Take the train for a short roll out to Eibsee, then whistle up the 12-minute cable ride to the 9730-foot crown of Zugspitze Mountain; it's an eyeful you'll never forget.

★★★ **Alpina** • reveals an alp's-worth of high-fashion hotel baubles in a low-profile, stucco-and-wood, chalet-style building. Exquisite garden and pool area; inviting public rooms; 40 deluxe bedchambers; superior cuisine.

★★★ **Post** • in the Partenkirchen part is also excellent, especially for its luxurious hunting lodge flavor.

Wittelsbach • has declined wittle by wittle and struck me as too tatty to recommend.

Ramada Sporthotel • is out at Riessersee and in a lovely alpine setting.

★★★ **Clausing's Posthotel** • back in the Garmisch segment, attracts chiefly a European clientele. If you are looking for that Old World atmosphere with scarcely a Colonist in sight, you'll most likely find it here.

Grand Hotel Sonnenbichl • has much to offer if you don't mind being somewhat out of the center. Service and cuisine are above average; lovely gardens; pool and tennis available. The excellent eyeful from its frontside balconied rooms might distract you from the glitzy interior. Dramatic, if not puzzling aesthetics.

★★ **Partenkirchener Hof** • is rich in alpine personality, and it boasts one of the best tables in the valley for the medium budget. Indoor pool, fitness center, and sauna.
Holiday Inn seems so out of sync with nature that it would appear to be a fine example of architectural future-shock. The accommodation, however, is reliable if not predictable. **Obermuhle** makes a splash with its indoor pool. **Garmischer Hof,** a breakfast-only hostelry, has had many improvements; approximately ½ of its units have private bath. **Neu-Werdenfels** also provides reasonably good shelter for budget travelers. Outstanding pensions are (1) **Leiner,** (2) **Schell,** (3) **Flora,** and (4) **Gastehaus Georgenhof.** More? Take your pick of the other 172 hotels, inns, pensions, and guest houses—and *viel Gluck!*
Want to get away from it all? Atop the 9730-foot Zugspitze, masons in crampons constructed the miraculous **Hotel Schneefernerhaus,** with its lovely winter garden overlooking the top of the world. Basic accommodations for ski buffs, scenic buffs, and yeti; a wonder of engineering.

HAMBURG

With approximately 1.6 million population, Hamburg is Germany's first seaport and second city. It spins an 890-foot-tall TV spindle that has a rotating restaurant. Dine in the famous Ratsweinkeller, stroll through Platen un Blomen Park, shop along Alster Lake, visit one of Germany's largest collections of fine paintings at the Art Gallery (50 showrooms!), take a whirl through that naked, rowdy Reeperbahn night district, visit a Doll Museum with 300 *puppen* and 60 tiny houses, see the early Sunday morning trading at the St. Pauli Fischmarkt, ride a steamer to Blankenese on the Elbe River, or to the war-famous island of Helgoland and see Hagenbeck's renowned zoo with its Troparium to display its apes, snakes, crocodiles, and other exotic critters in natural surroundings.

HOTELS

Please refer to the section "About the Stars" as a key to these personal rankings, which often differ from the local ratings.

☆☆☆☆☆ **Atlantic Kempinski** • is comfortable and elegant, providing a faintly robust air of executive domain. Its Poseidon is tall, amiable Karl Walterspiel. As you enter, the lobby is a gracious restoration of the *Atlantic* of 1909—and a pleasure to behold. You'll find Die Brucke restaurant for quick meals, the Edwardian-modern Rendez-vous Bar with piano music, a dining room with orchestrated dinner dancing, a superb grill, air conditioning in all public quadrants, an indoor pool-massage-sauna complex, and 320 rooms and some glorious suites. A 3-story garage adjoins; excellent concierge team; fine and traditional.

☆☆☆☆☆ **Vier Jahreszeiten** • is a salubrious choice for the discriminating voyager who prefers subtle tapers to bright lights. With an exquisite, lakefront setting, this is a dreamy haven for tranquillity seekers. A variety of rooms, so ask for the type you desire. Excellent cuisine; delightfully serene grill with open hearth. The Condi Cafe features split-level lunching and a candy shop on the ground floor. The Simbari Bar, with its own small loft, is an artistic and cozy corner.

★★★★ **Elysee** • brings a new zest to Hamburg's hotel scene. It exudes a youthful ambience that you will note in the lobby afternoons and evenings when live music stirs the air. Keen focus on art and exhibits; fitness facilities; two restaurants plus a Bodega and the toe-tapping Bourbon Street Bar. The Old Guard may be disarmed if not dismayed, but the "right now" folks love it.

☆☆☆ **Intercontinental** • resides a bit farther down the same lakeshore as the Vier Jahreszeiten, fronted by a few trees along the residential drive. The 9th-floor Fontenay Grill is one of Hamburg's high spots—both physically and gastronomically. The nautically inspired Hulk Brasserie is so popular that a reservation is a must nearly any time. While the Hansa Kogge bar is refined, the hardy Bierstube is far more fun for easy chitchat and casual imbibing. Attractive glass-lined pool; a casino; spacious suites; colorful but somewhat narrow-lined twin units.

SAS Plaza • spliced neatly into the municipal convention center, boasts of being the nation's highest hostelry. SAS, which caters chiefly to business travelers, now runs this show, which is plainly a massive commercial enterprise. Its restyled corridors lead to 570 look-alike units; most are cookie-mold-standard doubles or twins; there are 4 restaurants, a pool, saunas, a communications center, and bars; the abstract paintings remind me of a Creative Playthings school. The windowsills are a tall 4 feet above carpet level.

★★★ **Garden Hotel Posedorf** • seems aimed at almost the same audience as the Elysee—upward mobile young executives, models, theater people, and the frolicsome movers and shakers of modern Germany. The botanical feature in its name imparts a more residential than commercial tone to its overall aura. The area *(Harvestehude)* surrounding Magdalenenstrasse is likewise quiet and more private than the midcity precincts. Prices are reasonable too.

☆☆☆☆ **Prem** • is a renovated mansion peppered with antiques, oils, and tapestries, spiced with crystal chandeliers and well-maintained moldings, and festooned with acres of gathered curtaining. Tasteful entrance and lobby, with its adjoining paneled bar; chummy Stuberl for lighter fare; the garden-side *(sic)* La Mer presenting more serious and truly excellent cookery; warm service; parking lot and individual garages; all units bright. Very nice indeed.

☆☆ **Ramada Renaissance** • offers more than 200 rooms and several luxury suites, a commendable restaurant called the Noblesse, a piano bar, rooftop sauna, and a "club" concept for executives who require extra fillips for a supplemental charge. All units with eider quilts, TV, and video; well presented, as most Ramadas abroad are these days.

Bellevue • is a neighbor to the Prem and boasts 85 bedchambers and an 85% bath ratio.

Berlin • a Y-shape structure, is convenient for motorists who weary near the autobahn junction of Bremen and Lubeck-Kiel. Well maintained; the run-of-the-mill doubles are small and cluttered.

Maritim Reichshof • a station hotel, is smart while retaining very pleasant period decor.

Europaischer Hof • also comes up with a brightened yet stolidly traditional personality; 500 rooms with a high proportion of singles; groups use it a lot, but value is here.

Alster-Hof • has 80 varying accommodations, 2 so-called penthouse suites (possibly because one gets that pent-up feeling in them), and 21 of the most minuscule baths outside a U-boat; #211 and #212, among the latest batch of improved units, are exceptions, with twin basins and adequate tubs. Maintenance is good. This one's now right for the price.

RESTAURANTS

★★★★ **Ratsweinkeller** • pride of the municipality, is one of the best of its type in Germany—and it's priced at no more than a neighborhood restaurant back home. Elaborate, dignified, and cosmopolitan atmosphere; service careful and prompt for such a large establishment. Try its Nordsee-Steinbutt Gekocht mit Zerlassener Butter if you're a turbot fan.

☆☆☆☆☆ **Landhaus Scherrer** • a costly taxi ride from the center, is a low house facing the Elbe; this is for serious (and expensive) gastronomy. It features 2 rooms, of which I prefer the pale green salon dominated by a large Kokoschka painting. Dishes—and marvelously light they are—appear exquisitely under silver bells. The music is baroque; a rehoboam of Pauillac costs around $1800, with German wines ranging down to $15. You'll never suffer heartburn here, but the host might achieve heart failure when billtime rolls around.

☆☆ **Wein-Restaurant J. H. C. Ehmke** • is good but not grand; some of our vegetables were insipid; better for sea-faring than steer-age; closed Sun. Nice sampling of the Old World.

W. Schumann's Austernkeller • *Oyster Cellar, Jungfernstieg 34* • is a page out of the memoirs of Kaiser Wilhelm. Alas, the cookery no longer has the appeal of former times—at least to my taste. High-backed booths and chairs; stained-glass touches; 7 private dining roomettes with closable door for business conferences or monkey-business conferees.

Sellmer • *Ludofstrasse* • is a specialist in fish—and *only* fish. Very typical preparations of Hanseatic waters, but not inspiring visually.

★ **Jacob** • *20 minutes out at **Hamburg-Nienstedten*** • is a riverbank mansion that served its first guest on April 1, 1791. Now it wears a fresh wardrobe and is viewful and fetching when it is warm enough to dine on its terrace.

☆ **Landhaus Dill** • is across the roadway from Jacob and better skilled at handling pots and pans.

☆ **L'Auberge Francaise** • is where Gallic management create what sometimes is claimed to be the best of France in northern Germany—even to shopping twice weekly in the Paris markets! Locals lavish praise upon their efforts, but my own judgment is more tempered. Decoratively it is pleasant but not elaborate; modern cuisine is the main thrust from the kitchen; wines are *only* French. Expensive? Well, what do you think of $170 per twosome?

Le Canard • is another quacker from Gaul—a smidgen bigger, also with the latest fashion in French cuisine and some of the oldest wines, also on the costly side—but worthwhile if you hanker for *la belle France*.

Roma • *Hofweg* • and **Il Ristorante** • *Grosse Bleichen* • are two superb Italian choices. **La Vite** • *Moorweide* • also deserves attention for these specialties.

☆ **Bavaria Blick** • is a split-level, glass-lined aerie topping the St. Pauli Brewery. Suave reception; 25 flower-clad tables; dishes as appealing to the eye as to the palate; the house pride is northern fish; coffee comes up with a snooker of double-rich whipped cream; it seems to improve every time. Ask your waiter for binoculars, to put yourself right on the bridge of that freighter piloting up the Elbe.

☆☆☆ **Fischereihafen-Restaurant** • on a quay overlooking the busy Norder Elbe waterway, has excellent salmon, sole, and other fruit of the sea. Reserve in advance, especially at lunch when businessmen take over; go upstairs; don't order lobster or crab, unless you've just received fair tidings from your stockbroker. Downstairs is a pub called **Kapitansstube** for simpler fare; the "fisherman's breakfast" will keep you going until midnight.

Alsterschiff • a small ship permanently anchored in the Inner Lake (center of town), offers 11 tables in the tiny cabin for dining afloat; amusing experience, but the galley's not the best.

Schiffer Borse • opposite the station, is one of the most impressively tricked out maritime hideaways you'll find anywhere. The grub is not all that good, but see it even if you only invest in a beer or a glass of wine.

☆☆☆ **Muhlenkamper Fahrhaus** • *Osterbekstrasse 1, a few minutes out from the center* • prepares perfectly splendid gastronomy. Atmosphere almost homey in execution; padded red-leather booths for sink-in comfort; oil paintings, brass chandeliers, and warm wood paneling; excellent-to-extraordinary service. Delicious slivers of smoked salmon and sturgeon were delivered on individual wooden platters and garnished with fresh salad tidbits. The sweet-and-sour goose was tender, flavorful, and handsomely presented as was the lamb with chive and cream sauce. The raspberry Romanoff (a Hamburg specialty of smooth, tart gelatin folded in cream) is a dessert fit for the czars.

Blockhouse ● *Dorotheenstrasse is one location, but there are 6 others now* ● is named for Herr Block, its beefeating proprietor and the blockbuster behind the previously mentioned Elysee Hotel. Attractive interiors, usually rustic in nature; Western-style steaks; good baked potatoes and salads.

Among the hotels, the ☆☆☆☆☆**Atlantic,** the ☆☆☆☆Fontenay Grill of the **Intercontinental,** and the ☆☆☆☆☆**Vier Jahreszeiten** duel in mortal combat for a *touche;* I'd give the edge to the mood you are in at the time you dine, because each is distinctive and outstanding for gastronomy (see "Hotels").

Like so many other German metropolises, Hamburg has its own TV tower cum revolving restaurant, dubbed the **Fernsehturm.** The whip cracks for dinner at 6:30 sharp; then the herd stampedes in like bulls thundering through the streets of Pamplona. Just so much fodder.

NIGHT LIFE

The Reeperbahn and its sidestreets are brilliant from dusk to dawn with the neon enticements of dozens of girlie-joints. In these, generally 3–12 "artistes" perform solo or in tandem in the seminude or nude and to the outer limits of human imagination.

In this twilight zone, 3000 of the 13,000 residents are prostitutes. Then there are the local shills, pimps, strippers, and associated tradesmen who are confronted by a downturn in business due to the pervasive international fear of AIDS.

If you'll stick to the places recommended below, your wallet and your molars *should* be safe (no blanket guarantees). As a rule, there's a $10 to $12 entry fee (if there's a show), another buck for your coat check (never tip here); Scotch (much of it falsified) runs up to $12 per slug. *But don't wander elsewhere under any circumstances.*

Among the smaller strip depots, **Colibri** (Grosse Freiheit 34) is absolute tops. One of the few offering live music; coveys of girls. Jammed with lone males; continuous show; young, accomplished, good-looking strippers who work up their amorous themes with partners of all persuasions; unmonkeyed with whisky; beer plus schnapps for reasonable tabs (a mandatory combination not sold separately). **Salambo,** across the street, has it all—including what's happening on the banquette beside you. It's not for the timid, and it certainly has to be the most uninhibited community of carnality since Sodom. **Erotica,** next door, deals in free-reelers. Blue films; beer the most popular beverage; no entry fee; as raw as they come. **Travesti,** next to Colibri, lights up a small stage with the top transvestite acts in the city. Strangely enough, they can be more tasteful than many straight performances. **Black Market** offers a drag show; so does **Pulverfass; Ahrweller's Rendezvous** specializes in cabaret. **Safari** offers an expandable interior glazed by a colossal onstage sun. Good spirits; good shows; swinging for the broad-minded. **Tabu** mounts a non-stop show daily from 8 p.m. to 4 a.m. **Barcelona** features a carbaret in which it would be difficult for even a gynecologist to distinguish between the senoritas and the senores. **Moon-**

light is often loaded with transvestites, odd sexes, and nonsexes; here was one of the dirtiest, rottenest, most tasteless shows I've ever seen anywhere, anytime. **Blauer Peter** *is open from 4 a.m.–10 a.m. only;* no show; 5-piece combo for dancing; all kinds of light food and all materials for a nightcap.

You might like to visit the infamous Herbertstrasse, a 1-block street just off the main drag, where harlots sit in showcase windows facing the sidewalks. Here the prostitutes ask about $60 per encounter. Another is the Fish Market district, where the scales fall even lower for a squalid catch.

Casinos are located in the **Intercontinental Hotel** and on the **Reeperbahn** (#94–96); take your passport for entry. The first offers roulette, baccarat, and blackjack; at the latter there are other games, and your jackpot payoff could be a new Porsche or Mercedes.

HANOVER, the capital of Lower Saxony, has just celebrated its 750th anniversary. In the State Opera and at Herrenhausen Park you'll discover top-line music and theater. Explore the castlelike New City Hall and the Market Church, situated in the Old Town. Stroll along the Red Line, a unique sightseeing walk (guidebook available from the Tourist Information). Riflemen during the end of June or early July are pumped up by the *Schutzenfest,* the biggest marksmen-fair in the world. A bit quieter is the Maschsee-Lake-Festival in early August or the traditional Christmas Market around the Market Church in December. Shopping areas include the exclusive Georgstrasse, Galerie Luise, and the Kropcke Passage. Markthalle (market hall), in Karmarschstrasse, is interesting. Start early and take a champagne breakfast.

☆☆☆ **Intercontinental** • rates among the top modern-style hostelries on the Continent. Ideal situation, with the City Hall (magnificently illuminated at night), town lake, and shopping center almost at your doorstep; glittery lobby warmed by rosewood panels and glamorous movie-TV stars who make this their offstage greenroom; Calenberger Bar with candlelight, a terrific combo, and perfectly concocted drinks. Delicious cuisine in the dramatically decorated Prinz Tavern (lunch and dinner), the open-rotisseried grill segment, the cheerful Brasserie (6 a.m.–11 p.m.), and the chummy, rustic *Bierstube* (snacks and suds from noon to midnight). The sleeping accommodations contain many agremens.

Kastens Hotel and Luisenhof • formerly the leader, is now a distant second, perhaps even third after the **Maritim.** Very close is the **Schweizerhof,** better known for its fine restaurant than for the accommodations.

Next would come the **Stadtpark** (a congress hotel), **Mercure** (cool and commercial), and a **Holiday Inn** at the airport. About 25 miles northeast, at the medieval village of *Celle,* the **Parkhotel Furstenhof** is a boreal dream comprising a 17th-century baroque mansion and dwelling annex.

HEIDELBERG ("Heather Hill") boasts an enchanting situation astride a riverbank, the world's largest wine barrel (58 thousand gallons), Karzer Prison for obstreperous 15th-century students of its celebrated university, the Lion Gate, and the 127-foot TV tower (observation platform open to the public). Heidelberg is guilty of nothing except an excess of beauty and historic charm; the only thing wrong with it is the rabble of Japanese, French, Italian, Belgian, Scandinavian, Indian, Greek, North American, Latin American, and Hottentot tourists who spoil it in Season. But in good weather during the slowest months—*wunderbar!*

☆☆☆☆ **Europaischer Hof** • (sometimes called "Europe"). It makes continuous updatings in the most tasteful of traditional Germanic themes. Its latest bauble is a 33-room wing with shops, conference salons, and a cellar garage. Total of more than 120 units; terrace-dining (with huge windows that vanish into the floor at a button's touch), or Kurfurstenstube Grill (local specialties and beguiling color); attractive bar.

☆☆ **Holiday Inn Crowne Plaza** • is a large (232 rooms) and smart looking house with a pool and a fitness center, a well-regarded restaurant and a fair degree of elegance, especially in its public sancta. A very substantial option for a stopover.

Rega, with 125 units, is comfortable and contemporary and in the newer part of town, but if you are looking for antiquity, try the 15th-century **Hirschgasse** or the 18th-century **Schonberger Hof** or the **Hollander Hof** facing the Alten Brucke (Old Bridge).

Penta • owned by a consortium of European airlines, is a 250-room entry with color TV, minibars, air conditioning, a health club, and a pool. It deals a lot in bulk booking.

Ritter • which planted its first cornerstone in 1592, is growing newer by the moment. Except for the restaurant, almost every speck of its once-rich antiquity has been erased. Very central.

Neckar • on the waterside in the city, is an awkward building dappled with bright modern hues and functional furniture.

Kurfurst • offers 47 clean but spare bedrooms and some private baths or showers.

☆☆ **Europaischer Hof's** • mealtimes offer versatile facilities and fine cookery in its Kurfurstenstube.

☆ **Ritter** • comes up with above-average vittles and authentic Old German surroundings. Two adjoining rooms; blossoms on each table; informal ambience; inexpensive.

★★ **Museum Restaurant** • is a delight. Entry through large portals that face a court and a sylvan park beyond; interior with heavy beams supported by carved tree trunks; 2 rooms separated by red granite pillars and ancient arches; windows with stained-glass inserts; bronze chandeliers. The menu is enticing, the service sound, and the prices in the medium bracket.

Schinderhannes • *on Theaterstrasse* • is fun as a wine restaurant; it is open only for dinner and late revels. For light bites, there are miles of spaghetti factories and endless rounds of pizzerias along the Hauptstrasse in the center of town.

Simplicissimus • tends toward modern approaches in cuisine served in sophisticated surroundings. **Kupferkanne** is agreeable; prices are moderate. **Weinstube im Schloss,** reopened this season after a thorough renovation, used to decant. Teutonic atmosphere as thick as a dumpling. I hope it hasn't modernized too much.

HERRENALB

☆☆☆ **Post Hotel** • is 12 miles from Baden-Baden and into the fringing wineland of the Black Forest. Ideal for a pastoral excursion or a restorative holiday. Cuisine that satisfies; pleasant but not overdone decor, touched up with rich antiques; cozy 12th-century Klosterschranke Grill, with beams, stucco, and stone; 2 dining rooms and garden sipping nook; bar; heated pool; 50 comfortable units, most with shower and/or bath. Here is an isle of bucolic calm where the value of peace is understood to its very core.

HINTERZARTEN

★★★★★ **Adler** • *in the Black Forest* • steals the loving cup as one of the beauty queens of Germany. Glorious parkland and flower-girt setting; glass-enclosed swimming pool for year-round dipping; tennis, minigolf, *boccia* court, watersports on Lake Titisee, ice skating, curling rink, toboggan run, nearby ski lifts and golf course; owned by the Riesterer family since 1446; only 13 miles from Freiburg; an arcadia of *Hochschwarzwaldian* peace.

Thomahof • with its sills decorated with flowers is worth a try. The terrace is especially pleasing. There's a covered pool plus a charming fringe of garden. The dining is elegant and delicious. Wintertime is also enchanting in this setting once the snows fall.

LUBECK, "Queen of the Hanse" (the Slavonic name means "the pretty one") is so rich in monuments (Holstentor town gate is 1 of 7), antiquities, paintings, and antique salt-storage houses that it's a great favorite of serious-minded voyagers—and *Travemunde,* the neighboring Baltic resort, balances the ledger by offering a gambling casino and plenty of excitement in summer to the frivolous. The Town Hall first called together its council in the 13th century; 3 major churches date from that time or earlier. *Kiel,* nearby, was the marine host for the sailing contests of the Olympics. Worth a visit, particularly by old salts— and especially during Kiel Week in early summer when regatta sailors from all nations gather to compete. Other sights, if you have a car, should include the colorful Old Town of *Luneburg, Ratzeburg* with its Romanesque Cathedral, and pretty *Molln* boasting a lottery medieval market place. In Lubeck, our overnight choice would be the fresh **Movenpick Lysia** beside the Trave River. The

Kaiserhof is also worthy, as is the aptly named **Altstadt,** located in the enchanting Old Town. At *Travemunde* it's the seaview **Maritim** or the **Kurhaus.**

☆☆☆☆ **Schabbelhaus** ● the last word in Town House refinement and grace, is enchanting as a lunching and dining target. It is an ancient mansion with tall windows, massive beams, perfect service, and delicious cuisine. It's not destructive to the budget, either.

★★★★ **Haus der Schiffergesellschaft** ● is another stunner, which dates back to the dawn of Hanseatic maritime activity. The decor is authentic; dining is at communal tables; ships' models hang from the timbered ceiling—as do 3-tiered brass chandeliers with candles that are illuminated at dusk. A delight.

Ratskeller ● invites you to go in and have a glass of wine just to absorb the atmosphere of the Middle Ages.

MAINZ Hilton is by far the leading hotel locally. Open V-shape structure nipping at the banks of the Rhine; adjacent to the 3000-capacity Rheingoldhalle congress center; recent 195-room Cathedral wing, which includes 2 additional dining centers (the Bistro is French and fun) plus a health club. Specialty restaurant suggestive of a steamer (overlooking the Rhine too); brick-walled Weinstube; Bierstube; cocktail lounge; full air conditioning; garage; car rental facility; beauty parlor; barbershop. **Mainzer Hof** is a lazy second.

MONSCHAU is tucked away in the Eifel mountains, a dreamy little medieval townscape seemingly taken from a theater set. The rushing Rur bumps and froths among the tilting half-timbered, slate-roofed houses; delicious trout come from that stream. See the Rotes Haus of a prosperous wool merchant, the glassworks called Glashutte, eat a spice cake and take walks in the countryside and about the hamlet. For overnighting, the modest **Horchem** is center stage; **Burgau** offers a restaurant overhanging the river; **Muhlenberg** is also pleasant and inexpensive. All dining is in the hotels.

MUNICH

The Bavarian capital is the southern apex of industry, commerce, and at least one foreign visitor for every one of the 1⅓ million permanent population. The typical Bavarian is a hardy, fun-loving host; the city's booklet (*Munchen*) contains 6 full pages of museums for every period and interest. Taxis, buses, and a newly expanded subway system can deliver you almost anywhere in and around the town.

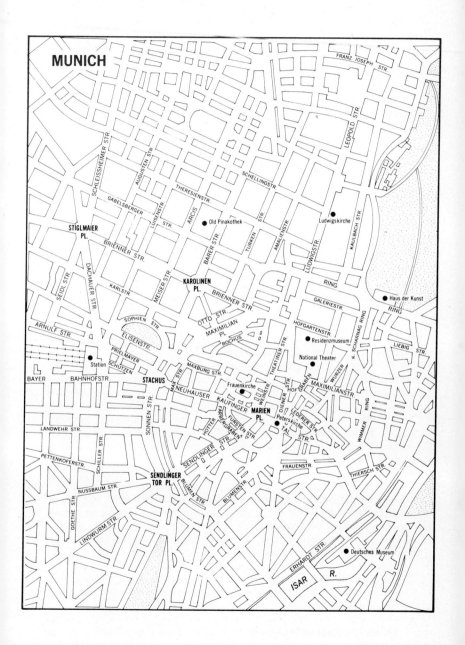

MUNICH

FRANZ JOSEPH STR.

LEOPOLD STR.

SCHLEISSHEIMER STR.

AUGUSTEN STR.

THERESIENSTR.

SCHELLINGSTR.

GABELSBERGER

STR.

STIGLMAIER PL.

BRIENNER STR.

LUISENSTR.

ARCIS

BARER STR.

● Old Pinakothek

TURKEN STR.

AMALIENSTR.

LUDWIGSTR.

● Ludwigskirche

KAULBACH STR.

DACHAUER STR.

SEIDL STR.

KARLSTR.

MEISER STR.

KAROLINEN PL.

BRIENNER STR.

RING

GALERIESTR.

RING

● Haus der Kunst

SOPHIEN STR.

OTTO STR.

MAXIMILIAN PL

HOFGARTENSTR.

K. SCHARNAG RING

LIEBIG STR.

ARNULF STR.

ELISENSTR.

ROCHUS

THEATINER STR.

● Residenzmuseum

PRIELMAYER

● National Theater

WURZER

● Station

SCHUTZEN

MAXBURG STR.

MAX STR.

WEINSTR.

HOF GRABEN

MAXIMILIANSTR.

BAYER

BAHNHOFSTR.

STACHUS

NEUHAUSER

KAUFINGER

● Frauenkirche

DIENER STR.

LEDERER STR.

WIMMER RING

SONNEN STR.

MARIEN PL.

● Peterskirche

LANDWEHR STR.

NOTTER

FARBERGRABEN

FURSTEN STR.

TAL STR.

SENDLINGER

PETTENKOFERSTR.

SCHILLER STR.

SENDLINGER TOR PL.

FRAUENSTR.

THIERSCH STR.

NUSSBAUM STR.

BLUMEN STR.

BLUMENSTR.

GOETHE STR.

LINDWURM STR.

ERHARDT STR.

● Deutsches Museum

ISAR R.

ATTRACTIONS

Peterskirche • *Peter's Church, Petersplatz* • Founded in the mid-1100s, this beautiful Gothic church is Munich's oldest. It has a 300-foot tower that can be climbed to view the Alps when a white disc is displayed on its front; a red disc means the visibility is limited.

Marienplatz • This charming medieval square has been the hub of Munich since the city's founding in the 12th century. Both the old town hall (**Altes Rathaus**) and the new town hall are situated here, and numerous important historic buildings and churches are clustered around the square in the immediate area.

Neues Rathaus • *New Town Hall, Marienplatz* • The world-famous **Glockenspiel** is housed in the lovely tower of this fine Gothic structure, which dominates the Marienplatz. Each day at 9 a.m., 11 a.m. and 5 p.m. from May 1 to Oct. 10 the mechanical figures perform. For the best view, find a window table in one of the 2nd or 3rd floor cafes in the building on the opposite side of the square.

Residenz • *The Royal Palace* • For close to 5 centuries these magnificent structures, which were built at various times from the 1500s to the 1800s, have been the home of kings, princes, and dukes of the House of Wittelsbach. The **Residenz Museum** offers a vast collection of paintings, antique porcelain, and tapestries, in addition to fine Renaissance, Rococo, and Neoclassical style exhibits. Another section of the palace houses the **Schatzkammer** (Treasury Chamber), in which are displayed masterpieces by goldsmiths and lapidaries from the Middle Ages to the baroque period. The **Alte Residenz** is the rococo, central section of the palace, and includes the Cuvillies Theater. The fourth section is the **Festsaalbau** (concert hall), plus the Hofgarten, a garden lined with pleasant arcades.

Bayerisches National Museum • *Bavarian National Museum, Prinzregentenstrasse 3* • Established in 1855, this interesting museum contains an extraordinary collection of Bavarian crafts, including gold and silver work, jewelry, porcelain, tapestries, and popular arts. In addition, there is the unusual Krippenschau collection of Christmas cribs.

Valentin Museum • *Isartorplatz* • A museum of "blooming nonsense" that delights practical jokers. Its hoard of collectibles, some very silly, pay tribute to a German comedian.

Deutsches Museum • *German Museum of Science and Technology, auf der Isarinsel* • Nicely situated on an island in the middle of the Isar River, this colossal institution is the biggest technological museum in the world. There are scale models of mines, mills, factories, dams and harbors, as well as separate sections that illustrate the development of cars, planes, rockets, trains, ships, and musical instruments. Also connected to the museum is the highly regarded **Zeiss Planetarium.**

Munchner Stadtmuseum • *Munich Municipal Museum, St. Jacobs Platz 1* • This elaborate 15th-century building houses a wide variety of objects illustrating Munich's history. One entire wing is devoted to the art of beer brewing. There is also a photography and film museum, which presents films daily at 6:30 p.m.

Frauenkirche • *Cathedral of Our Lady, Frauenplatz 1* • Constructed in 1488 in the Bavarian Gothic style, this beautiful building was almost totally ruined by bombs but has since been completely reconstructed. The lovely twin onion-shaped domes have long been Munich's city symbol and are frequently seen silhouetted on T-shirts, decals, and other notions.

Deutsches Jagdmuseum • *German Hunting Museum, Neuhauserstrasse 52* • Opened in 1966, this excellent collection of over 200 mounted hunting and fishing trophies, including antlers and other field-and-stream lore, will be of particular interest to the sportsminded. It's in midcity near the cathedral.

Tretauto Museum • *Westenriederstrsse 26* • contains antique autos of numerous nations. The models are in sparkling condition.

St. Michaelskirche • *St. Michael's Church, Neuhauserstr. 53* • Built in the 1500s, this austere Jesuit church houses the tomb of Ludwig II, sometimes known as The Dream King or Crazy Ludwig, as well as that of Napoleon's stepson.

Alte Pinakothek • *The Old Art Gallery, Barerstrasse 27* • With a display of over 900 works of art by every European master artist from the 14th to the 18th centuries, this fabulous museum is easily Munich's most important. The collection was started in the 16th century, and was greatly enlarged by King Ludwig I in the early 1800s. Among many others included in this extraordinary collection are Rembrandt, Durer, Altdorfer, Rubens, El Greco, Titian, Raphael, Da Vinci, van Dyck, and Tintoretto.

Neue Pinakothek • *New Art Gallery, Barerstrasse 29* • This one's a chronological complement to the Alte Pinakothek next door, concentrating on French and German impressionism and 18th-century English works.

Glyptothek • *Konigsplatz 3* • This solid, imposing building is the home of an excellent collection of ancient sculpture from the Egyptian, Greek, and Roman ages.

Lenbachhaus • *Luisenstrasse 33* • Just around the corner from the Glyptothek in an unassuming structure stands the Lenbachhaus, filled with highly regarded modern paintings. Included is perhaps the best single collection of the early works of Kandinsky and the works of the Blue Rider school, which revolted against the traditional styles of the late-19th century.

Theater and Music

Next to the combined Berlins, Munich boasts the greatest concentration of live theater anywhere in the nation. Nearly every night, 12,000 seats are up for grabs by music, ballet, opera, drama, comedy, and cabaret devotees. A monthly brochure put out by the Fremdenverkehrsamt (Tourist Office) has all the theater listings, and will help you decide which one to see.

National Theater • *Max-Joseph Platz* • Lovingly restored as a centerpiece for Old World grace and classic architecture, this is one of the city's proudest buildings. It is the home of the Bavarian State Opera, which performs Wagner and Strauss, among others.

Concerts • The Cultural Center Am Gasteig, housing 2400 visitors, is among the nation's more beautiful architectural creations; it is also home of the city's **philharmonic orchestra.** The city hosts an active chamber music schedule in June. The Opera Festival takes the spotlight in July and August.

Markets • Kettles, clothes, candlesticks—you name it—can be picked up cheap if you hit it right at the **Auer Dult,** a flea market that has been going on in one form or another here since the 12th century. It is held 3 times a year (one week at the end of April, one at the end of July, and one at the end of Oct.) at Mariahilfplatz. Also, on every workday morning the bustling stalls at the **Viktualienmarkt** are worth a look. Interesting displays of fruits, vegetables, breads, cheeses, and wines are presided over by rustic-looking but friendly Frauen.

Festivals • Two sprees you can't miss, if you're anywhere near Germany when they're running, are the fabled **Oktoberfest** (late Sept. through early Oct.) and **Fasching** (beginning Nov. 11—11:11 hrs. on the eleventh day of the eleventh month but at its most exciting period around Jan. 7). Another celebration is the Strong Beer Festival, known locally as **"Starkbierzeit,"** which is observed during Lent. The suffix "or" (Imperator, Salvator, Patronator, and more) refers to this extra-potent brew. Because Salvator is the most famous, we suggest going to their own beer hall at Hochstrasse 77 for a pre-Easter sampling.

Excursions

Schloss Nymphenburg • *Nymphenburg Palace and Park* • On the western outskirts of Munich you can visit this baroque palace and its 495-acre park with lakes, winding paths amid the trees, hunting lodges, a carriage collection, a porcelain museum, and a formal garden. Constructed between 1664 and 1745, Nymphenburg was for years the residence of Bavaria's rulers.

Tierpark Hellabrunn • *Hellabrunn Zoo, Siebenbrunnerstrasse 6* • Nib-bling at the banks of the Isar, this lushly planned zoo is Europe's largest. Small rivers enhance the park's natural forestland setting. Buses leave regularly from the Marienplatz.

Neuschwanstein • *Fussen* • Unquestionably one of the most photographed castles in the world, the fantasia of the 19th-century was built by Bavaria's eccentric King Ludwig II. About 2 hours outside of Munich by bus tour or car.

HOTELS

☆☆☆☆☆ **Bayerischer Hof** • is a midcity champion that keeps improving with age—a prizewinner that has garnered the *Prix d'Excellence* for European hotellery. Brightest baubles include a Trader Vic's restaurant, an 850-capacity festival hall, the Tirolian Stube adjoining the Palais Keller for local atmosphere and short-order regional cookery, a 200-ton sliding-roofed swimming pool, a health center with adjoining bar, saunas, a solarium, and the grill with its garden-terrace. There are 7 floors of delightful country-style rooms, many offered as junior suites. Color TV and in-house movies; fresh carpets throughout. The adjoining Palais Montgelas is an elegant classic serving as sort of a Bavarian cousin to the Waldorf Towers. The tariffs there are only slightly more than in the main building, but from private receptionist to golden bathroom taps, everything here is exclusive. In the cellar there's the finest and liveliest nightclub in Bavaria for 200. Highly professional Chief Concierge Walter Freytag has a vast and able team ready to help you. Owner Falk Volkhart merits kudos for his spirited supervision.

☆☆☆☆☆ **Vier Jahreszeiten** • is another splendid and fashionable stalwart provided you receive one of its premium rooms (ask to see your accommodation first). The white-and-gold Walterspiel restaurant is *the* focal point of the area's gastronomy. To one side is the intimate English bar serving soft dance melodies with sips and sups; on the other flank is the Eck ("Corner"), a window-lined nookery that has become famous for its Friday-Saturday buffets; the rooftop pool and sun terrace offer breakfast and lunch and the very same panorama provided by the ultraplush Presidential Suite. Other fillips include the sauna, massage center, hairdressing salons, and a 2-level underground garage. Concierge Alfred Graf is one of Europe's best. Recommended any season.

☆☆☆ **Rafael** • is a relative newcomer appealing to a highly discerning audience of world travelers. Consequently, most of its accommodations are devoted to luxury suites. Marks restaurant, piano bar, rooftop pool, and terrace. A traditional building given every nuance and comfort for the 21st century. The group in which it is a member is one of the prestige names of the world.

☆☆☆ **Continental** • is sumptuous too—if you can find a room that is big enough. (The interior ones overlooking the garden are tranquil.) Spacious lounges;

glorious azure-tiled winter roof garden bursting with flowers; 2 small outdoor parks for summer dining; corridors (some skylighted). Handsome popular Conti Grill with 2000-year-old fountain; cuisine that many residents and travelers praise.

☆☆☆ **Palace** • has come onto the Munich scene with zest, panache, and discreet high style. It's near the English Garden and the Isar, opposite the famous Kafer-Schanke fine-foods complex (see below). Happily, German traditionalisms are preserved; superior comfort; marble baths; rich textiles and decor. Only space for about 130 guests so a sense of personality exists.

Marriott • the American export, is 2.5 miles from the center of town and 20 minutes from the airport. It contains space for about 700 guests, a California Grill, bar, and a pastry nook off the lobby. Then you can take off the sweets in the gym, the sauna, or the indoor pool. A colorful choice, but not too handy to central events.

☆ **Holiday Inn** • is a 3-part giant in the Schwabing district. Its trio of buildings contains rather limited but colorful space for 600; all of the singles have been decked out with double beds. Modernistic interior; lobby and reception in the central edifice staffed with helpful knowing personnel; handsome Old Munich Bar under brick arches; dining salon, grill, and coffee shop; Yellow Submarine nightclub; beverage and ice machines on the various floors; swimming pool.

☆ **Park Hilton** • sited near the English Gardens and thus also a fair fling from midtown, greets guests with an attractive lobby and then charms them with a host of Bavarian bedchambers. The higher ones view the lovely Isar River and canal. Grill plus terrace dining by the waterside, all very appealing; year-round swimmery plus sauna. Bus service (for a fee) to and from the airport every 90 minutes. A **City Hilton** with an additional 750 pillows has just been fluffed up on Rosenheimer Str. Be sure to note the difference in locations when booking.

Sheraton • on the outskirts, has mellowed nicely, with vines covering its once raw concrete modular panels. Pool; Atrium restaurant; international plus tour clientele; sleek impression generally.

★ **Eden-Wolff** • boasts a fine plant with a wood-lined lobby, polished bronze-toned lounge, and adjoining well-architected corners in stone, glass, and sedate rusticity. Zirbelstube ski-lodge dining room with knotty timbers, stone arch, and Brueghel mural; colorful sleeping quarters, many featuring alcove beds; garage.

☆☆ **Excelsior** • hard by the train terminal, is a surprising island of quiet. Contemporary Christmas-card lobby in wood and stained glass; appealing Sankt Hubertus restaurant in 3 tiers and hunting motif; 100 spotless units, including penthouse suites, encircling a peaceful courtyard; most sancta cheery and others very smartly elegant.

☆☆☆ **Konigshof** • offers an attractive and unusual colorama; lovely mezzanine restaurant with a sophisticated mood and superior cuisine; cozy hideaway bar; every square millimeter revamped, upgraded, and buffed to perfection; bedchambers with a maze of convenience-gadgetry; air-conditioned.

★ **Intercity** • by the station, continues to win a following for Old World charm and modern comfort. All Chambers soundproofed and air-cooled; immaculate maintenance.

★ **Splendid** • would rank even higher if it had a restaurant and a bit more space. It is a 40-room house with antique furnishings, distinctive decor (with each unit different), and very amiable people. Quite nice if you are happy with breakfast only.

★ **An Der Oper** • takes its name (obviously) from its proximity to the Opera, which also affords the visitor a convenient address for general sightseeing and shopping. Restaurant with international selections; professional staff overseen by keen management; 55 rooms so there's no sensation of mass commercialism. Moderate prices; recommendable.

Penta • a 600-unit sister to the airline consortium of Europe, is functional. Happily, the subway (S-Bahn) stops at its door on Rosenheimer Platz.

Arabella • *on the street of the same name* • in a satellite suburb that's a costly taxi ride from the bright lights, is—like the Sheraton, its neighbor—probably too remote for holiday makers. A subway connection does make linkage faster and cheaper, however. There are three other Arabellas of this group (Olympic Park, Westpark, and Central) in or near Munich.

International • seemed too aggressively mod-minded to suit me, but the prices are fair; breakfast is the only meal served.

Austrotel • near the railroad station, is commercial and clean; 180 rooms within its 18 stories; reserve high for wide-window eyefuls and silence.

Drei Lowen • *"Three Lions"* • is a favorite of well-bred Bavarian gentry who visit the metropolis. Two attractive dining rooms; cheery retreats. Recommended for its warmhearted personnel and matching clientele.

Amba • hosts numerous tour packages within its 90-room shell; breakfast only.

Ariston • also serves breakfast only.

Metropol • is stiff, dour, and institutional; icy-cold lobby halfheartedly brightened by tropical flora; routine bedchambers.

Tourotel • is boxy. Distant location in an industrial forest of smokestacks; plasticky reception and lobby; Naugahyde-and-formica restaurant and bar; pool and sauna. While the kind staff remains the big plus here, in my opinion the minuses have it.

RESTAURANTS

☆☆☆☆☆ **Aubergine** • *Maximilianplatz 5* • is plainly sensational if quality is your object and price is not. Also, patience should be one of your virtues because a major repast can consume 4 hours for ingestion. Chef Eckart Witzigmann has created a haven of modernistic beauty (locals jestfully call it the "operating room" because of the sterility) with modernistic cuisine to match. There are a few windowside tables plus an inner alcove, all in white with brushed aluminum paneling, a curious blend of Empire and Star Trek styles. Reception and service are perfection; a gourmet menu of vast variety and whispy lightness totals close to $100; a la carte will come to nearly the same for a third the number of dishes. The city is rightly proud of this splendid contender.

☆☆☆☆ **Tantris** • *J. Fichte Str. 7* • a practitioner of similar gastronomy, is nearly as spectacular. Modular futuristic construction; orange and red color scheme; walls and ceilings carpeted; planter boxes, and tall floral displays; thoughtful yet peculiar illumination in keeping with its challenging architecture. The food, too, is graciously constructed with prices a smidgen below Aubergine's. Superb, and enthusiastically recommended.

★★★★ **Weinhaus Schwarzwalder** • *Hartmannstr. 8* • a few steps in front of the Bayerischer Hof Hotel, is one of my favorites in the nation for authentic German atmosphere and honest national fare. One room in rich wood tones, pewter decorative plates, brass chandeliers, oil paintings, candlelight—in other words, all the elements for true Old World flavor. Maitre Berghauser will kindly lead you through the menu choices and the generous wine list. My roasted duck was excellent; so were the turbot filets and venison ordered by others at my table. Memorable.

☆☆ **Boettner** • *Theatinerstr. 8* • is another fine choice, and offers only 9 tables in rear of a small wine and gourmet-item shop; pleasant but not ornate atmosphere; close attention by staff who *care;* shuttered on Sun.; very expensive but worth every pfennig. Be certain to make your advance reservation in this extraordinary nook.

★★★★ **Kafer Schanke** • *Schumannstrasse/Prinzregentenstr.* • is for the most fun along with overwhelming variety and sparkling culinations; the Barnum & Bailey & Bulgari of Munich gastronomy. Its enormous success springs largely from its quality. This one grew out of a patrician delicacy shop that now includes related gift items. Most of the tempters for first courses and appetizers are displayed in cafeteria-style chilling cabinets. Diners are invited to take their plate and select from the dozens of handsomely presented salads, gelatins, timbales, pates, croutes, coldcut tidbits, treasures of the briny, and a trove of other nibbles; pick as much or as little as your appetite or diet dictates; the staff keeps a running record for your billing. Later a flock of waiters serves the main dishes, beverages, cheeses, sweets or other platters at your table or at rustic counters. The atmosphere is gay with laughter and bustling with activity.

☆☆☆☆ **Vier Jahreszeiten's** • dining room unquestionably retains its high repute. Excellent soft music is rendered with the comestibles in the intimate bar annex. The Friday-Saturday buffets in the Eck ("Corner") of the lovely dining salon are becoming famous with German epicures.

★★★★★ **Bayerischer Hof** • rafts ashore with its Trader Vic's, which is keeping the jungle drums busy beating out exciting drinks, Polynesian fixin's, and amiable professional service; the traditional favorite here has always been the grill. The latter, with an intimate Stube, has nightly substantial cookery, zither melodies, and competent management.

★★ **Haxenbauer** • *Munzstr. 2* • nestles among the most antique buildings of Munich. Tantalizing roasts grilling in the windows; cozy, snug, dark interior—probably better in winter than on a summer's day. Noteworthy for its natural food and charm.

The steak houses **Ochs'n Willi** and **Ochs'n Sepp** mix up a nightly mess of old-fashioned Oklahoma spareribs. This same group runs the **Beim Haberer** local-style wine cellar, and the modern **Spatenhaus.**

☆☆ **Goldene Stadt** • *Oberanger 44* • whipped up one of the best meals of a recent teutonic trot—including those sampled at restaurants of infinitely higher cost and fame. Four adjoining rooms; main segment adorned with a photomural of the bridge over the Moldau in central Prague; respectful reception, the like of which one seldom experiences in this era; careful service by German-speaking waiters. The Slavic and local dishes are all prepared by highly skilled Dusan Hubacek, the white-smocked owner-chef. Be sure to top off his feast with a shot of Barack offered in a stovepipe glass. The finest Czech-point this side of Prague.

★ **Peterhof Gaststatten** • next to the ranking Ratskeller (see below) complex (Marienplatz), is recommendable for solid, moderately priced Bavarian fare. Two-floor Peterhof from ground level in clean-lined regional decor and with plenty of space between its tables and big booths; basement Peterskeller for beer and oompah band between 5 and 12:30; slightly more costly Hoch Cafe on 5th floor with lovely view of the square and of the historic moving figures in the Town Hall which enchant big crowds at 11 a.m. and 5 p.m. (summer only); both restaurants open continuously from 9 a.m.–midnight. Salt of the earth.

★ **Ratskeller** • is a splendid example of its genre. It's big, of course, and the food is regional, solid, and tasty. Low vaults; low prices; high value.

Zum Alten Markt • *Dreifaltigkeitsplatz 3* • edges the town's food market, a testament to the freshness of its wares. In nice weather dine at the courtyard.

☆☆ **Mifune** • *Ismaninger Strasse 136* • is run in conjunction with the local Japanese tourist office. Attractive Oriental flavored (and fragranced) decor; longish bar; large counter service section with Nipponese bell-shaped grills for the steak teppanyaki specialty; 2 western dens with about 7 tables; tea room for ceremonial purposes. Hours: 11:30–2 and 6–midnight the calendar round, except on Mon. when Mifune rests.

★★★ **Alois Dallmayr** • is fascinating. On the vast ground floor is one of the world's most distinguished food centers with a staggering variety of German and imported delicacies including an aromatic coffee department, a tea department, a marvelous selection of cheeses, fish, hams, vegetables, pastries—name your yum-yum. Upstairs is a 4-room skein of charming light-bite restaurants. Adjoining is a very distinguished gift boutique. The food is expensive but superb.

Kreutzkamm • near the Bayerischerhof on Maffeistrasse, is an excellent *konditorei* for nibblings; it is open the whole shopping day. Homemade desserts and candies are main features.

★★★ **Olympia Tower** • a 951-foot TV spike looming over the site of the Olympic Games and an enormous ice rink. From its upper tiers the Alps (65 miles away) are easily visible on a clear day. Small entrance fee; ground-floor Atrium Restaurant; rocket-thrust ascent via the fastest elevator in Europe (you might swallow your tummy as you rise 7 meters per second); revolving 3-speed, 32-table panoramic dining ring that is breathtaking; stationary snack bar; upper-level observation deck, plus a children's platform still higher (with low but thick walls to prevent parental coronaries when the little ones venture near the edge). For about $8 by taxi, pennies by tram (#3 or #7), or special bus from the station, visually rewarding for any first-timer to Munich. If it's a glaring or bright day, bring sunglasses.

Mathaeser Beer City • bills itself as the "largest beer-tavern in the world." The open-air garden upstairs normally operates during the 3 warmest months. Concerts in main section at 10:30–4 and from 4:30–12 with a bigger band; open every day except Dec. 24; good hearty food.

Nurnberger Bratwurstglockl • opposite the Dom, should be mentioned for an atmosphere-filled and gratifyingly inexpensive meal. The dumplings, as well as the wursts, are triumphs.

Platzl • opposite the Hofbrauhaus and a few steps from the Vier Jahreszeiten, might be called a Bavarian Music Hall; a lively show (in German) goes on throughout your dinner every day of the week except Sun. Also clean, also sound cookery, also typical.

Lowenbraukeller • a gigantic building and garden, can handle 7000 customers at a sitting. And if you want to sit with 'em, that's up to you. It's a genuine slice of life, however.

Hofbrauhaus • which has a capacity for 7000 tipplers, seems to have been the target for every tourist since Genghis Khan. Have a drink, a peek, and a listen to the oooom-pah band. If you do it just once, that's enough.

Weinstadl • *Burgstrasse 5* • an Old City tavern newly restored but virtually unchanged since the day it opened more than 5 centuries ago. Here is Munich's most ancient house, the site where town scribes scratched out the first municipal records at long wooden tables. Main floor plus cellar; vaulted ceilings of brick and mortar; nothing fancy and nothing pretended. Try only a platter of local cheeses and wine if you are not too hungry; open daily from 10 a.m.–midnight.

NIGHT LIFE

Munich has quite a variety of night spots. The No. 1 choice is the subterranean lode of the **Hotel Bayerischer Hof.** Split-level gem with the bar and wraparound tables mounted high and a dance circle below; brick and timber decor; central heating by some of the hottest bands on the Continent; appetizing snacks and good honest drinks. **Hilton** features pana-romantics and dancing on its 15th floor. Also in hotel circles, the Holiday Inn's **Splash** packs in a full house most nights. **Vibraphon** vibrates, too, in the Sheraton. **Eve** is a sophisticated lady who is tastefully ornamented. Continuous show beginning at 11:30 p.m.; the inevitable door snip; at tables, the house policy requires a bottle of champagne (expensive to astronomical) or a ½-bottle of whisky; individual drinks grudgingly served at bar; teetotalers find themselves in the squeezer, with orange juice at perfume price levels per cup (and it's been cut!). Among tonight's top disco hubs, **Sunset** attracts loyal nighthawks, as do **Canterville, Charley M,** and **Lenbach-Palast. Schwabinger Podium,** in Schwabing, draws the Smart Young Set. In this same nightlife district, **tomate, Doctor Flotte, Turbo,** and **Kauzchen** are diverting. **P-1** has a charming allure generally and is ideal for romancers. Inner sanctum with timber and oil paintings. Many seek solace from loud music by having a midnight snack at **Lilien's Affair** (Lilienstr. 51), which harks back to the twenties. It's "in" right now with all levels of local society.

The prostitutes parade along Landsberger Strasse, near the outskirts of the city, and Josephspitalstrasse, where they must remain in doorways or passages to avoid arrest for "streetwalking." They also advertise on a special page in the *Abend Zeitung.*

SHOPPING

SHOPPING AREAS: Briennerstrasse, Theatinerstrasse, and Maximilian-strasse are the most chichi. Kaufingerstrasse is a pedestrian's pasture. Between the Marienplatz and Karlsplatz are most of the large department stores. Leopoldstrasse—in fact, Schwabing in general—is not what it used to be. Forget it.

NOTE · · · Europe's largest underground shopping center is under the Stachus, Munich's main square.

CAMERAS AND ACCESSORIES: Kohlroser (Maffeistrasse 14) is our favorite camera shop in southern Germany—not only because the stock is so extensive, but also because Mr. Schindler and assistants Mr. Honig and Mr. Fischer are so honest, so kindly, and so interested in doing the best possible job for each client. They refund the turnover tax of about 12% through the Tax Free Shop Organization after the customs declaration form is returned. Every camera in the shop is guaranteed for a minimum of 12 months, even if shipped. On their shelves you'll find an extensive assortment of the absolute latest models of cameras, movie cameras, binoculars, opera glasses, Zoom lenses for German and Japanese cameras, automatic slide projectors and flea-size electronic computer flash units and keen knowledgeability. Furthermore, the house provides 2-day service on Ektachrome. Superb stocks, superb values.

FOOD DELICACIES: Feinkost Kaefer (Schumannstr. 1) and **Alois Dallmayr** (Dienerstrasse 14–15) offer so many items to tantalize your 5 senses that I won't even begin to encourage you on the path of sin here.

FURNITURE: Deutsche Werkstatten (Briennerstrasse 54) is the marketplace of many independent Bavarian artisans, with its accent on furniture, fabrics, lamps, and wooden paintings.

HANDICRAFTS: Wallach (Residenzstrasse 3) has 2 floors packed to the rafters with them, as well as a basement bulging with antiques.

HIGH FASHION: Maendler (Theatinerstr. 7) dresses the smartest ladies in Munich, a city noted for its tasteful womankind. Here are the people to see for evening gowns, designer sweaters, suits, and anything else for your wardrobe.

JEWELER: Hans R. Rothmuller (Briennerstrasse 1) is the most distinguished—with the most distinguished price tags, too.

MARKETS: There is no **Flea Market** in Munich. The so-called **Farmer's Market** (Auer Dult) runs its frenzied course 3 times per year—early April, early Aug., and Oct. 15–23. It's a huge rummage sale which is such fun that we urge you don't miss it if you're there when it's in action.

OPTICS: **Sohnges** (Briennerstrasse 7 and Kaufingerstrasse 34) is one of the 2 or 3 top optical complexes in the world today. Excellent contact lens department; sunglasses and other eye aids available; cordial service and noteworthy precision.

TABLEWARE: **Nymphenburg** (Odeonplatz 1) is Rosenthal's only German rival for quality porcelains; this singular brand is made at the Munich factory.

NURNBERG   is a charming example of the once-moated medieval metropolis. Its walls, towers, and ancient landmarks have been almost completely restored (one tower stands 1000 feet tall beaming TV pictures thoughout the area); the impressive **Kaiserburg** (Imperial Palace) dominates the local landscape, but without the "Iron Maiden" and other historic instruments of torture; the **Meistersingerhalle** is handsome. Durer's 5-century-old dwelling and the St. Lorenz and St. Sebaldus churches are the most popular sights. On the first Sat. of every month you can hop aboard Trolly #701 which predates World War I; its a fun way to tour the city's landmarks.

As for its hotels, **Maritim** is fresh and well managed with a cheerful dining salon of polished rusticity. Next would be the **Atrium;** the **Grand** is still the Old Guard leader. **Victoria's** exterior and downstairs, on the other hand, belie what you'll find when you open your bedroom door: sterile and heartlessly grim cells. **Moat House** is a reasonable buy and the **Carlton** offers similar rewards for like prices. **Am Ring,** situated in the eye of an interesting traffic hurricane, is bright, clean, and satisfactory; breakfast only. **Reichshof** evokes a commercial feel, with furniture that looks as if it were borrowed from a nightclub. **Queens** is excellent if you are making a fast passage. Handy site for roadrunners near the exit to the Berlin–Munich and Frankfurt–Nurnberg autobahns; 6 stories containing a specialty restaurant, the Puppengrill for international fare, the Oldtimer Bar, and well-appointed bedrooms or suites.

When speaking of food in this town, I'd like to lead with my first choice of *the* place to avoid: The famous **Goldenes Posthorn.** This self-appointed temple of gastronomy claims to be both the oldest wine cellar in Germany (A.D. 1498) and very nearly the finest restaurant on both hemispheres. With as much charity as I can muster, let's just confess that my views hardly coincide with those of its management. Much better, in my opinion (and much cheaper too), is **Heilig Geist-Spital,** built over the water in midcity on arches placed in the 14th century. Yellowing walls, iron chandeliers, antlers; hardy bratwurst, liver, pork and dumplings, snail soup, and wonderful saurbraten in gingerbread sauce. Very friendly people. Pure fun and authentic local color? You'll probably have a grand old time at **Bratwurst-Herzle.** Community tables; standard pewter plate, heartshape platter of fingerling sausages, sauerkraut and horseradish, beer, cheese—and that's all; always packed. In the same category, **Friedl** and **Bratwurst-Hausle** are also worthy but offer less flair. **Nassauer Keller** has better cookery.

OBERAMMERGAU   The legendary *Passion Play,* portraying the last days of
Christ's life has made the town famous; it is given every decade and last year
was a performance year. Meanwhile whittlers feverishly carve out shelves (nay,
warehouses) of passionate souvenirs that are sold at prices higher than in the
neighboring villages. The leading hotel remains the **Alois Lang.** Quiet situation;
51 rooms; all units with private balcony and most with bath; carpeting throughout. Its 3 dining rooms serve up savory vittles. The **Wolf** offers more charm in
its bedchambers (especially the top-floor Bavarian rooms), but its central situation and busy-busy public areas give it a somewhat commercial feel. Flowers
and colorful touches everywhere; prices lower than the leader; very good value.
Alte Post comes up with cheery accommodations but a very low bath count.
Bold plays host to battalions of *G.I.*'s during ski season; not bad for basic-
minded sportsman. The **Wittelsbach** seems to have a love affair with package
tours. Independents might feel uneasy. In neighboring *Ettal,* also in Oberbay-
ern, the barnish **Ludwig der Bayer** has a big name locally, but it seems as cold
as a penguin's pinfeather; if you burrow into its icebergs, take the newer wing
only.

ROMANTIC ROAD   Along this ancient way what you seek, of course, is
preserved obsolescence. You'll discover exactly that. This fascinating route was
a vital and thriving lifeline during the Middle Ages, when a military link between fortresses was imperative for survival. The word "Hof," which is suf-
fixed to the names of so many modern German hotels, literally derives from the
walled and safe "courtyard" where travelers could rest while passing from
stronghold to stronghold. Initially, they slept in their carriages or under their
horses. Soon drink was provided. Later food was served. Finally overnight shelters were constructed. When the wars ended and transportation lanes were shifted,
these great installations became superannuated. Not until recent times did historic interest regenerate their unique touristic allure.

Wurzburg offers a spectacular beginning for your pilgrimage. The Franks
founded it in the 7th century and Irish monks gave it a Christian essence about
100 years later. Today its most noteworthy features emphasize the power and
riches of its once great economy and religious orders. The Prince-Bishops' Palace is a sightseeing must; the chapel is dazzling, with gold applique on marble;
Tiepolo paintings adorn the walls; the adjoining castle is awesome for its majestic chambers. Include a visit to Marienberg Fortress with its treasury of priceless
Riemenschneider woodcarvings, costumes, pewter and paintings of a like category, including Cranach's *Adam and Eve.* The Cathedral is a glorious manifestation of Romanesque style as is the Neumuenster, a basilica that was begun in
the 11th century. There are approximately 20 other sightseeing alternatives of
considerable interest spread throughout the town. Most of them can be visited
with determined footwork if you have a pedestrian nature, the midtown area
being convenient and attractive for walking. Should your spirits flag, adequate
regional restoratives can be found at the **Buergerspital,** which is a working
winehouse with roots planted in the early 14th century and many old-fashioned
culinary presentations of almost the same era. The **Ratskeller** offers a multitude
of dining segments including a beer cellar, the Shield Hall, and the colorful Old
Wurzburg room. Another amusing choice is the dining salon of the **Hotel Am**

Markt with its fantastic view of the Falcon House and ecclesiastical buildings. For overnighting, first-place honors go to the well-managed **Rebstock** with its extremely hospitable staff overseen by the Unckell family. International cookery in the restaurant and Franconian selections in the cozily rustic Weinstube; comfortable complement of 81 bedrooms. The **Maritim** is so large (more than 500 souls) that it slays the notion of visiting villages on this route. The **Steinburg** resides on its own *berg* overlooking vineyards and the city. The 7-century-old **Leicht,** out toward Kitzingen, is a charming haven of antiquity with superior regional cuisine. Spend a night in either *Mainz* (the **Hilton** is a far cry from a "Hof") or in *Wiesbaden* (see further along, where accommodations are better than anything you'll find en route, with the exception of Rothenburg ob der Tauber). *Bad Mergentheim* is no longer lauded as a scenic attraction; today it's more famous as a spa, with the top watering spot the modernistic **Viktoria** or the traditional **Park.** Now zip through *Weikersheim* and *Creglingen* to *Rothenburg ob der Tauber* for the best and most exciting overnight of the entire loop. This antique sparkler is the gem of the bracelet, so we urge that you concentrate most of your time, calories, and shut-eye here.

Rothenburg is one of the wonderlands of Europe, standing above the Tauber, which today is a nearly dried-up fiction. The streets are cobbled, the cottages and buildings lean toward each other, and painted signs and guilded windlasses glisten in the sunlight while bells chime hauntingly through the evening hours. Craftsmen work at the windows of their ateliers creating delightful wax figures, textiles or spice cakes. And what better place on earth to have 12 months of Christmas? The unique **Kathe Wohlfahrt's Christkindlmarkt** (Herrngasse 2) is a bewildering sight on an August day or any time of the year. Inside there is Christmas music, trees are alight, angels sing carols from loggias, toy soldiers bow and march, and if you count them you will probably notice as many as 50,000 different items in the inventory—a fairyland of toys, decorations, and gift ideas that provoke thoughts of everyone back home. While there are many historic things to see here or elsewhere on the Romantic Road, this particular emporium is unique in the world. Incidentally, if you show this book to Mr. Wohlfahrt or any other key personnel they will give you a Christmas ornament as a memento of your visit.

The hotels break down into two styles, both of which I consider 5 star in quality but different in mood: ★★★★★ **Eisenhut** ("Iron Hat") offers a stunning perch over the Tauber vale; it augments this with a terraced restaurant and windowfront dining room; an annex, beautifully antique, is across the street, but with no valley view. The mood here is Old World, with many new baths and comfort features to improve your stay. ★★★★ **Goldener Hirsch** also has viewful accommodations. Here the public rooms and accommodations put more emphasis on luxury. The staff is extremely warmhearted, the cuisine includes fresh venison any time of the year whether the chef must obtain it locally, from France, Austria, Hungary or elsewhere. There is a special menu just for snails (common to vinelands) with 15 separate choices of *Schnecken.* Your innkeeping pleasure in this town really depends upon your own personal taste.

☆ **Adam** ● has a *Weinstube;* far better bedchambers than the older ones in the Eisenhut at twice the bite.

Try also the **Tilman Riemenschneider,** the **Baren,** or the **Romantik Hotel Markusturm.** Moving on through *Feuchtwangen* to the walled city of *Dinkelsbuhl,* which is a glorious antique gem set among lakes. The painted houses are set among 20 towers and gateways. Here the **Goldene Rose** has been reperfumed petal by petal and is now quite recommendable; the nearby **Deutsches Haus** started life nearly six centuries ago, the dining room boasting illuminated legends and heraldic links to the past—and very acceptable cuisine too; the little **Palmengarten,** though without a restaurant, is pleasant as an alternate choice for sleeping. *Nordlingen* is not for lingering, and *Donauworth* also is hardly worthwhile; both should be daylight pauses only. In *Augsburg,* the most august is the **Drei Mohren** ("Three Moors") followed by a ho-hum **Holiday Inn; Augusta** and the **Dom** are breakfast-only shelters; the **Alpen** is fair enough, but none will really wow you. The city itself is rather large, known for its Fuggerei (named for a powerful local dynasty), the Rotes Tor for open-air opera and Mozart summer festivals. In *Landsberg,* the pleasant **Goggl** has augmented its basic allure, with a handsome timbered interior, gay textiles, and much improved gastronomy. In *Regensburg* (off "The Romantic Road" but in the same district), the tiny **Avia** is more intimate than the nicely restored and restyled **Parkhotel Maximilian.** *Rottenbuch, Wies, Steingaden,* and world-renowned *Schwangau* will never win prizes for creature comforts, but they are thrilling for rubbernecking. **Hirsch** in nearby *Fussen,* boasts 50 rooms, a listless restaurant, and a cozy country-style *Stube* for beer, wine, and trencherman fare. If you are heading this way for the purpose of seeing the Neuschwanstein and Hohenschwangau castles, opt for either the road-hugged, tiny **Lisl und Jagerhaus** or the **Muller** at the base of the path leading up to the summits. The latter with some chambers attractively finished in pinewood; snack bar; tavern; not bad if you can sweet-talk private plumbing from the reception people.

STUTTGART takes pride in its pleasant location, mineral springs, eye-popping 692-foot Fernsehturm (TV tower) restaurant, German Antiques Fair, Liederhalle for concerts, the stunning Daimler-Benz Museum, the Carl Zeiss Planetarium, "Sunny" (the performing chimp at the Wilhelma Zoo and Botanical Gardens), and such important factories as Daimler-Benz, Porsche, Kodak-Germany, and Bosch-Germany. The citizens are not too sure whether they are pleased with the expensive and architecturally bizarre Neue Staatsgalerie created by Britain's controversial James Stirling. See for yourself if they received their pound-stirling's worth in the rampant free form passages and colorful halls that contain mostly 20th-century works (especially those of Otto Dix, the expressionist). I find it more whimsical and witty than Paris' intestinal Pompidou Center. Literally translated, the name of the city is "Stud Farm," which harks back to an era of far less industry in this burgeoning district.

The young and spry 277-room **Intercontinental,** in the center overlooking the "Castle Garden," brings a new level of sophistication to town. (It even offers "nonsmoker" rooms!) Lovely Les Continents restaurant plus an Italian patio and some hardy wine and beer nooks. Indoor pool and sauna; basically sound and directed especially to the business traveler.

The 8-story **Am Schlossgarten** is an asset of innkeeping to this Detroit of Germany. Good cuisine in its glass-lined dining salon or parkside sun terrace; Swabian tavern with paneled, leather-ceilinged bar; adequate for short stays.

The **Graf Zeppelin** is a well-managed chain operation. Longer-term visitors may find larger accommodations here, plus a goodly supply of suites; informal to dressed-up dining in 2 fine salons with superior cookery; plenty of charm and personality recently added to rooms and lounges; indoor swimming pool plus a sauna. **Parkhotel,** 10 minutes out in Villaberg Park, offers restful surroundings, except when the tours pour in. **Schloss Monrepos** is a romantic lakesider at *Ludwigsburg,* a nearby playground of nobility and a charmer in every respect. **Schloss Solitude** is a 15-minute scoot from town via the highway that periodically becomes the world-famous sports-car racing course. Its main function (except to coddle Porsche-bred nostalgics who rally out to whip through a few gears) is to serve as a multinational arts academy instead of its former function as a hotel. **Airport (Movenpick) Hotel** glides in with a cargo of flair in its soft-toned, window-lined dining room, its adjoining bar, and the mod-mooded lobby. All 128 rooms with bath, radio, beds with vibrators, and telephone; bus and even a helicopter service for the Stuttgart environs. **Hotel Stuttgart International** raises its proud head just off Highway 27 at *Mohringen,* 5 minutes from the airport and a fairly expensive taxi hop from the center of town. Dining facilities galore; pool, sauna, bowling lanes, underground garage. Superb furnishings in all 200 bedrooms, demisuites, and full apartments. There's a **Ramada** at *Sindelfingen;* it's a nice one, used mainly by travelers related to the auto industries of the region.

By day or by night, the **Fernsehturm** (TV tower) is a sensation—for view, not for gastronomy. Atop a hill, it's a 692-foot-high needle, which impales a tapered aluminum and glass "cork" at the 558-foot level—and this cork is a 4-story restaurant, TV transmission point, observation platform, kitchen, and wine cellar (sic). Back in the city proper, most townsfolk seem to be addicted to the colorful and charming **Alte Post.** For regional cooking in wine restaurants, try either the **Schellenturm** or the **Schreinerei. Movenpick,** with its woodlined Rotisserie Baron de la Mouette, sizzles on the Kleiner Schlossplatz.

WIESBADEN is a scenic spa and an excellent springboard for your Romantic Road–running. There's a May Festival, a splendid Casino, the Kurhaus, thermal baths, museums, lovely old buildings, and the network of parks retained from Germany's most gracious period.

☆☆☆☆ **Nassauer Hof** ● retains the lead among innkeepers. For dining here try the deluxe Die Ente vom Lehel restaurant with exceptional duck specialties. The Orangerie, in a delightful, cheery setting, has lighter nouvelle dishes with a German approach. Bar with copper hearth; pool and sauna.

This would be followed by the old-fashioned **Schwarzer Bock,** the new-fashioned **Holiday Inn Crowne Plaza,** the **Aukamm,** the **Penta,** and the **Forum,** the last of which are utilitarian. The midtown **Badhaus Baren** provides a pool; only breakfast is served. Pretty good value.

★★★★ **Schwan** ● *in the outskirts of Ostrich* ● is one of the nation's best-known country inns—and it has country-style appointments rather than city-slick refinement; set-back Rhine-side location with enchanting view; savory regional cookery; *tastevin* cellar for wine sampling; friendly service. It is also one of the few places where you can order fine "ice wine" by the glass instead

of having an entire bottle (which can be expensive and too sweet). Ask for
room #207 or any riverfront unit for the view, or a back accommodation for
quiet. Operated by the Winkel-Wenckstern family since A.D. 1628; ideal for
tranquillity; legendary for its wines; open March 1 to December 1 only. Don't
confuse it with the one in *Walluf,* which is 4 miles closer to Wiesbaden.

☆☆ **Reinhartshausen** • in the same riverside neighborhood, is attracting
visitors to its stately and dew-fresh precincts. The location makes it ideal as a
pausing spot in your motoring explorations of this richly historic region.

★★★★ **Die Enle vom Lehel** • in the Nassauer Hof attracts food-conscious
international gourmets. Don't forget the Orangerie here too. Expect a hefty bill.
Hotel de France also boasts a fine kitchen.

Movenpick • is across from the Casino; it's okay for medium-priced dining in this high-priced town.

Alt Prag • produces some praiseworthy Czech creations.

While in the vicinity, avoid the wine-soaked streets of **Rudesheim,** but
instead visit riverside *Eltville* or roam in the vineyards above to the 850-year-
old *Kloster Eberbach.* It was here that Burgundian monks introduced their ex-
acting techniques, which resulted in quality control and German "kabinett"
wines. There's a small cafe for light bites and gauging the local viniculture at
the cloister. More formalized wine tasting occurs weekends only.

GIBRALTAR

USA: Gibraltar Information Bureau, Mr. Perry Stieglitz, 710, The Madison Offices, 1155 Fifteenth St. N.W., Washington DC 20005; Tel. (202) 542–1108; Fax (202) 872–8543.

SPECIAL REMARKS: The border between Gibraltar and Spain has been reopened for some time, but the future of this patch on the straits between two continents remains unsettled. Until negotiations are concluded between the United Kingdom and Spain other useful sources of information will be either the British Tourist Authority or British Airways.

"The Rock" is back in business. While Gib remains in British hands, the amnesty that was arranged with the Spanish government provides for a wide-open frontier—averaging 6000 visitors a day and at peak times as many as 18,000! While such volume, naturally, comes from the Spanish side by bus, it is also possible to have direct connections from London and several other European points. The airport boasts a 6000-foot runway that can accommodate Tri-Stars but that hosts chiefly Boeing 737s.

Gib is a mountainous promontory at the western mouth of the Mediterranean, 3 miles long, three-quarters of a mile wide, and 1396 feet high. There are 27 miles of narrow roads and approximately 30,000 souls who live or work here. You can drive in from La Linea on Winston Churchill Avenue, see the changing of the guard at the Governor's Residence, stroll among winding lanes, telephone from London-style kiosks, and knock back a pint at Ye Olde Rock Inn, a noted pub close to Assembly House.

While chambermaids fluff up only 2500 pillows per day, ambitious projections look to more than doubling that figure over the next several years—all in an area approximately the size of New York's Central Park. As a visitor, all you need are a passport and a pocket full of money; the latter, you'll find, will go a loooong way in purchasing cashmeres, tobacco, and other shopping bonanzas for approximately one third the U.S. sums. Returning to Spain, however, the duty-free allowance is only about $60 worth of goods. But as you leave Spain you'll also be permitted to obtain the Spanish rebate.

Apart from bathing, roaming up among the water catchments, and shopping, almost the only thing to do is to get acquainted with the 35 Barbary apes at their Den, visit the magnificent St. Michael's Cave, explore the Upper Galleries, tip your hat to the British bobbies, and spin away a few pesetas or pounds (both are accepted currencies) at the casino. Yachtsmen will probably enjoy yarnin' with the salts in the harbor.

For the moment **The Rock** is the grande dame of local hotels, residing in 9 acres of gardens on the western flank. The swimming pool is a delight, but by far the event no visitor should miss is cocktail hour on the terrace, a staple of British colonial establishmentarianism. The **Holiday Inn** (the best called **City Centre**), the **Bristol,** and the **Caleta Palace** follow in that order for other overnight choices. **Gibraltar Beach** is around at *Sandy Bay* (and it is aptly named) with all rooms facing the water. Facilities are not opulent, but the variety of accommodation makes this a unique choice for families; it offers full hotel service, self-catering apartments, bed-and-breakfast or half-board options. Furthermore, there's a beach bar, coffee shop, and the Trafalgar Restaurant.

As a military bastion that has hosted garrisons from Rome, Phoenicia, and Arabia, as well as modern European conquerors and defenders, there is a nostalgia hereabouts that is unique. Don't schedule a lot of your time on Gib, but as a travel curiosity it is again worth a visit.

GREECE

INCLUDING THE ISLANDS

USA: National Tourist Organization of Greece, 645 Fifth Ave., New York, NY 10022, Tel. (212) 421–5777

SPECIAL REMARKS: (1) Don't consider a voucher anywhere in Greece (hotel, ship, or air transport) sufficient to secure your reservation—especially during High Season. Only a "confirmed" document provides some assurance in the most popular touristic months. (2) Once abroad, you might find help at the **Greek National Tourist Organization,** 2 Amerikis St., Athens. In general bureaucratic buck-passing seems more tangled than Hydra's headdress, so don't expect too much efficiency. A pity, too, because this office used to be one of the most spirited and imaginative in Europe. (3) For travel arrangements, **Hellenic Tours,** 23/25 Ermou St., Athens, is one of the most ethical companies on the scene. President Nelson Melamed couldn't be kinder or more efficient. Since Greece and especially the islands are so jammed in peak seasons, an experienced travel agency can work wonders on your behalf, leaning on overbooked hoteliers, airline personnel, and cruising lines like a friendly elephant.

TELEPHONE: Access code to USA: 00; To phone Greece: 30; time difference (Eastern Daylight) plus 7 hrs.

By its very existence, Greece has to be one of the great sightseeing targets of Western Civilization. Athens itself can be seen rather quickly, so budget your time with that in mind.

Poetry, music, astronomy, philosophy, graphic arts, architecture, mathematics, medicine, law, politics, military science—almost anything that is important to us today, had its seed planted in the Plains of Attica centuries ago.

The shrines of these beginnings still exist—though they are too varied and numerous to list outside of an encyclopedia (and even that was invented by the Greeks: *enkyklios paideia)*. There's Athens with its crowning Acropolis, the Agora, the Temple of Zeus, the Parthenon, the Stoa, Theater of Dionysus, and enough museums to wear out 33 pairs of your stoutest shoes.

Then there are the great attractions of the Peloponnesus such as the Lion Gate and Tombs of the Kings in Mycenae where Agamemnon reigned; Olympia, Nauplia, Delphi, Sparta, and others, with historical sites streaming in tides from the local guidebooks.

Finally there are the islands that served as the womb of mankind: windblown Crete, romantic Mykonos, shimmering Santorini, Kos, lovely Patmos, the jewels of the Saronic bracelet (Aegina, Poros, Hydra, Spetses), Rhodes, Corfu, and a sparkling odyssey of aquarian destinations in the Aegean and Mediterranean seas. (These are covered individually.)

In season—the warm months—the crowding can be tedious. But fortunately the fringe periods are even more delightful than the hottest days of summer, and the attractions are beckoning longer into the spring and autumn than in more northerly climes. Try for May and early June or for September and through most of October.

TRANSPORTATION   **Airline Olympic** is better on transatlantic and European routes than it is within its own homeland. It calls in the U.S. 5 times a week. Pan Am had a thrice weekly non-stop New York-Athens route that it may have sold to another carrier by the time you read this; the linkage also involved an hour's stop via Frankfurt four times per week. TWA also listed a transatlantic route from Athens. Though marginally improved at Athens, the chaos at national airports in summer is numbing. If you plan a trip in High Season, be sure to have your tickets booked and confirmed.

Ferries Several ferries operate between Brindisi (Italy) and Patras. Stops at Corfu and Igoumenitsa; facilities ranging from airplane-type seats to deluxe cabins for both day and overnight sojourns; drive-on-drive-off gangways; space for 150 or more cars; running once every day of the week the year round and more frequently in summer. Additional routings reach Patras from Ancona. There is also piggyback railway service for autos through Italy, a sleeper-bus hookup between Naples and Brindisi in summer, and a viewful coastal highway at the threshold to Greece. The scenic drive between Patras and the capital takes a mere 3 hours.

Taxis Scarce—normally so absent that they should be considered an endangered species. Luckily, the "radio taxi" is an alternative choice. "Immediate" service (about 15 min.) costs 150 Drs. (roughly $1) extra and advance booking (e.g. 2 hrs. ahead or the evening before for an airport run) tacks on 250 Drs. Hotels, tavernas, and clubs have come to rely on these for their clients. Space is so short that passengers often double up and share a hack together. Frequently, a driver will pick up a second fare midway through your ride; he's supposed to ask your approval but seldom does. Expect to be drubbed the full rate; the pickup will pay only a proportion.

When the meter flag drops it registers 60 Drs., with the minimum ride set at 280 Drs. Luggage costs extra, the exact price depending upon the weight and zones covered—a hopeless complication unless you are carrying scales and a

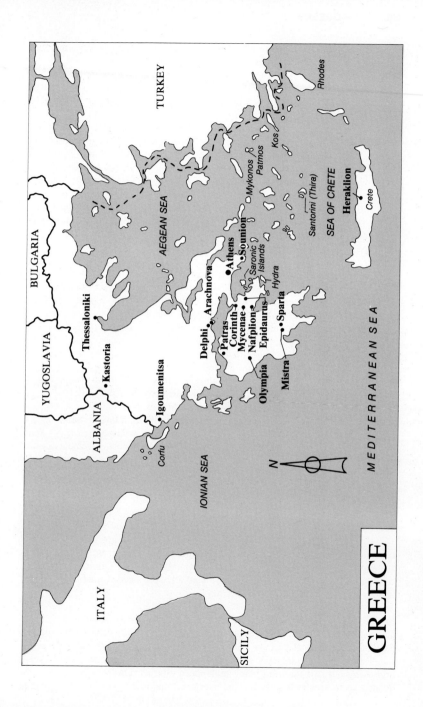

GREECE

city map. You also are charged 30 Drs. more between 1 a.m. and 6 a.m., with additions of Drs. 30 for airport, harbors, or the train and bus termini. As for tipping, don't bother. If you want to be generous, round out the bill by 5 or 10 drachmas—but no more. Thanks to the National Tourist Office, a driver who overcharges and is reported often loses his license. Now he is both more careful and more sly as a result.

To avoid problems, have your destination written out (in Greek letters if possible) and carry a map to indicate where you're headed. An Athenian friend advises "pay *only* the fare shown on the meter and if in doubt stay in the cab and shout for a policeman"—a situation that conjures up visions of meek Woody Allens begging of the rascal at the wheel: "What is the Greek word for cop?"

Buses and Trolleys Buy your tickets in advance. Kiosks near stops sell them (50 Drs. per ride), which can be cancelled by you aboard the trolley (honor system); busses also employ this system. You may purchase individual ducats or books of ten. Leading hotels offer scheduled bus shuttles to and from the airport. Some (Hilton, Marriott, Intercontinental, and Chandris, as examples) operate hitches between their portals and Constitution Sq.

Trains Greece is a member of the moneysaving **Eurailpass** system. You'll get much more for your dollar here, too, since Greek trains are so slow. The service is improving generally, but it's still spotty in quality. The international expresses through Yugoslavia to Zurich, Paris, Ostend, Germany, or other European points are comfortable. There is good diesel railcoach service from Athens to Corinth, Olympia, Nauplia, Tripolis, Levadia, Larissa, and Salonika. The roadbed to the Peloponnesus is narrow-gauge and rooted in a foundation of Jell-O. Travel by car (but be sure to read the "Hired Cars" warning below) or by bus if you can; the Pullman-coach buses are royal chariots by comparison.

Hired Cars and Motoring If you wish to drive yourself, the best rental agency I've found is Hellascars, with its vast fleet of well-maintained vehicles. Next, choose Hertz or Avis. Prices are extraordinarily high on the mainland and even higher on the islands, where you are a captive audience and can't shop around. This is largely due to taxation and the walloping cost of vehicles in this nation. Chauffeur-driven cars in Athens are a special breed of misery. Book *only through one of the recognized and reputable travel agencies in Athens,* such as **Hellenic Tours** mentioned previously. With them, you will at least know the established price beforehand. They have offered to serve as special watchdogs for readers of this book. For excursions, your only solution is to resort to an ordinary cab. Be sure to fix the price before you set out!

If you plan to motor extensively, join ELPA; that's not a Greek cry for assistance, but the initials of the Greek Automobile and Touring Club. There is a registration fee of Drs. 7000 plus an annual charge of Drs. 8000. Among other services, it gives road assistance, legal advice if needed, and discounts on various gas coupons *outside* the country.

NOTE · · · The traffic in the capital's narrow streets became so horrific that authorities are banning midcity circulation for certain vehicles on specific days of each week. If you are a self-driver ask locally for guidance on this.

Roads are not Greece's greatest selling point. On the mainland they are improving but still far from being high-speed arteries. On the islands they frequently seem to vanish entirely. The nation's 2 major highways run from Patras to Athens (limited access and a lovely 3-hour run) and from the capital north to Thessaloniki. The toll pike leading into Athens is very short, only 2 lanes wide in many places, and so poorly engineered as to be especially dangerous on rainy nights.

Don't start any motoring journey after dark. Few oncoming drivers have even heard of the headlight dip-switch; moreover, the countryside is so desolate that if a breakdown occurs you could be stranded till dawn. Trucks also begin their long hauls in the evenings; the pikes are clogged with them all night.

FOOD Stews, salads, roasts, and grills comprise the stereotypy of the Greek kitchen, but that can be as inaccurate as any generalization. There's a much wider variety which requires a sense of adventure and a degree of coaching. If you happen to be gastronomically timid, there are ample opportunities to swallow "international" recipes.

Regional dishes of deserved pride include dolmades (grape leaves stuffed with meat, rice, onion, and seasonings); souvlakia (a succulent facsimile of shish kebab, consisting of lamb, tomatoes, and peppers roasted on a spit); moussaka (chopped meat from some member of the animal kingdom, eggplant, tomato sauce, cheese, eggs, and spices); the magnificent red mullet, finest in the 7 seas; kalamaraki (tenderized squid); thalassina (clams); octopus (so delicious it tastes like chicken-lobster); and the local langouste (clawless crayfish). These are merely samples; there's a large choice of other specialties. Greek ice cream in general (not always) nearly vies with the finest Italian ice cream; try it at the G.B. Corner of the Grande Bretagne Hotel in the capital.

While Greece is in the midst of a sizzling pizza boom, I still prefer peinerli, which literally means "with cheese." It's a "sandwich" of crisp dough shaped like a Viking ship containing your choice of fillers: tomato sauce, chopped meat, chopped meat and egg, ham, ham and egg, sausage and egg, fried egg and ground meat—but *always* with cheese. When it comes piping hot to the table, mix the fillers on the "deck" so they soak into the underside of the crust. Then eat the center out, and finally polish off the whole. **Y Pighi Eleftheriatis** ("The Source") at *Drossia,* 14 miles northeast of Athens, is the original creator and king of this dish.

Meal hours are generally from 9 p.m. to 11:30 p.m. for dinner. As in Egypt, Spain, or Portugal, the later the hour, the larger the crowd.

DRINKS Brandy is the national hard drink; Metaxa, sharply sweet, is the most popular; Camba, far drier and smoother, is the closest contender. Ouzo, bless its jaunty heart, is the national aperitif; it is a thaumaturge's cross between French Pernod, Javanese arrack, and Turkish raki, with a faint licorice flavor. Order Sans Rival brand (its superiority to all others is notable); mix it with water plus lots of ice. No Greek whisky is made, but Greek vermouth is quite drinkable. The multinational brewers produce plenty of Heineken, Amstel, Lowenbrau, Kaiser, and Germania for you to cut the edge off a hot day.

If you are a first-time visitor, you'd probably better order your wine *aretsinato* ("without resin"), or your mouth will pucker so much you'll think you've eaten a basket of persimmons. *Retsina,* or resinated wine, has a distinctive flavor, in no way related to conventional wine expectations, a taste that is refreshing when well chilled. (Personally, I like it on a hot day.) Retsina is properly poured from a brass mug; nowadays you'll usually find it served in aluminum replicas. In *tavernas,* the protocol is to half-fill your cup, especially when quaffing the resinated ones.

Here are a few suggestions:

For the red—Boutari Grande Reserve

For the white—Tsantali, in the distinctive green bottle; a fine label from Macedonia.

For the rose—Caligas

Among dry-to-medium white wines, Elissar, Cava Kamba, Pallini, St. Helena, Demestica, King, and Minos are also especially favored; Port Carras Blanc de Blanc is fresh. Cava Boutari and Caviros reds (Burgundy-type) are heavyish but sound; both are good complements to extra-spicy or garlicky dishes. Montenero is another popular cup. From Rhodes, Chevalier de Rhodes is quite passable; Ilios is a pleasant white from Lindos. Mavrodaphni and Samos are sweet choices.

TIPPING   In luxury or first-class restaurants, although the 15% service charge is included, add 5% on the *plate* for the waiter or maitre and small change on the *table* for the busboys. In your hotel (if you are staying several days and it is deluxe category), give at least $5 to the concierge, $2 to the maid, and 50¢ per bag to the baggage porter.

AEGEAN CRUISES   The itineraries, which begin and end at the Athens port-suburb of Piraeus, are virtually standard. The 3-day wanderer will probably head to Delos, Mykonos, Rhodes, and Patmos, plus a pause at Kusadasi (Turkey) for a look at Ephesus. The 4-day sailor is almost sure of stopping at Crete, Rhodes, Santorini, Kusadasi, Patmos, and Mykonos. The 7-day pilgrim is even more certain—but not 100%—to disembark at Crete, Santorini, Rhodes, Patmos, Kusadasi, Istanbul, Alexandria, Delos, and possibly Mykonos. (Generally if Alexandria is on the list, then Istanbul and Kusadasi are off it and vice versa.)

Next, depending upon your option, any day can be sailing day. Since cruising is Greece's star attraction, early booking is recommended, nay, essential. Departures are usually scheduled for late afternoon or early evening. Long voyages weigh anchor between late morning and late afternoon. Current capacities vary between 200 and 750 berths. No company runs these cruises between the end of October and the middle of March. Most operators start later and end earlier.

For details and reservations on all of the vessels listed below, consult **Hellenic Tours,** which is mentioned under "Special Remarks" at the beginning of this chapter, or your travel agent.

On the better ships, you can expect to find stabilizers, full air conditioning, ample lounges, at least 2 bars, poor-to-fair institutional-style cuisine, a ship's hospital supervised by a doctor, a swimming pool (perhaps 5 postage stamps in breadth), a beauty parlor, a cinema, a sundeck (too often cruelly cramped), trap shooting, a nightclub with orchestra, and piped music. A few offer such extras as elevator, laundry service, telephones in the staterooms (the *Jason* and a couple of others feature a 10-button system throughout), a sauna, and a small gymnasium.

The Sun Line operates the 700-passenger *Stella Solaris,* an opulently lavish floating hotel with just about every amenity possible to imagine. She breaks the waves smoothly on the 7-day circuit in summer and brings happiness to Caribbean trippers in winter. Then there's the tasteful and dignified *Oceanis,* which takes shorter trips. The Epirotiki Line creates many smiles with the Golden Fleece Voyage aboard the 12,000-ton, refashioned *World Renaissance;* it also can be boarded on a 7-day whirl (as part of a longer 2-week swing out of Genoa) in Piraeus to cruise the Black Sea and such ports as Yalta, Odessa, Messebur (in Bulgaria), plus Istanbul, Rhodes, and Mykonos. As the ports-of-call vary slightly from season to season on these packages, consult your travel specialist for exact sailings.

The *Pegasus* is the Epirotiki flagship. Her public rooms reflect many happy surprises, including such extras as a heated inside swimming pool (not counting the big one in the sun), a cinema, and a fastness of open deck space. Nearly all of her cabins are relatively spacious vis-a-vis much of her competition. The 16,000-tonner operates on 7-day loops that include Israel, Kusadasi, and Egypt (with land tours) and also call at Patmos and Rhodes. Basically this is a slight variation on the Mediterranean Odyssey, mentioned above.

The *Jason,* who hastens for the Epirotiki Line, is on an ambitious 14-day program called Europe by Sea. She is imaginative in her ambience and versatile in her facilities. If you can afford her best, the Castor and Pollux suites on Apollo Deck are worth the extra investment. Next best are staterooms #A-1 to #A-6, equipped with tubs. Try #P-7 to #P-22 on D Deck for a less costly but satisfactory buy. Good value and a heap of history in a fortnight afloat.

Sun Line's *Stella Maris* (3- to 4-day cruises) is not too large and boasts excellent food and service on these half-week voyages.

The *Mistral* will be your only choice for one-day cruises from Crete to Santorini. The *Hermes* and *Aegean Glory* zip out to Aegina, Hydra and Poros. On Aegina there's an optional excursion to Aphaia Temple, considered the most complete in Greece. The *Saronic Sun* offers daily service from May 1 through October 30 from Athens to Mykonos.

Interisland hydrofoils of the *Flying Dolphins* company provide low-cost, high-speed thrills; they can cover a lot of sea (33 knots) in brief sprints. The Saronic playground (Hydra, Poros, Egina, Spetses) is their specialty, but these speedy Russian-built water-taxis can be found on other wine-dark waves more distant from Athens, too.

No scheduled ship unlisted above is recommended this year.

CITIES AND REGIONS

AKTI APOLLON, also known as Attica, is the beautiful coastline that travelers sometimes call the "showcase of Greece." With steering wheel in hand, motorists should begin at the small Mediterranean fishing port of Kanari; the drive ends at Cape Sounion, where you'll find the Temple of Poseidon.

ATHENS

Athens (Athina) with its port of Piraeus is the capital and by far the largest city in Greece, with more than 4 million people. Constitution Square (officially called "Syndaghma" Square), Omonia Square, and other landmarks have been revamped; 5 additional public plazas have been opened. The ancient, tavern-filled Plaka district is where you go after dark. Mount Lycabettus, its looming central hill, has a cable railway zooming through a 225-yard tunnel which whisks sightseers from Plutarchou and Aristippou Sts. to its crown in 2 minutes. Up top, a restaurant and snack bar provide forgetful fodder with forget-me-not vistas, plus possibly the purest air in Athens. P.S. Next year local authorities plan to control automotive emissions in the capital, the cause of 80% of the city's air pollution. If true, what a blessing!

Acropolis • The history of the limestone citadel rising above modern Athens reaches back to legendary pre-Hellenic times. On this site, Poseidon and Athena fought over who would be patron of the city. King Erechtheus constructed a royal palace and the first temple here where the clash took place. The Acropolis has been built and rebuilt many times; construction scaffolding and cranes will be on site probably until 1994 for current repairs, but still you can stroll around most of the buildings. During the Golden Age, it became an "Altar to Beauty" under the guidance of Pericles but was plundered by later Roman, Byzantine, and barbarian invasions.

Theater of Dionysus • At the foot of the Acropolis, its 67-tier semicircular amphitheater held 17,000 Athenians during the annual Dionysian spring festivals.

Theater of Herodes Atticus • *Dionyssiou Areopagitou Ave.* • It has been expertly restored and is again an active theater during the Athens Festival that takes place every summer. There are performances of classical plays as well as orchestral and operatic concerts.

The Pnyx • *Pnyx* means "tightly crowded together," an apt name because all of the 18,000 citizens of Athens during the Golden Age were entitled to participate in the legislative process here. In summer it's the site of sound-and-light performances starring the Parthenon.

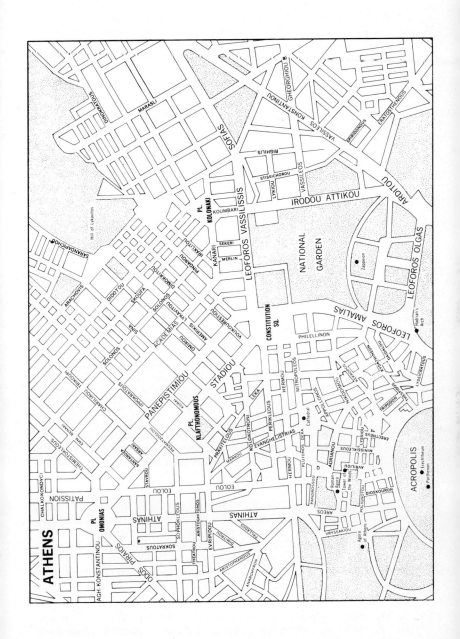

ATHENS

Parthenon • Built under the supervision of Phidias, the temple to the virgin goddess Athena was designed to endure, and its Doric exterior lasted nearly intact until 1687 when a bomb set off an ammunition cache the Turks had kept inside. Subsequently, Lord Elgin carried the western frieze away to England but replicas remain.

Erechtheion Temple • This is considered one of the most graceful products of ancient architecture, yet its Ionic style and tripartite form is in marked contrast with the symmetric, Doric Parthenon. One of the most famous parts is the **Porch of the Karyatides** where, instead of columns, six statues of virgins support the architraves. (Lord Elgin also took one of these maidens; all have been replaced by copies; the original damsels await a promised new museum to be constructed across the street at the site of the Makriyanni police barracks.)

Acropolis Museum • In 480 B.C. attacking Persians destroyed much of the Acropolis. Afterward, Athenians decided to extend the citadel by adding strong bastions. In his haste, the director of this project, Themistocles, used broken statues and columns in rebuilding the fortifications, unwittingly preserving the marvelous collection of art on display in the Acropolis Museum. Finds include the Frieze of Victories, a gift from Alcibiades that was on the parapet surrounding the temple of Athena Nike, and a wonderful bas-relief of Nike Unfastening Her Sandal. Open 8:30 a.m.–3 p.m.; closed Tues.

The Propylaea • It had a central chamber covered by a roof decorated with gold and two wings projecting on either side. It was used by the Turks to store ammunition and much of it blew up in a thunderstorm in 1656 when it was struck by lightning. Archaeologists have excavated the original stone to restore a substantial part of the ancient form.

Aghioi Apostoloi • *Polygnotou St.* • This 11th-century church, located just above the Agora, is among the gems of Byzantine ecclesiastical architecture. If you fancy ikons see the **Kanellopoulos Collection** in *Plaka* at Theorias and Panos sts., one of the finest in the nation.

Stoa of Attalus • *Thissiou Sq.* • The Athenian Agora was the city's busy commercial and administrative hub as well as the spot where Socrates and Plato met with their followers. Reconstructed by the American School of Classical Studies, which also carried on the excavations of the Agora, the stoa was named for King Attalus of Pergamos, who built it in the 2nd century B.C. The two galleries, which held over 20 shops on each floor, now contain the **Museum of the Agora,** open from 8 a.m.–2 p.m. but never on Tues.

Monastiraki • *Ifestou St.* • You'll find this Flea Market as you continue your walk down from the Athenian Agora—an amusing place for a cool drink at the umbrella-dotted cafes. Don't buy jewelry or furs in this fast-paced district and haggle your tongue off for any souvenir or antique that you wish to buy.

Hadrian's Library ● *Areos St.* ● The Roman emperor Hadrian (A.D. 117–138) was responsible for significantly enlarging the city of Athens. One of his contributions was a library erected on the edge of the Roman Agora.

Aghios Eleftherios ● *Pandrossou St.* ● When Athenians converted to Christianity, they often endowed the saints with the attributes of the Olympian gods and transformed pagan temples into churches. The 12th-century Byzantine Aghios Eleutherios was erected in the place where Eleutho, goddess of child-bearing, had been worshiped and is dedicated to Our Lady of Urgent Requests. Judging from the population of modern Athens, this must be one of the most successful shrines in Christendom.

Temple of Zeus ● Today this once-magnificent temple to the chief Olympian consists of only 16 columns, of which 13 stand together under their architraves. Begun in 515 B.C. and completed in the 1st century A.D. by Emperor Hadrian, it was once the largest temple in Europe.

Hadrian's Arch of Triumph ● On its eastern facade is written "This is the city of Hadrian," but on the western facade are the words "This is the city of Theseus." Take your pick from the modest pair.

National Archaeological Museum ● *Patission 44th* ● It covers the entire expanse of Greek civilization, beginning with Cycladic statuettes that are over 3000 years old. Open 8:30 a.m.–3 p.m. but closed Mon. (There's a special **Museum of Cycladic Art** in Athens if you wish to delve further; see it at 4 Neophitou Douka St.) Especially wonderful is the Mycenaean Treasure, rediscovered by Schliemann in the 1870s, which consists of exquisitely crafted gold funerary masks, ornaments, weapons, and vessels.

Historical Museum ● *Kolokotroni Sq. at Stadium St.* ● is the repository of the nation's crown jewels; it was the original palace. See artifacts of Greek life in the last century.

Heinrich Schliemann Mansion ● *Panepistimiou St., off Constitution Sq.* ● houses possibly the finest coin collection of its type in the classical world. It also offers a splendid opportunity to view how the legendary self-taught archaeologist lived.

Aghios Nikodimos ● *Philellinon St.* ● Constructed on the ruins of a Roman bath, this is the oldest and largest Byzantine church in Athens. It is built according to the traditional Byzantine plan of a cross enclosed in a square surmounted by a dome that is supported by an octagonal drum.

Benaki Museum ● *1 Koumbari St.* ● The core of the museum's holdings derives from the private collections of millionaire Emmanuel Benaki but has been greatly enlarged since the museum opened in the early 1930s. Displays include Islamic, Byzantine, and Coptic art, textiles and folk costumes, and some El Greco paintings. Like many, it closes Tues.; open 8:30 a.m.–2 p.m.

National Picture Gallery Alexandros Soutsos Museum • *50 Vas. Konstantinou Av.* • Historically, Greece has never gained much renown for painting, but here is a potent effort to right that wrong. Occasionally foreign artists are exhibited.

Excursions

The 1-day jaunts or hydrofoil taxi services out to the surrounding **Saronic Gulf** islands have been mentioned under "Aegean Cruises." These are splendid and ideal if time is limited.

Temple of Poseidon, Sounion • Sounion is 45 miles down the coast from Athens and easily reached by car or bus. It is worth a trip for its beaches in warm weather and for the **Temple of Poseidon** in any season. Mostly destroyed by the Persians in 480 B.C. and rebuilt by Pericles, the pure white of the temple's 12 remaining Doric columns is a striking sight against the brilliant blue of the sky. The temple is set on a cliff high above the water. It was a shrine to the god of the sea who controlled the destinies of sailors leaving on voyages on the open sea. Look for Lord Byron's initials carved into the marble.

Monastery of Daphni • The road leading to Daphni follows the Sacred Way that the annual procession of the Eleusinian Mysteries followed. The peaceful 11th-century monastery here contains remarkable examples of Byzantine mosaics.

Eleusis • Twelve miles from Athens, Eleusis was the center of worship of the Eleusinian Mysteries now the site of impressive ruins.

NOTE · · · Most newspaper kiosks, hotel desks, and travel bureaus carry *This Week in Athens* and *The Week* in Athens. They're in English and invaluable.

HOTELS

Basically, the leading establishments in the Greek capital divide neatly into modernistic and traditional brackets, your choice depending on which of the two concepts you prefer. In summer I personally would recommend the fresher mood of contemporary styles, while winter seems more appropriate for the heavier tones of older hotels. Let's begin with the newer ones.

☆☆☆☆☆ **Astir Palace** • is my choice for midcity even though it does not incorporate gardens or a swimming pool among its assets. Extremely handy location on Syntagma (Constitution Square); 8 tall glassy vertical tiers reflecting the activity of the city's focal point; fresh white marble lobby softened by tasteful textiles; colorfully golden dining salon and more clubby cocktail lounge.

Complement of only 77 accommodations, mostly suites; fully air conditioned, of course. This is an outstanding link in Greece's premier hotel chain, always recognizable by the Astir appellation. The complex at nearby *Vouliagmeni Beach* (below) is superb for fair-weather vacationing away from the city's hubbub.

☆☆☆☆ **Meridien** • sharing a similar location at the heartbeat of the city, also is young-in-spirit. Its tone is slightly warmer and somewhat more commercial, but the amenities are all there for high ranking in the international hotel world. Especially noteworthy are the cuisine and the pleasant atmosphere created in its dining and sitting areas. Clearly, the French heritage of this innkeeping organization is manifest in the finesse and lifestyle you will discover. In-house color TV and video, minibars, and a cargo of other pleasantries make this a rewarding choice.

★★★ **Ledra Marriott** • offers a dynamic vitality that many will admire. In my view, its primary attributes are the spectacular rooftop swimming pool with snack area (really breathtaking at sunset) and the unusually attractive Polynesian restaurant that is uniquely blessed with running-water statuary. The Grill is also a plus; all dining areas within are expensive by local standards. Soft-spoken marble lobby; light-toned bedroom stylings, a bit small in size; in-house movies; frigobars. Except for the location, which is on a busy boulevard some minutes from town—a neighborhood shared by the next entry—this is a very fine operation indeed.

☆☆☆ **Inter-Continental** • just down the block, is massive, but miraculously manages to maintain a certain intimate character. The open pipe girders and the golden globe in the lobby are hideous, in my view, but can be overlooked in consideration of the floriferous terraced architecture, tranquil pool area, and the ingratiating colors employed throughout the interior. My favorite dining spot is the Cafe Pergola, but your taste may run to the sophisticated Rotisserie, the jovial Taverna, or the poolside snackery. Very professional, but very large.

☆☆☆☆ **Hilton** • 5 minutes by taxi from the center and near the U.S. Embassy, resides on a knoll facing the Royal Palace. Captivating and animated Taverna and coffee shop plus the addition of the popular Kelari snackery for tea, cocktails, and piano lilts; cozy circular Polo Bar designed by the talented Maurice Bailey. Units with balconies and black Carrara baths; varying suites; air conditioning plus soundproof windows. Try to book facing the Acropolis.

☆☆☆☆ **Grande Bretagne** • frequently the choice of traditionalists, has been an internationally famous landmark for generations. Its far-flung clientele affectionately call it the "G.B." Enormous high-ceilinged lobby and lounges warmed up with acres of tapestry; chic, silken-suave bar for delightful relaxing; lovely dining room; double-glazed windows throughout plus air conditioning; prize chambers the 6th-level terraced perches overlooking Constitution Square; concierge staff renowned for its friendliness and savvy. There's the popular GB

Corner with wood and leather decor, which dispenses excellent snacks, meals, and drinks continuously from 10 a.m. to 2 a.m.

Now for an assortment of hotels of varying distinction and styling:

☆☆ **Royal Olympic** • is located across from the Temple of Zeus (or Jupiter, if you're a Roman). Coffee shop that doubles as a poolside barbecue; convention hall; ballroom; automatic phone system. The cuisine in the darkly handsome medieval Templar Grill is generally not too distinguished. Whisper-soft, individually controlled air conditioning plus double-glazed windows as noise shields; pleasant oh-ing and ah-ing at Mt. Lycabettus and the Stadium; upper floor peeks at the Acropolis. Bedchambers with full carpets; multichannel consoles for music and radio; well-appointed baths.

Holiday Inn • *50 Michalakopoulou St., back of the Hilton* • offers a spacious, sterile ground floor with the faint ambience of a casino; 24-hour coffee shop and tatty bar adjoining; first basement with small Bistro Grec Taverna, a hairdresser, and a disco; second basement with 16 bowling lanes, a snack nook, and screaming music; rooms with TV, radio, air conditioning, and 2 double beds in the twin accommodations. The rewards seem lower than the price tags.

Herodion • is sited on the lower slopes of the Acropolis. Splendid sweep from the upper 2 tiers to the rear; bright accommodations that complement the charm of the public rooms; very reasonable price structure and ultra-kind staff attitudes. Many travelers like it—and so do I.

☆ **Divani Zafolia Palace** • nearby, also appears to be winning friends. Extensive use of marble; merry colors employed in textiles and pigments; remnants of the ancient Themistoclean Wall and its cellar (you are invited to take a look); *taverna* plus conventional restaurant; attractive public areas; swimming pool. The upper bedchambers offer excellent panoramics, but their closets, which resemble gymnasium lockers, are almost too short for anyone bigger than a jockey.

★★ **St. George Lycabettus** • sits high over the city in the Kolonaki residential enclave, which is so quiet that it is a lovely retreat. Two-tiered rooftop pool; appending terraces with snack tables; L-shape lobby with many gracious touches; lower-level restaurant with appetizing color blends; intimate grill, plus a coffee shop that is a knockout for design and rendition; attractive Tony's Bar; bank, shop, hairdresser, and barber; garage. The suites are striking; the normal twins are clean lined and charming but somewhat short on space for this category; the singles are neat and adequate.

☆ **Park** • is a neat package that unfortunately is situated at an inconvenient distance from midtown, facing the Gardens of Areas. There's a penthouse pool, bar, and sun deck; a pizzeria; a tartan lounge, restaurant, coffee shop, and well-appointed bedchambers with prices that vary with the desirability of the views.

☆ **King Minos** • structural scheme highlighted cleverly by marble and wood; indirect illumination; 100% air-conditioned; beauty parlor and barbershop; 5-stool bar; next-door lounge with ornamental birdcage; balconies on all front units; reasonable tabs for reasonable living space.

Esperia Palace • looks good if you crane your neck over tour groups to see it. Ingratiating Athineos Restaurant and cafeteria; large parquet-floor lounge; library and card room; blithe little bar. All zestlessly wall-papered accommodations with veranda and private bath, mostly with squat-down tubs; air-conditioned. Try to get a high perch for the view and to avoid the traffic din.

Attica Palace • has an ideal address and a so-so oft-crowded downstairs. Pencil-thin aluminum-and-glass structure in central location; loooong and narrow rooms with baths and showers; simple lobby up one flight. Noisy, but much improved in its housekeeping standards.

Caravel • is a 520-unit, large triangular edifice near the Hilton. It's the only hotel I know of with a mosque on the roof. Prairie-size lobby frequently ajam with chattering mobs awaiting their room numbers or tour leaders; air conditioning; rooftop pool; sauna; 2 bars, a 24-hour cafeteria, a pizzeria, and a *taverna;* convention halls. A hotel metropolis, with all that implies.

Athens Chandris • is situated far out by the racecourse and planetarium where it is often difficult to find a taxi. There are all of the facilities one would expect in a project of this size. But as it caters so devotedly to groups, I believe the independent traveler might feel lost in the herds.

Astor • introduces itself with a functional lobby and pleasant bar adjoining; cheerful rooftop restaurant open until midnight; conventional baths totaling 35%; other 65% (a nice one is #710) featuring 2-step tubs that will give you the feeling you're Rodin's *Thinker*. This same group inaugurated the **President,** not too far from the U.S. Embassy. Somehow the various elements don't jibe.

Stanley • is unabashedly aimed at package tourism. Sited on Karaiskaki Square with a pleasant greensward at its front door, it is too far from the hub of the city for most hikers to hoof it to the center. Attractive public rooms; top marks for the rooftop pool, solarium, and relaxing zone; lower scores for the utilitarian bedchambers; premium accommodations air chilled.

Dorian Inn • is another contender tailored for conducted tours. Three main columns mark its 13-story triangular ground plan, again with a swimmery at penthouse level. All rooms air-conditioned; restaurant, grill, bar, shop, the usual bag of tricks with a few surprises.

★ **Electra** • crackles with a full bath count, full air conditioning, ½ of its bedchambers facing inside; and a restaurant plus cafeteria. The cheeriness in decor, the finger-lickin' savor of its cookery, the perfect midtown situation for active travelers, the try-harder attitude of management and staff, and the low rates all meld to make this one a prize in the Athenian grab bag.

★ **Electra Palace** • is up in the Plaka district. In addition to similar decor and similar bedchambers, this same group offers a rooftop Eden overlooking the Acropolis, a garage, and a swimming pool.

Arethusa • comes up with a viewful roof garden, an inviting mezzanine cafeteria, and 87 quiet panel-windowed bedchambers that are becoming tatty and worn. Ask for any nest ending in "01" or "08"; while these are in the same moderate price range as the standard twins, they provide an extra dividend in scenery and space.

Titania • is frigid in the most gelid context of a sleeping factory. It has all the basic ingredients—except warmth.

Acropole Palace • despite its deluxe classification, caters almost exclusively to conducted-tour bookings and airline crews. Fair lobby; brightened public rooms; big bedchambers that seem rather gloomy. Its chief assets are its A-plus table and a staff that seeks to please.

Diomia • resides on a quiet, narrow lane about one block off Constitution Square. Scandinavian-style lobby and minibar; airy dining salon; snack bar-drink bar a split level below the ground floor. If offers honest-to-goodness rugs and honest-to-goodness pictures in the bedchambers, warm touches that are almost nonexistent among its confreres.

Athens Gate • has some front units that provide Olympian views of the Temple of Zeus. Ground-level public space limited, but plans include utilization of the rooftop; cookery said to be worthy; friendly service; clean.

Golden Age • not far from the Hilton, reveals a stark lobby and a somber mien. Excessively small doubles; appealing cellar *taverna;* a mixture of pluses and minuses, with the emphasis on the latter.

Ilisia • with 85 rooms, seems run-down, beat-up, and flawed-out.

Ilyssos • offers good value for your drachma.

Atlantic • rides on a tide that's commercial and noisy; preponderance of conducted groups; cramped space; strictly functional; sparsely furnished.

Achillion • is run well as a commercial-grade tour-oriented hostelry. Although its situation is unattractive, this one is superior to many in its classification.

Alpha • provides a restaurant, a bar, a cocktail lounge—all better downstairs than in the sleepers.

Minerva • *across from the King George* • occupies the top 3 floors of an office building. All 60 rooms have bath. It caters in good part to a heavy traffic of local businessmen.

Omonia • boasts a full bath-or-shower count but not much else to lift your spirits.

Pythagorion • has much more heart—and for almost the same outlay.

Lycabette • *on a quiet street* • is air-cooled throughout; chummy bar; nice lounge; well furnished; radio in every nest. Not bad.

Hermes • *on Apollonos Street* • has 45 plain and inexpensive accommodations. Heaven-scent roof garden for summer dining; full pension plan pushed during peak periods.

Imperial • has no lobby—but it does have 21 chambers and an owner who is especially hospitable.

★★★★★ **Astir** is the prestige assemblage of distinguished country hotels standing majestically above the *Vouliagmeni* shores (15 miles from Athens) where the privileged city dwellers disport themselves; where shipowners, yachtsmen, and sybarites of all callings tan their burnished hides and nourish their recreational ids and itches. Hotel facilities are divided into 3 separate enclaves: the **Palace** (most exclusive, oldest, and possibly the least cheerful now that age has provoked a few gerontic wrinkles); the **Nafsika** (intermediate cost with even more decorational chic than the playground of the Old Guard; all units with balcony and seaview; gorgeous swimming pool and terraces plus beach and gardens; fabulous luncheon buffet but with meal exchanges with others in the group); **Aphrodite** (on a cliff above a man-made sea basin for swimming, also with pool; glass-lined marble lobby viewing the shipping lanes; bar facing perfectly situated tiny islands on one side; pool on inner court surrounded by rock-bound restaurant; shops; 169 rooms with balcony, some with their own gardens, which are breathtaking). The last hostelry is the cheapest and one of the best bargains in the nation. Within the Astir region are tennis, watersports, and interchanges of every sort; Glyfada golf course is 5 miles away. Your choice of residence depends largely on your individual taste. Personally, I would choose Nafsika for beauty, Aphrodite for economy, and the Palace for people-watching. In their separate ways, each is a winner. advance reservations are advised (Tel. 896–0211; Telex 21–5013; be sure to specify your preference).

Astir Bungalows • *at Glyfada Beach* • 10 minutes closer to town but under the screaming jet approaches to the airport, is operated by the same company. It's more villagelike in concept. Hillside perch dotted with 100 one-room chalets, 7 two-room, and 7 three-room villas, all with private bath or shower, refrigerator, wide flower-girt terraces, and central heating. Bigger units cozied up with working fireplaces; room service; Asteria Tavern for let's-go-out dinners; 3 other restaurants or cocktail and snack bars; both rocky and sandy beaches at the bottom of the grassy slopes; pool and imbibery a-bubble. Recommended for families or more thrifty travelers.

Cape Sounion Beach • has a panorama that is plainly glorious; there's a huge pool beside the remains of a 2000-year-old silver mine; a 7-sided glass-enclosed bar adjoins its delightful restaurant; another dining salon plus a *taverna* also are available. When finally completed, it will comprise 400 rooms and 400 bungalows—virtually a village in itself.

Xenia Lagonissi • because of its situation on one of the most breathtaking headlands (Lagonissi) on this enchanting coast, could be a marvelous money-mill. Personally, I much prefer its spacious beachside cottage accommodations to the cramped main-building lodgings. Most of the amenities are here for a tiptop holiday at reasonable prices.

PLM Porto Heli • in the district from which it takes its name (35 miles from Epidaurus with ferry connections to Athens), offers a private beach, a swimming pool, and 2 restaurants. The group that runs it is experienced and reliable in providing upper-medium accommodation.

Holiday Club Poseidon • is a moderately priced holiday village in both hotel and bungalow style at Loutraki (50 miles from Athens on the Gulf of Corinth).

RESTAURANTS

Except in the most sophisticated establishments, it is a national custom for patrons to saunter directly into kitchens to select their fish or to examine the other comestibles before giving their orders to the waiter. Similarly, many *tavernas* have counters, often in the rear, where all of their main wares are displayed so that their menus can be ignored. To neophytes some of the concoctions in these pans or on these platters look poisonous—but you might be surprised how good even the most evil-looking ones taste!

Menus generally carry 2 columns of figures. One is the price set by the management. The other is the total when the taxes and service are included. As an example, a barbecued half chicken with trimmings might be listed in the first at 490 Drs. and in the second at 550 Drs.

Don't miss the enormously colorful lineup of restaurants at the crescent-shape base for fishing boats in *Mikrolimano* ("Small Port") across town near the Piraeus harbor for private yachts. Almost all of these are still simple and unspoiled. Choose your shellfish (as many and as varied as you wish); then ask the chef to open the stainless-steel drawers where the catches of the day are stored. Watch his scales as he weighs your picks and ask to see the government-regulated rate per kilo (2.2 lbs.). Fish is surprisingly costly (you'll spend about $40 for 2 for a simple meal), but items such as squid, octopus, and other creepers are cheaper. Crustacea or any critter vaguely related to a lobster will be the most expensive, of course. If you want a prepared platter such as a fisherman's stew or something unpronounceable, have no compunctions about going out to the kitchen and pointing to the items you wish. A nice complement is Greek peasant salad; garlic fans should bid for the piquant and unusual skordalia sauce.

Along this row, **Zephiros** repeatedly has turned on high-tide comestibles; shellfish are cunningly presented. **Kanaris** is another fat catch; sitting by the yachts at its fringe and under the awnings on a warm day or evening can be pure bliss. **Kokkini Varka** ("The Red Boat") is less polished, but still a winner. The balance, navigating from the southwest and moving northeast along this short avenue are **Mourayo, Prassina Trehandiria, Kranai, Trata, Poseidon, Psaropoula, Kuyu-Kaplanis,** and **Zorba's** (of course)—most of them good.

★★★★ **Dionysos** ● among the much more expensive and soigne institutions, at the foot of the Acropolis, is almost as important as the Parthenon to the tourist trade. Despite certain drawbacks, it is worth a visit, if only to dwell upon the 3000-year-old architecture and to watch the Sound and Light spectacles flickering on the historic next-door mountain as you dine. About 30 tables and alfresco terraces upstairs (best view); more below for snacks and libations; heavy-ish and sometimes greasy international cuisine. Evenings it is nearly always jammed, so reserve well in advance. The branch on Mt. Lycabettus also provides a feast for the hungry eye. Again the staff attitudes are often cool, but this seems minor compared to the glories surrounding you.

☆☆☆ **Gerofinikas** ● *10 Pindarou St.* ● Entry through a narrow alley; 2-tier dining room with sun terrace on one side; delicatessen-style display case stretching the entire length of a wall with a dazzling galaxy of viands; cheerful and bustling mien; hearty, gregarious maitre who circulates to welcome his guests; expensive by Hellenic standards.

☆☆☆ **Nine Plus Nine** ● *Platia Stadiou* ● is where *dinner only* is served, and it revels late in its disco sector. Charming understated ambience employing bentwood chairs, an Ecuador of greenery, intimate dimensions, and laudable cuisine; nail down your table in advance.

☆☆☆☆ **Bajazzo** ● *35 Ploutarchou St.* ● occupies a site in a converted stately home, masterly supervised by Klaus Feuerbach, the cordial chef-patron. Cuisine is international rather than Greek, costing roughly $100 per person for a beautifully presented repast with wine or champagne. Always in demand, so be sure to reserve. (Tel. 729–1420.)

Hotel Dining

By far the top quality otherwise in international cuisine will be found at the leading hotels in the capital. Tavern dining, while exciting and adventurous at first, soon becomes tiresome and routine, so if your visit is to be an extended one, it is probable that your yearnings will move toward conventional gastronomy. Hence, let's begin with some of my favorite hotel choices:

☆☆☆☆ **Meridien** ● offers the sparkling **Brasserie des Arts** overlooking Constitution Square and serving perhaps the most noteworthy French cookery in town. Service is outstanding and the mood is decidedly sophisticated. Becoming illumination warmed with copper sheaves hanging from the ceiling; a

376 · · · GREECE

background of excellent live music from the small combo. Some dishes to remember are the avocado with crab, the breast of duck with green peppercorns, the salmon in pastry on a bed of seaweed, and scrambled eggs in a shell with caviar. Not too costly but certainly rewarding.

☆☆☆☆ **Ledra Marriott** • has set the pace for unusual dining with its **Kona Kai** Polynesian restaurant, which also features Teppaniaki cooking at your own table. Exotic cocktails add to the splendor of this cooling atmosphere, enhanced by falling waters into a central pond. Other facilities include the spectacular rooftop pool for lighter dining as well as the Ledra Grill. Prices here are possibly the highest in town, a factor that has in no way impaired its popularity.

★★★★ **Hilton** • continues to produce wonderful meals and a delightful ambience at its lavishly refashioned **Taverna Ta Nissia,** which is basically Greek, but is so refined that this tamer version could almost be considered "international." The **Byzantine Cafe,** also given a dash of decorative spice, is noteworthy for its snacks and delicious *mezethes*. The **Kelari,** in the lower lobby, also offers light-biting in a mood more like a lounge or piano bar.

★ **Astir Palace** • boasts one of the most ingratiating settings for midday business lunches, but my several attempts at agreeable digestion seemed futile. Moreover, the service was downright punk. Possibly my luck was poor because the dining facilities at the other Astir installations at Vouliagmeni are consistently good. An anomaly.

★★ **Grande Bretagne** • can be proud of its **G. B. Corner,** which seems to have hosted every visitor since Pericles. It is a perfectly ridiculous concept that simply works—an ornate snack center where the hamburgers, salads, and club sandwiches are deified under Belle Epoque globe lighting, polished wood paneling, taproom accouterments, and tartan carpeting underfoot. Lunch will cost about $20. It's good and, strangely, it is satisfying visually.

☆☆☆ **Intercontinental** • offers a full panoply of choices ranging from the cosmopolitan **Rotisserie** to the panoramic rooftop **Premiere,** the atomspheric **Kubla-Khan,** and the **Cafe Pergola.** For consistent dining, I think this one tops the quality list.

Templar Grill • in the **Royal Olympic** is appealing to the eye but variable otherwise.

Attica Cellar • No, it's not a contradiction in terms. It's a very up-market restaurant that the **Attica Palace Hotel** decided to locate in its basement.

Othello's • *45 Mihalakopoulou, behind the Hilton and in front of the Holiday Inn* • produces steaks with first-class sizzle; also Cypriot specialties such as fried *chaloumi* cheese and the sparkling white Bella Pais wine. Noteworthy for your rambles.

☆☆ **Three Brothers** ● *7 Elpidos St.* ● is a fraternal import from Corfu. Nondescript, smoke-filled front room; passageway with bustling kitchen on the left; 14,926,344-calorie showcase of comestibles on the right (pick your share before sitting down); gardenlike sanctum to the rear containing perfectly awful seacoast paintings, lanterns, and maritime riggings. No English spoken; fish plates especially fresh and well prepared; not at all fancy; no fancy tariffs either. A winner in its fraternity.

Tabula ● *40 Pondou St., about 10 minutes by foot from the U.S. Embassy* ● is an easy target for Hilton guests. Its garden dining is pleasant under summer skies.

Steak Room ● *4 Aeginitous St.* ● also is a short walk from the Hilton in the direction of the U.S. Embassy. Dual sectors: one for the namesake product, the other for omelets, chicken, and hamburgers. The most expensive cuts of steer, though often tough, are reasonably priced and come with trimmings. Not bad.

Vladimir ● *12 Aristodimou St.* ● perched on a steep hillside a short climb from the Hilton, offers a curious melange of Russian, Greek, French, and Oriental specialties—even "American Hamburger." Terrace munching in rear garden during the warm months; immaculate kitchen; pleasant ambience.

In the high-rent district of Kolonaki, 3 are noteworthy: **Vegera,** Aristipou St., **Act One,** Academias 18 (where local politicians, literati, and theater folk mingle all night at the outdoor terrace), and **Prunier,** 63 Ypsilantou St.

Corfu ● *6 Kriezotou St.* ● appeals more to the stomach than to the eye; this one is simple, spotless, and enormously popular. If you don't mind the rush-rush atmosphere, it's a worthwhile low-cost choice.

Delphi ● *13 Nikis St.* ● is a midcity favorite among businessmen because of luscious lunches, tiny tabs, and ΦΑΣΤ service. The front segment is rustic in aura while the rearward enclave seeks to appear more refined. There's also another layer upstairs.

Kentrikon ● is an excellent midcity choice. My recent lunch was unusually good, low in cost, and the staff was smilingly efficient.

Vassilena ● *corner of Etolikon and Vitolion Sts., port of Piraeus, 20 minutes from the heart of Athens* ● This funny little grocery-shop-restaurant has about 14 tables in a clean but simple room with wine bottles and canned tomatoeš on shelves. No menu is offered; you merely sit down and your waiter will start the no-choice parade of 18 heavenly dishes that will take you 2½ hours to consume. Price of this gargantuan repast, including coffee and all the open wine you can pour down? Less than the cost of one fine bottle if you were at home! *Dinner only;* closed every Sun. Reserve in advance. Don't be detoured by the ridiculous deceit evinced by the people at any concierge's desk. Since the restaurant is too small to give them a cut of your business, their attitude is easily explained—but don't *you* swallow this nonsense.

Tavernas

Every traveler should pay at least one visit to a typical Greek *taverna*. (Ta Nissia in the Hilton is much too urbane to be classed as such.) These famous institutions, most of which operate on a cold-weather basis *only*, feature rotisserie-type grills, hearty menus, wine from huge barrels, folk music that is often deafening, and informal, family-style hospitality. Within the city (not the environs), most do not serve lunch; evening is the time to go.

Palia Athina • *4 Flessa St.* • reslicked rustic decor; orchestra and dancing; vague aura of a transplanted German *Bierstube;* outdoor frolics adjoining during summer.

Steki tou Yanni • *1 Trias St.* • is a perpetual favorite—with good reason. Motif—if you can call it that—trending toward a shambling stew of reed mats, bamboo fixtures, pastel-washed stucco, eclectic odds-and-endless ends; clangorous, busy, and stuffy; leather-lunged singers backed up by guitarists; hustling service. Here, unless you make an emphatic point of ordering just what you desire, a huge, multicourse, set meal will appear automatically.

Xinou • *4 Geronta St.* • To the eye, it's a tumbled-down shack divided vaguely into 3 rooms and a tree-covered patio. To the palate, it's much better. Plank ceilings; exposed pipes; coal stoves; the inevitable cretonne curtains; genre paintings on cracking walls. Its trio of musicians wander from room to room playing folk melodies with expressionless visages. Very inexpensive for the rewards.

Neo Rigas Taverna plays out its Greek floor shows at two addresses: Hatzimichali 3 (Plaka) in summer and at Andrianou and Ypridou streets in winter.

Costoyannis • *Zaimi St. 37, opposite Green Park* • has caught on with the theatrical throng; its best shows are the shrimp and crab salads, mussels with rice; standard meat and fish acts aren't bad either.
La Bussola for Italian fare, **Psaropoulos** for fish and **George's** for steaks are bettable bets in the Glyfada district, about 9 miles from town. **Themistocles** • *Vas Georgiou 31, Pangrati* • welcomes you to an intimate summer courtyard; Greek cooking that is outstanding; low prices; usually open Sundays. Refashioned interior for winterizations. **Belle Maison** • *Victoria Sq.* • appeals to locals chiefly; they come to hear the guitar pickin's and to dine on its finger-lickin' vittles. **Erotokritos** • *in the Plaka* • is another popular target, as is **Seven Brothers. Bacchus Taverna** offers a small show in its ancient nook of the Acropolis. **Kritiku** • *24 Mnissikleous St.* • in 4 rooms, is an escape from the sidewalk cracklings of shishkebab. Along this same street there are more kebab joints than you can shake a shish at.

French?   ★★★**L'Abreuvoir** and **Je Reviens** ● *51 and 49 Xenokratous St.* ● are next-door neighbors up in the Kolonaki district. While the cuisine is high-level in both year-round, you'll probably prefer their summer wiles at parkside tables. It's peculiar that the two are almost identical, but that the former is nearly always full and the latter is clearly left field. On a warm eve, the experience is quintessentially romantic. **Remezzo,** in the same vicinity, is one of the chic-est spots in town, but mainly in winter when the famous Remezzo of Mykonos closes and returns to the capital. **Le Foyer,** near the Caravel Hotel, is another fair choice. .

Italian?   **Al Convento** ● *in Kolonaki* ● is recommendable, as is **Da Walter.**

Fish houses?   If you don't go to the previously mentioned *Mikrolimano* area, in midtown try either **Bouillabaisse** ● *28 Zisimopoulous St.* ● or the nearby **Boutsaris.** Both somewhat costly, but very worthwhile for wiggling-fresh seafood and ocean stews.

Game for game?   Shoot for the modest, galleried, shoplike **Zafiris** ● *4 Thespidos St.* ● where you can top your boar, pheasant, partridge, or luscious pigeon with a dessert of quince jelly or a pool of golden honey flecked with walnut chips. Good hunting!

Jimmy's Cooking ● *at the steps of Lycabettus, 36 Loukiano St.* ● is fun in summer when tables nuzzle the curbside. Owner James spent much of his career cooking in the USA. Go for drinks (or if you can stand the snacks!) around 12:30.

NIGHT LIFE

Bouzouki?   The devil-may-care custom of breaking cheap saucers when the excitement reached a climax has risen from the simple and inexpensive merriment of yore to a startlingly expensive pastime. First, the customer has no trouble in spending up to $50 per person for the dinner. Second, the crockery and the small baskets of flowers that are thrown are purchased by the piece— and the cost of the latter averages from $35 to $40 per unit. Here's why these places draw such a large proportion of the local patronage among young spendthrifts and the *nouveaux riches.* If you go, sit well away from the stage or protect your eyes from flying fragments. The heavy action generally starts after midnight.

If you are not in one of the speakeasies, all entertainment must cease by 2 a.m. on weekdays and an hour later on Sat. and on the eves of holidays. **Fantis** ● *in the Plaka district* ● is fair, but you'll have to forgive the management for spoofing up the evening with electronic musical assists. My meal was routine-to-poor. One dancer carried a table clenched between his teeth—more tender, I'll wager, than my beefsteak. **Dilina** • *at distant* **Glyfada** • ranks in the top league at the moment. **Kalokerinos** • *Kekropos St.* • meets the finest requirements as an aspiring clip joint.

Mostrou • *Mnissikleous St.* • also in the Plaka district, pulls at the strings of many an Athenian heart with its own show backed by the national folk music; a professional operation. Others include the popular **Palia Athina** • *4 Fleesa St.* • and **Plakiotiko Saloni** • *15 Dedalou St.* • Both feature Greek cabaret.

As is the case with most nightspots, they rise and fall rapidly. Athenian nighteries seem to be particularly fickle, so for your convenience, below is a list of the top *bouzouki* players and singers currently in vogue. If you can pinpoint where they are at the moment of your visit, you'll probably enjoy your evening. They are as follows: Doukissa, Alexiou, Argyrakis, Miropanos, Sakellariou, Parios, Bithikotsis, Hadji, Poulopoulos, Voskopoulos, Marinella, Moscholiou, Kokotas, Mitsakis, Tsitsanis, and Zabetas.

The continuing popularity of the taverns has caused a nightclub debacle of major proportions. Of today's scepter bearers, **Galaxy** is one of the front-runners. Big time entertainment nightly; high but value-filled tabs; nearly always crowded. Be sure to reserve ahead. **Copacabana** • *behind the Royal Olympic Hotel* • produces the biggest floor show of all. It's sort of a Levantine version of any gin mill or bump-and-grind emporium one might find in any big city. **Athinea** • *6 Venizelou Ave* • offers winter-only dancing; in summer it gallops to an enchanting open-air site at the racecourse. No cover charge; no cabaret; passable vittles; dinner reservations mandatory.

Discotheques? Platters spin at **Ergostasio, Nine Muses** (out at **Glyfada**), **Nine Plus Nine, 14 Disco** in *Kolonaki,* **Agora Herodium** in *Maroussi,* **Akrotiri** near the airport, **Video Disco** and **Barbarella** • *on Syngrou Ave.* • and **Seychelles** in *Ilioupoli.* A new twist is the combined disco-diner, two outstanding examples of which are said to be **Papagayo** • *Patriarchou Soakim St. 37, Kolonaki* • and **Studio 54** • *Philelinou St. 13, Constitution Sq.*

Places to see-and-be-seen at this instant include **Montparnasse** (Ratka's) for pre- and after-theater frolic, **Piccolo Mundo,** with superb piano melodizing, **Gallery,** with 88 more keys plus excellent singing (usually), the previously mentioned **Act One,** often with jazz-piano, and the somewhat pretentious **Shangrila.**

Gambling: At **Mont Parnes,** 3500 feet above Athens and 25 miles north of it, the National Tourist Office operates a posh gambling casino—every day but Wednesday. The cuisine is above average, the accommodations are comfortable, and for gamesters it can be an excellent target for an evening, a weekend, or the "full-house" treatment. Be sure to take your passport.

SHOPPING

SHOPPING HOURS: They vary on alternate days. Currently on Mon. and Wed., they are from about 8:30 a.m.–4:30 p.m. On Tues., Thurs., and Fri. they operate from 8:30 a.m.–2 p.m. and 5–8 p.m. Because this awkward system might well be temporary, please check upon your arrival. Many tourist-type stores in the Plaka throb daily till 10 p.m.

BEST AREAS: The streets surrounding Constitution (Syndagma) Square and the Plaka district are the two prime targets. The former displays more quality merchandise, the latter is stuffed with smaller shops and cheaper wares.

DEPARTMENT STORES: Minion (Patissia St.) and **Lambropoulos Bros.** (Aeolou and Stadium Sts.) are the national pacesetters. None of these appeals to me.

FLEA MARKET: Near the Plaka at Monastiraki, Pandrossou St. is the start of its Athens equivalent. Good fun for the shophound, if you strike it right. Open daily from 9 a.m.–1:30 p.m. and 5–8 p.m., weekends from 8 a.m.–2 p.m.; bargaining isn't easy.

FURS: Dora Furs (31–33 Voulis St.) has the bargains! Lower prices reflect Greece's low-cost labor, but there is nothing lost in quality. A 55-pelt female Emba mink coat that might be sold for $14,000 in the U.S. sells here for between $5000 and $6000. Dora offers about a dozen luxury hues from pale Apollo to Autumn Haze to all the fashionable shades of American Emba. Even car coats in leather and Persian lamb (about $2000) and that wonderful reversible rainwear (about $850) with lynx, lamb, beaver, Swakara, or whatever your choice are part of the versatile collection. Ask Dora to guide you through the unusual opportunities in her smart midtown boutique.

GOLD JEWELRY: Lalaounis (6 Panepistimiou St.) is recognized worldwide as the greatest proponent of the antique styles of ancient Greece and the classic Byzantine period. The collections extend to modern concepts as well. Branches at Tower of Athens, Hilton, and Grande Bretagne hotels.

STERLING CREATIONS: At **4 Lamda** (''Tower of Athens'') silver is mixed with crystal, plastic, and semiprecious stones.

GREEK SOUVENIRS, PAINTINGS, HANDICRAFTS: Attalos (3 Stadium St.) is the *only* place in the downtown area for these items. The mendicants in this precinct and along Karageorg; Servias St.—in fact, all of the Constitution Sq. zone—border on hucksterism at its most blatant. The **National Welfare Fund** (24A Voukourestiou St., plus boutique in the Hilton) offers lovely needlepoint, woven or Persian rugs, pillowcases, and other well-chosen items. **Pandora** (behind Athenee Palace, plus a downstairs shop at 1 Filellinon St.) is also worth a stop. **Kori** (13 Mitripleos St.) has expensive peasant-type garb for the younger group.

JEWELRY (UNIQUE CREATIONS): **Petradi** (Voukourestiou 20), inspired by designer Kate Tasedakis, raises personalized decorative jewelry to a fine and novel art. Much of the distinctiveness is in the selection of materials: semiprecious stones, gold-plated brass fittings, forms following the alluring contours of nature so that no two pieces are alike.

READING MATTER: **Eleftheroudakis** (Nikis St.) carries a mouthwatering supply of American and English books, originals and reprints. **Samouhos** (Amerikis St. 23) and **Pandelides** (11 Amerikis St.) are also versatile and worthy. **Les Amis du Livre** (Valaoritou 9) specializes in rare books, engravings, and maps of Greece. Open Mon.–Sat. 9:30 a.m.–3 p.m.

RUGS: **Karamichos-Mazarakis** (31–33 Voulis St. and 3 Mitropoleos St.— right on Constitution Sq.) carries a wide range of handcrafted Greek carpets that include kilims, minoan, fur, and rag rugs, plus their newest venture, called Artline—rugs that are copies of designs of 20th century masters such as Klee, Dali and Magritte. For at least 400 years (probably 1000!) the Karamichos family has crafted *flokati*—gorgeous, fluffy, 100% virgin wool floor coverings. It is officially classified by the government-sponsored National Organization of Hellenic Handicrafts as their No. 1 creator in the nation. Sold by weight— which provides a measure of their purity—these top-line Karamichos carpets are handloomed to last a lifetime. Bred in water, visibly they improve with both washing and wear. Chris Karamichos is so justly proud of these creations that, as far as we have learned, he is the sole dealer in the land who gives a money-back guarantee. These handwoven beauties are sold exclusively here; the extra-thick category (''Karamichos Anniversary Flokati'') is the Rolls-Royce of the art. If miracles could happen, Karamichos is the only place I would know where they just *might* produce a magic flying carpet if I were sufficiently serious! Well-stocked sales center at the end of the main quai in Mykonos (Harbor Road).

DELPHI

This classic sightseeing target, 105 miles from Athens, draws countless excursionists—and well it should, because were it not for the teeming mobs that overswarm this target, few travel rewards in Greece could be richer. A new cultural and spiritual center also may bring even further crusades of pilgrims and scholars to its heights in the very near future.

Transportation CHAT offers a bus tour from the capital; the loop includes lunch; the ride is 4 hours each way. Key Tours, the cooperative enterprise of Athens travel agencies, also provides worthy packages aboard air-conditioned coaches. Private operators base their tariffs on the number of passengers—and prices are positively cutthroat. For one person, the rate is plainly outrageous; for 5 occupants the split fee is merely paralyzing—for a simple one-day outing! There are magnificent vistas peppering this road, all buses pause frequently for picturetaking. Many visitors prefer to drive themselves at a leisurely pace and hire a guide when they arrive. The highway itself is not the best.

Points en route The **Monastery of St. Luke** boasts a trove of outstanding eleventh-century mosaics. *Levadhia,* 1¼ hours out, comes up with a striking panorama of Mt. Parnassus and the Thebes Plain. Its principal restaurant, featuring the usual specialties plus peasant bread and beer, is unattractive. For sunny-day lunching, you might prefer the charming little establishment at Falling Water, on the edge of town. Its scads of rug shops should be completely avoided. *Arahova,* 6 miles before Delphia, nestles in a hillside; the humble houses and ancient buildings have a distinctive style. You'll enjoy the photo opportunities.

Sights The **Oracle, Museum,** and **Theater**—the why-and-wherefore of your trip, of course—are in the near suburbs of Delphi. On full-moon nights, Athenians run up here to see the moonbeams on the ravine and the lower plain containing 9 million (!) olive trees. The reflections are such that it is impossible to discern where the land ends and the Gulf and Corinth begin. If you go, be sure to book a seafront room, of course. The settlement itself has 2000 permanent residents and is perched at an altitude of 2132 feet.

Hotels Amalia garners the local laurel wreath. Modernistic, wood-stone-and-glass-lined lobby, almost Danish in concept; lounge, dining room, and bar; efficient, color-toned bedchambers; air conditioning; small but light baths. Viewful.

Xenia offers a dining room with a wide terrace. Fresh lounge; 45 rooms, all with bath and a vista of the gulf; door numbers on tiles with flower patterns; 4-story ranch-design construction; simple but tasteful.

Vouzas situated on the main thoroughfare; 60 units with 60 baths or showers; many outsiders with private terraces; roof restaurant with glorious sweep of the mountainscape. Also good, but not quite up to the leaders.

Hermes and **Baronos** are side-by-side, looking at the splendid scenery; both are okay. The **Parnassus** and **Pythia** are fair. **Castalia** is more frenetic and less inviting. Avoid all other lodgings in this area.

Dining The **Amalia,** the **Xenia,** and the **Vouzas,** plus the 2 tourist pavilions (Mr. Damigos has the **Belvedere**), are open all day; tea, sandwiches, and beer are served in the latter.

Shopping Don't bother to buy anything either en route or at the destination. The merchants are so cynically tourist-oriented that generally the quality is shoddy and the prices are much higher than those in Athens.

EPIDAURUS The world famous Drama Festival draws as many as 50,000 visitors each year in June and July. Greek theater at its purest; marvelous acoustics; top caliber stars. You can also enjoy this stop while on the Argolis tour, which includes Corinth and Mycenae.

MISTRA   The Byzantine mosaics are at the root of its only fame—and amply deserving of it too.

MYCENAE   Here the **Lion Gate** and the **Tombs of the Kings** are the big attractions. This playground of Agamemnon reached its high point in the thirteenth century B.C. The marvelous excavations are a compulsory lure to any student of antiquity. If you are traveling independently, avoid the **Ifigena** restaurant on the highway a couple of miles east of these proximate relics, as well as all others in the area, which are inferior even to this massive culinary factory for tour groups. Drive farther along to either of the **Xenia Hotels** in *Nauplia.*

NAUPLIA   Here, possibly, is the most lustrous gem among all of the towns in the Peloponnesus. Although it's a l-o-n-g haul for a 1-day excursion from Athens, legions of travelers take it in stride. Start very early, comb the principal inland sightseeing classics during the morning, have a late lunch, and then return via the spectacular coastal highway. This lovely little port is the most southerly settlement of importance on what is technically the Greek mainland. (Actually this province is an island which is connected only by a single bridge at Corinth.) The **Amalia,** with its large garden, pool, a pair of restaurants plus a cafeteria and bar, is the most impressive hotel locally. Very attractive. Both of the air-conditioned **Xenia Hotels** are sited high on a hill, which blesses them with glorious panoramas over the harbor and sea. The lower one, with sound cuisine and comfortable rooms, is Class A. The upper one, in the luxury category, is more striking and elaborate. The exhilarating indoor-outdoor restaurant is 2 levels below the entrance.

OLYMPIA   Once it was thronged by visitors from every cranny of the ancient world who came to participate in or to view the original Olympic games. The Olympiads were devoted not only to athletic contests, because poetry and prose readings, lectures, philosophical debates, and musical and dramatic competitions were also held. While the **Stadium,** of course, is the main focal point, the **Museum** is one of the most important in the nation. Sculptures of the pediments of the Temple of Zeus, Paionios' "Victory" statue, and the statue of Hermes by Praxiteles are among its many masterpieces. **Hotel Amalia** provides air conditioning, its coolest feature. Greek and European-style fare without much flair; open-air bar; swimming pool; intimate tea room; convention hall for 350; smallish but comfortable quarters.

SPARTA   Above the plains of the modern but dull town, the **Temples of Athena and Artemis,** as well as the **Circus,** rise against the snow-banked crags of Taiyetos. You may also inspect a worthwhile museum in midvillage; a number of Byzantine churches and palaces, and a fortress built by the Franks.

THE ISLANDS

No two are alike. They are scattered in their infinite variety from the Ionian to Aegean Seas, and Crete rises from the Mediterranean.

Although the larger islands are available by air as well as by sea, it is recommended that you pay your calls by cruise ship. (See previous descriptions.)

Now for an alphabetical rundown of some of the better known tourist hubs in the surrounding seas. The nearer **Saronic Isles,** which almost can be considered as day-excursion destinations from Athens are collected as a group at the end of this section.

CORFU

It's off the northwest coast on the sea route from the Italian port of Brindisi. The island measures 48 by 20½ miles and boasts 150,000 residents—half of them in the city proper. Motoring from Athens is arduous work. If you think you're seeing green spots before your eyes, you are, because this isle sprouts more than 4 million olive trees.

Venetians left a strong influence here (venetian blinds as one example). George Palace, having been built by the English, is appropriately Georgian. There's a wonderful Museum of Asiatic Art, too, and, naturally, an archaeological museum for earlier roots—even though Corfu offers no major digs for antiquarian prowls.

Almost all visitors pass through Corfu Town, where the only hotel of note is the **Corfu Palace,** with beautiful gardens but without sea bathing. About 6 miles outside of the capital, the **Astir** rates highest for waterside leisure followed by the **Chandris** at *Dassia Bay.* The large and splendidly isolated **San Stefano** at *Benitses* resides on a remote forested hillside that's awesomely romantic. The **Kontokali Palace** is about 3 miles from the city; it's on a charming lawn site that juts into the sea, offering a small man-made beach. The **Hilton** at *Kanoni* is not too exciting except that it now contains the island's only Casino; fair but no rave.

Restaurants Generally, your hotel will sock you for 2 meals or 3, so tourist restaurants don't really thrive here. The **Corfu Palace** and the **Hilton** produce the most up-market cuisine. Out at *Achilleion* the **Bella Vista** specializes in seafare and *bella vistas.* **Tripa** offers more variety plus Greek music;

it's at *Koinopiastes*. **Spiti Prifti** at *Gouvia Bay* is reliable and fun. In town, try **Bella Napoli** or **Xenichtis**.

Night Life Achilleion Casino Within this Pompeiian-style oasis you'll find roulette, baccarat, and boule. Gaming rooms, nightclub, restaurant, and snack bar open from 5 p.m. to 2 a.m.; park and museum available from 9 a.m. to 1 p.m.; operates year-round.

Shopping Four places for starters: **Aris** (74 Nikiforou Theotoki) offers spectacular hand-painted dresses; **Music House** (same street at #92) specializes in Greek tapes and disc recordings; **Costa Marollas** (Evieniou Voulgareos 61) creates Byzantine and ethnic silver masterpieces; and the **National Welfare Organization** displays the best in handicrafts.

CRETE

Geography? It is 160 miles long but never more than 36 miles wide. Its variegated terrain ranges from beaches and plains to rolling foothills to the rugged mountains of up to more than 8000 feet which form its central spine. *Population?* About 460,000. *Climate?* So beneficent that its planners are striving to transform it into the principal market garden of Europe. As one example, the average yield of 1100 square yards of land is 15 tons of magnificent tomatoes per 40 days from roots to shipping boxes. The winds are too strong for commercial quantities of bananas. *Industry?* Olive oil, wine, nuts, citrus fruit, dairying, and small mineral workings. At this point of development, raisins are the main export. *Culture?* Western civilization was born here about 3000 B.C. when the Minoans migrated from Asia Minor. Through causes still unknown to archaeologists or historians, this great power mysteriously vanished 1600 years later. Since then it has been occupied by the Dorian Greeks, the Romans, the Genoese, the Venetians, the Turks, England, France, Russia, Italy, Germany, and Thomas Cook. The influence of its Venetian occupiers is strongly evident today. *Connections?* Between an assortment of ports on Crete and various points on the mainland or other islands, there are several daily **Olympic** flights plus more than a dozen ferries. Early reservations are strongly advised. *Wines?* Try **Dilanda Minos,** a delightful, very palatable white bottling.

Cities and towns? Iraklion ("Heraklion" in English, with its name changed from Candia in 1823), the capital and principal port with 100,000 residents, is the hub of its wheel. In my view it's sleazy, strident, and graceless. Because tourism is just *too* good in this sellers' market (there are 65 travel agencies and 85 rent-a-car offices), with very rare exceptions its facilities are dismayingly crummy. As a curiosity, more sidewalk cafes are clustered around Eleftheria ("Freedom") Square than in any other municipality you are likely to see anywhere. *Ierapetra,* in the Lassithi county, has Roman heritage and Venetian as well; there's a fortress, a fine beach, and plenty of sun late into the autumn.

Worthwhile sightseeing targets include the absolutely splendid **Archaeological Museum** (midcity), the **Historical Museum,** and the world-famous ruins of the **Palace of Knossos** (10 minutes out of town; closed Mon.). **Phaestos** is second only to Knossos in Minoan culture, so try to see it, too. Also in this Mesara Plain is the Bronze Age palace of **Aghia Triadha.** The site at **Samaria Gorge** is chiefly Byzantine; you'll find chapels in the Levka Ori range on the western part of the island. In general, my preference is the northeast coast, which is described farther along.

Hotels: Within *Iraklion,* the hotels run the gamut from production-belt mediocrity to wretched. My suggestion is that you spend only one night here and base yourself in one of the country hotels along the lovely shoreline if you wish to stay longer. Both **Elounda Beach** and the **Astir Palace** (see below) are the pacesetters for the island.

Galaxy • *67 Dimocratias Ave.* • is a U-shaped building on stilts erected around a polyangular pool. Group-filled multileveled lobby; 2 roof gardens; coffee bar; big pastry shop; total of 144 rooms with shower and 28 with bath, all simply decorated, small, functional, and with individual terrace.

Xenia • is in the middle of the city. It benefits from having a modern structure, but follows suit by being filled relentlessly by package tours.

Astoria Capsis • on the main square, goes it one better in the air conditioning of its chambers. Otherwise I found it even more dreary. The 90-room, C-grade **El Greco,** just off a small square a few blocks from the seafront, serves breakfast only. Small, amiable lobby backed by a little garden; friendly bar-let adjoining. Here's an unusually satisfactory family operation for this low-priced category.

Restaurants: You'll probably be stuck having to feed with the pack in the herd of groupies. If you can escape the pension plan, your best meal could be found at the **Kiriakos,** on the same street and 50 yards from the Galaxy.

Shopping: Tourist junk is rampant. **Zacharopoulos** in the Knosos Palace is worth exploring for jewelry and handicrafts. **Andreas Fanourakis** (Psarom-ilingou St. 2) has some attractive pieces of bijoux. **Helen Kastrinojianni,** opposite the Iraklion Museum, features local handiwork plus attractive woven fabrics. **Midas,** on Freedom Square, displays some gold and silver table pieces and picture frames of excellent quality. **Ariane** has two stores: On Dikeosinu St. and at the Astoria Hotel. Information? Smraryanakis Evangelos at the **Greek National Tourist Office** is tops as an official source. Otherwise write to or visit the **Creta Travel Bureau** at 25th August St. They will plan your tour, whistle up a self-drive car, and in general be your guide.

Other Targets: The only other city of importance is *Hania* ("Canae" in English), which is 85 miles due west and about one-half the size of Iraklion. Except for a far lesser flood of foreign visitors, in atmosphere and facilities it rather closely resembles its larger sister. **Kydon** is the only Class A hostelry. Among the 7 Class B entries the little **Doma** is the overall leader in attractiveness. This neoclassical mansion facing the water, with 29 rooms and showers, has been maintained charmingly. Restaurants? The most colorful are those around the old harbor that are crowded with habitues on summer evenings. There is a large, unadorned cafe in the Public Gardens.

Ag. Nikolaos ("St. Nicholas" in English and often spelled "Ayios Niko-laos" in Greek) is a delightful port town 44 miles east of Iraklion. Although its overnight accommodations are Spartan (try **Minos Palace** or **Minos Beach;** then you might consider **Mirabello** and the more expansive **Mirabello Village**), its restaurants, *tavernas,* and discos are a lodestone in season for vacationers from complexes that dot the hills. Out at ***Chersonissos,*** the **Nana Beach** has a certain appeal for seasiders. The best place to eat is the **Cretan Restaurant;** next down our list come **Rififi** (for view) and **Limni; Argo** is good for pizza. Why not scout around to find your own preference? Normally there is a lovely air of languor here, particularly on sun-drenched days.

From here (or from the Astir Palace) take a short boat trip to the tiny abandoned fortress island of **Spinalonga,** formerly Venetian and latterly a leper colony. Many visitors also drive up to **Kritsa,** a hilltown 6 miles into the mountains; it features 40 churches—and so much millinery and embroidery hanging over the architecture and out for sale that you probably can't distinguish an altarpiece from a dolmada joint.

Arina Sand • *5½ miles out of* **Heraklion** *near the village of* **Kokini Hani** • has 83 chambers and suites in its main building plus a complex of 141 accommodations. Properly managed; it's lively and well-maintained.

Creta Maris • *"The Massive,"* a 12-mile run at **Limin Chersonisou** • has been laid out as a Cretan village. This 1200-bed compound, with a staff of 400 and 11 beautifully landscaped gardens, is one of the largest hostelries in the nation. The 360 nests in its simple but colorful bungalows with large verandas are the choicest. The range of its facilities for its clients is enormous. Its poor European-style cuisine is balanced by its Greek culinary offerings. Despite its size, clients can easily find privacy if desired.

Kernos Beach • *near* **Malia** • is designed diametrically opposed to standard planning, with its center of activities adjoining the beach rather than the reception area. This requires a great deal of unnecessary walking. The ruins outside of Malia, not incidentally, in some ways are more impressive than Knossos. The setting by the sea, with mountains on the inland rise, is majestic. The restoration here was less ambitious than Evans' somewhat fanciful if not overly zealous rebuilding of Knossos. The town itself is to be avoided, but this hotel is pleasant enough and the archaeology is richly rewarding.

Minos Beach • *a 44-mile drive* • is on the skirt of a bay within walking distance of **Ag. Nikolaos.** Inaugurated in '61 as the granddaddy of them all, it has been restyled extensively, air-conditioned and given plenty of attention as a born-again host. Beautiful setting; 106 twin-bedded bungalows with porches; 2 beaches; clean. The same management runs the opulent 300-bed **Minos Palace** across the bay.

★★★ **Elounda Beach** • *near* **Elounda** • 5 miles beyond Ag. Nikolaos via a spectacularly scenic route, is a knockout. Lovely setting on a promontory above 2 semicircular beaches; main building spacious, attractive, and spotlessly maintained; masterful settings directly below of individual bungalows and a big pool cunningly landscaped among carob trees; replica of a Greek minivillage with a blue-and-white chapel, an art gallery, a *taverna,* a cafe, boutiques, a hairdresser, a newsstand, and more; open-air cinema with English-language films. Elounda itself has the **Elounda Mare,** which is satisfactory but should not be confused with the Elounda Beach.

★★★ **Astir Palace** • comes so close to the setting and comforts of the nearby Elounda Beach that your choice must depend only on personal taste. Both are superb. Here's another luxury hotel and bungalow resort on 20 acres which stands sentinel over 2 sandy beaches and a small cove. In or around its tastefully blended green area at its base are a main pool, a children's pool, an enclosed heated pool, a *taverna,* a bar, a beauty salon, boutiques, and 2 floodlit tennis courts. One of its most popular drawing cards is the staggering daily 52-platter lunch-buffet.

Lyktos Beach • (and Tennis Club) at *Ierapetra* on the southern coast is a recently created project from the design studios of the tasteful Maurice Bailey. The tallest structure is two floors high so there's a village feeling to this purpose-built resort community. Superb credentials, so it will surely catch on.

Capsis Beach • is located at *Aghia Pelaghia* A V-shaped nexus on a narrow peninsula with sea scenes on both sides. Almost every imaginable amenity can be found here.

Rithymna Beach • is also above average. An attractive feature is the swimming pool with a floral island in its center.

KOS

North Europeans have long favored this expansive, sunny representative of the Dodecanese Islands, which lies within sight of Turkey. Agriculture vies with tourism as the chief money crop. Historically, it is held in almost sacred reverence because the founder of modern medicine, Hippocrates, lived and taught here. The legendary plane tree under which the doctor lectured stands as a focal point in the harbor area—one of the more attractive ports of the myriad that exist in Greek seas. Near the center is the beautifully preserved **Aesculapium,** the ruins dedicated to the ancient god of healing. Still very visible are the Departments of Anatomy, Pathology, and even a building housing medical prescriptions hewn onto stone tablets. Though the shrines date back to the 4th century B.C. they have remained in remarkable preserve. Fittingly, an international medical movement has been founded in the region devoted to the science of gerontology, with its target the extension of man's normal lifespan to 150 years.

Fringing the port's inner core, with its stately **Mosque of Loggia** and a rambling but attractive commercial hub, are the ruins of a Hellenistic **Agora,** the **Sanctuaries of Aphrodite** and **Hercules,** and a **Basilica** from the Christian era. Other *musts* are the **Temple of Dionisus,** the **Odeon,** the **Roman villa,** and **baths,** plus the **Gymnasium** of the Hellenistic period. Kos is probably one of the most convenient cities anywhere for archaeological browsing; most sites are within easy walking distances of the center. Apart from the scholastic rewards, the architecture is mellowed with a scintillating patina of golden light, tumbling vines, billows of bougainvillea and hibiscus, magnificent royal palms, cool gardens, and tasteful restorations. Even ordinary pedestrian lanes are patterned with black and white stones in artistic motifs. The port itself was created within the colossal fortification ramparts built in medieval times and known as the **Chateau des Chevaliers** or **Castle of the Knights of St. John.**

Unfortunately, the bad news is that the hotels are clearly geared for bulk tourism—an anomalous situation when 40% of all visitors to Kos are members of the medical profession. You can completely ignore the official rankings of these establishments because they are based upon statistical ratings rather than on subjective elements of comfort and beauty. My top choice would be the **Oceanis,** out of town by the sea; there's a sandy beach; tennis; stucco-and-wood lobby with white marble floors; 2 pools; private balconies. It is warmly decorated and well appointed. Next would come the **Sun Palace,** the **Hippocrates Palace,** and the **Ramira. Continental Palace** is large but uninspired. The little **Kos** (with pool) and the **Titania** are excellent low-cost choices. For sightseeing, **Norida Beach** at *Kardamena* (south coast) is a massive white city for group tourism, also with bungalows. *Tigaki* and *Marmari* (north littoral) are also developing to honor similar traffic. I prefer the former settlement, where the **Tigaki Beach** and the **Toulas** are reasonably good but simple hotels. For dining, your hotel will probably expect you to contribute to its coffers and your indigestion, but escape if you can and take light refreshment at one of the many cafes overlooking the port. For more exclusive gastronomy in Kos, I found the **Chevaliers** better than average. **Platanos** was fair. At *Kardamena,* **Andreas** seems to serve the best seafood, but if you came to Kos for culinary adventure you can consider yourself well off course in any direction.

MYKONOS

This dazzling white islet in the Cyclades is tourist-conscious—but not quite spoiled. Aside from its topographical attractions and its 300 tiny churches (you may see 3 individual chapels side-by-side-by-side), it is most famous for its pet pelicans—the island's chief mascot being furnished by a German travel agency. Long ago the original bird, who flew in from the unknown, was credited as the talisman who relieved the islanders' financial woes. Just as Gibraltans pin their faith on their lucky Barbary Apes, the Mykonos folk believe they will prosper as long as a pelican is in residence to freeload on the community. *Area?* 32.5 square miles. *Population?* About 10-thousand. *Terrain?* Largely rocky. *Climate?* Usually windy but sunny. *Industries?* Fisheries and tourism. *Towns?* **Mykonos,** a small, whitewashed, windmilled village clustered in the center of a bowl-shape bay, is the only important one. *Beaches?* Excellent, especially along **Plati Yialos Bay** in the direction of **Psarou.** The swimming is wonderful. Nudism is becoming a popular pastime at 3 beaches. Their names? Paradise, Super Paradise, and Hell. In summer campers pitch their tents here or unroll their sleeping bags under the open sky. *Things to see?* Practically nothing—and nearly everything. It is a town to stroll through. Don't miss sunset among the incredibly cozy jumble of seafront houses at **Little Venice.** If you are looking for 19th-century atmosphere, **Lena's House** is an authentic preserve. Nearby is the modest **Aegean Nautical Museum,** which can be fully absorbed in 4 minutes flat. Though the sights sound spare, Mykonos is one of the richest rewards visually of any island in Greek Seas. Since the roads are poor and they go almost nowhere, it stands to reason that there is practically no motor traffic. Greek Easter is nothing short of spectacular here. You'll see the outdoor services at midnight, with boys tippling in the belfries ready to haul on the bell cords, skyrockets going off, and the magnificently robed priest calling out "Christ is Risen!" while parishioners try to toss lighted firecrackers under his skirts. (Most of the explosives, not all, are wrapped in rope to prevent injury.) Then come processions, incense, plenty of imbibing throughout the holiday weekend, and so much lamb to eat that you'll think your hide is coming up in white fleecy tufts.

Hotels: No recent changes. Since officials are worried about insufficient water supplies, an embargo was imposed on new construction. Thus what was, is—and probably will be for a long time to come.

Theo Xenia • is the favorite of the mini crop. It is on a promontory above a bay, a picket line of windmills, and the white-on-white townlet of Mykonos. Comfortable, motel-like accommodations; abundant and sometimes even appetizing cookery; extremely nice people who run it.

Cavo Tagoo • a short hike from town, is a whitewashed pueblo of 40 rooms overlooking mountains, sea, and a handsome vari-form pool. It is about as close to luxury as anything on the island and its smallness is an asset. Quiet and reasonably intimate.

Leto • nibbles at the edge of the main tour boat and fishing harbor, so bathing here is not the best. Its uninspired decor might leave you cold.

Mykonos Beach Bungalows • provide lots more charm; the amenities are satisfactory, too. Superb views from here.

Kouneni • is an old-fashioned homestead in the center with vine-clad patios and cool nooks for intimate relaxing. Even if it doesn't sparkle like a new product, the nostalgia quotient is appealing.

Petassos Beach • at *Plati Yialos Bay,* offers the top living accommodation near the best beach. But a small car will be required unless you don't mind the 10-minute bus ride into town (it leaves and returns frequently). The **Kohilt** and **Koralt** are run by members of the same family.

Santa Marina ● also requires a car, but once you are in its secluded tranquility you may give up the idea of moving at all. It's like an expanded private villa; well-furnished; a pool, beach, marina, tennis court, and oooodles of peace.

Aphrodite ● about a 30-minute bus jog-and-jostle across to the desolate end of the island, maintains a romantic lonely vigil over some of the most breathtaking sea-and-landscapes in the Cyclades. Two beaches enfolding twin coves; all rooms are joined in one stair-step structure; all with bath and balcony facing the waves; swimming pool; tennis; ample recreation hubs for the groups to which it seems to cater; careless service, as might be expected in so remote a clime. The solitude is the thing here—good or bad. Shoppers will find it too far from town; peaceniks will probably love it.

Restaurants: The hotels will likely require that you have breakfast and one other meal with them. **Filippi** offers a tree-shaded garden in a wonderful warren of whitewashed walls. This bower is best at night. **Katrin,** on a lane facing a chapel, has rock walls with stucco and half-timber. Cuisine is reliable and a bit more international than the regional Filippi. **Eden** is worth a try; a pleasant setting for romance in a garden. For typical food, I like **Alekandra, Spyros,** and **Antoninis.** Every turn in the lane seems to have a cafe, so never fear starvation.

Night Life: The very air lilts with Greek music wafting with forlorn softness from the myriad bars. The best places to weep or fall in love with its infatuating melodies are at the **Mykonos.** It has a rush ceiling (the only thing hurried about it) dancing, and someone is normally on hand to give informal instruction in the *bouzouki*. Next come the **Montparnasse** (go to the back room for more meaningful hand-holding), the **7 Seas** (near the harbor and strong on atmosphere), and **Meltemia; Castros** can be gay. The **Remezzo** leads the discotheque file. It offers an incredibly beautiful harborside patio. The **9 Muses** is much more of a swinger; it's recommendable for old married couples who are enjoying their 2nd week anniversary. Because lots more await, the fun is to wander and discover.

Excursions by Sea: The most popular is the ½-hour voyage on stout fishing launches over to the small island of **Delos** with its famous museum, its extensive ruins, its mosaics, and its famous stone lions. Quickie low-cost trips can be had, leaving at 9 a.m. from the main harbor and returning from the rocky uninhabited archaeological sites by lunchtime. *Other sightseeing?* Walking, drinking ouzo in the port, and viewing the **Archaeological Museum** plus **Mykonos Folklore Museum** overlooking the dock.

Shopping: Lalaounis has a jewelry branch here. Be sure to visit **Panos,** where Joan Kousathanas will show you her hand-loomed wares. The **Present Shop** weaves a tale of local blouses, jerkins, and lump-knit sweaters. Don't forget that **Karamichos-Mazarakis** (see "Athens") has a splendid store for *flokati* and other Greek rugs at Harbor Road, the end of the main quai in the port; same shipping facilities available. **Petradi** (also of Athens), near the famous Pierro's Bar, similarly has a branch here on the island displaying Kate Tasedakis' stunning jewelry. The **Mykonos Art Shop** purveys some of the better quality souvenirs on the island. Prices are low by U.S. standards; even so, you should bargain.

Mykonos is unique. Since the aforementioned water shortage has placed a

governor on its growth, it offers the rare mixture of rewards that so many vacationers seek but seldom find in combination: sun, sea, and relative solitude.
Clever, those pelicans!

PATMOS

This minuscule island is relatively undiscovered by migratory tourism, but
still it gets its share from the cruise traffic or the hydrofoil excursionists who
zip over from Kos (1½ hrs.). During the warm months an increasing number
of backpackers are finding its warm dunes and beaches to be excellent sites for
bivouacking. Elitists such as the Aga Khan and about 100 shipowners have long
been aware of its Dodecanese charms, having constructed their villas here almost within the cultural influence of Asia Minor. While Cariens appear to be
the early inhabitants, the island's greater fame comes from its association with
St. John of the Apocalypse who dwelled and preached on the remote, windswept isle. Indeed, the high point both spiritually and physically of any visit is
the mountaintop **Monastery of St. John,** filled with magnificent ikons, scrolls,
frescoes, paintings, and books from the 12th-century onward. It was built in
1088 over the ruins of a still older structure. Since it closes between noon and
2 p.m., plan your taxi excursion accordingly. (Shorts are considered inappro-
priate dress; the doorman, however, will rent you some baggy pants for a nominal sum in the same way that ties and jackets are provided by fancy restaurants
in American metropoli.) The upper village is a maze of perfect strolling townscape. Seek out the colorful but intimate **Patmian House** for lunch; it also can
provide apartment shelter. **Scala,** with no sea view, offers satisfactory accommodation down by the beach. **Xenia, Chris,** and **Astoria** are passable hostelries
in this part of the harbor.

RHODES

The "Isle of Roses" now has more tourist beds than Athens. (Astonishing,
but true!) Yet the parade of hotels cheek-by-jowl has not seriously affected the
basic charm of the capital or its environs. Battalions of buses? Yes. Regiments
of new lodgings? Yes. Alien hordes of migratory invaders? Yes. But these have
not made serious dents on the island's historic radiance.

Location? Largest of the Dodecanese Islands, roughly 16 miles off the
Turkish coast and 280 air miles southeast of Athens. *Size?* 54 by 27 miles,
shaped like an ocarina. *Population?* Nearly 70 thousand. *Cities?* **Rhodes** proper,
with 30-thousand people, is the capital and the only important settlement. *Lindos,* a whitewashed village with its own Acropolis, is about an hour away. In
fair weather this charming coastal hamlet is a *must* for sightseers. *Connections?*

From *Athens* (Piraeus): *Kamiros* and *Ialysos* are large, comfortable, air-conditioned ferries run by a Dodecanese co-op with daily noontime sailings; also in the 18-hour itinerary are the isles of Kos, Patmos, Leros, and Kalymnus. The cost is less than flying—and what a fine way to sneak in a Greek Island cruise! From Athens airport 50 weekly Olympic Airways flights which take a little over an hour; from other islands thrice per week. Caution: In peak periods, traffic is so heavy that normally you will be asked to show your confirmed return ticket before Olympic will permit you to board in Athens. *People?* Lovely; overwhelmingly kind. They have a sense of humor that is easygoing and filled with chummy banter. *Best season?* Late spring or early fall. Summer is fine when the breezes blow, but when they don't, it can be hot; winter is comparatively mild, but some spells are unpleasant; prices from November through February in many hostelries have been slashed 50% as a spur to Off Season tourism.

Hotels

Rodos Bay • looms up as one of the loftier buildings on the island, allegedly 30 feet higher than the vanished Colossus of Rhodian legend. Sited 2 miles out toward the airport, this entry fronts the beach from a slight rise. Rooftop saltwater pool; bar and restaurant sharing a twinkling tableau of southwest Turkey; excellent fish and barbecued meats; shops, tennis, minigolf, and sauna; *taverna;* nightclub; cavernous, granite-girt lobby punctuated by wooden beams and paved with gray marble; 28 air-cooled bungalows; 35 split-level suites; 175 bedchambers with white stucco walls, pastel-tiled decking, telephones, baths or showers. Have a look at the high-ceilinged duplexes on the 5th level.

Olympic Palace • a daring architectural flow of 8 floors in concentric semicircles, overlooks Trilanda Bay from a lovely slope of forested mountain. Butterflys flutter in the vales in summer; there are 3 pools; space for 700 souls; a well-divided dining zone (for so many feeders); simple bedchambers. Plenty of nightlife and a shopping arcade. If sun and sea are your calling you'll find them here.

Grand Hotel Astir Palace • 100% air-conditioned, bows welcome to nearly 800 courtiers, all of whom may make their individual splashes in any of the 3 swimming pools, including one indoors for cooler months. Oases of snacking corners and alfresco lounges; 2 restaurants with nearby cocktail bars, popular self-service snack bar; English pub; Isabella nightclub; casino for year-round gambols from 9:30 p.m.–2 a.m. Some units with verandas facing gardens and pools; other seafront accommodations slightly more expensive; winter reductions about 50%. The situation is its primary asset.

Dionysos • is probably next. This also-superbly-sited entry consists of 2 separate air-conditioned buildings, tennis courts, minigolf, and 3 swimming pools. The first structure, in the deluxe category, is limited to suites that offer a 2-bed room and bath, a sitting room, a kitchenette, and a big veranda also with a magnificent view of the sea. There is a garden cocktail bar plus an adjoining snack installation featuring regional specialties. The second structure is a complex that embraces the main dining room, the main bar, a cinema, a lecture hall, and a nightclub.

Miramare Beach • an ambitious project 3 miles from the city on the airport road, offers a central edifice, 152 1- and 2-storied bungalows, and a bevy of 2-bedroom deluxe cottages. Beachfront ambience in a lovely setting; swimming pool; international cuisine with Greek specialties; windsurfing; tennis; minigolf. Homey and friendly; particularly good for traveling families.

Paradise • may be gained (or so the management attests) just a bit south of Rhodes, where 1200 fellow vacationers experience sun worship and seasiding from a complex of one central slabular building and a pair of smaller annexes. The beach is vast—and so is the restaurant. Functional bedchamber; *taverna,* night club, and bar. Overwhelming in volume, but well executed for its mass-minded purposes.

Des Roses • has been refreshed. Its central location and views recommend it.

Mediterranean • offers a pleasant sidewalk terrace but otherwise it's blatantly commercial.

Rodos Palace Resort Complex • consisting of a deluxe tower hotel for 800 plus chalet accommodation for nearly as many. The decor makes handsome use of marble and panels, with ample space and the clever employment of trickling water to add a note of solace. Cheer-packed grill, huge restaurant, colorful nightclub, pink coffee shop, shops also for shopping.

Oceanis • with a relaxed composure, is sited out near the Miramare. Inviting swimming pool; fair public rooms; air conditioning; well-appointed bedchambers. If you prefer a noncentral address (across the highway from the breakers), this is it.

Metropolitan Capsis • across from the Dionysos, is an imposing structure. Roof garden, pool, sauna, and gym; seaview rooms with air conditioning; food and service geared to the throngs of tour registrants who roll in as waves to the shore.

The **Cactus, Sirabas,** and **Ibiscus** line up side by side side, revealing equal proclivities for boredom. **Chevaliers Palace** may lack an apostrophe, but it offers an air-conditioned welcome to some 300 pilgrims and sun worshippers. Decoratively, it jousts merrily with its own image: flags, armor, chain mail, and other hokum of ages gone by. **Plaza** is pleasant. **Park**'s best feature is its nightclub. You won't miss much if you avoid the **Belvedere, Golden Beach, Imperial, Thermai,** or the distant **Elafos.**

Restaurants Most hotels impose a full-pension plan, but a few independents have had the courage to serve the more adventurous public. Try the **"13",** which to Europeans is a lucky number. It's very close to the Hotel Mediterranean. Then drive out (or by taxi it's 20 minutes) to *Tris,* a village that is gaining local fame for its **Kioupia.** The excursion alone is fun and the food is excellent.

Fotis, in the Old Town, creates a magical potion of tiny shrimps that are boiled to such tenderness that they are devoured shells and all. The sea fare is noteworthy. **Kon-Tiki,** moored at the extension of a marina that overlooks a small bay, is another tight little ship on the horizon. All the nautical trimmings come with this one: Hurricane lamps, tarpaulins, ship's tackle, and the fetching charm of a cozy bark. **Alexis** is for seafood stalkers, while **Casa Castellana** caters to steak hounds. **Maison Fleuri** fits into the luxury category; the cuisine is French. As for local *tavernas,* the colorful **Vrachos** huddles by the shore; it is haunted by burly sailor lads and assorted toughies.

Night Life: Nearly all of the deluxe and first-class hotels have nightclubs that function from time to time. In the New Town **Akteon** is tops, followed by **Highway, Playboy, La Scala,** and a zippy disco called **Laser.** For typical dance (read *bouzouki*) go to the unlikely-named **Copacabana** and the likely-named **Zorba; Diogenis** is also an honest choice.

Sightseeing The site of one of the Seven Wonders of the World, the **Colossus** of Rhodes, which once straddled the harbor and which was destroyed by an earthquake in 224 B.C. (a group of sculptors and archaeologists plan to erect an aluminum replica of the original); a 1-hour tour of the ramparts and defenses of the **Old Town** (a *must* for every visitor), built by the Crusaders; the magnificent medieval **walled city** of the Knights Hospitalers of St. John of Jerusalem (today the Knights of Malta), with its castles, palaces, and fairy-tale ruins; the **Acropolis** for the city of Ancient Rhodes; the **Archaeological Museum** and the **Palace of the Grand Masters;** the **Thermal Springs of Callithea,** 6 miles out, with Moorish architecture, a grotto restaurant, a spring house, 3 kinds of beneficial waters, and a challenging array of 120—count 'em 120—toilets; the splendid cellar **Aquarium** with an amazing variety of rays, moray eels, turtles, brilliant starfish, and local sea denizens in a series of tanks; the **Acropolis** of Ancient Ialyssos at Filerimos Hill; **Ancient Kamiros,** an abandoned town on the romantic western shore; the **Valley of Butterflies** at Petaloudes, 15 miles out, where clouds of pinkish-gray beauties rise by the thousands as you walk along the little cascades (season only). For other types of sightseers, a nudist colony for 500 bare-skin buffs was undraped in the coastal region opposite the airport from the capital. Finally, try not to miss a drive out to **Lindos,** an hour from your metropolitan doorstep. This ancient, lime-washed, seacoast village is nestled in a rugged meander of an age-old ravine. Park your car in the town square and take the 20-minute hike up the footpath to the cliff-high fortress and the quietly eroding sandstone Acropolis. The awe-inspiring vistas of the sapphire water, the cubistic white-on-white jumble of houses, the fishing harbor, the still lagoon in a bracelet of volcanic rock, and the far-ranging sweep of a golden sandy beach, are breathtaking. If you pack a picnic lunch, nibble and daydream on the flower-covered slopes below the ramparts; you will be much happier than if you had dined at the handful of rawboned *tavernas* in the town. On the way down, take the path leading to the small but gemlike Byzantine chapel. Be sure to give a moderate tip to the 212-year-old woman who explains in perfect Greek just what every statue, painting, niche, and curlicue means (to her, not to you, unless you speak the language). If you *must* overnight, the **Pallas** and **Electra** boardinghouses are just about the only pads available.

SANTORINI

The beauty here is incredible. Santorini not only yields its name to the chief island but to the profoundly deep, dark basin composed of 5 surrounding Cycladic isles that form the *caldera* or "kettle." It is regrettable that so many visitors only see this whitewashed poem briefly when the cruise ships are in port—a criminal loss for anyone who has traveled so far and who will be denied the inner secrets of one of the Hellenic world's most breathtaking attractions.

Phoenicians and Dorians settled as early as 2000 B.C., probably one of the first Minoan colonies. In 1520 B.C. a shattering volcanic eruption destroyed the civilization, simultaneously creating yet another legend to add to the string of Lost Atlantis myths. In recent times archaeologists discovered **Akrotiri,** a Bronze Age town of approximately 30,000 inhabitants. But since there were no human remains or precious artifacts such as jewels or gold, it is presumed that the citizens had been forewarned. In my view, Akrotiri must be considered one of the most important finds of Western civilization, tying together many of the mysteries of our earliest ancestry. In *Thira* you will see reproductions of the magnificent frescoes that have been swept away to the Athens Museum—as much an affront to Minoan culture as the limp excuses England has made for appropriating the Elgin Marbles. To a sensitive American, this would be as offensive as finding our own Miss Liberty one day guarding the entrance to Yokahama harbor. Here is a splendid excavation of monumental importance that should be preserved for the people who occupy its historical presence and where the art should haunt the memory of earlier periods and inspire visitors and residents alike. (If you are here sightseeing during lunchtime, try a meal at **Kastro.**)

Most arrivals are brought in by lighter from the ships and make the half-hour climb by foot or by burro to the upper village, where they arrive with faces of puce and bathed in sweat; if you're a sissy, the cable car ride takes only minutes. Viewful terrace restaurants along the higher shelf are ornamented by displays of drying octopus and squid; lamb and fish also generally are available. The better choices for mealtiming include **Lichnari, Leonidas,** and (of course) a **Zorba's.** Additionally, **Babis** and **Fantasia** are recommendable. So is **Camille Stafani,** but it does not overlook the sea. Be sure to sample the soft mellow Santorini Lava red wine, a product of the volcanic ash.

If there is time, one *must* experience sunset from the promontory village of *Oia* (also **"Ia"**), one of the most soulfully romantic settings to be found anywhere. There are cafes and restaurants along the clifftop (the **Kyklos** is best followed by the **Petrus.**). Other sightseeing targets might include the black sand beach of **Kamari** (have lunch at the **Sphinx**) and the **Monastiri,** which peeps impishly from between the legs of towering communication spires on the 2000-foot mountain that soars above the valley and shore.

The top hotel in the capital is the small and viewful **Atlantis;** otherwise you'd probably be snug in the **Atlantis Villas** at Ia (traditional houses restored and comfort-ized) or at **Perivolas** in the same village. The **Tennis Club Apartments** and the **Altana** in *Merovigli* also are recommendable.

Shoppers will find themselves in a cliff-high paradise. On the steps spiraling down to the port, don't miss **Robos** for hand-woven dresses, floppy shirts, rugs, vests, and bedspreads. Ladies will go bonkers-in-Greek for the **Aris** hand-painted dresses; the colors are zesty and ideal for summer. An address will do no good; it's in the high town. Jewelry is always an area of caution, but **Greco Gold** (also in midvillage) appears to be the most reputable and have the highest quality stocks. Ask for Yanis or Stefanos Keramidas. Antiques? Go to **Athanasios Papatheodorou,** not far from the Atlantis Hotel—many beautiful items, including the *akrokeramo* (decorative finials). If you're still not magenta from walking up and down the mountain lanes, go to step 566 where you'll find **E. Youkas,** the specialist for carpets and wall hangings and pillow covers. All are hand-loomed and surprisingly inexpensive.

By all means try to arrange your visit to include more than the few hours the ships' anchorages provide.

SARONIC ISLANDS

These oft-neglected gems lie in a J-shape form running south and west from the Athenian port of Piraeus. They are accessible by both standard ferries as well as hydrofoils. If you want to see them all, you can do so in a day on the Flying Dolphins that skim through these beautiful seas at 30–36 knots. While there are many islets and salt-and-pepper rock dots within the group, you are probably going to visit only the chief ones mentioned here—that is, unless you are a scholar or have some other specific calling. In general, accommodation is less than luxurious, but more than adequate and you can enjoy an enriching cultural experience by spending a night or two at each of the 4 major ports.

Aegina, closest to Piraeus, offers splendid beaches and a history that goes back to Neolithic times. The temple of **Aphala Athena** is the dominant architectural target from the 5th century B.C., predating the Acropolis in Athens, for which it served as the model. Other ruins include a **theater** and **stadium.** Excellent bathing at *Agia Marina* (8 miles from the port) and lovely scenery at the fishing village of *Perdika.* For overnighting, try the **Apollo** in *Agia Marina* or the **Aegina Maris** (hotel and bungalows) at *Perdika.* In the port, **Danae** is satisfactory, followed by the bungalows of **Nafsika** or the **Pension Pavlou.**

Poros is really one marvelous whitewashed dream, with yacht moorings strung along a lane of open cafes and wind-tossed patios. Across the strait is the mainland town of *Galatas.* There is not much to do except hold hands, stroll, and fall into a blissful Hellenic reverie. For romancers on limited budgets it is a paradise. Another **Pavlou** serves for shelter; the **Neon Aegli** is the largest hostelry, followed by the **Poros.** The main thing here is to try to find an accommodation overlooking the water and the boats that pass through the channel.

For shopping notions, speak to Stacy Soloyanis at **Apollon** beside the Fountain Square.

Hydra is at the very bottom of the "J." Certainly the busy port, which stairsteps up the steep mountain chalice, is one of the most frequently photographed frames of scenery to be found anywhere in Homeric waters. Fishing as well as recreation vessels create a cheerful atmosphere of activity; all town life fringes the harbor under awnings or in the shade of the pastel buildings. The prestigious **School of Fine Arts** is located in **Villa Tombazi.** The mansions sprinkled around the bowl reflect the 19th-century heyday, when fleets sailed in and gave the island the nickname of "Little England." While its topography is rock, good beaches exist at *Kaminia, Molos, Palamida,* and *Bisti* on the western flank, as well as the **Miramare** strand at *Mandraki.* Both **Miranda** and **Miramare Beach** (Mandraki) control the top hotel ranking, while **Hydrousa, Delfini, Cavos,** and **Amaryllis** provide reasonable comfort in a lower category.

Spetses is the most distant from the capital—approximately 2 hours by hydrofoil. There is no special archaeology here, but islanders are proud of Bouboulina, their heroine sea captain who led her small fleet against the mighty Turkish armada and defeated them with such a trouncing that the Turks never again returned. Minuscule water taxis take bathers to nearby private beaches for small sums and retrieve them at appointed times. No cars function after 3 p.m.— only charming horse-drawn fiacres. One *must* is to have an exotic cocktail at sunset on the roof of the **Hotel Ilios** (Soleil). The **Spetses** is modern; **Possidonion** is old-fashioned, but in a good position; **Kasteli** offers hotel and bungalow accommodation. **Roumanis** and **Myrtoon** are also worth considering in a lower bracket.

In all of these a limited pension plan is possible at your hotel, but I would by far recommend that you dine along the port frontages where dozens of attractive tavernas serve precisely the same thing in far more bewitching surroundings.

For reservations, travel arrangements, or a helping hand, Ioanna Nicolareisis has offered to assist readers of this book. She is the attractive young manager of Dapia Tours in the middle of the town of Spetses; Tel.: 0298–72040.

IRELAND

USA: Irish Tourist Board, 757 3rd Ave., New York, NY 10017, Tel. (212) 481–0800; **CANADA:** 10 King St. East, Toronto M5C 1C3, Tel. (416) 364–1301

SPECIAL REMARKS: (1) The master organization is called **Bord Failte Eireann;** its Bord Chairman is Martin Dully. The Information Office in Dublin is located at 14 Upper O'Connell St. In addition, there are more than 70 regional branches. For a small charge they can also find accommodation for you almost anywhere in the nation.

TELEPHONE: Access code to USA: 16. To phone Ireland: 353; time difference (Eastern Daylight) 5 hrs.

Ever heard of an entrancing, beguiling, little nation named Poblacht na hEireann? Pronounce it *"Pub*lockt nah *Hair*-un," but call it the "Republic of Ireland" if you don't speak Gaelic. The island is smaller than Pennsylvania but larger than South Carolina; you could drop its entire area into Lake Superior.

One-sixth of the seagirt land mass is Northern Ireland, administratively part of the UK and scene of most of the political fireworks which locals refer to as "the troubles." There is a vast difference between the men of the North (containing Derry, Antrim, Armagh, Down, Tyrone, and Fermanagh counties) and the more tranquil South. Occasionally violence spills over the border, but wise voices from both segments urge an end to the quarreling.

Here is the sod on which to relax. As *Time* stated so pungently, "The Irish have always cultivated the art of living, and they still have time and space for the slow perusal of race horses, the thoughtful consumption of stout, and the weighty disputation in rich, foamy periods that make English English seem like verbal porridge. . . . Ireland has in abundance the qualities that often seem to be disappearing elsewhere: kindliness, an unruly individualism, lack of snobbery, ease, style, and, above all, sly humor." Dublin today—not to mention the even cheaper rural Irish targets—can provide one of the lowest-cost holidays in Europe. But if you want floor shows, superhighways, strip joints, recreation

IRELAND

ATLANTIC OCEAN

N. IRELAND

Boudoran

Belfast

Sligo

Ballynahinch
Newry

Ballina

Castlebar

Carrickmacross

Dundalk

Westport

IRISH SEA

Clifden

Cong

Mulingar

Oughterard

Cashel Bay

Galway

Athlone

Dublin

Ballyvaughn

Wicklow

Shannon

Limerick

Adare

Kilkenny

Tipperary

Cashel

Tralee

Cahir

Wexford

Killarney

Waterford

Glenbeigh

Waterville

Cork

Bantry

N

ATLANTIC OCEAN

directors, subways, nightclubs, and the frenzied, taut scurrying of the mass-produced vacation, here still isn't your answer. Ireland will offer you a good chair and invite you to enjoy what John Burroughs once called "the Beautiful Foolishness of Things."

SHANNON INTERNATIONAL AIRPORT   Shannon is the airport and Limerick (see separate listing) is the town. Transit passengers generally have time to refuel in its outstanding Lindbergh Room restaurant, to polish off a quickie at its friendly bar (amazingly low prices), and, *if not bound for Dublin or domestic points,* to load up with tax-free spirits, U.S. cigarettes, French perfumes, Swiss watches, English pewter, Irish linens, and other treasures at the Tax Free Airport Store, which has been dramatically redesigned. The Souvenirs Department, with ½-million customers annually, does a turnover Macy's would envy. Shannon Mail Order, by the way, is an exciting armchair answer to your shopping headaches. It can save you money, time, and trouble by selecting from the wonderful brochure. Even with postage and U.S. duty added, you will realize considerable savings. To obtain a catalogue, enclose $2 and direct your request to Mr. Michael O'Gorman, General Manager, Shannon Mail Order, Shannon Free Airport, Ireland. Great for birthdays, Christmas, anniversaries—or to avoid carrying bulky parcels that strain your temper and your back.

Within easy reach of the Airport are 3 banqueting castles: **Bunratty** (open year round), **Knappogue,** and **Dunguaire** (both functioning summers only). Within the **Granary** adjoining the Tourist Office in town, the **Captain's Table** offers maritime tavern entertainment, mandolin and banjo music, and shantys; a 2½-hour show and dinner for about £18.

Adjoining Bunratty, the reconstructed 19th-century Irish village complex called the **Folk Park** has cottages, a forge, and a souvenir and craft shop in the original site. Now that enclave has been expanded from 6 to 20 acres; there's a post office, a potter's shed, a printer, and—as you might expect in Ireland—a sweet shop. Bunratty House, built in 1804, is also now incorporated into the general admission. A "horizontal mill," used by the Irish since the seventh century, is on display, suggesting distinct trading links between Asia and Europe in those early times. You can observe busy fingers weaving, basketmaking, and following the same pursuits of 150 years ago. There's also the wonderful **Avoca Handweavers** shop beside Bunratty Castle for knitwear, glass, linen, and Irish crafts that follow those rich traditions. (In fact, it's the *only* commercial enterprise of its type worth visiting in the immediate Bunratty vicinity, in my opinion.) Within a few steps is **Durty Nelly's,** which first started as a pub more than a century ago. After careful restoration and expansion in the late 1960s, it has 4 rooms with stone walls, sawdusted floors, and 2 peat fireplaces. Typically light food is served inexpensively at all licensed hours. Its friendly atmosphere and convincing authenticity make it definitely worth a stop-in for drinks before the banquet.

Nearby is the **Craggaunowen Project** with replicas of lake dwellings and forts of the early Christian Irish. The leather *Brendan* boat which courageously sailed across the Atlantic to duplicate the route of navigator monks is on show here too—fascinating for salty types. A number of attractions (castles, prehistoric huts, ring forts, and museums) reflecting the natural history and culture of the area can be absorbed on day tours by coach from Limerick City. The neolithic settlement at **Lough Gur** is another attraction for amateur archaeologists. To visit either site, check the Tourist Office, which is located in a restored 18th-century Georgian warehouse in Michael St., for details.

Weathered-in passengers may take the 2- to 3-minute walk from the terminus to the **Shannon International Hotel,** which has a first-rate restaurant, a sauna and gym and color TV in the bedrooms and a free baggage transfer service. **Fitzpatrick's Shannon Shamrock Hotel** glows with administrative savvy. Motel mood with warm touches of dark stone and wood; bar-lounge; pleasant dining room flanked by enclosed pool with a view of Bunratty Castle; sauna and massage; courtesy shuttle to airport; ice machines; TV plus in-house movies; among its 100 accommodations with bath, the 8 end rooms (4 in atelier style) are very much more appealing if you're splurging a bit.

SIGHTSEEING   In the countryside, the drive through the extreme **southwest** of the nation (*Bantry–Ballylickey–Kenmare* and around the legendary "Ring of Kerry" to *Killarney* or the nearby *Dingle Bay*) is particularly stirring, beautiful, and worth adventuring. The L54 *coastal* road up to *Ballyvaughan* (County Clare) is even more breathtaking—a parade of glorious seascapes and landscapes in wild and unforgettably impressive terrain. Many of the hotels in this area are closed during Off-Season.

And while in Killarney, don't miss the extraordinary excursion up the mountain road to "Ladies View" and "Moll's Gap." If you don't use your own car or take a conducted bus tour, you may proceed by jaunting car, pony trap, or pony-*back* up, in, out and around, to the upper lake. Here a filling picnic lunch may await you. Your return may then be made by big comfortable rowboats, with 4 brawny oarsmen pulling you down the 14-mile channel through the 3 lakes. This is a 6-hour trip. Also in Killarney, **Muckross House Folk Museum** is well worth a visit.

Tralee, County Kerry, is the base of **Siamsa, the National Folk Theatre,** where the traditions of the countryside—the thatching, weaving, butter-churning, story-telling—are brought alive through mime, music, song, and dance.

The *Naomh Eanna,* a handsome little steamer, handles the Aran run all year round and is assisted by *The Galway Bay* from June 1 to mid-September. Arrival and departure times are such that you will have to spend 2 nights in Galway. The *Naomh Eanna* trip takes about 2½ hours to the main island and after a stay of approximately 1½ hours (depending on tides) returns via the other islands, taking about 5 hours. *The Galway Bay* calls on the main island and returns on a direct route, taking about 2½ hours each way. From Rossveal (20 miles from Galway) there are also regular voyages. If you can't spare that much time, regularly scheduled 20-minute flights zip out of Galway; they're very reasonably priced.

For amateur sailors the appeal of a delightful vacation option is escalating in eye-popping proportions. Today hundreds of smart-looking and safe, comfortable cabin cruisers are available for self-operated exploring along the Shannon River, where you can get away from it all by enjoying the peace, quiet, and scenery of one of the world's most unpolluted and beautiful freshwater streams where all commercial traffic is banned. Eleven companies handle the charters out of Carrick-on-Shannon, Athlone, Banagher, Belturbet, and Killaloe. Before launching you'll be briefed on handling and navigation. Easily spotted signs mark its channels and with the aid of charts most pilots reach their chosen ports. Periodically the river broadens into serene loughs (lakes). At night you tie up at a village of your choice and spend the evening quietly, often enjoying the amenities of the local pub or visiting with the friendly rural folk. All standard craft are available. One class, for example, sleeps 6 in 3 private cabins, has 2 heads, a shower, a refrigerator, and a stove, plus plenty of living and sunning space. If you don't care to take the helm yourself, there are river circuits aboard tour boats. There's also the *Shannon Princess,* a floating hotel for a dozen cruisers who may spend a week on the nation's longest river; passage on the 105-foot vessel runs close to $1700 based on a double-occupancy cabin—food, wine, fishing gear, and bikes included. Contact Bord Failte Eireann to put you in touch with the booking office nearest you.

Perhaps the most famous single tourist landmark is **Blarney Castle,** near the city of *Cork* (75 miles from Shannon, 160 miles from Dublin). To kiss the stone, admission is now about $1; children are less than half price.

TRANSPORTATION   **Aer Lingus** flies the Atlantic and connects to other routes out of Shannon, Dublin, Galway, Sligo, or Cork. Its U.S. gateways are New York, Chicago and Boston; from Dublin it flies to 8 regional airports. Should it be a choice between Shannon or Dublin, pick the one most convenient to your travels because the road link between them is 136 miles long. (If your connecting times are appropriate, Aer Lingus offers a daily flight between the two major airports.) Delta (via Atlanta) now utilizes the Shannon facilities and provides excellent service that I would use in preference to the Irish carrier over the Atlantic. Premier class on Aer Lingus is, however, recommendable if you care to pay the premium. Shannon has a splendid duty-free facility (as mentioned).

Trains If you plan to wander for any length of time, the $58 8-day **Rambler Pass** can represent quite a saving. There's also a rail and bus ducat and a plan for youths, and these can run on up to 30 days. Ask your travel agent about them.

Taxis Several fleets of radio-contact cabs: **Blue Cabs,** tel. 761111; **Metro Taxis,** tel. 683333; **National Cabs,** tel. 772222; **VIP Taxis,** tel. 783333. In addition, the **independents,** recognizing competition, have perked up their cars and services and even have a central telephone of their own; 766666. Call any of these and you may expect to have a metered taxi within 10 minutes, regardless of where you are.

Jaunting cars (the Irish "dogcart," a one-horse affair) are lots of fun. In Killarney, as one example, there are a multitude of tours that range in price from $26 to $57 for 4 people. **Bicycles** cost perhaps $11 per day, a fine investment. But the most exotic transportation available has got to be the **Gypsy Caravan,** a horse-drawn trailer capable of accommodating 4 persons. These brightly painted wagons are equipped with foamrubber berths, a bottled-gas stove, heat, light, sheets, and blankets—and they're all yours for between $450 and $800 per week, depending on the time of year. (There's an off-season weekend quotation of $233 for hardy types.) You don't even need to know one end of the beastie from the other, because they'll cheerfully give you free lessons in harnessing and driving—something which you should accept as insurance against mishaps. Check the Irish Tourist Office for details.

If you are motoring, the efficient **Sealink** ferries can carry you to and from convenient points on either side of the Irish Sea. Frequent drive-on services during all seasons, so pick up a timetable or consult a travel agent.

Short-run trains are showing great improvement. All the **Irish Railways'** local lines are now dieselized. Among the blue-ribbon runs, the *Enterprise Express* and the *Dublin-Cork Express* are outstanding.

Ireland is in the Eurailpass system; connections from Rosslare in the southeast to Cherbourg and Le Havre by ships of the Irish Continental Line.

Long-distance **bus** hauls—and some of the newer short-haul links—are as modern and speedy as our Greyhound routes. But when you climb aboard the average rural Irish bus, prepare yourself for An Experience. A few pick up passengers every 42 feet—but you'll get a kick out of your ride, and you'll probably arrive on time. The friendliness and banter are worth the price of admission.

The **C.I.E.** (35 Lower Abbey St., Tel.: 300777), a big-time organization with large and comfortable vehicles, operates 2- to 15-day tours with prices varying with your choice of accommodation. One-day and ½-day circuits start from Dublin's Bus Station; rail excursions also are available linking with bus or a jaunting car along the route. Book early to insure your space.

FOOD AND RESTAURANTS   Irish regional cuisine is superb—and so, too, are grills, roast beef, steaks, salmon, or simple dishes. The stews of yore are disappearing and chefs are more inventive. What you'll note immediately is the freshness of products for the table.

Fresh salmon is a staple—and Ireland is one of the last places on earth where you can still taste it "wild" in restaurants. Institutions elsewhere usually serve "ranched" fish, which lacks the texture of the real McCoy. In better establishments the menu will specify the origin. Mashed potatoes are called "creamed potatoes"; paper napkins pop up even in some of the most elegant establishments. Milk is rich, plentiful, and pasteurized; soda fountains are dubbed "cafes" or "milk bars."

Personally, my enjoyment in this nation comes not from seeking out the international cuisine that is often just another gastronomic cliche, but looking for the unique flavors and treatments given to local foodstuffs. You might try the fine home-grown beef flamed in Irish whiskey, Kerry scallops, Donegal crab, the briny Galway oysters, or special mussels of Wexford and Kinsale. If you insist on a stew, then why not try one steeped in Guinness or grow stouter with a filet stuffed with oysters? Even the cliche can be delectable—if you order Dublin Bay prawns.

DRINKS   A taste of Irish whiskey is often better than a raincoat. No potatoes at all; it's triple-distilled from barley (Scotch is merely twice distilled!). Put about a pound on the bar, ask for "a half one," and up will come this unique, potent, and healing libation.

A consortium called Irish Distillers Group now produces all of this category of spirits in the country, despite the continuing competition between individual brands. John Jameson's (Holinshed's "Sovereign Liquor At Its Finest"), John Power's ("Enjoy That Gold Label"), D. E. Williams at Tullamore ("Give Every Man His Dew"), and Cork's, makers of Paddy ("Will 'oo have a Paddy?")

means your host is a true-blue Cork man. Bushmill's Black Label, a long-aged premium offering, is extra-full-bodied and malty. Many people regard it as the best of all; coming from the oldest licensed distillery in the world, its birth certificate is dated A.D. 1608!

Generally speaking, the average Irish toper is not a natural consumer of hard booze. He is a devotee of stout—a dark, very rich, very special beer. This dedication is so important that the price of the pint is chronically a dominant issue in political elections. Guinness comes in both bottle and draught. This brewery landmark, on which the original Arthur Guinness took a 9000-year lease, has merely another 8767 years to go before expiration; the same yeast strains have been continuously under cultivation and in use since its founding. The brewery stands on 60 acres, the largest in Europe. Visitors are welcome any time (except on bank holidays) between 10 a.m. and 3 p.m. from Monday through Friday to see a film of its operations and sample the product. Murphy's stout is particularly popular in the Cork area. It is a bit lighter and sweeter than Guinness. Many Americans take these diluted with beer or ale; "Black Velvet" (50% champagne and 50% stout) holds vast appeal.

Beer flows in Niagaras, of course. Harp lager twangs a tangy note. In your sweetest Irish tenor, warble for an extra-cold one. Otherwise it may be served to you at skin temperature.

Irish coffee (also known as Gaelic coffee) is one of the pleasantest beverages possible to sample. To make it, add a jigger of Irish whiskey to ⅔rds of a glass of steaming black coffee; add sugar to taste; float thick, rich cream on the top without stirring. Every bar makes it; most licensed restaurants, too.

For your after-dinner liqueur, Irish Mist is to Ireland what Drambuie is to Scotland. Interesting and different; increasingly popular. Bailey's Irish Cream, Carolans, and Waterford Cream are liqueurs composed of the native elixir and rich squeezings from Elsie the cow.

NOTE · · · As in the United Kingdom, the police have cracked down mercilessly by applying the roadside "Breathalyser" test to anyone they suspect. If the crystals in the plastic bag turn green (even that 2nd pint of beer might do it for some people), the offender will face fines up to $1000 or 6 months in the pokey (or both) plus loss of driving license. There is no recourse for either resident or visitor.

TIPPING · · · In many hotels and restaurants a 10–15% service charge is added in lieu of gratuities and no additional outlay is expected. When it is not included, you should add about 10% to your bill. Tipping is not customary in pubs and never in movies, theaters, shops, or stores. Ten percent is usual for taxi drivers for a normal ride; 50p is okay for porters and your cloakroom attendant.

CITIES AND REGIONS

ADARE (County Limerick, 10 miles southwest of Limerick City) prides itself on the famous little **Dunraven Arms.** Within striking distance of Shannon Airport; decor of antiques, soft colors, and serene character; pleasant dining room with improved cookery. Long Bar swarming with families including small fry on summer weekends; ramps for wheelchairs; 24 rooms with bath or shower, spotless in maintenance.

ATHLONE (County Westmeath, halfway between Dublin and Galway on the main road) **Athlone Castle** is open to public viewing during the summer months. **Shamrock Lodge** and the **Prince of Wales** are useful for motorists but no more than utilitarian.

BALLINA (County Mayo)
    Mount Falcon Castle • if the truth be told, is more of a semi-stately home than a castle. Salmon fishing on the Moy or Lough Conn; woodcock and other fowl for shooting; tennis plus a seesaw and 2 tire-swings hung from a shade tree for those who can't live without constant entertainment. The house is so full of joviality created by Proprietress Aldridge and her rollicking band of family, dogs, and friends that a jolly-good evening around the hearth and table is almost guaranteed. Creaky but cheerful.

    Belleek Castle • is in the same county about an easy hour's drive southwest of Sligo. Great Hall very impressive for its antiquity; savory gastronomy; many antiques throughout its 16 bedchambers and spacious public rooms.

BALLYNAHINCH (County Galway)
    ★★ **Ballynahinch Castle** • with 20 simple, no-frills rooms and bath, is smaller than its more famous neighbor, Ashford Castle, but from the sportsman's point of view it's even better. Excellent salmon and trout fishing, both river and lake. Owned by a syndicate of American sportsmen who have no intention of spoiling the fun of its loyal clientele.

BALLYVAUGHAN (County Clare)
    ★★ **Gregan's Castle Hotel** • 4 miles from this coastal hamlet on the Lisdoonvarna road, is seemingly hell-and-gone from everywhere—but actually it is in beautiful country only 30 miles around the bay from Galway. (If you are

proceeding northward, be sure, *double sure,* not to miss the glorious coastal drive along L54, one of the most magnificent ocean panoramas in the nation.) In no way is this country inn a "castle." Sited on a slight promontory, with a sweeping view of the countryside down to the distant bay; Corkscrew Bar; Tudor-style dining room with noteworthy cuisine based on regional viands; 2 lounges; with distinctive antiques; 16 rooms, 12 with private bath, all named for Irish towns or counties instead of numbered. There's a cozy air about the house.

BANTRY (County Cork, extreme southwest) **Ballylickey House** has been rebuilt as an 11-room facility, all with private bath. There's also the **Seaview.** Next, try the **Westlodge Hotel** with 106 rooms and baths, heated indoor pool, squash and tennis courts, and a pitch'n'putt course.

BUNDORAN (County Donegal, northwest coast) **The Great Northern** resides on 130 acres of treeless "parkland" bordering a small sand beach and rocky shoals; large Victorian building serenely surrounded by an 18-hole championship golf course (free to guests); heated indoor pool; ambitious dining facilities; viewful lobby and lounge. Its 96 bedchambers and baths are in good shape; some are small, so request a large one; some have superb sea views.

CAHIR (pronounced "care," County Tipperary) **Keane's Cahir House** is not bad for a brief stay. Its rural-style welcome is warming and its restaurant amiable. There are 3 private baths for its 14 rooms. **Kilcoran Lodge Hotel** is 5 miles outward toward Cork. This one also radiates a happy family atmosphere. It has been spruced up considerably, now offering an indoor pool, gym, and health center. Homey furnishings; spotlessly kept; flowers throughout; try for your reservation in the shooting lodge from which it was converted, rather than in either wing. There's rewarding angling in the area, and the Lodge is only 3 miles from *Ballyporeen,* the ancestral matrix of a gentleman named Ronald Reagan.

CARRICKMACROSS (County Monaghan) is globally famous for its lace. The 40-room-and bath **Nuremore,** with its own 9-hole golf course, indoor pool, tennis and squash courts, is also drawing praise for its kitchen. **Markey's Pub,** on the central drag, is another reliable dining choice, notably for its grills.

CASHEL BAY (County Galway, not to be confused with Cashel of County Tipperary, below)

★★★★ **Cashel House** ● is possibly the most sophisticated address you'll discover in northwestern Galway; still it is as intimate as a familiar lodge or favorite weekend country home. The enchanted garden is a deserving prizewinner, one of the best in the nation; cuisine is based on local sea and land fare; lounges crackle with turf fires; smiles abound. To use this as a base for exploring the rugged bayscapes, hills, and strands is ideal. Not much to do unless you like deep breathing, nature worship, golfing (nearby), fishing, tennis (one poor court) or relaxing at a 19th-century pace. Some high excitement in seeing the site where Alcock Brown nosed in after the first transatlantic flight and where Marconi built his first transoceanic radio station. As "firsts" go, I much prefer to be first by the fireplace with a good book and a Paddy.

☆☆ **Zetland Arms** • was built by the Guinness family as a fishing hotel. It stands on 5 acres of garden overlooking Cashel Bay, surrounded by bog, lake, and estuary landscape for rough shoots and angling. The dining room affords magnificent vistas across the water as do 4 premium doubles that are extremely spacious. Approximately a quarter of the registry is given over to fishing enthusiasts.

CASHEL (County Tipperary, roughly ⅔ along the Dublin–Cork highway)

Scholars might enjoy a browse through Bolton Library, adjoining the town's cathedral. It is a major repository of medieval books, manuscripts, charts, and maps.

★★★ **Cashel Palace** • a converted 18th-century bishop's manse is owned and managed by Ray Carroll who put Sandy Lane of Barbados on the Caribbean charts. Flowering soul-soothing gardens and lawns; 20 rooms and 20 baths, all attractively done; #2, #7, and #1 are own favorites, in that order. Reserve early.

Chez Hans • in a converted church, whomps up choice meals for wanderers in this domain. Irish critics number it among the better bets in the country for culinary performance.

Alternative dwelling space of reliable quality can be found at **Dundrum House,** or you might like to rent the American-owned **Clashleigh House** all for your own, a handsome Georgian redoubt with space for eight. **Bailey's** is both a guesthouse and restaurant in the town center. Inexpensive, genial, and good value.

CLIFDEN (County Galway)

★ **Crocnaraw House** • is informal and made ingratiating through the cheery ministrations of its hostess with the undeserving name of Mrs. Fretwell. A bright white exterior is in vivid contrast with the emerald lawn and the greystone gardens. Lounge with a painted hearth; big cottage windows. Only 10 rooms, evoking a homey sort of atmosphere. Good taste and good value.

★ **Rock Glen** • a former shooting lodge, perches in bright white splendor above its own sea lake. The comforts still reflect a life where more time is spent outdoors than in. But what views! Prices are surprisingly low for the more than adequate accommodation. In town, the ☆☆ **Clifden Bay** steals the metropolitan thunder (population 800); while it is a charming village and the capital of Connemara, I'd always go to the Rock Glen first.

CONG (County Mayo)

★★ **Ashford Castle** • usually is considered the No. 1 hotel in Ireland—a view I am not willing to dispute too vigorously, but one which does not win my full enthusiasm either. It is dramatically sited on the shores of Lough Corrib. The turreted walls and its baronial furnishings, including incredible 3-dimensional paintings, are straight out of the pages of a fairytale book. It's a 4-hour drive from Dublin directly across the island to this former home of the Guinness family. Given more decorative sparkle, it could be among the zestier choices of the nation. While some guests are awed, I tend to yawn.

CORK is 2nd in importance in the nation. It's on the River Lee, way down south; Blarney Castle is 6 miles from the center. Cork Airport serves an increasing tourist traffic to the Southern Counties. Its citizens—Corkers to their core yet officially known as Corkonians—radiate a special vitality that you'll adore. The small-boat harbor (called the "Sailing Centre") of *Crosshaven,* around the river's bend nearby, is much more scenic and tranquil for overnighting.

★★ **Arbutus Lodge** • indubitably leads the parade, with Jurys more effective in its quarters but far less so in its comestibles. The former is a converted house that overlooks the River Lee and Cork city below—best seen from its Gallery Bar, as well as from the accommodations directly above.

☆☆ **Jurys** • occupies an airy location a few minutes from the center. Fastnet Restaurant for elegant mealtimes; convivial Corks Bar; Pavilion with 2 dining spots, pools, lounges, dancing, and abundant foliage to create an indoor garden. The service is attentive, kind, and willing. Good.

Fitzpatrick Silver Springs • also a short haul along the Dublin highway from the nexus, is a 7-tier, waffled structure of contemporary design. Bamboo-clad lobby; spectacular hexagonal dining room with large panes for its river view; Blarney Bar directly underneath, also hexagonal and also attractive; big carpark. All sleeping quarters quintagonal in shape to offer maximum vistas.

Imperial • on the main street, and the **Allied Metropole** both have appealing public rooms. The former has very nice bedrooms; it also boasts a first-rate chef. The latter has been refurbished totally and is now a substantial choice.

On the outskirts, the **Cork Airport Motel** occupies 4 acres of hillside with a wonderful view. Postage-stamp lobby with glass-sided 10-table dining room adjoining and bar to rear; air-conditioned; central heating; piped music. Its 20 sleeping quarters, all standard, are Lilliputian, with trickle showers. **Ashbourne House** at *Glounthaune,* 6 miles along the Waterford road, is a converted private mansion which comes up with 24 rooms with bath, TV, radio, and video, a solar-heated pool, 2 tennis courts, 10-acre garden, and good cookery.

Dining choices in town would be either of the three following eateries.

☆☆☆ **Arbutus Lodge** • This colorful oasis, with an elaborate pub-type ambience and open terrace service in summer, offers light fare. In its famous dining room such superb cuisine—much of it seasoned from its galaxy of spices grown in its own versatile herb garden—regularly wins prestigious gastronomic awards. As one sample of its magic skilletry, order the drisheen with creamed tansy sauce—tansy being a plant which thrives only in the Cork area and to my knowledge nowhere else in the world.

☆☆ **Cliffords** • *23 Washington St. W.* • is the fresh modernist created by Michael Clifford. The cuisine is contemporary.

If you are looking for a pub experience, **Annie's** is fun; the pub is at her sister's **Levis,** across the lane where you have your drink first. They are on Main Street, *Ballydehob.* *An Sugan* is another choice; it's in *Clonakilty.*

☆☆ **Lovetts** • a fish specialist off Well Rd. in *Douglas.*

☆☆ **Ballymaloe House** • takes its name from its setting, not far from the fishing port of Ballycotton, the address from where most of the sea denizens on your table will derive. The cookery's among the most intelligent in the nation, blending cottage ingredients with modern gustatory finesse. About £90 per night per twosome; 30 simple but adequate bedrooms. Best for gustation and relaxing.

DINGLE (County Kerry) Do you recall the beautiful classic film *Ryan's Daughter?* Most of it was filmed on these breathtaking rugged shores. You can dine at either **Doyle's** or the **Half-Door.** You might like to overnight at the **Skellig** or **Benners.** Don't expect the Ritz.

DONEGAL (County Donegal) has the **Abbey** and the **Hyland Central,** both of which provide fair comfort at a fair price.

DUBLIN

Settled by Danes in A.D. 852, counting the suburbs it has grown since then to almost a million people; quaint and colorful, it's a fascinating blend of bustling metropolis and dusty one-horse town. Dublin was dubbed as Europe's "City of Culture" recently, and the rub-off effect is enduring. Museums, gorgeous parks, dance halls, movies, a million things to see, including a 94-foot-wide fountain, which the city commissioned to celebrate its millennium. Wags have named the reclining nude as "our Floozie in the Jacuzzi." The airport, once a sleepy bump on the heath, is atingle with activity as a result of improvements to accommodate large jets. Aer Lingus-Irish Airlines runs internally to Shannon, Sligo, Galway, and Cork, and it also flies direct to various cities in England and on the Continent. (Other carriers crossing the Atlantic must first touch down at Shannon as well as depart from that western gateway.)

ATTRACTIONS

Merrion Square • This stately and historic square, considered one of Dublin's most beautiful, offers a quintessential display of fine Georgian architecture. As you wander through compare the great variety of pillared, fan-lighted doorways. Oscar Wilde spent his youth at No. 1, and the Nobel Prize-winning poet, William Butler Yeats, lived in No. 82.

St. Patrick's Cathedral • Built in the 12th century by a dissenting archbishop from nearby Christ Church, its the national cathedral of the Church of Ireland. See the Cork Memorial, the Geraldine Door, and the monument to Dame St. Leger. Jonathan Swift, author of *Gulliver's Travels,* was dean here for over three decades.

The National Museum • *Kildare Street* • The Irish Antiques Division houses a collection of gold objects dating from the Bronze Age to Early Christian times; don't miss the Ardagh Chalice and the Tara Brooch. The other segments are the Art and Industrial division, with objects from 1916 to 1921, and the Natural History section, which has its own entrance on Merrion Street.

Dublin Castle • At least two previous castles—one a wooden Viking fortress—are believed to have stood on this site before John of England erected the present structure in the 13th century. For 400 years it was the center of English rule in Ireland.

St. Stephen's Green • With 22 acres of splendidly laid-out trees and flowerbeds, a waterfall and an artificial lake, this is a fine place to relax. In July and August bands play in the bandstand.

Leinster House • *Kildare Street, Merrion Square* • Built as a sumptuous mansion in 1745 by Lord Kildare, Earl of Leinster, this house became the official home of the Dail (House of Representatives) and the Seanad (Senate). It is a grand building, which is thought by many to have been the model for the White House. When the Dail is in session you may audit the proceedings from the visitor's gallery.

The National Gallery of Ireland • *Merrion Square West* • The works of every school of European painting are included. Under the same roof is the excellent **National Portrait Gallery,** which has a remarkable assemblage of drawings, watercolors, and miniatures.

Trinity College Library • *College Green* • With nearly a million volumes, and the best collection of illuminated manuscripts and early printed books in Ireland, this is an attraction not to be missed. The library's most famous and

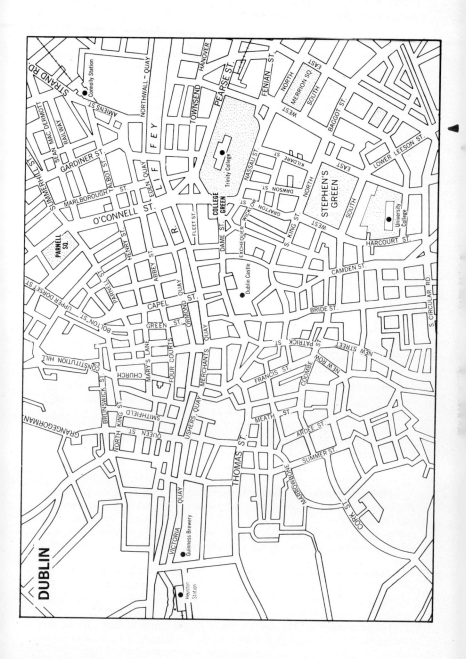

DUBLIN

STRAND RD
Connolly Station
AMIENS ST
RAILWAY
SEAN MAC DERMOTT
GARDINER ST.
SUMMERHILL ST.
MARLBOROUGH
TALBOT ST.
O'CONNELL ST.
PARNELL
SQ.
HENRY ST.
ABBEY ST.
PARNELL ST.
UPPER DORSET ST.
BOLTON ST.
CAPEL
GREEN ST.
ORMOND QUAY
CONSTITUTION HILL
BRUNSWICK ST.
CHURCH
MARY'S LANE
FOUR COURTS
NORTH KING ST.
QUEEN ST.
SMITHFIELD
USHERS QUAY
MERCHANTS QUAY
GRANGEGORMAN
VICTORIA QUAY
Guinness Brewery
Heuston Station
THOMAS ST.
FRANCIS ST.
MEATH ST.
ARDEE ST.
SUMMER ST.
MARROWBONE
COOMBE
NEW STREET
NEW ROW
CORK ST.
S. PATRICK ST.
BRIDE ST.
DUBLIN Castle
DAME ST.
EXCHEQUER ST.
WICKLOW ST.
S. KING ST.
GRAFTON
DAWSON ST.
NASSAU ST.
WEST
NORTH
STEPHEN'S GREEN
SOUTH
EAST
CAMDEN ST.
HARCOURT ST.
University College
LOWER LEESON ST.
S. CIRCULAR RD.
BAGGOT ST.
KILDARE ST.
MERRION SQ.
NORTH
SOUTH
EAST
WEST
FENIAN ST.
HANOVER
PEARSE ST.
TOWNSEND
NORTHWALL – QUAY
EDEN QUAY
LIFFEY
R.
FLEET ST.
COLLEGE GREEN
Trinity College
QUAY

valued treasure is The Book of Kells, an illuminated manuscript from the 8th century which has been described as "the most beautiful book in the world."

Phoenix Park • Within its bounds are the lovely People's Gardens and the **Dublin Zoo.** Also, the residence of the President of Ireland is here, as is that of the U.S. Ambassador.

Guinness Brewery • *St. James's Gate* • Established in 1759 by Arthur Guinness with an initial investment of £100, this world famous brewery has become the largest exporter of stout beer in the world. Tours of the brewery are not available, but a film presentation can be seen, after which visitors are welcome to sample the product.

Whiskey Corner • *Bow St.* • tells the story of *Uisce Beatha* ("Water of Life") in the 2-century-old Jameson Distillery. After a sobering tour refreshment is offered in the woody Ball O'Malt pub to confirm that Irish efforts in these skills were not in vain. A splendid museum, indeed, sir.

The National Theatre • *Lower Abbey Street* • Both the famous 625-seat Abbey Theatre and the 157-seat Peacock Theatre make their home here. The Abbey primarily performs Irish plays (in English), while the Peacock concentrates on experimental theatre.

Gate Theatre • *Parnell Square* • This fine company, founded in 1928, specializes in an international and classical repertory not included in the Abbey playbills.

Excursions

National Botanic Gardens • *Botanic Road, Glasnevin* • Splendidly situated outside the city, these lush gardens cover 50 acres and contain a huge variety of trees, flowers, flowering shrubs and tropical plants.

Chester Beatty Library • *20 Shrewsbury Road, Ballbridge* • This magnificent collection of Oriental manuscripts and miniatures is widely considered to be the finest and most valuable in existence.

Malahide Castle • *Malahide, County Dublin* • Directly north of Dublin, in the coastal suburb known as Malahide, stands this majestic 12th-century castle. For 800 years it was home to the Talbots of Malahide; it's open to the public. Fine 18th-century furniture embellishes the castle's interior. If you're of a mind to escape the inner city for a day, this makes a worthwhile excursion.

James Joyce Museum • *Sandycove* • Fanciers of the great writer will enjoy a trip to this place where Joyce once lived—known as Martello Tower. The collection includes numerous objects associated with the author and his life.

Glendalough • At this place, south of Dublin some 30 miles, lie the fascinating ruins of a monastery that dates to the 6th century. Glendalough means "the glen of two lakes," and it is known as much for its beautiful rolling green hills as for the ruins.

HOTELS

A limited economy has not allowed Ireland's hotel industry to flower as it has in some other European countries. Your greater rewards are more likely to be found in smaller establishments where you meet and chat with the personnel. Staff people everywhere, despite professional shortcomings, have hearts of gold; treat them as friends and you'll discover a new dimension in the art of innkeeping.

An ingenious twist is the **Rent-An-Irish-Cottage** program; a total of 133 dot the map. These thatched-roof houses, extremely simple in execution and in furnishings, embody the flavor of a small, traditional farmhouse. Rental rates are astonishingly low. Each is complete with half-door and open peat-burning hearth, traditional furnishings, all-electric kitchen, central heating and all modern conveniences. Cottage types A and B sleep 8 and 7 persons, respectively. Types C and D sleep 6 and 5, respectively; prices vary with the season. Ask your travel agent for details. The minimum rental must be for 7 nights (or weekends in off seasons); extra days are charged pro rata.

The *Discover Ireland Hotels and Guesthouses Guide* indicates stopping places that furnish baby-sitting service up to midnight for about $7 per hour. Since most already offer a 10% to 33⅓% discount for children under 10 years of age, this supervision is a built-in bonus.

Law requires that tariff sheets be displayed either at or close to all Reception Desks.

★★★ **Shelbourne** • a town house dating back to 1824, is proud of a recent refurbishing that fluffed up the luster of its 19th-century foyer and lounges. The Horseshoe Bar is one of the chosen spots in town for chitchat. Authors from Thackeray to Elizabeth Bowen have fondly sung its praises in their books; the Constitution of the Irish Free State was framed within its venerable walls. Two dining salons; younger 6-story wing; 14 suites; high ceilings throughout; parking lot for 50 cars. Its Victorian facade commands a splendid view of St. Stephen's Green. The hands-on management has initiated an "Early bird" guarantee for transatlantic zombies who wing in with the dawn and don't relish sitting around lobbies until noon; if you book a deluxe unit you are assured occupancy within 30 minutes of check-in; just preadvise with your date of arrival and flight number.

☆☆☆ **Berkeley Court** • is set amid 3 acres of gardens. The site of the 8-story edifice is on Lansdowne Road in the fashionable Ballsbridge district. Communication is so efficient between this suburb and midtown that its location will not represent an inconvenience. Fancier international restaurant plus grill; cocktail bar and lounge; indoor swimming pool; saunas; hairdressing facilities;

boutiques; in-and-outside parking. Sprinkled among its 200 bedchambers is a handsome complement of suites.

☆☆☆ **Westbury** • is a newer product from the same group that runs the above hotel, the ubiquitous Doyle dynasty. While the accommodations are fairly predictable, the dining quadrants are more of an adventure: one Chinese cookie that's the city's best and the instant-antique Sandbank Bar where oysters and stout are the talk-o-the-town. Especially recommended for food and beverage.

☆☆☆ **Jurys** • is clearly a 20th-century efficiency hotel while its kissin' cousin called the **Towers of Jurys** (and on the same corporate sod) is a more deluxe Jury verdict. The first accommodates nearly 300 souls while the "towering" throng—a third as many—pay a third more for the up-market label. Gracefully and freshly modernized, busy lobby, extremely attractive Dubliner Bar in pseudo-antique Irish motif; Embassy Restaurant; smashingly successful snack bar (open from 6 p.m. to 4:30 a.m. except Sun. when it snoozes from 11 p.m. until Mon. morning); hairdresser and barber. The Pavilion houses the Kish fish restaurant, a pyramidal bar, a lounge, a swimming pool, a hot whirlpool massage unit, a children's zone, all set amid waterfalls, rocks, and greenery; a musical group adds a special zesty charm here.

★ **Burlington** • seeks to blend traditional decor with modern comfort. Airy lobby with busy adjoining bar and popular lounge; ground-floor Sussex Room, its premier restaurant; President Bar; partly closed parking space a big bonus to motorists. The accommodations provide space, light, and efficiency; the 4 large executive suites are exceptional. Busy and basically sound.

★★ **Sachs** • is a 10-minute drive from the center. It has gained a reputation for chicness which is supported by refined decor, smartly outfitted bedchambers with sophisticated materials; there's the not-too-exciting Bistro plus the Raffles nightspot, and an inviting Library Bar. Because 1 Regency house and 5 adjoining Georgian houses in a row were connected, it is replete with short stairways and intimate corridors. This, coupled with the ambitious updating, gives it a special personality that many travelers will prefer to larger commercial institutions.

Royal Dublin • greets guests with a lobby painting of Sitric, the Viking king, and "raths" (plans) of fortresses in sandstone and pebble. Its Oyster Bar features bivalves shipped fresh from Galway Bay each dawn in season. Cool-tinged yet appealing grill, bar, and dining room; underground carpark; gray brick corridors; front units with balconette-bay windows; velvet headboards; matching curtains; emerald carpets; radios, telephones, and thermal shower taps; inviting Queen Gormley suite.

Bloom's Hotel • was named after Leopold Bloom, hero of Joyce's *Ulysses*. All rooms with bath, radio, and color TV; lots of brightly polished glass, brass, and mirrors in public areas. Yesterday's Bar, Bogies Bar, and the Blazes Boylan Grill Room complete the picture.

Gresham • has a fine midtown location, a pleasant grill, and a few attractive suites. It seems so totally devoted, however, to package tours that independent visitors might feel they are on the sidelines.

★ Lansdowne • is a Georgian house with homespun attributes, open fires in the lounges, a restaurant, and 2 bars. The friendly air is a strong selling point for checking in.

Skylon • resides about 10 minutes by car from both the airport and the center. Low, rather extensive lobby with simple furnishings, piped music, and buried baby spotlights in an acoustic ceiling; bizarre hodgepodge bar-lounge; Rendez-vous Room for grills; fetching dining room with Cecil King murals and well-planned illumination. Its 88 keys unlock 88 rooms which are identical; terribly cramped baths and insufficient storage space.

Tara Tower • described by a bellhop as having "an evocative name for the Irish," refers to a hallowed spot in County Meath, 20 miles northwest of Dublin, which was the capital of the Celtic Empire and the site from which St. Patrick began his evangelizing mission in the 5th century. This one could almost serve as a carbon copy of the Skylon. Quick-service coffee house with Dublin Bay prints. Pick a high waterfront unit, which might render evocative moments for you, too—Irish or not.

Clarence • is located on a historic riverview site overlooking the Liffey. That's the best I can say about it.

Buswells • is a mixed bag. The central location is a singular (perhaps *the* singular) advantage.

International • at the airport, offers a fresh entrance, foyer, bar, coffee shop and restaurant, plus color TV and direct-dial phones in all rooms. Executive accommodations have private bar facilities.

Royal Marine Hotel • at *Dun Laoghaire* ("Done Leery") lies on a harbor 6 miles south of the capital. Here's a viable candidate for pilgrims taking the 3-hour car-ferry hop to Holyhead. It is a gingerbread structure (vintage 1865) with high ceilings. The restaurant/grill offers excellent food, pleasant ambience, and good service at reasonable prices; 5 acres of lawns and flowers; boating, swimming, yachting, sailing, golf, tennis, racing, hunting, and dancing; pick your weather carefully here.

☆ Fitzpatrick Castle • at Killiney, 9 miles out, is a spacious private residence dating back to 1741 which has been reconstructed and redecorated by Paddy Fitzpatrick and his wife Eithne; 9 acres of ground overlooking Dublin Bay; candlelit Victorian dining room; inexpensive but good Jester snackery made from church pews; inside pool; 3 squash courts; tennis; minigolf. The 94 bedrooms and 3 executive suites, all with baths, are adequately furnished; many of them have four-posters; all now feature TV with closed-circuit movie choices.

Montrose • in the *Stillorgan* residential district, offers a vast panoply of sleeping combinations that can accommodate almost anything from an eremite to a Ringling Brothers troupe. Every unit with TV; radio, direct-dial phone, and central heat; Belfield Grill for light appetites, open noon to midnight; active Robert Room restaurant for table d'hote and à la carte; huge bar; health studio; hairdresser and gift-shop-newsstand-book-counter; parking lot.

Green Isle • beside the Naas Road just off the Shannon turnpike is 4 miles from the center. Its lodgings are split between its main building and its motel section, both of which are routine.

Grand • at *Malahide,* a 9-mile skip, resides in its own quiet seaside estate, near to several important golf courses. The "Island" (restaurant) is noted for its saltwater fare. Tranquil.

RESTAURANTS

★★★★ **The Lobster Pot** • *9 Ballsbridge Terrace* • is easily the leading restaurant of the city, and one of the finest in the nation. As if you hadn't guessed from the name, the specialties come from the Atlantic: marvelous bisques, scallops, crustacea, and fish that are so fresh they are still twitching. Normally in Ireland I am hesitant about ordering complicated preparations, but here the sauces are masterful, the presentation is delicate, and the comprehension of gastronomy is thorough. Extensive wine list (somewhat rare in this country); attractive, rich, clublike atmosphere enhanced by subtle illumination, fresh flowers, polished copper and brass, and warm textiles. Closed Sun.

☆☆ **Le Coq Hardi** • *35 Pembroke Rd., in Ballsbridge* • draws heavily from the local embassies and top hotels in this tenderloin district. It is located in an attractive town house; salon a few steps down for relaxed predinner drinks and conversation; 2 dining quadrants in brown with soft materials and polished mahogany. Professional reception; service by waiters in swallowtail coats; candles reflecting in golden place plates; valiant efforts at reproducing French cuisine; house wine cheap—and it tastes it! A meal for 2 would absorb approximately $110, but spend more and order one of the better bottled vintages.

White's • *119 St. Stephen's Green* • traditionally one of the leaders for sophistication, went over the seas to France and imorted a new chef whose wares I've yet to sample personally. Local friends, however, praise his *fin bec*. The mood inside is refined country life. Not at all costly for what you received in the past, but perhaps the Gallic experience will rectify that little nuance.

★ **The Grey Door** and **Bistro** • *23 Upper Pembroke St.* • is an engaging combo in a converted house. Victorian salon upstairs with dishes drawn mainly from the Slavic repertoire, including those of Russia and Finland; guitar music and songs from the Steppes. Downstairs the Bistro presents less expensive meals to the tune of live piano music. An amusing meld of concepts.

☆ **Celtic Mews** • *109a Lr. Baggot St.* • has been a success for a number of years. Reception and service warmly hospitable. Ground-floor lounge with upstairs room for dining; candle illumination. An altogether enjoyable night out.

☆☆ **Patrick Guilbaud** • *in the same district at 46 James's Place* • specializes in *nouvelle cuisine,* a *nouvelle* fillip, indeed, in hardy Dublin Town. Fresh floral atmosphere and delicate, lovingly presented dishes. But decidedly not traditional Irish fayre.

Oisin's • *31 Upper Camden St.* • is so Irish that even the menu is in Gaelic; it is explained, however. Go here for corned beef and cabbage, Irish stew, Bailey's carraigeen, coddle, and a larder of ethnic fixin's. Lobster and shellfish also find their way to the tables. Live music nightly, except Sun. and Mon., when it rests.

Ernie Evans or simply **Ernie's** • *Mulberry Gardens, Donnybrook* • is the jovial chef-patron who put Glenbeigh (of the Ring of Kerry) on the gastronomic map. Now his skillets sizzle here, his artworks adorn these walls, and his sole bonne femme is as succulent as it ever was from Dingle Bay.

Ospreys • *42/43 Shellbourne Rd. in Ballsbridge* • provides a cottage atmosphere with open fires and candlelight for dinners. Open for lunch Mon.– Fri. and for evenings through Sat. Charming, so be sure to reserve in advance.

Lord Edward • *23 Christchurch Place* • is rightfully known for its fine seafood. A small lunch is served in its bar, which is up one flight. Above this is the restaurant which contains only 10 tables. Dark wood predominates in this atmospheric veteran, with odd chairs, wall plates, and prints of Lord Edward grace-noting its charm. No meat is served and the tariffs are medium. As an incidental tip, because commercial fishing is inactive on weekends, Monday is not the best time to patronize such specialty restaurants. Here, however, the management has a hook baited every day of the week, so his stocks are fresh. The staff is unusually kind. Recommended.

Shrimps • *1 Anne's Lane* • is for light biting and observing the new fashions.

A pleasant expedition is a ramble through the zoo at **Phoenix Park** and an inexpensive meal in its lovely setting of lawns and flowering shrubs; worth the trip when the sun is out.

An ethnic romp? Try **Gallaghers Boxty House** • *20 Temple Bar* • where— to name a few—you can choose from Chinese, Cajun, Lebanese, Indian, Japanese, Creole, Greek, or several other specialty restaurants.

Pocket-size excursions?

In nearby *Stillorgan,* a residential suburb, the **Beaufield Mews** offers antiques and nutrition to those who hunger for a quiet haven similar to our own popular northeastern Red Barns, White Turkeys, or Spinning Wheels. Softly illuminated converted stable; 5-course menu nightly; operative 7 p.m.–10 p.m., but never for lunch, Sundays, bank holidays, or Christmas and Easter weeks. Oodles of charm. In *Howth,* a fishing village only 20 minutes north of midcity, the **Abbey Tavern** draws raves from almost every quarter. Old-style tavern to which a restaurant has been added; cookery composed mostly of shellfish; other landed specialties also on tap; upstairs serving more exclusive moods and nutrients; traditional Irish entertainment nightly in the barnlike room to the rear. Touristic, to say the least. There's a more refined sort of seafood restaurant called the **King Sitric** (named for the famous ninth-century Viking sovereign of Dublin) around the corner on East Pier. Brick facade looking to the harbor; upstairs bar done out preciously in florals and ruby; sea-level restaurant with waiters in black tie. Both of these anchorages can be reached by bus from town. By taxi, the ride is expensive, so go only if you have a rented car. **Roundwood Inn** is still turning out noteworthy Irish and continental cuisine. You might also try the **Glenview Hotel** near *Bray.* For seasiding, *Dun Laoghaire* offers **na Mara** (overlooking the water and specializing in seafood) and the family-run **Trudi's** (1920s decor and an unusual but tempting menu including delicious orange and carrot soup). **Digby's,** the same district, overlooks Dublin Bay. It is decorated with Batik tenting; cozy wine bar. **Oliver's** also shares this locale; very fresh vittles in a relaxing atmosphere. This town makes an excellent excursion point.

Rolland • in *Killiney* is the creation of Henri Rolland who cooked for palates named Kennedy, Nixon, de Gaulle, and MacMillan. So much for Chief-of-State-dropping. The food is also tops.

PUBS

My favorite in the **Mooney's** chain • *on Parnell St. around the corner from the Royal Dublin* • is colorful and cheerful in the modern mode, with a 15-stool bar, perhaps 7 tiny tables within each of 3 banquettes. Its offerings of hot dishes include steak-and-kidney pie and cottage pie, plus a selection of sandwiches, salads, and desserts that are unfancy but big and filling. Go from 12 to 12:30 before the crowd descends in force. **Slattery's Terenure House** • *Terenure Rd.* • consists of 3 sections in a large building. The first is a ground-floor lounge-bar that could be mistaken for an expanded version of a typical Irish hotel installation. The 2nd is a spartan ground-floor bar for the serious male toper. The 3rd is its *piece de resistance:* An upstairs cabaret-bar (small admission charge) which holds 400 revelers. Stage and orchestra; electric organ; lone singers or small groups airing their adenoids in tandem; public address system twisted up to its maximum. Thurs.–Sun. are its only scheduled nights of operation. **Kitty O'Shea's** • *23 Upper Grand Canal St.* • does magical things with its grilled black sole (black magic, perhaps, and delightful). Brothers Kevin and Brian Loughney have given new meaning to the sabbath with their Bloody Mary Sunday Brunches. See if you don't become a born-again follower. **William Searson** • *42 Upper Baggot St.* • is a suavely decorated contemporary complex of 3 bars with lounges; while 2 are modern, the Public Bar is done in fake turn-of-the-century. Crowded by students. In atmosphere, here could be a cocktail lounge in any American city. **Bartley Dunne** • *Lower Stephen St.* • offers an unusually versatile selection of booze drawn from its wines-and-spirits shop adjoining. Dim lighting; candles on tables; piped music (softly so, for a change); 2 arched, cozy, corner rooms to rear that encourage romance. Also popular among the Junior Set.

Classic types?

★★★ The **Bailey** • *Duke St.* • has been for ages one of the city's most celebrated haunts of the literati. Ground-floor bar with leather booths and slat-faced walls; upstairs salon, again wood lined and touched up with old mirrors, prints, fans and hanging plants. The air of conviviality is manifestly inviting; so is the splendid quality of its foodstuffs. Richly recommended for blue-ribbon pubbery. **Brazen Head** • *20 Lower Bridge St.* • has a history going back to the 17th century; a staunch redoubt of rebellion and liquid spirits. **Davy Byrnes** • **Duke St.** • draws more than its share of very earnest young authors. **Stag's Head** • *1 Dame Court* • weaves its spells among stuffed namesakes, old clocks, stained glass, and surroundings which seem best in semidarkness. **Patrick Conway** • *Parnell St.* • with its panels and semi-partitions, is authentically old-school Hibernian. Ham cooked in red wine plus the ubiquitous steak-and-kidney pie are its best-known specialties. Typical charm in somewhat faded surroundings. **Ryan's** (Parkgate St.) and **Mulligan's** (Poolbeg St.) should attract Irish blood by their names alone. **O'Donoghues** • *15 Merrion Row* • and **Dohery & Nesbitt** • *5 Lower Baggot* • are a couple of stalwarts of the old school. **Neary's** • *Chatham St.* • with a tiny cocktail bar on one side, is friendly and unpretentious; it is reminiscent of a U.S. corner tavern. **McDaid's** • *Harry St. off Grafton St.* • not long ago was restyled, but is still atmospheric. **Peter's Pub** is fun and distinctive. Finally, you might like to try **O'Dwyers** and **The Pizza Cellar** at Lower Mount St. What? You've never heard of classic Irish pizza? For shame!

After dark? Apart from the hotel lounges or dance floors, try **Midnight at the Olympia** or the rollicking **Bad Bobs** (34 E. Essex St.) for late music and booze. Otherwise, there's **The Waterfront** (14 Sir John Rogersons Quay) or **The Point Depot Bar** (North Wall) for a rich Dublin atmosphere.

SHOPPING

SHOPPING HOURS: In the capital, generally from 9 a.m. to 5:30 p.m. In some parts of the country, 1 p.m. closings are made on Wed. or Thur.

BEST AREAS: Grafton St., Nassau St., and Dawson St., are where the better shops are located. Henry St., Mary St., Talbot St., and South Great George's St. are second rank.

SAVINGS ON PURCHASES: As in a number of countries abroad, the VAT system—10% on clothing and 23% on everything else—deeply permeates the economic lives of the citizenry. It is included in retail prices but deducted for all non-European Community residents on goods, whether they are taken away or mailed. A note for those who do live in an E.C. nation: VAT is payable on goods carried out of the country but *not* on items that are shipped.

ANTIQUES, BRIC-A-BRAC, AND SILVER: Butler (14 Bachelor's Walk) gets our nod of approval. Other leaders in the field include **R. McDonnell** (16 Kildare St.), **Dillon Antiques** (27 South Anne St.), **Mitchell's** (40 Clarendon St.), and **Saskia Antiques** (43 South William St.). A stroll along the North Quays starting at O'Connell St. Bridge or Francis St. in the old part of town might prove fruitful. Quite a few old silver and jewelry dealers are along South Anne St. too.

BOOKBINDER: Antiquarian Bookcrafts Ltd. (Marlay Craft Courtyard, Marlay Park, Rathfarnham, Dublin 14) is a joy for the aficionado. These craftsmen work on governmental gifts and invitations, valuable first editions, old manuscripts, special presentation books, and other *rarae aves*. There is a large range of bindings and especially handmade papers for endpapers. Mail orders are welcomed. Fine—and a find!

CRAFTS: Some of the best can be found at **Marlay Park Centre** in Rathfarnham. However, don't miss the **Kilkenny Design Workshops** (Setanta Center, Nassau St.), **Fergus O'Farrell** (60 Dawson St.), the **Powerscourt Town House Centre** (South William St.), and **IDA Enterprise Center** (Pearse St.).

DEPARTMENT STORES: Historic **Switzer & Co. Ltd.** (Grafton St.) and **Brown Thomas & Co.** are almost directly across the street from each other. Both are excellent.

HAUTE COUTURE: Pat Crowley (14 Duke St.) is on network television in the USA almost every night. (Her clothes are anyway.) Society figures and celebrities from all over the globe are beating pittypat paths to Pat's now famous doorstep. **Thomas Wolfangel** (158 Pembroke Road, Ballsbridge) offers fashionable designs and well-cut day suits, coats, dresses—both made-to-measure and ready-to-wear.

HERALDIC ARTISTS LTD. (3 Nassau St.) already has over ½ million names in their roster. They'll undertake to trace yours further, or, through the extensive facilities of their Genealogy Bookshop, supply you with the aids to do your own research. Their artists will create shields, crests, family trees, and parchments in a variety of designs; excellent brochures and mail-order service; write to owner Martin O'Beirne. A quiet air of scholarship pervades its precincts, unlike the hurly-burly of many of its ilk.

IRISH AND INTERNATIONAL SPECIALTIES: House of Ireland (37–38 Nassau St.) says it *all*. From woolies to Waterford, from Celtic crosses to Claddagh rings, from Foxford blankets to Hourihan tweeds—the whole bright realm of Hibernia is represented in its finest manifestations. Go here first for *any* shopping notions—Irish *or* European—because this house is a stimulant and an inspiration.

JEWELRY: Weir (96–99 Grafton St.) is almost a museum in itself, a 3-story period piece overflowing with distinguished merchandise. The unusual old world windows and vitrines contain modern jewelry, gold, silver, typical Tara brooches, Claddagh rings, and many exquisite antique and rare secondhand pieces. Weir also custom designs trophies for sporting and commemorative events.

TWEEDS: Kevin & Howlin Ltd. (31 Nassau St.) is a specialist with great standing, merit and reliability. Look carefully in order to find exactly the pattern, color, and texture which best strike your fancy. There's the nobby Donegal tweed of traditional fame and the lighter weight but still full-bodied new mixture of wool, cashmere, and mohair for more temperate climes—all done in the subtle techniques that blend hues of the moorlands, hills, sea, and sky. You will also find tweed hats and caps (some to match the jackets and suits). Sara and Noel Kevin, a mother-and-son team, are usually on hand to greet you personally.

DUNDALK (County Louth, directly south of the Northern Ireland border on the coastal highway)

★★★ **Ballymascanlon House** • about 4 miles down a side road north of the center, is enchanting from its exterior. Its long, winding entrance of prize-winning lawns and gardens, and its steeds wandering in their green pastures whet the appetite for its handsome structure. Some of the art exhibited was made available through the Arts Council of Ireland. There's a heated indoor pool, sauna, gym, tennis courts; all 36 units with bath have been updated recently. The same people also operate the modern **Imperial** in Dundalk.

ENNIS (County Clare; about 14 miles north of Shannon Airport) The ☆**Old Ground** is a charmer. Its venerable interior has been smartened up radically. Mellowness of lobby typified by its well-rubbed grandfather clock and other serene antiques; lovely rose-hue, wallpapered dining room; Celtic Lounge with touches of tweed, oil paintings, and woven river rush, opening to a walled garden; 63 fresh rooms with bath, I prefer the older section. The 116-unit **West County Inn** is a comfortable choice, too. Its kitchen is noteworthy.

GALWAY is the capital of western Ireland, a city of consequence that has been energetically freshening up its public face of late. An effort is being exerted to add some additional cultural notes to those voiced melodically each night at the King's Head Pub (gratis). One noble effort is the busy calendar of the **Druid Theatre Company** (Chapel Lane), which includes lunchtime performances in summer. Also, because of improved ferry connections from Galway and neighboring Rossaveal, here is a convenient gateway for exploring the Aran Islands.

The **Great Southern** is far and away the local leader—and it is getting better every season. Its Claddagh aerie complex incorporates a penthouse restaurant, cocktail bar, swimming pool, and sauna. Another bar and restaurant also now welcome guests. The 100-room **Galway Ryan** is on the Limerick highway perhaps a mile east of the center. Dramatic space-age main building, centered by white-brick, orange-chaired cockpit which is its sunken lounge; red-carpeted, cream-walled, red-chaired dining room divisible with sliding panel; tasteful low-ceilinged bar; piped music. The 115-unit **Corrib Great Southern** works a lot with tours so there is a commercial tone about it. Structurally and decoratively, however, it is a recommendable stopping place. All accommodations with private bath; pool and sauna. **Flannery's,** about 400 yards south of the Galway Ryan, has 98 rooms with bath, plus color TV and direct-dial phones. The beach resort area of *Salthill*—only minutes from the center—might be summed up in 3 words: A cleaner Blackpool. The totally refashioned **Ardilaun House** nestles on 5 acres of Irish landscape known as Taylors Hill. Dining salon with Waterford chandeliers, 91 units with bath, lounges with open fires. Nice in its Victorian mood. At mealtimes, the newish **Blue Raincoat** in Spanish Arch is said to be pleasant, but I haven't tried it personally.

GLENBEIGH   (County Kerry) a comely village on the Ring of Kerry, has 2 little treasures.

☆ **Towers** ● an intimate, family-style haven, owned by Brendan Sweency, is predominantly a center for sportsmen; fishing with ghilies available or rough shooting; bedrooms modernized; restaurant specializing in seafood and shellfish. Here is a fine Irish country hotel—simple, friendly in its welcome.

Glenbeigh ● is a 1½-century-old mansion. Reservations policies can be careless, according to readers who were disappointed here. Viewful dining salon; some bedchambers are quite small, all are different and all are attractively decorated.

Caragh Lodge ● at the lake of the same name, is a recommendable guest-house with low rates and a beautifully tended garden.

GOREY   (County Wexford) ★★★ **Marlfield House** is the country home you've been looking for in this district. It is restful, tasteful and replete with fine antiques. As an added bonus, the cuisine is among the finest in the land. Reserve with Mary Bowe, Tel. 55-21124; Fax 21572.

KENMARE   (County Kerry) Modernists should opt for the **Kenmare Bay.** Traditionalists looking for a warm greeting in intimate surroundings would be happier in the Victorian-style ★★★ **Park** which is noteworthy for its cuisine. The atmosphere is so captivating that you should not use it for mere overnighting; plan a weekend or longer if you can.

KILKENNY, often called the Medieval Capital of Ireland and only about 2 hours from Dublin on the Waterford road, presents the **Newpark** as a pleasant stopping spot for visitors to the city's castle, Rothe House, the Tudor buildings, and craft center. Set on the edge of rich meadows and a lawn dotted by oaks, this modern entry is very well run and genuinely inviting. **Lacken House** boasts the prize-winning cookery of Eugene MacSweeney. **Butler House** was the 1760 dower residence of the Dukes of Ormonde; 13 suites; central location. **Edward Langtons,** facing the 12th-century John's Priory, is one of the leading pubs in the nation.

KILLARNEY AND ENVIRONS (County Kerry)

★★★ **Dunloe Castle** • 6 miles out on the *Gap of Dunloe,* offers the greatest luxury, even though its architecture is, in my view, a grave disappointment. It is not a castle, but it "borrows" its name from the site of a vanished 15th-century fort. The large separate building opposite its entrance is its convention hall, the center of its many congresses; there's also a swimming pool, a sauna, 2 tennis courts, a putting green, a driving range, a 1-mile jogging track, open meadows for riding Haflinger horses, and a hairdressing parlor. Burnished modern lobby warmed by Persian rugs over ceramic tiles; vast dining room seating 180; pleasant little grill adjoining; 12-stool, 4-table bar nicely done; spacious lounge up one flight. This 140-bedchamber, 8-suite extravaganza is operated by the same German entrepreneurs who run the Hotel Europe (see below).

★★★★ **Aghadoe Heights Hotel** • about a mile toward Tralee, is spellbinding, richly viewful, and ever-friendly. Its hilltop setting offers a 360° sweep of the lakes and countryside—wow, *what* a glorious situation! Rooftop restaurant and cocktail bar to take maximum advantage of its unique panorama; 60 rooms with bath, all on the smallish side. The cuisine, the warmhearted Hibernian attention, the sink-in modern comfort, and the solace of those fairyland hills and silvered lakes beckon your spirits.

★★★ **Europe** • is the harnessmate of Dunloe Castle. Open lakeside location, about 3½ miles from town; formal dining room plus the Tyrol for specialties; heated pool, 2 tennis courts, and pitch'n putt course; sauna; fishing rights; enormous, well-used parade ground for trotting out the vast stable of horses. Efficient, viewful, but somewhat institutional.

Great Southern • is in town, yet with a golf course at its doorstep. The ornate, flavorful lobby, with its high ceilings, masses of filigree, and melange of furniture, is as Celtic as a leprechaun. There's the Malton Room for serious gastronomy; Irish cabaret from May to Oct.; the bar is called The Punch Bowl; the huge, white dining room with its rotunda overlooks green, green lawns; stunning heated indoor pool and sauna.

The Torc • (meaning "Boar Mountain") is a cool motel-style structure just out of the city on the Cork highway. Modern-as-next-week main building; hollow-square interior containing reception at entrance, bar to rear, dining room on other side and broad corridor, all enclosed by floor-to-ceiling glass. Piped music; live entertainment in season; heated pool; sauna; delicious food for its reasonable tabs. The adjoining bedrooms section displays better taste than the competitive Ryan's houses, but its luggage space and baths are inadequate for overseas guests. Okay for solo trippers or for couples, but a brannigan is virtually guaranteed when more adults are squeezed in.

Killarney Ryan • is a few hundred yards farther along the same road as the Torc. Open-plan central block with reception, small bar, and lounge seating 100, shamrock-green dining room seating 200; piped music; Telex; occasional evening entertainment in season. A no-nonsense value for the bargain hunter.

Castlerosse • on the Kenmare Estate 1½ miles along the lake, is a frequent choice of golfers since an excellent 36-hole circuit is only a club-head away. Far from fancy, but ample comfort for the dedicated sportsman. Swimming pool; tennis; games room; bountiful table of salmon, meats, and homegrown vegetables; car service available. Its 40 bedrooms, including 3 "duplex suites," all have baths. Pleasant in the simple country style.

White Gates • is big on warm half-timbered charm and small on its tabulations. A winsome nest.

International • has been overhauled extensively, melding modern touches with tradition. Sun terrace for bright times; grill, 3 bars, dining salon, plus the Whaler for seafood selections. Satisfactory for an overnight.

Cahernane • perhaps one mile along the Muckross road, occupies a 100-acre park through which there is a long driveway to the century-old converted mansion. Today it boasts 35 refitted bedrooms and baths; fine staircase, fireplace, and other antiques in its lobby, plus the amiable Wolfhound Bar with its handsome vaulted ceiling. Dining choice in either the select Pembroke Room or in the larger salon. There's tennis, pitch'n'putt, croquet, and reserved fishing on the River Flesk.

LETTERKENNY (County Donegal) There's the 56-room, 56-bath **Mount Errigal** at Ballyraine, sited ¼-mile from town in a park setting; modern in execution; rooms are small. **Gallaghers,** in the center of the village, is a fair alternative.

LIMERICK (County Limerick)

Jurys • 96 units lead the local pack. Riverside situation; U-shape layout and central service building housing the handsome Copper Room restaurant, an 18-hour-per-day coffee shop, and a bar lounge. Its accommodations are unarguably the choicest to be found in this busy junction.

Royal George • on the main street, greets you with a small lobby with smartly turned-out hall porter; alcove restaurant, bar, and snack corner on ground floor. Bunkers a standard 12′ x 12′ in dimensions, which is obviously too snugglesome except for honeymooners; judicious employment of colors almost throughout. Ask for a corner room overlooking the river.

Limerick Ryan • draws the 3rd-place ranking—a significant illustration of the paucity of attractive shelter here. This complex is sited in an 8-acre park on the outskirts beside the airport highway. Because of the juxtaposition of hyper-moderna with Victoriana, maintenance appears to be slipshod when, in fact, it is satisfactory. The buffet lunch is popular. Budget oriented.

Cruises Royal Hotel • in the center, is a perfunctory choice. **Two Mile Motor Inn** (guess how far outside of town it is) has been given a thorough renewal; now a reliable oasis for nomads.

★★★★★ **Dromoland Castle** • near *Newmarket-on-Fergus,* is an 8-mile skip-and-jump from the airport and is considered to be in the Limerick area. This baronial fief can be proud of its grandiose park setting; 18-hole golf course; tennis court; fishing and shooting facilities; 2 lovely lounges; cozy main bar; a second downstairs with one or two instrumentalists in summer. Meals consisting of selections such as lamb chops, sauteed chicken, turkey and ham and corn-on-the-cob; production-line service by kind but overworked staffers. The major-ity of its 67 bedchambers and 67 baths are spacious; a few mother-in-law rooms are uncomfortably small; avoid #11 and #12 at all costs. One of the most expensive stops in Ireland, but visually unforgettable.

★★★ **Clare Inn** • a few hundred yards down the highway on a corner of the Dromoland estate, was launched as supposedly "a less costly option." Nevertheless, "less" is a relative term. Hilltop situation; white building remi-niscent of high-class motel; more subdued decor; golf course privilege, riding, fishing, and other facilities of its sister house extended to all guests. Small but pleasant reception area; panoramic bar in tartan (where you'll be asked to have a sandwich and/or soup for lunch if you arrive in fringe seasons); dining room with wild purple-and-rouge circus colorations; serene lounge and solarium in light greens and whites. Its 121 bedchambers in 4 different color schemes are large and handsomely furnished, and have walls so thin that you should ask for an isolated room if one is available. This venture depends heavily on high-bracket tour groups. A commercialized Dromoland Castle, without the fan-fare—and priced way, way up in the fluffy clouds, too.

★★ **Limerick Inn** • is a worthy alternative. Six tall arches on the facade; stone and glass central entrance; health and leisure center plus indoor pool; floral decorative themes; ample living space; red-damask bar; burgundy restau-rant with soft red decor on the walls; basket-weave wool carpets; a high level of cheer everywhere.

Carrygerry House • at *Newmarket-on-Fergus,* is new but in a two-cen-tury old manor which keeps its traditions. The cuisine is noteworthy, too, ac-cording to friends who have tried it. We'll drop in soon.

Restaurant

Oliver's • *Parkway Centre* • is on the Dublin Road and seems to be on the highway to culinary pleasure. Intimacy in a Dickensian mood—all of which provokes the query: "Please, sir, can I have some more?"

MOYARD (County Galway)

☆☆ **Rosleague Manor** • resides on a knoll above a boggy vale with its own sea lake (*Bearnaderg Bay*, 7 miles north of Clifden). It is also at the edge of the 5,000-acre *Connemara National Park*. All 13 doubles with private bath; 3 gracious lounges; home-style appointments; reasonable rates for the substantial rewards. Within the snap of a line, you will find salmon and sea trout angling, deep sea fishing, pony trekking, golfing, and hill climbing.

OUGHTERARD (County Galway; 17 miles northwest of Galway city, directly across the lake from Ashford Castle at Cong) is a sleepy hamlet with perhaps 900 inhabitants.

★★ **Sweeney's** • garden fronted and with 21 rooms, is my choice in this village. It fairly oozes charm, conviviality, and tasteful homeyness. Two-century-old lounges; lawnside dining salon; tiny elevator; laced from cranny to nook with brassware, oil paintings, and highly polished hospitality.

Connemara Gateway • is an elongated structure of gray paneled concrete about a mile from the center, sited on 10 acres of lawns and pastoral land, with a view of Lough Corrib in the distance; functional lobby; lounge-bar with intimacy the keynote; restaurant; heated swimming pool brightened by umbrellas and complemented by a snack bar; putting green; croquet; tennis. All 62 units come with bath, clip shower (telephone style), electric kettle, coffee, tea, sugar, and 2 cups.

Egan's Lake Hotel • where the action is, is not on the water but smack in the center of the settlement. Although it is a hodgepodge in architecture and in furnishings, the brass shines as brightly as the staff. Salmon and lobster are specialties at the table. Fishermen generally find this a happy haven.

Sportsmen also frequently bunk in at the **Corrib Hotel.** At nearby *Clifden,* the imposing ☆☆☆☆☆ **Abbeyglen Castle,** owned by Paul and June Hughes, is highly regarded for its gastronomy as well as for its comfort. The crenelated towers overlook a swimming pool (not the moat, sire) and restful green undulating countryside. Set in its own 12-acre valley; great for fishermen and golfers; heated pool; tennis court; comfortable rooms.

PARKNASILLA (County Kerry; roughly 35 miles from Killarney and 15 miles from Kenmare) has ★★ **Great Southern** hotel that sits in a 300-acre park on the shores of an island-dotted Atlantic fjord. Lush subtropical vegetation nurtured by the Gulf Stream, which hits the coast at this point; azure cove with

sweeping view of the bay, fronting rock-clad beach with patches of sand, and a toy wharf with its tiny boathouse; tennis, golf, deep-sea fishing, shooting, pony trekking, boating, water skiing, swimming in the cove or in the glasslined pool; sauna. I rate this high on the Ring of Kerry for tranquil lazing in the region. Not far away at Tahilla Cove is a charming little guesthouse; limited accommodations; satisfactory food. Incidentally, at nearby **Sneem,** the **Blue Bull** is an ambitious restaurant effort that combines top quality cookery with a literary atmosphere. Traditional Irish music in the evenings.

RATHMULLAN (County Donegal) ★★★ **Rathmullan House** is an inviting inn on the fringe of Lough Swilly. Take the beautiful Atlantic Drive to Horn Head. At nearby *Dun fanaghy,* the **Port-na-Blagh** or at *Marble Hill Strand,* the **Shandon** are adequate. At *Rosapenna,* also here in the far northwest, the **Rosapenna** is fair; recommended mainly for its golf links. Most everything up in this corner of Eire functions only from April to Oct.

ROSSNOWLAGH (also in the northwest) The 40-room **Sand House** resides on a dune bank above a 2-mile-long beach. Use it as a touring base only for Donegal rovings because the adjoining settlement has nothing to offer except pinball machines. Pleasant meals and helpful staff, but unquestionably the boondocks; it functions from Easter to Oct.

SLIGO (County Sligo) This is rugged Yeats Country. While the poet was born in Dublin, he lived, wrote, and was buried in the Sligo region, with most of his references within the framework of Rosse to Ben Bulben, a prominent mountain that you'll pass while touring. The **Silver Swan,** next to Hyde Bridge in the center, offers the soothing and pleasant sound of rushing waters on 2 sides. Air-conditioned lobby in modern colors; horseshoe-shape bar. Total of 24 small rooms and 16 baths or showers. The **Yeats Country Ryan** is 5½ miles out at *Rosses Point,* overlooking the bay. It is 200 yards from the County Sligo Golf Club (one of the best courses in the nation); guest cards are available to all clients. A fine beach (arctic-temperature ocean!) is a 5-minute walk from its doors. Lobby and lounge with cream and white brick walls plus red and brown carpeting; dining room in original Yeats House; bar attractively blended to conform with the modernity of the housing wing. Another good buy for the thrifty traveler. The 20-room-and-bath **Ballincar House** is on a tangent to *Rosses Point,* perhaps 2 miles from the city. It is sited on a tranquil park. Dining spread overlooking the garden; cozy drawing room; bar; squash courts, tennis courts, sauna, and sundeck. **Sligo Park Hotel** occupies a 7-acre chunk of scenic Irish turf. The grand design is that of a motel, while it offers the facilities of a first-class hotel.

TIPPERARY (County Tipperary) Yes, it's a long, long way . . . so while you're here you should try to visit the Rock of Cashel, Cahir Castle, the High Crosses, and some of the other forts and abbeys of the historic region. The town itself is pretty colorless. The **Royal** is clean, and its food smelled country-good. I'm told that the secluded forest-bound **Aherlow House** and **The Glen** in the *Glen of Aherlow* are worthy stopping places.

430 · · · IRELAND

TRALEE (County Kerry) has most of its appeal on the fringes of the town itself. Its beauty is in its name and in its famed "Rose" of song. **Brandon** is adequate for brief stays. Modern and usually jammed with tours; nice staff. **Benners,** on the main street, bespeaks its 1¼ centuries of careful use. Attractive entrance with shining copper, plus peat fire burning in winter; neighborly bar to the right; old-fashioned lounge to the left; 49 grandfatherly rooms; 27 private baths. Clean, plain, friendly, and very Irish. Out on the Killarney road a few minutes by car, the modernistic **Earl of Desmond** commands an eyeful treasure of land, sea, and sky. It offers tennis and a putting green on the grounds; many safe beaches are nearby. **Ballygarry House** is an intimate, well-run address; moreover, the food is above average in quality.

WATERFORD (County Waterford) Why not try **Waterford Castle**? It's on an islet reached by a ferry that runs day and night and only takes five minutes for the crossing. A very pleasant change and most agreeable. The **Ardree** ("High King") sits high across the river with a sweep of the port. This massive modern structure contains 100 rooms with bath, a restyled restaurant, and an amiable bar. Its competition comprises the 50-room **Granville,** the **Tower,** and the family-run **Dooley's.** Of course, this is the home of the famous glassworks, so you may wish to take a look at the factory, studios, and exhibition halls. There are five tours per day; book in advance by phoning 051–73311.

WATERVILLE (County Kerry)

★★★★★ **Waterville Lake** • is a superdeluxe fisherman's paradise that wets its line only between May 1 and Sept. 30; otherwise it is closed. This inspired enterprise is handsomely situated on the shores of island-studded Lough Currane. It offers one of Europe's finest 18-hole championship golf courses, an indoor pool and spa pool, a games room, sauna, and sun bed. Ask your travel agent if it is functioning close to your time of departure.

The promontory that you can see from here is host to the links- and lough-side **Waterville Beach** which has an Irish pub, an indoor heated pool, a tennis court, and oodles of real estate for children to play on. In the village, **Butler Arms,** a tiny nest for sportsmen, would be the choice of the modest candidates that line the single trail along the shore.

WEXFORD was created where the Slaney flows into the harbor, an ancient Norse settlement with crooked lanes. The National Heritage Park is at nearby *Ferrycarrig,* where you'll find riverside replicas of early Irish dwellings, forts, and monastic remains. Comfortable overnighting at the **Ferrycarrig, Whites,** or the peaceful and amusing five-room **Newbay Country House.**

ITALY

~~~~~~

INCLUDING CAPRI, SAN MARINO, SARDINIA, and VATICAN CITY

USA: Italian Government Tourist Office, 630 Fifth Ave., Suite 1565, New York, NY 10020, Tel. (212) 245–4961, (also known as "ENIT"); 360 Post St., Suite 801, San Francisco, CA 94108, Tel. (415) 392–5266; 500 North Michigan, Suite 1046, Chicago, IL 60611, Tel. (312) 644–0990; **CANADA:** 3 Place Ville Marie, Montreal, Quebec, H3B 2E3, Tel. (514) 866–7667

SPECIAL REMARKS: One of the most helpful touring organizations in the world is located in Italy. It's called **Compagnia Italiana Turismo (CIT)** with 50 offices in Italy and 49 in foreign cities. The Rome headquarters are located in piazza della Repubblica. Address any inquiries to Dr. Cesare Della Pietra, General Manager. For escorted tours or group arrangements CIT is peerless.

Italy's ingratiating climate is as diverse as its landscape. Along the Italian Riviera, it's subtropical, similar to upper (not lower!) Florida at its most delightful. Around Sicily and the southern coast, you'll bask in typical Mediterranean surroundings. The Adriatic side is cooler than its western twin. The Po Basin, across the North, has seasonal extremes, and is similar to the mid-Atlantic climate. Around Rome, Naples, Pescara, Bari, and Taranto, conditions are fairly pleasant throughout the year. But keep out of the high Apennines and Alps from September to May, unless you've got skis. April to October are the best tourist months.

Apart from the sometime government of Italy itself, 3 independent domains, each with its separate leader, laws, and diplomats, function within the borders of Italy—the Vatican, the Sovereign Military Order of Malta, and the Republic of San Marino.

Patriarch of the **Vatican** is the Polish-born Supreme Pontiff, John Paul II. His papal state of 108 acres and 890 people operates under extraterritorial rights; as spiritual head of the Catholic Church, he is responsible only to his tenets, his followers, and himself. The flag is white and yellow, charged with crossed keys and triple tiara. A complete coinage is struck every year; examine your change in Rome for Pius XII coins, because the early ones are collectors' items. (For further information turn to the Vatican.)

The **Sovereign Military Order of Malta** (better known as "Knights of Malta"), with headquarters on via Condotti, and a villa—its demesne—on Aventine Hill in Rome, sends its own ambassadors to many Catholic countries, issues its own "SMOM" license plates, and performs many other functions of separate statehood. Its total population is 40. The nation now boasts its own stamps, which are prized by many collectors. It is smaller than Vatican City, but potent both ecclesiastically and politically.

In thumbnail form here are some jottings about **San Marino,** the world's most ancient and smallest republic, which is now almost 17 centuries old; its birthday is September 3. *Location?* Only 23.4 square miles of real estate in the Apennines, entirely surrounded by Italian soil, 20 minutes by car from Rimini and the Adriatic Sea via the Superstrada. The District of Columbia is 3 times as large. *Altitude?* More than 2200 feet, with a glorious view as far as the Venice lagoon and Yugoslavian coast when the sky is clear. *Population?* About 19 thousand (its out-of-country citizenry is even more voluminous—22 thousand). *Industries?* Postage stamps, fingernail varnish, furniture, and tourism. *Public debt or unemployment?* Zero. *Armed Services?* There's a standing army of 180 stalwarts—but because it's such a peaceful nation, sometimes they sit. You'll also be relieved to know that the republic's Grand Council ratified a pledge not to acquire nuclear weapons. *Number of foreign tourists?* Roughly a million non-Italian sightseers per year; 2,500,000 if you include their Latin neighbors; in High Season, between July 15 and August 15, approximately 10 thousand per day (but as many as 80 thousand have arrived within 12 hours). *Odd facts?* (1) Every U.S. President since Lincoln has been made an honorary citizen of this land. (2) The magnificent aqueduct, plus the lovely circular fountain below Government House, were a gift from the U.S. (3) Though landlocked, San Marino has arranged a toehold of Adriatic beach at **Riccione**—15 miles by your car's odometer, but almost 2 hours distant on a busy Sunday afternoon in August. (4) The Casino, closed as a gambling hall, functions as an occasional dance center or sports arena. (5) The cost of running such a vast government keeps soaring, with practically no end in sight. The heads of state, 2 Captains Regent, receive $10.15 per diem for the upkeep of their uniforms and for ceremonial pocket money. Italy has stepped in to award the republic $3.7 million each year for not becoming a tax haven or a gambling enclave. (6) In July, don't miss the biggest, most colorful national contest of all—the crossbow championship. *Currency?* Italian lire. On request you may buy San Marino's copper, silver, and gold coins, which are minted for collectors. *Language?* Italian. *Connections from Rimini?* In addition to the high-speed Superstrada, ordinary buses, and special excursions, there's a 5-flight-daily helicopter in summer only. The Funivia terminus is also a cable-car stop. *Formalities at Border?* Absolutely none; no passport or credentials demanded, but they'll sell you a souvenir visa on request—*if* you can find a customs official.

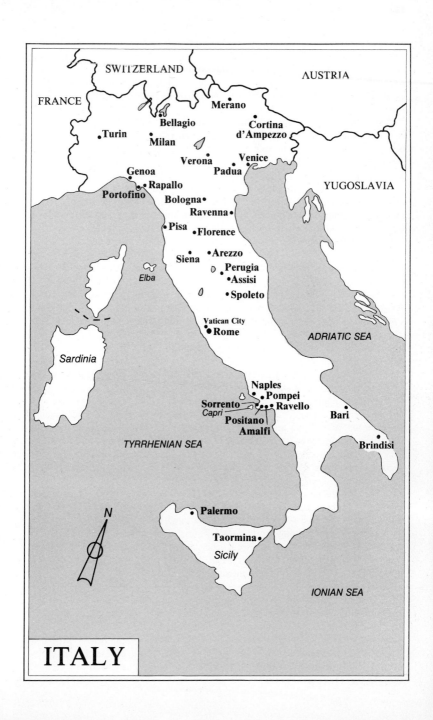

SWITZERLAND
AUSTRIA
FRANCE
• Merano
Bellagio
Cortina
d'Ampezzo
• Turin
Milan
Verona
Venice
Padua
Genoa
YUGOSLAVIA
• Rapallo
Portofino
Bologna •
Ravenna •
• Pisa
Florence
• Arezzo
Siena
Elba
Perugia
• Assisi
• Spoleto
Vatican City
• Rome
ADRIATIC SEA
Sardinia
Naples
• Pompei
Sorrento
• Ravello
Capri
Bari
Positano
Amalfi
Brindisi
TYRRHENIAN SEA
N
• Palermo
Taormina •
Sicily
IONIAN SEA

ITALY

TRANSPORTATION   **Airline Alitalia** has a wonderful flair for hospitality and graciousness once you get aloft, but the desk services and the support systems are *average* (at best) or certainly below the levels of excellence displayed by flight crews. The carrier is trying hard now to improve matters at ground zero.

If you fly in or out, you'll probably use Rome or Milan airports. The first is a long haul from midcity, and transport can range from 40 minutes to 1¼ hours, depending on traffic and rush-hour congestion; agree on your taxi fare beforehand—always! Milan, sometimes in a state of chaos, is beginning to realize it is one of the most important business hubs in the world.

Taxis: The fares are jumping so fast and so often that sometimes a legitimate boost is correctly added before the meters can be adjusted to tally it. To avoid being conned (which nears attempted standard practice), be certain to look for the *official* notice which by law must be prominently displayed.

Important: *From 10 p.m.–6 a.m., there is an extra charge per vehicle* (not per passenger).

Unless your driver is extraordinarily patient or kind, 10% should be his maximum tip.

Metro: The capital boasts its own subway systems. Line A scoots from Anagnina (Cinecitta) on Tuscolana to via Ottaviano near St. Peter's. Midtown stops include Termini, and piazzas Repubblica, Barberini, and di Spagna. There are others, of course, so study the route map. Line B begins at Rebibbia Termini Station and pauses at via Cavour, Colosseum, Circus Maximus, St. Paul's, and several more key points before heading for the outskirts of town. Some even romp out to the popular beach at Ostia. In such a crowded city, it can save you *tempo, lire,* and *frenesia.*

Trains: Your best chance of getting a seat is in first-class. *Make sure of it by reserving in advance, whenever reservations are possible.* If you have no reservations, and if you are leaving from the point where the train is made up or cars are being added, plan to arrive at the station 30 minutes before departure time, to assure yourself of a space when the gates are opened for entry. In second-class, there's an excellent chance you'll stand. First is definitely worth the difference.

Some of the single-compartment sleepers are the best around. The cheapest sleeping accommodation is called the *Carrozze Cuccette*—ordinary coaches fixed up with bunks. Again—be certain to reserve them beforehand.

You may save money by buying a Tourist Ticket (valid for 8, 15, 21, or 30 days and permitting advance seat reservation), a "circular" ticket (a minimum of 600 miles within 60 days), or a "family" ticket (minimum of 4). And don't forget to check into the Eurailpass.

FOOD   Discounting the North, where rice is king, Italy loves its pasta. If you are budgeting, either of these plus a salad can serve as a pretty filling meal.

And if you are not economizing, Italian white truffles are the most scrumptious in the world—infinitely superior to the coarser black variety grown in France. Specially trained dogs are used in Alba, south of Turin, the global capital of this delicacy, to sniff out their earthen hiding places and to root them up.

Risotto is marvelous. It has innumerable versions. The basis is towel-rubbed rice, simmered in bouillon or chicken broth until the kernels are dark and tasty. With this are mixed mushrooms, peppers, onions, saffron, butter, and cheese; veal, chicken, pork, lobster, beef.

Polenta is a staple of the North. It's a cornmeal porridge, white or yellow, so heavy in texture that it stands up by itself. It isn't particularly interesting in taste, but it comes into its own when used to mop up a rich gravy. Incidentally, northern cooking leans heavily on butter; the prime ingredient throughout the South is olive oil.

Prosciutto, dark spicy local ham served in wafer-thin slices, is an excellent cocktail appetizer. It's wonderful with fresh figs or a slice of melon—but be sure to order it "crudo" (raw), or they might served it "cotto" (cooked).

Other specialities worth trying are scampi alla griglia (grilled crawfish resembling large grilled shrimp), sea crab cocktail (eat the delicate "coral" separately), carpaccio (heavenly paper-thin slices of raw sirloin spiced with ground pepper and dashed with oil and vinegar), scaloppine San Giorgio (veal stuffed with ham, cheese, and mushrooms), pansoti con salsa di noci (a Genoese specialty of pasta with a walnut filling), gateau Saint-Honore, purely Italian, despite its French name, and the fashionable cream-spun dessert that most sweets trollies display today, Tiramisu.

Don't forget that extraordinary Venetian crab, either. Listed as la granseola, it's a lobster-size crawfish with tiny claws and a huge, meaty body. The favorite way to serve it is in the shell, reinforced with piquant seasonings. Venice is the center; summer is the season; try any good seafood restaurant for a succulent sample.

NOTE · · · Stick to bottled water in rural or village areas of Italy. In the larger cities, tap water is pure. Most people are never bothered by the water but invariably blame it for indigestion after downing cocktails, wine, cognac, and gigantic repasts served in tropical surroundings. Popular sparkling brands of bottled water are San Pellegrino and Crodo; Fiuggi and Sangemini are the best bets without gas (said to be *the* remedy for kidney stones).

You may order half (*mezza*) portions of pasta—a useful gimmick to save money while saving room to sample more new dishes.

If you are traveling by car, the *autostrada* pit stops are clearly the pits. The huge Pavesi pull-offs even offer public microwave ovens so that you can heat you own grub. (At one recent feed near Orvieto, the only thing that had warmth was my Coca-Cola.) Agip can't do much better. So, should you want to enjoy a meal, you'd better drive off the superhighway and into a town.

Meal hours: In Rome and the South, breakfast, 7–9 a.m.; lunch, 1–3 p.m.; dinner, 9:30–11 p.m. From Rome northward, dinner is often earlier.

DRINKS Grappa, vermouth, and brandy are the national hard drinks. Grappa, popular in the North, is a raw, harsh, high-proof beverage made from the leftovers of the ordinary distillation process; Friuli is one of the best. If you are tired of the enamel on your teeth, try Centerba, made as the name implies, from 100 herbs and a generous supply of alcohol. It's a digestif from Tocco Casauria near Pescara. A more mellow one (perhaps because it is made from only 79 herbs) is Amaro Siciliano. As for brandy, Vecchia Romagna and Rene Briand are the only brands we can recommend. A drink that delights most visitors is Sambuca (*anisette*) when it is served *con mosche* (with "flies," which are floating coffee beans).

Italy is a wine country. She has moved ahead of France as the largest producer in the world, even though the Gauls still drink more on a per capita basis; she dedicates 55% of her farmland to the glories of the grape.

Taste, of course, is a very personal thing. The "fashion" of the instant is Prosecco, a cheerful sparkling white from the Veneto district; it's wonderful as refreshment or with shellfish. I often order a chalky red called Villa Antinori or the softer Tignanello (also Antinori) as quality Chiantis which are reliable and universal. (Pay no attention to the irrelevant fact that the Antinori production is not registered in the regional "Classico" category; the house provides some of the greatest rewards to be discovered in a corked bottle.) Soave Bertani, though common, is a gentle white while the ever-popular Bolla company produces a soothing rose beverage.

Bardolino (a red from Verona), Verdicchio (a white from the Adriatic slopes), and Rosatello (a rose) are excellent alternatives. If you favor greater softness in a red, try a Torgiano Rubesco from Umbria. Most bottlings beyond 5 years of age are fine companions for meat or fowl. Picolit, from the northeast, is a cheerful white. Barolo, a rich ruby pressing from the Piedmont, is not too flexible, but it is satisfying given the complementary foodstuffs. Some would opt for something lighter, like Barbera, for instance. The Lambrusco from Emilia and the Recioto from Verona are bubbly reds that drinkers of American sparkling burgundy might enjoy. Asti Spumante is similar to a sugar-fed champagne; the dry types called *spumante metodo champenois* are rapidly replacing French imports these days.

If you don't choose a light white wine as is the custom today for an aperitif, the customary standbys remain Martini and Cinzano (red or white), the mellow dark Punte Mes and the Ferrari-red Campari (try the last mixed with orange juice and ice on a summer day).

NOTE · · · The best tonic in the world for overeating, flatulence, gas pains, picking yourself up off the floor when you've mixed oysters and bananas—practically any stomach ailment up to chilblains or ulcers—is an Italian bitters called Fernet Branca. The taste is horrible, but the effect is atomic. This hideous black liquid can save your digestion and your temper. Try any bar; it's less than soda pop.

TIPPING Aside from the hotels and restaurants, a nearly general 10%.

Hotels automatically add 18% to your bill for a "service charge." This is sometimes a racket, because the employees who have helped you don't always see it, despite union laws which insist that they must. Give the concierge from $1 per day extra and small amounts in person to your maid, baggage porter, room waiter, and valet, if you use them. At sit-down cafes, the tabs *always* include service, but many villains stamp the required *Servizio Compreso* so lightly it's almost illegible. In restaurants, a flat 15% is added to the bill; give your waiter half of the service charge in addition, the minimum being 1000 lire.

Always tip everybody for small services, because Italians consider it gainfully earned income.

CITIES AND REGIONS

AMALFI An important maritime republic during the Middle Ages, Amalfi is also the target of dozens of daily bus tours from Naples, which pause here for refreshment on the spectacular (but not too difficult) coastal drive between Salerno and Sorrento. Small, increasingly inviting village with reminiscent links to Wagner and Ibsen; handsome yet modest hotels; definitely worth a visit or even a stopover.

If you do pause, the **Santa Caterina** evokes sighs with a patio 150 feet above the sea. Viewful units for 90 guests in the main building, plus accommodations for 30 more in villas spotted along the lemon grove slopes. Balconies for all; elevators to the beach plus rippling swimmery; well-prepared food with vegetables grown on the premises; service as crisp as the lettuce. The 50-sancta **Luna-Torre Saracena** also rises proudly above the coastline; you'll find a lift from the street to the hotel, a pool, a fresh dining room and terrace, a summer-only nightclub and a notable kitchen. **Excelsior** at *Porgerola,* a twisty 15 minutes up, teeters viewfully above the town. If awards are ever given for tranquillity, this one should win a Peace Prize. First-class category; modern ambience in a sawtooth layout; extensively updated in the strange Italian meld of 19th- and 12th-century themes; all 90 seafront units have bath; most have private terrace. The service and kindness are hallmarks of its success. The **Cappuccini-Convento,** by far the most famous (a marble plaque here recalls the visit of "Enrico Wadsworth Longfellow"), has a fantastic setting in a 12th-century monastery. The atmosphere is clearly touristic and the house needs more perk and sparkle. **Pensione Sole** is a clean, quiet, family-run house with a bounty of comforts for its extra-low tariffs. A fine buy for the money. The second-class **Residence** is not recommended. **Caleidoscopio,** about 2 miles from the center, overlooks (but is not on) the sea. Every room with bath or shower; all front accommodations with balconies; large pool; substantial cuisine; a happy choice, in a modest way, for travelers who seek calm. The well-situated **Miramalfi** is budget class, with a good building but mediocre food and service; it, too, has a concrete-lined swimmin' hole. Staircase construction with ample parking space at the uppermost rung; outstanding view. The first-category **Saraceno** courts posh pashas from its perch just below the highway at *Conca dei Marini.* Here's a cliff-hugging structure linked by mirrored elevator to a private beach and jammed-crammed with gimmickry. Whitewashed lobby and lounges; more Middle Eastern memorabilia than Suleiman the Magnificent's tomb; vaulted restaurant-grill with tiled floor; gilt cave-dwelling bar; lower-level pool and mini-chapel. In addition to the so-called "Royal Apartment," there are 60 adequately sized doubles with showers, chilled air, TV's, Frigobars, more Arabesque accouterments, and waterfront terraces. The nearby second-class **Bellevue,** a 5-minute drive toward Positano, is a better than average roadside spot—if you don't face that noisy roadside. It offers only 24 bedchambers, each with balcony, terrace, and bath or shower; nice pool; easy parking (very important in Amalfi). Good news for money-savers.

ASSISI is a wonderful little place with scenery that will bedizzen the most crusted traveler. If you haven't much time, plan at least a half day here. That should be sufficient to briefly admire the renowned Basilica of St. Francis, to be wooed fleetingly by its gothic romanticisms, and to drink in the view of the plains below. If possible take a bit longer to be humbled by the Basilica of Santa Chiara and the Cathedral of St. Rufino. There's also a Roman Forum, the Temple of Minerva, and an Hermitage (Eremo Carceri). At the Basilica of St. Mary of the Angels, you can actually enter the Portiuncola, a chapel where the Franciscan order was born. If you'd like a scholarly and pleasant guide, the brothers at the San Damiano Convent are beloved by many North Americans; no charge for visiting their own sanctuary, of course—just alms to the church, which are voluntary. Excursionists have discovered it, of course, so you can expect some souvenir shops in the ancient streets. If you do sleep over, the **Fontebella** is substantial and its restaurant is one of the best among hotels. Otherwise, the **Subasio** has the eyeful views, but the **Umbria** has the best rooms; **Windsor Savoia** and **Giotto** are both passable. All are chilly in the cool months due to their high altitude and low heating standards. **Hotel Giotto** is the culinary choice followed closely by the **Umbria**. **Subasio Hotel** provides fair vittles plus a magnificent vista. **La Taverna dell'Arco** is the pick of independents.

BELLAGIO

☆☆☆☆☆ **Grand Hotel Villa Serbelloni** ● a national monument that has operated as a hostelry since 1872, resides today in an enclave of land belonging to the Rockefeller Foundation. Lakeview terrace flanked by palm trees in its park; small sandy *lido* plus a heated pool; main salon with frescoed ceilings, parquet floor, and working fireplace; spectacular garden vista from the restaurant; outstanding kitchen with superb wines. Venetian and Florentine bedchambers come with home-style comfort; about half boast waterfront reflections; only 4 feature balconies. I prefer the north wing, especially suite #160, a corner choice. Operative Apr. to Oct. annually.

BOLOGNA, boasting about 500-thousand residents, is the seat of the oldest university in the world (the word "university" was invented here) and the richest, highest-caloried fodder of the nation. Bologna is famous for its kitchens. Busy modern pace in the embrace of a marvelously antique atmosphere; more than 20 miles of arcaded walks; leaning towers; splendid palaces designed by a master such as Vignola; 10 museums with treasures from Etruscan to modern times; National Gallery with works by 56 great painters, including Raphael's "St. Cecilia"; villa and mausoleum of Guglielmo Marconi. "Baloney" originated in Bologna; if you'd like to sample the original article, ask for Mortadella.

Incidentally, if you arrive by train, be certain to take the West (Ovest) exit—*not* the more remote East (Est). There are no taxis at the latter.

☆☆☆☆☆ **Royal Carlton** • The taste overall is an exquisite meld of modernity and tradition, with every comfort available and every convenience provided. Well run kitchen; excellent cave with the accent on Italian vintages; superb Royal Grill that is truly regal; handsome American bar backed by a breakfast room. Total of 250 bedchambers including 22 suites; colors varying from powder blue to cognac to olive green to salmon; extravagant artwork.

☆☆☆☆ **Baglioni** • was the leading light here for several generations. Then it was closed and later reopened with most of its opulence carefully restored. Now with 130 rooms, 4 suites, and fine marble baths. Lavish is the word for it.

☆ **Internazionale** • a 2-part structure dating from the 16th century and 1972. Of its 140 units more than half are singles; both of these hostelries come with ample garage space—an important factor in this cluttered town.

Residence Elite • well below the others, offers many suites, some with kitchenettes; charming restaurant with bottles in vitrines for decor; copious buffet popular with Bolognese.

Milano-Excelsior • opposite the station, is a good buy. Shiny, dirt-free throughout; 109 bedrooms, all with radio, telephone, and bath; 6 very pleasant suites; double windows on the front side; amiable personnel who aim to please.

Alexander • is a solid value at an even lower tab than the Milano-Excelsior, which owns this place.

Jolly • facing the rail station, is more commercial in tone. Chilly ambience; 2 dining rooms; spacious lounges; 200 units, all with bath; fully air-conditioned. Always booked solid by visiting salesmen, so be sure to nail down your reservation.

Roma • remains satisfactory for physical amenities. Midtown situation, one block off the central piazza; covered parking area; intimate public rooms; 91 units, all with telephone and many with large private terrace; 55 baths or showers.

Holiday Inn • on the outskirts near the congress center, offers 164 clean and cheerfully simple shelters. All's here for a pleasant repose.

Kennedy • which is second-class, is out of the center, but it is air-conditioned.

Tre Vecchi's • has 92 fresh rooms and an adequate dining salon.

☆☆☆ **Bitone** • *via Emilia Levante 111* • is an *osteria* with lots and lots of charm and many of the city's chic-est guests. The antipasto and the wild mushroom salad (in season) are fine light starters. End it all with a marvelous zabaglione.

★★★ **Al Cantunzein** • *piazza Verdi 4/d* • has one of the most favored reputations in the city for dining and hosting theatrical and political celebrities. The risotti are splendid.

★★★ **Dei Cacciatori** • *piazza Marescalchi 1* • is a joyful house for typical gastronomy in the country mood. The pastasciutte is exceptional.

Cordon Bleu • *via Saffi 38* • is more for international (read French) cuisine in a contemporary mood.

Rodrigo • *via della Zecca 2* • features international cookery. It is popular with after-theater and post-operatic calorie hunters.

BOLZANO **Park Laurins** is the choicest for overnighting. This one is smack-dab in the middle of town, but it is peacefully embraced by tall shade trees and a somnolent garden with a private swimming pool. Quality furnishings in many of its 190 accommodations and 4 suites; lovely terraces for breakfasting or bucolic lounging; open all around the calendar. If you opt for silence and the amenities of 1910, look no further. The faster-paced **Grifone,** under the same management and with the same rates, draws a livelier clientele. Three restaurants plus a large, coolish bar; 101 unfancy units and 100 baths; garniture in Tyrolean Baroque and Biedermeier. Tops for the young in heart. The flamboyant **Alpi** boasts 100 bedchambers—each with bath or shower. Ceramic-and-marble lobby, somewhat cramped dimensions; air conditioning. The **Scala** and the **Luna** are okay for medium-cost hostelries. The **Citta** has updated bedroom styles. The public sancta always have been attractive and the pasta is above average in the restaurant.

CAPRI

Capri and the upper-level Anacapri are born again to the "in" scene with such resounding *eclat* that the results for the island as well as its visitors are gratifying. By spending millions on comfort and style, augmenting its droll charm, and never losing the unique *Caprice* that historically has lured emperors as well as daytrippers, the island's success is secure. And even with their prosperity, the inhabitants are not spoiled. The cuisine is Mediterranean and varied, the shopping is on the leading edge of international chic, the hotels are among the finest in the nation (yet cheaper than many on the mainland), and the scenery is as unspoiled as when the ancients first scrambled up its cliffs—or tossed their enemies off of them. The hypnotizing Blue Grotto, reached by skiff from Marina Grande or by bus from Anacapri, remains an eternal attraction. Among antiquities, there's the 14th-century Certosa di San Giacomo, Tiberius's Villa Jovis, and the church of Santo Stefano (17th century). There's a funicular from main port to main village; chair lift to mountain peak above Anacapri for a spellbinding view; from May 1 to September 30, private cars banned from the tiny isle; taxis and buses available throughout the year; one small, so-so beach at Marina Piccola; fast inexpensive hydrofoil service (40 minutes) which skims atop the waves from Naples to Capri and returns in half the time of the even less expensive—but much more crowded—regular service. In summer there's a hydrofoil link daily from Fiumicino (Rome) for fly-ins—and a genuine fly-in by chopper on a regular basis from Naples airport, 10 minutes away. Other helicopter flights can be arranged on request. In spring or fall there's greater tranquillity, but many visitors richly enjoy the hubble-bubble of humanity in midsummer. It snoozes in idle repose during the windblown winters. Up at Anacapri the big draw is Axel Munthe's Villa San Michele. If you feel inspired, mornings are best, before the throngs roll in from Naples and Sorrento.

HOTELS

Please refer to ''About the Stars'' in the introductory material. Ranking in this book does not necessarily follow the ''official'' local listings, which may employ different criteria.

☆☆☆☆☆ **Grand Quisisana** • never diminishes in its mandate for excellence. Attractive lobby often open to the patios and terraces; romantic restaurant by the palm-grove pool; 2 tennis courts; gym plus covered pool; handsome bar (with live music), nightclub; superb professional management by the Morgano family, masters of their trade. Bid for the seafront units only; the back ones face the footpath just off the town square. Zestful and luxurious.

★★★★ **Luna** • beams with honors. Marvelous view of the Faraglioni cliff on the seaside and L-curving for a townscape panorama along the other shank; one of the quietest sites of any Capri hostelry; entrance via a 100-yard vine-covered path bordered by cascades of blossoms; full air conditioning; swimming pool. Top first-class (not deluxe) category: 50 rooms; extra-good plumbing in all the better accommodations; somewhat clashy Italian provincial furnishings, but agreeable nonetheless.

★★★★ **Punta Tragara** • a casually sprawling cliff-hugger in persimmon hue, was designed by Le Corbusier. It's at the end of the footpath (about 15 minutes' walk from midvillage) overlooking the majestic Faraglioni. Lovely pool, patio, and multi-tier sun deck; panoramic restaurant; rich to almost heavy furnishings mixed with 16th-century antiques. Eden Rock night club; hydro-massage and other fitness facilities. Sitting on the private balcony at twilight is pure bliss.

★★★ **La Pineta** • also on a viewful spot, is a sweetie. Excellent rooms, some even handsomer than those in the Quisisana; heaven-sent privacy; superb view from the heart of a pinewood facing the sea; lovely pool area with sauna and bar, just right for lunch, surrounded by 1- or 3-bedroom units; breakfast on your terrace (or in the nibble-nook if, saints forbid, it should be raining); beach strip at Marina Piccola with cabanas, provision for watersports and lunching facilities at Gloria's Ristorante delle Sirene.

★★★ **Flora** • is just as nice, with roughtly the same upper-level rates—but it's a smidgen more formal. Both prime for tranquillity and comfort.

★★★ **La Scalinatella** • resides next to La Pineta. It's just as melodic as the sound of its name. With the latest additions, it now embraces 12 suites with terrace, Frigobar, and safe, 16 doubles, 3 singles, air conditioning, no restaurant, an oooolala garden and pool, a bar, a wide lobby. For romancers only.

★★★ **Tiberio Palace** • commands a wonderful vista at one of the most convenient perches on the island; no restaurant; pleasant bar; spick-and-span furniture throughout; air conditioning, radio, and TV.

☆☆ **La Palma** • stands in stacked-arcade fashion in a very central position but with no sea view. Alfresco terrace for sipping and sunning; sauna-solarium complex; wide corridors; superb maintenance. All 80 amply proportioned chambers provide air conditioning, bath or shower, balcony, and Frigobar. The lounge areas—both inside and out—are among the most inviting on the island for comfort.

Regina Cristina • despite the attractive pool it shares with the Villa San Felice, is rather old-fashioned. Present total of 55 bedchambers, all with showers; 27 with terraces; high decibel level; furniture either tiki or taki.

La Residenza • next to the Regina Cristina, comes up with a floorload of late-model pads, plus some of its older traditional units; 16 balconies, and Mother Nature outside your window at her most exquisite.

Gatto Bianco • with many terraces, is a melange of conventional and supermodern decorative concepts. Colorful, maybe even flagrant!

Villa delle Sirene • is a comfortable first-class hotel. Newer floor with 4 suites, large terraces, and simple decor; lounge with lemon-grove vista; flower-filled balcony restaurant; 20 rooms in neighboring annex; clean, attractive, recommendable.

Bellavista • is a sister operation but dull by comparison. Both cater heavily to groups.

Villa Margherita • in second class, offers a lovely quiet garden at its entrance, a neat little lobby, and some excellent rooms with terrace and bath; it is an odds-on choice as a residence house, serves breakfast only.

Pensione Esperia • enlarged and updated, has sensible rates and is good for the bracket.

A'Pazziella • with its splendid garden and thoughtful touches is also for close budgets.

Florida and **Floridiana** are hives for economy package tours. Nix.

Vittoria Pagano • is inexpensive and that's about all.

Pensione Terminus • is a third-class, pocket-size bargain if you don't mind parking at a busy, noisy midcenter address.

Anacapri

★★★★★ **Europa Palace** • is rewriting the deluxe history of Anacapri, the higher ground of this lovely island. The hotel has become pure loveliness since its total reshaping and beauty treatment by Dr. Antonio Cacace, its proprietor and nonstop host. Concierge Eduardo Esposito also is one of the most helpful and savvy of souls to be found at this highest of hotel perches on the isle. There's a grand penthouse suite with its own vast terrace and swimming pool (it's called the *Megaron*), a quartet of vineyard-and-garden suites with their own pools, junior suites with new fine marble baths and viewful balconies, 100 air-conditioned rooms, many with balcony or terrace, the fine Alexander restaurant plus one by the pool, 3 nearby tennis courts, piano bar, and La Cabala nightery. There's also an ultra-chic fitness and beauty center and a new indoor pool. A masterful and enticing renaissance.

Caesar Augustus • on a cliff 1000 feet above the sea, offers one of the most spectacular vistas found in any European hotel. The facilities are ghastly— and that's being charitable.

San Michele • almost across the road, has modern furnishings, a fabulous terrace, and the same disadvantage of this suburban location. A bus stop on the Anacapri-Capri route is immediately outside, however, and this transportation is easy, cheap, and frequent.

RESTAURANTS

First a word about the food, much of which is brought to the island by ship. Fish is mainly frozen—even though you will watch sailors netting their catches from your restaurant terrace. When it is fresh, the price is spine-tingling by the time it reaches your table. Seafood *antipastos* are staples; try local *caciotta* and *maggiorana* cheeses; and don't miss a sip of the Capri liqueur made from laurel.

La Capannina ● *via delle Botteghe 15* ● is always rewarding. The 3 interior dining rooms are lovely, and the patio is beautiful. The house wine, from their own vineyards, is excellent. The prices, while not inexpensive, are competitive. Superb value overall. Closed Wed. and 4 months in winter.

Ai Faraglioni ● *on the footpath called via Camerelle* ● is variable. Scenic, terraces for people watching but staff who seem too casual.

Da Gemma ● perhaps 50 steps up the arch-covered footpath from the Central Plaza, is the artists' and writers' favorite. There are 2 sections, one a year-round tavern and the other a seasonal patio; the former comprises a series of rooms enclosing an open, sunken kitchen.

Da Paolino ● is my favorite for cuisine, but it's a short taxi ride (near Marina Grande). It resides in a lemon grove. Pasta dishes—especially ravioli and spaghetti with raddicio, basil, and cheese—are among the best to be found in the south of Italy.

La Sceriffa ● near the funicular, is also superb for regional yums. Try not to miss it.

Quisisana's ● garden is particularly attractive at night; for indoor munchers, its French restaurant effects elegant tones. The quality of the cuisine is noteworthy; prices are high.

Grotta Verde ● near the funicular base in the port, is strongly *caprese*— rough but fun, with excellent typical cookery and reasonable tabs. Closed Mon.

La Pigna ● *below the taxi rank off the main piazza* ● is a family operation which has everything going for it except the cookery. Shame on the chef.

La Piazetta ● is down at **Piccola Marina,** the sea-bathing pebble beach. The fish is the dish; the vista is intoxicating. There are a few other similar shacks here, but this is the most reliable, in my opinion.

Cucciolo ● is tops in the Blue Grotto region.

Among the outdoor cafes most frequented at the cocktail hour, the **Caffe Caso** seems to draw eager conversationalists while the **Gran Caffe Town and Country** attracts fashionplates; **Piccolo Bar** is more for every *uomo*. **Tiberio** resides in the cellar of a local church; touristic in *extremus*.

SHOPPING

Capri

JEWELRY: **Alberto e Lina-La Campanina** (via Vitt. Emanuele 18) is on the most traveled lane on the island. (The path leads to the Quisisana Hotel.) You'll pass it hundreds of times on your visit—and be tempted at each passing. Their splendid work graces many of the world's celebrities but prices are kept very reasonable since almost all of the inspiration and composition originate from this amiable and enterprising family. Meet the namesake parents and their delightful Filippo and Marioli.

LADIES' AND MEN'S WEAR: **La Parisienne** (on the square), featuring Livio de Simone's inspired apparel, is the acknowledged fashion arbiter. **Caprisport** and **La Petite Parisienne** also capture the flavor of this chic resort. **Yves Dupuis** (via Camerelle) makes his own exciting fashion statement. It seems as if **Canfora** (via Camerelle, across from the Quisisana) has been making sandals since Tiberius took his holidays here. **Chantal** (via Camerelle 10) and **Russo Uomo** stock stylish clothes for Him.

PERFUME: **Carthusia-Profumi di Capri** is the *only* one to visit (3 shops) because no matter what they claim, this is the finest—and the original. (Another latecomer even bills itself as "Profumi originali di Capri".) Carthusia, begun in 1948, employs distilling methods first used by 16th-century Carthusian monks. The scents embrace the floral spectrum of the Mediterranean—"Caprissimo" being one of the most captivating. "Carthusia Lady" gained international acclaim when it launched the 40th anniversary of this house. There are also bolder creations for men. Visit the laboratory-shop at via Matteotti 2A–2B, the boutique at via Camerelle, and the Anacapri shop on via Capodimonte (a.k.a. via San Michele). Forget the rest.

POTTERY AND CERAMICS: **The Sea Gull** (via Roma 25) says it all for garden, conservatory, kitchen, or any household that needs a note of cheer. Ceramic furniture (indoor or outdoor), urns, fountains, wall decorations—even to masks, birds, fruit, and other ornaments.

Anacapri

Mariorita is a playground for shoppers. It's the spacious and tasteful complex at the garden entrance to the deluxe Europa Palace Hotel. Every fashion nuance is here—all the irresistibles from scarves, belts, sweaters, leather; for summer, fall, or spring. Be sure to see the intricate inlaid furniture, the cameos, the fine Capo di Monte porcelain, the pool-and-beachwear. You can combine this with a visit to Villa San Michele or the chairlift to the island's highest peak.

CAMOGLI This is what Portofino must have looked like before tourism flooded in. Every house, chapel, spire and fisherman's hut is a different muted shade of pink, ochre, buff, persimmon, and pastel blue, surrounding a crescent beach of black volcanic sand. Here's an enchanting mix of antiquity, cultures, and sun-burnished *Mare Nostrum* charm. Only one hotel offers first-class comfort and that's the pleasantly creaky **Cenobio dei Dogi** at the nadir of forested hills by the sea. Lovely pool and waterfront terrace. For dining, the **Vento Ariel,** just a hutch over the fishing port, has excellent cuisine, but I found my billings enriched by perhaps 20% beyond the menu prices. The **Gatto Nero** is a worthy alternative, but not quite so romantic. **Golfo Paradiso** is also a worthwhile choice. Next would come **Rosa** on a balcony facing the frontage. **Bar Primula,** overlooking the pebbled beach is where everyone goes for ice cream and coffee. Renato has several times been voted the nation's best barman. His ices are famous. The nearest exit to Camogli from the *autostrada* is **Recco.** If you can, rent a fishing smack and cruise around the cliffs to *San Fruttuoso* in the Tigul-lio Gulf, one of the most exotic excursions you can have in the district.

CERNOBBIO (LAKE COMO)

★★★★★ **Villa d'Este** • is world famous. Built in A.D. 1568 as a private residence for Cardinal Tolomeo Gallio and later occupied by the Dowager Em-press of Russia, the Princess of Wales, the Princess Torlonia, and other no-tables, it has been operated as a hotel since 1873. Alas, more than a century later, a frightening number of bus tours have "discovered" it. About 110 rooms in the main building; 51 comfortized ones in the neighboring annex; a quartet of junior suites plus many upgraded standard units; terrace restaurant; glorious setting; 6 tennis courts and 1 for squash; nearby 18-hole golf course; heated pool with 2-style saunas and gym; outdoor restaurant for bathers; private beach; horses available; slot-car track; nightclub plus discotheque; woody grill in the Sporting Club for informal meals; open early-April to late-October.

Regina Olga • is a pleasant alternate choice; much less expensive too.

COMO, of course, is the pivotal town of the Italian Lake District.

Barchetta Excelsior • is a highly inviting medium-priced stop. Piazza lo-cation facing the water; modern building; sidewalk cafe; 80 sky-bright func-tional rooms, all with cramped baths or showers; very clean and now quite a good buy.

Villa Flori • has come up notably under the guidance of Antonello Pas-sera, a talented professional who is performing wonders of restoration in this elegant converted home. Most units overlook the lake, many with balconies; the Raimondi restaurant boasts a bit of fame locally.

Como • sited in the center, is a sound bet for those who don't like too much Como-tion.

Metropole e Suisse ● is a fine investment in second-class. The piazza setting faces the lake.

A bit to the east is *Lake Garda,* with its charming lakeside **Locanda San Vigilio** (only 7 rooms in which a long list of celebrities have stayed), the **Grand Fasano** (once an estate of the Habsburgs), and **Villa del Sogno** (also on the Gardone Riviera). All are intimate, tasteful, and tranquil.

CORTINA D'AMPEZZO

This is the most lively, fashionable, and sporting of the Dolomite resorts— the unusually beautiful mountain range that rises to slender spires surrounding this vale. Topographically, it comprises rare and dramatic scenery. The skiing is superb; so is the hiking in summer. After April prices sink by at least 30%.

☆☆☆☆ **Miramonti Majestic** is sited in an outskirts situation surrounded by a golf course, tennis facilities, fitness and beauty salons, indoor swimming pool, and the well-tempered chords in the Tiger Club; excellent grill; 130 spacious accommodations, most with balcony; open mid-Dec. to March, and June to Sept. Very good indeed.

☆☆☆☆ **Cristallo Palace** ● is another fine choice. Except for a golf course, it has all the recreational features of the Miramonti, plus an outdoor pool. Complement of 98 rooms with Tyrolean decor; 90% with private balcony; operative from mid-Dec. to Mar. and from June to Sept. This CIGA-chain hotel is in many ways warmer and more friendly than the M-M.

☆☆ **Savoia** ● is a merry address with 2 buildings, connected by a tunnel under the main street; roof-terrace with pool; tennis; rustic grill. Lively and gaily traditional.

Corona ● picked by many discriminating wanderers—is in a special category. It is more of a high-grade, expensive guesthouse rather than a conventional hotel. It's filled with costly contemporary paintings. Chalet-style exterior; 64 rooms; 40 with bath or shower.

De la Poste ● is fresh, popular, and worth the outlay of close to $80 to $160 per person, all meals included. The chalet style is particularly attractive.

Europa ● remains open all year. Rooms about as tight as the inside of a ski boot; good food in its below-stairs restaurant. Central and very good.

Splendid Venezia ● just a few doors away, is a smart buy if you can snatch one of its back-corner doubles with balcony. Fine for the price.

Menardi • should be ranked in a higher official status, but the owner prefers it to remain a quiet "sleeper" value at budget rates. Excellent dining room; 41 units; spotless maintenance.

Ampezzo • is another bargain, despite its growing age. Like most of the above, it is open all year.

FLORENCE

Florence is the Athens of Italy. The metropolis is aburst with works of art bearing such signatures as Fra Angelico, Michelangelo, Botticelli, Donatello, Ghiberti, Cellini, and Leonardo da Vinci. Unlike in Rome, you can easily walk to almost every major monument or attraction in this gracious center of culture. (A good thing, too, since cars of non-residents are being banned from midcity.) Italian museum hours change more often than the temperature, so always inquire before setting out for the day.

ATTRACTIONS

Piazzale Michelangelo • *At the end of the viale dei Colli* • On a hilltop on the opposite bank of the Arno from the bulk of Florence, the Piazzale Michelangelo, with its copy of *David,* affords a fine panorama of the city.

Duomo (Santa Maria del Fiore) • *piazza del Duomo* • When you try to picture Florence in your mind's eye, the towering dome of Santa Maria del Fiore is bound to dominate your picture, as it does this glorious city. One of the largest cathedrals in the world, the building was begun in 1296 and is a composite of many contributing architects. Don't miss Michelangelo's *Pieta,* in the nearby Museo dell'Opera del Duomo. The church offers two lookout points with incomparable vistas of Florence: one is the unique **campanile** designed by Giotto; the other is atop Brunelleschi's 90-meter-high dome.

Baptistry of St. John the Baptist • *piazza del Duomo and piazza San Giovanni* • It is famous not only for its geometric form and the marvelous black-and-white marble revetment of the facade, but also for three doors: the bronze-paneled eastern door known as the "Door of Paradise," (Ghiberti's masterpiece, 1425–1452); the northern door also by Ghiberti, and the southern door

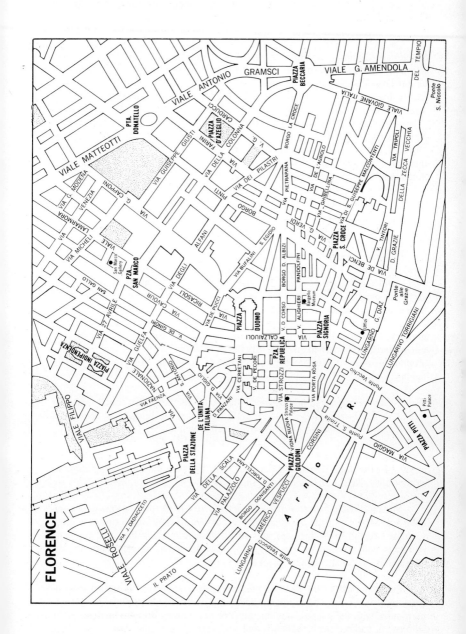

by Andrea Pisano (1336). Some of the original panels are in the nearby **Museo Opera del Duomo.**

Cappelle Medici • *Medici Chapels, piazza di Madonna degli Aldo brandini* • Adjoining the presbytry of San Lorenzo, these consist of the **Princes' Chapel,** an elaborate baroque mausoleum containing the tombs of six Medici Grand Dukes and built on an octagonal plan, and the so-called **New Sacristy** (Sagrestia Nuova), built by Michelangelo (1520–1557) to complement Brunelleschi's "Old" Sacristy in San Lorenzo. Begun in 1604, the domed Princes' Chapel is decorated with semiprecious stones, marbles, and gilt bronzes. The New Sacristy has Michelangelo's famous sculptured tombs: that of Lorenzo, Duke of Urbino, and of Giuliano, Duke of Nemours. The artist also began a monument for Lorenzo the Magnificent but finished only the sculpture of "Madonna and Child," which you'll see on display.

Galleria dell'Accademia • *Academy Gallery, via Ricasoli 60* • Here you'll find Michelangelo's *David* and other sculpture as well as paintings by Florentine artists from the 13th through 16th centuries.

Palazzo Vecchio (Palazzo della Signoria) • *piazza della Signoria* • Constructed between 1298 and 1314, the Palazzo Vecchio was once a Medici residence and the seat of government. The exterior, with its slender tower jutting above an overhanging battlemented gallery, is a monument to the secular life of medieval and Renaissance Florence. In contrast to the austere facade, the interior of the palazzo contains lavishly decorated rooms. The largest and most important is the Salone dei Cinquecento (The Hall of the Five Hundred). The gilt coffered ceiling is filled with frescoes—huge frescoes adorn the walls, and around the sides of the chamber are sculptures, including Michelangelo's "Genius of Victory."

Ponte Vecchio • It first spanned the Arno in the 10th century and was rebuilt in the 14th century. Since the 16th century, the bridge has been lined with shops that specialize in gold, silver, and jewelry.

Palazzo Strozzi • *Strozzi Palace via Tornabuoni* • Here's a classic example of Florentine Renaissance architecture. Today it's used for important art exhibitions, like the *Biennale dell' Antiquariato.*

Museo di San Marco • *Museum of St. Mark (Fra Angelico Museum), piazza San Marco* • Inside the Renaissance convent of San Marco that was renovated and rebuilt by Michelozzo, this small museum contains the most important paintings and frescoes of Fra Angelico, who decorated its cells and cloister. Ghirlandaio's "Last Supper" is set here too.

Palazzo Pitti • *Pitti Palace, piazza Pitti* • Brunelleschi designed this architectural boast for Luca Pitti, an adversary of the Medici family. Grafted to harmonize with the palazzo, the magnificent and famous **Boboli Garden,** which adjoins, is adorned with fountains and sculpture. Today, the Pitti houses three museums: the **Galleria d'Arte Moderna** (Gallery of Modern Art); the **Galleria**

Palatina (Raphael, Titian, Lippi, Veronese, and others); and the **Museo degli Argenti** (Jewel Museum), filled with Medici acquisitions and containing the Medici living quarters—more's the Pitti! In July and August, there are evening concerts in the palazzo courtyard.

Galleria degli Uffizi ● *Uffizi Gallery, loggiato degli Uffizi* ● The museum contains the full range of Italian painting through the Renaissance. Among its most famous holdings is Botticelli's "Birth of Venus," plus antique sculpture, works by Durer, Rembrandt, Rubens, El Greco, Goya, and Cranach, and a collection of self-portraits in the Vasari Corridor.

Galleria Corsini ● *via di Parione 11* ● This baroque palazzo contains the most significant private collection in Florence: works by Lippi, Raphael, Hans Memling, Andrea del Sarto, and others. Visits are by appointment only, so phone 55/218994 for viewing Mon., Wed., or Fri. from 2:30 p.m. to 5:30 p.m.

Markets ● The **Straw Market** in the 16th-century Loggia del Mercato Nuovo (near the Palazzo di Parte Guelfa) offers straw and raffia items as well as leather. The big market is the **Centrale** on the Borgo San Lorenzo; morning is the time to go. An interesting fruit and vegetable patch at **Piazza Santo Spirito** functions until around noon every day but Sun. Among the line of pushcarts along the **via dell'Ariento** (near the Medici Chapels), the bulky fishermen's pullovers and cardigans and other sweaters have mixtures of wool and synthetic yarns that enable them to stretch. This market is closed on Sun. The **Flea Market** is at piazza dei Ciompi near the loggia del Pesce, which was the fish market of the 16th century; closed Sunday.

Excursions

Fiesole ● *just beyond Florence on a hillside* ● In ancient times the site of an Etruscan community and then a Roman town, it is less than a ½ hour by bus from piazza San Marco. After visiting the 11th-century cathedral, it's a short walk to the Roman amphitheater, still in use during the Fiesole Summer Festival (June–Aug.). The walls of the old Etruscan town are still in evidence. For hotels see the "Outskirts" report further along.

HOTELS

Please refer to "About the Stars" for my personal (not official) ratings of hotels and restaurants.

☆☆☆☆☆ **Excelsior** ● boasts many rooms and suites among the loveliest in Europe; of the latter, each outside charmer with its own massive penthouse terrace overlooking the Arno or a townscape of gloriously untouched antiquity; Donatello Bar with buffet service, very popular; rooftop patio for sipping and dining; enchanting and viewful barbecue area. This 5-star show is run with vigor and savvy by softspoken Paolo Guaneri.

☆☆☆☆☆ **The Grand** • *across the piazza Organissanti from the Excelsior* • is owned by the same great hotel chain as the Excelsior. It had been restored in part, offering about 36 rooms, a winter garden, and a restaurant. Still thriving and obviously still growing.

☆☆☆☆☆ **Regency** • *piazza M. d'Azeglio 3* • is a poetic and elegant little house of only 31 rooms; Mussolini's sister once lived here in what remains the finest residential district of Florence. It is fronted by a park which is close to the romantic Donatello Cemetery. While space is limited and there's no elevator, the decor is so strikingly beautiful that few could carp at such trifles. Patrician main salon with crystal chandelier, stain-glass panels and textiled walls; courtly lounge; rich, darkwood-paneled dining room with fine china on casement shelves; delicate flower-dotted table settings; comfortably furnished accommodations with homey atmosphere; extensive use of mirrors to effect an air of greater space both in the main house and gardenside annex. Unique and not for everyone, but with qualities that are unmatched in large establishments.

☆☆☆☆ **Villa Medici** • always with distinctive physical charm, once-again boasts deluxe-level service standards to match its eloquent architectural and decorative graces. Air-conditioned; lobby glowing with fresh flowers; more than 100 comfortable quarters all with bath or shower, some in traditional style and some very assertively modern, so be sure to specify your wishes; captivatingly landscaped street-level pool and garden with buffet lunch served (which gives this hotel added cache in summertime). The back rooms and penthouse perches command the best view and most tasteful decor. A building worthy of any modern-day Medici.

★★★★ **Torre di Bellosguardo** • *via Roti Michelozzi 2* • is across the river, out Porta Romano, on a hillside overlooking the gems of Tuscany. A noble house with ancient tower; vaulted gallery and salon; painted ceilings; deeply inset windows; many four-poster beds. The walled garden is an added fillip of patrician calm.

★★★★ **Villa Cora** • *in a park above the town* • offers a dinner-only restaurant (flanked by a swimming pool), a tavern, and 56 fully-bathed accommodations which are very beautifully furnished. The frescoed ceilings and public sancta are marvels of their time and a joy to observe. The large suite #333 is perfect for family use. The concierge is one of the city's finest.

☆☆ **Savoy** • is a fine but not too exciting midtown *palazzo;* high-ceiling corridors; spacious dimensions; air conditioning; walnut, mahogany, or painted Venetian-style furnishings; all baths renewed nicely; liberal scattering of antiques and ancient chandeliers, bar and dining room rather heavy and old-fashioned. Back rooms are best for quiet.

★★★ **Brunelleschi** • is a young hotel in a Renaissance robe. There's also a Byzantine tower (housing a breakfast nook), a bar with piano tinkling, a dullish restaurant, antique bricks and polished open beams. The 94 bedchambers are in schemes of green, orange, and cream; very good baths with marble-top basins; air conditioning. A convenient and historic midtown location.

☆ **Jolly-Carlton** • maintains a firm footing at the entrance to Cascine Park. Unquestionably, the reasonable tariffs and contemporary luxury amenities give it a special demand status. Spectacular, modernistic lobby; glorious 6th-floor roof garden for alfresco apertifs, backed by 2 glass-fronted interior restaurants and bars for service year round; open-air 7th-floor pool and sun terrace; austere main dining room with open spit and a chef under the tallest cap in Tuscany. All 145 units with bath, air conditioning, piped music; 32 good-size front doubles with balcony, alcove, bathroom, and lavatory. As a guideline for preference when booking, the 3rd-floor units are modernistic in decor, while all other levels are traditional.

★★★ **Lungarno** • is a beauty. Its extra-choice situation beside the Arno, a few steps from the Ponte Vecchio, possibly makes it the most expensive real estate anywhere on the river. Of 70 accommodations, 22 suites, including one atop the 13th-century stone tower; some excellent balconied riverfront units; back rooms disgracefully small, as are many other pockets of this miniminded house; cozy bar but no restaurant. Very colorful, tasteful, and comfortable if you pick a proper-size habitat.

☆ **Kraft** • offers most rooms with balcony and these are best. Air conditioned; efficient units with good baths. Roof terrace with panoramic view and swimming pool; fair dining salon; management has brought this house up again after a spell of listlessness.

☆ **Michelangelo** • a hypermodernistic 140-room structure, goes all out to say it is with it, *really* with it! Corridor floors, walls, even doors, are carpeted in the same gray-brown wool that cloaks the bedrooms; beds have sleek striped spreads; prints provide color; all in all it is a creature of its time—from small baths to a plenitude of panache. Units on first and second levels with private terrace.

☆ **Park Palace** • is lord of its hilltop. Total of 21 units in main building and 9 in the annex; private baths and air conditioning throughout; swimming pool; downstairs Taverna restaurant and bar adjoining. While each ingredient is attractive, it doesn't seem to jell as a whole. You may prefer this at lunch rather than for overnight.

★★ **Porta Rossa** • is the city's oldest hotel—and so it appears. Comfort is adequate, but chiefly you go for the unique atmosphere, which cannot be duplicated in modern hostelries. It's in midcity, so some rooms could be clamorous.

Berchielli ● cheerfully greets guests with a black and white polished marble lobby; good space concepts and fresh appearance; colorful baths. A worthwhile investment, close to the major sights.

Minerva ● very central and with a pleasant piazza in front, comes up with 85 doubles with bath and 35 with shower. Cool-ish lobby; attractive restaurant with glassed-in garden; coffee shop; air-conditioned; topside pool; interior wall surfacing of harsh and dismal marble-dust gesso; front units more spacious but noisy; newer wing, overlooking a quiet cloister, with cell-size sleeping quarters. Overall verdict? Fair.

Astoria Pullman ● has increasingly stiffer tariffs for spotty rewards. The palatial breakfast room is one of the most spectacular one can imagine. (Instead of "Breakfast at Tiffany's," it suggests "Eggs Benedict in the Sistine Chapel.") Your happiness here will depend on the room you take since quite a few are cramped and dark; others, however, are grand.

Plaza Lucchesi ● *up the Arno near Santa Croce Church* ● has an entrance in glass and brass. Top marks in maintenance; cordiality from every staffer. Getting better.

☆☆ **Anglo-Americano** ● is an old-timer that still has flair. The stately reception corridor and entry hall set its tone of dignity and warmth. Hospitable welcome; 40 floral-tile baths (almost a full ratio now); 35 rooms very handsomely furnished; beds in gold leaf or white; serene. More a made-over homestead than a metropolitan hotel.

Continental ● fully air-chilled, is sited beside the Arno. One of the most romantic little 12th-century tower suites in Christendom; roof garden plus bar and breakfast room; no dining facilities; plunked smack in the center of the city's worst traffic snarl. Not bad for pedestrians and the slightly deaf.

Augustus ● with 71 rooms, nestles beside its *sorella,* tucked slightly off the main drag. Again, no restaurant; sunken, Nordic-style modern bar under a gently arched white ceiling; self-control air conditioning (which aids as well in sound proofing); singles with showers; all twins with baths.

Londra ● is in the same group as the Minerva; public space is appealing; accommodations somewhat restricted.

Principe ● is just adequate. Arno-sited; 24 rooms with bath; centrally air-conditioned.

OUTSKIRTS:

★★★★★ **Villa San Michele** ● *at Fiesole, 4 miles out of town, overlooking the Arno and the Florentine valley* ● has been expensively and oh-so-generously refashioned by the stellar Cipriani doges of Venice. This one is a tastefully converted 15th-century monastery originally designed by Michelangelo. The garden, with its waterfall and pool area, is surrounded by 200-year-old oaks. Splendid panorama; a guest book that boasts more blue blood than the registry for a royal coronation. Its 27 variegated bedrooms, all with bath and all former cells, have been lavishly and comfortably outfitted. Many units with working fireplaces; fine frescoes and oils as well as antique furnishings; presidential suite at $800 including half-board; junior suites around $350. Here is a Deluxe bell ringer (sweetly muffled, of course). The hotel provides a bus shuttle to Florence if you don't wish to drive. Once autumn begins, inquire if it is open before going up.

★★★ **Villa La Massa** has gained an ardent following as a country-estate-type hotel in neighboring *Candeli*. The rooms are comfortable, immaculate, and tastefully furnished. Engaging dining salon; sleekly rustic, blue-clad-and-gold-gilt, October-to-May La Cave nightclub for cellar-brations; touch-ups numerous and well done. There's a tiny pool, and anglers can borrow the gardener's pole for compleat relaxation on the Arno banks. The best route for the "carriage trade" to reach it is by the Viale Europa, not the Lungarno.

Relais Certosa ● in *Certosa* at the edge of Florence on the route to Siena ● nestles into an open park setting; arched ceilings in many units; antique-style furnishings; 4 tennis courts; pool. Okay, especially for the view of Certosa Monastery looming above.

~~~~~~

RESTAURANTS

☆☆☆☆ **Enoteca Pinchiorri** ● *via Ghibellina 87* ● has gained international acclaim for its spotlight on wines; gastronomy is also generally praised. On a very recent visit, I found the service spotty and an attitude that seemed to suggest that Americans all arrive directly from Hicks-ville. In any case, my meal (food and beverage) was fine. The house presents its brace of elegant salons in a dignified town house where refined polychrome mouldings surround the ceilings. Homespun effects incorporating plants, a hearth, aristocratic stemware, and even colorful Majorlica porcelain are evocative of high times and old times— only the cuisine is nouvelle. A mere 10 tables, supervised by Giorgio Pinchiorri and Annie Feolden; generous variety in both its gustatory presentations as well as from its 60,000-bottle cave. If you order a landmark vintage, request that the opening of the bottle be done at tableside, a practice that is customary where wines are costly. Closed Sundays—as are most of the following restaurants.

☆☆ **Al Lume di Candela** ● *via delle Terme 23* ● is a long, inviting room with a bar at its entry, walls paneled in a rough wool twill, beamed ceilings, candle beams and beaming customers. The Franco-Italian culinary efforts were commendable—especially the pasta mixed with shellfish; duck with orange sauce also was something to quack about.

☆ **Oliviero** • *via della Terme 51R* • is a 3-room string of nooks, the first containing a bar and melodious piano tinkler and the next pair for calories only; flamingo-hued cloths on extra-tiny tables; matching banquettes; greengage textiled walls; coffered ceilings. Very attentive service. Substantial, miles from cheap, and moderately elegant, but not a true aristocrat in any sense.

☆ **Sabatini** • *via Panzani 41* • is a local classsic carefully run by proprietor Angelo Schiavi. The interior has always been an attractive, busy, rambling affair that first looks nice but pales under the too-bright-lights. The panzarotti alla Sabatini is a luscious hot cheese and pasta starter. Don't tell anyone but the chef is in love with his salt shaker. Waiters seem to push the high-price items. Closed Mon.

☆ **Harry's Bar** • *lungarno Amerigo Vespucci 22R* • is a Florentine landmark; it's only a long olive-pit throw from the Excelsior. Still small, still intimate, still cozy. The waiters are now all Harry's since they bought the original out; happily they have maintained their mandate on quality. Animated, cosmopolitan, fun. Closed Sun. and Dec. 20 to Jan. 15.

☆ **Pierrot** • *piazza Taddeo Gaddi 25R* • does magical things with fish, especially the mixed grill or sole and a splendid octopus salad; grilled mushrooms also are delicious accompanied by Russiz Superiore. If you have questions, ask amiable Enrico Bolognini, one of the brightest lights in Italian gastronomy and oenology. He's always on hand.

★ **Cantine Antinori** • *piazza Antinori* • is on an offshoot of via Tornabuoni, a courtyard and palace of the chianti moguls who have created this nook as a showcase for their excellent wines. Ground floor plus balcony with a few tables; moderate-priced food of the region with which you can sip some delicious vintages; friendly woody atmosphere in an historic building. A reasonable choice if you are sightseeing near the Duomo or browsing along Florence's main shopping via. It's a pity it closes over the weekends.

★ **Bordino** • *via Stracciatella 9R* • is a gladsome hideaway peeping under richly bold stone and stucco vaults, beckoning with soft illumination, and displaying appetizing and artistic culinary spreads on a central table. Ceramics, wrought-iron, banners, and cooking utensils deck the walls. It is so Tuscan down to its toenails that it is built right into the foundations of the town in a square that nudges the Ponte Vecchio. Regional cuisine; outstanding red wine; closed July, also Sun. Highly appealing for color, antiquity, and value.

Icche C'E' C'E' • *via Magalotti 11R* • is one of the most honest, forthright, and altogether pleasing trattorias I know in Italy. There is nothing spectacular about it, but Tuscans love it and its cuisine—as do I. Not expensive but awfully good.

Giovacchino • *via dei Tosinghi 34R* • is noted for its roasts. Self-service downstairs; dancing on the upper level. Fast service and often packed with Americans.

Corsini • *Lungarno Corsini 4, next to the British Consulate* • is in the experienced hands of Mario Pucci, who used to be *maitre* at the world-famous Doney. Now working for himself, his smiles are even wider. High-vaulted salon; air-conditioned; try *risotto con frutti di mare;* closed Mon., but open Sun. Reliable cookery at reasonable prices.

Ottorino • *via delle Oche 12–16R* • near the Duomo, is a linkage of interesting stone-lined rooms, but otherwise not very decorative. The "hay & straw," carpaccio and skewered mozarella garnished with toasted anchovy are splendid. Moderate price tags.

Alla Vecchia Bettola • *viale L. Ariosto 32* • is well-known to well-fed Tuscan families. Try the mortadella combinations or alone (Bologna style) and the stuffed chicken as well as the veal stew. Cuisine that sounds heavy and rich but is easy to digest.

Buca Mario • *piazza Ottaviani 16* • should give you a good dinner for a low tab. Three rooms in cellar; clean, attractive, and plain; heavy local trade; increasingly popular with foreign visitors. Closed Wed.

Buca dell' Orafo • *"Goldsmith," tucked in behind the Ponte Vecchio* • is a family *trattoria* with savory cookery. It has continued to improve to the point that it is now frequented by the elite of Tuscany and their guests. Only a dozen tables; no decor; specialties include stracciatella alla buccia di limone, bistecca alla fiorentina, bollito, and stracotto. An amiable choice, but never on Sun. or Mon.

Sostanza • *behind the Excelsior at via della Porcellana* • is a highly touted *trattoria* among Florentines. Rough, amusing atmosphere; go noonish for lunch or at 7 p.m. or 10 p.m. for dinner, to avoid the peak of the throng; otherwise it's frenzy in Firenze. Best bets were the breast of chicken, local beefsteak that is enormous and vegetable soup. A popular stop. Closed Sat.

Taverna del Bronzino • *via delle Ruote 25R* • was Bronzino's home and his home-cooking has hardly changed here since the 16th century. In autumn the Italians go manic for its mushrooms (very few tourists); authentic and rewarding. Closed Sun.

Ruggero • *near the Roman Gate* • is another trattoria that trades well on its honest, no-nonsense fare. Traditional T-bone steak and *bollito* (boiled meats) are staples. Prices are moderate.

★★★★ **La Loggia** • *at piazzale Michelangelo* • is a municipally owned century-old former art gallery. Its dramatic hillside site commands a 180° panorama of the city. Alfresco terrace lunching or dining among portico columns or an open patio bordered by stone balustrade; about 90 tables; pleasant, small glassed-in restaurant for wintertime. As a capricious little fillip, you may ride by carriage to this happy spot. Enchanting—*if* a surfeit of tour groups doesn't spoil the atmosphere. Closed Wed.

Camillo • *borgo San Jacopo 57–59R* • remains one of the most talked-about and visited trattorias. Throngs of U.S. buyers continue to pour in here; they are on generous expense accounts or being treated by rich Florentine purveyors. While the prices knock it out of the *trattoria* league, the atmosphere is still that of a rough-and-tumble hash-house. The food can be outstanding, especially if you arrive with somebody who is known to the management. On Wed. and Thurs. it is shuttered.

Mamma Gina • *from Camillo* • a few doors away is more of the same, but I usually prefer the cooking here to Camillo's variable style.

Otello • *near the station* • often a host to tour groups, is for those with the appetite of a ravenous panther, and the stomach of a hippo. A barrage of howitzers couldn't be noisier—but that Big Gun in the kitchen couldn't possibly mow you down with a more walloping charge of fodder. Even the pepper mills are 5-feet tall! Sit in the hut-style room. It won't be the best meal you've ever devoured, and far from the cheapest, but I'll bet you a wheel of Gorgonzola it'll probably be the biggest. Closed Thurs.

La Rucola • *via del Leone 50* • does its cooking in the Florentine way; it does it very well indeed—every day but Sunday. There's a garden and a dull interior room. What matters is on the plate and that's splendid.

Al Campidoglio • *via del Campidoglio 8R* • *can* have fine vittles and service to match. But when it's crowded, it's a different story: hurry-hurry, busy-busy, gobble-gobble, brrrrp-brrrrp. Rest on Tues.

Mario • *on the main square, in Fiesole* • served the best fare locally. It's very inexpensive; the view (why you came) does not exist. Ask to sit in the upstairs dining room in winter and the courtyard garden in summer. Also closed on Tues.

★★★★ **Villa San Michele** • (see ''Hotels'') is by far the top restaurant in Fiesole. It is also the most expensive. But the summer view from the terrace is matchless, the service is impeccable, and the cuisine is among the finest deluxe offerings in the nation.

★★★ **Vecciolino** • requires a car too. But the trip (10 min.) is worth it. Rustic glass-lined terrace; inner hall with farm tack and forestry tools; colossal antipasto table (about 50 choices!); hams hanging from rafters; shelves of cheese, sweets, pies, custards, and fruit. A brilliant performance by its kind and helpful owner. Drive to **Monte Morello (Sesto Fiorentino)** and take the hilly road to **Colli Alti.** Marvelous and inexpensive.

NIGHT LIFE

The city's darkling hours are darkling even more; nightclubs are sparser and sparser in this city. **Jackie-O** remains the heartthrob for the bar-and-disco set. **La Cave,** in the Hotel Villa La Massa (Candeli), is sophisticated. **Full Up** currently is the fullest straight discotheque. Comfortable and highly agreeable for its type. **Space Electronic** is the leading edge when it comes to mod sounds. **Energia,** going the other direction, is agreeable as a piano bar. The **River Club** is well located, but no longer recommended. As night clubs go, **La Caditale** is probably the better choice. **Arcadia** lifts spirits with its piano bar, cabaret, and disco doin's. Closed Aug. 1 to Sept. 15.

SHOPPING

SHOPPING HOURS: 9–9:30 a.m. to 1 p.m. and 3:30–7:30 p.m., Mon. closing; summertime 4–8 p.m., with closures on Sat. afternoons instead of Mon. mornings.

BEST AREAS: Along the Arno (Lungarno Corsini, Lungarno Acciaiuoli); on the Ponte Vecchio; along streets running from the Ponte Vecchio toward the Duomo such as: Via Por S. Maria, Borgo S.Apostoli, Via Porta Rossa, Via Calimala and Via Calzaiuoli; from Piazza S. Trinita along Via Tornabuoni to Piazza Antinori; on the other side of the Arno, the Borgo S. Jacopo and Via Guicciardini.

ALABASTER, MOSAIC, AND SEMIPRECIOUS STONE OEUVRES: **Balatresi** (Lungarno Acciaioli 22 R) is so fascinatingly different that no one should fail to visit here. Lots of their treasures are one-of-a-kind. Head first for their eye-popping alabaster collection, all created by skilled craftsmen exclusively for them. Also importantly featured are magnificent pieces in hard stones such as malachite, lapis lazuli, rodonite, and other specimens, as well as exquisite enamelware including the famous Faberge reproductions. The crown jewels of their vast array are the gorgeous original works of art which are sold only here, such as those created by the last pair of great Florentine mosaicists alive today. Proprietor Umberto Balatresi, his wife Giovanna, and his sister Daniela are totally trustworthy. As a bonus, these dedicated experts take delight in giving geology lessons on whatever objects intrigue their customers. Safe shipment is made to anywhere in the world; their guarantee is their sacred bond.

ANTIQUES: **Via de' Fossi** (cheaper) and **Via Maggio** are the best streets—but take care!

BELTS: **Infinity** (Borgo SS. Apostoli 18A) hugs your waist in an unforgettable way, decorating the leather with copper, brass, silver (coins too), turquoise, and numerous other elements. From casual use to ultra-high-fashion themes, this is a place to visit, especially since it is situated in a fascinating 14th-century tower near the Ponte Vecchio.

BOUTIQUES: **Raspini** and **Beltrami** (both on Via Calzaiuoli) offer the latest in chic and trendy Italian fashions. The multinational operation called **Benetton** (Via Calimala) has inexpensive sweaters and trousers in great crayon colors. You'll find their shops in every major European city now with branches in the States as well.

BRIONI FASHIONS: **Brioni** (via Calimala 22R) has come to Florence! Now if you are traveling between here and the capital you can arrange all sorts of extra appointments, fittings, and pamperings. The stocks are superb. (See ''Rome.'')

CRYSTAL, PORCELAIN, AND STERLING: **Armando Poggi** (Via Calzaiuoli 105R and 116R) carries all the great world-class brands in these various fields. Poggi does its own silver designs too; everything for the fine home and gifts at all price levels; savings from 30–50% of U.S. tabs for the exact same wares.

EMBROIDERIES: **Cirri** (Via Por Santa Maria 38–40R) has enchanting babies' and children's wear, lingerie, linens and handkerchiefs. As a second choice, the **Rifredi School of Embroidery** (Via Carlo Bini 29) is a 10-minute ride from town.

FLORENTINE-STYLE PAPER PRODUCTS: **Il Papiro** (Via Cavour 55R) has a wide selection of articles bound in this unique and decorative covering. At **Giulio Giannini & Figlio** (Piazza Pitti 36–37r.) and **Bottega Artigiana del Libro** (Lungarno Corsini 38–40r.), there's so much to choose from that you'll wonder if you should buy another suitcase first.

GALLERIES: **Masini** usually offers the best selection of paintings at reasonable tariffs. Handsome salons at piazza Gololoni 6R; excellent reputation.

GIFTS: **Ducci** (Lungarno Corsini 24R) One of the great collections of Alinari reproductions of masterpiece paintings—on boxes, trays, lampshades, and platters. Fabulous, inventive carvings in wood; items in leather and stone; variety in several media. **Tarzia** (Piazza dei Pitti 32R) leans more toward tables, office, den, and garden decorations; cheerful artisanry applied to bronze models of animals.

GLOVES: **Madova** (Via Guicciardini 1R) and **Chris Gloves** (Por Santa Maria 42R) are both excellent and will handle all the mailing of your purchases back home.

JEWELRY: Try **Aurum** (on Lungarno Corsini between John F. and Miraposa), which carries gold and silver items plus precious and semiprecious stones. Much of it is in the distinctive Florentine style and finish, some in Etruscan, a lot in a wide variety of contemporary and classic moods. Director Domenico Palomba also can make up special designs for you personally.

KNITWEAR AND SILK DRESSES: **Romei Boutique** (Lungarno Acciaioli 32-R) is a bijou which is the highly successful creation and namesake of an enormously talented queen of local knitwear, Lori Romei. These as well as her wools, silks, cottons, linens, and certain accessories are designed and manufactured through her own virtuosity; when you buy here you'll automatically get wholesale prices with which nobody else can begin to compete.

LADIES' SHOES: **Lilly of Florence** (Via Guicciardini 2R) is one of the best bets—and bargains—within 7 leagues of the Arno. These shops are the sole distributor of world-famous Sesto Meucci and Petra designs; the dressier ''Lily of Florence'' line is also featured, as well as Switzerland's celebrated Bally assemblage for men. All U.S. sizes; tariffs which run 30% to 50% less than those you'd pay back home.

HIGH-FASHION LEATHER: **John F.** (Lungarno Corsini 2)—this family firm wins this sweepstakes in a walk. Here in its section of a historic *palazzo* is a small, intimate, and convivial reserve of a broad and ultrafashionable range of handbags, attache cases, leather coats and jackets exclusively made for this shop, as well as small leather articles. The craftsmanship is superb—and all merchandise is at ⅓ of their U.S. and Canadian prices!

MAJOLICA CERAMICS AND ITALIAN HANDICRAFTS: **Soc. A. Menegatti & Co.** (Piazza del Pesce 2R, close to the Ponte Vecchio) and **S.E.L.A.N.** (Via Porta Rossa 107–113R) offer good browsing.

MARKETS: The charming **"New" Market** (Porta Rossa and Santa Maria) and the **San Lorenzo "Central" Market** are good for strolling and casual buying. The rather poor **Flea Market** (Piazza Ciompi) operates from Mon. through Sat.

SILVER: **Sacchi** (Lungarno Acciauoli 82R), while absolutely tops, has items at every price level: frames, candlesticks, trays, pillboxes, plus goldsmithery and works in semiprecious stones. Tell them I sent you.

GENOA (Genova) is perhaps the least publicized and visited center in the country. It's suffering from a continuing depression of its overall economy, but urban renewal, a new airport, and a boost in its economy could turn things around. As a commercial port and industrial hub, it is not one of the nation's major tourist attractions. From the time it rivaled Venice as an independent maritime republic, *La Superba,* as it was labeled, retains art treasures waiting to be rediscovered by today's public.

Colombia, once the undisputed leader, may soon reopen after total reconstruction.

Starhotel President • is a new 200-room candidate that will be functioning for your arrival.

Eliseo • also has caught the renewal fever, so by the time you are traveling, you'll probably have a reasonable choice.

Savoy-Majestic is now quite a bit better; it is followed by the sister operation, **Londra Continentale.**

Plaza, centrally but quietly situated, provides appealing shelter with a small hint of luxury.

Bristol Palace is a living period piece; the baths on the 2nd floor, for example, could be in a showcase of Italian design crafts; they are so dated, but so beautiful. Public rooms vary between tasteful opulence and gaudy neon color schemes in plastic textiles; its 6-person white Formica elevator must have been built for a dozen Goliaths; it's the biggest seen outside of the U.S.S. *Enterprise.* If you enjoy indoor tennis, push aside the easy chair in room #244 and you should have just about enough space.

Restaurants

Giacomo • *Corso Italia 1* • is modern, well above average in price, well above average in quality, and featuring careful attention by a friendly staff. There's a tendency toward contemporary concepts in cooking.

Zeffirino • *via XX Settembre 20* • still draws the local cognoscenti—and those Genoese know their vittles. Some prefer the upstairs section, which offers live music; others for the plain and rustic downstairs feedery. Vast open-for-the-eye wildlife refrigerator at entrance; yawning tile oven where the game sizzles gamely; boar, venison, or other season-only choices aboard a rolling "hot counter" to serve you at tableside.

Le Fate • *via Ruspoli 31* • offers some of the best cuisine locally. The problem will be obtaining a table when you want one.

GROSSETO The most alluring target in this area is slightly to the northwest at beautiful *Punta Ala* where the **Hotel Alleluja** is the "inn" place in a zone that is known more for villas, golf links, bridle paths, and sun, sun, sun—also for honeymoons with other bridal tack and other grooms.

★★★★ **Gallia Palace** • has scenery much in common with the land-and-waterscape around Port'Ercole to the south. Architecturally and spiritually, everything is oriented toward the great outdoors—although the great indoors is unusually felicitous, too. Elba is just 10 miles to the west.

LUCCA   is a beautiful and highly sophisticated walled city maintained in excellent preserve. (I much prefer it to Pisa for overnighting in this region.) **La Principessa** is a noble home in its own park; excellent comfort and manifest aesthetic rewards. For dining, **Antico Caffe delle Mura** is an elegant choice with its own piazza in front, covered porch, wrought-iron chandeliers, lovely mural, high-falutin' waiters, and piped music such as you hear in only the best elevators. Try the tagliate (a Tuscan steak, usually for two).

MENAGGIO,   the little town about an hour from Como, is proud of its **Grand Hotel Victoria.** This one is tricked out with turn-of-the-century spaciousness, a lovely lake vista, 100 old-style rooms and 53 private baths with reluctant plumbing. The second-category **Bellavista** is tops in its category.

MERANO

☆☆☆ **Kurhotel Palace** • receives the top reviews. It's a deluxe haven. Naturally there are pools and fitness facilities; the gardens are lovingly maintained; the cookery is outstanding. Don't think it's a clinic only because of its name, but indeed it is good for the nerves.

☆☆ **Meranherhof** •   is also worth attention. Rates are somewhat lower because it is not so specialized, but quality remains first rate.

★★★ **Schloss Rundegg** • is actually a beauty farm *(kurhotel)* with stunning hotel facilities in a marvelous parkside castle. Pool, gardens, gorgeous surroundings—all served up with heaping dollops of cold cream. Also in the castle category are the luxurious **Castel Freiberg** and the moderately priced **Castello Labers.**

Parkhotel Mignon • is now a worthy alternative in the first-class category.

When the meal gong sounds, Merano offers little, because most hotels require full pension. **Andrea** is intimate and regional. **Flora** would be my alternate option.

MILAN

Milano is second in size in Italy, with nearly 2 million people. Primarily commercial, with a non-Latin aura of hustle and bustle, it is the financial and industrial center of the nation, boasting 37% of all Italian businesses; with less than ⅟₂₅ of the country's population, it accounts for ⅕ of all wages and pays 24% of the national tax bill. North American buyers rattle in by the planeloads to snap up next season's fashions. Still, it has one of the most disgraceful hotel pictures of any major city in Europe—and at teeth-shattering prices. The reason is that the hoteliers possess a classic "captive audience" of business clients who *must* come here. So—as you might expect—it's a ripoff situation. My advice is to move out of Milan as soon as you've seen its proudest buttons.

ATTRACTIONS

Duomo • *Piazza Duomo* • This most famous landmark on the upper half of the Italian Peninsula, concentrates 224 statues and some of the world's finest stained glass in two treasure-filled acres. Construction on the Gothic cathedral began in 1386. Walk around the outside; you'll notice all the gargoyles (96 of them) peering out from the heights. The third largest church in the world and Italy's largest Gothic building, this magnificent cathedral is crowned with 135 spires, the central one of which bears a gilded statue of the Madonna (known as La Madonnina). For a really good look at the details, take along binoculars.

Palazzo Reale • *Royal Palace, Piazza del Duomo 12* • The 18th-century facade of the Royal Palace is by Piermarini. The Royal Apartment and the Hall of the Caryatids house art exhibitions. The palazzo also contains the best of contemporary works and the **Museo del Duomo** with models and drawings of the Duomo during its 427-year construction, plus rare art objects collected over 6 centuries, that can help orient you on your tour of the cathedral.

Galleria Vittorio Emanuale • *Piazza del Duomo* • Designed by the same architect who put the finishing touches on the Piazza del Duomo, this freshly restored 195-yard-long arcade is a huge glass-and-iron structure dating from the Victorian era when these were considered architectural marvels. Inside is an array of boutiques and shops where anyone with an appreciation of Italian design and craftsmanship will enjoy browsing, if not buying.

Pinacoteca Ambrosiana • *Ambrosiana Gallery and Ambrosian Library, Piazza Pio XI 2* • There are works by Titian and Botticelli, several by or attributed to Leonardo da Vinci, including his *Atlantic Codes*. The Library holds 400,000 volumes and 30,000 original manuscripts.

Palazzo della Ragione • *Piazza Mercanti* • The palazzo dates from 1233. During medieval times, it was at the center of Milan; it's worth a walk now.

Palazzo Clerici • *Via Clerici 5* • Renowned for the Tiepolo fresco *The Sun That Lights the World*, this 18th-century palazzo is a rare gem—one of the few that did not require reconstruction following World War II.

Teatro alla Scala ● *La Scala Opera, Piazza della Scala* ● The elegant interior of the auditorium attains acoustical perfection; music from the stage will reach you whether you have a hard-to-get orchestra seat or are perched high up in the balcony. The season runs from Dec. 7 through June 30, with intermittent performances in summer.

Museo Teatrale ● the theatrical museum of La Scala, is a must for opera buffs. The documentation of the colorful history of La Scala includes posters and rare photographs as well as paintings and sculptures.

Pinacoteca di Brera ● *Brera Gallery, Via Brera 28* ● An excellent collection of paintings by Piero della Francesca, Raphael, Bramante, Correggio, Carpaccio, Titian, Tiepolo, Mantegna, and others.

Parco Sempione ● Looking for a bit of greenery and a place to relax? Behind the Castello Sforzesco, you'll discover Parco Sempione, with plenty of shade and spots just right for a picnic. On summer evenings, you are likely to come across an outdoor concert here.

Castello Sforzesco ● *Sforza Castle, Piazza Castello* ● When the Sforzas fell from power in 1525, the castle became a fortress for 250 strife-torn years until 1893 when its buildings were restored and transformed into not one but several museums. **Civiche Raccolte d'Arte Antica,** the museum of ancient art, houses substantial collections of paintings, sculpture, ceramics, glass, textiles, furniture, and bronze. The most famous work in the museum is the *Pieta Rondanini,* Michelangelo's final sculpture. Also within this complex is **Museo degli Strumenti Musicali Antichi** ● *Museum of Ancient Musical Instruments* ● The museum contains hundreds of medieval and Renaissance instruments.

Archaeological Museum ● *Corso Magenta 15* ● Stop here for displays of Neolithic and Bronze Age artifacts, Greek vases, and Roman art.

Basilica of Sant'Ambrogio ● *Piazza Sant-Ambrogio* ● The ancient core of this church goes back to the 4th-century lifetime of St. Ambrose, while the enlarged basilica is a prototype of Lombard Romanesque architecture.

Museo Nazionale Scienza e Tecnica "Leonardo da Vinci" ● *Leonardo da Vinci National Museum of Science and Technology, Via San Vittore 21* ● This museum is roughly in the same genre as the Smithsonian Institution except that it includes something special that no North American museum has: a gallery with models constructed from sketches by Leonardo. It also contains early machines, metallurgical and telecommunications exhibits, an especially interesting railroad collection, plus a Museum of Physics and a Naval Museum.

Museo Poldi Pezzoli ● *12 via Manzoni* ● Getting jaded? Not yet, *per favore.* Stop here to absorb Bellini's poignant *Pieta,* della Francesca's *San Nicolo,* Pollaiolo's *Portrait of a Woman,* or a processional cross by Raffaello. Not only is the collection wondrous, but the decorative scheme is richly rewarding.

Santa Maria della Grazie • *Piazza Santa Maria Della Grazie* • Here you'll find Leonardo da Vinci's *Last Supper* (1494–1497), although the church is interesting for other reasons. Built in the last half of the 15th century, Bramante later added the large, triple-apsed tribune. On the left side is the entrance to the former Dominican convent where, on the refectory wall, is *The Last Supper.*

Sant'Eustorgio • *Piazza Sant'Eustorgio* • The present edifice is the result of reconstruction that began in the 13th century and continued for several hundred years. One of the extant chapels, however, dates from the 7th century but is embellished with 15th-century frescoes. According to legend, the large tomb inscribed "Sepulcrum Trium Magorum" contains the relics of the Three Magi.

HOTELS

Pierre • is a recent addition to this very old city, and it is as lovely as anyone might expect from this Rafael Group candidate—one of the best hosts in the hotel business globally. Only 47 rooms (small closets, hi-tech touches, fine textiles), intimate dignified restaurant, piano bar, sedate and tasteful—and, naturally, expensive. I also like the location bordering Santa Maria della Grazie; a car or taxi will be necessary, however, since it is out of the center on via de Amicis.

Principe e Savoia • Expense accounters in this businessman's hub seem drawn to this old standby as the executive hotel of choice. Manager Roberto Bucciarelli has his able hands full. With ample funding he could restore this establishment's former mandate on elegance. You might prefer the **Annex,** which contains only suites and evokes the air of an upper-crust residence.

Palace • was updated recently, reverting from a thoroughly modern mien to a pleasant traditional mood. The Casanova Grill also has been nicely refreshed; the roof garden is delightful. Its 200 rooms have balconies, many facing the public park.

Hilton • extends a hearty welcome to contemporary travelers. You might like the freshness and calm that pervades this Hilton—from the penthouse "Executive" floor to the chummy Trattoria da Giuseppa at mezzanine level; 335 units; off-lobby London Bar, nursery. Twin units somewhat cramped but extra-brightly decorated; maintenance so listless that you could get a fine room or a disappointing one; radio, TV, massage vibrators. For those who can afford the walloping tabs, it's a fine if not predictable stop.

Excelsior Gallia • handy to the rail terminus, put on fresh raiments at the time of its Trust House Forte takeover. Under the direction of Manager Bertolini, every floor has been renewed and every room respiced. Public sectors retain the mood of opulence; a restaurant has been built. Now 100% air-conditioned but not 100% efficient, according to some heated readers; 280 units, all ample in size, adequate in comfort, and clean. The modern bar with tiny spotlights is especially appealing; so are the prices. (Be sure you have the booking confirmed in writing along with the agreed tariff.)

Diana Majestic • goes back to the "liberty" period for its decorative scheme; very inviting it is too. The lounge mixes pilasters and potted palms, tall windows with modernistic bentwood chairs, and ample space and light. A sound choice, if you like that style.

Splendid • also is spiffy; it can rate among the fashion leaders of Milan—such as they are.

Grand et de Milan • harks back to the last century. Close to the Duomo and remembered by nostalgic musicologists as the place where Verdi went out on a final gracenote.

Plaza • serves breakfast only. Futuristic, cantilevered lobby; heavy use of chrome and glass; semicircular bar; angular construction; interesting colors. A bit odd but you may like it.

Jolly President • mixes Empire highlights with an egg-crate ceiling in its lobby and lounge. Air-conditioned; small chambers with floor-to-ceiling windows; 200 totally refreshed rooms; competently run in a commercial way.

Michelangelo • has set up its modern easel near the tracks and is highly touted by local *dilettanti*.

Grand Duomo • shines in spots—but the trick will be to find those spots. The duplex suites and "VIP rooms" would be the top choices, so ask for these first and then request that they show you around if some other accommodation is desired.

Milano Fiori • is located in the Convention Center. Businessmen who come for the numerous commercial fairs in Milan will appreciate its location and the helpfulness of its energetic management.

Rubens • in the Fair district and recently updated, is quite good.

Nasco • in glass and concrete, is a product of our modern times, rendered smoothly in a chipper meld of Italo-Scandinavian concepts. Bar-lounge that doubles as a foyer; new Grill with recommendable cookery; 7 color schemes; snug accommodations, but good ones; 150 rooms. A lively candidate with numerous virtues.

Carlton Hotel Senato • offers 80 cramped but efficient bedchambers, all with bath, shower, stocked refrigerator, and micro-TV sets; facial tissues, shoe-shiner, silent valet, scales, and other functional gimmicks; garage, restaurant, and bar. Mercantile but convenient.

Cavour ● comes up with a nice lobby, 100 appealing but smallish rooms, and 73 private baths. Choose your location on the courtyard side away from the clattering street; you'll find a tub with every room, radiant heating here and there, and modest features in general.

Concorde ● is modern; it's a first-category house that's nicely maintained.

De la Ville ● boasts 93 baths for 104 breezy nests; it is soundproofed and sound for medium budgets.

Andreola ● a toot from the station, is attired in up-to-the-era stylings.

Manin's ● claim to fame are the Colombo brothers who own it and try to greet every guest by name; garden dining, air cooling, Telex, and proximity to the city's zoo are its fringe benefits.

Cavalieri ● refashioned many of its units—but oh, those retailored prices! A bit too *cavalieri*.

Jolly Touring ● does a far better job now that it belongs to the Jolly chain. The service and the accommodations show perk and pride.

Ramada offers its shelter about 15 minutes out of the city.

RESTAURANTS

☆☆☆☆☆ **Gualtiero Marchesi** ● *via Bonvesin de la Riva 9, in a ho-hum business district* ● is simultaneously the most modern, elegant, and the most expensive restaurant in this most expensive Italian city. If you worship at the shrines of such French chefs as the Troisgros, Guerard, and Bocuse, then you will probably find this Italian version of the nouvelle cuisine (e.g., spaghetti salad with chicken lobster and creamed red pepper sauce) equally exalted in its genre. The interior also reflects the avant-garde tendencies even down to the handsome sculptures by contemporary artists that decorate each table. If you don't choose one of the house's special wines (with which the cellar is very well stocked) a superb repast is likely to cost at least $95. Closed Sun. and Mon. at noon.

☆☆☆☆ **Scaletta** ● *piazzale Stazione di Porta Genova* ● casts a mood of exclusivity and *richesse* that evokes faint stirrings of romance in dim places— just the nookery where two Beautiful People might meet for a private tete-a-tete. The cuisine is a happy blend of Franco-Italian mastery, and the billings might make you think of unnumbered Swiss bank accounts. Try a risotto with pumpkin as a novelty, or the persimmon mousse. It is shuttered on Sun. and Mon. as well as Aug. Delightfully suave.

☆☆☆ **Romani** • *via Trebazio 3* • is a favorite nip-inn for the city's top executives. Though traditionally outfitted, there is an air of vital animation that belies the sedate interior. Undeniably this is prompted by so many disciples expressing satisfaction over the superb culinations, the splendid amiable service, and the surprisingly moderate prices. Incidentally, if you have a sweet tooth, the overwhelmingly caloric dessert trolley could probably make a millionaire of your dentist. Closed Sun.

☆☆ **Savini** • *Galleria V. Emanuele II* • remains the chosen rendezvous of La Scala artists. Slightly formal atmosphere; happy little bar; too-bright illumination; a landmark operation. After performance is the best time for people-watching. Closed Sun.

☆☆ **Alfio-Cavour** • *via Senato 31* • is a honey that seems to get sweeter. Midway down the entrance stairs you spy a huge open freezer shelf, overhung with garlands of fruits and vegetables and groaning with a magnificently colorful preview of what you'll be swallowing. The cuisine is excellent; the specialties are antipasti and fish, but a huge menu boasts almost everything that grows or wiggles; the prices are medium.

☆ **El Toula** • is decidedly up-market and often peopled with Milanese society. Location behind La Scala in the city's "Wall Street" district; spacious; gracious decor; advance reservation suggested, especially during the opera season.

★★★ **Riccione** • *via Taramelli 70* • is a simple, reasonably priced fish restaurant—one of the best in Italy. A skiff at the entrance sets the tone; helpful waiters who can explain the vast catch; no need to order bottled wine because the open house variety is excellent. Very professional but a happy place where you won't be stunned when you reel in the bill.

★★★ **Trattoria Aurora** • *via Savona 23* • does its ever-lovin' best to provide a panoply of Piedmont cuisine. How well it comes off, too! You can nibble and sip until your eyes roll back in your head and never fear any pain in your pocket. Each of our several samplings was so delicious, so natural, and so honest that I could as happily dine here on a regular basis and never tire of the gastronomy. Wonderful.

☆ **St. Andrews** • *via Sant' Andrea* • is a first-category entry that is beloved by locals. Mockwood ambience; central hearth the main decorative feature; bookcases on walls; leather chairs and love seats around low tables; subtle lighting from overhanging hooded lamps; rust carpets; lime-green textiles; profession-proud waiters in formal attire. The cookery was much better than average; it was much costlier than average, too.
Much quieter but very solid is **Bice,** with many Milanese. **Torre di Pisa** caters to bevies of models—and students who come to gawk. **La Collina Pistoiese** isn't fancy but it is a superior value. **Da Aimo e Nadia** is rather Tuscan in its touch and moderate in its prices; go for dinner when its mood is best. **Il Mazzetto Guarnito** goes back to the last century for its recipes, providing a relief from nouvelle cuisine while still being genteel and light.

Giannino • *via Amatore Sciesa 8* • remains popular and that disturbs many visitors—possibly because it seems to cater so heavily these days to tourist traffic. Several modern dining rooms; glassed-in kitchen; winter garden; initial reception sometimes lax, but table service usually (not always) attentive and thoughtful.

La Nos • *"The Walnut,"* at *Via Amedei 2 in old Milan* • is "camp" in concept. Diners walk up some stairs to find 2 main sections and 2 smaller nooks. Whirring fans; suspended Tiffany-style lamps; a church pulpit used as a bottle rack; a menu in the shape of a walnut tree—all in all, Grandma's rummage sale decor that just doesn't click. Minstrels who look as if they've been wandering since Justinian's court play softly and pleasantly. Closed Sun. and Aug.

★★★ **Taverna del Gran Sasso** • *pizzale Principessa Clotilde 8* • looks like the warehouse on the MGM studio lot marked: "Storage #67, Italian Restaurant Scenery." And has it got it—*mamma mia!* Your eyeballs are poked by wagon wheels, garlic strands, corn clusters, brass pots, wine jugs, cheese wedges, cattle yokes, oaken barrels, sausage, hams, chickens, salamis, ceramics, breads, even a sewing machine—plus checkered tableclothes, natch. The dishes are chiefly from the Abruzzi province.

★★★ **Il Canneto** • *or Osteria del Vecchio Canneto, via Solferino 56* • is the seafood version of Gran Sasso; it's under the same decor-happy ownership. Greetings to all comers with a foghorn and ship's whistle; cellar site; huge room decked with brass musical instruments, an ocean-liner's anchor, sails, a winch, and fathoms of chain; singing waiters in shipwreck costume; leviathan 16-course meal for a white bait price tag. The only items not from the briny deep are the pasta, the fruit, the wine, and the bib tucked under your proliferating chins. Not dressy (very little *is* in this metropolis).

Boeucc Flavio • *piazza Belgioioso* • was ardently recommended by a Milan exile of exceptional taste. I followed it up personally and agree with our correspondent. It's an honest place, near chic redoubts, and is reasonably priced. **La Vittoria, La Libera, La Briciola,** and **Solferino** are excellent but difficult to get into unless you have pull. **Il Piccolo Teatro** and **Rovello** also win plaudits locally. For pizza and inexpensive fare **Le Specialita** • *via Pietro Calvi 31a* • is a midcity winner. Attractive, too, with copper pots and farm implements on the walls; closed Sun.

Scoffone Bottega del Vino • *via Victor Hugo 4* • is one of the most ancient wine houses in Italy. Scrumptious hot and cold dishes are available at a do-it-yourself counter or in a more modern cafeteria-style dining room in the rear. I prefer the front segment with its painted walls and ceiling, black dado, wrought-iron chandeliers, and earthly atmosphere. A bottle of Barolo, slices of cold suckling pig, pickled vegetables, and floating mozzarella (it should come in its whey when it is properly kept and served) were admirable straightforward fare. Prices are low; the quality is high. Hundreds of varieties of native wines await experimenting oenologists. Very plain—but just plain wonderful for what it is.

NIGHT LIFE

After dark, top honors for *summer* operation go to **Rendez-Vous.** Garden ambience, with tables both inside and alfresco; good cabaret (for Milan!); dancing nightly; high-grade attention to cuisine and service; frankly expensive by national standards. Unrivaled during the warm months. For *winter* shenanigans, **Astoria** (piazza Santa Maria Beltrade 2) is currently the most elegant. Rich, large, and brightly illuminated; entertainment and lively orchestra; tiny "music fee" but robust booze bill; closed June through Aug., when the staff migrates en masse to Nord-Est in Santa Margherita. **Taverna dei Sette Peccati** (via Imbonati 52) presents an outstanding fixed-price dinner with its show; a quality meal is quite rare for this kind of establishment, but here's an exception. Closed Sun. **Maxim** (Galleria Manzoni) offers coral-velvet banquettes, double-candle lamps on tables, dancing, a modest cabaret.

Discotheques? **Bang-Bang** (via Molino delle Armi), followed by the **Old Fashion** in the Park. **Nepentha** (near Plaza Hotel) presents a black lacquer and Chinese red ambience; tableside whisky service at tabs that trim the plumage of fine-feathered night owls; cagelike dimensions. **Santa Tecla,** behind the Royal Palace, demonstrates its jazz interests through myriad record jackets on its walls.

SHOPPING

SHOPPING HOURS: 9–9:30 a.m. to noon or 12:30 p.m. and 3:30–7:30 p.m. (winter); 4–7:30 or 8 p.m. (summer), however, some close for a shorter lunch break and reopen between 1:30 p.m. and 2:30 p.m. or don't close at all, Mon. mornings most are closed, too. Department stores such as Rinascente and Coin stay open 9 a.m.–7:30 p.m.

BEST AREAS: Via Montenapoleone is the local peak of chic. If you begin on its lower end and stroll through the short pedestrian mall of via della Spiga, and then cut back down via Manzoni, this U-shaped trek will show you the choicest galaxy of merchandise in this center; or draw a one-mile radius around the *Duomo* and start from this bulls-eye in any direction, and you'll discover some of the city's tiptop shops.

NOTE · · · Milan spells fashion! But prices are astronomical. It seems to be, more and more, a city for expense-accounters. Along the via S. Gregorio (between the piazza della Repubblica and the Central Station) you'll find store fronts which announce *"solo grossisti."* This is the wholesale district for the rag trade. Many manufacturers are producing knockoffs of the hottest designers of the moment from Paris, Milan, and Rome. If you have cash in hand and determination, look in the windows, take your pick, walk in and ask if you can buy. They might say "no," but it's likely, if they aren't terribly busy, that they'll say "yes." You'll probably try the garment on between packing cases, but it's worth it.

A QUICK WRAP-UP: Some of the better *boutiques* to look for are **Giorgio Armani** (via S. Andrea 9), **Missoni** (via Montenapoleone 1), **Gianni Versace** (via della Spiga 4), **Trussardi** (via S. Andrea 5), **Fendi** (via della Spiga 11 and via S. Andrea 16), and **Sharra Pagano** (via della Spiga 7). For *shoes* try **Raphael-Rossetti, Tanino Crisci,** and **Santini** (all on the via Montenapoleone, the latter being very trendy). Don't miss **Peck** (via Montenapoleone and via Spadari 9) the Italian answer to the Fauchon's. In addition there's **Jesurum** (via Leopardi 25), which has an enticing selection of dentelle. Turn to "Venice" for more details.

L'Utile e il Dilettevole (via della Spiga 42) is a wellspring for gift ideas. The taste and uniqueness are special.

Galtrucco (via Montenapoleone 27 and piazza del Duomo 2) is the combined Saks-Bergdorf-Macy for yard goods. Branch in Rome.

La Rinascente, the big department store, is at via San Raffaele 2 on Piazza Duomo. **Coin** (piazzale Cinque Giornate) is also popular.

SECOND-RATE FLEA MARKET: The **Fiera di Senigallia** (via Calatafini) every Sat. morning. Haggle your hardest! **Via Fiori Chiari** jumps with its fleas the last weekend of each month.

MONTECATINI, 25 miles from Florence, catches much of the overflow when Florentine hotels are overbooked. The waters are famous for their beneficial effects on the liver. Within the immediate area are over 300 square miles of parks and gardens which tend to keep things cool during the hottest months.

It's **Grand Hotel e La Pace,** known as "La Patch-eh" to its international clientele, is the luxury-class leader. Total 170 rooms, 170 baths; pool; April–Oct. only. You may be happier at the **Bellavista Palace & Golf** which is also deluxe. The **President** is a delight. The predominant color is palm green—fresh, happy, modern, and totally inviting. **Croce di Malta,** next down the line, has been extensively face-lifted. Very good, too; alfresco pool; well sited among the thermal parks; open all year. **Tamerici & Principe** is one of the smartest addresses in the area between April and Nov. **Nizza e Suisse** has been thoroughly remodeled and boosted up to first class. If you don't like these, there's a choice of more than 50 others.

NAPLES

Napoli, the nation's 3rd city, continues to provoke both irritation and pity. With all its exquisite natural assets, this could be *the* gemstone in the Tyrrhenian tiara. Instead, corruption has taken a toll and prevented progress for citizens who would like to see their city at its best. The airport has improved and many features cast a spell of sunlit invitation. Poverty is more visible here than in northern cities, so you an expect to witness those side effects.

Attractions include **Vesuvius,** the new digs at nearby **Oplontis, Ercolano,** one of the world's most magnificent bays, the **Castel Nuovo** (Anjou Castle) and the former **monastery of San Martino,** the **Museo Archeologico Nazionale** (Greek and Roman art, and some of the best since it was so subject to theft at the digs that the finest articles were taken here for protection and viewing), the **Museo e Gallerie di Capodimonte** (paintings by Botticelli and Michelangelo among many others), the **San Carlo Opera House,** 499 churches—a score of wonders. **Pompeii** is covered separately.

HOTELS

☆☆☆ **Excelsior** ● is so far ahead of other hotels here that no other house is in any way competitive with it. From the tallest eaves to the deepest wine cellar, it is a Koh-i-noor diamond that glitters dazzlingly over the rather glum choices elsewhere in the city. All lodgings in classic elegance and nearly the entire hotel recently refashioned; full-house air-conditioning; there are soundproof double windows on all sides; a dozen stunning suites plus the splendid "Royal." The cuisine is sumptuous; the service is flawless. Director Di Nunzio is a great help to any traveler to this city and shows concern for his guests.

Royal ● also facing the bay, is gold and blue and glass; the lobby is its best feature, with comfortable leather armchairs and soft lighting; the clientele is very mixed. Warm-weather penthouse pool; cramped dimensions. A mass hostelry that packs 'em in and out at tariffs considerably lower than those of the Excelsior.

Continental ● *via Partenope* ● and **Grand Hotel Parkers** ● *corso Vittorio Emanuele* ● are other passable choices in this category.

Vesuvio • is air-conditioned. Tons of plastic and Formica; range of lodgings from Archaic to Zesty; tabs pegged at about half those of the leader. It tries to look prim beside the wreckage of a decaying building.

Santa Lucia • next to the Excelsior, is a mixture of fair to grim. Sleeping units restyled in part so be sure to ask to see one before agreeing to stay.

Jolly • is proudly called the *Grattacielo* (''Skyscraper''), and it will provide an altogether heebie-jeebie, knee-knocking sensation when the bay-borne winds make the edifice sway in the breeze. It occupies the 16th to 30th floors of an office building, with a separate entrance. Very groupy.

Britannique • boasts a viewful perch above the city; its 80 rooms have been totally refashioned. Location alone makes it worth considering.

RESTAURANTS

☆☆☆☆ **Hotel Excelsior •** is the most consistently dependable choice in its Casanova Grill for lunch or dinner in the entire region. Cuisine is Mediterranean in style. All of the rigidly top-quality cookery, service, and hygienic standards maintained throughout the great CIGA chain are scrupulously observed here, with the consequence that the fare is uniformly excellent. The bar is good for snacks.

La Sacrestia • *via Orazio 116* • choicely positioned on a hillside 15 minutes from the center, draws bevies of smartly attired sophisti-cats. Alcoved main dining room in neo-baroque decor; more intimate subterranean chamber with tiny bar; outside terrace for viewing the crescent-shape metropolis while sampling the Assaggi (''Mixed Pastas to Test''); dignified but not warm service; closed Wed.

Giuseppone a Mare • *discesa Capo Posillipo* • on the sea perhaps 10 minutes from the center in the vicinity of Masaniello, is relaxing on a sunny day. Extra-fresh fish every day; average meal up to $35 per person. Specialties of oysters and shellfish, vended from table to table by a blue-sweatered *ostricaro*, or ''oysterman''; on the simple side in furnishings; open terrace; clean, bustling, busy; pizza a dream; not much English spoken; don't go on Sun. Add up your bill here before paying.

La Bersagliera • *in the Santa Lucia Basin (marine cove opposite the Excelsior and Vesuvio hotels)* • is still an unabashed tourist-hooker—but, regardless of this drawback, it is now definitely worth a visit. The waterside terrace is a delight, despite its pushy waiters. Spotlessly clean, enormous kitchen, which you may inspect; fresh sea denizens. Prices are on the high side, but in line with the brutal official tariffs on seafood. Closed Tues.

Ciro • *same basin area, on the first mole* • is a bit more refined; indoor and alfresco seating; very proper service. Try the spaghetti with clams and the grilled shrimp. If you don't favor olive oil, be sure to advise your waiter to go easy.

PADUA is the city of St. Anthony, Giotto, and Donatello with roots that go as far back as the 4th century B.C. and the paleovenetian civilization. As a reminder of the Trojan War and its influence, you must see the beautifully carved Wooden Horse in the richly painted 13th-century Palazzo della Ragione. The Church of Sta. Sofia and the frescoes at the Scrovegni Chapel are other major inclusions in any visit to this pre-Christian fishing village. If you do overnight here the commercial-minded **Plaza** is a substantial bet. Then you might consider **Le Padovanelle,** the **Europa,** the **Milano,** and the **Monaco.** Other choices: **Toscanelli, Donatello,** and **Leon Bianca.**

PALERMO, full of art treasures and beautiful historic buildings, is Italy's 6th city and Sicily's largest center; the lion's share of commerce, however, is concentrated, around *Catania,* on the East Coast. Labeled by its promoters "The Golden Shell," it has some pleasant aspects including Moslem ruins, Norman heritage, and baroque beginnings. There's a daily overnight ferry link with Naples, a Genoa connection 3 times a week, and runs from Catania and Siracusa to Naples and Malta frequently; these ships are proud vessels of the Tirrenia Line.

   Grand Hotel Villa Igiea, in its own back-o-town park by the sea, is a shining oasis in this hotel-poor region. It's rambling, aged, and cool—a traveler's reward. Seawater swimming pool; 100% air-conditioned; erratic service. **Jolly,** severed from the sea by a wide avenue, nonetheless gets blasted by highway noise *all night l-o-n-g.* It's still better than much of the competition— especially if you're a heavy sleeper. **The Grande Hotel & delle Palme,** owned by the Villa Igiea, is a fair choice despite the fact that it's showing its age virtually everywhere. Midcity situation in the throbbing eye of the 4-wheel hurricane; overweening institutionality despite some recent renovations; air-cooling now cooing a Grandiose sigh of welcome relief; clean but zestless bedchambers. If you stop, please ask to see the modest little corner where Wagner composed *Parsifal.* The **Politeama Palace** and the **Jolly Foro Italico** are reasonable alternatives. Apart from the nostalgic dining spread at **Villa Igiea,** your most memorable meals probably will be at **Gourmand** or the **Charleston.**

PERUGIA, like Assisi, draws floods of excursionists to absorb the well-preserved antiquity and renaissance beauty. This ancient hill town is the site of the University for Foreigners. The Collegio del Cambio has some fine frescoes (by Perugino, of course); Town Hall houses the National Gallery with a selection of famous paintings, and the panorama of the valley is lovely. You'll also want to visit its Gothic Cathedral and probably the Etruscan-Roman Museum, one of the finest assemblages of this elusive period anywhere; don't forget the Etruscan well and 3 tombs. Stroll through the Oratorio of St. Bernard, and don't miss the 15th-century Campanile at the Church of St. Peter where the octagonal shape will live in your memory. The Church of St. Domenico is another important target, not to mention the medieval hamlet built inside the Paolina Fortress and Marzia Gate. And if you really want to feel young, see the Tempio di St. Angelo, which goes back to the 6th century. An incredible city!

For greater convenience, the Rocca Paolina is reached by a cleverly engineered system of moving staircases that link the center with the lower part of town that is utilized for parking.

If you need an official guide for any Umbrian site, be in touch with Associazione Guide Umbria, via Fani 14, Tel. (075) 65124.

In hotel circles, the **Brufani** maintains a gimpy lead over a still more slow-footed field. Old, Old, Old World flavor; still renewing its rooms; central situation. Fair. The **Plaza** is not too inspired either. The **Grifone,** of a similar ilk, would come next, since it has been completely air-cooled and pepped up. The little **La Rosetta,** down the street from the Brufani, is a lot cheaper and it now provides many renewed units. **Locanda della Posta** also has been given some modern touches, although it is the oldest hostelry in town; bed and breakfast only. **Le Tre Vaselle** in the nearby town of *Torgiano* is one of the most attractive retreats in the region. Cuisine and accommodation are tops.

The best dining bets are at the **Brufani** and the small, less-expensive **La Rosetta.** Among the independent restaurants, I favor **La Taverna** and the viewful **Del Sole. Osteria del Bartolo** is best for regional food. Have an espresso at **Ferrari.**

PISA   Naturally, any first-time visitor must run to see its legendary Leaning Tower, venerable Duomo, baptistery, and exquisite Gothic church by Nicola Pisano. You can take in a lot very quickly here because the main sights are highly concentrated in one central area. Of course, scholars could pass lifetimes in the shadows of these timeless monuments; there's so much to study if you care. The 8-century-old Tower leans 17-feet off the perpendicular and is tipping at a quicker and more perilous rate each season. By the time of your arrival, visits may be restricted in the immediate surroundings. Visits into the tower were curtailed some time ago. A restoration program of nearly $100 million will be under way. June (*Giugno Pisano*) is best, when *Il Gioco del Ponte* (tug-of-war on the bridge) and other pageantry bring it alive.

Dei Cavalieri   is Neo-Italian-Modern, with 102 air-conditioned rooms, a bright-red American bar, and a better-than-average restaurant. Now that it is being managed properly, the improvements have been legion. Otherwise the hotel picture is so lackluster locally that I would suggest you drive 10 miles over to lovely *Lucca* and stay at the palatial **La Principessa.**

Golf • at *Tirrenia* (on the coast, 10 miles from the steps of the Tower) • might be an answer to your vacation prayers if you want to escape the summer crush. Pine grove situation set back from the sea; adjoining golf course, tennis, swimming pool, and full resort amenities; modern tone with ornate fillips; all 100 units with bath, balcony, and air conditioning.

POMPEII   If you can remember back to A.D. 79, you will see the splendid excavations from Vesuvian wrath. A quick trip involves a full day in the digs, but several days would give you time to pause at the forum, the open and covered theaters, as well as in the earliest research areas. Later archaeology uncovered such beauties as the Vettii House, the Villa of Diomedes, the Golden Amorettes, plus "The Mysteries" and yet another amphitheater. The paths are endless and each mosaic, shop, or hearth is fascinating. Herculaneum (Ercolano) also was victimized and preserved by Vesuvius. It is nowhere near as impressive as Pompeii. A museum now exists even if work has slowed due to hardening earth. (This city was covered by mud rather than ashes and, hence, is very well preserved.) A lingering tour also should include the sites at Paestum (south of Salerno) and Cumae, in the vicinity. If you tire of antiquity, about 10 dozen villas of the 18th century are being restored at **Campolieto,** which is nearby on slopes overlooking the bay.

Many visitors breeze in to ramble in an archaeological stupor all morning, hoping to pause for a decent meal at midday. **Ristorante Turistico** is suitable for a perfunctory meal. **Tiberio** is equally punk. The former closes on Tues.; the latter is open the week around. **Anfiteatro,** a bit out of the center, is, without doubt, "the best place to eat in Pompeii," according to Mario Scisciola. He's the owner and he wrote me to say so. Most of these stops involve themselves in the parking ploy: little or no charge for diners and about $7 for leaving your vehicle while you visit the digs. Some fringe lots are totally untrustworthy, so try to park in a free public slot near the police rank at the main entrance.

The highway from and to Rome is loaded with souvenir shops and cameo vendors, most of which are not only second-rate but trashy. Only one place, as far as we know, offers top-class stocks and is reliable. **M. & G. Donadio** is the largest and oldest, with a good reputation, locally and internationally. Don't bother with any of the rest. **G. Apa** is certainly not recommended by me.

PORT'ERCOLE is a quiet harbor of *snobismo* on the Argentario promontory opposite Orbetello, 103 miles north of Rome toward Grosseto). The village itself isn't much; its few hostelries are often inconvenienced by an inadequate water supply. Island-hopping can be fun aboard hired boats; best destinations are *Giglio* and *Giannutri* (the last was not the American movie cowboy). *Sciendum est.*

☆☆☆☆ **Il Pellicano** ● has a beak full of charm. Seaside location; Pompeiian-red manor house with a glorious patio for sipping and munching; novel pool; 18 original rooms, plus 5 cottages and an 8-unit annex; fine, highly polished rusticity cooled by full air conditioning; very high all-inclusive tariffs. There's an air of elegant hominess.

The pick of the restaurants in the area is **Egisto** in neighboring *Orbetello* for its well-above average Peninsular cookery. **Il Cacciatore** features game (hence its name) in season; **Armando** is tops in *Porto S. Stefano.* Next, in the Porto itself, it's a toss-up among **La Posada, La Ribotta,** or **La Lampara.**

PORTOFINO has one of the dreamiest natural settings—a tiny, cliff-lined harbor of unsurpassing charm and intimacy, over which broods a castle and the Splendido Hotel. It's about 75 minutes by road from Genoa. Spring and fall are the best times to go; in summer it's often akin to Times Square, so crowded that the excursionists, the gays, and the souvenir vendors nearly trip over one another along the quay. Even driving into the port area can absorb an hour to cover 200 yards of roadway. A *must* to visit—but pick your season.

★★★★ **Splendido** • *perched on a mountainside* • offers one of Europe's most gracious vistas. A pool is splashing for your pleasure and a barbecue area nearby; there's a tennis court. Total of 80 units, not all of them too spacious, but they are air conditioned; much glass and mirror in the decor; quality appointments almost everywhere. Structurally and from a landscaping point of view it's glorious; management by Antonio Marson is taut and service is efficient and warm—as might be expected from the same conductors who run the *Orient-Express* and the Cipriani interests.

San Giorgio • is poorly situated but fairly well run.

Piccolo • the only remaining choice, is tiny; facilities are perhaps too regional for the average North American.

Il Pitosforo • holds the lead for dining candidates. Situation farthest out on the bayfront; 2 stories above street level, with a small interior restaurant, a 20-table, semiopen terrace, and a lovely view; service friendly; menu regional and substantial; very costly by local standards. Bianco Secco Portofino wine, dry and agreeable with an amusing label. Best in the village.

Tripoli • whomps up flavorful seafood risottos.

Puny's • best dish is fish baked in crusted salt.

Splendido Hotel • cuisine is deluxe in every respect, and its setting is magnificent. A recent lunch was excellent from soup, to service, to Saltimbocca.

La Gritta • is a Turkish-style bar replete with sports-car-height chairs, cushions, and diners in blue jeans; it's only for special tastes.

POSITANO, in the opinion of many, is the star attraction of the Amalfi Drive and of the entire area near Naples. The houses of this highly paintable village climb straight down the mountainside, like mountain goats; so will you, every time you go for a swim in the sea. (Happily, many hotels now boast pools and/ or cliffside elevators). If you're planning an overnight in this region, it's a sensible stop.

★★★★★ **San Pietro** • girt by flowers, aproned by sea, and showered with love by proprietor Attanasio is one of the nicest spots of all. This canon takes its name from the chapel on its cliffside. Pool and tennis court lately unveiled; private beach awesomely set among stone caverns and linked to a sun terrace with bar service; plant-lined restaurant with 2 grills and a pizza oven; exquisite taste in its clean-lined accommodations; floral displays rampant; balconies and terraces cushioned by bougainvillaea. A dream spot—but not from mid-Nov. until Easter when it shutters.

★★★★ **Le Sirenuse** • also clings to a hillside, with 7 floors staggered in staircase fashion, and with the main entrance on the 4th. All living quarters facing the sea; door keys featuring a mermaid suffering a severe bellyache; *taverna* and barbecue sizzling brightly; private steps to the waves. Very colorful to the eye and to the spirit.

★★ **Miramare** • with the same ownership as the San Pietro, has a superb position over the sea, with a full panorama to the south; enchanting restaurant; 15 rooms with bath, in 2 buildings; glassed-in goldfish swim merrily in some of the bathroom windows while you bathe; facilities simple but adequate; good but not outstanding, except for the magnificent location; be prepared to climb steps until your ears turn cartwheels.

Villa Franca • down the scale, has a similar personality. All of these are intimate and oriented toward vacationers rather than transients.

Royal • a first class entry, is not directly on the briny but its 5 levels offer an excellent vista of the coast and the Mediterranean. Seven-minute walk from the center, with bus service available; elevator; 50 unadorned rooms, all with bath or shower and private balcony, radio, telephone; some units enlarged and modernized; nice pool.

Poseidon • has an off-beach setting, with an 11-room addition facing the Gulf of Salerno. Good parking space; viewful terrace swimming pool; above average cuisine.

Montemare • with the same breathtaking sea view as the Miramare, is second class, clean, and unpretentious; there are 15 rooms with bath or shower. **Pensione Pupetto** is a budget bet and a good one. On the beach, the **Covo dei Saraceni** sails away with salutes. Also second-class; convenient for bathing; pleasant. Low man on the local totem pole is the **Savoia,** with a heavy Italian trade. Locals who don't dine in hotels often use **Cucina Casareccia de Vincenzo,** followed by a nightcap at the viewful beachfront **Bar de Marino.**

At neighboring *Praiano* (2 miles away) the 70-room **Tritone** is fresh and worthy as a hotel stop; all units with balcony; pool, dining salon, and terrace with sea-and-coast commands. **Le Agavi,** at the entry to Positano, is a clean-lined cliff-hanger where the rocks are sometimes the walls of your room. Nice pool too.

RAITO, the alluring cliffside village 2½ miles from Salerno up the Corniche from the main Amalfi Drive, boasts the first-class **Raito** which is tip of this top. Good kitchen; recommended. The nearby **Lloyd's Baia** is also a worthwhile stop.

RAPALLO, a short hop from Genoa, is nestled in a chalice of lovely mountains that hold the sun most of the year.

Pick of the luxury hotels is the **Bristol** • *2 miles out along the Gulf of Tigullio* • with large seawater pool and direct elevator service from building; private beach; spacious terraces; open-air restaurant. **Eurotel** is a 50-room apartment house that rents by the day, week, or month. Appealing restaurant;

bar; pool; gardens; excellent for its type. **Savoia** reminds us of an old crone with too much makeup; although seriously in need of a face-lifting, it is still popular. **Rosa Bianca** is now the leading hostelry in the superior second class. **Bel Soggiorno** ● *on the coast* ● offers reasonable value to families. While the **Miramare** is a winner for food, it lacks spice in the bedroom stew. Thoughtful, nice people who run its basic plant very well indeed. With a generous bank loan, this could be one of the better bets in town.

RAVELLO is above Amalfi, and it is almost as attractive—one of the more popular targets, in fact, on the peninsula. Its Villa Rufolo gardens are famed (here Wagner was purportedly inspired to compose *Lohengrin*—sorry, but a more enlightened reader corrects us and avers that it was *Parsifal,* second act, the magic gardens of Klingsor). Its Hotel Caruso and Hotel Palumbo are agreeable, and its wines are well regarded by Italian connoisseurs (a viewpoint I personally cannot share).

The village, 1000 feet above the sea, offers the totally revamped and charming **Palumbo,** a 12th-century palace with 40 units in the main building plus 2 annexes, respectively rated in categories I and II. Daring color schemes; 20 private baths; rooms identified by the colored tilework as well as numbers; #28, #32, and #34 offer stunning 3-directional panoramas and plenty of breathing space. **Caruso Belvedere,** a converted castle, has an enchanting garden and terraces, 26 old-fashioned rooms (some with fireplaces), and pure serenity. **Rufolo,** with exquisite gardens, is more modest. The 25-unit **Graal** is a third-category sweetheart with limited space; you will be rewarded with the same eye-popping view as is offered by the 2 leaders—but at only about half the tariff. Open the year round for thrifty wanderers with acumen. **Parsifal,** next to the C-B and very good for value, is the leading pension. Thanks to the Patron Saint of Tired Travelers, a road now wiggles directly up to this highland enclave where Wagner quilled the opera that gave it its name.

The feederies here are almost entirely limited to the innkeepers' kitchens.

RAVENNA, halfway between Venice and Ancona, is a culture seeker's paradise—historically and artistically, one of the outstanding smaller sites of the Western world. No other city can compete with its wealth of Byzantine architecture or its unique mosaics. Ecclesiastical treasures; Dante's tomb; Theodoric's tomb; a scholar's heaven. Giant ENI rubber-and-fertilizer plant; indifferent hotels, limited touring facilities; 6 miles from the sea on the Corsini Canal. If you can take the time, you'll want to visit St. Vitale of Galla Placidia for its purity of Byzantine art. Travelers cross oceans to view the famous mosaics of St. Apollinare Nuovo (take a strong flashlight to bring out added luster and sparkle). Nearby is the oratorio di St. Giovanni—just one more of the architectural gems of this rich historic port.

Bisanzio, with its rather gaudy decor but hospitable personnel, receives hotel honors. **Jolly** is basic and sound. **Argentario** is next. **Gallia,** 25 miles out at *Lido di Spina* in the Ferrara district, is on a beautiful beach with pool, gardens, and delicious homemade pasta daily. You can cruise the Po basin from here and dine on the catch your crew prepares.

ROME

Roma is said to have been founded in 753 B.C., when Romulus, son of the god Mars, yoked a bullock and a heifer to a plowshare, marked out a boundary, and built a wall. Be that as it may, the city has at least 2500 years of unparalleled cultural accomplishment. I, for one, regret the present trend of removing the rich persimmon, buff, red, ochre, and russet shades of ancient architecture and repainting the walls in white, a misguided effort by city planners to copy the mood of the 18th century. Hence, you should visit Rome soon if the blanching program offends your aesthetic senses. Larger than Philadelphia, it now totes up close to 3 million *Romani*. Since the banning of vehicles from 5 of its main piazzas, the Eternal City is becoming a much more pleasant place to stroll. The Traffic Commissioner has sealed off a whopping 25 acres in the Trevi Fountain district for pedestrians (hotel guests, residents, and employees excepted). It has more envoys than any other metropolis since diplomats maintain embassies or missions to 3 separate states within the city limits.

ATTRACTIONS

You may wish to view many of the following sites from an **Acquabus,** which plies the Tiber when water levels are sufficiently high. The tour takes less than an hour and carries about 40 passengers from Tiber Island to Duca d'Aosta Bridge (or the reverse journey). Climb aboard on the right bank facing the island (that's the Vatican side) or from the left bank just beyond the Cavour Bridge. How quiet and sleepy the city seems from the river's surface.

Janiculum • *Near Porta San Pancrazio* • For a splendid view of the Eternal City, stroll on the Janiculum Promenade where you can see the Tiber with the Castel Sant'Angelo, the Colosseum, and much more. The equestrian statue is of Garibaldi, the patriot who fought for the unification of Italy.

Colosseo • *Colosseum, piazza del Colosseo* • Known to citizens of ancient Rome as the Flavian Amphitheater, the Colosseum was built during the years A.D. 72–80 under emperors Vespasianus and Titus. The present structure's original marble facade was mined for constructing other monuments, including St. Peter's. In the 18th century, Pope Benedict XIV declared the Colosseum sacred, which stopped further destruction.

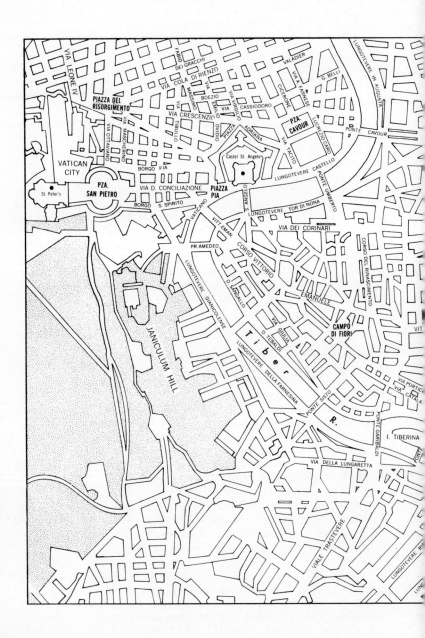

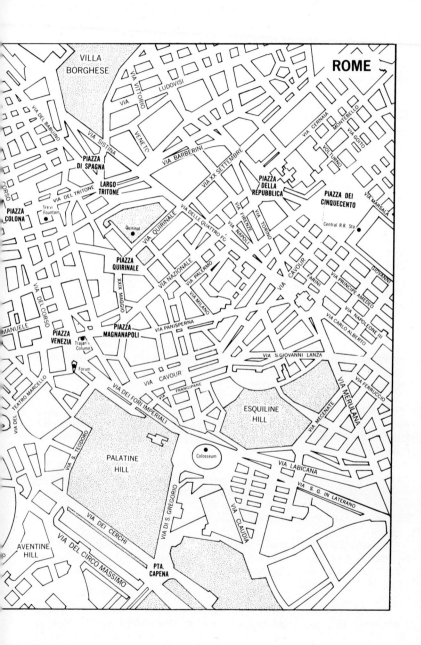

ROME

VILLA BORGHESE

VIA VITTORIO

VIA LUDOVISI

VIA DEL BABUINO

VIA SISTINA

VIA VENETO

VIA CERNIA

MONTEBELLO

VIA GOITO

PIAZZA DI SPAGNA

VIA BARBERINI

VIA XX SETTEMBRE

VOLTURNO

LARGO TRITONE

VIA DEL TRITONE

PIAZZA DELLA REPUBBLICA

PIAZZA DEI CINQUECENTO

VIA MARSALA

CORSO

PIAZZA COLONA

Trevi Fountain

Quirinal

VIA QUIRINALE

VIA DELLE QUATTRO FC

VIA FIRENZE

VIA NAPOLI

VIA TORINO

Central R.R. Sta.

GIOVANNI

PIAZZA QUIRINALE

XXIX MAGGIO

VIA NAZIONALE

VIA PALERMO

VIA MILANO

VIA CAVOUR

FARINI

VIA PRINCIPE AMEDEO

VIA NAPOLEONE III

VIA DEL CORSO

EMANUELE

PIAZZA VENEZIA

Trajan's Column

PIAZZA MAGNANAPOLI

VIA PANISPERNA

VIA CARLO ALBERTO

VIA S. GIOVANNI LANZA

Forum

VIA CAVOUR

FRANGIPANE

VIA FERRUCCIO

VIA TEATRO MARCELLO

VIA DEI FORI IMPERIALI

ESQUILINE HILL

VIA MERULANA

VIA MECENATE

VIA DEL

VIA S. TEODORO

PALATINE HILL

Colosseum

VIA LABICANA

VIA DI S. GREGORIO

VIA S. G. IN LATERANO

AVENTINE HILL

VIA DEI CERCHI

VIA CLAUDIA

VIA DEL CIRCO MASSIMO

PTA. CAPENA

Arco di Constantino • *Arch of Constantine* • Next to the Colosseum and erected in A.D. 315 to commemorate a victory by Emperor Constantine, this was the largest of many triumphal arches in ancient Rome.

Foro Romano • *Roman Forum, via dei Fori Imperiali, near the piazza Venezia* • Just behind Rome's Campidoglio (city hall) are the ruins of the Forum of ancient Rome. It contained shops, temples, and various public institutions, and was not a single forum but several. The **Trajan Forum** is easy to spot. Over 120 feet high, the column is covered with a frieze picturing the military experts of Emperor Trajan. (A genteel way to enjoy it is with a meal at **Ulpia**, facing the basilica of the same name.) The statue of St. Peter on top was added in the 16th century by Sixtus V. There are also forums of other caesars; to distinguish one group of ruins from another, a specialized guidebook is helpful. Personal (licensed) guides also are useful; they are in the vicinity of all major monuments or you can engage one beforehand by phoning 6789842.

Capitoline Hill • *piazza del Campidoglio* • The bronze equestrian statue is of Marcus Aurelius; when restoration is completed it may move to a museum and a copy put in its stead. In the palazzos designed by Michelangelo are the Capitoline Museums; this 500-year-old collection focuses on Roman sculpture as well as on Oriental art, including religious objects from conquered provinces and the famous statue "The Dying Gaul," which is a replica of a 3rd-century bronze. If you are hill-hopping among Rome's greater seven, see the **Palatino** too. And a pair of museums not to miss are the Etruscan one at **Villa Giulia** and the classical art one at **Palazzo Barberini.**

Palazzo Venezia • *piazza Venezia* • It looks more like a fortress than what it was: a papal ambassadorial residence. It now contains paintings, sculpture, and varied objects by Italian artists.

Trastevere • This popular quarter of Rome has been a residential area since ancient times. If you are walking, you can reach the Trastevere by crossing the Tiber by the 2000-year-old Ponte Fabricio to the Tiberine Island and then on Ponte Cestio to the other side of the river. The main street in the district is the viale Trastevere, where you can soak up some of the human flavor of this colorful part of Rome. **Santa Cecilia** is one of the quarter's most visited churches, also frequented for its musical performances. **Santa Maria** in **Trastevere,** especially lovely at night when illuminated, presents a facade containing very early mosaics and its Romanesque campanile.

Palazzo Farnese • *piazza Farnese* • Now the French Embassy, this beautiful Renaissance palazzo was commissioned by Pope Paul II in 1500 but not completed until 1589—giving you some idea of the labor problems faced even by the Bishop of Rome.

Pantheon • *piazza della Rotonda* • It was begun in 27 B.C. by Agrippa as a temple of Mars and Venus and rebuilt in the 2nd century A.D. by Hadrian after it had been damaged in a fire. The facade sports Corinthian columns, a deep porch, and domed roof. Inside is a huge, acoustically perfect rotunda lighted naturally from a 9-yard-wide central oculus high above in the cupola. The marble floor of the rotunda is empty, but around the curvilinear sides of the immense enclosure are chapels containing the tombs of Italian kings, including that of Victor Emanuel II, the first sovereign of a unified Italy. To many people, however, the most important tomb here is that of the painter Raphael, who is buried between the 5th and 6th chapels.

Piazza Navona • This elongated, elliptical piazza was built over the site of the Circus Domitian, which was a race course during the Roman age. Of today's trio of monuments here, the central one is the celebrated Fountain of Four Rivers (1651) by Bernini.

Fontana di Trevi • *Trevi Fountain* • A coin tossed into what is probably the world's most visited fountain is supposed to guarantee your return to Rome. The Trevi Fountain squirted slowly into life from 1732–1751 by Nicolo Salvi from a design by Bernini. Most warm afternoons and certainly evenings, the youth of Rome gather on its flanks for socializing.

Museo Nazionale Romano o delle Terme • *National Roman Museum (Terme Museum), via delle Terme di Diocleziano* • This extensive collection contains many inspiring pieces of Greek, Roman, and Christian art. The rooms incorporate some of the remaining walls of the baths (from A.D. 305), which could accommodate 3000 people. Michelangelo worked on the redesigning of the building; entirely of his inspiration is the perfectly square Great Cloister with its 100 arches.

San Pietro in Vincoli • *piazza San Pietro in Vincoli* • Michelangelo's striking sculpture "Moses" is here.

La Scalinata di Piazza di Spagna • *Spanish Steps* • These (137 in all) often serve as a starting-out point for visitors to Rome. At the foot of the Steps is the boat-shaped fountain by Pietro Bernini, father of the prolific Gian Lorenzo Bernini. At the top is the Trinita dei Monti with yet another fine view of the city.

Piazza del Popolo • In the center on a pedestal embellished by lions spouting water from their mouths is the **Flaminian Obelisk** (1232–1200 B.C.) The piazza has three churches; **Santa Maria del Popolo** (reputed to stand over Nero's tomb; frescoes by Pinturicchio and paintings by Caravaggio); **Santa Maria in Montesanto;** and **Santa Maria dei Miracoli.** No vehicles are allowed, but there are vast migrations of tourists day and night.

Galleria Borghese • *via Pinciana* • In the Villa Borghese, this is among the finest museums in Rome, with works by Titian, Correggio, Caravaggio, Botticelli, Raphael, Canova, Bernini, and others. It is surrounded by Rome's loveliest park, a car-free refuge with artificial lakes, bridle paths, and a zoo.

Castel Sant'Angelo • *Largo Castello* • This unique battlemented structure began in Roman times (A.D. 135–139) as Hadrian's mausoleum and was made into a fortress in the 3rd century. Having shown its value as a stronghold during barbarian invasions, it was later used by the popes, who connected it to the Vatican by means of a tunnel. Some of the ugliest crimes in Italian history took place here.

Terme di Caracalla • *Baths of Caracalla, via delle Terme di Caracalla* • You'll hear splendid opera here in summer—outdoors, of course. Next to the Baths of Diocletian, the Baths of Caracalla were the largest in ancient Rome. During their heyday, they were valued for their beautiful marbles and decorations.

Basilica of San Giovanni in Laterano • *St John in Lateran, piazza San Giovanni* • Before the papacy was installed in the Vatican, St. John in Lateran was the residence of the pope and still is the Cathedral of Rome. And as long as you're basilica-hopping, don't miss two other fine ones, possibly even of greater interest: **Santa Maria Maggiore** and **San Paolo Fuori le Mura.**

Keats-Shelley Memorial House • *piazza di Spagna 26* • This building was a temporary residence for many traveling writers and artists; it is where John Keats died. On display are a collection of Keats's original drafts as well as mementoes of Byron and Shelley.

Excursions

Via Appia Antica • *Appian Way* • Extending from Rome to the port of Brindisi, it was a direct link with the Orient. Alongside the Appian Way are tombs and monuments in various states of preservation—and, of recent date, the villas of film stars and other notables. A pleasant way to enjoy it is with lunch in the garden of the **Antica Roma** (closed Mon.) or at night when the 2000-year-old walls are illuminated showing the burial niches of slaves set free from the time of Augustus.

Catacombs of San Callisto • *Via Appia Antica* • Before the Christian era, these deep, winding catacombs served as a burial place. The early Christians used them for meetings and hiding places. Originally, St. Cecilia was buried here, but her remains are now entombed at the church named after her on the Tiberine Island.

Hadrian's Villa • Emperor Hadrian was among Rome's most active builders and one of his pet projects was a magnificent villa begun in A.D. 120 that was intended to be a self-contained world with recreations of the most beautiful and/or the most luxurious examples of architecture that Hadrian had come across in the course of his many journeys throughout the empire. What's left of this imperial dream—in the same direction as Tivoli—are ruins and a few reconstructions.

Villa d'Este • This creation in Tivoli (20 miles from Rome) was built for Cardinal Ippolito d'Este around 1550. With hundreds of fountains and luxuriant, irrigated landscaping, it was meant to reflect the glory of one of the great families of the Renaissance. Try to include a sumptuous lunch at **Sibilla,** a villa commissioned by Hadrian. (Tel. 0774–20281; closed Mon.)

Ostia Antica ● This was an early port settlement; nearby modern Ostia remains a beach resort of summer-izations for today's Romani. The archaeological sites can be visited by boat *(Tiber I)* leaving from Ponte Sublicio (Ripa Grande) each day around 9:30 a.m.

HOTELS

While your room rate may be quoted to you as a fixed sum, many places have sharply jacked up the prices of amenities such as drinks, laundry, and room service items. Ask what is included; generally, it is a Continental breakfast, but often you'll be socked extra for air conditioning.

The ratings below do not necessarily correspond with the official listings. Mine are personal evaluations, as described in "About the Stars" in the introductory text of this book.

☆☆☆☆☆ **Hassler** ● favorite of many for its intimacy and flair, is expertly run by Roberto Wirth, whose family has been at the helm here for generations. If you want a viewful and convenient address in Rome's finest quarter, then look no further. The subtle hominess here is hard to duplicate anywhere in the city. It offers a wonderful roof garden and refashioned window-wrapped dining paradise now with Roman cuisine, an outdoor patio with the Imperial bar in its court, a genteel interior bar with large adjoining lounge, a reading room in soft greens, perfect maintenance, and extra-smooth service. Magnificent view from the upper floors; full air conditioning; fine hair-dressing salon; all front units restyled; many widened by clever architectural techniques and built-in furnishings; hand-painted murals added to some walls; top spreads are the San Pietro, the Presidential and the Medici Suites, all with glorious views of the city. The effort here is so cordial and zealous that the Hassler even will arrange golf and lunch for guests at a beautiful nearby club. Hosting at its best by Manager Silvano Pinchetti and his skillful staff.

☆☆☆☆☆ **Grand** ● 100% air-conditioned, is the home of diplomats, dignitaries, and lovers of top traditional European hotelkeeping; urbane, spacious, and luxurious, it is the capital showcase of the CIGA chain. Now more glamorous than ever, with a reshaped lobby, containing an attractive bar-buffet with piano music; there's the freshly styled restaurant with Mediterranean cuisine; 2 squash courts, sauna, Turkish bath, massage, and gym. Each floor has been graciously refitted and baths renewed in marble. It is operated by capable director Massimo Rosati. Highest recommendation for this Grand old landmark.

☆☆☆☆☆ **Eden** ● commands a viewful midcity situation atop a small ridge, with the added bonus that 70% of its bedchambers overlook the Villa Borghese and the Pincio Gardens. Like the Hassler, it is small and reserved rather than large and bustling. Since its purchase by the Trust House Forte group, almost everything from its penthouse restaurant to its wine cellar has been revised. Director Lorenzo Giannuzzi will have completed the updatings by the time of your arrival.

☆☆☆☆ **Excelsior** • CIGA-owned cornerstone of via Veneto, is perfectly suited to its midstream location. A lot of updating has gone into the huge house over the past several seasons. It is a beautiful, ornate and palatial building; but since it is so large, much of its elegance is lost in the busy-ness of its lobby, lounges and public sectors, which are so often filled with tour groups. Savory food in its small off-lobby restaurant; soundproof double windows wherever you peek; enlarged baths, including twin basins, separate nonskid tub and shower rooms; immaculate maintenance. Tariffs range from the reasonable group levels to the stratosphere for rooms and suites that outshine even those of the Grand.

☆☆☆ **Flora** • is excellent for location, smack on the via Veneto. The exterior has been smartened nicely, but the interior needs pep to jolly up the mood of the public rooms. Genteel aura; cuisine pleasant but not memorable. All of the restyled bedrooms have high ceilings, quasi-portable-unit air conditioning, plenty of closet space, and lots of Lebensraum.

☆☆☆ **Ambasciatori Palace** • *"The Palace of the Ambassadors"* • is also on the jump under the ambitious administration of personable Giancarlo Polesel. Lovely flower-girt entrance with fountain, one of the most convenient addresses in Rome; refashioned lobby and reception; wonderful Embassy suites (facing the enclave of the U.S. ambassador). Attractive shaded dining terrace; a favorite of business types during the week, which makes the establishment unusually peaceful for tourists in town over the weekend.

★★★★★ **Cavalieri Hilton** • is a 400-room, air-conditioned, fully balconied hostelry facing the Vatican and the Alban hills, an 8-layer-cake structure that adds dazzle to the Latin scene. Sited in a 15-acre park atop Monte Mario, it is about 15 minutes from via Veneto by the Giuseppe Mazzini route and about 30 minutes by the piazza di Spagna-piazza del Popolo-via Flaminia route. Extensive gardens; lobby in Italianate boldness with 6 shops; adjoining cocktail lounge; penthouse 90-seat La Pergola restaurant with bar and dinner dancing where advance reservations are advised; colorful Trattoria del Cavalieri that is a delight; a pool for all seasons; sauna; frequent free bus shuttle service to the center of the city. All of the remade and enlarged sleeping quarters are graceful, tasteful, and outstandingly comfortable, with numerous thoughtful touches; in-house movies; marble baths with vanity tables and makeup mirrors. Good, but so far from midtown that many travelers may feel divorced from the action while others may prefer it.

☆☆☆ **Mediterraneo** • is not as luxurious as some of the above, but the management shows such alert interest in North American tastes and preferences and the staff is so friendly that most wanderers seem to feel at home here. Behind its tremendous success is Angelo Bettoja (pronounced Bet-toy-yah), the

president of the Rome Hotel Association, whose wife is American. Restylings
include 8 new penthouse suites with private terraces, a piano bar, new dining
salon, new marble baths, new elevators and a reformed lobby. One block from
both the central railway station and the airline terminus; 120-car garage—and
what an asset that is here; air conditioning. You'll find greater lushness and
plushness elsewhere, but not quite the same friendly attitude.

☆☆☆ **De la Ville** • a first-class-category house atop the Spanish Steps next
to the Hassler, boasts an ideal address. It too has a breathtaking view plus a
marvelous cool inner courtyard for summer dining and sipping. Quiet lobby,
uncluttered and uncommercial; calm Patio Bar with light meals; 6th-floor solarium with all of Rome at your feet; air conditioning; most lodgings with TV
(with English programs), radio, direct-dial phones and private baths. The staff
goes all out to make your stay a happy one. Here's a splendid value for vacationers.

★★★ **Jolly** • *fringing the Sylvan park and Borghese Gardens* • in modernistic contrast to—but not in conflict with—the nature and antiquity which surrounds it. The visitor benefits from living on one of the capital's prime parcels
of real estate; bronze-tinted windows; subterranean lobby, bar, and dining spread;
200 units in the 21st-century mood, all with a goodly supply of formica veneer,
a microscopic bath and shower, a music console, a TV, and double-glaze windows. The balconied treetop accommodations are heaven-sent abodes of tranquillity. The service standards and cuisine in this backyard of princes are typically
Jolly—the antonym of the name. (It has one of the lowest staff-to-client ratios
in the city for its category.)

★★★ **Parco dei Principi** • *near the Aviary of the Borghese Gardens, an
8-minute stroll from via Veneto* • Aesthetically it evokes a sense of freshness
that is more appropriate to summer than to winter vacations. Very standardized
interior; enormous downstairs dining rooms for everyday patronage or for ceremonial occasions; air conditioning; skinny hear-through walls; clean-lined furniture; 18 showrooms for seminars, fashion shows, and other money-spinners.
A rustic snack bar and cabanas are snuggling next to its handsome irregular-
shape outdoor pool. An island of quiet and suburban calm in the midst of one
of the world's busiest metropoli.

☆☆ **Victoria** • *sedate but convenient location overlooking Borghese Gardens, around the corner from via Veneto* • pulls in attractive clientele of profes-
sors, musicians, artists; refined dining salon in white, mustard, and gray; 115
rooms with 115 baths; optional air conditioning up to 90%; some accommodations lovely and some more simple; radios that tune in to English broadcasting;
color TV; frigobars; colorful roof-garden for sunbathing and sipping. Swiss-
owned by Alberto H. Wirth, a splendid host.

Bernini Bristol • seems to have lost some of its head of steam. The earlier
upliftings now are becoming dated and the textiles especially seem dismal in
colors and motifs. Full air conditioning; refrigerators in all bedchambers; most
rooms small; more space and flair in units ending in "06" and "07"; 75% in

contemporary decor; double windows installed wherever needed. What it lacks is a dash of inspiration.

Hotel Quirinale • *connected to the Rome Opera House* • has been an imposing landmark in the Eternal City. The lobby and many of the other segments have been rebuilt. The spacious, open patio-garden is a beautiful oasis with alfresco dining and its own bar. Overlooking this is a restaurant in the reopened corridor to the artists' entrance of the Opera. Its 200 air-cooled rooms, all with bath, are still mixed in their quality and appeal.

☆ **Gregoriana** • *via Gregoriana 18, just below the Hassler* • is a little gem for little people (who must be petite to enjoy its miniature dimensions). It's a beloved magnet for Italian fashion designers and models—not known for their bulk. Completely air conditioned; virtually no lobby; no restaurant; breakfasts served in bedchambers; apartment across the street for shows. Their wall-to-wall rugs and white-painted bamboo furniture are highlighted by the same vividly hued accents in their curtains, bedspreads, and towels. The maintenance is superb, as is the hospitality of its staff. Here's an elfin, fun-filled inn—formerly a convent—for travelers to whom these special surroundings appeal.

☆ **Borromini** • *via Lisbona 7* • is a few minutes from the action in a residential zone. Cheerful, softly lit, peaceful lobby in dark blue and orange; no restaurant; snack facilities from noon to 6:30 which carry over to main bar from 10 p.m. to midnight; garage. In addition to 5 suites, there are 85 dark-blue doubles with wall-to-wall carpeting, Frigobars, cramped bathrooms, and no bedspreads. Above average.

☆ **Cicerone** • *via Cicerone 55* • in a relatively quiet district near the Vatican, is a strong candidate as the leading first-class inferior (an official grading) hotel in the city. Angular lobby in brown and yellow; subdued ambience; large coffee shop seating 250 open from 6:30 a.m. to noon; light fare available in American bar during the afternoon and evening. Agreeable bedchambers with small bath, Frigobar, and thoughtful touches such as shower caps, shoeshine cloths, and more but with inadequate storage space; garage. Commercial? Yes—but it's good.

☆ **Massimo d'Azeglio** • *opposite Mediterraneo near the station* • is a solid value. All 300 comfortable but unfancy rooms with smart marble baths or showers; fully air-conditioned; double windows to s-s-s-s-s-s-sh street exposures, but some facets still noisy; modern lobby; bar'ette; serene, cozy, attractive dining room with cuisine which is just plain *terrific* (top quality at decent prices).

Londra & Cargill • *Sallustio 18, 2½ blocks from via Veneto* • reminds us of the Little Girl With the Curl. On the ground floor its muted modern lobby in white and heather green, its adjoining 20-table restaurant with freshly white-grilled walls, canary cloths, and coordinated carpeting, and its subtle pinpoint spotlight ceiling illumination are all stunning. Upstairs, however, the burnt oranges and greens are so screaming that they might knock your eyeballs for a loop.

Fleming • *piazza Monteleone di Spoleto 20, way out beyond the Olympic Village* • the largest second-class hotel in Rome, so strongly impresses me as cold, impersonal, and mechanically tour-oriented that I cannot commend it in any way.

Leonardo da Vinci • a link in the Jolly chain, has begun to take on a more commercial air. Nonurban situation on the murmur-quiet via dei Gracchi; entrance flanked by awning-covered terraces for sipping and alfresco chatting; restaurant, grill, and bar; underground garage. Accommodations generously equipped with 6-channel radios, Venetian fixtures, excellent furniture, tile flooring, double windows, and 100% air conditioning.

☆ **Sitea** • *opposite the Grand Hotel at via Vittorio Emanuele Orlando 90* • is a second-class hostelry with unmistakably first-class comfort. Its progress has been so laudable that, without jack-rabbiting its prices unfairly or unduly, it now vies with the big fellows in more respects than simply value for money. Pleasant little dining room, bar, and lounges, all immaculate; savory snacks; parking garage. Its greatest asset is the friendly welcome.

☆ **Carriage** offers a unique personality. Antiques, chandeliers, mirrors, brocades, and thick carpets adorn its foyer-style lobby, ornate salon, and TV lounge. This candidate has no restaurant and almost no other public amenities. However, its irreverent bar was formerly an altar in a 17th-century Sicilian church, and 2 panels on the wall come from an 18th-century library. All bedrooms come with bath, telephone, radio, floral wallpaper, combination bed-table-bar wagons, and curious triangularly shaped corner wardrobes. Fuchsia-tone #36 wins our prize among our twins, while rooftop #47, with its wraparound terrace, is a splendid single for the price.

☆☆ **Lord Byron** • greets you with a fresh, cheerful visage and a lobby soothed by soft music; handsome appointments and American Bar; praiseworthy Le Jardin restaurant, which could be a set from an Antonioni masterpiece: glossy white walls warmed by pastel rose broadloom and cream-colored furniture.

☆ **Inghilterra** • *near the Spanish Steps* • is a former palace annex in the finest shopping district of Rome. An historic stop for writers from H.C. Andersen to E. Hemingway (also for a king or two). F. Mendelssohn (another guest) would have noted the graceful counterpoint between fine antiques and modern comforts. The recent restyling was a smash hit.

President • *near St. John Lateran Basilica* • steers a reasonable platform to its group-minded electorate. La Hacienda restaurant with woven tablecloths, Andalusian paintings, Tiffany-style lamps, and a nibble nook devoted to authentic Castilian pizza; woody bar; colonial breakfast room.

Forum • named for the Imperial Forum which it overlooks, is tucked into a small restored *palazzo*. Intimate, pleasant, wall-to-wall carpeted lobby; neo-Edwardian decor; air-conditioned; double windows for sssssssilence; tasteful little roof-garden restaurant; interior dining salon for rain-outs; small but agreeably furnished bedchambers.

Cardinal • began life circa A.D. 1400. In this century it finished a massive renovation which didn't help too much.

Eliseo • *just off the top of via Veneto* • has a small entrance lobby; adjoining bar; roof-garden restaurant; copper-sheathed rotisserie. Okay, provided you draw one of the prime balconied units rather than the several mother-in-law rooms.

Visconti Palace • provides comfortable modernistic shelter, trim uplifting decor, a roof garden (gone to seed on our visit) and an overall mien that would seem to attract conducted tours; 250 rooms.

Villa Pamphili • about the same size, has a location convenient to the Vatican; otherwise it is too far out of the shopping center for many visitors. Huge pool; 2 tennis courts; terrace dining plus main restaurant; fair amenities.

Midas Palace • is somewhat bigger but similar in concept since the same firm also designed the Pamphili. It, too, boasts a large swimming pool. Not bad if you prefer lounging to gadflying around the town. Many groups.

Atlante Star • and the **Atlante Garden** • *300 yards from St. Peter's* • are attractive medium-price twins if the location is suitable for you. By prearrangement they offer free pickup service from the airport.

Boston • *almost in the shade of the Borghese bowers* • is a mixture of Beacon Hill nabobery and baked-bean basics. Seventh-floor units with terraces, the aristocrats of the Back Bay Society; other accommodations simpler but still very appealing with textile wall coverings, Frigobars, TV, radio, air conditioning, and good baths throughout. The midcity site is a distinct asset.

Ritz • *in the Parioli district* • has a remote location for sightseers to the city. Heavy patronage by groups that are often carted thither by bus.

Residence Palace • is more central but sad in aspect.

Napoleon • *a 10-minute walk from the station* • has a piazza location in full view of a public market. All 100 units with bath or shower and "Massage Boy" bed vibrators; about half with radio; 40 singles; 2 tiny suites per floor; full air conditioning; tasteful traditional decor.

Michelangelo • *a few steps from the Basilica of St. Peter and the Vatican border* • offers a fading modern tone and an ultra-efficiency motif. Scuff marks in many places; 100% artificially cooled; 200 rooms with dark "interior" full baths or showers; many chambers with floor-length glass doors or windows, but 50% with individual balconies.

Commodore ● boasts 70 bedrooms with bath or shower, a sprinkling of balconies, sitting rooms, air conditioning, bright and clean appointments, quality furnishings, a helpful staff kindling a friendly atmosphere, and a central setting. Demipension is not demanded. Pleasant as a midtown haven.

Savoia ● was given a major overhaul. A lot went into cosmetics in the public rooms and facade. Lovely Venetian glass chandeliers; fine antiques; cheery coffee nook; bedrooms a bit stark but adequate in comfort. Excellent location bordering via Veneto.

Claridge ● *on a tramline in the Parioli district* ● offers 200 air-conditioned, wallpapered rooms, all with bath or shower. Small, rugless, severely modern decor that seems a bit pinchpenny in its rendition; high ratio of tiny individual terraces; chipper dining salon with patio for outdoor ruminations.

Metropole ● comes with air conditioning and double windows throughout; modern, plastic-chaired lobby, about as sterile as the inside of a Band-Aid box.

La Residenza ● *a few steps off the via Veneto at via Emilia 22* ● is a charmer. It has only 27 rooms, most with bath but all with quiet homespun character; #25, #35, #51, and #55 are excellent havens. Snack service only; off-lobby bar. Here's a decently priced stop, with one of the most convenient (and even quiet!) locations in the Eternal City.

Panama is tranquil and also as cozy as the back seat of a Fiat; colorful lobby; attractive restaurant, bar, and downstairs grill; parking area plus a small garage; 42 small, well-groomed rooms and 40 baths or showers, most overlooking a shady little garden; #101 the largest double; service unusually good for its informal style.

San Giorgio ● has a lobby and restaurant connection with the Massimo d'Azeglio; 200 rooms with baths, 25% of which are fresh; air-conditioned throughout; double windows for quiet; 2 modern automatic elevators; bar with handsome Roman murals; lovely breakfast nook; all immaculate, and all modestly but amply furnished.

Lloyd ● has a handsome exterior with orange-awning trim, a pleasant, amiable atmosphere, and an efficient concierge. Small lobby with adjoining bar; bedchambers large, but many lack warm decor; bath or shower with most rooms. A good buy.

Regina Carlton's ● refitting program was, in my opinion, a flop. I believe that it still leans too heavily on its wonderfully convenient via Veneto site.

Porta Maggiore, fronting the best preserved of Rome's gateways (from which it takes its name), is a splendid money-saver and is easily reached by trams #14 or #516. Substantial dining facilities; a bargain.

Tiziano • is a mixed bag of airline-terminal and traditional trappings. Beautiful ancient stairwell; some updatings; in general, furnishings not to my taste and the noise from traffic can be deafening.

Degli Aranci • in a quiet residential district, offers its dining terrace suspended in an orange bower. Improved lobby and bars; 47 rooms with 80% bath count. The better accommodations can be plucked with private balconies for the same price as the lesser ones.

Colosseum • offers a nice lobby, a slick-rustic lounge, a handsome breakfast corner, and 50 bedrooms with shower; the units are decorated in Castilian moods; each seems smaller than a Spanish fly.

Giulio Cesare • provides a splendid view of the Vatican and the Borghese from its roof garden. In addition to the successful refurbishment of its salons and many of its bedchambers (both somewhat on the overdelicate side), the service and cuisine have improved notably. Avoid its basement lodgings.

Anglo-Americano • winks hello with an electric-eye door. The lobby has midnight-blue, textiled walls, plus lots of leather and wood. Upstairs the bedchambers and baths are so narrow that I'd bet you'd find it easier to squeeze between the hyphen in its name.

Columbus • *in the shadow of St. Peter's* • Vatican-owned, was once a convent. Its 115 rooms, 60 with bath or shower, are painfully impersonal, with furnishings that amplify their sterility; in doubles pick #345 or #221. A favorite journey's end for religious pilgrimages or tours from all over the world. For the ecclesiastically inclined only.

Majestic • *on via Veneto* • comes up with a charming outdoor terrace for summer meals. But inside, the beauty fades. Clean but darkish atmosphere; puffy old chairs; similar clientele.

Atlantico • *joined to the aforementioned Mediterraneo* • has the advantages of Bettoja administration, full air conditioning, and a kindly staff.

Plaza • *on the busy Corso (around the corner from the deluxe shopping oases of via Condotti* • has changed only a whit, structurally or in decor, since it opened more than a century ago.

Mondial • has a chilly modernistic lobby, air conditioning in its restaurant and in a scattering of bedchambers, and an overall cast of stark functionality.

Hermitage • has an unlived-in feeling. It's spacious enough, but the violent color contrasts of flaming roses and poisonous cretonnes are eyeracking.

RESTAURANTS

Some of the best dining currently to be found in Rome will be in a selection of leading grand hotels or discreet intimate ones. Because of labor problems and spiraling costs, these better-organized institutions can provide outstanding service, refinement, quality ingredients—and very often the settings and panoramas will be much more inspiring than at the independent entries; advance reservation will be necessary at all of the following. Let's lead off with several of today's top contenders:

★★★★★ **Hassler Roof** • *piazza Trinita dei Monti* • is something (luckily) that money *can* buy! After its sparking redesign and fresh decoration, here is easily *the* most breathtaking perch to occupy at any time of day (it also serves breakfasts) or night in the Eternal City (see ''Hotels''). And since the attention is so professional and the cuisine is so exquisite, why not marry aesthetics and gastronomy in the best match since Adam and Eve? Almost singlehandedly, proprietor Roberto Wirth has brought back Roman cuisine to Rome. The emphasis here is eternally delicious.

★★★ **Eden Hotel** • also with a scenic penthouse, provides high-style atmospherics to Roman high society. Not too spacious but very select.

☆☆☆☆☆ **Grand** • has taken one of the most historical corners in Rome and turned it into its dining parlor, which is simultaneously fresh and elegant. This hotel has always drawn the aristocracy of the globe, so on almost any day you will find its tables occupied by front-page personalities. They have come for good reason because the cuisine, attention, and character are insurmountable. The view, however, is rather limited.

☆☆☆☆☆ **Lord Byron** • offers only a few tables at its **Le Jardin,** but they are always filled with the gustatory *conoscenti* of Rome and visitors of world renown. There is a graceful, lighthearted cheer that pervades—obviously egged on by selections from one of Italy's most prestigious wine cellars. While many dishes tend toward Italian *nuova cucina,* I remain hooked in the house *gnocchi.* I must confess, however, I also admire the French *chefs d'oeuvre,* which appear from the kitchen with frequency.

★★★★ **Hilton** • though well out of the center, presents masterful gastronomy at **La Pergola** (nights only). The setting alone is worth the journey to this hilltop of such overwhelming panoramic beauty. Dinner dancing is available and the evening can be carried on late into the dark velvet night. My last encounter with a scampi here was memorable. For a summer lunch, the poolside buffet (antipasto at $14) is inventive and nicely done—both for cold *and* hot dishes. The sandwiches, however, are disastrous.

☆☆☆ **Massimo d'Azeglio** • is probably the leader among the lower-priced hotel dining salons. There is no pretense here, but the quality is legendary, especially for traditional Italian cooking.

☆☆☆☆ **Excelsior** • Dine *only* at the small and gracefully ornate restaurant, which is at the back of the main lounge and up a few steps. Put yourself in the hands of the cherubic maitre who will help you select the finest and freshest choices of the day's market. His spaghetti (or other pasta) with tart lemon flavoring is a delicious starter; so are the sparkling shellfish on the center display. As mentioned, these great hotels often consider their dining facilities as loss-leaders or necessary services to their resident clients. This guarantees top quality for you at extraordinarily low billings.

Independent Restaurants

☆☆☆☆ **El Toula** • *via della Lupa 29* • Here's a moss-green nookery where the walls are covered with velvet and the carpet is earth-hued; there are vegetables and flowers on the tiny tables; at night everything would dissolve in an instant if illumination were not by candles. The heaven-sent Tagliatelle and South Tyrolean Sondbichilar white wine were outstanding. The dominant theme here is subtle seduction. If that certain someone shares your mood, you'll probably love it, him or her, and everything in sight.

☆☆☆ **Sans Souci** • *via Sicilia 20* • occupies a site a few steps from via Veneto; blackamoor to greet your entrance; cunning, softly illuminated little bar in separate room; necklace of split-level nooks and crannies fetchingly strung with their walls in green, yellow, and white tapestries and their banquettes in handsome light leather; melodizing by singer-pianist with guitarist. Comprehensive, original menu offering outstandingly savory national and international dishes; *dinner only*. Open at 8 p.m. but shuttered Mondays and *sans souci* in Aug.; always reserve in advance. You can well expect to pay up to 100% more than in almost any other dining oasis in Rome. And don't be too surprised if your waiter regards you as doltish; they can be prize snobs at times.

☆☆☆☆ **La Graticola del Jackie O'** • *via Boncompagni II, ½-block from via Veneto* • consists of complementary twins. "The Grill," down one flight, is an elaborate, plushly decorated restaurant, while Jackie O' is a glittering ground-floor disco-nightclub. A showcase for theatrical personalities, gold-disc rock stars and other self-styled Beautiful People who come to see and to be seen. Impressive canopy-corridored entrance; winding staircase to large, quietly voguish, segmented premises in tavern motif; immaculate open kitchen and king-size grill firing to greet clients as they step inside; cunning adjoining bar. Go late—not before 10:30 ever—and reserve in advance; closed July 25–Aug. 25, but otherwise in action 7 days per week; *dinner only*.

☆☆☆☆ **La Clef** • *via Lazio 22/A, also ½-block from via Veneto* • smaller, more intimate, more reasonably priced, is a major contrast to the above trio. This little siren has the comfortable, cozy milieu of a select private club. Bar at entrance with piano; 2 adjoining rooms; paneled walls with tasteful modern paintings artfully placed; subtle to dark illumination; deft, sophisticated client attention; limited but carefully chosen menu; good wine list. Also *dinner only* from 8 p.m.–1 a.m.; also go late; also with a nightclub annex. A benison for Rome's quiet swank set who wish to relax, to talk, and even to hold hands.

☆☆☆ **George's** • *via Marche 7* • is an old standby. Gallic rather than Italian in tone; satin-lined ceilings; lamps and flowers on tables; lovely garden terrace; smooth dinner music; attention sharply honed. A moderate lunch can casually wave *ciao* to $75. Usually closed from Aug. 10–Sept. 10.

Hostaria dell'Orso • *via di Monte Brianzo 93* • hobbles on as a place for a dining and/or dancing rendezvous. It occupies Dante's 14th-century home, an official National Monument. Piano Bar, with a pianist and 2 guitarists; princely Borgia Room with its lapis lazuli pillars and gold utensils; La Cabala now merely a noisy, thumping discotheque.

☆☆☆ **AL 59** • *via Angelo Brunetti 59, near piazza del Popolo* • is run by the founder of the famous Cesarina, who whomps up delectable Bologna-style cookery. Noisy after 1:30 or 9 p.m., so go earlier if you prefer its more tranquil moods. Be *sure* to try a tiny cup (not bowl) of Mamma's heavenly Passatelli first, followed by the tri-plate—bite-size samplings of 3 different types of pasta called Misto Cesarina—while sipping her Albana white wine from the North. After this, sample the Giambella, a featherlight lemon-flavored cake dipped in the Albana before application to your soul. Closed in Aug. and each Sun.
The same group which bought **Cesarina** also took over the once-proud **Fontanella, Toscana,** and the **Girarrosto Toscano,** none of which can be recommended by me today.

☆☆☆ **Cucurucu** • *via Capoprati 10* • is a rust-colored building fringing the Tiber, about 5 minutes by taxi from the center. In the summer the garden dining is captivating; in winter the stucco-walled interior spreads over several rooms, the nicest being before a crackling hearth. Shelves with bottles and artifacts line the rustic salon; fantastic antipasto display greets you at the entrance; you'll be rewarded with very honest Italian cuisine coupled with helpful and generous attention. Here is one of the most reliable bets in town.

☆☆☆ **Taverna Giulia** • *vicolo dell'Oro 23* • is a linkage of 3 rooms in a lovely white house beside the river. The dark-wood beams and the animated atmosphere are a perfect setting for the delicious Genoese preparations. One of Rome's top gathering places for good food and good value.

★★★ **Vecchia Roma** • *18 piazza Campitelli* • near the Capitol, also hosted a current Capitol Hill personage but long ago: Sig. George Bush. Typically Roman in mood, a noble house sprawling with many rooms and corners; passage beside an open kitchen; traditional gastronomy of this city. It can be dressy but the baroque atmosphere also tolerates casual attire. Honesty is a present virtue.

☆☆☆ **Passetto** • *piazza Zanardelli 14* • is a standby of the Old Guard. Kind reception; warmhearted professional attention; boat-shape rolling cart containing shellfish and crustacean appetizers in nests of shaved ice; high-quality ingredients; knowledgeable preparation. On the costly side, but very reliable.

☆☆☆ **La Maiella** • *piazza S. Apollinare 45* • can be an amusing alternative if Passetto is full. It's very nearby, with a hedge-lined terrace and parasol-topped tables. Grilled flat mushrooms are superb; so are the fish dishes. Italians love this house and I found they are more appreciated here than are foreigners.

Alfredo alla Scrofa • *via della Scrofa 104* • impresses me as highly over-priced and distinctly tourist-happy, with cuisine which I thought was definitely substandard. To lure visitors, just about every gimmick on the list seems to be there, including the corny hamming with the spoons when they mix the fettuc-cine (the quality of which reveals no legerdemain from the chef either). The illumination is overbright, the noise level can be deafening, and the harem-scarem "service" was straight out of a Chaplin scenario.

☆☆ **St. Ana** • *via della Penna 68* • still radiates debutante grace. Cellar site with steps leading past a food display; long semidivided room (I prefer the pink-toned right side); paintings and sculpture adorning the stucco walls; white furniture. The ravioli was served in a huge porridge bowl; grilled quail was fair game; after the repast, a house *digestif* was offered free of charge. It was a composition of—hold your breath—Creme de Cacao, Tio Pepe sherry, French cognac, and Grand Marnier, floated with whipped cream and garnished with a cherry. (Horrible as it sounds, you'll probably find it *delicious!*) Closed Sun.

☆☆ **Domus Aurea** • *Giardini al Colle Oppio* • rambles across a small hill overlooking the Colosseum. Inviting open terrace for 150 diners, many of them from bus groups; air-conditioned interior salon; music nightly; sparkling kitchen producing so-so to ho-hum cookery. Easily accessible to midtown sightseers and panoRomantically rewarding.

Il Pianeta Terra • *94 via Arco del Monte* • is oh-so-refined—from its gilt-edged baroque decor to its gilt-edged billings. Very imaginative modern cuisine that also can be rich: venison in red wine, turkey livers in apple sauce, and zabaglione with caramelized framboise topping. Not everyman's dish.

★★ **La Lampada** • *25 via Q. Sella* • is a 4-seasonal specialist in mush-rooms (if they are not current, they are preserved). Any salad, meat, pasta, or other dish may be garnished with *funghi, porcini, tartufi,* or rarer forest growths. (I'll bet you could even get a dessert with such upstarts.) Rustic room in cozy style; nice people; English menu available; easy location 3 blocks behind the U.S. Embassy.

☆☆ **Giovanni** • *64 via Marche* • is a solid contender in the midcity area, an old-timer that continues to give pleasure and value. Entry up a few steps to a simple, modern L-shape room; talkative atmosphere; wide selection of native dishes. For everyday dining this provides quality without fanfare. Very handy and very good.

☆☆ **"31" Al Vicario** • *via Uffici del Vicario 31* • has attractive rooms in beige and white; comfortable banquettes; thick carpets; rich textiles in salmon and complementing pastels; Picasso, Marini, and other modern-art treasures on the walls; outdoor patio dining during warm months; closed Aug. This one is a genuine asset to refinement in Roman culinary circles.

★★★ **Mastrostefano** • *diagonally across from Tre Scalini (see next)* • Extensive 2-part terrace with rows of parasoled tables; one interior room; abuzz with many North Americans.

★★★ **Tre Scalini** • *piazza Navona 28* • is named for the "Three Steps" that were immortalized by Garibaldi. Since all but walking traffic has been banned from this large and lovely square, it is a delight on a beautiful day or evening to sit under the awnings of the sidewalk "terrace" here and contemplate the magnificence of the Bernini Fountains. A very recent meal was passable but presented and served listlessly. The allure of the setting remains, however, so why not just pause here for coffee or a dish of its famous ice cream? The specialty is the luscious chocomania called Gelato Tartufo, about $6. Taxi drivers might try to take you to **Ai Tre Scalini Rosanna e Matteo** • *via S. Quattro 30* • but this is not the famous one.

4 Fiumi • *directly next door to Tre Scalini* • is a similar setup, as the name suggests. But whether it's Three Steps, Four Rivers, or Five Continents, the final results are almost identical. Perhaps the floods of tourists in this pedestrian hub of Rome have dampened the local service standards.

☆☆ **Bolognese** • *piazza del Popolo* • is a favorite meeting place of lovely budding movie stars, painters, and creative arts people. Their choice is well founded, because the cuisine is superb, the personnel are warm, and while the house isn't opulent in any respect, the prices are right. Closed every Mon., willy-nilly; open the other 313 days of the year. Best in good weather on the terrace. Now—*please don't take dessert, coffee, or liqueurs here.*

Pasticceria Rosati • *piazza del Popolo 5a* • is expensive and highly a la mode. On a sunny day it could be heavenly to laze here almost within the shadows of the Bernini Fountain, the Ramses Obelisk and the 2 beautiful churches on Valadier Square, with the Borghese Gardens directly above. You decide, but, personally, I detest the overblown self-importance of its waiters.

Il Matriciano • *via del Gracchi 51–57* • replaced Bolognese for some but *never* for me. Remote outlying location with no scenic charms; sidewalk dining; superswift and cheerful attention.

★★ **Sabatini** • *vicolo Santa Maria 18* • is one of the most popular trattorias on the Trastevere banks. Largish hedged terrace on piazza Santa Maria; front door facing a handsome open grill glowing with charred wood and sizzling with roasts, chops, fish, and fowl; interior hall with leaded windows and 3 enormous ancient timbers supporting a raftered ceiling; aging walls topped by a rich but fading painted molding.

Galeassi • *piazza Sta. Maria in Trastevere* • with a similar outdoor-indoor layout but a bit smaller, faces the same *piazza*. It has its host of loyal adherents, too—and its tariffs are slightly lower.

☆☆ **La Tana del Grillo** • *"The Cricket's Nest," on Salita del Grillo* • is one of the top spots around Trajan's Forum these days. It offers Bolognese dishes for the first reel of cinematic personalities.

La Capricciosa • *largo dei Lombardi 8* • is a sound, budget-level *trattoria* for serious feeders. No bar; 3 clean dining rooms and one basement corner in modern tone; open 9 a.m. till after 2 a.m. every day of the year. The food is good, the ladles are generous, and the prices are right.

☆☆☆ **Taverna Flavia** • *via Flavia 9* • lines its walls with photos of celebrated clients while lining its clients with celebrated cookery. Simple interior of several interlocking rooms; bottle-green color scheme; generally folksy service. The pasta, white truffles, grilled scampi, sauteed brains with a light garlic flavor, and the house wine were all above average. If fresh peas are in season, be sure to order a side dish. Very good—but always total up your bill here.

★★ **Scoglio di Frisio** • *via Merulana 256* • in the low lire league, gets better every year. The Frisio's "Rock" motif is expressed in rough papier-mache boulders which project from the walls as from the interior of a cave; fishnets, Bowery Art Shop murals, and stalactites pull hard against one another in polychromatic contrast. The pizza (evenings only), the spaghetti with clam sauce, the filet of sole with peas, mushrooms, and olives (ask for "alla Frisio") are a dream. Closed Sun.; evenings only.

☆ **Piperno a Monte Cenci** • *via Monte Cenci 9* • a nonkosher pride of the Jewish-Italian ghetto of the Eternal City, has been famous since 1844 as The Artichoke Capital of the World; its specialty *(carciofi alla giudia)* comes in Jewish-style only (opened, flattened, and sauteed in some deliciously secret fashion). Operated by a vigorous and competent young couple who have improved it so dramatically that now at nearly every meal the house is full. Friendly, noisy, and bustling; old-fashioned furnishings; closed last half of Aug. and various holidays; wine and beer only. I'm told (but don't know personally) that a trio of Kosher restaurants in Portico d'Ottavia, near the main synagogue, are better than sliced *matzos*. These are **Da Luciano, Alfredo** • *via Principe Amedeo* • and **Fratelli Pepi** • *via Sistina.*

Trattorie

Al Chianti • *via Ancona 17* • also known as "Ernesto & Mario," has a Tuscan ambience, with about 14 Lilliputian tables in Italian-rustic. Its motif employs enough raffia, straw, and flotsam to titillate the heart of Trader Vic. The substantial viands lose some of their savor under the high-pressure rush-act of the waiters. Nice tone for the price range.

Memmo • *piazza Cavour 14* • does memmo-rable things with traditional home cooking.

Luigi and **Polese** • *within an olive's toss of each other on piazza Sforza and Cesarini* • seem to be *mano-a-mano* in the quest to produce the city's finest veal. Either way, you'll come home a winner.

Romolo • *via di Porta Settimiana 8 in Trastevere* • is still popular among local socialities for its down-to-earth Roman atmosphere. Clean; big garden which once belonged to La Fornarina ("The Bakery Girl"), who was Raphael's mistress; sound food; low, low tariffs.

Da Mario • *via della Vite 64A* • comes up with one room, one waiter, and wonderful Tuscan cuisine; clean, inexpensive, and so crowded my elbows are still contused.

Augustea • *via della Frezza 5* • offers 2 plant-lined rooms, a free fish dish to start, a good meal in the middle, and a gratis liqueur at the end. Seafood is the mainstay; closed Mon.

Something Different

★★★ **Ambasciata d'Abruzzo** • *via Pietro Tacchini 26, up in the Parioli district* • is usually crammed to the rafters with laughing locals, a jovial proprietor, and his staff who keep bellowing, "Mangia, mangia, mangia!" ("Eat, eat, eat!") and similar encouragements. Even as the host carries platters to his patronage, he spoons free bites to other clients along his happy route. The moment you sit down, a basket with 17 types of sausage is placed on your table, plus a cutting board, bread, cheese, and knives. Then you are given a stack of plates and told to take anything (and as much) as you want from the terraces of antipasto; I counted 35 different preparations and were they ever delicious! Serious gourmands then go on to roasts, fowl, trout, and a menu so long that our vision blurred just glancing at it. Absolutely imperative to reserve in advance, especially on a Sat. afternoon. The entrance, incidentally, is so narrow that you may squeeze in, but if you "Mangi, mangi, mangi!" as the man says, I'd bet you won't be able to squeeze out.

NIGHT LIFE

The previously mentioned **Jackie O'** (via Boncompagni 11, less than a block from via Veneto) is the most ostentatious dazzler. Ground floor above La Graticola (see "Restaurants"); large room with walls and ceilings in shiny black plastic plus mirrors almost anywhere one looks; ultramodern tables and trimmings; small bar plus bandstand for 4 musicians; whisky around $12 per cup all-in, with no cover charge; go very, very late. The cinema, theater, and rock-music, Big Name, Big Talk Set finds it Heaven.

La Clef (via Marche 13, also near via Veneto) shares its name and address with a dining spot. (See "Restaurants.") Here you will find a cozy hand-holding rendezvous in a richly modern and discreet milieu. Subdued strains of a singer-pianist from 10 to 12; rock with dancing from 12 to 1; disco gyrations from 1 to 3:30; cover charge and first drink about $10.50; subsequent drinks about $6; open end of Sept. to end of June only. So skillfully conceived that the top of the night-owl society love it and flock here.

Gil's (via Romagnosi), very dressy and exotic, and **Bella Blu** (via Luciani 2) are trendy with upper-crusted discophiles. Both are costly and clique-ish.

La Cabala (via dei Soldati 25), resides on a rooftop near piazza Navona. A summer night passes agreeably here.

L'Arciliuto (piazza Monte Vecchio 5) is the love nest created by the renowned musician, Enzo Samaritani. His romantic den is tucked in a former studio of Raffaello. (Please note the great artist's fresco plastered into the arch just inside the entrance—a priceless windfall which Sig. Samaritani discovered through private research.) The inner structure has been left almost exactly as originally designed by the 16th-century Maestro. Vaulted ceiling; sienna-colored walls mellowed by flickering tapers; beige carpets; provincial woodwork. Comfortable leather chairs and divans for sipping, listening, and between-song conversing; lutes and rare stringed instruments forming the decorative motif; piano for intermission tinkling or for accompanying the proprietor as he strums, chants, or softly whispers the melodies of Calabria, Sicily, and other provinces of his musical land. Excellent and expensive drinks; canapes available; suave service; honest accounting. Be sure to get *exact* directions before you set out, because it's in a hard-to-find, tiny courtyard about 3 minutes' walk from Passetto restaurant. If you wish to reserve a table (it is small), telephone 65–94–19. Warm endorsement for seekers of that tranquil evening.

Scarabocchio (piazza dei Ponziani 8) has capitalized on its living-room structure. Angular bar; ring of chairback stools around the piano occupying one corner and most of the spotlighting; divans kneeling at squat tables; illuminated glass floor for dancing; subtle lighting; an audience that works strenuously at getting with it.

Club 84 (via Emilia 84) is still plugged into the elegance circuit. High voltage prices; year-round operation; L-shape, raucous, close, and intimate; small band; no cabaret; companions available but not graspy; slide projections of resort scenes. A nice spot that is honest.

Piper Club, far out at via Tagliamento 9, now features discotheque-nology and roller skating. It remains the top-o-the-pops "megadisco" followed by the punky **Mais** (via Cesare Beccaria 22) and the 3-story **Much More** with banks of pinball machines for the youth patrol.

SHOPPING

SHOPPING HOURS: There are so many local variations that it's wise to check first with the concierge of your hotel. Wherever the siesta custom is observed (Rome, Naples, the South), most stores are open from 9 a.m.–1 p.m. and from 4 p.m. to 7:30 or 8 p.m. Everything is open at 3 or 3:30 p.m. in Milan, Turin, Genoa, Bologna, and Venice. Often shops are closed in Aug.; frequently during summer months Sat. p.m. closings substitute for Mon. a.m.s.

BEST AREAS: The piazza di Spagna and all the streets off of it such as via Condotti, via della Croce, via Borgognona (now a delightful pedestrian mall), via Bocca di Leone, via Frattina, via del Babuino and via Due Macelli; at the top of the Spanish Steps the via Sistina; via del Corso (running from piazza del Popolo to piazza Venezia); via Veneto and the many streets that crisscross it on either side; via Barberini; via Bissolati; via Nazionale (cheaper shops) and via Cola di Rienzo (extending, on the other side of the Tiber more or less across from the piazza del Popolo, to the Vatican) where prices are on an even lower scale and bargaining is common.

ANTIQUES: Via Giulia is a good street for general hunting, so are via Margutta, via del Babuino, and via dei Coronari (with a *Settimana dell' Antiquariato* three times a year). Piazza Fontanella Borghese also offers jewelry. Watch out for counterfeits.

ART GALLERIES: **Gallerias Schneider,** owned and operated by Americans, handles some of the top Italian painters. **L'Obelisco, Barcaccia,** and **Il Camino** are well known. There are more than 50 salons in the capital.

BOOKS: **The Lion Bookshop** (via del Babuino 181) has large stocks of reading matter—or try either the **American Book Shop** (via delle Vite 57) or the **English & American Bookshop** (via Torino, close to the Opera House), which are also versatile.

BOUTIQUE: **La Mendola** (piazza Trinita dei Monti 15, atop the Spanish Steps) has been taken over by **Albertina,** one so highly respected that her knitwear creations were chosen to be part of a permanent collection at New York's Metropolitan Museum of Art. Now, in addition to the beautiful silks that have always made up the elegant and exclusive day and evening wear of La Mendola, there is an impressive line of unique Albertina knits available. Albertina's masterful suits, dresses, coats, and embroidered specialties continue to be sold at via Lazio 20, close to the via Veneto.

CLOTHING FOR BOTH GENDERS: **Brioni** (via Barberini 79) is a pacesetter for the man-of-the-moment. It collaborates directly with top textile manufacturers in producing exclusive Brioni silk, wool, cotton, and linen designs, creates a complete parallel line of shoes, ties, and accessories to blend with the colors and stylings of its models, and influences world style trends. This establishment is Italy's oldest and most famous High Fashion center for men. If you want conservative lines, they'll stitch them, of course, but if you really want to knock them out, choose one of their stunning black silk dinner coats or other custom-made beauties which are their badge and their seal. Normal 3-to-4 day delivery on custom garments; ask for Dr. Ettore Perrone-Brioni. The adjoining Ladies' Boutique, run by the maestro's daughter, Gigliola, is a trendsetter of its own. Now they have a branch in Florence at Via Calimala 22R.

Angelo (via Bissolati 34/36) is equally magnificent. Angelo Vittucci with his partners, Aldo Uggeri and Carlo Illari, made an instantaneous success when they opened this elegant house in 1963. And with their taste, imagination, and own special dash, how well they deserve it! Superior handworked suitings in silks, worsted, tropicals and others; unique foulard linings; additional full line of chic ready-made suits at lower prices; all haberdashery imaginable; finished delivery in 3-to-4 days. Also just as stupendous.

In this same luxury bracket, **Cucci, Caraceni,** and **Cifonelli** are all master cutters, too—but Brioni and Angelo are tops. Move warily among the smaller, less famous, less costly stylists, because they are all too apt to victimize you. In all custom-made garments, always, *always* find time for 3 fittings. A minimum of 2 fittings normally does not work.

DEPARTMENT STORES: La Rinascente (via del Corso at piazza Colonna and piazza Fiume) is the leader. They even carry some designer labels in their clothing sections. **Coin** (piazzale Appio), **Standa** (with lots of branches in the city), and **Upim** (piazza S. Maria Maggiore and others) follow. None is really special. It's far more amusing to do your buying in individual shops.

FLEA MARKET: Be careful! This operates on Sun. from 6 a.m. to midafternoon; stretching from Porta Portese to Viale Trastavere; it is a tourist trap to end all tourist traps. If you absolutely *must* see it, go very, very early, as the dealers do, bargain fiercely, and try to take along an Italian friend to protect your interests. Completely avoid all "genuine Etruscan" articles, because they're fakes. It's worth knowing that pickpockets have a field day here.

GLOVES: Catello d'Auria (via Due Macelli 55) is the leader, without doubt. The stocks are vast and the quality is peerless.

HAUTE COUTURE AND DELUXE READY-TO-WEAR DESIGNERS:
Valentio, Princess Irene Galitzine, Fontana, Mila Schon, Lancetti, Versace, Krizia, Biagiotti, Genny, Trussardi, Complice, Basile, Ferre, Armani, Riva, Tiziani, and **Albani** have exalted reputations currently. **Capucci, Andre Laug, Soprani, Balestra,** and **Antonio de Luca** are also in there pitching. You can expect to be rocked an Arabian Princess' fortune. **Emilio Pucci** is enjoying a renaissance. **Fantasia** has lovely accessories at high tariffs.

JEWELRY AND OBJETS D'ART: **G. Petochi** (Piazza di Spagna 23) Here's the heart of Rome for shoppers and the nation's finest jeweler. There are classic pieces, period gems, corals and pearls, contemporary stylings, and even such rare items as Russian icons and splendid Roman miniature mosaics; you'll also find Italian, French, and old Enlgish silver as well as antique Sheffield. Petochi has been the leading name in Roman jewelry for more than a century.

KNITWEAR: Our choices are **Missoni** (via Borgognona 38B), **Albertina** (via Lazio 20), **Laura Biagiotti** (via Vittoria 30), and **Trico** (via delle Carozze). **Laura Aponte** (via Gesu e Maria 9) had a small and poor selection when we were there.

LEATHER: **Skin** (via Due Macelli 87 and Capo le Case 41/44) has the zestiest stylings and marvelous quality in suits, pants, coats, jackets, skirts, handbags—some items with fur trim. Also a great leather wardrobe for men. There's a custom tailoring service as well if you want an original or something copied. A sister company, **Renard** (via Due Macelli 53), does excellent work in the same medium, but at much lower prices. At #49/53 on the same street, look for **Bizan,** which is highly innovative in its leather ready-to-wear plus smart choices in silk and wool. **XL** (via Due Macelli 59A) is the hottest blast for the young: lots of studs applied to leather—printed styles too—and suede, bomber jackets, skirts, and pants. Hopped up and great fun. **Gucci** (via dei Condotti 21) is the most plush. Its 2-floor premises are rich and its stocks are elegant, but I think that its merchandise is grossly overpriced. **Fendi** (via Borgognona 36A, 36B, 41) is another address where cost must be no object. **L. Righini** (via dei Condotti 76) is more down-to-earth. **Pier Caranti** (piazza di Spagna 43–45) is the sole purveyor of Bottega Veneta creations in town. **Giuseppe Belmonte's** (via Emilia 36) cupboards are full, too, of the latest in handbag fashions. **Prado** (via Sicilia 26–28) is also fine.

RELIGIOUS ARTICLES: **Al Pellegrino Cattolico** (via di Porta Angelica 83) offers complete stocks for the devout. They will have your rosaries blessed by the Pope and delivered to your hotel at no extra fee. Honest, 100% dependable, and fine; none better.

SHOES: For ladies **Lily of Florence** (via Lombardia 38; see "Florence") is the exclusive purveyor of the famous Sesto Meucci and Petra lines. Mrs. Power, herself an American, is the director of this branch. **Raphael** (piazza di Spagna and via Veneto) and **Fragiacomo** (via Condotti 35) are pacesetters. **Tanino Crisci** (via Condotti) is a classicist. **Grilli** (via del Corso 166) and **Giust** (via Sistina 79) are somewhat less costly. **Tradate** (via del Corso) is definitely cheaper and displays some good models. So does **Cardinali** (via di Propaganda Fide, near the Spanish Steps). Via dei Giubbonari and via Arenula near the Ghetto boast over 20 shoe shops.

SILKS AND OTHER MATERIALS BY THE YARD: **Galtrucco** (via del Tritone 14) has everything. **Polidori** (via Borgognona and via Condotti) and **Bises** (via Fleming 53, via del Gesu 63, and at "Valentino Piu" via Condotti 13) carry the wonders of the Italian textile industry—many couture fabrics.

SUNGLASSES: **Ottica Bileci** (via due Macelli 83) is Italy's fashion house for what bridges some of the world's most beautiful noses. All the leading brands are on display plus their own designs; all normal optometry services available. Sunglasses are considered apparel in this country so don't miss this collection.

TIES: **Giofer** (via Frattina 118) has models in crepe de chine, wool, silk twill, reps and jacquard silk. There are literally hundreds to choose from.

TREASURES FOR THE HOME: **Fornari** (via Frattina 71) has an artfully chosen collection of Italian and international charmers.

SALERNO   is in one of the most scenic regions of the nation and handy to archaeology buffs, being a key feederpoint on the *autostrada*. **Lloyd's Baia** is glued to the cliffside viewing the Amalfi shoreline. Air conditioned; terrace dining; a dreamspot. **Jolly,** on the seaside, is another possibility; all units have bath or shower and air conditioning. Okay.

SAN GIMIGNANO   Of the 72 medieval towers that once punctuated the local heavens, only 14 still exist, but they are worth the ½-hour drive from either Siena or Florence (Poggibonsi exit). Excellent frescoes and paintings in the cathedral and chapels. Only 2 so-so hotels: **Cisterna** (viewful restaurant on main piazza) and **Bel Soggiorno.**

SAN REMO,   9 miles from the French border toward Nice, is regaining much of its bygone sophistication; its scenery remains breathtaking. As a study in Mediterranean architecture and once-resplendent luxury, here is a period piece that recalls gentler times. *Ospedaletti*, 3 miles away, is startlingly cheaper.
 The century old **Royal,** long the Queen, offers comfort and high-tone nostalgia. Lovely vista with terraces, flower beds, tables, and pool marching down toward the sea. Total of 15 suites and 140 bedchambers, nearly all with handsome marble baths (those dozens of corridor cupboards disguise the plumbing facilities); newer accommodations furnished in Italian-modern that is skimpy and garish; old ones antique but in less harsh ambience. In first-class, the **Miramare** commands a viewful seaside and palm-garden domain. Some units even better than some deluxe nests, at a lower price; 70 rooms, including its *dependance* in the greenery; recommendable kitchen; cordial staff; closed end-Sept. to Dec. 20. The imposing white-faced **Astoria and West-End** • *across the avenue from the water* • is less tasteful in decor; singles are the better bets here. The **Londra** displayed gaudy flamboyance coupled with broken walls, cracked baseboards, and furniture suggestive of a hoochy-cooch act in a 2-bit flesh parlor. The central **Europa E Della Pace** is clean, commercial, and nice for what it is—which is ''adequate.'' Here is a careful operation. You might prefer to push along to the modernistic **Grand del Mare** • *near Bordighera* • than stay in this city. Otherwise, on Cape Nero, between *San Remo* and *Ospedaletti,* the very modern **Rocce del Capo** has another beautiful view and another swimming pool. Private beach, nightclub, and restaurant; very Italian resorty in tone, with possibilities of so-so fun in season.

SANTA MARGHERITA has smart hotels worthy of such a glittering resort, an interesting fish market and a pleasant situation on the water. It is booming today—perhaps because it can accommodate more visitors than lovely, neighboring Portofino.

Imperiale • offers a rococo turn-of-the-century building, a lushly refurbished decor in the Grand Tradition, a private park and gardens, a vista of Tigullio Bay, an open-air restaurant, and a courteous staff. A must if you consider yourself a classic conservative.

Park Hotel Suisse • has arresting angular architecture of the ultramodern school, self-control air conditioning, a twisted-torso-shape seawater pool, and electric-bright color contrasts throughout. Roster of 75 smallish rooms, all with bath or shower; bay view and quiet hillside situation; interior and alfresco dining or imbibing; charcoal grill. You'll either like it or loathe it, depending upon your receptivity to its progressive ambience.

Miramare • on the beach, is a middle-age structure that has been modernized in a pleasant way. Traditional tone retained but brightened; baths in expensive *imported* opaline marble (why this was done in marble-rich Italy I'll never comprehend—but they are lovely); gardenside quietest in summer; excellent cuisine.

Continental • cops all honors as one of the select bargain paradises along this stretch of coast. Wonderful perch nesting cozily in a park of southerly-exposed flora and palm; romantic private beach; open terrace for breakfast and dinner; simple dining room; 64 good-size bedchambers, including the annex, all with private bath and seafront balcony. Operative year-round.

Regina Elena • is almost as good, but it is more modern and it lacks the marvelous situation of the Continental. Glass-lined dining room under a geodesic dome; double-plate glass doors on all bedroom balconies. Superb for the category.

Laurin • down a notch from Regina Elena (in our book) operates under the Park Suisse aegis. It has been to the beauty parlor, though, and now twinkles. **Metropole** is sound in basic amenities and geared to European tastes. **La Vela** ("The Sail") pulls well. **Tigullio,** inside the city, is okay for budgeteers or for seaside vacationers who hate the sea.

Dei Pescatori • the port's top independent kitchen, is on the fringe of the yacht harbor. It's long and narrow, with no outdoor service; fish, of course, is the specialty.

Nanni • also harborside, is very popular with the boating crowd.

Cesarina • calls itself a trattoria, but the prices put it in the luxury category. If you can swallow that the rest is easily digested.

SARDINIA

On the northeast coast you'll discover the breathtakingly savage, sea-lapped **Costa Smeralda,** a 30-mile necklace of wild, lonely, *ponete*-blown coves. Along this glorious villa-specked littoral—more extensive, incidentally, than the entire Belgian seaboard—are no less than 80 powder-white beaches. It's a land of twisted cork trees, soughing pines, and glistening juniper, with a boscage of rosemary that scents the Mediterranean sailor's wind. The angular mountains are of granite and basalt. The vales are dotted with nuraghi (prehistoric fortress-shape structures). Its primitive inhabitants speak a Low Latin, with dialect overtones of ancient Genoese, Lybian, Phoenician, Spanish, and Carthaginian. The inlets and quiet corners along this row are far too numerous to mention; a typical one has been described accurately as "a Pacific bay on a Brittany coast." There are 5 hotels of varying categories, co-crowned by the magnificent Cala di Volpe and the equally luxurious cottage-style Pitrizza.

Cuisine? Much of it is about as exciting as a hangnail. The local fare, based ponderously on pasta, is even worse. In the posh hotels it is costly, contemporary, and clearly not concerned with Sardinian origins. The yacht basin at **Porto Cervo** is one of the best, most expensive, and most scenic in the western world; the local marina, skipper's club, and nucleus of cozy-corner night spots swing with those who wing in or cruise over from the nearby thickets of Rome. Winter, when few hotels stay open, can be as lonely as a doxy at a revival meeting—bringing just enough rawness to evoke an avid interest in timetables. The easiest way to arrive is aboard the turboprop airline, Alisarda, which calls regularly at Rome, Nice, and Milan from the home base, **Olbia.** Alitalia zips in daily from Milan and Rome to **Alghero** and **Cagliari.** The latter is hopelessly far away; the pull from the former is a tediously long ride. British Airways has a London link with Alghero. Passenger and car ferries steam 4 times a day in summer from the port of Rome (Civitavecchia) to Olbia and the adjoining **Golfo di Aranci.** A loop with Genoa is also possible aboard the *Canguro Rosso,* the so-called Red Kangaroo that hops with its pouchful of passengers between the north of Italy and Sardinia. Genoese luggers drop anchor at both Olbia and **Porto Torres.** (The latter is about 80 miles from your hotel.) As islands go, the land of the Sards is so vast that if you head to this chip of emerald paradise, don't plan to land anywhere else but Olbia.

★★★★★ **Cala di Volpe** • nestles almost village-style by the sands of a glorious bay. Surrounding the pueblo enclave is a toy harbor. Here you will find hotel boats bobbing at their moorings, tennis courts, a huge swimming pool, and a parcel of what might be called beach-lets. Entrance across a bamboo-covered footbridge to a timber-toned lobby; main restaurant and bar under giant wooden beams and plaited stalks, both overlooking the teal waters and the 100-yard-long pier; 44 rooms in the older segment, each in different dress (bid for these since the newer wing is only so-so and can be hotter). Rates surpass deluxe standards almost anywhere in Italy—but, because of its relative isolation, the frolicking night life, and the fun-filled ambience of play-filled luxury, a pair of pilgrims could easily work through $500 per day, including normal meals (not caviar, plover's eggs, and the like). There's one all-encompassing word for this Eden—*fabulous!*

★★★★★ **The Pitrizza** • is in the same deluxe category. This one is nearer to the coastal heartbeat of *Porto Cervo,* a 10-minute panoramic ramble by car. Although it is more private in concept—about thirty 4-to-8 person bungalows— it is equally glorious, equally comfortable. Rates here can run to $750 per night. Each yard-thick roof of the villas and main building has been given a rich blanket of soil, an independent irrigation system, and a magnificent assortment of Mediterranean flowering plants and shrubs. The pool, hewn from native cobble, first flows through hillside pockets and then cascades over a rocky weir into the sea. Central clubhouse with restaurant, bar, and coveside terrace; candlelight dinners twice weekly; dancing a regular feature; all chalets with air conditioning plus working fireplaces; individual patios under vine-draped, rawwood lattices; stable-type doors; agrestic Sardinian handicrafts; colorful, nature-toned decor. A splendid 18-hole golf course designed by Trent Jones is teed up.

★★★★★ **Romazzino** • with 100 rooms, also is in the deluxe bracket. It commands the most scenic site of all—a hillside perch above a bay twinkling with salt-and-pepper islands. Every unit with seaview balcony and air conditioning; North Wing best; modern lobby and lounge with ceramic "trees"; Juniper Bar; dining salon; beachside "Wooden Leg" barbecue hutch; Alfonso's Pizzeria; private boat dock; hairdresser and barber; free baby-sitter service; Sunfish sailboats for rent; full range of watersport facilities; newspaper kiosk and a few shops. Its generally spacious bedchambers have colorful tile floors and raffia carpets. Selected antique furnishings mixed with contemporary comfort-insurers; baths, showers, and individual peignoirs; private balconies; single bedsteads from a nunnery.

★★★ **Cervo** • smack in the center of the port, is the nucleus of the social, boating, and night life whirl. It is the only area in the close-knit community that stays open year round, encompassing a marina, the neighboring Tennis Club, a swimming and barbecue area, restaurant, bar, supermarket, equestrian club, shopping arcade, plaza for star-sprinkled galas, real estate agency, post and telegraph office, and ultra-exclusive Yacht Club. Simpler accommodations than Cala di Volpe and Pitrizza; correspondingly lower tariffs; same administrative aegis; full air conditioning; more than adequate comfort; convivial people; usually full in season—and with good reason.

★★ **Luci di la Muntagna** • with 80 rooms and a distant view of Corsica, also hops with carefree abandon. Architecture that suggests it came out of a plaster-of-Paris mold; active floating jetty for sport boats (6 for rent by guests); good beach with free deck chairs and umbrellas; restaurant; rooftop solarium; swinging discotheque; all units with bath or shower; narrow dimensions; 5 pastel color schemes. Except for the cell-size accommodations, here's a laudable medium-bracket candidate.

Residence Liscia di Vacca • is a worthy second-class stop with its own pool. Quiet, pleasant, and money-saving.

Cinesta • is a young contender also in the second-class category. **Pevero** ("pear tree") chipped in by the golf links has 420 rooms; first class. **Dolce Sposa** ("sweet wife") makes up more than 100 beds. Additional hostelries may be found along the shores (perhaps a ½-hour drive) and in a dreary town of *Olbia*.

For meals, you'll probably be on a house plan at the hotels. Don't bother with any of the local wines except Vernaccia or Fundata Olia; if needful of more adventure, try Vermentino, Moscato, Cannonau, or Anghelu Ruju. Regional culinary specialties are spit-roasted suckling pig and wild boar ham. **El Toula** in the **Sporting Club** on the half-island of *Punta della Lepre* is the only notable independent restaurant in the entire area. The golden spread here (but with only room for 3-dozen super-yachts) is called *Porto Rotondo,* and it is by far the *most* chichi of all the chic-eries in Italy in summer. **San Marco** (the little brother of the Sporting Club) in *Porto Cervo* is its number one candidate followed by **Il Pescatore, Il Pomodoro,** and **La Fattoria.** The main piazza here serves as its central "nightclub."

Finally, 80 miles from **Cagliari** in the south, Trust House Forte created the **Forte Hotel Village.** It comprises 600 spacious red-tile-roofed brick cottages (2 bedrooms). **Hotel Castello,** 114 units and air-conditioned, is housed here. Lighted tennis courts; 18-hole links nearby; 5 pools; Colosseo buffet-style restaurant; seafood-specialty Beachcomber; Torre Steak House; multiple snack and pizza bars; more. Its piazza Maria Luigia, said to be a fair copy of the Centro in Porto Cervo, has shops, pubs, and nightly entertainment.

SESTRI LEVANTE (about 30 miles south of Genoa). The far-and-away leader is **Grand Hotel dei Castelli**—3 linked castles that occupy their own high-perched peninsula up a first-gear-only road. Gorgeous antiques scattered through its 43 rooms and 6 suites—plus its exquisite panorama and good facilities—merit salutes and salaams. **Vis a Vis** is simple-modern but has a fine bay setting for meditations and quiet pursuits. Pleased reports have come in about the 16th-century **Villa Balbi.** One 20th-century wing; "fine service and food"; "excellent attention."

SIENA supplies a mesmeric passageway to the Renaissance; it is probably the only city in Italy to retain so much ancient charm. As an illustration, filmmakers found Verona's complexion had changed so radically over the years that they came here to shoot *Romeo and Juliet*. The **Duomo,** the **Pinacoteca,** the **Town Hall,** and the **Music Academy** are musts; the capper is the spectacular **Palio** ("the world's craziest horse race"), a pageant climaxed by hell-for-leather riding in the huge piazza del Campo; this event is held twice annually on the

Festivals of the Madonna, July 2 and Aug. 16. For peace-lovers, the prime attractions nestle in the surrounding hills.

Park • *1½ miles out* • is a landed estate with 69 rooms and an annex surrounding a flowered terrace and pool. Totally renovated in questionable taste; *e.g.* hideous modernistic lamps illuminate a gracious old vaulted salon; enchanting dining patio but chilly dining room; elegant lounges; 2 hard surface tennis courts; rich textiles. Sixteenth-century furnishings and quiet mien. Tranquillizing and very recommendable indeed. Year-round management by able Antonio Esposito.

Villa Scacciapensieri • *"scatter your cares,"* a careless mile or more from the center but only 5 minutes from the station* • was transformed into a hostelry with 19 units in the Villa, 9 in the Villino, and 2 in the poolside Villetta; all accommodations are regaled with loving attention to detail; the dining room reflects the devotion to cuisine and wines of Francesco Pallasini, a connoisseur of heroic stature. A truly international and discriminating clientele returns with regularity to this country estate. One good reason: Emma Nardi, the owner and a gracious hostess for for more than 4 decades, shudders at the mention of mass tourism. She also shutters it tightly when winter winds blow.

Certosa di Maggiano • *on the Certosa pike* • is a peaceful garden-girt throwback to Old World grace. Only about a dozen rooms but all choice. Very well recommended.

Garden • in second class, presents a magnificent terrace view over the entire city. The spacious grounds are an asset for travelers with children.

Excelsior • was revamped recently and it is now a satisfactory member of the Jolly chain.

For dining, **Al Marsili** • *in the Old Town next to the Questura (Police) and the Duomo at via del Castoro 3* • is an exceptional wine house with superb gastronomy of the region. Brick arched room and high ceiling; careful service; game in season and delicious autumn mushrooms. Try the guinea fowl and the luscious tiramisu. One of the finest cellers in Tuscany, so here's the place to test your enology. Monday it rests.

Guido • offers a stone-and-brick vault on the main street of the Old Town. Rugged rusticity lined with photos of opera and theatrical personalities; spitted meats spinning over licking flames at the entrance; hardy fare that is superb for what it is; service variable-to-negligent; some legerdemain on the billings, so compare prices with the menu and add totals; closed Mon.

Medio "Evo" • *via del Rossi 40* • may lure you. It's a handsome ancient brick-lined room with worn staircase, sculpture, banners, and arms; but for all this, the food ranks as just about the most assertively repulsive of any sampled in the entire republic.

Al Mangia and **Alla Speranza** • famous tourist meccas; both have outdoor terraces facing the magnificent piazza del Campo; both are oh-so-geared for bulk tourism.

La Taverna di Nello • *28 via del Porrione* • is very good and not too heavy on the pricing. Here's another one that takes Monday repose.

SIRMIONE (midway between Milan and Venice). The theater-set town juts out into Lake Garda with canals meandering among the ruins. Most cars are left at the fringes and visitors must walk in. (Guests at hotels with parking zones may drive.) The romantic, pillared **Villa Cortine** overlooks the water from the center of a large park; it's tranquil and pleasant but very expensive, especially for its mediocre dining choices. Still, it's a period piece of extraordinary distinction. The **Continental** is in the inner town while the **Grand Hotel Terme** is outside, opposite the Information Center. The area offers about 5-dozen additional hostelries. Everything is seasonal here.

SORRENTO The town is set high along Mediterranean cliffs. In winter it's sleepy; in summer it crackles with visitors. Its only penalty is its overwhelming beauty.

You'll find manager Enzo Acampora of **Acampora Travel,** a CIT affiliate, an extraordinarily resourceful and competent lifesaver in solving any lodgings or similar problems which might arise.

Excelsior Vittoria • which stays open year-round, is the resort's most renowned spot. Its Old World furnishings are so quaint they're almost a Bemelmans caricature—but the staff are warm human beings instead of unsmiling robots. Ideal situation; parkland setting with large pool; relaxed atmosphere; excellent food; professional guidance by Ugo Fiorentino.

Tramontano • now the largest, has a commanding situation. It's fusty in spots but passable if you are happy in large establishments. Ask to see your room before booking it.

Parco dei Principi • is by the sands, with its entrance at the end of a verdant grove. Perfect setting; air conditioning; 105 good-size rooms with private baths and terraces. The saddening thing here is the pinchpenny attitude displayed in its clashy Formica-clad furnishings, in its frequent absence of pictures, in its stagnant-looking swimming pool, and in its stark, Woolworthy decor.

Royal • damaged seriously by an earthquake, has been refitted expensively by proprietor Renato Scarpato and manager Antonino Esposito. A fine comeback.

President • *on a pine-dotted hill overlooking the town* • has credentials which include a heavily marbled rotunda lobby; a long lounge warmed by intricate tilework and Persian-style rugs, a sedate dining room adjoining an outside terrace, a woody bar in the mod mode, and a solarium-pool complex. From its contemporarily furnished upstairs precincts there are panoramas of Vesuvius, Ischia, and the azure Tyrrhenian Sea.

Cesare Augusto • *100 yards behind piazza Tasso* • 125 rooms; fully balconied; it's a beauty for modern metropolitan tastes rather than for resort-sort amenities. Conscientious staff; enormous dining salon with mediocre cookery; woody, almost Scandinavian, Taverna dei Mulini; ice-cool bar. Rooftop pool, plus solarium with snack service. Bid for the 4th or 5th floors, the only ones high enough for a sea view. Excellent, if you don't insist on a waterfront address.

Ambasciatori • *on a cliff over its own stretch of sand* • has 105 nests perched up high. Heavily wooded and tiled lobby in avocado; matching bar with sloping ceiling; airy seaview dining room; lush enclosed garden; rippling pool; alert maintenance throughout. While all of the bedchambers are reasonably proportioned, their bathrooms are almost absurdly cramped; all sport balconies, with the 40% bordering the briny the most choice. Recommended.

This city is the largest, greatest, and most celebrated center in the world for inlaid furniture and similar artistic accessories. The range of its products is astonishing. Utilizing skills which flowered here ages ago, every single piece from the most modest fruit basket to the most elaborate baroque highboy is 100% inset by hand. To see these displays is a unique experience.

As for shopping, the cornucopia of exquisite, exclusive masterworks in the enormous 3-level showrooms of century-old, 400-employee **A. Gargiulo Jannuzzi** (hub of main square) stops us in our tracks: The monumental collection of everything from dining sets to chests of drawers to ladies' desks to tea carts to 3-table nests to cigarette, music, jewelry, and cigar boxes to a plethora more. Beautiful, moderately priced embroidered table linen, blouses, handkerchieves, and the like, hand made in convents or by orphaned children, a strong alternate magnet and statues by famous sculptors. Free brochures; worldwide shipment; guaranteed delivery; continuously open 365 days (summers until 10 p.m.). We salute matriarch Gargiulo and sons Peppino and Apollo. Wonderful!

SPOLETO is known for its Festival of Two Worlds comprising theater, opera, concerts, films, ballet, and art exhibitions. Science is also being spotlighted with relevant congresses. The town is rich with antiquities and so are the shouldering Umbrian hills. Among the top hotel choices, the **Albornoz-Palace** is the newest (many groups). The **Barbarossa, Dei Duchi,** and the **Gattapone** are also suitable.

TAORMINA is the garden spot of Sicily, clinging to a headland almost 1000 feet above the outer Straits of Messina (above the bathing beach too, which is good to know in advance). The view of the town and sea from inside the Greco-Roman theater is one of the most inspiring anywhere; the summer concerts draw musicians of stellar significance. Mount Etna, the volcano of Ulysses, thrusts its snow-capped cone through the clouds to the rear; in '62 this off-again, on-again boiler built a new 120-foot hill beside its crater; CIT will take you there on a fascinating all-day excursion. The highlight of the city's social glitter is its annual mid-July David di Donatello Film Festival, Italy's most important event in the motion picture industry. Strand-hounds, young and old, prefer to stay at Mazzaro Beach, directly below, to which there is a funicular. Naxos is also popular.

★★★ **San Domenico Palace** ● once a huge convent. This spectacular 16th-century landmark (a hotel since 1880) is perched on the rim of a 1000-foot cliff. Long, white-tiled pool decanted 3 terraces down into the flower-decked garden; Romanesque outdoor bar plus a cluster of changing cabins; fully air-conditioned; almost every suite, bedchamber, and bath in excellent taste, each different from the next. Spacious rooms with magnificent vistas; extraordinarily fine Sassari tilework and 1984-style fixtures in most baths. Indisputably the leading house on the island.

Capotaormina ● a large, crescent-shape structure, perches 150 feet high along the edge of the most advanced promontory on the coast (its namesake), which blesses it with a sweep of the most breathtaking seascape of any major hostelry in the region. Totally contemporary design and ambience; 200 air-conditioned rooms and baths, all but 12 with balcony; 2 bars; beauty parlor; boutique; sauna; underground garage and parking space above; convention facilities for 350; special elevator to the private beach in its own cove.

Diodoro Jolly ● air-conditioned, claims a sea-and-volcano vista. Ten-minute hike from town; modernistic furnishings; facilities for alfresco dining and drinking; 300-seat inner salon with gold carpet, wooden beams, and green velvet chairs; huge swimming pool for summer and winter dipping; sauna; tennis court; all 102 diminutive units with private bath and big balcony; first-class rating for deluxe physical standards (this commercially oriented chain bought it after it was built). Recommended.

Bristol Park ● is older in fashion. Similarly breathtaking panorama from a site that is neither in the village nor at the beach (a car would be an asset, but there's free minibus service to the shore); sprightly dining room with pink napery; pleasant terrace for breakfast and apertifs; 100% air-conditioned; snail-like elevator. Every accommodation with its own attractive balcony; simply but tastefully furnished; demipension required in season. Its warm-hearted family touch is everywhere in evidence.

Excelsior Palace ● is the center but with views of the sea and a warm-hearted volcano. Swimming pool surrounded by a wonderful garden, overlooking Naxos Bay; full air conditioning; reputable restaurant.

Mediterranee ● in a tranquil urban location, is a solid first-class candidate. Modern; 70% air-conditioned; rooftop swimming pool; all rooms with bath or shower; most with terrace; panoramic site. Less expensive, naturally.

Continental ● offers an excellent position, many modern amenities, reportedly good food and service, and extraordinary popularity. No elevator, but full air cooling; 43 units with bath or shower, plus terrace or balcony. A fine budget choice.

Villa Paradiso • 33 rooms, is officially designated a pension, but it offers comforts that few first-class hostelries do in this resort. Whitewashed salon divided by arches and gladdened by foliage; penthouse terrace restaurant; extensive use of wrought iron; most perches with vistas of Mt. Etna, the public gardens, and the hamlet of Giardini.

Villa Riis • recently was refurbished. Now it is open from April–Oct. This charmer is well liked by just about everybody.

Down at *Mazzaro Beach*, a lazy 5-minute amble by car, the **Mazzaro Sea Palace** has its deluxe portals at a site almost adjoining the funicular terminus (connected to this station by a tunnel). This ultramodern, high-cost entry features a round "superstructure" lounge for 360° pan-o-ramics, a restaurant with tinted glass and white molded tables, a bar to match, a seawater pool, and private beach. Its 80 air-conditioned bedchambers are only a pillow's toss from the breakers. They have expansive terraces, quality twin beds, beige carpeting, and adjustable lighting.

Villa Sant' Andrea • is a sparkling anchorage with a light cargo of wiles. Lovely garden terrace a tier above water level; dining patio and outdoor bar; 40 homey rooms, all with bath; 7-unit annex; nice clientele; open March–Oct. Just the retreat for sun-worship, park-strolling, sea-bathing, and lazing up a daydream.

Lido Mediterranee • with 73 rooms, and the centrally cited but quiet, 59-unit **Vello d'Oro** are another pair to consider.

Most hotels expect you to dine with them. Independent ones are not too interesting.

TURIN (Torino), is a busy foothills metropolis in the Piedmont near the French border (readily discernible in the local dialect) that is close to the heart of Europe and has drawn its culture from the many peoples who have left their traces here—from the Celts to Hannibal, to Romans to Goths, Franks and Charlemagne's followers. Today there are close to a million citizens in this wide, verdant valley formed by the Po and the Dora Riparia. About 30,000 work in the Fiat auto works, largest plant in the world outside the Detroit area; the unique **Museum of The Automobile,** containing 370 vintage models, is fascinating. They are equally proud of their city's art treasures, **Museo Civico d'Arte Antica, Egyptology Museum** (second most important in the world), **Cinema Museum,** the overwhelmingly sumptuous former **Royal Palace,** and **Palazzo del Lavoro.** Based on a Francophile influence, here is a way of life which, like Milan's, differs from that of the rest of Italy.

For pausing, the **Turin Palace** leads the luxury parade with ample flair, coupled with a graceful rich tradition. A bit less costly but also appealing are the **Sitea** (116 air conditioned rooms) and the dashingly cheerful **Meuble.** Of the several Jolly-chain candidates, I prefer the more intimate **Ligure,** only a totter from the Porta Nova Station. Jolly also drives the famous **Excelsior Grand**

Hotel Principi di Piemonte, a hostelry appropriate for its targeted client—the businessman who wants grand style with turbo-charged efficiency. The **Jolly Ambasciatori,** more modernistic in decor and mood, seems to function on approximately the same principle and, insofar as its audience is chiefly commercial, it serves its purpose very well indeed. **Conte Biancamano** is a modestly priced aristocrat with lovely Old World features. **Boston** is full of personality, but in a clean-lined contemporary tone. Very good for its moderate prices. The arresting **City** is proud of its futuristic architecture—and well it should be, because it is an agreeable combination of comfort and imagination that required courage on the part of the proprietor.

Villa Sassi • 4 miles out on the Genoa approach road, is a stately and tranquil haven for those who prefer the lush countryside. Only 12 rooms in this 2-century-old mansion overlooking the river; 5-acre park setting; dining room and terraces that are sometimes commandeered by banquet parties; bedchambers pleasant but not outstanding. A favorite hideaway for many let's-get-away-from-it-all Torinesi.

The metropolis has fine gastronomy and fine vermouths. **Cambio** • *in the Teatro Carignano building* • is our lead choice. Nineteenth-century aura featuring crystal chandeliers and velvet-swathed banquet rooms; noteworthy food, friendly staff, and decorous dining. **Al Saffi** • *via Saffi 2* • and **Montecarlo** • *via S. Francesco da Paola 37* • also must be considered among the better tables of Turin. **Tiffany** is intimate; added to its charm, you can count on well-prepared cuisine. **Al Gatto Nero** • *corso Unione Sovietica 14* • Entrance through a cozy bar; clublike atmosphere with red brick walls and hanging flora; open 12:30 p.m. to midnight. Reserve in advance. Highly recommended. **Vecchia Lanterna** • *21 corso Re Umberto* • does very attractive regional cooking. My lamb with alpine herb was delicious. And if you have wheels, don't overlook the peaceful setting of **El Toula** out at Villa Sassi. It's expensive, but usually worth it.

VATICAN CITY

Standing on the side of a hill on the west bank of the Tiber, it is separated from Rome and Italy only by a wall. The Pope is absolute monarch, with full legislative, executive, and judicial powers. (Please refer to the introduction of this chapter for further comments on this enclave.)

Dominating the City is the **Basilica of St. Peter,** largest in the world and sited in the smallest independent state in the world. Close by is the Apostolic Palace, home of His Holiness and site of the famous **Vatican Museum;** while many go only for the religious art of classical periods, don't pass up the 55-

room modern art section with acres of beauties by Matisse, Marini, Shahn, Kokoschka, Miro, even Lurcat tapestries. It is the biggest residential castle in existence, with 1400 rooms that cover some 13½-acres. Within are also the City Governor's Palace, a post office, a tribunal, a mosaic factory, a barracks, an observatory, a railway station, a power plant, a newspaper, a pharmacy, a TV station, and the super-radio station over which are broadcast the Pope's messages to 6 continents. A self-service restaurant for visitors is located in the basement in front of the main picture gallery, with a tree-shaded terrace at ground-floor level; there's a snack bar in the modern art segment too. *Sampietrini* is the name given to those who maintain the Basilica but do not live here. The ranks of the famed Swiss Guard, a colorful and elite corps whose red, yellow, and blue pantaloons were designed by Michelangelo, is being phased out; their replacements are the plain-blue-uniformed Vatican *gendarmerie*. The papal apartment is newly opened in the **Lateran Palace.** Robes, uniforms, and arms are on display; the frescoes are in splendid condition from the 16th century, the period before the pope took up residence in the Vatican.

St. Peter's is the core of the enclave. The dome, Michelangelo's work, is almost as high as the tallest Egyptian pyramid; from doorway to altar, you could tuck in the towers of New York's Waldorf-Astoria with room to spare. In the museums, chapels, and libraries of the Vatican you'll find Raphaels, Michelangelos, Peruginos, Botticellis, tapestries, liturgical vessels, priceless manuscripts. An elevator will whisk you to the base of the dome; from there you can climb the winding stairs to the pinnacle for a splendid view of the meandering Tiber and Rome. Then take the walk around the inside upper periphery, put an ear close to the wall, and listen to people talking hundreds of feet away. St. Peter's alone is worth a special trip across the ocean. The Sistine Chapel—now magnificently refreshed, revealing vibrant original polychrome—is closed to visitors on Saturday afternoon and Sunday as well as on holidays.

Audience with the Pope: The best way to arrange this is through a letter from your Bishop to Rt. Rev. Msgr. Benjamin Farrell, J.C.D., Casa di S. Maria dell'Umilta, via dell'Umilta 30. Small group or individual meetings are becoming more and more difficult to arrange, though His Holiness grants a few almost daily. Apply as soon as you arrive in Rome; the Casa is only 2 blocks from the Trevi Fountain, a bonus to sightseers who are in the area. I'm also told that the Paulist Fathers at the Church of St. Susanna are extremely helpful in this respect.

On Wednesdays an enormous audience is held in St. Peter's for which tickets are usually available a day ahead, provided you don't require reserved seats. There are 3 classes: The first 2 permit you to sit in grandstand structures flanking the main altar, while the 3rd is simply admission for standing room. For tickets to this (as well as to the excavations beneath St. Peter's), apply to the same source mentioned above. Thousands flock to these gatherings, so get there early. For special audiences (*Baciamano*), ladies should wear black dresses, high necklines, long sleeves, and veils (now optional, but more courteous), while men should appear in dark suits with dark ties. Dress requirements for the Wednesday services are nearly as rigid, although they are constantly violated by scores of unknowing travelers. The Papal address is condensed and translated in English, French, German, and Spanish. The big assemblages are scheduled from October to July, moving to the summer residence in Castel

Gandolfo from July to late September. Transportation to St. Peter's is provided at nominal cost; hotel pickup and round trip are available through SITA (the "coaching" arm of CIT), American Express, and Thomas Cook, also for relatively few lire.

Note: · · · You'll hear cheers, loud handclapping, and cries of "Viva Il Papa!" from European student priests and other spectators when the Pope is carried into the Basilica by the *uscieri*. It provokes the same effect as the final bell in a heavyweight championship fight at Madison Square Garden.

VENICE

Venezia is an absurd and wonderful dream. To protect themselves from the approach of armies by land, a group of staid and somber citizens many centuries ago carved for themselves a slice of sea and proceeded to erect buildings on top of the waves. This fantastic conglomeration of houses, churches, gardens, factories, streets, and squares rests on piles sunk deep into the mud. It has been called "a kind of poem in stone accidentally written by history on the waters." The main boulevard, most of the important arteries, and many of the small streets are paved with *acqua* instead of asphalt—and sometimes this H$_2$O bears no resemblance whatsoever to *Quelques Fleurs* or *Chanel No. 5*.

Note: · · · Taxis, buggies, rickshas, bicycles, roller skates, and all types of transportation which can't dance on the water are forbidden. Visitors can count on the *circolare* (in all other Italian towns a tram or bus, but here a boat), and that, with the vessels of about 500 gondoliers (about a dozen now motorized) plus about 200 launch operators, is IT; the fastest of the *motoscafi* is the *diretto* variety. A canal ride ticks off 45 minutes in travel time between the Marco Polo airport and the center of town. Ask about the *Collegamento*, or Airport Connection. This terminus, built on reclaimed land, can accommodate only jets without full fuel loads at takeoff. It is from Venice that the super-posh antique train, *The Orient Express*, all polished, air conditioned, and comfortized, departs for London on a sybaritic journey that recalls the glories of an earlier transportation era; an Alpine linkage also is available on a daylight schedule.

Ample funds are available to fight flooding, pollution, and decay. In addition, Dutch hydraulics experts have teamed up with Italian engineers to seek a lasting solution to the city's permanent wave problem. These specialists have checked the tides by employing removable barriers at the 3 sea entrances plus industrial controls within the lagoon. Many wells have been permanently capped, providing a cushion upon which Venice can "float," the collapse of the city already has been markedly reduced, and prospects are good that the Venetians will enjoy a new and long lease on life.

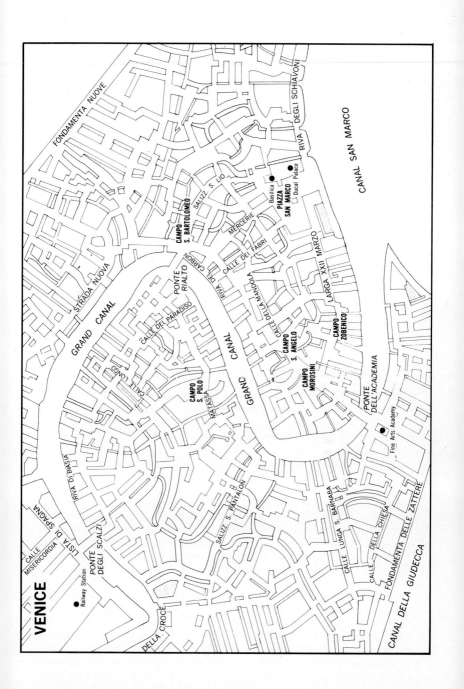

ATTRACTIONS

Piazza San Marco When St. Mark's was first built, the square was a garden with a canal running through it. In the year 1000, the canal was filled in and the square enlarged, allowing the area to fulfill its inevitable function as the religious and political center of Venice. The tall, majestic **campanile** began as a lighthouse and was not built up to its 300-foot height until the 16th century. That structure lasted about 300 years, collapsed, and was reconstructed in 1912. An elevator was installed to enable visitors to have a matchless view of Venice from the tower heights. Don't miss the **Museo Correr,** which covers Venetian life and art from 1300 to 1700.

Basilica di San Marco • *St. Mark's Basilica, piazza San Marco* • In A.D. 829 the remains of St. Mark the Apostle were shipped from Alexandria to Venice, and soon thereafter work began on the basilica. The current structure with its domes and arches has its beginnings in the latter part of the 11th century— Venetians wanted the cathedral of their patron saint to reflect the wealth and power of their state. The facade of St. Mark's is a synthesis of Byzantine, Romanesque, and Gothic elements; a dividing gallery in the center displays four bronze horses of 4th-century Greek origin. Everywhere there are marble columns, sculptures of sacred personages, and mosaics (400 square yards of them), all unified according to a complex inconographical plan. Spend some time, too, looking at the gem-encrusted Pala d'Oro, or **Golden Altarpiece,** which took centuries to complete and shows the Byzantine influence on a uniquely Venetian work. The **Treasury** has a sumptuous collection from many periods of vases, reliquaries, and liturgical items, jewelry, and other handcrafted objets d'art.

Palazzo Ducale • *The Doge's Palace* • The Doge's Palace is one of the world's most beautiful public buildings. The unusual exterior has two beautiful loggias. The columns of the lower arcade have 38 capitals carved with allegorical figures and heads. Here is the famed **Staircase of the Giants** (1567) by Sansovino. The opulent rooms are adorned with paintings, frescoes, sculptures, and carvings by scores of Italian artists, including greats like Tintoretto, Veronese, Titian, and Tiepolo. After you are dazzled by this monument to Venetian wealth and vitality, visit the **prisons** that are reached via the **Bridge of Sighs** (not yet built in the days when the Doge's jails were most active).

San Stefano • *campo Morosini* • This large Gothic church, quiet as it seems to the visitor, had to be reconsecrated six times because blood was shed within its walls. In the sacristy are two late works by Tintoretto (circa 1580): "The Agony in the Garden," and "Christ Washing the Disciples' Feet." Fine churches are so numerous in Venice that you must have a "short list" or otherwise plan weeks for your sifting and browsing. Here are my top choices: **San Giovanni e Paolo, Santa Maria Gloriosa dei Friari,** and **San Giorgio Maggiore.** These are noteworthy not only for their distinctive period architecture but for the art contained within them. A local guidebook can fill you in on details.

Gallerie dell' Accademia • *Academy Gallery* • Housed in the former Convent and Church of **Santa Maria della Carita'**, the Accademia is a cornucopia of painterly riches from the 14th through the 17th centuries. You'll find works of Bellini, Giorgione, Titian, Tintoretto, Canova, Tiepolo, Vivarini, as well as of lesser Venetian artists and foreign artists who settled here.

Ca 'd'Oro • Try to see it first from the Grand Canal and then absorb the splendid paintings contained in its **Franchetti Gallery.** This "House of Gold" was begun in 1224.

Ca' Rezzonico • also is on the Grand Canal and also has golden associations: the Golden Century of Venice (18th), where you can relive the ultimate moments of this city's power and glory.

Scuola di San Rocco • *campo San Rocco* • Itself an impressive Renaissance structure (built between 1515 and 1560), the Scuola di San Rocco contains a cycle of 56 paintings by Tintoretto, who did these works between 1564 and 1581. But apart from the oils, your eyes may be torn between the magnificent gilt coffers on the ceiling and the polychromatic marble floors underfoot. It has to be one of the most ornate parlors in Christendom.

Rialto • The ancient Rialto district, which is still the busiest part of Venice, cannot be seen or experienced except by foot. Even if you are prepared to spend a small fortune in Venice to travel via gondola or *vaporetto*, take advantage of the filled-in streets and see the city by foot. Start at the 16th-century shop-lined Rialto Bridge spanning the Grand Canal, making sure you stop to survey all the activity below on the waterway. On either side of this landmark are numerous grand palazzos, many new municipal buildings and, always, crowds of Venetians buying and selling food, leather goods, and other products. This is also where you'll find the colorful daily marketplace early in the morning.

Fondazione Peggy Guggenheim • *Calle San Gregorio* • Housed in the architecturally discordant Palazzo Venier, this private collection features modern art beginning with the Cubists. As one of the biggest touristic drawing cards for Americans, you'll probably want to go, but personally I find both the building as well as her artistic sensitivity third rate—sculpture excepted. Open daily except Tues., 2–6 p.m. Closed in winter but possible to have special showings at announced times.

Palazzo Grassi • A Fiat-sponsored art center with modern themes only.

Excursions

Torcello • One of Venice's "out islands" and 40 minutes away by *vaporetto*, Torcello makes an interesting trip for its vast contrasts with Venice. On this sparsely populated island whose importance was eclipsed by the rise of

Venice, you'll see not only farmers' fields, cypress trees, and palms, but also an 11th-century cathedral with 13th-century Byzantine mosaics and the Church of Santa Fosca, originally built in the 7th-century and reconstructed in circa 1000.

Burano • Burano is a charming island with canals and narrow streets where the inhabitants make their living as lacemakers and fishermen. The 16th-century church of San Mattino has an early painting by Tiepolo, "The Crucifixion." Take along a picnic lunch and some extra *lire* if you expect to purchase some of the lace for which the island is famous.

Murano • This island is primarily known for the products of its glass factory, which makes for an intriguing visit (when you arrive at Murano, disembark at Colonna, the first *vaporetto* stop). If you still have time, visit the 12th-century Basilica of S. Maria e Donato.

Palladian Villas can be seen by bus every Thurs., with a lunch stop at *Bagnolo's* Villa Pisani. For details, speak to Countess Maria Pia Ferri at St Mark's 2814; telephone 8 5343.

HOTELS

★★★★★ **Cipriani** • *let's begin outside of mainstream Venice on this magical island of Giudecca, 5 minutes from St. Mark Square by hotel launch (free)* • Aside from being a wonderland of extraordinary luxury, this establishment also features its own intimate harbor for independent yachtsmen, fully supplied with electricity, water, and services. Set apart from the busy whirl of the town itself, this tranquil deluxe enclave is materminded by Natale Rusconi, one of Europe's premier hosts. The heated, Olympic-size, filtered salt water pool is a lovely centerpiece for the health club and surrounding garden suites, with a tier of luxury apartments crowning these; cuisine is among the finest to be found in Italy and is known and praised by cognoscenti the world over; spacious, beautiful modern units with their own Jacuzzis are the last word in pampering. If greater exclusivity is desired, ask about the 14-suite annex in a nearby palace, which views Venice across the lagoon. Travelers who have utilized this hotel's link to the nostalgic Orient Express will find a boutique with items from the train. Closed for part of midwinter, so be sure to reserve in advance. Incomparable as a vacation isle. PS: If you arrive by car, many of the top hotels recommend the vaguely reliable Mattiazzo garage in piazzale Roma, where endless tips are expected and where you are bludgeoned by an 18% surcharge if you wish to pay for their cherished services by credit card.

☆☆☆☆☆ **Gritti Palace** • of Ernest Hemingway fame, just across the river and into the trees from the gondola park is in the skillful hands of the highly professional Dott. Nico Passante who is overseeing even further renovations. This house traditionally has been one of the number one stopping places in the world. It is operative year-round. First, it is small, gladsome, and almost club-like. (Indeed, the restaurant, with its canalside terrace, is called the Club del Doge.) Second, nothing has been spared in decor, in staff, or in the attributes of pure luxury. All units, incidentally, come with stocked bar-type refrigerators; the entire house, of course, is air-conditioned; all baths are now in marble. If expense is no object, try to reserve Suite #110; it's one of the finest hotel accommodations, in taste and in feeling, to be seen anywhere. In season there are free boat shuttles to the Lido (Excelsior's pool or the park-sited Des Bains).

☆☆☆☆ **Palazzo del Giglio apartment colony** • is almost next door. It is an exquisite union of bright, joyful colors, modern comfort, carefully selected antiques, and works of art to complement the whole and create an enchanting homey atmosphere. Just 16 suites in varying sizes to accommodate couples or families or friendly migrants; full air conditioning plus TV, radio, beautifully equipped kitchens; the works. Laundry, maid, and other services are available. The cheer, the privacy, the luxury, and the economics make it almost irresistible for travelers who plan to stay a week or more in Venice. Administration is by the Gritti people, who are always at the beck or phone call of their neighboring apartment clients.

★★★★★ **Danieli Royal Excelsior** • evokes an Old-World magic that can never be repeated in modern-day structures. The view from the glass-fronted rooftop dining room also is enchanting. More than a third of this house has been superbly renovated; entirely air-conditioned; roughly 245 rooms in 3 separate "generations," coupled by short passageways: the "Palace" building (architecturally gorgeous; double-pane windows in front; quietest units on Rio del Vin side); the "New" building (less classic and also appealing); and the "Danielino" building (used chiefly by groups). Different in concept from the Gritti or the Cipriani and very fine, indeed.

☆☆☆ **Europa & Regina** • which links two former independent neighbors is first class and offers an extra feature in its sprawling construction; the guest can view the big canal from 4 sides. Main floor restyled and most bedrooms updated very recently. Beautiful garden restaurant; fully air-conditioned. Vast changes recently—all of them highly beneficial structurally.

★★★ **Londra Palace** • has become a charmer through careful, tony updatings and ceaseless additions for comfort. The Do Leoni waterfront restaurant—managed by kind-hearted American Silvia von Block—is also a fine reason for making this your Venice redoubt. The piano bar is a snug harbor at night and a solarium terrace overlooks the lagoon by day. The position is perfect, the people are hospitable, and the prices are very reasonable.

★ **Bauer Grunwald** • boasts parts of a five-century-old cloister and a houseful of Medici-style furnishings, but the increasingly heavy group traffic diminishes its appeal for independent travelers. Units ending in "52" or "53" cast wonderful glances at the canal; most of the building is air-conditioned. Public rooms with modern decor melding softly through a rich antique haze.

Grand Canal terrace; roof garden; opulent Royal suite; ordinary accommodations "inside" and somewhat cramped; expensive, and less lively than most.

★★ **Metropole** • boasts an excellent address a few steps away from the ferry landing, facing the Lagoon. Canal entrance for gondolas and water taxis. Complete air conditioning; sumptuous interior, a modern adaptation of the classic Venetian style; compact restaurant and American bar; generously outfitted bedchambers. For situation and decoration, this proud house is loaded with appeal. Its service standards are another story.

☆☆☆ **Monaco** • nestles dockside on the Grand Canal just across the walkway from Harry's Bar. The house has a quiet traditional mien, lovely furnishings, and numerous fine antiques; bar-lounge with one of the finest vistas in Venice. Sumptuous dining room plus alfresco mealtime terrace. Rooms with satellite color TV, radios, minibar, and safe. Manager Gianni Zambone is an expert hotelier and host.

★ **La Fenice** • is above the restaurant of the same name, but is not associated with it. Located in the wings of the famous Fenice Theatre; cozy-elegant lounge with silk wall coverings; beautiful antique furnishings; no restaurant, but a bar 10 seconds away; 70 rooms, most with bath but some of the "sitz" style. A decent bet within its second-class ranking.

Luna • Venice's oldest hotel (dating from 1474, but a religious retreat even prior to *that!*), claims a central but quiet locale. Fully air-conditioned; waterside bar on tiny canal facing the Royal Garden; comfortable bedchambers; most baths replete with marble. There are an attractive rose-toned dining room and open terrace; ambitious billings and dining edicts sometimes cause irritation among visitors.

Pullman Park • quietly situated across from the railway station and city parking garages, has 100 medium-size rooms, the back ones facing Papadopoli Park. Straightforward comfort, kind minions, and homespun hospitality.

Patria Tre Rose • is somewhat less than a honey for the money; readers' opinions are sharply divided on this one.

Cavalletto & Doge Orseolo • has been mightily improved. Public rooms refashioned; 80 units with bath or shower; well-respected dining salon; commercial but worthy for its reasonable tariffs. Closed in winter.

Boston • near St. Mark's Square, serves breakfast only. Inexpensive and solid. **Ala** has 80 chirpy nests; only breakfast is required. **Carpaccio,** on the Grand Canal, steps forward with a generous helping of flair for its bracket. Large rooms, generally clean; simply furnished; situation excellent; moderate terms. One of the best *quids* for your *quo* in the city. **Pensione Seguso,** fronting the Canale Della Giudecca, bobs up with 50 units, ½ with bath or shower; #23, facing the trees across the water, should double your pleasure. Top value.

Country living near Venice

☆☆☆ **Hotel Villa Cipriani** • *in Asolo, about 50 minutes out on the main Venice-Verona highway* • is in the town that boasts of the celebrated former home of both Eleonora Duse and Robert Browning. Beautifully operated; 35 rooms all with private bath; 4 deluxe suites; huge garden; full pension—with a la carte menu! Here's a fine stop for lunch or for rest.

☆☆☆ **Excelsior Palace** • *in the Lido, a few minutes by motorboat from Venice* • has made this island the legendary summer resort that it is. Guided by Sig. Balaudo, the hotel is in good hands. The strand of beach is more beautiful than ever. A pool also is splashing and a waterfront Taverna is sizzling. There are a beach bar and 360 luxury cabanas. Air conditioning murmurs throughout this 380-room house. (You can't open the windows because of the mosquitoes.) The best units are the cheerfully modernized ones on the ground level and the 5th and 6th floors.

Grand Hotel des Bains • is gifted with a warmed seawater pool, 3 tennis courts at its Sporting Club, a discotheque, a bar, and full air conditioning.

Villa Mabapa • believe it or not a contraction of mamma, bambino, and papa of the Vianello tribe who run the place, has 75 rooms. Except for the location, which is far from the casino and other Lido action, this one competes favorably with the Four Fountains.

RESTAURANTS

☆☆☆☆☆ **Harry's Bar** • *San Marco 1323* • remains faithful to the Hemingway cult. It's intimate, friendly, sophisticated, and cheerful, but decoratively of no particular distinction. Great fun for people-watching; limited but excellent menu with many stateside delicacies; shockingly high prices that Ernie probably never would have tolerated. **Harry's ★★★★★ Restaurant** twinkles happily too; 60 can be nourished in ★★★★★ style at one sitting. Try a batch of homemade ravioli and a plate of scampi carlina. Always reserve in season. ★★★**Harry's Dolci** • *on Giudecca Island at Santa Eufemia 773, a 15-minute walk from the Cipriani Hotel* • is an informal addition for light refreshment, carafe wine, sweets, and ices; canalside romantics at the outside tables and woody bistro intimacy inside. If you have a sweet tooth, try the chocolate cake made at the nearby Cipriani bakery.

☆ **Antico Martini** • *San Marco 2007, in the piazza facing the famous Teatro La Fenice* • is both a nightclub and restaurant; luxury-leaning interior with French curtains, gilt mirrors, and crystal fixtures; professional service. Dinner only; very costly; closed Tues., also Dec. and Jan.

★ **Madonna** • *San Polo 595, near the Rialto at Calle della Madonna* • is hardy, noisy, and jostling with voluble citizenry. The vivacity is catching (except Wednesdays, when it closes). Sprawling precincts where fish, risotto, and you are the star attractions.

★★ **Il Cortile** • *via XXII Marzo 2402, near S. Marco* • is a romantic midtown spot for summer-izations; it resides in a walled courtyard and under a lovely undulating awning; relaxing shade with fresh greenery; delightful at night too—whether indoors or out. The Venetian fare is light and appetizingly presented.

☆☆☆ **Corte Sconta** • *calle del Pestrin 3886* • is a *trattoria,* which many may think cannot merit 3 stars simply by definition. It's hard to find and obviously ugly, having been a cow stall and not having changed much since used for its original purpose. You sit in a spartan room or a lackluster courtyard with brown paper mats on bare tables. But *Mamma Mia*!!! Is the food delicious! Start with a chilled Prosecco lively white wine, then Spaghetti in Three Ways, shellfish or sepia in its own ink, or just anything—and you'd better go before 9 p.m. or risk missing the best catch in all Venice. A meal for two will nudge $50 and it is certainly not an aesthetic experience. It's an adventure. Closed Mon. and Tues.

★★ **Da Ivo** • *follow Calle dei Fuseri to San Marco 1809* • is noted for its waterside traffic of gondolas and its interior decoration of T-bone steaks, more suggestive of Florentine beefeating than typical Venetian calories. I enjoy the mood here. Very central, too.

★★ **Taverna La Fenice** • *San Marco 1938* • for Italian dining and a romantic atmosphere this is usually a winner. Begin with a pasta dish; the house spaghetti is special, spiked with niblets of cuttlefish. Handsome, timber highlights; covered terrace in summer; versatile kitchen; tariffs very lofty and I've also found—and some readers too—that the waiters are in love with addition. Check your bills carefully and ask before you order. Closed Sun.

★★ **Caravella** • *calle XXII Marzo* • is even higher, but in its way it is more beautiful, too, and the culinary preparations are unusually savory. Bar at entrance with cozy tables; interior room on 2 tiers; wood-lined walls resembling an ancient bark: brass lamps imparting a soft glow; gay explosions of flowers everywhere, and all dew-fresh. Specialties include lobster, spaghetti Venetian-style (that's with a mixture of sauteed onions and anchovies that might be too seasoned for many palates), spider crab, and sole. In season, the larded hare is exceptional on a cool day. Closed Wed.

☆☆☆ **Locanda Cipriani** • *a 35-minute speedboat ride to the island of Torcello* • has a peaceful terrace; gourmet fare at fixed price in the opulent area; try *both* gnocchis—gnocchi Torcellano and a gnocchi Santa Fosca—each featherlight, different in concept, and guaranteed taste treats.

★★★ **Antica Locanda Montin** • *Fondamenta Eremite,* behind *Acemia* • is a favorite of mine from way back. Picture-lined, raw interior; vine-lined summer garden; simple cookery; basic tariffs; frequented by artists, nobility, and a grateful travel writer or two. Try the house filet in a rich sauce. Closed Tues. nights and Wed.

☆ **Do Forni** • *calle Specchieri 468* • features 2 of the 3 rooms in medieval Venetian style; tented motif for summer dining; comestibles medium to expensive. Sample spaghetti all'Isolana and spiedino do forni guarnito (a brochette of 7 meats). Be sure you are clear on the meaning of the fine print on the menu, because some readers have complained of misunderstandings when the bill was presented. Closed Thurs.

☆ **Da Fiore** • *San Polo 2202* • is a family spot where the fireworks are in the value, not in the atmosphere or antics of the waiters. Honest Venetian cooking is the theme and risotto is the staff of life. Don't mix its name up with the one above.

Caffe Florian • *piazza San Marco* • began life as far back as 1720. It offers 6 little rooms, each with its own entrance, plus 7 rows of outside tables; a seasonal band gently massages the eardrums of anybody in the entire square. The pick of the esplanade. **Quadri,** just opposite and also born in the 18th century, seems faded and listless. Nevertheless, it's a valid antique.

Trattoria La Colomba • *Frezzeria 1665* • and, to a lesser degree, **Al Graspo de Ua** • *San Bartolomeo 5094* • offer substantial regional cookery; no terrace at the latter. The former, by the way, is the well-known establishment displaying paintings on its walls. **Al Colombo** • *San Luca 4620* • is often confused with it; this one is less colorful but reliable for *trattoria* cookery. Mon. closure.

Al Teatro • *on piazza Fenice adjoining Teatro La Fenice* • still gets first ranking as the top pizzeria in town. The entrance rooms contains a counter, a bar, an open grill, and a frenzied trade; the second room offers about 15 tables, 24 ceiling lights, celebrity-photo-lined walls, and a cheerful, relaxed atmosphere; between the 2 is an open kitchen with a pizza oven that's home base for 16 types (available only during mealtimes, when the stoves are hot). Super for its category; we tout it heartily.

NIGHT LIFE

Four suggestions: (1) the Casino at the Lido, (2) **Chez Vous** at the Excelsior-Lido, offering all-out competition, (3) a drink, a dance, or a pitch at the **Antico Martini** or (4) go to bed with a good book. Pleasant dinner-dancing on the **Bauer-Grunwald** roof in season only. Venetians usually end their evenings (in summer) sitting outdoors in piazza San Marco—far more entertaining, in my view, than any nightclub could ever be.

SHOPPING

Buyers will find that this lodestone is teeming with guides, concierges, gondoliers, and other fast operators hungry for commissions on their purchases. The usual bite is 20% to 25% on glass and 15% on lace. Don't tell anyone where you're going, inform the shopkeeper immediately that nobody directed you to his establishment (except a guidebook or other distinterested source), that you're paying cash, and that you want the above scale of discounts for yourself.

NOTE · · · To counter the fringe operators, the Chamber of Commerce and the legitimate old-line merchants, such as those mentioned below, set up the **Venetian Crafts Association** to attest to both product quality and business ethics among its members. Be sure to look for the Association's 4-leaf-clover symbol displayed in all these companies.

ARTS AND CRAFTS: **Union of Venetian Artistic Artisans** (Calle Larga San Marco 412/13), just behind the piazza San Marco, is an exposition-sales outlet for some of the best local talent in all media of materials from glass and wood to the elegance of Countess Foscari's brilliant frames tipped in silver or brass. Vast variety and excellent prices.

CREATIVE JEWELRY: **Paolo Scarpa Primitive Jewelry** (San Marco-Merceria San Salvador 4850) is small but mighty. The creations of the couple who scour the globe for unusual materials offer absolute uniqueness in every piece. But prices for all this worldwide adventure start at only $100 (rising to $10,000). Like a museum and not be to be missed.

GLASS: We suggest that you avoid the island of **Murano** and the swindlers or seamier merchants throughout Venice itself and do 100% of your buying only in the 2 oldest, largest, and soundest houses—**Pauly & Co.** (Ponte dei Consorzi, 3 branches in piazza San Marco) and **Salviati & Co.** (San Gregorio 195, across the Grand Canal from the Gritti Palace, Campo S. Maria del Giglio 2461 next door to this hotel, plus 2 branches on San Marco). These 2 establishments are impeccably honest and reliable; both glitter with beauty and are as much a part of the Venetian spectator's scene as the Square, the gondolas, and the cathedral. We list them in alphabetical order because of their equal ranking.

The venerable **Pauly & Co.** products have won 25 Gold Medals, 16 Notable Award Prizes, 33 Award Diplomas, the French Legion of Honor, the Crown of Leopold, and the Crown of Italy. In their archives, you'll find more than 800-thousand one-of-a-kind sketches of antique, classical and modern patterns. A team of celebrated Glass Masters create exclusively for them. At their

Ponte dei Consorzi headquarters there is a demonstration furnace and budget shop on the ground floor; upstairs you may wander through perhaps 20 glorious rooms full of treasures for the table, the home, and the eye.

Salviati, dean of the field, recently captured the celestial "Golden Compasses" award, the bi-annual "Oscar" presented for Italy's most noble designs in manufactured output. Their pioneering has had a profound influence on the evolution of glass all over the world. Salviati mosaic panels or murals have been commissioned by world-famous institutions. Don't miss a visit to their magnificent display mansion where you will find 2 of the most exciting museum collections of ancient and modern glass in existence. You'll revel in chambers full of objects that shimmer as did the Pleasure Dome of Xanadu.

Both firms guarantee safe arrival to your home of everything they ship— and you can absolutely trust them on this. But have limitless patience about shipment delays (months are par for the course, due to Italian export red tape and the monumental backlog snarls at U.S. docks)—and be sure to find out approximate delivery costs to your area, because port brokers' fees are sometimes wicked through no fault of these good artisans. Please remember that nobody is permitted to pay U.S. Customs duties and handling before our American officials can evaluate these foreign purchases upon entry, so it is impossible for these companies to estimate the levy accurately.

LACE AND LINEN: **Jesurum** (Ponte Canonica 4314) is famous for its lace, lingerie, delicate embroidery, and boudoir fashions. The lovely old palace is brimming over with layettes, wedding veils, tablecloths, and placemats. Don't miss the antique lace collection! There's a branch in Milan (Via Verri) and one in Parma (Via G. Tommasini 6).

LEATHER GOODS: **Vogini** (4 shops on 4 corners of San Marco-Ascensione) runs the gamut in fine merchandise in this field. Everything from shoes and boots to purses, attache cases—even clothing. The prices are stunning values compared to those in the U.S.

VENETIAN JEWELRY: In quality, in fame, in the distinction of its worldwide clientele who seek these treasures, the unchallenged King of this City of Palaces is **Nardi** (piazza San Marco 68–71). Since 1920 it has specialized in designing and creating exquisite *bijous* in gold and precious stones, all handmade and all signed as originals with the famed Nardi name. Full line of gems, including impressive antiques; the shop at No. 68 contains exceptionally fine rarities; at No. 71 there are hard semi-precious stones and watches (especially Piaget); no purchase tax ever. Ask for the knowledgeable Mr. Sergio Nardi, or for Messrs. Semenzato or Zambon.

VERONA, the city of Romeo and Juliet, provides a whirl of ancient byways, tiny piazzas, hill and valley vistas, an open market, superb opera at the open Arena in summer or in its 18th-century *Teatro Filarmonico* in winter, and trade fairs galore. Here's a charmer that you really should visit.

☆☆☆ **Due Torri** • For more than 1000 years there has been some kind of inn, tavern, or hostel on this site (Mozart stopped here in 1770); it's a showplace, one of the most unusual hotels in the nation. Within its rooms there are 50 different motifs of exact period-furniture combinations of the 18th- and early 19th centuries, both Italian and French; a sufficient supply of excess antiques is in storage to equip 200 additional rooms! Dignity and richness everywhere; cuisine vastly improved and very well presented; rates especially moderate for such opulence.

☆☆☆ **Gabbia d'Oro** • an expensive stop in midtown, spealizes in suites. Luxurious it is and worth considering if big spending presents no problems.

Victoria • would be the next choice.

Colomba d'Oro • has improved; restaurant and breakfast room renewed; firm-sprung beds throughout; nice baths; brass lamps and flowered wallpaper installed; 60% air conditioning sealed-in silence with double windows; garage. Fresh, clean, and tasteful.

Grand • has been perked up brightly. Public rooms smartened; lobbyside patio sweet for summer dining; most ceilings so high you'll think you're sleeping in a square silo. Comfortable, nonetheless, and getting better.

Nuovo San Pietro • *on the Autostrada exit from Venice and Milan* • is so-so for go-slow motorists who prefer Verona from afar. Each unit with private balcony; most with bath or shower; clean as shining tile.

San Luca • in the second file, comes up with first-class amenities. Alley situation, which detracts from its status but adds to its tranquillity; cool but appealing lobby with adjoining bar; mezzanine breakfast deck; rooftop solarium; good, modern air conditioning; extra-kind concierge and back-up staff. All 40 smartly appointed contemporary bedchambers with wall-to-wall carpets, muted color blends, and small but efficient baths. For its low rates and relatively high-style rewards, it's a sensible buy.

Accademia, Giulietta e Romeo, and **Milano** are alternative second-class bets.

For dining, **Le Scrigno** and **Convivio** are recommendable, followed by **Torcoloti Il Cenacolo** and **La Lampara.**

LIECHTENSTEIN

> **TELEPHONE:** Access code to USA: 001. To phone Liechtenstein: 41; time difference (Eastern Daylight) plus 6 hrs.

Liechtenstein, like Andorra, Luxembourg, Monaco, and San Marino, is a storybook land that frequently seems to get lost by Europe cartographers. It is a cozy matchbox principality with matchless scenery and openhearted people. I openly confess a love affair with this tyke—and I think you'll fall for it, too.

Vaguely the shape of Idaho (and about the size of an Idaho potato), this midget Elysium sprawls between the east bank of the Upper Rhine (near Lake Constance) and a towering range of 7000-foot peaks that provide ski slopes for winter sportsmen and ski champions for World Cup competitions; it is the historic buffer state, 16 miles long and 4 wide, which separates Switzerland from Austria. St. Gall is only a hop, skip, and jump from the capital; Zurich is an easy morning's drive, and Innsbruck (Austria) isn't much farther by crack train. The main railway line to Vienna, one of central Europe's greatest arteries, cuts across the heartland and then passes on Austrian soil within rods of the bordering river (international transfer points: Sargans or Buchs/SG, both in Switzerland).

Founded in 1719, it has proudly cherished its independence since then; the reigning monarch is Prince Hans Adam II. The national language is German, and the monetary unit is the Swiss franc. There is no standing military might; 55 policemen do the job of the army, navy, air force, and marines. There are no labor unions, no poverty, no unemployment, and practically no taxes (to discourage fugitives and financial-angle guys, however, citizenship papers are almost impossible to obtain). Crime is virtually unknown and in 1986 women earned the right to vote.

Industries include postage stamps, textiles, tools and fastening systems, space age insulation, false teeth (producing 70 million molars a year, here's a big chomp in the economy!), and optical instruments; agriculture has lost ground, while banking and commerce have roared ahead. The postage stamps boast some of the finest engraving in the world; oddly enough, they have the same value to philatelists whether they're canceled or uncanceled.

Vaduz (pronounced Vah-dootz), the capital, crams 5000-odd living human beings (national census: 28,452, composed of 18,098 citizens and 10,354 foreigners) into one metropolis, if you can imagine such staggering overpopulation. *Schaan* and handsome little *Triesenberg,* with its proud local museum and community center, are the only other villages of importance. In winter almost everyone and his ski partner evacuate the centers for the higher slopes. The isolated hamlet of **Malbun** is the capital of the snowflakes. It's no more than a porcelain-white chalice in a cul-de-sac where several hotels and guest houses provide shelter, food, and a fair degree of comfort. If you look carefully, you may recognize the royal sitzmark of Prince Philip, Prince Charles, Lady Di, or Princess Anne, who make this a scheduled winter wonderland.

HOTELS

Let's consider the ones in **Vaduz** first. The Elfin **Sylva** at **Schaan** and the **Engel** (near the Austrian border at **Nendeln**) are somewhat distant alternates.

★★★★★ **Sonnenhof** • on the mountainside, easily captures top honors not only as the finest hostelry in the land, but also as one of the leading choices in the entire region—in or out of Liechtenstein. This is the happy domain of Emil Real and his beautiful wife, Jutta (pronounced "Utah"). There is a lovely view from its front-facing rooms; the tranquillity is heavenly; you'll discover a splendid woody dining room in 2 tiers which peeks at the Rhine Valley; glass-wrapped swimming pool and wood-wrapped sauna are fully operational, a dozen fine suites, each with color TV, frigo bars, and its own private lawn or terrace—the last word-and-sigh for contentment. Awaiting you are wall-to-wall carpeting, excellent furniture, well-conceived baths, and the feeling that the house is in certain harmony with its peaceful surroundings. Since these warmhearted hoteliers try so hard to create a cozy, friendly "family" atmosphere, all guests are encouraged to enjoy their cups together in the homey main-floor lounge. Its extrasavory cookery, worthy of gastronomy's top laurels, is reserved for residents (and their guests), which keeps the flavor up and the maddening crowds down (another Real-istic guarantee of solace). Closed mid-Jan. to early March; tons of bucolic charm; perfect for a rest in every particular. *Wunderbar!*

★★ **Real** • the centrally located brother of the Sonnenhof, is the 10-unit (5 singles, 5 doubles) extension of Liechtenstein's most celebrated restaurant. The staff's warmth of hospitality is truly overwhelming.

★★★ **Schlossle** • a mock castle in a bluff buff hue, has done lots of revamping recently; smart management has created a pleasant and homey atmosphere. And now, too, its restaurant is one of the tops in the region. The carpeted bedchambers have been refashioned under vigorous, attentive supervision. Nice as a mini-apartment address.

★★ **Engel** • (this one in town) is adequate rather than fancy. Busy-busy location; flower-lined balconies along front; the first (and so far, only) Chinese restaurant in the principality; 17 rooms with baths or showers; minibar in each unit; sparkling clean, and appealing.

Vaduzer Hof • in improved dress, is quite comfortable; many rooms with balconies but only 10 of its 28 with bath or shower; reserve away from front of

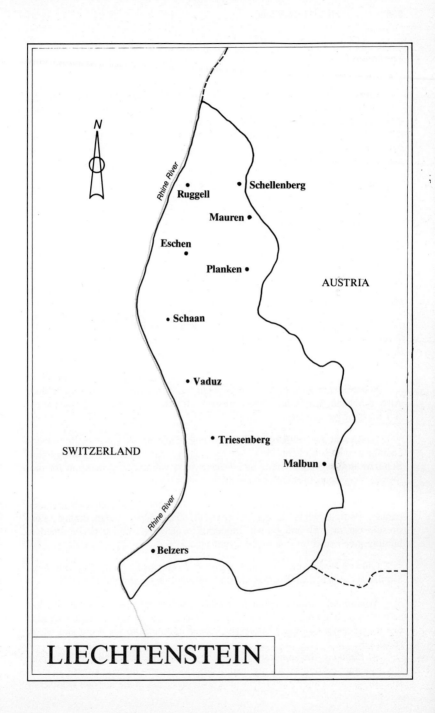

N

Rhine River

Ruggell •

Schellenberg •

Mauren •

Eschen
•

Planken •

AUSTRIA

• Schaan

• Vaduz

• Triesenberg

SWITZERLAND

Malbun •

Rhine River

• Belzers

LIECHTENSTEIN

house due to noise; warm, inviting dining room; open-beamed bar. Good. The **Landhaus Prasch** is nearby and also recommendable; it serves breakfast only ("garni").

Lowen ● offers its captivating and historical restaurant overlooking the vineyards to recommend it, featuring an open terrace for dining. Careful restoration has been rendered to preserve this delightfully antique national trust, which dates back to 1380. Bedchambers have been much improved; there are 7 with bath and shower, the singles being the best buys. A unique haven, but especially noted for its gastronomy.

Gasthof Au ● also experiencing a revamping spree, is a simple but typical country inn where you can sample local food such as *Kasknopfle*.

Hotel Meierhof ● has a restaurant downstairs and 23 bedrooms above, including some suites. Passable for serious budgeteers or summer-izing families who might enjoy the adult and kiddie pools in the back garden. High in the country, the inn in *Silum* is ideal for students or hard-driven economy-seekers from May through October only. Behind the Meierhof is the **Schlosswald** with 33 units and a quartet of studios with kitchenettes for longer stays. Rather modern in tone.

Muhle ● between Vaduz and Schaan, is a sweet little honeybunch of only 7 rooms that are compact but inviting. The low stucco building resembles a Spanish colonial *hacienda*. Charm-laden restaurants (1 for grills), bar, and polished-rustic lounges. Pert and proper.

Schaanerhof ● I'd pick this at *Schaan,* with the **Dux** waddling up behind. Also at Schaan, **Linde** has been refreshed; all units with bath or shower; superior inexpensive cookery.

Kulm ● in *Triesenberg,* is fairly young; chalet style; some of its wooden chambers with excellent views to the valley; fair restaurant. **Landgasthof Schatzmann,** between Vaduz and *Triesen,* is a warmhearted tuck-inn for motorists. Very peaceful here and excellent gastronomy.

Malbunerhof ● at *Malbun,* fully balconied, 30-room-and-bath leads the small parade. Pool, bowling, sauna for physical fitness types; tartan dining salon; fireside bar in gray and brown; modernistic paintings; alpine decor tuned to hunting green. Bid for one of the larger units.

Gorfion ● owned by the same team, is also a worthy choice for hillbillets. Similar and equally well managed. Both resemble hyperthyroid chalets.

Alpenhotel ● would be our next choice; it is more modest, but it also has an enclosed swimming pool as well as personality and comfort. The owner also has the 12-room **Galina;** visitors cluck over its fine little tea room and pastry selection.

At *Planken,* the smallest village in this miniland, the **Saroja** is a sweetie; the restaurant portion serves regional dishes. Moreover, did you know Liechtenstein has a Low Land? Two rather nice hostelries exist in the hollow: **Deutscher** da

Rhein at *Bendern* and the **Krone** (with pool) at *Schellenberg.* While at the latter be sure to visit the Russian Memorial.

A youth hostel beckons near *Schaan,* about 100 yards from the bus junction. You can have breakfast here, cook your own food if you wish or get a substantial cheap meal at the nearby Cafe Forum. About 80 beds with rates close to $12 per noggin. Clean, neat, and economical.

RESTAURANTS

★★★★★ **Real** ● on the main square in *Vaduz,* is definitely first, foremost, and finest in the land—in fact, one of the most consistently sound kitchens in Europe. You'll almost always find the Reigning Family dining here on the cook's night off at the castle. Small, not fancy; one of its working family will greet you with a smile and *"Gruss Gott!"* While I could suggest dishes to try, I would urge you to leave it to Martin Real to offer his prides of the season.

★★★★ **Sonnenhof** ● (see "Hotels"), which only serves to residents and their guests, is firmly in the big leagues of Continental gastronomic achievement. Owner-chef Emil Real shines with masterful brilliance in his presentations of Scampi Orientale, duck with green peppercorn sauce, poached salmon on a pallet of spinach and garnished with dill; the *fettucine al limone* and ravioli are marvels; the fruit gratinee in *Sabayon* is a delight. The real artistry of balance and flavor, as well as the aesthetic joys of this cuisine provide such a satisfying experience that any hedonist cannot do less than visit the Sonnenhof for a minimum of several rewarding days.

★★★ **Lowen** ● (the hotel-restaurant in Vaduz, *not* Schellenberg) is now one of the finest in this nation of gourmets. It's a very special building, beloved by the local citizens—and with good reason.

★★★ **Waldhof** ● at Schaanwald on the busy main drag between the Austrian frontier and Nendeln, glitters under the sterling management of Peter Meier and his charming wife, Ruth. In warm weather the outdoor terrace is a sylvan roadsider and restful when traffic is light. The wooden roof has heating elements to dispel the evening chill. Main salon in French international style; conscientious service. Traditional cooking laced with imagination; inventive combinations such as fresh mango and parma ham or individual cocottes filled with shrimp and pasta napped with the lightest of cream sauces and then whisked under the grill; game and wild mushrooms when the forests permit. Comfortable, innovative, appealing.

☆☆ **Torkel** ● site of a 3-century-old winepress, is pleasant enough for the rustic-toned flavor of Old Liechtenstein. It belongs to the Prince but is designed for Everyman on a princely salary. Winepress dominating the interior; a few alfresco tables on the edge of a vine-covered slope.

Engel • as mentioned before, has a Chinese restaurant. It's expensive but worthy.

Lowen • at *Schellenberg*—only a grapeseed's toss from the Austrian border—is about as old as the historic Liechtenstein Charter. The outside suffers from a severe case of shingles (they are new); the inside is cozy; the menu features such local syllables as Kasknopfle, Schwartenmagen, and Sauerkase. Its quiet, viewful and oh-so-easy on the budget. **Sele** in *Triesenberg* serves local fare as well as light conventional dishes.

☆☆☆ **Schatzmann,** the previously mentioned hotel, also features one of the best kitchens in the land.

Berggasthof • at *Masescha* serves a good table; so does **Schachle's Weinstube** at *Nendeln.* The latter has a huge selection of vintages available; it's also a hotel in case you care to tuck in overnight.

If you have a car, take the 20-minute ride to wonderful *Maienfeld,* a Swiss fortress.

☆☆☆ **Schloss Brandis** • the restaurant, is in an ancient tower with chevroned shutters; rugged all-wood ceiling; iron chandeliers; stone walls and terracotta floors; leaded windows with etched glass. Delicious Bauernwurst (red sausage); highly ambitious menu that's rich in its selection of international treats; mellow local Maienfeld red wine, my happy choice; friendly, smart service. A very rewarding excursion through beautiful forested terrain.

SHOPPING

For attractive gifts and artistic handicrafts, visit the ultrakind Helene Demarchi at the midvillage **l'Atelier** (Stadtle 36). It's a tiny boutique, but the level of taste is tops in town for my value-seeking Swiss Francs. Be sure to visit the Stamp or Art Museums and other high points such as the **Walser Museum** *(Heimatmuseum)* at *Triesenberg* (showing an interesting collection on the cultural history of the settlers plus a sound and slide presentation on alpine topics), a drive up to Masescha, and later a mountain excursion to the lofty wintersports resort of Malbun (5000 feet), with 9 hotels, 4 ski tows, and 2 chair lifts that zip up to 7500 feet for a fascinating survey of Austrian real estate to pop your eyes. As a warm-day alternative, plunge in the ultramodern swimming pool between Vaduz and Schaan or play tennis in the 4-court hall of which the citizens are so proud.

Measure-for-measure, the country may be small, but its pepper-hot **National Tourist Office** director, Berthold Konrad, is a purebred Texan in his vision and wide-angled approach to hospitality. A team of 20 smiling hostesses is available to arrange museum tours, special interest visits, or guided romps all over the country. If you yearn for anything at all, write to him at P.O. Box 139, FL 9490, Vaduz, Principality of Liechtenstein. What this land lacks in girth, it more than makes up for in zeal.

LUXEMBOURG

USA: Luxembourg Tourist Information Office, 801 Second Ave., New York, NY 10017

TELEPHONE: Access code to USA: 00. To phone Luxembourg: 352; time difference (Eastern Daylight) plus 6 hrs.

Luxembourg is a Grand Duchy, a never-never land of castles, turrets, swords, gold braid—a 20th-century Camelot with toy trimmings. Anno Domini 1963 marked its 1000th anniversary. There's a romantic sort of aimlessness about it. If a citizen gets mad at his vested officials, he has only to dial 478–1 to hear a voice reply, "Good morning! The Government!" It's a happy, serene, fat little community of 365,000 people, a quarter of whom are foreign-born; Chicago is said to boast more Luxembourgers than the homeland. It's a prosperous tyke, too—so fond of finance that there is one bank for every 1100 citizens in the Duchy. In the Middle Ages knights and barons controlled the destiny of the nation. Their homes were tremendous strongholds—fortresses the ruins of which dot the countryside at Vianden, Beaufort, Bourscheid, and other locales. They were responsible for dubbing the domain "The Land of Haunted Castles." The country takes its name from the tiny palace of Sigefroi, Count of Ardennes, who 10 centuries ago erected his "Lucilinburhuc" ("Little Castle") where the capital stands today. The mantle of State is worn today by Grand Duc Jean. After settling the Kammerwald border dispute with Germany, and giving back 1200 acres, Luxembourg again boasts the easily remembered total of 999 square miles. One-third of its inhabitants raise crops or cattle; steel mills chuff as the prime industry, a bit less profitably of late. The army (600 professionals) is receiving higher pay than ever before. Illiteracy is unknown. The country is 96% Roman Catholic, but there is complete freedom of worship. There are 130 castles but no full-time university exists. Radio Luxembourg, which broadcasts in 5 languages to 10 countries, claims more than 50 million daily listeners, including 78% of the teenagers in Great Britain. A national showpiece is the Luxembourg Theater at Limpertsberg, where opera, drama, and ballet reach their peaks; the Grand Duchy also boasts a $16 million European Parliament edifice. The official as well as the *operative* tongue is a jawbreaking hash (derived from German) called Letzeburgesch. German and French also are common and, since it is so international, many speak English.

One of the most striking vistas in the country is the after-dark illumination of the Petrusse Valley bed, which winds its way crookedly through the heart of the once-impregnable, 1000-year-old Luxembourg City, a bastion which covetous generals of yore labeled the "Gibraltar of the North." Clervaux, previously mentioned Vianden with its enormous Hall of the Knights, and several other historic castles in the hinterland are now beautified by the same technique. On many evenings until 11 p.m. in summer (the schedule varies) cleverly placed spotlights and floodlights give the medieval bridges, massive ramparts, towering spires, and greenery the ethereal glow of a Victorian fairytale illustration. Here, in this capsule, is one of the loveliest creations of nature and man.

HOTELS

If you wing in by Icelandair and are booked on to another destination, the "Stopover Program" is a giant-size aspirin for flight-weary travelers who watch their pennies. This package includes pickup service at the airport, delivery to the hotel, all meals, a room with private bath, a citywide sightseeing tour, and transportation back to the airport. Should you nod "yes" to this bonus plan, you may tuck in a good chunk of Luxembourg as a low-cost extra during High Season.

☆☆☆ **Le Royal** • *12 bvd. Royal* • has established a commendable level of luxury for the center of the capital. New but nicely mellowed honey-colored stone facade; interior swimming pool; Arlequin nightclub; sedate, taper-lit Relais Royal restaurant blending modernistic freshness with quasi-French traditionalism; a second restaurant for groups, plus the informal Jardin and snack-time terrace; piano bar. Bedchambers (180) small but well outfitted, clean-lined to the point of institutionality; fully air conditioned. Free airport or terminal shuttles. A very welcome addition.

☆☆☆ **Cravat** • *in Luxembourg City* • has an overall view of the Petrusse Valley and all-over amenities. The Petrusse corner boasts 20 spacious, carpeted, twin-bed nests plus 2 suites perched high over the river gorge. Cozy ground-floor cafe, still the social umbilicus of the city; rotisserie in the restaurant; lunch and dinner menu includes delicious smorgasbord-type buffet at bargain tabs; popular bar. This family house is managed by the 3rd-generation Fernand Cravat.

★★★ **Intercontinental** • *Europa Park* • while almost double the size of the Royal, benefits from its tranquil woodland setting. Still, it is large, busy, and typically international (or intercontinental, if you will). Bedrooms are cheerful and vaguely Polynesian in tone. Handsome, masculine Cafe Stiffchen at the

BELGIUM

N

Clervaux •

GERMANY

Vianden •

Diekirch •

Echternach •

Larochette •

Ehnen •

• Luxembourg

Mondorf •

FRANCE

LUXEMBOURG

grill; elegant window-lined Les Continents gourmet restaurant; poolside snack bar and the gracious off-lobby La Veranda for tea-timing; tennis. Having your own car would be a benefit although shuttles and taxis are always on stand-by.

Sheraton Aerogolf • *4 miles from midtown* • is flanked by a splendid 18-hole golfcourse and the airport, which is 300 yards away. Total of 150 air-conditioned rooms all with wall-to-wall carpeting and private bath; grill plus lunch restaurant facing the gardens; 4th-floor cocktail lounge nodding at the treetops. Manager Keller oversees a pleasant rural address.

Pullman • entered its bid opposite the Common Market Center in outlying *Kirchberg,* perhaps 25 minutes from the train station. There's a restaurant, a swimming pool, 250 bedchambers, and ample parking for motorists. Private baths and phones in all single, double, and triple nests; tot-cots provided for a small extra charge; lofty tabs.

Central-Molitor • provides 35 centrally sited kips with bath and shower, carpets, private safes (we won't say where), double windows and soundproofed walls, bidets ("with hot and cold running water," reminds the administration proudly), automatic door openers, electronically controlled red warning-lights that glow "Do Not Disturb" in the corridor, and many other button-poppers.

Rix • with bed and breakfast only, offers 20 bright accommodations which proprietress Rix keeps rubbed to a state of immaculate polish. Crusty shell; simple lobby; friendly main-floor bar; well-outfitted rooms with full carpeting; front units with balconies; rear accommodations supersilent for serious snoozers; small baths with excellent ventilation. Clients frequently dine at the Cravat.

Nobilis • *avenue de la Gare* • comes up with 47 rooms and baths, two restaurants, a bar, and soothing tariffs.

Alfa • *place de la Gare* • has 100 units that are comfortable; prices are moderate.

Parc-Hotel • about 5 minutes along the Route d'Echternach, is a low-octane pit stop for motorists. Chalet-style building; 220 units; pool, play area, and private lake; camping ground with A-frame shelters; thatched-roof cafe-restaurant and dancing on occasion; simple accommodations with curtained-off baths. Not much when compared to the city slickers.

☆☆ **Hotel du Grand Chef** • in *Mondorf-les-Bains* is an Arcadian dream. Situated beside the huge rose-filled Kurpark (state operated, with 40 types of water treatment); back garden along a 3-foot stream, called the Gander River, separating Luxembourg from France. Handsome, imposing structure with modern comforts; 35 units in the old wing and 15 newer ones with rivate balcony, reputed to serve some of the most satisfactory vittles in the land. A charmer in every respect. Closed in midwinter.

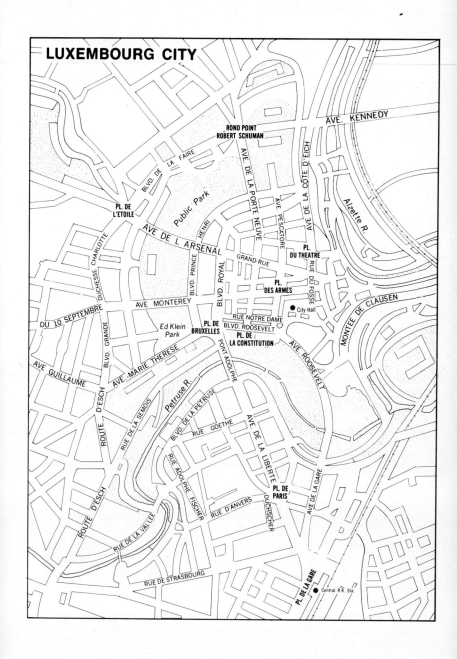

LUXEMBOURG CITY

AVE. KENNEDY

ROND POINT
ROBERT SCHUMAN

BLVD. DE LA FAIRE

AVE. DE LA PORTE NEUVE

AVE. PESCATORE

AVE. DE LA CÔTE D'EICH

Alzette R.

PL. DE
L'ETOILE

Public Park

AVE. DE L ARSENAL

DUCHESSE CHARLOTTE

HENRI

BLVD. PRINCE

BLVD. ROYAL

GRAND-RUE

RUE DU FOSSE

PL.
DU THEATRE

PL.
DES ARMES

City Hall

MONTEE DE CLAUSEN

AVE. MONTEREY

DU 10 SEPTEMBRE

BLVD. GRANDE

Ed Klein
Park

PL. DE
BRUXELLES

RUE NOTRE DAME
BLVD. ROOSEVELT
PL. DE
LA CONSTITUTION

AVE. ROOSEVELT

AVE. GUILLAUME

AVE. MARIE THERESE

PONT ADOLPHE

Petruse R.

ROUTE D'ESCH

RUE DE LA SEMOIS

BLVD. DE LA PETRUSE

RUE GOETHE

AVE. DE LA LIBERTE

RUE ADOLPHE FISCHER

RUE D'ANVERS

AVE. DE LA GARE

DUCHSCHER

PL. DE
PARIS

ROUTE D'ESCH

RUE DE LA VALLEE

RUE DE STRASBOURG

PL. DE LA GARE

Central R.R. Sta.

★★★ **Heintz Hotel** • in the lovely little town of *Vianden* personifies the gentle charm of Mme. Hansen, its owner. Thirty bedrooms, all with bath and private balcony (you may pay extra for the latter); decorative highlights include vaulted ceilings, timbers, and oodles of antiques. It's about 45 minutes from the capital, and it's the proud possessor of the only chair lift in the Grand Duchy—a low-cost ride to a forest-type chalet where you can have a drink on open-air terraces to spike the already intoxicating view. A former convent, here's one of the nation's oldest and most interesting buildings.

Bel-Air • in *Echternach,* smartly remodeled and expanded, is a garden retreat for weekending. The kitchen is praiseworthy.

Airfield Hotel • about a 3-minute walk from the terminus, has a country setting, simple amenities, a wide variety of dishes on its menu, a small bar, and a good location for a quick getaway.

Other havens?

Euro • is along the busy Route d'Arlon to Brussels. This one has decor to please any 40-year-old tot: drum stripes, checks, sworls, and animal wallpaper.

Dany • on this same road and with an antique carriage out front, is also good basic shelter. Its prize, however, is its charming little restaurant boasting charbroiled steaks, lamb on the spit, and other grills that pop right in front of your popping eyes. Expensive tabs here, but pizza and snacks are available in the Crazy Horse Bar, which adjoins the stables and is ricks of fun. For other rural hostelries, check with the Tourist Bureau or our Embassy.

FOOD AND RESTAURANTS

Quite a few of little Luxembourg's restaurants are outstanding.

St. Michel • (excellent turbot and salmon), **Au Gourmet** (trout with fresh herbs or entrecote au Roquefort), **Clairefontaine** (fabulous sole), the **Relais** at **Le Royal** hotel, **Les Continents** at the **Intercontinental, Cravat,** and **Patin d'Or** are tops for city dining.

★★★ **Hotel Hiertz's** nookery in *Diekrich* plus ★★★**Bonne Auberge** at *Gaichel* (about 25 minutes from the center by car) get my top vote for rural excellence.

★★★★ **La Bergerie** • and the ★★**Bel Air** are in *Echternach.*

Speltz ● refashioned not long ago, is a 60-second walk from the Cravat. It offers 2 main rooms plus a small nook to the rear. Ancient pewter highlights; attractive chandelier; comfortable chairs. Versatile menu of game, specialties, and stock dishes comprising perhaps 75 choices; full wine card. If the Ostend oysters are in season, please try them. Excellent.

Cordial ● is perched on a window-wrapped mezzanine in a commercial building, overlooking a routine square; it's packed at noon with somber businessmen: we find it tops in food but bottoms in service.

Rotisserie ● has a rustic ambience. Bar semidivided by greenery; walls partially paneled; cartwheel light fixtures, provincial gimmicks. Despite the obviously touristic outlook, it is chiefly favored by locals who think franc-ly about their vittles. Certainly this is one of the best dining bargain spots in the nation.

Roma ● featuring an Italian menu, is adequate. Of a similar ilk are **Bella Napoli, Rigoletto,** and **Vesuvio.**

★★★★ **Hotel Hiertz** ● in the sleepy town of *Diekirch* (half-an-hour north on Route 7). Emerald watersilk and wood-paneled walls; flowers and candles on tables; Limoges porcelain supplemented by tiny cloverleaf patterns on salmon-colored napery; smooth, friendly service. Always reserve your table.

Suburban or rural expeditions? **La Bergerie** at *Echternach* is the leader, followed, in *Gaichel,* by the charming **Gaichel,** and the **Bonne Auberge,** located so close to the border it's almost an immigrant.

Hotel du Grand Chef ● in *Mondorf-les-Bains* bordering the vineyard country, is convenient and pleasant for a short summertime safari.

Le Central ● a small hotel in *Ettelbruck,* with its restaurant up one flight, offers excellent cuisine.
Many dining places on the Moselle River are delightful.

Hotel Simmer ● in *Ehnen* and **Hostellerie des Pecheurs** in *Remich* are best bets.

Hotel Hallerbach ● in *Haller* (northwest of Echternach) is also special; the *patron* rattles the skillets, and live trout are stored in his little aquarium.
Check these and all other country places before leaving the capital, because most of them close down when business is slow.
Be sure to treat yourself to some wild game in fall and winter. The supply of partridge, pheasant, venison, and wild hare is usually ample. The hare is smaller and sweeter than the Belgian variety. My favorite is roast saddle of hare; the Luxembourgers seem to like theirs cooked, ears and all, in red wine. But the delight of delights—a dish fit for a palace—is Partridge Canape—a fat little bird served whole on toast, with baby mushrooms and a sauce of pan juices to crown it.
If you want a weekend of forests, brooks, trails, peace, and quiet, you

might like the aforementioned **Hotel Bel-Air** in *Echternach*. There's stream fishing and hiking for active souls, loafing for others. The building has been extensively renovated in a charming way; the locale is gorgeous and the reception is warmly hospitable. As an overnight stop, it is also highly recommendable.

NOTE · · · Coffee is inordinately expensive in Luxembourg—often twice the price of a piece of pie.

If you enjoy the tactile sensation of green persimmons, then try Letzburger Kachke's (cooked and aged cottage cheese) for breakfast or with cocktails. It's a proud specialty. You may detest it (as I do), or you may love it—but one thing is certain: your breath will never allow you to forget your holiday in Luxembourg, forever and evermore.

DRINKS

Luxembourg has now thrown the gauntlet at Milwaukee, Munich, and Copenhagen. To keep pace with the output of its 7 local breweries, each Luxembourger—man, woman, and child—downs an average of 33 gallons a year. Tops in white wines (reds or roses are not pressed in this land) for most American tastes is Gewurztraminer. Always ask for the '79 vintage, which is now the choicest year generally available. The '81s, '82s, and '83s (especially) are promising. You might find extra pleasure in a Riesling called Wormeldange Nussbaum. Next comes Riesling Sylvaner (pale, light, and flowered). The Muscat Othonel is too fruity and too sweet for most U.S. palates. Local gentry seem to prefer the fairly dry Riesling Wormeldange Koeppchen; ask for this one by the grower's name, the best of which bears the Schlink Hoffeld cachet. For a sparkling wine, the St. Martin, the Gales, or the Bernard Massard brand are quite drinkable. Additional local production—and it sounds like a tidal wave for such a little land—includes the 100-proof plum brandy (slivovitz-type) known as Quetsch, 2 others made from yellow plums called Prunelle and Mirabelle, and the Swiss-beloved, cherry-pit spirit: Kirsch.

NOTE · · · As a guarantee of quality and authenticity in selecting your wines, be sure to ask for those bottles with the ''Marque Nationale'' sticker. This control device assures you that what you order, you get.

CAPSULE JUNKETS

Here are suggestions for covering some of the lesser-known treasures of this little Duchy. You can pick up a map when you get there, and the strange names of these off-trail places will make sense. (Incidentally, I've been told (but never tried it personally) that Kemwell Car Rental is an excellent and inexpensive choice for week-long leases with unlimited mileage.) All of these are one-day junkets, based on residence in Luxembourg City:

Drive to *Clervaux,* take lunch at the Hotel Koener, continue to *Wiltz,* and backtrack to *Vianden.* From teatime at the Heintz Hotel you're only 45 minutes from the bright lights.

Or visit the **Hamm Cemetery,** where so many of our soldiers, including General George S. Patton, are at peace—continue to the Moselle River, have lunch at Simmer's in *Ehnen*—and get back to the capital in time for coffee and cakes at Namur's, a ceremony you shouldn't miss.

Or amble out to *Echternach,* where on each Whitsun Tuesday there's a renowned **Dancing Procession** that might be called the New York Garment District rumba (3 steps forward and 2 steps back). Splendid basilica, 8th-century tomb of St. Willibrord, and handsome forested surroundings. Then proceed to *Esch-sur-Sure,* swim, motorboat, or laze above its hydroelectric dam, and return.

For a longer outing, run up to the **Hamm Cemetery** via the road to Saarbrucken. After this stop, continue for 3 miles, turn left at *Sandweiler,* and skip on to *Ehnen* for coffee at the Simmer. As you leave the hotel, turn right along the Moselle and motor on until you reach a stone gate with a huge champagne bottle at the entrance. This is the **St. Martin Cave,** where some of the nation's finest sparkling wine is sleeping—and where, for a trifling sum including a glass of bubbly, you may watch it snooze. It's a fascinating tour into the cliffside cellars; afterward, you can sit on the river terrace (with Germany only 50 yards away) and sip the house product at factory tariffs. Now push on to *Remich* and cut in to *Mondorf-les-Bains,* where you can stroll in the lovely rose gardens of the **Kurpark** or take a hydrotherapy treatment in the modern bathhouse. Have lunch at the Hotel du Grand Chef (the backyard has a tiny footbridge to the other side of the fairyland stream, which is French soil). Then zip back to the capital by the main pike that passes through *Frisange* and *Hesperange.* It's a full circuit, but not tiring—and most rewarding for all it embraces.

For single-track gustatory excursions: Try for lunch or dinner (1) the **Hotel Hiertz** at *Diekirch,* (2) the Hotel Welcome at *Mondorf-les-Bains,* (3) the Hotellerie de Vieux Moulin near *Septfontaines,* on the Valley of the Seven Castles route, (4) the stops listed above.

At least take a look at *Larochette,* if you can. This lovely village is in the approaches of what is called the "Little Switzerland of Luxembourg," a beautifully wooded and hilly region with striking rock formations, between Consdorf, Echternach, and Beaufort. Here's a perfect example of the toy charm of the Grand Duchy.

MONACO

USA: Monaco Tourist Office, 845 3rd Ave., New York, NY, Tel. (212) 759–5227

SPECIAL REMARKS: In Monaco touch base with the **Direction du Tourisme et des Congres;** Director Gilles Noghes can open every door to his Principality. It's located at 2A Boulevard des Moulins (hours are Monday through Saturday, 9 a.m.–7 p.m.; Sundays and holidays, 10 a.m. to noon).

TELEPHONE: Access code to USA: 19 (dial tone). To phone Monaco: 33; time difference (Eastern Daylight) plus 6 hrs.

Monaco, 12 miles east of Nice, has a higher population density (over 40,000 per square mile) and smaller total area (425 acres plus 75 that have been added through land reclamation) than any other nation in the world. It is just about half the size of New York's Central Park. The correct pronunciation is "MON-a-co," not "Mon-AH-co."

Ruled by members of the Grimaldi family since the late 13th century, it has been an independent state—almost unbelievable in Europe—since 1415. This remarkable dynasty—"Seigneurs" until 1621, when they became "Princes"—has reigned for more than 5½ centuries.

The Principality is divided into distinct sections: Old Monaco (a tiny antiquated village that sits on The Rock), La Condamine (home of many amiable Monegasques), Fontvielle, a residential district on the reclaimed land, and Monte Carlo (named for Charles III in 1866). If you look closely you'll note that Fontvielle is putting on weight; it gained 54 acres (spreading into the sea) in recent years; it also boasts a stadium with a capacity for 20,000 souls.

Each year 2½ million tourists come to the terraced hills and azure waters of Monaco, to play golf or tennis, to tie up their yachts, or to laze in the gentle sun by day and to dine, drink, dance, or gamble by night. The Monte Carlo Golf Club perches on the 2700-foot cap of neighboring Mont-Agel in France. Its 18 holes are scattered in the mountains in such a spectacular way that if the

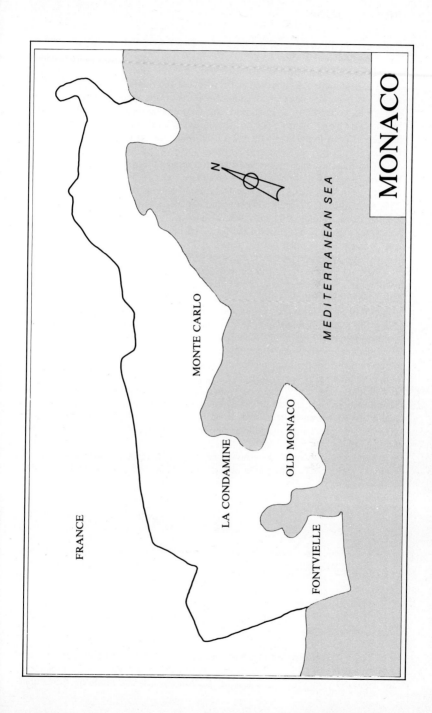

MONACO

FRANCE

MONTE CARLO

LA CONDAMINE

OLD MONACO

FONTVIELLE

MEDITERRANEAN SEA

N

player carelessly stepped off the fairway to search for a ball, he might suddenly find himself doing a slow breast stroke in the sea. The Monte Carlo Country Club offers 20 championship tennis courts, several squash courts and practice courts, an attractive clubhouse, and the fabled Internationaux de Monte-Carlo tennis tournament, one of the outstanding sports events of the year. For sailboat, motorboat, waterskiing, fishing, and skin-diving enthusiasts, the Yacht Club de Monaco has major interest. For skeet and electric-target fans, the Shooting Stand Rainier III is so fine that it's the site of the International Championship Meet in February.

The economy has blossomed into a diversity that old-timers find hard to believe. Chemicals, food products, chocolate, beer, plastics, precision instruments, beauty products, glass, ceramics, and printing now contribute between 25% and 30% of the total state revenue. Tourism and companion trades ante another 30%, stamps 8%, and taxes on tobacco and liquors, plus registration fees, provide the lion's share of the rest. The intake from the gambling concession, contrary to popular belief, makes up only about a 3% share—even when there's a good winning year.

The wheels of the world-famous Monte Carlo Casino, which start at 10 each morning (movie houses don't open until 2 p.m.!), have been spinning since 1856. Of all the gaming operations on the Riviera, this one is the unquestioned aristocrat, far better, in our view, than the American-style extravaganzas along this coast. Nevertheless, if you prefer Yankee gambols, the brand-new Cafe de Paris with its glitzy Jeux Americains caters to just that. Here one can play electronic poker, many new hi-tech slots, console roulette; catch snacks at the glass-lined modernistic nibble nook, outside at the shaded patio, or take a shopping breather in the arcade.

Radio Monte Carlo and Tele Monte Carlo, the local broadcasting and television stations, are powerful voices that are heard or seen throughout the Continent. A huge transmitter—said to be the world's most electronically potent commercial installation—is plugged in; oddly enough, France owns 83% and Monaco the remaining 17%.

Festivals, fireworks, dog shows, opera, ballet, fencing tournaments, international yacht races, automotive events (the Grand Prix is in May), swimming championships, lectures, the latest plays from Paris, religious pageants—these are but a few of the many activities and attractions.

HOTELS

The rankings below do not necessarily conform with Monaco's official system. They reflect personal opinion as outlined in "About the Stars" in the introductory section of this book.

☆☆☆☆☆ **Hotel de Paris** ● is generally considered the pacesetter and certainly chef Alain Ducasse has brought overnight fame—all of it deserved—to the beautifully presented and tasteful gastronomy. In this rambling Edwardian structure are housed sumptuous apartments complete with servants' quarters, the fashionable Louis XV dining realm, the Empire Room restaurant dominated by a colossal Gervais mural painted in 1909, and a cellar of 185,000 bottles of fine wines. Four additional stories of air-conditioned luxury suites ("La Rotonde"); 8th floor glass-wrapped Grill with nightly dancing; piano bar, smooth and distinguished; top-drawer boutiques in rear of the lobby. Another stunner is the huge, shell-roofed, oval, heated-seawater swimming pool niched on the cliffside augmented by 9 saunas and the so-called "California" Terraces. Administration by the courtly and warmhearted Dario del Antonio, who is also one of the brightest lights in the SBM organization that runs most of what is best in this nation.

★★★★★ **Hermitage** • is superb. The stately lobby retains the wood carvings of 1878; Princess Wing nobly outfitted; a top-line hotel restaurant; indoor/outdoor bar; 236 bedchambers radiating glamour; gleaming brass beds; elegant Belle Epoque trappings; modern, functional baths; full air conditioning. Try for a unit facing the harbor—lovely! A bouquet to manager Jean Rauline. Heartily recommended.

☆☆☆☆ **Loews** • hotel-apartment complex, a small city in itself, dips its toes directly into the Mediterranean at the foot of the cliffs below the Grand Casino adjoining the congress hall. It contains its own Las Vegas-style gaming room, 3 spectacularly outfitted restaurants including the Folie Russe supper club with cabaret, old-fashioned salon called the Foie Gras for its specialty and other lovely $-fed stuffings; an Argentine steak house with music of the pampas; Le Pistou for Monagasque food; 3 bars, a surprisingly small rooftop pool, sauna, a fitness club, boutiques, and terraces with every accommodation. The decor is almost dazzling in its effort to evoke zip, zest, and pizzazz throughout. To fill it management must accommodate many groups. For a large hotel, the hospitality level is superb.

★★★★ **Mirabeau** • is linked to an even larger apartment complex; both segments here face the sea, but some of the finest waterfronters gaze onto a freeway overpass that occludes the Med. The hotel is tastefully clad in costly raiments. Noteworthy *haute cuisine* in its La Coupole restaurant; cozy dining spread; smooth service; just great, if it weren't for that darned pike's peek.

☆☆☆☆ **Metropole Palace** • The 170 rooms are in the luxury category; its location above a chic midtown shopping complex provides plenty of appeal if you don't wish to be directly at the seaside. There is an overall feeling of being in a sophisticated metropolitan hotel rather than at a resort.

★★★ **Monte Carlo Beach Hotel** • boasts 46 rooms (all with air conditioning and bath or shower); 7 bungalows, 200 dressing cabins, 144 cabanas, 34 private solaria, a restaurant, and 3 snack bars. Guests in all the *Societe* hotels may use these facilities, but outsiders must pay an admission fee. Much better than it was. Closed Oct.–March.

★★★ **Beach Plaza** • is on Larvotto Beach, an ideal location beside the Sea Club; year-round, heated, saltwater pool; lovely, elegant public rooms; 316 air-chilled doubles with color TV and radio. A fortune has been spent to restyle and enliven this excellent resort property. Bid for a front room only, since the backs overlook a wall and a highway.

Abela • boasts 18 suites in a complex of 192 units; all with bath and fully air conditioned. A fresh entry at moderate prices.

Alexandra • occupies a noisy, midnation perch; no restaurant; gaudy appointments; 80% bath/shower count; clean but achingly small-dimensioned.

Balmoral • enjoys a superb vista of the bay and some refashioning; good value in the medium category.

Miramar • on quai John F. Kennedy, comes up with 14 smallish rooms that are almost in the mast rigging of the yachts tied up at its doorstep. The restaurant is 25 steps away. Convenient for docksiders and now very good for its class.

Siecle • near the station, used to be ideal for the student exile, but it has undergone a thorough renovation; now smart and clean and not too costly.

Terminus • also is in the station area and is very recommendable for economizers.

Du Louvre • offers 34 air-conditioned units and a cool price schedule for budgeteers.

RESTAURANTS

Most spectacular, of course, is **Le Cabaret** with its big-name international nightclub; it is downstairs at the **Casino.** Go for dinner or later; the cuisine is just fair; the music (provided by a 16-piece honey-smooth orchestra during a recent repast) is so delightfully danceable you'll forget that rock ever existed. In the same class is the **Monte Carlo Sporting Club,** which now is comprised of the Maona, La Salle des Etoiles, Jimmy'z and Parady'z, plus the gaming rooms and recreation facilities; glamorous to look at, but is it ever expensive. Among worthy hotel candidates, the aforementioned Folie Russe in **Loews** generates excitement and rubles with its high-cost cookery and cabaret; the Foie Gras is also a smoothie—and again quite costly. The Empire Room and the Grill of the **de Paris** are both outstanding, but the Louis XV room is the place to be seen. The last is the realm of the previously mentioned Alain Ducasse, who is one of the greats of our era. The room itself, decorated with Louis' mistresses (in cameo form) around the ceiling, is magnificent. La Coupole at the **Mirabeau** is just plain good—well, not so plain either. Try the salmon for a sea treat. **Monte Carlo Beach** also has a luxury restaurant with a pleasant atmosphere.

Rampoldi has a fine reputation for cuisine, and prices that have been levered downward. It can be trusted as one of the better independent restaurants.

Bec Rouge is also good, but here the tariffs have jumped upward. The atmosphere is softened by flowers.

Roger Verge's cafe is in the gallery of the Winter Sporting Club, with no natural light and a feeling of claustrophobia. There's a brasserie feeling here. The prices have a lot of brass too.

As for others, **L'Escale,** in the port area, serves good fish and ravioli on an open terrace. **Santa Lucia** is an Italian specialist and fun for few francs. **Chez Bacco** hides behind beveled glass windows overlooking an open patio by the port; it's tiny and highly enjoyable, and not too costly. **La Rascasse** is farther into the port by the recreation boat harbor; very pleasant for munching lazily on a sunny day or starlit evening. **Le Texan** rustles up Tex-Mex grub for homesick cowpokes. It's an amusing diversion. **Astoria** appealed for its quietly sophisticated ambience and recommendable cuisine. Bar at the portal with a lone cream-color room farther back; my meal was reasonably priced and appetizing; the house Bordeaux was outstanding; I experienced good service, too. Worth a try. On The Rock, the **Pinocchio** now seems to enjoy a rock-hard reputation. **St. Nicholas,** near the Prince's Palace, is not recommended. My steak was so thin that it better belonged on a microscope slide. The **International,** also close to the Regal Residence, is decked out in the rustic mood, highlighted by checkered tablecloths. I enjoyed its skillful skilletry and rejoiced in its modest price tags.

Short excursion? If you seek panaromantics at higher prices in an even higher setting, the restaurant of the **Vista Palace,** at nearby *Roquebrune* (described in the "French Riviera" section), may be your candidate.

Pissaladiera, Socca, Pan Bagnat, and Tourta di Ge are among the food specialties. The "blond" Monaco beer, 4-quart steins of which are sold near the Gate of the Royal Palace, is known all over the world for its excellence.

NIGHT LIFE

The **Monte-Carlo Sporting Club,** on a terrace over the sea, is by far the most chichi oasis during the warm months. During galas, 1000 guests are accommodated in this handsome (and expensive) social center. Now the terraced clubhouse is deftly screened by roof gardens. **Le Cabaret** at the Casino draws the elite of 6 continents. The **Empire Room** of the Hotel de Paris is also smart, swank, and glittering. **Loews** features its own casino plus the doin's in its supper club and discotheque. The **Living Room** evokes a club atmosphere; not loud, but cozy in a piano-bar mood. Don't forget the previously mentioned

Jimmy'z. For an informal beer, it's **l'Ariston** or the **Tip Top.** Finally the **Open Air Cinema,** miniskirting the Mediterranean, proudly advertises that it shows ''100 films in 100 days''—but who wants to go to the movies in Monte Carlo?

DAY LIFE

The ubiquitous fetes, galas, and sports already mentioned; the Prince's Palace (open to the public from June to Oct.; tapestries, art treasures, Napoleonic memorabilia, view of the bay); the National Museum (believe it or not, children will love it—that's because of the wondrous collection of 18th- and 19th-century puppets); the Oceanographic Museum (one of the world's oldest, finest, and most important, directed by commandant Cousteau of underwater-exploration fame, with an extraordinary aquarium, a deep sea exhibition, and a magnificent collection of nautical wonders and formalde-hideous freaks); the Zoological Acclimatization center of Monaco; the Wax Museum that waxes over the eloquent Princes of Monaco; the Museum of Prehistoric Anthropology (entered through the Exotic Garden). *The Monte Carlo Story* is shown in multivision at the parking terrace of Chemin des Pecheurs near the Oceanographic Museum; it's a 35-minute history about the rulers of this sunny domain. Big concerts are given in the Court of the Prince's Palace during the summer. Finally, the gardens of the Principality are famous for their beauty—Casino, St. Martin (bordering the Oceanographic Museum), Parc Princesse Antoinette (olive trees millennia old), and the strange Exotic Garden itself (thousands of plants, from semidesert countries, which cling to the slopes of the mountain, flourishing in their new environment). Their climax comes with the Monaco Garden Club's International *Concours* of bouquets in May—a beautiful ''do.''

splendid job at Amsterdam's Molen De Dikkert. Fancied-up (even ornate) farmhouse edging a pond and fountain; contemporary stylings complementing the modern cuisine; exquisite table settings with octagonal metal place plates, candles, flowers, and delicate stemware.

WITTEM, which is about 10 miles from the scenic town of Maastricht, offers the **Kasteel Wittem** where the welcoming Ritzen family knows no limits in hospitality (especially toward Americans). This grand house sits in its own park; drinks by a pond peopled by swans. The dining is superb and it is worth a night's pause only to enjoy a dinner here. Rooms, however, are only adequate. Not far away (even closer to Maastricht at *Valkenburg Aan de Geul*) the **Prinses Juliana** is well known for its table. The tone is more modern and so are the accommodations, if not somewhat sterile.

NORWAY

INCLUDING PEER GYNT MOUNTAIN COUNTRY

USA: Norwegian Tourist Board, 655 Third Ave., New York, NY 10017, Tel. (212) 949–2333, Tx 620681, Fax (212) 983–5260.

Special Remarks: In the Norwegian capital, the Oslo Tourist Information Office is located at City Hall.

TELEPHONE: Access code to USA: 095. To phone Norway: 47; time difference (Eastern Daylight) plus 6 hrs.

Europe's most northerly country is only the area of New Mexico, but it's so long and thin that distances are amazing. From top to bottom it stretches the same length as from New York to Omaha, Nebraska; from side to side, however, its width varies between 269 miles and 3.9 miles. The famous Skagerrak (same latitude as Scotland) separates it from Denmark; the northern tip rises far beyond the Arctic Circle.

Within its huge, sprawling area of more than 125,000 square miles there are slightly more than 4 million inhabitants—less than one half the population of New York City. Except for Luxembourg and some other tots, this makes it the least populated major nation in Europe—but one of the highest in the world in per capita income. Oslo, the biggest city, has only 450,000 people. Bergen comes second, with 210,000, and Trondheim third, with 135,000. It is so thinly occupied that killingly high taxes are a fact of life. Ethnologically 98.7% are dyed-in-the-wool Nordics; 0.7% are the 25,000 Lapps, and 0.5% are miscellaneous.

Crook by crook, the coastline measures 12,500 miles—½ the earth's circumference, twisting through a 2 x 4 area—and most of it is islands and fjords.

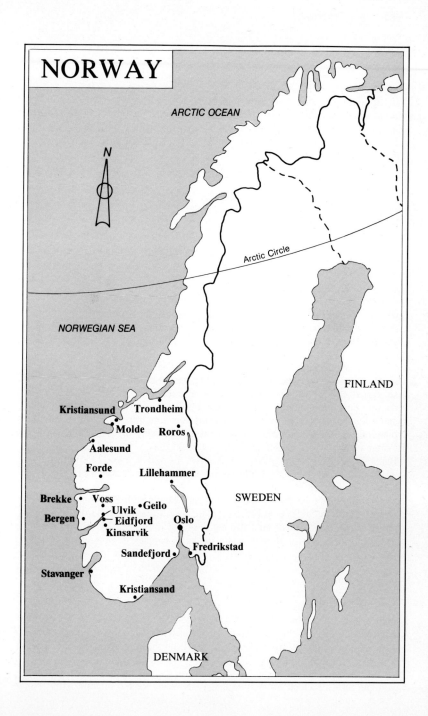

There's wonderful fishing everywhere; you can drop your hook off 150,000 islands!

While whaling is scorned for commerce, some Norwegians are trying to convert a bygone livelihood into a modern form of reverence. **Whale Safaris** are offered off Andenes in Vesteralen: half-day guided tours on whaling vessels to view the tooth whale, sperm whale, the sei, Rorqual, humpback, killer, Gray's, and other cousins of the deep. Rates (with a meal on board) are about 600 crowns per adult and 400 NK for children. For details contact Andoykontoret, Box 58, 8480 Andenes, Fax (88) 41326, before June 20; or afterward: Tourist Information, Andenes, Tel. (088) 42719. You can even fish aboard—but *not* for whale.

Don't worry about raccoon coats and red-flannel underwear; the Norwegian climate is duplicated in parts of Massachusetts. The Gulf Stream keeps it warm: In the summer, the means are 60° Fahrenheit at Oslo, 50° on the Arctic Circle; in the winter, they're 24° at Oslo, 10° where Santa Claus comes from. The midnight sun above the 66th parallel makes daylight last for weeks. There's no real darkness, even in the south, from May to August. On the west coast it rains so much you'll think you're in Waterville, Washington. Its flowers and cool green forest are profuse.

While in Norway, try to see everything you can. Get away from Oslo, which is beautiful but not typical; go west to the fjords or north to either the Peer Gynt Mountain Country (see our separate section) or to Finnmark, because you're not even scratching the surface of a magnificently scenic country if you don't.

One of the very best bets for the first-time visitor is the fjord region with some of the most spectacular water- and landscape on this planet. The tours are so varied and so well organized that it is impossible to single out any one circuit. First, you should budget your time. There are 4-hour boat excursions and 4-day loops by ship-train-bus transport plus a multitude of in-between combinations. The Bergen-Voss-Hardanger trio is possibly the most popular. Both Winge (1–3 Chr. Michelsengt., Tel. 5–901300, Fax 5–901305, Tx 42773) and Bennett (9–11 Ole Bulls plass, Tel. 323010, Tx 42098, Fax 313318) in Bergen are fine travel agencies with offices also in most Norwegian centers. They can show you the waterways and goodies available.

If you wish to strike out alone, the **Oslo–Flam–Stalheim–Norheimsund–Bergen–Oslo** circuit is possibly even more spectacular and rewarding for unescorted vacationers. This round trip can be done in 4 days, by train, boat, and bus, but extra time in Bergen would make it happier; logical en route stops would be the Fretheim Turisthotell at Flam and the Stalheim at Stalheim. A very similar pre-packaged tour has since been assembled under the name "Norway in a Nutshell," which begins and ends at Bergen.

The Gold-Plate Special is a tour of **Finnmark**—the land of Norway's fairy tales, where Kriss Kringle picks up his reindeer, and where the sun shines at midnight during the bountiful, green summer. Hammerfest, 944 miles above the Arctic Circle, is the "highest" town in civilization—and the ultimate is reached via a 22-mile highway from the world's most northerly village of Honningsvag to the North Cape itself.

Please note that *everything must be set up long in advance*. During the day you can turn the clock back some 200 years; seek out the migrant Sami (Norwegian for Lapps) in their tent villages and watch them lasso reindeer; drive on well-surfaced roads over the treeless Vidda (highlands), the stark beauty of which is matched only by the steppes of Russia. You can drop a line, if you have a license, in any stream and hook fresh-water salmon up to 50 lbs., trout up to 25 lbs., and several varieties of game fish.

An excellent independent itinerary is **Oslo–Tromso–Lakselv–Karasjok–Hammerfest**; it may be done in 3 ways. One tour of 6 to 8 days is by SAS plane to Lakselv, by hired car to Karasjok and eventually to Hammerfest, from there by Norwegian coastal steamer (clean, comfortable, cheap) to Bodo or Trondheim, and by SAS plane back to Oslo. (Coastal Express vessels are practically the only year-round links between the south, the north, and the lovely points in between. Take one of these island-skirting voyages if you can.) Karasjok is the Lapp capital, a few miles from the Finnish border; if the weather is pleasant, you can hire a colorful river canoe with an outboard motor and cruise through the wilderness to this remote frontier. If you have your car with you and enough time, another possibility would be to follow Route 6, the North Cape road, all the 1517 miles; this, however, becomes monotonous toward the end.

Do go to Finnmark or see those fjords farther south, no matter what. The Hardangerfjord, Sognefjord (fast boat service available), Sunnfjord, Geirangerfjord, and Nordfjord are wonderful.

TRANSPORTATION **Airlines** Norway, of course, is in the **SAS** partnership (see "Denmark"). The eternally reconstructed but still poor **Fornebu Airport,** the nation's chief gateway, is so near to Oslo that there is not much saving in taking a taxi or limousine instead of a bus into the city center. **Braathens SAFE** is an independent feeder company that wings to everywhere of importance and offers tremendous discount programs from May 1 to Sept. 30. For lesser destinations, lakes, and snowfields, there are many good **air taxi** services out of Oslo; the **Busy Bee** line is my own favorite and it is expanding in an impressive way.

Taxis They are readily available but rather costly. Oslo is a very concentrated city, so you can walk to most destinations. More distant sightseeing targets are easy to reach by inexpensive ferry, subway, or train—especially if you utilize the "Oslo Card" mentioned further along.

Trains Very good. The Arctic route runs 796 miles straight up to Bodo in the Land of the Midnight Sun.

NOTE · · · If you're traveling short distances (especially between Oslo and Bergen), pick tourist class rather than first. The tourist units are brightly decorated and divided into smoking and nonsmoking departments; windows are wide; seats are the big airliner type that can be made to recline; you can also reserve one of these chairs at a slight extra cost if you're traveling within Norwegian borders. First class offers 2 seats on one side of the aisle and a single on the other.

FOOD Although the accent is on fish—hundreds of varieties, hundreds of tricky recipes—that doesn't mean Nordics don't know a good beefsteak when they see one. As a rule, avoid piscatorial choices on Monday. In a culture where the critter is no longer considered fresh if it is 5 hours out of the sea, any stored fish is regarded as old. Nets, by law, cannot be put down on Sundays; thus, the Saturday catch, while preserved on ice, meets with no enthusiasm.

Distinctive northern items are ptarmigan (mountain or snow grouse), flat-bread (crisp cracker thinner than a dime), multer (delicious, all-purpose dessert or jam made from yellow mountain cloudberries with a unique flavor), tyttebaer (known as "lingon" or cowberries to Swedes, this is a small, tart, red berry— a cranberry with a difference), local cheeses of Port du Salut type (not the goat's milk cheese, which looks like kitchen soap and tastes like caramel) or the pop-ular Jarlsberg, kreps (succulent, 2-inch freshwater crayfish), reindeer steak (dark red, fine flavor), and the Norwegian "sandwich," which will haunt you pleas-antly wherever you go.

The first meal of the day, particularly in rural areas, is rightfully a world-famous institution. In addition to such normal staples as coffee, tea, chocolate, juices, hot or cold cereals, eggs, and the like, the buffet table normally displays a bonanza of such comestibles as assorted herring, cheese, cold meats, fruits, jams, jellies, a mini-bakery of breads and much, much more. Since food is so thunderingly expensive and since breakfast buffets are usually on the hotel bill anyway, canny nordics stoke up manfully on the morning comestibles and try to glide past the lunch hour.

Norway is a coffee-drinking nation; tea is mediocre. It is also the biggest cheese-eating nation in the world; per capita, each Oslo citizen (infants-in-arms included in this statistic) packs away nearly 25 lbs. per year!

Meal hours are cockeyed to foreigners. The residents eat a heavy breakfast at 8 a.m.; at noon they munch sandwiches at their office desks, working with possibly a half-hour interruption; between 4 and 6 p.m. they sit down to their big dinner, and a little later may finish the day with coffee and cakes.

DRINKS There's a government beverage control in Norway called the Vin-monopolet, and some of the vagaries imposed upon it (and the harried con-sumer!) by the legislature are the most mysterious in the travel world. John Law tells you how, where, when, and what you can drink; the regulations contradict themselves backward, forward, and sideways. Over-the-counter drinks are dis-pensed *only* in Oslo, Bergen, Trondheim, Stavanger, 7 small towns, and in the most popular tourist hotels of the hinterland. Spirits may be served only from 3 p.m. to midnight or 1 a.m.; not one drop can be served on Sundays or May 17 (Constitution Day) anywhere in the land. The aforementioned tourist hotels are the only establishments allowed to start pouring at 1 p.m. Beer may be con-sumed all day and all evening except on Sundays, when it is withheld until noon. While the larger establishments are generally fully licensed, almost all of the smaller ones can sell only beer and wine. Bottles up to any number may be obtained in the official Wine Monopoly stores. In the larger cities they function between 10 a.m. and 5 p.m. on Mon, Tues., Wed.; Thurs. till 6 p.m.; opening an hour earlier on Fri. On Sat. and days prior to national holidays (if they do not fall on Sun.) their hours are from 9 a.m. to 1 p.m. *Buy all liquor for weekend consumption or for any off-the-beaten-track excursions before leaving Oslo or the key centers.* Should you be forced to do so in the designated tourist houses, you'll be charged up to 50% more than the normal levies.

The prices are intoxicating. By the drink, they are so high that you'll quickly learn the virtues of dehydration. Beer is the most economical option. Though shockingly expensive, wines are splendid since the nation itself is the customer at Bordeaux, Burgundy, and elsewhere; hence, Norway receives preferential treatment over even the largest commercial vintners of other lands. (Sweden, with a similar set-up, is competitive in the bidding wars.) It's a great country for anyone who is on the wagon!

Linje Akevit or aquavit is the pride of Norwegian distillers, and distinctly palatable to most visitors. "Linje" means "line," and every bottle of this brand has been mellowed on a ship that has crossed the Equator. The action of the sea supposedly softens the aquavit. Always drink it with beer; this "keeps away the red nose," Norwegians say. (Danes say the opposite!) Whatever the truth, all Nordics assist their *snaps* with beer.

For the rites of the Skal ceremony, turn back to the "Denmark" chapter.

TIPPING Practically none. Only hotel baggage porters still linger after their task is done. About Kr.3 per piece should do it. Everything else is at your own disposition.

CITIES AND REGIONS

AALESUND, very scenic and dappled with a degree of art nouveau, is a calling spot for steamers on the Coastal Expressway. It is built on islands; when your ship pauses here for its usual 2½-hour docking, a run up to the summit of Aksla Mountain (only 625 feet high, but with a restaurant affording a breathtaking view of the waterways) is about the only show in town unless you can make time for the splendid Aquarium exhibits. If you need accommodations try either the **Rica Parken** or the **Scandinavie,** a remodeled oldster; the **Skansen** and **Havly** also are recommendable.

BERGEN

Bergen recently kindled its 900th birthday candle. The port is on the Atlantic side, directly across from Oslo. Here's Norway's 2nd largest city. Medieval charm will captivate you by day and enchant you by night. A magnificent panorama unfolds from Floien. There's a fish market, of course, and it's like a graduate course at Wood's Hole; there are turreted bastions, crazy little houses built before 1800, the Edvard Grieg home—called *Troldhaugen*—with its superb concert hall (especially nice in summer), the aquarium, the intriguing Hanseatic Maritime Museum (don't miss this one if you've got salt in your veins), good restaurants, and good comfort. Shipbuilding, trade, and harbor activities keep most of the people busy; don't believe the legend that "it always rains in Bergen"—it is only 99% true, and then only in 10- and 15-minute spells. For information, phone (313860) or call on the Bergen Tourist Board.

HOTELS

☆☆☆☆ **Norge** • has such a firm mandate on design, decor, appointments, cuisine, and administrative mastery, that it remains among the nation's leaders. Always well managed; expansive atrium; modern lobby in marble tones; remarkable complex of no less than 9 dining and drinking operations ranging from the elegantly deluxe luminary to a sidewalk cafe, all different and all splendid (see "Restaurants"); Corner Disco Pub; shops; bank; swimming pool making a splash too—and very luxurious it is. Try to bid for a lakeside view.

☆☆☆ **SAS Royal** • follows the pattern of others in this chain, providing amenities that are both imaginative and comfortable. Harborside houses with birthrights going back 9 centuries have been linked into a colorful architectural whole; a restaurant, cafe, tavern, bar, and shops. It also includes a sauna and pool.

★ **Admiral** • has a smart command. Very central and close to the city's fabulous fish market. Hence, its Emily restaurant is known for its sea fare.

Ambassadeur • (30 rooms and a small restaurant) is adequate.

Grand Terminus • near the station but still surprisingly quiet, has become more and more of a traditional favorite due to its elegance, space and reasonable prices. For many travelers, however, its ownership by a religious order and consequent lack of alcohol automatically drop it a notch as a holiday haven. The lunch buffet is splendid, as are many of the fine Old-World furnishings. Medium tariff.

Bryggen Orion • is a worthy alternative. The entrance affords a hospitable view of the cozy hearth and the nearby Bistro self-service snack bar with its scrubbed wooden tables. The dining-cum-breakfast salon is on the 3rd floor overlooking the harbor. Moderately good for the outlay. Low-medium to medium prices.

Neptun • remodeled and with an excellent restaurant, occupies the 4 top floors of an office building in midcity. The reception desk is at street level. Its quarters are midsize and very nicely equipped.

Augustin • offers color and a cozy atmosphere plus an inviting restaurant and patisserie.

Rosenkrantz • leans heavily to commercial traffic. Indifferent.

Out at *Os* (half an hour's drive from Bergen), the waterside **Solstrand Fjord** nibbles at the water's edge. The loudest noise you might hear could be the plop of a tennis ball or the kerflop of a leaping salmon. A fine choice for country life.

RESTAURANTS

The dining choices in Bergen offer surprising variety, though the emphasis, of course, is on seafood.

★★★★ **Bellevue** • is one of the most outstandingly spectacular restaurants in Scandinavia. Exquisite cuisine; stunning panorama of Bergenfjord and the city; aristocratically suave decor; background music; 16 candlelit tables; fixed-price repasts; a la carte expensive but not prohibitive for its exalted category; superb attention. Fresh main-floor bar and disco. It, with the Hotel Norge, constitute the *only* truly distinguished dining places in this second city of the nation. Reserve in advance. A rare and true joy.

☆☆☆☆ **Norge** • includes the crowningly sophisticated gastronomic Main Restaurant, the Rotisserie; the less-formal Baldakinen Restaurant on the open mezzanine (continuous service from noon until 11:30 p.m.); the Hjornet ("Corner") Pub in dark wood highlighted with copper and brass fittings; the cozy Ole Bull (named for the world-famous Norwegian violinist) with charcoal grills; the oaken Karjolen Bar with barrel stools active from 3 p.m. until 11:45 p.m. that turns into Norge Dancing to 1:30 p.m.; the glass-enclosed, all-year Pavljongen Sidewalk Cafe; and the Garden Room Restaurant from mid-June to mid-August, which has dancing. It is no wonder that these draw a remarkable 55% of *all* diners-out in Bergen—an obvious reason being that every one delivers outstanding values for its price range.

Holberg Stuen and the **Wessel Stuen,** under the same ownership, offer low-cost, tavern-style edibles that are appetizing for their category. **Zachariasbryggen** is located at the Fish Market and composed of **L'Etoile de Mer** and the more informal **Zacharias,** a cafe that often features live music. **Amorini Villa,** located near the Norge Hotel, has won awards for its wine list. Then you might like to try the charmingly informal **Trattoria Marco Polo** for home-style Italian cookery.

Gamle Bergen Tracteursted, for budget dining, is situated in an old house 5 minutes north of the center. Its Victorian furnishings and period atmosphere evoke the feeling of walking into an elderly grandma's living room. Time marches elegantly backward.

BOLKESJO The 240-pillowed **Bolkesjo** is worthy of bearing this resort's fair name. Reasonably priced, all rooms with baths.

BREKKE The amusing **Brekkestranda** comprises split-log construction with rooms and even beds fashioned to scorn rectangular patterns.

BUSKERUD The charm-laden **Sundvolden** is about 27 miles from Oslo on Highway E-68. A wooden-balconied house filled with antiques; warmhearted staff; delicious regional food; tranquillity by the carload.

EIDFJORD is a useful speck on the motorist's map because of the scenic drive via Fossli to glory in the waterway and the Voringsfoss waterfall. Your rooftop here will be the **Voringsfoss.** Very basic accommodations; low-medium range, all rooms with baths; its high point is the hand-painted dining room rendered for free drinks by the famous Norwegian artist, Bergslien. Worth a detour for a nip and a peek. For wheelborne travelers, the **Norheimsund Fjord** is a comfortable stop with a convenient motel segment. Nearby you'll find the dramatic Steinsdalsfoss fall under which you can walk on a footpath.

FORDE, naught but an angler's haven, offers the **Sunnfjord** shining with space for 330 keenly bent on early-morning fly-casting. Hardy's of London has hooked up a fishing school here with equipment for use by guests, plus experts standing by with baited breath to show how to use it. All modest-priced units have bath or shower; about $500 buys a week of shelter, food, instruction, and whatever you can catch. Indoor and outdoor pools, a tennis court, a solarium, and more recreation rooms.

FREDRIKSTAD is a tale of 2 cities: the New Town (35,000 modern-minded citizens) and the Old Town (cobbled streets, moats, and surrounding fortress walls. Here is the site of the famous Plus craft center (its ateliers are open to the public). When it's time for a meal, the best bet in the new town is the **City Hotel** (in the dining room, be sure to wear a coat and tie, gentlemen). All rooms with baths at medium rates. If you are searching for a restaurant in the older section, try (1) **Kongsten Fort** (almost exclusively for groups), (2) **Tamburen** (year round), and (3) either the **Stabbursloftet** or the **Gryta** (both outstanding cafeterias in Scandinavia's largest food center).

GEILO is on the main railway line halfway between Oslo and Bergen; it offers one main street, a handful of cozy hotels snuggling above the valley, excellent food on virtually every table, and an intimate spirit of holiday frolic. The ski runs are not as long as they are in the midriff of the Continent, and the cold (yet super-dry) air may be too brittle for all except the hardiest outdoor types. But, as a retreat from the hustle and bustle, this tiny gem is hard to beat.

Bardola steals the local thunder for travelers with modern tastes. Situation on a hillside glen above the town; private ski lift; spacious; sleekly rustic public rooms and lounges recently updated; glass-lined dining room with woody touches, cascading greenery; cellar nightclub; gameroom with minibillards, minibowling, and a toyland of diversions to keep the Small Fry out of mischief (free supervision, baby-sitting, and scheduled programs for kiddie pastimes); superb His and Hers sauna facilities; beauty salon; horseback riding available in summer; health center, gym, and solarium; swimming pool yet another lovely fluid asset. The expanded **Highland** has windows scanning Lake Ustedalsfjord. Slightly larger than my first choice and a lot cooler in tone. **Vestlia** is an ingratiating chalet with captivating window-wall frontages looking beyond your private balcony. Very cozy. The **Ro,** on the main drag, is lower in category; ground-floor cafeteria; pleasant Kro restaurant; not bad. **Geilo Pension** is fun for its Old Norway atmosphere. **Alpin,** on the outskirts, seemed stiff and flairless. The **Geilo Hotel** offers a modern flavor. The **Youth Hostel** is clean, neat, and reasonably priced; mostly English-speaking youngsters occupy its bunks.

KINSARVIK The 135-bed **Kinsarvik** is a nirvana for nature lovers. Especially convenient for ferry passengers crossing the Hardanger to Kvanndal. Medium priced.

KRISTIANSAND is on the lower tip of the nation; it is a thriving ferry point for Denmark, England, Germany, and Holland. The leading hotels are the fresh, newly smartened **Ernst Park** and the **Caledonien.** The **Christian Quart** is adequate. Kids will love the Setesdal Park, the railroad museum, and the assemblage of old farm houses.

KRISTIANSUND straddles 3 islands with connecting bridges. This center is a fishing port and the striking-out point for climbing tours to the Nordmore Alps. If you stay, check in at the **Kristiansund,** the **Rica,** or the **Grand.** And don't miss a cruise out (west) to the toylike fishing village of *Grip,* one island in a group of 80 rockdots where you will absorb the essence of Norwegian coastal life from its earliest times.

LILLEHAMMER This beautyspot on the lovely face of Norway is busy primping to become hostess to the 1994 Winter Olympics. The remote mountain setting offers the **Sjusjoen** in the hills above the village or the **Nordseter Mountain** with an indoor pool. Those in the town itself are rather spare. Be sure to visit the **Maihaugen Museum,** a settlement composed of about 100 wooden buildings filled with period furniture and lore depicting all facets of peasant life over a millennium plus the 900-year-old **Garmo Stave Church.** Here is the Norwegian version of Williamsburg. Then up at *Oyer* (where the Hafjell Olympic hills are located) take the kids to Lilleputthammer's miniature village and to *Hunderfossen* to quiver before the world's greatest troll. You may wish to see the hi-tech 180° film on Norway that is shown in a special theater here.

LOEN, in the Nordjord region and close to the grandeur of the Briksdalsbreen Glacier, offers the **Alexandra,** with a good kitchen; all rooms with baths in medium price range; it has pulled down most of its older limbs and built new ones. The drawback here is its bigness (space for 400 guests), which makes it something of a nordic beehive. For sightseeing, few can top the eagle's-nest **Videseter,** a perch high, high, high, above the Vide Valley.

MOLDE   is famed for roses and a panorama of 87 alplike peaks. For less tranquil types, the annual jazz festival is the drawing card. In the More and Romsdal fjord district, the **Viking** at **Orsta** is one of the newer hotels, but the older standbys still attract settled vacationers through their smooth-running portals. These are the **Union** at *Geiranger* (*what* a vista!), the **Alexandra** at *Molde,* and the **Grand Bellevue** at *Andalsnes.* The area is one of the most striking in Norway.

OSLO

Oslo is the capital, chief port (which is saying a lot in this maritime nation), and nexus of Norwegian society. Despite its aforementioned sparse population density, in area it is one of the largest cities on the globe; still, the center portion is so small that you will become oriented almost immediately. You might also become frustrated by unexpected traffic snarls; the town council is trying to control this by imposing 10 NK tolls on vehicles entering the midtown area.

Go first to City Hall, down by the port, and pick up an inexpensive **Oslo Card,** the price depending on whether you want a 1-, 2-, or 3-day version. It provides free admission to the nation's top sightseeing attractions, museums, free transport on buses and boats, discounts and bonuses galore. There's a 70-page booklet describing all of the goodies in detail, so forgive me if I don't repeat them here. The savings are phenomenal—and that can be important in a city that is considered one of the most expensive in Europe. (Ranked 7th in the world in a recent survey.)

ATTRACTIONS

Vikingskiphuset • *Viking Ship House, Huk Aveny 35* • These three most famous Viking ships—the Gokstad, the Tune, and the Oseberg—date back to 800, and all were found near the Oslo fjord. The trio probably comprise the proudest heritage of all the Scandinavian nations combined. Also on display is a fine collection of ceremonial sleighs, utensils, and various Viking objects.

Kon-Tiki Museet • *Kon-Tiki Museum, Bygdoynes* • This is about a 15-minute walk from the Viking Ships and an even shorter stroll to the next two

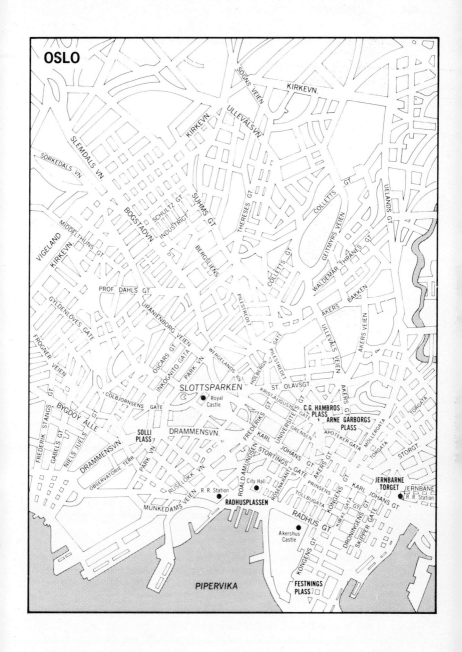

OSLO

SOGNS VEIEN
KIRKEVN.
KIRKEVN.
ULLEVÅLSVN.
SLEMDALS VN
SÖRKEDALS VN
THERESES GT.
COLLETTS GT
UELANDS GT
GETTMYRS VEIEN
BOGSTADVN
SCHULTZ GT.
SUHMS GT.
INDUSTRIGT.
VIGELAND
MIDDELTHUNS GT.
KIRKEVN.
BERGELIENS
COLLETTS GT
WALDEMAR THRANES GT.
AKERS BAKKEN
PROF. DAHLS GT.
GYLDENLÖVES GATE
URANIENBORG VEIEN
PILESTREDT
AKERS VEIEN
FROGNER VEIEN
OSCARS GT.
INKOGNITO GATA
PARK VN
WERGELANDS V
HOLBERGS GATE
PILESTREDT
ULLEVÅLS VEIEN
SLOTTSPARKEN
ST OLAVSGT.
AKERS
Royal Castle
KRIST AUGUSTS GATE
COLBJÖRNSENS GATE
C.G. HAMBROS PLASS
TORGATA
BYGDÖY ALLE
ARNE GARBORGS PLASS
FREDERIK STANGS GT
DRAMMENSVN.
UNIVERSITETS GT
MÖLLERGATA
SOLLI PLASS
APOTEKER GATA
GABELS GT.
FREDERIKS GATE
GRENSEN
TORGATA
NIELS JUELS GT
KARL JOHANS GT.
STORGT.
DRAMMENSVN
PARK VN
ROALD AMUNDSENS GATE
STORTINGS GATE
AKERS GT.
OBSERVATORIE TERR.
RUSELÖKK VN
ROSENKRANTZ GATE
PRINSENS GT
KONGENS GT.
KARL JOHANS GT
JERNBANE TORGET
City Hall
JERNBANE R. R. Station
R. R. Station
TOLLBUGATA
KIRKE GATA
MUNKEDAMS VEIEN
RÅDHUSPLASSEN
RÅDHUS GT.
DRONNINGENS GT
SKIPPER GATE
Akershus Castle
KONGENS GT.
PIPERVIKA
FESTNINGS PLASS

museums. Built in 1957, the museum houses the balsa raft *Kon-Tiki*, which Thor Heyerdahl used in his 1947 expedition across the Pacific Ocean from Peru to Polynesia; an underwater display; and statues from the Easter Islands. Later the museum added Heyerdahl's papayrus boat *Ra II*, sailed on his 1970 experimental voyage from North Africa to Barbados.

Norsk Sjofartsmuseum • *Norwegian Maritime Museum, Bygdoy* • Inside is a fascinating collection of Norwegian boats, as well as models of sailing ships and fishing harbor stations. Outside is Roald Amundsen's Polar ship *Gjoa*, the first ship to navigate the Northwest Passage.

Polarskipet Fram • *Fram Museum, Bygdoy* • This famous ship, designed and built by Colin Archer in 1893 for Fridtjof Nansen's 3-year Polar expedition, was used again in 1910–12 for the expedition to the South Pole.

Norsk Folkemuseum • *Norwegian Folk Museum, Museumveien* • 170 wooden buildings from all over Norway have been dismantled and reconstructed in this lovely park to create a representative semblance of Norway's past way of life. One of the most interesting of these buildings is a 13th-century church of hand-hewn wood. Indoor exhibits include tools and objects illustrative of Norwegian urban and rural culture.

Akershus Festning og Slott • *Akershus Castle and Fortress, Radhus gate* • Originally constructed around 1300 by the Viking King Haakon V, this is one of Norway's most prized Medieval relics. Akershus was transformed into a Renaissance palace in the 1600s by King Christian IV. Now, having been completely refurbished inside and out, the castle is used by the government for state festivities and occasions, but it is open to the general public and worth a visit.

Norges Hjemmefront Museum • *Resistance Museum, Akershus* • On the lovely grounds of Akershus Fortress, the museum presents haunting memorabilia that illustrates the German occupation of Norway from 1940 to 1945, the dark phase of the Quisling era, and the dauntless Norwegian resistance. The entire experience is a moving one and in dramatic contrast with the peaceful vistas provided by the ancient ramparts above the town and the shimmering Oslofjord.

International Children's Art Museum • *Lille Froensv. 4* • A unique new offering comprising ceramics, sculpture, tapestry, paintings and handicrafts from more than 130 nations. There's a workshop, too, if your tikes feel inspired.

Domkirken • *Old Cathedral, Stortorvet* • Though both the interior and exterior of this wonderful old church have been restored since its original construction in 1699, the altarpiece and pulpit are from 1699, and the organ facade goes back to 1727; beautiful bronze doors; magnificent stained-glass windows. The rustic stables that surround the church now house shops where artists, silversmiths, potters, weavers, and antique dealers market their wares.

Nasjonalgalleriet • *National Gallery, Universitete gate 13* • Here is where you'll find the nation's most important art collection. While the emphasis is on Norwegian painting, sculpture, and lithography, the collection also includes many European works, especially French Impressionism. A highlight is an important representation of the works of Edvard Munch.

Munch Museet • *Munch Museum, Toyengaten 53* • Norway's most famous, if not most lugubrious painter, Edvard Munch, bequeathed all his works to the city of Oslo in 1940, and most are housed in this center. The collection includes his paintings, drawings, watercolors, lithographs, and sculptures—all in all, more than 20,000 mournful pieces.

Contemporary Art Museum • *Bankplassen 4* • in the splendid former center for Norges Bank. An impressive collection of both international and Norwegian modern art. The bookshop is interesting too.

Gamle Aker Kirke • *Gamle Aker Church, Akersbakken 26* • This striking stone church, built in 1100, is Scandinavia's oldest such structure and is still in use. It may be visited throughout the year. Nearby, stroll through Damstredet, Bergfjerdingen, and Telthusbakken for a village atmosphere of the 19th century.

Vigeland Museet • *Vigeland Museum, Nobels gate 32* • Formerly the residence and studio of Norway's eminent artist Gustav Vigeland, it now displays thousands of his sculptures, woodcuts, and sketches. The museum is situated just outside beautiful Frogner Park, a showcase replete with almost every human activity that the sculptor portrayed in stone during his prolific lifetime. You may not like it, but you can't help being impressed. While in the area, see the **Bymuseum** in *Frogner Manor,* with its artifacts of the 1790s.

Concerts • Oslo is extraordinarily musical; there's something doing almost every day. The city boasts the multimillion dollar Concert Hall. Open-air performances grace the forecourt of the Vigeland Museum (Nobelsgate 32) in summer on Sun. at 1 and on Wed. at 7. Presentations inside the Cathedral on Wed. at 7:30 p.m. are equally notable. The Munch Museum schedules frequent recitals. The Norwegian Folk Museum has performances each Sun. at 5 from mid-May until mid-Sept. at its open-air theater; these same folk, incidentally, dance at 8 at the restaurant during weekdays.

Markets • The Youngstorget and the Stortorget lean heavily toward botanical items. Best time for all is in the early morning. You might also like to browse among Oslo's Cathedral Bazaars, ateliers housed in the adjoining crescent. Textiles, antiques, ceramics, and silver are inside; a flower market blossoms outside.

Excursions

An **Oslofjord cruise** can be had in a brief period and will be remembered for a lifetime. Departures from the port area fronting City Hall all through the day; durations from 50 min. ranging up to 2½ hours and some including a bus-tour component or a meal ashore or afloat. The waters are flat, the prices are low, but the rewards are high in scenic appeal.

Jeep Safari • *Tourist Information at City Hall* • This adventure on wheels gets in gear at 9 a.m. and pulls up the handbrake at 5 p.m. after a bouncy day of Land Rovering around the **Marka,** Oslo's expansive forest-and-lake suburbia. Lunch at a chalet in the woods; stops for refreshment; a fulfilling jaunt for landlubbers. If you are in a rush, half day romps are also available.

Holmenkollen Ski Museet • *Ski Museum, Holmenkollen* • Although in a contemporary building, this is the world's oldest ski museum. (How many can there be, Olaf?) A fascinating assemblage of skiing equipment and objects illustrates the history of the sport. Included is the tip of a 2500-year-old ski believed to have been used in the earliest Polar expeditions. Take the 20-minute ride on the Holmenkollen railway from downtown Oslo to the Holmenkollen Station, then walk 15 minutes to the museum.

Sonja Henie-Niels Onstads Kuntsenter • *Sonja Henie-Niels Onstad Arts Center* • Near Fornebu airport about 7 miles outside the city, this fine museum was built in 1968 to house the collection of 20th-century art donated by Sonja Henie, the great skating champion, and her husband. The permanent collection includes works by Picasso, Miro, and Munch. Exhibitions illustrating modern trends in music, architecture, film, and literature are regularly scheduled.

HOTELS

Please refer to "About the Stars" in the introductory chapters. It explains how the rankings in this book may differ from official judgments.

☆☆☆☆☆ **Continental** • is one of the proudest rigs in the port city. Dining room with the finest cuisine in the nation—a view I share with many others; superb Fortuna Pub Maritime Restaurant; chic hairdressing salon and barbershop; thoughtful touches such as in-house English-language movies over video, frigo bars, and "temporary" resting rooms for early-arrival guests whose regular accommodations are not yet ready. Air conditioning throughout plus sound-insulating windows; handsome corridors. "Caroline" breakfast room with a buffet table of tempters; the sidewalk-level Theatercafeen (the cultural hub of Norway), a ground-floor bar plus another one in marine motif, and The Loft, disco-bar. Professional administration by the owning Brochmann family aided by manager Mathis Berge.

☆☆☆ **Grand** • offers the captivating Penthouse Restaurant Etoile with deliciously authentic French specialties; Palmen Restaurant, traditionally one of the capital's most chic gathering places for lunch; Fritzner Grill in woody tones; Grand Cafe for chitchat and newspaper reading; celebrated Speilsalen Restaurant ("Mirror Room") with music from 9 p.m.–12:30 a.m. A fine indoor heated swimming pool and free sauna disguises its large bomb shelter, which is compulsory by law.

★★★ **Bristol** • welcomes you into a lobby that is most attractive and richly Old World in atmosphere—even the stuffed bear will agree. Adjoining is the Library Bar, separated only by a wooden divider. Pleasant Trafalgar Bar; paneled Grill; mawkish El Toro cellar restaurant seating 350 to 400; Disco in better taste.

☆☆☆ **Oslo Plaza** • is a member of the widespread Reso group and is said to be the largest hotel in Scandinavia. It is very much geared to the business traveler. Every amenity has been included from pool to sauna to solarium to a tower-top bar; from an exterior glass-bound elevator to a dizzying selection of dining and drinking nooks. It is in midcity near both rail and bus hubs. Accommodation for 1550 souls, so don't expect much intimacy. Nevertheless, it's good for what it is.

☆ **Scandinavia** • also is one of the tallest hotels in the land and as cold as a Grade-A Norwegian icicle. Spacious, low-ceilinged, pillared lobby is in sterile tones; cozy, 2-tiered Holberg Grill with piped music and streamlined traditional Rotisserie decor; 250-seat Brasseriet; strikingly handsome 21st-floor Summit Bar; Charly's cafe; indoor heated pool and saunas. Premium rooms are those with balcony.

★★★★ **Holmenkollen Park Rica** • resides at one of the capital's most historic sites—the mountain on which the famous international ski jumping championships are held. Hardly a more scenic location of forest, fjord, and Bogstad Lake-country could be imagined. The former modest but atmospheric hostelry, which dates back to 1894 and features turrets and Viking woodwork, has been expanded to 200 modern, but cramped bedchambers, the breathtakingly unique De Fem Stuer ("Five Rooms") restaurant, the hearthside and woody bakery snack alcove and the hypnotic, viewful Atrium Bar; when nighttime falls you can jump at the "Night Jump" club or simply hop into one of the quietest bunks in the North. The lobby features a colossal refrigerated snowflake sculpture that is always covered in frost—fascinating for its conception and technology! Guest membership at nearby golf course; jogging trails; indoor swimming pool; tennis courts; sauna; fishing rights; and cross-country ski trails. Though this is about a quarter-hour's drive from midcity or the airport, both limousines and minibus shuttles are frequently available. Middle price range, all units with private plumbing. Full marks as a skyland of utmost tranquillity.

☆☆ **Ambassadeur** • is a smart-looking town house with homelike accouterments. A neighbor of the Royal Palace in a quiet locale; pool and sauna; color TV; bar and dining room. Recently refreshed.

☆ **Europa** • in midcity, combines efficiency with tradition. I find the public rooms especially cheerful and fresh.

Rica Oslofjord • aptly named for its locality, is a 288-room candidate outside of town (hard by the highway to the Henie-Onstad Museum) that ties into the congress center. It features 2 dining areas, a health club, saunas, and a jogging track. The appalling pastel-green exterior glistens like a highly polished bathroom. What a hue and cry!

Scandic Crown • is clean but cool; all units with baths or showers, TVs, and minibars; handsome restaurant and bar; special children's menu. Many conducted tour groups stop here.

Helsfyr • is now a good buy; an excellent efficiency-style house.

Cecil • has space for 100 guests on a prime site very close to the Grand. New, fresh and moderately priced.

Gabelshus • is a converted manor house about 5 minutes from the bright lights; tiptoe tranquillity; flagstone pathway to its arched portals. Ingratiating ambience; dining room flanked by a window-walled summer "conservatory" for lunching and snacking; flamed dishes served from a 1911 pram; cellar wine-and-beer rendezvous; kindly personnel. Middle price range.

Ritz Hotell and Pension • a stately white town house, occupies a quiet situation adjoining Embassy Row, 5 minutes by tram from the center. Handsomely turned out lobby; rich wood, leathery glass-bound lounge; lovely dining salon opening to sylvan courtyard; Telex; wine and beer only but set-ups served. High on aesthetics and high on value. Low-middle prices; all units with baths.

Stefan • a Mission Hotel behind the Bristol, has a children's playroom in the basement. (Youths under 18 years may bunk free with their parents.) Rightfully its biggest boast is the upper-story restaurant, with cuisine and prices that attract knowledgeable locals, especially at lunchtime. There are ice- and snack-vending machines on every level. Medium priced.

Norum • is especially geared for traveling families. Turreted, vine-covered building about 10 minutes from the center; air-conditioned Bar Bistro that angles out to a tiny popular restaurant with an acoustical ceiling and ingratiating atmosphere. Homespun ambience; heavily patronized by Parliament members and NATO personnel. Prices as above.

Nobel • is totally refashioned and attractive. It has always had a fine reputation; now after its refreshment it competes handily with the sound commercial-grade hostelries of the city.

Rica Carlton • is for budgeteers or stoutish snackers; the special lunch table ladles out 16 self-service selections, including 1 hot dish.

☆☆☆ **Royal Christiania** • a rather glitzy, modern candidate, has a pub, a dance bar and lounge, sedate library that doubles as a coffee corner, a rotisserie, a reception hall, plus 456 bedrooms, most with private bath or shower and about a quarter of them as suites. There is a sauna, Turkish bath, plus a fine indoor pool. There is also a delightful summer garden restaurant.

West • Though I have not overnighted in the renewed structure, it is well supplied with modern amenities at moderate tariffs.

Triangel • a handsome, old-fashioned building, features quite a number of budget accommodations with shower or bath. There are many single units; it's popular because of its fortunate location directly behind the Hotel Scandinavia and hence at the City Airport Bus Terminus.

On the outskirts of the capital, the **SAS Park Royal** is one of the nation's most efficiently run hostelries. Set in parklike precincts overlooking Oslofjord, it is cozy and attractive. Grill with sound food and serene atmosphere; fetching bar and lounge; conference facilities for 4 to 130 participants; well-planned bedrooms with bath, 4-channel radio, and message service. Also near the airport, **Scandic Oslo** runs a motorists' stop at *Hovik*. **Gyldenlove**, in *Bogstadveien* behind the Palace, was given new raiments, but they seem to be heavy enough to be the costumery of an Ibsen play. The suites especially hark back to the Norway of Old even though they are virtually new; only bed and breakfast are provided. Okay for medium-budget historians.

RESTAURANTS

☆☆☆☆ **Feinschmecker** • *Balchens Gt. 5* • welcomes visitors with 2 wide cottage windows overlooking a handsome street in one of Oslo's better residential neighborhoods. Chummy lounge with banquettes for drinks before dinner; chiefly pink in its color scheme; soft upholstered wicker garden chairs with the occasional piece of rustic Norwegian furniture; attractive stemware and table accessories. The cooking is of the modern school, refined to the taste and appealing to the eye; gentlemen might say the same for the comely waitresses.

☆☆☆ **Kastanjen** • *Bygdoy Alle 18* • is another residential candidate that seems to be attracting Oslo's cafe society. A cursory check suggested that prices here are even higher than at the Feinschmecker but, of course, the dishes are not duplicated. While it's both comfortable and worthy, I feel that the haughty reception and coolish attitudes will make foreign visitors feel uneasy.

★★★★ **D/S Louise** is located in the new *Aker Brygge* shopping complex down at the ferry boat harbor. It's just plain fun for any little boy or girl under the age of 85 who has the slightest amount of salt in their veins. Purely maritime in tone from its red primer paint job to its steamship stack to its polished helms and myriad brass propellers decorating the precincts. Naturally, there is a predominant interest in the seafare here and very good too.

★ **Hos Thea** ● *Gabelsgt. 11* ● is a single room with an open kitchen in the back. Soft lighting from sconces and chandeliers; tile floors; menu in a loose-leaf notebook that carefully describes fish, lamb, beef, and game; small wine list. Especially recommended are the salmon stuffed with a delicate mousse and the venison. There's a nice feeling of honesty and simplicity here.

Hotel dining in this city is unusually good and some of the best values may be enjoyed in these establishments since the gastronomy is often used as a loss leader for local prestige.

☆☆☆☆☆ **Continental** ● is a masterpiece of refined service and gustatory excellence. The window-wrapped and elegant **Annen Etage** is its star; it features international dishes and rather *nouvelle* approaches to Norwegian tradition; in addition to its versatile a la carte menu, there's a superb 3-course table d'hote.

★★★★ **Holmenkollen** ● *see "Hotels"* ● certainly is one of the scenic and decorative wonders of the North. Have a drink in the modern Atrium with its glass roof before dining at one of "The Five Rooms" of the deluxe restaurant. Simpler grills are better than fancy dishes. The **Holmenkollen Restaurant** is a separate entity lower down the hill, lower in price, lower in quality, but also viewful.

★★★ **Grand Hotel** ● has its enchanting Penthouse Etoile, which parades French specialties in a strikingly urbane, modern milieu. Its Palmen Restaurant is a lodestone to the Smart Set at lunchtime, while its sprawling Speilen Restaurant ("Mirror Room"), with music from 9 p.m.–12:30 a.m., is more informal and easier on the pocketbook.

☆ **Scandinavia** ● has its stylish, 2-tiered Holberg Grill with piped music and updated Rotisserie decor. As additional lures there are: (1) the knockout 21st floor Summit Bar with a magnificent panorama; (2) the excellent, low-priced, 250-seat Brasseriet with breakfast buffet until 10:30, lunch buffet to 2:30, a la carte thereafter, and snacks continuously from 7:30 a.m. until 11 p.m.; and (3) Charly's for even more cafe-teering.

Ambassador ● is winning a devoted following with its Sabroso, where fish is the reason for going—and when seafood is prized in Norway it is *really* something memorable.

Bristol ● is variable. The main Trafalgar Bar with its suave ambience and the smaller Library Bar (which is in essence part of the lobby) are both hits. As for dining places, I find the quality at the Grill indifferent, at the Disco better than passable, and at the El Toro cellar restaurant depressing.

☆ **Stefan** ● near the Bristol, has an upper-story restaurant, with prices that appeal to canny residents especially at lunchtime, when a splendid Nordic buffet is presented. The main problem will be trying to find a seat, so be sure to book in advance.

NORWAY · · · 601

Frascati • *Stortingsgata 20, near the Continental Hotel* • is cozy and atmospheric; the food has regained importance in the city; now worthy of its following. Air conditioning in summer; charming little bar; piano-Solovox music for dancing; friendly service. Very central and handy to the major hotels.

★★★ **Najaden** • *on the peninsula of Bygdoy and in the Maritime Museum, 10 minutes by ferry from the Town Hall* • with 30 tables, oozes with Norwegian salty decor; the service plates bear a map design from A.D. 1539; picture windows open to the fjord and the legendary Polar ship, *Fram*. The major meal (euphemistically called "lunch" by foreigners), consists mainly of open sandwiches. A la carte service is available at prices that will make you think again about swallowing.

★★ **Molla** • *"The Mill," Sagveien 21* • started life as a nunnery in the 14th century, then became a flour mill, a textile factory, and now houses a business and recreation center. The spacious restaurant reveals the machinery of its active past; furthermore it has been cunningly charmed for snugness and warmth. Upstairs is a cafeteria where lower cost grist is milled in the same kitchen. Sacks of fun for solid value.

★★ **Blom** • *Karl Johansgate 41, a block from Grand Hotel* • a remodeled wine store, caters to artists, writers, and as many tourists as they can pack in among the colorful family shields, pillars, oils, and handsome medieval trappings. Rollicking fun, where seafare predominates but there is still extensive variety; most visitors like its regional flavor. If it's packed, try the offshoot right beside it called **Fru Blom,** which is dominated by a gigantic wine tun. (Here you can buy vintage cru by the glass.) Both are run by Inni-Carine and Gunnar Holm of Bergen fame. At #35 on the same street, **Sostrene Larsen** is a lot of fun and most appealing for cellar dining.

3 Kokker • *Drammensveien 30* • is considered one of the most expensive restaurants in town. And at least in that respect I agree with public opinion; that it is of prestige quality, I demur. Alluring cellar location with low-ceiling bar-lounge on one side (live piano music) and handsome open-kitchen dining room on the other. Pleasant rustic trappings; cordial reception; pretentious menu that fails in presentation (not-so-*nouvelle* cuisine, cool vegetables); some may find it claustrophobic. The associated **Cafe Felix** at ground level is a routine hub for motorbike clientele.

☆ **La Mer** • *Pilestredet 31* • on the other hand, suffers from a dreary location and unexciting decor; but its seafood is noteworthy for its freshness and honest treatment. Upstairs site in a fringe district near the center; whitewashed walls with murals; aquarium; waiters in pursers uniforms; only about eight main choices and two desserts; superior, reasonably priced house wine— always a sign that the management cares.

★ **Bagatelle** • *Bygdoy Alle 3* • costs perhaps two-thirds as much as better-known and fancier places, but its dishes are among the most savory under the Midnight Sun. The service is generally frenetic. Favorites of budgeteers with educated palates are Crevettes a l'Indienne and Volaille a l'Indienne. Exceptional value if you seek food and not frills.

Ludvik • *Torqgt. 16* • is limited to pub choices served with live music; possibly it's category is more appropriate under "Night Life." Decor somewhat funky, including Ludvik himself, a moose that announces the time every hour.

Peppe's Pizza • *Stortingsgata 4* • Norway's largest pizza house, with a clever interior design. In such an expensive culinary nation, this pasta can put welcome elastic into a tight budget.

Lanternen • *on the Bygdoy waterfront at Huk Ave. 2* • releases stacks of mouth-watering publicity about its "American" hamburgers and other "U.S." specialties. Unfortunately, however, the PR man isn't the cook. The location, however, is delightful for scenery and perhaps only for a cup of coffee; April 1 to mid-Sept.

Tostrup-Kjelleren • *opposite the Parliament Building at Karl Johansgt. 25* • is entertaining for lunch on Friday when many Ministers dine after the weekly Palace conference. Tempting Norwegian sandwiches; also open for dinner.

KongeTerrassen • *across from the Royal Palace* • beside the Haakon VII Statue, is a kingly setting in the open air for princely rewards.

★★★★ **Frognerseteren** • *25 minutes by funicular or 20 minutes by car up the mountain (1387 feet)* • is a municipally owned and privately operated sports-restaurant with a magnificent panorama from 2 tiers of open terraces; if you can tear your eyes loose from the succulent white grouse on your plate, you can see at least 20 miles down the Oslofjord on a clear day. Authentic Norwegian log house, interestingly decorated; crowded with skiers in winter and tourists in summer, so be sure to reserve ahead; gorgeous when the sun is shining or the stars are out.

NIGHT LIFE

As is frequently the case in Scandinavia, after-dark revels are either boisterous or highly provocative of yawns. There is little middle ground. **Come Back** combines a nightclub, discotheque, and restaurant under one roof, although the various sectors are divided. For couples, possibly the most reputable spot for dinner-dancing is **Grotten** (Wergelandsveien 5). The major hotels also have recommendable and attractive facilities: the **Bonanza** at the Grand, the **Galaxy** at the Scandinavia, the ever-popular **Loftet** at the Continental, and the fun-filled **Night Jump** way up at the scenic Holmenkollen Park Hotel. The

Summit 21 atop the Scandinavia is pleasant for cocktails and panaromantics. The Bristol has the **El Toro,** which I dislike, but the **disco club** is agreeable. Discotheques are more fluid than the Oslofjord. **Dancing Bar** at the Frascati restaurant is reliable. Youngsters like the **Barock, Waterfront,** and **Hospitalet.** Others might include **Night Cap** or the **Back Stage At Night** in the Bristol, but ask your hotel concierge first which ones you can trust because they change so rapidly that I don't feel too confident about offering you this guidance.

SHOPPING

SHOPPING HOURS: In most of the larger cities: Weekdays normally 9 a.m.–5 p.m. in winter (often with a late closing on Thursdays at 7 p.m.), sometimes to 4 p.m. in summer, and 9 a.m.–2 p.m. on Saturday, with no noontime closings.

BEST AREAS: Aker Brygge is a fresh shopping concept down by the port with everything spread through two adjoining buildings: boutiques, novelties, fashions for men and women, food stalls, and fanciful restaurants. Also browse along Karl Johans Gate, the side streets radiating from it, Hegdehaugsveien, and Bogstadveien; the last two begin behind the Royal Palace and run toward the Majorstua zone. In the East End, try Markveien and Thorvald Meyersgate.

SAVINGS ON PURCHASES: If you buy a minimum of 300 NK worth of goods at any one store displaying the sign "Norway Tax Free Shopping" you can get a rebate of 10–14% of the total. Ask the merchant to give you his "Taxfree Shopping Cheque," which is redeemable as you leave Norway; Sweden also will recognize this document upon departure in case you forgot to claim it in Norway.

ANTIQUES: Kaare Berntsen (Universitetsgaten 12) sets the pace, both for quality and price. Smaller **Wangs Kunst** (Kristian IV's Gate 12) and **Hammerlunds Kunsthandel** (Tordenskjoldsgate 3) sometimes offer good rummaging as well. We're particularly fond of **Bergfjerdingen** (Damstredet 20)—2 elves' rooms with copper molds, wood, glass, pottery, and a big fireplace.

ARTS AND CRAFTS: Norway Designs (Stortingsgaten 28—opposite the Continental Hotel) for shopping for the best in Norwegian ceramics, glassware, woodwork, kitchen items—even woolen shawls and candles. You can see the nation in a nutshell here. **Den Norske Husflidsforening,** popularly known as "Husfliden" (Mollergaten 4), has an old name and a large selection of items for the home.

BAZAAR: The butchers' stalls in the historic brick firehouse behind the Cathedral have been rebuilt into enchanting little shops that no interested visitor should miss. The whole complex is known as **Basarhallene.**

DEPARTMENT STORE: **Steen & Strom** has a representative cross section of Norwegian retailing. **Christiania Glasmagasin** (Stortorvet 9) is a great catchall.

JEWELRY: Norwegian artisans have developed fine enameling to the point where not even Venetian or Florentine craftsmen can successfully compete with them. **David-Andersen** (Karl Johansgt. 20), almost universally considered to be the leading house in the country for this work, produces gracious enameled demitasse spoons, cake forks, and solid-silver salt-and-pepper sets. Another big draw is their original collection of 11th-century Viking jewelry facsimiles. For enameling and silver, ask for Mrs. Njoten, and for jewelry ask for Mrs. Esser or Mrs. Spangebu.

Tostrup, across the street, also has an enviable reputation and sound merchandise—but I don't have quite the same enthusiasm for their displays as I do for David-Andersen's. Perhaps you'll disagree.

REGIONAL WEARABLES AND SOUVENIRS: **William Schmidt & Co.** (Karl Johansgt. 41) is excellent for clothing and articles with distinctive Nordic flavor. Here you'll find handknit sweaters in ancient Norwegian patterns—the largest selection by far on the Continent. There are models for ladies, men, and children—all shrink-resistant, color-fast, moth-proofed and wonderfully comfortable. They have added a line of machine-knitted garments of the highest quality, too, plus handbags, gloves, hats, ski boots, slippers, knives, and other togs. Collectors of curiosa will discover intriguing wood-cut figurines and naughty trolls as well as dolls in native costume; pewter fanciers have a big choice; and there are many handwoven mats and runners for the table. Generous savings on U.S. or foreign deliveries; sizable mailorder business; all shipments totally guaranteed.

PEER GYNT MOUNTAIN COUNTRY

Here is one of the few remaining lightly trodden touristic magnets in Western Europe. Scenic glory and tranquillity are the keynotes of what its dwellers have long called "Our Friendly Wilderness." Within this triangle of 2200 square

miles, with its apexes at Rondane, Jotunheimen and directly above Lillehammer, you may drive for an hour without encountering another car or seeing a
single billboard. It is so pristine, in fact, that you may safely quench your thirst
from any pool, brook, stream, lake or other body of water in the entire region!

The name springs from Ibsen's most acclaimed poetic drama, Grieg's opera, and the ballet that followed—one of which, incidentally, is presented hourly
somewhere in the world 365 days per year. They evolve around the picaresque
international adventures of this mythical Norwegian folk hero. Before starting,
the playwright tracked down the grave of farmer Per (one ''e'') Gynt, the crumbling headstone of which attracts legions of pilgrims to the serene little cemetery
in Vinstra.

This grid of diverse ranges and 5 valleys is about 3½ hours north of Oslo
by train or car. Bus excursions are made from both of the capital's airports and
from landings of ferries from abroad. Because of the shortage of taxis, through
prior arrangements hotel cars meet guests at the nearest station.

The winter season from December through April draws the majority of
visitors to the slopes for downhill and cross-country skiing. Conversely, the less
costly summer season from the end of May to Oct. 1 shows greater popularity
in the glades. During the latter you may enjoy the lovely skeins of carefully
marked and supervised walking trails, fishing, excursions, various sports including tennis (no golf)—but mostly relaxing to commune with nature at its sublime
peak.

Seven of the leaders, while operated independently, have loosely banded
together to form the Peer Gynt Hotels Groupement. (Tel: 62–96666 or Fax 62–
96–688 or Telex 78601 to reserve at any.) These are Skeikampen, Dalseter,
Gola, Fefor, Espedalen, Ruten Fjellstue, and Gausdal Mountain hotels (see below). Although full pension is required, clients may lunch, dine or use the
facilities of any of the other 6 without extra charge. All offer free entertainment
and live dance music. While these are fully licensed to serve drinks, some of
the less prominent ones aren't.

The **Skeikampen Hoyfjellshotell** • *2635 Tretten; Tel: (062)28505* • is my
favorite. This gracious, elegantly sophisticated, impeccably maintained house
commands a lovely sweep of lake and countryside. Flowers, candles, paintings,
colorful rugs, and antiques abound within its tasteful precincts. Unusually felicitous indoor pool lush with greenery, with adjoining gymnasium and saunas;
outdoor pool and sun terrace; tennis court; delightful Spanish-style Bodega, where
proprietor Alf-Christian Anderssen gives tasting parties of Bordeaux selected by
him in France, with special cheeses offered with his compliments; outstandingly
sumptuous Norwegian lunch buffet; international ski school; black tie 3 times a
week in winter; other attractions; open year round. Accommodations include
one suite, 3 junior suites, 50 rooms with bath, and 13 with shower. Expensive
but tops in the entire region.

The **Gola Hoyfjellshotell** • *2646 Gola; Tel: (062)98109* • owned by Hoeghs
Rederi, offers superb amenities. Cozy main building with 30 well-furnished
units (try for # 107); 10-room chalet wing in birch with its own brand of charm;
4 individual yesteryear and 25 modern double-party guest cottages, each simply
and practically equipped for 6 persons with cooking gear, refrigerator, shower,
toilet, electric clothes dryer, fireplace and wall-to-wall carpets; riding, tennis,

sailboats, fishing, minigolf, 3 neighboring ski lifts and cross-country ski tracks prepared by machine; closed Oct., Nov., and May. A happy oasis, especially for families in its cottages.

Dalseter Hoyfjellshotell • *2627 Svatsum; Tel: (062)99910* • also with a glorious panorama, comes up with a handsome lobby, an intimate Bar-Lounge with fireplace, a 230-seat dining salon, a heated indoor pool, 2 saunas, a well-equipped gym, horses for riding, a children's playground, and more. Its buffet table offers a viking-style breakfast from 8:30 to 10, as well as a versatile cold assortment with selected hot dishes at lunchtime. There are 83 chambers with bath or shower, and 9 with only a private toilet. Try to be lodged on its southern side for the scenery. Elsa and Erik Gillebo run this well. Worthy.

The most typical Norwegian style establishment in this group is the **Fefor Hoyfjellshotell** • *2640 Vinstra; Tel: (062)90099, Fax 91760* • Mountainside site over lake; ski lift, skating rink, tennis, minigolf, squash, horses, indoor and outdoor pool, fishing, saunas, dancing nightly; delicious country-style cuisine with marvelous breakfast buffet; well-maintained 1902 structure with Robert Scott mementos from training here for his South Pole expedition; public rooms with good fireplaces; 123 bedchambers and many baths rebuilt but backdated to the space and grace concepts of the birth of this century; about 15 new self-service chalets which are ideal for prolonged holidays.

Except for the glaringly large and out-of-key Coca-Cola sign plastered at the entrance, the **Kampesaeter Fjellstue** • *2643 Skabu; Tel: (062)95525* • offers a very plain but ingratiating rustic atmosphere and a panorama that is fantastic. Attractively extended dining room; nighttime stube that r-o-c-k-s in season; 34 rooms; furnishings somewhat tacky. There's a convivial feeling here a la comfortable clothes and old shoes.

The **Sodorp Gjestgivergard** • *2640 Vinstra; Tel: (062)91000* • architecturally a Norwegian chalet, is almost a straightforward American-style motel in its interior. A pleasant young couple named Austerheim attained their life's dream when they opened it in '76. Large dance hall with live music every day except Monday; 27 rooms with convertible beds, showers, and no frills; lunch stop for bus groups; open all year.

Gausdal Hoyfjellshotell • *2622 Skei-Gausdal; Tel: (062)28500* • is a member of the deluxe group with correspondingly deluxe rates. There's a wing above a congress center. Except when the chartered tours pour in for the noon-time meal, the ambience is notably relaxed—but so is the upkeep. The most felicitous feature is its indoor pool with its adjoining solarium; there's a tennis court, and also a ski school. The food makes up in quantity the gap which it lacks in quality. Open around the calendar.

The **Espedalen Fjellstue** • *2628 Espedal; Tel: (062)99912* • (complement of cottages, suites, or chambers and 60 beds for sportspeople; big-sky country outside your windows; starting point for the canoe-camping excursion) and the **Ruten Fjellstue** • *also 2627 Svatsum; Tel: 99911* • (stunning sweep of countryside; chalet-type construction; in a red barn style; woody denlike lounges; simple but viewful dining room; half the accommodations with shower and W.C.; fishing nearby; ski lessons).

Send your queries for brochures, any other information, and/or reservations to Oddvar Naess of **Peer Gynt Hotels** Box 115 (N-2647 Hundorp, Tel. (062)96000, Fax 96688).

ROROS is a historic mining town (on UNESCO's "preservation" list) and a cross-country skier's paradise; miles of rolling slopeland that stay under good powder until the end of April; strictly for sportsmen who love it in winter and antiquarians who love it in summer. A rare treat for music lovers is **Olavsgruva,** a subterranean concert hall. The choice stopping place is at the **Roros Hotel.**

SANDEFJORD, is a one-time whaling city. (This commerce once made its inhabitants the most affluent citizens per capita in Norway!)

☆☆☆☆ **Park Hotel** • This monument to Moby Dick and his descendants is so extravagantly constructed, so lavishly outfitted, and so generously maintained that it will never make a dime—and the beauty of it is that it was planned this way! As a result, here is not only one of Scandinavia's finest hostelries, but one of the top oases in all of northern Europe. For physical diversion there are the sliding-roof, saltwater, heated pool (with its very own grill and bar, no less), a gym, a solarium, underwater massages, 2 saunas, and a local hunting and fishing club where you can arrange to hook a salmon from late June through August. The main salon, the Restaurant (dancing nightly year round), the Bistro lounge (snacks, lunch, and sips), and the Jonas (a cellar hideaway where the freshmen-to-postgrad set congregate Sat. evenings). Stay only in the main building.

★★ **Klubben** • out at *Tonsberg,* is a mod-minded knockout these days. Umbrella-dotted and awning-shaded waterside terrace cracking with the snap of wind-kicked flags; stone-floor reception; window-lined dining spread with schoonerisms on the walls; double rooms with sitting areas; facilities for yachting, golf, congresses, and dancing nightly to combo music. A big plus for the region, so be sure to reserve well in advance. Medium price range.

STALHEIM

★★★ **Stalheim** • sweeps the local honors. Attractive lobby gladdened by rich woods and regional antiques; all rooms with bath; some beds in nook-style alcoves. Many amenities, but its brightest feather is the awesome view down the Naeroy Valley. Open mid-May to mid-September.

STAVANGER Petroleum has pepped up the vitality of this town to a lively octane content nowadays as well as nights. Even so, little has been changed in this old, bucolic, and lovely fishing port. (It was formerly the capital of the national sardine industry.) The normal oil strike pattern of hard-boozing boomers, honky-tonk joints with B-girls, con artists, pitchmen, grifters, and venal merchants does not exist. Nor has it become a resort, despite the fact that 10 of the country's 18 miles of beaches are in this area. It is a characteristically charming town where most of the 96,000 residents still smile in their encounters with other members of humanity. Due to the influx of outsiders, there are almost 100 restaurants reflecting the variegated international tastes and numerous night clubs keep the clocks busy for extended revelry. Incidentally, the people pronounce their town "Stah-VAN-grr." A "Siddis" is a person from here.

Traditionalists might prefer the slightly dowdy **Victoria,** which has a splendid locale right by the waterside. It offers five stories of red-brick hospitality. The **SAS Royal**, a modern house with oodles of conveniences, a pool, bars, and zesty decor, recently flew in with 196 rooms. **Skagen Brygge** offers 110 units in a cleverly architected linkage of Waterfrontage: 9 buildings that resemble lean Scandinavian houses. There's also the handsomely appointed and immaculate **Atlantic,** which is edging the water. Upper-middle price range. The rather large **K.N.A. Hotel** was built as an apartment house and converted. The Grill is a placidly pleasant room stretched to include an old-fashioned corner that has lots of intimate appeal. The motel-like **Scandic** offers an inviting grill and piano bar; small pool and gym plus sauna. Very reasonable price range for all rooms with showers. The hilltop **Alstor** offers a routine lobby; exceptionally attractive 100-seat dining room; dance bar; tiny rooms. Moderate prices.

Diners will find a collection of old wooden wharf houses restored and opened as restaurants. **Mortepumpen,** with antique fixin's, does wonders with fish and grills, but it is devoted solely to groups. The 17th-century **Sjohuset Skagen** is strongly maritime, rustic in tone, and entertaining. **Cartellet** is French influenced; rough brick walls and intimate illumination. The suave restaurant at the Victoria Hotel, **Steak House,** is outfitted in attractive mulberry and darkish-wood decor; open grill at entrance; comfortable banquettes; piped music; open continuously from 7 a.m. until 12 p.m., starting with a versatile Breakfast Buffet; Lunch Buffet on weekdays. **Cafe de France** is one of the city's finer independent restaurants, as is **Jan's Mat-og Vinhus.** **Straen** specializes in fish. (Could there be one in Stavanger that doesn't?) Joking aside, there is great variety—from a Chicago steak house to a Greek taverna to a Mongolian grill and even to Thai, Indian, and oriental restaurants.

TROMSO has a trio of winners: the **Grand Nordic,** the ever-expanding **Royal,** which is piloted by SAS, and the more economical 53-room **Saga.** Be sure to reserve in advance before mushing so far north.

TRONDHEIM, third in importance in Norway, is pronounced "Tron-dee-em" by most residents over 40 and to rhyme with Sondheim by the younger ones. Decatur, Illinois, is larger; timber, fish, and shipping are the chief industries. The cathedral is the finest of its kind in Scandinavia. Geographically, you'll find the setting delightful. It's on a fjord; the old name is "Nidaros," which means "Mouth of the River Nid"—and that's just what it is.

The **Britannia** is the only solid, gracious monument of hotellerie in this city. Large, lovely Palm Court in Moorish tones for dining; sizable and lively adjoining dance-bar; Victorian clublike charm. **Royal Garden** nestles among old warehouses along the river, lending a special personality to this establishment. I like its sense of adventure. Next on our roster is the **Astoria,** decorated in good taste. Intimate Bistro in the modern mood; TV room and lounge on 2nd floor; Disco dance-bar; 42 decent-sized Scandinavian-type units with bath; 10 singles with washbasins only. The breakfast-only **Ambassadeur** overlooks the river and a sylvan scene. All of the above are midrange in price. **Larssens** is a charmer for the moderate prices. Pleasant dining room lined with paintings up 1 flight; cozy lounges; restaurant and beer tavern on the main level. While the **Neptun** is considerably newer, it is the same type of house, with like tariffs.

Popular cafe; beer and wine served in dance-bar; 30 airy but somewhat cramped quarters, all with bath or shower. Fair **Gildevangen** is still braced intrepidly as a distinctive and imposing mini-fortress. The period 1905 inaugural aura is retained in its old-fashioned high ceilings and elsewhere; its attempts at dispelling this fall flat in heaviness and sadly do not come off. But while it is almost as grim on the inside as on the exterior, this aura is radically countered by the warm friendliness of its staff. An indomitable antithesis to today's sleeping factories. The 100-bed **Trondheim Youth Hostel,** on a hillock overlooking the sea, is one of the best of its type in Norway; dormitory style, of course, but clean as an Arctic breeze. The 98-room **Singsaker Studenthjem** is an alternate.

For dining and night life, the **Monte Cristo** is lively; it has a restaurant, club, 3 bars, and a wintergarden.

Tyholttarnet is a lofty communications tower with an observation platform plus a revolving (1 rph) restaurant at the summit. Reserve in advance (Tel. 07-513166).

The **Grenaderen** oozes with charm and urbanity. More than 2 centuries ago the structure was tenanted by a blacksmith; the old forge and other appurtenances are still there. Sophisticated rustic ambience; about 15 tables; little King's Room to rear with 5 more tables; adjoining bar delightfully reminiscent of an old-fashioned hunter's lodge; mini-attic with stools for imbibers; high standards of cookery; expensive.

ULVIK   offers the **Brakanes**—with its emerald lawn nipping at the skirt of the Hardangerfjord. This very reasonably priced hostelry is perhaps the most stunning of all. Long, white, fresh-looking building plus a set-back annex (take the former in preference to the latter); lovely waterside terrace; some front units looking straight down the ripples; limited living space; open mid-May to late September. Recommended. The **Ulvik Tourist Hotel,** functioning as late as Christmas, is chiefly for passersby rather than for lingerers. The **Strand** is a frostbiter's delight. Step out of bed into a skiff or a sailing dinghy at your doorstep. If your ancestors were penguins, waterskiing is also in the ice tap. Brrrrr! Shelter is not expensive in these ports.

VOSS,   birthplace of Knute Rockne, presented to the University of Notre Dame a handsome memorial honoring this immortal. Pilgrims to this burgeoning village will find a cableway and several ski lifts to haul an ever increasing number of Americans and Britons each snowtime; the trails for walking or slicing down the soft white hills are among the loveliest to be seen (be sure to go to the very top first). Fine headquarters for fjord motoring excursions or skiing patrols into the nearby wilderness; apres-ski activities for nocturnal upliftings, too.

Park tops our list for dwelling space. Year-round operation; main-street situation opposite a church built in A.D. 1150. Unhappily, the bedchambers lack even a smidgen of decorative verve. The gabled **Fleischer's,** so close to the station that every guest should automatically be issued a pocket watch, a fob, and a lantern with his door key, is so old-fashioned in its main building and so modern in its 18-room annex that the contrast is startling. Its "motel" afterthought, across the pike, is targeted for budgeteers, families, and—we suppose—"motorists." All units with bath. The **Jarl,** at the lower end of town, offers 90 basic chambers that are best in the newer wing; all rooms have showers. About the same range in tariffs as Fleischer's. The **Youth Hostel** is another of the splendid Norwegian shelters for undergrads; this one is one of the best in the land.

PORTUGAL

INCLUDING MADEIRA

USA: Portuguese National Tourist Office, 590 Fifth Ave., New York, N.Y. 10036–4704, Tel. (212) 354–4403. You may also obtain information from the Portuguese embassies or other government agencies.

SPECIAL REMARKS: (1) It's worth noting that State-operated *pousadas* or inns exist all over Portugal. These are rest houses often located in palaces or historic buildings; in 1990 the network won our annual *Fielding Travel Award* for excellence and value. Information can be obtained from the Portuguese National Tourist Offices in New York or in Lisbon from the Director General for Tourism (executive offices at Av. Antonio Augusto de Aguiar 86, with Travel Information facilities at Praca dos Restauradores 27). (2) The Portuguese State Tourist Office has developed what they call *"Turismo no Espaco Rural* (countryside tourism) now divided into *Turismo de Habitacao* (manor houses, palatial homes and buildings of special architectural value; $92 singles and $127 doubles), and *Agroturismo* (farm houses in agricultural areas) at amazingly low prices ($23 for singles; $30 doubles). Some of these manors (''solares'') date back to the 15th century; many are located off the beaten paths throughout the country. Contact Mrs. Maria do Ceu (Posto de Turismo, in the town of Ponte de Lima, Tel: 058–942335). (3) Another source for this is A.C.T. (*Assoc. das Casas em Turismo,* Torre D-2-3°A Alto da Pampilheira, 2750 Cascais; Tel. 2842901 and 2844464; Telex 43304 PITSAP); attention Mrs. Ines Pinheiro. This group contains about 30 houses, including 10 manors, all over continental Portugal. Also you may contact Mrs. D. Laura Acheman at PRIVETOUR, Rua Castilho 209-1°, Frt., 1000 Lisbon; Tel. 654953 and 2868232.

TELEPHONE: Access code to USA: 07 in the north, but varies with district. To phone Portugal: 351; time difference (Eastern Daylight) plus 5 hrs.

Portugal remains the least spoiled and one of the least expensive nations in the Western Alliance.

This historic republic, with fewer inhabitants than the city of Tokyo, measures only 350 miles in length and less than 150 miles in width. Yet, first spearheaded by Prince Henry the Navigator, Vasco da Gama, and other epic explorers, during the 15th and 16th centuries it was one of the mightiest powers on the globe.

The visible east-west line between **Lisbon** and the Customs point beyond **Elvas** splits the country into two markedly diverse conformations, including a less pronounced cleavage in their California types of climate. The South, which possesses a massive chunk of the overall 500 miles of beaches, has as its matrix the coastal **Algarve** as its crowning playground. In the interior you will find excellent roads with light traffic, tidy, serene, lovely landscapes, and sleepy, charming villages in which most of the dwellings carry their own hue among a large range of soft pastels. The North is far more industrialized and far less colorful, although its inhabitants in general are equally hospitable. Because of their narrowness and caravans of heavy trucks, the main arteries are despairingly overcrowded. However, multitudes of splendid cultural attractions await voyagers here.

As mentioned above, Portugal operates a skein of *pousadas* ("places to rest"), most of them country inns. These were followed by the network of *estalagems* and *albergarias,* which are privately operated; hence, their standards vary. A *residencia* has no restaurant and only breakfast is available. Many are located in converted fortresses, monasteries, and ancient mansions. They offer from as few as 4 to a maximum of perhaps 50 accommodations. The majority are simple but charming. Numerous examples are scattered through this text. The Portuguese National Tourist Office can furnish a full list.

The national method of listing currency comes as a mild shock to newcomers. The symbol "$" is placed *after* the escudos and *before* the centavos. Thus, at this writing 1 escudo is written 1$00 and is worth a fraction of a cent.

Among short trips offering the richest rewards, here are some suggested routes:

(1) From London, take an inexpensive one-week charter tour to Madeira and return. See "Madeira," below.

(2) **Lisbon**/day excursion to **Estoril** and **Cascais,** with lunch at the *Hotel Palacio* in Seteais/fly to **Faro** and lodge where you have chosen on the **Algarve**/the beautiful small road **Portimao-Monchique-Odemira-Beja,** with lunch at *Pousada dos Loios* in **Evora** and overnight in *Pousada da Rainha Santa Isabel* in Estremoz/north just before Mora to **Montargil-Chamusca,** lunch at *Estalagem de Santa Iria* in **Tomar-Coimbra-Mealhada**—overnight at **Bucaco/ Coimbra-Leiria-Nazare-Caldas de Rainha-Lisbon.**

Further information on all of these high points follows.

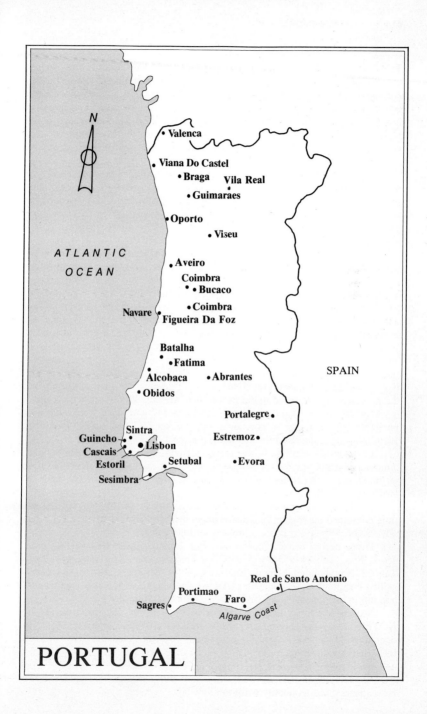

N

ATLANTIC
OCEAN

• Valenca

• Viana Do Castel
• Braga   Vila Real
   • Guimaraes

• Oporto
      • Viseu

• Aveiro
   Coimbra
   • • Bucaco
   • Coimbra
Navare • Figueira Da Foz

Batalha
• • Fatima
• Alcobaca   • Abrantes
• Obidos

Portalegre •

Sintra   Estremoz •
Guincho • • Lisbon
Cascais •
Estoril   Setubal
Sesimbra •   • Evora

SPAIN

Real de Santo Antonio
Portimao   •
Sagres •   Faro
          Algarve Coast

PORTUGAL

TRANSPORTATION **Airline Air Portugal** works hard, but facilities are not those of nations that have enjoyed longer prosperity. Aircraft are good (Boeing, Airbus, and Lockheed Tristar), but not posh; staff courtesy is uneven—usually better aloft than on the ground; cuisine can't be called inspired. You'll realize how precise the flying is when your pilot puts you down on that postage stamp at Madeira. Lisbon Airport is improving and it is handy to town, but it virtually needs more seating space in the lounges. The national grid is well served, as are the Azores and Funchal.

Taxis All cabs are metered and rates are reasonable for the plethora of free thrills. *Set your price in advance on all out-of-town excursions;* here you must pay both ways, from cabstand all the way back to cabstand. Tip 20 escudos for the average distance; if longer, 15% will do fine. He cannot legally carry more passengers than the number stipulated over the meter. From 10 p.m. until 6 a.m. there's a night supplement of 20% on the meter.

Trains Greatly improved under a generous development program. The ticket costs are so low, the distances are so short, and the differences in comfort are so pronounced that you should travel first class wherever it's available. There are special deluxe runs both ways between 3 cities daily, which levy a peanut supplement for their first-class facilities. They offer club chairs, sofas, a hostess and service for drinks, plus a communal dining car. On the 3-to-3½-hour run from Lisbon to Oporto (should be one hour less by this season), for about $34 you can bask through the countryside on the nonstop ALFA Service train. In either direction between Lisbon and Faro, the capital of the Algarve, reservations may be made for about $24 (first-class only) aboard the *I C Rapido.* The fixed-price meal is about $13. Since the road arteries between these hubs are the most heavily trafficked in the nation, here are delightfully relaxed escapes.

Tourist Ticket. You can buy one for about $12 entitling you to a week of public transportation in Lisbon, or a 4-day ticket for close to $9. Inquire at Escadinhas de Santa Justa for this money-saver.

Car Rentals While self-drive rentals are considerably steeper than in North America, the mileage you will normally cover is relatively so short that their tariffs shouldn't evoke too great pain. Hertz, Avis, and many of the other International Big Boys are active here.

But hired cars with drivers—wow! They work on the principle of the less time consumed the higher the rates. To avoid what might be startling surprises, always check the price before climbing into the vehicle.

If you need a driver, get in touch with Luis de Castro (rua Feio Terenas, 15–1, Esq., Tel: 8149536 or 539202) or Fredauto (Av. Ressano Garcia 36-E, Tel: 539202, both in Lisbon. English-speaking Mr. de Castro is a superbly skilled chauffeur and a fountain of knowledge about every worthy touristic attraction in his nation. He drives an air-conditioned Mercedes.

Seat belts are required for everyone occupying front seats in Portugal.

NOTE · · · In the next two years the Lisbon-Oporto highway should be operative (3½-hour ride) and the new bridge over the Guadiana River will link the Algarve with southern Spain.

FOOD Greatly improved. With increasing prosperity the Portuguese larder has expanded vastly; quality is tip-top nowdays.

In Portuguese cuisine the French influence is pronounced. The creations are unique, delicate and flavorful. The wonderful fresh fruits of the sea you will probably find are more appealing than earth's bovinity. Steaks and veal are staples. Cod is beloved; sole and all the brotherhood of the crustacean clan are still abundant; lobster (clawed or clawless) is snappingly expensive.

If you have a timid nature about certain flavors or styles of cooking, you'll have to remember 3 phrases: *sem azeite* ("without oil"), *com manteiga* ("with butter"), and *sem alho* ("without garlic").

Since Brazil is a cultural offshoot of Portugal, coffee is the pillar of almost everyone's diet. The local version seems muddy to many neophytes. Actually, the quality is higher than can ordinarily be found in the U.S.; they simply don't blend it, that's all. Some travelers find the "Carioca" style the most acceptable—equal parts of coffee and hot water; others like it *com leite*—coffee and milk, 50-50; after a heavy meal, most of us take it *bica* (plain)—but the wise follow the national custom of filling almost ⅓rd of the cup with sugar before consumption.

Cheese? Serpa, snappy and tangy, is outstanding. Serra is a lighter, creamier version that is pure heaven as a complement to a glass of vintage port. Queijo fresco, a butter substitute with overtones of cottage cheese, is liked by many foreign visitors.

Agua de Luso is the best-known bottled water, though my favorite one is Pedras Salgadas.

DRINKS Port is the major national wine, of course. Economic conditions have forced the export of virtually all of the most superior class. Your best chance of securing fine vintage stock will be at some outlet that caters chiefly to foreigners. There are 5 kinds. Vintage, which takes 20 years to reach its prime, is the best; Crusted, never dated, is excellent; Ruby and Tawny (favorite of most travelers) are blends of up to 40 separate wines; White, light and pleasant, is the only type served before a meal. (The rest are consumed at the end, with the cheese).

Madeira is the minor national wine—not as fashionable as it was when the clipper ships were sailing, but still as kind to the taste. It has the longest life of any. The 3 best types are Bual (my preference), Sercial (dry, characteristic flavor), and Malmsey (on the sweet side).

Portugal's stars for just about every second meal are the unique *Vinhos Verdes* from the old Minho region in the far north. Although they are called *verde* ("green") because their grapes are picked when young, most are white or straw-yellow and some are deep red. All of these light, dry, delicate, inexpensive bottlings, each with its official seal, which guarantees the contents as genuine, must be drunk cold. With virtually everything from meat to shellfish, the amber Gatao and Logosta are among the most popular brands. A traditional exception is the service of a red variety with freshly caught sardines. Literally dozens of vintners produce this different and delicious treat.

Among the standards, the leaders are Clarete, Ferreirinha (a very fine red), Quinta da Aguieira (excellent in red and white), Reserva Sogrape (another mellow red), Monopolio and Ermida (both exceptional whites), Bucaco (supply rather severely restricted) and Grandjo, if you prefer a very sweet white. The reds from the Dao, the second largest area of growth, are full-bodied and strong, with a translucent ruby hue and a taste closer to burgundy than claret. It is especially useful to ascertain their age before ordering these; between 7 and 10 years is normally their peak. Roses? Most of them, including the famed Lancers and Mateus, are noticeably effervescent—a far cry from their confreres in the Provence or Cote de Rhone. All of the still versions seem undistinguished. As for the naturally sparkling choices, you might find Caves da Raposeira "Bruto" to be the most acceptable local substitute for champagne. Be warned, however, that most Portuguese bubbly is cloying and unpalatable. Last, there's always the wine of the country, in "open" servings; order this as *vinho da casa;* sometimes they furnish it with your table d'hote (not a la carte) meal.

Brandy? Quite a few poor ones. The best I've sampled (and I confess that my experience in this area is limited) is Antigua, in a lovely, tall, green, fluted bottle. Also in the prime category are Antiquissima, Velhissima, Fim do Seculo, Avo, Dom Teodosio, and four or five others. In the more popular division, Marcieira Five Stars is a splendid black-label entry. A brand named Constantino is seen frequently, but I prefer the above choices.

All major Western spirits except American whiskey are available at very high prices due to heavy import duties.

Ginginha, the cherry liqueur first invented and distilled by local monks, is curious and worth a try.

Sagres, Super-Bock, Carlsberg, and Tuborg have become the ranking beers. Imperial seems to vary in quality.

TIPPING Give taxi drivers 15% on top of the meter reading; hairdressers, 10%; washroom attendants, 5 escudos; station porters should get their fixed charge only; and theater ushers, 5 escudos. For waiters, add only 5% inasmuch as service and a tourist tax are already included. In general, the Portuguese themselves tip in mini amounts, but as many are so strained economically, you will win their hearts and gratitude if you tip normally—which will seem generous to them.

CITIES AND REGIONS

ABRANTES Right in the epicenter of Portugal, this lively town is full of graphic history and colorful tradition. It is sited on a hillside a mere half mile from the right margin of the Tagus. From the **Castle** tower you can view a radius of perhaps 50 miles. The ancient streets were paved with rounded pebbles from the nearby river. In the upper town lies the **Hotel de Turismo.** Warmhearted director Manuel Alves is proud of this delightful 24-room hostelry; fully air-conditioned; TV and frigo bars. Panoramic restaurant with sweeping vistas over the surrounding valleys; regional cuisine. Moderate prices. **Tubuci** and **Central** are two of the only four other pensions.

ALCOBACA on the Lisbon-Oporto road about 87 miles from the capital, with a classic Cistercian monastery: **Real Abbey of Santa Maria.** This Gothic monument, begun in 1178, was made up of the church, cloisters, chapter house, and many other impressive sancta. Perhaps its most unusual feature is the brook that flows through its kitchen. The monks were thus able to catch their fresh meals and wash the dishes of the same repast. Worth seeing are the **Tombs of Dom Pedro** and **Ines de Castro;** a love story is depicted in the colorful rose window of the high altar. Only three pensions exist for overnighting: **Coracoes Unidos** ("United Hearts"), the **Santa Maria,** and the **Mosteiro** (within the monastery itself). All are modest. **A Curva,** a half-mile away toward *Leiria* is the best dining bet.

ALGARVE

This glorious maritime province, which forms the extreme southwest of the European Continent, is Portugal's lushest garden and principal playpen. It is a narrow ribbon 96 miles long that occupies the nation's entire southern coast, geographically separated by a barrier of hills. The name is derived from early Arab settlers, who called it *al-Gharb,* "The West." Summer never really finishes in this subtropical Hesperides. It is always ablaze with flowers, familiar and unfamiliar, for it basks in more sunshine than Mallorca, the French Riviera, or California. Spectacular rock formations of strangely eroded shapes enfold many of its golden sand beaches. The scenery is hauntingly serene when you escape from the occasional pockets of high-rise architecture. The only industries of importance are fishing and tourism. Over centuries its people have been known for their simplicity, their openness, and their great capacity for making friends.

Faro, the capital and site of its only commercial airport, is close to the center of the fine trunk road that runs from *Sagres* on the Atlantic tip to *Vila Real de St. Antonio* at the Spanish border. Its fortunate location almost halves the travel distances to the resorts both to the east and west of this most popular gateway.

Virtually every conceivable summer recreational facility abounds—chimney spotting (they are so unusual, travelers pick a "winner" for the day), swimming (because of fitful undertows, go only where there is a lifeguard), all water sports, tennis, riding, fado singing, folk dancing, 3 casinos, nightclubs, discos, hang-gliding, festivals, carnivals, name it and it's there. Today golfers wing in from all over the globe to enjoy its captivating courses, many of them edging the sea. There are three of 27 holes each, six with 18 holes and one with 9 holes. Two additional 18-holers are under construction. Their quality is becoming a legend for the region.

Albufeira This major resort is widely known as "The St. Tropez of Portugal." Prices copy those of St. Tropez, too; they're very high for the Algarve! While here is a colorful, hilly settlement with a good but crowded beach teeming with holidaymakers, its best quarters are in its environs. **Clube Mediterraneo da Balaia** has employed strikingly interesting and advanced architectural concepts in both its exterior and interior. Sextagonal lobby ascending to 7th-story skylight; urbane, viewful Grill and restaurant; big heated pool; adjoining "bungalows" in customary solid-block building; 186 air-conditioned accommodations somewhat sterile but facing the ocean; longish hike to splendid strand. The 250-room, 7-flight **Alfa Mar** also features the same straight-up lobby. Its less fetching units look down to a basement-level patio-garden. Parade of recreational facilities; total of 120 "bungalows" with sitting room, kitchenette, tiny bath, and either 1, 2, or 3 bedchambers; wonderful beach quite a haul by foot. **Montechoro,** one of the Big Boys, is down one notch in official classification. White entrance hall; blue lounge; dining room another extension of its Moorish theme; 2 pools; 2 tennis courts; 4 bars; 362 spacious, well-furnished, wall-to-wall glass-fronted chambers; 45 suites, some of which are lovely. An excellent buy. **Aparthotel Auramar** comes up with 282 pleasant but rather cramped double studio-type nests with kitchenette and terrace. Cheerfully decorated; superior pool en route to expansive sands; no room service. Worthy for the prices. **Aldeia das Acoteias,** with 300 studio apartments sited on its 100-plus acres, is a tourist complex that has been transformed into a paradise for sportsmen specializing in track-and-field athletics. In addition to a "tartan" running lane, it has a cross-country course plus paths for jogging.

Carlton is the latest addition to the local scene. Its 310 well-appointed nests are air-conditioned; spacious restaurant; grill; a typical Scotch bar; 2 heated pools (one indoor); health club plus other conveniences. A major benefit to the resort.

Among the independent restaurants, **Panorama** (Albufeira-Jardim complex) is the most elegant and comfortable. An outdoor terrace overlooks a swimming pool and the sea. **La Cigale** is the runner-up. It is on Olhos de Agua beach, and reservations are recommended. **A Ruina** is right on the beach; vaulted ceilings in a 3-level structure. One of the best buys for fresh seafood delivered by next door's fish market (where you choose from the counter).

Alvor The opulent, high-rise ☆☆☆☆☆ **Alvor Praia,** which commands a heavenly cliff-site panorama above a rock-and-sand beach, offers just about every imaginable provision for vacationers who seek comfort and recreational activities. Handsome white linear structure; full air conditioning; spacious and gracious lobby; split-level dining room with maritime vista plus candlelit Grill; heated pool the best on the whole coast; elevator to strand; 400-seat Convention Hall; 241 smallish balconied units and 16 very large suites. Reserve on the ocean side to escape the busy road in front. A pacesetter in the Algarve. Nearby is the ☆☆ **Delfim,** a top-grade, 18-story, 325-bedchamber giant. Both of the above are officially located at *Praia dos Tres Irmaos,* which is adjacent to Alvor and is generally considered an extension of it. The less-costly **D. Joao II** boasts fabulous golden sands and a huge pool—but very little else unless you can be happy in a blatantly overcommercial pleasure palace. If apartment dwelling suits you better, you might check at the giant **Torralta** complex, which rents 1, 2, or 4-bedroom units at surprisingly low rates, especially during the fringe and off-peak seasons.

Armacao de Pera lays claim to the largest beach on this entire coast. It's a pity that so many high-rise, cheapjack buildings spoil the village and that the strand remains so ill-kempt. The ★★ **de Garbe** is immaculate. Glorious clifftop situation; indoor pool, sauna, gym, and squash court; discotheque and snack bar; airy dining room; open terrace for seaside dancing; room capacity doubled to 220 sleek units. ★★ **Do Levante** dominates a lovely promontory. Soothing lounge; nice restaurant; 2 pools with bar and sun terrace; 41 smallish quarters; 90 steps to excellent strand. Same tariff ranges but less action and much cozier than the de Garbe. The avant garde **Viking,** 2 miles from the settlement, operates only from March to November. This 400-bed house, with its stamped-out modern aura of impersonality, is typical of its type all over the map. It gave me the chills. The **Vilalara Holiday Village** is a mile out. Although its setting is spectacular and its sports amenities are versatile, I don't think that this would hold strong appeal to the average vacationer. Restaurants? **Santola** steals the thunder locally for refinement and professionalism. A memorable repast will cost about $22. **A Grelha** (rustic and simple), **O Forno** (over the sea with outdoor barbecue), and **Panorama Grill** (clifftop) just about wrap up the picture.

Faro is the capital of the Algarve and its principal gateway since this is where the major coastal airport is located. Probably you will be overnighting elsewhere, so I'll only suggest some restaurants as transient pastimes. **Kappra** (Rua Brites Almeida, 45) is where I recently enjoyed what surely must have been one of the best soles (with almond sauce) on the Algarve. **Lady Susan** (Rua 1 de Dezembro 28) and **Cidade Velha** (Rua Domingos Guieiro 19) also are recommendable. If you still have time to kill, **Bones Chapel** might help; it is in the Church of Our Lady of Monte do Carmo and composed of 1250 human skulls. The **Se** (cathedral), formerly a mosque, is in Gothic and Renaissance styles. How's your appetite now?

Lagos, toe to heel with *Praia da Rocha,* means "lakes"—but there's nary a pond to be seen. Here was where the caravels were built that spearheaded the Age of Discovery; there's a 1000-year-old Moorish castle and the remains of Europe's first slave market. St. Anthony's Church features magnificent rococo gilt carvings, possibly the nation's finest; the neighboring museum has a fanciful chimney exhibit, cork creations, 16th-century vestments, old embroidery, coins, and heaps more to keep you busy. The ★★★★ **de Lagos,** centrally situated facing the harbor promenade, is officially classified as first class instead of deluxe only because a small segment of its rear rooms are too cramped to qualify. Sited on a 3-acre hilltop; 100% air-conditioned; spacious arched lobby; verdant interior courtyard; dining room, Grill, and Coffee Shop; comfortable, relaxing bar; 6 cozy lounges tucked at different levels; heated pool; English direction. Large expanses of white combined with orange, cooling blue, and vibrant green form its outstandingly attractive theme throughout. All clients are extended free privileges of its Duna Beach Club, 5 minutes by shuttle, with its clubhouse, sands, pool, and daily buffets. The 5-story, 259-room **Golfinho** is typical of the hurry-built hostelries in this area. Appealing vista from Penthouse Grill; ground-level restaurant crammed with 350 seats; clam-size space concepts that are far too spare for long-staying holidaymaking. Not bad, but far from exciting. You might prefer the eensy **Pensao D. Ana** around the curve of the coast, about 100 yards above a bathing cove. It has a mere dozen clean accommodations at lean tariffs. The second class **da Meia Praia** and **Sao Cristovao** are both far from the action and not worth the bother. Restaurants? **O Alpendre** ("The Shed") is one of the most sophisticated along the entire coast. Handsome paneled-stuccoed decor with clever touches that add richness and intimacy; about 20 tables in L-shaped main section and nook at rear; strikingly lavish food display in center; bar downstairs; fine tiled, stainless-steel, open kitchen with white-capped chef; dishes excellently cooked and presented. **Os Arcos** and **Dom Sebastian** are next in line. While the shopping in general is routine here, **Porches,** on the main Faro-Portimao road, stocks a large, unusual assortment of hand-made, hand-painted pottery in the traditional regional style, most of which is spun from the local red clay.

Penina The ☆☆☆☆☆ **Penina Golf** remains one of the most famous and illustrious golfing resort havens in Europe. This great estate, on which more than 400,000 trees have been planted since '64, is 2½ miles from the sea—an advantage for players who shun the wicked Atlantic-borne winds. Magnificent championship 36-hole links designed by Henry Cotton; fully outfitted clubhouse downstairs in main building a few steps from 1st tee; practice ground and putting greens; caddies, golf cars, caddy carts, and clubs available for hire; Olympic-size swimming pool in the garden; 2 tennis courts; sauna. Attractive interior appointments set amid modern Algarve architecture; clean-lined lobby with sumptuous adjoining lounges; spacious dining room; chic, intimate Monchique Grill with brass lanterns, touches of timber and glass-covered rotisserie; dancing nightly; total of 214 air-conditioned rooms, many with their own balcony. The plush **Alvor Casino,** only a 5-minute walk, is open every day from 5 p.m.–3 a.m. Good restaurant with dancing and floor show; 3 bars; the normal games of chance. Don't forget your passport if you wish to play!

Portimao is the second largest and second busiest settlement in the province. During its days and evenings it is constantly a-bustle with residents and visitors. Despite its numerous high-rise buildings and its public market, which covers the central plaza with racks of clothing, textiles, and other products—all sold to the strains of screeching rock music—a substantial portion of its traditional color remains. Curiously, the second class **Globo,** with a crisp lobby, panoramic 7th-floor restaurant, and 80 mini-mini-mini abodes, is the only hotel above the bottom-budget level. Its small, family-operated restaurants, however, are numerous. **A Lanterna** near the harbor bridge with no view, is the most popular eating place within many a mile. Modern in tone; open kitchen; 17 tables split by arched partition; midget greenhouse bar; blackboard menus on the walls. Fresh, fresh seafood is the staple of its delicious fare. Their delicate small clams steeped with mild onions in a white sauce are treats. The **Old Tavern** is charming in a British way. Pub-style interior; light, airy, enclosed garden with tables to rear; curries, spareribs, clam chowder, turkey a la creme, and vol au vent are typical standards. Closed Saturdays. This English-run house is a comfortable and clubby oasis. **Humphrey's** occupies a century-old mansion. Key Largo Lounge with live music; generous drinks in the African Queen Bar; dependable skilletry in the Casablanca Room. **Veneza** offers a bar and snack bar on the ground floor; dining room on mezzanine; passable but not notable. The **Dennis Inn** features a fetching bar and a snack-tea-coffee shop. Favored by the foreign trade. Shopping? Tourist junk abounds. Well above this in quality are **Vinda** (branch in *Albufeira*) for boutique items, celebrated **Vista Alegre** (see "Lisbon") for porcelains, and **Galeria Portimao** for Portuguese paintings, tapestries, and sculptures. All are on rua Santa Isabel. Enchanting *Monchique,* 14 miles out, is famous for its "Caldas" (spas), which date back to the Roman period. Its hot springs are reputed to cure rheumatism. Drive to the very top of Foia peak for a glorious panorama of the Algarve.

Praia da Luz ★ **Luz Bay Club Villas** is a colony of about 200 attached "villas" with 2 swimming pools and 2 garden restaurants. **O Poco** is a convenient beach dining spot; large outdoor terrace; good local food and friendly service.

Praia da Rocha This center is becoming zestless and mundane compared to other top-quality oases that have sprung up in the near vicinity. Its pride remains the famous 7-story, 220-room, white-and-blue, luxury ☆☆☆☆ **Algarve.** Although a king's ransom was poured into this landmark, perhaps Old-World enthusiasts would find it too flamboyant. It boasts almost every conceivable facility a deluxe hostelry could offer. Intimate azure-toned Grill; 2 heated pools; 2 restaurants (Zodiaco for more informal meals); nightclub; sauna; tennis; conference rooms and the works. The lower-category ☆☆ **Jupiter,** a few hundred yards away, is another attraction in this hamlet. Groupy in feeling and more commercial in general; heated swimming pool (covered in cooler months) at its entrance, too close to the traffic for comfort; restaurant with haughty service; nightclub; disco; 144 appealingly decorated bedchambers with bath. Satisfactory for its bracket. The 21-floor ☆ **Tarik,** 5 minutes from the sands, is firmly in the modern mood. V-ended pool; tennis; 2 restaurants; tiny "supermarket"; 120 doubles and 63 very small suites, plus 36 studio-type "suites" and 77 single-chamber "studios," both of the last with kitchenettes.

Sagres is a small harbor on the lee side of *Cape St. Vincent,* the magnificent harsh promontory that is the most southwesterly point of Europe and that for centuries has been called "O Fim do Mundo"—the End of the World. Because the Continent first meets the onslaught of the Atlantic here, anglers will find the best fishing grounds in Portugal and scuba divers can glide through a virtually unrivaled aquarium. The drive to its famous fortress and lighthouse is a *must* for every visitor. Whenever this road takes you close to the edge of its all-embracing cliffs, there are thrilling views of the sea pounding away hundreds of feet below. Many human flies with poles sit nonchalantly on its rim and play out their amazingly long lines into the swirling waters.

Pousada do Infante, with its stunning maritime panorama, is so popular that it is wise to book reservations at least 4 months ahead; 23 chambers with bath and balcony. Simple modern building; 2 sweet dining places with 200 capacity; garden terrace; pool; tennis; barbecue; reasonable tariffs as in all these government-operated *pousadas;* open all year. **Da Baleeira** is sited directly above a good sandy beach. This poorly maintained house caters frequently to German tour groups. Strictly routine, despite its viewful location. The little **Residencia Dom Henrique,** in town, is a mixed bag. Some of its limited number of abodes have private bath and some offer a small sitting room. So-so. The modest **A Tasca,** a typical fishermen's bar-restaurant with a lovely sweep of the bay, is the only independent eating spot of consequence.

★★★★★ **Vale do Lobo** is a completely self-sufficient world of its own. The Reception Center at its main entrance, operated 24 hours per day, has a pleasant multilingual staff. On arrival, passports or identification cards are required to be presented. In addition to its hotels and villas, you'll find a villa-flanked 27-hole golf course designed by Henry Cotton, the excellent Roger Taylor Tennis Center with year-round coaching, 6 independent restaurants, 6 independent bars or coffee shops, beach and water activities, 2 swimming pools, beauty shops, medical attention, 4 nightclubs, a drugstore, physiotherapy, and just about everything needed in resort community living. The luxurious ☆☆☆☆☆ **Dona Filipa** is a gem. Superb location close to 9 miles of golden sands; outstandingly tasteful decor; air conditioning that automatically shuts off when doors or windows are opened; Rotonda and Bistro its 2 gracious dining rooms; Kasbah nightclub with show; tennis, pool, and many other amenities. At neighboring *Quinta do Lago* ☆☆☆☆☆ **Hotel Quinta Do Lago** is one of the most luxurious resorts in Portugal, with 3 pools, a golf clinic, tennis, and all the amenities any sunseeker could wish for—including night life too. It resides on a 1600-acre estate containing 4 golf courses, the excellent Shepherds Restaurant, the Patio Club, and an apartment complex overlooking its own seawater lake.

Vilamoura claims to be Europe's largest and most completely privately owned vacation center. Its 1615 acres of beach and gently rolling hills—1200 of which are set aside as green zones—make it bigger than Monaco.

The facilities in this vacationers' playground are already vast. In addition to hostelries, apartments, and Holiday Villages, there are manmade lakes, excellent 18-hole golf courses designed by Frank Penninck, a casino, a private airport, a riding center, tennis courts, swimming pools, a 2-mile strand, and much, much more. The Marina will eventually shelter 2800 craft. In its area there are a number of private homes, rentable villas, a sizable shopping center, the moored floating **O Vapor** restaurant, and a pub. The Tourist Villages (**Aldeia do Golf, Golferias, Aldela do Mar, Aldeia do Campo, Le Clube, Monte da Vinha, Prado do Golf,** et seq.) consist of apartment blocks, "bungalows" in communal buildings, and small groups of villas, all clustered around their central clubhouse with their restaurant, bar, pool, and shared public precincts. Among the stopping places, the ☆☆☆☆ **Vilamoura Golf Hotel** boasts 52 nests with full bath, a terrace, and a subterranean parking area; airy suites are available. The international restaurant, bars, boutiques, and dining terrace are built around a handsome swimming pool. The 9-story ☆☆ **Dom Pedro,** 300 yards from the Casino and 2 miles from the Atlantic, has curvilinear structure; modern, rather cluttered lobby with overloud piped music; Grill with limited choices; simple, crowded Buffet; lovely sun area with pool and jumbo Gazebo Bar; 2 tennis courts. The 12-story, 400-room **Marinotel** is a deluxe newcomer with 2 pools (one heated), 2 restaurants (Grill Sirius overlooking the marina), tennis courts, putting green, private beach, shopping facilities, and worlds more. **Marina Dom Pedro,** about half the size, is a fresh and highly commercial competitor in the resort sweepstakes. Same ownership as the Dom Pedro (above); 2 pools (one with a sliding roof); Italian restaurant; tennis; boutiques; early success based on solid merits.

Also in the port you'll find ☆☆☆☆ **Vilamoura Marinotel** ● the largest in this city, with 399 luxurious bedrooms, and ☆☆☆☆ **Atlantis;** 266 bedrooms, 24 suites, indoor and outdoor pools, 4 tennis courts, a nightclub, and a very bright future. **Aldela do Golf** comes up with 150 quarters all built in attached groups of 3, 4, and 5. These range from single-level villas with 2 chambers to 2-level villas with 3 chambers to the so-called Golferias of 2-story "apartments." Unexciting. **Golf Hotel** jams 52 rooms in villas to its rear. The furnishings are well kept but cheezy in design and quality. Not very good, but its people were amiable.

AMARANTE knocks at the very door to the mountains, about 40 miles east of Oporto. Sao Goncalo, the local saint, is the patron of marriage. A splendid honeymoon target is 12 miles farther, along the spectacular drive to the *pousada* of the same name, a 15-room gem nestled on a hillside overlooking the Serra do Marao. Advanced reservations strongly recommended.

ARRAIOLOS This village—not too far from Estremoz—is famed for its distinctive carpets. I feel this center is a waste of time as a sightseeing target. There is no place to eat (not even a bar clean enough where you would want to sip a cup of coffee or a soft drink), and the town is run-down.

BARCELOS A mere 20 miles north of Oporto, in the richest handicraft region (which created the 13th-century Cock of Barcelos, legendary symbol of Portugal). Don't miss the ceramics of Rosa Ramalho, the "Grandma Moses" of the nation. Other folk art—especially visible during the popular Thursday market—includes brightly colored earthenware, carved wood ox yokes, embroidered tablecloths, and brassware. For accommodation, **Albergaria Condes de Barcelos** provides adequate shelter. So does the quiet, 27-room **Residencial Dom Nuno,** where a double costs about $37 per night with private bath.

BATALHA Famous for its imposing monastery of Santa Maria da Vitoria— the "battle abbey" of Portugal. King John I promised to build it if he conquered Aljubarrota in 1385. It took almost 2 centuries to complete, an indication of the labor problems in ancient Portugal. Considered the most important Gothic monument in the nation, it is also the largest monastic edifice, containing the tombs of Prince Henry the Navigator and Portugal's Unknown Soldier. For more than 100 years the monastery was utilized as a school for architects, sculptors, and glassmakers. An absolute must for history and art lovers. For overnighting I recommend the 21-room **Pousada do Mestre Afonso Domingues,** located near the abbey. Its restaurant is noteworthy too.

BRAGA This inland city 44 miles from the northern frontier is one of the nation's oldest Christian towns and among the most historic of shrines. When a Portuguese wishes to emphasize that something is *really* old, he says "As ancient as Braga Cathedral." Important monuments, churches, paintings, and tombs abound; it is also the seat of a small university. The 132-unit, air-conditioned **Turismo** offers comfortable lodging. Sterile, commercial lobby; Golden Bar as garish as a pinball machine; pleasant dining room and extensive lounge with terrace up 1 flight; probably the best cuisine and service in the region; some bedchambers merry with color. **Pensao Grande Residencia Avenida** is a giant step downward; only 11 of its 21 billets have private plumbing. Of the remaining 8 houses, I suggest only the two most recent additions: **Caranda** and **Residencial S. Marcos;** both are clean and functional. Besides the relatively sophisticated restaurant of the **Turismo** hotel, my favorite independent choice would be **Conde D. Henrique,** next to the Cathedral; decoration unpretentious; solid regional cuisine; attentive service. **Inacio** and **Terraco** serve international dishes; the latter offers panoramic views of the city. **City-Rio** specializes in Brazilian cooking. **Principe Negro** serves seafood. As an excursion target, delightful **Bom Jesus do Monte** (3 miles southeast) is noteworthy for its church, gardens, and granite double staircase. I've been informed that a new **Pousada** will soon open at the nearby **Monastery of Tibiaes.** Definitely worth a look if completed by your arrival time.

BUCACO (pronounced "Boo-SAH-Koh") is one of the most enchanting attractions on the Portuguese mainland. Its spacious, ultrarococo ★★★★ **Hotel Palacio,** crowning a huge forest-park, is straight from the pages of a fairy tale. This splendid palace in Manueline style—originally the hunting lodge of a Portuguese king—is adorned with a galaxy of works by notable artists and artisans, finely furnished, and embraced by extraordinary (though not private) gardens. Its public rooms are regal. There are 70 abodes, 8 of which are suites; the best: Queen Amelia; it costs about $420 for 2 suiteies per night. The excellent cuisine is matched by a cellar where reportedly 200,000 bottles of wine sleep. Service is amiable but s-l-o-w. Tennis; 2 pools less than a mile away, but they do not belong to the hotel. If time permits, and if you have a rented car, make an excursion from Lisbon to this gem for at least 1 overnight. Start at about 10 a.m. on the heavily traveled inland main highway north; stop for a leisurely lunch at the charming **Pousada Do Mestre Afonso Domingues** in **Batalha** and please don't miss the fantastic next-door 14th-century Gothic Cathedral; head for **Coimbra** and turn off at **Mealhada** to conclude this 145-mile jaunt. (To save money you could lodge at the Estalagem and visit the Palacio for the noon meal only—but your departure would have to be earlier.) Because both of these places are so popular, be certain to nail down your room reservations in advance.

CALDAS DA RAINHA, 50 miles north of Lisbon, is famous for its colored glazed tiles (*azulejos*) of Moorish influence, its pottery, and its bustling fruit market. It also boasts one of Portugal's most beautiful parks, with trees that are hundreds of years old. **Hotel Malhoa** is perhaps the only passable hostelry. **Patio da Rainha** is best for meals.

CASCAIS This resort is 14 miles from Lisbon. It is dominated by the colossal, 19-story, 400-room **Estoril Sol.** Towering mightily near Cascais Bay, it dominates the skyline for miles around. For youngbloods, group leaders, and modernists, it also dominates the social life of the area. Its vast skein of entertainment or pastime facilities include a terraced Olympic-size pool, kiddy pond, artificial beach with tunnel access under the road, bowling lanes, Turkish bath, sauna, discotheque, 5 bars, a beauty parlor, barbershop, and 2 banquet-conference rooms for 1200. Lobby and reception are effectively redone in Moorish style; 10th floor nerve center with spacious lounge, panoramic restaurant, bar, card nook, and ballroom; each level hued in different color schemes. Book away from the "front," because of the railroad and auto traffic noises. ☆☆☆☆ **Albatroz** is a tranquil retreat that has mutated from a cozy inn to become a 40-room air-conditioned hotel with pool. The site is one of the finest along the cliff-high coast. Moreover, the refinement and manifest sense of private luxury evoke an alluring mood for the traveler wishing to avoid the big, the brash and the highly bruited addresses. **Cidadela** is unusual in concept and fair in execution. You may choose between hotel-style living or private apartment-style living with connecting-door units stretchable from 1-to-7 person occupancy. (A small but well-stocked downstairs supermarket can furnish the comestibles for your fully equipped kitchenette.) Inside-outside dining area; glass-fronted and poolside bars; large terrace adjoining main floor; beauty salon; 2 boutiques; garage and parking space. For the wayfarer in search of Portuguese P. & Q., this haven probably will be suitable to most trippers. **Estalagem do Farol** is close to the sea at Estrada da Boca do Inferno 7; most of its 11 units face the tides. On this latest round, the 87-kip **Baia** seemed commercial, clangorous, and too well used. **Residencial Solar Dom Carlos** is an elfin haven in the town itself. Grand roster of 13 bedchambers, all with bath; chapel renovated; striking 18th-century dining room. **Residencial Na. Sra. Das Preces,** with the same ownership and prices but different management, is a converted mansion in the most elegant local residential area. The furnishings in its 17 nests, all with private plumbing, are also simple and practical. *Fado* is performed here nightly from 10 p.m. up to dawn, depending upon the clientele and the outside groups that come to listen. The whitewashed 53-room **Nau,** the tall and functional 120-nest **Equador,** the 19-apartment **Nuno Filipe,** and the humble **Albergaria Valbom** are the other choices.

Food? ☆☆ **Baluarte** is a haunt of monied sophisticates. Promenade-sited with sweep of harbor; avant-garde, semicircular bar at ground level; gracious, window-wrapped dining room with small terrace up 1 flight; music nightly, with dancing thrice weekly; versatile menu with costly tabs; closed all day Monday and Tuesday for lunch. A smoothly professional, upper-bracket operation. ★★★ **Pescador,** a 2-minute stroll from the port behind the fish market, is also superior. Trappings of rough nautical life cover the walls; the atmosphere is refined but almost sporting in its informality; the attention can't be faulted for a place of its type; and the cuisine—both in preparation and volume—is savory. Outstanding value in an outstanding fisherman's hut. ☆☆☆ **Beira Mar,** also on rua des Flores, is noteworthy for its sea-oriented gastronomy. On the same mall, **O Pipas,** a few doors farther into town, is perhaps even more attractive in a gimmicky fashion, but I found the cookery fourth-rate by comparison—and at very little difference in outlay. The garlands of garlic, the false wine tuns on the walls, and the maritime come-ons somehow seemed artificial here. **O Batel** (Travessa das Flores, opposite the fish market) is situated in a tiny courtlike square, also away from the sea. Two immaculate rooms (18 tables) divided by arches and colorful Portuguese draperies; beaming staff who fairly bust to please in their friendly but fractured English. **O Retiro,** located on Jardin Visconde da Luz, is noted for its Portuguese kitchen specialties and shellfish. **Beira Mar** (Rua das Flores) serves excellent fare in a cozy ambience, but be sure to ask prices if you order special items not listed on the menu.

COIMBRA, the fourth city, is ancient, beautiful, and serene. It spreads itself lazily over one big hill, rising from the banks of the Mondego River (the longest that has its source in Portugal) to a dominant clock tower at its cap. The nation's largest university, with more than 12,000 students, is here; its 150,000-volume library alone is worth a special trip for bibliophiles. The Old Cathedral, the Santa Cruz Church, and the spellbinding Machado de Castro Museum with relics dating from the 14th to 18th centuries, are sightseeing classics. The famous *fado* "April in Portugal" was composed as a tribute to this two-tiered town of the "miracle of the roses": When Queen Isabel was about to offer bread to the poor, legend has it that it was transformed into blossoms. Don't miss the *"Portugal dos Pequenitos"* (Children's Portugal), a park where you'll find miniature reproductions of regional buildings. Apart from the **Estalagem** in nearby *Santa Luzia* and the **Astoria** (Av. Navarro), there's the recently inaugurated **D. Luis,** with 100 rooms, restaurant, and ample amenities. Try the air-conditioned **D. Pedro** and **Pinto d'Ouro** for decent fare or the modest **Ze Manuel** or the **Democratica** for home cooking. (In any case, save the artistic *Penacova* toothpicks for a better occasion.) Archaeology fans should focus on the Roman remains of *Conimbriga* (9 miles south). Rediscovered in 1930, this formerly sumptuous settlement unearthed marvelous mosaic floors (some of which can still be seen), imposing temples, and a forum.

ESTORIL Gambling, swimming, yachting, golf, horseback riding, trapshooting, tennis, fishing, thermal baths, dancing—the works. Less than ½-hour by car or 45 minutes by Toonerville-type train from the center of Lisbon.

The ☆☆☆☆ **Estoril Palacio** has regained its former splendor. Traditional glamour and fine antique furnishings glisten; room count at 200 bedchambers. Beautiful pool in garden with thermal water; sophisticated Four Seasons Grill, sauna, terraced bar; 19-hole free Golf Club within 2 minutes' walk (plus additional 9-hole one). This legendary house is immaculate.

☆☆ **Lennox Country Club** is a hotel—not a club, as its title implies. Here is a perfect little gem for golfers and tranquillity-seekers. It is just a chip shot from the center, on a narrow, peaceful uphill lie. Two buildings resembling a private-mansion complex (10 bedrooms in the main structure, 22 in the annex); glassed-in dining room opening to a swimming pool with its own ranch-style imbibery; lounge with small bar (pour-your-own-drinks and write-your-own-bills policies). Only residents and their guests permitted use of the public rooms, bars, pool, or cinema; complimentary shuttle services to airport, golf course, and docks; free, unlimited supply of house wines, bottled water, fruit, mid-morning coffee, afternoon tea, and a welter of other kindnesses. Write to Henrique Dias and Dias de Sousa, the proprietors, *long* in advance, because the clientele consists chiefly of well-contented repeaters.

The inland **Sintra Estoril,** a short hop from the center, is the second largest hostelry in this resort. Avant-garde, semicircular, 3-story structure; fascinating metal collage stretching across entire long wall opposite reception; large public areas with a chill factor; dining room with small tables almost lost; 2 bars; 192 air-conditioned lairs; pool, tennis, mini-golf, and more. A superior first-class house that is striking but stark and impersonal.

Estoril Eden specializes in suites—and very nice they are. All resort facilities on tap, too.

The lower first-class **Lido,** in a quiet residential zone, offers a pool, a bar, and bright topside restaurant, and 62 accommodations (7 of them 2-bedroom suites). Nice relaxed family feeling here.

Atlantico is scissored from the sea by railway tracks. The formerly disgraceful maintenance standards here have been somewhat tightened at last.

Paris exudes a fresh persona throughout. Reconstructions, renovations, and repaintings galore; 2 pools (1 heated); disco; gym and sauna.

Food? The **Palacio** is the first choice for patrician dining. **Tamariz,** on the beach, is pleasant on a sunny day—especially since the installation of the pool and locker rooms. Attractive dining terrace, plain interior; seemingly slightly on the grimy side, but not enough to throw you. The **Estoril Country Club,** open to Palacio Hotel guests, is the luncheon favorite of golfers. Wonderful view, lovely surroundings, reasonable and attractive food. The cliff-dwelling **A Choupana** in Sao Joao do Estoril presents wide windows for coastscape vistas, courteous service, gentle-to-the-tummy but not outstanding cookery, and moderate tabs.

Big-time entertainment and gaming regularly are dealt out in the **casino.** Within this massive, modernistic, park-fronted structure, you will find: (1) A Las-Vegas-type nightclub-restaurant with a surprisingly inexpensive (albeit mediocre) dinner from 9 p.m.–1 a.m., featuring a floor show at 11:30 p.m., a prairie-size stage which ebbs and flows in independent segments, and a sizzling orchestra, (2) a small nightclub, (3) a cinema, (4) 2 bars, (5) a snack bar, and (6) the gambling rooms. There are separate salons for baccarat, U.S.-style craps, boule, and a regiment of one-arm bandits for lovers of levers. Other pastimes include roulette, chemin de fer, blackjack, and French Bank. Limits vary; $1.50 minimum play at blackjack is one example. Your passport is required (no exceptions!) for admission to the gaming rooms; the entrance fee is about $3, with minimum play around $3.50 to $7 on most games; 75¢ on slot machines.

ESTREMOZ This fascinating city—famous for Roman and Etruscan-style earthenware—is easily accessible from Lisbon by car over fine highways (which will also enable you to see Evora in the same day's excursion). Take time for at least a meal or night at the palatial ★★★★ **Pousada da Rainha Santa Isabel** (Tel. 22618). It overlooks the whitewashed stucco houses amid awesome beauty of an era that will never return to Portugal. The building is a living museum of aristocratic antiques, furnishings, paintings, and art. Directly adjoining are a glorious ancient chapel and the medieval apartment of a long-ago queen; ask Reception to arrange a quick visit to both, because they are fascinating. Another couple of choices (at lower rates) are the 15-room **Pensao Residencia Carvalho** and the smaller **Pensao Mateus,** which are clean, simple, and good for the budget. If the pousada is too full to take you at mealtimes, try **Aguias d'Ouro;** the high quality and low prices are appealing. Another worthy candidate is **Ze Varunca.** You might also like to take the 24-mile drive to the **Pousada Santa Luzia** in *Elvas,* near the Spanish frontier, for its famous 4-course lunch. This is by far the leading gastronomic center in the entire region. The prix fixe is about $27 per person.

EVORA This one's a sleepy little town near the Spanish border, with the 2nd-century Temple of Diana, quaint monasteries, all sorts of things dating back to the Romans. Here is one of the keystones in the development of Portuguese history. The ★★★★ **Pousada dos Loios** (Tel. 24051) is not only a sightseeing must but a great reward if you have time to spend the night. It is composed of ancient courts, thick walls, arches, and vaults—the former convent of Loios. A number of the rooms were cells in the fifteenth century. Some units with painted walls and ceilings, some with terrace, all with bath. The cuisine places its accent on dishes of the immediate region—very interesting, but not for anyone without a sense of culinary adventure. Otherwise, try the **Fialho** (Trav. das Mascarenhas 14) or **Cosinha de S. Humberto** (rua Moeda 39). Lower-priced places for overnighting include the **Planicie** plus the super-saving **Pensions Riviera** and **Giraldo** or the **Hotel Santa Clara.**

FATIMA Atop a mountain range called Serra d'Aire, this is the scene of the celebrated religious miracle in which Mary appeared before three peasant children on repeated occasions during 1917. The site is 107 miles from Lisbon, a strenuous one-day round trip. The **Shrine of Our Lady of Fatima** (built next to the Cova da Iria) attracts thousands of pilgrims from all over the world, especially on May 13 and October 13. The basilica, with its 200-foot tower, is topped by a crown of bronze weighing 7 tons, plus a huge crystal cross. Try to see the night procession when hundreds of pilgrims bearing candles or torches walk silently around the immense square. Multilingual Father Juan Villanova will be happy to be of assistance to you if you need further information or help. This dynamic and jovial priest enjoys conversation and promised special attention to readers of this guide. While here, don't miss the wax museum, composed of 28 religious scenes. You may stay at the 51-room **Pax,** the 59-unit **Santa Maria,** the similar-in-size but cheaper **Cinquentenario,** the **Tres Pastorinhos,** the **Hotel de Fatima,** the **Pensao Zeca,** the **Beato Nuno** (operated by the Carmelite Fathers; 8 rooms with bath, 60 with shower, 65 roomettes; many altars; English-speaking priest always on duty), or any of the 20 small, modest pensions of which the **Floresta** seems to be the brightest petal. Parasitic commercialism thrives at the outer fringes of this monument to faith.

FIGUEIRA DA FOZ, a major seaside resort, is 123 miles north of Lisbon. Splendid beach; imposing promenade; facilities include a gambling casino, a big open-air swimming pool, scads of hotels (the 70-room **Costa de Prata** and the 36-unit **Wellington** are the newest; the **Atlantico** and the **Soto Mayor** are good apart-hotels; of the older crop the **Grande Hotel da Figueira** is the leader, followed by **Estalagem da Piscina, da Praia,** and **Albergaria Nicola**). For a meal, hop over to the neighboring fishing village of *Buarcos* and try the sea fare at the oceanside **Teimoso;** you can swim from the fine beach here too. I recommend **Calema** for both Portuguese and French cuisine; it boasts its own orchestra and daily show. **Sagres** specializes in seafood; **Piscina da Praia** is a solid all-around bet; **Adega da Quinta** features grilled regional fare. The natives here are so proud of their mammoth strand that they claim this is the only place in Portugal where they could guarantee 10 or more square meters of beach per visitor. Summer attractions galore, informal and animated in season.

GUIMARAES "Aqui nasceu Portugal" (Portugal was born here) can be read in big characters on an ancient wall in the main square of this enchanting village. Here, 32 miles north of Oporto, was the nation's first capital and birthplace of its first king, Alfonso Henriques. Its **castle** (main tower built after the Norman invasion in 996) is regarded as the foremost monument of this nation while the 15th-century **Palace of the Dukes of Braganca** reveals the influence of various styles imported from Northern Europe. Its collegiate **Church of Our Lady of the Olive Tree** (of incredible beauty) served as seat to the former Royal Chapter. In fact, a stroll through the town is a time warp into the Middle Ages. Or you can travel further back into history by visiting the archaeological ruins at **Briteiros,** of pre-Roman origin. **Santuario da Penha** (Sanctuary of the Rock) is situated 1800 feet above sea-level. Adequate overnighting at the new 50-room **Pousada de Santa Marinha da Costa,** the **Pousada Santa Maria da Oliveira,** or the 63-room, modern, tall, functional **Fundador Dom Pedro. Nicolino** is recommendable for its amiable staff, good food, and low prices. Across the charming main square, unpretentious **Cervejaria Martins** will serve you a trencherman's beefsteak, fried egg, rice, tomato, ham, chips, and one beer for the princely sum of $6. **Vira-Bar** is also a fair choice, followed by **Jordao.**

GUINCHO, 20 miles from Lisbon and 4 miles beyond Cascais, is the site of Cabo da Roca, the most westerly point on the continent. Don't miss the exquisite ★★★★★ **Hotel do Guincho,** which commands one of the most glorious settings of any hostelry in the land. Its cliff-high perch is flanked on either side by bowls of golden sand rising from the breakers up into the gorse-covered dunes. It was restored in the 1600s, and later updatings to this sparkling antique gem were effected without altering the original tone or structure to any appreciable degree. Each of its 33 rooms is different—most with balcony, 3 large suites with fireplaces (#309, 310 or 312), all with air conditioning, many with carved vaulted stone ceilings. Some furnishings dating back 350 years. The lunch in its elegant seafront dining room was nothing short of superb, at a surprisingly reasonable price. Be certain to reserve long in advance *summer or winter*. The neighboring **Muchaxo** has 24 modest bedchambers. The **Estalagem** has 13 simple, clean rooms and the same view but far less color.

As said above, for dining it's the **Hotel do Guincho.** Elegance is the word. Very highly recommended for discriminating voyagers. Much more informal, the nearby combined **Muchaxo Restaurant** and **A Barraca Bar** draw knowledgeable excursionists from miles around and seat 400 guests of all descriptions, economic brackets, nationalities, and sizes; swimming pool adjoining; service excellent and friendly; food excellent for its inexpensive category. It is packed to the scuppers when the weather is right. **Porto de Santa Maria** is excellent for fish. **Arriba,** on the seaside cliffs before you reach Guincho, is nice for sunning and poolside lounging, but for little else. **Forte D. Rodrigo,** on the road to Sintra, specializes in fados.

LISBON

(Lisboa, pronounced "LISH-boa") is the capital and heartbeat of the Republic and one of the most international and charming metropolises in the world. It's relatively small for its importance—only about 1 million people—and there's a small-town air about it, particularly in the winding little streets of its Old Quarters. The contrasts are striking: luxurious hotels, an overcrowded airport, epicurian food, shops overflowing with opulent goods from 5 continents—and centuries-old poverty between the cracks in the plush facade. Historic treasures and cultural arts abound. The jewel in its crown is the 752-foot figure of "Christ the King," with arms outstretched, which rises on the opposite bank of the Tagus facing the city. As its nexus, here *is* Portugal—because this land has room for only one nerve center.

ATTRACTIONS

The most impressive and beautiful tourist sights in Lisbon and the suburbs are the Coach Museum (a unique collection of vehicles; usually functioning 10 a.m.–1 p.m. and 2:30–6:30 p.m. in June, July, Aug., and Sept. and to 5:30 p.m. during other months), the Old Moorish Castle (Castelo de S. Jorge), and that part of the Old City adjoining the Castle called Alfama. Go escorted to the latter, and in daylight; see the Popular Museum and a slice of life left over from the days of Columbus; the National Art Gallery is the repository for the historic talents of the land. Gulbenkian Museum offers Rembrandt, Rubens, and superb Middle Eastern artifacts; the Tower of Belem (the 16th-century starting block on the Tagus for many of the ancient explorers); Jeronimos Monastery (burial place of Vasco da Gama, kings, poets, and Portuguese heroes); the neighboring Naval Museum, which has many beautifully restored vessels as well as early aircraft; Se Cathedral (the capital's oldest church, built by Portugal's first king, D. Alfonso Henriques; a Romanesque resident of Lisbon since 1147); a trove of gold and silver objects can be viewed upon request). The National Costume Museum contains outstanding civil garments, a sparkling collection of the 18th century, and Coptic fabrics of the 4th and 8th centuries while the Madre de Deus Church displays not only its own beautiful self but one of the best assemblages of antique tiles (15th to 19th centuries) in Europe. The interior is incredibly resplendent and shouldn't be missed. Museums rest in the capital on Mondays, while Queluz Palace is shuttered on Tuesdays and Sintra Palace on Wednesdays.

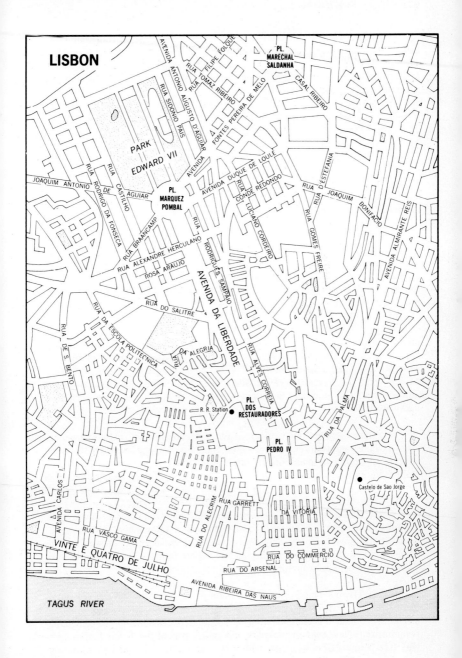

632 · · · PORTUGAL

From Dec.–June top operatic stars perform at the romantic 18th-century S. Carlos Theatre; concerts also are given here as well as at the S. Luis Municipal Theatre. There's dancing at the National Ballet Company and the Gulbenkian Foundation offers concerts and ballet by top artists from early fall through late spring at very low admission fees.

For a holiday in Portugal involving sun, swimming, dancing, all sports, old-fashioned loafing and/or big-league gaiety, Lisbon isn't your dish of tea. The experienced traveler, particularly during the hot months, splits his or her time between the capital and escapes to such neighboring resorts as **Estoril, Cascais, Guincho,** and **Sintra.** These areas are described later.

HOTELS

Today's room tariffs are appreciably below those of their North American counterparts—and dramatically below the scales in the hubs of Europe. Meals are also a great bargain if you dine on local products such as fish and fowl rather than on imported fancies.

☆☆☆☆☆ **Intercontinental Ritz** • is the most imposing hotel in the capital. Architecturally, its 300 air-conditioned, soundproofed rooms and 300 baths are sweeping in dimensions. In decor, it is a sumptuous contrast of old and new. A nonsmokers sixth floor is now available; attractive Grill with French cooking plus the Veranda and the Snack Ritz with piano and classical guitar; outdoor dining in summer. Excellent service by minions who have been here for many years.

☆☆ **Meridien** • within a block of the Ritz, boasts bold stairstep architecture, a white marble lobby with a tiered fountain, a glitzy mirrored Brasserie with clever illumination and quite a few snack and lounge corners, plus a health club. Bedrooms are not very large but textiles are appealing and the mood is attractive.

☆☆☆ **Sheraton** and **Towers** • is another sound choice for devotees of American-type living. New lobby and reception in salmon tones; interior Alfama Grill; Caravella Coffee Shop (very perky); penthouse bar. "Tower" means upper floors with executive rooms and breakfast lounges for floor residents. Well run and unusually inviting for such a large house.

☆☆☆ **Tivoli** • This Portuguese version of an American operation is commercial in tone, but its airy, fresh public rooms and its conservatively modern and well-maintained accommodations are so attractively done that impersonality is minimized. New entrance; carpark and garage part of the Tivoli-Jardim complex (see below); all units clean, with bath, radio, TV outlet, and air conditioning; varied color schemes; many handsome marble baths. A beautifully viewful rooftop terrace-grill-nightclub combination overlooks the slope to the river, with a cheery fireplace for cool months and a patio for summer tippling. Outdoor heated circular pool; tennis court. The service is keen; it is masterminded by veteran director Alfredo Coelho Fernandes.

☆☆☆ **Altis** • which gives the impression of a Scandinavian hotel transplanted intact to Iberia, has expanded and warmed up its welcome with a snack area and pool, a 1200-seat convention hall, a 400-seat auditorium, a health club, and a shopping center. Dark marble lobby in sedate burgundy tones; window-lined penthouse Grill; appealing Girassol restaurant at treetop level; Herald Bar; bedchambers with minibars, good solid furniture, satellite TV, and marble bath. Much enhanced by its building program.

★★★ **Lisboa Plaza** • has a subdued lobby with inviting cottage windows; sumptuous lounge; attractive adjoining Grill; soothing Bar in soft greens and whites; Coffee Shop; 100 small, simple, but well-done rooms; private car parking. Excellent use of colors is the highlight here.

Diplomatico • near the Ritz and Meridien, is another upper-category choice. It provides 90 latchkeys and plenty of appeal.

Novotel • part of a vast medium-priced chain, offers 250 units, an outdoor pool, both a restaurant and grill as well as a bar. This one is fresh and satisfactory for the reasonable outlay.

Avenida Palace • in midcity is struggling against so much antiquity that I have doubts that any New World voyagers can yet appreciate its creaky status. The excellent staff is kind and well-meaning in both the living sectors as well as in the Old World restaurant. Nevertheless, the few patches of modernity, such as the entrance, lobby, and several other areas, are not enough to warrant a position with others in its price grouping.

☆☆ **Alfa** • is located in the direction of the zoological gardens. Rooms divided into 181 singles, 21 doubles with large beds, 377 twins of varying types, 4 suites and one vast Presidential Suite, which has half the square footage of a normal private home. Ground floor with 18th-century Pombalino restaurant plus the rustic A Pousada room, the Labirinto bar, a shopping arcade and garden; barber and beauty parlor; garage; second floor with open-air swimming pool, 2 squash courts, sauna, gym, physical therapy, snack service. While the expansive congress facilities attract many conventioneers and business travelers, its scope is broad enough to encompass the full range of tourism.

☆ **Tivoli-Jardim** • is just behind its alma mater the Tivoli, and preferred by some travelers. Set-back construction insuring extraquiet and insulation; independent reception desk; easy parking; orange and blue lounge; woody snack bar with a magnificent Lurcat tapestry; cozy dining room with white bricks; mezzanine bar; rooftop solarium; full air conditioning. Very good for its category.

☆ **Holiday Inn** • offers a metropolitan air of sophistication rather than the motel ambience one might expect from this chain. Glass and beige marble lobby; handsome Vascoda Gama restaurant; rather spare bar; and ample size bedchambers with fresh color schemes. A reasonable buy.

Embaixador • ("Ambassador") is very central. Bandbox lobby; tasteful, quiet lounge up 1 flight with little bar; 9th-floor, L-shaped, self-service restaurant pleasant in appearance; hairdresser and barber; 96 rather cramped accommodations without special character but with air conditioning.

Roma • seems to be a rather crass sleeping factory. Very noisy location; commercial lobby with glass-lined boutiques, neon signs, and jazzed-up appurtenances; panoramic 10th-floor restaurant, bar, and solarium its best feature. At least it is air-conditioned.

Principe Real • comes up with a tranquil address in the upper town, an unimpressive entrance and facade, and some of the kindest hotel personnel you are likely to find on your travels. Viewful 5th-floor breakfast room with 10 tables—a knockout; A-plus maintenance from cellar to rooftop; 24 units, each with private plumbing, wall-to-wall carpeting, odd-shape configurations, and bolts of clashing cretonnes; TV in all units; lounge but no full restaurant. Except for the cramping of the sleeping segments, this one has a unique allure.

Miraparque • is agreeable enough in some ways, but the feeling of choppiness in its layout is such that everything seems distressingly squeezed to those who like s-p-a-c-e. The mood is sedate but dark, possibly even gloomy.

Florida • Portuguese textiles and regional hues throughout; lobby in gray, red, and blue, with adjoining wood-paneled bar; cool dining room facing plaza; Grill serving a la carte selections from 9 p.m.–3 a.m.; umbrella-dotted terrace for breakfasting or imbibing now buffeted by more and more traffic noises.

Dom Carlos • is a semicircular house, at the edge of a small park, offering reasonable amenities.

Fenix • provides full air conditioning, a Spanish-style Bodegon (taproom), a commercial patina, inadequate elevator service, and tiny, tiny rooms in jocular colors with equally small baths.

Mundial • is much in the middle of things—too much so, from the standpoint of noise. This house caters to tours and to business people. Pleasant roof-garden restaurant.

Presidente, the **Jorge V,** the **Flamingo,** and the **Impala** are not very inspiring. **Principe, Reno** (adjoining), and **Excelsior** (best of the lot) are typical representatives of the flock of smaller havens that sprang up to lure the mass influx of holidaymakers. Basically they do their jobs quite well. The **Lutecia, Metropole,** and **Rex** are all adequate; the cookery is often their weakest point.

The **Capitol,** with fair rates, draws many older clients; book on its air-conditioned 7th floor. It is sited on a cacophonous corner.

Praia Mar • *pried away from the water by a superhighway at distant Carcavelos (almost in Estoril)* • suffers from its off-the-sea location, but boasts compensatory comforts and amenities. Subdued ambience; public rooms air-conditioned; splashworthy pool; large 8th-floor glass-bound restaurant with a wonderful vista; 2 bars; lounges; small nightclub. Handful of little suites in its overall complement of 143 accommodations with confined dimensions; sparse furnishings. Except for its unfortunate situation, this one's basically sound.

★★ **York House** • *Rua das Janelas Verdes 32* • a converted 17th-century monastery plus a much newer annex, is very, very special. Homelike atmosphere within its cloistered confines; inconvenient suburban situation; hard-to-find, inconspicuous gate; tiny reception area; intimate, half-tiled main dining room; cozy bar. As an informal and friendly hideaway, here is one of the best "pension" choices you can find in the city. Make reservations long in advance.

Residencia America • *across the street from the Sheraton Shopping Center* • is another outstanding bet in this price group; 7-floor operation with lounge, bar, restaurant, TV room, and visual sweep; 56 nests with 1 to 3 beds and 54 baths ample-sized but not spacious; clean and tidy upstairs. Worthy for the outlay.

As we were going to press, a new hotel was about to be inaugurated on Avenida da Liberdade, 300 yards from Rossio Square. **Pullman** will boast 171 units (including 2 suites); 9 conference rooms, 2 restaurants, and a full panoply of modern facilities. A welcome upper-moderate addition smack in this city's heart.

Lisboa Penta • *2 miles from both the city and the airport* • is packed with nearly 600 rooms in 18 stories of building. This busy-busy bee is essentially patronized by multinational transient trade. Air-conditioned; massive lobby; dramatic Passarola Grill; 2 bars; partially self-service Coffee Shop; heated pool; shopping arcade; accommodations well planned, comfortable, and impersonal.

RESTAURANTS

☆☆☆☆ **Tagide** • *Rua da Academia Nacional de Belas Artes* • in the ancient Chiado district probably provides the finest independent cooking in the city. Moreover, the mood is that of a distinguished Old World establishment. Spotless polished brass banister leading to its entrance; long curved room with window tables viewing the Tagus; sparkling chandeliers; menu of international as well as national dishes. Professional attention that is also kind. Very reasonable prices for such high quality.

☆☆☆☆ **Intercontinental Ritz** • offers the beautiful Grill, which is far and away the most elegant hotel dining facility in its aura; savory too is its cuisine. Proper dress is *de rigueur*. Costly by local standards but a joy in its suavity and urbanity.

☆☆☆☆ **Tivoli** • penthouse is also outstanding. Woody, clublike atmosphere with huge windows viewing the town and the Tagus; excellent on every count.

★★★ **Altis** • offers a rooftop grillroom with a sweeping vista and less than breathtaking cuisine. Go only for the scenery—or when you have a cold.

☆☆☆☆ **Aviz** • *Rua Serpa Pinto, off Rua Garrett* • a legend among the independents, remains a beautiful spot and an impressive place for entertaining. Premises 1-flight up; handsome oak-and-quilted-leather bar with globe sconces, velvet upholstered chairs, green brocade wall-coverings, and a small vitrine displaying a novel pocket-watch collection; 3 dining rooms, 1 in beryl and 2 in gold; sophisticated atmosphere and fashionable clientele; somewhat haughty service standards. For Portugal it is very expensive.

★★★★ **Tavares** • *Rua da Misericordia 37* • is again among the city leaders. And now that it has refashioned itself, it sparkles but with no loss of traditional grace. Purported to be the oldest and most aristocratic restaurant in the capital (founded in 1784), it still maintains most of the same refined yet cozy ambience that originally made it so popular. The Lobster Montiverde is a gustatory delight—if price is no object. Extensive menu. Costly.

☆☆☆☆ **Casa da Comida** • *1 Travessa das Amoreiras, 5 minutes from Ritz* • gets the runner-up vote. Three of its glass-lined walls border a lovely interior patio with a blue-and-white pool and greenery. Down a few steps is its lush, richly decorated bar-lounge segment with the polished intimacy of a fine private club. The 13 tables make an L directly on the fringes of this central oasis. The Pate Ovas of red fish roe was unusual and very, very good; turbot was delicious—and its almond cake a wonderful sign-off to a marvelous meal.

★★★★ **Da Leone** • is atop the ramparts of S. Jorge Castle. Open only for lunch—but you can linger—and with the city's most enchanting vistas. Excellent cuisine at surprisingly low prices.

☆☆☆ **Bachus** • *Largo da Trinidade 9* • This one (with a Bachus statue to welcome you) maintains a prominent status on the capital hit parade. Chic brass and wood decor; small wine museum displaying, too, the house vintage. Lots of mirrors; intimate ambience. Ask for their delicious Bachus Beef, shrimp on the spit, or Espetada a Chiado.

★★★ **Cota D'Armas** • *Beco de S. Miguel 7* • in the heart of Alfama, specializes in *Pescada na Cataplasma* (hake cooked in copper pot) and *Bife do Lombo* (filet mignon) done in cream and coffee ($13 each). Delightful—and air-conditioned. Access by car is most difficult so I suggest you stop at Rua Terreiro do Trigo and then walk up a short distance through narrow Rua da Sao Pedro. Free Fado songs and guitar in summer. Closed Sun. and lunch Mon.

☆☆☆ **Escorial** • *Rua das Portas de Santo Antao 47–49* • is modern in concept. One room with a counter and quick service; the other with wood walls, vertical metal strips, globe lamps on polished steel brackets, and fireman-red tablecloths. Drinks cart for premeal sippers; shellfish specialties; attractive and clever presentation; rushed but smooth service. Reserve ahead, but still expect to wait in a cramped corridor until a table is cleared.

☆☆☆ **Gambrinus** • *Rua das Portas de Santo Antao 25* • is an old-timer that remains right up at the front of the pack. Entry to a seafood display; long bar leading to a split-level, arch-ceilinged dining room. Handsomely brightened; principal wall featuring a colorful Portuguese abstract painting; 23 tables; extraordinarily agile service; well-prepared cuisine. BUT since I was charged so much for shellfish here, I consulted Lisbon chums who avowed that neighboring houses were preferable for such dishes. On this same lane they recommended **Escorial** or **Sol Mar** for sea fare or **Solar Dos Presuntos** (top of the street) for popular priced Portuguese dishes, especially "shellfish rice." The window displays are equally convincing.

★★ **Caseiro** • *Rua de Belem 35* • seems to be Lisbon's favorite corner for young executives and media people. Convenient to the neighboring Coach Museum; usually crowded with customers patiently waiting to be seated at dwarfish, elbow-to-elbow tables. Rustic decor; superior Portuguese cuisine; overwhelming desserts; fast service.

Chester • *68 Rodrigo Fonseca, in the neighborhood of the Ritz* • is a steakhouse. Cellar bar with bold, diagonally striped carpets; fresh airy lounge; ground-floor restaurant with wooden coffers and paneled walls; placemats recalling scenes from the U.K.; engaging touches such as candles floating in vases surrounded by flowers. The service was superb, but alas, the meat can be tougher than a buffalo shank.

☆☆ **Michel** • *Largo de S. Cruz do Castelo 5* • is a converted artist's studio with white walls, terracotta floors, and piped classical music playing through its several rooms and bar-lounge. Interesting, ambitious menu; very low prices for the superior cuisine; friendly. You'll enjoy the meal and strolling through this hilltop area.

★★★ **Faz Figura** • *Rua do Paraiso 15-B* • resides high in the Alfama district (but low in cost) overlooking the harbor cranes and shipping channels of the Tagus River. Two rooms with leather Chesterfield banquettes, large windows, air conditioning, and a wonderfully posh, clublike atmosphere; expansive 14-table open terrace with an awning for summer diners; exceptionally kind reception; attentive service. Shrimp cocktail is delicious; the Steak Portuguese is cooked in a casserole with boiled potatoes and smoked ham; the tiny Squids Gratine are lovely.

Pabe • *Rua Duque de Palmela, 27-A* • means "Pub"; decoratively, it is one of the most stylish establishments you'll find in the land. Half-timber exterior with stained-glass leaded windows; first room with open beams, pewter plates, rich woodwork. Don't make the mistake of going to the rear chamber through the saloon doors, where the atmosphere oppressively suggests an Edwardian parlor.

Antonio • *Rua Tomas Ribeiro 63* • in the shadow of the Sheraton, is a corner site with two rooms; pick the one farther back. Ink-block molded ceiling in blue and white; inset planter boxes; always busy with schools of hungry Portuguese who swim in for its excellent piscatorial preparations.

Frascati • *Padre Antonio Vieira* • is where a former chef, maitre, and 2 captains of the Ritz decided to create their own restaurant 2 blocks from their hotel. Only about 30 seats; almost always a queue; moderate tabs for Italian-style cookery. It fully merits its high popularity.

Delfim • *Rua Nova de S. Mamede 23* • is low-priced and rewarding. Unpretentious white-and-blue-tile decor. I suggest fried pork with clams, grilled turbot with tartar sauce, and the house dessert. National cuisine and ambience; friendly staff. Excellent for its category.

Cortador ("Butchershop") • also known as "Oh Lacerda!" used to be okay—but no longer, emphatically. On my last look at this steak house in which the clients pick their own cuts of meat, the atmosphere reeked of contrived touristy "quaintness" and the meal was clearly substandard for the price.

A Primavera • *Travessa da Espera 34* • is a tiny budget favorite. This one has 2 long tables and 1 small table, tiled walls, an open kitchen, and stools for seats. Closed Sunday; a whopping meal (including wine and service) in down-to-earth surroundings for a song; excellent for the type. **As Velhas** • *Rua c. da Gloria 19/21* • and **Oriental** • *Rua Sao Juliao 132* • lunch only, also bat high in this league.

Bairro Alto (High Quarter) Restaurants

Ancient Lisbon can also be found in Bairro Alto, which, together with Alfama and Mouraria, is one of the capital's most typical quarters. Right at the heart of the city, it was founded in 1513, soon developing into the favorite spot of nobility. Afterward, especially during the last century, it was converted into the residential area of the working class. Its narrow, cobblestone streets and alleys, its *varinas* (fishmongers) and laden carts create a market atmosphere. It also has a nightlife that focuses on fado, a few streetwalkers, unpretentious restaurants, *tascas* (snack havens), and numerous small bars. The following "short list" (selected out of 120 candidates) comprises some of the better choices.

Tascas

Baralto • *Rua Diario de Noticias 31* • Cod minho style. **Primavera** • *Trav. da Espera 34* • Filets of hake Primavera. **Tasca do Manel** • *Rua da Barroca*

24 • Beef chops. Prices, house wine included, range between $7 and $12 at the three tascas.

Moderately Priced

Bota Alta • *Trav. da Quaimada 37* • Royal cod ($8–12). **Mata Bicho** • *Rua·Gremio Lusitano 18* • Rabbit Algarve style ($8–12). **Cocheira Alentejana** • *Trav. Poco da Cidade 19* • Roast suckling pig ($9–14).

Upper-Moderate

Adega do Teixeira • *Rua do Teixeira 39* • Grilled fish ($15–25). **Pap'Acorda** • *Rua da Atalaia 57* • Shellfish with bread soaked in their sauce ($12–20).

Fado

Lisboa a Noite, Arcadas do Faia, and **Painel do Fado** (see following "Night Life" section for a more complete description).

NIGHT LIFE

Fado. No traveler should leave Lisbon without visiting one of the world-famous *fado* restaurants—birthplace and home of the heartrending folk music so beloved by the people. These are the "taverns" (for want of a better word) where women in aprons or potbellied characters in sweaters will suddenly burst forth in these stylized, haunting, provocative laments. Informal atmosphere; adequate food; songs which will never leave you. *Reserve early everywhere.*

Machado (Rua do Norte 91), beneath its touristic skin, offers a personality and drive that carries it over into the dimension of captivating talent and genuine worth. Okay, so there are the usual manifestations·of nightclub artifice. But as a reward you will hear some of the nation's top performers for voice, instruments and mood. The pause between sets is minimal. Waiters don't push. The wine and cheese are good; the cuisine is routine. The music is what inspires and this they do very, very well.

Lisboa a Noite (Rua das Gaveas 69) is a solid candidate—but the key is to go late; after midnight is best. Whitewashed den under arches; open tile-lined kitchen at one end; guitars and copperware on the walls. Solid local fare; *fado* renditions every 30 minutes after 11 p.m. (the only carp is that one waits too long between sessions); the soul-buffeting voice of Fernanda Maria. **Senhor Vinho** (Rua do Meio a Lapa 18) is owned by one of the great *fadistas* of recent times, Maria de Fe. The cooking here seems to be above average—an easy achievement since in most Portuguese nightspots the grub is substandard. **Painel do Fado** (Rua S. Pedro de Alcantara 65/69, in the upper town) is a long downstairs room with a bar at a still lower level. The handsomely pillared sanctum displays oil paintings, carpets, colorful table settings, candles in pewter, and rose-toned lighting. Well-dressed waiters; excellent *fado,* with interludes of organ, guitar, or piano music. **Parreirinha d'Alfama** (Largo Chafariz de Dentro) is much lower on the musical scale although many tourists roll in here. Overcrowding and poor ventilation seem to be its chief drawbacks. **A Severa,** on the same street as Lisboa a Noite, is the monotonously insistent choice of almost every concierge and taxi driver in town. They've got a point, at least concerning the musical renditions. **O Faia** (Rua da Barroca) is where you will hear everything from "My Bonnie Lies Over the Ocean" in Danish to very beautiful native songs to the latest mod-*fado.* Check your bill and take your Tums. **Taverna del Rey,** at the base of the Alfama and near the waterfront, evokes the flavor of a neighborhood pub. Both male and female musicians with excellent instrumentalists; low prices; authentic, though rawboned. **Adega Mesquita** (Rua do Diario de Noticias 107) pans out favorable food and very occasional portions of *fado.* **Timpanas** (Rua Gilberto Rola 22–24), offers dances, songs, and piano melodizing; not bad. **Luso** (Travessa da Queimada) is usually crawling with rubberneckers; you can do better. **O Forcado** (Rua da Rosa 221) is yet another in the something-for-everybody category. Ths music is professional, but the gimmickry is overwhelming. Group pilgrimages seem to have sapped its viability.

Porao da Nau (Rua Pinheiro Chagas 1-D) has dancing as its big drawing card. **Cova da Onca** (Liberdad 248) means "The Jaguar's Cave"; it's popular for romantics; no show.

Nina (Rua Paiva de Andrada 11) is cavernous in size so you'll feel pretty lonely if you go in at the shank of the evening when traffic is slack. Small international cabaret (matinee from 6:30 p.m. to 7:30 p.m.; small show at 8 p.m.; reopens at 10 p.m.; more shows at 2 a.m. and 3:30 a.m.; closing 5 a.m.); untampered whisky and fair prices; don't trek there before 12:30 a.m. at the earliest.

Maxime (Praca da Alegria 58) comes up with tatty surroundings, plenty of solo gals for solo gents, wheezy shows, seminudes (1:30 a.m. and 3:30 a.m.), souvenirs, and drinks that might sharpen your choppers to needles.

A Cave (Avenida Antonio Augusto de Aguiar 88) is *the* quick turnover den in the city. Instead of having to build up the boy-meets-girl rapport by the usual routine of soaking up a ½-dozen drinks, here the lone fox can stoll in, sip a quickie, and toddle off with a vixen 5 minutes later. Cellar setup; peppery combo; no show; restaurant service if desired; tiny quaffs of questionable origin.

Fontoria (across the square from Maxime) teems with "hostesses" who usually announce their approach with "Cigarette, please?" (Actually, it is a pathetic scene because the tough economic conditions in this country have forced many women into degrading circumstances. Bar girls here really *need* the money.)

Hipopotamo (adjoining Hotel Eduardo VII) is where you might wish for (or grow) leather-lined eardrums. Combination snack bar (open all day) and dancing oasis (functioning until 2 a.m. *if* the traffic warrants it); records only; noise level only 3 bels lower than the amalgamated decibels of New York's subway. Closed Sunday; inexpensive. **A Lareira** (Praca das Aguas Livres 8) and **Calhambeque** (Rua Conde de Sabugosa 11) are rated highly by the local nocturnity. Both are colorful and moderately priced. **Millionaire** (Rua D. Francisco Manuel de Melo 30–B), naturally, is a bit more expensive. **Whispers**

(Av. F. Pereira de Melo 35) is not as soft-spoken as its name implies, but it's fun. **Banana Power** (Rua de Cascais 53) attracts a young following; good for singles. Other disco precincts include the modernistic **Mundial** (Rua M. Ferrao 12-B), where the tone is proper for visitors of any age, the ultra-private and ultra-costly **Stone's** (Rua do Olival 1), where you'll pay about $50 minimum, the **Beat Club** (Rua Conde de Sabugosa 11F), where you can beat it up daily, even on Sunday, **Charlie Brown** (Av. S. Cabral 39) and **Archote** (Rua D. Filipe de Vilhena 6D), which is the lowest in cost and possibly in value, too.

SHOPPING

SHOPPING HOURS: Mon.–Fri. 9 a.m.–1 p.m. and 3 p.m.–7 p.m. Sat. closings at 1 p.m. Shopping centers (see below) open 7 days a week until midnight.

BEST AREAS: The "Chiado" district encompassing Nova do Almada, Rua Garrett, and Rua do Carmo; the "Baixa" section running roughly from the Rossio Sq. to the Tagus River; and the Rua da Escola Politecnica. Now the **Bairro Alto** zone and the **Praca das Flores,** once the flower market, are attracting attention.

SAVINGS ON PURCHASES: The 17% **IVA** is refundable from each store where you buy goods that cost a minimum of 11,000 escudos. The Portugal Tax-free Shopping Service oversees this. Merchants working within the scheme display red and green stickers that say Tax Free for Tourists. Ask them about how the Tax Free Cheques are reimbursed. It is very easy. **IVA** on Madeira is somewhat less, ringing up at just 12%, but, of course, that's refundable too. You can get back 19% on any gold objects costing more than $98, which is irresistible.

NOTE · · · In August 1988 a fire raged through the Chiado precincts and nearly 50 businesses were destroyed in this historic neighborhood—Lisbon's worst tragedy since the 1755 earthquake. Shopping goes on normally now with the rebuilding well under way.

ANTIQUES: **Solar** (Rua D. Pedro V 68–70) is normally a fruitful first stop for the aficionado. **Xairel** (Rua D. Pedro V) could be another winner. If you don't find what you're after in either of these, browse up and down the same street through a number of interesting alternates.

ANTIQUE FURNITURE COPIES AND LEATHERWORK: For a unique experience, tour the magnificent **Fundacao Ricardo do Espirito Santo Silva** ("Decorative Arts School Museum" at Largo Das Portas do Sol 2), a glorious treasure house of perfect reproductions of 17th- through 19th-century European furniture plus Portuguese silver, tiles, Arriolos rugs, and other masterpieces. (It has been whispered that most of the copies in Versailles were manufactured here.) Deliveries take months; please be prepared for high-key hustle and bustle. Here's a landmark!

CERAMICS AND PORCELAINS: Lovely stocks at **Vista Alegre** (Largo do Chiado 18). They're worth the attention of any collector; artisans create contemporary stylings or re-create the traditional motifs of Portugal. **Sant' Anna** (Rua do Alecrim 91A) features, among other things, tiles that are faithfully reproduced from antique models. At your instructions, the borders on shades will be painted to match the design on any lamps that catch your fancy—a charming decorative fillip. **Viuva Lamego** (Largo Intendente Pina Manique 25) is into its second century in the ceramics realm. You can reckon on quality—continuity, too, obviously. **Fabrica de Loica de Sacavem** (Av. da Liberdade 49–57) offers handsome big tile pieces, and **Ana** (Hotel Intercontinental Ritz, 2nd floor) has an enchanting selection of pottery, antique tiles, and a small stock of Vista Alegre porcelain.

GOLD: the best bet in the country. The law says that 19 carats is the minimum weight that can be sold over the counter. Of the many purveyors here, the nation's oldest and most respected specialist is **W.A. Sarmento** (Rua do Ouro 251).

PORTUGUESE HANDICRAFTS: **Casa Quintao** (Rua Ivens 30) is known for its Beiriz and Arraiolos rugs. Other centers are **Casa Regional da Ilha Verde** (Rua Paiva de Andrada 4) and **Centro de Artesanato** (Rua Castilho 61). However, this last one would also be my last choice.

MADEIRA EMBROIDERIES, ORGANDIES, AND TAPESTRIES: **Madeira Superbia** (*Lisbon's* Av. Duque de Loule 75A and Hotel Intercontinental Ritz; in *Estoril,* Hotel Estoril Sol; also in *Faro*) is THE house, in our unqualified opinions. Every piece of its richly wrought stocks comes direct from its venerable studios and "factory" in the island capital of Funchal. This progressive enterprise has expanded its very extensive range of tableware to include full lines of linen dresses, silk and linen blouses, fine handkerchiefs for both genders, and daintily designed children's wearables. Also awaiting your inspection are floral needlepoint chair covers, and both petit and gros point evening bags. Colorful regional tapestries, into which every thread is hand-embroidered, have long been one of Madeira Superbia's most famous specialties. Art connoisseurs will find rugs and wall hangings that are remarkably duplicated tapestry copies of the paintings of classic and contemporary masters. Splendid!

SHOPPING CENTERS: There are numerous so-called commercial centers that have sprung up. They stay open from 9 a.m.–12 p.m., 7 days a week the year round, including holidays. The **Imaviz Shopping Center** is across from the Hotel Sheraton. Of more recent vintage is the **Centro Comercial das Amoreiras** (Avenida Duarte Pacheco), about a ten-minute walk from the Ritz. This one boasts over 300 establishments within its precincts, plus an exhibition hall.

Things NOT to buy: fabrics, perfumes, and any imports.

MADEIRA

This island is one of Europe's last unspoiled outposts. Here is the uncontested queen of the West Atlantic islands (there are 8)—far more ingratiating than the spoiled Canaries and the more starkly primitive Azores.

Now for some capsule facts to pinpoint this ocean fairyland: *Situation?* About 1½ hours' flight by jet from Lisbon, north of the Canaries and 300 miles off the coast in the warm current of the Gulf Stream. *Inhabitants?* The 280,000 *Madeirenses* are warm, outgiving, generally with ripe-olive eyes that reflect their sunlight and inner tranquillity. *Climate?* Benign almost year round. The mid-winter sweater-weather is only 15 degrees lower than the 78-degree mean of high summer. Early November to mid-December is when many northerners like it best (good sun, a few scattered showers and frequent winds to freshen the foliage, and no tourist mobs). Clouds are most likely to linger in June. No other European region—the Greek islands, Mallorca, Sicily, or elsewhere—offers such a salubrious aura and tempered clime. *Topography?* A bastion of rocky cliffs, soaring hills, and lustrous vales which burst with fruits and gay flowers. Mountains peak at well over 6000 feet. Ridges crisscross its 35 miles of length and 14 miles of breadth. The coastal loop contains 2300 curves, with its longest straightaway exactly ¾ths of a mile. (If car-sickness afflicts you, sit in the front seat, stop at *miradors* to break the trip, and take extra fresh air.) The profusion of wild and cultivated flora is breathtaking. Bananas, sugarcane, grains, blossoms, and tropical fruits blanket the rich earth near the coast. Thick forests mat and tint the higher reaches of the slopes. *Language?* Officially Portuguese, of course—but English is spoken in hotels, restaurants, and shops. *Connections?* All by air, except for calls by cruise ships. You can chug out to neighboring Porto Santo, however. The heaviest traffic is from and to England (see following "Note") and Lisbon; Air Portugal also maintains a lesser route between Las Palmas (Canaries), the Azores, and Funchal. Santa Catarina Airport is 15 miles from the capital and located on cliffs with the sea at either end of the runway—an exciting beginning and end to your Madeira vacation. *Food?* Pretty limited. Scabbard fish, often misnamed "black swordfish," is the most renowned and most exotic specialty. This extraordinary long and narrow critter is brought up from 3000 feet on drag lines. It is beautifully delicate and savory. The *caldeirada* is a piscatorial stew with dark minestrone undertones. *Espetada* is a local variation of a shishkebab with a maniacal affinity for salt, garlic, and bay leaves. *Lapas* are limpets that are grilled with butter and served in their mossy shells. Excellent! Especially delicious silver bananas are indigenous here. *Bolo de Mel* is the mouth-watering regional honey cake that will keep for a year. Cod, a dietary mainstay throughout this nation, now comes principally from Norway.

NOTE · · · If you are coming from overseas, try to break your trip in London and take a one-week charter tour to Madeira. Under normal circumstances, this adventure is worth far more than its very reasonable price. Thomas Cook (587 Fifth Ave., N.Y., NY 10017) or Kuoni (11 E. 44 St., N.Y., NY 10017) would make your arrangements.

CITIES? Funchal is the heart and capital. Magnificent bay; home base for ⅓rd of the populace; houses stair-stepping up, up, up, up the mountainside. Its dwellings accent the Portuguese addiction for vivid shadings and hues. The sidewalks are surfaced with intricately patterned small cobblestones. The world-famous fireworks display every New Year's Eve illuminates the great crescent of the bay in stunning and awesome cascades of flame. For many weeks beforehand nearly every householder plots his own pyrotechnic wizardry for this thunderous 15-minute climax of his year. An ambitious "Lido" project has been created in the hotel district with 2 pools, snack bars, and 5 levels of seaside facilities that accommodate 3000 sun-toasted hides. Given the Portuguese talent for architecture, this vies with the best strands in Europe.

HOTELS

In nearly every case except Reid's, the hoteliers have allotted between 90% and 95% of the rooms to tour groups and between 5% and 10% to independent trippers. Although this seems an anomaly, the great disbalance in mass traffic has not spoiled the capital or the outlands to any notable degree. Almost all of the hostelries require demi-pension, with full pension as a moneysaving alternate.

☆☆☆☆☆ **Reid's** • one of the last of the fabled Great Hotels of character, tradition, and elan. Commanding position crowning a promontory; ornate dining room; exquisite glass-walled Garden Restaurant gazing at 1 of its 2 pools and the sea; absolutely *superb* cuisine; glass-lined dance floor with wonderfully romantic view; tennis court; elevator to private beach. A masterpiece of innkeeping.

☆☆☆ **Albergaria Quinta de Penha de Franca** • is a walled enclave in the hotel district, a private home that gradually expanded to its present comfortable size, simultaneously improving its views in this neighborhood. Poolside service; lunches only; very cozy and very special as a nonhotel concept.

☆☆☆ **Sheraton** • belies its almost offensive facade with a warm and ingratiating interior. The Churrasco Grill, in terracotta tones, has the mien of an ancient tavern. A larger restaurant in 17th-century decor is well designed but seemingly swollen with group traffic. The tearoom seating 80 is a bit more chummy. Lobby on 6th floor; bathing plus 2 pools (one heated); sauna, massage facilities; amusing little indoor-outdoor pub facing the port; active night life in the Farol, a glass-lined drum-shaped rookery above the water. Three categories of bedrooms, all with balconies; gothic doors with wrought-iron hinges set into lava-stone arches; rich furnishings; baths with stall showers and tubs; superb illumination.

★★★ **Casino Park** • is the spectacular creation of the renowned architect Oscar Niemeyer, who positioned every brick and pebble of Brasilia. Vast glass-fronted linear building on stilts with literally acres of lobby and lounge fastness; restaurant so expansive it seems a part of the sea—and as cold; spacious greensward by the heated pool; 2 tennis courts, solarium and gym; 400 clean-lined, comfortable, and sterile units. Impressive it is; warm it is not.

Windsor, Raga, and **S. Joao** • are contemporary style, fresh, and devoted largely to group traffic. They are good but not very personalized.

☆☆ **Savoy** • is a huge rambling establishment turned out in a melange of decorative styles. There is a certain regal warmth that seems to please the British. Glass-bound 7th-floor restaurant—only slightly smaller than the state of Montana—eye-boggling in its *nouveau richesse;* lavish rooftop Fleur-de-Lis Grill with terrace; better skilletry than in many competitors; airy abodes; 2 heated pools; pontoon to island for Atlantic bathing and waterskiing; 2 tennis courts; more. If flamboyant is your bag, this one has it.

☆☆ **Madeira Palacio** • is a 9-level, twin-winged giant that is shielded in front by a restaurant and a heated pool. The decor and furnishings throughout are attractively executed in a tastefully modern mood. Within its deluxe precincts you will find a whopping list of amenities for its guests of all ages, from the hand-holding atmosphere of its Viceroy Grill, to its 3 bars, to its horseshoe-shaped pool, to its cheerful, air-conditioned accommodations, to its tennis courts, to more than a dozen other places. Although it is sited on a headland perhaps 1 mile from the center (free shuttle buses are provided), I prefer this fetching house to the Sheraton, Casino Park, and Savoy.

Quinta do Sol • a block up the hillside from Reid's, offers an attractive ground-level restaurant, an intimate bar, a panoramic rooftop "Garden" solarium with snackery and cafe for light fare, a pool, and 107 domiciles that include 2 suites on every floor. Good for its tariffs.

Villa Ramos • also is perched up on the mountainside. Pleasantly subdued lobby; amiable split-level dining room; heated pool with terrace and bar; full air conditioning. Among its 107 lodgings, the front ones are excellent except for their tiny baths and the rear ones are somewhat cramped.

For longer stays, you might prefer an apart-hotel. Three attractive ones of this ilk are the **Regency, Do Mar,** and the **Navio Azul.**

Baia Azul was about to open during my latest visit. It's located on Estrada

Monumental; a promising collection of 215 units as well as all the up-to-date facilities of a first-class candidate (including a heated pool).

The remainder are not very exciting; they are adequate at best.

★★★★ **Atlantis** • 18 stories and richly accoutered and one hour from Funchal beyond the airport at *Discovery Bay,* is gorgeous but fiscally it must be a hopeless White Elephant. Fully air-conditioned; suave, spacious, elegant lobby separated by glass from stunning indoor heated pool and to one side from b-i-g Z-shaped outdoor pool. Copacabana Bar, buffet lunch apex and saunas; attractive Madeira Grill; gaily colored Restaurant Algarve; Bar Madeira and more formal Bar Estoril; disco; tennis; nautical sports; much more. Its 300 comfortable, cheerful accommodations come with 2 king-size double beds, bath, balcony, and majestic views of the sea and surrounding mountains. Next to Reid's, unquestionably this is the best luxury hostelry on the island—but ask yourself if you want to be at a site so isolated from outside action.

Dom Pedro • is directly below the Atlantis at the edge of the village of *Machico.* First class and pleasant enough, it suffers the same difficulty of location.

RESTAURANTS

Agreement is virtually universal that the Grill Room and the Garden Restaurant of **Reid's** remain the most elegant dining establishments on the island. The Viceroy Grill of the **Madeira Palacio** plays upon charming intimacy. Its motif reflects contemporary stylings, with flowers on tables, nibbles of crisp salad, and embroidered overcloths. The attention is also superb. As for other hotel dining rooms, please refer back to the previous section for those descriptions.

The *independent restaurants* in the center of the capital range from fairly good to poor, probably because so many of the hotels require full pension. A friendly reader bids us try **Casa Velha** and **Casa dos Reis,** which will be high on our list for our next island sojourn. Dropping in quality, **Caravela** offers a minor bonus with its up-1-flight, glassed-in "terrace" and viewful midcity span of the harbor. Menu in 5 languages; Aveleda *vinho verde* excellent; solid but not outstanding. **Charola** might be more agreeable if you are looking for a bit more refinement. **Tonel** and **Avenida** also try for a tony mood. **Estrela do Mar** resides smack in the nexus of the traffic ebb and flow. Dark hole-in-wall lined with seaborne flotsam; candles by day and night; menu on a dried fish hide; seating at community tables. The next-door **Romana** is also pleasant. Its dishes are more international than local. **Montanha** has gained a following among meat eaters. **Boa Vista** and **Kon Tiki** are routine.

Up on the **Monte** slope, **A Seta** is noted for grills and visual thrills. And down at the seaside, the **Club de Turismo** is fun for a swim, a snack, or a more ambitious meal in the intimate dining rooms or on the veranda.

SIGHTSEEING

Flora, sea, and mountains are everywhere; you'll even find wildflowers growing between the cobbles in the roads and orchids cascading from construction sites. Most visitors give highest priority to the famous *Funchal* snowless sleigh ride. Take a taxi for the l-o-n-g climb to Terreiro da Luta. After drinking in the glorious panorama of the capital at your feet, climb aboard the wood-runnered sledge and bump down, down, down—2 miles of "tobogganing"—through the narrow and picturesque streets. There is absolutely no danger, because 2 men race alongside, guiding the clumsy vehicle in the proper direction (or pushing it whenever the going gets too slow). The price is about $10 per person. For motorboating along the coast, the *Amigos do Mar* is available for charter. Within the hub there are 4 more traditional lures: (1) The tiny Aquarium (in the Municipal Museum at Rua da Mouraria), (2) the Municipal Museum itself (regional natural history), (3) Cruzes (antique art, with a fine orchid house adjoining), and (4) Arte Sacra (religious art). You can arrange to look a big one through the Madeira Game Fishing Center; yacht chartering is available; just go down to the marina and ask, or speak to your hotel concierge. Whether you play or not, you'll certainly want to see the Casino, a wonder of modern architecture soaring stunningly beside the Casino Park Hotel. Open every day in the year except Christmas from 8:30 p.m.–3 a.m. or 4 a.m.; French and U.S. roulette, blackjack, craps, chemin de fer, French Bank, baccarat, and 120 slot machines; penthouse Panorama Restaurant with show; Boite-Nightclub Zodiaco with late cabaret for night owls. *Don't forget your passport!* Then there's the Public Market, which is a ball if you see it sufficiently early in the day.

One of the most delightful excursions is to *Porto Moniz* on the extreme northwest corner of the island—a *gorgeous* drive to a small, sleepy fishing village with a spectacular natural pool. (Avis rents good little cars for the twisty roads; the office is in front of the Sheraton.) Here you can lunch among the fjords and cliffs at the **Cachalote,** a breathtaking extraterrestrial setting. Take bathing attire and swim in the other-worldly chalices of rock—an experience of a lifetime! Hall porters often recommend a meal stop at the **Aquario** in *Seixal,* but I found it a dull and overpriced roadside rest. Another awesome target is *Curral das Freiras,* a tiny, primitive, fascinating hamlet cradled in a valley of towering peaks, where you might get the vivid impression that you are 3 days' journey from Lima, Peru, in the heart of the Andes; it is almost impossible to believe that this sanctuary from another century is less than *45 minutes* from the bright lights of the Big City. **Canical** is promoted as a whaling port. 'T'ain't so, and it ain't the least bit interesting either. If you take a round-the-island drive, a pleasant stop for a coffee is the **Cabana** at *S. Jorge,* way up in the hills of the north coast. Then a dash back to Funchal takes about an hour.

SHOPPING

SHOPPING HOURS: Same as Lisbon.

BEST AREAS: Camacha and Rua Dr. Fernao de Ornelas are just the ticket—many of the better establishments are ranged along here for serious purchasing or just plain window-shopping.

DEPARTMENT STORES: The Victorian **Maison Blanche** is small-townish in tone, quality, and styling. Its personnel couldn't be kinder.

EMBROIDERIES: The embroidery and organdy studios and "factory" of **Madeira Superbia** (Rua do Carmo 27-1, up 1 flight) make a serene, venerable complex of large, plainly decorated rooms in which are displayed for sale the hosts of beautiful products made by this ranking establishment. For further information, please turn back to the description of Madeira Superbia in the "Lisbon" section. Charming Sra. Farra at **G. Farra & Co. Ltda.** (Rua da Ponte S. Lazaro 8, with branches in most of the top hotels) also has a fine selection—different from the Superbia creations.

HANDICRAFTS: The very best shop in all of Madeira is **Casa do Turista** (R. Conselheiro Jose Silvestre Ribeiro 2), where you will find a cross section of Portuguese handicrafts that is unequalled even on the mainland—ceramics, porcelain, pewter, brass, copper, embroidery, wickerware, and lots, lots more. There are a wine-tasting room, reproductions of a country shop ("venda") and an old-fashioned rural living room, plus a thatched shed in the basket-weavers' tradition. Safe shipment to any part of the world is guaranteed. Ask for owner-manager Jose Barreto. Here is an absolute *must* that NO traveler should miss!

WICKERWORK: At the village of **Camacha** (about a half-hour drive from Funchal), virtually all of its 3600 inhabitants seem to be busy weaving wickerware for the store-factory in the main square. Surely somewhere in these sprawling premises you should find what you were looking for in this fantastic assemblage.

WINE: A call at the famous **Madeira Wine Company** is rewarding.

NAZARE (pronounced Nah-zar-ay), about 3 hours from Lisbon, is a colorful little fishing village and summer resort of whitewashed houses, tourist-conscious fisherfolk, and narrow streets which all run down to the sea. Unfortunately, it receives the expected tidal flood of rubberneckers. Legend ties the famous local tartan costumes to a crew of Scotsmen shipwrecked here centuries ago, while a more recent version talks of Wellington's troops, who stopped here during the Napoleonic wars. You may buy this unique hand-woven cloth along the beach.

Wonderful swimming; fishing—from sardines to fighting *carapau;* boats rentable at reasonable rates. There's a funicular to the Sitio (Upper Town), where you'll find a lighthouse, a church, and a glorious view. Lodgings? The **Hotel Mare** is fairly contemporary, the **Nazare** is pretty good, followed by **Da Praia,** the very plain **Dom Fuas,** the **Central,** and 11 pensions. **Mar Bravo** offers seafood; so does **Beira-Mar.**

OBIDOS   This totally walled city, a fascinating jewel, is an easy excursion hop up from Lisbon or a worthwhile overnighting point if you can secure accommodation in the **Pousada do Castelo** (Tel. 959105). The hostelry contains a mere 9 rooms, half of them with private bath, but it is so overwhelming in its beauty that we urge you to spend some time here if you can. This installation is built into the fortress tower—at the same time both intimate and grand. A visitor has the feeling that he is part of the court of a noble household. In the lower village, also within the crenellated walls, is the **Estalagem do Convento** for an emergency. Adequate inexpensive accommodation can be found at 2 *albergarias:* **Rainha S. Isabel** and **Josefa de Obidos.** A mildly athletic tourist can circumnavigate the entire village walking on wide tops of the walls. In the hamlet itself there are numerous bars, several churches, and, of course, the inevitable souvenir shops. As a possible alternative to the above stopping places, you might find space in the **Mansao da Torre,** 2 miles out of town toward Santarem, or at **Casa de Hospedes Madeira. D. Joao V, Alcaide,** and **Lidador** are discreet local restaurants.

OPORTO   through a curious twist, has long been the accepted name applied by *foreigners* to this nation's second city—possibly a relic of its heavy early British influence. The Portuguese, on the other hand, always call it **Porto.** This massively industrial gateway to the ocean, bustles with determined activity. It is built from top to bottom on a dome-shaped hill; exits of its famous 2-tier bridge hit the riverbank both high and low.

Don't fail to visit the wine lodges at *Vila Nova da Gaia,* across the Douro. Of approximately 30 such installations, I suggest the old and prestigious **Ferreira** caves, where a team of 8 multilingual guides will show you the cellars and explain the process of winemaking. Phone Mr. Fernando Xavier (Tel: 300866) in advance; readers of this guide will be shown the "old bin," the cooper section, and be privileged to sample the prize wines. Ferreira very likely will offer a house souvenir or, if you prefer, a rebate on a 45-minute "Three Bridges Cruise" along the river (April to Oct., except Sat. afternoons and Sundays).

The deluxe-grade **Sheraton-Porto** would be my choice today as the tops in town. It boasts 153 rooms, 2 suites, 2 restaurants, 2 bars, a health center, and amenities galore, while the **Meridien** offers 232 rooms and 9 suites (1 presidential, 1 diplomatic, and 7 junior), restaurants, bar, disco, health club. Both represent splendid contributions to this oft-neglected city. Contemporary **Porto Atlantico** is situated in the Boa Vista residential district. Full air conditioning; 3 floors; decor vaguely Scandinavian; adjoining Galeria restaurant; popular avant-garde bar; 2 pools (1 covered); 2nd and 3rd-level rooms with their own balconies. Next comes the antique but steadily improving **Infante de Sagres,** a block from the main square. **Ipanema, Dom Henrique, Castor,** and **Inca** come next in my list.

Food? Nothing north of Lisbon touches the **Restaurante Portucale** in its 13th-floor penthouse. Three walls of v-a-s-t windows to down-nose the city and river; decor striking but charmingly *intime;* sculptured walnut ceiling with buried spotlights; center service area; silken attention; open every day in the year. So sophisticated that it qualifies among the top rank anywhere in Europe. Next comes the restaurant at the **Infante de Sagres;** try the tenderloin if you are a beefeater. Another contender is the **Galeria** in the **Hotel Porto Atlantico.** The chairs are fitted with boxing-glove leather. Well above average cookery. Nearby, in the same Boa Vista area, you will find the **Steak House,** which specializes in you-know-whats. It is pretty good. Finally, **O Escondidinho** is a solidly established, no-nonsense local institution.

PALMELA   Situated 25 miles south of Lisbon and 5 miles from Stubal in the midst of a winegrowing district, this ancient village is renowned for its 8th-century Moorish castle, peaking 700-feet high on the summit of the Arrabida. Its age predates the nation itself. Within its fortified walls, ★★★★ **Pousada de Palmela** will delight your senses with its mysterious blend of austerity, coziness, and serenity; 20 impeccable rooms; magnificent salons; and a well-regarded formal restaurant. Director Monteiro-Marques, himself full of vivacity and cheer, is striving to add those elements to this imposing monument. His success is evident. Try not to miss this enchanting hamlet and its namesake fort.

SESIMBRA   Portugal's main resort for sea angling (especially swordfish) is located only 45 minutes from Lisbon via the gloriously panoramic bridge. The **Hotel Do Mar** nestles 75 yards above the sea and this still unspoiled fishing village. Vaguely Hawaiian-style construction; buildings stagger up a hillside for successively better vistas of the bay; entrance at top, with access to 4 tiers of rooms and terraces; glassy crown composed of a 2-section restaurant with a sweeping view. The shoreside **Espadarte** offers 80 modest rooms with private baths or showers—some with balcony. Its restaurant—quite naturally—specializes in sea fare. About 3 miles away, **Estalagem dos Zimbros** has the advantage of being closest to the imposing **Cabo Espichel.** It has 35 clean bedchambers, a swimming pool, and 2 tennis courts. **Angelus, Ribamar,** and **Pedra Alta** are simple eateries.

SETUBAL   fifth in size and the principal fishing port of the nation, is a sardine-factory center that is a half-hour ride from the capital on the express highway and within sight of the previously described *Palmela.* The Church of Jesus, in which the pillars are twisted to resemble fishermen's ropes, is so curious it shouldn't be missed. Above the town is the **Pousada de Sao Filipe** (Tel. 523844). It is built into a glorious, 16th-century mountaintop fort with a magnificent view of the area and surrounding hills. Only 15 small but pleasant rooms, 8 with Atlantic vistas (and some without windows due to the thickness of the walls); fine little tile-lined restaurant overlooking the port; bar under vaulted ceiling; covered terrace for tea and evening libations. Inspirational for observing, but simple in creature comforts. Down in the city, my choice is **Pensao Casa de Sao Joao.** Another worthy contender is the **Troia** in the burgeoning Torralta project, which contains several hotels on the adjoining peninsula, as well as one of the best 18-hole golf courses in the nation. This can be reached in 5 minutes by Hovercraft, 20 minutes by normal ferry, or several hours by car. For dining, **Roda** and **Setubalense** are relatively refined choices. Frankly, however, I prefer **O Beco** for its down-to-earth regional cookery and the limitless friendliness of its efficient staff.

SINTRA This one you must see; it's less than an hour from the capital. Drive out through Estoril and the spectacularly beautiful mountain road through a national forest preserve. (For the longer seaside route, go out to Guincho). When you near your goal, climb up and up through gardens and flowering camellia trees to the mammoth Pena Palace, straight from an illustrated fairy tale, perched on a peak. Also stunning is the medieval Royal Palace, which was the summer home of the last kings of Portugal. The road curls down past an old Moorish castle atop a neighboring crest to the little town in the valley. Some of the finest *quintas* (country estates) of Portugal are here, and they are a dream. Sintra also can be reached by train from Rossio Station in the capital, which runs to and fro about every 30 minutes.

The ★★★★ **Hotel Palacio de Seteais** has a wonderful setting, gorgeous gardens, lavish furnishings, and superb cuisine. This former summer residence of a king was converted into a classically luxurious country inn with elegant public chambers and 18 dwellings. Advance reservations are almost always obligatory.

The 7-floor, 75-unit, air-conditioned **Tivoli Sintra**—a protege of the excellent Hotel Tivoli in the capital—was inaugurated to the rear of the castle. It boasts a superb panoramic restaurant. This first-class house is coming on strong.

On the road to Sintra, the historic ★★★★ **Queluz** (pronounced "Kayloosh") **Palace** is a peanut-size replica of Versailles. In its ancient, enormous scullery the *Pousada* management group (Enatur) has built a full-scale restaurant called the "Cozinha Velha" ("Old Kitchen")—and that's exactly what it is. You'll see the original spits used for hundreds of years to roast whole oxen— plus enough utensils and gizmos in fine old copper to arouse larceny in the soul. Interesting and unusual; *Cozinha*-work focused on fine Portuguese dishes, perfectly served and elegantly presented. It's about 20 minutes by car from Lisbon and well worth the excursion.

Saint Peter, paradoxically, seems to hold a sybaritic status in Sintra: The two best restaurants (in this pilgrim's opinion) are **Cantinho de S. Pedro** and **Solar de S. Pedro.**

TOMAR This area is likely to draw motorists due to its lovely situation overlooking a dam and because of the Castle of the Templars, an interesting medieval military structure. **Pousada de Sao Pedro** seems to have regained its status as a first-class inn after a period of poor management. This one will soon have a new sister, the **Pousada Convent of Christ,** which was being reconditioned during my latest rovings in this region. The well-run ☆☆ **Dos Templarios** resides in its own park and gardens. While here you must visit the overwhelming Church of Christ, the ornate, Emmanuelene headquarters of the Knights Templar, a seat of riches, intellect, and politics in Christendom. Seldom have I been so stunned by architecture as I was at this shrine. The town also offers a famous synagogue and additional attractions that make it one of the chief drawing cards in Portugal.

VALENCA DO MINHO, 9 miles from the ocean along the northern frontier, is an ancient walled town with narrow, crazily winding streets jampacked with perhaps 150 small, variegated shops for the mass Spanish trade that floods across the border to buy Portuguese merchandise at substantially lower prices than those in their homeland. In majestic tranquillity above the maddening crowd sits the lovely **Pousada de Sao Teotonio** on the crown of a hill, with a beautiful vista over the Minho River, its long bridge ever chocked with vehicles and walkers during the daylight hours and a sweep of the foreign countryside. In July and August and during the Easter and Christmas holidays, reservations must normally be booked 2 months ahead. **Pensao Rio Minho** and **Pensao Valenciana,** the only other lodgings here, are quite basic; each has 2 private baths. If you are interested in driving 4 miles to the **Albergaria Atlantico** in Moncao for one of the best regional lunches in this part of the country, then you might prefer to base at *Viana do Castelo.* In the latter, the outlying **Hotel Santa Luzia** is probably your best bet.

SCOTLAND

FOR USA and CANADA see "England."

SPECIAL REMARKS: (1) The Scottish Tourist Board (23 Ravelston Terrace, Edinburgh) is your source for any kind of travel aid. It can even arrange to find you living space with crofters and cottagers almost anywhere within the nation. (2) For pamphlets and guidance on what to see from Edinburgh's Royal Mile to Sule Skerry or from salmon fishing to hang-gliding or skiing, phone or write STB's Information Department, P.O. Box 705, Edinburgh EH4 3EU, Tel.: 031–332 2433. (3) For special requests concerning places to hunt, golf, fish, ride, sail, or you-name-it, write to Mrs. J. Ball, Tours and Travel Promotions, 25 Brunstane Dr., Edinburgh EH15 2NF, Tel.: (031) 669 5344, Telex 72165. (4) Inquire at the STB concerning the discount cards for visitors. You can also find brochures and help at the Tourist Information Office, Edinburgh's main rail station on Princes St.

TELEPHONE: Access code to USA: 010. To phone Scotland: 44; time difference (Eastern Daylight) plus 5 hours.

Within an area roughly the size of West Virginia wee Scotland offers fjords, glens, moors, mountains, prairies, heaths, bogs, rills, alpine lakes, and even Gulf Stream-nourished palm trees on its Isle of Arran—just about everything in the geography book except Himalayan ice bridges and Amazonian rain forests. This scenic kaleidoscope, only 375 miles long and 150 miles wide, breaks down naturally into 3 divisions and several clusters of islands. The *Southern Uplands*, a wedge between the English border and the Edinburgh-Glasgow line, stretch in a number of moorlike ranges from south to north—the Lowthers (or Leadhills), Moorfoots, Cheviots, and others. Sheep-rearing and woolens keep these hardworking folk out of mischief; the fishing is extra-fine, because the Clyde, Tweed, and other rivers rise here. The *Central Lowlands*, that narrow band that belts the waist of the nation, contains ¾ths of Scotland's 5 million inhabitants and nearly all its heavy industries. Edinburgh, certain Clyde lochs and resorts, and the handful of its better attractions shouldn't be missed. Otherwise, this crowded ribbon, ravished by factories, is generally joyless for the tourist. The *Highlands,* on the other hand, are among the most glorious holiday areas in the world. These granite mountains and plains, split across the center by Loch Ness and Loch Lochy, sprawl over more than half the country's terrain. Grouse, deer, salmon, trout, ptarmigan, and hare abound in their purple moors, flashing streams, turquoise lakes, and cool forests. The once sleepy Shetland and Orkney island groups have grown richer as petroleum investments burgeon. The Hebrides, Skye, Arran, Bute, and other tranquil isles—each different, each fascinating to the off-trail explorer—round out the picture.

ATTRACTIONS *Edinburgh* is the traditional base for the traveler's Scotland. Nearly every visitor starts or finishes his Scottish explorations here. If you wish to begin looking into your own family past, this is also the touchstone for genealogical discovery. **Register House** at the east end of Princess Street probably has a record of every Scottish skeleton in every closet of your illustrious heritage. Anyway, here's the spot to commence digging up your ancestry. Turn ahead to "Cities" for more details on this wonderful metropolis of dark stone and light hearts.

The lower end of *Loch Lomond* is an everlasting favorite of travelers. *Balloch,* at the southern tip, is called the "Henley of Scotland." During the milder months, twice-daily steamer sailings across the loch originate from here; it's a 2½- to 3-hour trip each way, and a lovely one. This region shouldn't be missed. If you are driving, try to pause at **Drover's Inn** at the northern junction of 4 counties; this lakeside pub (Rob Roy's mum was born in the kitchen) has been a Perthshire nip-inn since the 17th century. And it seems untouched since the first mug of ale and platter of herring in oatmeal (delicious) were set before a herdsman.

Provincial Scotland breaks down into 5 main areas: (1) The Trossachs, called the "Rob Roy" and "Lady-of-the-Lake Country" (which, like Lower Loch Lomond, is crowded during holiday times), (2) the "Burns Country," dominated by Ayr and Dumfries, (3) The Highlands, lord and master of Scottish grandeur, (4) the "Sir Walter Scott Country," from Edinburgh to the English border, and (5) the Isle of Skye and the Hebrides.

Since most visitors follow jet-propelled itineraries, I recommend this 2-day trip, with 1-day optional extension. This 48-hour itinerary allows you to sample every type of terrain and view such major sights as Gleneagles, Loch Ness, Loch Lomond, Ben Nevis, and a score of others.

Edinburgh is the beginning and end of your loop, and *Inverness,* capital of The Highlands, is your midway stop. One day before departure, if you've never tried a real Scottish Haggis (see "Food"), ask your porter to telephone the Station Hotel in Inverness and arrange that this traditional treat be waiting in place of the fish course of your dinner here; 24-hour notice is generally required. Then on the following morning, leave *Edinburgh* at 8:30 a.m., point the nose of your car toward *Stirling,* and get the lowlands along the Firth of Forth behind you as briskly as you can. At nearby *Doune,* there's an unthinkably ancient fortress-castle plus a sports- and racing-car collection of the 1920s

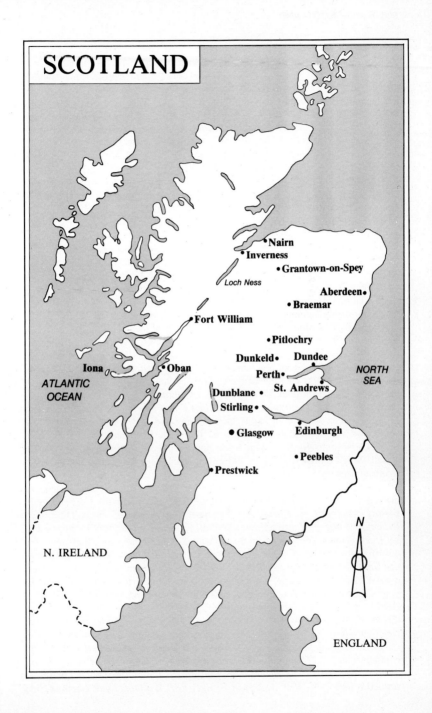

and '30s—but perhaps you'd rather push on to Gleneagles, Scotland's most fabulous hotel for a coffee break; this baronial country estate is something special. Then proceed to the Dewar's White Label town, *Perth,* for a friendly aperitif in the Highlander Bar of the Station Hotel, followed by lunch in the dining room here (the food is the best in the area). Now cut northwest along the river valley through *Pitlochry, Blair Atholl,* along glorious *Glengarry,* through *Drumochter Pass* and the *Forest of Atholl* down to *Dalwhinnie,* and onward. (Mid-April to early-Oct., the Pitlochry Festival Theatre draws crowds to its competent performances. Six plays ranging, say, from Shakespeare to Chekhov to Jean Anouilh to Noel Coward are presented Mon. through Sat.) By teatime, *Carrbridge* should loom up, and the simple, fishing-and-sporting Carrbridge Hotel should break out homemade dainties. You might want to take in the **Landmark Visitor Center** which capsulizes Highland history and lore. It has its own restaurant plus shops. One hour after you're roadbound again, you'll be in *Inverness,* where the austere but adequate Station Hotel—and your Haggis, we hope!—is waiting.

The second day you take a different, even more spectacular, route. Start no later than 8 a.m. After leaving the "Ceud Mile Failte!" sign (Gaelic for "100,000 Welcomes!") behind at the city limits of Inverness, you loaf along the *Caledonian Canal* until it opens into *Loch Ness*—and as you parallel the 24 miles of this landmark, keep every eye in the car peeled for "Nessie," the fabled Loch Ness Monster! *Loch Lochy* is next—and then, 2 miles before *Spean Bridge,* you'll pass the famed **Commando Memorial,** a stirring sight in a stirring location. Now it's time for coffee in the Milton Hotel in *Fort William.* Refreshed, stretching your legs almost in the shadow of Scotland's highest peak, *Ben Nevis,* you next take the bridge crossing at *Ballachulish,* then swoop across the magnificent *Rannoch Moor* and *Black Mount.* After the turnoff at *Crianlarich,* there's an interesting ride down *Glen Falloch* to the northern tip of *Loch Lomond,* and you now view this loch of song and story in its entirety all the way down to its termination at *Balloch.* Tea at the Buchanan Arms at *Drymen* will then be yours for the asking—and home you go to *Edinburgh,* in time for a well-earned dinner. Less than 400 miles, round trip—with about 4000 miles' worth of scenery!

For the 1-day extension, on the second morning of the trip, instead of driving to the Caledonian Canal, continue west and north from *Inverness* to *Beauly, Muir of Ord, Garve,* and *Braemore Forest;* turn off on A-832 around *Braemore Lodge,* go through *Dundonnell,* follow along the south shore of *Little Loch Broom* (not to be confused with Loch Broom and Ullapool to the north), and then sweep in a U-shape hook through *Aultbea, Poolewe, Gairloch,* and back along the lovely shores of *Loch Maree* to *Kinlochewe.* Turn southwest on A-890 at *Achnasheen,* and follow it to the turnoff for *Kyle of Lochalsh,* your destination. This is the ferry point for the *Isle of Skye* and its capital, *Portree.* (If you want unspoiled rural flavor and untouched scenic magnificence, this is it.) Round-trip bus excursions from *Inverness,* encompassing the enchanting *Isle of Skye,* operate selected days between May and September.

On the third morning, take off early for the *Kyle of Lochalsh* ferry and continue along A-87 through *Dornie, Invershiel, Cluanie Br. Inn* and *Tomdoun* to *Invergarry.* At *Invergarry,* pick up the route down *Loch Lochy* described in our 2-day tour (to *Spean Bridge, Fort William, Loch Lomond,* and eventually to *Edinburgh)*. The only thing you'll miss is Loch Ness, but honest to goodness, you'll never miss it.

These are fairly stiff hauls—but in 48 or 72 hours, you'll have a better cross section of the real Scotland than most travelers can get in a week.

Oban, a lovely little port, is one of the most convenient jumping-off points for scouting the Hebrides. Day excursions may be made to the islands of *Mull, Lismore,* and *Iona.* (The last is the birthplace of Scottish Christianity, where St. Columba preached, and where the first abbey has been restored.) Aboard the *RMS Columbia* you can take 3-day mini-cruises or hop on a car-ferry for a visit to the islands. Even shorter skims aboard 12-passenger motor launches leave at scheduled intervals from the *Oban Times* slip and glide out to *Seil Island.* There you may stroll the beach and actually pet the animals for which the isle was named. Caledonian MacBraynes' Steamer Services also run comfortable year-round circuits through both Inner and Outer Hebridean points; these include 2- or 3-day mini-cruises or a (Ho-ho-ho!) Island Hopscotch program in which you pick the places and the time ashore. Cars can be ferried, too. The vessels are solid; the comfort is sound; the food is hardy and substantial; the price is right. Local wags who thirst for a sea voyage remark that MacBrayne's steamers are all beautifully equipped "with quite a few engines" (local parlance for "bars")—and that they are, mon!

TRANSPORTATION **Airlines** Scotland is in with the excellent and widespread British Airways regarding its flying services (see "England"). Prestwick (see alphabetical listing) is the intercontinental terminus while Edinburgh Airport handles much of the European work. Prestwick offers a bus link to Glasgow and train connections onward through the British Isles. Scottish European Airways flies from Glasgow and Edinburgh to and from Brussels, Frankfurt, and Hamburg.

Taxis You'll pay about $3 for the first mile, and there's no supplement for baggage *unless it rides in front with the driver.* Tip is 15% on short jaunts, falling to 10% for lengthy hauls.

Trains Since Scotland is crosshatched by branches of the British Railways network, see "Trains" in the section on England. All facilities and equipment are pooled throughout the U.K. The popular Thrift-Tour Tickets and other bargains include the noted Circular Tours of Scotland, and Caledonian MacBrayne's Steamer Services in the West Highlands and Western Isles. *Most of these are sold only in North America.*

The *Royal Scotsman* is this nation's variation on the *Orient Express* theme. Distances are shorter, of course, but there's no shortage of luxury or scenery. A 6-day chug begins in Edinburgh and huffs and puffs all over this lovely land. Top billings: £1200 per person in a State Cabin. There are lower rates for simpler accommodations or shorter segments. Meals and beverages are included for all aboard.

FOOD The Scots love the table, and their approach to it bears little resemblance to that of the English. Specialties? Haggis (see below); Scotch broth; Cock-a-leekie (chicken and leek soup); roasted or stewed grouse or ptarmigan; fresh trout, salmon, haddock, cod, or sole; Arbroath Smokies; kippers; fried herring in oatmeal batter, or grilled herring with mustard sauce; Findon Haddock (finnan haddie) with poached egg; scones; pancakes; oatcake; shortbread; heather honey; Black Pudding (oatmeal, blood, and seasonings); White Pudding (oatmeal base); Black Bun (chewy with raisins and ginger); marmalade; many, many more. When you see the *Taste of Scotland* sign at a restaurant, it indicates participation in a program to offer many of the above specialties as well as an extra dollop of Scottish hospitality.

Meal hours: lunch, 12:30 p.m.–2 p.m.; tea, 3:30 p.m.–5 p.m.; dinner, 7 p.m.–9 p.m. or later in summer, but 6 p.m.–8 p.m. in winter. Chinese and Italian restaurants usually operate until or shortly after midnight, providing the only late-hour fare on any Main Street.

NOTE · · · No visitor can say he knows the real Scotland until he has gone through the Haggis Ceremony. This national festival dish of oatmeal, assorted chopped meats, and spices must be specially prepared, but that's easy; just call any good hotel on your itinerary 1 day before you plan to arrive, and ask them to give you a Haggis with your dinner in place of the fish course. Be sure to order hot mashed turnips on the side, and be doubly careful not to forget what the Scots call the "gravy"—straight Scotch whiskey (or malt) sipped between bites, the *only* liquid that complements this fascinating dish. Maybe you'll love it, or maybe you'll loathe it—but I'll guarantee you'll find it sufficiently intriguing for that low-cost gamble of buying it.

DRINKS   For nearly 500 years, distillers all over the civilized world have tried to imitate Scotch whiskey. But even with identical ingredients and methods—for reasons which are unclear—no foreign-produced product has ever come within hat-tipping distance of the original.

This Most Seraphic of Solaces of Gentlemen, as Samuel Johnson put it, is classified into 5 types—4 geographical (Highland, Lowland, Islays, and Campbeltowns) and the 5th chemical (grain spirits for processing). North Americans overwhelmingly prefer the Highland category, because its peat-fire-dried malt adds the distinctive smoky tang to which they are accustomed. After it is matured in casks for at least 3 years (usually 4 or 5), blending formulae are applied by each producer. There are about 3000 blends! The Scotch we drink usually contains from 17 to 45 different whiskies. The Royal Family of this kingdom are the pure Pot Still Malt runs which are *not* blended but remain in their virgin glow. Of these there are fewer than 100. Many Scots sip theirs with water; personally, I prefer it neat on a cold day and not at all on a hot day; soda is universally considered to be a sacrilege, and ice is also not quite cricket. Islay (pronounced Eye-lay) is mysteriously rich in peat, lacking in sweetness, and firmly in a class by itself; so is the smoky two-fisted 10-year-old Laphroaig (pronounced Laff-royg); Glenmorangie, at the other end of the scale, is one of the smoothest, softest, and most delightful elixirs I know. Glenlivet, Glen Grant, and Glengarry are all better known and fine. Ironically, it's sometimes a chore to find your familiar proprietary brand in the nation of its birth. Too much is exported. Bartenders, however, know their fluids intimately, so if you tell them the name of your usual back-home favorite they will pluck a similar choice off the shelf for you.

Drambuie is nectar from the Isle of Skye. Its base, of course, is Scotch, but the rest, except for mountains of sugar, is a secret. For saving his life during his attempt to regain the throne, Bonnie Prince Charlie gave the Laird of Mac-kinnon the recipe, and it's been guarded as carefully as the crown jewels since 1745.

Scottish brewers build brass knuckles into many of their products. "Prestonpan's 12-Guinea Ale" (delicately referred to, when ordered, as "a wee heavy" or "a dump") is one of the strongest ales made; it's dark, thinnish, and somewhat cloying. McEwan's, the most popular export ale, and Younger's, the leading beer, are on draft in the better pubs.

NOTE · · · When you drink with a Scotsman, say "Slans-Jevah!" (phonetic spelling) instead of "Cheers!"—and watch his eyes sparkle with surprise at hearing his traditional Gaelic toast from the lips of a stranger.

GOLFING GUIDELINES If you yearn to win a passel of Scottish pounds bet some patsy that Edinburgh is farther north than Moscow. Then if you need a follow-up, challenge your opponent to guess within 50% of accuracy how many golf courses there are in the capital area. There are eighteen 18-hole circuits *within the city limits* (located no farther than 5 miles from Holyrood Palace) plus five 9-hole rounds. And if that doesn't zap them hard enough, you can open the Edinburgh phone book and rattle off at least threescore more just for the record.

There are few things that can make you feel quite so "foreign" as teeing up on Scottish turf and not knowing the lore of the links. Soon enough you'll learn that Scots play golf with quite another style. In this windswept country, the high arc of a beautifully lofted ball is seldom observed—it might land behind you on a breezy day. Courses are seldom overwatered as in North America; either they are in a natural state or the wind dries off the rain, providing an added feature of a long bounce rather than our hit-and-stick techniques. On many courses I've trod, only the greens receive irrigation treatment. I've even entertained a notion that entire tournaments could be played with only a two iron and a putter!

Here are some tips that refer specifically to the nation's most noteworthy circuit, the Old Course at St. Andrews. The same form more-or-less applies elsewhere. Anyone can play, but you must obtain a tee-off time; in peak seasons this should be done 2 months ahead (better if its 6 months), offering several preferences (8 minutes between parties). The cost for "putting in your ballot" is £20 per round to the Starter (phone 0334–73393; Fax 0334–77036) or Club Secretary (Tel. 75757). These exalted personages are often mistaken for deities. (One wintry morning I watched as a neat, handsomely sweatered American golfer was scolded at Muirfield for not appearing in front of His Grace with a tie and jacket.) It is a waste of time to beg for space before such ridiculous pomposity, so this is why a detailed account here might be helpful. Now, you'll get back £10 when you show up, but the greens fee costs £20. September can be difficult if the Royal & Ancient is having its own meet. And even with all of the advice above, I've occasionally strolled down to the Starter Box, clubs in hand, forked over the £20 and begun to play—no fanfare at all. The same is true at other clubs, but please don't rely on that technique.

Other tips?

- Only use eight or nine clubs stuck into a pencil bag. Carts are often available and are not expensive. A few offer golf cars, but the courses are so delicate that strict maneuvering rules are applied. (A ranger has the power to evict you from the course.)
- Be prepared for the worst weather and pack along rain gear even on the brightest days.
- Don't display colorful sartorial fashions appropriate for Palm Springs. Dress like a grouse—in drab shades, tweeds, or wearing plus-twos. Un-chic is proper.
- On those blustery courses, don't speak loudly—unless you want to be overheard by someone at the next downwind hole.
- Don't believe Scottish handicaps; they're either too high or too low. (Only 3 scores are turned in each year!)
- Play with dispatch; 3 hours is par for 18 holes.
- There are no "Mulligans" in Scotland. That's an Irish term. Instead, ask for a free drive on the first hole.
- In Scotland a "foursome" means two balls and four players. To convey the American concept of a quartet of players teeing off together, you should refer to "four-ball" play.
- A "scratch" player is one who regularly makes par. Par and scratch are used almost interchangeably.
- Here are some don'ts at the 19th hole: No ice with your malt—and no soda either.
- Never display cash for bets at private clubs. Resist any urge ever to discuss business at the clubhouse.
- Women are often given special times to play and separate lounges (since they may not be invited into the mens bars or restaurants).
- In private clubs, gentlemen are usually expected to wear ties and jackets at mealtime or after play.

And now that you are armed with those disarming hints, here are some choices of links around the nation by category. Most are by the sea.

PUBLIC COURSES: Gleneagles (often considered the best parkland layouts; King's and Queen's courses here are the premium circuits), Turnberry (my pick for beauty), Gullane, Carnoustie, Dornoch, Cruden Bay, and St. Andrews (4 other fine circuits available besides the famous Old Course where golfing was born). In the Aberdeen region, tee off at Auchmill, Balnagask, Hazlehead, or King's Link.

PRIVATE COURSES: Muirfield, Prestwick, Troon, Blairgowrie, Bruntsfield, Crail, Elie, Ladybank, Deeside, Murcar, Royal Aberdeen, Royal Burgess, and Western Gailes. All accept visitors, but some tolerate women only on certain days or at certain hours of the day. That's the custom; so be it.

QUAINT GOLFING (ALL PUBLIC): Braids, Boat of Garten, Machrihanish, Stonehaven.

CITIES AND REGIONS

ABERDEEN, becoming well known as a year-round flower center, successfully blends medieval mellowness with the gaiety of a modern seaside resort. There is also a fever of prosperity as the region enjoys what might be termed a black-gold rush. Commerce and tourism are mated in creating better theater, more music, and a far more active cultural scene. Discerning admirers of whiskeys may stagger along the Malt Trail, which incorporates the glens of Livet, Fiddich, and a half-dozen more greats in the distillery realm, plus some of the most beautiful countryside of Europe. Additional trailblazers can troop the Castle Trail in the historic Gordon District running north and west of Aberdeen. Hotels are jammed with business visitors and petrodollars have caused local prices to skyrocket. The expanding limits spread along the banks of the Don and the Dee rivers and not far from the off-shore oil fields that are being developed by the nation. Between the mouths of these waterways, a 2-mile sandy beach has been dedicated to holidaymakers—perfect for Polar Club bathers who sprout walrus hair on limbs, back, and shoulders. Outstanding university, 15 lovely parks, numerous arts projects supported by the oil companies, venerable St. Machar's Cathedral; don't miss the Fish Market, one of the most interesting in the United Kingdom.

Caledonian's • zealous ownership swept in like a new broom not long ago to realize a promised renovation. Very central, edging Union Terrace; all units with bath and shower.

Royal • also in the center, offers 42 rooms, a welcoming mood, an active bar, and a substantial dining facility.

Amatola • has completed an ambitious refurbishing program. Very reliable in the upper-middle bracket.

Treetops • on Springfield Road in the west end, occupies a tranquil situation 5 minutes from the traffic nucleus; handsome dining room and better-than-average cuisine for the region; long, inviting, lantern-lit bar sided by intimate tables; fire-crackling lounge and TV nook; fitness and leisure center for hyperactive relaxers.

Dee Motel • 1 mile out on the river, deserves mention along about here. A steady construction program now puts the overall count at 75 plain but bright

662 · · · SCOTLAND

bedchambers, each with shower and toilet. Three bars, including a snack corner; pine and brick decor; comfortable lounge; motel-ish in concept.

New Marcliffe, Belvidere, and **Atholl •** are individually managed and for travelers who don't want the obvious sort of shelter. Each has a distinctive personality, more residential than hotel-like. If you don't wish to be in city center, these are outstanding choices—the order of preference being as listed.

Moat House • at *Bucksburn* plus a trio of **Skean Dhu** redoubts for motorists: one at *Dyce,* one at *Altens,* and one at the *Airport.* **Westhill Inn** also is at *Skene;* all are suburban. **Northern** and **Laurels,** both 10 minutes from the center and 5 from the airport, might fill the budgeteer's bill; the first offers chipper bedrooms in pastels with white furniture; restaurant; jigger-size bar. Both good bets at the price.

☆☆☆ **Meldrum House •** *Northwest of here, 2 miles out of Oldmeldrum •* is where Robin Duff, the Laird, is as respectful of his skillets as of his guests. Space for only 12 overnight couples, but 72 couverts for diners. Imposing gray-stone castle structure at the end of a drive lined with towering oaks and rhodo-dendron shrubs; wide greensward at its door; a deluxe target for which you should certainly reserve in advance.

Holiday Inn • has an inn-let at the Airport. Reliable for transient traffic.

For dining in the Scottish mood, the hotels seems to do a consistently high level of performance. My choices would include the **New Marcliffe** and **Ardoe House** in the upper crust, with **Tree Tops** and **Caledonian** recommendable in a more commercial grade.

ADVIE
☆☆☆☆☆ **Tulchan Lodge •** is writing a deluxe chapter in the Spey River anthology. Shooting and angling rights plus all the comfort and convenience that humanity can divine will cost you close to $2400 per week per person. It is so special that more space can't be devoted to it except to recommend it to the sporting set.

AIRTH This uninspiring village about 28 miles west of Edinburgh is proud of its pre-Victorian **Airth Castle Hotel,** which resides handsomely in its own syl-van park. What's more, it doesn't cost the Airth. Not bad in a pinch.

APPIN
★★ **Ardsheal House •** is the quiet domain of resident-proprietors Jane and Bob Taylor, eager Americans who open their 12 rooms (8 with private bath) and their great hearts to tranquillity seekers. Casual and homespun, it's on the shores of Loch Linnhe and has roots reaching back to the 16th century. Clearly, the greenhouse dining salon is one of its most arresting blossoms; the cuisine is interesting in choice and wins orchids locally for execution; ask to see some of the stunning locally made sweaters that are sometimes shown here for sale. There's a tennis court; boating nearby. For more information, write Kentallen,

Appin, Argyll PA 38 4BX. Take the long-cut drive (3 hours vs 45 minutes via the direct route) to **Timorran Castle.** What lake and seascapes! The hills of Morvern may kidnap you forever.

ARGYLL AND ENVIRONS   This region lies in the southwestern corner of the Highlands and Islands. It is the Garden Belt of Scotia, warmed by the Gulf Stream effect. Some of the most noteworthy estates that you can tour include the imposing Achnacloich and Ardchattan Priory of A.D. 1230 (both near Connel), An Cala (by Easdale), Barguillean (Taynuilt), and 24-acre Arduaine (Loch Melfort). The usual showtime for these is Apr.–Oct. They are magical. At **Kilchrenan,** sitting on a small bluff beside Loch Awe amid one of the great informal gardens of the west coast of Scotland, is the graceful ★★★**Ardanaiseig.** All of the main public rooms are viewful, and the bedrooms for its 28 guests, each with its own bath and telephone, are comfort-oriented but not fussy. The hotel supplies boats for fishing in the Loch—both rainbow or brown trout— and a picnic hamper, if desired. Also on the grounds are facilities for tennis, croquet, clay pigeon shooting; a liaison has been made in the neighborhood for golf, rough-shooting, or deer stalking. Closed from Oct. through the winter and so remote that you should be sure to reserve ahead. The **Bridge of Orchy Hotel,** 33 miles from *Loch Lomond,* is a reliable excursion stopover. You'll find friendly service and appealing cuisine. In the same county and just outside of *Strachur,* **Creggans Inn** wins hearts with its modest country charms. Situation just across the shore road on Loch Fyne; panoramic lounge; public rooms cloaked in chintz; pleasant flower-papered dining salon; adjoining woody cocktail lounge; exceptional cuisine. Of its 24 rooms and 5 private baths, ask for #22, a garret-style double. At *Inveraray,* the **Argyll Arms,** with its pier and grassy beach in front, is recommended for summer sojourns. The **George** is tops in winter, followed by **Lochfyne** at waterside. The town consists of a main street of perfect dimensions, white buildings and, above it, the Castle, which is occupied by the Duke and Duchess of Argyll. You can visit the clan's homestead (summers only) from 10 a.m.–1 p.m. and 2 p.m. to 6 p.m.—a rewarding experience, if only for the panoramic view. At the end of the Crinan Canal beyond Inveraray is the **Crinan,** an inviting port of call with delectable seafaring menus; excellent beds; oil-fired central heating. The crowning glory here is the kitchen. **Stonefield Castle,** a few miles away at *Tarbert,* offers 32 rooms with private baths. **Loch Melfort,** taking its name from its breathtaking location, is simple, substantial, comfortable, and worth a detour of any length to savor the view down the lake. Look for *Arduaine* between Oban and Lochgilphead.

BALLATER   This captivating townlet might be called the gemstone of the castle belt. Down the pike a few miles is the Queen's own **Balmoral,** where the gardens are open to public inspection (when she is not in residence). A bit farther is magnificent **Craigievar,** which was lived in until very recently and was left totally intact and furnished when the owners shifted to other digs so that everyone could share the beauty of their ancestral estate. Of course, **Braemar Castle** is next door (see our separate comments) and is viewable; the lecture tour here is superb. In the same region are **Crathes Castle and Gardens, Drum Castle,** and engaging **Banchory Museum.** There's the Z-plan **Castle**

Fraser with its extensive **Castles of Mar** exhibition. (The Z-formed structure was once widely acknowledged as the most modern defense system architects could devise.) This area is so sylvan and so enchanting that unless you had compelling reasons for settling in nearby busy, Aberdeen, I would overwhelmingly urge you to bunk here.

☆☆☆ **Tullich Lodge** • is fit for a baron. This 10-bedroom noble mansion sits tall in its own park overlooking the rushing Dee. Antiques and fine furnishings fill the twin first-floor lounges and spaciously comfortable accommodations. When they are at their best resident proprietors Hector Macdonald and Neil Bannister create an atmosphere of cheerful bonhommie; they also can produce some of the finest cuisine in Scotland and present it in one of the liveliest salons in Aberdeenshire. A beguiling retreat.

★★★★ **Kildrummy Castle** • not too distant, is surrounded by 15 acres of manicured nature and water gardens. In fact, the hotel has its name on all the fish along a 3-mile stretch of the River Don. Game for the table also frequently wears the Castle's name tag. Across the greensward is the original fortress dating from A.D. 1245. Your own comfort standards, however, are purely 20th century, while the mood is richly traditional.

★★★ **Raemoir House** • a 28-room noble mansion for sporting and relaxing types, is backed by the 1500-foot Hill of Fare plus legions of supporters who sing its praise from all quarters of the globe. The landscape around this hostelry is a chapter from *Field & Stream*. Excellent.

☆☆☆ **Craigendarroch** • is a lovely tawny-rose, towered structure with blissful Deeside scenery, ample luxury in its 23 accommodations and local game, beef, or seafood in its Oaks restaurant. Pool, children's room, beauty salon; golfing nearby at the Ballater Club.

★★★ **Invery House** • is at Banchory, almost midway between Ballater and Aberdeen (on A-93). It resides on 40 acres on the west bank of the River Feugh, a white mansion with stately-home appointments and the grace of ages. Only 30 guests tuck in, many of them devoted to sports and outdoor pursuits of the region.

☆ **Mar Lodge** • is a former royal hunting manse and judging from the clientele observed on a recent visit, its chief appeal is still for nimrods and anglers. If these are not your primary interests, you might be happier in one of the above establishments.

BANFF   is a former Royal Burgh, which means a bonus in scenic values for today's traveler. See Duff House for its Georgian Baroque mien and visit nearby *Portsoy* and *Fordyce* for their architecture, *Macduff* for its fishing atmosphere and cliffside villages such as *Gardenstown, Crovie,* and *Pennan*. The 30-room **Banff Springs** is on a lonely bluff overlooking a magnificent stretch of sea and coast. The modern lines suggest a suburban grade school; nevertheless its comfort is abundant. A car is a necessity, of course. The cozy, homespun **County,**

in Banff proper, the **Highland Haven** on Macduff Harbor, and **Fife Lodge** overlooking the River Deveron are other worthy stopovers. Drive over to *Cruden Bay* (wonderful golf course) and see *Bullers o' Buchan* and the clifftop ruins of **Slains Castle,** which inspired Stoker's *Count Dracula.* Two additional hotels of note in the region are the 100-room **Waterside Inn** at *Peterhead* and the park-surrounded **Saplinbrae House** near *Old Deer.* Then if you are up at the salty little port of *Pennan,* there's a water's-edge welcome from the Griersons at their snug little **Pennan Inn.**

BLAIR ATHOLL   This is the Perthshire stronghold of Atholl's dukes and earls. You can visit Blair Castle, which is rewarding, but try to push on rather than overnighting at the commercial **Atholl Arms** or the **Tilt,** both down on the main pike.

BRAEMAR   The leading house here is the 60-room **Invercauld Arms.** Cheery appointments; cozy lounges; many updatings; top dining spot in town; amusing Colonel's Bed buffet, with food displayed on the soldier's bunk. One of the worthier stops in the area. The **Fife Arms** pipes in next. Open all year; migrations of bus tours pause here. Creaky. The modern **Spittal** is an amiable lunch stop if you're running south through the *Satan's Slide* (formerly called Devil's Elbow; the crookedness has been removed and now it is wickedly slippery at icy periods). Inexpensive; tailored for budget ski buffs.

Near Braemar, the **Dalmunzie Hotel** on the 6500-acre Spittal O'Glenshee estate has an altitude of 1200 feet, making it Great Britain's highest hostelry. Rather bleak secluded location; facilities for tennis, golf, fishing, mountaineering, skiing, grouse shooting, and deerstalking. The **Spittal Hotel** is on the main route through Satan's Slide. Very satisfactory; no luxury.

CALLANDER   The turreted ★**Roman Camp Hotel** is on a 30-acre estate that is 38 miles due north of Glasgow, above Stirling. Formerly it was the 17th-century hunting lodge of the Dukes of Perth. Library, lounge, magnificent gardens, fascinating tiny Gothic chapel; 15 bedrooms, nearly all with private or connecting bath; 1 eminently relaxable suite. The shocking-pink annex across the drive is less luxurious. Numerous signs of corner-cutting and undistinguished nutrients. Locals love it for its tea and scones. Closed in winter.

CUPAR   This is the closest (4 miles) hamlet to **Fernie Castle,** a fresh, appealing, whitewashed fortress dating back to the 14th century. It is generally considered to be in the St. Andrews area; thus, 45 golf courses are located within its county. Lovely approach along a fir-treed lane; circular dining salon overlooking a small private loch; the Keep Bar in its own stone vault; 11 large bedrooms with TV and tea-making units. The Scottish menu and the international a la carte selections are well regarded locally.

DORNOCH   The **Dornoch Hotel,** in oddly named Sutherland (odd because Sutherland, with Caithness, is the most northerly tip of the mainland), gorges itself with tour packages. Now it is closed in winter. **Dornoch Castle,** the former palace of the Bishops of Caithness, overlooking the Firth, has been attractively converted. Both offer the celebrated facilities of the Royal Dornoch

Golf Club, plus loch-or-sea fishing, cold-water swimming, shooting, and deer-stalking. **Tongue,** in the townlet of the same name, comes recommended as a Victorian hunting and fishing retreat.

DRYMEN The **★Buchanan Arms,** Stirlingshire, is 5 miles from Loch Lomond, 36 miles from Glasgow, and 50 miles from Edinburgh. Country-house style; tartan carpets, colorful lounge, charming enclosed dining terrace; glass-sheathed rooftop cocktail lounge; 23 spotless rooms, 18 with private bath; cuisine inoffensive to mediocre.

DUNBLANE

☆☆☆ **Cromlix House** • resides on a hunting estate of some 5000 wooded acres about 4 miles north of this picture-postcard town. The Victorian mansion, with a heritage reaching to the dawn of Scottish history, has its own private chapel, antiques of museum quality, and heraldic needlepoint that enthusiasts cross the Atlantic just to view. Meals—and superb they are—are likely to be your most memorable dining experiences in Scotland. The 10 bedrooms (with private baths) are in the grand tradition of a great country house. Rates are high, but so is the quality for the rare privilege of visiting such a home.

DUNKELD

★★★★ **Dunkeld House** • (Perthshire) resides on one of the most romantic Tay-side stretches you're likely to find in all of Scotia. Entrance via an arched stone gate; a mile's drive through forest and garden to the ocher-hued mansion; lawns of Karastan neatness and lush vegetation; pitch-and-putt golf course; all facilities for fishing in that glorious river. My recent meal was pleasant but not outstanding. Sport is the theme and that it has.

★★ **Cardney House** • about 3 miles away, is a charmer in its more personal fashion. The atmosphere evokes more that of a Scottish house party rather than the cool austerity of hotel living. Everyone sits at a common table dining on farm-fresh pickin's and viewing the dales and glens of the estate. A whacky sort of place that I happen to like, but not so eccentric that any traveler with a sense of adventure wouldn't love on first sight.

EDINBURGH

ATTRACTIONS

Edinburgh Castle • Easily the most striking structure in the city, it stands majestically above the town on a huge jutting rock. At a height of about 270 feet, the castle walls offer the best panorama of the city and surrounding hills and coastline. There has been a fortress of some sort on this site since before the 7th century. When King Malcolm moved here in the 11th century, the castle was greatly enlarged. The tiny chapel on the east side of the castle grounds was dedicated to Malcolm Canmore's wife, Queen Margaret, and is now Edinburgh's oldest building; this explosive lady—and simultaneously a saint—also inspired **Mons Meg,** a 15th-century cannon. Today, the castle houses the **Scottish Regalia** (crown, sceptre, sword, and jewels) as well as the **Scottish War Memorial,** with a fine collection of historical weapons and costumes.

Royal Mile • This is the road that runs down the hill from Edinburgh Castle to Holyrood Palace, through the oldest part of the city and comprising Castle Hill, Canongate, High Street, and the Lawnmarket. Since the entire population of "Old Town" lived along these four streets, the "mile" is positively packed with wonderful historic places: The High Kirk of Edinburgh, with its beautiful crown-shaped spire, many fascinating museums, and enchanting 16th- and 17th-century houses.
P.S.: High Street used to be the headquarters for the Royal Mile Medieval Banquets, which are so popular in Edinburgh. Recently, however, they were given three days' notice to quit their premises to make way for a gay nightclub—neighboring John Knox's House, by Jove! Now all inquiries should go to Deborah Dickson (Tel. and Fax 031–663–1325).

Gladstone's Land • *483 Lawnmarket* • Something of a fancy 17th-century tenement building, this is one of the many arcaded structures that once lined the streets of the Royal Mile. Some of these buildings stood as high as 14 stories. Gladstone's Land was built in 1620, is now a National Trust property, and is open for public viewing.

Parliament House • *Upper High St.* • King Charles I had this building constructed in 1632 to replace the Collegiate buildings of St. Giles Cathedral as home to the Scottish Parliament. Today, Parliament House is used by Scotland's supreme court. In the Great Hall you will find an excellent collection of portraits by famous Scottish artists, including Raeburn. In the square: the equestrian statue of Charles II, the city's oldest.

Lady Stair's House • *off Lawnmarket, through Lady Stair's Close* • Built in 1622, this house has been turned into a monument to 3 great Scottish writers: Robert Burns, Robert Louis Stevenson, and Sir Walter Scott. Collections of letters, pictures, and interesting memorabilia of the authors are displayed here.

St. Giles Cathedral • *Upper High St.* • One of Edinburgh's greatest historical sanctums, the High Kirk of Edinburgh has not always been here as such, having boasted of cathedral status for only 5 years of its controversial history. For more than 1000 years a church has been standing on this location, earlier efforts having been burned, pillaged, and rebuilt. Here you will also find the extraordinary Chapel of the Most Ancient and the Most Noble Order of the Thistle, Scotland's lofty order of chivalry.

Anchor Close • *off High St.* • This is a fine example of the many such tiny alleys that once led to the quaint inns and public houses characteristic of the 18th century. Many of these taverns date back to the 16th century. If you ramble over to Grassmarket you'll see the **White Hart Inn,** a writers' retreat that rings with echoes of Burns and Wordsworth.

Museum of Childhood • *38 High St., opposite John Knox's house* • Here is a fascinating assemblage of toys, games, dolls, books, and costumes. Although most of the collection is from the mid-19th century, there are some primitive toys that predate the Christian era, as well as a few early-20th-century knickknacks. This museum is as fun for adults as it is for children.

Canongate Tollbooth • *Canongate* • Constructed in 1591, this is now a "People's Story" museum. Several turreted towers with outside steps characterize the medieval structure. Inside, you will review the pastimes, work and lifestyles of ordinary citizens through the last century or so.

Acheson House • *140 Canongate* • Sir Archibald Acheson, secretary of state to King Charles I, built this courtyard mansion in 1633, the same year Charles was crowned. The peak of elegance for its first 100 years, thereafter it became a huge brothel, then a home for approximately 15 families. It now houses the **Scottish Craft Center,** where you can buy all sorts of beautiful handmade articles.

The Palace of Holyrood House • *at bottom of Canongate* • Its roots go back to the 12th century as an Abbey. It became a guest house, founded by James IV, some three centuries later, and the structure was elaborately expanded to its present state by Charles II in 1671. Before Charles, Mary Queen of Scots lived here for 6 years of her exciting reign. The old part of the palace still contains her bedroom and the room in which David Riccio, the Queen's supposed lover, was murdered. Holyrood Palace is where Queen Elizabeth II

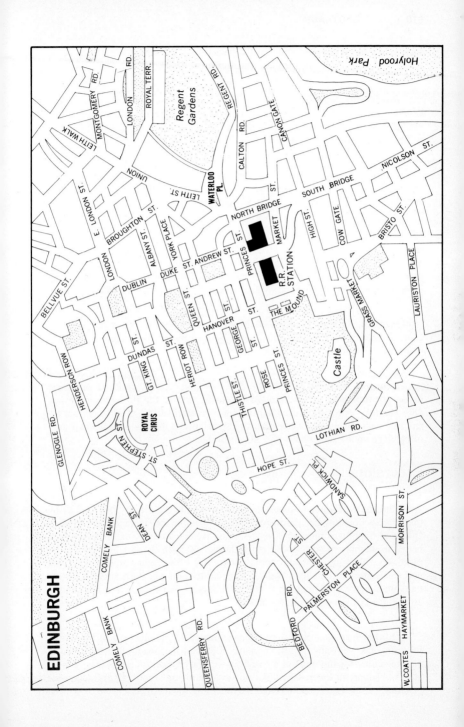

EDINBURGH

670 · · · SCOTLAND

stays when in Edinburgh. Tours of the palace (none offered during royal occupancy) are fascinating for their colorful historical detail.

Royal Museum • *Chambers and Queen sts.* • This is a vast and comprehensive museum, with exhibits covering a huge range of subjects including natural history, geology, archaeology, medieval war history, and cultural arts and crafts. A visit will require a fair bit of time.

National Gallery • *The Mound* • Here is an excellent collection of paintings by British and European masters from the 1300s to the early 20th century. A separate section houses the great Scottish artists.

Scottish National Portrait Gallery • *Queen Street* • Definitely one of the most interesting galleries in the city, here you will find lifelike portraits of Scotland's most famous and important citizens from the 16th to the 20th century. You'll become familiar with John Knox, father of Presbyterianism; poet Robert Burns; Sir Walter Scott; Mary Queen of Scots; and many more.

Scottish National Gallery of Modern Art • *Belford Rd.* • A fine 19th-century building with 20th-century works by such figures as Lichtenstein, Hockney, Picasso, and numerous greats of this expression.

Georgian House • *7 Charlotte Square* • Completely furnished in period decor, it offers a rare view into the lavish lifestyle of the rich during the late 18th century. Don't miss the kitchen, which is packed full of obsolete but interesting culinary objects. Audio-visual presentations on the topography and history of New Town are included in the admission fee.

Excursions

Linlithgow Palace • About 55 minutes outside the city by bus and 20 by train; as spellbinding for the history buff as it is for the average tourist. Mary Queen of Scots was born here in 1542, and Bonnie Prince Charlie stayed here between attempts to seize the English throne. In 1646 the last Scottish parliament was held here. The surrounding 16th- and 17th-century houses are worth noting, as are the Cross Well and the castle fountain. Also situated here is the 15th-century St. Michael's Church, the largest parish church in Scotland to escape damage during the Reformation.

Dunbar • A snug old fishing village situated 35 minutes east of Edinburgh by train. The surrounding Lammermuir Hills and the beautiful Firth of Forth are the setting for the ruins of a castle where Mary Queen of Scots was brought after her supposed lover, David Riccio, was murdered. Enjoy a stroll along the beautiful pebble beach and through the charming town streets.

HOTELS

☆☆☆☆☆ **Balmoral** • used to be known as the "North British" or "N.B." Now, along with a name change and a bright fresh facade on the city's main boulevard, a total renovation program has given it a new $15-million wardrobe. The quality, location, and history of this fine house assure the continuing prestige.

☆☆☆☆☆ **Sheraton** • Stately design in vaguely post-modern motif; fresh lobby in light tones; Cafe Beaumont glass-faced and dotted with foliage and palms; Atholl Bar with piano tinklings. You'll find a heated pool, sauna, and gym; well-furnished accommodations with uninspired textile selections (in this land of weavers); extra-fine suites. We suspect it will mellow like a heritage dram.

☆☆☆☆☆ **Caledonian** • facing Edinburgh Castle, glows with sparkle and interior grace. Plenty of private baths; some units stately (the quietest front the abandoned station, not the Castle), some only so-so; 5th floor with dormer windows. The popular Pompadour offers superior Scottish dishes; light meals are served in the Gazebo; attractive courtyard patio for summer.

☆☆☆☆ **George** • is a dramatically improved example of the finest neo-classical decor, in other words: Adam architecture; the rehabilitation not only includes revisions in the current facilities, but the grafting of extra bedchambers that join the main building. Chambertin dining room and wonderfully antique self-service Carver's Table restaurants; the Clans Bar; typical Scottish entertainment in High Season.

☆ **Carlton Highland** • resides up the bridge from the Balmoral. Apart from the extensive comforts for creatures, those same creatures can huff and puff in an extensive sports complex that adjoins.

☆☆ **Hilton National** • perches not beside but over the Water of Leith, a millstream that dances through the hotel and separates one of its bars from the restaurant. Two other bars also cater to raging thirsts.

☆☆ **Post House** • is one of the most appealing modern addresses in the nation if you have a car. It's a 15-minute drive from the center on the Corstorphine Road to Glasgow and backs onto the Zoo, raised above the highway and looking across rolling meadows toward the Pentland Hills. Dining and coffee shop plus lounge bar; superb comfort in its well-appointed bedchambers.

Royal Scot • 5 minutes from the airport, is physically more daring in concept. Wood has been handsomely melded into the interior design, which is basically modern; pool plus fitness center. Many business travelers use it.

King James • in town, an unusually busy host, is packing 'em in. Attractive Brasserie St. Jacques and Dunedin Suite. The smallish accommodations are thoughtfully outfitted. Okay as an up-to-date midtowner. The Scottish Dinner Show known as Jamie's Cabaret is one of the best acts in town.

★★★ **Roxburghe •** tranquilly situated and limply refashioned to a period mood, retains far more of a family air than its busy-busy colleagues. Traditional tones with Adam highlights preserved; light, airy, downstairs *à la carte* dining room; captivating ground-floor cocktail bar (which you might prefer for light dining) in Le Consort; self-serve luncheon buffet. Some of the nicest staffers in the city.

Mount Royal • also has had a renewal under its changed ownership. The results now make this an attractive choice for lodging.

Howard • similarly bristles with renewed vigor. All 40 units freshened and provided with private baths.

Rutland • across from the Caledonian, offers viewful accommodations and many proud updatings. A brewer has converted its mercantile character into more of a family haven. Total of 18 rooms; 10 baths; bar and grill noisy after nightfall.

Scandic Crown • is large, sterile, and well suited for group traffic. Prices are moderate, comforts adequate.

☆☆☆ **Dalhousie Castle •** is a noble address outside the city proper. The neighboring Jacobean Feast (at Dalhousie Courte, a few miles distant; see "Restaurants") is a highly bruited publicity come-on, but its soft-spoken luxury accommodations in the quiet isolation of the fortress are absolute charmers. Henry IV held the castle in siege for 6 months and many a modern traveler might happily bivouac here for a lifetime—or at least a fortnight. All 25 units are truly superb, but I'm especially fond of Bridal Suite in the Tower or #22 up on the battlements (no elevator). Something unique and spectacularly rewarding for 20th-century day-and-knight-hood. The official address is Bonnyrigg, Midlothian, a short haul from Edinburgh.

★★★★★ **Greywalls •** *at Muirfield, Gullane, 17 miles from Edinburgh •* overlooking the golfing shrine of Muirfield, is a masterpiece of architecture by Sir Edward Lutyens, Britain's preeminent Edwardian designer and my favorite housebuilder from any period. It is a joyful blend of coziness, elegance, and solidity. (Only the dining salon seems out of style; the cuisine, however, is excellent.) Gardens laid out by Gertrude Jekyll; engaging hearthside library; cheerful rooms. The "walls," incidentally, are not "grey" but a tweedy beige. It's Mecca for golfers: 10 courses in the immediate area, 4 of which are championship grade. Open April to Oct.

☆☆☆ **Houstoun House •** *at Uphall, about 20 minutes by car from the bright lights •* is another tranquil dreamland! This one is a converted mansion embraced with green lawn, guarded by a rolling 18-hole golf course. Handsome, refined dining salons on the 1st floor; glass-lined, linkside lounge; vaulted whitewashed bar with deep soft divans and crackling fire in the chimney; 19 bedchambers with private bath (or one immediately adjoining); added wing with modern conventional decor. For reservations, write to Houstoun House, Uphall, West Lothian, or if you want to telephone to book a table, the number is Broxburn 3831. One of the warmest recommendations in this book, but not at all for seekers of the fancy, the ritzy, or the pretentious.

★★★ **Johnstounburn House** • *40 minutes or 15 miles from the city at* **Humbie** • is again one of Scotland's brightest gems, having gotten back into business after a period of closure. Wonderful gardens and park; 17th-century mansion tone; splendid lounges; richly paneled dining room. Surely (and happily) on the comeback trail.

★★★★ **Borthwick Castle** • *20 minutes from the capital at* **Gorebridge** • is a product of the early 15th century where 10 rooms are available to paying guests. Candlelit dinners are served by the log fire in the Great Hall beneath a 40-foot gothic arch and minstrel's gallery. Today you'll find a cozy snuggery from which Mary Queen of Scots once escaped custody. Had she waited until it was refashioned, she would have changed her mind. From step number one of the spiral staircase to turrets, here's a tidy tower of taste and comfort.

Prestonfield House • *out on Priestfield Rd.* • is mentioned under "Restaurants," the category on which its esteem is more properly based.

Donmaree • *21 Mayfield Gardens* • also can be recommended as a restaurant, but the gardens, the score of large, comfortable, homespun rooms with duvets, and the delightful hospitality of the Gelts who own it urge me to list it primarily as a hotel. Go for either purpose and you won't be disappointed.

Forth Bridges Moat House • *at the headland of the famous firth* • casts a commanding sweep over the wind-chafed waters. Efficiency-style bedchambers; 107 rooms with bath; some with TV (who could watch it with that magnificent sea outside your window?); each unit with its own teamaker set and all the fixin's; health center and pool. For motorists and wide-eyed wanderlusters. Especially useful if you are playing golf courses on that side of the firth. Rush hour traffic across the bridge can ruin composure and tee time.

★★ **Hawes Inn** • *nearby at* **South Queensferry,** *is down by the water opposite the old pier* • Here is where (room #13 to be exact) Robert Louis Stevenson blocked out the plot for *Kidnapped* and began writing the novel; it is also where Sir Walter Scott penned his *Balfour*. Only 7 bedchambers, 3 baths, a darned good dining room, and a cozy cocktail lounge and bar. For nostalgics, excursionists, and overnight adventurers, but not for long stopovers—or Norman Mailers.

Crest • *3 miles north of Edinburgh, out in the same direction* • Six floors of 120 lookalike cells; 6 so-called suites; 2 levels of public rooms; wide windows that don't allay the narrowness of the dimensions. Sheltering arms, but not inspired.

★ **Braid Hills** • *south of town on Braid Road* • weaves much more flair. Total of 70 units split equally between singles and twins; reasonable rewards; pleasant as a suburban address.

Ellersly House • *about 2 miles from the center on Ellersly Road* • was updated very recently and remains a worthy choice for tranquility seekers. Garden situation and croquet green enhancing the converted private home.

RESTAURANTS

At long last Edinburgh's dining establishments are beginning to recognize that the 20th century is hard upon us. Young and daring entrepreneurs are making a noble effort to enliven the tablescape of their capital town, but it remains to be seen whether the crusted Old Guard will support those gallant whipper-snappers. Perhaps the tourist traffic alone will be enough to keep them alive—and indeed they do merit the outlanders' attentions. Let's hope they keep up their inspired kitchenwork. Hotels, in the meantime, are redoubling their efforts and the results are heartening.

☆☆☆ **Cousteau's** • *Hill St. Lane, North* • is—as if you hadn't guessed—a breath of sea-fresh air. Outside hang colossal iron swimfins and a giant diving mask suggesting a link with the great French naturalist (which doesn't exist except for the proprietor's esteem for the deep). There's a bar downstairs, with dining above. Well-made cane furniture with leaf-green upholstery. Main dishes range from £6 to £17; excellent mussels; splendid grilled fish. But the show-stopper is the spectacularly attractive cold seafood platter served in a rugged scoop of cork bark almost a foot long and radiant with marine critters. Closed Sundays; dinner only. Very good.

Vito's • *55A Frederick St.* • is a bright touch of Tuscany in the heart of the city. (You'll probably prefer this Vito to the original one at 109 Fountainbridge, which is hued in gray and brown.) Down a few steps to a bewitchingly colorful cellar; unusual heavy white-pine tables and chairs with red backing; terra-cotta floors; gaily painted tiles; front wall composed of beehive wine racks; two small rooms plus a bar and lounge. Amiable Italian waiters; muscular seasonings in the ample selection of Latin dishes; sweets rolled out on an amusing trolley carved as a wooden horse. Different and uplifting.

☆☆☆ **Caledonian** • is known for excellent standards of cookery at the Pompadour.

Balmoral • As mentioned earlier this hotel (formerly called the North British), fully renovated, is functioning fully and is a beautiful example of a born-again dowager in gamin's garb. Top gastronomy and gracious surroundings have been staples here for generations. I expect you will find those attributes repeated.

★★★ **George** • turns droves of visitors into calorie-counters (see "Hotels"). Have drinks in the colorful Clans Bar, which is a living history of Scotland. Chambertin caters to continental tastes. The Carver's Table combines turn-of-the-century decor with 20th-century self-service in an amiable and economic way. All segments recommended.

Cafe Royal & Oyster Bar • *17 W. Register St.* • has always prided itself on its seafood. The place itself is a period piece to be savored.

☆☆ **Howtowdie** • *27A Stafford St.* • is appealing, especially for game, steaks, and salmon; vegetarians also avidly nibble here. About a dozen tables aflutter at lunch and dinner with well-presented table d'hote and a la carte creations. Closed Sundays (Sept.–May); costly but rewarding.

Doric Tavern • *15–16 Market St.* • is a friendly sort of haven having only 9 tables with blue-and-white-checked cloths; cozy, informal, "family" aura; food superior.

★★★ **Hunter's Tryst** • *Oxgangs Rd.* • a delightfully former coaching inn, once hosted Scott and Stevenson—and if their roast beef was as good as mine, they must have been regular customers. The name aptly embodies its romantic candlelit mien. A lover's tryst, too.

Beehive Inn • is abuzz with a loyal colony of diners. A nice couple are the drones who supervise the steak and seafood fare (which are superb).
    For elegant dining in the suburbs, please look at our "Hotels" section for the description of **Houstoun House** at Uphall, one of the top tables in the British Isles.

Prestonfield House • *10 minutes from your midtown doorstep* • has been the prestige oasis. Here's a beautiful converted estate gentled by somnolent grace, fanning peacocks, Highland cattle, grazing lambs—and, gulp, fleets of buses on summer evenings with tourists trouping into the neighboring festival center. (Only the idea is disturbing, but still it affects the mood generally.) Fireside bar for friendly persuasions; a few bedrooms for visitors with lingering ambitions; large menu and somewhat pretensious cuisine; chic clientele who find it wiser to reserve in advance. Open all year for lunch and dinner.

Cramond Inn • *8 miles (20 minutes by #41 bus) from the center, where the River Almond meets the Firth of Forth at Cramond* • This 300-year-old village tavern and adjoining pub is again well-regarded after a brief dip in popularity. I think you may like it.
    La Potiniere, at Gullane, bordering the golfing shrine of Muirfield, has

only about a half-dozen tables, but its fame goes well beyond its capacity so be sure to book—sometimes *months* ahead—if you're going this way. The tiny Scandinavian-minded **Howgate Inn** (40 minutes out of the center) is another winner; rich dining on copper service; medium tabs for superior rewards.

Don't forget the previously mentioned Jacobean Feast out at **Dalhousie Courte** (3 miles from the Castle) in *Bonnyrigg*. Eat with your fingers or a hunting knife; lusty singing by medieval troubadours; free double-decker bus service from Edinburgh Monday through Thursday; find your own way out and back Friday and Saturday; always book ahead. Inclusive banquet, serving about 170 vassals, for about $28, and no tipping. Nearer to the city you might try **Royal Mile Banquets** (9 Victoria St.) if you've got an abiding love for humanity. These robust spectacles have become pretty popular all over—but not with gastronomes.

★★ A dinner afloat? Try **Pride of the Union,** a 60-foot barge which ambles along the Union Canal, leaving Bridge Inn jetty at Ratho (near the airport) before (7:30) sunset and returning around 11 p.m. An accordionist adds a few more notes of charm. The mini-cruise and galley works cost about $30 per passenger; tea-time voyaging also available. Reserve by phoning 333 1320 and allow about 30 minutes (and £10 or so) for the taxi run from midtown.

NIGHT LIFE

Weeknight dancing at some of the better hotels, but no strip or girlie cabarets. Folk singing and dancing are pervasive as family entertainment.

When the sun goes down in Scotland, you've got your choice of hotel dancing, pub crawling, the handful of casinos in Edinburgh and Glasgow, or washing your drip-drys 5 or 6 times. Edinburgh offers a few discotheques: **Buster Brown's,** the **Red Hot Pepper Club, The Amphitheatre, The Network,** and **Calton Studios** are responsible for most of the next-day redeye in the capital.

PUBS

As in London and Dublin, the pub of yore is rapidly being replaced here by a hybrid that is part saloon and part discotheque. Today it's rare to find a thoroughbred stall where hairy-chested males gather for purposeful drinking. The oldest and best examples, physically unchanged for decades (when you can find one today), are rich with color, flavor, and charm. Routine neighborhood-corner-tavern examples, on the other hand, are often painfully plain and colorless.

Edinburgh offers several enchanting establishments. For the authentic feel of the Old City, the canopied rectangular bar and ornate woodwork of **The Abbotsford** (3 Rose St.) will transport you to mellow Victorian days. You may lunch here or nibble its snacks; noon to 2:30 p.m. and 5 p.m.–11 p.m., jam-packed on Saturday night; delightful but no food downstairs in the evenings. Upstairs it provides traditional Scottish fare Mon. through Sat. Equally beguiling is **The Volunteer Arms** ("Canny Man"), about a 15-minute taxi ride from the center at 237 Morningside Road. Its Public Bar is stuffed with mementos accumulated over nearly a century. Go between 7 a.m. (if your liver functions at that hour) and 8 p.m.; Saturdays are best. **Scott's** (202 Rose St.) is a family institution with a loyal following. Drinks only; an exceptionally amiable spot. The **Golf Tavern,** 10 minutes out at Brunstfield Links, faces the pitch-and-putt course of one of the world's oldest golfing centers. Sporting clientele; friendly Public Bar and higher-toned Cocktail Bar. Lunch or beverages from noon to 2:15 p.m.; evenings from 5 p.m.–11 p.m.; go Saturday, if possible. The **Laughing Duck** giggles for gaggles of gay quackers. Beware of the goose.

SHOPPING

SHOPPING HOURS: Weekdays, 9 a.m.–5:30 p.m., Saturdays the same but with some 1 p.m. closings. Late (8 p.m.) shopping Thursdays along Prince's St., George St., and in Waverley Market (a.k.a. Waverley Shopping Centre).

SHOPPING AREAS: Prince's St., George St., and the Royal Mile (from Castle Esplanade to Holyrood Palace); also Waverley Market—St. James' Centre.

SAVINGS ON PURCHASES: Please see "England" chapter since the system is the same.

NOTE · · · Avoid the phony "white heather" peddled as a "rarity" and shun the typical tourist claptrap worth about half what is asked for it.

ANTIQUES: In Scotland, most zealots look first for Portobello pottery jugs and copper or brass candlesticks. **Wildman Brothers** (54 Hanover St.) is dependable for silver, jewelry, china, and the like.

DEPARTMENT STORES: **Jenner's** (Princes St.) is the local pacesetter.

HANDICRAFTS: **Living Crafts Centre** (12 High St., Royal Mile) for the whole regional gamut.

JEWELRY, GOLD AND SILVER: **Hamilton & Inches** (87 George St.) is about as well known to discerning Scots as their own clan tartan. It has been an institution of the nation for almost a century-and-a-quarter—purveying to landed families as well as visitors unique, hand-fashioned Scottish items so fitting for Highland Dress and casual use.

TARTANS AND TWEEDS: Geoffrey (Tailor) purveys his stitches next to the John Knox House at 57-59 High St. **Kinloch Anderson** (Commercial St. corner Dock St. in Leith) is top of the peerage of this elite field. It makes kilts for the Royal Family. You can watch them being made.

ERISKA   This is a flat, water-girt island about 15 minutes by car from Oban.

★★★★★ **Isle of Eriska** is the stately home that has stood above the Firth of Lorne since 1884 and that is reachable via a modern bridge today. The personable, hard-working couple Robin (he) and Sheena (she) Buchanan-Smith have wrought wonders in providing such a discriminating panoply of enticements in so remote a clime. Crackling fires, oak panels, deep snooze-away chairs, a well-stocked bar, restful vistas, books, books, and more books all conspire to giving up thoughts of ever wearing a wristwatch again. The exceptions are just before mealtimes when telltale cooking fragrances hint of grand things to come. Rooms are named for Hebridean Islands and my own favorite twin mooring is "Skye" with its vast vaulted wooden roof, its rich antique appointments, its color-keyed linens, its excellent carpeted bath, and its own large Skye-light in the ceiling. Closed winters; distinguished and costly.

FORT WILLIAM is an important junction for motorists that is halfway between Inverness and Oban. Castle ruins dot the hills and there are museums recounting the dramatic past of Lochaber. It's a place of extremes—the highest mountain in Britain being *Ben Nevis* with the deepest sea loch in Europe and the fresh water *Loch Morar,* plus the shortest river in the UK. About 15 minutes north of town there's a splendid gondola lift to 2300 feet for an eagle's eye view of the surroundings; there's also a restaurant if you care to linger. You can take the vaunted West Highland steam train to Mallaig from here and carry on further, making Skye the limit, if you wish. As a town, it impresses me as being primarily intent on catering to mass tour movements that pour through. On a sunny day hop aboard the sightseeing boat that chugs out to *Seil Island;* the scenery en route is wondrous and the seals offer excellent fellowship (even if they can't spell their own name, which derives from Middle English and Celtic roots).

☆☆☆☆☆ **Inverlochy Castle** steals not only all the local innkeeping thunder but, to an ever-growing number of devotees, it is now considered one of the brightest lightning bolts in the national welkin. Exquisitely appointed baronial estate surrounded by 50 acres of garden within 500 acres of farmland; only 14 supersumptuous luxury accommodations; skilled skilletry with predinner drinks in the richly outfitted salon; coffee and libations in the lounge; billiards in the trophy room; blue-ribbon price tags; open May through October normally, but they will welcome special parties throughout the year if requests are made. Please reserve way, way, w-a-y in advance with personable young director Michael Leonard. Wonderful. P.S.: Within the grounds is the simpler, cheaper, and yet amply comfortable **Factor's House,** which can be a worthy alternative if the castle is full.

The first-class **Milton** is a solid bet—but not for the victuals. The ranch-style **Croit Anna Motel,** 3 miles out, has become a close contender, with solid comfort and cookery. The **Alexandra** is much improved since it spent a packet on modernizations. These are followed by the **Imperial** (for bareback riders only) and the busy-busy **Highland.** Down the pike at *Ballachulish,* the **Ballachulish** comes up with home-style comfort, waterside dining, and year-round availability. Convenient, but not posh. The **Onich,** a few minutes away, offers more color and charm. Stone-and-stucco house that grew, g-r-e-w, and G-R-E-W; 2 cheery bars; tartan-toned dining room with a reputation for savor; 20 well-appointed bedrooms, with private bath. The **Lodge on The Loch** at *Onich* has a remarkable location overseeing Loch Linnhe; rooms have been modernized and many expanded, with their own bay windows and sitting areas. Overall, it is tranquil, inviting, and nicely outfitted as a country house. At nearby *Glencoe* (scene of the massacre of Macdonalds by Campbells), the **Kingshouse** is a pleasantly updated coaching inn at the edge of Rannoch Moor. The dining room is outstanding for the vicinity—that is, if the chef isn't a Campbell and you are a Macdonald.

Arisaig House resides west of town on the "Road to the Isles," among flowered gardens running to woodlands and lake vistas. It's a lovely part of the world and this greystone mansion represents one of the high points of Scottish country life. The culinary art here will keep you walking off calories for months.

GLASGOW   What a transformation! And it's still going on in a city that recently was dubbed the Cultural Capital of Europe. Quite a change from its former gloomy past. The dynamic boostrap recovery is due entirely to talented administrators and dedicated citizenry. With nearly 725,000 inhabitants, here is the center stage of commerce for Scotland and the 3rd-largest city in Great Britain. Despite the decline in shipbuilding and heavy engineering, business is burgeoning. The famous cathedral dates back to 1197 and the University to 1450. Yet there's a born-again sensation coupled with a vigorous civic drive hereabouts. Just look at the gleaming glassy St. Enoch's Centre, or the young-at-heart shopping enclave called Prince's Square. After 4 decades of searching for a proper showcase, the dazzling Sir William Burrell art collection now has a museum base at Pollok Park, 3 miles from midcity. It's an eye-opener because the 8000 items—rivals of the Hearst trove—lay unseen in crates for so many years waiting for a window on the world. (Even so, only 40% of the works can be displayed at one time.) The Kelvingrove Art Gallery, City Chambers, Hunterian Museum, the engaging Transport Museum, Provand's Lordship 1471 house, Botanic Gardens, and Zoo are among attractions. The city has 50 public parks, 15 art galleries, 20 smart new office buildings, and 5 newspapers. Out at *Kilbarchan* (8 miles, off A737) you can watch 200-year-old looms at work at Weaver's Cottage; Tues., Thurs., Sat. in season. Crookston Castle predates Columbus. The airport is now second only to London's Heathrow in its traffic of British skywaymen. The hotels, drab and mercantile until recently, are improving; a tough, rigidly enforced antismoke campaign has dispelled the one-time grim, grimy, franchise on smog; its newly scrubbed face as well as the city's beautiful antiquities are at last being revealed in a more flattering light. Convenient jump-off point for many interesting excursions.

The modern, 9-story, 250-nest **Albany** is the top hotel in town, in my view. Its Four Seasons dining room is a delight for formality while the red-and-black Carvery sizzles with open banks of grills; a trapper's cabin hides in the cellar for light biting; accommodations throughout are well conceived and smartly attired. Also in this jumbo class are the huge **Hospitality Inn** and Convention Centre, the modern **Holiday Inn,** the chain-operated **Moat House International,** and the sleekly contemporary **Crest**. Next come the attractive **Central, Copthorne,** and the **Kelvin Park Lorne.** More intimate is the Victorian, 8-room **One Devonshire Gardens** with homelike comforts. The gastronomy is noteworthy too.

For dining, your hotel will provide a reasonable meal, if you stick to the ones mentioned above. The **Holiday Inn** offers the L'Academie, which is reliable; evenings only and never on Sundays. The Terrace is the lunch spot here. Among independents, the **Ubiquitous Chip** features Scottish dishes of superior quality and fine wines while **The Buttery** is into nouvelle cuisine. **Le Provencal** isn't bad as a wine bar for light meals and sips. **Rogano** is an old standby; I like the seafood here. For refreshment try on the **Willow Tearoom,** a restoration of architecture from MacKintosh, one of the greats of Glasgow's past.

GLENEAGLES

★★★★ **Gleneagles Hotel** • *Perthshire, 1½ hours from Edinburgh* • is undoubtedly one of the top stopping places in the nation—and also *undoubtedly* every golfing tour in the land stops here for tee. It is more popular than ever— both a blessing and a curse. Wonderful pastoral setting and lovely gardens; splendid golf facilities including four 18-hole championship courses, one pitch-and-putt 9-hole course, and one 18-hole putting run; computer banks often filled with golf reservations years ahead; tennis, riding (arranged through Mark Phillips, no less), and fishing; heated swimming pool and indoor games room; saunas; squash courts; tennis (hard courts and grass). Strathearn Restaurant, Country Club Brasserie, plus Dormy House Grill; several more nibbling nooks and bar-lounges. Central heating; color TV in every room; conference center; and leisure complex. Open year round and most of its 241 rooms booked well into the future. If you are out this way, for a change of pace you might try a meal at the highly respected **Nivingstone House** at *Cleish*. Be sure to ask for directions and since it is so small, be certain to reserve in advance.

GRANTOWN-ON-SPEY

☆☆ **Grant Arms** • has marched smartly to the fore. It's an easy hour's drive south from Inverness or Nairn. White-leather furniture commanding attention in the parade-ground-size lounge. Winter-garden restaurant reconnoitering the Cromdale Hills; elaborate menu forecasting superior fare. You'll also discover a licensed snack bar, a sauna, and a beauty parlor. **Muckrach Lodge** at *Dulnain Bridge* is a haven for sportsmen, walkers, and anglers. The Sunday evening meal is so enriching that you'll pick up your ergs for the week right here—and delicious they are.

☆ **Craiglynne Hotel** ● —pure Walden for the nature lover, the sportsman, or the world weary. Tumbling, salmon full Spey only a toddle from your doorstep; daily (or overnight, if you wish) pony trekking across fells and mountain slopes; shooting parties arranged; hardy tartan bar with peat fire usually smoldering; friendly, home-style service.

Nethybridge Hotel ● *15 minutes south along the river at the hamlet of the same name* ● offers less zing in its more ancient amenities. But fishermen go into ecstasies over its 6-mile reach of private Spey. Strictly for dedicated anglers.

HADRIAN'S WALL This is roughly in the *Carlisle* area, where one of the best bases for exploring the region would be **Farlam Hall** near *Brampton,* a country house with links to John Wesley and steamy George Stephenson. Comfort and gastronomic standards are tops so you can dine and rest assured.

INVERNESS Here is the capital and one of the key touring centers of the Highlands. The **Caledonian** offers 100 units with private bath; swimming pool, sauna, and fitness center. Modern rather than traditional tone. Peppy, fun-filled atmosphere. **Hospitality Inn** provides 118 latchkeys to contemporary dwelling space. The linkside and youthful **Kingsmills** is a mile from the center; its ways are traditional while its amenities are modern. The level of gastronomy is also superior for the region. You can work it off in the gym, pool, spa or hot rooms. The generously recharmed ☆**Culloden House,** 2 miles out, has the same name as the battleground nearby where Bonnie Prince Charlie was defeated in his attempt to capture the British throne for the Stuart kings. In fact, the "House" existed as "Culloden Castle" before the famous punch-up and served as the Duke of Cumberland's HQ at the time of the battle. Never mind. It will capture your heart and soul more than 2 centuries later. Everything about it bespeaks the easy comfort of Country Life. Back in town, the **Station** is noteworthy for its kitchen. **Glen Mhor** overlooks the River Ness. It rambles in houselike fashion, employs chenille and cretonne by the square mile, and creaks and squeaks from its welcoming floorboards. Call me addled, but I like it even for its faults. **Glenmoriston** has had all of its 19 bedrooms refurnished and redecorated. The **Palace** occupies a quiet location on the Ness—a stately, old-timey, Establishmentarian establishment with 2 tall towers and tariffs not too steep for the ample comforts. The **Cummings,** with a fresh white facade and windows outlined in brown, is moving up in quality. Many private baths have been added, too. Both **Loch Ness House** and **Dunain Park** are homespun delights set in pastoral frames. Very traditional and heartwarming. Dunain is especially known and admired for its table.

IONA A short cruise in the Inner Hebrides? Here, facing the New World, is the rockdot where St. Columba landed and began to christianize the north of Britain in the 6th century. Macbeth also found his final resting place here. It is a 1¾-hour whisk via ferry from Oban, skirting the vast, lonely, and hauntingly beautiful island of Mull. (You also can hop to Mull by boat, take an overland transfer, and cross to Iona at the western extremity.) Within easy walking distance of the small dock is the ancient Abbey, the Nunnery, a coffee shop and, naturally, a golf course. Of the 2 tiny hotels, I prefer the **Columba** to the **Argyle,** but both afford reasonable comfort and restful vistas of the Sound and Fionnphort on the Ross banks. Shoppers can visit charming "Fiona of Iona," mistress of **Iona Scottish Crafts** where woolens, jewelry, and pottery of the isles are purveyed.

KINROSS   The engaging **Windlestrae House** is a charming overnight stop. Only 4 bedrooms, but they are pleasant; attractive dining salon where you shouldn't miss a try at the Duckling Seychelloise or the Chicken Jan van Riebeck if they are still on the menu. A pause that refreshes.

KYLE OF LOCHALSH   The **Lochalsh Hotel,** 80 miles west of Inverness at the ferry point to the Isle of Skye, features an admirable view across the strait, modern appointments, and genuine Scottish flavor and color. Well-supplied bar; 45 rooms, about ⅓ with bath; service spare; book long, long, long in advance, because this mini-house is always crowded. While it is open all year, the biggest crush comes during High Season when visitors are heading Skye-ward. Here is the most important way station en route. The viewful **Balmacara,** 6 miles south of *Kyle,* is a worthy alternative.

MELROSE   The **George & Abbotsford,** near Galashiels (Roxburgh), drops its lure to fishermen and to scholars hooked on Sir Walter Scott. (He's buried at nearby Dryburgh Abbey.) Rights on the River Tweed to 4 private pools; groups never sheltered; 22 rooms and 13 baths; solid comfort with abundant touches of grace and charm; room #19, with 4 windows and a view of the ancient abbey, is our favorite. Very Scottish; recommended. **Waverley Castle Hotel,** also is recommendable.

NAIRN
        ☆☆ **Newton** • *30 minutes northeast of Inverness on the Moray Firth* • was described to us by a good Scotsman as "a civilized place"—and that it is. Here is a favorite quiet hideaway of prime ministers, industrial colossi, and Very Old Families. Vintage 1850 structure surrounded by 35-acre parkland; castle architecture; 2 championship golf courses; tennis courts; trout and salmon fishing; central heating and open peat hearths; numerous lounges; cocktail bar oriented (or is it "occidented"?) toward the most glorious sunsets in the Highlands. The cuisine is above average for Scotland. Not posh, but deeply satisfying. I like it.

   Golf View • is bigger, more modest, and less expensive. Waterside situation; also with tennis facilities, also near the links; commendable cookery; attentive service; the best corner units are #106, 207, and 307. Both of these are open year-round.

   Royal Marine • with 47 kips, most with private plumbing, is kept in fine trim. Recommended, but seasonal only.

NORTH BERWICK

☆☆ **Marine Hotel** • *20 miles from Edinburgh* • is on the march again. This disciplined, taut, bright-eyed Marine—which stood so long at parade rest—is now snapping smartly to attention.

Blenheim House • is so tiny it's almost an afterthought; pleasant decor; savory a la carte selections; perky.

☆☆☆ **Open Arms** • at *Dirleton, 3 miles from North Berwick* • with only 7 rooms and baths, is well regarded for its kitchen. Though it began life in the 17th century, it appears as a contemporary structure edging the town green and neighboring the 13th-century castle. Golf, fishing, and riding nearby; Edinburgh is a half-hour's drive to the southwest.

OBAN   The traditionally front-running **Caledonian** offers a midtown waterfront situation just a toot from the Hebridean ferry slips; old exterior; spacious public rooms; vista-oriented dining salon. Coming up with gratifying speed. The **Park** has reappeared from a reconstruction spree with fresh amenities and a beckoning mien. Lots of work and many rewards. **Great Western,** beautifully perched on the Esplanade, is an imposing gray-and-white Georgian building with a viewful lochside command. Glass-fronted terrace and adjoining bar; excellent position. **Manor House** has fewer than a dozen rooms and a reliable kitchen. The **Alexandra,** less appealing for comfort, boasts a better down-the-loch panorama; it is older in tone, despite recent refurbishings. The **Lancaster,** on the Esplanade, offers a magnificent vista! It operates all year. So does the **King's Knoll.** The **Columba** and the **Regent,** back at dockside, are fair choices in the upper-middle range. Here is the springboard for cruises out to the Hebrides. For 5-star elegant country living, please check our report on *Eriska.* For gift hunters, look at the distinctive Highlands jewelry at **The Iona Shop** (2 Queens Park Place, on the waterfront). The Celtic patterns, silver, staghorn cutlery, and local minerals are so different and so appealing that you are bound to succumb; the prices, too, are surprisingly low. Ask for the proprietors, Mr. and Mrs. Dennis Cathro.

PEEBLES   If you're dead set on staying in "Sir Walter Scott Country," the **Peebles Hydro** is the logical selection. Sprawling structure; vast dining room, in which you're asked to use the same napkin for several successive meals; a la carte restaurant; cool, uninspired bar; dancing nightly. Recreational or health facilities include steam baths, massage parlor, swimming pool, 8 tennis courts, badminton, a pitch-and-putt course, Tweed River fishing, and nearby golf and horseback riding. The sprightlier **Tontine** is younger in spirit; studio-style accommodations facing the river and Newby Uplands; older bedchambers more spacious; cozy, clean, and filled with warmhearted cheer. The **Park** is colorful and inviting. Both inexpensive, both for travelers younger than typical Hydrophiles, and both very pleasant indeed. ★ **Cringletie House** is a country place on 28 acres of greenery. It has a distinguished air of privacy and solid homespun comfort, plus a fine table.

PERTH's berths are cozy and most of them have enjoyed recent renovation sprees. My first choice today would be the **Royal George,** a riverbank tieup that was once the local haven of Queen Victoria. Nice views of the Tay and Perth Bridge; especially tempting grills; handsome lounges; solid in comfort; appealing in concept. The sparkling clean **Station Hotel** is also a sound bet. Midcity garden with lime-treed border; ambience so cheerful you'll immediately feel your spirits lifting; lounge with plenty of Perthshire perk. The commercial, ultrabasic **Salutation,** in midtown, greets its guests with traffic noises about the level of a 3-gun salute. Some windows have been double-glazed so ask first if you are a light sleeper. The **Isle of Skye,** at the bridgehead across the Tay, is a money-saver. White stucco and wood facade; captivating sipping lounge; firelit parlor. Ladies may wish to visit **The Scottish Pedlar** *(sic),* otherwise known as Mrs. Patrick Henderson, who stocks designer sweaters and knitwear at phenomenal prices. Her home is about 10 miles out of town, but phone first (082–15–219) and make a date.

PITCAPLE
★★★ **Pittodrie House** • north of Braemar in Aberdeenshire, is one of the most historic and well-appointed estates in the nation. The antiques are collectors items (please don't) and the library is superb (it can be used for private dining). By contrast there is color TV in every bedchamber. Superior homelike comfort with an elegance that only time and grace can provide.

PITLOCHRY,
Perthshire. This is where a very singular enchantment of Scotland can be discovered. Mountains, lochs, and rivers merge into spectacular scenery surrounding a storybook town; salmon leaping by the famous Dam & Salmon Ladder; distilleries; woollen and tweed shops; the Pitlochry Festival Theatre with a summer-long program of plays, concerts, and foyer events. Blair Castle is home of the Duke of Atholl and the Atholl Highlanders, Britain's only private army. As for hotels, **Scotland's** offers hospitality, comfortable rooms, a new swimming pool and fitness center, and praiseworthy cuisine. **Green Park,** on the edge of Loch Faskally, provides sumptuous country house manor-isms along with magnificent views and "Taste of Scotland" menus. Attractive **Pine Trees** cossets guests in estatelike elegance. **Atholl Palace** crowns its dominating position with baronial interiors. **Pitlochry Hydro** flexed its muscles by focusing on its fitness facilities; gym, sauna and indoor pool. Tasteful furnishings; ask for a corner suite. For fishing or golf as well as other touring pastimes in the district, obtain guidance at the town's Tourist Information Center. At nearby *Aberfeldy* (20 minutes), **Farleyer House** with its homey **Atkins Restaurant** is a twin-bill winner. It's Scottish country life at its best, but not at its most luxurious. Solid, honest, and deeply rewarding on every score.

PORTPATRICK
☆ **Knockinhaam Lodge** • Wigtownshire, is not only the best but it's almost the *only* fine address in southwestern Scotland, a region that is indeed

lovely but in fact neglected. Simon and Caroline Pilkington are warm-hearted hosts.

ST. ANDREWS is, of course, the place where golfing put down its roots. For tips on the special lore that surrounds this mystical sport and your chances of obtaining a starting time, please see the special section on golfing guidelines earlier in this chapter. Don't be disheartened or dissuaded if you can't tee off on the almost-sacrosanct **Old Course** because there are dozens of other links—some even better—in the immediate vicinity. Within the town are the Old Course, The New, The Eden, The Jubilee, a 9-hole circuit, and the latest 18-hole tormentor named **Strathynum,** which may be maturing by the time you're searching for another alternative. This is a lovely city—one of Scotland's oldest—and the University was born at the dawn of European higher education. It is even possible to obtain accommodation (very inexpensive) at this revered institution; available on a daily or weekly basis; some houses also for rent by writing to: Bursar of Residences, 79 North St., St. Andrews, Fife.

As for hotel space, hardly anything in the nation can now rival the spectacular and newly outfitted (in-fitted too) ☆☆☆☆ **St. Andrews Old Course,** which stands in modernistic splendor at the edge of Scotland's prime golfing real estate beside the infamously tricky Road Hole. Glorious views from the Swilcan Lounge; superb international dining; expanded suites and bedroom facilities in brown, peach, white, and blue; patchwork quilts; dozens of ingratiating touches such as silent valets, flowers, fruit, and even (sometimes) whisky. Every golf facility is available through the in-house stewards (tip them generously) or the pro shop. ☆☆☆ **Rusacks,** bordering the links, recently was given an entirely new tone while maintaining its enviable traditional atmosphere. It boasts lockers and changing rooms so that "outsiders" may play the local courses without struggling into or out of their wardrobes beside their parked cars. Beautiful high-ceilinged lounge; upgraded cuisine; excellent comfort; a delightful 19th hole. Open year-round. ★★★ **Rufflets** offers only 20 bedchambers; naturally they are almost always booked. Outskirts situation about 10 minutes by car to the tee; substantial cookery; homespun rewards—except for the sourpuss reception wardens. The well-known **Scores,** on a hillock overlooking the course, is ideally situated; now that the maintenance has improved, I think you'll enjoy it. The **Argyle** is good for budgeteers; it provides bed and breakfast only. Three miles out, **Kincaple** offers 9 pine lodges available to 4-person parties—ideal for families or golfing foursomes all year round. Rates run under £300 (including linen) per duffer for a week, and shorter holidays can be had here if bookings are slack. Facilities are excellent if you don't expect the Ritz. The **St. Andrews Golf Hotel,** with the same sea-and-course view as Scores, has undertaken some updatings and is an adequate shelter for golfers.

When the golfing is done and evening light lingers in these northern skies, the **Old Course** is lovely for dinner or leisurely bar snacks. Then, the upstairs spread of the **Niblick** often chips in with tasteful gastronomy. The **Grange Inn,** an outskirts address used a lot by sporting types, is appealing for atmosphere. The open fires and antique intimacy conspire nicely at the end of the day. The **Russell** is a useful name to remember. Outside of town, both **The Cellar** at *Anstruther* (excellent sea fare) and the **Peat Inn** are intimate and up-market.

For shoppers, the **St. Andrews Woollen Mill,** adjoining the Old Course

Pilmour Links is *the* knitwear outlet for me. Manager Jimmy Stuart warmly encourages visitors to wander through the rambling building, to browse in the Tartan Gallery (over 600 tartans), the collection of Knitting Stitches, and to enjoy the view from their huge picture window overlooking the 18th Green! Among their additional tempters are top-name cashmeres, tartan travel blankets, sheepskins, mohair throws, stoles, and yard goods (including cut-priced ends-of-batches, factory seconds, discontinued lines) and a category amusingly dubbed "Frustrated Exports." Packing and mailing are flawlessly provided. Don't miss it!

ST. FILLANS

★★ **Four Seasons** • certainly must occupy one of the most eye-catching patches of Perthshire open to the tourist. Loch Earn, worthy of a volume of poetry, is at your doorstep. Vaguely Scandinavian in tone; nice people; good food; moderate prices. What more could one ask?

SELKIRK

SELKIRK resides in a fetching parcel of the Yarrow Valley, Borderland real estate where many frontier disputes exploded in centuries past. Its sheriff for 33 years was Sir Walter Scott, who also managed time to write between scrapes with outlaws. ★★ **Philipburn House** is an easy drive from Edinburgh, but still provides the peace and local color of small-town lifestyles. The hospitality combines the grace, charm, and pure human warmth of Jim and Anne Hill, one of the nicest couples I've met in my Scottish travels. Only 16 rooms but what a heart!

SKYE

SKYE Though the season may be brief, the rewards are abundant, especially if scenery is your quest. It's the largest of the Inner Hebrides, reached by a short ferry ride from Kyle of Lochalsh. In *Portree,* the capital, top hostelries are the **Rosedale, Coolin Hills,** or the **Royal,** plus a number of comfortable bed & breakfast inns. **Skeabost House,** outside of town, is another reliable choice. *Always book in advance before going off on a Skye-lark.*

STIRLING

STIRLING Haughty, noble Stirling Castle gazes at the Grampian Mountains from above the town; the valiant 17th-century fortress guards the gateway to the Highlands. You may visit it for a fee and there's an audio-visual film prior to the tour. The **Golden Lion,** 1 hour from Edinburgh, has long been one of the most popular centers for excursionists to Loch Lomond, the Trossachs, and the Southern Highlands. ★ **Park Lodge** is a more luxurious Georgian parking spot with just a few rooms. About 20 minutes southwest, the 33-room efficiency-modern **Falkirk Metropolitan** also is available as an en route stopping point.

TROON

☆☆☆☆ **Marine Hotel** • *a quick skip from Prestwick Airport and 26 miles from Glasgow* • offers an unprecedented 20 miles of golf courses in a row. (At the Royal Troon Club, women may play *only* on certain days.) Almost 2-dozen units in attractive decor; dining room with sea-and-links panorama; handsome cocktail bar. Heaven for golf bugs, but becoming a frequent target for short-stay excursionists and package trippers.

TURNBERRY

☆☆☆☆ **Turnberry Hotel** • *Ayrshire, 50 miles south of Glasgow and 15 miles from Ayr* • is the favorite of the "Burns Country" excursionist, as well as many dyed-in-the-Shetland golfers. Each of its 121 units with private bath or shower plus TV sets; color-matched textiles to offset the stark-white walls; fresh bar; spacious and viewful lounges, dining room, and bechambers. The selected grounds sanctified for British Open Golf Championships; tennis courts; indoor pool; dancing and movies; snooker room; minibus service to Prestwick and other getaway points; smoothly operated from check-in to *adios*.

The **Carindale** at *Dumfries,* less expensive, also draws heavily among the Robbie Burns pilgrims.

SPAIN

INCLUDING MALLORCA

USA: Spanish National Tourist Office, 665 Fifth Avenue, New York, N.Y. 10022, Tel. (212) 759–8822; 845 North Michigan Ave., Chicago, IL 60611, Tel. (312) 944–0216; 8383 Wilshire Blvd., Suite 960, Beverly Hills, CA 90211, Tel. (213) 658–7188; 1221 Brickwell Ave., Miami, FL 33131, Tel. (305) 358–1992. **CANADA:** 102 Bloor St. West, 14th floor, Toronto, Ontario M5S 1M8, Tel. (416) 961–3131

SPECIAL REMARKS: The well-known Parador system consists of 86 inns and mountain lodges, ranging from remodeled ancient castles to modest shelters in remote areas. They used to be among Spain's hottest bargains, but now tariffs have skyrocketed and basic rates run from $50 to $150 per person, exclusive of meals, service, taxes, and extras. The food is usually typical of the region. Some of the nation's finest architects, archaeologists, and scholars have cooperated to reproduce accommodations that are representative of the period in which they were built. This chain has an American representative: Marketing Ahead Incorporated, 433 Fifth Ave., New York; it handle reservations. Once you arrive in Spain you can make your bookings at the Paradores Madrid headquarters (Velazquez 18, Tel: 91–435–9700; Fax: 91–435–9944; Telex 44607 RRPP).

TELEPHONE: Access code to USA: 07. To phone Spain: 34; time difference (Eastern Daylight) plus 6 hrs.

For the first-time visitor, the face of Spain is like that of an ornate clock: The numerals on the perimeter are noteworthy and Madrid, in the center, is the heart of the movement. Starting at ''XII'' you have Santander with a history going back to the Cantabrians and a might that reflected the power of ancient Rome.

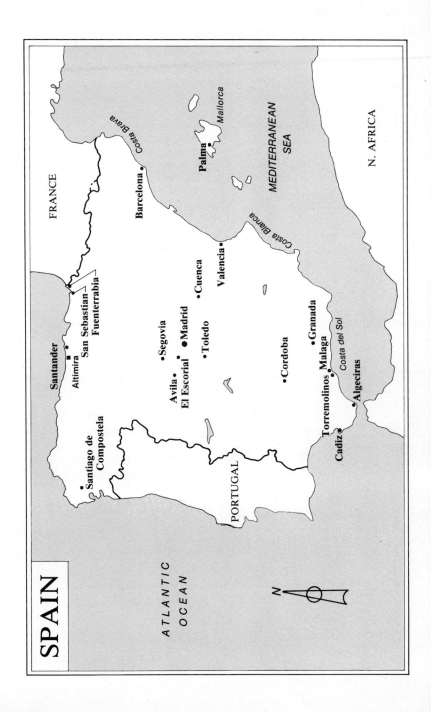

Moving east there is San Sebastian at the edges of the Pyrenees like a jewel couched in green velvet facing the wind-tossed Bay of Biscay. Then down to mountainous Pamplona, the pulse beat of Navarra where each year at the *Feria de San Fermin* brave souls still expose themselves to the "running of the bulls." The hands sweep through the throbbing tourist sectors of the Costa Brava to burgeoning Barcelona, pride of Catalonia, which boasts the Cathedral and room where Queen Isabella celebrated Columbus's triumphant return from the Americas. Then comes the gaiety of Valencia with its *Fallas* and the ever-present smell of citrus groves and roses. Granada and the fabulous Alhambra strike "VI," one of the most rewarding moments in the passage of your time abroad. There's the slow and easy, sunlit Costa del Sol for lazing, golf, and aquatic sports—not to mention the continuous nighttime activities for which the area is famous. Into Andalucia and sun-baked Seville with its Moorish antecedents, neighboring Cordoba standing in the shimmering heat, up to lovely Salamanca, to the rugged Atlantic fjords of Vigo, Pontevedra, and Arosa, to land's end, jewel-like La Coruna, and finally to the stately antique grace of Santiago where so many other pilgrimages have ended. There are many important "minutes" in between and fascinating, fairy-tale towns in the interior—yes, even castles in Spain—but if time is pressing, the "clockwise route" probably includes the greatest variety in this vast and variable peninsula.

TRANSPORTATION   **Airlines** As I live in Spain, **Iberia** and I are long-term acquaintances, but our friendship runs hot and cold. Schedules, both domestic and global, are good, but ground services and labor strife can sometimes upset the smooth flow of traffic. Supervisors are understanding even if the system is burdened by forces beyond their control. It's a busy carrier and does a lot of airwork very well, usually. **Aviaco,** a sister operation functioning on a highly localized basis, is more of the same.

Several times in past seasons I have bought a ticket for an Iberia flight and found myself sitting on an aircraft I'd never heard of and attended by staff in non-Iberia uniforms. When I asked stewards why this should be, the reply was "We are just as good." Then I requested an explanation from the airline's chief public relations executive; there was not even the courtesy of a reply. By the small print on every ticket, a carrier (ship or plane) has the right to make such switches. But if you ordered a Lincoln and the car salesman delivered a Ford, would you be satisfied with a retort that the Ford is "just as good" as the Lincoln?

Madrid's Barajas Airport, about 35 minutes from town in normal traffic, is one of the least inviting in Europe—in either the domestic or international termini. Barcelona offers a train ride (only 150 pesetas) from town to tarmac, but on rainy days it is not always reliable; there's no bus connection and a taxi costs about 1800 pesetas.

Taxis Fares inching up to match fuel and other dollar-based inflation, but still a bargain compared to U.S. rates. Avarice seems to be the inevitable handmaiden of upward economic movement nationwide. Many cars now have fancy digital meters on which there are 4 buttons the driver presses: #3 is used within the major city limits. As soon as these are passed he presses #2, which ups the rate; #1 is for Sundays and holidays only, and #4, at this writing, is a dummy.

Result: Exactly the same distance could cost 25% more than it should on a purely distance basis.

Subways In the capital, you can often avoid the hassle with hacks by opting for this fast, clean, and efficient public transport. It will set you back all of 65 pesetas per ride. A timesaver and a moneysaver in an increasingly traffic choked metropolis.

Trains Improving in comfort, but several recent accidents put the safety standards in question. Border-to-major-city and major-city-to-major-city schedules are convenient, but be sure to pick the fast trains only (strange as it sounds, the *expressos* are among the slower ones). The *Talgo,* the top performer and pride of the line, links the capital with Irun, Barcelona, La Coruna, Malaga, Cordoba, Granada, Seville, Murcia, Santander, Bilbao, and (across the border) with Lisbon, Paris and Geneva. Passenger fares are very modest by U.S. standards. For luxury lingering you might like to sample the slower *El Andalus* or the *Transcantabrico,* updated antique trains that stop often for cultural browsing, even with entertainment aboard each evening.

You can save 15% buying a pass called *chequetren* that can be used by a maximum of 6 people with no time restrictions or validation period. The value of the coupons also applies to Talgo or sleeping surcharges. Passengers over 65 receive a 50% reduction through the purchase of a *Tarjeta Dorada* (Golden Card); a passport is required for proof of age. The Eurailpass is a better bet— if you're traveling in other countries as well.

FOOD Regional specialties are surprisingly good, and their varieties are enormous. Since the nation is chiefly agricultural, chefs have a heyday in the marketplace. Through swift transport systems, fish gets to interior towns on the same day it is netted. Beef, once scorned for its toughness, is now tender and flavorful. Salads and fresh vegetables are safe wherever you go.

The *nouvelle cuisine* has its practitioners here, as well. The movement began among Basque chefs and is spreading throughout the nation. Catalans claim they taught the French how to cook—a morsel of hyperbole, perhaps, but many swallow it.

The spellings and translations on the menus can be, well, spellbinding. Women visiting the Catalonian fishing ports have been known to swoon over the "Rape (a fish) Sailor Style," while others wonder if "Amotic of Squalus" isn't some ancient hero of Iberia. Readers report squinting at "Pork Chok mit Peepers," or being put off by "Braised Spit" or "Gudgeons of Golden Bream George Sand."

Roast lamb (cordero asado) and roast suckling pig (cochinillo) are generally the finest meats. Spanish hams, like those from Jabugo, Trevelez, and Teruel deserve their worldwide admiration. Poultry? Usually delicious, especially when grilled on open fires. Spanish eggs, incidentally, are like those from dim memory in North America: real color in the yolk and genuine flavor, not the washed-out production-line pills that we are fed by industrial poulterers.

Exquisite fruit of all varieties, including the world's best oranges (winter only); honey with the fragrance of rosemary, marjoram, and orange blossoms; almond, nougat, marzipan, and tons of confections. As for cheeses, the better types include the Tetilla (soft and greasy), Cabrales (fermented and piquant),

Burgos (all cream), Asturias (smoked-cured), and Manchego. Try the last, which has been molded in matting and preserved in oil; it's my favorite. Your friends might avoid you for 2 weeks afterward, but it's worth the gamble. If you have *real* courage, order a Teta, which literally means "breast" and which comes in that shape and of varying dimensions. It's soft and creamy.

Spanish meal hours call for heroic belt-tightening and self-discipline on the part of the visitor.

Breakfast is at your option, generally as early as or late as you choose. Lunch is from about 2 p.m.–3:30 p.m.—so it might be 4:30 p.m. before you stagger away from the table to your siesta. Dinner usually starts at about 9:30 p.m. at the earliest—which often brings the dessert and demitasse swinging down the aisle after midnight.

DRINKS   Sherry, the national wine, comes in 7 major types, some with a number of subclassifications; like port (Portugal), it is always bottled blended rather than "straight." Call it Jerez (pronounced Hair-eth) if you want to please the bartender. Through the revolving *solera* system of mixing, the old and the new vintages are combined to produce a product that is always standard. Years ago, a small inner circle of British pukka sahibs made superdry sherry a mark of social elegance in England; this foible, based on snobbism far more than on actual taste, quickly spread. Manzanillas and Finos are examples; now many are served chilled to soften the bite. San Patricio when it's very cold is very nice, but some Spaniards shudder at the thought of cooling sherries. Tio Pepe ("Uncle Joe" in Spanish) has the big reputation and international markets; Long Life (or any similar Oloroso blend) is old, soft, and golden, with just enough dryness and richness of body to give pleasure to those who pucker up with the dryer varieties.

Spanish red table wines are perhaps the most underrated of any in Europe. Countless gallons flow over the border each year to be sold as "French" types in France and elsewhere. Most of these reds resemble Burgundies rather than Bordeaux in their heaviness and fullness; the whites, not as fine, are most often too sweet. The other extreme is the type with no body, but they can be pleasantly refreshing. Some of the roses (*rosados* such as Marques de Riscal or Senorio de Sarria) are commendably dry and crisp.

If I were forced to pick out 1-of-a-kind for comparatively expensive daily consumption, I'd take Vina Tondonia or Marquis de Riscal for red, Monpol for white, Cepa de Oro for Chablis, and Codorniu N.P.U. for Spanish "champagne." *Cava,* incidentally, on labels of Spanish champagne means that it has rested in lodges (French style) and is of superior quality. Vina Pomal and Federico Paternina remain superior rubies in their "Reserva" class. Many "Reserva" and "Gran Reserva" types have deteriorated. Aside from N.P.U., the "champagnes" range from sweet to cloying to sick-making. You'll pay from $4 to $7 for all of these save the N.P.U., which runs perhaps $10 per bottle.

During the summer, sample the cooling, refreshing wine punch called Sangria. Choose your own base (red, white, or champagne); as at home, it will be served in a pitcher with orange slices, lemon slices, seltzer, and sugar, but here you often also get a tiny glass of cognac for flavor. Available anywhere at any mealtime; light, delicate, and delicious.

Fundador is by far the leading *cognac* because it's the only truly dry, champagne-type brandy on the local market. You'll pay perhaps $1 per glass or about $6 per bottle in the average bar or grocery shop. (It's around $18 in the States, now that it is sold on our side of the Atlantic.) Spaniards like Carlos I, Gonzalez Byass Lepanto, Larios 1866, and similar distillates, but they're much too rich and too heavy for the typical stranger. The lighter brands are Fundador, Soberano, "103," Terry, and about a dozen more.

Liqueurs? Just name your favorite, and chances are good that they'll have it. Any big bar stocks at least 30 or 40 varieties. The prices are so low (since they are made under license in Spain) that you should ask only for the original, not the cheaper copies with names that sound like Perry Herrink, Quandro, Shardroos, and other phonetic phonies.

Beer? All of the leading brands on the Continent are now imported, and 40 breweries spread over 25 of Spain's provinces. Almost everyone agrees that San Miguel has taken over the leadership among domestic labels.

TIPPING   Give your taxi driver from 5% to 10% of the fares. Hotels extract their own service charge, usually 15%; to this, add the following: Baggage porter, 45 pesetas per person per suitcase and now some have their own scale of payment; maid, 70 pesetas per day; room waiter, if used, 110 pesetas per day; concierge, minimum of 110 pesetas per day, not exceeding $10 per week, unless special services have been rendered; valet, if used, 50 pesetas per call. Restaurant waiters should be given 5% to 10% over and above the check, depending upon the quality of the attention. Theater ushers get 25 pesetas—or 50 pesetas if you are generous.

CASINOS   Spain has given the nod to more than a dozen provinces to build casinos (20 so far). Their number within each region depends on the judgments of the autonomous governments. The restrictions include the stipulation that they be located in the outskirts of major cities (of more than 300,000 inhabitants). Naturally, tourist zones are favored, so if you are gamboling around Iberia this year and are looking for games of chance, be sure to check with your hotel concierge to learn where the nearest one is. Don't forget to bring your passport or entrance will be denied. As the government monitors all activities related to gambling, you can be pretty sure you will get a fair shake or shuffle.

CITIES AND REGIONS

ALGECIRAS,   traditional gateway to Gibraltar, has grown to a city of 100,000 souls; it is an important fishing port and a tie-up for many cruise liners as well as container ships. Festivals and fairs occupy her time in June and August;

there's a sleepy old town and a bustling new metropolis. In its environs, no fewer than 3 major tourist centers are either already perking or are preparing to lure merrymakers with sun, sea, sand, and salubrious *saludos*. Archaeology buffs will find their digs only 6 miles out of town. There's also a Roman aqueduct, some curious ancient furnaces *(Rinconcillo)*, and the lovely Chapel of Our Lady of Europe; the former two are not open to the public, unfortunately. As the chief springboard to North Africa, Transmediterranea has hydrofoil (1½ hours) and ferry (2½ hours) links to Ceuta and Tangier, which further enhance holiday rewards.

★★ **Reina Cristina** is the traditional choice for traditional living—a graceful morsel of yesteryear. Gardens, tennis, minigolf, seabathing, beautiful heated pool in blue and gold mosaics, dancing, shopping, elbow-bending in its Patio Bar—all are on the premises or within easy reach. Cuisine vies with the finest hotel fare in Spain. Suite-niks like #246 and #346, which face the pool; both have working fireplaces. **Octavios's,** with 80 units, seems eager to please— and except for its urban situation facing the bus depot, it achieves that end pretty well. Airy mezzanine restaurant; classic furnishings with marble highlighting; soundproofed accommodations; eye-soothing blues, reds, greens, or gold predominating on each floor. A reasonable value. Nearby, **Las Yucas** boasts a more recessed location but not quite the same elan. All 33 rooms with bath or shower, piped music, and air conditioning, and a few of them (such as the "01" and "09" series) with terraces. Groups win the restaurant while independent explorers are shunted over to the cafeteria—so how's *that* for revealing its priorities? **Alarde** and **Al-Mar** follow suit. **Guadacorte** resides at *Los Barrios,* on Algeciras Bay about 12 miles toward Sotogrande. It still has many God-given assets in its favor. Man, however, has managed to infect the placid scene with a busy highway and a noxious petroleum cracking tower crowning the crest of a nearby knoll.

For dining in the region, a sensible choice is the **Reina Cristina,** with its lovely summer garden and soothing music, or the independent romantic siren on neighboring Getares Beach, with its fish so fresh they'll practically leap off the plate to insult you, its sardines grilled on an open fireplace, its big steaks, and its view of "The Rock" (Gibraltar) across the bay. Full-pension guests of the hotel may dine at the first without extra charge. **Los Remos** ("The Oars") is noted for the quality of its basic food products, even having recently won an award for such selectivity. It's located in the Municipal Terminal of *San Roque.* **Marea Baja** (Trafalgar 2), under the same administration, is cozy and highly maritime. **Pepe Moreno** (Murillo) is popular for its sea specialties, whereas **El Bosque** (Somosierra 5) serves meat dishes.

ALICANTE For sightseeing, allow time for the 17th-century San Nicolas de Bari Cathedral, the Santa Cruz district, Santa Maria Church, museums of Archaeology and 20th-century Art, La Asegurada, and Santa Barbara Castle. The **Melia Alicante** boasts 545 rooms and its sawtooth eminence fairly dominates the sprawling metropolis. You'll find 2 restaurants, a snack bar, 2 heated pools, and other sound amenities. Massive in concept—as Melia's projects usually are. Then I'd select either the **Gran Sol** or the **Maya.** The former, in midcity, offers a quiet lobby as a retreat from the frenetic street, a snack bar-restaurant on the

26th floor, a sparkling and viewful bar-lounge, and pleasant, splendidly maintained kips, some of which proffer kitchenettes in their studio enclaves. The Maya, a 198-200-room, 10-story, chocolate-brown edifice overlooking Santa Barbara Castle, tilts heavily to an Aztec motif and tribal migrations from heap-big travel agencies. Ample facilities; 3 pools, Patio Andaluz flamenco stage, solarium; basement cafeteria; restaurant on first floor. At **Residencia Covadonga** your happiness will very likely depend upon your luck in drawing an acceptable bedroom. If you snag a spacious one facing the plaza and the Lucerios fountain, your stay might be delightful. Otherwise, we're not too sure. Next comes the 108-room, air-conditioned **Leuka,** perched up the hill and away from the worst effects of the madding crowd. This would be followed by the **Almirante** on Playa de San Juan and **Melia Alicante** on Playa del Postiguet. Up the coast near *Villajoyosa,* **El Montiboli** offers a romantic cliffside setting, gardens, tennis, terrace dining; one of the best around.

For diners, **Delfin** provides an eye-popping harbor view and a belt-popping Supreme de Pularda; the Sole Poseidon also is memorable. **Nou Manolin** spotlights tauromania; try the rice with onions or artichokes with clams. **Pizzeria Romana** (a.k.a. **L'Auberge de France**), located on the Finca Las Palmeras, is at *La Albufereta;* cookery is a delight. Even though it's not Italian, please try the Mouclade Charentaise, which is heavenly. Tiptop, in any language. **Ranchito Veracruz,** at Playa Muchavista, El Campello, blows hot and cold. Can be fun. **Currican** offers sea delicacies in a maritime environment. Ambitious **Darsena** boasts more than 30 different rice dishes daily.

BARCELONA

This, of course, was the starting point for the Age of Discovery, and five centuries later this Old World port will harbor new surprises. Already the metropolis is experiencing the feverish and joyful challenge of hosting the Olympic Games. Vast changes are underway to turn global spotlights on a brighter, fresher, and more prosperous Catalonia. Already one of the most densely populated cities in the world, Barcelona (after Madrid), is considered second in importance—a point that any good Catalan will heatedly refute. It's on the Mediterranean coast, northeast of Madrid, about 100 miles from the Pyrenees, sitting on a rich plain between 2 rivers and 2 towering mountains. Catalans feel a very special identity with their metropolis, which proudly produces so much of the nation's wealth; since 1980, it has had its own provincial government called "La Generalitat." Artistic activities abound; cultural attractions are numerous; it conducts business in an energetic style and is a huge commercial port. One detriment is the occasional throat-rasping smog from its booming industries. While restaurants are superb, the hotels have gone price happy while remaining below continental standards for a city of such significance.

ATTRACTIONS

You may choose from the **Fine Arts Museum** (Medieval, Renaissance, Baroque Paintings and Sculpture), **Archaeological Museum** (prehistory of the Moorish invasion), the **Natural History Museum** (stuffed animals and specialized 7000-volume library), the **Scenic Art Museum** (theatrical memorabilia in a Gaudi-designed building), the **Numismatic Museum** (coins of all periods), the **Municipal Museum of Music** (musical instruments, manuscripts, and effects of celebrated composers), the **Maritime Museum** (ship models and nautical lore), and other displays. The **Modern Art Gallery** features collections of 19th- and 20th-century paintings, sculpture, and drawings; even more timely, the expanding **Picasso Gallery** was inaugurated in a 15th-century palace; it houses early paintings and sketches, later experiments in ceramics, plus the artist's 2 gifts of his assembled personal collection totaling more than 2000 works done between the ages of 9 and 22, plus a set of canvases finished when he was 36; there's also a **Miro Foundation** on Monjuich honoring the artist who Catalans revered so passionately—an affection returned with many great Catalonian topics in Miro's art. **Antoni Tapies,** often called Spain's greatest living artist, now has a Foundation too. Antiquary hounds may visit, under the street, the excavations of the original city as it stood from Christ's time to A.D. 400. Antonio Gaudi's **Templo Expiatorio de la Sagrada Familia,** a colossal, ⅕-completed (it was started in 1882) cathedral that resembles a 300-foot-tall tower of gingerbread, is a must. Architecture buffs have been arguing about this edifice for nearly a century; you'll find it wondrous or a nightmare, but certainly you won't be apathetic. There are a fairly good **Zoo,** a **Terrarium,** and an **Aquarium.** The Young and the Brave have great fun riding the aerial railway and the Ferris wheel on **Mount Tibidabo.** As for the world-famous Monastery of **Montserrat,** about 30 miles out, you'll find a glorious vista and strange mountains formed in a fanciful pattern; at the foothills there's a theater for productions of a local **Passion Play** (in the local language). **Empuries** is another excellent fairweather excursion target, on the coast road heading north. Greeks settled here first; later Romans used it as a retirement resort for Imperial military officers. Reconstruction reveals fine homes, mosaics, statuary, and all the signets of classical town planning and organization. It can occupy a full morning or afternoon; so-so meal stops in nearby villages; snacks at the site; vistas worthy of an empire.

HOTELS

The capital of Catalonia is all dressed up for the Olympics. Among the new hotels to be ready for your visit (but yet untested by us since they were being constructed at this writing) is the modern, atrium-style, deluxe **Rey Juan Carlos I.** This handsome 425-room stalwart, built by Barcelona Projects, was spearheaded by the master hotelier Raoul de Gendre, long the director of the famous Dolder Grand in Zurich, the city of bankers. And, appropriately, this one is situated on the famous "Diagonal" boulevard in the financial district, with quick access to midtown and the airport. It offers the peace and beauty of overlooking the Polo Grounds, lush gardens, and the Turo Tennis Club. Polo restaurant plus a buffet, a Japanese salon (even Japanese breakfast), Chukker Bar, a champagne nook, transparent elevators and a generous slice of splendor. I'd guess this will be the pick of the new crop. The **Arts,** a creation of the Ritz Carlton group, offers space for almost 1000 souls in Villa Olimpica. **Havana Palace** has a stylish modern tone and a fine location on Gran Via; 150 rooms. **Gallery** is also smallish (120 units) and on the Rosellon; first class rather than deluxe. **Palau Vedruna** promises to be a smart luxury candidate. **Gran Hotel Catalonia** is on the busy Balmes Avenue. Then come the **Bailen,** the **Plaza Espana,** the attractive little **Llanca,** followed by the **RENFE** candidate, **Valle Hebron,** and the **Redding.** Obviously, there will be no shortage of space in Barcelona in future years, but if you want to attend the Olympics this season, be sure your reservation is confirmed and absolute.

☆☆☆ **Princesa Sofia** • is the leading choice out of the large institutional type of hotels. Totally air-conditioned; today-style marblesque lobby illuminated with baby-spots; commodious lounge up 1 flight; Le Gourmet restaurant in rust and black; rustic Bavaria room for more informal dining (a peculiar selection of Spanish rather than Teutonic dishes that were not impressive); relaxing Mayfair Bar; Top City penthouse rendezvous for dinner dancing; light biting in the Snack 2002. To burn off some of the built-in calories there's a glass-fronted interior pool, a sauna, and a small gymnasium; there's also a hairdresser plus massage facilities. Bedrooms limited in space concepts but efficiently executed; tariffs rather high for Iberia. Its location, about 10 minutes from midcity, may be a disadvantage to travelers who seek urbanity at their doorstep; but if you don't mind the $3 taxi ride, here, indeed, is a pleasant 21st-century address.

★★★ **Condes de Barcelona** • is a house of a totally different personality. It is quiet, tasteful and patronized by a discreet following of international loyalists. It's located in the ancient *Casa Batllo* building of special beauty. Fully air-conditioned, with conference facilities. The *Brasserie Condal* restaurant is devoted to regional cuisine. Try to obtain a bedroom overlooking the garden or the superb Dali suite on the top floor. Young but cordial and efficient staff.

★★ **Ritz** • has spent a fortune to bring back its traditional splendor. This fine old house boasts one of the most dedicated and efficient staffs in Europe. Its location, too, is superb for sightseers and shoppers. Most rooms are spacious and all have private bath. Manager Juan Domenech and Concierge Pasqual are splendid professionals and human beings. As some of the accommodations are totally revamped and flower-fresh, be sure to shop for your room here to secure top-grade lodgings.

★★★ **Gran Derby** • provides a flair and panache that is cheerful the moment you see its facade. Inside the decor is visually exciting as well. The tone, comfort, cleanliness, and spirit provide a most welcome address in one of the nicest quarters of the city. It's cousin, the **Derby** just across the street, is less inspired aesthetically, but the prices are more modest and the basic facilities are good. The rustic bar is especially inviting.

☆☆ **Hilton** • is newly functioning in this district (Diagonal) this season with 285 luxury units, 5 suites and an Executive floor. Prices are rather lofty, beginning at over $230 per twin occupancy. In the concept of modern hotels, it no longer evokes the Hilton Export magic, but joins a long list of other good reliable Catalonian stalwarts that are similar in tone and likewise overpriced. Nevertheless, I recommend it.

☆☆ **Diplomatic** • also in the center, also may have appeal for modernists. Los Borrachos Grill with a full, rich menu, a wine bin, and piano music nightly; Restaurant Chez Diplomatic; snack plus drinking bar; The Scotch disco hub; writing room and sumptuous lounges; TV nook; barber and beauty salon; garage; travel agency; news kiosk; Telex hookup. The 10-story, setback structure contains a thimble-size swimming pool and solarium on the 8th level with beverage and light-bite service; office facilities available for businessmen who live out of a briefcase.

☆☆ **Gran Hotel Calderon** • provides a rooftop swimming pool with small bar and separate solarium affording a magnificent view of the city; hypermodernistic entrance and lobby; extremely handsome, spacious mirrored lounge; cocktail nookery with comfortable upholstered chairs; calm, tasteful dining room; piped music wafting through the public sancta; 100% air-conditioned. All 244 rooms with bath, double basins, and your own TV; varying arrangements for its smallish accommodations; 12 amply sized suites; rather dark decor.

Melia Sarria • is contemporary in mood in a high-rise style. Cleverly conceived restaurant; executive floor with so-called "Elite" fillips for business travelers; some beds not anchored well so that suspicious noises haunt the nightscape; small but efficient interior baths. A chain operation, but with its own personality.

★★ **Avenida Palace** • is best likened to a well-shined and comfortable old shoe. Courteous concierge; most of the floor personnel are adept. Busy lobby in marble, glass, brass, and wood; listless dining room with glassed-in fountain and better than adequate cuisine; plain bar; air conditioning; immaculately maintained; blond-wood furnishings. Good solid solace without glamour at a purse-satisfying price.

☆ **Presidente** • is in a very noisy locale on the thoroughfare called the Diagonal. This 15-story structure is of white stone, steel, and glass; a small hook-shape swimming pool-terrace on the 9th floor overlooks another outdoor sipping patio at the 4th-floor level. Simple but smart glass-lined restaurant with ebony leather chairs, globe illumination, and a maritime mural; wood and tartan bar adjoining the spacious mezzanine lounge; tiny concierge's desk, which results in client logjams during rush hours. All of its 150 modernized doubles and 8 suites come with individually controlled air conditioning.

★ **Colon** • is scenically sited face-to-face with the ancient Cathedral in the Old City. Air conditioning and private bath or shower; pleasant subterranean Carabela Restaurant; smartly renewed corridors with brass lamplights of low wattage; demisuites ending in #06 are among the best buys in the province. The 6th-floor units with wide-open terraces will put you eyeball-to-eyeball with one of the oldest churches in Christendom. Handsome decor highlighted with velvet furnishings, gold-leaf mirrors, and lovely prints; fusty in some quarters. Many European travelers of taste choose this one for its grace and homey atmosphere.

☆ **Majestic** • at a convenient address on Paseo de Gracia, is proud of its majestic (well, handsome) raiments. The finery is almost deluxe although the official category (and prices, too) comes lower. Efficient staff and pleasantly functional.

Regina • handily sited on Plaza Cataluna, is a queenly choice and good value for money. It's comfortable, clean, and central. Though air-conditioned, front units can be noisy if the French doors to balconettes are open.
The 60-unit **Regencia Colon,** near the Colon and with the same ownership, offers bare shelter at greatly reduced tariffs. Poor for view, but reasonable for peseta watchers. **Cristal** isn't recommended. The 76-room **Regente** offers better maintenance. Panoramic rooftop solarium, plus open terrace, restaurant, and tub-size swimming pool; newish restaurant at salon level; 2 floors with private balconies; well-outfitted bedchambers with individual air conditioners, 2 phones, door chimes, night bins for shoeshining, wall-to-wall carpeting, and cleverly designed bedlamps that won't disturb the other snoozer. Modern, functional, but too small in its twins for long-staying visitors; the singles, however, are ample. **Balmoral** is more of a residential stop than a full-blown hotel; parking facilities for motorists; very recommendable as a midtown hitching post. The **Dante** has rebounded and is worthy again. So is the totally refashioned **Royal,** which is one of the slickest glass-and-marble chicks on the old Ramblas.

RESTAURANTS

☆☆☆☆ **Via Veneto** • *Granduxer 10-12* • is a gemstone. Professional greeting by a liveried doorman who also parks your cars (rare in this country); small cocktail nook at entrance with a standup minibar; main dining room on 2 tiers; flowered carpets, *fin de siecle* decor, lavender-hued globe fixtures; plum leather chairs and banquettes; about 20 tables and several back rooms for satellite service; flower-embraced silver candelabra. Imperial attention from a sharp-eyed battery of carefully trained waiters; staff sometimes inclined to effect snobbish airs now that its success with Catalonia's nabobbery is assured. Grand presentation from merlon-cut melons to stuffed feathered pheasants to flaming crepes.

☆☆☆☆ **Azulete** • *via Augusta 281* • is the charm bomb of radiant proprietess Victoria Roque. It's expensive, very inventive (even with oriental influence), somewhat Catalan (if you know France is the next county), and fun. In any case, King Juan Carlos seems to enjoy it, as do many well-heeled citizens of this toddling town. You'll probably like it most if you go with Spanish friends.

☆☆☆☆ **Jaume de Provenca** • *Provenza 88* • is becoming one of the city's oh-get-me-in dining spots. Crowded every day; satisfying and happily boisterous; always enthusiastic clientele. My sole stuffed with mushrooms was delicious; prices are reasonable. Closed Sun. evening and Mon. Bring an avid hunger—and perhaps some earmuffs.

★★★★ **El Dorado Petit** • *Calle Dolores Monserda 57* • has won national awards for its kitchen, which is as tasteful as is the refined mood of the restaurant itself. Upper level lounge for sipping before meals; Catalan menu relies on the day's market choices; abundant wine cellar. The meatballs with crayfish and shrimp are superb for a regional concoction, but many dishes reflect international trends too. Don't confuse this one with *La Dorada*, mentioned further along.

☆☆☆☆ **Reno** • *Tuset 27* • is another member of the silk-stocking bracket. Air-conditioned heptagonal room, with suave decor highlighted by comfortable black banquettes, paneled walls, and oversize windows; 15 tables inside, plus 10 smaller ones on glassed-in sidewalk terrace; deft, discreet service that oh-so-smoothly tends toward the "hard sell" approach.

☆☆☆ **Neichel** • *Av. de Pedralbes 16 bis* • is fronted by the swimming pool of a smart apartment edifice. If you are known to the staff you might be treated like a member of the human race; otherwise, I think the whelps who pass out Big Macs have a greater sense of courtesy. (At least that's been my experience; going incognito, of course.) Minimal decor with pale gray walls and no artworks; modern lighting; only 11 tables. The superb gourmet (fixed) menu at $60 is thoughtful and rewarding—and a bargain! Lobster and crawfish in pasta was noteworthy; so were the seafood terrine and the cold shellfish cream soup. Rather swank.

★★ **Agut d'Avignon** • *Trinidad 3* • tucked away in an obscure cul-de-sac off Calle Avinyo in the Old Town, is another regional bell ringer. Romantic 3-story residence divided into quintet of working segments; antique roundings highlighted by huge turn-of-the-century murals. Fair regional cooking, plus indifferent international selections. Lunchtime jammed with businessmen; dinner hours crowded with legions of society settlers; functioning 1–5 p.m. and 9–11:30 p.m.; closed *Semana Santa* (Holy Week).

☆☆ **Orotava** • *Consejo de Ciento 355* • has been a favorite of loyal Catalonians for decades—so much so, in fact, that many regard it as their private club in Barcelona. The beaten-copper facade graphically depicts the wild game specialties that are featured inside. The service is swift and kind; the cuisine and the presentation are highly laudable. The raw salmon in marinade and sauces is delicious. A topflight bag, but bring along your money belt loaded with ammo.

★★ **Casa Isidro** • *Flors 12* • is a yumptious small restuarant; go only for their superb regional dishes.

★★ **Botafumeiro** • *Gran de Gracia 81* • is gaining note as a first-class seafood redoubt. Amiable service and growing popularity among foreigners. Heartily recommended.

★★ **Florian** • *Bertran i Serra 20* • is gaining more visiting clientele due to its solid reputation locally and an everygreen approach that shows a continuing innovation trend. (You may not, however, care about one of its classical dishes based on meat from bullfights, but the rest of its menu is as interesting from a gustatory point of view as it is attractive to the eye.) I suggest their *rolle crujiente de rape al estragon* as an example of the chef's best work or any of their delicious mushroom creations. Closed Sun.

☆☆ **Azulete** • *Via Augusta 281* • boasts one of the most appealing decorative schemes in the Catalonian capital. Frequented by international celebrities who crave Toia Roque's innovative, and often controversial, Mediterranean cuisine—dishes such as "crepes Vunnasiens," duck with honcy and sherry vinegar, and cold-and-hot orange "corona." Worth a try. Closed Sat. afternoon and Sun.

Quo Vadis • *Calle Carmen 7* • is simple but often very good. On other occasions, however, the chef goes wild with his salt shaker and condiment shelf. You'll find a decorative scheme employing stonework and bright tones; a host of fast-paced waiters; meats and regional dishes, mostly. Tip: The smooth verbal pitch here to order the costliest items (*French* oysters, crab, and the like) is an irritant. Closed Sun.

☆ **Beltxenea** • *Mallorca 275* • was called Ama Lur (meaning "motherland" in Basque). Unfortunately, this once favorite of mine now has declined dismally. My recent gratin of fish with a garnish of lobster appeared cool, the vichyssoise was poor, the drab-looking stuffed crab had a delectable flavor; the service was not superior to the kitchen performance. Its atmosphere remains beguiling, with bay-windowed niches overlooking a flowering garden where you may dine on soft summer evenings. Let's hope it can recapture its former glories in gastronomic terms because visually this one is a treasure. Closed Sat. afternoon and Sun.

☆ **Carballeira** • *Reina Cristina 3* • faces the port. Possibly $5 have been invested in fancying up this noisy joint, but the cookery is what counts here. The long lines of happily anxious clients waiting to dine here vouch for the values. Kind, considerate service (daily Spanish stock-market report on each luncheon table).

★★★★ **Casa Bofarull-Los Caracoles Bodega** • *Escudillers 14* • is colorful and charming, with so much regional flavor that many less hardy clients consider it unsavory. Not so at *all!* Caracoles means "snails"; this is the specialty, but everything under the sun is available. The entrance looks discouraging, but once inside, you pass the huge woodstove to find yourself in a hive of nooks on 2 floors. The walls are lined with wine casks, peppers, garlic clusters, and drying spices; the snail pattern is followed in the shape of the special bread. Daily recommendations of the chef are written on the back window, in bright chalk; all tables are generally full during the rush hours. The roast-chicken-on-a-spit is worthy of an award—which it once received in Paris (order *pechuga* if you want white meat). Menus are in 4 languages, including English—and their listed prices are still simple for this simple type of place. Use a cab instead of your own car, because the streets are too narrow. Open from 1:30 p.m.–1:30 a.m. every day of the year.

★★★ **La Dorada** • *Travessera de Gracia 44–46* • is a first cousin of the seafood realm of the same name in the capital (see our Madrid entry). The menu is similar and the quality of the catch is always reliable. Closed Sun.

★★ **Siete Puertas** • *Paseo de Isabel II 14* • is architecturally the distillate of turn-of-the-century Spain. It has been a Barcelona fixture for more than a century. Nowadays it's more of a brasserie. By all means go for its Old World-liness at any time, day or night.

☆ **Can Fuste** • *Gran Via de Carlos III 50* • is a festival of excellent comestibles in a boisterous ambience. Rustic wooden decor with dozens of dried hams hanging from the ceiling; seating lacks intimacy; extremely fast service; loud but courteously sassy waiters. I enjoyed my seafood chowder, grilled *rape* (that's a fish, not a felony) and *crema Catalana* (cool custard with toasted caramel crust), but had to complain about the overstuffed bill.

Can Fayos • *Loretto 22* • Holy be! Here is one of those throwbacks to the quaint era when waiters prepared your meal at tableside on chafing dishes. They wear starched aprons adorned with something resembling angel wings. Fish dishes, stews, and other Gallego fixin's are the pride.

Finesterre • *Av. Diagonal 469* • with its forest green exterior, used to be the city's top restaurant; it has gone through recent restoration but still displays an atmosphere of a bygone era. Service suave to meet the standards of this emerging neighborhood of banks, shops, and hotels. Upper-moderate prices. Closed Sun. during July and August.

★★ **Casa Costa** • *in nearby Barceloneta* • is a Catalan-style picnic pavilion for fish that opens directly onto the beach. There's a baker's dozen of similar establishments along this row, all with hawkers out front and some with similar names. But this one is tops; you can be sure you are at the right stop because it is the *only* one that is contiguous to the strand. Moderate prices; plain white walls, but attractive sea view; rough but friendly service; savory preparations in the plebeian manner. This entire region is due for razing and rebuilding for the Olympics so ask locally before going.

★ **Can Majo** • *Alm. Aixada 23* • Try this one if you are not in a hurry. Its rice dishes are the reason for its popularity among locals. Closed Sun. night and Mon.

San Jorge • *out at the airport* • is an almost hidden nook beside the main restaurant. A dozen tables; charming decor; polished, attentive service. Although its prices are virtually double those of the main establishment, it's worth the difference to the tired traveler in transit who seeks blessed quiet and who doesn't mind the higher costs. *Open noon to 4 p.m. only 7 days per week.*

NIGHT LIFE

In this nocturnal city, the Smart Set highsteps smartly out to **La Scala** (Paseo San Juan 47), a spectacular theater restaurant. Next is **Belle Epoque** (Muntaner 246), where you'll enjoy a decent Music Hall show. **Tres Molinos** is located out at the end of Av. Diagonal. This "Three Windmills" offers interior, patio, and teatime dancing; poor cookery; highish prices; open year-round. In the smart Eixample district, north of the Old Town, **Nick Havanna** draws the sleek night hawks. Simple room with pillars, video screens, and high-tech effects. These are followed by—*at this instant only*—**Up and Down, Otto Zutz Club, Ciro's, Snob, Le Clochard,** and **Regine.**

The hottest corner for *winter* play is the famous overcrowded **El Molino** (Vila Vila 93), which specializes in raw eroticism. **Las Vegas,** where local socialites gambol, sip, jiggle, and yak, places second in this hierarchy. *Nouvelle vague* singer, usually French; fairly expensive; no pickups. Closed during the *caliente* months. The **Planeta 2001** is a novelty. The highlight here is in your highball—an illuminated drinking glass! After you've closed this one (*if* you're single that evening), down your nightcap at **Chez Charley** while sizing up the battalions of distaff talent.

Flamenco? **Los Tarantos** (Plaza Real 17) is a V-shape room with a raised platform at the bottom of the V; ambience that tries valiantly to resemble a gypsy camp; lantern illumination; shows at 10 p.m. and midnight; every performer a serious artist in this ethnic specialty. Other candidates are **El Cordobes** (Rambla Capuchinos 35) and **El Patio Andaluz** (Aribau 242).

Bodega del Toro (Conde del Asalto 103) also can be a delight to lovers of this form of Iberian art—as long as they (1) have flaps on their pockets, and (2) learn the Spanish word for "no." Attractive mien; small stage; no food; terrific musicians and performers; painfully expensive for the Catalan league. Watch out for this smoothly executed swindle here: after 10 or 12 gypsies have come to your table to show their stuff, they'll coolly invite themselves to 1 or

2 rounds of drinks at your expense—and suddenly you'll wake up with a $100 tab clutched in your moist palm. To avoid this slick charade, your best protection is to glue yourself to the bar from the time you enter; you can see and hear all the doin's from there. Closed Monday.

Gambling? There are 3 centers in the region: **Gran Casino de Barcelona, Casino Castillo de Perelada,** and **Casino Lloret de Mar.** Opening times, meals, and shows vary, so inquire through your concierge before going.

SHOPPING

Barcelona's **Paseo de Gracia** between Plaza Cataluna and the Diagonal has the best shops; if you stroll along each side in turn, you'll probably find what you're after. For local color, try the U-shape walk from **Plaza de Pino** through **Calle Petritxol,** around the corner of **Puerta Ferrisa** to **Galerias Malda,** and back again to Plaza de Pino. This street offers a gaggle of shoes, watches, candy, and staple items. **Loewe** (Paseo de Gracia 35, Diagonal 574, and Hotel Princesa Sofia) has no rivals for handbags and traditional Spanish leather goods. **Yanko** (Paseo de Gracia 100) is one of the leading names for ladies' and men's shoes. **El Corte Ingles** (Av. Diagonal and (Plaza Catalunya) is the leading department store.

BURGOS, the home of El Cid and the early capital of Spain, was a major stop on the pilgrimages to Santiago. Now the main highway north misses it, but anyone interested in early Spanish history should take the easy detour to see its imposing structures. The focal point is the great white limestone Cathedral, which dates from the 13th century.

★★★★ **Landa Palace** • 2 miles south of town on N–1. For lingering, it's one of Spain's finest hotels. **Almizante Bouifaz** • *Vitoria 22* • and **Condestable** • *Vitoria 8* • also are recommended.

Meson del Cid • is located at Plaza de Santa Maria 8. It is more modest in tone and in price.

Ojeda • *Vitoria 5* • is my favorite restaurant in town. Here you'll enjoy exquisite regional dishes in a typically Castilian atmosphere. **Fernan Gonzalez** • *Calera 19* • displays a more innovative cuisine in a more luxurious milieu.

CHINCHON This wonderful scene of rural antiquity is less than an hour from Madrid and is convenient as both an excursion point or for an overnight in the **Parador Nacional.** The central square is an ancient *plaza de toros,* ringed with low, wooden-balconied buildings, shops selling the local anis liquor, garlands of garlic, and the unusual breads in amusing shapes that can be kept for years as household ornaments. If you have time see the castle ruins and the 16th-century church. Dine at the **Meson Cuevas del Vino** (Benito Hortelano 13) at the top of the town; it's built into an olive press where enormous ceramic crocks line one room; rough-and-ready service; country cooking; tremendous fun in the spirit of Old Castile. Other choices would be **Meson de la Virreina** (Plaza Mayor 28), **Meson Quinones** (Quinones 29), and **Meson del Duende** (Jose Antonio 36). All of them serve solid regional dishes.

CORDOBA is changeless and beguiling. Its colossal Mezquita (1000-year-old mosque which is now the Cathedral) is one of the show places of the nation; its Romero de Torres collection (the 20th-century eccentric who painted prostitutes as saints) is intriguing; its narrow streets in the Old Town and ghetto have color and charm. About 4 miles out, the fabulous ruins of the Medina Azahara are breathtaking; this palace (almost a mile long and more than a ½-mile wide) was built at the same time as the Mezquita, by the Caliph Abd-Ar-Rahman III. The nearby Monasterio San Jeronimo (vintage 1405), with its enchanting primitive cloister, is also worth a visit; try to talk your way into its privately owned precincts. Also worth seeing is the Palacio de Viana with its 11 patios and superb art collections.

Locally, the **Parador Nacional de la Arruzafa** is not in the center but some distance from midcity. Lots of polished marble; 56 doubles; air conditioning and central heating; highly dunkable pool; telephone in every room *and* bath; private terraces overlooking the city and Guadalquivir Valley; kiddie-corner for children's dining. A passable choice in the independent league is the **Melia Cordoba.** Though its physique is handsome, its grooming looked slack to me. Enclosed dance terrace overlooking the swimming-pool patio; dining salons getting oldish; TV lounge; every suite with a refrigerator; cunning desk-table tops disguise the air-conditioning ducts. Only fair. Facing La Mezquita, the town's chief tourist attraction, **Residencia Maimonides** welcomes pilgrims with gracious arms, clean appointments, and a friendly mien. The Caballo Rojo snack stall subs for a fuller restaurant. All chambers with private bath; plenty of living space; good taste on display from cranny to cranny. In short, a *mitzvah.* **Adarve** is conveniently situated in the Old Town. **Sol Los Gallos** crows about its rooftop pool, terrace, and bar; a viewful patio; an attractive, somewhat spare lounge; a red and white diner in the cellar; 97 doubles, 6 singles. The **Husa Gran Capitan** offers the finest view imaginable of the railroad yard. Five-tiered structure enfolding 100 look-alike units; commercialized 2nd-floor reception; limp garlic-spiced restaurant; bar-lounge. Maintenance overall seemed pauce to me. That aside, the main demurrer here is the roundhouse location. **El Califa** and **Selu** also are worthy contenders.

Among the restaurants, **El Caballo Rojo** ("The Red Horse") is the winner by a length, especially if you order the ox-tail stew, the mazarabe lamb, or the eggplant with cream of prawns. Always jammed. **El Churrasco** also stews up some rich kettles: trigueros, beef, lamb, plus noteworthy grilled kidneys. It's in an antique, graceful mansion offering patio dining in fair weather. For a sunny-day excursion, **Castillo de la Albaida** is a modest but deserving choice. One mile out of town, on the road toward Trasierra; tranquilizing 270° vista of the plains and distant mountains; country manse atmosphere, with the best feature its open terrace for viewful munching. **Ciros** is quite popular for its regional cuisine and **Oscar** serves meritorious fish creations.

COSTA DEL SOL

The "Sunny Coast" with Torremolinos, Marbella, El Rodeo (an urbanization), and other resort settlements strung along the 106-mile strip of seacoast on the Algeciras-Estepona-Malaga road, is geared to package tourism as well as to independent voyagers. Contrary to her neighbors, Marbella is much more select and sedate; the sea bathing is excellent, the golf courses are perfect, and the atmosphere is sportingly chic. For do-it-yourself holidaymakers, apartment rental (and there are many) can represent a sizable saving in the peseta department.

HOTELS

Almeria (Officially listed now as part of the "Costa de Almeria," but still generally thought of as a Costa del Sol address): This province is known as the "Hollywood of Spain" because of its pure light; the town itself became the focal point of film folk from all over the celluloid world. (Most of the sets actually were located out at *Tabernas* where more than 400 movies were reeled out in a matter of months.) And to coin showbiz terminology, the **Gran Hotel Almeria** is the best show in town. The modern edifice stands at the junction of the port's 2 main streets, offering a pool. It is followed by the **Torreluz VI** in midcity and **Playaluz**, at *El Palmer* bay, 3 miles away. Other unpretentious choices are **Costasol**, the **Indalico, Torreluz II** and San Jose at *San Jose*, by the sea, 25 miles away.

Fuengirola boasts the sumptuous, starkly white ★★★★ **Byblos Andaluz** with every sybaritic pleasure from gourmet cuisine to thalassotherapy to two stunning golf courses by Robert Trent Jones. For sport and relaxation at tiptop prices, here's your Spanish oasis.

Malaga is more of a hub for pausing rather than for lingering. For your vacation, pick some of the other more resort-style stops further along the coast. Its aeronautical welcome includes a modern building and control tower. There's also a slightly sunnier note in the hotel and restaurant scene. Should you decide to overnight here, then your best choice would be the **Guadalmar** on the road to Cadiz, 7 miles distant. Nice setting at the foot of the mountain range, on the sea—but that's about all, touristically.

Malaga Palacio • reveals expensive and frequently kooky construction; attractive lobby and lounges, more French than Iberian in tone; shopping bazaar;

disco-cellar for all age groups; popular dark-paneled, brass-highlighted bar; coolish but urbane glass-lined, marble-pillared dining room, stunning rooftop swimming pool, with an apron for food service and a marvelous vista of the port, the sea, and the cathedral; fully air-conditioned. Parking remains a headache despite an 80-car garage nearby. The best (if only) Palacio in town. (Out of the center I much prefer the Parador Nacional Gibralfaro, but more about that later.)

Don Curro • fits into the next slot in my today's rankings. Rustic dining room, plus another in simpler motif; complete air conditioning; all 49 sun-shy doubles with private bath.

Los Naranjos • smiles at its only tiny fruit tree (orange) in its front garden. Salon with TV and small bar at entrance; 42 air-conditioned rooms. Cheerful, clean, and certainly adequate within its bracket. It serves only breakfast—and guess what juice?

Las Vegas • has gone through a renovation program recently and is now an adequate choice with modern amenities.

★★★★ **Parador de Gibralfaro** • *just 2 steps below the welkin and 10 minutes from the center of Malaga* • in the Gibralfaro complex, is a heavenly choice. Only a dozen rooms, but each features a special panoramic slice of earth, sea, and sky; rustic decor; huge double accommodations; wide-angled terraces with folding louvered doors. So superior a value, with such a rewarding billion-dollar vista, that it's even worth renting a little car just to take advantage of this dreamland.

Marbella leads the pack of Costa del Sol resorts. Like all the others, it has skyrocketed in growth and popularity, but its maturity seems to have arrived more gracefully and its following seems more tasteful than the elbow-to-elbow mob scenes associated with many of the throng centers. For one thing, it is more spread out. For another, it now boasts a gambling casino that enhances its tone as a playground of sophisticates.

☆☆☆☆☆ **Los Monteros** • is a delightfully ingratiating suburbanite which beckons only a ½-mile from the first tee of the famous Rio Real course; free private bus to the greens; original stucco-and-wood structure surrounded by 3 lovely pools (one heated); it has Pavillon Mediterraneo complex with 50 hyper-deluxe units plus 7 suites; Abanico section in duplex form with splendid vistas (#'s 178, 278, and 378 are my choices); 7 superb tennis courts, and informal gardens; thatched-roof beach club, one of the loveliest in Southern Europe; 5 excellent horses and acres of cantering space; pleasantly rustic feeling with 20th-century comforts. Dining at either the beach haven, the Sportsmen's Clubhouse, the Grill Room (open all year with piano music nightly), or the salon; the lavishly redecorated English Bar (orchestra every night) and a 2nd one in the hotel, plus another at the banks of the Med; management and staff fairly bubbling with kindhearted efficiency; friendly, clubby atmosphere.

☆☆☆ **Don Carlos** • *a fast 15-minute drive from Marbella itself* • This 150-foot-tall, 17-story, 236-room slab of eye-shocking architecture boasts fantastic coastal vistas, especially from the upper levels; 2 beautifully designed swimming pools and covered terrace with snack service and a marine theme; 5 restaurants; a handsome interior court surrounded by boutiques, a hairdresser, a cosmetics corner, and a newsstand; a charming Moorish fountain in the center of the main patio; 11 tennis courts; 21 acres of estate with a vast palm and cypress grove spreading to a thatched-roof beach hut offering bar and nibble wares.

☆☆☆☆☆ **Puente Romano** • ("Roman Bridge"), deluxe, a 198-room entry that's not far from the next contestant, just a short hop from the town center. The location is lovely, edged by gardens and patronized by the chic-of-the-chic on the coastal circuit. La Tasca is fun for dining, but do try the appetizing buffets at poolside or at the beach. Tennis available next door at Bjorn Borg's racket club. Nightclub queen Regine, of Paris and international fame, has one of her money mills here. Very much a winner.

★★★★ **Marbella Club Hotel** • is composed of 2 parts—the "New" and the original one. I prefer the "New" M.C.H. with its 117 rooms, its handsome beach baskery, and its myriad recreational facilities both on the premises and nearby. Decor varies between modern simplicity and mock Andalucian; 80% of all units with private terraces; ample space; better as a lingering base than as an overnight stop. The original **Marbella Club,** farther up the pike, stands on 11 acres of outskirts terrain. The attractive but expensive grill offers large windows, central hearth, and a clubby atmosphere. Veranda Bar; a trophy room for more loving cupfuls; a beach retreat; a small pool plus aviary in the garden. The newer suites are modernistic; the older cottages reflect Iberian traditions; rooms vary from spacious to cramped; all were clean. Very social.

★★ **Golf Hotel Nueva Andalucia** • is the leading handicapper of a trio which also comprises the groupy **Andalucia Plaza** and the apartment-style **Torre de Andalucia,** which caters almost exclusively to golfers. My personal choice in this threesome boasts only 14 doubles and 7 singles—plus 2 golf courses, the Las Naranjas Golf Club, a handsome pool, and such a loyal following of links buffs that advance reservations are an absolute must.

★★★ **Golf Hotel Guadalmina** • *near the hamlet of* **San Pedro de Alcantara** • also is such a mecca for the mashie set that links addicts are often required to book as far ahead as 1 year. Two courses at your doorstep plus the clubhouse; riding; tennis; 3 pools (one heated) and cabanas; restyled lobby; 100 rooms, each given a personality course and now very inviting indeed; each with its own bath and balcony; 6 bungalows plus another privately owned cluster that is rapidly becoming a subdivider's paradise; varied cuisine in its restaurant; Grill air-conditioned; more informal than Los Monteros. Tee-rrific for players who can also enjoy exchange privileges with the Los Monteros and Atalaya courses.

☆☆ **Melia Don Pepe** • Aside from the nearby mountains, it's the tallest thing around—and to me, it gives a vivid impression of being architecturally out of joint. Vast list of resort amenities, including 204 bedchambers, a nice private beach, circular, all-weather pool, watersports, gardens, seasoned Almirante Bar, El Farola grill in green and mocha, sauna, nursery, hairdresser, shops, and scores of terraces for sunning by day or murmurs by moonlight; 2 tennis courts, and a movie theater.

Marbella Club 24 ● *adjoining **Puerto Banus*** ● with its tennis, golf (by bus shuttle), and bathing facilities on tap. Reservations can be made through the Holiday Inns organization, so you might check with them. One thing about this Puerto Banus area: It is thunderingly expensive, far out of line for the values but so "in" with the Spanish *nuevos ricos* that an attitude of "anything goes" seems to prevail.

Atalaya Park ● *9 miles toward **Algeciras** and officially in the **Estepona** district* ● is heavily group-oriented. Lap-of-the-sea location, beauty and health farm pamperings available; 18-hole golf circuit teed up; handsome Clubhouse with a timber-lined restaurant, a snack bar at the first tee, lovely lounges, and free bus service to and from the hotel; billiard room; bowling alleys, swimming pool and bathers' restaurant; riding and water-ski facilities; plus catamaran sailing and windsurfing; 11 tennis courts; snack bar, grill, and nightclub; shops; full air conditioning. All 200 rooms with bath and terrace; 25 bungalows for quieter vacationers or families.

★★★ **Rincon Andaluz** ● has gobbled up the cottage concept. Miniature village of about 100 tiny houses, all with private terraces and tiny baths; swimming pool and cabanas; Teheran Room for Middle Eastern vittles; managed by a deposed Persian prince who is also an art collector. A fairly amusing beat-the-heat stopover. It is shuttered in winter.

Las Chapas ● *on the main highway in the settlement of **Las Chapas*** ● is a startler: The restaurant, bar, and some of its living quarters semi-enclose a tiny bull ring instead of the conventional patio. Swimming pool; tennis courts; mini-golf; on many Sundays, small but jet-powered cows are released for the *tienta*, and YOU can be the matador for free.

☆☆ **El Fuerte** ● and ☆**Bellamar** ● the only 2 major candidates in *Marbella*, itself, are simple and adequate. The former has had many renewals; pool; tennis court; mini-golf; cool dining hall; comfortable but not inspired; open all year. The latter offers efficient public rooms, fair bedchambers, and a pool; open March to October only.

★★★★ **Golf El Paraiso** ● *along the path to **Estepona**, in the Patio El Alcornocal development* ● is a knockout. Gary Player played a major part in the sporting side. Situation a ½ mile from the beach; heated pool plus children's paddler; 2 tennis courts; playground; revolving rooftop restaurant; discotheque; beauty center; space for nearly 400 guests in air-conditioned luxury.

Otherwise in this vicinity, **El Mero** wiggles in with a fish-shape pool and an irregular-shape facade. Two minutes from the breakers; pleasant glass-lined dining room air-conditioned; reasonable tariffs; open March to October.

★★★★★ **Sotogrande del Guadiaro** • complex (in the *Cadiz* province) for its physical attributes, almost nothing in the nation can touch it. Huge holdings of 3200 acres in view of the Rock of Gibraltar; magnificently manicured, cork-and-olive-tree studded, 18-hole championship course, plus smaller 9-hole circuit; ruggedly handsome Clubhouse with restaurant; 3 bars, pro shop, 2 boutiques, and L-shape heated pool; 200-yard-wide sandy beach sweeping for ½-mile along the private shoreline. Bungalows plus Tennis Club Hotel with very comfortable inn-type atmosphere; pool, stable, a bull ring, tennis, its own 18-tee links, Fronton Club by the shore, shops, restaurant, and discotheque. The British proprietors plan many changes. The star-rating remains high because the natural beauty and architecture conspire to create such a beguiling atmosphere.

Torremolinos? Vast changes in this boom-boom-BOOM town. Both in the hamlet itself and along its coastal approaches, new hostelries until very recently were popping up as rapidly as bubbles in a pitch-pot. So many in this roiling caldron are house-of-cards affairs that the older generation of leaders, which gave way to these bright-and-shiny buttons for a while, have now come back into their own glory. Others that could not keep up with the double-time pace have converted to apartment dwellings. Many of the giant new structures, too, trend toward the residential concept—either renting their space, or leasing or selling it under a cooperative arrangement. For the tourist who plans to spend a week or longer, this can be a big money-saver, because (1) they are cheaper to run, (2) building codes are more relaxed than for hotels per se, and (3) service standards are low to nil. Typical rates in these can range from $180 per person per month (winter) including breakfast and house cleaning, to $375 for the same renderings in High Season. The very best we saw—and it stacked up well against any luxury hotel accommodation in the vicinity—drew about $1200 per month for a 3-bedroom spread (6 beds, no service). Within its living complex were 2 swimming pools, shops, gardens, and a minigolf course; the apartments all had telephones and were efficiently air-conditioned. Some of the leaders in this bracket are: (1) **Castillo de Santa Clara** deluxe resort boasts 244 rooms, 350 apartments, and any conceivable type of facility to entice your leisure time, (2) **La Nogalera** (excellent furnishings; accommodations of all sorts), (3) **Eurosol** (more metropolitan in concept), (4) **Alay** (smartly clean-lined; a refreshing production by Jose Sendra, one of the most likable and skillful innkeepers on the coast, the best buy around), (5) **Las Cascadas,** (6) **Aloha,** and (7) **El Congreso** (a stack of 3500 units in 8 edifices looking like columns of Paul Bunyan's poker chips; a good bet, providing you get a map with your key). **El Remo** also is noteworthy but I haven't inspected it personally.

☆☆☆ **Guadalmar** • at the city's airport gateway, presents 200 nests spread over 8 floors of white stucco. Spacious dining terrace overlooking pool complex and gardens; restful Andalusian decor with all-American undertones; cozy green-clad Retiro cafeteria; grill plus La Bodega restaurant; Corrida Bar in black and red. Accommodations featuring 2 double beds, wall-to-wall warp-and-woof, twin-sinked baths, and a generous cargo of comfort standards; the "16" series of suites is especially inviting.

☆☆ **Pez Espada** • ("Swordfish") keeps on improving. Structurally, it is in the modern tower concept. Precisely 100% of its 149 double accommodations offer an angular sea view. It is big, with full air conditioning, large terraces. Grill Room with dancing, a nightclub, 4 bars, inviting pools (summer and winter), sauna bath, private beach (one of the best on the shore), tennis court, minigolf, water-skiing, and a garden with a tropical bar. Everyone is working hard to give it more personality and zest.

☆☆ **Don Pablo** • surrounded by well-manicured gardens, shows a combination of Spanish and Moorish styles in its decor. Its air-conditioned accommodations: 367 twins, 36 doubles, 11 suites, and 16 minisuites. Two heated pools, 7 tennis courts, a shopping arcade, health club, Cordoba restaurant, Patio bar, disco, a giant video screen, and a daunting conference center. Though not in the deluxe range, it is a worthy candidate indeed.

☆ **Triton** is nicely sited out at Benalmadena-Costa. Management has updated baths, improved the gallery between the 2 buildings, and enlarged the barbecue patio at poolside. Many resort fillips including 2 tennis courts and 2 saunas. Try for a garden room, not one facing the fortress of apartments.

Melia Torremolinos, the **Al-Andalus,** and the **Cervantes** • all concentrate on group bookings and for that market, they are satisfactory.

Nautilus • features a glass-enclosed heated pool; tastefully decorated seaview bar and lounge; indifferent cookery and dining-room service; clean but cheerless marble corridors; billiard parlor, kiddy nook, tennis court, boutiques. Most of its accommodations have been revamped; these now sparkle.

★ **Tropicana** • in the next less-costly category, is an informal atmosphere that is homey and cheerful. Its brightest baubles are the Trader Victorian dining room and the romantic pool that suggests an attractive Seminole campsite. The kindness of the staff and the warmth of their attention show the epitome of Spanish hospitality. Adequate (but not sparkling) maintenance; comfortable rooms with good-looking rustic touches; appetizing meals. Recommended as a happy house with lots of heart.

Sol Las Palomas • is a mammoth, 5-storied habitational lump that suffers from a 99% invasion by group tourism. It's popular among the local hotel family but . . . no, thanks.

Parador del Golf • is a better-than-par challenger to the top group for out-and-out living comfort (especially for golfers who don't mind taking a few extra swings at the sparrow-size mosquitos that strafe in from the neighboring swamp; there's air conditioning, so they don't attack by night); low, low tariff for a handsome double lodging. This 40-unit project, architected in the rustic *ranchero* style, occupies the center of an 18-hole golf course 5 miles out on the main road toward Malaga and beneath the airport's approach lanes. Impressive circular swimming pool; attractive public rooms; outdoor dining May to September; private beach 100 yards from the doin's; rough-hewn wooden planking in the bedchambers; motel atmosphere with do-it-yourself-dammit service standards. Here's a perfect hitching post for motorists, links buffs, or wayfaring families.

~~~~~~

RESTAURANTS

Let's start with *Almeria,* where gastronomy certainly was not born, but where it is given a decent foothold at **Anfora,** the newest and already most popular restaurant; specializes in sea fare. At **El Rincon de Juan Pedro** the decor makes no pretensions; it is purely and simply regional, clean, attractive, and relaxing. You could say exactly the same for the food. Other candidates are **Club de Mar,** next to the harbor, **Imperial,** and **Bellavista.** The last is gaining an increasing number of followers.

Estepona turns up quite a variety of restaurants, the **Yellow Book** being the top choice on the bestseller list of independents. It is located at Km. 167 on the Malaga-Cadiz pike. Taped music and decor of the twenties; baby lamb carved at tableside and quiche lead the gustatory parade; reserve ahead (Tel: 800484); closed Mondays. **Le Nailhac** in the **Byblos Hotel** is known along the entire coast as being one of the most exclusive centers of gastronomy in the region. **Salas Chef** (Puerto Deportiva) serves international dishes with an inclination toward seafare. **El Molino,** same ownership as El Libro Amarillo (''Yellow Book'') offers so-so French cuisine while **Antonio,** at the local marina and **Marcues** (Puerto Duquesa) serve sea critters. Just between ourselves, we have a hunch that the budding *Puerto de Estepona* complex will one day knock the spots off its Banus competitor. The **Club Nautico** is quite good too for fish and grills.

In *Fuengirola,* **Los Marinos I** (Paseo Maritimo) is tops for seafood, while **Oscar** (Cruz 15) offers a more international cuisine with emphasis on fowl dishes. **El Jardin Escondido** (Acapulco 28), **Ceferino** (Valencia), and **La Langosta** (Los Boliches) complete the roster.

Marbella's waves have rolled up a crester on a hill named **La Hacienda** (Las Chapas) at kilometer stone 193. It's a white adobe structure composed of a small bar at its entrance leading to a T-shape room with a fireplace where the T is crossed. Beamed ceiling; bleached walls; terra-cotta floor; wooden tables; cushioned chairs; elegant place settings with gargantuan wineglasses. Roquefort Salad and veal baked in aluminum foil were superb, as were the Roast Partridge in Vine Leaves and Quail Flambe. Phone ahead (831 267 or 831 116) for reservations. Closed Mondays. Recommended. One of Madrid's leading restaurateurs, Horcher, operates **La Fonda** at Plaza de Cristo 9–10, a former hotel that has been lavishly redesigned with the sleeping portions removed. Nouvelle Epoque interior with 16 tables and twice as many on its summer patio; lush botanical decor; menu featuring many original Horcher creations plus some regional homestyle dishes; average meal around $45 without wine. Dinner only; closed Sundays. **La Meridiana** • *Camino de la Cruz (next to the Mosque)* • is famous for its ''sesos con setas'' (brains with mushrooms) and other sophisticated specialties created under the supervision of Paolo Ghirelli. Try the 6-course sam-

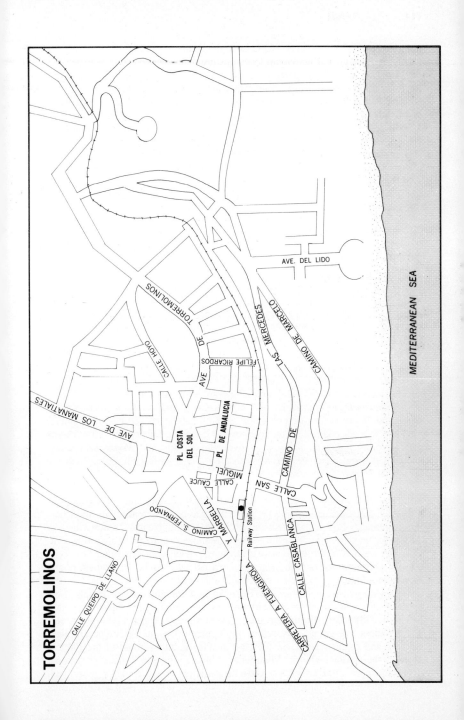

TORREMOLINOS

MEDITERRANEAN SEA

AVE. DEL LIDO

CAMINO DE MARCELO

LAS MERCEDES

FELIPE RICARDOS

AVE DE TORREMOLINOS

CALLE HOYO

PL. COSTA DEL SOL

PL. DE ANDALUCIA

CALLE MIGUEL

CALLE CAUCE

Y MARBELLA

CAMINO S. FERNANDO

AVE DE LOS MANATIALES

CAMINO DE

CALLE SAN

Railway Station

CALLE CASABLANCA

CALLE QUEPO DE LLANO

CARRETERA A FUENGIROLA

pling menu at approximately $45 per couple. Some might find certain creations daring in concept, but its overall standards are noteworthy.

La Dorada (at kilometer 176, Coral Beach complex) is recommendable for its seafood specialties in a somewht yuppie atmosphere. Also yummie. **Casino de Marbella,** open for dinner only, is located at Hotel Nueva Andalucia. With staff trained at Madrid's El Amparo, this new addition is rapidly gaining a solid reputation. Try the *dorada* with oranges and marinated lemon. Delicious. **Marbella Club,** at kilometer 178, is another gem. Chef Martel's *paella* is a gustatory delight. Other worthy contenders are **El Corzo** (at kilometer 187 toward Cadiz), which happens to be Los Monteros' restaurant, **Triana** *Gloria 11* ● for savory regional cuisine, and **Marisqueria Santiago** (at Paseo Maritimo) which is the natives' favorite spot for fish and shellfish creations. Feel like taking exquisite preparations for a picnic? Scamper off to **Semon** ● *Ortega y Gasset* ● where Miss Montse will entice you with a rich selection of pates, salmon, and other delicacies.

Out at fashionable *Puerto Banus*—so expensive that wags are beginning to call it the *Costa Tu Much*—Madrid's Clubs Jockey and "31" have extended their capital gains to this coastal venue. The **Club 31** hosts 200 guests in the main establishment with seating for 26 more in a private salon. Decor similar to the Madrid "31"; cuisine and its cost also following suit; functioning 7 days per week save in November, when it hibernates. Very chic. Other choices are **Cipriano** for fish, **Red Pepper** for Hellenic dishes, **La Taberna del Alabardero** for Basque creations, and **Don Leone** if you prefer Italian fare.

San Pedro de Alcantara, midway 'twixt Estepona and Marbella, can be proud of **Los Duendes,** which offers a cool terrace in summer, a crackling fire in winter, and chilling price tags the year round for its refined French-inspired cuisine. Service, cookery, and atmosphere are all deluxe calibre.

Sotogrande, of course, has the various dining and snack facilities of the 2 hotels, but if you are in quest of simple Spanish fish dishes and no-frills platters, then hop in a car and roll up the road toward Estepona. Otherwise, **Cabo Mayor** offers worthy nouvelle dishes in a lovely inner patio and **Midas** serves less sophisticated but adequate cuisine with after-dinner drinks till dawn; both are located at *Puerto Sotogrande.*

Torremolinos has an indifferent lot, the only exceptions being **El Roqueo** ● *Carmen 35 (Carihuela beach)* ● for international cuisine, and **Casa Guaquin** ● *Carmen 37 (Carihuela beach)* ● where Sr. Carmona is faithful to his fisherman's heritage. Lovely sea view and excellent cuisine. Nearby **Juan** ● *Mar 11–14* ● is the second most rewarding choice. Sample their pepper salad to accompany the fresh fish. **Moncho** will try to lure you into his beach lair. It's only so-so if you muncho, but the location is marineland. **Maria, El Comedor,** and **Frutos** at kilometer 235 are passable candidates only.

In *Malaga,* the state-operated **Hosteria de Gibralfaro** (see "Hotels") offers one of the most stunning panoramas of any restaurant in Spain. It's atop Monte de Gibralfaro, 10 minutes out; heavenly terrace, especially at night; cuisine tasteless but prices reasonable; don't miss a trip up here. For excellent cookery and sophistication, on the other hand, the dining room of the **Palacio Hotel** is the patrician choice. **Malagueto** is big locally; you'll discover regional dishes at upper-moderate prices. **Cafe de Paris** (as if you couldn't guess) specializes in French cuisine. If you like Italian food don't miss **La Romantica**

(Carcer 3), which claims to be the Costa del Sol's "most prestigious pizzeria"—and they might be right. For an amazingly low outlay you'll enjoy abundant quality foodstuffs in a clean and—yes—romantic ambience. For a sunny-day lunch, the seaside, pueblo-style **Antonio Martin,** near the bullring, is a relaxing noontime choice. Here you'll find the best general level of cookery in the town; sit only in the waterfront patio; its inside dining room seemed a mite less inviting and is always packed. Finny fare is best (especially the *chanquetes,* if they are running—inch-long white fish that resemble fat needles and are kissin' cousins to anemic eels); tabs are low; go early or reserve in advance. Very popular. Otherwise, **Casa Pedro** (Paseo Maritimo), **El Figon de Bonilla** (Cervantes, Edificio Horizonte), and **Bistrot** (Cervantes 10) come next in my listing.

CUENCA   This is one of Spain's most spectacular attractions, reachable from Madrid by car in about two hours. The thriving **Old Town** has been clinging to the rocky cliffs above its solemn gray gorge since the 14th century. The **New Town** is still growing—and uglier by the minute. Ignore the latter except for the excellent and reasonably priced **Hotel Torremangana** and **Alfonso VIII,** and center your attentions on the Plaza Mayor (main square) from where you can begin your strolling. The architecture is a mixture of fortress and residence, as if medieval hives for humans were once attached to the raw stone. Replicas of the "skyscrapers," "hanging houses," the Torremangana (tower), and other features of this unique hamlet are produced in red clay and glazed porcelain by potters in this artists' quarter. In the upper tier of the town you'll find the **Museum of Abstract Art** containing many of the finest contemporary masters in Spain today—names such as Tapies, Zobel, Muro, Rueda, Chillida, Torner, and about a score more. The building itself is as engaging as this challenging art. Next door is the town's most celebrated restaurant, **Meson Casas Colgadas,** which advertises itself as "typical," one of the locality's most vigorous exercises in false modesty. The view is nothing less than breathtaking, the food is outstanding as regional cuisine, the prices are low, and the service is courteous. Dishes include stuffed partridge, trout from the local streams, and an almond-honey pastry called *alaju.* Other mealtime possibilities are **Marlo** (Colon 59), **El Figon de Pedro** (Cervantes 13), famous for its local specialties, and **Los Claveles** (18 de Julio 32) but none can touch the vistas at the Meson.

The **Museum of Archaeology** is worth about an hour unless you are a scholar; visit the **Cathedral,** but the **Treasury** at the **Museo Diocesano** is of little interest except for its pair of jeweled gold crowns.

One of the top sights of my travel lifetime resides about 45 minutes by car from Cuenca—and very few foreign tourists seem to know about it. It is called **Ciudad Encantada** (Enchanted Town), but go only if you can walk over rough paths for about an hour and only if the skies are clear. Fantastic rock formations created by weathering cover an area of about 25 acres. The shapes are awesome—and even astonishing when you consider that the film industry has not yet discovered them as a backdrop for *Planet Zorro* or some other futuristic movie. Perhaps these forms are too unbelievable and, hence, have been ignored. Only a simple hutch with a wheezy fire, a bowl of soup, and some skinny lambchops is on the property, so you may prefer to bring a picnic.

GRANADA

Granada is lovely. Allow plenty of time to browse through the world-famous Alhambra and the Generalife. They represent high moments in Arabic architecture and the government is currently dedicating enormous funding for their preservation. Alhambra means "red house"; its glow is especially dramatic toward sunset. The gardens command half a day alone to view properly. The 13th-century Alcazaba, Carlos V's palace, the Cathedral with the royal chapel and tombs of the Catholic monarchs, the Albaicin, and the Cartuja are only starting points. Then, as evening closes, look across the violet flat *vega* to the rise of the Sierra Nevada, only 20 miles away. This sports center is a wonderful excursion point if you need refreshment from artifacts of 2 great ancient civilizations.

HOTELS

Most visitors' first choice for overnighting is the state-operated ★★★★**Parador San Francisco** up in the Alhambra complex itself. The building was originally an Arab palace and mosque; lately it was converted into a Franciscan convent and finally into a parador. ("Lately" in the Granadino's mind means circa 1492!) This officially declared National Monument is a unique repository for many of the region's greatest artists and artisans. It is literally crammed with rare iron and copper pieces, rugs, tiles, mosaics, and embroideries. Its 38 air-conditioned nests are always booked 6 months in advance. Just plain wonderful.

Among the privately owned hostelries, the ☆☆☆☆**Luz de Granada** provides by far the best accommodations and service. Clean modern structure; spacious lobby with tentacles of lounges radiating from one side; masculine bar and wide-angle dining room up 2 flights; delicious cuisine on our belly-busting luncheon; perfect attention from a well-trained squadron of maitres and waiters; different ownership El Cadi disco on the premises. Bedrooms not too big, but thick in comforts and thin in price. Then comes ★★★**Carmen,** a 205-room, air-conditioned entry. Centrally situated in the main shopping district and a most welcome addition to this city's hotel family. The 121-unit ★★**Alhambra Palace** offers perhaps the best position of all for sightseeing. Rooms perked up; full air cooling; fresh facade. Portions remain dreary, but efforts are being made to restore its grace. Midtown **Melia Granada** was thoroughly renovated and the **Washington Irving,** where the wordsmith once stayed, is going through a revamping program too. Its progressive abandonment was a pity for a hostelry that holds such an excellent position edging the Alhambra. Nearby, **Residencia Macia** offers 40 fresh, clean, attractive kips in the low-priced category. **Hostal America,** within the walls of the Alhambra, displays 14 cozy nooks in a most convenient location. It has a lovely patio for alfresco dining. I enjoy its family atmosphere and recommend it wholeheartedly. Also in the Alhambra district, **Alixares del Generalife** is devoted to group tourism. Modern layout; 148 fresh bedrooms, convention hall; swimming pool and private garden. Cool ambience, but well maintained. **Princesa Ana** and **Triunfo Granada** are two worthy additions to the local scene. **Brasilia** turns on its greatest appeal at the 7th floor, where the front accommodations boast Sierra-view balconies. Midcity situation, sparkly, air-conditioned, and worthy for the outlay. The **Guadalupe** welcomes numerous groups to its Alhambra arms. If you can snag either #407 or #426, do.

RESTAURANTS

Granada's top choice is **Baroca** ● *Pedro A. Alarcon 34* ● English decoration; refined cookery, often utilizing avocados inventively presented; big, too, on mousses, crepes, and hardy grills. The garden at **Parador San Francisco** is lovely in good weather. The inside is pleasant, too. For regional dishes nothing tops **Alacena de las Monjas** ● *Plaza Padre Suarez* ● situated in a 16th-century palace. **Ruta del Veleta** ● *Carretera de la Sierra 50 (km. 5,500)* ● also serves excellent local fare. **Horno de Santiago** ● *Plaza de los Campos 8* ● specializes in Basque and Castilian cuisine. **Carmen San Miguel** ● *Torres Bermejas 3* ● **Pilar del Toro** ● *Hospital de Santa Ana 12* ● and **Velazquez** ● *Emilio Orozco 1* ● serve adequate local creations. For day-in-dine-out consistency, you could keep going back to the **Sevilla** (Oficios 12), where you'll see nothing spectacular and you'll swallow nothing spectacular. Nevertheless, for this city, it's darned good—and it seems to stay that way year after happy year. If you feel like driving 16 miles to **Durcal,** don't miss **El Molino** (Camino de las Fuentes). This 18th-century building houses the Andalusian Center for Gastronomical Research. Here you can not only enjoy interesting Moorish dishes but take with you homemade cheese, jam, and fruit preserves.

Before dinner, try to find sophisticated **Jardines Aben Humeya,** hidden at the heart of the Albayzin (Carril de las Tomasas 12) and accessible only through steep, narrow, winding, cobbled roads. Sipping a sherry on its secluded and romantic terrace while you admire the imposing "night look" of the Alhambra might constitute one of your most cherished remembrances of this enchanting town.

~~~~~~

NIGHT LIFE

The gypsy dancing remains a disgusting racket. The sucker is levied the fixed price for a package deal, and the tour operator then selects the cave that will yield the most profit for the least effort. Average performance less than 30 minutes; "artists" so untalented no top operation would hire them (the best migrate to Madrid, Barcelona, or Seville); one free eyedropper of rotgut *manzanilla* for "refreshments"; spectators packed in too tight for anyone to escape before completion of the show. You'll be sorry if you don't avoid this travesty; it's a cosmic low in tourist-racketeering. Away from the city, there are the nightly 2-hour performances at the poolside **Jardines Neptuno,** where the entrance fee of around $15 includes one quaff and the show. The flamenco sessions in **La Cueva de la Golondrina** (advance notice necessary) have been sterilized, dehumanized, and left bereft of any cultural significance. As a curiosity, however, they still may be worth a jaunt. If you can stand a so-so dinner and dance "sevillanas" till dawn, go to **El Corral de Principe** • *Campo del Principe.* Otherwise, **Zocalo** • *Granada 7* • 4 kilometers out of town at Ogijares provides a soothing ambience in its lovely garden while you enjoy classical music.

JEREZ DE LA FRONTERA, home of sherry and Iberian-style "cognac" (in Spanish, *conac*), revolves around these palatable products to the exclusion of all other interests. Make the fascinating tour of one of the major *bodegas* (Gonzalez Byass, Pedro Domecq, Harvey's, Sandeman, or Williams), which extend all the way down to the oceanside village of *Puerto de Santa Maria* to see how these potables are produced; advance booking mandatory. Try not to miss Alvaro Domecq's Equestrian School on Ave. Duque de Abrantes, where he runs his world-famous show "How Andalousian Horses Dance." Charming little country town, with lots of color.

Among hotels, the **Jerez,** already *numero uno,* is now run by the Aga Khan's excellent CIGA group. It should become even better. Spanking-white 3-story structure; cool, carpeted reception and sunken lounge; clean, airy dining den abutting an alfresco terrace and pool; chummy equestrian bar. Recommended. Alternate choices might be the **Royal Sherry Park,** the newish **Avenida Jerez,** or the **Capele.** Finally, there is a parador at **Arcos de la Frontera,** about 18 miles from Jerez, that's a good option.

But what this sherryland lacks in hotels, it more than equals in its absence of good restaurants. Jerez, for some strange reason, seems almost a gastronomic desert. One possible oasis is **Venta Antonio,** at kilometer 5 toward Sanlucar. It specializes in fresh sea fare with the accent on shellfish. **La Posada** • *Arboledilla 1* • is becoming more reliable. **El Bosque** • *Av. Alvaro Domecg* • 1 km from the center along the Seville highway. Has a big name locally. **La Mesa Redonda** • *Manuel de la Quintana 3* • and **Gaitan** • *Gaitan 33* • offer regional cuisine in a homey atmosphere, while **Tendido 6** • *Circo 10* • specializes in fish.

MADRID

This capital of more than 3 million people is right smack in the middle of the country. In size it ranks just under Philadelphia; in temperature, hotels, food, and gracious living, it's hard to find an equal in Europe. May and October are the best months; midwinter is sometimes surprisingly cold, due to the city's situation and altitude. It's uncomfortably hot for only about 2 weeks per annum—and many hotels are now fully or at least partially air-conditioned.

ATTRACTIONS

Unlike London, Madrid is a tale of at least 4 cities. It also is the cradle of the Spanish Empire's *Siglo de Oro* ("Golden Century") when writers such as Lope de Vega, Calderon, and Tirso de Molina stood as towering figures in the world of letters. The traveler probably will be most concerned with the following:

MEDIEVAL MADRID: The best examples of this period are the **Torre de Lujanes** (Plaza de la Villa), the **San Nicolas de los Servitas** (Plaza de San Nicolas), and the church of **San Pedro El Viejo** (Puerta del Sol).

MADRID OF THE HAPSBURGS: The Austrian influence is best seen in the **Casa de Cisneros** (Plaza de la Villa) with its wonderful collection of tapestries, the **Casa de las Siete Chimeneas** (Plaza del Rey), a "House of the Seven Chimneys" from the 16th century containing important works of art, and the church of **San Sebastian** (corner of San Sebastian) where the dramatist Lope de Vega is interred. As this is one of the richest time frames of Spanish architectural prowess, the list of exemplary buildings is extensive. You shouldn't miss the **Plaza Mayor,** a fortification erected in 1617 that is a Madrid landmark, or the baroque cathedral of **San Isidro** where the remains of the city's patron saint are located. I am also fond of the church of **San Antonio de los Alemanes** (Corredera Baja de San Pablo) containing the works of Carreno, Ricci, and Giordano, among others, and **San Gines** (Arenal 13) with paintings by El Greco and Ricci. For students of *Don Quijote,* the **Convento de las Trinitarias** (Lope de Vega) is where Cervantes is buried and the **Hospitalillo del Carmen** (Atocha 87) is an ancient hospital—later turned into a print shop—where the first edition of the famous book was published.

MADRID OF THE BOURBONS: Even if you don't understand Spanish, a visit to the **Teatro Real** or Royal Theater (Plaza de Oriente) is rewarding. It was constructed in 1818 by Antonio Lopez; the district also contains the **Royal Conservatory** and **Concert Hall.** The **Academy of Fine Arts** (Alcala 13) is an excellent example of neoclassical architecture. Every citizen is in love with the **Cibeles fountain,** a grand show by day or night. **San Antonio de la Florida** (Paseo de la Florida) contains some important frescos by Goya as well as the remains of the artist himself.

MADRID OF THE 19TH CENTURY: The **National Library** (Paseo de Recoletos 18), the **Bank of Spain** (Plaza de la Cibeles), and the **Stock Market** (Plaza de la Lealtad) are perhaps the most imposing edifices of this period. A more thorough tour would include the **Parliament** (Plaza de las Cortes) and the romantic **Apollo Fountain** (Paseo del Prado).

Of course, Madrid has a modern side; possibly the most controversial structure in the town is the wildly ornate **Palacio de Comunicaciones** (Plaza de la Cibeles), which just squeezed into the 20th century in 1904. Today there are innumerable banks and office towers reflecting the most daring architectural innovations in Europe. And one of the nicest areas of counterpoint to high-rise construction is the network of parks throughout the capital. The finest is **El Retiro** with its lake, fortress, gardens, and statuary. The **Botanical Garden** preens in front of the Prado. The **Casa de Campo** was formerly the private hunting grounds of Felipe II; it includes a lake with rowboats, a pool, a zoo, and an amusement park. The **Sabatini Gardens** are on the north side of the Royal Palace; the **Campo del Moro,** established by Felipe III, is in the same area. Others include **Alameda de Osuna, Fuente del Berro,** and **Parque del Oeste.** Now for a few of the standard attrractions:

Teleferico • *Paseo del Pintor Rosales* • Although there are no hills to climb in order to look down on Madrid, you can provide yourself with a bird's eye view of this sprawling metropolis while riding the *teleferico* linking the paseo del Pintor Rosales and Casa de Campo Park.

Museo del Prado • *Prado Museum, paseo del Prado* • One of the foremost museums in the world, the Prado shows not only works of Spanish origin but also masterpieces from Flemish and Italian schools. A new wing doubles the original display space. Treasures include works by El Greco, Velasquez, Goya, Rubens, and other Spanish artists from the 12th through 18th centuries, plus examples of work by Titian, Van Dyck, Hieronymus Bosch, Tintoretto, Murillo, and scores of others. Behind the museum, you'll find the **Cason del Buen Retiro** and the **Villahermosa Palace;** the former shows Pablo Picasso's stark, emotionally charged *Guernica,* which at the artist's behest was not permitted to be displayed in Spain during the long years of the Franco regime, as well as Spanish 19th-century art; the latter will soon become Goya's museum. The Prado also houses important classical sculpture, coins, enamels, and goldwork—the last among the "Jewels of the Great Dauphin" (Louis XIV, whose grandson was Felipe V); Napoleon snatched them but Spain finally got them back. Closed Mondays.

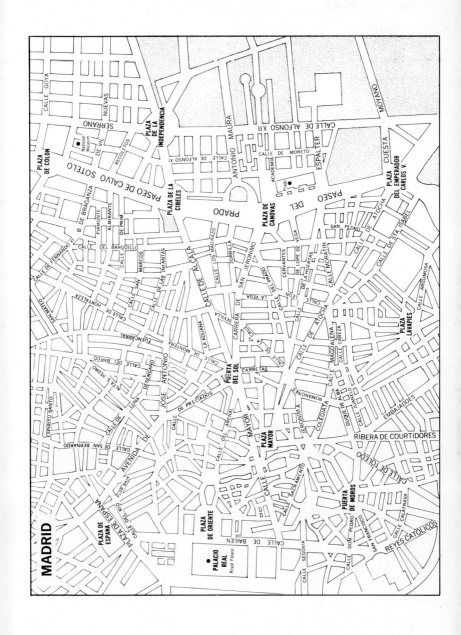

Palacio Real ● *Royal Palace, plaza de Oriente* ● One of Madrid's main tourist attractions is the Royal Palace, which is open to the public. (King Juan Carlos resides in the more modest Zarzuela Palace.) This huge 18th-century neoclassical building is considered one of Europe's finest palaces. Itself a museum with its hundreds of Gothic tapestries, throne-room ceiling by Tiepolo, and Royal Pharmacy, you can also visit a Museum of Carriages on its grounds as well as the living quarters of former Spanish rulers (filled with priceless furniture) and the Royal Armory, with an exceptional collection of instruments of torture and old weapons. The palace is surrounded by beautiful grounds.

Museo Arqueologico ● *National Museum of Archaeology, calle Serrano 13* ● The Altamira Caves are closed to the public, but you can see replicas of them here. The museum also has a significant collection of Greek vases and Roman art and artifacts as well as prehistoric finds, more ancient art, medieval art, coins, and ceramics. Closed Mondays.

Museum of Contemporary Art ● *Juan de Herrera 2* ● This recently opened museum of modern art has works by Miro and Picasso. Closed Mondays.

Museo de Lazaro Galdiano ● *Lazaro Galdiano Museum, calle Serrano 122* ● This modest-sized museum (30 rooms) makes up in quality and variety what it lacks in quantity. Installed in a lovely villa, it contains choice works by Zurbaran, Goya, Velasquez, and El Greco, a rich tapestry collection, a noted display of enamel and ivory, furniture, coins, and silver and gold. Closed Mondays.

Centro Cultural Reina Sofia ● *Santa Isabel 52* ● A most interesting and modern exhibition center that since its recent inauguration has become one of Madrid's most important cultural magnets. Closed Tuesdays. When you arrive in the capital, ask what's on.

El Rastro ● Madrid's Rastro is one of the prototypes of the flea market. If you have an eagle eye for antiques, you might succeed in sorting out something of value from the masses of secondhand goods and odds and ends of every description. But you need not spend a peseta to enjoy mingling with the crowds of shoppers and browsers in a holiday mood.

Excursions

El Pardo ● *Pardo Palace* ● For 40 years, Generalissimo Francisco Franco ruled Spain, outlasting his Facist counterparts in Germany and Italy by more than a generation. During his time as Head of State, Franco lived in the 16th-century Pardo Palace, a few miles outside the capital city. Recently, the Generalissimo's successor, King Juan Carlos opened this residence to the public. On view are Franco's personal effects, uniforms, and photographs, as well as memorabilia of his tenure in office.

Surroundings of Madrid? Bus excursions are operated on various days of the week to 5 popular suburban targets; check with your concierge for schedules and details. ***Toledo,*** 44 miles to the south, has often been called "the most perfect and brilliant record of genuine Spanish civilization." The walls and crenels are intact; if you can arrange to be here before or after the bus excursions pour in, there's a pervading mood of ancient Castile. The setting is magnificent, the **Cathedral** is a treasure house of art, the **Sephardic Museum** at **El Transito Synagogue** is a flight into history, **El Greco's** house is routinely interesting (his best works have gone elsewhere)—but so many souvenir hawkers and curbstone promoters greet the swarming armies of sightseers that the atmosphere at midday can be tinny, mechanical, and cheap. *Don't buy a single piece of merchandise in this city;* the sharks who run some of the supposedly most respectable shops charge up to 40% more than you'll pay in Madrid for the identical item. ***El Escorial,*** 18 miles out, has Felipe II's famous castle-monastery filled with paintings, royal tombs, and royal antiquities. Still standing boldly since the 16th century, it remains one of the finest Renaissance edifices in Europe today, with 12,000 windows and doors, 7 handsome towers, and 15 gateways. The library (open to view and close scrutiny of ancient manuscripts) was once considered the world's largest and in the forefront of early science. The village is simply a Spanish hilltown, but adequate for finding a tavern meal or pausing under the shade trees for a cool drink in summer. The surrounding Guadarrama mountains are rugged in greystone and scrub pine that turn to indigo at sunset. Nearby, ***Valle de los Caidos*** ("Valley of the Fallen"), Generalisimo Franco's tombsite and monument to casualties on *both* sides of the Spanish Civil War, is colossal in scope. A mountain of rock, topped by a cross 500 feet high and 300 feet across the arms (elevator inside), has been converted into a gigantic basilica and great nave large enough to hold 4 good-size churches with space to spare. Approximately 30 miles from the capital; lots of buses cover both Los Caidos and neighboring Escorial for honest fares that include the usual third-rate lunch. ***Avila,*** 70 miles to the northwest of El Escorial, is a fairy-tale city with 86 towers and a medieval wall rising starkly from the landscape; it is an essential part of the Spanish picture—to see it is to capture a capsule image of Iberia.

Try to make the ***Segovia–La Granja*** tour. The latter was the summer residence of Spain's first Bourbon monarch; it's in a glorious parkland with tended gardens, fountains, and architecture that resembles Versailles. If you wish to view the famous tapestries, phone first for the opening times at the palace itself. At the entrance gates there are 3 simple restaurants, but all along the route there are beautiful forested picnic sites. (See "Segovia" for futher information.) If you're on your own, you can easily pause for an inspection of the Valley of the Fallen, which is roughly in the same area. Then continue on via the road that tunnels 1½ miles under the Guadarrama Mountain Range; the small toll is negligible for a look at this engineering marvel.

Art lovers will certainly find it rewarding to visit **Museo Picasso** in *Buitrago*—47 miles northeast of Madrid. Opened in 1985, it displays 48 works given by the genius to his friend and barber, Eugenio Arias.

HOTELS

☆☆☆☆☆ **Ritz** • is elegant and smallish. Skillful administration by keen-eyed John Macedo has given it greater beauty and glory than it possessed even in former times. The outside now shines with fresh pride and so do an increasing number of interior facilities; there's a 1910-style terrace under awnings; refashioned dining salon is a gem; cuisine is again among the finest in the capital; the bewitching garden segment for summer meals has been magnificently relandscaped, partially covered, and insulated from street noises; lounges are nicely revamped; the bar is fresh, white, and formal—and protected by a statue of Diana the Huntress. Bedrooms, too, again reveal a stately grace. You'll find one of the most willing staffs on the Continent. The highly competent chief concierge Prudencio Diaz-Agero typifies the topflight personnel—people who have served loyal clients for more than a quarter-century.

☆☆☆☆☆ **Villa Magna** • is a midcity oasis, a quiet haven of Spanish *richesse* and refinement. Extravagant garden fronting its set-back entrance; balconied 9-story structure of polished marble, glass, and stainless steel; breathtaking Carlos IV lobby by world-famous Jansen of Paris; opulent restaurant downstairs; Mayfair Bar in English motif plus burgundy-banquetted Bonbonierre imbibery; aristocratic lounge; shops, hairdresser, and secretarial services; sauna; subterranean garage. All accommodations amply proportioned; 2 large easy chairs; double-glazed windows; individual thermostats; radio and TV; compartmented baths with twin basins. A *magnum opus* that is beautifully directed by Eduardo Cruz del Rio; now under Hyatt management and Japanese ownership.

☆☆☆☆ **Palace** • across the plaza from the Ritz, has come back with unrestrained zeal—and pesetas. The restoration is stunning and many Madrid visitors are returning to it with the same loyalty that was manifest in the past. Welcome by liveried doormen; exterior freshened; entrance and rotunda sparkling with Old World grandeur; Neptuno Grill restyled and trellis restaurant (11 a.m. to 2 a.m.) added; corridors updated smartly; most bedrooms raised to "superior" status by its CIGA proprietors. Today this is almost a totally new hotel retaining the best traditional features. Director Juan Berges is doing a commendable job here.

☆☆☆☆ **Miguel Angel** • (Spanish, of course for "Michelangelo") is a masterpiece of more contemporary hotel arts. The lounges are vast, with icelands of chandeliers—even with crystal balustrades; the Farnesio bar pulses quietly under a smoked-mirror ceiling; the Zacarias restaurant-cum-discotheque is down a few steps off the lobby; a garden court offers aperitif tables and stone sculpture by Assler (reminiscent of Lipchitz); the indoor pool is airy, with cheerful white furniture on its apron; there's a Finnish sauna, a Turkish bath, hairdresser, and a shopper's lane. Upstairs, the corridors are sedate but dark; the small bedrooms feature silk spreads and textiled walls, brass sconces, silent valets, deep carpeting, TV-music consoles, air conditioning, and superb furnishings.

☆☆☆ **Melia Madrid** • offers a lobby cleverly architected to kindle warmth in an essentially cool milieu; Don Pepe Grill up 1-flight, bigger, impersonal, less ingratiating Princesa Restaurant in the same level; Ebano ("Ebony") Bar with dimensions too open for intimacy; adjoining lounge; discotheque. Rooms comparatively commodious and air-conditioned, all with TV, refrigerator, piped music, wall-to-wall carpeting, and handsome fabrics; baths small but efficient; showers over nonskid tubs. The 3rd floor is devoted to a quintet of deluxe suites, with a hand-picked staff to coddle their occupants. Superb value.

☆☆☆ **Castellana** • offers one of the capital's friendliest staffs. By recapturing the grace of the fifties, innkeeper Jacques Chevasson is going backward in a forward-looking way. All public rooms and bedchambers refreshed; high-priced Oxeito nook for *marisco* (seafood) niblets from noon to midnight, a Turkish bath, and some impressively viewful double suites. You'll also find an 80-car garage and other supplementary facilities. Now excellent.

☆☆ **Luz Palacio** • stands 9 stories above a residential block of the Paseo de la Castellana. Totally air-conditioned; effective, gracious entrance and lobby; cleverly illuminated adjoining bar; attractive food displays; evening dancing in the spacious yellow-hued dining room; a pervading atmosphere of soft, modern luxury befitting its deluxe station.

☆☆ **Mindanao** • makes its deluxe headquarters in the University District; air-conditioned. L-shape lobby; coolish Domayo restaurant; evenings-only Club Mindanao; adjoining Coffee Shop; dimly lighted, lazy-S-form bar; somewhat uninviting P-shape swimming pool in the basement. Predominance of twin units; a few suites and singles available; small bedchambers for stout rates.

☆☆ **Plaza** • fully air-conditioned, is one of Europe's tallest hotels and boasts a wonderful penthouse. On its 25th and 26th floors, you'll find dancing in a disco-pub, a swimming pool for summer splashing, and roof-garden dining, plus an unparalleled view of the city. Spanish flavors both in decor and in its all a la carte cuisine; huge panoramic windows; an urbane bar with a small lounge; no groups ever accepted in this area. Swarming lobby; boutiques, a drugstore, and travel agency on mezzanine; downstairs Coffee Shop; big dining room; brightened corridors. Motorists have access to the underground garage across from the entrance.

★★ **Eurobuilding** • is composed of 2 attractive, angular edifices of laminated white marble. While the 8-story wing contains the posher pads, another 15-floor segment is devoted to more cost-conscious voyagers and convention groups. A quartet of restaurants, with the Balthasar, in Arabian reds, offering the most elegance; 4 distinctive bars; massive congress quarters; concourse of shops; sauna and garden-sited pools; barber and hairdresser; 700-car garage. Generous spread of 150 suites in the high-priced plush section; 450 bedchambers in the other block. Full air conditioning; balconettes; TV and piped music; pastel color schemes; modern furnishings; good baths.

☆☆ **Princesa Plaza** • makes a dignified bow to modernity, nicely blended with an amplitude of well-chosen deluxe amenities. Vast, stalwart edifice; spacious lobby and lounges; yellow-toned Margarita restaurant; Triangulo cafeteria; Bar Chic; hairdresser; saunas and massage facilities; underground parking. I find it restful and efficient—in the better traditions of the 21st century.

☆☆ **Monte Real** • seems to have made a marvelous recovery after suffering from a severe case of love-loss and neglect. It is in a special category because of its outskirts situation at Calle Arroyo del Fresno 1–15 minutes out by taxi and just a potent mashie shot from El Pardo. Crescent-shape swimming pool; summer bar; garden-bowered with bouquets of color; nearby golf course. Within, you'll find a cheerful dining room, a downstairs Grill with impressive artwork, and other appurtenances. Once again a desirable retreat from the big-city jitters.

★★ **Wellington** • is fashionably moored on the fringes of sylvan Retiro Park. Continuous updatings; rose and white fittings; all units now have air conditioning, taped music, TV, hand-stitched broadlooms, and attractive *seregrafia* tiles in the baths; dive into one facing the pool if you can. English pub, cafeteria, plus the none-too-inspired El Fogon grill. This is the traditional dwelling of *toreros* and breeders. Say *ole* to *Cucharito,* the stuffed bull in the lounge, which was dispatched by Paco Camino (but not in the hotel).

☆☆ **Villa Real** • is a recent and most welcome addition to Madrid's distinguished hotels scene. Conveniently located at *Plaza de las Cortes,* next to the Spanish Parliament, it offers all sorts of facilities and amenities. Exquisite decoration in traditional style. Sumptuous Royal and Imperial Suites and well-appointed rooms throughout. Heartily recommended.

☆ **Melia Castilla** • one of the most massive shelters abroad, is an "aparthotel" run as a concession for a multitude of investors. Three-level brick-toned Hidalgo Grill plus a cafeteria; attractive La Marisqueria seafood nook; everything under the sun for the wanderer, especially if he and she are business oriented. Despite efforts to the contrary, the lobby, the public rooms, and the ambience are as *intime* as Grand Central Station. Upstairs, the pinched "efficiency" bedchambers each offer radio, TV, and an elfin bath. This monster is frankly designed and operated more and more for the conventioneer—and not the lavishly open-pursed one, either. With it has come a high chill factor.

★ **Pintor-Goya** • named, of course, for the great Spanish artist, makes its address appropriately at Goya 79, a brushstroke from picturesque Retiro Park and the Serrano shops. A tableau of tourist comforts fills its 9-story canvas. Lobby verdant with cascading flora; glass-hemmed garden; restful peacock-blue salon; small dining room that seems an afterthought; good barber; partly submerged garage. All quarters are tastefully blessed with pleasing pastels, chilled air, and commodious baths.

☆ **Suecia** ● ("Sweden"), conveniently sited behind the Cortes, is a reasonable bet. Except for the ground-level lobby, the first 4 floors of its building are occupied by Swedish offices (a bonus in silence for the upper tiers of bedchambers). Entrance on a tiny street; sauna (men only); small rooms, all with old-fashioned baths, all air-conditioned, and all with Swedish-style furnishings; Bellman Restaurant. Here's a nonfancy operation.

Hotel Residencia Florida Norte ● greets you with a handsome high-ceilinged lobby lined with light gray marble. Strikingly lighted salon to right with coffee-brown wall-to-wall carpeting; harmonious furnishings, and huge gobelins; Bar Goya on open mezzanine communicating with cafeteria; world-of-tomorrow subterranean restaurant; TV lounge; gift shop; hairdresser and barbershop; 100-slot garage. All units come with air conditioning, taped melodies, and a contemporary mien; all but the smallest singles have an independent seating area and ample dimensions.

☆ **Velazquez** ● air-conditioned and looking very smart today, has bounded back with renewed vigor; many renewed baths and rooms. Very good location and now recommended.

Colon ● is commercial and not handy to the shopping district.

☆ **Alcala** ● near Retiro Park, is a quiet retreat with a small lobby-lounge and circular iron hearth, a better-than-average restaurant (under outside concession and with Basque specialties), cheerful halls, discreet lighting, and a kindly staff. Air conditioning throughout; dual-glaze windows on the front to blunt the din of the busy street; TV and piped music for further soothing. Cozy bedchambers, full-length mirrors, and walnut-paneled walls.

☆ **Mayorazgo** ● welcomes visitors with a Castilian lobby. It is soothingly and conveniently set back from the street. A fresh lounge, replete with fireplace and stained-glass windows, also offers a warm welcome. Units here are sized on the small side and range in ambience from adequate to pleasant.

Residencia Breton ● has a pleasantly modern lobby from which a booze bar, snack bar, and breakfast nook are separated by screens. For the price, it's okay.

Emperatriz ● was a total disappointment but I am told that the **Victoria** is quite good for the moderate category. I don't know the latter.

Principe Pio ● is too routine to inspire much enthusiasm.

☆ **Sanvy** ● features an English Club (attractive as an extra residents' lounge), an American-style cafeteria with Spanish-slanted vittles, a ballroom, the violet-and-white Victor Bar-Discotheque, a beauty salon, and a barbershop. Pool still a popular puddle for Madrid's summer heatnicks; every unit with private plumbing; 4 suites on each of its 6 floors; no singles, but doubles rented at lower rates to lone wanderers. Interior units better than exterior ones; staff not too helpful in my experience.

Claridge • is a long haul from the city's heartbeat. Corner situation rising 15 floors above the portals; modern dogleg lobby with a coffee shop, a small food stall, and a cocktail lounge at the paw's end; noise level heightened by bar music; unfancy but adequate cellar dining room with open kitchen; dimensions inclined to be dwarfish.

Menfis • once was an appealing address, but not enough care has gone into it lately.

Serrano • is only a hop from the U.S. Embassy and around the corner from one of the most fashionable shopping avenues in the city. Small structure with no restaurant, but a cozy pub with snacks; spotless chambers in contemporary Iberian motif; all doubles with Frigobar; administration by young, shy, and competent Don Jose Prados; extra-careful maintenance; eager and kindly staff.

Carlton • in a noisy, unattractive situation beyond the railway station, is gradually becoming fuddy-duddy and spiritless. Small dimensions with onion-skin-paper-thin walls; plain, uninspired decor. Tolerable only.

Hotel Zurbano • A vast palette of browns from sand to chocolate prevails from the lobby to the dining room to the upstairs corridors to the furniture and textiles of the accommodations and probably to the house cat (if there is one). Most units are not only decent in size but present 2 closets; each has its viable bath which, even without the ring around the tubs, is brown.

Cuzco • is quite a stretch from the center. Large characterless lobby; no restaurant; brightly lit snack bar and cafe; clean and efficiently executed, but sterile and impersonal in tone and atmosphere.

The **Barajas,** on a hillock overlooking Madrid's busy airport, is a spacious perch for your capital fly-over. The 4-level, red-brick, linear structure contains 230 air-conditioned and jet-proof bedchambers, all with bath—and many with private balcony too. It also boasts the Toledo and El Porche restaurants (the latter is alfresco), El Patio Coffee Shop, Las Brisas Club (by the pool), Discotheque 747, a shaker of bars, a beauty salon, a sauna, a gymnasium, and convention facilities; a heated pool also gushes an invitation to relax. **Alameda,** newer and with the same ownership, is a neighbor and a worthy alternate.

RESTAURANTS

☆☆☆☆☆ **Las Cuatro Estaciones** • *General Ibanez Ibero 5, corner of San Francisco de Sales 41* • means the "Four Seasons," a reflection of the exquisite cuisine here, which changes with nature's finest and freshest provender. This is one of the most attractive establishments I have seen (and normally I dislike restaurants without windows). In this case, however, masterful artifice has been employed—vines, mirrors, flowers, burgundy tones, and cork ceilings. Interesting presentations such as soup served in a hollowed-out pumpkin (autumn) conspire to further enhance the mood. Midday occupancy chiefly by executives; mixed clientele in the evenings; director Jean-Pierre Vandelle is the host and genius behind this operation. Be sure to quote the full address because many taxi drivers are puzzled by the first street only. Closed Sat., Sun., and Aug.

☆☆☆☆☆ **Zalacain** • *Alvarez de Baena 4* • is currently one of the most sought-after dining meccas in the capital. It is approached via an illuminated lawn off the Castellana. Rust-tone bar; textile walls, some hung with game paintings; rich woodwork; beautiful floral arrangements; Basque kitchen in the *nouvelle cuisine* style; elegant appointments in concord with its 5-star classification. Little ole Spain demonstrates how modern it can be here; prices now, gulp, run close to $300 per couple. It is at rest noon Sat., Sun., and all of Aug.

★★★★★ **Cabo Mayor** • *Juan Hurtado de Mendoza 11–13* • is a specialist in seafood but also contains an enviable larder of meat, fowl, and game. Downstairs location with entrance to a foyer and small wine cellar; wooden interior with nautical panels and white strakes; copper lamps, blocks, tackle, brass portholes, and carved wooden statuary. The *besugo* (sea bream) with green peppercorns and a salmon steamed with saffron were delicious. One of the most interesting maritime menus in Europe with its focus on northern-water rather than Mediterranean fish. Closed Sun. and Aug.

★★★ **La Dorada** • *Orense 64* • is also a devote of marine life, but this time mainly Mediterranean creatures. Decor composed of polished wood, ships lamps, binnacles, and all manner of chandlery; waiters in blue middy jackets and striped undershirts; extremely fast service that some clients dislike and other prefer. I am told that the waiters operate on commission, so they hustle the traffic and frequently push the high-ticket items. Try the dorada in a baked crust of salt—heavenly! This fast-paced candidate also boasts branches in Barcelona and Seville. Closed Sun.

☆☆☆☆ **Cafe de Oriente** • is located across from the beautiful Oriente Palace, containing only 9 tables in a high, brick, vaulted room that is the last word in exclusivity. The *maestro* here is King Juan Carlos's private confessor and profits go to the cleric's charity. If you don't like the Basque-style food, just jot a note to His Majesty. The buck stops there. Next-door's **Horno** features a brasserie atmosphere and popular-priced gastronomy. Though the 2 are totally different in character, they are mentioned here together for your convenience.

☆☆ **Horcher** • *Alfonso XII 6* • is very well known, intimate, and, of course, very traditional in its gastronomy—a fashion that may be fading elsewhere in Europe but that remains intact in the Spanish capital. While most of the Old Guard still swear by it, I am finding the cooking uneven and faulted by not keeping up with the leading edge of culinary trends. The atmosphere remains luxurious. Very expensive and accordingly (but unnecessarily) haughty.

☆☆ **Jockey** • *Amador de los Rios 6* • is small (21 tables only), highly exclusive, and expensive. *Always crowded,* so arrange with your hotel concierge to book in advance. Closed all of August; open daily and Sunday, otherwise. The chief demurrer here is that sometimes the ''regulars'' get too much good attention, while the newcomers are given the impression they're out in left field; when no table reservations are made at peak times, the neophyte almost surely will be shunted into the listless lofts upstairs, without even a hope of experiencing the real Jockey. Go late (2:30 p.m. or 10:30 p.m.). Closed Sun. and Aug.

☆☆☆ **Alkalde** • *Jorge Juan 10* • is not much to look at but the cuisine is honest and memorable. The crab-cream soup would have to travel lightyears to find a rival. In fact, most dishes are far ahead of competitive efforts in similar upper-middle-class peerage. Ground-floor room with typical standing bar for snacks, plus a few tables; downstairs with brick arches and several segments; rough walls and tile floors; easygoing atmosphere but always busy. Outstanding. Closed Sat. and Sun. afternoons and Aug.

Club 31 • *Alcala 58* • is cool to the point of registering a chill factor. But it remains popular. Abundant and fine wine choices, interesting game dishes during hunting season in the autumn. Closed Aug. (when it's warm).

★★★★ **O'Pazo** • *Reina Mercedes 20* • the nostalgic heartbeat of romantic Galicia in the capital, offers an elegant greeting with its dressed-stone facade, coach lamps, and Georgian windows. Marblesque English bar to the right of entrance foyer with green banquettes, hunting prints, and shelves of Toby mugs; L-shaped, 3-segment, large dining room pleasantly outfitted with homeland paintings, patterned carpet, and moss and coral tablecloths; intimate seating despite the spaciousness of the salon. My party's seafood cocktail, medallions of octopus, croquettes, and grilled whitefish were uniformly succulent, revealing careful preparation. Closed Sun. and Aug.

★★★★ **El Amparo** • *Callejon de Puigcerda 8, corner of Jorge Juan* • is fashionable today; it also is one of the capital's more charming spots. To arrive at its portals is an enchanting experience, along a narrow aisle of old Castillian buildings. Multitiered interior; table settings in the new fashion with wide-brim plates as an appetizing showcase for the *nouvelle cuisine;* great attention to culinary presentation and color. As at Zalacain, the cookery is derived from Basque fundamentals with light modern variations on this theme. Advance reservations mandatory. Enjoyable, especially to the hungry eye. Closed Sat. and Sun. afternoons and Aug.

☆☆ **Jaun de Alzate** • *Calle de la Princesa 18* • is the workplace of chef Inaki Izaguirre, a genius and philosopher of gastronomy. Think about the following: a vichyssoise of white truffles, a tepid salad of scallops with cider vinegar and bergamot aroma, or a bass in *txacoli* (white Basque wine) with saffron. Here's a thoughtful inventor who honors a noble tradition in cooking.

★★★ **Casa Lucio** • *Cava Baja 35* • is beloved by *Madrilenos,* always having been considered the classical tavern of the city's Royal Court. Lucio's loyal followers include artists, politicians, high-ranking personalities, plus numerous Juan and Juanita Does of the capital. Tempting classical Spanish fare: fresh fish, shellfish, famous Jabugo ham, the popular *carne roja* (red meat), and a different stew daily; sip the economical *vino de la casa.* A branch called **El Viejo Madrid** is just opposite, whomping up exactly the same goods. Very, very popular—perhaps too much so. Closed noon Sat. and Aug.

Luculo • *Genova 19* • offers an innovative French influence in a luxurious setting. Smart, professional service. Closed noon Sat., Sun., and Aug. 15–Sept. 15.

☆☆ **La Trainera** • *Calle Lagasca* • is a nook for nautical niceties; the shellfish are superb. Service, too, is of the first water with platters on wooden tables. Closed Sun. and Aug.

★★★★ **L'Hardy** • *San Jeronimo 8* • which is sequestered atop an antique bar and takeout shop. Dark interior; embossed leather walls; parquet floors; heavy framed mirrors, burgundy velour banquettes; globe lighting, ancient waiters in tails. The cuisine is less important than the distinctive atmosphere. Here is a unique holdover from a graceful era that we believe conservative diners will relish. A touch of Victoriana that I love. Closed Sun. and Aug.

☆☆ **Principe de Viana** • *Manuel de Falla 5* • gets a big play from local luminaries as a site to be seen. The food and presentation seem to be secondary—a shame because they deserve attention and respect. It's best enjoyed in the company of capital-ists. Closed Sat. noon. Sun., and mid-July to Sept.

★★★★★ **Botin** • *Cuchilleros 17* • always a tourist mecca, is a tried-and-true standby, famous all over the world for its bullfighting guests and its roast suckling pig. This is the restaurant where Jake Barnes, hero of *The Sun Also Rises,* plays his last scene; Hemingway gave the place considerable attention in *Death in the Afternoon* as well. Nancy Reagan was Queen Sophia's guest of honor here when she last came to Spain. Cooking is still done in the original oven, dating from A.D. 1725. Be sure to order the Cordero Asado or the Cochinillo Asado because this baby lamb and this juicy little piglet are too good to miss. Ask for Don Antonio, the hospitable son of the owner (and the 4th generation to be represented here). Try to ignore the pesty gaggle of trippers who insist on exploding flashbulbs to record their big occasion at a Spanish table.

☆☆ **El Bodegon** • *Pinar 15* • remains a solid contender. The staff is alert and friendly; the food is substantial; high segments of Madrid society often may be found within its precincts. Closed Sun. and Aug.

★ **Senorio de Bertiz** • *Comandante Zorita 4* • is gaining fame among *Madrilenos* for its home cooking of Basque origin. Try the smoked goose salad with duck liver. The yums! Closed noon Sat., Sun., and Aug.

★ **Casa Paco** • *Puerta Cerrada 11* • in the old part of town, zings with color for the eyes, peasant-style flavor for the tummy, and noise for the ears. Two floors (go upstairs); always busy, if not hectic; steak's the main thing and it's usually ordered by weight; Cebon de Buey is also delicious, as are some of the seafood platters. Don't worry if the meat is not done quite well enough for you; the plates are literally oven-hot, so simply slice off a slab, touch it to your heavy porcelain platter, and it will be brown in a jiffy! Some travelers find its ambience too "authentic" to suit them. Not for the squeamish. Closed Sun. and Aug.

★★★ **Taberna del Alabardero** • *Felipe V 6* • is one of the most beloved informal hideaways for *estar al loro* (the "in" people). Located near Oriente Palace; 2 stand-up bars for cheerful and highly animated conversation (as well as snacks); a pair of small dining quads down a corridor that passes the open kitchen. I prefer the back room in authentic art nouveau. Tendency for Basque cuisine; try the fish casseroles, the stuffed hake, or the oxtail carnage. Excellent in a chummy way.

★ **La Parra** • *Monte Esquinza 34* • is one of the old standbys for smart Madrilenos. Single room with Moorish tiles, ceiling fans, potted plants, and a decibel level that advertises the happiness of its clients. Wholesome Andalusian food without any attempt at grand cuisine. Very clubby for Madrid's cafe society.

☆☆☆ **El Cenador del Prado** • *Prado 4* • is elegant, designed for bankerly types. One trellis salon plus another more stately tier in salmon tones; vitrines with flowers and porcelain statuary; waiters in formal attire. Suave, costly, and reflecting the sophistication of Castille in its nouvelle form.

Combarro • *Reina Mercedes 12* • is *the* shrine for Galician cooking in this capital. Excellent value for your pesetas, but I'd be happier if its staff would slow down a mite. Closed Sun. evening and Aug.

★★ **Ainhoa** • *Barbara de Braganza 12* • is for aficionados of Basque cookery. (The restaurant is named for a town in that French district.) Long room on 2 elevations decorated with iron firebacks and peculiar coils of candle wax normally used in church ceremonies. very friendly people and superb seafood concoctions.

Korynto • *Preciados 46* • is hardly spellbinding. In fact, it is aggressively undistinguished to the eye. The value is on the table, where the shellfish and other saltwater preparations are generous and uniquely satisfying. The atmosphere is salubrious, generated by a throng of joyful regulars.

El Lando • *Plaza Gabriel Miro 8* • Don't miss this popular establishment if you hanker to savor authentic Castilian cooking; it's in the typical *La Vistillas* suburb. Closed Sun. and Aug.

TASCAS FOR TAPAS

If you want a truly Spanish experience, be absolutely certain to try the **tascas** (taverns) on or near the Calle de Echegaray—just an olive-pit's throw from the Palace Hotel. Here's where Madrid's lively hordes huddle for snacks and aperitifs from 7 p.m.–10 p.m. The word *tapas* literally means "covers" and the gentle art of creating and serving them began in Andalusia where it was simply too hot to face a full meal. Today tasca-hopping is practiced all over Spain, usually in stand-up bars where heated trays or display counters afford you an opportunity to glimpse the wares before you buy them.

Each stop banners its own specialties. **La Casona,** which can pack in 400 nibblers, is noted for its potatoes and mushrooms. **La Chuleta** draws ham and *mariscos* (shellfish) fans. **Gayango** is renowned for its *bacalao* (cod), steaming casseroles of baby shrimp and oysters. **Posada del Enano** comes up with a trove of *boquerones* (a very special anchovy); **O'Pote** serves delicious *vieiras* (scallops); **Motivos** offers *chanquetes* (oh-so-good sea minnows); **Espuela** purveys *pinchos morunos* (barbecues); **La Trucha** is good for heavier fare, and **Taverna Toscana** has other palate tempters. **Los Corsarios** (Calle de Barbieri 7) projects a swinging atmosphere beloved by the Younger Set; cellar-sited **Sesamo,** where the Fielding gypsies usually throw in the towel, features the reviving *Sol y Sombra* ("Sun and Shade," half anis and half Spanish *conac*). Drink either the house wines or common sherry; beer is too filling, but some prefer its cooling effect (tiny bottles called "botellines" are available, as are small drafts). Scads more places may be explored in these Tidbit Alleys. They are very, very inexpensive, and they provide a scrumptious experience for travelers in ALL economic brackets.

NIGHT LIFE

The after-dark scene in Madrid offers tremendous variety; many revelers declare that today this capital is where it all happens. Generally, *flamenco* is "out," discos and cafes are "in," and there are many other combinations that are commanding attention from all segments of the public.

Speaking in the broadest terms (specifics later) here is where you'll find 'em:

▪ Barrio de Arguelles: this is in the university district mostly given over to the young.

- Barrio de Malasana: scores and scores of bars devoted to punk, rock, hippies, and night-freaks of every description in one of the city's oldest quarters. Literally wall-to-wall frolic from sunset to dawn.
- Plaza de Chueca and vicinity: Madrid's gay scene.
- Calle de Orense (Azca): high-quality discos.
- Calle Huertas: mostly pubs and music bars.
- Plaza Mayor district: typical bars and taverns.

The *espectaculo* or "live show," usually with a dinner that is almost inedible, is coming back (or up) with vitality. **Escala Melia-Castilla** (Rosario Pino 7) seems to lead the pack for Lido-type galas. This is rivaled by the shows at **Vanity** (Miguel Angel 3), **Sala Windsor, Pasapoga Xenon, Macumba,** and a host of others that may fade by the time of your arrival. Check locally regarding this highly perishable nighttime commodity; these open around 11 or 11:30 p.m. and yawn shut around 4 or 5 a.m.

An amusing oddity that has caught the city's imagination is found at **Las Noches de Cuple** (Palma 51), which recalls the gaslight era. Pianer players in ostrich boas hammer away at melodies suggesting composition by a Spanish Scott Joplin. Music hall singers reminiscent of Iberian Jeanette MacDonalds lustily air their adenoids in funfully comic mockery of cafe society. Matching the mood of the late 19th century is the cuisine, which seems to be a holdover from that period—without refrigeration. The most charitable thing to say about it, in my view, is that it is miserable. Never mind, the evening is a great success. Go late to avoid the dinner and order only drinks and nibbles.

Striptease, while phasing out in other European capitals, has found new life in Castile. The most ardent proponents at this instant are **Chat Noir, Alazan, Candy,** and **Don Q.** Their supremacy changes so swiftly that serious followers should find out from their hotel concierges about the leading house of the moment.

Gay haunts include the **Leather Bar** (Pelayo 28), the neighboring **Manhattan Pub** (Pelayo 37), and **Cueros Pub** (Pelayo 2). **Rey Fernando** has to be admired for its address: Prim 9. Transvestite shows at the **Fantasy** (San Diego 3).

Alfresco sipping: (summer months only) **Castellana Terraza** (Castellana 8). **Sky Garden** (Pl. España atop Edificio España) is Madrid's highest terrace; impressive views.

Authentic flamenco: Since most neophytes to Madrid usually want to see the world-famous and historic flamenco dancers, here's a sampling of the most prominent names currently on stage. **Casa Patas** (Cañizares 10). **Zambra** (Velazquez 8) has made a comeback after several years of retirement. Locals agree it is good again. It was always the most refined of this type of club. **Corral de la Moreria** (Moreria 17) means "Corral of the Moorish Quarter." L-shape main room with small stage show; about 10 performers, all much more attractive than those in other flamenco parlors; corner bar; capacity for about 80 show-viewers; popular for dinner; food miles from great, but edible; your first libation painfully high and your later ones less. **Cafe de Chinitas** (Torija 7), a long room with a stage at one end, today resembles an elegant Spanish salon, but the original cafe was a far more modest Malaguenian *tablao* of the 1850s. Red-framed portraits of renowned matadors; tomato- and avocado-colored bar; chairs, tables, and other trimmings carrying out the Andalucian motif. Smaller flamenco ensemble than at the Corral; performances better conceived but far less spontaneous; excellent costumery; top guitarists and singers; honest drinks; no groups. **Las Brujas** ("The Witches") is at Calle Norte 15 in the Old Town, a narrow street that's hard to find and virtually impossible for parking. Dogleg bar at entrance facing a huge blue-and-white mural; l-o-o-o-n-g arched main room to the rear resembling the tunnel from Grand Central to 125th Street; small stage way up front with about 20 wee (if you're in the back) performers; intermittent shows from 11:30 p.m.–3:30 a.m. Don't go for dinner, even though it's served. **Torres Bermejas** (Mesonero Romanos 15), formerly the Taberna Gitana, has perhaps the most attractive setup of all. The ceiling is coffered in gold; the walls are brightened by Moorish tiles; a loggia bedecks a corner beside the raised stage; numerous small package-groups tumble in.

Select pubs: **Cafe de Paris** (Santa Teresa 18). Cats (Julian Romea 4) is huge and has live music. **Impacto** (Campoamor 1) is a genuine classic. **La Vaqueria del Carmen** (*Ave.* Filipinas 1) is an old dairy converted into a glamorous and luxurious pub. **Balmoral** (Hermosilla 10) has a more traditional slant.

Cocktail sancta: **Chicote** (Gran Via 12) is a revival of the most famous "drinks museum." **Henry's Bar** (Blasco de Garay 59) is where World Champion Enrique Bastante will delight you with his creative cocktails. **Universal** (Fernando VI 8) is a favorite of artists and scholars.

Yuppies and modernists: **Archy** (Marques de Riscal 11). **Cafe de los Artistas** (Martinez de la Rosa 3). **Fabrica de pan** (San Bartolome 21). **Hanoi** (Hortaleza 81) serves snacks till very late at night. Add to your late list **Kitsch** (Galileo 32) and **Pacha** (Barcelo 11).

Discos for the young: **Abre Vilma** (Pº Habana 41). **El Callejon** (Nuñez de Balboa 63) incorportes a giant video screen. **Jaccara** (Principe de Vergara 90) features modern music concepts every fortnight.

Jazz: **Cafe Berlin** (Jacometrezzo 4) and **Cafe Central** (Pl. del Angel 10) are my two favorites.

Oddities: **Baja Epoca** (Ventura Rodriguez 24) looks like the interior of a pyramid, with additional Egyptian themes. **Cafe del Foro** (San Andres 38) offers Arab dancing mixed with humor and pop rock. **Voltereta** (Princesa 3) is Madrid's "latest" disco scene; it's really alive from 5 a.m. *onwards!*

Among the other "respectable" places in Madrid that are fun for everybody, the leader tonight is **El Biombo Chino** (Isabel La Catolica 6), a former movie house that was converted into a fairly attractive reeler without cinematics. Alluring entrance, with flowers and plants and running water bordering the stairs; balcony with handsome bar and a few tables at street level; main seating area and dance floor 1-flight down. Sizzling orchestra of 14 to 16 musicians; cabaret not an extravaganza but excellent in quality.

Flamingo (Av. Jose Antonio 34) draws a lively young clientele, well-dressed, well-mannered, and nonbeatnik. Good Italian band and soignee female vocalist.

Bali Hai (Flora Alta 8) is a South Sea-soned cellar specializing in Polynesian nutrients, both in the glass and on the plate. Some exotic beverages sipped out of distinctive containers through 2-foot-long straws; decor suggesting a Malayan longhouse; high-backed Malacca chairs; waiters in glossy dinner jackets; enough flotsam and jetsam on the walls, hanging from the ceilings, and stuffed into vitrines to evoke the envy of Old Vic—Old *Trader* Vic, that is.

In winter, **Cubaclu** (Virgen de la Alegria 9, near the bullring) swings best to a Latin beat; dancing; low tabs; weekends are the jumpingest if you love humanity. **Camaguey** (Desengano 16, just off the Gran Via) does not feature dancing, but the atmosphere is nice, the music is excellent, the cookery is recommendable, and the drinks are good; go late.

SHOPPING

GUIDELINES: This is a rather special Fielding service, being given a pilot run in Madrid and later perhaps in other European capitals. Our collegue Barbara Ham (Tel: 3084709) will help you shop, find designer collections, visit private salons, go to cultural exhibits, or tailor your time in the capital to your exact preferences. The chauffeur-driven vehicle will accommodate from one to five persons (no more); it can also return packages to your hotel. Normal hours are 10 a.m. to 2 p.m. and the price depends on how many are going. Call Barbara for arrangements.

SHOPPING HOURS: Most shops selling anything but food: From 9:30 a.m.–1 or 1:30 p.m. and 4:30 or 5–7:30 or 8 p.m. (even 8:30 p.m. in summer) weekdays, with Saturday afternoon closings (usually in summer, but this isn't standard either). Department stores stay open till 9 p.m. Public markets: From 7:30 a.m.–2 p.m. These are merely a rule of thumb because now that Spain is part of the E.E.C. the nation's shopkeepers have been told they may keep *any* hours they wish.

BEST AREAS: Calle Serrano, Av. Gran Via, and Plaza Cortes district (for antiques).

SAVINGS ON PURCHASES: I.V.A. is Spain's designation for a "value-added tax" of 12% and 33%, depending upon the category of merchandise. If your shopkeeper participates in the program and is cooperative you could receive a significant rebate. There are several provisions: (1) the item must cost more than 25,000 pesetas including the tax; (2) you must receive a triplicated form from the shop; and (3) upon departure from Spain you must show Customs your purchase or purchases and leave the documents with the officials. Be sure your sales receipts show the price of each item and that its **I.V.A.** has been noted as well. If there is only one grand total the authorities will not reimburse you. If you spend over 100,000 pesetas per article you are eligible for the larger reduction, since you will have been buying luxury goods. In time the tax should be sent back to you, but as the system is so new and the nation's adjustment to this complicated commercial administration is so vexing I wouldn't rely on a rebate for some seasons to come. Other countries with greater experience and a longer history of tax-refunding are, for the moment at least, more reliable.

NOTE · · · Wherever you wander in today's Iberia, please be extremely leery of any of the stores or so-called "factories" where tour guides might lead you. The commissions they collect on *your* purchases with *your* money normally average 25%. We clearly state that our **Guidelines** service (described above) does not take any commissions, ever, from stores. Fees come from you, its clients. You'd be wise to comparison shop and then to patronize ONLY reliable independent merchants.

Please DON'T buy: Spanish shawls. The only real ones are antiques from China. This has become a tourist racket.

ANTIQUES: Try your luck along Calle del Prado (off Plaza Cortes) and Carrera San Jeronimo. Bargain like crazy!

ART: Despite the tremendous renaissance in Spanish art, it is still much less costly than French, Italian, American, and other *oeuvres*. Nowhere in existence is there anything comparable to this school. (See below.)

ARTISANWARE: **Artespana** is a capsule of Spain's finest craftsmen working in the media of ceramics, hides, glass, copper, bronze, furniture, wood, cane, raffia, straw, textiles, rugs, and other handicrafts for the home, office, or garden. You'll find branches at Ramon de la Cruz 33, Hermosilla 14, Plaza de las Cortes 3, and Centro Comercial Madrid 2 La Vaguada.

BOOKS: **Miessner Libreros** (Jose Ortega y Gasset 14) probably contains this city's largest selections.

CLOTHES: Spain is still a paradise for the affluent clothes-conscious gal. Only the wealthy, however, can now afford to patronize the Big League houses— **Pedro del Hierro, Agatha Ruiz de la Prada, Miguel Rueda,** and a few others.

Well-known and respected men's tailors are **Ongard** (Av. Jose Antonio 34), **Cutuli** (San Jeronimo 29), **Gregorio Ruiz** (Zorrilla 23), and **G. Cristobal** (Castellana 53).

COLOGNES AND COSMETICS: **H. Alvarez Gomez** (Sevilla 2 and Serrano 14) is a long-established local landmark and has large and versatile stocks. The prices are aromatic to many visitors' noses. Sample the scents produced by a Spanish company called Puig (pronounced "Pooch"). They have a delightful range of eau de colognes and flowered soaps.

DEPARTMENT STORES: **Galerias Preciados** is stuffed with merchandise at lower-cost levels. **El Corte Ingles** is extremely popular with the Madrilenos. These are open during the usual siesta hours. Now that **Marks & Spencer** (Calle Serrano 52) has come to Madrid a lot of people have given up their periodic forays to London.

EMBROIDERED LINENS AND NEEDLEWORK: **Casa Bonet** (Nunez de Balboa 76; see "Mallorca") is the world's mightiest name and greatest exponent in this field. Its exquisite handworked pieces are sold at prices still so low

738 · · · SPAIN

that you won't believe them. All its glorious Palma stocks are available. Make this your first stop, ask for Miss Pilar, and don't miss it!

FLEA MARKET: **El Rastro** ("The Thieves' Market") is an interesting jumble of junk—some good, some dreadful. Haggle hard; go from 10 a.m.–2 p.m. on Sunday, and leave all your valuables (including passport!) in your hotel. Its so-called antique stores are also open on weekdays. Pickpockets are rife; trust *nobody*.

NOTE · · · The Toledo Gate Market ("Mercado de la Puerta de Toledo") near the "Rastro" is in the former Madrid central fish market. Art galleries, antique stalls, jewelers, craftsmen and fashion boutiques rub shoulders—quite a few restaurants, too. It's a fun excursion.

GALLERIES: **Galeria Kreisler** (Hermosilla 8) features exceptional traditional Spanish art. Here's the place for time-honored expressions of Iberian culture in more figurative form. **Jorge Kreisler** (Calle de Prim 13) fills out the spectrum by exhibiting on a regular basis the avant-garde creations of leading Spanish artists. They range from the oils, graphics, and sculptures of such masters as Miro, Picasso, and Juan Gris, to those of virtually all talents of special note within the nation, to those of the younger group who show exceptional promise for later dividends. Most are permanently represented in Madrid's National Museum of Contemporary Art and in prodigious foreign showcases.

Next best known art gallery is **Biosca** (Genova 11) with scads of new ones continuing to pop up.

HUNTING AND FISHING: **Diana Breton** (Serrano 68). Iberia has always been famous for its field and stream sports and Diana Turba is really the goddess of all hunt and angling needs. Shotguns of national production—and I have owned several—are among the most beautiful produced anywhere, with exceptional tracery, high-grade mechanisms, satin-smooth stocks, superb balance and, best of all, prices that are stunningly lower than those of other nations. For any equipment, clothing, or advice about sporting pursuits in Spain, ask Mr. Jose Lopez Matilla; he can also guide you pleasantly through the jungle of Spanish tax rebates for your purchases and consult with you on ordering from the Diana Turba catalog.

JEWELER: **Jesus Yanes** (Goya 27) has the finest collection of distinctive modern creations on the peninsula. Outlays for such imaginative gems and settings will surprise you when you compare this quality with other notable continental houses. Yanes has been a major name in the art since 1881. Especially creative (and inexpensive) are the expressive gold-and-enamel Nautical Initials, a colorful alphabet for pendants that make unusual gifts. Ask personally for either Mr. Jesus Yanes or his son, Juan.

SHOES: **Bravo-Calzados de Lujo** has some of the proudest footprints in the world on its various Madrid doorsteps—movie stars, nobility, and luminaries from all walks of achievement. Apart from their own luxury inventory, they carry such international brands as Magli, C. Jourdan, Di Sandro, Barker, Lanvin, Bally, Sebago, Timberland, Church's, Loake, and numerous others. Styles and materials are the very top to be had in their leather-bound realm. Additional temptations in handbags, clothing, and accessories. Midtown shoppers will find the following outlets convenient: Serrano 42, Hermosilla 12, Gran Via 31 and 68, Goya 43, and Princesa 58. Other branches in Seville, Torremolinos, Marbella, Fuengirola, Valencia, Bilbao, San Sebastian, Santa Cruz de Tenerife and Las Palmas de Gran Canaria. If you are traveling extensively, ask for exact addresses at one of the Madrid establishments.

MOJACAR Down on the coast about 50 miles from Almeria, this shoreliner boasts the modern **Parador de Los Reyes Catolicos,** not to be confused with the antique Hostal of the same name in northwestern Santiago de Compostela. Enormous pool; broad vistas; superb comfort; interesting textures—a common feature of the parador system. The neo-Moorish, 145-room **El Moresco** hangs on a cliff higher up toward the whitewashed town. The octagonal rooftop pool is a marvel; the bedchambers, however, were somewhat disappointing. **Palacio** is my first choice for a meal, followed by **Terraza Carmona** (*Vera,* 15 km out of town), and **La Lubina,** on the beach.

MURCIA This sun-toasted province between Valencia and Andalusia is aptly named *Costa Calida* (Warm Coast), extending along 155 miles of pearl-white strands, snug little coves, and hidden inlets. Highway and air connections are excellent. You'll probably want to see the unique Cathedral with its Velez Chapel and the neighboring castles of Los Velez and Monteagudo. Recreational facilities, including a casino and golf links, center around the 94-square mile *Mar Menor,* so called because it is embraced by the elongated, 300-to-2000-foot-wide flatland called *La Manga* ("The Sleeve"). This sea-and-landscape phenomenon means you can choose between calm lake waters and occasionally rough Mediterranean sea bathing. Top hotel choices run from the **Cavanna** to **Doble Mar Casino** to **Galua,** to the recent newcomer **Arco de San Juan.** **Borsalino** serves decent French-style cooking while **Dos Mares** specializes in regional fare; try the latter's Caldero al ajo (stew with garlic), a richly seasoned mullet and shellfish dish with boiled Calasparra rice and ali-oli (oil and garlic sauce). In *Murcia* (the capital) itself, there's reasonable shelter at **Siete Coronas Melia, Conde de Floridablanca, Hispano, Majestic, Churra,** and **Fontoria.** For a meal, don't miss **El Rincon de Pepe,** famed for its fish pies, stuffed peppers, and sinfully fattening desserts.

NERJA A tiny place, but with noteworthy caves, fabulous panoramas, and plenty of archaeology to keep you digging. The **Parador** is tops for seaside lazing. The **Balcon de Europa** (named for this extraordinary viewpoint) is also friendly and comfy. Both are for seekers of absolute tranquillity. **El Ancladero Capistrano Playa,** on the road toward *Motril,* is perhaps the best mealtime spot. Owners David and Pamela Toft are exceptional hosts. **Casa Luque** at Pl. Cavana is my second choice.

OVIEDO This Asturian capital is rich in pre-Romanesque art, much of which can be seen in the vicinity of the captivating 9th-century San Julian de los Prados Church (Gijon-Oviedo highway). Don't fail to visit the Sacred Chamber of the Cathedral as well as the Old Palace of Santa Maria del Naranco. Antiquarians should pencil in the Archaeology Museum. For overnighting, tuck in at the majestic **Hotel de la Reconquista,** which incorporates within a *hospicio* (children's refuge) built by Carlos III, a restored ancient chapel, a restaurant, grill, coffee shop, tearoom, and a host of hospitable nests for today's wayfaring pilgrims of any age. Fully air-conditioned for the heirs of yesteryear. **Gran Hotel Espana,** near the Cathedral, is recommended, too. As for restaurants, the three best bets are **Casa Fermin** • *San Francisco 8* • **Trascorrales** • *at the Plaza of the same name* • and **La Goleta** • *Covadonga 32.* All specialize in regional cuisine. Other candidates are **Pelayo, Marchica, La Gruta, Del Arco,** and **Casa Conrado.**

PAMPLONA Hemingway recorded for all time the Fiesta of San Fermin, which occurs from July 6–14 and is kicked off by the running of the bulls. (Remember, the number 7—the 7th day of the 7th month.) Chances are you won't get into harm's way with bovinity since the authorities discourage foreigners from joining the throng of young Spaniards who hurtle along the town streets and into the bullring. The 8-story, curvilinear **Hotel de los Tres Reyes,** with its 3 crowns shining over the fringes of the city, is a godsend in this community. Total of 168 units including 8 suites, each with private terrace, bath, telephone, and radio; all public rooms and bedchambers air-conditioned; summer swimming pool plus patio dancing; good food in its modern-tone restaurant; 3 bars; barbershop and beauty salon; garage for 40 cars. **Iruna Park,** inaugurated recently, is a welcome addition in the upper category bracket. Also worthy is **Hotel Maisonnave,** near to the Plaza del Ayuntamiento and Estafeta St., where the running of the bulls occurs. **Ciudad de Pamplona, Sancho Ramirez,** and **Europa** come next down the ladder.
    When it comes time to eat Pamplona's pride and joy is **Josetxo** • *Principe de Viana 1* • situated in the city's most central and elegant suburb. Their Cordero Chilindron (heavenly stewed lamb) is a gustatory delight. Next comes **Hartza** • *Juan de Labrit 19* • with access through a small garden. The Hartzas are the heart throbs here, sisters who double-team on cooking and hospitality. I suggest their Ensalada de la Huerta (colorful salad) as a preface to other savory fowl and fish dishes. **Sarasate** • *Garcia Castanon 12* • is another of my favorites. **Hostal del Rey Noble,** also known as "Las Pocholas," offers a broad menu selection; high prices for the district. **Rodero** • *Arrieta 3* • offers excellent regional fare.

S'AGARO, about 70 miles from Barceloná, is my only choice today on the tawdry Costa Brava.

    ★★★★ **Hostal de la Gavina** • is sited there with 56 rooms, 16 suites, gardens, a pool and snack terrace, tennis courts, and a fair beach. Most units with silk-clad walls and terraces for breakfasting; lunch by the pool in summer; Candlelight Club in winter for dinner. This one is a jewel for Catalonia, but it stands alone in a dismal setting of packaged bulk tourism.

SALAMANCA This is Spain's "Golden City" and you'll see why when sunset dusts the turrets, towers, and domes of the cathedrals and the famous ancient university. A Chicago friend writes, ''I would be hard pressed to think of a more entrancing experience than walking across the Plaza Mayor (now closed to traffic) when the bells are sounding at midnight.'' Columbus consulted the scholars prior to his New World voyage. (They advised him to stay put.) The Roman Bridge still spans the Tormes, the architecture is varied and everlasting. If you can get in, try for the **Parador** for an overnight. If not, then come to **Castellano III, Monterrey** or **Regio.** The **Gran Hotel,** smack on the truck route, is too noisy. **Chez Victor** • *Espoz y Mina 26* • **Chapeau** • *Gran Via 20* • and **Rio de la Plata** • *Plaza Peso 1* • are the most noteworthy restaurants. Outside of town, see the Castillo del Buen Amor, where one amused reader is tickled by the pair of horns mounted on a wall directly above a chastity belt.

SANTANDER is a cultural and museum center with great interest in prehistory, ethnology, and maritime subjects. It offers the **Real** as its leader among hostelries. You'll find deluxe accouterments plus 124 comfortable bedchambers. Tops. Next comes the ultracommercial **Bahia.** It counts 179 tiny cubicles with baths, but I can't wax enthusiastic over any of 'em. **Maria Isabel** would be my next choice followed by the **Santemar.** Farther out, at *Santillana del Mar,* the **Parador Gil Blas** is a sweet medieval complex in a wonderfully intimate dairying hamlet. Don't miss this touch of arcadia if you are within 100 miles of the village. **Los Infantes** is in the same settlement, blending old-world decor with modern times. Simple but nice. At *Fuente De,* along the route of the Picos de Europa mountains, there's the 4-star **Parador Nacional del Rio Deva.**

Don't hesitate to drive to *Puente Arce* (barely 7 miles away) to enjoy a quiet feast at bucolic **El Molino.** It's a baroque country mansion with fresh, even daringly imaginative, cuisine. If you prefer marine fare, then I suggest you anchor at **Bar del Puerto** • *Hernan Cortes 63* • which is good but quite expensive, **Canadio** • *Gomez Orena 15* • or **La Sardina** • *Doctor Fleming 3* • where you'll savor some of the best dishes of Cantabria.

SANTIAGO DE COMPOSTELA This is poetry in stone, one of Europe's most dramatic architectural creations and the destination—often tragic—of numerous religious crusades through the ages. The gray spires, rainy esplanades, richly ornamented portals, and purity of the church edifices conspire to recall the very essence of the Middle Ages. A modern airport now brings it closer to the heart of Iberia. The multimillion-dollar ★★★★ **Hotel de los Reyes Catolicos** (''Hotel of the Catholic Kings'') is a fantastic monument—so opulent, so grandiose, and so extravagantly conceived that it's a wonder to the eyes. Spacious public rooms, 4 dining salons, concert hall, auditorium, bar, and hairdresser. There are 122 doubles, 5 with salon, 1 suite, and 13 singles; the cuisine is appealing. Worth a special detour to overnight here, because there's nothing else like it in Spain. Other much less impressive choices would be the **Araguaney, Los Tilos,** and the uninspired **Peregrino. Vilas** • *Rosalia de Castro 88* • and its younger sister **Anexo Vilas** • *Av. Villagarcia 21* • are by far the best restaurants in town, followed by **Don Gaifero** • *Rua Nova 23* • a true cosmopolitan.

SEGOVIA, 50 miles from the capital, boasts the most impressive Roman aqueduct to be seen in Iberia. It's plainly colossal; locals believed it had been built by a devil in the course of one night. It's almost half a mile long, as high as a 9-story building, and contains 167 arches. **Granja de San Ildefonso,** an 18th-century palace (7 miles out of town) is best seen on Tues., Sat., or Sun. when its eight fountains splash at 5:30 p.m. The 12th-century **Alcazar** and the Cathedral are admirable too. Apart from the **Parador Nacional,** the modernistic **Los Arcos, Acueducto,** and **Los Linajes** (the latter overlooking the Parral monastery) are the best hotels in the community. The **Meson de Candido** (on the main plaza) is practically a national institution and for itself alone justifies a lunch excursion from Madrid. Several room levels; stupendous roast piglet and roast lamb; colorful, not too expensive, and fine. Service is fast, if not abrupt. *Phone for your table in advance.* **Jose Maria** • *Cronista Lecea 11* • is another local sancta; regional cuisine, extensive wine list, and swift attention. Otherwise, you may wish to try **La Cocina de Segovia** • *Ezequiel Gonzalez 24* • **Casa Amado** • *Fernandez Ladreda 9* • or **Duque** • *Cervantes 12,* • which lay claim to being Segovia's oldest ''meson''.

SEVILLE

Seville is glorious, with its wealth of archaeology and art. It is gearing up for the 1992 Expo (Columbus Day five centuries down the line), spiffing up its riverfront (9 new bridges) and a new rail station. Be sure to give yourself time to see the cathedral, the 12th-century Giralda, and the centuries-spanning Alcazar of King Don Pedro. There are churches, spacious parks, convents (La Merced is exceptional), tombs, museums, and galleries on practically every block; palm and orange trees line the winding streets. Either walk to the sites or ride in the gradually vanishing horse-drawn carriages with their bright yellow wheels (an air-conditioned coach is too sterile). The *Feria,* held soon after Holy Week, is the biggest, most frenzied, most colorful traditional celebration in Spain. Every soul in town pulls out his regional dress from the mothballs, and for 144 dizzy hours all work is forgotten. This event alone is worth a special trip to Europe—but reserve your space months in advance, because every pallet in the district is sought after by the hordes of outside visitors.

HOTELS

★★★ **Alfonso XIII** • is almost a shrine for nostalgic visitors to Andalusia. Now that it has been totally restored and is in a prestige hotel chain (CIGA) owned by the Aga Khan, it must be rated as the leading period piece in the region. The overall air of historic grace is so pervasive that merely walking in is a travel experience. The lobby and fountained atrium remain a museum of Spanish and Moorish art; the lavish workmanship, the specially baked tiles, the tapestries, and the priceless gold service for royalty will never be duplicated.

★★ **Tryp Colon** • has come back and fully regained its former charm and glamour. Total of 218 units; exquisite service. *Bienvenido de nuevo!*

☆☆ **Dona Maria** • Midtown situation squinting at the Cathedral from the narrow Calle don Ramondo; vaulted lobby with brick pillars; restaurant in Moorish decor; rooftop swimming pool with bar and snack tables; 100% air-conditioned. Total of 50 doubles and 12 singles—and no 2 alike; full carpeting; 12 units with canopied beds; Simmons mattresses for all snoozers; attractive paintings; many baths with double basins; some with French doors leading to balconettes. Very tasteful; very comfortable; very highly recommended.

☆☆ **Pasarela** • gaily terraced, exudes good taste, modern tones, expensive garniture (marble trim in baths, as one small example), a garage (which is a blessing in this town), and such highlights as potted gardens hanging in front of your picture window. You'll also find a cafeteria for putting on weight and a sauna for taking it off.

Melia Sevilla • is a blip in a critically massive Spanish hotel chain reaction. Tours pour in where individuals fear to tread. It's *the* spot for shelter if you've celebrated excessively: the fitness center is life-saving.

☆ **Porta Coeli** • is situated on the outskirts—which means you need a taxi or your car. Fully air-conditioned and functional in decor; 217 doubles, 26 singles, and 3 suites; piped music, frigobar, and optional TV; cafeteria; Ascot Pub; 4 convention halls (wow); parking facilities.

☆ **Los Lebreros** • opposite the soccer stadium, is a contemporary colossus catering to group traffic. Nevertheless, the facilities are sound, the decor is handsome, and the comfort is abundant. There's an outdoor swimming pool, full air conditioning, English bar, discotheque, and dining for all budgets. The twin units usually come with 2 beds and a studio sofa.

☆ **Gran Hotel Lar** • offers 137 units with most of the necessary mod-cons. Marble lobby cheered by a small aquarium; restaurant for intimate dining near entrance; larger banquet hall up a flight; staff on the cool side but well trained. The bedchambers are meticulously maintained; patterns are at war with each other but the colors overall formed an amnesty pact; book units ending in "18" because they are much more spacious than others.

★ **La Macarena** • is beside the old wall of the city—a nice touristic touch that later seems merely tedious when you are saddled with the effort of getting to or from midtown. The glassed-in patio is a plus as is the rooftop, L-shape swimming pool. In sum, however, you can do better closer to the doin's than way out in the ruins.

Hispalis ● is modern and comfortable, with moderate prices and an efficient staff. Fully air conditioned and convenient location at the *"ensarche."* A sound choice.

Murillo ● is sited on a charming, lamplit, hard-to-find, pedestrian-only street (Lope de Rueda 3, 5, and 7) in the Old Town. Slaphappy, informal administration, overseen by funloving proprietor Miguel Linares, a brother in the family that operates Spain's largest chain of art and antique shops. Colorfully decorated with pieces of his Linares collection; 64 small rooms with bath or shower; all front units with private balcony; best buys in the 14-suite annex. At *Carmona*, 30 minutes by car, the **Parador Nacional** is a converted ancient convent with a splendid view of the surrounding plains.

Also in this town is the 16th-century palace of 30 luxurious rooms called **Casa de Carmona**, a gem by any standards and quite expensive.

Don't forget that Seville will be brimful of visitors this year for the Expo. Among the newer hotels to be built to accommodate the throngs are the **Betania**, the **HUSA, Alcora, San Ignacio,** and a congress (congresos) whopper in the airport district. For more modest budgets, newcomers include the **Bellavista, Monte Triana, Oromana,** and some nice apartments, **Mairena** on C. San Juan Mairena (Tel. 4813011).

RESTAURANTS

Seville will never exactly out-dazzle Paris as a Temple of Gastronomy; there's an old Spanish saying that the people of Andalusia think too much about living to waste time on food. Frequently the sauces—and usually they come in pool-size quantities—cover up (but only wistfully) the indifferent cuisine.

☆☆ **The Alfonso XIII** seems to turn out the best meal (see "Hotels"). Moreover, the decor is lifted from the stuff of Moorish fairy tales.

Egana Oriza ● *Calle San Fernando 41* ● near the ancient courthouse, caters to the legal eagles and politicos. New and immediately successful. Conservatory theme with arches taken from a Seville bridge design, originally from Eiffel's Gallic drawing board. Basque-inspired cuisine and plesantly light.

La Albahaca ● *Plaza Santa Cruz 12* ● also reveals a supply of wrought iron, but this time more delicate. Happy, frisky mood; colorful; a complement to the local lamb specialty.

Figon del Cabildo ● *facing the Cathedral at charming Plaza del Cabildo* ● offers international cuisine. The mood is clearly patrician. My filet of sole

Cleopatra was fit for an emperor; top it off with the red currant "sorbete" for dessert.

San Marco • *Cuna 6* • comes next as a bright light among the local independents. The Ramacciotti brothers entertain Seville's jet set with sophisticated Italian creations, surprisingly enough. Try the distinctive salted salmon with anchovy sauce.

La Dorada • *Virgen de Aguasantas 6* • is, as its name implies, a house that specializes in sea fare (rush from the coast daily). Service in the popular establishment also can be a bit rush-rush. Dorada a la sal (in a jacket of baked salt) is the favorite dish here, but my turbot was indeed a gustatory delight. You may agree that their hard-chilled white wines are of questionable reward.

Jamaica • *Jamaica 6* • boasts what could well be Seville's most distinguished wine cellar. Fish and met specialties continually draw the city's business community.

Rincon de Curro • *Virgen de Lujan 45* • is about 5 minutes by foot from the Alfonso XIII, and worth every footstep.

Bailen 34 • *Bailen 34* • is a cozy and homespun den where you'll enjoy perhaps the most imaginative Sevillian dishes. Don't miss it.
Other possible candidates: **Bodegon el Riojano** • *Virgen de las Montanas 12* • regional cuisine in 14th-century surroundings; **Don Raimundo** • *Argote de Molina 26* • local cooking in what looks like an antique shop; **El Burladero** • *Canalejas 1* • heavy atmosphere beloved by bullfighters and their following; **Florencia** • *Avda. Eduardo Dato 49* • the focus is on cosmopolitan dishes, but do try its "ham salad" if you wish to savor something really special. This restaurant is soaring in popularity.

NIGHT LIFE

The city's leading exponent of flamenco is the **Patio Sevillano** (Paseo de C. Colon 11a) owned by the enterprising Juan Cortes and Matias Garrado. Excellent *tablao,* clean surroundings, and a polka-dot nebula of whirling Andalusian atmospherics for the $10 entry fee. Every tourist who has ever been to Spain has looked in, so don't expect a "discovery." **La Cochera** (Av. de Menendez Villajos) dances close on the heels of the first—it might even have fractionally more chic. Rustic bar and restaurant in front serving regional fare; 3-alcove back room under a beamed ceiling; raised platform for the excellent young dancers and singers; honest drinks. **Turin** (Asuncion 21), reputedly, is very popular as a discotheque; so are **La Torcha, Piruetas** (Asuncion 1), and **El Dragon** (Betis 60); the last two for young discophiles. For economy nightowling, **Garbanzo Palace** (Menendez Pelayo 18), which means "Chick Pea

Palace'' is well regarded. Fun and folksy as a bar and nothing more. **El Coto** (at Hotel Los Lebreros), **La Recua** (a half mile away toward Cadiz), and **Abades** (Abades 13) are meant for the general public. Other ''tablaos'' are **El Arenal** (Rodo 7), **Patio Sevillano** (Paseo Colon 11), **La Trocha** (Ronda de Capuchinos 23), and **Los Gallos** (Plaza Santa Cruz).

TOLEDO is a *must* for its Gothic cathedral (13th–15th centuries), synagogues, and religious shrines, as well as for its El Greco Museum. (One of his most famous paintings, however, is in the Santo Tome Church.) The town has skyrocketed in its hospitality offerings of late. The duet of national paradors make it unique in Spain, for nowhere else to our knowledge are there 2 in such a small area. The ★★★★ **Conde de Orgaz** affords an almost orgaz-mic (ouch!) view of Toledo—especially from its summer terrace where you may also take lunch. Room count of 77, 61 with balcony. The ★★★★ **Parador del Virrey Toledo** actually resides within the 14th-century Oropesa Castle. It's about two hour's drive, incidentally, from midcity. If you can snag some digs high in the older section, you will have found your castle in the Spanish sky. Among the privately operated houses, the ★★ **Hostal del Cardenal,** within the ramparts, stands above any other independent inn in sight. Fountains, hearths, flowers, elegant staircases, and a salon sheathed with intricately carved wood form a proud cloak of refinement for this cleverly antiqued house. Two-tier restaurant; suite, 3 singles, and 2-dozen doubles whisper their Castilian heritage. **Carlos V** leads the also-rans; if you should hear strange sounds as you walk through the Tombs of the Spanish Kings in the Escorial, they might be wails of protest from this great Emperor for this calumny on his name. **Alfonso VI,** with its updated interior and kind personnel, is a sounder bet today. Otherwise, you may wish to try the newcomers **Maria Cristina, Mayoral** and **Beatriz.**

When you're ready for a meal, the ★★ **Hostal del Cardenal** has an enchanting garden, a marvelous arbor-covered dining-terrace, a cleverly ''aged'' 2-story restaurant (pick the upper level), and a score of attractive features. The cuisine is less appealing however. **Asador Adolfo** • *Granada 6* • comes next on my list; pleasant interior and worthy Castillean cookery, followed by **Anticuario** • *on Kilometer 2.6 to Avila* • famous for its salmon salad. **El Abside** • *Marques de Mendigorria 1* • offers chiefly international fare. **Casa Aurelio** is a sort of Spanish bistro; simple and worthy in its three premises: two on Calle Sinagoga and a third at Plaza Ayuntamiento. **Venta de Aires** • *Circo Romano 25* • is not a favorite of mine in spite of its popularity. Instead, for regional cooking I suggest **Hierbabuena** • *Cristo de la luz 9* • which is becoming quite popular amonng locals as well as visitors.

VALENCIA (touristically known as Costa de Valencia) has a special charm. Its lifeline, water, is held in such reverence that the 1000-year-old Arab ceremony of electing a tribunal to regulate the flow to the orchards is still practiced and still recognized under the Spanish legal system. (You can see the judges in session every Thursday outside the Apostle's Door of the Cathedral.) The twin high spots of the year—the famous *Fallas* fiesta on St. Joseph's Day (mid-Mar.) and the magnificent Battle of the Flowers (early Aug.)—shouldn't be missed by any vacationer who is footloose in Spain during these times.

The 314-room **Melia Valencia Rey Don Jaime** is out of the center and fringed by its own park, gardens, and swimming pool. Full air-chilling; marble lobby in beige and brown with highlights of polished wood and crystal; English-style bar, darkly handsome; cheerful dining facilities; nightclub with circular brass dance floor; comfortable suites but smallish doubles, all equipped with TV and direct-dial phones. The **Astoria Palace** presents 208 spacious but stark rooms; La Bruja nightclub; terrace dining-and-dancing; a chilly marblesque lobbyette, an uncozy lounge, an unattractive restaurant, and all of its accommodations air-conditioned. Hospitable staff attitudes; better than ever. The **Excelsior** is coming up once again—but there's still a long climb ahead. Fully air-conditioned with individual controls; American Bar with adjoining summer-winter terrace; 65 rooms and baths; 12 corner suites; fresh wall coverings and paint make it much brighter than it was. The ancient and seedy **Reina Victoria** had a piecemeal renovation job that still lacks flair. Except for the **Renasa's** situation at the edge of town near the soccer stadium, it is one of the better buys in Valencia. Fresh clean-lined personality. The **Llar** specializes in heavy group patronage. Bustling, genial staff; clean modest surroundings. **Ingles** is stark. "Give a man a landscape and a passion," said Jesus Gomez Escardo, "and you give him everything!" That last word nicely sums up what this master host and his charming wife Dona Alicia provide the fortunate guests of the ★★★ **Hotel Monte Picayo.** This hostelry is not actually within the city limits of Valencia, but 14 miles down the pike in *Puzol-Sagunto.* Sprawled over a large hill are the central building, 10 cottages, swimming pools, and 2 championship tennis courts. The lobby is stunning in concept, unusual in design, and flawless in execution: It consists of 4 descending tiers, housing respectively the reception area, the library, the bar, and the lounge overlooking the cascading main pool. Within easy strolling distance are the Grill, the sauna, the shopping gallery, the discotheque, and the 83 hypersumptuous chambers in the principal edifice. More? Much, much, much more. The **Lehos, Expo, Husa Dimar,** and **Feria Sol** comes next in my listing.

Out at *El Saler,* the **Parador Luis Vives** provides peaceful duals in the sun. All 58 accommodations doubles; clinical taste; pool fringing the golf links. Fair-ways. **Sidi Saler Sol** is *the* region's deluxe hostelry and displays the standard assets of its category. In *Torrente,* 14 miles from the port, the **Lido** is better as a dinner-and-dance stop than as an overnight hitch. For motorists, **La Pinada,** at kilometer stone 28 on the Zaragoza highway, has a pleasant pool, a routine restaurant, and so-so sleeping quarters.

As to restaurants, **La Hacienda** (Navarro Reverter 12) specializes in fish and fowl and displays the richest wine list in the city; impeccable service. **Ma Cuina** (Gran Via Germanias 49) follows lead with an imaginative blend of Basque dishes and nouvelle cuisine. If you prefer fish **Ismael** (Burriana 4) will delight your gustatory senses with fresh seafare. **El Gourmet** (Taquigrafo Marti 3) offers a more international choice while **Eladio** (Chiva 40) is becoming very popular for its Galitian creations. **L'Estimat** (Ave. Neptuno 16) is more inclined toward regional cuisine and very inexpensive. **Les Graelles** (Arquitecto Mora 2) enjoys lovely surroundings while **El Plat** (Conde Altea 41) boasts a different rice dish every day. **Lionel** (Pizarro 9) facing the Plaza del Pais Valencia, is genteel, discreet, and chicly intimate. The cuisine is French, *mais oui!* The **Real Club Nautico** (Camino del Canal 91) overlooks the port entrance. From your table you can toss a line to that passing boatswain. Outdoor terrace and glassed-in, flower-lined dining salon; separate bar; wonderful seafood, especially shellfish and fish-rice (a southern specialty); courteous service; physically raw in appearance; teeming with local folk in season; inexpensive. **El Timonel** (Felix Pizcueta 13) also specializes in seafood. Finally, if you are outward bound from the airport, the **Azafata Sol,** off Highway N-III, is better than any terminal cookery (that phrase is almost 100% accurate) you are likely to ingest before you fly.

VIGO   This is Spain's salty old girl of the north. Its Berbes fish market is Spain's leader in sales volume. The ancient quarter invites hours of strolling. Among its hotels, the **Bahia de Vigo** leads the convoy. It's on the waterfront a few steps from the docks; there's a modern commercial atmosphere throughout; ocean-wide restaurant on the 2nd floor as well as the Corsair's Bar; all 107 staterooms come fully plumbed. Shipshape. The modern **Coia** would rank next in the Vigo regatta, followed by the **Ciudad de Vigo** and the beachfront **Gran Hotel Samil. Sibaris** (Garcia Barbon 168), **Puesto Piloto Alcabre** (Av. Atlantica 194), and **El Castillo** (Monte del Castro) are the three top restaurants in the area, followed by **El Canario** (Av. de Vigo 218) at **Chapela** and **La Oca** (Purificacion Saavedra 8).

In the Vigo vicinity, the environs almost bristle with those wonderful government-run paradors. Pick of the neighboring trio is the ★★★★ **Conde de Gondomar** at *Bayona,* a true beauty spot created by God and man. It nests in an L-shape fortress bathed by the same winds that drove the ships of Sir Francis Drake along these shores. Infinite variety of pastimes, sports, recreation—even a genuine dungeon in which to drop the kids when they get cantankerous. Then there's the 50-room **Parador Casa del Baron** in the town of *Pontevedra* (20 miles from Vigo). The situation is not so maritime, but the regional cuisine is seasoned by the sea and the comfort and aesthetic standards are high. Nearby you'll find the tiny but charming **Parador del Albarino** at Cambados, directly facing the waves. Finally, there's the **Parador de San Telmo** at *Tui* (17 miles from Vigo) which gazes at Portugal across the Rio Mino. It's a nice stop if you wish to dawdle a while longer in Spain before hopping the frontier.

VITORIA   is a mix of medieval and modern. The Santa Maria Cathedral is its centerpiece. **Canciller Ayala** (deluxe category; 200 rooms; by far the most imposing in the region). **Gasteiz** and **General Alava** come next. **Dos Hermanas** (Madre Vedruna 10) is my choice at mealtime. Otherwise, you may wish to try **Ikea** (Paraguay 8) for fresh seafare or **Zaldiaran** (Av. Gasteiz 21) for regional cooking.

ZARAGOZA   strikes first-time viewers with its towered Basilica del Pilar; the facade and domes are decorated with Goya and Bayeu frescoes. **Gran Hotel** offers 138 units in a magnificent ancient edifice; professional staff and refined atmosphere. The 10-story **Melia Zaragoza Corona** provides space for 520 guests in deluxe surroundings; 2 restaurants featuring American, French, and Spanish cuisine; excellent and colorful grill; active bar; patio, solarium, sippery, and swimming pool on the roof; dark but spacious bedchambers. **Palafox** follows with 184 deluxe accommodations. Then come a covey of question marks: **Rey**

Alfonso I (120 rooms; reportedly nicely furnished), **La Romareda** (90 units in deluxe quality), and **Don Yo** (170 door keys). Bringing up the wagon train, we have **Goya** (Statleresque in atmosphere; 100 newer rooms, all air-conditioned; 60 older units revamped; 100% bath count; clean, fresh ambience; garage). The newish **Cesar Augusta, Conquistador,** and **Oriente** come next.

This city has dozens of bars for tidbits—but a paucity of full-fledged restaurants. **Costa Vasca** (Tte. Coronel Valenzuela 13) is considered the top dining choice in town, followed by **La Casa del Ventero** (at Villanueva de Gallego, 14 km away), which can produce good French cuisine. **Los Borrachos** (Paseo de Sagasta 64) is high in the pecking order for its fowl. For strictly regional cookery in colorful Aragon surroundings, the **Meson del Carmen** is tops. Busy-beehive atmosphere; U-shape room with nibbler-and-sipper's bar down one side and tables down the other; smoky; full of rich Spanish life and vitality; excellent skilletcraft in the manner they know best; reasonable tariffs. Seafare lovers might enjoy **Riskomar** (Francisco Vitoria, 16) and **La Mar** (Plaza Aragon 12).

MALLORCA

This island was last year's prizewinner for the *Temple Fielding Travel Award,* the island where the late founder of this guidebook series made his home.

For the last two decades Mallorca has projected a tawdry image of mass tourism, but more recently international travelers are discovering **The Other Mallorca.** The harbors are filled with spectacular yachts from San Francisco, Dubai, Monaco, and other redoubts of the very rich. Simultaneously, marinas, hotels, and golf courses have emerged with such a degree of luxury that they represent the forefront in today's escapes to leisure, sun, and natural beauty. As the economics of this has not yet caught up with the eloquent statements in architecture and design, prices for the outlander seem significantly below those of other international resorts. All of this is due to a dynamic tourist council that said "Okay, enough is enough! From now on we legislate a better grade of everything." Not easy to do, and it took political courage to turn the trick.

Mallorca, roughly 60 miles by 50 miles at its widest points, is the capital of the Balearic Islands (Menorca, Ibiza, Formentera, and scores of rock-dots; persnickety islanders claim that only the 2 largest bodies form the Balearics, while Ibiza and Formentera should be known as *The Pitiusas*). Lying almost exactly 100 miles southeast of Barcelona, it is accessible from there in 25 minutes by air and from 8 to 9 hours by modern car ferry. The connections to and from every Western European capital and a number of other major cities are fast and frequent. With its 5000-foot mountains, lush plains, magnificent beaches, horses, tennis courts, rapidly expanding golf courses, benevolent climate, warmhearted people, colorful background, and moderate prices, it has become one of the most popular resorts on the Mediterranean.

July-August is High Season, with practically flawless weather. Spring and fall are normally lovely in the main; May, June, September, and October have more than enough balmy days to offset gray ones. November-December and March-April are chancy—sometimes glorious, sometimes awful; parts, but only parts, of January and February are chilly. The legendary false spring called *Las Calmas de Enero* ("The Calms of January" which sometimes occur in February), like our Indian summer, bring for 2-or-3 weeks heavenly weather and the blossoming of nearly 10-million almond trees attired in petals of pink or white. There's good swimming from late spring to middle fall.

Mallorca has the profile of a goat's head: *Palma,* the capital, is at the throat, and is home to almost half of the island's 650,000 resident population. *Soller* is near the eye, and *Formentor* is on one of the horns. The heartbeat of the island lies in Palma. Here is *the* center of the action where you will find most of the good restaurants, hotels, nightclubs, shops, the nearby Casino and most of the frenzy. At the peak of the season (not so noticeably in the spring or fall), the capital is packed so tightly with French, English, German, and other nationals who are flown or ferried in on bargain tours like so many cattle that it's grossly tinny and crass; strike out during July and August for the tiny villages to find the real charm of the Balearics.

Car Hire For self-drive autos, one and only one is recommended in the capital: **Empresa Garaje Vidal** (Rover Motta 11, near the seafront; Tel. 46–17–00); new or nearly new vehicles at moderate tariffs are the specialty. The cheerful English-speaking owner, Jochen Brill, will see you receive conscientious service.

NOTE · · · If you have any problems concerning car ownership in Spain (or Europe), shipment home of your vehicle, technical specifications, or retirement abroad and the most economical way to go about licensing your family vehicles, go immediately to the previously mentioned Jochen Brill who makes an extra-special effort to help readers of this book. This gentleman has gone so far as to provide his personal office telephone number (Palma 46–36–00) for your convenience. His town headquarters, where he is the Ford agent, is **Motor Balear S.A.** at Aragon 2; he also can arrange purchase of other makes of autos. For anything from Spanish tourist plates to a brass ooga-horn, this brilliant administrator is the accelerator who will speed you to your destination with the least possible trouble.

Trains Blown-up Lionel-type miniatures are electrically operated to and from Soller and by diesel on the Palma-Inca route. The lead coach on the former is so reminiscent of the original Toonerville Trolley that it's great fun, especially if you're bound at excursion rates for a lunch in its port. While this portion will continue as narrow-gauge, a vast chunk of the new rejuvenation program is fast converting the tracks of the longer run to standard width and adding a second parallel line. New rolling stock also has joined the railroad; departure frequency is every half-hour between Palma and Inca).

Air and Sea Travel Iberia, with its **Aviaco** division, provides most of the muscle in Mallorca's air bridge, lots of it stretching between Madrid, Malaga, or Barcelona and Palma. British Airways, SAS, Lufthansa, Swissair, KLM,

Sabena, Air France, Air Algeria, and many more offer direct service from their respective capitals to Palma; some are summer only. *Every flight on every airline is nearly always crowded;* nail down your tickets early, or you might be stuck for several frustrating days. Also try to have your flight confirmed by an Iberia representative and noted on the Iberia computer; all too often they have failed to honor my bookings on Air France or other carriers flying into Spain— an infuriating practice.

Transmediterranea provides most of the surface transportation between Mallorca and the mainland. Its sizable fleet of steamers plies between *Palma* and *Barcelona, Valencia,* as well as *Sete* on the French Mediterranean. At this writing hydrofoils are being given sea trials for short runs along the coast or for possible island ferry exchanges; Palma-Ibiza is one proposed skimmer route. While the following schedules are accurate as we go to press, sailings are altered continuously, so it would be wise to doublecheck your calendar with a professional, up-to-the-minute travel agent. From Barcelona the ships sail nightly plus 7 daytime voyages per week. From Valencia there is a departure every day but Sunday. Service from Sete (June to September) departs every Saturday. The ports of call are Palma, Ibiza, and Valencia, with returns every Friday. There is also a 4-day cruise leaving Barcelona for the Balearic Isles; departure every Friday (mid-June to early September, except during Easter).

Don't, for heaven's sake, take deck passage on *any* overnight sailing, regardless of circumstances. The bigger ships offer airline style chairs (120 to 250 of them!) in enclosed dormitory-like salons; they're clean enough, but when full they're a jungle. Get a stateroom. For daytime crossings, the cheaper seat ticket is perfectly adequate because a lot of your time will be spent in lounges, pacing the decks, or at poolside. Try to purchase this in spite of vigorous efforts by some independent agents to bludgeon you into taking a ''required'' cabin. Several times this seamy ruse has been pulled on me. I've been told that all low-cost day passage had been snapped up, so if I wished to sail I'd have to take a gilt-edged stateroom. Of course, once I was aboard, I saw oodles of available space at the economy level.

Drinks Mallorquin specialties are either sweet or dry *hierbas,* an anise-flavored slugger highly favored by fishermen, laborers, and sophisticates as well; it is absorbed as a pre- or after-dinner nip, neat or served with ice-and-soda in summer. Others are *palo* (originally made from the bark of the Peruvian quina tree), which I prefer presented highball-style, and *anis* (the Tunel brand is marvelous). Hunters (probably of dragons and other such perilous game) swallow *mesclat* or *canya* on chilly mornings. Embalming fluid is kinder to the system. All major international spirits are available on the island.

ATTRACTIONS

The number one sightseeing attraction traditionally remains the **Caves of Drach** at *Porto Cristo,* 40 miles on good roads from the capital. The music is so corny you'll probably have to stifle your giggles; a gimmicky boat ride on an eerie underground lake; worth the time, if you don't get stuck in one of the interminable queues that sometimes stack up at its water section. Bus excursions from Palma at regular intervals. *Arta* also has awesome caves; *Campanet* has them in miniature. For natural splendor, take a run up to *Formentor.*

A **medieval joust?** You can enjoy it as performed by daredevil stuntmen at the ancient palace of **El Compte Mal,** 7 miles from Palma (Tel: 403611) on a spur that joins the Soller and Valldemosa roadways. While it may seem unabashedly touristic, this is one of the best performances of Middle Ages theater you are likely to find. Though the games of competition, acted out on the earth-covered enclosed court, begin at 9 p.m., you are advised to be present at 8:30. Dinner, served on heaping litters by page boys, consists of consomme, finger-licken' flambeed chicken, and interesting side dishes plus wine; the meal and show cost approximately $18. After the repast, a large orchestra plays dance music in the adjoining lounge for guests who wish to lengthen the evening. Tickets are available in Palma at major travel agencies, many of which provide bus transportation; otherwise you may have to commission a very expensive taxi for the jaunt. It functions all weeknights in summer and 4 days weekly in winter. A socko spectacle which is a splendid value for children and adults.

In the capital, the magnificent, privately financed, multimillion-dollar **Auditorium** is the most impressive cultural magnet of the Balearics. If you're music-hungry, be sure to check the programs and schedules during the time of your visit. Here's a fabulous *coup* for the island—and you! Also on your must list for the city are the **Cathedral** (second largest in Europe), the spectacular **Bellver Castle,** overlooking the town, and the small but exquisite **Museo de Mallorca,** which graphically reveals the rich artistic heritage of an oft-conquered island (much of it religious in nature).

In the north, the village of *Pollensa* sponsors a **Music Festival** during the summer months. Such virtuosi as Segovia, Szeryng, Spierer, Ricci, Rubinstein, Stern, and Richter have given concerts in the charming art-filled cloister of the Santo Domingo Church. Any concierge on the island probably can arrange tickets for you. The prices are laughably low and the rewards are memorably high.

Marineland makes a glorious splash on the Costa den Blanes, a few minutes out of Palma on the Andraitx road. Trained sea lions, dolphins, and parrots, plus a zooful of other critters, are on hand for the splendid shows, the exhibits, or for just strolling around and chatting with the animal kingdom. Within this seaside compound are myriad recreational facilities, rides, play parks, a restaurant, a snack terrace, an aquarium—enough to keep mom, dad, and all the brood engaged for many happy hours. Public relations director Roberto Bennett knows very well that the best show on earth is the earth and its residents. Some of our globe's most lovable companions are here just waiting to extend a paw, a claw, or a flipper in everlasting friendship. Recommended.

Petra, about 1½ hours by car from the capital, offers a dot of territory that until 1982 was an official part of the State of California—the house of the great Junipero Serra, who founded 21 missions on our west coast and who changed the history of our Pacific area. It was turned back at the request of the Spanish government. The home is surprisingly small and sparsely furnished, but it reflects an interesting picture of 18th-century Mallorquin living; the nearby Museum Center of Studies contains paintings and books referring to this indomitable pioneer. If you've got time on your hands and adventure in your blood, you may take the aforementioned mini-railway that pokes through the heart of the island to this little village; culture-minded motorists find it a convenient detour en route to the Drach Caves excursion. Especially appealing to Californians. Hollywood is doing a film on Fra Junipero; rumor has it that Dustin Hoffman is playing the lead.

Valldemosa, the monastery where George Sand and Chopin once wintered, is a 21-carat tourist trap but, nevertheless, an attractive one. While this famous couple were here, there was such mutual antipathy between them and the natives that they left the island under a cloud; now, however, the shrewd locals have "recreated" (to use a kind word) a shrine to these historical characters—almost 100% for foreigners, who swarm through the premises. The view is magnificent. Clever job of "reconstruction," though, so long as the spectator realizes the width of the gap between "legend" and fact. Only 11 miles from Palma; plenty of bus trips that stop here and continue to Soller, which is pleasant from a scenic point of view. The Chopin Festival runs the whole of August with an international piano recital on Saturdays or Sundays in the delightful surroundings of a 12th-century cloister just in front of the cell where Chopin once lived.

The top **beaches** are at Formentor, Alcudia, Magaluf, Paguera, Cala d'Or, and San Vicente (beware of undertow at the last during certain sea conditions).

Golfing Suddenly Mallorca has emerged as an important center for evergreen swingers. Even during the worst months, the weather is benign enough to attract the dedicated sportsperson and in most cases conditions are ideal. In every instance the natural beauty is spellbinding.

The most well-known course is the 18-hole circuit associated with (but no longer owned by) the **Son Vida Hotel.** It's the oldest and the most popular, providing for the visitor a promenade along the frontages of some of the island's most impressive mansions. The restaurant, terraces, and bar are very attractive; the food is very good too. **Roca Viva** is new, major, and with vegetation that will attract many TV cameras for future tournaments. Probably one of the nation's more noteworthy circuits. For pure unadulterated exquisiteness **Golf Pollensa,** 30 miles north of Palma, is breathtaking and boasts the finest clubhouse of them all; the restaurant fulfills only snack hungers. From almost every point the sea is visible, a monastery peers down on the valleys of olive, carob, and almond trees, and the conditions are manicured to perfection. A second nine is scheduled. **Santa Ponsa,** a long course about 10 minutes from Palma's center; it was cleverly designed from the technician's point of view; a second 18-hole circuit is just opening. The challenges are well considered, there's a hotel and restaurant that are passable, and the situation is far enough away from urban congestion to sooth the aesthetic senses. **Vall d'Or** is on the southeast coast, blessed with Mediterranean views; dining facilities available plus other amenities. **Poniente Golf,** in the Magalluf region, is a toughie designed by Severiano Ballesteros, the great Spanish champion. **Bendinat,** associated with the ultra-exclusive resort complex on the south coast, is designed for strong-legged mountain goats. It's short, beautiful, and not very horizontal. **Canamel** is a beauty spot held within a chalice of mountains; the first 9 holes are tight and the back nine are open. Nearby, **Son Severa** is a fine 9-holer; lots of club activity here. These are only a few of the sporting chances available. Before long you may see pins in the greens at Calvia, Capdepera, Campos, Arenal, Marratxi, Establiments,

Valldemossa, Vilafranca, Alcudia, and Formentor—some of them will-o'-the-wisp pipe dreams that will never get off the drawing boards, but others that certainly will materialize over the next several years.

~~~~~~
HOTELS

Mallorca has the highest concentration of hotels and pensions per capita *of any major resort area in the world*. The isle now has a grand total of *approximately 1700 hostelries*. Naturally, the facilities and service in most of this crop are amateurish in the extreme. And, just as naturally, many sectors cater 99% to tour packagers. The places mentioned below still aim to please the independent traveler.

★★★★★ **Formentor** • is bewitching for its natural beauty—and that alone can sell it. In addition to a lovely nearby ribbon of golden beach, you'll find 2 exquisite swimming pools (one heated) tiled in Valencia-style patterns and sited in a palm grove almost at your doorstep. Fully air-conditioned; panoramic lobby and new reception; 3 dining rooms plus a high-priced Grill in sterile Art Retro, but in midsummer the grill patio is blissful; Beach Bar with buffet lunches; indifferent bedchambers, the best with sea view; a handful of suites and just a few balconies; good hard-surface tennis courts. London-Savoy-trained concierge Don Francisco Borras is a gem. The taxi ride to or from the capital or the airport takes about 90 minutes and costs around $55. Closed in winter.

★★★★★ **Son Vida** • nestles less than 15 minutes from Palma in a breathtaking mountaintop showcase. This totally converted castle had been renowned for centuries for its priceless collection of medieval arms. It is surrounded by an 18-hole golf course that is now under independent management. Completely air-conditioned; handsome public rooms; fantastic 250-foot poolside terrace partially awninged for outdoor lunching and supping; spacious main dining salon; 3 bars; muted disco largely patronized by adults; 175 excellent accommodations; tennis. Not by the sea but a delight for deluxe vacationing.

★★★★★ **La Residencia** • *at Deya on the western flank* • resides on 40 acres of some of the most beautiful mountain country in the entire Mediterranean. The concept is for exclusivity and special attention in Mallorca's oldest art colony. The hotel itself is a linkage of two 400-year-old farmhouses plus a new wing (which I hope will not bulk it out too much). Restaurants in a restored ruin and beside the pool (the former is bruisingly expensive; the latter is picnic level); 4-poster bed in many units, 8 suites; antique furnishings. Reserve by contacting Mr. or Mrs. Axel Ball the young and enterprising proprietors (Tel: 639045; Telex 69570 Deya).

★★★ **Vistamar** • *at Valldemosa* • Finally, there is a hotel-and-restaurant of quality near this popular center. It's a captivating loggia-fronted mansion of

8 rooms and 1 suite; 3 with balcony; romantic glassed dining terrace; pool set among rocks. Intimate, restful, and ideal for country living.

★★ **L'Hermitage** • *at Oriente* • is in the center of the island with savage cliffs rising above it and lovely orchards surrounding. A few rooms in the ancient farmhouse; more in a converted library; attractive alfresco lunches or evening dining in an old olive mill. Take a bathing suit in summer. Very romantic and intimate for inlanders rather than seacoasters.

IN PALMA

☆☆☆☆☆ **Melia Victoria** • remains the unchallenged sachem of city hotels. Quietly inviting lobby with glass-enclosed wild-duck pond and fountain; 100% glass-walled stretch commanding the seaside fronts of the lounge, dining room, and leather-and-paneled bar; mammoth open terrace dotted with pine trees and flora; circular 3rd bar plus card and TV/writing rooms; striking bayfront pool with snack service and dancing until 1 a.m., smaller heated pool. All of the 150 smartly outfitted bedchambers with bath, air conditioning, and individual balcony; 115 bayside units and 35 facing the garden. General Manager Antonio Perez, crack chief concierge don Miguel and his colleague Gabriel radiate kindness. Tops in town.

☆☆☆ **Valparaiso** • Breathtaking view; acres of polished marble floors; extravaganza of costly and showy appurtenances in public precincts; formal dining room plus window-lined grill of no great distinction gastronomically; patio for outdoor snacking; 24-hour bar; vast ternate pool area; second pool inside with saunas; handsome discotheque; 3 styles of bedchambers, all with balcony, air conditioning, compartmented baths, TV, and high quality furnishings; stunningly expensive by Spanish standards. Impressive it is; cozy it isn't.

★★ **De Mar** • *about 15 minutes from the center in **Las Illetas*** • occupies a lovely suburban hillside that cascades in terraced gardens down to a rocky shore. The pool and palm fringed patios are a design for sunlit days and romantic evenings. This electrifyingly modern contestant—its daring brown ceramic exterior has given it the nickname ''Villa Chocolate''—sails extensively in the lanes of bulk commercialism.

Bellver Sol • *facing the bay from Palma's Paseo Maritimo* • is a hard-bit victim of the touristic boom-bug. All 15 floors air-conditioned; swimming pool; cinema; nightclub; coffee shop. Conventions and mass bookings compose the majority of its roster of registrants.

Palas Atenea • *with a similar bayfront setting* • the same pack-'em-in attitude, and the same administration, which provides an unusually kind staff in both hotels. If you book one of its 400 look-alike cubicles you may experience how truly boring a hotel can be.

☆ **Saratoga** • *also in midtown* • is amiably executed and not expensive. Three lounges and dining room adjacent to heated pool and balconied bedchambers above; another pool and bar topside; colorful contemporary furnishings; doubles with baths and singles with showers. Again good for midtowners.

In the busy-busy *Illetas* suburb, the **Bonanza,** with its neighboring (and cheaper) **Bonanza Playa,** is a sheltering corner. Two pools (one heated), mini-golf links, and private beach; garden with ancient cloister decor; evening meals outdoors in summer; bar in bamboo tones; 10 Moorish-mooded "villas" on the grounds. **Gran Albatros** is a standout on this part of the coast. A private beach and heated swimmery add to its attractions.

The **Son Caliu** takes its name from the cove where it is sited. Adequate beach plus pool; waterside snack bar; maintenance slipping perilously. In danger of overdeveloping.

Not far away, the **Punta Negra** distributes its dual personality of a 40-room hotel and 13 bungalows between the twin beaches at its doorsteps. Sea or pool swimming available; dining room with savory offerings; cozy in tone.

In *Magaluf,* the 15-story, cliff-sited ☆ **Coral Playa** is king of the mountain. All 200 sea-seeing bedchambers with terrace and private bath; cooled public rooms and heated swimming pool; dancing nightly in Season. Very attractive. **Cala Vinas** usually is booked solid with British clients. Not very exciting but passable. The 161-room **Pax,** while second class, offers heart and warmth. Not directly on the water but across the road from it; nice heated pool; bar, salon, and dining room; Iberian-tone bedrooms, each with terrace and private bath; plenty of color; quiet and economical for the right traveler. Open April to mid-October. **El Caribe,** in the same category as the Pax, comes up with a better seaside situation, but with far less elan than its spiffier competitor. It's okay— but if you don't insist on quartering at water's edge, choose the Pax.

All of these are within about a ½-hour radius of Palma.

For fun-and-games at a soothingly reasonable price level, *Puerto de Pollensa* offers the most—especially to unmarrieds and young-marrieds. This is the nearest village to Formentor, with frequent inexpensive boat service to the Formentor beaches for swimming (less spectacular but much improved bathing and beautiful maritime surroundings in the Puerto). The outskirting ★ **Illa D'Or** has my first slot now, especially if you snag a balconied unit in the newer wing. (The set-back apartments around the pool also are nice for longer stays.) Seaside situation about 10 minutes from town by foot; waterfront patio plus facilities for bay bathing; snack bar for swimmers; tennis court; handsome lounge; Valencia-style dining room; largely filled by well-mannered British clients and young families. Now functioning through most of the year. Recommendable, if you don't mind its distance from the port action. The midtown **Daina** operates from April to late October. Its proudest asset is the large swimming pool with sundecks that extends into the fronting bay. Comfortable, glass-lined off-lobby salon; pleasant lounge-bar plus outside terrace for sips and studying the passing parade; seafacing rooms the best but not the quietest in midsummer. Well-run and a solid value. The little **Sis Pins** has a homey personality. Improved seafront apron for swimming or sunbathing; earplugs suggested if you draw a rear window in summer; now offering bed and breakfast only in a formula that clients seem to appreciate. The ★ **Miramar** is a relic of a bygone era. Yet it is very well maintained and sparkles as an island period piece. Elderly travelers or novelists who might wish to insinuate themselves into a quiet colonial setting undoubtedly would preen in its rocking-chair mood. Closed November to March.

Pollentia, a bit more out of the center, also features Old World grace and authentic Mallorquin atmosphere. The people are especially warmhearted here. The 66-room **Uyal,** about a mile along the same Alcudia road, continues to deliver the goods for its summer patronage. Seaside swimming and sunning terrace across the highway; swimming pool fringed by the salon and bar; 2 fine tennis courts; large annex facing the seaside; now unfreezing commendably.

CASINO

The tastefully sleek **Casino Sporting Club of Mallorca** gambols in a stunning building on the Carretera Cala Figuera at *Mallorca Sol,* about 25 minutes by car east of the capital. Soft illumination, tons of fine marble, a galaxy of paintings, rich textiles, and gracious furnishings make its ambience warm and attractive. Among its facilities are full air conditioning, a nightclub, a low-priced coffee shop, restaurant with special bargain buffets, cafeteria, bars, discos, an art gallery, tennis, golf, squash, a gymnasium, 2 swimming pools, a sauna, a bank, a winter garden beach club, and a solarium. Free shuttle buses for the one-armed-bandit players only have been installed to and from the capital. Unlike in many of its sister establishments in Spain, the dress standards are informal. At this writing, the admission charge is approximately $4.

The ceilings of the gambling area glitter with a forest of hundreds of shimmering lights. The 32 tables accommodate a capacity of 600 players. The action is split among slot machines, American roulette, French roulette, Blackjack, Craps, Punto Banco, Chemin de Fer, and Boule. This area is open daily and Sundays through Thursdays 6 p.m.–4 a.m. and Fridays, Saturdays, and holidays 6 p.m.–5 a.m. *Please be SURE to take your passport* if you wish to try your luck.

RESTAURANTS

☆☆☆☆☆ **Samantha's** • *Francisco Vidal Sureda 115* • is easily the top choice within the Palma limits, a gathering spot for top royalty and just ordinary bon vivants who love the food, the mood, and the gracious hospitality of the Newmans. The attractive renovated private house stands above the city, still higher than the Valparaiso Hotel on the same street. Parking apron in front; grand windows by the bar-lounge; comfortable spacious salon. There's a splendid feature here in that most dishes come in full or half portions so you are able to sample a larger selection or tailor your order to your appetite. Casual or dressy patronage; easygoing, friendly tone. Be sure to try it.

★★★★★ **Anchorage** • is in the *Bendinat* suburb (10 minutes out), the exclusive dining facility of Mallorca's finest subdivision. The setting is a distillate of Mediterranean dreaming—pastel buildings, seaside terraces, fountains, cordiality, and finesse. Maritime bar and delightful sea-theme lounge; food pleasant but not attempting to be grand cuisine. Be sure to reserve ahead (Tel: 405212) because residents have preference here. Nearby, its golf club also features a dining salon and lovely terraces overlooking the links. Skillful chef for such informal pastimes.

☆☆☆☆☆ **Tristan** • is nearby the Anchorage at ***Portals Nous*** in a marina called Cala Portals. Here the chef is a dedicated professional in the modern mold; table presentation is fresh and contemporary; prices are for the yachting set. Both individual selections as well as a fine gourmet menu available. Its position by the pleasure boats and in a charming complex is ideal for spendthrift romancers (Tel. 675438).

☆☆ **Caballito de Mar** • *Paseo de Sagrera 5* • faces the city's harbor from beside Naval Headquarters. Simple decor, but one of the best seafood selections to be found in Spain; northern fish flown in 3 times per week; kind reception and service. The bream or other catch of the day baked in rock salt is deeeelicious; have it with Olara white wine.

☆☆ **Penelope** • *Progreso 39* • in the interior of the capital, is one of the most consistently reliable kitchens on the island, producing superior international dishes and tantalizing catches from the Mediterranean. Attractive marine theme enhanced by the sound of rushing water from its own cascade; glasslined tank for fish and crustacea; warm, clublike ambience; amiable attentive service masterminded by warmhearted Don Juan Bonet. A charmer.

Xoriguer • *C. Fabrica 60* • is an enigma. With its grim interior, incessant din of the ventilator fan, and timid attempts at *nouvelle cuisine* that is no longer *nouvelle,* it is peculiar how it hangs on. Incidentally, this is the *only* restaurant I've come across where I was *under*charged. *That* I did like!

★★★ **Club de Mar** • *nexus of the yacht basin in the **Puerto Pi** section of the capital* • today draws by far the largest segment of the illustrious and the Beautiful People. Its strikingly attractive premises, including the luxurious bar, are open the calendar around, but meals are served in its dining room and on its handsome terrace *from July 1 to August 31 only*. When the King and Queen spend their annual holidays in Mallorca, a table is reserved nightly in case they should wish it. Although it is a very exclusive private club, if space is available, for about $4 you may procure a one-time guest courtesy card which would entitle you to all of its copious facilities. Splendid vista overlooking thickets of anchored crafts; stunningly modern, airy decor in blue-and-white nautical rigging; mixed dress from conservative suits and long gowns to seagoing informal wear on the boaters. Don't, incidentally, confuse this one with a restaurant called **Porto Pi,** on the hillside above. The latter is in a townhouse of modest distinction. A new chef handles the skillets now and he is gaining fame in cooking competitions. The aura of snobbism puts me off. Very chic.

★ **Mediterraneo 1930** • *Paseo Maritimo 33* • is a casually rendered study in art retro. The harbor view, the excellence of the sea fare, and the service, which is as polished as its period mirrors, conspire to make this one very, very enjoyable.

★ **Le Bistrot** • *Teodoro Llorente 4* • is a tiny corner of France transplanted into the heart of Palma. Marble-topped tables; Tiffany wall-lamps; sizable open kitchen; Nouvelle Epoch chairs; limited menu; excellent food; terrible acoustics. The family of operators doesn't have enough members to provide fast service. We still salivate for their *profiteroles* with chocolate sauce. Closed Sunday.

☆ **Casa Gallega** • *Pueyo 6* • in midcity is changeless. The ground-floor counter is always jammed; down here you'll also find a few tables; upstairs is for more formal dining. Some of the Galician platters are super (such as toasted, seasoned medallions of octopus or the tiny eels called *angulas* in oil and garlic), while others are merely excellent. Rudeness is par for the course in the service here—but for such gastronomy, try to forget it.

Horchateria C'an Juan de S'Aigo • *Calle de Sans 10, behind Plaza Santa Eulalia* • was established in 1700. It remains THE place for Mallorquins to drop in for hot chocolate, ensaimadas (a light super-appetizing pastry), or almond ice cream. I applaud the tradition and follow the crowd.

Gran Dragon • *Calle de Ruiz de Alda 5* • leads for Chinese food. Tastefully modern premises with plenty of room between tables; air-conditioned; wide array of comestibles; attentive service; savory wok-work at competitive tariffs. If you're splurging, order Peking Duck 24 hours in advance for a truly memorable treat. Excellent. Don't bother with the **Peking,** next to the Auditorium. I did and would rather have dined on duck feathers.

Shogun • *Camilo Jose Cela 14* • is Mallorca's first-rate Japanese offering. Main floor plus lower level overlooking a garden; black enamel decor contrasted with white; attentive reception; all service personnel in oriental costume. The cookery is superb; highish prices.

★ **S'Altell** • *Avinguda Antoni Maura 69, at Pont d'Inca* • is about 10 minutes from midcity. The name refers to a rustic loft common to Mallorquin farm buildings in antiquity. The cookery matches the strong regional flavor of the architecture: angler fish custard garnished with prawns, eggplant tart, partridge with a dusting of hazelnuts and other inventive creations from its innovative chef. An average repast will total about $25, a painless outlay for a memorable experience. Closed Sun. and Mon.

Club Nautico Cala Gamba • in the cove that gives it its name, is a safe (and enchanting) harbor for—well, *gambas* (shrimp), fish and shellfood. The site alone is worth the trip on a balmy day or evening.

At the absolute center of the island, *Inca* offers ★★★ **C'an Amer,** unarguably the best cellar restaurant on Mallorca. The vast wine tuns are still filled each autumn with new pressings. Regional cuisine that is outstanding and reasonably priced.

Pollensa, 20 minutes further to the northwest, offers the delightfully cozy ☆☆☆ **Font del Gall** in the center facing the Coq Fountain from which it takes its name (symbol of the town). The radiant Christine, owner and hostess, keeps this house in perfect trim, but in a friendly clublike way. Always full, so phone for a table (530396). Open for lunch and dinner; Sunday lunch, when roast beef with Yorkshire pudding is the specialty; closed Mon. ★ **Farina** boasts a French proprietress, a French chef, an amusing atmosphere of a made-over flour mill, and very reasonable prices. Ask for Francoise. In this area you'll also find ☆ **Ca'n Pacienci,** a tiny *finca* (farmhouse) tucked at the end of a short driveway on the left-hand side about ⅓rd of the way from Pollensa to Puerto de Pollensa. Fixed-price meals for about $35 per person. *Advance reservations are absolutely necessary;* your concierge can make them by calling 53-07-87. Closed for 4 months in winter, and Sundays in summer.

On the northeast coast, ★★ **Ses Rotges** in *Cala Ratjada* leans to French cookery since the chef and his hostess-wife are from Lyon. The garden dining in summer is a romantic treat, but there is no sea view. The gastronomy is quite refined for the region. At the port itself, **Ca'n Maya** looks directly at the Med. Excellent fish and very simple in mood.

NIGHTCLUBS

In *Palma,* **Tito's Palace** disco commands a truly palatial view of Palma Bay. With laser shafts and moonbeams, it is the capital's pride of the night. Dancing until dawn. **Victoria Center,** attached to the hotel, is another worthy contender in the top bracket.

Abaco (just off Apuntadores) is one of the most dazzling bars that you are likely to find anywhere. Open from 8 p.m. into the wee hours, it occupies both the Great Room and the open garden-patio of ancient town house. Only beverages ($4 per) and small bowls of complimentary snacks are served. Two unique features heighten its drama: Its daily displays of at least $1000 worth of fresh flowers with fruit and an estimated minimum of 100 lighted candles from small to mammoth. (The owner is also a florist.) Beautifully balanced classical music, mostly symphonies, flows from the numerous speakers as background.

Broadway, in a basement across from the Victoria Hotel, lights up with strip shows and cabaret.

Piano Bars are increasingly spreading on the nightscape. Good examples are **Victoria Bahia, Azzurro,** and (for youth) **Arcadia;** these three are neighbors on the Paseo Maritimo; then come **Rodas Pub** (Av. Magalluf-Plaza next to Ses Palmeres), with a discreet atmosphere, and **Napoleon** (Juan Miro 322 in Cala Mayor), also with dancing.

Among the less glamorous entries on the disco scene, **BCM Disco Palace** in Magaluf is tonight's leader. **Abraxas** and **Colapso** seem to be edging out **Alexandra's.** The young **Acron Discotheque-Boite** is coming along strongly as another choice. All do their zingy thing in the latest mod mood. **Villa Rio** (Juan Miro 105) offers the bonus of alpine style restaurant upstairs. **Black Cat** is said to be gay at times. **Kiss** is keener than most on promotion. Out toward *Arenal* (the crass mass-tourism beach resort) the expensive 2000-seat **Riu Palace** is the latest "mega-disco" with laser beams and the most modern sound and light equipment.

SHOPPING

Palma is the shopping center; the choicest merchandise is here. If you want to find ancient-style hand-loomed textiles that are distinctive of the "Isle of Calm" you'll have to travel north to Galerias Vicens in Pollensa—a wonderful excursion in any case (see below).

SHOPPING HOURS: See "Madrid."

BEST AREAS: Paseo del Borne, Av. Jaime III, Calle Puigdorfila, Calle Constitucion (just off the Borne halfway up on the right), Calle San Nicolas (and just off this, the renewed Calle Veri, with its art galleries and super-chic boutiques) and, in the district of Plaza Cort, Calle Colon and Calle Jaime II.

SAVINGS ON PURCHASES: See "Madrid."

ANTIQUES: **Linares** (near the Cathedral) rules the roost. It is a branch of the celebrated Madrid pacesetter. Both its stocks and its physical plant are in exquisite taste.

The **Casa Bonet** (Plaza Federico Chopin 2) is to needlework what the Rolls-Royce is to cars—except for its fantastic price values. For nearly a century, Casa Bonet has won consistently every Exposition Gold Medal in sight and has spread the fame of Mallorquin hand embroidery all over the globe. The artistry of its 350 island specialists cannot be duplicated anywhere else today; its museum is an Aladdin's Cave of musical scores, Chinese calligraphy, and intricate etchings exquisitely duplicated by needle. The array of bridge sets, tablecloths, placemats, and the like—every stitch done by hand, in plain or colorful patterns—is (adjective applied literally) sensational. New pride of the house is its even-lower-cost, exclusive, perfectly executed line of machine-made linens of highest quality. For men or for women, one special suggestion: Class AAA linen handkerchiefs, *with your own signature or choice of 200 monogram styles* for one-quarter of U.S. prices. Don Alfredo Bonet, the global King of Embroidery, will be happy to greet you. Lovely branches in Madrid and Marbella (see "Shopping" earlier in chapter). Super-super.

FOOTWEAR: Ladies' and men's shoes are one of Mallorca's biggest exports, and **Yanko** (General Mola 3) is a pacesetter of this key industry. Its boots for both genders are simply *beautiful*—and their prices are from 35% to 50% less than the best on Fifth Avenue! A reliable and excellent money-saver.

GLASS: Gordiola (Calle Victoria 2 and Jaime II 26) is internationally famous for its regional glassware of all types. Here is the finest quality and most outstanding selection on the island. We do not like the prices, attitudes, or swarms of bus traffic at the much-advertised *Campanet* center.

JEWELER: Nicolas (Av. Antonio Maura 14) is one of Spain's leading creators, as well as being one of the oldest and finest in Europe. **Gregory** (Constitucion 1) is splendid, too, and with great variety. **Relojeria Alemana** (Jaime III 26) is a showcase for watches chiefly, but also for personal jewelry. **Karatti** (Plaza Pio XII 9) is more general in its inventory. All are outstanding and prices are below most other European markets.

NEWSPAPERS: The *International Herald Tribune* is available at better hotels and newsstands. Also helpful is the English-language-American-idiom *Mallorca Daily Bulletin*. Jammed with island happenings. Here's a colorful souvenir of your Mallorquin meanderings.

PEARLS: Caution!! There is only one—we repeat, *one*—founder, developer, and leader of this industry: **Perlas Majorica,** with 3000 artisans the largest in the world. Don't confuse it with "Majorca" or "Mallorca"—and be SURE to look for its "Official Agency" seal. Others are rank imitators, but at first sight these inferior ones so closely resemble the originals that it's difficult to tell them apart. Every individual Perlas Majorica piece carries a unique 10-year (!) International Certificate of Guarantee which you may present in the U.S. or 50 other countries. Their sizes, also flawless, run from 4 to 14 millimeters in diameter—offering so many hundreds of combinations that many North American pilgrims end up buying several pieces. And the prices! For *exactly* the same Perlas Majorica exported globally, you'll pay a mere fraction here at the source. If you're making an island excursion to Manacor don't fail to visit the factory at Via Majorica 48 or its shop opposite. But if your sojourn is limited to Palma, its succulent shop is at Av. Jaime III 11, where you should ask for manageress Antonia Girbau. Buy *only* Perlas Majorica to be safe.

SUEDE AND ANTELOPE WEARABLES: After years of searching, I have yet to find one outlet that completely satisfies me. None of the loudly touted factories and shops for antelope or suede in *Inca,* center of this industry, appeals to me much. Incidentally, most of the cheaper lines are so poorly dyed that the color will stain your hands and your body.

WROUGHT IRON: Casa del Hierro (Calle Victoria 6) yields a striking assortment.
Pollensa, about an hour's drive north from Palma, offers the world-famous **Galerias Vicens** (at the crossroad to Puerto Pollensa), where the Artist Martin and Antonia Vicens re-create the patterns of island textiles on hand looms. Decorators from the finest houses shop here among the scores of colorful bolts that bear a resemblance to *hongroise* themes. In addition, there are handicrafts, antique decoys, irons, urns, decanters, keys, furniture, silk cassocks, and oil paintings. Plan to have lunch in the area and make a day of it.

SWEDEN

USA: Swedish Tourist Board, 655 Third Ave., New York, NY 10017, Tel. (212) 949–2333

SPECIAL REMARKS: (1) **Stockholm Information Service** has its headquarters at Sweden House plus a summer tourist bureau at City Hall and a hotel booking office year-round at Central Railway Station. It provides a telephone service concerning local events. Dial 22–18–40. (2) The **Swedish Tourist Board,** also located at Sweden House, deals mainly with people in the communications world and officially is not open to the public; however, it can offer advice and assistance to a limited extent. If you are going to visit the capital, Malmo, or Gothenburg inquire about the special discount opportunities for admissions, transport, and other tourist-related pastimes. (3) Youth Hostels comprising some 270 shelters, farmhouses, and historic buildings function chiefly during the summer months. For details write to Svenska Turistforeningen (Swedish Touring Club), Box 25, S 10120 Stockholm. Hitchhiking, incidentally, is sternly discouraged in Sweden.

TELEPHONE: Access Code to USA: 009–1. To phone Sweden: 46; time difference (Eastern Daylight) plus 6 hrs.

Here's a land of lakes and streams; much of it is flatter than Ohio. Thousands of pools and rivulets glitter on the placid, green landscape of the south; the summer sun there is warm, fields burst with ripe, golden wheat, and gentle pastures are brilliant with flowers. One-tenth of the population tills the dark soil on these plains, the coastal terraces, the lake shores, and the northern valleys; in this balmy bottomland climate, warmed by the Gulf Stream, everything flourishes from peas to sugar beets to long-stemmed roses, even to strawberries; but, of course, the season is short. The mountains, sentinels shared with Norway, rise in the north and west.

Democracy and socialization have far outstripped most other western countries. This northern wonderland also happens to be one of the most "capitalistic" nations on the globe (above the per capita income in the U.S.)—while still being the most civic-conscious of major countries. To support this, taxes are murderous. Some by-products of this state paternalism are startling to the stranger. Parents are no longer permitted to spank their children. Few jails in Sweden have iron bars. Smoking is relatively low on a per-capita basis, but legislation has gone through to virtually create a nonsmoking nation over the next decade or so. Except for expense no country in Europe is better suited for tourists—as holidaymakers are beginning to discover more and more.

ATTRACTIONS In the **suburbs of Stockholm,** dozens of resorts and maritime beachscapes afford the visitor fascinating glimpses of coastal Sweden. You may charter a fishing boat and crew to poke at your whimsy through Stockholm's archipelago of 25,000 islands and skerries. Green shores, smiling beaches, pastures and groves, sunbaked isles, and foaming bays; a delight.

Should you proceed independently, go by commercial steamer and return by rail or bus. *Saltsjobaden,* a short ride from the city, is the best known beach; take your bathing suit and plan on luncheon at the local Grand Hotel. If you are young, rugged, and want to get away from the crowds of this popular resort, get off the Saltsjobaden train at the station nearest *Erstaviksbadet,* a wooded beach with fewer people and wonderful swimming. You used to have to undress behind a tree, a matter that was supremely unimportant to everybody but yourself. Now cabins have been provided for the modest. *Flatenbaden* is another fine alternative for sea bathing.

Sandhamn, the largest yachting center, has perhaps the best overall seaside atmosphere; the ride takes 3½ hours each way—a long haul but definitely worth it. You'll ride on a steamer that chuffs through some of the most enchanting island realms on this globe. *Vaxholm* is a pretty trip and excellent for a quiet lunch. The fortress and town are charmers; it's on the same route as Sandhamn, but not as far. Swimmers can take a dip at nearby *Erikso.* Package tours can be purchased at the Excursion Shop, Sweden House, Hamngatan 27, Stockholm.

Away from Stockholm, there are dozens of organized expeditions that range far afield—going up to the top of the world, to reindeer country, to Christmas in Lapland, even to polar safaris by dog sledge. Swedish Touring Club (Svenska Turistforeningen—STF, Drottninggatan 31, 10120 Stockholm, Tel: 7903200) sponsors any number of treks from 1 to 10 days to fit almost any wanderer's whims or budget, including visions of Scandinavian coastal areas, lowland track areas, Swedish glass factories, Norwegian fjords and mountains, lake districts, the Isle of Gotland, Western Scandinavia, capital cities, and many other tempters. Your travel agent has details on all of these—and more.

If these don't appeal to you, a quick tour of *Ostergotland* might. About 2 hours by train from Stockholm, on the main line to Copenhagen, it's Sweden in a capsule, with rolling fields, sweeping forests, lovely lakes, and miniature mountains. High point to most visitors here is the excursion on the Gota, or Kinda, canal—charming at every bend in the route. You can also play golf, sail on the lakes, fish for salmon or char, go to horse races or county fairs, or do

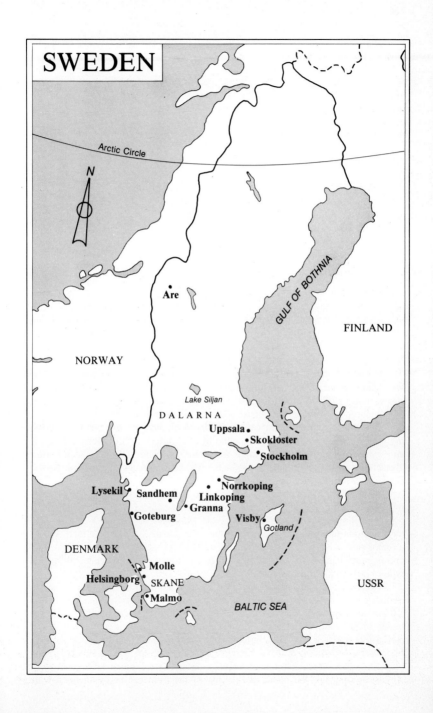

SWEDEN

Arctic Circle

N

NORWAY

FINLAND

GULF OF BOTHNIA

• Are

Lake Siljan

D A L A R N A

Uppsala •
• Skokloster
• Stockholm

Lysekil • • Sandhem
• Norrkoping
Linkoping
• Granna

• Goteburg

Visby •
Gotland

DENMARK

Molle •
Helsingborg •
SKANE

• Malmo

BALTIC SEA

USSR

practically anything you like. This is rural living, but it is usually busy and always urbane.

Farther down in **Skane,** Sweden's southernmost province, the late Dag Hammarskjold's farm near Loderup is open to visitors during summer months. The lovely white farmhouse, with its enclosed cobbled courtyard, reflects this great mediator's wide cultural interests and world travels. All of his personal possessions are here. It is a fascinating stop—one well worth a detour.

Sharing the same bucolic enticements is **Dalarna** province. This round requires at least 2 days, and preferably 4. You'll get a glimpse of a way of life different from anything else in Scandinavia. Go first to **Rattvik** (4 to 5 hours from Stockholm)—and then proceed, if you like, to the entrancing little village of **Tallberg,** beloved of so many of Sweden's overseas guests.

From Rattvik it is 3 hours by car or hotel bus to the strikingly different terrain around **Salen.** Here are the high mountains and deep valleys of the West. The **Hotel Storlien** is situated on an Alpine plateau near the Norwegian border. Its 200 rooms and 150 baths make it one of Scandinavia's largest resort hostelries; tiny accommodations; modern decor; unusually happy for children.

Want a full day's excursion to keep the tykes out of mischief? Drive east to **Lake Storsjon** and search for the Swedish brother of the Loch Ness Monster, which was sighted again recently by 4 workmen. King Oscar I long ago commissioned an official hunting party, and his ancient beast-snaring equipment can be seen in the Ostersund City Museum. Accounts vary about this uncaught but oft-seen fellow. Some say he's black, others say he's brown. Some measure his length at 15 feet, some swear he's not an inch under 70 feet. But they ALL agree on one observation: He wears a *very* sinister smile.

Or how about a cruise? Steamers depart from Stockholm bound for the semi-autonomous **Aland Islands,** halfway to Finland. The 12-hour round trip allows you to fill up on tax-free stores aboard, sights galore, and a pretty fair smorgasbord on some of the ferries. Inquire locally for details.

The world-famous glass center of **Orrefors,** just off the main east-coast highway between Denmark and Stockholm (220 miles north of Helsingborg), is an especially interesting little detour for motorists. Here you may watch master glassblowers turn out exquisite products. Alternate choices might be at Kosta, Boda, or Strombergshyttan in the same district.

Skokloster, which dominates a large lake about ¾ of the way toward Uppsala from Stockholm, is one of the most magnificent palaces in the hemisphere. It was built in the mid-17th century for Field Marshal Carl Gustaf Wrangel—and the gorgeous interiors bear witness to the splendor of Sweden's Golden Age as a major power. If you're wheeling toward the University City of Uppsala, this one is more than worth the short turnoff to any rover who appreciates its special type of beauty and magnificence.

No tourist should miss **Visby.** This insular capital, the only walled town in northern Europe, is one of the most worthy sights in Scandinavia. You'll find Viking remains such as you have never seen before; occasionally you'll see traces of Minoan, Greek, and Roman cultures. The wall is about 2 miles in circumference; there are 100 churches that stood before Shakespeare donned his first pair of long trousers. Now Visby is a vacation center. Broad beaches, good bicycling, good tennis, gorgeous scenery; impressive Medieval Week in early August recapturing the mood and events of the 13th century with town-wide pageants. One night from Stockholm by boat, or about 50 minutes by the interior air carrier Linjeflyg (6 flights daily).

TRANSPORTATION   **Airline** Refer to "Denmark" for comments on SAS. There is a discount program called the "micro-price," but it must be booked 2 weeks in advance. If you are staying for a while, ask a travel agent. Arlanda Airport, the Swedish gateway, is far from Stockholm's center. SAS runs buses between Arlanda and the city terminal (next to the rail station). It also operates an efficient limousine service with town pickup and delivery *guaranteed* for your SAS flight. You can ride it into the city, too, so inquire upon arrival or book it when you buy your SAS flight. Ask also about the luggage delivery, which relieves you of your baggage through a system devised by SAS. Incidentally, on an experimental basis, no smoking is permitted on domestic flights; this includes the departure hall at Arlanda.

Taxis Gone are the days when taxis were plentiful. Now they are too often excruciatingly difficult to obtain. The wisest method is to ask your concierge, restaurateur, or shopkeeper to telephone 15–00–00 for one—and plead for the help of your personal shepherd while this is being done. If it doesn't work, then you are forced to other means of transport such as buses, trains, or your own legs. This acute shortage is a disaster. Although the minimum rate is fairly low, the meter goes up like a missile. A trip across the city can cost you $10 or more. "Ledig" means "For Hire." If you can spot this on his car flag and wave with appropriate vigor, it's yours. Waiting time is very, very expensive, so beware.

As in many other countries, scores of jockeys "don't happen to have change"—trusting you'll let them pocket the difference. Watch this racket.

For Stockholm sightseers: For about $15 you can buy a 3-day, unlimited-travel ticket valid on all buses and subways, including the lines to Drottningholm Castle and Lidingo Island.

From 6:30 p.m. to 6 a.m. one taxi company has lowered fares for women by 15%, a gesture offered so ladies can avoid travel on subways at night. Subways are properly illuminated, clean, and the capital's crime rate is relatively low, but this kindness reduces after-dark anxieties for some women.

Trains Superior. There's a continuous program to hitch up new rolling stock. First-class smoking compartments often come equipped with twin banquettes of 3 seats each, plus a table flanked by 2 sink-in adjustable armchairs—all in the same roomy, handsome, and practical salon area. Other compartments (always including second class) are conventional but also relaxing and well designed. Many trains feature half-coach snack bars instead of fullfledged dining cars. They're immaculately clean; limited menus in 4 languages; soft drinks, wine, export beer, tea, and coffee are the only beverages; the food attracts the eye but is lackluster to the palate.

The Swedish Railways, known as "SJ" (Statens Jarnvagar), operates 95% of the nation's railroads, 22% of its buses, and 5% of its highway freight, plus a network of travel offices. While most visitors hold close to the coast, the *Inlandsbanan* covers some 800 miles of north-south interior terrain that is lovely. A 2-week pass from Lake Vanern to the Arctic, with stopover privileges in 2-dozen towns, costs about $75. For the visitor who wants to see a lot and whose funds are limited, SJ and its Danish, Norwegian, and Finnish counterparts offer

(1) train "circular tours" around Scandinavia (interrupt your journey wherever you wish, and save 10%–25%), (2) a sliding scale of prices which decrease as the distance increases (if you buy all your tickets at once, this arrangement will earn dollars for you), (3) a 30% discount—regardless of nationality—for seniors, and (4) "Red Departures" is a new discount program that adds to the bargain opportunities, so ask a travel agent for details. Fares are low; sleepers are very cheap.

Boats As Sweden is a paradise of islands, ask about the **KustLinjen** program, which ranges through the eastern isles—300 miles of archipelago, 25 ports of call, and miles of used-up film footage to give you pleasure for years.

FOOD Until a few seasons ago, smorgasbord was nearly extinct in its own homeland. It wasn't a case of smorgasboredom. It developed because restaurateurs found they could heap up bigger piles of kronor from straight dining, which involves less wastage—less waistage for you, too, if you make a habit of it. Thank goodness there are a few keepers of the flame. Smorgasbord goes full blast at the Operakallaren and the Stallmastaregarden restaurants (see below), most days both for lunch and dinner, but be sure to phone in advance to confirm this as there is some time variance with the seasons. Don't miss it! Elsewhere in the capital, this type of service can be found at the Grand Hotel (on the Veranda), at the beautiful and superb Ulriksdals Wardshus and at Solliden in *Skansen.* Some city restaurants offer their items individually on small plates, tailored to the customer's girth and pocketbook; these are known as *assietter.*

Cardinal rule with smorgasbord: Eat all fish on the 1st plate, meats on the 2nd, and hot appetizers on the 3rd (optional). Never mix fish and meat.

As a curiosity, try the delicious tiny crayfish called *kraftor*—a freshwater toyland lobster. It's expensive but you'd be wrong to miss this important ceremonial dish; the season is most of August. Odd facts department: Since a disease recently killed many of them, a fresh crop is being bred from those of our own Lake Tahoe.

DRINKS Package sales today are unrestricted. The Swede is the world's 2nd-thirstiest tippler, lining up at the counter right behind the Yugoslav. You may buy unlimited amounts of whatever you choose at any state liquor store from 9:30 a.m.–6 p.m. Mon.–Fri. and from 1 p.m. Sun. Restaurants keep the corks out of the bottles from noon until closing time.

Aquavit, the national drink, is also called "snaps," "brannvin," and "aqua vitae." But no matter by what name it slides down the gullet, there's enough heat in 1 glass to turn all the radiators in the Empire State Building cherry red. The base is potatoes or grain. It is flavored with berries, seeds, leaves, herbs, flowers, and spices. Drink it well chilled with smorgasbord (not with the entree or by itself), gulp the potion in 2 or 3 swallows (don't sip!), and chase it quickly with 5 or 10 gallons of beer. The best brand, in my view, is Skane; Ahus is slightly lighter and more like Denmark's Aalborg. Swedes prefer others, such as Overste (slightly spiced, slightly sweet) or O.P. (aroma of cumin).

Swedish Punch is a happy beverage. The ingredients are Java arrack and a special rum; float Remy Martin or another good French cognac on top of the glass; you'll find a drink fit for the gods. Expensive but worth it.

Beer comes in the following grades (based on their alcohol content): *Starkol* (4.5%), *Folkol* (2.8%), and *Lattol* (1.8%). One Swedish wag quips that the first leaves you in no doubt as to whether you are drinking beer and the last in some doubt as to whether you're drinking water. Pripps and Spendrups are the most popular brands for middle-of-the-road drinkers (not drivers). Now that the government controls the nation's largest brewery, it is curbing the outlets of the stronger types and limiting many of their former ones to only the weakest variety. Spendrups Gold is one of the world's most delicious luxury beers. Limited production, so you'll have to ask for it in better restaurants.

TIPPING Due to socialization and high salaries, this custom has almost disappeared here. Since most restaurants automatically add a service charge to the bills there is no need to leave more. In hotels, a supplement appears when it has not already been included in the room rate (virtually all the prestige houses now bury it in your bill). Give hatcheck girls 5 kronor and taxi drivers 10% of the fare. The hall porter in the hotel gets a separate bite on top of your automatic service charge; it's not customary locally to tip him when you check out unless he has given special service to you. Railway porters have, alas, vanished. Have 5-Kronor pieces on hand for carts and lockers.

CITIES AND REGIONS

First, are you ready for a delightful off-beat expedition? The **Diplomat Aregarden,** 425 miles north of Stockholm, is very special in its deep-heart-of-Sweden atmosphere and beautifully selected deluxe facilities. It is divided into 3 sections: The Diplomat (14 singles, 28 doubles), the Aregarden (18 singles and 25 doubles), and the Sporthotel (40 doubles). In summer there is white-water canoeing, mountain hiking with guide, water-skiing, fishing, swimming, sauna, tennis, table tennis, dancing, riding, boating, and film shows. In winter there is downhill skiing (numerous lifts), cross-country skiing with teacher, a ski school, curling, fishing, sauna, table tennis, dancing, disco, film show— and even gliding. Highly recommended to the adventurous traveler who seeks sport in beautifully pampering tranquillity.

DALARNA AND LAKE SILJAN In the Dalarna province of central Sweden, not far from the Norwegian mountains, there are 3 prime regional targets. *Tallberg* has by far the most color and charm with its mountainside spread, lake view, pine groves, and scattering of barn-red cottages in the lap of Siljan forests. Its silent mystique is periodically upset in High Season by reindeer-like herds of tourists. *Rattvik* also radiates lure, but it is more urban and physically less enticing. The outskirts should not be overlooked. *Leksand* is relatively commercial and dull; not worth the transatlantic fare to see it, but if you are in the area it has its points. As for hotels in this birch-and-pine heartland, here's a detailed town-by-town breakdown: In *Tallberg,* the **Green** boasts lovely buildings and an enchanting situation. In many respects—especially physical allures—it reeks with Dalecarlian appeal from its gables to its tables; dozens of nooks for cozy chats; Rumpus Room; tiny Picasso lounge; 17th-century library; brass place settings in its viewful woody dining room; gracious young hostesses; indoor-outdoor swimming pool with temperature control; minigolf and badminton. All rooms (named, not numbered) now have tub or shower and fresh furnishings; "Gesunda," with its arched ceiling, sublime little balcony, warming hearth, and gay colors, is my personal pick; open all year. The **Dalecarlia Turisthotell** offers 60 rooms plus 21 cottages sleeping 6 each. Its tiny 16th-century reception hall is engaging; very large glass-fronted dining room with a heavenly command; earthly dancing once or twice weekly throughout the year; casino; bar; minibowling. This one demonstrates a certain flair for mass appeal, suburban-style—but it is spectrums below the Green for sheer color. The **Langbersgarden,** a farmstead occupying 10 hilltop acres of ancient cattle-grazing land, boasts 55 rooms—25 in the main building and 30 in sleepy little cottages dotting the rumpled terrain. Poma-type ski lift for winter sports; 3 chalets, which Americans seem to love for their peaceful seclusion. *Rattvik*'s leader is, in my view, the **Lerdalshojden,** which is out of the hurlyburly above the lake. Rambling central structure plus annexes and individual chalets. All bedchambers, while tight-dimensioned, are ultra-clean and attractively furnished. Very pleasant. The **Motell Rattvikshasten's** 36 doubles are woefully cramped. *Leksand* (about 6 miles from Tallberg) has as its leader the ancient 40-room **Tre Kullor.** The **Furuliden** is next. The **Siljansnas** (on the lake, 9 miles west) lists a pool, sauna, curling, and scenery, plus 30 rooms, 22 baths, and 20 balconies. At *Mora,* the **Mora Hotel** deserves mention with 92 moorings. I haven't yet seen the **Siljan;** 37 units with toilet and TV; 9 with shower; sauna. **Tomteland** (Santaworld) is a year-round charmer with whimsy, good nourishment, and fun for the family in a fairy-tale setting. The celebrated **Salens Hogfjallshotell** at *Salen* has an annex that functions on a variable schedule, so check before going.

GOTEBORG (Gothenburg), pronounced "YOTE-ah-borg," where Volvos are born, is on the west coast facing seaward. There are many historic canals here, and the Gota River ends the famous Gota inland waterway that winds cross-country to Stockholm. Several hotels are available. Dining spots are now more engaging than before. There are ample tourist facilities. The city is an interesting one, and the inland boat ride across the peninsula is a relaxing and pleasant journey. It boasts an international airport; you can fly back to Stockholm by fast, frequent SAS service. A new private airport has relieved pressure on the main commercial terminus.

   SAS Park Avenue is one of the leading hotels of the nation. Traditionally attractive decor; wonderful Lorensberg Restaurant with orchestra music; beguiling Belle Avenue Grill; mezzanine bar and snack loggia; self-service breakfasts. Pool and sauna; of all the twins, ¼ have private verandas; top floor (10th) is entirely in elegant balconied large suites. **Sheraton** has 343 units opposite the central station. **Gothia** offers another 300 linked to the Trade Fair complex (Svenska Massan). **Tidbloms** leans more to intimacy, personal service, and quality cuisine. Those trying to avoid institutional dwelling and mealtiming will probably prefer this choice. **Lilton** is also a little charmer, only 10 rooms and a peaceful, personalized mien. It's at Foreningsgatan 9; ask for Eva Kjerulf. **Scandinavia** devotes most of its 323 rooms toward the convention trade. **Panorama** also sheds a businesslike aura throughout its 352-room shell. Speaking of shells, its Yarrawonga dining salon is noteworthy for its seafare. For modernists, the Reso-owned, 10-story, crescent-shape **Opalen** is as fresh as a fjord breeze. Careful planning of the bedchambers gives these comfortable and tasteful accommodations the edge over the cool-tempered public rooms. Clerestory restaurant (dancing except Sun.); quick-lunch den converting to a roulette rank at nightfall; hairdressing and barber facilities. All 230 rooms with well-equipped baths (good ventilation, soap flakes, peignoirs, Kleenex, bidets). There are artful touches in the displays of 20th-century tapestries and the handicraft vitrines in the corridors. The **Rubinen** stands a few doors away from the Park Avenue. It features 5 "executive" floors (each with its own concierge), a wine-tasting club in the cellar, a handsome restaurant plus the Bistro Chez Charles for lighter nutrients and imbibing. The 480-room **Europa** presents accommodation of no special distinction, usually small and dreary; several dining quadrants; a bar; gym, sauna, and pool; pedestrian passage connecting it to the shopping mall. **Eggers** was totally rescrambled not long ago and eggs ever onward. Seriously, it is a good bet today. **Ramada** is located on the E-6, about 10 minutes from midcity. Pool and sauna; fresh restaurant and appetizing food presentation; a formula for sleeping but a pretty good one. **Novotel** is built into an ancient brewery; it offers 150 rooms and special units for the disabled as well as for allergy victims. **Scandic** operates a motel at the entrance from the Malmo highway and another one on the Oslo highway. Cozy restaurants; modern comforts; better-than-average pitstops for traffic shunners. In *Kungalv,* 13 miles north of Goteborg, the 130-room **Fars Hatt** wears the sylvan crown. Two comfortable wings and a swimming pool; 2 saunas, tennis, bowling, and a golf course nearby; 2 popular restaurants and an active bar. Very solid accommodations, as a motel-type stop, excellent.

For dining in this city, the **Park Avenue Hotel** is a knockout. Fashionable clientele; attentive courtesy but staffing insufficient; chic, lively, and delightful. Among the independents, traditionally the best known is **Kajutan,** 10 minutes from the center. Glorious view of the harbor and busy cargo cranes; veranda; dancing downstairs in the nautical Kajutan Room in season; friendly, fast, and deft service, but is it ever expensive! **Sjomagasinet** is a red loft on the piers specializing in shellfish and other denizens of the deep. Interior with open beams; beguiling cocktail corner in off-white with plants and modern art; boardwalk terrace for outdoor repasts during long twilight summers. Altogether pleasing to the senses. **White Corner,** a 2-minute walk from the Rubinen, is much less costly. Ground-level snack center, bar, and popular-price restaurant; downstairs Grill with steaks the feature; crackling rotisserie and hearth at one end; comfortable armchairs and booths; blue- and gray-checked tablecloths; pewter place plates; illumination by candles; excellent service by waiters who present the meat choices on plaques. Highly recommended—especially downstairs.

GRANNA   For honeymooners, the favorite is **Gyllene Uttern,** 1½ miles south of the village on the Stockholm-Jonkoping-Malmo route. Two hotels (1 first class, 1 for country living); Tudor-style architecture; grass growing on the roofs; lake view; guest cottages with 1-or-more bedrooms, a bath, and a sitting room; exquisite Wedding Chapel to make it legal; lovely setting and enchanting decor; not overexpensive and now open around the calendar. Just the dish for lovebirds who want bucolic scenery and less-than-zero chatter from anybody.

HALMSTAD, SOUTHWEST COAST   This region has recently enjoyed a touristic boom period. *Tylosand* (the seaside resort on a cape facing Denmark, 5 miles from Halmstad on the Malmo-Goteborg road) comes up with a cluster of summery hotel buildings, several bungalows for transients, 1 restaurant seating 700, 2 smaller dining establishments, Finnish steam baths, a wonderful beach (cold water—brrr!), and 36-hole golf courses, tennis courts, dancing, and many other attractions. The **Nya Hotel Tylosand** is open year round. At *Halmstad,* the **Grand** and **Martenson** are quite good. For pilgrims from Denmark, the Lion Ferry makes the daily run between Grena and Varberg or Halmstad.

LINKOPING   (pronounced "Lin-sho-ping") is a good land base for exploring the Gota and Kinda canal locks; interesting cathedral and neighboring Air Force Museum at *Malmstatt.* The town produces the delightful little **Frimurarehotel-let,** provincial but comfortable. Its newer section is best; there's a bath provided with every unit. Good dining room under a slat roof; ancient Grill with hunting scenes in stained-glass windows; chef laboring happily under a copper hood; off-lobby bar. Inviting in a clubby fashion. The 135-room **Rally Motel** is just a fair bet for motorists. Squash court, Finnish bath, barbershop, grill-restaurant, and 24-hour coffee shop with help-yourself snack bar. The **Scandic Hotel** is also on the scene with 96 gleaming reasons to pause for the night. In the center, the **Stora Hotellet** is adequate for emergency shelter if all else is filled.

LULEA   is far up north. **SAS Globetrotter** welcomes you with an efficient and pleasant 213-room hostelry.

LYSEKIL,   2 hours north of Goteborg just off the trunk road to Oslo (Norway), has the well-known seaside **Lysekil** with 50 rooms, some with bath and all with private toilet; 3 restaurants, a nightclub, a bar, and a gaming room adjoin. Facilities are amiable without being plush. In this very Swedish summer mecca, you'll find fishing (no licenses or restrictions), an open-air cafeteria on the beach, an Aqualung Diving School, an International Youth Club, dancing nightly at the **Nautic** restaurant, and other drawing cards.

MALMO,   Sweden's third city, resides down on the southwestern tip, closest to Germany and Denmark. This is the jumping-off point for excursions to the Swedish chateaux country; there are at least 200 fine ones from the 16th and 17th centuries. You are also handy to **Lund,** which King Canute created in 1020 and which became the hub for Scandinavia's religious, commercial, and cultural activities. Good hotels and interesting restaurants, plenty of shops, and plenty of bustle; 6 miles of quays, Sweden's biggest man-made harbor, and one of Scandinavia's largest and most modern theaters are here. Immaculate and comfortable ferryboats make the crossing to Copenhagen in 1–1½ hours, and 30 hydrofoil and/or hovercraft services per day in both directions nip the time to a mere 45 minutes.

Among hotels, the **SAS Royal** boasts some of the largest rooms in Europe—quite a turnabout for Scandinavia, where accommodations usually are minuscule. All 240 units well outfitted with contemporary fixin's. The **Savoy,** mellow, charming, and carefully maintained, has an enviable location overlooking the canal and maritime docks. Cozy, popular Grill, French dining room and Cafe, all noteworthy for cuisine. **St. Jorgen** is a sterling example of the modern crop. Centrally situated and thoughtfully planned; built-in tranquillity surrounding 2 garden courts, effectively designed restaurant and cafeterias, wine cellar and music bar; roulette room where you can play for your meal chits; sauna and gymnasium. **Kramer** carries on as a traditional Malmo address. Pleasant lounge; Kramersalong for dinner and dance; 2 nightclubs; handsome bar in mahogany tones plus the Pub. A penthouse lords over 4 suites plus 100 lesser pads with 64 baths; each floor features a different shade of linens. The 270-room **Skyline** is sleek, linear, and near to the congress center. More intimate is the fresh **Noble House** with about half as many beds, an inviting restaurant, and a cozy bar. This is my favorite of the smaller places. The 216-unit, supermodernistic **Scandinavia** provides a surprising amount of elbowroom for a contemporary north-country enterprise. Beguiling roof garden; cheery restaurant, bar, and casino; sauna and gymnasium; billiard parlor; 44 bowling lanes (site of a World Championship); all bedchambers with 2 windows, alarm clock, radio, telephone, silent valet, and full bath, plus telephone-style shower in each; soothing color schemes. The centrally sited, 175-room **Garden** flowers on 2 floors atop an office building. Fresh restaurant plus enclosed tea and breakfast room surrounded by flora; small modernistic units; dull colors; commercial but economically priced; adequate for brief stays. **Teaterhotellet,** across from the Stadsteatern, and the **Plaza** are both pretty routine. Adjoining the racetrack is the ultrabasic **Jagersro Motell.**

Malmo's best bet in restaurants is the ★★★ **Kockska Krogen,** the vaulted cellar of Jorgen Kock's palace. (He was the city's powerful mayor in the 15th century, when the port was Danish.) As an example of authentic period architecture, I'd call it an *absolute sightseeing must;* it's a happy haven for gastronomy as well. One main sanctum with several radiating brick-arched rooms; wonderful cheese bar at the entrance for munching with beer or wine while you wait for your table; benches with stuffed coffee bags for cushions; interior units with comfortable banquettes; leather-backed armchairs with brass studs; wooden place platters and bread plates; candles in wrought-iron bases; rich brown carpet to warm away the basement chill. The menu is in Swedish, but a maitre in chef's costume helps with the translations; food bills—presented in a music box—are very reasonable for the quality. An extraordinary tourist attraction that rings true, without the slightest spoilage by gimmicks. ☆☆ The **Borshuset** is fairly young but already gaining fame for its kitchen. ★★ **Radhuskallaren** is in (as the name suggests) the Town Hall. Dramatic cellar vaults and intimate mood. Another worthwhile eye-pleaser, providing a panoramic view of the town and of Copenhagen (across the sparkling strait), is the penthouse **Kronprinsen,** a spellbinder crowning a residential structure. It contains a garage, a 2nd-floor nightclub, and enough ground-level shops to keep you busy until you're hungry again. Heavy food odors; cuisine not special; clientele drawn from every quarter; go for the vista and the relaxing ambience, not for the cookery. For a browse and more nutrients, try Malmo's indoor **Food Market,** which houses 5 restaurants and the surroundings to whet any appetite. In nearby *Skanor* a few minutes from Falsterbo, **Gastgifvaregard** offers the perfect village diversion for city-tired travelers. Cozy old house converted into a restaurant in 1910; 3 rooms inside a flag-lined building; geese by the gaggle greet the guests; white-hatted chef doing wonders with each and every goose. Try this and the smoked eel (the latter cut with sheep shears and presented on a special server with scrambled eggs and rye crisp). Another treat is a delicious bitters called Malort, extracted from a local plant. Lovely for a fair-weather excursion.

MOLLE This is a convenient stopping place for touring the pastural beauty of *Skane,* about 20 miles north of Helsingborg, which, of course, is opposite the Danish port of Elsinore. In neighboring *Kullaberg,* **Kullagardens Vardshus** is an historic inn with homey comforts and hushabye surroundings. It's the soul of Sweden's *House & Garden* country.

NORRKOPING Here's the beginning of the Gota Canal, an area with rock carvings going back to the Bronze Age, and Kolmarden, the largest animal-nature park in Europe. At the cliffedge of the Baltic, you can find viewful shelter at the **Vildmarkshotellet.** In the center both the **Grand** and the **President** are pleasant.

SANDHAMN Sweden's age-old sailing center is not unlike the whaling towns along New England's rocky coast. It is an island due east of Stockholm and easily accessible via public transportation and frequent ferries. Its crooked pastel-painted cottages nestle among humpback basalt mounds that historically have afforded dozens of inlets for the safe protection of sailing ships. Tall masts and firs are reflected on the still waters of the harbor. The heartbeat of the sporting port is the Royal Swedish Yacht Club, which also contains a public dining room with surprisingly refined cuisine for such a tiny and remote island. A crewman's snack bar and cafeteria are in the same charming Old World building. The front apron displays some of the finest competition vessels in Scandinavia.

For overnighting the best bet is **KSSS Seglarhotellet,** located behind the yacht club. Beds are bunkstyle; space is limited (but vast if you've just stepped off a Maxi racing sloop); service is kindly but unseasoned—in fact, perfect for the informal life of a yacht harbor. Prices run close to $56 per night for two. For dining, try the **Sandhamn's Vardshus,** which began life in 1672 as an inn and has not closed a single day since its birth. It is a wooden klinker-built building with some of the most delicious fresh fish—especially flounder—that I have ever sampled. The island bristles with cozy corners but, naturally, most of the activity centers around the yacht club. For travelers in a hurry—and I don't recommend any rushing here—there is an air-taxi service to Stockholm that lands and takes off from the harbor. Very salty and recommended to anybody with a maritime bent.

STOCKHOLM

To many world travelers Stockholm is Europe's most attractive capital. It's difficult to disagree with that. Spires and stately buildings, boats, and green parks abound. Somewhat larger than Washington, it has 1.3 million people, a subway system that is practically a museum of contemporary artistic endeavor, an excellent hotel picture, plenty of restaurants and shops. There is enough to do here to keep any tourist busy any time of the year—from canoeing through midcity to cycling around royal hunting grounds that fringe the midtown district to cultural attractions galore to browsing among some of the most attractive stores anywhere in the world to people-watching where many consider Adam and Eve were at their best. What a good-looking collection of human beings they are! This 700-year-old city of islands is spick-and-span, modern, efficient, and beautiful to the eye.

ATTRACTIONS

Kaknastornet • *TV Tower, at Kaknas, Norra Djurgarden* • This is the best possible view of Stockholm from on high. Kaknastornet, with its 400-foot-high tower, is Scandinavia's tallest building.

Stadshuset • *City Hall, Hantverkargatan 1* • The other way to get the lay of the land (and water) in Stockholm is from the 348-foot tower of the City Hall. (An elevator will take you part of the way up.) The building itself is a masterpiece of early 20th-century civic architecture. Made of red brick with marble colonnades, the Stadshuset incorporates the Golden Hall. If like most folks you associate Swedish design with simplicity, the opulence of the Golden Hall will surprise you—it is gilded with over 18 million pieces of gold-leaf mosaic. The Blue Hall is the venue for the annual Nobel Prize Banquet.

Kungliga Slottet • *Royal Palace, Gamla Stan* • Don't miss the Royal Palace if you want to see how the *very* wealthy lived in centuries gone by, for within the deceptively plain exterior of this former king and queen's residence (the current royal couple maintain their official residence at Drottningholm Palace) are endless treasures. Many, but not all, of the royal riches are concentrated in the Royal Treasury. Among the dazzling regalia on display are a crown, scepter, orb, and key made in 1560 for the coronation of King Eric XIV. Also open are the Festival and Bernadotte Suites with collections of art and historic furnishings as well as the fabulous living quarters belonging to former King Gustav III when he was a mere crown prince. No less striking are the art-filled Chapel Royal and the elegant Hall of State with a silver throne. Watch the **Changing of the Guard** at 12:15 on Wed. and Sat. off-season and daily during July and Aug. Don't plan your day, however, around this event. While the marching band booms and tootles along with gusto and precision, the guardsmen are so drably outfitted in stone gray uniforms and white helmets that they resemble a platoon of button mushrooms set out to dry. If there is one single manifestation to demonstrate the difference between the splendid theatrical sense of the Danes and the pragmatic expression of the Swedes, this is it in a nutshell.

Riddarholmskyrkan • *Riddarholm Church, Riddarholmen Island* • This church with 13th-century origins has been the burial place of Swedish royalty since the 17th century (except for Catholic Queen Christina, who's entombed at The Vatican).

Nationalmuseum • *National Museum, Sodra Blasieholmshamnen* • Here is the fine state-owned collection of art, Swedish and foreign, ranging from the 16th century through the 19th. The museum usually has one or two interesting temporary exhibits and frequent classical concerts. Not incidentally, this edifice is said to contain the largest ikon collection outside of the Soviet Union.

Nordiska Museet • *Djurgarden* • A time capsule of Nordic life that should not be missed if your visit to Scandinavia is a brief one. The Lapp exhibits are especially engaging, illustrating that the herdsmen and hunters of the far north were and are much more than mere survivalists.

Ostasiatiska Museet • *Museum of Far Eastern Antiquities, Skeppsholmen Island* • This is not a huge museum, yet an hour or two here will leave you with satiated senses, for here is one of the best permanent exhibitions of Oriental art outside of Asia. The heart of the museum's holdings is its early Chinese arts and crafts, beginning with Stone Age ceramics, but you'll also find treasures from Japan, Korea, and India.

Moderna Museet • *Museum of Modern Art, Skeppsholmen Island* • The conservative collections of many important modern-art museums sometimes give one the impression that artists stopped producing in the 1950s, if not earlier. Not so Stockholm's Museum of Modern Art. There you'll see outstanding examples of cubism, Dadaism, and surrealism from Europe and North America, a selection of Edvard Munch paintings, and avant-garde works from the 1960s by American and European artists. There is also an important photography collection.

Wasamuseet • *Wasa Museum, Djurgarden Island* • To the misfortune of much of its 150-man crew, the man-of-war *Wasa* sank in Stockholm's harbor in 1628. The disaster, which occurred on the ship's maiden voyage, caused the ship literally to be pickled in saltwater for over three centuries until it was rediscovered and salvaged. Visitors to this marvelously well-preserved relic of Sweden's maritime history watch a film about the 5-year-long salvage opera-

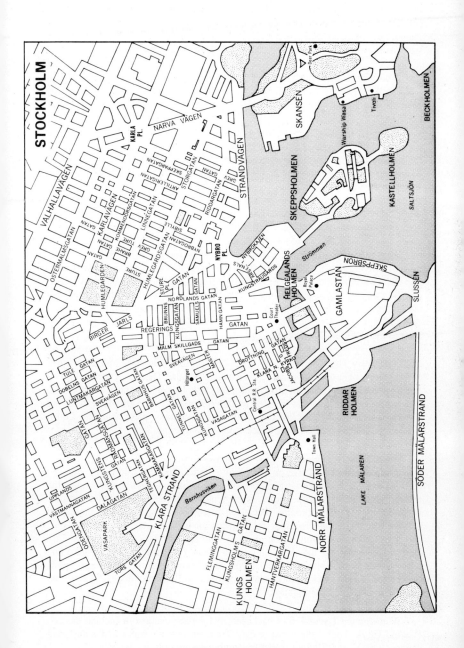

STOCKHOLM

VALHALLAVÄGEN

KARLA PL.

NARVA VÄGEN

STRANDVÄGEN

ÖSTERMALMSGATAN

BRAHE GATAN

KARLAVÄGEN

GATAN

KOMMENDÖRSGATAN

GREV TURE GATAN

LINNÉGATAN

NYBROGATAN

GREV GATAN

SIBYLLE

ARTILLERIGATAN

STORGATAN

SKEPPARGATAN

RIDDARGATAN

KARLA PL.

HUMLEGARDSGATAN

STURE GATAN

STURE GATAN

NORDLANDS GATAN

NYBRO PL.

HUMLEGÅRDEN

SKANSEN

Deer Park

Warship Wasa

Tivoli

SKEPPSHOLMEN

KASTELLHOLMEN

BECKHOLMEN

SALTSJÖN

JARLS

BIRGER

BRUNNS

KUNGSGATAN

SAMUELS GATAN

HAMN GATAN

KUNGSTRÄDGÅRDS

NYBROKAJEN

ÖSTRA TRÄDGÅRDS

Strömmen

ÄELGEALANDS HOLMEN

REGERINGS

MALM SKILLGADS

GATAN

GATAN

Court Theater

Royal Palace

GAMLASTAN

SKEPPSBRON

TULE GATAN

DOBELNS GATAN

LUNTMAKARGATAN

SVEAVÄGEN

BARNHUS GATAN

TUNNEL GATAN

SVEAVÄGEN

MASTER GATAN

MASTER GATAN

DROTTNING GATAN

KLARA N. KG.

JACOBS

GATAN

KLARA N. KYRKO

STRÖMMEN

SLUSSEN

GATAN

GATAN

RÅDMANSGATAN

KUNGSTENS

Högtorget

VASAGATAN

KUNGSGATAN

Central R.R. Sta.

RIDDAR HOLMEN

UPPLANDS

VÄSTMANNAGATAN

ODENGATAN

DALAGATAN

TEGNÉRGATAN

KAMMAKARGATAN

KLARA STRAND

Barnhusviken

Town Hall

NORR MÄLARSTRAND

LAKE MÄLAREN

SÖDER MÄLARSTRAND

VASAPARK

TORS GATAN

FLEMINGGATAN

KUNGSHOLMS GATAN

HANTVERKARGATAN

KUNGS HOLMEN

NORR MÄLARSTRAND

tions that began in 1956 and then go on a guided tour. The *Wasa,* one of Sweden's biggest tourist attractions, recently made her final voyage to this new anchorage. Soon all the galleries will be filled with exhibitions. In the same waterfront district you may also visit a lightship and an icebreaker.

Thielska Galleriet • *Thiel Art Gallery, at Blockshusdden on Djurgarden Island* • Amassed by banker Ernest Thiel, this collection contains paintings by Edvard Munch, plus 19th-century art from Scandinavia and France.

Skansen • *Djurgarden Island* • Scandinavians have a thing for open-air museums, and this one, built in 1891, is the mother of them all. Established for the preservation of crafts and dwellings from all of Sweden, including Lapland, Skansen provides a panorama of life during the nations past few hundred years. It has more than 150 buildings from the 1700s and 1800s, among which are a manor house, a Lapp hut, and an active glassworks. There are traditional crafts workshops and demonstrations, too, plus an open-air theater, gardens, and a zoo. On summer evenings, you'll find dancing and concerts.

Markets • **Hotorget** is the public market in the center of the city. Here, by early Sept., you'll find foodstuffs and flowers. Morning is the best time to go. **Ostermalms Saluhall,** on Ostermalmstorg, is a colorful old covered market that bears comparison to a giant smorgasbord. Stock up here on smoked fish and gourmet items for your picnic. There are also salad bars, health food counters, and stands. **Lisa Elmqvist's** is a reliable restaurant here where you should sample the esteemed "Delicacy Plate."

Theater • The Court Theater at Drottningholm Palace (see above) features 18th-century ballets and operas. The Royal Dramatic Theater is where Ingmar Bergman and other Swedish artists got their start. Its performances are in Swedish, naturally. However, at the Regina they're in English. **Confidencen Court Theatre,** next to lovely Ulriksdal Wardhus, is actually older than the Court; similar programs of music and dance from May through Sept.

Boat Tours • With so much water in and around Stockholm, you are missing an important perspective on this Nordic metropolis if you don't try your sea legs at least once. Ferries travel from island to island, and tourist boats, the aquatic equivalents of tour buses, wind regularly through Stockholm's waterways during the warm months. Packaged motorboat outings include the Grand Scenic Tour under the Bridges, the Royal Canal Tour, the Archipelago Tour, and a waterborne version of the evening tour you can take by bus. Near City Hall at Klara Malarstrand, you can catch a steamer to Drottningholm Palace and other points along Lake Malaren. If you want high speed, book a luxury whirl on *Lisa* or *Sluggo,* two beauties that zip along at 35 mph. Phone 7830010 and arrange the day and the pickup.

Motorcoach Excursions • Packaged motorcoach excursions include the two "Grand City" Tours, the nonstop City Tour, an evening loop, and a day-long trip to Uppsala and Sigtuna. Most bus tours operate only in summer.

Ballooning • Yes, it's possible and it puts you over some of the most breathtaking land- and waterscapes to be witnessed on this globe. Telephone (08) 7303485 or (08) 343410/524200 to get yourself properly inflated.

Excursions

Drottningholms Slott • *Drottningholm Palace (Queen's Palace), Island of Lovon* • Built during the years 1660 to 1690 for Queen Hedvig Eleonora, Drottningholm Palace is a treat to visit. While it is often dubbed the Versailles of Scandinavia—and indeed the architecture and formal gardens are of French inspiration—Drottningholm is a Swedish phenomenon. Located on an island, the baroque palace contains a plethora of Gobelin tapestries and period furniture. Nearby, on these exquisitely manicured grounds is a beautiful summer house called the Kina Slott, or China Pavilion. Also in the vicinity you'll discover the Court Theater. Exceptionally well-preserved because it lay idle between 1792 and 1922, using much of the original 18th-century stage sets and machinery, the 350-seat theater specializes in ballets and operas from its own epoch. Tickets can be hard to come by. They are often available on the day of the performance an hour before curtain time.

Milles Garden, looking across the water toward Stockholm, was the home of master sculptor Carl Milles, many of whose pieces adorn New York City architecture. The art collection in his house and the garden with his colossal creations will easily absorb a full morning or afternoon.

Run Away for a Day • *Sweden House* • The **Inter-Skerries Card** (approximately 125 Kr.) is a 14-day wonderland pass of unlimited travel on ferries throughout the archipelago. A booklet describes the multitude of things to do—from a Skipper's Feast to cabin accommodation in blissful countryside to walks through nature preserves. With 25,000 islands in the vicinity, forgive me if I leave out a few details. Operative June through August.

HOTELS

☆☆☆ **Strand** • with the most convenient site in midcity and beautifully commanding a waterfront view, offers imaginative public rooms combining tasteful traditionalism with cheerfully fresh Scandinavian decor. Inventive touches such as charming hand-painted bouquets on corridor walls indicating the color scheme of the respective accommodation; space a bit pinched and maintenance not too uniform. Original art throughout; antiques, chandeliers, rich textiles, and large beds; color TV and refrigerators; 7th-floor singles exceptionally good buys. The whimsical Strand Piazza for breakfast, cocktails, or late nibbles; elegant, clean-lined dining salon. Sky Bar in the panoramic tower with a lower level devoted to sauna and fitness facilities. The staff are perfectly groomed, unusually cordial, and evoke an atmosphere of welcoming you to a very fine home—which it is, indeed. A convenience for air travelers: an SAS check-in counter right at the main portal.

☆☆☆☆ **Grand** • more imposing as a structure, also provides a waterside venue; vintage 1874 lobby area with tall columns; bedchambers expensively comfortized. Its famous front verandas, one of which is now serving the city's best reasonably priced smorgasbord (at both lunch and dinnertime), has been restyled, broadened, glassed in, and air-conditioned for all-year operation. Restaurant and cozy British-style bar felicitous and very elegant. Spegelsalen ("Hall of Mirrors") a genuine period piece. The personnel take a sincere interest in guests, with more hospitality offered than ever before.

☆☆☆☆ **The Diplomat** • housed within a classic art nouveau downtown structure, projects warmth and small-hotel intimacy. The prevailing decorative schemes range from Swedish-birch freshets to English open hearthside. Richly woody paneled bar; cheery garden-toned Teahouse serving the breakfast buffet, lunch, afternoon tea (of course), and dinner; pastel-hued corridors. Individual decor in lovely bedrooms; Stockholm Suite with its own sauna. General Manager Christina Ekstedt is a charming hostess.

★★★ **Royal Viking** • is a major midtowner of 400 rooms with plenty of modernistic flair. The expansive atrium with its vine-clad balconies is a keynote of its daring architecture. A pleasant breakfast room occupies this inner court; suave and elegant dining in a hearth-front salon; seafood and salad bar for snacks; simulated rock-bound swimming pool; Sky Bar on top with viewful supper club. Superior comfort, especially in the duplex suites.

☆☆ **Sheraton** • is also a 9-story midcity slicker. Banquet and convention facilities for 425; restaurant and lobby bar, both very successful; casino; telex; on-the-spot banking; expense-accounter room tariffs; high quota of attache cases among its luggage check-ins. All walls and fabrics in an especially lovely shade of blue brilliantly blending with its orange-and-brown carpeting; sauna; top-floored balconied units its premier spreads; 6 lakefront suites; business suites outstanding, moving up to bigger executive suites and the Texas-size presidential spread; many twins with 2 double beds surrounded by teal, rouge, and other rich colors in modern themes; TV plus music console; small but well-equipped baths. In sum, here is a fine example of the American mood.

☆☆ **Sergel Plaza** • not to be confused with the next entry, caters heavily to business travelers. It is in a complex of metallic office buildings near the Sergel Tower. Pleasing 18th-century Anna Rella restaurant with a splendid tile oven; compact but well-appointed bedrooms; prices very good for the tiptop value. Though it contains more than 400 rooms, this large, sleek house in the former parliament building seeks to create an ambience (in some quarters) of an earlier mood in Stockholm.

★★ **Plaza** • is housed in a Swedish-traditional edifice; all the finest classic touches have been retained or enhanced. The Cecil restaurant is gaining popularity, but without loss to the small-hotel personality that is so prized here. Bar, cafe, plus Alexandra nightclub; sauna in the cellar, handy address in midcity.

★★ **Lord Nelson** and (of course) **Lady Hamilton** • are companion editions of the same innkeeping yarn. Both richly decorated in maritime themes pertinent to the era of this loving couple. Folk art of Sweden to fill in the cross-cultural gaps. Both are a lot of fun and as cozy as a sea captain's stateroom or a lady's boudoir. You'll be paying quite a lot for the cuteness, however. If roughly $140 per lord-and-lady is acceptable, you'll probably enjoy their see-worthy appeal.

★★★ **Victory** • (as if you hadn't guessed already) is yet another sister ship in this fleet. All rooms named for sea captains with much of their personal keepsakes on display; unique restaurant in the foundations of early Stockholm. Similar maritime theme as the two previous entries, but presented in a more substantial package.

☆ **Anglais** • overlooks Humlegarden Park. Facade dotted by flaming gas lamps; Swedish-modern lobby; candle-brightened Grill Room; attractive cocktail bar; enclosed court accessible to first-level guests. Every unit with bath, an alarm-clock/radio, an individual thermostat control, a centigrade thermometer for readings of the outside weather, foldaway luggage racks, and 3-way vanity mirrors; the poorest 41 units in the basement.

☆ **Park** • greets its guests with a lemon-colored lobby that adjoins a salty restaurant and a merry-time bar. Excellent sauna; pool; kitchenettes available. If you can snag a sleeper overlooking the lovely Humlegarden you will be rewarded with a majestic sylvan tableau smack in the center of the city.

★ **Reisen** • is a pert combo linking 5 homes and 3 warehouses that date back to A.D. 1639. From topmast to keel, the milieu here is nautical. The lobby exudes warmth. Both the Piano-Bar and the 13-table Clipper Club Restaurant, separated from each other by an artistic brass grill, have been decorated in matching paneling, comfortable leather armchairs, indirect illumination, and softly piped music. Guest-rooms incorporating the rugged brick walls of the original structures; cellar with 2 saunas; swimming pool; vaulted clubroom. Fine value.

★★★ **Clas Pa Hornet** • is more of an exclusive inn than a hotel. It also offers one of the best kitchens in Stockholm—and, again, the salon decor is more homespun than institutional. Try this historic gem if you dare to avoid the conventional. The location is not the most convenient.

Continental • is close by the main station in midtown. Air-conditioned; handsome lobby; large-but-cozy, low-ceilinged, wraparound Cafe on the mezzanine overlooking the entrance hall; quick-service cafeteria in the cellar by the subway exit; Steak House; split-level, split-personality dining room, ingeniously highlighted by striking use of Orrefors glass insets on pillars and lamps for decorative effect. Seven types of rooms, all with wood floor-to-ceiling panels backing the beds, and offbeat employment of textiles and colors; all baths su-permicroscopic. Commercial and solid.

Amaranten • is one of the best investments for your travel dollar if you can weather its tempest of convention and other groups. Noncentral but not inconvenient location (subway station in the block); spacious lobby; adjoining Brasserie with room dividers, hanging lamps, and excellent cafeteria-type food service; sumptuous restaurant with both tables and booths. Spacious 200-seat nightclub; saunas. Rewarding for the outlay.

Prince Philip • boasts remote control color TV, frigobars and telephones in the baths, plus hair dryers and extra radio speakers. It is up-to-the-instant in modern comfort and convenience gadgetry.

Birger Jarl • features a lounge that is somewhat cluttered by vitrines and TV; self-service cafeteria with homey fare from 7 a.m.–3 p.m. converts into Coffee Shop from 3 p.m.–9:30 p.m.; gymnasium, sauna, and plunge pool; compact studio-type rooms, all with bath, shower, and alarm-radio unit; ice machines and 2 shoeshiners on each floor; 200-car garage with elevator to ground floor. Since this house is owned by a religious organization, beer is its only alcoholic beverage (or wine for groups).

Wellington and the **Mornington** • are sister houses. Each offers simple but colorful amenities, dining rooms that are continuously open between 11:30 a.m. and midnight, and saunas. Some of their chambers are conventional in design while others are studio-style. The 7-floor Wellington has 6 suites and 46 units, some of them with a fine view. The Mornington occupies the 3rd, 4th, 5th, and 6th floors of a structure otherwise occupied by members of the Swedish Dentists Association. Although neither is in the deluxe category, they are proud of the personal touches that are reminiscent of a small-town rather than of a metropolitan hostelry.

Palace • occupies 4 floors of a fringe-area commercial building (the prem-ises of a local automobile dealer); with such ample garage space, its main oc-cupancy target is the motorist. The chambers are triumphs of architectural planning for children, elves, or midgets.

Malmen • is a streamlined, starkly modern factory of mass-production tourism. Dining salon; Club Malmen for night owls; 265 minuscule rooms; ser-vice for minimum essentials only.

Stockholm • occupies the 6th and 7th floors of an office building; lovely view; some bedchambers agreeable; breakfast room but no restaurant.

Alexandra and the **Bromma** • (near the domestic airport with 143 cham-bers) are both truly basic.

Flyghotellet • is reasonable enough as a medium-priced landing field.

Arlandia • is a worthy choice if you must overnight far out at Arlanda, the international airport that's 35 minutes from town.

City • might be called the Salvation Arms; it's run by the Army and it's far more opulent than you might think. Nice mood of marble polish and pink tones; dry, of course.

Royal Star • is a good investment for short stays.

Esplanade • in a courtyard next to the Diplomat, advertises itself as "an informal hotel for diplomats, businessmen and tourists." After viewing this two-story plant of 32 bedrooms, 3 baths, 26 showers and no restaurant, I found only two accommodations that were amply big and to my taste. Yet because of its official rating, its tariffs come close to those of its plush and handsomely equipped neighbor. Nix.

Kom • centrally sited, breakfast-only, is open all year. Fully air-conditioned; sauna; conference rooms; parking facilities; somewhat cramped quarters including mini-pantry with refrigerators and all with shower but no tub. Routine.

Flamingo • might be termed a supermarket hostelry. No porters, so you load your luggage into a grocery cart provided in the lobby and wheel your cargo to your bin; no reception minions even to show you to your address. Restaurant, grill, bar, and cocktail lounge similarly impersonal; clean, ultra-modern, and oh-so-sterile.

Sjofartshotellet • possesses a quick-frozen lobby, a nautical dining room, and monotonous corridors. Within the 6 stories are 183 modern, utilitarian rooms with glass-front masks; efficient for group bookings.

Jerum (June-Aug.) and the **Domus** • (open all year), are students' dormitories in winter and equally sterile, institutional-style hotels in summer.

Kristeneberg • about 10 minutes out in a residential district, lacks zip, zest, or zing.

Scandic • a motel, offers 153 rooms at *Ulriksdal,* north of the city, and yet a newer one on the route to Arlanda Airport. Both are located inconveniently in very unattractive surroundings.

RESTAURANTS

Capital dining, which has always been excellent if not expensive, is better than ever in Stockholm. Fine, intimate establishments are proliferating, but there is one drawback in my personal view: most of them are based on French rather than Swedish culinary concepts. This seems to be a needless and heedless fad when the Swedish kitchen is capable of producing such memorable feasts. Hence, if you want to sample the native cookery chiefly, it would be best to avoid the restaurants listed below with obviously Gallic names.

As mentioned earlier, Sweden was already one of the most expensive nations in the world for dining when last year the politicians doubled the VAT (Value Added Tax), which now stands at an alarming 25%! This is having a thunderous effect on dining establishments (as well as other industries). Hence, by the time you read these words some of the restaurants below may have folded, thus providing no revenue at all for the state coffers. It's a pathetic situation that will produce drastic results for tourism for many, many moons.

★★★★★ **Operakallaren** • *part of the Royal Opera House* • with its window-lined **Cafe Opera** is probably the most celebrated proponent of Nordic cookery anywhere in Scandinavia (although this one and the next two are owned by Italian interests who vow not to alter the northern lifestyle here). It is an awesome and impressive complex in *fin de siecle* raiments. Undeniably, the smorgasbord is unique, both for its volume and for the presentation in one of the most ornate salons of Europe. A la carte available as well as snacks in the adjoining parlors.

☆☆☆ **Riche** • *Birger Jarlsgatan 4* • is in the same administrative circle. It, too, is distinguished. Enclosed sidewalk dining terrace with windows and flower boxes; 18th-century accouterments; opulent Riche Bar sparkling with gold-leaf frescoes. Its intimate **Theatre Grill** opens the curtain on apple-red upholstery, glass-and-gold partitions, attractive synthetic marble pillars and matching tables. The service is flawless.

★★★★ **Stallmastaregarden** ("Royal Stablemaster's House") • *15 minutes by taxi from the center* • is in the same group; the Swedish cuisine is meritorious; the staff attention and presentation are commendable too. Best of all, the setting by the edge of a lake is beguiling. Patio garden enhanced by a picturebook gazebo where you can take coffee by candlelight after dinner (reserve this very special place for your meal or beverages); rustic atmosphere tinged with urbanity and world-class sophistication.

★★★★ **Stadshuskallaren** • *downstairs in City Hall* • is a beautiful, darkly majestic salon with perfect service and impressive gastronomy—from the same chefs who prepare the Nobel banquets served upstairs each year. (See "Attractions" for *Stadshuset*.)

★★★ **Diana** • *Brunnsgrand 2, in the Old Town* • is a more informal cellar with an open kitchen at the end of an ancient vaulted brick hall. Candlelight and antique effects evoke a bewitchment of the senses that is augmented by beautifully presented Swedish dishes. I think the shrimp bowls as starters and the *Gravlax* (marinated salmon with sweet mustard sauce) are among the most professional displays to be found anywhere.

☆☆☆☆ **Nils Emil** • *Folkungagatan 122, in south Stockholm* • is the name of the former owner of the Diana, now with this very different yet superb enterprise in an apartment sector of town. Not much to see, but the quality is noteworthy. Ask the staff to guide you in selection. The talk of the town for gourmets. Not too expensive for such exceptional cooking.

★★★★ **Djurgardsbrunns Wardshus** • *behind Skansen in the famous Deer Park (15 minutes from the center by Bus No. 69)* • is well worth the brief but beautiful journey from the center. This converted 18th-century, Gustavian-style mansion suffered a fire recently, but most sections have been rebuilt; it resides over verdant greenery and a lovely canal. Its cuisine is superb. In summer a self-service open-air cafeteria operates at lunchtime and is so popular that it attracts up to 1000 persons per day. Beautiful and distinguished. **Brunnspaviljongen,** if you want similar scenic rewards but lower cost vittles, is the neighboring house, and okay for a simple dish and coffee.

★★★ **Kallaren Aurora** • *Munkbron 11* • sited beneath the vaulted ceilings of a 300-year-old cellar, interweaves historical and culinary traditions. Italianate entrance; collection of hideaways including Gustafva's Salmon Cellar, The Cadet Corner, The Little Society, and other intimate nooks; fowl suspended from ceiling rods; charcoal rotisserie grills; the Table of Plenty with a bountiful display; wine from Patron Herman's *cave;* refurnished bar. Costly but agreeable.

☆☆☆ **Grappe d'Or** • *Tyska Brinken 36* • is a study in French refinement, with its gustatory focus firmly on modern feather-weight creations. Very pleasant soft-spoken surroundings; open weekdays for lunch and dinner but Saturdays for dinner only; closed Sundays.

☆ **Hedwig** • *Storgatan 6* • is fresh and springlike in appearance, with pale prints and paintings hung on white kitchen tile walls; black ceiling; candles and flowers as well as plants in all directions. The cuisine is as light as the atmosphere.

☆☆ **Coq Blanc** • *Regeringsgatan 111* • is in the avant-garde of the parade of French candidates. Broad glass door at entrance; corridor lined with posters and attractive artwork; inner sanctum of booths illuminated by tapers. I enjoyed the blinis with egg and salmon roe followed by the assorted fish plate with tomato sabayonne. The lone attempt at Nordic gustation (filet of smoked reindeer) turned out a bit austere, so I would guess that the chef feels more at home in Gaul than in the Swedish archipelago.

☆☆ **Gourmet** • *Hornet Tegnergatan-Dobelnsgatan* • is the highly professional expression of the young and enterprising team: Bjorn Svensson and Kurt Schultes. Their domain is warm and intimate with a slight tilt toward the more southernly regions of France. Expensive it is, but usually worth the outlay if your tastebuds are so inclined.

☆☆☆ **L'Escargot** • *Schelegatan 8* • also is one of the most talked about Frenchies on the Stockholm scene. Here, however, the gastronomy points slightly farther north and, naturally, is devoted to the almighty totem of *nouvelle cuisine*. I like the atmosphere and the dedicated people. I am not so fond of the prices or the fact that it is closed in August when so many tourists are on the ground.

★★ **Paul & Norbert** • *Strandvagen* • is extraordinarily *intime*. Woody fixtures set into stucco; small hearths; copper pans on whitewashed walls; most main dishes in the $16 range. Two outstanding samplings: salmon in pastry shell and calves liver ragout.

Eriks • *Osterlanggatan 17* • is in the Old Town. A ship bearing the same name and serving a similar choice from the galley is berthed at *Strandvagen 17*. Both enjoy an esteem locally that ranks close to idolatry. I remain unworshipful, however, for a multitude of reasons. First of all, I think it is too costly for the unproven pudding. Guests are often directed to the bar and encouraged to have expensive drinks before being seated when their places are actually available when they arrive. My scallops in lemon butter as a starter were far too sweet, assaulting the palate and reducing my appetite for further dining. While the halibut in pistachio sauce was top quality, the turbot with trout roe and diced vegetables in cream was lackluster.

Fem Sma Hus ("Five Small Houses") • is strongly reminiscent of the Aurora. Here, again, the bar is utilized to encourage drinking while the guests are waiting to be seated; during this lag, however, I saw numerous tables that were too obviously ready inside. I wonder, therefore, if this isn't a ploy—if so, a clumsy one—to extract a few extra kronor from its innocent trade. Extremely engaging atmosphere but the attitude toward the client just might border on being naughty.

Ostergok • *Kommedorsgatan 46* • comes up with a fine net of fish. Side by side are two completely separated restaurants. The piscatorial segment on a street corner is the quintessence of simplicity, with unadorned marble tables and utilitarian furnishings; potted plants; painted tiles and appetizing food displays make up for the starkness. Directly adjoining is a cozy, tavern-y establishment for grills and other meats. The price levels in this duet are virtually identical and very reasonable. The adjoining pizzeria is disappointing. The steakhouse is closed in July. Be certain to reserve in advance.

Sturehof • has been a midcity fixture for almost a century. It was recently redecorated and spiritually rejuvenated. An old reliable in new attire.

La Brochette • *Storgatan 27* • is very appealing to the eye, but my luck has been so wretched here on several tries that I'm beginning to wonder who's jinxed, the chef or myself. The same seems to be the case with **Latona** • *Vasterlanggatan 79* • where there's been a mighty falloff in quality lately.

SWEDEN · · · **787**

★★ **Stortorgskallaren** ("Cellar by the Market") • *Stortorget 7, on the Great Square in Old Town* • It offers a cozy ambience with candlelit tables; 3 sections under vaults shoulder the wine cellars of former monarchs; very courteous people; the halibut and salmon in chablis is a delicious combination.

Malardrottningen • *near the Riddarholm Church in the Old Town* • For a diverting meal aboard a ship. Ordinary cookery but a pleasant ambience if you like boats. If you've put on too much ballast, you can anchor here for the night; it's also a hotel. For fish exclusively, try **Wedholms Fisk** for a net gain in any sense. Seafood is its magic preserve.

Branda Tomten • *Stureplan 13* • is a 50-year-old colorful drop-in landmark that has recently been refashioned in an inviting way. Service glitches but basically okay.

NIGHT LIFE

On special application, licensed restaurants may stay open until the wicked hour of 3 a.m.; alcohol must cease to flow at 2:30 a.m. And that's that!

The **Hamburger Bors** is a hot contender, presenting top bananas of show biz. Some semblance of movement might be found in the **Strand Hotel** and perhaps at the **Nya Bacchi. Cafe Opera** is popular for dancing. **Daily News** is young and frisky as a discotheque-cum-oyster bar. Strange combo, but it works. Also, the **Grand Hotel** is consistently dependable. **Golden Days** throbs with British piano and banjo pickin's on the merry mock-stern of a ship. **Konstnarshuset** and **Alexandra's** (a discoperation) plus a molting covey of pipits, warble for a woeful welter of night hunters. **Baldakinen** and **Aladdin** also draw an array of thwarted insomniacs. **Engelen,** a converted pharmacy, stirs out beer only with a dash of jazz for members—but you probably can wiggle in. **Stampen** is great fun for Dixieland rebs like us'ns. The ceiling and walls are hung with whimsical junk items: an upside-down Christmas tree, a bib-and-tucker, a baby carriage, and one of the most forlorn sights I've ever seen—a stuffed dog. Only beer is served along with some of the happiest sounds in the North.

SHOPPING

Swedish quality is renowned. In integrity of merchandise, you won't get stung. Price is a major consideration since almost nothing shoddy is even offered.

SHOPPING HOURS: Standard shops are normally open from 9:30 a.m.–6 p.m. from Monday through Friday and from 9:30 a.m.–4 p.m. on Sat. in winter but 1–2 p.m. in summer. Some are open on Sun. from noon–4 p.m. Check locally for the later evening closings of department stores.

BEST AREAS: Drottninggatan, Kungsgatan, Hamngatan, and Sergelgatan are all fairly close to the Central Station. There is an open market at Hotorget. In the Old Town browse around Vasterlanggatan and Osterlanggatan and visit the summer open market at Stortorget. The Hotorget Station (subway) and Central Station (basement) feature a cluster of stores that are open until 9 p.m. daily, plus Sunday afternoons and evenings.

SAVINGS ON PURCHASES: Many capital-ist stores now participate in the Sweden Taxfree Shopping Service. (See the blue-and-yellow sticker on their doors.) At these, you'll be given an extra export receipt which you present at the Servicecenter, up one flight at Arlanda airport. You will be reimbursed about 15% of the 25% VAT or "Moms" levied on all products, but you must spend at least 101 SEK to be eligible. This is operative at all airports and border crossings as well as train and ship departure points.

NOTE · · · DON'T buy: Perfumes, cigarettes, and similar luxury imports except at the airport tax-free shops, because heavy duties make them prohibitively expensive in town.

CERAMICS: Galleri Birger Jarl (Birger Jarlsgatan 2) is a delight, with grace and charm in its gorgeous table and decorative pieces. This is the showcase for the inspired Gustavsberg products as well as additional Swedish creations by Rorstrand. From Finland you'll find the bold designs of Arabia as well as the glassware of Nuutajarvi and Iittala. Very special.

DEPARTMENT STORES AND SHOPPING CENTERS: NK is one of the world's greatest department stores. **PUB,** a cooperative, is lower-level and not so interesting. Very modern **Ahlens** (Klarabergsgatan/Drottninggatan) is one of the largest. The 5-block **Gallerian** and the 3-tiered **PK,** across the street, have now become the most important, with **Hotorgscity** following right behind. At the **Sture Gallerian** (Grev Turegatan) you can even have a swim since it was the site of the Turkish Baths. The **Hotorget Station** (subway) and **Central Station** (basement) feature a battery of merchandisers that stay open until 9 p.m. daily as well as Sunday afternoon and evening.

FURNITURE: Mobel-Shop (Renstiernasgatan 24) has a full and handsome line that is hand-fashioned from old pine. Because they only work on logs that have been lying in the forests for a long time, the wood takes on a lovely sheen in the Nordic 16th-to-18th-century manner.

GLASSWARE: Svenskt Glas (Birger Jarlsgatan 8) is the outstanding specialist for Orrefors, Kosta, and other producers, which has supplied the Royal Families of Sweden, Denmark, and the United Kingdom for more than 40 years, as well as armies of foreign guests such as you and me. The dazzling advantage here for Yankee and Reb shoppers is that with ALL costs included—purchase price, shipping, and insurance—you'll still pay about half the American retail price for precisely, identically the same articles. What fantastic bargains!! The most popular categories among pilgrims are their tableware (monogrammed if you wish), engraved art crystals, and barware. Mail Order Department; expert export shipping with VAT discount. Here is *the* target for *the* discerning shopper.

HANDICRAFTS: **Svensk Hemslojd** (Sveavagen 44) is the marketing center for many of the nation's best artisans of their genre. **Konsthantverkarna** (Master Samuelsgatan 2) belongs to 70 freelance creators and serves as a permanent exhibition of their efforts. **Sameslojden** (Sjalagardsgatan 19), in the Old Town, offers wares from Lapland. **Panduro Hobby** (Kungsgatan 34) sells the raw materials from which you can create your own Scandinavian arts and crafts.

HOME FURNISHINGS: **Svenskt Tenn** (Strandvagen 5A) is almost a museum of Swedish design—a place for gift-gathering or creating a mood for your own creative home. If you go, set aside at least a full morning or afternoon to browse. When you purchase the shipping of goods is made oh-so-easy.

SWEDISH SILVER: **Atelier Borgilia AB Lars Fleming** (Sturegatan 24) has been serving this nation's most illustrious families for decades.

VISBY's leaders are (1) **Snackgardsbaden,** and (2) **Visby,** rebuilt and enlarged some years ago. The former has a pool, minigolf, badminton, and dancing during the evening; its big drawback is its paucity of private baths; June 1 to August 31 only. The latter comes up with a considerably higher bath count; open all year.

SWITZERLAND

USA: Swiss National Tourist Office, Director Helmut Klee, 608 Fifth Ave., New York, NY, Tel. (212) 757–5944; Director Eric Buhlmann of Western USA at both 222 No. Sepulveda Blvd., Suite 1570, El Segundo 90245, Los Angeles, Tel. (213) 355-5980 and at 260 Stockton St., San Francisco, CA, Tel. (415) 362–2260. CANADA: Director Dino Dulio, Commerce Court West, Suite 2015, P.O. Box 215, Commerce Court Postal Station, Toronto ONT M5L 1E8, Tel. (416) 868–0584

SPECIAL REMARKS: (1) In Zurich for everyday travel questions you can rely on the Tourist Office at 15 Bahnhofplatz. (2) Be sure to ask about the **Swiss Card** for 50% discounts on rail, boat, or bus travel within the nation.

TELEPHONE: Access code to USA: 001. To phone Switzerland; 41; time difference (Eastern Daylight) plus 6 hrs.

Switzerland has everything. It's got mountains, lakes, snow, the sort of thing you've been taught to expect, of course—but it's also got immense sophistication, castles, fondue, wild ibex, and, with few exceptions, one of the most honorable collections of human beings on the globe.

Amazing people: To the eye, there are enormous regional differences, but at the core there is an admirable sameness. It's not true at all, as the jibe has it, that when a Swiss wants to laugh he runs down to the cellar where he won't be seen. There is abundant joy, freedom, and even frivolity—but always with a pervading sense of responsibility, security, and appropriateness. The Italian Swiss in the South (Lugano, Locarno) seem the softest, gayest, and merriest; the French Swiss in the West (Geneva, Lausanne) seem most urbane and they also are rather volatile; the Alamannic Swiss in the East (Zurich, Berne, Basel, Lucerne, St. Gall) seem the most businesslike and, possibly, rather stiff. (After all, that's where most of the banks are located.) The way in which the "same-

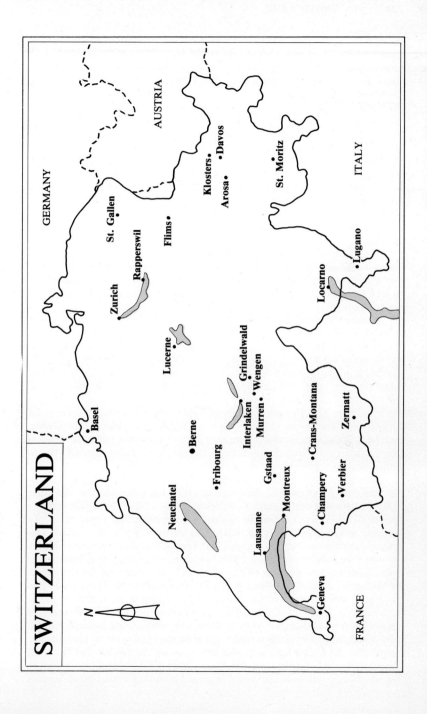

SWITZERLAND

N

GERMANY

AUSTRIA

ITALY

FRANCE

Basel

Zurich

St. Gallen

Rapperswil

Flims

Klosters

Arosa

Davos

St. Moritz

Lugano

Locarno

Lucerne

Grindelwald

Wengen

Interlaken

Murren

Crans-Montana

Zermatt

Berne

Fribourg

Gstaad

Neuchatel

Lausanne

Montreux

Champery

Verbier

Geneva

ness'' applies is in their generosity, correctness, and deep sense of humanity no matter which canton you visit. Swiss neutrality, in fact, is not so much a defense but a statement of respect for everyone's individuality. No wonder this nation is the home of the International Red Cross.

ATTRACTIONS   If you're after a region that few vacationers know and that hasn't been "civilized" beyond repair, the 2-day or 3-day circuit from *Zurich* through the Principality of *Liechtenstein* and *Die Ostschweiz* (Eastern Switzerland) is an enchanting choice. Spend your first night in *Vaduz,* the capital of this rustic little border state on the Rhine (see separate chapter); the second night might be spent in *St. Gallen.* If you stop here, there will be time for a look at the Abbey Library, neighboring *Appenzell,* and other points of interest. And the return to Zurich should be made around the other leg of the loop, through *Romanshorn, Kreuzlingen, Stein am Rhein, Schaffhausen, Winterthur,* and *Effretikon*—with a pause at *Neuhausen's* Rhine Falls if you're not in too much of a hurry.

From *Zurich,* should time be too pressing for such extensive coverage; a junket to the aforementioned Rhine Falls makes an interesting one-day safari; you may lunch comfortably in the ancient Sonne Restaurant at *Stein am Rhein*— or take the repast at the Fischerzunft in *Schaffhausen* (excellent cuisine), with tea at Stein.

If mountain driving is not too daunting for you, try this 7-hour loop from **Interlaken** (or *Andermatt*): East to *Brienz* and *Meiringen* (see Sherlock Holmes' falls) and on to Innertkirchen; take the **Susten Pass** through *Goeschenen,* then the famous **Furka** to the Rhone Glacier, and the fabulous **Grimsel** back to *Innertkirchen.* Three Passes not to be missed—but only, of course, in summer when they are open. This can also be done on the comfortable yellow postal bus.

There are 22 well-equipped mineral spas in the country. *St. Moritz* is the highest in altitude—and possibly in price. *Baden, Bad-Ragaz, Rheinfelden,* and *Tarasp-Vulpera* are characteristic. Each is a center for particular types of illness; some are purely for rest and relaxation. The Swiss National Tourist Office publishes a free Guide about them.

August 1 is the big Swiss national holiday—the Bundesfeiertag—with bonfires and dancing all over the country. The nation has now celebrated more than 700 birthdays since it became a confederation in 1291. Annual folk festivals include Good Friday at *Mendrisio,* Camellia at *Locarno,* Blessing of the Alpine Pastures at *Lotschental* (a great folklore experience; you'll also see the grotesque carved masks of the region), and Escalade at *Geneva;* everything on snow and ice from horse jumping, golf, and dog-sled racing to traditional winter sports. **Zurich** pops its fuses twice: once during the traditional Spring Festival of Sechselauten, when Old Man Winter (a mammoth dummy stuffed with fireworks) is publicly burned at the stake, and again during the June Festival weeks, with concerts, opera, exhibitions, theater, and other gala events. *Lucerne* toots its whistle from mid-August to early September, with enough concerts, choirs, plays, and cultural exhibits to make you positively unlivable to your friends, neighbors, and even casual acquaintances at home. *St. Gallen* also blows off the lid at the end of June *every third year,* when 9000 children march through the streets in the triennial Children's Festival, consuming as they go the legendary 29 miles of Bratwurst; check during the spring of your particular journey. Do you yearn for a barrel-organ festival, an antique-jewelry auction, a hot-air balloon congress, gliding, bridge, yodeling, or a toy-train exchange? All you have to do is want something and the Swiss National Tourist Office can point you in the right direction and tell you what time it starts.

The **Jungfrau** and *Interlaken;* the **Schilthorn** and the high surrounding triad corona seen from *Murren;* the **Lake of Constance** with its castles, orchards, and quaint villages; the **Graubunden,** land of 150 valleys; **Burgenstock;** the **Bernese Oberland,** with its lakes, glacial valleys, and high-Alpine landscape; the nearby **Jura** (which recently became the nation's 23rd self-governing canton with Delemont as its capital), delightful sites incorporating Biel, Tavennes (a district known for its horses, which you can rent by the hour), Bellelay, Porrentruy's Castle, ancient St.-Ursanne, and back to Neuchatel via La-Chaux-de Fonds; the glorious French-and-German **Valais**—everywhere in Switzerland you'll find something quaint and beautiful.

TRANSPORTATION **Airline Swissair** offers Geneva, Zurich, and Basel as termini, the first two being chief gateways for transatlantic flights. Zurich and Geneva airports have their own rail links into the city as well as into the nation's intercity network—and, hence, into the full European grid. The airports are superb and well-organized; First and Business lounges even offer laptop computers; planes on the European circuit offer onboard telephones. Furthermore, Swissair provides check-in services at the train stations of 18 city or resort destinations; at these points you're able to pick your seat and obtain your boarding card for later flights. Food is better than average; terminals are clean, comfortable, and convenient; everything works—in a typically perfect Swiss way. Incidentally, I recently flew the important Zurich-Los Angeles hop and it was one of the most convenient and enjoyable long passages I've every experienced aloft with *any* airline. See the "NOTE" further down about checking your luggage through and onwards via rail to your destination.

Within Switzerland distance are short but Crossair is especially useful on flights such as Lugano–Basel, or between Bern, Geneva and Zurich. Swissair links Basel, Geneva and Zurich, too. I recommend Swissair-ways anywhere on the route map. Efficency and cordiality are virtually peerless.

Taxis *Geneva* has a **Taxi Telephone Center.** Simply dial 141, and one of a fleet of 150 cars will be at your disposal. In *Berne,* it's 24–24–24; in *Zurich,* it's 44–44–41.

There's no need to tip since your bill already includes a 15% service chomp.

It's smart to use buses for short hauls in any Swiss city; conductors will steer you to your destination in a friendly way—and you'll save plenty.

Private Motoring As you cross the frontier by car, a guard will ask you if you plan to utilize the main roads of his nation—a silly formality because you *must* use them and a loaded question worth 30SF for the calendar year. This inhospitable highway robbery was passed by national referendum, so it must be enforced even in the face of wrathful Europeans, truckers, and bus companies (the latter are socked $2000 per vehicle!) for the privilege of bringing commerce and vast additional revenue to Swiss coffers. Switzerland's incensed neighbors view this as avaricious and insulting.

Trains Excellent. The SBB's (or CFF's, if you prefer the French initials to the German) national network is 100% electrified; they run like Swiss watches. They keep their split-second schedules; they are usually clean; they usually go like a bat out of Helvetia. One of the fastest runs is made by the noon flier from Geneva to Zurich.

Ticket prices are quite reasonable considering the value received for your franc. (Those francs, incidentally, can be dropped directly into automatic ticket dispensing machines—a timesaving innovation that is beginning to blanket the nation.) Don't forget that if you buy a **Swiss Card,** you can do *all* of your internal travel (boats and buses too) at a 50% discount.

And don't forget first to look into the Eurailpass if you are touring other countries as well.

An interesting statistic: If the 5000 bridges and 700 tunnels of the Swiss Federal Railways were stretched out in a line, they would reach over 275 miles.

Incidentally, the Swiss are swollen with pride because they now own the world's longest car tunnel—a 10.1-mile passage at the St. Gotthard Pass which brings the Mediterranean countries about 2 hours closer to northern Europe. This connects with another all-weather sub-alpine autoroute and with Helvetia's longest bridge, running beside the beautiful Lake Lucerne—the whole package costing its citizens about ¾ billion dollars!

Tourist Trains? These are marvelous pastime conveyances. Try the hypnotic *Glacier Express* between **Zermatt** and **St. Moritz** or the *William Tell* between central Switzerland and the Ticino in the south. The 2-hour chug between **Interlaken** and **Lucerne** is eye-popping, too, as is the slightly longer *Bernina Express* connection joining St. Moritz with **Tirano** in Italy. Finally, the *Golden Pass* route zigzags among lakes and peaks that dapple the passage between **Montreux, Zweisimmen, Spiez,** and **Interlaken.**

NOTE · · · An excellent time-, sweat-, profanity-, and worry-saver is to arrange with your hotel concierge (give him plenty of advance notice) for your heavier luggage to be shipped ahead of you, carrying only a light piece for overnighting. The thoughtful service applies to train, bus, and boat passage and is a *wonderful* help, particularly if you must make changes (Geneva to St. Moritz, for example, involves 2). Very inexpensive and 99½% dependable.

Children under 6 years of age ride as guests of the conductor and engineer; children 6 to 16 pay ½-fare or with a Family Card the transport is gratis.

Lake Steamers Every major body of water has them (some paddlewheelers) and many minor lakes also offer quaint smaller versions. Usually they make frequent rounds of the ports at the periphery—an excellent inexpensive and comfortable way to see Swiss country- and waterscapes. The big ones serve meals, so you can time your tour accordingly.

Stage Coach Journeys This is a great clip-clop backwards in time: last-century equine travel through glorious scenery in 3- and 5-day versions. Overnight stops at alpine post hotels; groups usually of 8 (or smaller coaches for special services); liveried drivers; beautifully outfitted teams and wagons. Check in with ITO Reisen, CH-6002 Luzern, Tel. 41/502233, Tx. 868154 Itolu CH. The U.S. hitching post is through Europe Train Tours in Mamaroneck, Tel. 800–551–2085 or 914–698–9426.

FOOD Switzerland has a superb cuisine and unfailingly cosmopolitan service standards in the major cities or resorts. In fact, there are today many, many restaurants that outshine the one-, two-, and three-star firmaments of France. Countless times we have seen *grands chefs de cuisine* of neighboring Gaul seated at Swiss tables on their days off—and often taking notes surreptitiously. (Later when I'm testing *their own* praiseworthy creations I'm amused to discover fragments of Helvetia in those splendid "French recipes.") It's not all chocolate and cheese, as many visitors suppose. Being a crossroads nation, it offers a tremendous variety of international fare—plus culinary masterworks of its own, of course.

Fondue is a common family dish that also is popular in restaurants since it is filling and money-saving. From Valais comes raclette, another melted cheese dish even more delicious than fondue.

Sausage is a national specialty, and each region has its own types. The big, fat Zurich version, a bologna with a Napoleonic complex, is one of the most succulent. Even more famous is the St. Gall Bratwurst. Order *any* kind of sausage—*any* time—with the fluffy, hashed-brown potatoes called Rosti, and you are in for a deeeeee-licious treat. Other typical offerings of this region include Geschnetzeltes nach Zurcher Art (thin-sliced veal with a cream sauce), Zurcher Leberspiessli (liver strips with sage seasoning, spit-roasted and served with beans), or Ratsherrentopf (mixed grill on a bed of rice or noodles). If you're only mildly hungry, order *Tellerservice,* which are snacks or hot items on one plate.

Dinner in top places runs perhaps $55 without wine; prepared blue-plate specials can be had for about $10. At the other end of the scale, both the tearooms and the Movenpick restaurants (an interesting combination of drugstore and cosmopolitan cookery, with branches in key cities) offer snacks and light meals for $10 or so. It's simply a matter of choosing your own category and spending what you please, because the range is ample. Prices are generally lowest in small villages or at train-depot eateries.

DRINKS *Swiss wines?* If you want to economize, order a glass of white wine instead of harder stuff; you'll find it refreshing. Almost any wine lover can instantly set them apart from good French, Spanish, or Italian vintages, even when blindfolded. They have a unique character of their own: A slight effervescence, a distinct tang to the tongue that is missing from all others. They take learning before true enjoyment can come. Most should be ordered young.

The majority of visiting North Americans seem to prefer Johannisberg as their white and Dole as their red; more particular drinkers pick Dole Fin Bec. You'll always be reasonably safe if you order either of these sound old standbys. Personally, I happen to prefer the Cortaillod of Neuchatel to the Dole, but that's merely a matter of taste. Other satisfactory types, at random, are Oeil de Perdrix (Geneva area and an excellent rose), Maienfelder, Altstatter, and Churer-Schiller (St. Gall and Graubunden), Crepy, Mont d'Or, Dezaley, and St. Saphorin (Lavaux), Fendant and Torrente-Chateau la Tour (Valais), and Cru de Champreveyres or the sparkling whites of Bienne or Neuchatel. Muscat is light and fresh; Armigne and Arvine have distinctive characters; Ermitage is one (perhaps the only) sweet wine in the press. If you can find it, Heida-Glet-scherwein from near Visp's glacier zones comes from Europe's highest vines. Here are the best of the land.

Swiss beer is cheap—and probably should be. All brands I've tried share a watery, milquetoast spinelessness. The Cardinal brand seems to embody the most zing. All major European beers are available.

For teetotalers, the noncarbonated, natural white or red grape juice called Grapillon is wonderfully uplifting, if you like a sweet drink; about $2, but be sure it's served icy cold. Apfelsaft is a pleasant and soft apple cider; the milk-based Rivella product is still taking the country by storm. Domestic cola types are preferred to U.S. colas by many Swiss, mainly for reasons of thrift.

Kirsch, made from the juice of compressed cherry pits, is one of the national hard drinks. It is to fondue what an embrace is to a lover. Don't miss a sample of this fiery, rather bitter spirit, especially with cheese or fruit. Pear liqueur is equally characteristic and even more delicious. Pear brandy (Eau de Vie de Poire Pure) is powerful and can be sharp.

The most astonishing Swiss liqueur is Appenzeller Alpenbitter. Appenzell is the town and Alpenbitter is the product—"Alpine Bitters," made up of the essences of 67 different flowers and roots. In taste it is vaguely reminiscent of gin-and-tonic consumed in a perfume factory, but don't let this stop you from sampling a genuine curiosity among potables.

TIPPING   An automatic service charge of 15% across-the-board in all cafes, restaurants, and hotels is in operation. This means you can greatly reduce or eliminate your individual gratuities. Even taxis now include a 15% supplement automatically, so the tab alone is what you should pay.

CITIES AND REGIONS

Please remember to refer to "About the Stars" in the introduction, since my rankings below do not necessarily conform with the "official" ratings of local tourist offices or hotel and restaurant associations.

AROSA   is a spellbinder for looks; it's a chic competitor that resides 68 miles north of St. Moritz. Now you can have a bird's-eye overview of the range and valley up, up, and up in the *Arosa,* a hot-air balloon that can take you above the peaks. Below are woodland trails, ski slopes, ski lifts, aerial cableway, and chair hoists; a cross-country ski school at Maran; glorious 2-hour excursion up to 7600 feet over the famous Arlenwald Circle by horse-drawn sleigh; summer 9-hole golf course, horseback riding, tennis, squash, fishing, rowing, Alpine bathing "beach"; superb sport accommodation; all varieties of cookery, from refined hotel cuisine, to a good selection of restaurants in the town, to tavern meals high up on the slopes. If you should need any help here, the hard-working, local tourist chief, Florenz Schaffner, is a mighty good man to see or to know; he does his job with utmost efficiency, and he's always ready with expert assistance.

In the upper crust of hotel circles, 3 houses—each with its own personality and appeal—are outstanding.

☆☆☆☆☆ **Tschuggen** • under German ownership, is stunning if your taste runs to rich modernity. The public rooms are vast and handsomely outfitted; there's a pool on the roof, plus a sauna, massage parlor, and panoramic snackery; there's a full ski shop in the basement, a bowling center, and a sweet little *Stubli*. The dining room is airy; the grill adjoining the ballroom-bar is inviting; there's dancing to an orchestra every night. The 20th-century bedchambers—replete with every conceivable comfort while providing hectares of space—focus their wide-angle windows on a Kodak kingdom of natural beauty.

☆☆☆☆☆ **Kulm** • directly on the ski slopes, is one of the friendliest luxury houses in the alps. All rooms renewed in a cozy way; new night club; an excellent fish restaurant, believe it or not; Taverna with more landed Swiss specialties plus a bowling alley. Other fillips include n indoor pool, fitness center and a beauty council. Most major ski runs at your doorstep; ice rink; an all-out Swiss welcome in every respect.

★★★★ **Park** • captures the crown for pure alpine esthetics. The woodwork, the carefully hewn polite rusticity, the costumed staffers, the mandate on coziness—all conspire to give this house a mellow glow of a deluxe Arcadia. Unfortunately, however, its situation in a viewless bottomland makes this the least appealing of the Big Three. Perhaps you'll disagree.

★★★★ **Savoy** • Rich open timbers counterpoint the white stucco walls; antiques dot the lounges. Pool and sauna; dancing, bowling, high living at reasonable prices.

☆☆ **Hof Maran** • turns on 85 rooms, most of which claim private baths. The vivacious will find a 9-hole golf course, ice skating, tennis, children's recreation, skiing, and curling. Dining room, grill, cafeteria, and separate restaurant; comfortable bedchambers with ample space and good baths.

☆ **Bellevue** • is an excellent bet—franc-ly speaking. Keen administration; attractive Arven Restaurant downstairs; English style pub; orchestra for apres-ski terpsichore; 75 balconied rooms and 66 baths. Try for its corner units. Very good.

Valsana • draws a lively young set; its bar glows with robust revelers when the snowflakes fall; there's a pool to add to the splash. Major renovations keep it on a continuing upbeat cycle.

Alexandra • offers space for 200 sleepyheads; a fair investment.

Merkur • for the economy-minded, is also excellent.

Excelsior • has begun to come up again since its restyling. All 80 units with bath; swimming pool.

Central • is also very worthy; moreover, it is noted for its kitchen. Many Arosa hotels are closed during part of April, all of May, part of June, and all of Nov.; exceptions are one 4-star hotel, two 3-star establishments, and two boardinghouses that operate throughout the year; all of these are clean and comfortable. As in most mountain areas, dining is usually at your own hotel.

ASCONA   Here is one of the gems of the *Ticino,* the romantic hillbound heart of Switzerland's Italian border.

★★★★★ **Giardino** • assuredly lives up to its botanical boast, being surrounded by lovely parks, forests, and flower beds. Inner beds are charming too (many are four-posted); terrace dining, tennis, swimming, golf, and fitness facilities; special diets if desired; elegance, peace, or animation (as desired) in a noble setting. Hosting by Hans Leu, one of the nation's most respected hoteliers and a friend to every traveler. A charming blend of taste and beauty.

BAD RAGAZ

☆☆☆☆☆ **Grand Hotel Quellenhof** • boasts 3 indoor thermal swimming pools and an 18-hole golf course; rambling, classic spa style; setting of refinement and blissful nature in season; lovely for serenity.

☆☆☆☆ **Grand Hotel Hof Ragaz** • also has an indoor splasher.

Touring Mot-Hotel Schloss Ragaz • conventional hotel, with motel in gardens; good but not luxurious.

BASEL

Here's a cultured dowager who is so cosmopolitan that she shares her roots with both France and Germany; she is also a major financial, pharmaceutical, and chemical center. The confluence of these social and economic wellsprings provides the city with a unique richness that discriminating voyagers appreciate. The Kunstmuseum, as one outstanding example, offers art in such variety and quality, that it alone warrants a visit to this riverbank town; its many antiquities, its Holbein collection plus 28 other museums, its university (which was in operation before Columbus weighed anchor), its zoo, its Roman ruins, and its skyline on the Rhine are additional lures for adventurers. The Carnival in Feb. or Mar. is so spectacular for costumery and revels that it daunts the imagination, if not the stamina; the music and festivities are literally nonstop; the atmosphere is merry; the air is spiked with jovial toasts night and day. Most of the gaiety occurs in the Old Town where auto traffic is prohibited. The Swiss Industries Fair draws many visitors in March.

HOTELS

☆☆☆☆ **Drei Konige** ("Three Kings") • at Rhine-side, founded in A.D. 1026, is Switzerland's oldest hotel and solidly in the forefront of the nation's innkeeping fraternity. The dining room, bar, and many public sectors have been restored to aristocratic splendor. Chandeliers, fine carpeting, burnished panels, polished crystal are but a few of the graceful hallmarks. Dining at the riverfront salon or terrace is a pleasure; suites and ordinary bedchambers are proudly furnished.

☆☆☆ **Hilton** • occupies a pleasant residential situation and functions efficiently—albeit without much personality. Lobby so small that it really should be termed a foyer; dignified, darkwood Wettstein Grill with candle illumination, orange textiles, brass-trimmed dividers, friendly service and good cuisine; Bora Bora Bar and Polynesian-style discotheque; poorly executed Cafe de la Marine Suisse, which labors to achieve a lakefront theme; pool facing inner court; sauna; ample parking. Bedchambers are well outfitted and colorful, with narrow dimensions and inside baths. The staff reflect the courtesy and cheer of Basel itself.

☆☆ **Euler** • near the station, is a midtown classic. You'll find an underground shopping passage connected to a cafeteria, a spacious carpark, and a rear courtyard. The dining salon somehow seems stuck in a dreary time warp halfway between French Regency and post-War Scandinavian. The service is tops, but it just lacks flair.

☆ **International** • provides plenty of color in the Modern Convention Hotel approach; pool, sauna, and gymnastic facilities very well architected and maintained; main dining room with appetizing rotisserie and chummy tavern; full air conditioning; a few viewless cubicles; others crackling with flair. Very good in the medium-to-high bracket.

Le Plaza • is a 250-room purpose-built hotel designed to serve the needs of the Congress Hall. Standards are often quite low but prices are not. Service personnel need smartening up. Complaints about the kitchen too.

Metropol • next to the Euler, provides fresh, clean-lined accommodation, color TV, minibar, direct-dial phone, and room rates that are not startling. Very agreeable for its bed-and-breakfast purpose.

Europe • is divided with 4 floors in the main building and 3 in the annex; an uncovered walk through a garden joins the independent units; the whimsical Bajazzo restaurant features a harlequin theme. Rooms are compact, but overall it boasts an upbeat package of hotel wares.

Basel • is in the old quarter; it generally carries out the antique motif with modern comfortizing touches. Stone-lined restaurant with crackling grill; amusing bars and cozy corners; historic corridors; fitness room; space limited in bedchambers, with the most imaginative ones on the 5th floor. A good mixture.

Schweizerhof • more than a century old, is fully contemporary in comforts. Rates hover in the welkin zones for the earthy rewards; #36 is one of its best maximum twins. Okay, but a bit steep.

Victoria • welcomes guests with an artful lobby. Limited in space but very prim and assuredly proper; 40% with bath and shower; double-glazed windows on the noisier front; 5th-floor units with balconies on the facade.

Alexander • cozily conceived, boasts many winning charms. The restaurant focuses on provincial recipes. Space limitations are a problem, but they are so cloaked in attractiveness that for brief stopovers I don't think you'll mind.

Merian • is a modern 60-room inexpensive find, with its riverside Cafe Spitz and breathtaking Old Town vistas.

Krafft • inexpensive and on the waterfront, also has a charming Rhine-lapped restaurant. Good buy for good living.

RESTAURANTS

☆☆☆☆☆ **Bruderholz** • one of the finest practioners of traditional cooking arts in the nation but still not so set in its ways that owner-chef Hans Stucki does not venture occasionally into fresh fields of gastronomy. The house (a mansion really) occupies a residential address with several salons providing different moods—all of them distinguished, rich, and exquisite. Immaculate reception; perfect service; deluxe accouterments featuring polished crystal, brass chandeliers, candles, flowers set in vitrines; decor chiefly derived from 19th-century furnishings and paintings. For summer there is a cheerful terrace through French doors for sipping and chatting. Menus at 3 prices or a la carte. It was a galvanic joy to experience such extraordinary quality for such reasonable tariffs. This one is a *must* for any traveling disciple of *haute cuisine*. Closed Sun. and Mon.

★★★★ **Donati** • garners a loyal following, many of whom come away full of admiration as well as full of Donati's varied and select Italian preparations. The lasagne was so blissful that it should serve as the definition for all lasagnes. The saltimbocca also was superb—and Parma ham just doesn't come better. Kooky (almost Dada-ist) theme drawn from the 1930s (Dada is said to have been born in Switzerland—and, perhaps, in this restaurant); highlighted with works by Chagall and Calder plus some rather ornate sculpture; one section with wood paneling and another suggestive of a brasserie; prices as easy to swallow as the excellent cookery. An experience that any follower of the arts should not miss if he ever claims to have visited Basel.

Schutzenhaus ("Ranger's House") • has color, good skilletry, and high-ish tabs.

Walliser Kanne • is rustic and attractive. Regional dishes of the *Valais*.

Casino • deals out so-so fodder.

★★ **Schloss Binningen** • *in a park setting a few minutes from the center* • is a renovated 13th-century castle (Junior Prince size), with a small Wine Garden at its entrance, a *Gaststube* in its front room, an enchanting medieval-style *Trinkstube* upstairs (private parties only), a quiet and intimate dining room, and a knockout of a terrace for warm-weather dining (lunch or dinner). The cookery could be improved, but the atmosphere makes it worth the short ride. Medium expensive.

BERNE

The capital is one of the few undestroyed medieval cities of Europe, and it's charming. The Aare River divides it twice, in a horseshoe, and the turreted buildings on its banks look like an illustration from *Grimm's Fairy Tales*.

ATTRACTIONS

Cathedral • In the heart of the Old City. There are 344 steps to the viewing platform at the top, but the hike is well worth this particular climb to the Bernese Oberland.

Barengraben • *Bear Pits* • This has been the forum for the city's mascots since 1315. Legend has it that Duke Berchtold V decided to go hunting and to name the city for the first animal killed. Hence, the bear that appears on the city coat of arms and the hundreds of flags that drape the colorful arcaded streets. For centuries bears have been kept in the Barengraben, except for the span when Napoleon took the critters to Paris.

Zeitglockenturm • *Clock Tower* • Ever since it was built in 1191, this has been the hub of the city, and its clock was for centuries the official measure for all tick-tocking in this horological district. The timepiece itself has been embellished through the years: the bell was added in 1405, and the automated dancing figures were installed in 1530. (Pretty little guides are added almost every year.) The charming mechanical show, with horsemen, jesters, knights, and (of course) bears starts at 4 minutes before the hour.

Kunstmuseum • The city's main fine arts museum includes paintings from a variety of eras and styles. The impressive Paul Klee collection and works by Modigliani and Picasso are perhaps more notable than that of the older schools.

Einstein Museum • *Kramgasse 49* • An apartment where physics was at home with Albert. He lived and wondered here from 1903–05.

Bernisches Historisches Museum • *Helvitiaplatz 5* • You'll discover relics dating back to the Stone Age as well as many objects from medieval times and the Renaissance. Local costumes of periods and 15th-century tapestries are the highlights.

Fountains • Berne just might have more fountains per person than any other city in Europe. Although many began their careers as early as 1550, today's examples are almost all reconstructed from the original wooden structures. Most are crowned by statues paying tribute with little squirts to bigshots locally.

HOTELS

★★★★★ **Schweizerhof,** with the most convenient location for shoppers, is ever-luxurious and just downright interesting as a place to reside. It is far, far ahead of anything else in the city proper—but do look at the comments on the out-of-towners further down. This house blends the fabulous Gauer-family antique collection with up-to-the-minute streamlining in living facilities; each hallway, for example, offers almost priceless collections from different periods (3rd floor in 17th century, 4th all-Swiss floor with ancient rifles, harness, a sleigh, *et al.*). When you pick up the direct-dial phone in your room it automatically switches off the radio, turning it on again when you put down the receiver! One of the most captivating innovations is the Simmental Stube, a dining salon of a fine old house that was dismantled and reassembled to the last splinter as a cozy restaurant; moreover, there's Jaylin's, an ultra-posh nightclub featuring live orchestra music, the Arcady Snack-Bar, and a Japanese restaurant. The outstanding Horseshoe Grill adjoins. General manager Jean-Jacques Gauer, personable son of the founders; concierge Louis Ackermann surely one of the best in Europe; a few suites with 2 tubs and 2 showers in the same bathroom. The favorite hotel abroad of scores of travelers.

☆☆☆☆ **Bellevue-Palace** • high on the riverbank, commands a view of the Alps. About 100 rooms have been added to the original 200. Restaurant and grill vast in size and appealing in a grand fashion; gastronomy befitting this elegant station; nightclub and bar plus restyled lounges; fine and spacious rooms.

★★★ **Belle Epoque** • is of a period indicated by its name; only 17 rooms, an elegant bar, antiques from eminent collections. This, of course, is unique as a hotel and for an especially discerning clientele.

★ **Metropole** • may be short on bedroom space, but its public sancta are a cheering delight. Colorful, woody Brasserie with beer-wagon theme, Vieux Moulin grill with a working waterwheel, gaily decorated President-Club bar. Lots of fun in an altogether odd-ball fashion—which foreign visitors will love.

Savoy • is located in midtown. Of its 56 bedrooms, 25 have full-tub baths, 25 have showers, and all have essential plumbing and radios; just a few attractive accommodations are available (#230 is an example).

Alfa • has a snack bar and a restaurant within its poured-concrete hull. Efficiency is the word, but this gets dressed up nicely in the bedchambers. Book the larger doubles for comfort and away from the busy Seilerstrasse for peaceful slumber.

Nydeck • is an inexpensive choice in the city's antique district. Very nice people running it; spare but prim; especially good for singles.

Baeren • romps in with 60 rooms, 30 baths, and 30 showers; bright decor; its only fancy quarters are #215, #315, and #415. Adequate.

Krebs • is sprightly and very clean; 42 rooms, many with bath or shower— and these are the better bets; breakfast only; a value for the price.

Wachter Movenpick • is in the same bracket as Krebs; #209 is a pleasant wood-lined twin.

Regina • 10 minutes from the center in a residential section, is also petite; breakfast is the only meal; good bet when the kids are along.

Bristol • centrally sited, is colorful in a modern plaid-and-plastic fashion. Not bad for mid-range budgets and breakfast-only overnighters.

City • has experienced an urban renewal program under the Gauer aegis (of Schweizerhof fame); it is moderate in cost and useful for short stopovers.

Continental • can easily be missed—at least by me.

★★★ **Le Vieux Manoir au Lac** • just ou'side of *Morat* (or *Murten* in German) is about 20 minutes by car from Berne on the route to Lausanne; it's a small paradise. It sprawls lazily across a greensward that slopes to the lake and peeps through the trees at the Jura Range. Structure of wood, stone, and stucco; tiny boat harbor at the garden's edge; dining salon with brocade panels, paned windows, and an aristocratic yet cozy bearing. The cuisine was outstanding as was the ultra-friendly service. Try the perch from the lake, also the local wine, which is distinctive.

Schiff • at the lakeside, is also in *Morat.* Surrounded by its own park, the umbrella-dotted terrace is ideal for sipping; open terrace with fish specialties; decor fussy but nice.

★★ **Goldenes Kreuz** • at *Gerzensee,* which also studies a lake scene, meadows, and vine lands in the Bernese valleys, is another inviting country house. The neat, 28-room hotel is separated from the restaurant section. The latter is composed of a popular-priced hunting segment on road level where locals sip wine and spin yarns; down a handsome flight is the luxury category grill with elegant decor, wood panels, and explosions of flowers in season; flowing from this is an open terrace commanding a vista that will make you think you've been transported to your Maker.

RESTAURANTS

★★★★ **Schweizerhof** • is the famous home of the Simmental Stube (a.k.a. the Schultheissenstube) and the famous Horseshoe Grill. They are unquestionably above everything else in the city limits. The former is the dining room of an old mansion, transplanted intact. The Horseshoe Grill has *gemutlich* dimensions, versatile menu, wine list so staggering that the printing probably costs a bottle per copy. There's also a fine Japanese restaurant on the property.

★★ **Zum Lowen** ("Inn of the Lion") • is at the nearby suburb of *Worb* where this establishment has been in continuous operation for more than 600 years. You'll probably love this ancient tavern; it's a taste of old Berne. Patinated stucco walls; tile *Kachelofen* (oven); cozy alcoves; delicious simple regional cookery at modest prices. Try it.

Lorenzini • underscores the theorem that some of the best cuisine of Italy is to be found in Switzerland. The chef tilts toward Tuscan gastronomy, blessed be he.

Charley's Beef Corner • slices into you-know-what on its main floor, which resembles a woody sort of brasserie. Excellent grills, steak sandwiches, and huge bowls of mixed salad for surprisingly moderate tabs. The service could have been better, but the atmosphere doesn't seem to require highly trained minions. Downstairs is the Cadillac discotheque in upbeat modern tones, a den for young executives. A successful package.

Churrasco • an Argentinian chain-bred hoofer that appears with frequency in German grazing grounds these days is popularly priced.

Roessli • in *Sariswil* (15 minutes by car) is where you can grill your own meat in the rustic farmhouse.

Frohsinn • near the cathedral, is small but good. The prices are moderate.

Pomodoro • has frolicsome decor and inexpensive pizzas; it's not bad for a quick meal.

Galaxy • rigged out as a ship, nets a fair catch of water-bred denizens.

Mistral • blows in with the cuisine of Provence served in an ancient cellar. Vaulted brick ceiling, stone walls, terra-cotta floors, hanging lanterns plus fat spluttery candles on polished dark-wood tables. The ground floor breezes in with a nice bar and lounge for lighter refreshments and freshets of conversation.

Klotzlikeller • a typical subterranean student hangout, is an antique at 400 years old.

Kornhauskeller • is a baronial German-type beer cellar, dominated by a massive wine barrel and made glad (evenings only) with an oomp-pah band; trencherman's fare, substantial cookery, horrible service, moderate tariffs; try the home-grown Berner Platte; recommended to sausage-and-sauerkraut fans.

Landhaus • *Altenbergstr. 6* • and **Zimmermania** • *Brunngasse 19* • are a pair that can be recommended for food and mood. Both are worthy choices at reasonable prices.

Movenpick • chain now boasts 4 capital branches, and "capital" they are, as drop-in feederies. They all sport the usual handsome decor and the characteristically huge range of prices. The one with the Gade Restaurant is tops, in my opinion.

NIGHT LIFE

For the carriage trade, of course, **Jaylin's** in the Schweizerhof Hotel wins every honor from Mon. through Sat. nights. Great names in jazz have appeared here, but chiefly it is a sophisticated haven for dancing, gentle persuasions, and imbibing. As one might expect from the brilliant Gauer proprietors, a way has been found to cleverly display their antiques in softly back-lighted vitrines—a touch unique to this hosting family. The next stop on your short list might be the **Mocambo.** Its Scotch Bar is at street level; reasonably attractive and very busy on Sat. night. Main enterprise in the cellar; spacious, multitiered sanctum, wrapped on 3 sides by tables at the balcony stratum; small bar in one corner. Dramatic Braille-provoking cell with 1-watt illumination and blue-and-white paneling; 5-piece band, with organ-inspired music straight off the corncob; dance floor more jammed than a Virginia turkey farm in early Nov. Hour-long cabaret at 10 p.m. and midnight. **Hollywood East** (within a block of Mocambo geographically, but perhaps 10 blocks down in quality) draws a younger crowd; you might see only 2 or 3 old men of 27 or 28. The **Babalu** makes its night-beat along the Gurtengasse. Two bars adjoin, including the local **Playboy Club.**

BURGENSTOCK There's no place like it in the world—but you have to pick sunny days to enjoy it in top form. This 500-acre sky empire over the Lake of Lucerne (25 minutes from Lucerne proper) must be seen to be believed. Three hotels are recommended. All have been newly renovated; only one will be open during the midwinter period.

★★★★★ **Grand**

★★★★ **Palace**

★★★ **Park**
All hung with Van Dycks, Brueghels, Tintorettos, and other titans, and all with a magnificent view; Mountain Inn for light refreshments at the 3000-foot peak, reached by one of Europe's fastest and highest elevators; 6-minute funicular to lakeshore bathing; Guest Club entertainment center; nightclub; 9-hole Golf Club; tennis courts; swimming pool with dancing at Poolside Cafe; and Underwater Bar for oglers; Golf Grill, Sporting Club, 2 orchestras, gala evenings, concerts, shopping center, beauty parlor, fashion shows, private chapel—this cloud-kissed community offers just about everything but harp solos by the neighboring angels. There's an athletic club with an indoor pool (white marble set amid black marble terraces), a sauna, massage facilities (dry as well as underwater types), and a restaurant—all reached via a tunnel leading to a cliff-side elevator. An ancient Tavern was remodeled and restored to use.

CRANS-MONTANA is experiencing a boom. From a resident population of around 5000 in the tranquil Off Season, the crescent of hills which has lengthened on both ends of town can accommodate some 35,000 sun-worshipers or snow-bunnies. To reduce alpine traffic jams, the clever hillfolk inaugurated an efficient public transportation. This Valais perch, 5000 feet above sea level in a glittering chalice, deserves a ranking a few rungs below St. Moritz and Gstaad. Virtually every major resort amenity is available: a championship golf course plus 9 holes designed by Jack Nicklaus, heated swimming pools, horses, a casino, helicopter service, curling, and enough ski lifts (40 on a late count, capable of hauling up 38,000 people an hour) and runs to befuddle an athletic centipede.

☆☆☆ **Royal** • overlooking a fir-flecked 9-hole golf course, offers the greatest rewards. Viewful, hearth-warmed main-floor lounges, bar, and dining room lined with glass; charming, lodgelike Caveau du Roy for Valais cheese specialties; cordial administration. All 80 havens with bath or shower; 50 bedchambers facing south, each with sunny balcony. Very sound.

★★★ **Golf & Sports** • chips in with a tranquil setting at the edge of the major links. From your doorstep it's a putt to the first tee, a 5-minute hike to the ski lift, a totter for a splash in the covered swimming pool, and a 15-minute wait between bus shuttles to the village. This one is the social heartbeat of the hillfolk.

☆ **Excelsior** • presents a modernistic lounge; nice bar; convenient play-room; balconies on the southern exposure; fresh-to-the-eye but cramped dimensions in the latest segment. Not bad.

☆ **Des Melezes** • an 8-iron shot from the Golf Club, is also on par. Here's an eagle in comfort for budgeteers.

★★★ **Rhodania** • took the rhode to recovery by refashioning itself in Art Deco style. Looking backward has paid off handsomely here. The **Etoile** is agreeable for accommodations.

The modern little **City** provides one of the best hotel kitchens in the region, for my money. The **Robinson** and the **Mont Blanc** are the best of the year-round operations. **De l'Etrier,** a good-looking A-frame structure in wood, comes up with 150 door keys for rentals on a monthly (perhaps on a weekly) basis. Tiny bar; no lounge; pool; superior for its type of apartment-hotel complex. The **Beau Sejour** is adequate; its pool is an asset. There are 3-dozen additional hotels or pensions on this mountain perch, plus a throng of guesthouses and apartment dwellings that are available. Most of the bigger ones are strictly seasonal. At *Montana* itself, the most impressive edifice for miles around is called **Supercrans**—and as an apartment citadel with a swimming moat that is just what it is. Super! The **Crans-Ambassador,** also with an aquatic spread, is a chalet-style beaut. *Anzere,* a budding resort nearby, can provide additional kips in its tiny but ultracozy **Hotel de Masque.** It remains a quiet village that is bound to wake up and roar very soon.

Crans-Montana nourishes most of its visitors either in its hotel dining rooms or in private chalets. Among the independents, only one really shines: the **Channe Valaisanne. Rotisserie de la Reine** offers an impressive international table.

DAVOS Here is one of Europe's leading centers for winter sport. Its visitors are often youthful and purposeful on the slopes rather than fashion-oriented and idle.

☆☆☆ **Belvedere** • is one of the brightest lights of the Alps. Many-balconied, block-long building; fresco-walled dining salon with carved wood ceiling and brick arcade; 2-level peasant-style grill; play lounge for tots; 200 units and 120 baths. Most North American ski buffs are as happy as seal pups here.

☆☆ **Derby** • also gleams with an inviting warmth. Approximately the same tariff level; chic clientele; atmospheric Paluda Grill; sauna, indoor pool, and health center; kindergarten. It's only 200 strides from the famous Parsenn funicular.

☆ **Schweizerhof** • is standing proud; you'll find a Bel-Etage, balconies for its southern facade, and an indoor pool.

☆ **Fluela** • next to the railway terminal, continually effects bedroom improvements, with uplifted public areas, a sizzling grill, a pool, a gym, and other recreational facilities.

Sunstar • is in a quiet part of the vale, a short walk from town. Ask for the balconied rooms on the south or southwest sides. Very tranquil and pleasant.

The Post swings with fun and frolic. There's a pool and a dapper 25-apartment wing called the Postli. The renewed and scenically sited **Waldhotel-Bellevue,** which is aptly named, deserves abundant praise. It's mighty inviting. The refashioned **Europe** is a popular action station with the Young Set, who frolic in the Cabanna and Grischa Cava night spots. Glass-lined swimming pool; sauna and fitness center; 3 restaurants; comfortable accommodation. **Davos Face,** on the main drag, has been freshly renovated and aims at the actively young market. Nice idea for the spry. **National** is noteworthy for the kindness of its staff.

If you are not bound to your hotel vittles, try chicken curry and other Oriental specialties at **Meierhof.** The **Waldhotel-Bellevue** cops the honors for scenery; the kitchen is top of the mark, too.

FRIBOURG is simultaneously rustic and refined, with possibly the largest and most variegated assemblage of medieval buildings in the nation deep in the canyon of the Old Town. (The newer city rims the upper cliffs.) Children will come unstrung at the charming Marionette Museum. Culturally it is a feast, so plan time to enjoy the banquet. Here are some choices: (1) **Le Parc** (with about 70 units and a fresh feeling). (2) **La Rose** (nightclub; 35 rooms, all with bath). (3) **Duc Bertold** (outstanding architecture; lovely appointments; top cuisine). (4) **Eurotel.** (5) **Elite** (small and, well, elite). While **Morat** (or **Murten** in German) is officially in the Fribourg canton, we have included **Le Vieux Manoir au Lac** and the **Schiff** at the end of the "Berne" section; this is because many travelers drive between the capital and Lausanne and, hence, might pass them by without being forewarned that they are on this route.

GENEVA

Geneva sits like a gem at the bottom of a sparkling alpine chalice. The lake is fantastically blue (except for the white plume of the world's best-known fountain—the Jet d'Eau). A walk among the ramparts of the Old Town, with its great walls, narrow lanes, and ancient shops is a step into the Middle Ages; do make the easy climb because many visitors miss this most colorful segment of medieval Europe that still thrives vigorously. The atmosphere is French, the buildings are handsome, the gardens are bursting with color, and the streets are a blaze of Ferrari-red, Porsche-silver, Jaguar-green, and other hues of the international Sporting Set. If you want gaiety, action, and healthy smiling faces, it's a fine place as a base for western operations.

ATTRACTIONS

Cathedrale St. Pierre • Perhaps the finest viewpoint in the city is the North Tower of this extraordinary 12th-century church. The beautiful interior—pulpit known to John Calvin—has recently been restored; visit also the archaeology site here.

Rhone Cruise • From April to early-Nov. there are departures from Pont-sous-Terre down to the Verbois Dam; the chug to and fro takes 2½ hours and couldn't be more enchanting on a fine day. There also are inexpensive **lake cruises** taking in the small ports and Castles of Leman which push off from **8 Quai du Mont Blanc** (opposite Grand-Casino). Perfect as Swiss pastimes.

Jet d'Eau • This spectacular 425-foot-high fountain, which functions from May to October, has become a symbol for the lovely city. The complicated 1400-hp pumping mechanism requires 3 full-time engineers to operate it.

Musee d'Art et d'Histoire • *2 rue Charles Galland* • Here you'll find works by European masters and emphasis on Switzerland's finest artists. The historical section includes a collection of medieval furniture, armor, and sculpture.

Musee de l'Horlogerie et de l'Emaillerie • *15 route de Malagnou* • Geneva has for centuries been the world's capital of clock- and watch-making; this excellent collection represents the history of the industry—from the 16th century to the present. The exhibit includes many examples of miniature enamelwork incorporated into watchmaking.

Palais des Nations • *ave. de la Paix* • This is now the headquarters of the European arm of the United Nations. Larger than the palace at Versailles, the plans for this impressive building were chosen from those of 10,000 architects who competed for the commission in 1926. In additon to a wide variety of multinationally designed conference rooms and lecture halls, there is a small museum of diplomatic history and a Philatelic Museum.

Le Petit Palais • *2 rue Terrasse St.-Victor* • The approximately 150 Impressionist and Post-Impressionist paintings hang in the drawing rooms and basement of a beautiful, large town house.

Maison Tavel • *6 rue du Puits-St.-Pierre* • is a historical museum for the city; it happens to be in the oldest private house in town.

Musee d'Instruments Anciens de Musique • *23 rue Lefort* • The former owner sold his private treasures to the city. The instruments are still playable. Musicians occasionally are invited to use them.

Institut et Musee Voltaire • *Voltaire Museum and Institute, 25 rue des Delices* • During his exile from France, Voltaire lived in this house for 8 years. Filled with his manuscripts, correspondence, furniture, sculptures, and paintings.

Red Cross Museum • *near the U.N. Headquarters on av. de la Paix* • From 1863 until today this humanitarian organization has been on the front pages of every newspaper in the world. Here you can see a dramatic illustration of its services.

HOTELS

☆☆☆☆☆ **Richemond** • is a prizewinning nominee in fine hotel circles. Direct credit for this can be traced to Jean Armleder, the supercharged proprietor, of the 3rd successive family generation to hold this post; he is assisted by a personable representative of the next legacy, his son Victor. Almost 90% of the establishment is furnished with traditional Continental softness and appeal; the Presidential Suite could well be fit for a King; the canton called the Royal Suite—merely $2500 per night with breakfast—is, quite obviously, one of the finest redoubts in hoteldom. Le Gentilhomme offers refinement in both its dining and bar segments, with dancing at the latter. I am especially fond of the belle epoche Le Jardin and adjoining sidewalk cafe, both bursting with flowers; here the emphasis is on light refreshment. L'Omnibus is the hotel's up-market bistro (nicely answering a growing trend in the city). A smart beauty salon for

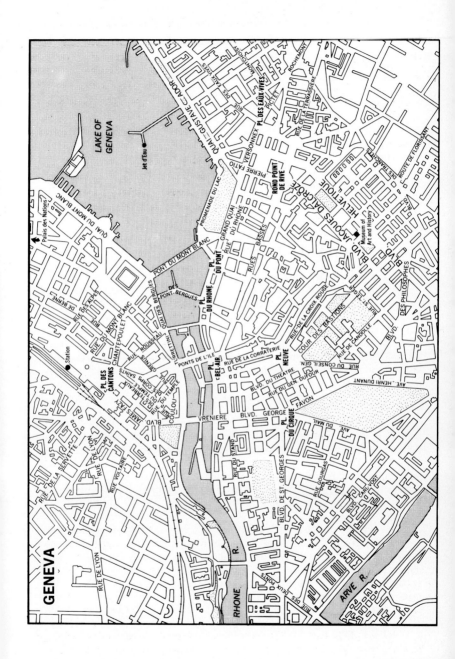

GENEVA

LAKE OF GENEVA

Jet d'Eau

Palais des Nations

QUAI DU MONT BLANC

QUAI GUSTAVE ADOR

RUE DES ALPES

RUE DE BERNE

RUE DU MONT BLANC

CHANTEPOULET

Station

PL DES CANTONS

RUE DE LAUSANNE

QUAI DES BERGUES

ROUSSEAU

RUE DE L'ILE

PONT DU MONT BLANC

PONT DES BERGUES

PONTS DE L'ILE

DES PONT. BERGUES

PL DU PONT

PL DU RHONE

RUE DU RHONE

GRAND QUAI

PROMENADE DU LAC

PIERRE FATIO

VERSONNEX

PL DES EAUX-VIVES

PICTET

RUE DE LA TERRASSIÈRE

ROCHE-MONT

VERSONNEX

ROND POINT DE RIVE

BLVD. JACQUES DALCROZE

HELVÉTIQUE

Museum of Art and History

ROUTE DE FLORISSANT

DES TRANCHÉES

BLVD. DES PHILOSOPHES

RUE DE LA CROIX ROUGE

COUR DES BASTIONS

RUE DE CANDOLLE

RUE DU CONSEIL GÉN

AVE. HENRI DUNANT

PL NEUVE

BEL-AIR

RUE DE LA CORRATERIE

BLVD. DU THÉATRE

RUE DU GÉN DUFOUR

BLVD. GEORGE FAVON

PL DU CIRQUE

AVE. DU MAIL

RUE DU STAND

VRENIÈRE

CORNAVIN

RUE DU TEMPLE

RUE DE COUTANCE

RUE DES CORPS SAINTS

JAMES FAZY

TURRETTINI

BLVD.

RUE DE LYON

RUE DE LA SERVETTE

RUE DE VOLTAIRE

RUE DE LYON

BLVD. DE ST. GEORGES

RUE DES DEUX PONTS

RUE GOURGAS

RHONE R.

CARL VOGT

ARVE R.

ladies. Parking space for 350 cars within 100 yards of the hotel. Highly recommended.

☆☆☆☆ **Du Rhone** • with an excellent riverside situation, and more of a contemporary mood than the Richemond, comes on stronger and stronger as a zesty address for globe-trotters. The freshness and comfort standards are superb; service is matchless—some doubles even include twin bathrooms instead of merely twin basins! Direction is by globally experienced and affable Marco Torriani while day-to-day operations are in the capable hands of personable Eric Glattfelder, one of the most admired hosts in all Helvetia. The sumptuous 6th floor (Bel Etage) was reduced and spaced out from 48 rooms to 30; this tier contains the ultra-exclusive Presidential quarters and the charm-laden but smaller suite #636–37. The updated Le Neptune is secure in its fame as one of the top dining spots in Europe; a new salon was created. There's an animated international atmosphere with smartly refashioned lounges a-chatter with clients from all 4 corners of the earth; underground garage (what a blessing) on 3 levels, and covered with greenery. Very strongly recommended to readers who seek discerning cosmopolitan taste and modernity.

★★★★ **Beau Rivage** • at lakeside, is sparkling as brightly as Leman's waters. Smartly updated lobby, reception, lounges, and bar maintaining the gracious style of its period architecture. Its fine rustic-toned Chat-Botte (Puss-in-Boots) rotisserie is respected for its cuisine and admired for its Louis XIII decor. In addition, there's the Quai 13 in soft green and yellow for light meals and a flowered terrace on an upper level. Interesting family museum of innkeeping; grand suite in which dwelled the Empress of Austria (the bath is the last word in luxury); a host of bright front rooms; all back units—many of them the most attractive in Switzerland—are preening proudly this year; the lakefronters are the latest gems to be polished.

☆☆☆☆ **Metropole** • one of the city's oldest and most stately lakeside addresses, is managed by talented Andre Hauri. Traditional exterior; joyfully rich interior combining creamy polished marble, glass, woodwork, and textiles; floral patterns of opulent cheer; 2 restaurants, one on the waterfront with terrace and another more formal salon inside; cuisine in the *nouvelle* style—dainty and tasty; walnut and brass bar; massive beds and posh comforts. The reception and service are skilled and warmhearted. Very fine indeed.

☆☆☆☆ **des Bergues** • functions smoothly as one of the prestigious addresses in this most international of international cities. Ambitious revisions everywhere; inviting lounges, a bar with both perky and soft live music; main dining room with balconied tables overlooking the lake spillway; beautifully sedate Amphitryon restaurant in rouge and gray, very popular with the Diplomatic Set; gustatory offerings among the finest in the country. Traditional gathering place of Swiss bankers, coupon clippers, and The Oldest Families.

★★★★ **de la Paix** • is one of the most distinguished smaller hotels in the nation. Lakefront situation; dignified lobby; restaurant *a la francais;* TV now in every haven; Picasso prints; colored tiles, up-to-the-minute fixtures, and scales added to practically all bathrooms; dispensing cabinets in case you've forgotten toiletry items. While some of its lodgings are small, others are ample in breadth. Worldwide reputation meriting every iota of its fame.

★★★★ **de la Cigogne** • is another retreat with generous personality. Each suite is a statement in originality; furniture is individually appropriated (the bed, for example of Cary Grant and Barbara Hutton); Chateau Suite with royalist accoutrements. Fireside lounge; wood paneled restaurant with superb food and reasonably priced wines; bankers, jewelry magnates, and fashion tastemakers gather here. Director Bischoff has created a masterpiece.

☆☆☆ **Noga Hilton** • resides on the Quai du Mont Blanc—one of the more glitzy and costly links in the worldwide chain. The architecture is modular, with sheets of glass to exploit the waterfront view; each floor is color-keyed throughout in a basic scheme; the ground level is stronger on design than it is in warmth. There's an indoor-outdoor pool, a fitness center with sauna and massage, plus the cosmopolitan Le Cygne restaurant as well as the Chinese Tse-Yang tables for putting back any weight you might lose. You'll find a shopping lane, dancing, a modest casino, a piano bar, and grand suites, smaller apartments, and well-appointed bedchambers with polished woods, rich textiles, color TV, frigobar, and the reassuring Uniqey security system on a housewide basis. So sleek that it's almost jazzy.

★★★ **President** • under the administrative wing of Swissair, accepts a limited number of group tours. Lakeside setting; white marble facade; French restaurant, with adjoining bar, grill, tea room, and cocktail retreat; rich downstairs decor a startling contrast of Gobelin tapestries, showy period pieces, and Lunar Missile modernity; lounge with sliding roof; 100-car garage. The handful of apartments, 30 suites, and 160 rooms all have bath, radio, 2 or 3 telephones, and floor-to-ceiling windows. Swissair is doing a good turn for the traveler here.

☆☆ **Intercontinental** • is a 16-story giant located about 5 minutes along the Lausanne Speedway. Immense marble-ized commercial lobby, 1-flight up by escalator; rich, cunningly decorated Les Continents Restaurant with nearby La Pergola Bar; coffee shop. You will also find a galaxy of shops, a swimming pool with summer barbecue for lunch and candlelight dining, a 170-car underground garage, and full air conditioning. Extensive bedroom revamping with colors and styles varying by the floor; 8 suites include separate dining salons.

★★★ **La Reserve** • is at the fringe of the city, boasting its own pool, tennis courts, and lakeside harbor. This ultra-quiet rural beauty dominates a spruce-dotted, 4-acre domain near the outskirting hamlet of Bellevue. A nice touch is the availability of motor launches for excursions on the lake or for shuttling to and from downtown Geneva. Open-space-concept lobby with crackling fireplace in winter; window-lined split-level dining room with a glorious view of lawn and trees. Continental plus oriental cooking available. All bedchambers with private loggia or terrace, marble bath, shower, radio and TV; color-keys in beige and salmon; some 3-person units available in its 120-room total; all third-floor units air-conditioned (but rarely necessary in Geneva). Both cuisine and dwelling space come at premium rates, but new director Bryand is providing excellent value for your francs.

★★★ **Les Armures** • is located at St. Peter's gates; the Cathedral, that is, at the top of the Old Town. Meticulously restored 17th-century building; intimate bedrooms. A deluxe romantic snuggery that resists the idea that it is a hotel in the conventional sense.

★★ **Ramada Renaissance** • is a happy surprise. Color, zest, and tasteful vitality are its stock in trade. The Ragueneau is its lobbyside tea room; the Cortille is a cellar nook for dining while the Toquade is a deluxe realm for the hungering; all the bedrooms in dark wood with fitted furniture, lockboxes, minibar, and mosaic-tile baths; there's ample parking space for your car, too. A good buy in the medium range.

Movenpick-Radisson • is a new arrival on the way to the Airport, on route de Pres-Bois. It's a luxurious, freshly styled titan with space for more than 400 guests. Flyers will relish the fitness center to unkink from their travels.

Holiday Inn Crowne Plaza • is also close to the Airport. Super-modern architecture; similar in size to the above; smallish rooms that are very well outfitted for a transit hotel; pool and health facilities; free bus shuttle to and from the tarmac.

☆☆ **Bristol** • offers a viewful restaurant, a bar with piano lilts, 32 traditional bedchambers, 4 duplex units, attic rooms with open beams, a fitness center with sauna, steambath, whirlpool, aerobics (whew), massage, and facials. If you sleep lightly, avoid any kip near the elevator shaft. There is an appealing meld of tradition and modernity here—including a video library (in various languages) for film viewing in your own room.

★ **Pullman Rotary** • welcomes guests with a gustily ornate Empire lobby; the elaborate motif is carried throughout the house, with each accommodation different and each well presented as a period piece. Downstairs restaurant, in a French regency mood, offering a menu that is small but select; rooms are thoughtfully equipped with color TV, radio, frigo-bars, and automatic telephone. The 8th-floor attic units are in duplex style and feature skylights; baths come with heated laundry rails and built-in hair dryers. Management of this deluxe gem is in the capable hands of George Hangartner Jr.

☆ **Royal** • devotes most of its 145 accommodations to group bookings, which usually means the guests only pause here for brief stints. Some of the units, however, incorporate kitchenettes, which make them ideal for longer stays—especially in a city where food costs in restaurants are so high. Pleasant decor, quality carpeting; a few cork walls; ample shelf and desk space; full-house air conditioning. King's Bar plus City restaurant with Old Geneva Tavern and Swiss Corner. Very sound and recommendable.

☆ **d'Angleterre** • boasting a restyled entrance, lobby, and reception area, offers 66 sound-proofed rooms, all with private bath, most of them amply dimensioned. Pleasant setting, with its excellent dining sections fronting the waterside; friendly people; heartily endorsed as one of the best candidates in its medium-price category.

☆ **Balzac** • is youthful; its restaurant, bar, and brasserie are independent; there's private parking in the adjoining Gulf station. All 40 unusually large bedrooms with efficiency bath or shower; comfortable armchairs or divans in some units; a few dressing alcoves; night tables with radios and telephones; TV on request; wide-angle windows affording townscape vistas.

☆ **Cornavin** • has garage facilities near its portals and numerous modernizations inside, including effective sound-proof windows. Prices very reasonable; not bad if you say "okay" to the station area.

☆ **Grand-Pre** • has been remodeled, given a wider lobby, and a more commodious bar. All 85 units tiny but tastefully outfitted; singles in front and doubles in back; only 6 singles without bath or shower; no restaurant. There's a crisp, happy atmosphere here. Excellent for budgeteers.

☆ **Century** • seems designed almost exclusively for male patronage. All sizes, shapes, and lines for masculinear appeal are here, without a single frill. Large lobby with comfortable chairs functionally arranged; 140 rooms with 120 baths or showers; 50% of the accommodations with kitchenettes. Deservedly popular.

☆ **California** • has a chummy cellar bar and a roof-garden snackery. All 67 units with bath or shower; good desk space for working types; 7 with kitchen facilities plus dining counter; 25 others with kitchenettes only.

☆ **Du Midi** • boasts an excellent central address, a spiral entrance stairway beside a gurgling fountain, the cellar Carnotzet for fondue, a sidewalk terrace, à breakfast room, and 82 accommodations, all with bath or shower, a refrigerator, radio, telephone, alarm clock, scales, and an air of no-nonsense functionality. Very solid for the modest outlay.

Ambassador • on the quai des Bergues, was somewhat of a disappointment. Woody lounge with modernistic padded easy chairs; corner restaurant and bar; 90 contemporary-style bedrooms, all fully carpeted but extremely small and with virtually no baggage space; tiny baths, and 28 units with only w.c.'s. The brochure looks better than the real thing.

★ **Warwick** • has much to recommend it, including this book. French-style les Quatre Saisons restaurant with seasonal accent; sun-dappled breakfast nook; coffee shop with daily menu; piano bar; sauna; nearby carpark; well-outfitted chambers (with refrigerators) with back views of Lac Leman and the Jet d'Eau.

Cristal • is well polished, very central but quiet. Bright colors and solid comfort; TV and video; Swiss breakfast buffet included in the moderate pricings.

De Berne • was initially planned as a haven for tour groups. Expansive lobby; color TV plus free video; soundproof windows; full air conditioning; dining room in harmonious beige and pink tones; small bar; improved hallways; fresh, simple quarters, each packed with minibar, direct-dial telephone, radio, mahogany furniture, and private bath.

Windsor • offers 56 bedchambers. Small lounge, small bar, small cells, small recommendation.

Excelsior • a station hotel, has space for 75 snoozers with very thin wallets. Fair shelter.

Rivoli's • sleeping quarters are even more minuscule, but then the prices are accordingly low.

Penta • largely held by a consortium of airlines, is sited in the vicinity of the airport. Artfully conceived grill room; coffee shop; cocktail lounge; bedchambers resembling studio design. Excellent value.

Only 11 miles across the border from Geneva (20 minutes by the Speedway), *Divonne-les-Bains* offers resort thermal-spa facilities, 3 aging but adequate hotels, an 18-hole golf course, a racetrack, occasional polo matches, and the richest gambling facilities in Gaul. The Casino—with roulette, baccarat, American games, boule, and chemin de fer—is the town's main attraction and almost its reason for being.

☆☆☆☆ **Chateau de Divonne •** is just outside of town on a commanding perch overlooking its golf course. It is a beautifully maintained structure dating from the second half of the 18th century. Captivating terrace; 23 period rooms with 5 suites; swimming pool; closed early Jan. to mid-March. Noteworthy cuisine; try the light ravioli of foie gras or the Bresse chicken. This Divonne world is as tranquil as the inside of a bubble, so don't expect fireworks. Recommended only for lazing, gazing, and gaming.

RESTAURANTS

☆☆☆☆☆ **Du Rhone •** its Neptune segment, currently is a bellringer. If it is in season, try flan aux truffes or the lamb kidney in basil. One dish is truly a work of art: tresses de filets de sole et salmon aux morilles or braided pink and white fish slivers with wild mountain mushrooms—a creation that should become a classic. Or try the Ravioles stuffed with truffles. Truffles are a specialty of the house; the season is Jan.–Mar. This unit is closed on weekends, but the adjoining dining salon is equally appealing and it remains open the week through.

★★★★★ **Beau Rivage's Chat-Botte** • is a hot item among gastronomes. There is an air of well-bred rusticity here and a friendly professional manner in the way its outstanding cuisine is served.

★★★★★ **Noga Hilton** • can be proud of its Le Cygne, a long glass-lined salon overlooking the lake and its tiara of lights. All the elements of refinement are here: candle illumination, burnished wood, piano melodies, impeccable service. The sweetbreads garnished with vegetable shavings and served with a billfold of spinach was in the mood of nouvelle cuisine as was the duck with three peppers. Every morsel was dressed with flair. The bill was dressed to kill.

☆☆☆☆☆ **Richemond's Le Gentilhomme** • with soft lighting and rich coloring, continues to draw fashionable clientele, many of whom arrive early to dance to the live music in the adjacent bar. As an alternative, Le Jardin, with its connected sidewalk cafe, comes up with thousands of flowers, skillful after-dark illumination, and music piped from Le Gentilhomme; a happy focal point for visitors and residents alike, from breakfast to after-theater snacks; U.S.-styled table d'hote lunch (consomme, hamburger-steak platter, ice cream) for hurried trippers, plus self-service hors d'oeuvres table.

☆☆☆☆☆ **Hotel des Bergues' Amphitryon Room** • retains one of the most joyful moods in Europe, especially at lunchtime.Deft service to match the exquisitely presented meals.

★★★ **La Reserve's** • view from La Closerie is enchanting. A recent dinner was a gracious bow toward light French cuisine.

☆☆☆ **Tse Fung** • is the best Chinese restaurant I have ever found in Switzerland—and it vies for my top ranking in all Europe. Elegant setting, furnishings, and tableware; large selection of Cantonese and Peking specialties, beautifully prepared; open 365 days for lunch and dinner. More expensive than average Cathay establishments, but infinitely better in its suavity and quality.

☆☆☆ **Le Bearn** • *quai de la Poste 4* • remains as good as ever. *Fin-de-siecle* decor; reliable menu combining modern style continental cuisine plus traditional cooking; sedate attention bordering on stiffness; highly professional in every respect, which accounts for its everlasting success in this demanding city of gourmets. All-out recommendation for this little gem; *don't miss it!*

★★★ **Au Vieux Moulin** • *89 rt. d'Annecy in* ***Troinex*** • features silk textiled walls, mismatched porcelain (on purpose and very nice, too!), kind Chef Gerard Bouilloux who has made a comely residence into a fine little establishment of the nouvelle school.

☆☆ **Le Boeuf Rouge** • *7 rue des Paquis* • is a major contender under the skillful handling of Daniel Huvet.

☆ **Griffin's Cafe** • *36 Blvd. Helvetique* • is a spinoff from the fashionable Griffin's nightery (see next section). Very correct to be wearing sunglasses after last night's bash at the next door disco.

☆☆ **Le Marignac** • at Grand Lancy is stirred by Louis Pelletier. **Le Curling** at Petit Lancy where the Top Broom is Daniel Ficht.

☆☆ **Hostellerie de la Vendee** • *also in Petit Lancy* • is one of the tops in the region and certainly worth the short journey to the sleek precincts of Daniel and Joseph Righetto. Try their ballotine of lakefish or the warmed salad of duck livers. In fact, almost everything sampled was extraordinary with the exception of the uninspired offerings from the sweets trolley.

★ **Au Fin Bec** • *rue de Berne 55* • is an unpretentious old-timer that used to specialize in game and is now concerned mainly with Italian cuisine. Enclosed-garden entrance; begonia-bowered, arch-lined, tree-covered patio for fair-weather meals, plus 3 inside dining rooms; neighborhood drop-in atmosphere.

★★ **Mere Royaume** • *rue Corps-Saints 9* • dating back to 1602, seems to be bouncing back to life under the Doldi leadership. My *omble* (lake fish) in butter sauce was not good, *it was fantastic!* More nouvelle cuisine dishes being added to up the quality without up-ing the price tags. Chummy brick and timber personality enhanced by kind, efficient service, and splendid value in the culinary output.

☆☆☆ **La Perle du Lac** • *on the lake* • has a lovely terrace, and an impressively agreeable alfresco atmosphere. The chef is aiming at gastronomic recognition—and, happily, he's achieving it. The prices, of course, are astronomic, too. Closed when winter winds blow.

Cafe-Restaurant de la Pointe • *6 rue de Villereuse* • is known for its steak au poivre; inexpensive and amusing.

Roberto's • *10 rue Pierre Fatio* • invites you to grow more and more Fatio on its Italian flavors mainly. At #15 on this same *rue,* you'll find *La Coupole,* a French connection that has caught on with Geneva's late-nighters.

Brasserie Lipp • has come to town, the Old Town, to be exact: in the Confederation center, where you'll also find **Harry's Bar,** another trendy import.

☆☆☆☆ **Restaurant du Parc des Eaux-Vives** • *across the far waters on the lake bank opposite the Richemond Hotel* • is an impressive graystone chateau which the city owns. Iron gate entrance; lovely landscaping with the Geneva Tennis Club courts behind; portal canopied with a blue- and white-striped baldachin; umbrella-lined terrace for tea or aperitif sippers, without food service; 6 huge windows in the main dining room with magnificent views of the water and the distant UN enclave. The quality of the gastronomy is now spiraling upward, so that it stands today as one of the city's more sophisticated and worthwhile dining targets. Try the souffle d'omble and see why. Closed Mon.

★★ **Auberge des Grands Bois** ● *at* **Buchillon** *2 exits short of Lausanne on the auto route, near St. Sulpice* ● turns out some of the best lake-fish cookery in the nation. The trout, perch, and *omble* (deep-water critters) are heavenly, the prices are relatively low, and the drive into the country is lovely. The set menu is a genuine bargain by rich Swiss standards. Typically rustic atmosphere with no pretensions. Very popular, so do call ahead to reserve. Closed Wed.

NIGHT LIFE

The **New Velvet Club** mixes modernity with Retro art forms through several comfortable tiers of delight. High ceilings, warm velvety tones, dance music, late dinner available. Another gathering place for the socialite and sophisticate is the Le Gentilhomme at the **Hotel Richemond;** no show, cocktails, gourmet dining, dancing to Latin strains, and Diors the main attractions. **Le Club 58** and **The Pussy Cat Saloon** share a common entrance; turn left for the former, right for the latter. Admission chomp on weekends; Edwardian interior with patterned carpeting on walls; rouge and black color scheme; excellent strips, similar to the Crazy Horse in Paris. Better for Him than for Her. The **Griffin's** is one of the most fashionable discotheques in the land. It's private, but membership can be purchased; frequently, generous proprietor Bernard Grobet or Maitre Joe Panarinfo invite newcomers to join on a gratis basis. Highly stylized, modernistic downstairs retreat; with sumptuous orange and gray upholstery; lofty mirrors; adjoining rustic dining room serving from 8 p.m. to dawnish (meats are best); very comfortable surroundings. **Regine** lures some of the night traffic to her digs in the **Noga Hilton.** It's a membership club, but usually the concierge can fix you up with a temporary card. Things are dear at dear Regine's so expect billings to be neck-snapping. At more humane price levels, **Le Petit Palais** is a split-level cave with alternating combos. Crowded dance floor; good ventilation; attentive service. Worth a Tour. **Ba-Ta-Clan,** wickedly fashioned in French tones, grinds out set after set of seminude shows. Tom Thumb tables in music-hall arrangement. **Maxim's** swings in with an ornate glass, brass, and iron entrance; wood and burgundy tones in its cellar salon; multilevel seating for better views of the jugglers, strippers, and crooners. **Moulin Rouge** is easy to live without. **Le Grillon** is agreeable for dancing; perky combos; small cabaret at 11 p.m. **Piccadilly** is smaller, more *intimo,* and okay for avoiding that certain someone. A bit of strip; everything closed Sun. **New Mylord** is a disco-haunt for youngsters. Finally, **rue des Etuves,** 200 yards east of Hotel du Midi, is lined with amusing working people's cafes.

SHOPPING

Quality is the byword here. You may be sure that anything you buy will stand up, if you can afford it.

SHOPPING HOURS: They vary wildly throughout the nation. During the tourist influx there's no usable rule-of-thumb. Stores open from 8–9 a.m.; some fold up for lunch anywhere from 12-or-12:30–1:30-or-2 p.m., while others stay open all day; most (not all) close at 6:30 p.m. on weekdays and midday or 4 p.m. on Sat. In winter, however, nearly every merchant goes home between noon and 2 p.m. on Sat. Large department stores and often other shops are closed Mondays until 1:30 p.m.

BEST AREAS: rue du Mont-Blanc (heading up towards the Central Station at place Cornavin); the streets running along either side of the Rhone; on the Old Town side, the rue du Rhone (stretching from place Bel-Air to place Eaux-Vives); the next street parallel to it which changes its name five times before it reaches the Carrefour de Rive (rue de la Confederation, rue Marche, rue Croix-d'Or, rue de Rive, Cours de Rive); Confederation Centre (rue de la Confederation) up in the Old Town, from the place Bel Air to the place du Bourg-de-Four (rue de la Cite, Grand-Rue, and rue Hotel-de-Ville).

SAVINGS ON PURCHASES: Many luxury items carry a 6.2% federal tax known as **WUST** that is refundable if you've spent a minimum of 500 S.Fr. per item. Check with the store where you make your purchases for details on procedures for recouping it.

ANTIQUES: Stroll along rue de la Cite, Grand Rue, and rue Hotel-de-Ville. The quality is generally good, but oh—those prices! How about a nice excursion, some 25 miles along the lake to *Rolle,* where there's a house called **Argentum** (Grand rue 52): Here Mme. Gutowski can lead you through a wonderful collection from all over Europe. Also new silver gift items.

CHOCOLATES: Always my first and last errand is to load up on **Lindt, Zeller** (13 pl. Longemalle), and **Pierre Moreau** (12 rue du Marche) chocolates. **Bonbonniere** (11 rue de Rive) and **La Chocolaterie du Rhone** (3 rue de la Confederation and Intercontinental Hotel) are two more mouth-watering addresses. Sadly, *no candies containing alcohol are passed by U.S. Customs.*

CUTLERY: Coutellerie du Mont-Blanc S.A. (7, rue du Mont-Blanc). Here you will find every possible model of Victorinox Swiss Army knife from the one actually used by the Swiss foot soldier (without corkscrew) to the mammoth "Swiss champ," which is probably capable of everything from brain surgery to tank repairs. Moreover, if their engraver is available, they will carve your initials on it free of charge while you wait. Beyond these is a virtual armory of knives for the kitchen, the hunt, decoration, and self defense. Stocks also include flatware by Christofle, fondue sets, chafing dishes, and dozens of easily carried low-cost presents. Additional branches at Centre Balexert and Cointrin Airport (open every day including Sun. for last-minute purchases).

DRUGSTORE: Pharmacie Principale (Confederation Centre 1), is one of the largest in Europe. It stocks everything from dried pimpernel flowers to maternity garments to neon-lit bikinis—you name it. If you look hard enough, you'll also find toiletries and medicines.

EMBROIDERY: Langenthal (rue du Rhone 13) is the unquestioned leader nationwide, with locations in a dozen other cities and resorts. Linens and handwork for dining room, bedroom, bath, and kitchen.

FASHIONS AND ACCESSORIES FOR LADIES, MEN, AND CHILDREN: Bon Genie (place du Molard, with branch in Lausanne), is the celebrated luxury specialty store that markets close to 100-thousand different manifestations of the latest styles and designs, through glamorous boutiques and departments headlining the greatest names in the industry.

GOLD: Not all the gold in Switzerland is in banks. The best of it is at **Lalaounis** (23 rue du Rhone), where it has been fashioned into fabulous Greek jewelry. (See "Athens.")

OPTICS: Wiegandt (10 Quai General-Guisan) is the city's leader, both for fashion as well as for precision and special needs in glasses or contact lenses. Here's where you'll find the finest in Europe.

GOTTLIEBEN (see also *Constance* under "Germany") This is a fairyland where the **Drachenburg** is one of the most atmospheric ancient hotels to be found anywhere. It's a study in painted ceilings, old timbers, bottle-glass windows, and romantic natural scenery. The **Annex,** more contemporary, is on the same waterfront nearby. It, too, is captivating. **Waaghaus,** with its own share of antique brass chandeliers and leaded peepholes, is less intimate but still very worthy. Meals within this complex are superb as high-grade tavern fare. **Krone,** a bit more commercial, has a lovely waterside patio restaurant plus good solid accommodation. More modest dwelling can be found at the nearby village of *Ermatingen;* the whimsically painted **Adler** is best, followed by the water's edge **Hirschen** and another **Krone;** both serve superb *felchen* and *egli* lake fish. Be sure to visit the neighboring **Napoleonic Museum,** too, where Queen Hortense lived; it looks as it did in her day.

GRINDELWALD, 13 miles up the valley from Interlaken, is a tiny toenail on the foothills of the magnificent Bernese Oberland. Europe's longest gondola lift will set you atop the point called First for a fantastic First-hand view of the spires above and the Lilliput below. A rack-railway scrambles—usually packed with group tours—up the 2-mile-high Jungfraujoch—"Top of Europe"—to the loftiest station in the Alps. Flanking this is the infamous Eiger "North Wall," that formidable barrier of stone and ice that has taken the lives of so many climbers. The Monch and Jungfrau are next door. Three transportation hookups now link the most important round-the-valley slopes into a skier's dream-come-true. The usual accouterments are thoughtfully provided by The Lord and His angels for hiking, skiing, fishing (the last in the glacially formed Lutschinen River); man-made facilities for heated-pool swimming, tennis, and sleigh-riding; 49 hotels or pensions. If you need any guidance whatsoever, go directly to Joe Luggen, the local Tourist Office Director who is one of the nation's most astute and warm-hearted ambassadors of good will.

☆☆☆☆ **Grand Hotel Regina** • rejuvenated by Fred Krebs and his son, Hans, on a cost-is-no-object basis, a queenly choice. Annex—a luxury chalet-style edifice with 29 suites, tiled stove, color TV, and even some baths with tubs for twosomes and a view of the Eiger; penthouse suites in older segment. His 300-piece collection of antique local prints (on display throughout) and fine clocks have consumed a small Alp of francs. Numerous standard units restyled with built-in furniture and hip-deep wall-to-wall carpets; plenty of flowers around; big, open-air, heated pool with colorful umbrellas on lawn, against one of the most glorious Alpine backdrops imaginable; adjoining Health Pavilion with a covered pool, solarium, sauna, massage parlor, and clubroom, plus a beauty parlor. Folklore Fondue Dinner Parties from time to time featuring a yodeling quartet (delightful in winter after a community sleigh ride); Candlelit Dinner Dances occasionally. Pianist or live combo in the attractive Hotelbar.

☆☆☆☆ **Belvedere** • has been soaring up in quality due to the ceaseless efforts of the friendly Hauser family, who own and care for it while also pampering their guests. New spectacular entrance with a bubbling fountain; refashioned lounges, one in Louis Philippe style, another modern with open hearth and both with Eiger views; totally rebuilt kitchen (6 course dinners are the norm here). Mostly suites and junior-suites and, of course, the ultra-luxurious spread called the "Eiger" with 2 bedrooms; beautifully outfitted accommodation throughout. The indoor pool, Bio-health sauna, and fitness center are ideal in a sporting atmosphere. An excellent house that continues to improve.

★★★★ **Spinne** • spins a wondrous web of entertainment and comfort. The dining and snacking sectors are filled with alpinisms, excellent fare, and jovial people. Fine bar, nightclub, and public facilities; bedchambers newly equipped with thoughtful touches.

★★★ **Sunstar** • also teetering above the deep valley, is a chalet-style structure. Garden, tennis; glorious vistas from practically every window; extensive revamping; indoor pool; woody dining tavern; cheery bedrooms; amiable personnel. Very sound.

★★★ **Parkhotel Schonegg** • offers cozy public rooms—especially the chummy bar—and overall there is the pervading warmth of Thomas and Christine Stettler, the fourth generation of proprietors who provide so much for their clients. All bedrooms recently restyled; private baths throughout; ask for a southfacing room with balcony—and you may never leave Grindelwald.

Bel-Air Eden ● for budgeteers, next to the Regina, is spic, span, and snappy. A lot has been done lately to perk it up still further—and the location is smack in midvillage. I consider it superior for the modest outlay.

Bernerhof Garni ● adjoining the Central Wolter, is also a tidy choice for tidy, uncluttered wallets. Not the choice for light sleepers when there is traffic, but overall a pretty good buy.

For dining, most hotels offer a full or half-pension plan. You'll eat well, but if you spend a lot of time on the slopes or walking, take some of your meals in the mountain huts.

Gift Ideas? **Langenthal** has one—a new one—of its legendary embroidery boutiques here. Don't miss a Grindelwald spree for linens, table dressings, the bath or bedroom. There are personal items too.

At **First,** the last stop on the 7220-foot-high chair lift, there's a spellbinding restaurant and terrace for plain fare and fantastic viewing. Never mind the provisions; you'll never see what's on your plate, anyway.

GSTAAD Socially, this is the hub of the winter whirl. Not as high in altitude as it is in society, the skiing is not always the best on the lower slopes. There are other compensations, however. The Swiss Open tennis championships occur here in July, followed by a summer of classical music and concluded in late September with a Country and Western Festival. Here, the international set does most of its dining, dancing, drinking, gossiping, and so-forthing in the merry surroundings of glamorous hotels—but it retreats to privately owned or rented chalets for its beauty sleep and repairs. Splendid natural setting where the Bernese and Vaudois Alps meet in an open valley that absorbs more hours of sunlight than many of its competitors; slick-rustic atmosphere. The 69 mountain railways or lifts cover nearly 150 miles of marked ski trails in Saanen country and on to the Diablerets Glacier fields. In summer this makes rapturous walking terrain.

☆☆☆☆ **Palace ●** is a traditional attraction. This castle-style hotel, Swiss flags flying from its truncated ramparts, dominates the village. It draws an ultrachic, sophisticated, international clientele, which is bolstered by fashionable residents of opulent chalets who make it their social fulcrum; many guests wear black tie every night at dinner. (But for those who don't wish to, there's a restaurant adjoining the grill playfully named Le Sans Cravatte, where the dining is cozy and, of course, *sans cravatte.*) The lobby and many of its public rooms were magnificently restyled very recently. Proprietor Scherz keeps everything running as smoothly, as quietly, and as sumptuously as a Rolls-Royce. Hi-Fi Club in basement for teenagers or young marrieds, jumping from 4 to 6:30 p.m. and from 8 p.m.–1 a.m.; large skating rink, curling, 2-lane "automatic" bowling, tennis, heated pool, beauty parlor, and table tennis room; instructors for all sports; sauna and massage; cable TV (over a 20-mile line!); within call (off premises), everything from golf to riding to ski lifts to mumblety-peg.

Residence Palace ● a complex of privately owned apartments (many of celebs) that are rented out under hotel supervision. Hence, these sumptuously grand suites also can be obtained as part of the Palace's ever-expanding services with all guest privileges included and many additional conveniences as well.

☆☆☆☆ **Grand Hotel Park** • Here's a new luxury candidate facing south from its own hilltop, two walking-minutes from the village. Exclusive restaurant facilities ranging from the Greenhouse with winter garden for breakfast and light snacks, to the Grand for tradition and panache, to Le Grill for a la carte choices in cozy painted-wood decor beside the open fire. Indoor saltwater swimming plus a heated outdoor pool; sauna, whirlpool, steambath, massage, solarium, workout room, and squash. Whew! Also a beauty center by Estee Lauder, hairdresser, anti-stress center by Dr. Gillet-Cantova, and a sports shop. Feeling exhausted? It also offers 93 wonderful bedrooms or suites, so have a rest.

★★ **Bernerhof** • is a solid midtown choice and ably hosted by its affable owner-manager Leonz Blunschi. A fine indoor pool, sauna, and fitness unit; playroom for children (useful since it's open winter and summer); garage parking; Swiss and Chinese dining options, plus a coffee shop and bar. The 45 accommodations are thoughtfully outfitted and well appointed. A reliable address if you want to be in the thick of things.

☆ **Bellevue** • at the approach to the village and structurally similar to the Parkhotel, is set in its own garden just off the main highway. Also seasonal.

Alpina • near the Palace but on higher ground, offers a sparkling view of Gstaad Valley and has its own spacious park. Well regarded for its kitchen; very relaxing; properly managed.

Olden • in season, is appealing more as a merry perch for night owls than for its lodgings. Attractive cafe and restaurant; popular La Cave night life activities; substantial and simple bedchambers; some refashioning achieved recently.

Post-Rossli • offers an appealing selection of rooms, 7 of which are in an annex; good cuisine; homey atmosphere. The location is noisy but handy (no taxi required to get to the doin's), and the price is right.

★★★ **Le Grand Chalet** • is a bit out of the center in glorious farm country. Wonderful homespun decor and an abundance of luxury—especially in the fine Bagatelle restaurant, one of the tops in the region.

★★ **Hotel Christiania** • is clean and well situated; all rooms with bath and WC; TV and radio; minibars and balconies. Restaurant with small bar. A chalet that's snugful of Alpine cheer.

Chesery • a special category, is an exquisitely executed chalet-style building with 3 handsome dining areas—but with a total of only 1 suite and 3 double rooms for overnighting. Its 4 accommodations are tastefully and imaginatively done in what might be punned as late Cantonese. During months of winter sport, live concerts by big-name jazzmen are a regular feature. If this one had more door keys, however, it would definitely rate as #2 in the region. Others in the chalet motif that are very worthy alternatives include the **Arc en ciel** (space for 45), the **Alphorn** (orchestrated for 30), and the 160-pillowed **Gstaaderhof** (excellent Saagi Stubli for regional food; indoor pool; superb indoor-outdoor tennis center; cozy fireside lounges); additionally, the **National** and the **Victoria** (both for about 50 guests each) are recommendable.

Sporthotel Rutti • is a couple of minutes out of the center and is handy to several ski lifts and a sports center with indoor tennis and pool. Folk evenings enliven the mood; colorful mountain-style carnotzet.

Steigenberger • is out at *Saanen,* a fetching assemblage of chalet-style, timber-clad buildings that form a pleasant sort of sport colony.

Chalet du Bon Accueil • at *Chateau-d'Oex,* 8 miles away, is a little place we hear mighty alluring reports about.

Caprice • is the easy choice in the captivating town of *Rougement,* which offers the 6600-foot Videmanette as its key scenic attraction. If you pause, the hospitable Montabon family will proudly tell you about this attractive corner of Switzerland.

INTERLAKEN is the most fun if you hanker for nostalgia. The real-life clock seems to have stopped back when this century was in diapers. Speaking of timepieces, it has a noteworthy Flower Clock; the legendary view of the Jungfrau from the hotels lining the Hoheweg, the annual Mozart Festival, and medieval Unterseen are other reasons to be here, not to mention the outright romance of "the valley between the lakes." Hop the funicular up the Harder Kulm, go to the Ibex Preserve, and take the circle trip to the Jungfraujoch (Lauterbrunnen and Kleine Scheidegg, returning via Grindelwald)—marvelous! As one gateway to the hauntingly beautiful Bernese Oberland, pause only briefly here while reserving most of your time for the majesty of the hills. The drive from Berne to Grindelwald and Lucerne via Interlaken threads along the shores of 5 lakes and through innumerable Alpine vistas. Major efforts, such as the addition of a community swimming pool, the teeing up of a golf course, and the inauguration of open-air plays in summer, are being made. While groups, of course, still pour in during high season, many individual travelers are returning to the revitalized town.

HOTELS

☆☆☆☆☆ **Victoria-Jungfrau** • is sparkling with vigor under the expert guidance of Emanuel Berger, its personable managing director. Nothing was spared in refashioning this *grande dame* in sumptuous raiments. It boasts 7 tennis courts (4 indoor), an enclosed pool, beautiful fireside lounges in rustic tones, sophisticated terrace dining, a cozy Swiss grill, a disco-bar and nightclub;

bedrooms are spacious, gracious, and lovely. A bevy of fresh new duplex suites are among the smartest in Switzerland and the penthouse apartment with its own cupola and open terrace is the stuff of mountain dreams, with big-city comfort and sophistication for both winter and summer enjoyment.

Beau-Rivage • near the Interlaken-Ost station, is a period piece that has been resurrected while retaining its Old World aesthetic values. It can do the same to you with its gym, sauna, massage, and solarium. Savory a la carte temptations and excellent dining-room service; the Ambiance beside the Aare River is lovely for easygoing mealtimes. Attractive pool and snack terrace. Nicely reclaimed from the Belle Epoque.

★★★★ **Hirschen** • is what you've always dreamed about as a Swiss chalet—with overhanging farmhouse eaves, wooden balconies, tumbling flowers, open beams, and unpretentious solid comfort at very reasonable prices. Add to that the delicious regional cookery by its owner-chef and the hospitality of the Graf-Sterch family (Peter and Marian) and you have all the ingredients of a wonderful holiday in the Alps. A charmer.

Metropole • is a modern, lofty, glass and concrete edifice almost next to the V-J but totally different in tone and concept. Beautiful vistas from the upper floors; superb cuisine in its several dining segments; careful management by Charles Zimmermann. Superior value if you prefer the 21st century to the 19th.

Krebs • has a variety of rooms, and a friendly welcome; while the mood is antique and traditional, the comforts are very modern; the chef wears his cap proudly with good reason. Management by the respected Koschak-Krebs family.

Beau-Site • operated by the warmhearted Ritter family, is a fine, well-located, medium-price choice in the traditional context. Excellent comfort and space; a fine reputation for good cuisine at reasonable prices; ideal for children, too.

KLOSTERS

☆☆☆☆ **Vereina** • is operated by Eva and Stephan Diethelm who fret personally over the needs of every client. Baronial atmosphere in public rooms and lounges; Le Duc French dining salon; Pizzeria; Scotch Bar in tartan, with a piano tinkling during the busy hours; ski school at the back doorstep; cross-country tracks nearby; ice rink. Fresh superior-grade twins and suites; many have their own balcony (the views overlooking the slopes are superb); #'s 23-, 24-, and 25-type units extra-spacious, a perfect combo for a couple with a small child. Sauna; massage; game room; kindergarten; swimming pool. All-in-all, a happy feeling pervades this wholesome family retreat.

☆☆☆ **Piz Buin** • in the heart of the town but near the cableway and rail station, is loaded with blue-ribbon amenities. Three restaurants (Swiss and Italian cuisine); the Funny Place for dancing; fitness center with swimming and whirlpool; sauna and massage; cosmetic treatments. Smooth management by Richard Rotheli. Most agreeable.

☆☆☆ **Pardenn** • indisputably steals the local thunder for modernistic good looks. Long, balconied, 5-story building bordered by lawns; open grill but hardly distinguished; glass-bound heated swimming pool; sauna plus beauty and health facilities; bar-lounge; sumptuous suites; spacious twin units with seating alcoves. Excellent for physical assets—and definitely among the frontrunners.

★★★ **Chesa Grischuna** • another highland jewel, exudes a rustic-style ambience. Total of 30 accommodations in knotty-pine *arvenholz* style (10 with bath and 3 with shower), including a 14-room annex with larger bedchambers—and that's all! But if you'll search the premises, you'll also uncover a restaurant, subterranean bowling lanes, a sportsman's bar, music, and barrels of animation. Here indeed is a pint-size prodigy.

★ **Walserhof** • is a Grissons-style offering with ample comfort and plenty of heart. Also in this category and very recommendable for comfort, alpine-type accouterments, and flair are the **Albeina** and **Steinbock;** both superbly managed. The former even has been suggested by local friends as a worthy alternative to the Vereina.

LAUSANNE, quieter and smaller than neighboring Geneva, is another popular center for holidays in French Switzerland. It is sheltered on the south slopes of hills that gradually fall away to Lake Leman. The climate is unusually beguiling, with a record of 1912 hours of sunshine per year. Its university and schools are world-famous. It offers good sports, entertainment, and food, along with the world's shortest subway, the peculiar Musee de l'Art Brut, museums on pipes, iconographics, and the Olympics, a generally well-ordered aura, and the homes of many international celebrities.

☆☆☆☆☆ **Beau-Rivage Palace** • *in the Ouchy district 5 minutes from the center* • is where you'll discover a plenitude of treasure—from a swimming pool (heated and in the shape of a grand piano; in winter it is wrapped in sliding glass walls) to a health club to saunas to a huge oval lakeside terrace that converts into a winter garden to some suites that are the last *mot* in luxury. Exquisite Cafe beneath the arcades with a la carte specialties, informality, and musical entertainment; La Rotonde gourmet restaurant; wine bar, disco club with all-night snacks and frolic. Lovely gardens; tennis courts; 80-car garage. One of the crown jewels of Switzerland.

☆☆☆☆☆ **Lausanne Palace** • born an aristocrat many decades ago, continues to reveal its *pur sang* breeding. All accommodations in the Palace Building have been refurbished; the grill is one of the 2 most fashionable hotel restaurants in the city; there's an attractive bar off lobby with pianist. The Brummell nightclub is operated by an independent company. The connecting Beau Site Building adds 50 rooms to the overall total plus shops by Gucci, Ferragamo, Saint Laurent, and Gerard, plus a sleeky modern barber and beauty salon, plus a sauna and massage parlor, plus a garden court, plus, plus, . . .

plus! Many accommodations feature shadowless reading lamps, pillow-side command consoles for adjusting everything in the room except your bedfellow (wanna try?), electric blinds, infrared bathroom heating and piped music as you bathe, Frigobars, thermal taps, and—wow!—I'm breathless. You might be, too, when you see this palatial Palace.

☆☆☆ **Royal Savoy** • reveals a modern entrance to this old-fashioned establishment; well-respected restaurant overlooking garden; bar; 2 conference quadrants; swimming pool plus skating rink and tennis courts 200 yards away. The staffers are especially warm and kind here.

☆☆ **Mirabeau** • is clean and comfortable; central location and traditional in tone with certain modern touches that could be viewed as advantageous or distracting. Ask for a waterside room on the 4th floor; these are the quietest and most viewful. The garden is splendid in summer.

☆ **Hotel de la Navigation** • 15 of its 39 bedrooms face the lake, the pleasure-boat harbor, and the distant mountains. Attractive grill and cafe; mustard-color velvet wall in its small lobby; carpeted corridors with doors of wood planking; double-glaze windows. The flexibility of having 3 beds in some rooms makes it an excellent choice for traveling families.

★ **Aulac** • also in Ouchy, conjures up a delightfully nautical theme in Le Pirate, an amusing restaurant that resembles an old sailing ship; waiters are dressed in black trousers, white shirts, red cummerbunds, and ascots. All-in-all a comfortable and whimsical package.

☆ **La Residence** • adjoins the estate of the luxurious Beau Rivage, its richer kith and certainly one of the best buys in suburban living. There is also an excellent restaurant in its spacious lakeside garden for summer dining; bar removed from the lobby and more cozy now; outdoor pool. A reasonably priced and intimate sylvan domain.

☆ **Carlton** • recently refashioned, is maintaining its vigorous elan. The Grill remains one of the better gustatory bets in the city; fresh and lively bar; some excellent suites if you are looking for space.

Victoria • greets incomers with a lovely Lurcat tapestry behind the reception desk. Attractive Le Paddock nightclub; snack bar; 65 units with bath.

De la Paix • is conveniently located in midcity; the upper floors offer a magnificent command of the lake. The restaurant and bar are added pluses.

Continental • hard by the station, chugs in with space for 180 overnighters. Within its slick core are Le Beaujolais Restaurant for French cuisine and grills, snack center, nightclub, and the Natacha bar with dinner and music. Front units air-conditioned; 5th-floor attic rooms spun up as demisuites; decor highlighted with paneling or stonework in soft brown, yellow, or orange tones.

Convenient, comfortable, and functional; better for Hiltonites than for Old Worlders.

City • is plain, stark, and distressingly plastic-ridden. Bare lobby; narrow but fresh-looking corridors; bright accommodations, some with bath or shower.

Alpha • is a clean, 240-bed house. Glazed-concrete lobby; cellar-situated Carnotzet for raclette, fondue, and other Alpine specialties; ground-level Caleche restaurant for more conventional dining; extensive bedroom revampings with wide windows, colorful linens, radios (which I like) and nonclosing closets, low beds, and eensie baths (which I don't like).

Agora • is in an excellent state; space for more than 200 guests, conveniently sited about 300 yards from the main station.

Bellerive • a converted apartment house, offers a micro-lobby, a black-red-blue-yellow-brown-white miniature bar, and tiny, cramped, functional, sterile bedchambers; not the nest for tall, rangy, or long-shanked travelers.

Novotel • boasts a grill and a swimming pool and this chain's usual clean efficient, low-cost accommodation. Also on the outskirts are the **Raisin** and the very appealing and rather costly **Debarcadere.**

Chateau d'Ouchy • is a bulky antique whose site dates back to the 12th century. Today all bedchambers come with shower and private bath; some suites only slightly smaller than Burning Tree Golf Course. Tourist-oriented, but different.

Restaurants

☆☆☆☆ **La Rotonde** • is the gastronomic creation at the **Beau-Rivage Palace;** it boasts a mighty reputation. The **Cafe,** in a neoclassic mood, faces the lake and is further cheered by greenery; many will like the "neoclassic" cooking too—clearly more classic than neo.

☆☆☆ **Lausanne Palace** • grill is also good, but the mood is cooler. A favorite of the local establishment.

☆☆ **Rotisserie de la Grappe d'Or** • maintains a dubious lead among the independent restaurants. Enormous open grill; beamed ceilings, and sophisticated rustic ambience. *Entre nous* atmosphere; well-schooled, attentive staff; many of the choicest selections limited to 2-person portions; priced for guests with big, fat, unnumbered accounts in those big, fat Swiss banks.

☆☆☆☆ **Hotel de Ville** • also known as **Girardet** for its chef-owner, in the tiny hamlet of *Crissier,* remains one of the most talked about shrines on the continent—certainly a recommendation, but so much in demand that you must book long in advance. It is worth it, however, if you've got $250 to spend on a monumental twin meal with a decent wine. You may choose from a set repast

or a la carte, but either way you will be transported to gastronomy's heaven—
and either way your bill will total nearly the same amount. Modern main room
with brown textile panels, autumnal paintings, soft lighting, beige-cloaked tables with fresh flowers, service on vast floral-etched platters; smaller inner room
that is also attractive but feels like left field. Closed Sun. and Mon. (Incidentally, Americans have been so casual about booking and not showing up that
you might be asked for a deposit to secure your seating.)

Voile d'Or ("Golden Sail") • offers a reed-lined lakeshore situation;
pleasant split-level lounge, bar, and restaurant in stonework and Douglas fir,
with icicle-thin ceiling fixtures in serpentine pattern; rope carpets, and scatter
rugs; orange-and-white-fringed umbrellas dotting the snack terrace.

The chef at the **Royal Savoy** is earning his numerous orchids. Le Beaujolais in the **Continental Hotel** turns on a reasonable meal for the outlay. La
Caleche, ground floor in the **Alpha Hotel,** is fun for rusticity in the city. Steaks
of all dimensions and cuts; cafeteria-style service; downstairs Carnotzet for cheese-
whizzing. Fair returns for the outlay; very popular. Down the line comes the
more modest **Pomme de Pin** • *Cite Derriere 15* • with its renowned chicken
specialties, also good, but far from cheap. **Cafe du Jorat** • *place de l'Ours 1*
• is famed for fabulous fondue-fondling. **Mandarin** • *avenue du Theatre 7* •
wins our fortune cookie for Chinese delights. **Kwong Ming** • *av. de Cour 74* •
is a worthy alternate. **La Cravache** • *a pub next to the Palace Hotel* • is simple
and cozy for a nip 'n sip.

☆☆☆☆ **Auberge du Chasseur** • *Preverenges near* **Morges,** *on the road
to St. Sulpice* • certainly qualifies as one of the unsung gastronomic shrines of
Switzerland. The owner trained at the previously mentioned Girardet establishment in Crissier, so many of the creations reflect the immaculate standards of
the famous Hotel de Ville. I was particularly taken by the oysters baked in a
light pastry and garnished with thinly shaved vegetables; the fresh duck liver,
the escalope de saumon in the chef's sauce, and the carre d'agneau were also
evoked by the divinities. The dessert trolley is so colorful that it would make
any self-respecting rainbow blush with shame.

★★★★ **Restaurant du Cerf** at *Cossonay* • *20 minutes west of Lausanne*
• is more attractive to the eye, residing in a single room with arches of stone
and a heavy timbered ceiling; a candelabrum provides soft luminescence while
candles and roses decorate the 10 glittering tables. On a recent sampling, again,
every morsel was bliss.

Le Debarcadere at *St. Sulpice* • is known as a hotel, but the restaurant
also deserves attention. The display of finesse is rewarding. Lakeside and lovely.

Hotel de Ville d'Echallens is said to be one of the top dining stops on the
outskirts of Lausanne. Personally, I haven't had a chance to try it.

After dark, Lausanne offers nightowls the lavish **Beau Rivage Palace's**
clubland, while the Continental features **La Griffe.** The **Chateau d'Ouchy** of-

fers darkling revels indoors only. **La Tomate, Le Placid,** and **Voile d'Or** are popular discotheques

LENZERHEIDE-VALBELLA   Here are 2 toy villages snuggling together in a mile-high Grisons' valley. There are almost 100 miles of ski runs obtainable via 38 ski lifts and cableways; in summer it is a leaf-green dimension of paradise with a multitude of activities for sporty types. Its 2700 beds are divided among 6 top-grade hotels, 9 of medium class, and 11 that offer only bed and breakfast. The picks locally? (1) **Kurhaus,** (2) **Schweizerhof.** The newer **Post-Hotel** (Valbella) provides ultracozy rustic appointments; handsome Grill, lounges, and terraces; indoor glass-wrapped swimming pool; all units with bath or shower; southside ones with private balcony. You'll also want to know about the nearby **Guarda Val,** which some consider to be Switzerland's most unusual country inn. It's a first-class hotel by official standards, uniquely composed of 7 renovated farmhouses, each room individually decorated. The **Valbella Inn,** the **La Riva,** and **Sunstar** all win praise from ski buffs, too. Each has a swimming pool.

LOCARNO,   the lowest city in Switzerland (with only a 600-foot elevation), is an ideal stop for the traveler to or from Italy. It has a lovely setting on the shores of Lake Maggiore; the Ticinese here are among the most warm-hearted and hospitable people in Europe. Reasonably good accommodations and fine restaurants; several swimming pools down by the Lido plus one covered; plenty of good shops; International Film Festival in August; theater, casino and night club at the Kursaal; friendly atmosphere.

★★★ **Esplanade** • offers a lovely lake view, open-air dining, dancing, a heated pool, tennis court, airy lobby, and a rekindled spirit that has it glowing radiantly. Here is a bucolic country address to keep in mind, especially if you are on a lazy trip by car to or from Italy.

★ **Reber** • *along the promenade where the Palma au Lac also resides* • is liked for its location. Swimming pool; tennis courts; nightclub next to the grill; 3rd and 4th floors featuring private refrigerators, safes, and furnishings that are a cross between classic and avant-garde; balconies jutting from each waterside .unit; corridors sheathed in mock-wood.

Pavilion Reber • *adjoining the Reber* • offers 14 rooms and 14 baths—a pleasant outbuilding with motel privacy but hotel-room service. Better every year.

★★ **Orselina** • *at the top of the funicular winking down at the slope, the town, and Maggiore* • is a honey. Recently renovated; kips for 150 relaxers who can probably be heard zzzzz-ing on any quiet afternoon.

☆ **Muralto** • *close to the station* • overlooks the lake from midcity. Within its shell is a snack center, a terrace restaurant, a heated pool, a metropolitan post office, a newsstand, 2 levels of shops, and an arcade. The decor is a blend of 20th-century and earlier themes that, paradoxically, meld well. Spankingly clean and eye-stimulating; bar and refrigerator in lake-front units; good baths with twin basins; huge towels; service primarily for do-it-yourselfers.

Remorino • with a swimming pool, provides space for 44 sleepers; full bath ratio; breakfast only.

☆ **Beau Rivage** • was refashioned a while back and is functional.

Excelsior • *next to the Tennis Club* • serves up 25 rooms with bath or shower, clean, unadorned simplicity and budget tariffs; sun worshipers will revel in its roof-garden solarium.

Zucherhof • *on the lake promenade* • is similar; all rooms with bath or shower.

LUCERNE

Its traditional star attractions are the Lion Monument, the year-round Glacier Gardens with its museum, the covered bridge, the famous August–September International Music Festival, plus the Easter concerts. Its 2 pet mountains are supplemented by a scenic 18-hole golf course, a fascinating Transport Museum (historic and/or modern locomotives, cars, airplanes, plus a steamer; a star-bright planetarium has twinkled on the scene and there's a restaurant) and a suspension cable-car system to the top of Mt. Pilatus. In town, the Kursaal-Casino spins for penny-ante gamesters (boule only), dancers, and diners. The Casino Chalet stirs in a dash of local flavor with fondue, local color with flag-throwers, and local sounds with yodelers. As in Florence, tourism makes 99% of its wheels go around; into this center of 60,000 inhabitants, from 10 to 30 thousand foreigners pour *daily* off the boats, trains, and cars; there are now at least 55 hotels with 5300 beds. If you're a first-tripper, naturally you won't want to miss the landmark. But hit it in the spring or fall, if you can—because in peak season it's so jammed with sightseers that its atmosphere, normally so alluring, becomes tinny, mechanical, and production-belt in feeling.

HOTELS

☆☆☆☆☆ **Grand National** • ranks among the key stopping places of the nation for appointments, luxury, and attention to the guest. For ultra-pampering

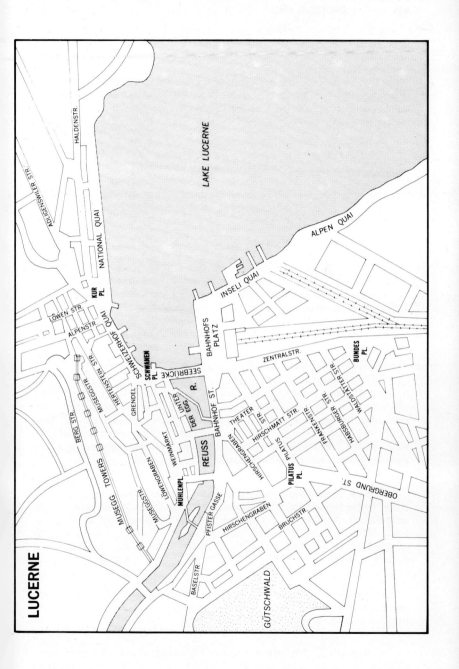

LUCERNE

LAKE LUCERNE

HALDENSTR.
ADLIGENSWILER STR.
NATIONAL QUAI
KUR PL.
LÖWEN STR.
ALPENSTR.
SCHWEIZERHOF QUAI
HERTENSTEIN STR.
GRENDEL
SCHWANEN PL.
SEEBRÜCKE
ALPEN QUAI
INSELI QUAI
BAHNHOFS PLATZ
ZENTRALSTR.
BUNDES PL.
BERG STR.
MUSEGGSTR.
MUSEGG TOWERS
MUSEGGSTR.
LÖWENGRABEN
WEINMARKT
MÜHLENPL.
UNTER DER EGG
R.
REUSS
BAHNHOF ST.
THEATER
HIRSCHMATT STR.
STR.
FRANKENSTR.
FRANKENSTR.
HABSBURGER STR.
WALDSTÄTTER STR.
PILATUS STR.
PILATUS PL.
HIRSCHENGRABEN
OBERGRUND ST.
PFISTER GASSE
HIRSCHENGRABEN
BRUCHSTR.
BASELSTR.
GÜTSCHWALD

there are 6 penthouses; a *Residence* created with 30 lakefront apartments for longer stays; there's a beautiful wood-roofed indoor swimming pool with sauna, solarium, and terrace, barber and beauty salon, travel agency, and boutiques. There are also the Promenade (a quayside tea room; you can rent lakeboats right at the doorstep); Von Pfyffer French restaurant with hearthside dining and lovely Belle Epoch atmosphere; the Viennese Cafe, and piano bar. All in all a bewitching combination.

☆☆☆☆ **Palace** ● is for young-in-heart wayfarers who might enjoy it just as much as the neighboring Grand National. Mignon for the light graces of cuisine; engaging bar; nearly every bedchamber and bath spiffed up, most of them boasting fabric wall coverings underlined with foam-rubber matting for silent nights; raw-silk curtains usually mated to upholstered headboards. A modern-style wing plus a pool, solarium, massage parlor, steam room, and a sauna. Also open year-round.

☆☆☆☆ **Schweizerhof** ● claims an excellent lakefront location. Since funding and clever management combined to restore and preserve the attractive elegance of this period piece, here is a marvelous cache of Old World charm. Certainly dining in the Rotonde can be one of the high points of any visit to Lucerne. There's a dated grace to living here. In the younger wing, every accommodation is air-conditioned, double doors are installed, and all appurtenances have been reupholstered or replaced. The older wing is now comely in the fashion of the turn-of-the-century. A winning blend.

★★ **Carlton-Tivoli** ● offers a roof-garden restaurant with lakeside dining in addition; Grill and expanded terrace; 3 luxury suites, 120 rooms, and a full bath count; high incidence of refurnishings and updatings including the addition of TV and refrigerators for many units. Private bathing and water skiing; 4 tennis courts; dancing in 1 of its 2 popular bars. Now youthfully zesty; a very good bet at the price. Closed in winter.

★★★★ **Wilden Mann** ● in the Romantik Group, is one of the nicer family hotels in the region, run by kindhearted Fritz and Mady Furler, who are top professionals. Antique style; decor joining 7 tiny old houses into one; new entrance hall and fresh facade; refashioned restaurant (and very good too); new suites added; well-outfitted rooms. A house that dates back to 1517 and is as modern as tomorrow.

☆ **Astoria** ● *on the main Pilatusstrasse thoroughfare* ● has a fine location and a splendid view. At night the traffic noises diminish, but still can be an irritation to light sleepers. Now well maintained.

☆ **Monopol & Metropole** ● *in midcity* ● is substantial and worth every franc. Good medium-price dining room called Albalete; busy bar; 5th-floor units never given to groups; #314 especially pleasant twin in Tirolean theme. Solid value.

★ **Montana** • *250 feet above the Palace* • is reached by funicular or road. Glass-and-aluminum entrance; 75 rooms and 45 baths; most units with balcony; 80% of them face the lake; I'm fond of #114; closed in winter. Fair.

☆ **Luzernerhof** • has cozy rooms and picture windows with Venetian blinds; improved lobby, reception, and fancy French-style bar; 12-room annex; good dining salon consistently serving up some of the most rewarding cuisine in the region; all accommodations clean and bright. Two floors restyled but prices are just as reasonable as always.

Royal • looks adequate for its category (I've never stayed there); closed Nov. to Easter.

Hermitage • *5 minutes out at Seeburg* • has been rebuilt in an attractive way. Road noise can be a problem.

Balances & Bellevue • one of the antiques of the city, was given a facelift that brings it almost up to the 21st century, give or take a dozen years. It retains the distinctive painted facade commanding the Weinmarkt (Wine Market Square) and the River Reuss, on the more tranquil postern side; decor light and airy with extensive use of marble; scenic La Vague riverside restaurant; attractive Zur Ratslaube dining room with abundant artwork, red curtains, and chain-held chandeliers; enchanting vine-lined terrace that will level you, eyeball-to-eyeball, with inquisitive swans. When Zur Ratslaube overflows its capacity, clients may take their meals in the mural-clad Rotes Gatter, in which hangs a portrait of this very room painted 8 centuries ago.

★★★ **Gutsch** • is also in a singular bracket. This interesting castlelike structure is located 5 minutes above the city, with an enchanting vista of the lake and the huddle of pitched roofs below. Authentic iron battle masks flanking the entrance, plus such decorative carry-overs inside as lances, suits of armor, and mounted deer heads; swimming pool in the forest garden; open patio with terrace nibbling in summer; elaborate dining salon. Its 45 rooms include 4 extra-charming duplex apartments in split-level arrangement for intimate hideaways, some units with four-poster beds, open ceiling beams, soft carpeting, and the atmosphere of a medieval fortress.

RESTAURANTS

★★★★ **Old Swiss House** • remains the first choice for a refined and colorful repast. Its decor and ambience are still Overdone Swiss, with too much aimed toward the tourist trade (waitresses in costume, antique crucifixes, and the like)—but here is such a tight ship that the cuisine is excellent, the service kind, and the welcome warm. The price scale is substantial by national standards.

★★★★ **Zum Raben** • *in the Kornmarkt of the colorful Old Town* • is on a terrace above the river, one of the most attractive sites in Switzerland. I like the air of authentic antiquity here and the honest kitchen. Try the Lucerne specialty: chugelipastete, sliced veal and meatballs with cream sauce in a pastry shell; or try chicken with morels—superb; the sorbets and fruit desserts are luscious. Chef-hostess-author Marianne Kaltenbach is masterful.

★★★ **Wilden Mann** • dates back to the 16th century with 6 salons in a complex of 7 contiguous houses. Regional cuisine; careful service; very enjoyable.

☆☆ **Le Manoir** • is highly sophisticated in the nouvelle style, totally different from any of the above. The gastronomy, of course, is international rather than local.

☆☆☆ **Rotonde** • *in the Schweizerhof* • is reckoned in the top category of Swiss hotel dining rooms.

★★★★ **Von Pfyffer** • *in the Grand National* • is in the same category as Rotonde but it's cozier.

☆☆ **Luzernerhof** • for delicious, unfancy wares, this chef and brigade can fill my bill any morning, noon, or night with their honest creations. Here vegetables taste like vegetables; food tastes like food; there's no trickery. The service is so sweet that the waitresses urge you to finish the huge portions; the dining room is attractive; the prices are very reasonable. What traveler could ask for more? Highly recommended.

☆ **Schwanen** • is a fixture in town and a good one.

★ **Stadtkeller** • pipes out Swiss music, Swiss food, Swiss alpenhorn tooting from special stage—almost more Swiss than the Swiss, to please its big foreign trade. This city lives for the tourist in season and here is one of its magnets.

☆ **Hotel de la Paix** • is where the Lapin Restaurant hops. Split-level dining room in sleek rustic-modern; waitresses in provincial costumes; moving-color-slide gizmo for selecting your dishes; some counter service; choice of 7 types of sausage, the house specialty; my Bratwurst and Rosti were delicious.

☆☆☆ **Li Tai Pe Chinese Restaurant** • *Furrengasse 14* • has been converted into a Jade Pavilion of the Orient. Breathtaking collection of rare Cathay artworks; 5 Far Eastern cooks mind the Soo-Gaw pots; savory cuisine and lovely presentation, but expensive even by Swiss measures. If you're a party of 4, be sure to order the Peking specialty variously called Chrysanthemum Pot or Chue Hua Kuo or Steamboat; this cauldron of Oriental treasures is, as far as I know, unequalled in Europe. It must be ordered 1 day ahead.

Galliker's is redolent of an English pub atmosphere. Hardy fare for these hardy Alpine rancheros; Pot au Feu seems to be the favorite choice. For light but full meals, **Cafe Arcade** is just the ticket; inside tables, plus a ringlet of alfresco *couverts* bordering the waterside and the Open Market; excellent pastries. Colorful as a ham-and-eggery. **Da Peppino** works up Italian specialties. *Buono!* Calories afloat? Try the good ship **William Tell,** moored in front of the American Express office. It carries a cargo of tea, snacks, and full repasts. *Bon voyage!*

SHOPPING

SHOPPING HOURS: see "Geneva."

BEST AREAS: Here's a good walking tour that will give you an opportunity to see this colorful city and go on a buying spree at the same time. Start strolling up the Schweizerhofquai to the Schwanenplatz, follow Grendel and Weggisgasse around to Weinmarkt, then Kornmarkt and come down Kappelgasse. Cross either Chapel Bridge (the world-famous covered bridge of a jillion photos) or the Seebrucke and head for the station. Wander up Pilatusstrasse to Pilatusplatz, turn right and follow Hirschengraben until you reach Kasernenplatz and the Mill Bridge. Cross this delightful span and continue along Lowengraben and Grabenstrasse until you come back out along Grendel.

CAMERAS AND OPTICS: **Ecker** (Pilatusstrasse 5) is one of the most complete shops in Europe. It stocks the tops in still cameras and lenses, plus all the other tack. When you see the town and the Swiss Alps you will probably want a video camera, too. There are alp-size savings in the purchase-tax refunds. P.S.: On the same street at #14, Ecker can develop your color photos in only 2 hours. They'll be done while you are having lunch!

EMBROIDERY: **Langenthal** (Weinmarkt 19) is the leader in this important hub as well as in the nation generally. While the work is superb, the prices are reasonable.

JEWELRY AND WATCHES: Now for watches in this center-of-centers. **Bader,** with two fine stores, is especially strong on intimacy, care, and showing their pieces in a time-honored fashion. Indeed, time is honored very well at the 16th-century **Bader-Huus,** which faces the exquisite Town Hall across the historic Kornmarkt. Apart from timepieces of fame, Peter Bader is probably the world's foremost elaborator of platinum (at this address). The second establishment on Pilatusstrasse (near the station) adds further to the watch collection and to contemporary expressions in gold and silver; these are spread through a wonderfully unconventional display area that invites casual browsing. Ask for Peter Bader at the first address or Daniel Rey at the second.

SOUVENIRS: **Casagrande** (Kapellgasse 24, branches at Hertenstein-strasse 35 and Schwanenplatz 6) is the place to find anything and everything in the souvenir line—and at a quality that can't be matched anywhere. If you want carved nativity scenes, lovely embroidery including fascinating lace pictures, delicious Lindt chocolates, Hummel figurines, cuckoo clocks (that work, for a change), music boxes, Noblesse Crystal, Lladro porcelain, beer steins or Casy Boys—typical Swiss models made at Casagrande's own factory here—this is a trove for gift items or curiosities. Ask for Mrs. Casagrande, brothers Robert or John, Eiko or Veronika. They ship all over the world and are totally dedicated to helping you. PS: If you show any of them this book, you'll receive a gift from the house.

LUGANO is on the lakeside in the mild southern flank of the nation, back-stopped by the mountains and bristling with temperate and even subtropical vegetation. It has been taking giant strides recently to improve its hospitality facilities. The bustling modern Congress Center herds conventioneers from all over the world. One of its biggest drawing cards is the gambling casino at Campione d'Italia ("Sample of Italy"), almost directly across the lake by frequent ferry service—an isolated chunk of Italian territory, 1.8 square miles in area; apart from the gaming, it's pretty dull. Shopping in Lugano has a decid-edly Italian fashion tilt. The steamer excursion to Gandria is mobbed in summer. About 120 hotels or pensions, almost all of them on the jump; funiculars, chair lifts, and cable cars galore. One thing that shouldn't be missed is the fabulous Thyssen collection of Goya, El Greco, Holbein, Dutch masters, and Italian Renaissance artists that is housed in a private museum adjoining this family's Villa Favorita; it is open to the public from early March until late October (Tues.–Sun. from 10 a.m. to 5 p.m.). If there's time, you might also enjoy the Cantonal Art Museum in the town center or the Museum of Non-European Culture at Villa Heleneum.

Near Lugano at Melide (lake bridge on main highway from Italy), a unique exhibition called Swissminiatur has already wooed more than a million specta-tors. Towns, hamlets, castles, mountains, automatic railways, remote-control steamers, and other real-life things are reproduced in exact dimensions and de-tail, on a scale of 1 to 25. Surely worth a stop if you're staying in Lugano or driving the southern route—or if you're an elf.

★★★★ **Eden** • *at lakeside, in town* • is vivaciously colorful and modern-istic. Sunbursts, arcs, bangles, painted rainbows, dyed leather, cheery textiles, sprightly plastics, and other gladsome inspirations of fanciful artistry give this house a decorative character unmatched anywhere in contemporary Europe. To-tally upbeat lobby, lounge, and public rooms; relatively sedate grill and mod-ernistic bar; adjoining waterside terrace for dining, sipping, or dancing; heated pool plus another one filled with salt *(sic)* water—in landlocked Switzerland. Bedchambers also flairfully attired, with balcony, radio consoles, TV, and re-frigerator; predominating schemes of olive, blue, or red; open year-round.

☆☆☆☆ **Splendide-Royal** • *in the city* • (deluxe class) boasts a classic re-sort mien, with all the traditional appurtenances of pillars, marble, Persian car-pets, and crystal chandeliers; handsome entrance and excellent recent wing with several dozen modernistic rooms; fine enclosed pool; location on the main boulevard facing lake (a traffic pattern shared by all other major hostelries except the Arizona); waterfront bar; excellent cuisine. Open all year.

☆☆ **Europa** ● features a broad patio with bubbling fountain and awning arcade; heated covered pool with hanging garden and bar; parking for 50 cars; street-level shops and Cafe Boulevard where snack-meals appear. Sleeping accommodations are pleasant; front corner doubles are best.

☆☆ **Bellevue au Lac** ● offers the following: a fresh lobby; tasteful dining salon plus open-air grill; bar; most rooms in modern tone; color TV on request (but you'll probably prefer the lake view from the balconies; Swiss television is so exciting that it schedules high-school trigonometry lessons at prime-time); extra-efficient kitchen. Closed during the winter.

☆☆ **Olivella Au Lac** ● *in the shoreside village of **Morcote*** ● melds clean-lined luxury with rural tranquillity. Viewful French restaurant; tavern-style snackery; glass-fronted indoor swimmery plus garden-sited pool; massage and beauty parlors; nursery. The bedchambers are smart and freshly decorated. Very worthy as a hideaway, if you don't mind the distance from the center.

☆ **Du Lac** ● *hard by the water* ● is a fine choice in the First-class category. Swimming pool in attractive setting; managed smoothly. Very pleasant.

☆ **Arizona** ● *high on a hill overlooking the town and the water* ● is a friendly and comfortable oasis for the weary motorist. Casual mood; all rooms with bath or shower, balcony, and angular walls in irregular directions. Offbeat but surprisingly pleasing.

Motel Vezia ● *10 minutes along the St. Gothard highway* ● is a steadily improving possibility for the roadbound. Adjoining restaurant; heated pool—red-hot sauna, too; low rates; 120 beds; most units with bath or shower.

Excelsior ● *on the lake promenade* ● is a first-class offering; 150 beds; grill room. It has an active conference trade.

Schmid ● *midvillage in **Paradiso** (foot of the San Salvatore funicular)* ● a white-balconied old-fashioned house is clean, quiet, and comfortable; rates are low for its full-pension rewards.

☆☆ **Admiral** ● sails in as an imposing member of the local flotilla. Handsome dining, sipping, and snacking areas; indoor and outdoor pools; good and fresh comfort standards. Very trim indeed.

☆☆ **Pullman Commodore** ● offers a fine situation and many up-to-date riggings to recommend it.

☆☆ **De la Paix** • in *Lugano Paradiso,* provides a heated open-air pool around which meals are sometimes served if the weatherman is kind. The last two hotels are very nice for their category.

☆☆ **Villa Castagnola** • in outlying *Cassarate* is warmly recommended following its extensive renovation; attractive swimming pool; numerous baronial touches. The flower-girt, costly ★★★ **Villa Principe Leopoldo,** in *Montalbano,* resides within its own Hohenzollern principality of a parkland. It's certainly a realm of opulence, with two dozen small suites, a heated pool, and tennis facilities. Behind it is the less luxurious **Montalbano,** both being superb choices and under the same management; the latter has no restaurant.

Al Portone rumbles all the thunder locally for gastronomy. **Huguenin,** on the lake promenade, is a splendid Old World independent restaurant. The city's best kitchen used to be the **Hotel Splendide-Royal,** but it has been colorfully upstaged by the flairful **Eden** in its Oasis Grill. Full meals or snacks are available at the latter. The **Capo San Martino** is on a promontory that is medium-high over the water; vast terrace service; clean; cheaper and quieter; very popular for lunching and gazing.

Within the city, **Bianchi** remains a winner for gastronomy. It is old-fashioned and solid, with gold-silk walls, high ceilings, a fireplace, and no-nonsense fare. **Galleria,** in an arcade off via Vegezzi, comes up with good vittles at fair prices.

MERLIGEN **Beatus** is on Lake Thun midway between Thun and Interlaken; modern in concept; indoor pool; 140 rooms with baths and balconies; private beach; this one's an absolute peach; definitely worth a detour to pause here—or even to dine here.

MONT-PELERIN is hiiiiiigh above Lake Geneva on such a lovely morsel of cloud that you may never come down once you've gone up. The reason for going up is **Le Mirador,** where everything from your liver to your toenails can be pampered. Health and beauty and relaxation are the tripartite themes. Add to that gastronomy, scenery that tingles and finally numbs, willing service by a multitude of minions, and prices that also nip at the troposphere and you probably get the picture. To find all this, travel first to **Vevey** and then point your vehicle toward the Welkin—roughly 2500 feet above sea level.

MONTREUX is forward-looking and lively, nowadays luring the big-fish traveler. The modern, enlarged conference and exhibition center hosts congresses in winter, fall, and early spring. The Casino includes a stunning array of restaurants, night spots, a movie house, and a recording studio. You should also take in the dramatically medieval Castle of Chillon, the lakeside promenades and roads, the heated pool, tennis, golf, the International Television Symposium (biannually), the Jazz Festival (July), and the Classical Music Festival (late Aug. to early Oct.). The Great St. Bernard Tunnel (coupling Germany's autobahn and Italy's Autostrada) is nearby, so in high season there's a certain funnel effect; at other times the town snoozes peacefully.

HOTELS

☆☆☆☆ **Palace** • a study in Art Nouveau that first came on the scene in 1906 has a born-again comportment after several years of renewal. This deluxe dowager certainly is worth the francs in value. Bright entry and lobby; informal dining salon; *Salle de spectacles;* Harry's N.Y. Bar; noteworthy kitchen; virtually all of its 270 rooms totally freshened, with the best facing the lake and with balcony; tennis; lovely pool with Bather's Bar and cabanas. Commendable on every score.

★★★ **Grand Hotel Suisse et Majestic** • maintains traditions of the turn-of-the-century; lovely period furnishings; space concepts that are indeed Grand and Majestic; gracious dining salon; best of all is that wondrous lake view from the terraces and balconies.

☆☆ **Hyatt Continental** • *lakeside* • is the next-door neighbor to the Convention Center. The American Hyatt group has a management arrangement with the 7-story establishment on the shore of Lake Geneva. More than half of its 160 units face the water; the remainder peek at the mountains; there's an indoor pool and health club, a French restaurant, a coffee shop, and a private terrace.

☆☆ **Eden au Lac** • *by the waterfront promenade* • is a Victorian dowager of excellent grooming; the small restaurant at terrace level is justly proud of its fish specialties; the lobby and another dining spread are one flight up.

☆ **Villa Toscane** • is a superb choice for a small, intimate hostelry in the Art Nouveau mood. Breakfast only, but some units with kitchenette.

☆ **Eurotel** • makes a vigorous splash with an indoor-outdoor pool plus sauna and massage facilities; 2 handsome dining areas; many units with kitchenette; rooms ending with "5" featuring lakefront balcony. For modernists chiefly.

★★ **Excelsior** • *on the lake* • is blessed by blissful vistas. Every room has been cunningly redone; additional major works also have been wrapped up, including a lobby, bar, expansion of the grill and terrace, redecoration of the dining room (with delicious food as a standard bonus), a new wing of apartments with its own pool, sauna, and sporting club. The southwest corner doubles are extra-beguiling in taste, brightness, charm, livability, and space.

Other worthy choices include the **Bonivard,** the 100-pillowed **Helvetie,** a little pearl if you are looking for a charming family-run Swiss shelter. The **Splendid** is well regarded for its ground-level pub. **Pension Masson** is a neighbor of Chillon castle, which means it's a long, long hike into town; the house is fresh and worthy, as is the **Villa Germaine** which is immaculate but has a low bath count. **Bon Port,** with 2 dining rooms, and **Bon Accueil** are both

842 · · · SWITZERLAND

modern in taste. **Victoria,** at *Glion,* now has its own swimmery. The **Alpes Vaudoises** is for traditionalists chiefly; I like it.

RESTAURANTS

★★★ **Le Montagnard** ("The Mountain Man") • is my top choice. About 15 minutes up by taxi you'll find this former old stable. The main hall is a split-level woody area with a slate-roofed bar to one side (note especially the all-wood clock at the door). Lights in brass bells, old-fashioned farm implements, chamois pelts, waiters in regional costumes, a mural, a loft, and several tables outside for warm-weather dining complete the picture. Don't fail to try "riz montagnard," the big specialty of the house; it's superdelicious.

Plein Roc • is a bit higher—this one at an altitude of 6500 feet on the west wall of *Rochers-de-Naye.* It is reached by a 650-foot long tunnel, quite an experience.

Now back to the town itself: The recently and lavishly redecorated Grill of the **Casino** is extra-pleasant for elegant dining. If your tastes run to the *nouvelle cuisine,* try the above average **Le Pont de Brent** or the Hyatt's **Regence.** The **Caveau du Museum** harks back to the 13th century when it was a wine cellar. Entry via an antique arch to subterranean nooks for atmospheric sipping and dining; old pots and pans decorate the walls; music and dance available in one segment. Fun and different. **La Vieille Ferme** is a rustic farmhouse panning out Swiss and French platters; don't fail to sample the chef's own homebaked ryebread. Yum. Don't bother with Chillon Castle. Ugh!

MORAT   (or **Murten** in German): **Le Vieux Manoir** is excellent as are other choices in the nearby area, so please refer to our full report under the hotel listings for Berne.

MORGES   **Fleur du Lac** (and it's smack on the *lac*). Other choices: **Mont Blanc au Lac** or **La Couronne.** Usually I stop here only for a meal while en route to another bedroom. The **Union, Auberge du Port,** and the **Leman** are recommendable.

RAPPERSWIL   A lovely waterside town with a castle overlooking it on the Swiss "Gold Coast." You can reach it by car from either side of the Lake of Zurich or by frequent lakeboats to its doorstep. (1) **Schwanen** (up-to-date rooms overlooking the *See;* food, service, and bar above average; medium prices; un-ruffled and good); (2) **Du Lac,** (3) **Speer,** and (4) **Hirschen**—all 3 routine.

REGENSBERG   This is a bewitching village about 25 minutes by car from central Zurich.

★★★★★ **Krone** • with roots back to the 13th century, is one of the most attractive restaurants in eastern Switzerland. Superior cuisine at deluxe prices. Go early and stroll around the hamlet.

ST. GALLEN This mountainous pocket is a lovely piece of Switzerland. Here's how I'd rate the hotels locally: (1) **Einstein** (Berneggstr. 2, close to the Old Town) was built in '83; all 65 rooms with private facilities; first-class amenities; (2) **Santispark** has 2 large beds in all 77 units; near to sport and leisure park; good for motorists. (3) **Walhalla** (opposite railroad station; commercial but well run; popular grill). (4) **Metropol** (across from the terminal; 36 rooms, all with full bath or shower). Below these are the **Sistar** and the **Dom Garni,** both fine as money-savers.

The stucco-and-timber **Fondue-Beizli Neueck** is tops for regional dishes such as fondues, raclette, and other cheese-whizzes. Taverny atmosphere; hanging lanterns; smoky air; extensive menu. **Baratella** is an Italian *trattoria* that many wanderers like. For conventional dining, best choices are the **Gallusplatz, Stadtkeller,** and **Alt Guggeien;** more informal are **Weinstube Neubad, Baumli, Goldenen Leuen,** and **Goldenes Schaefli.**

Swiss embroideries and handworked appliques have been famous for centuries; so have the St. Gallen linens and organdies, the most distinguished in Europe. For the best values and most tasteful stocks, try **Langenthal** (Multergasse 35), where Mrs. Lebrument will show you the nation's wonder in this art.

ST. MORITZ, roughly 6000 feet high, is the most celebrated winter resort— and a delightful summer resort, too. It is a cluster of 4 small communities strung along a mountain valley like glistening pearls on a green or white string; the Village, the Spa, St. Moritz-Suvretta, and St. Moritz-Champfer are its components. (*Pontresina,* just down the pike and devoted heavily to group traffic, lacks the glitter of its famous neighbor.) Winter traditionally has been very elegant and sophisticated, while summer, more sedate (and ideal for children). St. Moritz remains The Queen of Swiss Resorts, despite its accelerating influx of packaged tours and clubmanship festivities. If any gems have toppled out of her crown of late, it surely is the result of the hardness of the Swiss franc and the softness of the economies of the other nations. Train, bus, and air-taxi connections with most principal cities; nearly 50 hotels, from super-plush to simple, clean and amply comfortable pensions; scores of restaurants, from chi-chi, black-tie establishments to holes-in-the-wall; probably the most fabulous winter sports facilities of the world, from the Cresta run to the Olympic bobsled run to Olympic ski jumps to 17 ice rinks to almost 3-score ski routes to curling lanes; plus hang-gliding on skis, plus an aerial cableway extension to 11,000 feet which combine to hustle a capacity of nearly 50,000 snow-bunnies up the slopes every hour; championship regattas for summer sailors; tennis; dancing, fashion shows, bridge tournaments (plus lessons in 4 of the top hotels), lectures, concerts, horse races, polo, or golf on frozen lake surfaces, ice parades, "skeleton" races, every imaginable type of social activity; handsome terrain, not as breathtaking as Zermatt or even Arosa, but more pruned and polished.

Go between Dec. and Apr. 15 or mid-June to end-Sept., because these are the seasons; at other times, however, you'll be rewarded with healthy discounts on your hotel bill and might even be able to bargain down the price you yourself suggest.

☆☆☆☆☆ **Suvretta-House** • a short bus ride (or longish hike) from the center, is one of the loveliest addresses in the Engadin. This glamorous landmark occupies its own distinguished niche as the ideal family-type hotel. Everything is here: The Suvretta ski runs, ski lifts, ski school (140 instructors), skating rinks, stables, nursery, curling rinks—a complete plant for every holiday need, including a glass-lined swimming pool, brightly facing the sunny south. Free bus service to the village every 30 minutes. Handsome wood-lined entrance hall; arched corridors; exquisite nightclub in rouge hue with gold trim; bars everywhere you tipple. Attractive dining room with topflight skilletry, lovely dining-terrace, bowling, private club for regional residents, splendiferous boutiques by Hermes, Zegna, and Pucci, playgrounds, orchestras, many social events and galas; garage. Helen and Vic Jacob are warmhearted hosts in a spectacular establishment. P.S. Don't think of it only as a winter base. In summer the walks, riding, golf, tennis and warm weather pastimes are glorious.

☆☆☆☆☆ **Palace** • is almost a national shrine. The building is Wedding Cake, with nothing left off in the way of spires, V-shape gimmicks, and architectural frosting that could possibly be glued or screwed on. Inside, however, it is a triumph of urbanity. The swimming pool, glassbound and set among rocks and a waterfall, might qualify as the 8th wonder of the hotel world. A marine bar overlooks it from the mezzanine. "Regular" bar with dancing and nonstop zip; elegant little Renaissance Bar, a hideaway for quiet cocktailing and gossiping late at night; "Grand" bar always with the swingingest bands in Europe; Engadiner *Stubli* for more easygoing merriment; *intime* a la carte Grill; regular restaurant; King's Club discotheque full, full, *full* (reserve in the morning); superb service throughout. There are 4 tennis courts, squash, a gym, whirlpools, and even an indoor video golf-training center with the Pebble Beach Course recreated for intercontinental duffers. Total of 200 rooms, most with bath and all furnished in classic-style comfort and livability; extra-sumptuous suites; south side completely balconied; sauna and masseuse; organized bridge games and tournaments; every plush facility imaginable. An annex beckons across the street with a shopping arcade, a floor of "sports type" rooms for youngsters on limited allowances, and a top tier with 3 large apartments for longer lingerers.

☆☆☆☆ **Kulm** • the earliest major hotel in the resort and still a mainstay of tradition and fun, is managed by friendly and energetic Heinz Hunkeler with the aid of his sparkling wife Erika. It offers a breathtakingly beautiful view from its glass-fronted, heated swimming pool. Ballroom; baronial Rotisserie des Chevaliers; French restaurant; Sunny-Bar nightclub with live music in winter; snack-bar; sun terrace. Superb in every way and easily one of Switzerland's top resort hotels.

☆☆☆☆ **Carlton** • is also an institution in this community. Lobby majestic, almost to the point of being awesome; Grill-Bar one of the best in the region; attractive lounge for dancing; indoor pool, tennis, sauna and solarium;

renovations by new German owners. Splendid professional direction that can only keep pushing it ever higher in the rankings.

☆☆☆ **Monopol** • is a midtowner with a woody Grischuna Grill, filled with animated couples dancing nightly to its peppery combo; adjoining Barengraben room for specialties and fondues; rustic bar popular with chattering bench-sitters; covered rooftop pool; solid comfort, pleasant decor, ample space in most accommodations; some units too cramped, however. Tariffs hovering between those of the middle bracket and the luxury entries; excellent for the outlay; getting better every year.

☆☆☆ **Schweizerhof** • is maintained in smart and snappy style. All south-facing rooms being rebuilt with balconies added; entire floors freshly updated and new corridors created; frequent tasteful use of Art Deco in many accommodations (some units even with "cathedral" radios). Giardino patio restaurant in summer; winter-only piano bar; picnic club on the Suvretta slope; wood-lined Acla Grill. Good space and good value.

☆☆ **Crystal** • is a midcity, midpriced entry with many fine facets. Most rooms with handsome wood decor; quite a nice bet.

Hauser • features a restaurant-tearoom at ground level and 50 wood-toned, brightly decorated bedchambers above.

★★★ **Chesa Guardalej** • near Silvaplana and the Suvretta slopes, is a study in alpine architecture and coziness. Stucco and wood exterior with painted coins and window recesses; intimate dining and lounge areas; cheerful and viewful accommodations. Very sporting in mood.

Steffani • in Class 1-B, has an amusing discotheque; self-service cafeteria; cozy Cresta Bar; bowling, terrace-dining, other features. There's a fresh penthouse level; most other nests have been refluffed; a garage adjoins; very central and swinging in its youthful way.

La Margna • is small and economy-level, but all units have bath and furnishings are excellent; the hottest news concerns its super-steamy Turkish bath.

Languard • is our choice of the *garni* bets. Same view as the Palace.

Bernina • is in the same league; it's very economical and well situated for moving about.

Belvedere • also well-situated, and well-outfitted, serves only breakfast; solid bedchamber comforts; small indoor pool; reasonable tariffs. Not at all bad as a respectable money-saver.

Dining can be costly in this chic mountain paradise.

Chesa Veglia • owned by the Palace Hotel, is the local "21." Here's a glorified Engadine chalet with a marvelous (yet low-price) pizzeria. Heart of the enterprise is the vastly more exclusive, dressy, and expensive Chadafo Grill. The outstanding house is mastered by Reto Mathis (son of Hartly; see below); there is piano melodizing in the Chadafo, with dancing. All couverts should be reserved at least 24 hours in advance (48 hours on High Season weekends). Even for an apres-ski in the Patrizer Stuben, it is almost impossible to snag a table between 4 p.m. and 7 p.m., when C-V hops to tea dancing.

Hotel dining naturally dominates the town. The above leaders all feature first-rank kitchens, and when you are on a half- or full-pension plan, the economies realized are certainly worthwhile.

Salastrains • *halfway up the slope* • has snacks for skiers; packed tightly on sunny days. Steam in at noon for lunch and begin schussing earlier for maximum pleasure.

Acla Clavadatsch • *the nearby alpside hut for Schweizerhof guests* • has outdoor grills; piano player by the hearth; noontime only; meal chits in lieu of francs; a chummy bonus if you are staying in this hotel.

Corviglia Club • mecca of society sportsmen, is restricted to members and their guests; uncrackable, unless you're invited. It is not related to the next entry.

☆☆☆☆ **Corviglia Marmite Hartly Mathis** • has got to be one of the most unusual restaurants atop the world—high on an alp and so high in quality that it vies with the finest anywhere in Europe. There is even a special caviar menu to start you on the parade of pheasant, partridge, venison, chamois, or domestic critters; then to cassis ice cups, wild blueberries and egg brandy, pine-nut desserts, and many more splendid creations. Lunch only; lower priced diner adjoining also highly recommendable.

Lunch expedition on a balmy day? The trip up the **Diavolezza aerial railway** to 8800 feet can be enormous fun. It's a leap-and-a-skip past Pontresina, a drive which takes perhaps 20 minutes. At the top, the panorama from the terrace of the mountain restaurant is fabulous. You'll eat locomotive-size hot dogs and typical farmer fare—and love it.

★★★★ **Roseggletscher** • is not to be missed. Go to the Pontresina station and reserve on the horsedrawn carriage (or sled in winter) for the hour's clip-clop to the bottom of this magnificent glacier. The ride is lovely and the reward of arriving at the farmhouse restaurant at the end is bliss itself. If you have a sweet tooth, you'll think you've expired and gone to heaven when you see the overwhelming color-dotted dessert buffet with more than 30 spectacular offerings. Better walk back down the valley (1¾ hrs.) instead of riding.

SHOPPING

ARMS: **Haus des Jagers** (Via dal Bagn 53) produces some of the most beautiful, personalized hunting weapons in the world. They are gems so you can expect numbing price tags to hang from their triggers.

CASHMERES: **Lamm** (Via Maistra 15) preens with the biggest selection of sweaters (many exclusive designs), shetlands, tams, and assorted sportswear.

CHOCOLATES AND PATISSERIE: **Confiserie Hanselmann** clomps along with legendary fame, but on several recent visits I've found even the pastry to be as pedestrian as its ragged service standards.

EMBROIDERY AND LINENS: **Ebneter & Biel** (Hauptstrasse) is the un-questioned sachem in producing breakfast sets, tablecloths, napkins, handker-chiefs, comforters, and dozens of personal items for the elite of Europe.

FASHIONS: Both the **Palace-Arcade** and **Gallaria Caspar Badrutt** fea-ture doorways gilded with outstanding name boutiques; they will afford you glittering hours of delightful browsing.

FURS: **Victor Goldfarb** (Palace-Arcade) cuts the leading edge in styles. **Lindner** (Chesa Tuor Pitschna) is also good, but you'll find a better selection in the larger cities. Trends here, naturally, run to sporting models.

JEWELRY: **La Serlas** (Palace Arcade, opposite Palace Hotel) is the distin-guished name of these highlands. Their own collection is stunning.

SPORTING GOODS: **Corviglia Sport** seems to have the most fashiona-ble choices.

ZERMATT Here, a full mile above sea level and 2 miles below the tips of towering Monte Rosa, you will find one of the most breathtaking creations of Providence. For snow-buffs, it is Paradise on Skis. Counting the Italian descents (Breuil-Cervinia): 100 slopes ranging up to more than 6½ miles, with an alti-tude differential of over 7000 feet; 73 lifts totaling nearly 80 miles in length in 6 varieties of transport; almost 150 miles of officially maintained ski courses, plus oodles of deep-powder zones for off-trail adventurers; skating and curling facilities; seasonal trails to the rooftop of the world; a Hollywood director's Elysium of photographic possibilities (don't forget your ultraviolet or skylight filter). A system of skyhooks pulls skiers up to the lofty Klein Matterhorn, which scratches the belly of Heaven at a smidgen over 12,500 feet! This is now linked to an even newer feeder system from the valley which cuts overall wait-ing time to shreds. Meanwhile, a 6-jillion dollar funicular rockets through a solid stone tunnel in about 5 minutes to increase capacity to Sunnega on the Blauherd by 2600 skiers per hour—an F–4 could hardly climb any faster. (There are 3 systems of interconnecting mountains: Blauherd, Gornergrat, and Theodul Glacier, plus 2 links from the last over to Italy [Cervinia] via the Testa Grigia runs. Soon, one comprehensive ski pass may open snow trails in both nations.) Narrow-gauge trains pull from Visp to Zermatt in 65 minutes with 14 hauls a day each way. An auto route from Visp stops at Tasch (maintaining the traditional no-motor-driven-vehicle policy; expansive parking facilities are now at Tasch, 4 miles below Zermatt a rather expensive taxi, a minibus, or the cheaper train service, running every 15 minutes, provide the final leg). The Vergers have wound up a fine modern multiplane chopper service as an aid to mountain rescue and as a lure to well-heeled go-it-alone skiers. If you have any questions about the trove of possibilities here, address them to the dynamic Amade Perrig, director of the Zermatt Tourist Office. He and his staff are tiptop for efficiency.

Summer (also for skiing on the glacier) is a lovely time to come, too, because it turns into an arcadian garden of wildflowers, rippling streams, and clear blue light. The walks on the shelf of the Matterhorn are inspiring and the area is easy to reach.

If you are *really* a trailblazer, sign on for a week-long **Haute Route** passage (walking, climbing, and skiing) that runs from early April to early June. The top-of-the-world tour includes accommodation in huts, transport where necessary, most food, and expert leadership by tough, smart, and friendly Franz Schwery. The entire package costs roughly $720 (including liniment). For details: Franz Schwery, Bergfuhrer-Skilehrer, 3920 Zermatt (Tel: 028/672880).

HOTELS

Your place of residence in this village really should depend more on your desired lifestyle and less on the official category. Zermatt hostelries—most of them very good anyway—are strong on personality, so your ultimate happiness will depend on how you meld into the local architecture and mood of the hotel you choose.

★★★★★ **Alex** • is a charmer—and now it stays open both winter and summer. (Good news for mountain walkers who come for the flowers!) It is sited on viewful Matterhorn frontage, connected by a direct ramp from the railroad station. Chalet-motif building; enhanced entry with cookshed for outdoor meals in summer; captivating rustic lounge with crackling fire, snack service and cozy corners in 3 separate sectors; two dancing pods, the most popular in after-dark Zermatt; a score of luxury suites that are beauts, which have their own working fireplaces and artistic doors of cast Italian bronze; sumptuous Presidential Suite, formerly the owner's private apartment; vast, variform indoor swimming pool; saunas (both of these and the pool are free for hotel guests); tennis hall for year-round volleys plus one on the roof for outdoor play; 2 squash courts; exceptional Tavern Chez Alex in cellar, delightfully regional in dress, with old beams and all the trimmings. A conference facility is the latest addition. The rooms are outstandingly good for the price bracket. Sweater-clad Alex Perren, a 4th-generation mountain guide, is the cheerful personality who will go all out for your welcome and comfort. His delightful wife and helpmate Gisela is another bonus.

★★★★★ **Alex Schlosshotel Tenne** • belongs to the same Perren team—daughters Christine and Sonja, both radiating charm—but the building has a totally different personality from the Alex. It has been lavished with love and Swiss francs, a "castle" decorated in Art Nouveau, intimate, luxurious and clublike. Only 30 rooms, each different and most with working fireplace; 3 duplex suites with skylights; splendid baths with whirlpools. Softspoken lounge and bar with open hearth, vaguely Syrian pillars and pilasters, spiral staircase pulpit as a conversation piece, exquisite illumination, and soft music (often live) in evenings. Restaurant in Alpine mood—the one spot nearly everyone visits in Zermatt no matter where they are staying. They all come away smiling.

☆☆☆☆☆ **Mont Cervin** • (French for "Matterhorn") • for decades has been the most famous hotel of the Canton. It is still growing—in size *and* in quality. Now there's a fine southeast-facing wing with spacious suites (about $425 with half-board) and conference facilities. The atmosphere is more sedate than at the Alex, which some travelers may prefer. It boasts a covered swimming pool plus sauna and massage facilities. There's a supervised area for children aged 2 to 10 with a nurse from 9 a.m.–6 p.m. each day. Ingratiating and peaceful Matterhornstube, in attractive bleached timbers, with excellent adjoining bar-lounge, superb cuisine and professional service. The High Season Friday night buffets are nothing short of spectacular. Dignified, warmhearted, and perfectly managed on every score.

☆☆☆ **Zermatterhof** • is owned by the town's citizens. Handsome entrance has been given a smart copper canopy and polished marble in its immaculately pruned lobby; split-level lounge a casebook example of period gentility; L-shape dining room with one leg old-fashioned and the other brightly blended (a curious combination that comes off). Tons of gleaming chandeliers give you some idea of the mood and tone. Indoor swimming pool partially glass-lined, a fitness center, and 2 saunas (extra fee for use). The ground-floor U-shape section, fronting lawn and street, contains (1) the glass-wrapped Grill, (2) an ultramodern cafe with live and discotheque music, (3) an urbane dining salon, and (4) a sterile, brassy rotunda bar. The 100 rooms come with appealing Swiss-rustic decor, with burnished and slightly darkened natural wood ceilings, doors, bedboards, wardrobes, and trim; ⅓rd have a pleasant classic mien; all offer the identical yardsticks of quality and upkeep.

★★★ **Alpenhof** • near the Sunnegga funicular, is an excellent glass, timber, and stucco chalet-mood freshet. Luxury and informality are combined in bright textiles, wide windows (some triangulated in attic units), skylights, a sparkling dining salon, an intime bar, fitness center, sauna, and sun terraces. The situation is convenient for skiers; extra-kind personnel.

☆☆☆ **Monte Rosa** • an antebellum period piece, was born in 1855 and very recently was given its latest major remodeling, affording it nearly a full private bath count, 4 suites, and balconies on its south side. Today it flowers with bouquets of appeal without any serious loss of character. Smallish lobby and 3 lounges; popular expanded bar, one of the nicest in town for quiet exchanges.

☆☆☆ **Nicoletta** • young at heart and growing younger and more pert every season, offers an exceptional view-bound north-facing bar and lounge; refined dining room on the southern Matternhorn side; first-rate cuisine; restyled lobby; ideal location for skiers—equidistant from all major lifts. It turns on a solarium, a pool, and a sauna; the rooms are large and superbly furnished; the #503 and #504 suites are tip-top, featuring TVs over the tubs for leisurely soaking; some have private balconies; the colors add vim; the baths are carpeted—and so is the underground tunnel that leads to the Mont Cervin pool (open to Nicoletta guests). Mr. and Mrs. Merckaert are professional hosts with a fine modern house.

☆☆ **Schweizerhof** • boasts a swimming pool, sauna and fitness room, a formal dining salon, a grill, and a rustic *stubli* for snacks. A ground-floor arcade features a jeweler, kiosk, souvenir boutique, and a shop specializing in cross-country skiing items (a "first" for this town). Doubles all with private balcony; singles without and with showers only; some attic junior suites, and a few studio units with kitchenette (practical if you opt for bed and breakfast instead of demipension); radiant heating throughout. Good comfort at a price level slightly below the Mont Cervin, of which it is an ally along with the above two candidates.

Schonegg • is a newcomer reached through a long tunnel and up through a shaft in the solid rock to a cliffside shelf looking straight at the Matterhorn. Beautiful dining room and viewful bar, but my meal and service lacked polish during its first full season of operation; let's hope this one matures smartly. An exquisite setting if you don't mind the effort to reach this alpine aerie.

★★ **Walliserhof** • is a Zermatt landmark. All public sancta and every one of its bedchambers in a mood of rusticity. Accommodations with bath or shower, phone, radio, and Frigobar; many feature wooden ceilings. The grill is reliable and the Weinstube remains one of the most popular social hubs of the Valais—making this truly a *Walliser-hof*. The weekly buffet during ski season is mighty alluring—and its flavor lives up to its stunning eye appeal.

★★ **Julen** • is intimate, woody, and evocative of mountain themes. Balconies with all rooms; many units quite small; excellent public sectors; rough timbers and soft lighting prevail to create a highland mood. Very reasonably priced.

☆ **Beau-Site** • is a Grand Old Warrior, which has been made more youthful through an outside cleaning, an interior pep-up, and the addition of a swim-

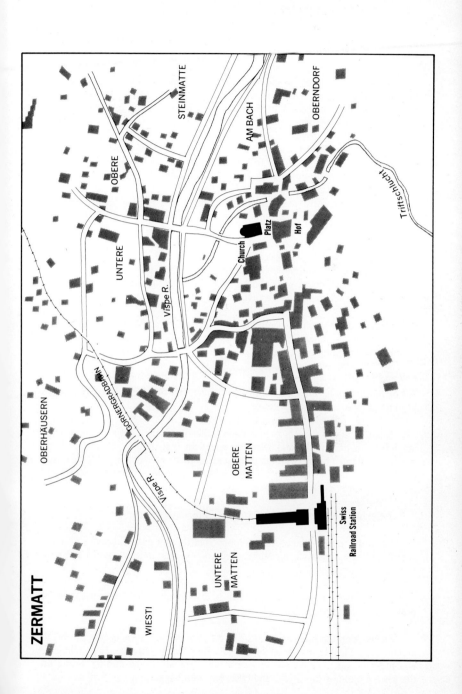

ZERMATT

STEINMATTE

OBERE

AM BACH

OBERNDORF

Triftschlucht

UNTERE

Vispe R.

Church
Platz
Hof

OBERHÄUSERN

GORNERGRADBAHN

Vispe R.

OBERE
MATTEN

Swiss
Railroad Station

WIESTI

UNTERE
MATTEN

ming pool. Its adjoining chalet was sold to become the not-unpleasant **Garni Christen.**

Alpenblick • closest to the Matterhorn, is at the extreme edge of the settlement. Lovely open terrace to one side (20 tables; drinks, snacks, or full meals), with a magnificent unbroken sweep of this mountain. Service and facilities are spare, however.

★★ **Albana Real** • is new and also at the southern end of the village. Inviting lounge and bar leading to a maritime-theme restaurant. Nice reception by the Lingg-Kronig family. Very appealing and intimate.

Bristol • features dancing in its neo-gothic cellar grill, a favorite spot for apres-ski romancers. Minisize cells, most with bath or shower. Fair pickin's for small-bones clients.

La Couronne • provides a central situation at the end of the river bridge across from the Zermatterhof. Old Zermatt Restaurant-Bar-Grill and hairdressing salon in front (count your change extra-carefully in the former); so-so accommodations; fair but hardly a rave.

Christiania • seems awfully casual. Adequate plant and a proper kitchen for its expanded dining facilities, but I simply don't tune into its wavelength. Adjoining swimming pool, sauna, fitness center, and an apartment-hotel.

BUDGET
All of the following are Garni (breakfast only), but full meals can be arranged in most of them, on separate terms.

Eden & Rex • form a twin combo under the same administration. They are joined in the middle and share an excellent indoor pool. Unusually large accommodations, many with balcony and all with breathtaking Alpine vista; public rooms and corridors highlighted with copperware, spinning wheels, and regional touches; chalet-annex nearby plus sauna. Nice.

Jagerhof • is clean, airy, informal, and recommendable.

Darioli • in midvillage, has no lobby, but its tiny grill and *Stubli* weave a gypsy spell. Peasant-style furniture in bedrooms; attic units without bath; simple, but winsome.

De la Poste • is globally noted for its discotheque complex in the cellar. I prefer the nonsleeping quarters to the kips.

Derby • on the main street next to the Walliserhof, sprouts typical upland architecture. Sizable restaurant on ground floor that is intimate, low-ceilinged, and pleasant; open-air terrace service a few steps above the milling throng on the road; bedrooms tiny, tidy, and cheerful, with baggage space sufficient for 1 small attache case; appealing, nevertheless, in their fully paneled walls, small streetside balconies, and color touches. Noisy in front, of course.

Biner • is okay. Chummy staff here.

Chesa Valese • is a warm, cozy 30-room villa with 6 baths, 6 showers, many balconies, and a feeling of "Welcome Home." Very ingratiating in its quiet fashion.

Excelsior and **Aristella** • are production-line plants a la Chalet School of architecture and appointments; these are also passable for their category.

Bahnhof • a summer bunker for rough-and-ready climbers, is as raw as they come. The prices are ultrabasic, too. Shelter here often means 6 to a room and "Everybody up at dawn!"

Above the village on the surrounding highlands are the following:

★★★ **Berghotel Riffelalp** • is up on a glorious terrace reached by the Gornergrat cog-wheel train. The site is superb as is the legendary Seiler management by Cecile and Thomas Moor. The 20 rooms are the last quiet word for tranquility. This hotel with its fabulous outdoor terrace serves some of the best country-style regional cookery in them thar hills. I love it and can't stay away. The final train from Zermatt is at 7 p.m.; after that, s-i-l-e-n-c-e and the rapture of the hills.

Augstkumme • is Seiler's apartment development on the same nearby alpine tier. All luggage transfers for both of these is handled by the above hotel.

Riffelberg • across the valley and on a different mountain and lift system, is for total isolationists. The views, of course, are magnificent, the rates are low, but I prefer it chiefly at mealtimes since my preferences are not so solitary.

RESTAURANTS

★★★★ **Tenne** • This is the "in" spot (in the Alex Schlosshotel Tenne) where people come to see and be seen. They also dine very well, needless to say. The mood is rich in mountain flavor—so is the saddle of lamb grilled on the open fire. (Sophisticated cuisine is available if you seek the modern taste trend.) Costly, but worth it.

★★★★ **Taverne Chez Alex** • the cellar of the **Hotel Alex,** is always busy at nightfall. Rusticity by the carload, with old beams, Alpine architecture, and the flavor of the hills.

☆☆☆☆ **Matterhorn Stube** • is the grill of the Mont Cervin Hotel and a very distinguished place it is. Bleached timbers, wood floors, paintings of Old Zermatt, and refined rusticity are here and in the intimate bar which adjoins. Excellent cooking.

★★ **Casa Rustica** • a few steps away from the station, is a sophisticated woody concept that recaptures a tavern mood at grand salon price tags. Very well decorated, food carefully presented in contemporary fashion, but as to value-for-money, I'll leave that question to you to answer.

Spycher • features a tiny intimate quadrant in the back of a multisection room. Lodge decor; typically overheated, as only the Swiss can overheat a restaurant. This one is always pleasant aesthetically, but the gustatory output is variable.

★★ **Stockhorn** • *near the Eden & Rex* • is quite a warm and cozy nook today. Ski instructor Emil Julen is the owner, and his taste for winter sport, climbing, and good solid cookery is reflected on its walls and tables. Ropes, crampons, picks and other lore of the mountains for decor; intimate ground-level dining room plus a charming dark raclette *Stube* in the cellar. Now definitely recommendable for its type.

Burgener • is a pleasant lunch stop in the village, on the main street. Soups and pastries are best.

Couronne • is best for apres-ski *Gluhwein* and snacks when the slopes have been retired for the day.

Elsie's place • *a few steps from the Hotel Zermatterhof* • is a very ancient house where you'll find 6 tables, a small semicircular bar, knotty walls, casement windows, and a friendly atmosphere. Elsie's prides: Irish coffee (very costly but *delicious*), ham and eggs, hot dogs, other light snacks. Closed May, Oct., and Nov.; otherwise it goes full blast from 10 a.m. to midnight, 7 days a week.

SHOPPING

SHOPPING HOURS: 8 to 12:30 and 2 p.m.–7 p.m., Sun. (in season only some open) 8–noon and 2 p.m. to 6:30 p.m.

BEST AREAS: Right up the center of the town from the station to the church square along the Bahnhofstrasse.

BOUTIQUES: **La Cabane** has 3 shops and among them they cover every need or whim. The one across from the Post Office is the fashion center, with both apres-ski and smart apparel for both sexes. **La Cabane Sport Shop,** opposite the church, is where you'll be outfitted for outdoor pursuits, summer or winter; great advice on ski rentals or purchase plus all the gear for climbing. **The Fun Box,** facing the Broken Ski Bar, is a whirl of novelty sportswear, snowboards and, well, fun things—a boxful!

CHEESE AND CHEESE RELATED GIFTS: **Chas Josi** (a few doors from the Nicoletta Hotel) is such a cheese-lover's paradise you'll forget your cholesterol count.

EMBROIDERY: **Langenthal, AG** (Bahnhofstr. 35) captures the local laurels.

GIFTS: **Haus der Geschenke** (across from the Hotel Schweizerhof) has a wonderful selection of carved Aosta coffeepots which make a cozy way to end an evening. We'll say no more. You can watch a whittler at work in the rear. **Geschenke Boutique** (near the church) is brimming over with candles, glassware, brass items and other present ideas.

JEWELRY AND WATCHES: **Bucherer** (on the main street near the station) is the commanding choice—whether it's for a handsome Bucherer quartz timepiece for as little as $60 or on up to the Rolex heavens where the sky's the limit. Numerous brands are on hand plus a treasurehouse of gems. This is a link in one of the biggest chains in the world, so price benefits are passed on to you—including the purchase tax refunds which might pay for your airfare.

MINERAL OBJECTS: **Etoile des Pierres** (past the church and a few doors along over the bridge) has one of the most creative displays of semiprecious stones we've ever seen. Set on tables faced in rock, the large, rough "befores" are side-by-side with the shining "afters." Rings, pins, necklaces, ashtrays, keyrings—they abound.

PHARMACY-PERFUMERIE: **Testa Grigia,** on the main street, is the first spot you should know about if you ski, hike or just expose your city hide to the Alpine weather or high-mountain sun. For bumps, bruises, sniffles, or sore muscles, the kindhearted English-speaking pharmacists are endless fonts of knowledge and caring. For beauty products, gifts, accessories and items in the luxurious lines of Dior, YSL, Trussardi, Karl Lagerfeld, Gucci, Jil Sander, Christian Lacroix, and an alp of other great names, this is a treasure house. Ask for our friend Pharmacist Christine Gentinetta, the proprietress, or if you are at the sister branch, Pharmacy Gentinetta, ask for Mrs. Claudine Petrig. These places are the finest of their type in the village.

SOUVENIRS: In Zermatt that's spelled **WEGA** (Shopping-Center am Bahnhof, Schweizerhof Hotel Arcade where it's known as Souvenir Shop, and facing the Post Office—"PTT"). They carry dolls in regional dress, postcards, packets of Alpen flower seeds, cow bells, Alpen horns, music boxes, a wide selection of foreign language books and specialized books on skiing and mountaineering, Swiss Army knives and any other gadget or gimmick that you can think of.

TRACHTEN: **Alex Boutique,** in the Alex Hotel, purveys the distinctive and now-fashionable regional dress of Bavaria and the Austrian alpine districts. Don't miss a visit because the assemblage of this tasteful apparel is unique.

ZUG In this delightful medieval town a local friend and food-savvy gastronome recommends the cozy little **Akim am Zytturm** to the high blue-Swiss heavens. Closed Thurs. At **Hecht,** at lakeside, I was presented with a marvelous fish platter, a glorious waterfront panorama, and a delightful wedge of Kirschtorte (a Zug specialty which was invented by the gods). The **Rathaus** is okay for light bites and atmosphere and the **Ochsen** leads the hotel herd.

ZURICH

Zurich is the largest and most business oriented metropolis in Helvetia; commerce, industry, and culture are centered here. You'll find the leading banks and insurance companies; biggest shops, factories, markets; excellent hotels, restaurants, and amusements. A speedy rail service now zips between airport and midtown in only 10 minutes—quite a saving over the taxi fare. From the tops of the encircling hills, the city is a stunning sight: Villas and gardens stretch down to the silvery inland sea, with snowcapped mountains always in the background. The people here are supposed to be the greatest boasters in the country—and why not, when 1 out of 275 residents is a millionaire (so who sneezes at millionaires in Swiss francs). Make Zurich and Geneva your excursion centers, for everything worth seeing in the nation can be covered from these 2 bases. If you can, plan to be in Zurich in June; the month-long Festival here is one of the most famous on the Continent.

ATTRACTIONS

Fraumunster Church • *Munsterhof* • The original structure was a convent church built in A.D. 853 from a donation by Ludvig, grandson of Charlemagne. The church that stands today was constructed in the 1100s, notable for its exquisite narrow blue spire and lovely cloisters. Don't miss the stained-glass windows that Marc Chagall created.

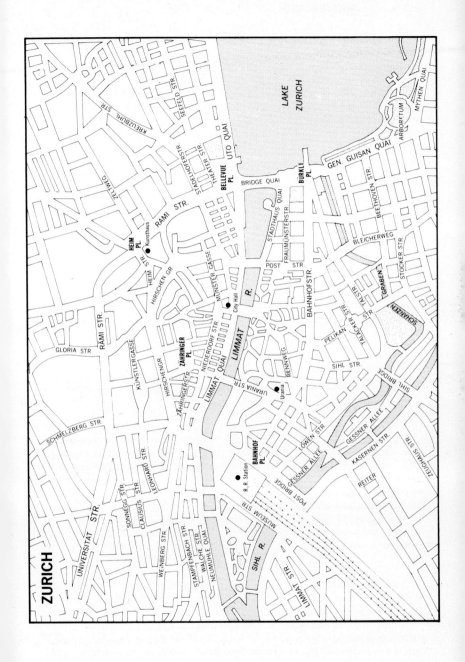

ZURICH

LAKE ZURICH

KREUZBUHL STR.

SEEFELD STR.

ZELTWEG

RAMI STR.

STADELHOFERSTR.

THEATER STR.

UTO QUAI

BELLEVUE PL.

BRIDGE QUAI

BÜRKLI PL.

GEN. GUISAN QUAI

MYTHEN QUAI

ARBORETUM

HEIM PL.

Kunsthaus

HEIM STR.

HIRSCHEN GR.

MÜNSTER GASSE

STADTHAUS QUAI

FRAUMÜNSTERSTR.

POST STR.

BAHNHOFSTR.

BEETHOVEN STR.

BLEICHERWEG

GRABEN

STOCKER STR.

SCHANZEN

RAMI STR.

GLORIA STR.

KÜNSTLERGASSE

ZAHRINGER PL.

HIRSCHENGR.

ZAHRINGERSTR.

City Hall

NIEDERDORF STR.

LIMMAT QUAI

LIMMAT R.

PELIKAN STR.

TALACKER STR.

SIHL STR.

RENNWEG

SCHMELZBERG STR.

LIMMAT QUAI

URANIA STR.

Urania

LÖWEN STR.

GESSNER ALLEE

KASERNEN STR.

SIHL BRIDGE

ZEUGHAUS STR.

UNIVERSITAT STR.

SONNEGG STR.

LEONHARD STR.

CLAUSIUS STR.

WEINBERG STR.

BAHNHOF PL.

R. R. Station

GESSNER ALLEE

POST BRIDGE

REITER

STAMPFENBACH STR.

WALCHE STR.

NEUMUHLE QUAI

MUSEUM STR.

SIHL R.

LIMMAT STR.

Kunsthaus • *Heimplatz 1* • The collection covers periods from the Middle Ages to present, with some emphasis on Impressionist and Post-Impressionist works by Monet, Rodin, Chagall, and Munch.

Rietberg Museum • *Gablerstrasse 15* • One of the world's most important collections of non-European art; interestingly housed in Wesendonck Villa, which overlooks Lake Zurich. The Chinese exhibit represents roughly 3000 years of cultural development, from the Shang dynasty (1500 B.C.) to the late-17th-century Ming dynasty. Other exhibits offer fascinating pieces from India, Africa, Japan, and South and Central America.

Schweizerisches Landesmuseum • *Museumstrasse 2* • Here is the biggest and most comprehensive collection of Swiss history; more than 100 rooms laid-out in chronological order—from prehistoric times to the late 17th century.

Toy Museum • *Rennweg 26, in the center* • will engage children of all ages any Mon.–Fri. afternoon. The dolls, soldiers, and full panoply of whimsy cover 300 years of playfulness.

Boat tours • A grand variety of boat tours is available on either the lake or the Limmat River. Any one you choose is bound to be a major highlight of your visit. Go to the pier at the end of Bahnhofstrasse for the lake tours. River tours depart just outside the National Museum.

HOTELS

☆☆☆☆☆ **Dolder Grand** • has a mountainside location, 10 minutes by car from the heart of the city. Breathtaking panorama; the last word in elegance today; viewful crescent-shape La Rotonde restaurant; awkward piano bar; 200 rooms and 200 baths; TV plus video option; volume-governed radios; tiptop concierges in Mr. Soliva and Mr. Follonier. Hotel limousine service to town is much cheaper than ordinary taxi, incidentally; you also can ride down or back on the inexpensive funicular. Spacious gardens and woods; 9-hole golf course, ice rink, and tennis courts nearby. Director Heinrich Hunold, formerly of the Sheraton in Stockholm, has one of the world's greatest hotels under his supervision.

☆☆☆☆☆ **Baur au Lac** • boasts a superb downtown lakeside setting and slightly higher tariffs than the above entry. The lobby and lounges are gathering places of wealth, nobility, and chic; there's an impressive Men's Club (with everything from the latest stock market quotations to a private secretary; women guests are admitted after 6 p.m.); in its cellar is the Petit Palais discotheque; there's an excellent telephone system throughout, a boutique plus barbering and hairdressing salons, air conditioning for the public rooms, and a panoply of posh accommodations. You'll snooze in a velour-upholstered bed, park your luggage on slide-out shelves, and use an improved bathroom (still smallish, but equipped with dressing tables and illuminated mirrors for the ladies). The grill-bar remains one of Zurich's top spots.

☆☆☆☆ **Savoy** (also called Baur en Ville) • oldest in town, looks as young as the day it was born—after a hypercostly reconstruction by its banking proprietors and co-directors Manfred and Christina Horger. Midcity location in the eye of the shopping hurricane; restyled freshly opulent lobby; Grill totally revamped and lovely, with excellent international cuisine; colorful and fun Orsini Italian restaurant adjoining; lounge/bar; simple Cafe Baur; 15 bedrooms renovated handsomely; a few units with balcony; substantial comfort; restful color scheme leaning toward golds, beige, and buff tones. A cheerful deluxe traditionalism pervades this born-again contender.

☆☆☆ **Eden au Lac** • just across the boulevard from the lake, is a splendid house. It turns out the imaginative fare in its intimate restaurant. The aura, bathed in a Trianon gray, is on the old-fashioned side, in a nostalgically serene way; the 53 rooms, all with bath or shower, are comfortable while not being luxurious; many have been updated and given air conditioning. Service unusually attentive; the value is here—and intimacy, too.

☆ **Carlton-Elite** • is smack in the center. Its Pub, decorated with saddles, bridles, and raw bricks, is more popular than ever even though I found the service in it as bad as ever. It is sited in a charming little cul-de-sac. Colorful Locanda Ticinese Italian-Swiss tavern; attractive Flower Terrace for open-air summer meals; communal plus private bar for guests; 10 split level accommodations in natural wood and textile motif, with color TV, refrigerator, "silent valets," twin washbasins, and up-to-the-minute gadgetry; other units on the smallish side, with wall-to-wall carpeting and modernistic tone.

☆ **Waldhaus Dolder** • splits its structure between apartments and rooms for transients while sharing its mountain address with its neighboring alma mater, the Dolder Grand. It is a 10-story *eminence grise* (gray concrete) which is first class, not Deluxe. Engagingly decorated restaurant and dining sectors; grill under iron hood with leaded glass and outfitted with woodsman's tools; Dolderbahn Bar for nostalgics; glass-lined pool area that can be opened in summer; sauna. Bedchambers as well as the longer-rental apartments rely heavily on formica and other coolish effects. Space is ample; comfort is abundant; tranquillity is assured. We suspect families will find it perfect for their needs.

☆ **Zum Storchen** • which occupies one of the better midcity situations, offers a timber-lined waterside rotisserie, a dining terrace over the water, a soulless bar with piano-tations, and superb concierge service. Total of 80 rooms, all with radio, TV, minibar, direct-dial telephone, and most with bath or shower; singles facing the town; the choicest streamside doubles #323 and #423 (often held for loyal clients); demipension required in summer.

☆☆ **International Zurich** • offers a convenient scenic location overlooking the river and a magnificent townscape; waterfront restaurant with cyclopean ceiling lights; inviting Grill; bar, pool, gym, shops, garage; handsomely furnished bedchambers with a heavy inclination toward white Formica surfaces; color-brightened baths. Somehow this brand of subdued modernity has a certain appeal. Costly by local standards. If you are fond of railroading inquire about the antique Orient Express cars which start from here and range from 1-day excursions up to journeys to the French Riviera and to Rome.

Ascot • is near one of the train stations. Tastefully refashioned; front rooms with balconies and deck chairs; 2nd floor Bel Etage with special flavor; 6 suites (2 with kitchens) in velvet, silk, and flowered decor; 60 rooms, all with bath, radio, and most with picture windows; many with color TV; enlarged lobby; high-in-the-stirrups, rouge-toned, intimate Jockey Club restaurant (microwave kitchen); sidewalk cafe; busy Turf Bar.

★ **Atlantis Sheraton** • *15 minutes by taxi from the center* • is sited in a suburban office complex. Spacious lobby in Scandinavian motif; 2-tier rotisserie plus intimate pinewood *Stubli;* nightclub; glass-fronted swimming pool covered by a sail; sauna with snoozzzzable easy chairs; hair dressing salon; fine Grieder boutique; Avis agency plus garage. The well-furnished rooms are efficient in the modern theme, highlighted by photomurals and generously outfitted with phones at bedside and in the bath; radios and TV (some in color and all with remote-control switches), refrigerators, infrared heat lamps; ample space; individual terraces. The penthouse units are especially laudable.

Europe • *in town* • glows with Old World charm and crackles with 20th-century convenience. Winningly attractive French-provincial lobby; beverage salon under crystal, embraced by ruby velour walls; patterned corridors; delightful accommodations with such touches as rheostat lighting, humidifiers, refrigerators, electric bed controls plus radio-TV consoles, air conditioning (in some units), wall safes, silent valets, shaving mirrors, drying racks in baths and much more—even to bowls of fruit placed in the rooms.

Opera • *behind its namesake* • offers rooms but no meals; it also serves no alcohol. Sounds austere, but it is really quite nice.

Nova Park • is large, aggressively commercial, and about as inviting as a bus terminal. Moreover, the rooms are so poorly illuminated that I expected to find bats searching for a roost. Give up the notion of reading here.

St. Gotthard • *1 block from the main station* • is in a district that is now a pedestrian zone. This landmark is best known for its Hummer ("Lobster") Bar, its cosmopolitan sidewalk cafe on the Bahnhofstrasse, and its Rotisserie; its 110 rooms and 8 charming luxury suites show commendable improvement plus a notable trend toward gaiety and decorative flair. One wing of 28 bedchambers twinkles with white brick, rustic textiles, rich wood, and floral patterns; all units with color TV and frigobar.

Glockenhof • isn't bad as a family stop.

Pullman Continental • a glass-and-steel edifice that started life as an office building, exorcises its commercial origins with a cunning use of lovely Valais antiques. A later restyling has made it even more ingratiating. Accommodations with radio, bath or shower, and makeshift closets; full air conditioning; attractive restaurants serving unusually high-grade cuisine.

Rigihof • is a converted apartment house on a clangorous street. Full bath count; homey atmosphere; excellent kitchen for reasonable outlays; for budgeteers and travelers with children superb for its special type.

Kindli • with no views from its inner-canyon site in midtown, is, in my evaluation, a conglomeration of good and bad. You pays your money and you takes your choice.

Krone • built on the Limmat Quai in A.D. 1599, is well situated for sightseers; intimate and vaguely French in tone.

Adler • with 50 rooms and 18 baths, is fair.

Schweizerhof • has made some heroic attempts at restylings. One of the best is the marble-slick Quick restaurant, gleaming under crystal chandeliers. The rooms are now well outfitted, comfortable and offer good value. Nice people too.

Alexander • *across the lake in Thalwil* • is not to be confused with one of the same name in Zurich proper; it has gone into a such a slump that the charm is gone for me.

Ermitage • *10 minutes by car (or 30 by boat) at the lakeside suburb of Kusnacht* • has been in a state of flux. Here's the residential wing of the well-known restaurant of the same name, with 28 rooms and 28 baths; tranquil and agreeable setting. The desk personnel are among the kindest to be found in this very kind nation. I like this house and wish it well.

Ramada • was due to open a 200-room hotel on the route to Kloten (the airport), but delays put it beyond inclusion in this edition. Usually, the European Ramadas are very good and with attractive dining facilities. A swimming pool was in blueprint.

Airport Hilton • roars in with topflight public quarters, a viewful swimming pool and sun deck, and a newer wing of 125 rooms. Fabulous Sutter's Grill that's a gold mine for beef-hungry U.S. prospectors; honky-tonk piano music nightly; salubrious dark-toned Bonanza Bar; coffee shop maintaining a spur of Old West flavor; bedchambers adequate but not up to the flair of the lobby and restaurant decor. Across the highway is the fortresslike **Movenpick Hotel Zurich-Airport.** The sister **Movenpick Hotel Holiday Inn** at neighboring *Regensdorf* has somewhat more architectural style, but both are intended to be only functional flyway-stations.

Hotel Airport • *5 minutes from the jet blast and 20 minutes from the city* • offers 47 adequately appointed units for one-nighters. All accommodations with bath or shower; attractive 9-tabled grill room plus Japanese restaurant; pleasing main-floor bar. Incidentally, all of these airport hotels are quiet because after 11 p.m. local air traffic is prohibited until morning.

Novotel • with 260 units plus a bar and restaurant, is a link in a reliable chain that offers clean medium-price shelter.

RESTAURANTS

☆☆☆☆ **Chez Max** • is in the suburb of **Zollikon** (Seestrasse 53). Proprietor-chef Max Kehl is assuredly one of the luminaries of European gastronomy. First, the atmosphere: It's brown-toned sanctum is darkly intimate, lovely, and joyfully relaxing—with contemporary paintings mixed with polished copper, flowers, and a delicate easygoing theme woven into every feature. Next, cuisine: It might have been prepared in the kitchens of Kingdom Come, and the selection depends on what's best at the markets. Even if you don't fancy sweets, ask to see the artistic dessert trolley. Wines span the Swiss hillsides to extraordinary French vintages. Prices are the only items that are hard to swallow, often giving hosts from soft-currency nations (e.g. USA) a permanent wince. Always reserve in advance.

☆☆☆☆ **Kunststube** • *in Kusnacht near Chez Max and Zurhohe* • also known by the chef-patron's name, **Petermann,** shares his precincts with the adjoining art gallery. L-shaped dining room with many oil paintings; strong inclination toward fish dishes; gastronomic menu approaching $100 with moderate a la carte meal about 20% less. Kind attention from Iris, the chef's lovely wife. Closed Monday; evenings only on Saturdays and Sundays. Highly regarded locally.

☆☆☆☆ **Zurhohe** • just up the hill above Max at Hohestr. 73, is far less costly and in some ways better. It is more animated (without wonder since one fine set lunch begins at about $13) and the atmosphere is popular. The revamped farmhouse contains several salons; enormous a la carte choices plus fixed-price meals at several levels. Fresh Atlantic fish flown in from Brittany; my scallops salad, wild duck, and exotic fruits sold for only $20 (wine extra) and was one of the best repasts of recent recall *anywhere*! Chef Robert Haupt really knows his pots and pans—*and* his audience. Closed Tues.; always book ahead.

★★★★ **Agnes Amberg** • *Hottingerstrasse 1* • is a lovely, fresh cosmopolitan redoubt for imaginative high-cost gastronomy. Pale-green color scheme; wooden floors; plants; attractive table settings. The restaurant takes its name from the chef who has created such a stir in local circles. I happen to be one of her admirers.

☆☆☆ **Rosa Tschudi** • *Gasthof zum Baren, Nurensdorf* • is another towering female personality in the realm of Swiss cuisine. Exquisite place plates, stemware, and presentation of dishes. Her creations incline more toward classic concepts than those of Agnes Amberg. Also expensive, also excellent.

★★★ **Kronenhalle** • *Ramistrasse 4* • varies a lot in cookery, but the service remains staunchly consistent—always rotten, at least on my oft-repeated tries. It remains popular possibly because of its unusually fine and vast assemblage of paintings in every cranny. Two floors; old-fashioned ambience, enlivened by the Picassos, Dalis, and Matisses on the walls; rendezvous of journalists, authors, painters, and people in the arts; miserably rushed attention that nearly always borders on negligence.

☆ **Haus zum Ruden** • *Limmatquai* • built in 1295 and restored in 1936, preserves the charm of the traditional Guild House. Proprietor Peter Halter and his lovely wife offer a friendly welcome. Handsome furnishings, fair cooking, and adequate service. Still solid.

★★ **Zunfthaus zur Waag** • *Munsterhof 8* • is in a more colorful antique square. Upstairs dining rooms with leaded windows, cream-colored panels, thick carpeting, candles and flowers on tables, and ultrakind attention by staffers who have a limited facility with English. The grilled meats are hewn from rancher's dreams.

★ **Kropf** • *just off Paradeplatz* • goes back before the turn of the century—as perhaps do some of its waitresses who bellow orders across the hall to its kitchen. Wooden floors, wonderful no-nonsense cooking, low prices, jovial in the best tradition of an honest tavern-type hideaway. Filled with Swiss. (Privately, one of my favorite corners in Zurich.)

Casa Ferlin • *Stampfenbachstrasse 38* • sometimes called Chiantiquelle, has the biggest name among Italian restaurants—and some of the most stunning price tags, too. Wall panels of red damask; ceiling decorated with ceramic denizens of the Mediterranean; delicious fettuccine; adept service. The owner sometimes plays the organ—sometimes too loudly.

Piccoli • *Rotwandstrasse 48* • is priced more modestly. The Veronese proprietor is the host, as well as the hunter who often shoots the game which is served; his wife commands the skillets with exquisite grace.

Investor's Club • *across from the Carlton-Elite* • markets light refreshment (rolls and coffee) along with ticker-tape replay of the stock market report. Savvy hostesses help you with your share selections, give advice, and answer your bids. Please don't step on a gnome, however.

Vegetarian munching?

Gleich • *9 Seefeldstrasse* • is as slick as a polished tomato. It is very attractive, modern in manner, and fully soundproofed to tone down the clack of healthy teeth crunching crispy-krinkly carrot steaks. The service is superb; a recent meal here was so surprisingly delectable that I returned on a later day to enjoy an even better one. It has become extremely popular, especially at noon. Closed Sunday.

Hiltl • *Sihlstrasse 26–28* • is another leaf in this botanical brotherhood. Its fashion is also modern and the cuisine is top-of-the-stalk. Ground-floor for groundling cookery; upstairs featuring an Indian plate, but in either place please finish your graze with the delicious mango ice cream.

NIGHT LIFE

In Zurich, the night spots can stay open until the wicked hour of 2 a.m.

Until the nocturnal wheels really start rolling and new challengers enter the nightscape, your most lively choices (partners often available, if desired) are (1) **Mascotte** and (2) **Cafe de la Terrasse. Birdwatcher's Club** in the Simplon Hotel is a quiet, elegant lounge where nighthawks preen for their well-feathered chicks. **La Puce** also is another colorful and comfortable contender. If you have a monumental thirst, **The Pub** boasts a bar that's almost 60 feet long. (On slow winter nights it's inclined and used as a skijump.) **Le Paragraph** (Kreuztrasse) is only a few steps from the Eden au Lac and Bellerive au Lac hotels, and it's catching on among the city's discophiles. The **Boite de Nuit** is the spinner of Jo Roland, the famous chansonnier. Musical shows nightly; elegant clientele; very a la mode. **Roxy** attracts a young crowd. **Blackout** blinks near the airport.

SHOPPING

SHOPPING HOURS: See "Geneva." Check locally about Monday closings.

BEST AREAS: Bahnhofstrasse is the heart, but there are some good pickings on the arteries that fan off from it. Browse among the web of lanes in the old section behind the Limmatquai near the Grossmunster Church.

ANTIQUES: The center of the action is on Schlusselgasse around St. Peter's Church. Rindermarkt, Neumarkt and Kirchgasse are also good bets.

EMBROIDERY: **Langenthal** (Strehlgasse 29) is suggested here in case you don't get to any of its chain-link sister operations across the nation. It is tops for lovely linens and delicate Swiss handiwork that simply cannot be found elsewhere.

HANDICRAFTS: If you seek honest-to-goodness regional craftsmanship instead of souvenir-stand junk, **Schweizer Heimatwerk** might warm your shopping soul. There are 7 of them. The headquarters is at Rudolf Brun-Brucke (ask for Manageress Miss Brassel); branches are at the National Bank Building at Bahnhofstrasse 2 (see Manageress Mrs. Butler), at Renweg 14 where you'll find a gallery featuring modern craft, in the National Gallery, main station, the *Zurich* Airport (Transit Halls A and B), the Glatt Shopping Center in *Wallisellen,* Hinterlauben 10 in *St. Gall,* and Understadt 38 in *Stein am Rhein.* In all you will encounter only the finest handwrought products from Alpine farm families and small artisans all over the national map—original costumes of the Swiss cantons, colorful Toggenburger wooden articles, ceramics, woodcarvings, dolls, handloomed textiles in gay patterns, fondue dishes, Swiss Army knives, basketware, Swiss semiprecious stones—and these are only the beginning. When you have examined this most exciting harvest of exclusively Helvetian rural treasures in any shops anywhere today, will you have finished your adventures in this particular field? For your sake we hope not, and here's why:

Remarkable Director Wettstein has applied his decades of specialized expertise to purchase, to expand, and masterfully to streamline his second related creation **Spindel** (St. Peterstrasse 11). His taste and professionalism have converted this 3-story structure into one of the best commercial assemblages of *international* hand-wrought arts and crafts from every European nation in existence. Your oracle here is Manageress Mrs. Akhrif-Hartung. Here's again a fascinating crossroads of far-flung cultural triumphs which pops the eyes!

HIGH FASHION AND ALL ACCESSORIES: **Grieder** (Paradeplatz) No fashion conscious visitor should miss an opportunity to enter the dazzling world of Grieder (rhymes with "leader"). Its epithet as "The Neiman-Marcus of Europe" fits it as perfectly as the stunning clothes, both ready-made and couture, which you'll try on. Branches at Zurich Airport and Lucerne. While in the main store, be sure to visit the **Lalaounis** boutique for the stunning Greek and Byzantine gold jewelry.

JEWELRY AND WATCHES: **Meister** (33 Bahnhofstrasse) is *the* prestige house of the city. Moreover, it occupies one of the prime spots on Zurich's "Fifth Avenue" of shopping. It's totally reliable, of course.

LEATHER GOODS: **Madler AG** (Bahnhofstrasse 26) is an illustrious, historic, and widely renowned firm. This fine old house, launched in Leipzig by gifted patriarch Mortiz Madler in 1850, has maintained its priceless name, traditions, and skills ever since. Awaiting you in these precincts is a sumptuous scope of strikingly beautiful, hard-to-find originals. The workmanship is exquisite, the styles have their distinctly illustrious cachet, the quality is superlative, and the cost range for the artistry is appealing. Proprietress Stephanie Madler, the only descendant of five generations still in this traditional trade, does credit to the fine company she owns and directs.

SILVER: **Meister** (28 Bahnhofstrasse) This is the tableware specialist of the previously mentioned jeweler. Glittering temptations that will brighten any home.

YUGOSLAVIA

USA: Yugoslav National Tourist Office, 630 Fifth Ave., New York, NY 10111, Tel: (212) 757–2801.

In general, this lovely Adriatic realm is having its troubles—chiefly political ones in drawing itself together into a single government. At this writing the most dramatic conflicts pertain between the peoples of Serbia and Croatia, but this could only represent a flashpoint and by the time you are ready to travel the fire could spread and the nation might be too volatile for holiday-making. Watch the news events carefully and judge for yourself.

While Yugoslavia has dedicated commendable energy to luring tourism from abroad, it is not yet geared to those luxuries that experienced travelers have come to expect from posher European lands. That might be both appropriate and anticipated from a socialist state. And even a capitalist can recognize an outright bargain when it is offered so guilelessly. Where else in today's Europe can you have a week's skiing holiday for under $850—including transatlantic airfare? You can take a fortnight on the coast for approximately $1200, also counting your air passage. The mainstream of visitors—and in summer that stream is a flood—wash in from Germany, Italy, Austria, and neighboring Slavic precincts. Obtaining a 3-month visa is easy, free, and almost automatic, but changing money on a summer day can be a grueling, time-consuming ordeal; it is not alleviated by the surly treatment from bureaucratic clerks who willingly reveal an impatience with North Americans. That, however, may change as the nation accommodates to further transoceanic commerce.

Strangely, almost spookily, everywhere you turn you find photographs of Tito; one's suspicion is that this is some haunting holdover of bygone government policy. When you look closer you notice that Marshal Josip Broz was portrayed in a variety of poses: in his youth, as a dauntless hunter, as a soldier, as a statesman or as an aging dictator, Tito's ubiquitousness is not evoked by officialdom; instead these pictures showing him at various stages in his career recall a national love for their hero and a nostalgia for the *only* personality in recent history who has united the separate states that now compose a single but agitated nation. Since his death the divisive bickerings of Croatia, Serbia, Dalmatia, and other regions have degenerated into separatism, jealousy, and wholesale irritability. The people from Zagreb have little time for those of Belgrade;

those near the Albanian frontier are voiceful and disruptive politically; like examples exist in every corner of the land (although this generalization is bound to be riddled by exceptions).

The single destination that I can praise to visitors is that splendid gem of the Adriatic, **Dubrovnik.** Naive and uninitiated zealots will aspire to a drive down the 500 miles of glorious coast from Venice to the medieval fortress city. I recently made this journey and don't recommend it to anyone during the summer months. While the first 100 miles from Italy are on *autostrada* and spin off rapidly, the remaining tableau is one of awesome natural beauty but unconscionable frustration, consuming more than two arduous days of wheelborne crawl. As soon as spring begins, almost the entire distance is bumper-to-bumper with mobile homes, trailers, broken-down vehicles, motorcycles, and campers.

While Venetian travel agencies may assure you that stopping places exist, almost all are filled by 3 p.m.; these are poor; therefore, you are left with *sobe* (single rooms) for rent in private houses. *Trieste,* sadly fading, is too near Venice for consideration as a stopover. Horse fanciers may prefer to take the spur to **Lipica,** a 4-century-old stud farm where stunning white Lipizzanners are raised, trained, and shown; a variety of hotels and boardinghouses provide indifferent shelter in the several neighboring villages. About halfway down the route at **Karlobag** I can recommend the seaside **Hotel Zagreb** (Tel. 051–894032 to reserve). **Zadar,** a promontory town of incredible antiquity, is often promoted as a resting spot, but its tourist complex is far from the city and third rate at best. Some adventurers split at **Split,** where the **Marjan** and the **Park** are possibles for overnighting.

My ardent advice is to fly in or arrive by cruise ship (preferably Italian). As grim as the preview may sound, the main feature, **Dubrovnik,** is a Baroque dream with High Renaissance overtones. The fortress is home to about 5000 residents. The modern city, the port, and the important hotels for tourists are built outside the massive walls, where they cling to the cliffs and overlook waters that Jacques Cousteau claims are the purest in the world. The towers face *Lodrum,* a tiny islet where Richard the Lionhearted ran aground. Apparently, the conqueror missed approximately 4000 other larger islands in the enchanting archipelago, which emerge like dark beads in the shimmering sea. All day life (apart from bathing) and most of the night life occur inside the fortress, where only pedestrian traffic is permitted. Buses and taxis arrive at the main gates to the Old City. Houses, shops, and restaurants intermingle along steep stone steps that finally arrive at the lower Stradun or Placa, a long, wide central avenue lined with art galleries, stores, and tourist-oriented boutiques with goods that probably won't interest you one whit.

Although I was told that there were several exceptional restaurants, I tried them all and found little to distinguish between them. Therefore, I'd suggest that you find a tavern with a view you prefer and dine there on grilled fish, simple meat preparations, and salads. An ample meal for two will come to about $30 with wine. As for hotels, by far the best is the architecturally dramatic **Belvedere,** probably the most luxurious hostelry to be found in the nation; a double runs close to $120 per day. The pool area gazes at ancient Dubrovnik and down the breathtaking coast. It's glorious, but even though the hotel is fairly young, it is showing some wear. (Maintenance generally is just so-so.)

The **Argentina,** formerly the leader, is now only adequate, followed by the **Excelsior.** Even these, however, have an overused air of commercialism about them that does not generate much enthusiasm.

Be sure to take an inexpensive half-day cruise along the nearby *Riviera* (the *Atlas* is a fine little coastal boat), which includes a 3-island jaunt and an endless quantity of fabulous scenery. *Cavtat,* founded by the Illyrians, is a bewitching destination about 12 miles by road from Dubrovnik, or 5 miles by sea. It nurtures an atmosphere of what the French Riviera must have looked like long before it was "discovered."

If you arrive during the summer's **Dubrovnik Festival,** be absolutely certain your reservations are secured. Some of the best music in the world is available at prices so low that you will think you are purchasing tickets to a neighborhood movie. Concerts are presented in the courtyards or on the balconies of magnificent palaces, sometimes on the battlement walls—spellbinding experiences with a new cultural dimension.

If you have time for roaming (and the nation is at peace), you might like to visit the capital, *Belgrade,* which resides in Serbia (approaching Romania), where the Danube and Sava rivers join. I find it commercial—as it probably should be, since it is the banking and administrative hub of the land. The three leading hotels are the **Intercontinental,** the **Metropol,** and the **Jugoslavia,** but there are about three dozen more in the city plus a burgeoning crop of motels and even "floatels" on the rivers. Wander into the Bohemian quarter of *Skardalija* for colorful tavern life and dining. The best shops line Tetrazije and Knez Mihailova streets. *Zagreb,* the Croatian capital, is known for its trade fair. Check in at either the big, white, linear **Intercontinental** or at the **Esplanade.**

Emphatically, Yugoslavia shines best away from its cities, Dubrovnik being the exception. *Bled* is a captivating lakeside redoubt crouching beneath the Karavanke and Julian Alps. Tito called it home for many years. You can stay at the lakeside **Grand Toplice** or the **Park,** which is near the water. **Vila Bled** is the conversion of Tito's estate into 21 suites and 10 rooms; high prices but very posh. *Ohrid* takes its name from the lake that it shoulders just at the Albanian frontier. It is old and charming and worth visiting if you can spare the travel time. Overnight at one of the several boarding houses, the **Metropol,** or the **Grand Palace.** *Mostar,* in the Neretva vale, has a strong eastern flavor, and *Pula*'s personality is drawn from the conquering Romans. I haven't paused at either town.

World-class skiers all know *Sarajevo,* host not long ago to the Winter Olympics. Quite a few hotels were opened for that showcase event. The **Holiday Inn** is modernistic. The **Jadran & Hercegovina** and the **Srbija & Bosna** offer thermal bath facilities and cures. **Terme** does the same. Snow bunnies and hares also gather at the resorts of *Krajnska Gora* in Slovenia, and in the Serbian purpose-built resort of *Kopaonik.* Your best bet for checking out details and prices for these places or other villages in the country is through the centralized headquarters of **Yugotours,** which also holds hands with the national airline; JAT can whisk you to its homeland from New York, Los Angeles, or Chicago. Yugotours is located at 350 Fifth Ave., New York, NY 10118; phone 800–223–5298 or (212) 563–2400.

Apart from occasional irritability manifest by socialist peoples resentfully hosting capitalist visitors, there is nothing to suggest any political abrasiveness toward westerners whatsoever. Yugoslavia—to the touristic eye—appears to be a completely free, if not grouchy, society. You can listen to the BBC, read British and American newspapers purchaseable at local kiosks, go anywhere and speak with anyone about any subject you like. But how will it remain?

HOTEL QUICK REFERENCE CHARTS

*Prices given are for average single accommodations unless otherwise noted.

AUSTRIA
Vienna

Hotel	Telephone Area Code: (222)	Telex	# of Rooms	Page
EXPENSIVE (AS 1200–2500)				
Ambassador Neuer Markt 5	527.511	111906	105	44
Bristol Karntner Ring 1	529.552	0112474	128	42
Hilton Am Stadtpark	752.652	136799	620	43
Imperial Karntner Ring 16	651.765	01/12630	160	42
Intercontinental Johannesgasse 28	563.611	131235	496	43
Marriott Parkring 12a	533.611	112249	304	43
Palais Schwarzenberg Schwarzenbergpl. 9	784.515	136124	42	43
Plaza Wien Am Schottenring 11	31.390	135859	223	43
Sacher Philharmonikerstr. 4	525.575	0112520	123	42
SAS Palais Weihburggasse 32	630.805	136127	165	43
UPPER MODERATE (AS 950–1350)				
Am Parkring Parkring 12	526.524	113420	65	44
Am Stephansplatz Stephansplatz 9	635.605	114334	69	44

Astoria Karntner Strasse 32	526.585	112856	116	44
Capricorno Schwedensplatz 3–4	633.104	115266	46	45
Clima Favoritenstrasse 12	659.605	132699	31	45
De France Schottenring 3	343.540	74360	150	44
Erzherzog Rainer Wiedner Hauptstrasse 27–29	654.646	132329	85	44
Europa Neuer Markt 3	521.594	112292	100	44
Konig von Ungarn Schulerstrasse 10	526520	7/7526	64	44
Kummer Mariahilfer Str. 71a	573.695	01/11417	108	45
President Wallgasse 23	573.636	112523	77	44
Prinze Eugen Wiedner Gurtel 14	651.741	132483	106	44
Ramada Linke Wienzeile-Ullmannstr. 71	850.40	112206	309	44
Regina Rooseveltplatz 15	427.681	07/4700	127	44
Royal Singerstrasse 3	524.631	1/2870	66	45
Strudlhof Pasteurgasse 1	312.522	135256	48	44
Tyrol Mariahilfer Str. 15	575.415	111885	35	44

MODERATE (AS 850–1200)

Arenberg Stubenring 2	529249	01/12692	23	45
Elite Wipplingerstrasse 32	632.518		30	45
K&K Maria Theresia Kirchberggasse M6–8	935.616	111530	123	45
Schneider Lehargasse 1	577.604	76004	70	45

ENVIRONS

Parkhotel Schonbrunn Hietzinger Hauptstrasse 10–14	822.676	132513	359	44
Trend Kurbadstrasse 8	681631	133361	256	44

BELGIUM
Brussels

Hotel	Telephone Area Code: (2)	Telex	# of Rooms	Page
EXPENSIVE (BF 5000–8200)				
Alfa Sablon 2–4 Strostraat	513.60.40	21248	32	73
Amigo rue de l'Amigo 1–3	511.59.10	21618	200	71
Hilton bd. de Waterloo 38	513.88.77	22744	373	71
Mayfair av. Louise 381–383	649.98.00	24821	100	72
Metropole pl. de Brouckere	217.23.00	21234	379	72
Royal Windsor rue Duquesnoy 5–7	511.42.15	62905	265	71
SAS Royal Rue du Fosse-aux-Loups 47	5118888	22202	240	72
Scandic Crown rue Royale 250	219.46.40	61871	364	72
Sheraton pl. Rogier 3	219.34.00	26887	600	71
UPPER MODERATE (BF 4200–6000)				
Bedford rue du Midi 135	12.78.40	24059	284	72
Europe Brussels 107 rue de la loi	2301333	25121	240	72
Jolly Hotel Atlanta bd. Adolphe Max 7	217.01.21	21475	240	72
Pullman Koningsstr. 103	217.62.90	25040	125	72

Ramada ch. de Charleroi 38	539.30.00	25539	200	72

MODERATE (BF 3000–3500)

l'Agenda rue de Florence 6–8	530.00.31	63947	42	73
Arlequin Rue de la Fourche 17	514.1615			73
New Siru pl. Rogier 1	217.75.80	21722	101	73
President Centre rue Royal 160	219.00.65	26784	73	73
President Nord bd. Adolphe Max 107	219.00.60	61417	116	73

AIRPORT LODGINGS

Holiday Inn Holidaystr. 7	720.58.65	24285	288	73
Mercur	242.53.35	65460	120	73
Novotel Airport Olmenstr.	720.58.30	26751	165	73
Sheraton Zaventem	725.10.00	27085	298	73
Sofitel Bessenveldstr. 15	02/720.60.50	26595	125	73

DENMARK
Copenhagen

Hotel	Telephone Area Code: (1–2)	Telex	# of Rooms	Page
EXPENSIVE (DKr 1100–1650)				
d'Angleterre Kongens Nytorv 34	120095	15877	144	94
Plaza Bernstorffsgade 4	149262	15330	106	95

UPPER MODERATE (DKr 950–1400)				
Grand Vesterbrogade 9	313600	15343	113	97

Kong Frederik V. Voldgade 23–27	125902	19702	127	95
Neptun Skt. Annae Plads 18	138900	19554	66	96
Opera Tordenskjoldsgade 15	121519	15812	66	97
Palace Raadhuspladsen 57	144050	19693	159	95
Royal Hammerichsgade 1	141412	27155	300	95
Scandinavia Amager Boulevard 70	112324	31330	550	95
Sheraton Vester Sogade 6	143535	27450	474	95

MODERATE (DKr 650–1000)

Alexandra H.C. Andersens Bd. 8	142200		65	96
Astoria Banegardspladsen 4	141419	16319	91	97
Copenhagen Admiral Toldbodgade 24	118282	15941	366	96
Imperial Vester Farimagsgade 9	128000	15556	176	96
Mercur Vester Farimagsgade 17	125711	19767	110	97
71 Nyhavn Nyhavn 71	118585	27558	81	95
Richmond Vester Farimagsgade 33	123366	19767	133	96
SAS Falconer Falkoner Alle 9	198001	15550	162	96
Sophie Amalie Sankt Annea Plads 21	133400	15815	134	95
Vestersohus Vester Sogade 57	113870		60	96

LOWER MODERATE (DKr 600–750)

Ascot Studiestreade 57	126000	15730	58	97

AIRPORT

Bel Air Lojtegardsvej 99	513033	31240	215	97
Sara Hotel Danmarkt Kastruplundgade 15	511400	31111	272	97
SAS Globetrotter Engvej 171	551433	31222	156	97

ENVIRONS

Hvide Hus Strandvejen 111 (Koge)	03653690	43501	118	88
Marienlyst Ndr. Strandvej Helsingor	211801	41116	213	101
StoreKro Slotsgade 6 (Fredensborg)			49	101

ENGLAND
London

Hotel	Telephone Area Code: (1)	Telex	# of Rooms	Page
EXPENSIVE (£135–200)				
Athenaeum 116 Piccadilly	71–499.34.64	261589	112	142
Berkeley Wilton Place	71–235.6000	919252	152	139
Claridge's Brook St.	71–629.88.60	21872	208	139
Connaught Carlos Place	71–499.70.70		106	139
Dorchester Park Lane (closed temporarily)	71–629.88.88	261802	300	139
Dorset Square 39–40 Dorset Square	71–7237874	263964		142
Fenja 69 Cadogan Gardens	71–5897333	934272	14	141
Halcyon 81 Holland Park	71–7277288	266721	44	141
Howard Temple Place	71–836.35.55	268047	111	147

Inn on the Park Hamilton Place, Park Lane	71–499.08.88	22771	228	142
Intercontinental 1 Hamilton Place	71–409.31.31	25853	500	144
Le Meridien Piccadilly Piccadilly	71–734.80.00	25795	290	148
Hilton on Park Lane 22 Park Lane	71–493.80.00	24873	431	144
Londonderry Parklane	71–493.72.92	263292	150	145
Marriott Grosvenor Square	71–493.12.32	268101	229	144
Montcalm Great Cumberland Place	71–402.42.88	28710	112	144
Norfolk Harrington Road	71–589.81.91	23241	97	150
Park Lane Piccadilly	71–499.63.21	21533	324	140
Ritz Piccadilly	71–493.81.81	267200	100	140
St. James Court Buckingham Gate	71–834.66.55	938075	400	150
Savoy The Strand	71–836.43.43	24234	386	140
Sheraton Park Tower 101 Knightsbridge Road	71–235.80.50	917222	300	144
Westbury New Bond St.	71–629.77.55	24378	225	144

UPPER MODERATE (£100–140)

Beaufort 33 Beaufort Gardens	71–5845252	929200	28	144
Blakes 33/35 Roland Gardens	71–370.6701	21879	50	143
Brown's Dover St. & Albemarle St.	71–493.60.20	28686	127	142
Cadogan Sloane St.	71–235.71.41	267893	320	142
Capital Basil St.	71–589.51.71	919042	60	143

Cavendish Jermyn St.	71–930.21.11	263187	255	146
Churchill Portman Square	71–486.58.00	264831	489	143
Dukes 35 St. James's Place	71–491.48.40	28283	52	140
Gloucester 4 Harrington Gardens	71–373.60.30	917505	539	145
Grosvenor House Park Lane	71–499.63.63	24871	478	142
Hyatt Carlton Tower Cadogan Place	71–235.54.11	21944	270	143
Hyde Park Knightsbridge	71–235.20.00	262057	182	141
Hilton Intl. Kensington	71–603.33.55	919763	611	147
Kensington Palace De Vere Gardens	71–937.81.21	262422	319	149
Langham Hilton 1 Portland Place	71–6361000	21113	410	141
Lowndes 19 Lowndes St.	71–235.60.20	919065	75	146
Royal Garden Kensington High St.	71–937.80.00	263151	442	145
Royal Lancaster Lancaster Terrace	71–262.67.37	24822	435	145
Royal Westminster Buckingham Palace Rd.	71–834.1302	916821	130	150
Stafford St. James's Place	71–493.01.11	28602	65	140

MODERATE (£85–105)

Basil Knightsbridge	71–581.33.11	28379	103	150
Bedford Southampton Row	71–278.78.71	263951	182	147
Belgravia Sheraton Chesham Place	71–235.60.40	919020	110	150
Chelsea Inn Sloane St.	71–235.43.77	919111	217	149

Chesterfield 35 Charles St.	71–491.26.22	269394	120	148
Cumberland Marble Arch	71–262.12.34	22215	880	150
Elizabetta Cromwell Rd.	71–370.42.82	918978	83	149
Embassy 150 Bayswater Rd.	71–229.12.12	27727	193	150
Forum 97 Cromwell Road	71–370.57.57	919663	914	146
Holiday Inn Marble Arch 134 George St.	71–723.12.77	27983	243	146
Hyde Park Towers Inverness Terrace	71–229.94.61	267465	110	150
Imperial Russell Square	71–278.78.71	263951	465	147
Kennedy 43 Cardington St.	71–387.44.00	28250	317	147
Leinster Towers 25 Leinster Gardens	71–262.45.91	27120	160	149
L'Hotel 28 Basil St.	71–589.62.86	919042	12	148
Londoner Welbeck St.	71–935.44.42	22569	121	150
London Metropole Edgware Rd.	71–402.41.41	23711	555	147
May Fair Intercontinental Berkeley St.	71–629.77.77	262526	390	140
Novotel 1 Shortlands	81–741.1555	934539	640	147
Portman Intercontinental 22 Portman Square	71–486.58.44	261526	287	145
Portobello Stanley Gardens 22	71–727.27.77		26	146
President Russell Square	71–278.78.71	263951	417	147
Regent Palace Piccadilly Circus	71–734.70.00	23740	1,244	150
Royal National Bedford Way	71–278.78.71	263951	556	148

Royal Trafalgar Whitcomb St.	71–930.44.77	24616	108	149
St. George's Langham Place	71–580.01.11	27274	85	149
Selfridge Orchard St.	71–408.20.80	22361	296	146
Strand Palace The Strand	71–836.80.80	24208	795	150
Tower St. Katharines Way	71–481.25.75	885934	826	147
Washington Curzon St.	71–499.70.30	24540	161	147
Wilbraham Wilbraham Place, Sloane St.	71–730.82.96		62	149

LOWER MODERATE (£45–90)

Averard 10 Lancaster Gate	71–723.88.77		60	150
Bloomsbury Crest Coram St.	71–837.12.00	22113	250	147
Dolphin Square Chichester St.	71–834.38.00		166	148
Mt. Royal Bryanston St.	71–629.80.40	23355	634	150
Mandeville Mandeville Place	71–935.55.99	269487	164	150
Park Plaza Bayswater Rd.	71–262.50.23	267465	282	150
Post House Bayswater Rd.	71–262.44.61	22667	176	150
Ramada 10 Berner's St.	71–636.16.29	25759	240	149
Regent Crest Carburton St.	71–388.23.00	22453	350	147
London Ryan Gwynne Place, Kings Cross Rd.	71–278.24.80	27728	213	150
Swallow International Cromwell Rd.	71–370.42.00	27260	424	150
White House Regent's Park	71–387.12.00	24111	600	149

ENVIRONS

Copthorne Effingham Park Gatwick Airport	0342–714994	—	122	152
Gatwick Copthorne Crawley Gatwick Airport	0342–714971	95500	260	152
Gatwick Hilton Gatwick Airport	293–518080	877021	333	152
Holiday Inn Swiss Cottage Adamson Rd.	71–722.77.11	267396	297	146

HEATHROW AIRPORT

Ariel Hayes, Middlesex	81–759.25.52	21777	185	151
Crest Bath Rd., Longford	81–759.24.00	934093	360	152
Edwardian Intt. Hayes, Middlesex	81–759.63.11	23935	441	151
Excelsior W. Drayton, Middlesex	81–.66.11	24525	660	151
Heathrow Penta	81–897.63.63	934660	680	151
Holiday Inn West Drayton	81–8954.45555		281	151
Post House West Drayton	81–759.23.23	934280	594	151
Sheraton-Heathrow West Drayton	81–759.24.24	934331	440	151
Sheraton Skyline Hayes, Middlesex	81–759.25.35	934254	360	151

FINLAND
Helsinki

Hotel	Telephone Area Code: (0)	Telex	# of Rooms	Page
EXPENSIVE (Fmk 650–900)				
Arctica Marski Mannerheimintie 10	641.717	12-1240	164	193
Hesperia Mannerheimintie 50	441.311	12-2117	285	192

Intercontinental Mannerheimintie 46	441.331	12-2159	600	192
Merihotelli Cumulus Hakaniemenranta 4	711.455	122999	87	193
Ramada President Etelainen Rautatiekatu 4	6911	12-1953	500	193
Rivoli Jardin Kasarmikatu 40	—	—	55	194
Strand Intercontinental John Stenberginranta 6	39351	—	200	192

UPPER MODERATE (Fmk 550–620)

Klaus Kurki Bulevardi 2	602.322	12-1670	75	193
Olympia Lantinen Brahenkatu 2	750.801	12-2101	100	193
Palace Etelaranta 10	171.114	12-1570	58	193
Seurahuone Kaivokatu 12	170.441	12-2234	114	193
Torni Yrjonkatu 26	644.611	12-5153	162	193
Vaakuna Asema-aukio 2	171.811	12-1381	290	193

MODERATE (Fmk 375)

Metrocity Kaisaniemenkatu 7	171.146	54	194
Ursula Paasivuorenkatu 1	750.311	46	193

LOWER MODERATE (Fmk 230)

Academica Hietaniemenkatu 14	(90) 440.717	12-1444	217	193
Hospiz (YMCA) Vuorikatu 17B	170.481		141	193
Satakunatalo Lapinrinne 1A	(90)6940311	12-2192	64	193

ENVIRONS

Dipoli Otaniemi	(90)461.811	12-1642		193
Torppa (Kalastajatorppa)			235	194

FRANCE
Paris

Hotel	Telephone Area Code: (1)	Telex	# of Rooms	Page
EXPENSIVE (FF 1450–1850)				
Bristol Faubourg St-Honore 112	42669145	280961	200	228
Crillon Place de la Concorde 10	42652424	290204	211	228
George V Av. George V 31	47235400	290776	315	228
L'Hotel Rue des Beaux-Arts 13	43252722	270870	27	230
Intercontinental Castiglione 3	426037800	220114	474	229
Lancaster Berri 7	43599043	640991	67	229
Meurice Rivoli 228	42603860	230673	160	228
Paris Hilton Av. Suffren 18	42739200	200955	470	229
Plaza-Athenee Av. Montaigne 25	43598523	650092	213	227
Prince de Galles Av. George V 33	47235511	280627	203	229
Ritz Pl. Vendome 15	42603830	220262	162	227
San Regis Jean-Goujon 12	435.94.190	643637	30	231
Tremoille 14 Rue de la Tremoille	43599721	640344	117	229
UPPER MODERATE (FF 980–1400)				
Concorde-Lafayette Pte des Ternes	47581284	650892	975	230

Grand Scribe 21	42603350	220875	600	230
Holiday Inn Pl. de la Republique	413554434	210651	335	233
Lutetia Bd. Raspail 45	45443810	270424	288	234
Meridien Bd. Gouvion-St-Cyr. 81	47581230	290952	1023	230
Meridien Montparnesse Cdt-Mouchotte 19	42603511	200135	964	233
Napoleon Av. Friedland 40	42277420	640609	140	232
Pullman St.-Jacques Bd. St-Jacques 17	45898980	270740	812	230
Raphael Av. Kleber 17	45530770	610356	90	231
Royal Monceau Av. Hoche 35	45619800	650361	250	229
Le Warwick Rue de Berri 5	45631411	642295	150	231
Westminster Paix 13	42615746	680035	102	232

MODERATE (FF 750–1000)

Alexander Av. Victor Hugo 102	45536465	610373	62	234
Ambassador Bd. Haussmann 16	42469263	650912	300	233
Aramis Rue de Rennes 124	45480375	205098	42	234
Bradford St-Philippe-du-Roule 10	43592420		49	233
Brighton Rue de Rivoli 218	42603003	217431		231
California Berri 16	43599300	660634	170	233
Cambon Rue Cambon 3	42603809	240814	44	231
Chateau Frontenac Rue Pierre-Charron 54	43593507	660994	100	231

Grand Hotel Littre Littre 9	4548771	270557	120	23?
Hotel de la Bretonnerie Rue Ste. Croix de la Bretonnerie	48877763		31	232
Hotel de Castiglione Fg-St-Honore 40	42650750	240362	100	233
Hotel de Castille Cambon 37	42615520	213505	55	233
Hotel de l'Universite Universite 22	42610939	260717	26	233
Hotel France et Choiseul St. Honore	42615460	680959	135	232
l'Abbaye St. Germain Rue Cassette 10	45443811		45	231
Lido Passage Madeleine 4	42662737		29	232
London Palace Boulevard des Italiens 32	48245464	642360	49	234
Lotti Castiglione 7	42603734	240066	129	231
Madeleine-Palace Cambon 8	42603782	211009	116	233
Madeleine-Plaza Pl. Madeleine 33	42652063		50	233
Nikko Quai Grenelle 61	45756262	260012	784	232
Normandy Echelle 7	42603021	670250	130	232
Regent's Rue P. Demours 6	47543940	640127	39	234
Royal Hotel Av. Friedland 33	43590814	280965	57	232
St. Simon St. Simon 14	45483566			234
Scribe Scribe 1	47420340	230024	200	233
Sofitel de Paris Louis Armand 8	45549500	200432	635	232
Terminus St-Lazare Concorde St-Lazare 108	42615120	650442	335	233

Vendome Pl. Vendome 1	42603284	680403	50	233
Vernet Vernet 25	47201670	29347	63	232
Victoria Palace Blaise-Desgoffe 6	45488040	270557	120	232

LOWER MODERATE (FF 520–750)

Astor Astorg 11	42665656		140	234
Cayre Bd. Raspail 4	42221082	270577	135	234
Chomel Rue Chomel 15	45485552	206522	23	234
Edouard VII Av. Opera 39	42615690	680217	95	234
G. H. du Mont-Blanc Huchette 28	40336388		41	234
Madison Bd. St-Germain 143	43265712		59	234
Mapotel Pont Royal Montalembert 7	45443827	270113	76	234
Massena Tronchet 16	40732560		30	234
Montalembert Montalembert 3	45486811	200132	65	234
Regina Pl. des Pyramids 2	42603110	670834	150	234
Richmond Helder 11	48247527	290574	56	234
Tronchet Tronchet 22				234
Vermont Bois-de-Boulogne 11 bis	45000497		29	234

ORLY AIRPORT

Air Hotel	7260310		56	235
Frantel Av. C. Lindbergh 20 (Rungis)	(1)6773909	260738	206	235

Hilton Orly Aerogares	7264000	842- 250621	388	235
Holiday Inn Av. Ch. Lindbergh 4 (Rungis)	(1)6872666	204679	180	235
Novotel	(1)36002010	670216	600	235
PLM Orly-Aerogare	(1) 6872337	204345	200	235

ROISSY AIRPORT

Arcade 95701 Roissy Airport Cedex	8624949	212989	360	235
Holiday Inn Rue de Paris 54	9859611	695143	121	235
Sofitel Charles de Gaulle Airport	8622323	691777	352	235

GERMANY
Berlin

Hotel	Telephone Area Code: (30)	Telex	# of Rooms	Page
EXPENSIVE (DM 225–400)				
Grand Esplanade Lutzowufer 15	261011	185986	402	305
Intercontinental Budapester Str. 2	26020	0182894	600	304
Kempinski Kurfurstendamm 27	88.10.91	0.183.553	335	304
Steigenberger Ranke-Marburger Str.	21080	181444	400	305
UPPER MODERATE (DM 175–210)				
Ambassador Bayreuther Str. 42	24.01.01	0.184.259	119	305
Excelsior Hardenbergstr. 14	31.991	0.184.781	320	306
Palace Budapester Str.	26.20.11	0.184.825	180	305
Schweizerhof Budapester Str. 21	2.69.61	0.185.501	400	305

Seehof Lietzensee-Ufer 11	32.10.51	0.182.943	77	306
Sylter Hof Kurfurstenstr. 116	21.200	0.183.317	131	306

MODERATE (DM 150–190)

Am Zoo Kurfurstendamm 25	88.30.91	0.183.835	144	306
Arosa Lietzenburger Str. 79	88.20.11	0.183.397	127	307
Berlin Kurfurstenstr. 62	26.92.91	0.184.332	225	306
Bremen Bleibtreustr. 25	881.40.76	0.184.892	48	306
Queen's Crest Guntzelstr. 14	87.02.41	0.182.948	110	306
Hamburg Landgrafenstr. 4	26.91.61	0.184.974	240	306
Hervis Stresemannstr. 97	261.14.44	0.184.063	73	307
Ibis Messedamm 10	30.20.11	0.182.882	189	306
Penta Nurnberger Str. 63	24.00.11	182877 BEPEN	425	306
President Au der Urania 16	213.80.61	0.184.018	72	307
Savoy Fasanenstr. 9	31.06.54	0.184.292	115	305
Steglitz International Albrechtstr. 2	79.10.61	183545	220	306
Studio (Am) Kaiserdamm 80	30.20.81	01.82.825	77	306

LOWER MODERATE (DM 100)

Franke Albrecht-Achilles-Str. 57	892.10.97	0.184.857	75	307
Lichtburg Paderborner Str. 10	891.80.41	0.184.208	72	307
Plaza Knesebeckstr. 63	88.20.81	0.184.181	132	307

| *Savigny* Brandenburgische Str. 21 | 881.30.01 | 0.184.053 | 60 | 307 |

ENVIRONS

| *Gehrhus* Brahmsstr. 4 | 826.20.81 | | 35 | 307 |
| *Stossensee* Glockenturmstr. 30 | 304.55.95 | | 45 | 306 |

Frankfurt

Hotel	Telephone Area Code: (69)	Telex	# of Rooms	Page
EXPENSIVE (DM 220–380)				
Arabella Grand K.-Adenauer Str. 7	29810	2981-810	378	321
Frankfurter Hof Am Kaiserplatz	2051	411806	400	320
Gravenbruch Kempinski Frankfurt/Neu-Isenburg 2	5050	0417673	315	321
Hessischer Hof Friedrich-Ebert-Anlage 40	7540	04-11776	161	320
Intercontinental Wilhelm-Leuschner Str. 43	230561	0413639	814	320
Park Wiesenhuttenplatz 28	2697	0412808	280	321
Plaza Hamburger Allee 2	770721	412573	591	321
UPPER MODERATE (DM 230)				
National Baselerstrasse 50	234841	0412570	130 beds	322
MODERATE (DM 150–210)				
Continental Baselerstr. 56	230341	412502	80	322
Excelsior-Monopol Mannheimerstr. 11	230171	413061	100	322

LOWER MODERATE (DM 160)

Luxor Am Allerheiligen Tor 2	293067	414136	50	322
Wurttemberger Hof Karlstrasse 14	233106		67	322

ENVIRONS

Airport Hotel Flughafenstr. 300	69851	413112	350	321
Arabella Lyonerstr. 44	66330	04-16760	400	322
Holiday Inn Mailaenderstr. 1	680011	0411805	190	321
Queen's Niederrad	069-67840	800 44 Utel	300	322
Ramada Oeserstr. 180	39051	416812	236	322
Schlosshotel Kronberg Hainstr. 25	503355	0415424		322
Sonnenhof Kurhotel Falkensteinerstr. 9	3051	410636	45	322

Hamburg

Hotel	Telephone Area Code: (40)	Telex	# of Rooms	Page
EXPENSIVE (DM 260–310)				
Atlantic Kempinski An der Alster 72	248001	2163297	320	328
Intercontinental Fontenay 10	441081	211099	299	329
SAS Plaza Marseillerstr. 2	351035	214400	570	329
Vier Jahreszeiten Neuer Jungfernstieg 9–14	34941	0211629	200	328
UPPER MODERATE (DM 170–195)				
Bellevue An Der Alster 14	248011	2162929	81	329

Berlin Borgfelderstr. 1–9	257211	0213939	96	329
Prem An der Alster 9	245453	2163115	50	329

MODERATE (DM 115–135)

Alster Hof Esplanade 12	341781	02-13843	144 beds	330
Europaeischer Hof Kirchenallee 45	248171	2162493	350	330
Maritim Reichshof Kirchenallee 36	248330	2-163396	350	330

Munich

Hotel	Telephone Area Code: (89)	Telex	# of Rooms	Page
EXPENSIVE (DM 210–300)				
Bayerischer Hof Promenade Platz 2–6	21200	23409	390	341
City Hilton Am Gasteig	—	—	500	342
Continental Max Joseph Strasse 5	557971	522603	150	341
Park Hilton Am Tucherpark 7	340051	5215740	481	342
Rafael Neuturmstr.	290980		74	341
Vier Jahreszeiten Maximilianstr. 17	228121	523859	365	341

UPPER MODERATE (DM 185–230)

Arabella Arabellastr. 5	92321	29987	260	343
Drei Loewen Echillerstr. 8	595521	23867	145	343
Eden-Wolff Arnulfstr. 4–8	558281	523564	220	342
Excelsior Schutzenstr. 11	557906	22419	120	342

Holiday Inn Leopoldstr. 194	340971	5215439	400	342
Palace Trogerstrasse 21	4705091	528256	73	342
Sheraton Arabellastr. 6	924011	522391	650	342

MODERATE (DM 165)

Konigshof Karlsplatz 25	558412	23616	120	343
Metropol Bayerstrasse 43	530764	22816	370	343
Penta Hochstrasse 3	4485555	529046	581	343

LOWER MODERATE (DM 90–110)

Intercity Bahnhofsplatz	558571	523174	209	343
Tourotel Domagkstr. 26	381000	215533	230	343

GREECE
Athens

Hotel	Telephone Area Code: (1)	Telex	# of Rooms	Page
EXPENSIVE (Dr 10,000–21,000)				
Astir Palace Constitution Sq.	3643112	215013	78	368
Athenaeum Inter-Continental Constitution Square	9023666	221553	600	369
Athens Hilton Vas Sofias Ave. 46	720.201–9	21-5808	518	369
Grand Bretagne Constitution Square 1	323.02.51	21-5346	450	369
Ledra Marriott Leoforo Syngrou	9525211	221833	500	369
NJV Meridien Constitution Square	3255301	210568	182	369

UPPER MODERATE (Dr 8000–12,000)

Acropole Palace Patission St. 51	522.38.51	21-5909	170	372
Astor Kar. Servias St. 16	322.49.71	21-4018	133	371
Athens Chandris Syngrou Ave. 385	941.48.24	21-8112	380	371
Attica Palace Kar. Servias St. 6	322.30.06	21-5909	78	371
Caravel Alexandrou Ave. 2	790.721	21-4401	471	371
Divani-Zafolia Palace Alesandra Ave. 87/89	644.24.11	21-4468	193	370
Electra Hermou St. 5	323.21.04	21-6896	110	371
Electra Palace Nikodimou St. 18	324.14.01	21-6896	120	372
Esperia Palace Stadiou St. 22	323.80.00	21-5773	185	371
Golden Age Michalakopoulou St. 57	740. 861	21-9292	122	372
Herodion Rovertou Galli 4	923.68.32	21-9423	90	370
Holiday Inn Michalakopoulou St. 50	748.322	21-88703	200	370
King Minos Piraeus St. 1	523.11.11	21-5339	178	371
Park Alexandras Av. 10	883.27.10	21-4748	146	370
Royal Olympic Diakou St. 28	922.64.11	21-5753	335	370
St. George Lycabettus Kleomenous St. 2	790.710	21-4253	154	370

MODERATE (Dr 5000–6500)

Alpha Chalkokondyli St. 17	522.12.53	21-5067	88	372
Arethusa Metropoleos & Nikis Sts.	322.94.31	31-6882	88	372

Athens Gate Syngrou Ave. 10	923.83.02	21-4202	106	372
Diomia Diomia St. 5	323.80.34		71	372
Dorian Inn Piraeus St. 15	523.97.82	21-4779	146	371
Ilisia Michalakopoulou St. 25	744.051	21-4924	69	372
Ilyssos Callirrois Ave.	921.5371	21-0537		372
Lycabette Valaoritou St. 6	363.35.14	21147	39	373
Minerva Athens Stadium St. 3	323.09.15	21-5838	50	372
Stanley Odysseus St. 1	522.00.11	21-6550	400	371
Titania Panepistimiou Ave. 52	360.96.11	21-4673	396	372

LOWER MODERATE (Dr 2000–4000)

Achillion Ag. Konstantinou St. 32	523.09.71		56	372
Atlantic Patission St. 35	523.53.61	21-5723	158	372
Hermes Apollonos St. 19	323.55.14		45	373
Imperial Metropoleos St. 46	322.76.17		21	373

IRELAND
Dublin

Hotel	Telephone Area Code: (1)	Telex	# of Rooms	Page
EXPENSIVE (IR£110–125)				
Berkeley Court Lansdowne Rd. Ballsbridge	601711	30554	200	415
Shelbourne St. Stephen's Green	766471	25184	166	415
Westbury Grafton St. 2	791122	91091	158	416

UPPER MODERATE (IR£70–90)

Bloom's Hotel Anglesea St.	715622	31688	86	416
Burlington Upper Leeson St.	605222	25517	420	416
Gresham Upper O'Connell St.	746881	25308	179	417
Jurys Pembroke Rd. Ballsbridge	605000	25304	310	416
Royal Dublin Upper O'Connell St.	733666	24288	110	416
Sachs Morehampton Rd. 21	680995	31667	20	416

MODERATE (IR£40–50)

Skylon Upper Drumcondra Rd.	379121	25517	88	417
Tara Tower Merrion Rd.	694666	25517	84	417
Buswells Molesworth St.	764013	Inter- hotel 24858	68	417
Clarence Wellington Quay	776178		70	417

ENVIRONS

Fitzpatrick Castle Killiney Hill Rd.	851533	30353	48	417
Grand Malahide	450633		48	418
Green Isle Clondalkin	593406	25517	56	418
Montrose Stillorgan Rd.	693311	91207	190	418
Royal Marine Dun Laoghaire	801911		115	417

AIRPORT

International	379211	24612	187	417

ITALY
Florence

Hotel	Telephone Area Code: (55)	Telex	# of Rooms	Page
EXPENSIVE (L 220,000–350,000)				
Excelsior Piazza Ognissanti 3	294301	570022	217	451
Grand Hotel Villa Cora Viale Machiavelli 18–20	2298451	570604	55	452
Regency Piazza M. d'Azeglio 3	245247	571058	32	452
Savoy Piazza della Republica 7	283313	570220	100	452
Villa Medici Via il Prato 42	261331	570179	105	452
UPPER MODERATE (L 160,000–190,000)				
Berchielli Lungarno Acciaiuoli 14	264061	575582	76	454
Brunelleschi Piazza Sta. Elisabetta	212810	575805	94	453
Jolly Piazza V. Veneto 4	(55) 2770	570191	162	453
Kraft Via Solferino 50123	284273	571523	60	453
Lungarno Borgo S. Jacopo 14	260397	570110	71	453
MODERATE (L 140,000–160,000)				
Astoria Pullman Via del Giglio 9	2988095	571070	90	454
Continental Lungarno Acciaioli 2	282392	570110	62	454
Grand Hotel Minerva Piazza Sta. Maria Novella 16	284555	570414	108	454
Londra Via Jacopo da Diacceto 16–20	262791	571152	100	454
Michelangelo Viale F. lli Rosselli 2	278711	571113	140	453

Park Palace Pizzale Galileo 5	222431		30	453
Plaza Lucchesi Lungarno della Zecca 38	264141	570302	105	454
Principe Lungarno Amerigo Vespucci 34	284848		21	454

ENVIRONS

Villa La Massa Candeli 50010	630051		39	455
Villa San Michele Via Doccia 4, Fiesole	59451		31	454

Rome

Hotel	Telephone Area Code: (6)	Telex	# of Rooms	Page
EXPENSIVE (L 160,000–350,000)				
Bernini Bristol Piazza Barberini 23	463.051	610554	128	489
Borromini Via Lisbona 7	841321	680485	90	490
Cavalieri Hilton Via Cadlolo 101	3151	610296	400	488
Eden Via Ludovisi 49	4743.551	610567	120	487
Excelsior Via Vittorio Veneto 125	4708.031	610232	374	488
Grand Via V.E. Orlando 3	4709.011	610210	221	487
Hassler Trinita dei Monti 6	679.26.51	610208	120	487

UPPER MODERATE (L 150,000–190,000)

Cicerone Via Cicerone 55	3576	680514	250	490
De La Ville Via Sistina 69	6799241		197	489
Flora Via V. Veneto 191	497.821	680494	200	488

Leonardo Da Vinci Via dei Gracchi 324	382.091	611182	264	491
Londra & Cargill Sallustio 19	473871	680412	105	490
Lord Byron Via G. de Notaris 5	360.95.41	611217	50	491
Mediterraneo Via Cavour 15	464051	610556	350	488
Palazzo Degli Ambasciatori Via V. Veneto 70	473.831	610241	152	488
Parco dei Principi Via Frescobaldi 5	610.517	61517	203	489
Hotel Quirinale V. Nazionale 7	479.901	610332	190	490
Savoia Via Ludovisi 15	474.41.41	611339	111	493
Victoria Via Campania 41	4739311	610212	110	489

MODERATE (L 90,000–180,000)

Anglo-Americano Via 4 Fontane 12	472.941	608118	115	494
Atlante Garden Via Crescenzio 78	3598884	680258	150	492
Atlante Star Via Vitelleschi 34	6564196	680258	150	492
Boston Via Lombardia 47	473951	680460	120	492
Cardinal Via Giulia 62	6542719	612373	68	492
Carriage Via delle Carrozze 36	679.51.66		25	491
Claridge Viale Liegi 62	868.556	610340	200	493
Colosseum Via Sforza 10	475.12.28	611151	45	494
Columbus Via della Concilizaione 33	6565435	613010	100	494
Commodore Via Torino 1	475.15.15	612170	65	493

Degli Aranci Via Barnaba Oriani 11	870202		42	494
Eliseo Via Porta Pinciana 30	460.556	610693	60	492
Fleming Piazza Monteleone de Spoleto 20	3276741	610640	280	491
Forum Via Tor de Conti 25	679.24.46	680252	83	491
Giulio Cesare Via degli Scipioni 287	310.244	613010	65	494
Gregoriana Via Gregoriana 18	679.42.69		19	490
Hermitage Via Eugenio Vajna 12	(06)870454	680195	100	494
Inghilterra Via Bocca di Leone 14	672161	614552	102	491
Jolly Corso d'Italia 1	8495	612293	200	489
Lloyd Via Alessandria 110/a	862.977		48	493
Majestic Via Veneto 50	486.841	680463	100	494
Massimo D'Azeglio Via Cavour 18	460.646	610556	230	490
Metropole Via Principe Amedeo 3	(06)4774	611061	285	493
Michelangelo Via Stazione S. Pietro 14	631.251	680414	200	492
Midas Palace Via Aurelia 8	6506	680414	360	492
Napoleon Piazza Vittorio Emanuele 105	737.646	611069	100	492
Panama Via Salaria 336	862.558		42	493
Plaza Via del Corso 126	672101		207	494
President Via Emanuele Filiberto 175	770.121	611192	149	491
Regina Carlton Via Vittorio Veneto 72	475.88.41	611684	134	493

Residence Palace Via Archimede 69	878.341	612291	191	492
Ritz Piazza Euclide 43	481047	610570	350	492
Sitea Via V. Emanuele Orlando 90	474.36.47	614163	40	491
Tiziano Corso V. Emanuele 110	655.087		50	494
Villa Pamphili Via della Nocetta 105	5862	611675	255	492
Visconti Palace Via F. Cesi 37	3684	680407	246	492

LOWER MODERATE (L 65,000)

La Residenza Via Emilia 22	6799592		27	493
Mondial Via Torino 127	472.861	612219	75	494
Porta Maggiore Piazza Porta Maggiore, 25	7598751	612612	120	493
San Giorgio Via G. Amendola 61	475.13.41	610556	186	493

Venice

Hotel	Telephone Area Code: (41)	Telex	# of Rooms	Page
EXPENSIVE (L 180,000–350,000)				
Bauer Grunwald Campo S. Moise	707022	410075	210	523
Cipriani Giudecca 10	707744	410162	100	522
Danieli Royal Excelsior Riva Degli Schiavoni	26480	410077	254	523
Europa & Regina San Marco	700477	410123	239	523
Gritti Palace Campo S. Maria del Giglio	26044	410125	101	522
Palazzo del Giglio San Marco	705166	410125	19	523

UPPER MODERATE (L 130,000–220,000)

La Fenice San Marco	26403	70164	150	524
Luna St. Mark's Sq.	89840	410236	128	524
Metropole Riva Schiavoni	705044	410340		524
Monaco San Marco	700211	410450	80	524
Patria Tre Rose San Marco	22490		32	524
Pullman Park G. Panadopoli	83394	410310	100	524

MODERATE (L 80,000–125,000)

Ala San Marco	708333	410275	130 (beds)	524
Boston San Marco	87665		46	524
Carpaccio San Toma	35946		24	524
Cavalletto Doge Orseolo San Marco	700955	410684	150	524

ENVIRONS

Excelsior Palace Lungomare Marconi 40	760201	410023	275	525
Grand Hotel des Bains Lungomare Marconi 17	765921	410125	272	525
Villa Cipriani Via Canova 298	52166	411060	40	525
Villa Mabapa Rivera S. Nicolo 16	760590	440170	70	525

NETHERLANDS
Amsterdam

Hotel	Telephone Area Code: (20)	Telex	# of Rooms	Page
EXPENSIVE (Dfl 260–470)				
Amstel (check reopening date) Prof. Tulpplein 1	6226.060	11004	115	564
Apollo Apollolaan 2	6735.922	14084	240	565
Barbizon Centre Leidseplein	6851351	12601	242	566
Barbizon Palace Prins Hendrikkade 59	65564564	10187	264	566
de l'Europe Nieuwe Doelenstraat 2	6234.836	12081	87	564
Dikker en Thijs Prinsengracht 444	6267.721	13161	25	567
Doelen Karena Nieuwe Doelenstraat 24	6220.722	14399	90	567
Hilton Apollolaan 138	6780.780	11025	376	564
Marriott Stadhouderskade 21	6835.151	15087	395	564
Memphis Lairessestraat 87	6733.141	12450	90	565
Okura Ferd. Bolstraat 175	6787.111	16182	411	565
SAS Royal Rusland 17	6231231	5208200	247	565
Sonesta Kattengat 1	6212.223	17149	360	565
UPPER MODERATE (Dfl 240–320)				
American Leidsekade 97	6245.322	11379	185	566
Rembrandt Crest Herengracht 255	6221.727	15424	99	566
Caransa Karena Rembrandtsplein 19	6229.455	13342	66	567

Garden Hotel Dijsselhofplantsoen 7	6642121	15453	100	566
Holiday Inn Crown Plaza Nieuwe Zijds Voorburgwal 5	6200500	15183	270	568
Jan Luyken Jan Luykenstraat 58	6764111	16254	65	566
Jolly Hotel Carlton Vijzelstraat 2	6222266	11670	150	567
Krasnapolsky Dam.	65549111	12262	254	567
Parkhotel Stadhouderskade 25	6730961	11412	184	567
Port van Cleve Nieuwe Zijds Voorburgwal 178	6244.860	13129		567
Pulitzer Prinsengracht 315–331	6228.333	16508	176	566
Schiller Karena Rembrandtsplein 26	6231.660	14058	80	567
Victoria Damrak 1–5	6234.255	16625	140	566

MODERATE (Dfl 200–240)

Amsterdam Ascot Damrak 95–98	6260066	16620	110	570
Capitool Nieuwezijds Voorburgwal 67			148	568
Ladbroke Park Hotel Stadthouderskade 25	6717474	11412	200	567

LOWER MODERATE (Dfl 90–185)

Marianne Nicolaas Maesstraat 107	6797.972		14	567
Owl Roemer Visscherstraat 1	6189.484	13360	31	567
Trianon J. W. Brouwersstraat 3–7	6733.918	14275	48	567
Von Wehde Korte van Eeghenstraat 8	6762.131		10	567

AIRPORT

Ibis Schipholweg 181 (Badhoevedorp)	602968.1234	16491	384	568
Pullman Schiphol Oude Haagseweg 20	6179005	15524	144	568
Schiphol Hilton Schiphol Centrum	6511.5911	15186	181	568
Golden Tulip Barbizon Schiphol Kruisweg 495 (Hoofddorp)	02503.15851	41646	168	568

ENVIRONS

Amsterdam Altea Joan Muyskenweg 10	6658.181	13382	128	568
Novotel Europaboulevard 10	6442.851	13375	600	568

NORWAY
Oslo

Hotel	Telephone Area Code: (2)	Telex	# of Rooms	Page
EXPENSIVE (NKr 1100–1700)				
Continental Stortingsgt. 24	419.060	71012	179	596
Grand Karl Johans Gate 31	334.870	71683	510	596
Oslo Plaza Sonja Henies Pl.	2171000	11059	689	597
Royal Christiania Biskop Gunnerusgt. 3	336.470	71342	313	598
Scandinavia Holbergsgt. 30	113.000	19090	476	597
Rica Oslofjord Sandviksvein 184	545700	74345	228	598
UPPER MODERATE (NKr 800–1000)				
Ambassadeur Camilla Collets vei 15	441.835	71446	50	597
Bristol Kristian 4's gt. 7	415.840	71668	143	597

Helsfyr Stromsvn. 108	672380	16776	115	598

MODERATE (NKr 675–850)

Cecil Stortingsgate 8	415840	71668	112	598
Scandic Crown Parkveien 68	562.690	71763	115	598
Nobel Karl Johansgt. 33	337.190	11915	61	598
Norum Bygdoy Alle 53	447.990		100	598
Stefan Rosenkrantzgt. 1	336.290	19809	130	598

LOWER MODERATE (NKr 600–750)

Carlton Parkveien 78	563.090	71902	50	598
Gabelshus Gabelsgate 16	562590	19668	48	598
Gyldenlove Bogstadveien 20	601.090			599
Ritz Fr. Stangsgt. 3	443.900	19668	49	598
Triangel Holbergs Plass 1	208855	19413	107	599
West Skovveien 15	562.995	18754		599

ENVIRONS

Holmenkollen Park Kongeveien 26	(02)146090	72094		597

AIRPORT

SAS Park Royal Fornebuparken, 1324, Lysaker	120.220	18745	150	599

PORTUGAL
Lisbon

Hotel	Telephone Area Code: (1)	Telex	# of Rooms	Page
EXPENSIVE (Esc 18,500–33,000)				
Alfa Av. C. Bordalo Pinheiro	775876	18478	544	633
Altis R. Castilho 11	560071	13314	219	633
Diplomatico Rua Castilho 74	562041	13713	90	633
Intercontinental Ritz R. R. da Fonseca 88	684131	12589	300	632
Lisboa-Sheraton R. Latino Coelho I	575757	12774	400	632
Meridien R. Castilho 149	690400	64315	353	632
UPPER MODERATE (Esc 15,000–23,000)				
Avenida Palace R. Pr. Dezembro 123	360154	12815	100	633
Holiday Inn Avda. A. Jose d'Almeida	735222	60330	169	634
Lisboa Plaza Av. da Liberdade	370331	16402	100	633
Lisbon Penta Av. dos Combatentes	740141	18437	592	633
Lutecia Av. F. Miguel Contreiras	897021	12457	151	634
Tivoli Av. da Liberdade 2	41101	1588	320	632
Tivoli-Jardim annexed to Tivoli	539971	12172		633
MODERATE (Esc 8000–13,000)				
Capitol Rua Eca de Queiroz	536811/5	13701	58	635
Embaixador Av. Duque de Loule 73	530171	12660	96	634

Fenix Praca M. de Pombal 8	736161	12170	125	634
Florida R. Duque de Palmela 32	554171	12256	120	634
Mundial R. D. Duarte 4	863101	12308	150	634
Praia Mar (Carcavelos suburb, near Estoril)			143	635
Principe Real R. dal Alegria 53	360116		24	634
Rex Rua Castilho 169	682161		77	634
Roma Av. de Roma 33	767761/3	16586		634
York House R. das Janelas Verdes 32	662435		48	635

LOWER MODERATE (Esc 6500–8500)

Dom Carlos Av. Duque de Loule 121	539071	16468	73	634
Excelsior R. Rodrigues Sampaio 172	537151	14223	90	634
Flamingo R. Castilho 41	532191		35	634
Impala R. Filipe Folque 49	58914		35	634
Jorge V R. Mouzinho da Silveria 3	562525		56	634
Metropole Praca Dom Pedro IV 30	369164		57	634
Miraparque Av. Sidonio Pais 12	54181	16745	100	634
Presidente R. A. Herculano 13	539501		59	634
Principe Av. Duque D'Avila 199	536151		55	634
Reno Av. Duque D'Avila 195	48181	15893	50	634
Residencia America Rua Tomaz Ribeiro 47	531178/9	13701	61	635

ENVIRONS

Novotel	250	633

Other suburban hotels often associated with Lisbon are covered separately under our alphabetical listings for "Cascais," "Estoril," "Guincho" and "Sintra."

SCOTLAND
Edinburgh

Hotel	Telephone Area Code: (31)	Telex	# of Rooms	Page
EXPENSIVE (S£75–100)				
Caledonian Princes St.	2252433	72179	212	671
Edinburgh Sheraton Festival Square 1	2299131	72398	263	671
George George St.	2251251	72570	212	671
Balmoral Princes St.	5562414	72332	193	671
UPPER MODERATE (S£70–85)				
Carlton Highland North Bridge	5567277	778215	98	671
Hilton National Belford Rd.	3322545		146	671
King James St. James Centre, Leith St.	5560111	727200	160	672
Post House Corstorphine Rd.	3348221	727103	208	671
Roxburghe Charlotte Square	2253921	727054	78	672
Royal Scot	3349191	727197	244	671
Scandic Crown 80 High St.	5579797	727298	238	672
MODERATE (S£60–75)				
Howard Great King St. 32	5561393	727887	26	672
Mt. Royal Princess St. 53	2257161	727641	153	672

Rutland Rutland St. 3	2293402		18	672

ENVIRONS

Braid Hills Braid Rd. 134	4478888		50	674
Dalhousie Castle Bonnyrigg, Midlothian	0875.20153	72380	24	672
Ellersly House Ellersly Rd.	3376888	76357	57	674
Forth Bridges Moat House Forth Rd. Bridge	3311199	724430	108	673
Hawes Inn South Queensferry	3311990	53168	6	673
Houstoun House Uphall	(Broxburn) 853831	727148	29	672

SPAIN
Madrid

Hotel	Telephone Area Code: (1)	Telex	# of Rooms	Page
EXPENSIVE (Pts 18,000–28,000)				
Luz Palacio Paseo de la Castellana 67	4425100	27207	200	725
Melia Madrid Princesa 27	5418200	22537	248	725
Miguel Angel Miguel Angel 29	4420022	54134	307	724
Palace Plaza de las Cortes 7	4297551	22272	526	724
Princesa Plaza Princesa 40	5422100	44377	44378	726
Ritz Plaza de la Lealtad 5	5212857	22272	175	724
Villa Magna Paseo de la Castellana 22	2614900	22914	200	724
UPPER MODERATE (Pts 14000–19000)				
Castellana Castellana 57	4100200	27686	378	725

Eurobuilding Padre Damian 23	4577800	22548	570	725
Plaza Plaza de Espana 8	2471200	27383	354	725
Villa Real Plaza de las Cortes 10	4203767		115	726
Wellington Velazquez 8	2754400	22700	325	726

MODERATE (Pts 9000–16,000)

Carlton Paseo de las Delicias 26	2397100		150	728
Claridge Plaza de Conde Valle Suchil 5	257300	22058	150	728
Colon Doctor Esquerdo 117	5730800	22984	350	727
Melia Castilla Capitan Haya 43	2708003	23142	1000	726
Mindanao S. Francisco de Sales 15	4495500	22631	300	725
Pintor Goya Goya 79	2254521	23281	170	726
Residencia Florida Norte P°–de la Florida 5	5416190	23675	338	727
Sanvy Goya 3	5760800		109	727
Serrano Marques de Villamejor 8	2257564	54134	36	728
Suecia Marques de Casa Riera 4	5316900	22313	64	727
Alcala Alcala 66	2251650	48094	153	727
Cuzco Av. Generalisimo 55	4560600	22464	331	728
Mayorazgo Flor Baja 3	2472600	45647	204	727

ENVIRONS

Monte Real Arroyo Fresno 17	3162140	22089	80	726

AIRPORT

Alameda Ctra. de Ajalvir, Km 12	2055040	43809	150	728
Barajas Aeropuesto	2054296	22255	730	728

SWEDEN
Stockholm

Hotel	Telephone Area Code: (8)	Telex	# of Rooms	Page
EXPENSIVE (SFr 1100–1500)				
Clas Pa Hornet Surbrunnsgatan 20	165130			781
Diplomat Strandvagen 7-C	635800	17119	120	780
Grand S. Blasiehomshamnen 8	221020	19500	355	780
Royal Viking Vasagatan 1	141000	13900	400	780
Sergel Plaza Brunkebergstorg 9	226600	16700	408	780
Sheraton Tegelbacken 6	142600	17750	476	780
Strand Nybrokajen 9	222900	10504	100	779
UPPER MODERATE (SFr 850–1200)				
Amaranten Kungsholmsgatan 31	541060	17498	363	782
Anglais Humlegardsgatan 23	249900	19475	212	781
Birger Jarl Tulegatan 8	151020	11843	259	782
Continental Vasagatan	244020	10100	250	781
Park Karlavagen 43	229620	10666	240	781
Plaza Birger Jarlsgatan 29	145120	13982	155	780

Reisen Skeppsbron 12	223260	17494	126	781
Victory Lilla Nygatan 5	143090	14050	48	781

MODERATE (SFr 300–800)

Alexandra M. Ladulasgatan 42	840320		90	782
Esplanade Strandv. 7	630740	12442	33	783
Kom Dobelnsgaten 17	235630			783
Malmen Gotgatan 49	226080	19489	254	782
Mornington Nybrogatan 53	631240	10145	115	782
Palace S:t Erikgatan 115	241220	19877	215	782
Wellington Storg. 6	670910	17963	50	782
City Slojdgatan 7	222240	12487	167	783
Domus Korsbarsvagen 1	160195	12642	200	783
Flamingo Hotellgatan 11	830800	10060		783
Jerum Studentbacken 21	635380	12642	120	783
Prince Philip Oxholmsgrand 2	7405100	14402	224	782
Sjofarstshotellet Katarinavagen 26	226960	19020	184	783

ENVIRONS

Arlandia Arlanda Airport	0760/61800	13018	300	783
Kristineberg Hjalmar Soderbergsr. 10	130300		146	783

AIRPORT

Bromma Bromma 1	252920	13125	139	782
Flyghotellet Bromma	262620			782

SWITZERLAND
Berne

Hotel	Telephone Area Code: (31)	Telex	# of Rooms	Page
EXPENSIVE (SFr 190–240)				
Bellevue Palace Kochergasse 3	224581	911524	221	803
Schweizerhof Schweizerhoflaube	224501	911782	120	802
UPPER MODERATE (SFr 100–125)				
Metropole Zeughausgasse 28	225021	33144	110	803
Savoy Neuengasse 26	224405	911863	60	803
MODERATE (SFr 90–110)				
Alfa Laupenstrasse 15	253866	33428	40	803
Baeren Schauplatzgasse 4	223367	33199	56	803
Bristol Schauplatzgasse 10	220101	33199	76	803
City Bubenbergplatz 7	225377	33232	55	803
Krebs Genfergasse 8	224942		42	803
Nydeck Gerechtigkeitsgasse 1	228686		18	803
Regina Mittelstr. 6	230305		45	803
Wachter Movenpick Gentergasse 4	220866	33232	45	803

LOWER MODERATE (SFr 80)

Continental Zeughausgasse 27	222626	33611	35	804

ENVIRONS

Goldenes Kreuz Gerzensee	980836		28	804

Geneva

Hotel	Telephone Area Code: (22)	Telex	# of Rooms	Page
EXPENSIVE (SFr 190–275)				
d'Angleterre Quai du Mt. Blanc 17	7328180	22668	110 beds	815
Beau Rivage Quai du Mont Blanc 13	7310221	23362	180 beds	812
De la Cigogne Place Longemalle 17	7214242	421748	50	813
Des Bergues Quai des Bergues 33	7315050	23383	173 beds	812
Holiday Inn Crown Plaza Voie de Moens 26	7910011	415695	305	814
Metropole Quai General-Guisan 34	7211344	421550	230 beds	812
Movenpick Radisson Rue du Pre-Bois 20	7987575	415701	350	814
Noga Hilton Quai du Mont Blanc 19	7319811	289704	446 beds	813
De la Paix Quai Mont-Blanc 11	7326150	22552	156 beds	812
President Quai Wilson 47	7311000	22780	410 beds	813
La Reserve Rte. des Romelles 4	7741741	23822	105 beds	813
Du Rhone Quai Turrettini 1201	7319831	22213	415 beds	812
Richemond Jardin Brunswick 1211	7311400	22598	200 beds	810

Bristol Ruc du Mont-Blanc 10	7324400	23739	140 beds	814
Intercontinental Petit Saconnex 7–9	7346091	23130	704 beds	813
Pullman Rotary Rue du Cendrier 18–20	7315200	289999	139 beds	814
Ramada Renaissance Rue de Zurich 19	7310241	289109	357 beds	814

MODERATE (SFr 100–170)

Ambassador Quai des Bergues 21	7317200	23231	134 beds	815
California Rue Gevray 1	7315550	23560	100 beds	815
Century Av. de Frontenex 24	7368095	23223	227	815
Cornavin Bd. James-Fazy 33	7322100	22853	175	815
De Berne S.A. Rue de Berne 26	7316000	22764	130	816
Penta Av. L. Casai 75–77	7984700	27043	496 beds	816
Royal Rue de Lausanne 41	7313600	27631	300 beds	814
Warwick Rue de Lausanne 14	7316250	23630	314 beds	815

LOWER MODERATE (SFr 85–115)

Balzac Rue de l'Ancien Port 14	7310160	289430	70 beds	815
Excelsior Rue Rousseau 34	7320945	289304	100 beds	816
Du Midi Place Chevelu 4	7317800	23482	140 beds	815
Grand-Pre Rue du Grand-Pre 35	7339150	23284	130 beds	815
Rivoli Rue des Paquis 6	7318550	22091	100	816
Windsor Rue de Berne 31	7317130	27742	90 beds	816

Zurich

Hotel	Telephone Area Code: (1)	Telex	# of Rooms	Page
EXPENSIVE (SFr 230–300)				
Baur au Lac Talstr. 1	2211650	813567	225 beds	858
Dolder Grand Kurhausstr. 65	2516231	816416	300 beds	858
Eden au Lac Utoquai 45	479404	816339	75 beds	859
Savoy Baur en Ville Poststr. 12	2115360	812145	150 beds	859
UPPER MODERATE (SFr 160–250)				
Atlantis Sheraton Doltschiweg 234	4630000	813338	320 beds	860
Carlton Elite Bahnhofstr. 41	2116560	812781	115 beds	859
Continental Stampfenbachstr. 60	3633363	55393	250 beds	861
International Am Marktplatz	3114341	823251	700 beds	859
Nova-Park Badenerstr. 420	4912222	822822	1000 beds	860
St. Gotthard Bahnhofstr. 87	2115500	812420	200 beds	860
Schweizerhof Bahnhofplatz 7	2118640	813754	150 beds	861
Zum Storchen Weinplatz 2	2115510	813354	110 beds	859
MODERATE (SFr 130–170)				
Europe Dufourstr. 4	471030	816461	65 beds	860
Kindli Pfalzgasse 1	2115917	812426	35 beds	861
Opera Dufourstr. 5	2519090	816480	100 beds	860

Waldhaus Dolder Kurhausstr. 20	2519360	816460	114 beds	859

ENVIRONS

Airport Hotel Oberhausenstr. 30	8104444	53287	70 beds	862
Alexander Am Postgebaude	2518203	57735	82 beds	861
Hilton	8103131	825428	400 beds	861
Movenpick W. Mittelholzerstr. 8	8101111	57979	570 beds	861

INDEX

NOTES